THE SAS AND LRDG ROLL OF HONOUR 1941–47

VOLUME I – DEEDS SHOW
North Africa, the Middle East and New Zealand

EX-LANCE-CORPORAL X, QGM

Published in the UK by SAS-LRDG-RoH
http://www.sas-lrdg-roh.com

First Published 2016
Second Imprint 2018

British Library Cataloguing in Publication Data
Data available

ISBN 978-1-5262-0332-8

Project managed, printed and bound by Cedar Group. UK Main Office: Unit 1 Triton Centre, Premier Way, Abbey Park Industrial Estate, Romsey, Hampshire, SO51 9DJ
Tel: 01794 525 032. Email: design@cedargroup.uk.com

Design by Ex-Lance-corporal X. Artwork and illustration by R. Chasemore and R. Farnworth

Typeset in Palatino Linotype. The text follows *New Hart's Rules – The Handbook of Style for Writers and Editors* published by Oxford University Press

Freedom is the sure possession of those alone who have the courage to defend it.
Pericles

CONTENTS

ALGERIA

On 8 November 1942 British and American troops landed along the Vichy-held French Moroccan and Algerian coastline during OPERATION TORCH. This Second Front, which went some way to providing much-needed relief to the Soviet Union on the Eastern Front, also improved Allied naval movement in the Mediterranean and set the stage for an Axis-free North Africa as well as the forthcoming invasion of southern Europe.

TORCH was three-pronged: a Western Force landed at three locations, the objectives being ports and airfields in the region of Casablanca and Rabat, the capture of which would safe-guard an Atlantic supply chain if required. Although opposed by Vichy ground and naval forces the area was secured by 10 November. Simultaneously a Central Force landed at three beaches close to Oran, the objectives again being the key port and airfields. Here the Vichy French also resisted but were eventually subdued by naval gunfire on the 9th. An Eastern Task Force landed at three beaches around Algiers on the 8th, met only light resistance, and had forced troops under General Juin to surrender that evening. Thus all Vichy resistance in North Africa had ceased by the 10th, largely due to a controversial deal made with Admiral Darlan, a member of the pro-German regime and, by chance, senior Vichy officer in situ. Although this precipitated the German occupation of Vichy France it paved the way for a rapid Allied advance eastwards towards the strategically important port of Tunis. However, it also prompted the Axis to fly in reinforcements. Despite Allied parachute drops, First Army's thrust was subsequently halted just short of the Tunisian capital before being pushed back by German forces.

To the east Montgomery's Eighth Army drove the Afrikakorps from Libya into southern Tunisia in early 1943. Here the enemy reinforced the Mareth Line, a formidable series of pre-war defensive strongpoints linking the sea with the Matmâta hills that blocked any northwards advance. In late March, after the Long Range Desert Group had pioneered a flanking route around this line, the Allies attacked on both fronts. Simultaneously they cut off both naval and air support from Sicily thereby trapping the enemy between the First and Eighth Armies. Tunis fell on 6 May and by the 13th all Axis troops in North Africa had surrendered.

During February 1943 David Stirling's brother, Bill, who himself had been involved in unconventional units since the beginning of the war, had brought the majority of the Special Operations Executive's Small Scale Raiding Force (under its cover name of No.62 Commando) into theatre. This was the foundation on which 2nd SAS was raised on 13 May 1943. Recruiting began in earnest. Many well-trained and battle-hardened veterans of the 1st Parachute Brigade, which during the North African Campaign had earned the respect of the enemy (as well as the nickname the 'Red Devils'), volunteered for the Regiment. They were joined by volunteers from Malta who were eager, now that the island's siege had abated, to balance the scales and take the fight to the enemy.

With its lengthy beach enclosed by hills 2nd SAS' base at Philippeville in north-east Algeria appeared an ideal training area. However, it was soon found to be a breeding ground for malaria, a factor that influenced the direction of more than one operation, sometimes, as will be seen, with fatal results. Before this was fully appreciated a troop from the Special Boat Squadron's L Detachment was sent from the Middle East to bolster 2nd SAS operations. This was complemented by a cadre of experienced men from 1st SAS that helped train their sister Regiment. With forthcoming raids on Mediterranean islands, and the planned invasions of Sicily and mainland Italy, the emphasis was on parachute and small-boat work. Three cemeteries within Algeria, containing a total of seven SAS casualties, graphically illustrate the inherent dangers of such realistic training: there are five members of 2nd SAS at Bône War Cemetery and another at Dély Ibrahim War Cemetery whilst one member of 1st SAS is buried within El Alia War Cemetery.

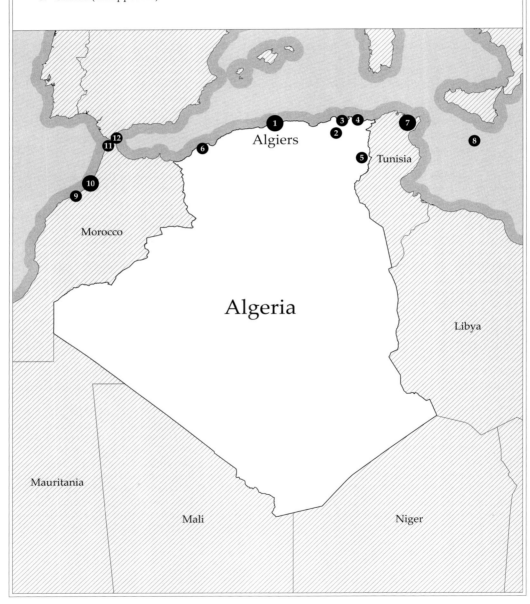

1. Algiers
   (Dély Ibrahim and
   El Alia War Cemeteries)
2. Constantine
3. Skikda (Philippeville)
4. Annaba
   (Bône War Cemetery)
5. Tebessa
6. Oran
7. Tunis
8. Malta
9. Casablanca
10. Rabat
11. Tangiers
12. Gibraltar

BÔNE WAR CEMETERY

Bône, prized for its port and airfield, was occupied by advancing Allied troops on 12 November 1942, 70th General Hospital being located here in the early part of the following year. The cemetery contains 868 Commonwealth graves of the Second World War and one First World War Mercantile Marine burial. In addition, there are fourteen non-war graves, mostly of merchant seamen. The town's name was changed from Bône to Annaba after Algeria gained its independence.

The cemetery is located 5 kilometres west of Annaba at the southern end of route du Sidi Achour. It is set back from the road next to a police station and 400 metres from the junction with the N44. GPS co-ordinates: Latitude 36.87218, Longitude 7.71793

GUNNER ARTHUR **BETTS** [876020] ROYAL ARTILLERY AND 2ND SAS (G SQN)

Born on 25 July 1919 in Sheffield, Arthur Betts worked as a miner before enlisting into the Royal Artillery at Doncaster in late December 1937. After training he was posted to the 22nd Field Brigade and in December 1938 decided to extend his service with the Colours to six years. At the beginning of 1939 he was posted to the 25th Field Regiment and served in India, although by the outbreak of war that September it had moved to Egypt. The regiment subsequently followed the 4th Indian Division to Sudan, arriving on New Year's Day 1941. Having crossed into Eritrea that month the 25th helped break up an Italian-led, Ethiopian cavalry charge at the mouth of the Keru Gorge. Driving forward as part of Gazelle Force it laid down a bombardment key to the capture of Cub-Cub late in February. After Italian forces in East Africa were defeated it returned to Egypt and went up to the Western Desert, most notably taking part in OPERATION CRUSADER during which it successfully repelled an armoured counter-attack on the Gazala Line in December 1941.

The following March Betts was re-posted to the 12th Field Regiment on Malta and married a local girl, Mary Rose Borg, that November, just as the Axis air attacks began to abate. Having been interviewed on the island by officers of 2nd SAS he volunteered for the Regiment, disembarking in Algeria on 25 August 1943 to join it at Philippeville that day. He subsequently drowned during a training exercise on 11 January 1944 along with Gunners Leonard Garnham and 'Taffy' James (see their entries within this section), and with Bombardier John Holmes who is commemorated in Italy (see his entry under Cassino Memorial within Volume II). 2nd SAS' training officer, Captain Felix Symes, who had recently returned from leading G Squadron in Italy, stated at the subsequent court of inquiry:

On the 11th January 1944, I organised a night boating scheme to practice my squadron in landing on a beach near the mouth of the Saf Saf River just east of Philippeville. NCOs were to command the landing and officers of the squadron to act as observers. The landing was to take place as follows: two canoes were to go in first to recce the beach. They would then signal in the dory [a small, shallow-draft boat] containing HQ Troop, who would take up positions just off the beach. HQ Troop would then signal in the other two troops. Each troop was in a separate dory containing approximately ten men. The enemy was provided by the third troop of the squadron, who had orders to oppose, if possible, the first attempt in landing, by firing live ammunition in the air out to sea.

On the way to the harbour from camp we passed the beach in question, and noted that the sea was calm. This was at about 1800hrs. On leaving the harbour, I noticed that one of the canoes was not visible, and on asking Captain Fenning in the dory behind the one I was in, where it had gone, he replied that he had sent it back to harbour as the occupants were not capable of handling it well enough. This canoe contained the signalling torch.

We arrived off the beach at approximately 2000hrs, in the order HQ dory (containing myself), the canoe, and then 1 Troop dory followed by 2 Troop. As the sea appeared slightly choppy then, I told the canoe not to attempt a landing, if there was any surf. The canoe left, and returned in about ten minutes time, the occupants stating that their canoe was leaking, and that there was a certain amount of surf. I asked them if they considered it was alright to land in a dory and they replied 'Yes'.

I then called to Captain Fenning in the second dory, and told him that I was going to have a look at the surf in my dory. We arranged that the signal would be five matches struck on the beach, if he was to come in, in the absence of the torch. If he did not see the signal he was not to come in.

On approaching the surf the enemy fired their rifles. I decided that it was not advisable to land, as we were not wearing life-belts that evening. If we had been doing so, I should have landed.

I then told Sjt Haley, who was commanding my dory, to return to the others. On arrival at where we left them about 6,000yds out, there was no sign of them. We then noticed them making for the beach further eastwards. We tried to catch them up, at the same time shouting to them and lighting matches. When about 300yds behind the No.2 Troop dory, we heard shouts in the water, close to shore, and realised that No.1 Troop had upset.

I then asked for strong swimmers in HQ dory and 2 Troop dory, transferring weak swimmers into 2 Troop dory. There remained in HQ dory SSM Puttock, L/Cpl Bigdon, Pct Curtis and myself [see Private Len Curtis' entry under Graffigny-Chemin Communal Cemetery, France, Volume III]. We approached the shore where a large group of people were now standing. We shouted, asking if everyone was all right. The only answer received was 'No, don't come in – go back', which was repeated half a dozen times. As we got no other answer we assumed all the occupants were safe, and as the steering couch had been snapped in the surf I decided not to risk another landing and pulled out.

We returned to the harbour where Sjt Woede informed me that there were four men missing, and there were still people searching the beach. I then went out in a French motor-boat, but by the time we arrived off the beach, which was about 1½ miles away, the surf had risen considerably, and we were not able to approach very close to shore. We cruised around off the beach for about ½ hour, shining lights on the water, but found no sign of anyone. On returning we met the French patrol which had previously been summoned, and they continued the search. We returned to the harbour.

Up to the present, midday the 14th January, the bodies have not been recovered, although a search has been made.

I believe that Captain Fenning's decision to land further up the coast was due to his assuming that I had landed, had been captured, and that therefore no signals would be visible. In my opinion this decision was reasonable owing to the circumstances [court of inquiry statement, 14 January 1944 – see Symes' own entry under Graffigny-Chemin Communal Cemetery].

Captain Robert Fenning, who was in command of the dory that capsized, stated:

On coming in I saw the breakers ahead and I did not think we would have any trouble in getting ashore. At that moment the stern lifted and we were carried forward like a surf-board. I looked round from my position in the bows and saw that the boat was at an angle of about 30 degrees, and a large wave about to break over the stern. The next thing that happened was that the boat swerved to the right in front of the wave being half swamped by the wave breaking. The dory did not overturn, but six of the crew were washed out. I ordered the remainder to continue paddling, and shouted to the others to swim back to the boat. At that moment another wave hit the boat and filled it completely, washing another man overboard who could not swim. After I helped him back into the boat I saw four or five men in the water, about 20 yards away, and heard one of them say 'I can't swim'.

Owing to my heavy clothing, I was wearing a parachute jacket at the time, I was unable to go to their help. The remainder of us stayed with the boat, and I was out of the boat clinging to the bows. I then found I could stand, removed my clothing, and swam ashore with the bow line. There was a very strong current flowing in the direction of Philippeville.

I immediately organised a search party for 200 yards on either side of where we had beached. I saw that there were seven survivors and went in search of Captain Symes whom I thought had landed further along.

Of the four men who were drowned Garnham and James were excellent swimmers, whereas Holmes and Betts were not. It is quite possible that the latter were aided by Garnham and James but struggled, and the current and broken water resulted in the loss of all four. These men were wearing denim or American overalls, felt soled boots. They carried no equipment and consequently should not have been unduly weighed down. In my opinion the boat was about 100yds from the shore when it upset [court of inquiry statement, 14 January 1944].

Sergeant Joe Coulson, coxswain of the upset dory, was able to expand on events:

I was washed out of the boat and when I came to the surface I was still grasping the steering sweep. There were two others in the water about 6 feet away, and the nearest one shouted that he could not swim. I could not see the boat. I heard James, who was the furthest away of the two, shout to the nearest one 'Here, take this paddle'. I then recognised this man as Holmes and lifted the sweep up and dropped it on front of him, still retaining hold of it, and he clung to it. We two swam towards the shore like this, with James on Holmes' right, swimming with a paddle in front of him. When nearing the shore, I became tired, and had to let go the car, which I had been clinging with one hand, and told Holmes, to keep going as he was only 20 yards from the beach. I continued and finding I could stand, waded ashore. When I last saw James and Holmes they were together, and apparently alright. I saw no sign of Betts and Garnham. I knew James to be a good swimmer, and Holmes could swim a bit, what happened in the last few yards I have no idea [court of inquiry statement, 14 January 1944].

The temporary Commanding Officer of 2nd SAS of the time, Major Ralph Milbanke, MC, concluded: 'in my opinion the accident occurred owing to a change of weather, which could not have been foreseen.' The Divisional Commander's opinion was that, although training needed to be realistic, Mae-West life jackets should have been worn.

Son of Henry Betts of Kings Road, Askern, Doncaster, Yorkshire (his mother's maiden name was Owen) – Husband of Mary Betts, also of Kings Road, Askern – Father of Henry Betts who was born shortly after his father disembarked in North Africa.
Age 24.
No inscription.
Grave 7.C.2.

GUNNER LEONARD **GARNHAM** [846776] ROYAL ARTILLERY AND 2ND SAS (G SQN)

Leonard Garnham was born on 29 January 1919 at Broomhead in Sheffield where he worked as a blacksmith and coal miner. He joined the Royal Artillery (TA) in April 1935 before serving with the regular 16th (Java) Heavy Battery from January 1936 until February 1937 when he was discharged on compassionate grounds. His exit report noted: 'a hard and conscientious worker. Cheerful, obedient and well behaved. He is honest, temperate and trustworthy.'

Whilst working back down the mines Garnham joined the 282nd Field Battery (TA) but re-enlisted into the regulars in August 1938. He was posted firstly to 20th Anti-Tank Regiment that December, and then to the 26th Anti-Tank Regiment with which he disembarked on Malta in April 1939. Three months later he was awarded a B Class Swimming Certificate, his unit being redesignated the 13th Mobile Coast Defence Regiment in July 1940 in response to the first enemy air attacks and the threat of amphibious assault. In February 1941, as the Axis onslaught developed, it was again redesignated, this time as the 17th Defence Regiment before Garnham was posted to the 26th Defence Regiment that July. The island's resistance during 1942 formed, in Churchill's own words:

> … the keystone of the prolonged struggle for the maintenance of our position in Egypt and the Middle East. In the bitter land fighting in the Western Desert the outcome of each phase was measured by a hand's-breadth, and frequently depended on the rate at which supplies could reach the combatants by sea. For ourselves this meant the two or three months' voyage round the Cape … For the enemy there was only the two or three days' passage across the Mediterranean from Italy … But athwart the [enemy] route to Tripoli lay the island fortress of Malta …
>
> The reduction of Malta to impotence, or better still its capture, was the main objective, and for this purpose an ever-growing German air force was gathered on the Sicilian airfields [*The Second World War, Volume IV: The Hinge of Fate*, by Winston S. Churchill].

Although the Axis assault was formidable, and the island's inhabitants and garrison pushed to their limits, the bombing began to ease during the second half of 1942 and more still after OPERATION HUSKY, the July 1943 Allied invasion of Sicily. Soon after Garnham volunteered for the SAS having been interviewed on the island by officers of the Regiment. He disembarked in Algiers on 24 August and joined 2nd SAS at their camp at Philippeville that day. He subsequently drowned during a training accident on 11 January 1944 (see Gunner Arthur Betts' entry within this section for full details).

Son of Samuel and Francis Garnham (née White) of Morgan Avenue, Parsons Cross, Sheffield.
Age 24.
Resting from his earthly labours in peace
Grave 5.F.8. As with some other casualties within this section Garnham's headstone, which replaced the original cross marker, is incorrectly inscribed 'Army Air Corps' under which the SAS did not fall until 1 April 1944.

GUNNER TREVOR JOHN JAMES [4077394] SOUTH WALES BORDERERS, WELCH REGIMENT, ROYAL ARTILLERY AND 2ND SAS (G SQN)

'Taffy' James was born on 22 December 1919 at Mynyddiswlyn near Blackwood in Monmouthshire where he worked as a colliery engine driver. Having served since March 1938 in C Company of the 1st (Rifle) Battalion, Monmouthshire Regiment (TA), South Wales Borderers, he transferred to the Supplementary Reserve of the Welch Regiment at Cardiff that August and reported to its training depot. Two months later he enlisted into the regular Royal Artillery and was initially posted to the 2nd Heavy Regiment before being re-posted the following February to the 26th Anti-Tank Regiment at Woolwich. As such he was a contemporary of Gunner Leonard Garnham (see his entry above). The pair disembarked on Malta in April 1939 where their regiment was redesignated the 13th Mobile Coastal Defence Regiment the following July. By December 1940 James was serving at Tal Handaq as a member of the 40th Defence Battery, although he was later absorbed into the 17th Defence Regiment. Having been posted to the 26th Defence Regiment he and Garnham were interviewed on the island by officers of 2nd SAS and were accepted as volunteers. They subsequently disembarked in Algiers on 24 August 1943, joining 2nd SAS at their camp at Philippeville that day.

James drowned during a training accident on 11 January 1944, most likely whilst helping Bombardier John Holmes, a weak swimmer, towards the shore (see Gunner Arthur Betts' entry within this section for full details and Holmes' entry under Cassino Memorial, Italy, Volume II).

Son of William and Elizabeth James of Pont Garn Terrace, Ynysddu, Monmouthshire.
Age 23.
No inscription.
Grave 8.E.8.

PRIVATE JACK WILLIAM SMITH [6344773] QUEEN'S OWN ROYAL WEST KENT REGIMENT, ROYAL ARTILLERY, ROYAL ARMY SERVICE CORPS AND 2ND SAS (D SQN)

Known as 'Smudge' or 'Smithy' to his comrades, Jack Smith was born on 18 October 1921 at St Mary Cray in Kent. His mother died when he was 7 years old leaving him the eldest of three children. Having attended the nearby Central School he took an apprenticeship as an electrical fitter for the Electro-Dynamic Construction Company and in July 1937, aged 16, he joined his father's unit, the local 4th Battalion, Queen's Own Royal West Kent Regiment (TA). At the time he was a keen football player, goalkeeping for his work team, The Dynamics, as well as boxing as a light heavyweight for the Royal West Kents.

At the outbreak of war Smith's father refused to take him to France with the rest of his company saying that he was too young. However, he did not prevent others of the same age going and as a result the young Smith swore that he would never allow his father stop him from volunteering for anything else. He subsequently transferred to the Royal Artillery in May 1940 and was posted to the Hampshire Heavy Regiment, serving on the Isle of Wight and at ports in the Solent. He married Annie Rosina Colyer that December at St Joseph's Catholic Church in St Mary Cray before returning to the 4th Battalion, Royal West Kents, in May 1941. Transferring to the Royal Army Service Corps in March 1942 he qualified as a Class III Electrician that month, obtained an A grade on an endurance course at Barrhead in April, and attended parachute course 19 at No.1 PTS Ringway that July. He may have then joined the 3rd Battalion, Parachute Regiment, although this is not clear from his records. What is certain is that before embarking for North Africa in January 1943 Smith went AWOL to attend his sister's wedding and see his wife and son. For this he spent

his passage at sea in solitary confinement. His movements on disembarking are also unclear although it appears likely that he served within the HQ of 3 Para before volunteering for 2nd SAS on 9 June.

Smith was admitted to 100th British General Hospital at Philippeville on 29 September 1943 and died from smallpox on 12 October. Veterans recalled that they had been out on one raid and in the run up to the next Smith began to feel ill. By the time they returned from their next operation he had died. That November the *Orpington and St Mary Cray Kentish Times* reported:

> Mrs Smith of 191, The Greenway, Orpington, has been officially notified that her husband, Private William Smith, aged 22, has died after a short illness in North Africa. He joined the Orpington and Crays B Company of the Queen's Royal West Kent Regiment (Territorials) in July 1938, and was mobilised with them in August, 1939, before the outbreak of war. In March 1942, he transferred to another corps and was sent to North Africa last January.
>
> After leaving the Central School, St Mary Cray, he was apprenticed to the electrical trade with the Electro-Dynamic Construction Co., at New Cross, and was in the firm's football team. He also played football for the Territorials. He is survived by his wife and 18-month-old son.
>
> His father, Colour-Sergeant W. G. Smith, who for fifteen years was in Orpington and Crays Territorials and went with them to France after the outbreak of war, and who also served for three years on the Western Front in the last war, is well known for his valuable work in the Odd-fellows at St Mary Cray and in the Orpington and Crays British Legion.

During December 1943 Captain Roy Farran, MC, of 2nd SAS, wrote to Smith's wife: 'He was one of the best men in the squadron, well liked by everybody, completely fearless and altogether an asset to the Regiment. I remember him for his beautiful style with a rifle, the smoothest action I have ever seen in the whole of my soldiering career' (Smith family collection).

Smith was originally buried at Philippeville Anglo-American Cemetery but was reinterred to his current resting place soon after. For years his father held himself responsible for the way events had unfolded (personal interview with Terry Smith, 2012).

Son of William and Alice Smith of Orpington, Kent – Husband of Annie Smith of Lower Road, St Mary Cray, Orpington, who never remarried – Veterans recalled how photographs of his son Terry had adorned the inside of their tent in North Africa.
Age 21.
Eternal Rest Give Unto Him, O Lord, And Let Perpetual Light Shine Upon Him
Grave 7.A.7. Also commemorated on Orpington's war memorial.

LANCE-BOMBARDIER ROGER WHITE MM [833924] ROYAL ARTILLERY AND 2ND SAS

Roger White was born on 23 March 1915 in the small village of Holytown just outside Motherwell in North Lanarkshire. Having worked as a van driver for local merchant, Andrew Clark Ltd, he enlisted into the 20/9th Field Brigade, Royal Artillery, in January 1934. Posted to the 61st Field Battery in February 1935 he was serving in Egypt by the end of the year. The following August he sustained a 'traumatic' knee injury 'whilst taking part in voluntary gymnastics'. This was deemed to 'interfere with [his] future efficiency as a soldier' and in 1937, at the end of his three-year engagement, he therefore left the army. His release documents noted: 'a thoroughly reliable and trustworthy man. Smart, honest and intelligent. He is a good and careful motor driver who has had a good deal of experience and has a good working knowledge of mechanical transport.'

Although White toyed with the idea of joining the Palestine Police Force he married Sylvia Jessie Stevenson at Finsbury, North London, during 1938, the couple soon producing a daughter they named Audrey. Having remained on the Army Reserve list he was called up the following June, subsequently serving in France with the 5/2nd Anti-Aircraft Regiment from the outbreak of war. Manning forts that surrounded Calais this regiment was forced to abandon its guns in the face of German attacks, its men being used as reinforcements to the two infantry battalions that were defending the port thereafter. White was one of the lucky few to be evacuated back to the UK.

Having manned anti-aircraft posts in London during the Blitz, White disembarked at Malta in July 1941. He was awarded the Military Medal whilst serving as an acting lance-bombardier in the 4th Heavy Anti-Aircraft Regiment during the height of the Axis bombing:

At [illegible] position during a period of intense dive-bombing attacks from the 15th March to [illegible] April 1942, this NCO was a gunner. On the 19th April the position was dive-bombed on five separate occasions, during the first of which both NCOs at his gun were wounded. He immediately took charge of the gun and kept it in action during the remainder of the day, coolly and efficiently engaging subsequent dive bombers [*London Gazette* 16/02/43, Supplement 18/02/43, WO 373/29].

Having been interviewed on Malta by officers of 2nd SAS White was accepted and disembarked at Algiers on 26 August 1943, joining the Regiment at Philippeville later that day. He was killed in a

parachute training accident on 26 October 1943. No further details can currently be located, although his former officer on Malta wrote to his parents in December 1943:

I may tell you that we thought so much of him that he was recommended for accelerated promotion. He was a most excellent NCO and what is more, he was a brave man. I am sure he enjoyed his time with us; he was always cheerful and nothing ever seemed to get him down. He was for some time my dispatch rider and I could not have wished a better. He volunteered later for another job which I cannot describe here, but it was a job for a brave man [*The Motherwell Times*, 24 December 1943].

Son of Henry and Winifred White of Sunnyside Avenue, Holytown, Lanarkshire – Husband of Sylvia White who served in the ATS – Father of Audrey White – Brother of Frank White.
Age 28.
On Whose Soul, Sweet Jesus, Have Mercy. May He Rest In Peace, Amen
Grave 4.C.10.

DÉLY IBRAHIM WAR CEMETERY

This cemetery contains 494 Commonwealth graves of the Second World War, eleven graves of other nationalities including one Russian and three Yugoslavs, and twenty-five non-war burials, mostly of merchant seamen.

The suburb of Dély Ibrahim is located 10 kilometres south-west of Central Algiers, just to the north of the N5 main road. The cemetery is situated on the hillside on the north side of the N36, between the Salle des fêtes Olympic and the German Military Cemetery. Opening times are Sunday to Thursday, 0800–1600hrs. GPS co-ordinates: Latitude 36.751045, Longitude 2.987723

LANCE-SERGEANT ALBERT DOUGLAS **POLLARD** [T/91402] ROYAL ARMY SERVICE CORPS AND 2ND SAS

Albert Pollard was born on 13 July 1916 in the small village of Elham, East Kent, although his family later moved to Ilfracombe in North Devon where he worked as a driver. Less than a week after the outbreak of war he enlisted into the Royal Army Service Corps at Exeter and was posted to 27 Company. By 27 September 1939 he was serving in France as a driver within II Corps Petrol Park and having been evacuated from Dunkirk on 30 May 1940 was re-posted to 2nd London Division's Petrol Company. He was promoted to lance-corporal during June 1941 whilst serving with the 47th (London) Division's Petrol Company. From the beginning of 1942 he was posted to companies attached to various tank brigades and was promoted through the ranks to lance-sergeant. He embarked for North Africa in January 1943 and on, or soon after, the formation of 2nd SAS on 13 May volunteered for the Regiment at Philippeville, a coastal town in north-east Algeria.

According to his service record Pollard 'died as a result of injuries sustained in [an] accident' on 21 July 1943. Although no detail can be found a Devon newspaper later reported:

Sergt Albert Douglas Pollard of a Special Air Service Regiment, attached to the First Army in North Africa, who has been killed in an accident in the Mediterranean theatre of operations, was a son of Mr and Mrs W Bruce Pollard … Sergt Pollard went through the Dunkirk evacuation and a letter the parents have received from an officer says that Sergt Pollard was one of the first to arrive in Sicily and displayed great presence of mind during operations. The tragedy is deepened by the fact that after going through extremely dangerous operations he met his end in an accident, which the officer described as 'one in ten thousand' [*Exeter and Plymouth Gazette*, 6 August 1943].

Operations on Sicily were on-going at the time of Pollard's death and it therefore seems likely that the one referred to above was OPERATION NARCISSUS. The object of this amphibious raid was to capture the lighthouse and surrounding high ground on the Isola delle Correnti in the early hours of 10 July. Lying just off the south-east coast of Sicily the island posed a threat to the Allied invasion that took place a few hours later (OPERATION HUSKY). The SAS party found the area to be clear of the enemy and withdrew once it had established that no threat existed.

Son of Walter and Ethel Pollard of Hillsborough Road, Ilfracombe, Devon. Age 27.
In everlasting remembrance of Douglas. Mum, Dad, Ian, David. Beloved by all
Grave 4.K.B. Also commemorated on Ilfracombe's war memorial.

EL ALIA WAR CEMETERY

This war cemetery was originally used solely for Allied casualties resulting from the OPERATION TORCH *landings of November 1942. It has since been added to by the municipal authorities into what is now a large walled area consisting of many different cemeteries. The plot contains 368 Commonwealth graves of the Second World War, eight graves of other nationalities, and fifteen non-war burials, mostly of merchant seamen.*

El Alia is located 13 kilometres south-east of Algiers. The cemetery lies on the route d'el-Alia that runs through the walled area described above. Access is controlled by guards via the rue des Frères Ouddak and is only gained by the public during daylight hours. GPS co-ordinates: Latitude 36.71974, Longitude 3.16472

TROOPER CHARLES WILLIAM **PRICE** [7953828] ROYAL ARMOURED CORPS
AND 1ST SAS/SBS

Charles Price was born on 22 January 1920 in the village of Withington near Hereford where he grew up at Veldo Farm. Having worked as a heating engineer he enlisted into the Royal Armoured Corps in March 1942 and was posted to the 57th Training Regiment at Warminster. Re-posted to the 52nd Training Regiment that August he embarked for the Middle East soon after, arriving in Egypt in October. Here he volunteered for 1st SAS on 14 January 1943 from the Middle East RAC Depot. His service record notes that on 3 June that year, i.e. after fighting in North Africa had ceased, he moved to Tripoli and that he was 'accidentally killed' on 18 August 1943 being 'on duty and not to blame'. There are no further details although presumably he was serving in Algiers at the time.

Price's service record also contains an entry stating that he had been posted to the Special Boat Squadron that May. At the time a troop from L Detachment, SBS, had been loaned to 2nd SAS for operations in the Mediterranean. The remainder of 1st SAS, its parent regiment, had been redesignated as the Special Raiding Squadron in March and was fighting on Sicily at the time of his death. This entry is, however, crossed out, either because it was recorded in error or because Price was loaned in some other capacity to 2nd SAS. Despite the fact that the SBS troop was operating from the submarine flotilla associated with HMS *Maidstone* within Algiers harbour it cannot currently be confirmed which formation he was serving with at the time of his death. His cousin, Able Seaman Frank Price, was posted missing, presumed killed, two weeks before when his ship, HMS *Arrow*, was caught in an explosion from an adjacent ammunition vessel in Algiers harbour.

Son of Albert and Isabella Price of Veldo Farm, Withington, Herefordshire. Age 23.
Peace, perfect peace. With loved ones far away? In Jesus' keeping we are safe and they Grave 12.D.34. Also commemorated, alongside his cousin, within St Peter's Church in Withington and on the village war memorial.

EGYPT

Confident that Britain was preoccupied with the defence of her own shores, Italy invaded Egypt from Cyrenaica, the coastal region of eastern Libya, on 13 September 1940. Correctly judging that their adversary had overstretched her supply lines, British forces struck back against superior numbers, virtually destroying the incumbent Italian Army. This, coupled with reverses in Albania, severely dented the prestige of Mussolini, Germany being forced to come to his aid in the form of Rommel's Afrikakorps and the Luftwaffe. Over two years of offensive and counter-offensive were to follow with ports, airfields, desert outposts and oasis alike regularly changing hands and taking on key importance. At stake was dominance of the Mediterranean, control of the Suez Canal linking the latter to the Indian Ocean and the East, access to Persia's oil reserves and the supply route to Russia. Although the Axis pushed Allied forces back to Egypt three times, their final offensive threatening Cairo itself, Commonwealth troops prevailed and eventually forced the last of the enemy back into Libya on 11 November 1942.

Throughout the North African Campaign the desert expanse to the south, impassable to heavy armour, formed a vulnerable flank difficult to both defend and attack from. Small, lightweight patrols, initially of the Long Range Desert Group and followed by those of the Special Air Service, made good use of this terrain. Although the former was based in Cairo, and the latter at Kabrit on the Great Bitter Lake, both units operated over vast distances from forward bases in desert oases such as Kufra, Jalo, Siwa and Jarabub.

Volunteers for the LRDG were initially trained during short desert patrols, their skills being honed 'on the job', although a more rigid training programme was later employed as the Group expanded. Many volunteers for L Detachment, one of two 'subunits' of the then mythical Special Air Service Brigade, came from the Middle East Commando Depot at nearby Geneifa but also included a squadron of Free French parachutists and later members of the Greek Sacred Squadron . All were trained at Kabrit, the adjacent RAF Station, which later assumed the title No.4 Middle East Training School, providing air assets for parachute courses.

The intensity of the campaign in the Western Desert is reflected by its casualties: memorials and cemeteries in Egypt commemorate twenty-two members of the SAS, two members of the SBS, six of the LRDG and two members of the Special Interrogation Group who were attached to L Detachment. Twenty-four of their names are recorded on the Alamein Memorial, their bodies either having been committed to the desert whilst behind enemy lines, having been lost at sea whilst prisoners of war, or posted missing in Eastern Europe during the last days of the war.

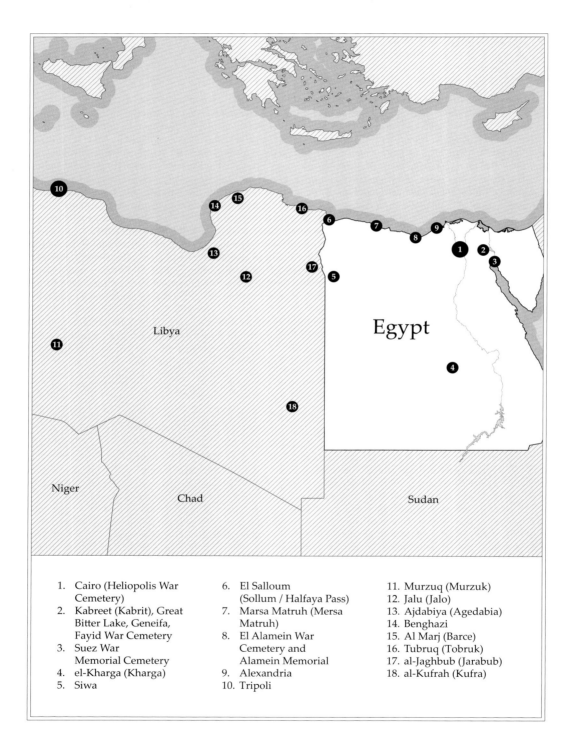

1. Cairo (Heliopolis War Cemetery)
2. Kabreet (Kabrit), Great Bitter Lake, Geneifa, Fayid War Cemetery
3. Suez War Memorial Cemetery
4. el-Kharga (Kharga)
5. Siwa
6. El Salloum (Sollum / Halfaya Pass)
7. Marsa Matruh (Mersa Matruh)
8. El Alamein War Cemetery and Alamein Memorial
9. Alexandria
10. Tripoli
11. Murzuq (Murzuk)
12. Jalu (Jalo)
13. Ajdabiya (Agedabia)
14. Benghazi
15. Al Marj (Barce)
16. Tubruq (Tobruk)
17. al-Jaghbub (Jarabub)
18. al-Kufrah (Kufra)

ALAMEIN MEMORIAL

The memorial forms the entrance to the El Alamein War Cemetery and commemorates over 8,500 Commonwealth servicemen who have no known grave having lost their lives in Egypt, Libya and during the Eighth Army's operations in Tunisia up to 19 February 1943. It also commemorates those without known graves that died whilst serving in Syria, Iraq, Lebanon and Persia. The Air Forces panels commemorate more than 3,000 Commonwealth airmen who died in campaigns in Aden and Madagascar, Crete and the Aegean, East Africa, Egypt, Ethiopia, Eritrea and the Somalilands, Greece, Iraq, Lebanon, Libya, the Sudan and Syria. Those who died serving with the Rhodesian and South African Air Training Scheme and who have no known grave are also commemorated here. The memorial was unveiled by Field Marshal the Viscount Montgomery of Alamein in 1954.

One of David Stirling's brothers, Lieutenant Hugh Joseph Stirling, killed in action just west of Sidi Barrani on 20 April 1941 whilst serving in the Scots Guards, is commemorated on Column 53. Private Augustus George Evans, MM, of P Patrol, S Detachment, SBS, who was murdered after capture in the Aegean is erroneously commemorated here on Column 66. His name will be removed when a new panel is erected (see his entry under Athens Memorial, Greece, Volume II, for full details).

El Alamein is located 130 kilometres west of Alexandria on the road to Mersa Matruh. The cemetery, set back from the road behind a ridge, is signposted. GPS co-ordinates: Latitude 30.83819, Longitude 28.94707

GUNNER PATRICK JOSEPH **ALLEN** [1610059] ROYAL ARTILLERY, L DETACHMENT SAS BRIGADE AND 1ST SAS (A SQN)

'Paddy' Allen was born on 17 March 1921 in the town of Fermoy, County Cork, Eire, but later lived in Blackburn where he worked as a farm labourer. In February 1941 he enlisted into the Royal Artillery and after a month's reserve service, during which he finished his duties on the farm, he was posted to the 211th Anti-Aircraft Training Regiment. Having qualified as a driver he was posted to the 87th Heavy Anti-Aircraft Regiment and embarked for the Middle East in July 1941. Arriving at Basra in Iraq he volunteered for L Detachment, SAS Brigade, on 12 June 1942 and took part in OPERATION BIGAMY, that September's large-scale raid on Benghazi. Having passed his jumps course at Kabrit he was granted parachute pay at the end of November, contemporary records noting that he took on the duties of cook when behind enemy lines.

Allen took part in OPERATION PALMYRA during which A and B Squadrons were tasked with the destruction of enemy 'transportation facilities', namely shipping, the Misurata–Tripoli railway line, fuel depots, vehicles and administrative units in the area between Sirte and Tripoli. Having crossed the Great Sand Sea from their operating base at Kufra in south-east Libya the squadrons were ordered to establish forward bases in the area of Marada. They were making their way towards this area when Allen was killed in action. Although his date of death is officially recorded as 5 December 1942 the regimental Intelligence Officer's report appears to imply that Allen was killed on the 7th:

On 6 Dec both our party and Major Oldfield's [both elements of B Squadron] got through the Sand Sea closely followed by A Squadron.

We drove all that day and all through the night passing about 20 miles W of Zella. We lost three Jeeps to mechanical breakdowns. At dawn the next day we hid in the edge of an escarpment. There were then reconnaissance planes over our tracks, but we were not spotted. A Squadron was bombed and one man killed [WO 218/97].

In 1985 Mr R. Hodgson, an English seismologist, wrote to the former Commanding Officer of the Long Range Desert Group, David Lloyd Owen, CB, DSO, OBE, MC. He disclosed that in 1983, whilst prospecting in the Libyan Desert, he had found the wreckage of four Jeeps near what used to be the main Zella-Marada road: 'close by was a shallow grave, containing a skeleton which had been badly mutilated, presumably by the explosion'. Lloyd Owen contacted a former LRDG patrol sergeant, Alf Ollerenshaw, who confirmed that he had passed through this area when returning from a Road Watch operation to the north and had seen the destroyed vehicles and a grave marked 'Trooper Allen'. His patrol commander, Captain Alastair Timpson, had confirmed in the LRDG's War Diary of 1942: 'December 20th. Found SAS Jeeps. One evidently much damaged by aircraft [seen here], and the grave of a certain "Paddy Allen". The other, I.1 Patrol [Indian Long Range Squadron] were eager to salvage, and took it on tow' (WO 218/91).

Due to troubled Anglo-Libyan relations, followed by the internal security situation post-2011, there has been no reinterment.

Son of John and Mary Allen of Fermoy, County Cork, Eire.
Age 21.
Column 33.

Captain Christopher Sidney **BAILEY** [141129] Royal Army Service Corps, 4th Queen's Own Hussars and L Detachment SAS Brigade

Chris Bailey was born on 12 February 1915 in London, attending Marlborough College, Wiltshire, from 1928 to 1932. Whilst managing the Boghaz Hotel at Famagusta on Cyprus he registered as a member of the Palestine-based Army Officer Emergency Reserve. He was subsequently commissioned into No.2 Pack Transport Company, Royal Army Service Corps, at Polymedia Camp in Limassol at the outbreak of war. His service record notes that he spoke Greek, French and Turkish, and that as well as a hotelkeeper he was a professional chef and former Gloucestershire publican.

In January 1940 Bailey arrived at Moascar in Egypt but within a month was serving with the Cypriot Pack Transport Company at Mory near Arras in Northern France. Evacuated to the UK on 1 June he was posted to Swindon until returning to Egypt that September. Having been promoted to lieutenant at the beginning of November he was appointed Aide-de-Camp to the Commander of the Western Desert, Lt-General Richard O'Connor, DSO*, MC. He subsequently served in Greece as an acting captain from March until May 1941 and was appointed Staff Captain to Commander Royal Engineers at Force HQ. He was evacuated late that April and promoted to temporary captain in June, his past finally catching up with him when appointed catering advisor to Middle East GHQ. This was obviously not of his choosing and ten days later he transferred to the 4th Queen's Own Hussars, Royal Armoured Corps, in Cairo. At the beginning of 1942 he was appointed GSO III (Ops) at HQ Eighth Army and volunteered for L Detachment, SAS Brigade, on 21 August 1942.

The following month Bailey was wounded in action during Operation Bigamy, the Regiment's abortive, large-scale raid on Benghazi: with the front line stabilised at El Alamein the German supply chain was stretched, most of Rommel's equipment making the long journey from the Libyan ports of Tobruk and Benghazi. Simultaneous raids were therefore planned to put these out of action, the former being allotted to the 1st Special Service Regiment (Operation Agreement) and the latter to L Detachment (Bigamy). Bailey was tasked with capturing Fort Benito, a wireless station on the escarpment overlooking Benghazi that might provide advance warning of that night's attack. In addition, he was allotted further objectives of Benina airfield and whatever merchant shipping lay at anchor. Leaving the main force in the Wadi Gamra around midday on 13 September his small band was given two hours to capture the fort. However, having tried to bluff its way in the Italian occupants opened fire:

> One of Bailey's party appeared out of the darkness, running down the side of the wadi. He wanted a doctor quick. He was the only one unwounded. The Italians in the fort had surrendered after EY rifle grenade fire. As Bailey's party entered the building the Italians opened fire. Bailey had been shot through the chest and Bob Mélot, who was with him, badly hit in the shoulder [*When the Grass Stops Growing: A War Memoir*, by Carol Mather – see Mélot's entry under Brussels War Cemetery, Belgium, Volume III].

The post-operation report notes: 'The Fort was duly destroyed and the wireless installation destroyed, but one member of the garrison was unaccounted for. Of the remaining eight, five were killed and three taken prisoner of war' (WO 201/748). Meanwhile the LRDG War Diary quotes Lieutenant Ken Lazarus who commanded S.1 Patrol assigned to the attacking force:

> 14 Sep … OC S.1 Patrol with the two remaining trucks one of which was a wireless truck, carried a badly wounded SAS officer back to the RAP [Regimental Aid Post] in Wadi Ftilia. After giving up the wounded officer back to the doctor, the two trucks hurried on towards S Patrol RV just as day was breaking [WO 218/91].

The Medical Officer, Captain Malcolm Pleydell, who later wrote under the pseudonym 'James', took over Bailey's treatment beginning with an examination of the wound:

> … it was very small … and there was no apparent bleeding … the left lung had collapsed; he had a sucking pneumothorax and his condition was serious. In the normal course of events, with early hospital treatment, he should have recovered, for there was no evidence of internal haemorrhage. Here, however, with a journey of about 800 miles back to Kufra, the future did not look so good. Even now he was breathless on the slightest exertion. How, then, could he stand the long bumping journey on the back of a three-ton lorry? [*Born of the Desert*, by Malcolm James].

Meanwhile, the SAS column had been ambushed on its way into town, Fitzroy Maclean, CBE, later recalling the subsequent withdrawal from the area:

> When I was not driving I sat with Chris, who was lying on a bedding roll perched up on the top of the petrol cans and paraphernalia with which the truck was filled. Though every jolt and lurch of the truck hurt him, he was as cheerful and gay as ever [*Eastern Approaches*, by Fitzroy Maclean].

However, Pleydell noted that Bailey's condition had deteriorated during the overnight journey and that he was now short of breath and exhibiting signs of cyanosis. Operating conditions had also deteriorated - Located by enemy aircraft the force was repeatedly bombed, the available transport being reduced as the number of wounded rose. With a more hasty retreat required to prevent further casualties the party reached its RV and a decision was made to leave behind those whose wounds meant that they would not survive the arduous journey ahead. They would remain there under the care of two Italian prisoners captured at Fort Benito and an SAS medic who had been allotted to stay (see the entry for 'Johnson' under the Unknown Identity section within Volume III). Pleydell later wrote that despite his condition Bailey 'found it a bitter pill to have to swallow.' Joe Plater, former L Detachment, recalled that the group shook hands with the wounded men and continued their withdrawal at 1900hrs on the 15th, the medic having been ordered to wait until 0700 the following morning before going back into Benghazi with one of the prisoners to get help (personal interview, 2013).

Whilst the Italians are alleged to have reported the whole group as having 'died of wounds', even though some were not seriously wounded and the medic not wounded at all, it now seems likely that they were not picked up by the enemy and were murdered by locals that October (see AQMS Arthur Sque's and Corporal Anthony Drongin's entries within this section for further details). The War Office wrote to Bailey's father in June 1943 stating: 'Information has now been received, through the International Red Cross Committee at Geneva, from prisoners of war, to the effect that your son died of wounds sustained during special operations at Benghazi and is buried at Sidi Moies [a shrine 100 kilometres south-east of Benghazi that was not manned by the Italians], Jebal, Cyrenaica.'

Bailey is officially recorded as having died of such wounds on 15 September 1942. A personal tribute appeared in *The Times* the following year:

> A fellow officer who was with him at the time writes: 'He was one of our best officers, and had done extremely well on these and previous raids. He combined exceptional intelligence and organising ability with great dash and courage; this and his personal charm made him popular with all ranks. I was with him myself after he had been wounded, and he bore the pain that he was in with the greatest fortitude' [17 September 1943].

Third son of Colonel Percy Bailey, DSO, OBE, veteran of the Boer War and First World War (12th Lancers), and of Dorothy Bailey of Mangersbury, Stow-on-the-Wold, Gloucestershire – Brother of Commander Richard Bailey, OBE, RN, of Major T. Bailey of the 12th Lancers, and of Anthony Bailey, a test pilot who was killed in a flying accident in 1941.
Age 26.
Column 15. Also commemorated within the Memorial Hall at Marlborough College.

Guardsman Stanley BOLLAND [2696934] Scots Guards, No.8 Commando and L Detachment SAS Brigade

Stan Bolland was born and grew up in Liverpool, enlisting into the Scots Guards at the outbreak of war. By November 1940 he was a member of No.8 (Guards) Commando, recently redesignated, albeit temporarily, as the 4th Special Service Battalion. Lodged at Largs in Scotland this undertook arduous pre-deployment training on the Isle of Arran before embarking for the Middle East on 31 January 1941. It arrived at Suez at the beginning of March as B Battalion, Layforce, an amalgamation of several Commando units assigned raiding duties in the Eastern Mediterranean. Sent forward to Mersa Matruh towards the front line an unsettled period ensued, the men of No.8 feeling that they were both underused and misused. Although it is not known exactly when Bolland volunteered for L Detachment, SAS Brigade, he was an early member, appearing on a nominal roll of September 1941 as a member of 3 Section, H Group.

Bolland was posted as missing in action on 29 November 1941 after Operation Squatter, the first SAS raid that aimed to destroy aircraft behind enemy lines at Tmimi and Gazala in Libya. Parachuting into the area on the eve of a British offensive, Operation Crusader, both men and equipment were scattered by a storm. With offensive action rendered impossible the survivors were forced to withdraw, Dave Kershaw later recalling:

> After a couple of days and nights we came to the Makele [Mechili] and Masous [Msus] track, that cut right across our front, and we saw four or five bodies, which was [sic] going completely away from the direction that we were going. I got the glasses on them – I had binoculars with me – and it seemed that they were Sergeant Yeats [CSM Yates, later captured] with Tranfield [Parachutist 'Tubby' Trenfield, later captured], Bolland, Calhoun [Lance-sergeant Colquhoun, later captured], and maybe a couple more. So we whistled and I got my .45 out and fired a few rounds but they took no notice. So we carried on [*The Originals: The Secret History of the Birth of the SAS in Their Own Words*, by Gordon Stevens].

Nothing further was seen of Bolland and with no other detail available he was subsequently presumed to have been killed in action on 20 November 1941.

Son of Mr and Mrs Bolland of Newstead Road, Liverpool – Brother of Vera, Edna and Norman Bolland (a wartime RAF navigator).
Age 21.
Column 54.

Sergeant John CHEYNE [2876138] Gordon Highlanders, No.11 Commando and L Detachment SAS Brigade

'Jock' Cheyne was born on 1 May 1914 in the parish of Auchterless to the north of Aberdeen where he later worked as a farm servant. He enlisted into the Gordon Highlanders in October 1932 and was posted to

the 2nd Battalion's D Company. Serving on Gibraltar from October 1934 he arrived in Malaya in March 1937 and on completing his engagement returned to the UK in May 1939. Posted to the Army Reserve he was subsequently called up that August, mobilised at the outbreak of war that September, and whilst at the regiment's infantry training centre was promoted to corporal. In October 1940 he volunteered for No.11 (Scottish) Commando (soon to be temporarily reorganised into the 2nd Special Service Battalion) and was promoted to sergeant.

On the last day of January 1941 No.11 embarked for the Middle East, arriving at Suez in Egypt at the beginning of March as C Battalion, Layforce. At the end of April, having been stood-to (and dropped from) a raid on Bardia earlier that month, the Commando moved to Cyprus in readiness for OPERATION EXPORTER, the campaign against the Vichy French in Syria. In the early hours of 9 June it subsequently landed close to the mouth of the Litani River in an attempt to seize locations key to the Allied advance, Cheyne taking part in the fighting at Kafr Badda Bridge. He soon took command of B Section, 8 Troop, after his officer, Lieutenant Bill Fraser, who later joined the SAS himself, had been concussed by a round hitting his helmet. Cheyne subsequently swam over the Litani with Sergeant Charlie Nicol, fixing a line so that the remainder of the troop could cross. After Australian troops had arrived from the south to relieve the Commando Fraser commended both men:

> During the whole action, 2873369 Sgt Nicol, Charles, and 2876138 Sgt Cheyne, Jack, behaved with extreme coolness under fire and repeatedly went alone into the woods to search for snipers. In addition, after I had been hit, they carried on with their subsections, and organised the withdrawal across the river, which was completed successfully [WO 218/171].

On returning to Egypt Layforce was disbanded and Cheyne posted to the Commando Depot at Geneifa. He volunteered for L Detachment, SAS Brigade, on 28 August 1941, the day it was officially raised (the unit had been proposed the previous month, some men arriving at its camp at nearby Kabrit prior to August). The following month Cheyne was noted on a nominal roll as being a member of 3 Section, A Group. He was posted missing in action after OPERATION SQUATTER, the Regiment's first raid that aimed to destroy aircraft at Tmimi and Gazala, Libya, on the night of 16–17 November 1941. His fate remains unclear: although Lance-corporal Jimmie Storie found him after they had parachuted into the area and thought that he must have died of the injuries he received during the drop Corporal Bob Tait, DCM, a member of the same stick under Captain David Stirling, noted that they had not been able to locate Cheyne. He is officially recorded as having been killed in action between 16 and 27 November 1941.

Son of George and Helen Cheyne of Todfold, Kemnay, Aberdeenshire – Known to have had two brothers serving in the army.
Age 25.
Column 69.

CORPORAL ANTHONY **DRONGIN** [2695218] SCOTS GUARDS, NO.8 COMMANDO, MILITARY PROVOST STAFF CORPS AND L DETACHMENT SAS BRIGADE

Anthony Drongin, the son of Lithuanian immigrants, was born in Craigneuk, a suburb of Wishaw in north Lanarkshire, on 14 February 1915. Growing up in nearby New Stevenston he was well known locally for his prowess at athletics and swimming. Having worked as an apprentice turner he enlisted into the Scots Guards at Glasgow in June 1935 and was posted to the 2nd Battalion. The following year he was promoted to lance-corporal and having passed a stretcher-bearer's course saw service in Palestine from September 1936 at the tail end of the Arab Revolt. Based at Balaclava Camp in Jerusalem the battalion carried out patrols until the end of the year when it returned to the UK. In November 1937 Drongin was promoted to lance-sergeant and the following year instructed at the regimental depot where he passed his sergeant's exams. Extending his service in March 1939 his character was described as 'exemplary'.

At the outbreak of war Drongin was promoted to sergeant and in June 1940 attended a course at the Small Arms School at Hythe. By that November he was serving as a sergeant in No.8 (Guards) Commando (under the temporary title of the 4th Special Service Battalion), which at the time was training at Largs on the west coast of Scotland. He was promoted to WOII (CSM) that December.

On 31 January 1941 No.8 Commando embarked for the Middle East, arriving at Suez in Egypt at the beginning of March as B Battalion, Layforce. The following month its men were at Mersa Matruh, towards the front line, although with operations drawn up and then cancelled an unsettled period ensued. When Layforce disbanded that July Drongin was nominally posted to the 2nd Battalion, Scots Guards, but was subject to a compulsory transfer to the Military Provost Staff Corps, the body responsible for guarding POW camps and military prisons. Although he reverted to the rank of sergeant he was promoted to acting staff-sergeant two months later and was posted to 307 POW Camp at Fayid, only a few kilometres away from L Detachment at Kabrit. Between January and April 1942 he was briefly re-posted to a camp at Khataba, north-west of Cairo, before rejoining the 2nd Battalion, Scots Guards, early that June with the rank of sergeant.

Drongin volunteered for L Detachment, SAS Brigade, on 22 June 1942, Sir Carol Mather, MC, a former officer of both No.8 Commando and L Detachment, later writing:

> One of my most admirable men, Corporal Drongin, had been a pre-war regular Scots Guardsman. He had also been my troop sergeant in No.8 Commando. Together we had scrambled up the braes of Loch Fine in crisp wintry weather – two years ago it must have been, but it seemed like an age. Drongin, well-built, with the looks of a Norseman, had been promoted to Commando RSM. He was a hard man and hard with others too. Feats of endurance were his speciality. He had travelled in bare feet all the way from Kharga. Although he was a loner he seemed completely selfless, in fact Stirling's 'ideal man'. In order to join Stirling's detachment he willingly reverted to the ranks, but was persuaded to accept the rank of corporal [*When the Grass Stops Growing: A War Memoir*, by Carol Mather].

Mather also noted that Drongin had taken part in the mass Jeep attack on Sidi Haneish airfield on the night of 26–27 July 1942. That September he was wounded in action on the night of the 13–14th when a large SAS column was ambushed on the approaches to Benghazi during OPERATION BIGAMY, Reg Seekings, DCM, MM, later recalling:

> And a chap named Drungeon [*sic*], and another chap, they were in a Jeep. I was talking to him actually when the first bursts of fire hit him. He was knocked off the Jeep. I went down with him, and that's when they thought I'd copped it as well. The armoureds had gone through the roadblock, the fire hit Jim [Almonds, who was captured], turned him over, set his Jeep on fire immediately. I got Drungeon up and it'd gone all through his hips … and Doug Beard had his arm blown to hell. I loaded those two up into the vehicle [IWM Sound Archive 18177].

During the subsequent withdrawal Mather jumped into Captain Bill Cumper's Jeep: 'Corporal Drongin was slumped in the back, shot in the groin. We travelled too fast for the wounded man's comfort I'm afraid, but we had to reach cover before dawn' (*When the Grass Stops Growing*). Seekings continued:

> Then along the side of the road we came across Drungeon. I'd loaded him onto a vehicle and they'd dropped him off [presumably Cumper's crew due to the discomfort the drive was causing him]. I couldn't take him because I knew this vehicle was clapped out. We couldn't take any chances. He was in a bad way, so I took him off the track, covered him up, saw he was alright. He was conscious – he wanted me to shoot him. If he'd have got it [Seekings' sidearm] he would have shot himself. I told him what the situation was, that I couldn't take the risk of taking him, but I would send people back with a good vehicle to pick him up and take him in [IWM Sound Archive 18177].

This was done and, having been treated, Drongin rejoined the main group that had been subjected to intense bombing by enemy aircraft. Due to the amount of transport destroyed, and the need for a speedy withdrawal, it was decided that the stretcher cases would be left behind with two Italian prisoners, one of whom was a medic. 'Johnson', an SAS medical orderly, was also allotted to stay behind having lost the spinning of a coin. The following morning, the 16th, 'Johnson' was to leave the Italian medic with the wounded and drive back into Benghazi with the other prisoner under a white flag in order to fetch help. Captain Malcolm Pleydell, the unit's Medical Officer, later wrote under the nom de plume of 'James' that Lt-Colonel David Stirling, DSO, stayed in the area for several days and reported seeing:

> … an Italian ambulance on its way to our rendezvous to pick up our wounded …
> I have since learned, with deep sorrow, that the British party who were left behind at Benghazi, died later as a result of their wounds. I can understand why Dawson died [Drongin – name changed for publication]; the outlook for Longland was uncertain [Captain Chris Bailey – see his entry above]; Cox, I had expected to recover [Sergeant James Webster – see his entry below]; while the cause of Wilkinson's death must remain a mystery [AQMS Arthur Sque – see his entry below]. Finally Johnson, the medical orderly who accompanied them, also died some eighteen months later, although no reason for this is known [*Born of the Desert*, by Malcolm James].

However, the exact fate of the five men remains unclear, a report in Drongin's file noting that a 'Private Watson' witnessed his burial at 'Sidi Moies (Jebel, Cyrenaica)' on 'about Sept 19th 1942'. Sidi Moies, unmanned by any Italian forces, is near to where the men were left. Indeed a sitrep of 5 October makes note of '1 offr and 4 Ors who may possibly be rescued later' (WO 169/3801). The four wounded are officially recorded as having succumbed to their wounds between 15 and 19 September 1942. 'Johnson' remains a mystery (see his entry under the Unknown Identity section within Volume III).

Son of Anthony and Annie Drongin of Stevenston House, Carfin Street, New Stevenston – Older brother of Vincent who was evacuated from Dunkirk and later demobbed, Alexander and of Francis Zigmund Drongin, MM, a Royal Engineer who died of wounds in Burma during April 1944 whilst attached to HQ 77th Indian Infantry Brigade (Chindits) and who is buried at Taukkyan War Cemetery. His Military Medal was awarded in November 1941 at Tobruk, Libya, for, amongst other acts, bringing in wounded men from no-mans-land after a night raid on enemy positions.
Age 27.
Column 53.

PRIVATE ELIAHU **GOTTLIEB** [PAL/30767] ROYAL ARMY SERVICE CORPS AND SIG (MIDDLE EAST COMMANDO) ATT L DETACHMENT SAS BRIGADE

Eliahu Gottlieb was born in Berlin on 26 November 1922. Although it is unknown exactly when his family migrated to Palestine it was likely to have been during the rise of National Socialism and subsequent persecution of the Jews. Having settled he found work as a garage hand and driver. Although a German national he enlisted into the Royal Army Service Corps in January 1942 at Sarafand, a modern-day suburb of Tel Aviv in Israel. That April, having been recognised for his language skills, he volunteered for the Special Interrogation Group (SIG) and was transferred to the Middle East Commando's Holding Squadron at Geneifa near to Kabrit.

The men of SIG, attached to the Middle East Commando and then L Detachment, SAS Brigade, were recruited and trained by Captain Herbert Buck, MC. Their role was to masquerade as German troops, thereby facilitating attacks on Axis camps (see Buck's own entry under Reading Crematorium, UK, Volume III). Impersonating the enemy, a breach of the Geneva Convention if combat is engaged, obviously entailed increased risk, Ariyeh Shai, a SIG veteran, later recalling: 'Captain Buck had warned that our lives would depend on our ability to wear disguises faultlessly, to learn to perfection the slang prevalent among the soldiers of the Afrika Corps and to drill in accordance with all the German methods' (*The Times*, November 2000). He also recalled how Buck had told them: 'If your true identity is found out, there is no hope for you.' By the summer of 1942 Buck's party consisted of two Germans recruited from POW camps, two Czechs and seven Palestinians, five of the latter having served with No.51 Commando in Abyssinia (WO 201/727).

In early June 1942 Gottlieb, now dressed in German uniform, was escorting a party of 'prisoners' behind enemy lines in Libya. They were, in fact, a group of Free French parachutists also attached to the SAS, tasked with destroying aircraft at Derna aerodrome. With Buck and one section of French having already peeled off to attack Martuba airfield Gottlieb and fellow SIG member, Corporal Petr Haas, successfully ascertained the monthly password from a checkpoint near to their own target. The driver of their truck was Bruckner, one of two German pre-war French Foreign Legionnaires captured at Tobruk the previous November who had allegedly extracted information from fellow Afrikakorps POWs. Advancing very slowly, then stopping, he complained firstly of engine trouble and then of a flat tyre. Claiming that he had lost the universal key to the tool chest he went to fetch a spare from a nearby German post. Minutes later the vehicle was surrounded by the enemy who demanded the party descend with their hands in the air. As they did so a fight ensued and the men scattered. All were later captured bar lieutenant Augustin Jordan, the French commander, who reported seeing the truck explode. He believed Haas 'had seen that he was hopelessly trapped, and while still in the lorry, had flung a grenade into the pile of ammunition in the back.' The interrogation report of Leutnant Friedrich Koener, a Luftwaffe fighter pilot shot down the following month, appears to confirm this:

P/W Koener states that on the night of 12th/13th June he was encamped at Martuba. The Germans have been aware for some time that a group of English saboteurs, who would carry out raids on German aerodromes in Cyrenaica dressed in German uniform, was being organised by an English Colonel.

As a result a state of alarm had been ordered as from sundown on all aerodromes. P/W had heard that on the night of 12th/13th June a German lorry stopped in front of the Aerodrome Command Offices on Derna aerodrome, the driver got out, saluted the CO, and stated that he was a German soldier acting as driver of a German lorry containing a party of heavily armed English troops [*sic*] in German uniform with explosive charges to destroy a/c. The CO was rather suspicious at first, but the driver pressed him to organise as many men as possible with all speed and as heavily armed as possible to disarm the raiding party. The lorry was immediately surrounded and the occupants forced to get out. A few seconds later after the last one had got out [?] there was an explosion inside the lorry and it was completely destroyed. A melee developed and it was believed that all the raiders had been shot. However, on the following morning a wounded man presented himself at Derna hospital saying he was a wounded German soldier needing treatment. For some reason the doctor became suspicious and on examination it turned out that he was not a German soldier but a Jew from Palestine [presumably Gottlieb].

The driver [Bruckner] is said to have been awarded the German Cross in silver.

[Another] P/W, who was encamped at Derna on the night of 12th/13th June, stated that a warning was issued in advance that a British raiding party would appear to carry out sabotage on the aerodrome that night. The party would consist of British troops in German uniform, driving in a German truck [WO 201/727].

Having been captured and his identity discovered Gottlieb was either tried and executed as a German national, or murdered without trial, his date of death being officially recorded as 13 June 1942.

Son of Mr and Mrs Norbert Gottlieb of Jerusalem.

Age 19.

Column 80.

Lieutenant The Hon. Robert Brampton **GURDON** [99183] Coldstream Guards and LRDG (G.2 Patrol, B Sqn)

Known as 'Robin' to his friends, Gurdon was born on 21 June 1904 in London, growing up at the family home, Grundisburgh Hall near Woodbridge in Suffolk. Having been educated at Eton and Magdalene College, Cambridge, he worked as a bill broker and banker, marrying popular society girl The Hon. Daisy Yoskyl Consuelo Pearson in the Church of St Margaret, Westminster Abbey, in January 1932. Granted an emergency commission in the Coldstream Guards at the outbreak of war he joined the 3rd Battalion in August 1940 and disembarked in Egypt the following month to serve as a platoon commander in No.2 Company. That December the battalion took part in Operation Compass, helping to push the Italians back into Libya before being withdrawn to the Nile Delta. Here it joined the 2nd Battalion, Scots Guards, in forming the 22nd Guards Brigade. Gurdon was promoted to lieutenant in March 1941, his motorised battalion being moved back into the line the following month to carry out joint patrols with the 4th South African Armoured Car Regiment on the escarpment between Halfaya Pass and the Libyan border. Having advanced during Operation Crusader that November it settled down to patrolling the area of Agedabia before taking up positions on the new front line at Mersa Brega. On 6 January 1942 the Coldstream broke through to Agheila but had outrun their supply line. When Rommel counterattacked the battalion, impotent against armour, had no option but to carry out a fighting withdrawal. Overtaken by Axis troops by day, and breaking out by night, it finally linked with the remainder of the brigade and concentrated south of Gazala.

On 26 February 1942 Gurdon volunteered for the Long Range Desert Group whilst it was refitting in Cairo. That May he commanded G.2 Patrol when it provided transport for Captain David Stirling's raid into Benghazi harbour. Earlier in the month he had led the patrol during Operation Humourist, an intelligence-gathering mission south-east of Benghazi: dropping Captain Bob Mélot and Lieutenant Segal, firstly in the area of the Wadi el-Gattara, then a little way north of the Wadi Ftilia, he arranged for a patrol of the Indian Long Range Squadron to pick them up a month later (WO 201/813 – see Mélot's entry under Brussels War Cemetery, Belgium, Volume III). In June his patrol provided a taxi service from Siwa, enabling groups from L Detachment, SAS Brigade, to attack the Benina and Berka aerodromes. Whilst the SAS attacks went in Gurdon mined the Benghazi–Barce railway with 50lb of ammonal before recovering the raiders.

G.2 met a combined force of LRDG and L Detachment at Qaret Tartura on the northern edge of the Great Sand Sea on 6 July 1942, their objective being to destroy enemy aircraft as prelude to a forthcoming British offensive. Having moved north Gurdon's patrol dropped off an SAS party on the night of the 7–8th for what was to be an abortive attack on one of the three Fuka landing grounds, G.2 destroying between thirty and forty vehicles at a staging post before it picked up the raiders. The following day the combined force moved west to Bir el Quseir, although the landing grounds in the area of Fuka remained the principal targets on which further attacks were made on the night of the 11–12th. Major David Stirling, DSO, then received a message stating that the aerodromes at el Daba should be attacked. On the 12th G.2, less two trucks, therefore escorted two Free French SAS parties towards the area, its vehicles being spotted by enemy aircraft during the early evening. The LRDG War Diary contains Sergeant John Stocker's subsequent report:

> The position and view was checked with the map. The party were 17 miles short of their next objective and approximately 15 miles from the nearest LG [landing ground - the location is variously described as 'in the neighbourhood of Minqar Sida (787267)' and 'near dunes 10km east of Gallal 10km south of coast at 1700hrs']. At this moment (1715 hours), three [Italian] aircraft, subsequently identified as Macchis, were seen approaching, about 1½ miles to the west.
>
> The patrol leader endeavoured to avoid action by waving, but, following closer inspection, one plane cleared its guns overhead of G.7 and G.8. Firing broke out from the rear trucks, and under this cover an effort was made to move G.7 and G.8 from their open positions. Unfortunately, G.7, which had caused trouble in the morning, would not start, and Lieut Gurdon ordered his gunner and driver to abandon the vehicle temporarily, and he came on to G.8, the navigator sitting behind him on the spare wheel, the vehicle being driven in eccentric swings between the planes towards the broken ground to the south. One Macchi was now placed in good position for attack, firing all its guns from about 20 feet high and 20 feet away at the front seats. The burst first caused the navigator to fall off, being hit very lightly, and he ran to a bush, from where he saw Lieut Gurdon fall off and run to another bush, and hold his stomach. The vehicle then stopped, after 20 yards, and continued to burn steadily …
>
> The navigator [of G.7], Sgt Stocker, went over at the same time and saw Lieut Gurdon had been badly hit, and found Gdsm Murray with a serious wound in his arm. He then directed Cpl Wilson to Lieut Gurdon, with Morphia from G.7 – the patrol's medical kit being burnt on G.8, and also directed the Free French, who had then arrived, to Gdsm Murray. The French removed Murray and withdrew to cover, and shortly after, while Cpl Wilson was still with Lieut Gurdon, the planes returned, and the driver took the vehicles away. The planes searched the south side of the hill, but did not see anything in the failing light, and finally passed over Lieut Gurdon and Cpl Wilson without seeing them, on their final departure.
>
> The navigator, Sgt Stocker, then proceeded over the hill, directed Gdsm Vaughan to assist Cpl Wilson with Lieut Gurdon, and conferred with the French officers upon his position. They wanted advice on whether to proceed, and it was eventually decided to completely fix up the wounded and check up all personnel, and, if possible, obtain Lieut Gurdon's opinion [this was to carry on with the operation regardless] …
>
> Lieut Gurdon had died at 1200 hours [the next day, 13 July 1942]. It was then decided to leave the cooking truck with the party, and, proceeding on G.12 (the Breda truck) contact was made with the main party and the doctor attached to the parachutists brought to Gdsm Murray about 1300 hours. Lieut Gurdon was buried here – map reference 702268 [Spencer Seadon, a former guardsman of G.2 Patrol, later recalled that they buried Gurdon within his sleeping bag in a shallow grave carved out of very rocky ground, IWM Sound Archive 19044]. Cpl Wilson and Gdsm Vaughan looked after Lieut Gurdon throughout; he was entirely lucid, and understood the actions taken by the party. This NCO reported the extent of the injuries to the MO, which were caused by two cannon shell over the abdomen, and one in the right lung. The MO stated on this evidence that it would not have been possible to have saved Lieut Gurdon's life without an operation the previous evening [WO 218/91].

At the time of his death Gurdon was due to transfer to, and become Second-in-Command of, L Detachment, SAS Brigade (IWM Sound Archive 13039 – Lord Jellicoe, KBE, DSO, MC, a former fellow officer of the 3rd Battalion, Coldstream Guards, and of L Detachment). Alistair Timpson, a fellow LRDG officer, later wrote:

> Robin's manner of authority and humour was of the kind that made anyone do what he wanted … practically all situations were natural to him, though he injected a good deal of his own preferences into what he did and whom he did it with. He hated the war, but he was determined to take an active and effective part in trying to win it. When most of his contemporaries, 38-years-old or more, were seeking ways of making warfare not too dangerous or

arduous, he had different ideas. Like his father who had fought with distinction in the first war and had to neglect for a long time his farm in Kenya, Robin surrendered his directorships in the City and of Imperial Airways and became a platoon commander in the desert.

I have often considered how Robin would have taken such changes as we have had since 1945, had he survived. He represented all that was best in the English way of life, with its fairness, good manners and good humour. His patrol thought the world of him and when they disobeyed his last command they could scarcely do otherwise [*In Rommel's Backyard*, by Alistair Timpson].

Only son of The Lord Cranworth (Bertram Francis Gurdon, KG, MC, 2nd Baron Cranworth) and of Lady Cranworth, CBE, of Grundisburgh, Suffolk – Husband of The Hon. Daisy Yoskyl Consuelo Gurdon of Cotswold Park, Gloucestershire – Father of Jeryl, Charles and Philip (Charles was tragically killed, aged 9, in an accident at his prep school in 1945) – Older brother of Camilla and Judith Gurdon.
Age 38.
Column 51. Also commemorated, alongside his son, within St Mary's Church at Grundisburgh.

CORPORAL PETR **HAAS** [PAL/15500] THE BUFFS AND SIG (MIDDLE EAST COMMANDO) ATT L DETACHMENT SAS BRIGADE

Petr Haas was born on 28 March 1920 to Austrian Jews living in Brno as naturalised Czechoslovaks. Although it is not known when he emigrated to Palestine, he enlisted into The Buffs (Royal East Kent Regiment) on 11 November 1940 at Sarafand, a modern-day suburb of Tel Aviv in Israel, stating that he had previously been a student and driver. After training he was posted to No.6 Palestinian Company, one of a number of Jewish and Arab companies that would later form the basis for the Palestine Regiment. In August 1941 he was promoted to lance-corporal, then corporal, and on 24 April 1942 volunteered for the Special Interrogation Group. Moving from Palestine to Egypt that day his service record merely notes that he had transferred to the Middle East Commando's Holding Squadron.

Haas was posted missing in action, later presumed killed in action, as of 13 June 1942, the day his party attempted to attack Derna airfield (see Private Eliahu Gottlieb's entry within this section for full details, including the suggestion that Haas committed suicide rather than be captured).

Son of Wilhelm Haas of Lidická, Brno, and Dr Gerta Ungar of Hes Strasse, Tel Aviv.
Age 22.
Column 87.

LANCE-CORPORAL SIDNEY JAMES **HILDRETH** [3657806] SOUTH LANCASHIRE REGIMENT, NO.7 COMMANDO AND L DETACHMENT SAS BRIGADE

Sidney Hildreth was born on 24 October 1916 in the parish of St Johns, North Shields, and grew up a short distance away at Percy Main where he later worked as a coach painter. He enlisted into the 1/4th South Lancashire Regiment (Prince of Wales Volunteers) in April 1940, volunteering for No.7 Commando at Girvan that July. Later that year this was temporarily restructured as part of 3rd Special Service Battalion but arrived at Suez, Egypt, in early March 1941 as A Battalion, Layforce. The Commando subsequently carried out a largely abortive raid on Bardia along the Libyan coast on the night of 19–20 April, the majority of the targets having been incorrectly identified by intelligence. On their return the men were held aboard HMS *Glengyle* until the beginning of May when they were finally allowed ashore, much disgruntled, at Alexandria.

Later that month A and D Battalions disembarked at Suda Bay on the north coast of Crete to help evacuate Commonwealth troops after the German invasion. They joined the 5th New Zealand Brigade and the 7th and 8th Australian Battalions in a strong rear-guard action, fighting a running battle that enabled other survivors to make their way to the embarkation point at Sphakia on the south coast. Hildreth was one of the lucky few to be taken off to Egypt, the majority of his comrades going into captivity. When Layforce disbanded that summer he was subsequently posted to the Middle East Commando Depot at Geneifa near to Kabrit.

Hildreth volunteered for the newly-formed L Detachment, SAS Brigade, on 30 August 1941, two days after it was officially raised, a nominal roll of the following month recording that he was a member of 2 Section, E Group. He was fatally injured parachuting into the SAS' first raid, OPERATION SQUATTER, an abortive attack on airfields at Tmimi and Gazala in Libya. Trooper Roy Davies saw him die of his wounds on 19 November 1941 (see Davies' own entry under Hanover War Cemetery, Germany, Volume III). Records note that the pair had been on the fourth aircraft under Lieutenant Eoin McGonigal (see his own entry below).

Son of James and Florence Hildreth (née Coe) of Woller Avenue, West Chirton, North Shields. Age 25.
Column 63.

GUARDSMAN ALBERT **HOPTON** [2657737] COLDSTREAM GUARDS AND LRDG (H PATROL)

'Hoppy' Hopton, as he was known to his comrades, was born on 12 March 1918 at the inland port of Goole in East Yorkshire. Having worked as a driver he enlisted into the Coldstream Guards in Sheffield in February 1937 and was posted to the 3rd Battalion. He subsequently served first at home and then in pre-war Egypt from November 1937, in Palestine during the Arab Revolt from October 1938 and back in Egypt with HQ Company from April 1939. He was therefore a contemporary of Guardsman 'Beppo' Matthews (see his entry within this section), the pair volunteering for the newly-expanded Long Range Desert Group on the same day, 6 December 1940. Arriving at the Citadel in Cairo they and other volunteers from both the 3rd Battalion, Coldstream Guards, and the 2nd Battalion, Scots Guards, were formed into G Patrol that inherited the vehicles and equipment of the former W Patrol.

At the end of the month, after a brief period of training, the Guards joined the more experienced New Zealand T Patrol to attack Murzuk Fort in Central Libya: on 11 January 1941, having picked up Free French troops at Kayugi in Chad, the combined party closed on both the fort, that resisted heavily, and the adjacent Italian airfield at which aircraft and a hanger were destroyed. It then withdrew, briefly stopping after a few kilometres to bury two casualties, Sergeant 'Squib' Hewson and the French commander, Lt-Colonel Jean Colonna d'Ornano (see Hewson's entry under Tripoli War Cemetery, Libya, within this volume). On the 12th the patrols forced the surrender of Traghen and its Carabinieri outpost before going on to attack two further such positions at Um el-Araneb and Gatrun. They then intended capturing the oasis of Kufra en route to Cairo. However, having been spotted by enemy aircraft they were forced into the cover of Jebel Sherif late in the morning of the 31st. Early that afternoon they were attacked by the Compagnia Sahariana, their Italian equivalent, losing trucks and Corporal Rex Beech killed in action (see his entry under Knightsbridge War Cemetery, Libya). When Italian aircraft joined the fight the patrols withdrew, three men being captured (see Lance-corporal Clarrie Roderick's entry under Bolseno War Cemetery, Italy, Volume II, for details). The attack on Kufra was subsequently cancelled, T and G eventually returning to Cairo on 9 February.

At the beginning of June 1941 Hopton was posted to H Patrol, a temporary composite of G and Y Patrols under Lieutenant Jake Easonsmith (see his entry under Leros War Cemetery, Greece, Volume II). Using Siwa Oasis as a forward operating base H set off on the 10th and the following day dropped two Arab agents to gather information on the enemy airfield at Gambut. That night, having made a recce of the area's main tracks, the patrol took two prisoners and destroyed twelve vehicles before returning to Siwa on the 13th. The following day it went out once more, acting on intelligence to pick up Pilot Officer Pompey, a Frenchman hiding at Bir Bidihi, on the 15th before returning to Siwa (WO 201/809).

On the 19th the patrol drove behind enemy lines again, this time dropping off a British officer and two Senussi agents in the Jebel Ahkdar on the 22nd. They then began a recce of the Mechili area, circling the town to check for traffic. Early on the 24th, having completed their circuit, they stopped amongst abandoned British vehicles approximately 48 kilometres north of Mechili. Easonsmith's report takes up the narrative:

> About 0800hrs sun-time took my truck over to examine Bedford 30cwt abandoned in good condition (Helmet and Plumes? Armd Div). Stopped 20yds away my crew went to left of truck and I to the right. About to look in cab when there was an explosion. Found Gdsm Hopton badly mutilated, he died within a few minutes and Tpr Wise wounded in the foot. Wise informed me that Hopton picked something up and then opened the door of the cab of the Bedford. The explosion was instantaneous upon the latter action. I could see no thermos bombs but found two tops some ¼ mile away. The Bedford caught fire immediately, my own truck had two punctures. Hopton was buried (Map Ref T9275 Bengasi 1/500,000 Map) and a rough wooden cross erected. The grave is to the east and within a few yards of another unnamed one. I then hurried away as black smoke from the Bedford was advertising our posn [WO 218/94].

Hopton's grave was visited the following month by S Patrol. Presumably it could not be located at a later date. He is officially recorded as having been killed in action on 27 June 1941. 'Lofty' Carr of the same patrol noted; 'poor chap paid with his life for breaking the rule "never open an abandoned vehicle"' (personal correspondence, 2015).

Son of Bertram Hopton and May Patch of Montague Street, Goole, Yorkshire.
Age 24.
Column 54. Also commemorated on Goole's war memorial.

PRIVATE DOUGLAS **KEITH** [2882330] GORDON HIGHLANDERS, NO.11 COMMANDO AND L DETACHMENT SAS BRIGADE

Douglas Keith was born on 8 December 1921 in the small village of Auchenblae near Laurencekirk, Kincardineshire. Whilst working as an apprentice joiner he joined the local 5/7th Battalion, Gordon Highlanders (TA), in May 1939 and was called up late that August before being embodied at the outbreak of war. The following August he volunteered for No.11 (Scottish) Commando, this being temporarily reorganised as part of the 2nd Special Service Battalion soon after. It embarked for the Middle East on 31 January 1941, subsequently arriving at Suez, Egypt, at the beginning of March 1941 as C Battalion, Layforce. Stood-to, then stood-down from, a raid on Bardia in mid April No.11 moved to Cyprus at the end of the month in readiness for OPERATION EXPORTER, the campaign in Syria against the Vichy French. In the early hours of 9 June it subsequently landed close to the mouth of the Litani River in an attempt to seize bridges key to the Allied advance. Although these were destroyed by the French and the Commando suffered heavy casualties, it effectively tied down Vichy troops until Australian forces arrived from the south.

On returning to Egypt Layforce was disbanded and Keith posted to the Commando Depot at Geneifa. He volunteered for L Detachment, SAS Brigade, on 28 August 1941, the day it was officially raised (the unit had been proposed the previous month, some men arriving at its camp at nearby Kabrit prior to August). Keith appears as a member of 1 Section, B Group, on a nominal roll dated four days later. When writing the history of L Detachment in 1943 Brigadier 'Kid' Cator, MC, recorded the unit's rigorous training regime: 'Average training 9–10 hours daily plus night schemes – very primitive equipment locally constructed and no qualified instructors available. During training Pte Keith walked 40 miles across the desert in stockinged feet with 75lb load rather than fall out after boots gave way' (WO 201/785).

Keith is often recorded as having died of wounds during or after OPERATION SQUATTER, the SAS' first raid that targeted airfields at Tmimi and Gazala in Libya during November 1941. However, Dave Kershaw, MM, later recalled that, after jumping into the operation and being blown across the desert:

We had a discussion of what to do and then we started whistling and cat-calling and eventually we found Keith. He had hurt himself and we decided to leave Arnold with him … [Kershaw's group attempted to continue with the raid but realised it was pointless without its arms from which it was separated during the drop]. So we laid up and sat up smoking, no sleeping or anything like that, until dawn broke the next day when Paddy [Lieutenant Blair Mayne] decided to withdraw to the rendezvous. So we started hiking back. Unfortunately, we missed Keith and Arnold. I don't know what happened – either we misjudged the distance or … it could have been my mistake, but I doubt it. They could have decided to wander off. And even now I still don't know what happened to them. Don't know whether they were taken prisoner [IWM Sound Archive 18173].

Doug Arnold, a lance-corporal at the time of SQUATTER, later clarified events:

It was decided that they would have to leave me behind with another fellow [Keith] who was also rather badly injured and that they would go in and try to do their best. And I thought there was a good chance that I would be able to walk with this other fellow due south into the desert to where the Long Range Desert Group was likely to be, waiting for us to pick us up. The others went in. They had no success really.

And the remainder of my stick having failed in their attack, turned south to look for the LRDG, walked past us in the dark unfortunately and the following morning I saw somebody on the skyline, hoped it might be the LRDG, waved my hands towards him and ran toward him but unfortunately it was an Italian gentleman, an Italian soldier, out for an early morning stroll from his camp which was just over the sand dunes and he came racing towards me waving his gun and I hadn't got a gun of course, and he was waving his gun and I sat down promptly so did my colleague and he wasn't sure what we were but he knew that he had to keep pointing his rifle at us and people who say that the Italians were not good soldiers and that they were scared stiff etc well, they hadn't met this gentleman.

He took us both back to his little camp and it turned out that they were kind of pioneers and that they were doing a road back there and they were grade three troops but they'd taken me prisoner, you know.

I'd given all this stuff [weapons and explosives] to those that were going on. It was more use to them. All I'd kept were my emergency rations and my water bottle so I didn't think it was worth having a fight with this gentleman with a very, very long rifle out in the desert. He took us back to his camp and they treated us with great amusement. Once they found out that we were British we said we were engineers and that we'd fallen off the back of a truck. That was a carry on, and luckily they were so far behind the lines that they should have known that this was a blatant untruth but when we said that we'd fallen off the back of a truck and that like them we were building roads they thought: 'By crikey, we shouldn't really be here'. So they packed up and took us back to their lines and handed us over to people who fortunately didn't realise what they had in their possession. If they'd known that they had a couple of SAS fellas … but no they didn't. We told them that we were engineers, that we'd been taken out into the desert to do some recce work, that we'd fallen off a truck, that the truck had driven off into the distance and had left us there and that we were very, very sorry to be of trouble to them, and if they cared to send us back they could do, you know. But they treated us very, very kindly [IWM Sound Archive 17286].

Keith was initially reported as missing as of the night of OPERATION SQUATTER, 16–17 November 1941, his next of kin being informed as such that December. However, although there is no further reference to Keith in Arnold's report, it is now known that he was also put on transport for Italy: Private Allkin, Royal Army Medical Corps, stated that Keith was aboard the SS *Sebastiano Venier*, also known as the *Jason* or *Jantzen*, which left Benghazi on the night of 8 December 1941. She set a direct course across the Mediterranean towards the Greek coast from where she intended to reach the Italian mainland. The following afternoon she was attacked by the British submarine, HMS *Porpoise*, her captain unaware that 2,000 Commonwealth POWs were battened down in his target's five holds:

At the time that I knew Pte D Keith he was in the Paratroops after the No.11 Commandos were disbanded at Alexandria in Oct 1941.

1.   Pte Keith told me that he was in that particular hold for'ard and was making his way there as I left him.

2.   Yes, there were survivors from that hold for Pte Keith was seen on a raft with some English sailors and Italians after the ship had been torpedoed. I also saw New Zealand, African troops etc from the same hold.

3.   Dis-embarkation was not orderly, for nearly everyone was in a panic until assurance was given by a German officer that the ship would not sink. In my opinion there was a possible chance of escaping by personnel on the raft [WO 361/133].

After the Italian captain and crew had immediately abandoned ship the German bosun took control. Seeing that there was a possibility that the holed vessel would not sink he steered her towards land, running the ship aground at Kastelli Methoni on the Peloponnese. He then organised the landing of prisoners during a severe storm. Unfortunately, some were lost in the heavy sea adding to those initially killed in the explosion and those that were thrown into the water to drown later.

Information was eventually received from the Italians confirming that Keith had been captured, his family being informed accordingly in May 1942. That September the Infantry Record Office wrote to his father: 'I deeply regret to inform you that your son, the above named soldier, previously reported a Prisoner of War, has now been reported by Italian Authorities as missing, following the sinking of the enemy vessel in which he was travelling.'

Foster son of Mr and Mrs Charles Keith of Myreside, Auchenblae, Fordoun, Kincardineshire.

Age 22.

Column 70. Also commemorated on Fordoun parish war memorial on top of Gilbert's Hill at Auchenblae.

TROOPER STANLEY VINCENT **KENDALL** [557709] WARWICKSHIRE YEOMANRY, L DETACHMENT SAS BRIGADE AND 1ST SAS (A SQN)

'Darkie' or Stan Kendall, as he was known to his comrades, was born on 18 April 1920 at Stoke in Coventry. His father owned a local garage close to where he attended Stoke School. In January 1938, whilst working as a dyce sinker at Smith Stamping Works Ltd, he joined the Warwickshire Yeomanry (TA Corps of Hussars). However, when called up at the outbreak of war he was deemed 'unfit for embodiment and sent home.' Although the reason for this is not specified he was re-examined three months later and found suitable, subsequently embarking for Palestine in late December 1939. The Warwicks were posted to Iraq in 1941 and Jim Smith, a one-time member of the regiment and also of L Detachment, SAS Brigade, recalled that Kendall had been involved in a sabre charge in Syria, more than likely whilst fighting the Vichy French that July. What is certain is that when the unit was mechanised late that year, and therefore reorganised as part of the Royal Armoured Corps, Kendall was serving with C Squadron.

It seems likely that Kendall volunteered for L Detachment during June 1942, Smith recalling that his friend took part in that September's OPERATION BIGAMY, the large-scale raid on Benghazi. In October, with the SAS having been granted regimental status, Kendall was a member of Captain Bill Fraser's A Squadron party that destroyed a section of railway behind the lines east of Fuka before returning to Kufra later that month.

Fraser took the same group out again, Major Paddy Mayne, DSO, signalling Lt-Colonel David Stirling, DSO: 'Fraser intends to blow road tonight 29/30 [October 1942] on escarpment between minefield north of Charing Cross. If there is traffic on road he hopes to strafe it until one hour before dawn.' This was followed by a second message on 2 November: 'Fraser returned. He lost one Jeep and Kendall was killed by fire from a road block at Charing Cross. Matruh perimeter apparently defended. He was unable to get through' (WO 201/767). Ginger Adamson, former L Detachment, later recalled that this was 'near Oxford Circus' and that Kendall was 'presumed buried by enemy'. Meanwhile, a further report states the 'heavily armed road block' was located 'at [the] north end of Siwa-Mersa track'. Kendall's date of death is officially recorded as 30 October 1942.

Youngest son of Edwin and Lizzie Kendall (née Crofts) of Ansty Road, Wyken, Coventry.
Age 22.
Column 30.

Lieutenant Douglas Stewart **KENNEDY** [106690] Royal Artillery
and 1st SAS (A Sqn)

Douglas Kennedy was born on 3 March 1920 at Calcutta in India to a Scottish bank manager and New Zealand mother. From September 1933 until July 1938 he attended Loretto School in Musselburgh near Edinburgh where he was a prefect, captain of boxing and fencing, and held the rank of sergeant in the OTC. Having applied to join the army he entered the Royal Military Academy, Woolwich, in January 1939. Posted to the Army Reserve he enlisted into the ranks of the Royal Artillery at the outbreak of war that September (service number 1479319). Eight days later he was posted to 132 OCTU from where he was commissioned into the 57th Light Anti-Aircraft Regiment (*London Gazette* 07/11/39). His final report notes: 'Very sound and intelligent with plenty of self confidence and common sense and ability to organise.' Having been attached to 405 Company, 52nd Searchlight Regiment, he was posted to the 220th Searchlight Training Regiment at Yeovil later that year. In May 1940 he unsuccessfully applied to join the short-lived 5th (Special Reserve) Battalion, Scots Guards.

Having disembarked in Egypt in late April 1941 Kennedy was attached to the 4th Indian Division and served in the Syrian Campaign and then the Western Desert. At some point during the autumn of 1942, after postings to the 169th Battery (8th Battalion, Gordon Highlanders) Light Anti-Aircraft, and to the 100th Light Anti-Aircraft/Anti-Tank Regiment, he volunteered for either L Detachment, SAS Brigade, or its successor, 1st SAS.

After Operation Bigamy, the large-scale raid on Benghazi during September 1942 L Detachment had returned to Kabrit. Here it was granted regimental status, the newly-formed A Squadron, including Kennedy, setting out on 7 October for Kufra. Arriving on the 13th it split into two, both parties making their way to the northern edge of the Great Sand Sea where they established a forward operating base. By the 22nd, with ammo and fuel dumps in place over a wide area, raiding parties were ready to attack enemy road and rail traffic. An anonymous application for Operational Wings records that during this period Kennedy led a group that 'blew up petrol found at Sidi Barrani. Strafed road block.' Setting out again on 3 November Kennedy commanded a party that carried out a short patrol before returning on the 5th having delivered a Jeep to Lieutenant MacDonald and stripped another whose engine had seized.

The following day Kennedy set off once more to strafe petrol points near Sidi Barrani. On the afternoon of 8 November his four-Jeep patrol arrived at the eastern side of the Sollum escarpment and at dusk moved north towards the target area. As they approached they were detected, the enemy repeatedly sending up flares. However, the patrol carried on to the Buq Buq-Sidi Barrani road turning east towards the latter until they came across a check point. Having been fired upon the party became stuck in a rocky wadi on its withdrawal, the sump of one Jeep being smashed on a boulder and engine oil rapidly draining away. Forced to wait until dawn before finding a way out two enemy armoured cars followed their tracks and their damaged vehicle had to be stripped and blown up when constant re-oiling became impractical. The patrol arrived at the RV without further loss that evening.

On Friday 13 November 1942 Kennedy led a three-Jeep patrol, consisting of 'Sgt Sharman, O'Reilly, Briar, Wall, Cpl McDiarmid, Tillyer', to retrieve a Jeep from the Sand Sea and to carry out operations in the area of Martuba. On the 20th the patrol was returning to the main party when Kennedy's vehicle drove over a mine. He was killed instantly, Corporal Allan Sharman and Gunner Thomas Wall later dying of wounds (see their entries under Knightsbridge War Cemetery, Libya, within this volume). Loretto School's Roll of Honour notes that Kennedy:

… was on his return from the completion of a very difficult operation when the Jeep in which he was travelling ran over a mine, and he and the two other occupants of the car were killed.

'He showed himself to be an officer of very fine qualities, not the least of which was his great courage in action.

His behaviour in the face of the enemy always showed a complete disregard for his personal safety' [*Loretto School Roll of Honour 1939–1945*].

Only son of the late Cecil and Elsie Kennedy of Townhead, Glencairn, Moniaive, Dumfriesshire – The CWGC records his parents' address as Nelson, New Zealand.
Age 22.
Column 41. Also commemorated on the Moniaive 1939–45 war memorial plaque within the village Remembrance Hall.

WARRANT OFFICER CLASS II DAVID **LAMBIE** [2696787] SCOTS GUARDS, L DETACHMENT SAS BRIGADE AND 1ST SAS (B SQN)

Dave Lambie was born in Glasgow on 3 June 1915 attending Lady Jane Hamilton School in Ayr. As a keen body-builder he alternated between running the Health and Strength Club in Newton-on-Ayr and working as a labourer before enlisting into the Scots Guards in October 1939. Having passed through their depot at Chelsea Barracks he was posted to the Holding Battalion at the Tower of London in January 1940. That month, having heard that her son was coming home on leave, Lambie's mother went out to buy groceries and was killed in a road accident. Re-posted to the 2nd Battalion he appears to have been en route for Egypt late in April 1940 before his vessel returned to the UK for an unknown reason in late May.

Lambie embarked for the Middle East a second time in August 1940, joining his battalion in Cairo where it remained until moving to the Canal Zone for air defence duties the following January. As of March 1941 it came under the newly-formed 22nd Guards Brigade and training in the area of Kabrit commenced. Almost immediately the Afrikakorps launched its first offensive and the brigade was moved into the line just to the west of Sidi Barrani. It was here that the battalion suffered its first casualty, Lieutenant Hugh Stirling, brother of David. From June Lambie served with Brigade HQ although he returned to the 2nd Battalion at Daba in time for November's offensive, OPERATION CRUSADER. The battalion was either in action or at the front line until April 1942 when it was granted three weeks' rest at Buq Buq. Lambie subsequently volunteered for L Detachment, SAS Brigade, on 3 May 1942 and was promoted to corporal the following month.

After a month's training at Kabrit a large SAS party, including Lambie, drove behind enemy lines to mount raids from a temporary base at Querat Hiremas on the northern edge of the Great Sand Sea. One such action, a mass Jeep attack on Sidi Haneish airfield on the night of 26–27 July, resulted in the destruction of an estimated twenty-five aircraft as well as enemy aircrew. On the return journey Lambie's party, led by Captain Lord George Jellicoe, was strafed by three German fighters at the cost of two Jeeps. The men returned with great difficulty in the remaining, badly damaged vehicle.

In September 1942 Lambie took part in OPERATION BIGAMY, the large-scale raid on Benghazi. Having returned to Egypt he was promoted to WOII (CSM) on the 21st, the day that the SAS was granted regimental status, although he was content to serve within the Regiment as a corporal. He and Lance-sergeant Reg Seekings were loaned to the newly-formed B Squadron that November for operations along the Libyan coastal road between Buerat, Misurata and Homs. Leaving Kabrit the squadron reached the road close to an enemy convoy parked up for the night. They attacked under the guidance of Seekings, destroying trucks and supplies before making further use of the opportunity: 'I took Dave Lambie and three or four others and quickly destroyed four or five telephone poles, also laid a few anti-personnel mines around', recalled Seekings. The squadron commander, Major Vivian Street, MC, then moved off to a separate operating area taking Lambie with his party. Although both men were subsequently reported as missing, then prisoner of war, as of 30 December 1942, Street was rescued after a Royal Navy destroyer depth-charged the submarine on which he was being transported to Italy. Returning to the Regiment he reported that he and Lambie had been held together, later breaking unwanted news to Lambie's father:

> You will, I expect, have heard that your son died in prison. We heard this from another prisoner who was with him and wrote to one of our people. It is very sad news indeed, and a terrible blow to you. I hope you will let me offer you my deepest sympathy.
>
> He was a very fine chap, and liked by officers and men. We are all very upset that he is gone.
>
> Although we have no news of how he died, I imagine he had a go at escaping and was wounded, because as I wrote and told you, he was perfectly fit on January 13 [1943] when I saw him last, but he was always discussing with me the chances of escaping and I know that he pledged to get away. He was just like that. Nothing would get him down and he was determined to get away and have another go at the Germans.
>
> If I hear any more news I will let you know. But in the meantime we all offer our condolence. We shall miss him very much.

During October 1943 the War Office wrote to the Scots Guards clarifying events:

> A further report which seems to confirm that this Warrant Officer has died has reached the department. This report by a prisoner of war states:- 'We had the misfortune to be torpedoed on the way across and it is with deep regret that I have to tell you that Company sergeant-major Lambie went down with the ship.'

In February 1944 his fate was finally confirmed to his family:

> CSM D Lambie was taken prisoner on 12.12.42, and was being transferred to another Prisoner of War Camp when the ship on which he was travelling was torpedoed in the Mediterranean on 18.1.43. Therefore CSM D Lambie must be recorded as 'Killed in Action at Sea whilst Prisoner of War'. This information has since been confirmed by the German authorities [through Official Totenliste No.136].

Although Lambie's date of death is officially recorded as 18 January 1943 the most likely ship on which he was being transported appears to be the Italian destroyer RM *Bombardiere*. She was sunk by HM Submarine *United* on the evening of the 17th when 20 nautical miles north-west of Isola Marettimo off the west coast of Sicily.

Son of James and Elizabeth 'Lily' Lambie of Wallace Street, Ayr – Younger brother of Daniel Lambie – Older brother of Thomas (who later served in the Royal Navy), and of Elizabeth Lambie.
Age 27.
Column 53. Also commemorated on Ayr's war memorial and his parents' gravestone.

LIEUTENANT JOHN STEEL LEWES [65419] GENERAL LIST, RIFLE BRIGADE, WELSH GUARDS, NO.8 COMMANDO AND L DETACHMENT SAS BRIGADE

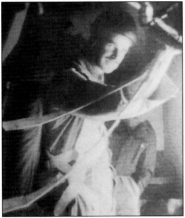

'Jock' Lewes was born on 21 December 1913 in Calcutta where his father was working as a chartered accountant. He was, however, brought up in Australia, his mother being from Sydney, and was educated at King's School, Parramatta, New South Wales. Going up to Christ Church, Oxford, he read Politics, Philosophy and Economics, was an active member of the OTC, and trained and led the 1937 boat crew to victory against Cambridge. Having been commissioned onto the General List (TA) in July 1935 he was attached to the 3rd King's Own Hussars, although he relinquished his commission in late 1938 with the intention of returning to Australia overland. However, in the run up to hostilities he was offered a job at the British Council that gave him new purpose: 'I have great faith in Britain. I swear I shall not live to see the day when Britain hauls down the colours of her beliefs before totalitarian aggression' (*Jock Lewes: Co-Founder of the SAS*, by John Lewes).

At the outbreak of war Lewes was embodied into the 1st Battalion, Tower Hamlet Rifles, Rifle Brigade (TA), as an ensign (*London Gazette* 16/09/39), before receiving an emergency commission in the Welsh Guards the following month. Having been posted to the Training Battalion he was noted as an excellent instructor and volunteered for No.8 (Guards) Commando at the beginning of August 1940. After being temporarily reorganised as the 4th Special Service Battalion, and after Lewes had undertaken arduous pre-deployment training including a sniper's course, the Commando disembarked at Suez in Egypt in early March 1941 as B Battalion, Layforce.

Although frustrated with the Commando's lack of activity Lewes, who had been promoted to lieutenant, began to train a select few from No.8 for an operation. At the end of May 1941 he wrote to his fiancée, Mirren Barford: 'I have been very preoccupied lately with a special task allotted to me: it is frighteningly exciting in preparation but gives me just that for which I have longed all my soldier days – a team of men, however small, and complete freedom to train and use them as I think best' (*Joy Street: A Wartime Romance in Letters*, by Mirren Barford and Lieutenant John Lewes). He received permission to train the men in parachuting, Lieutenant David Stirling of the same unit asking to be included and it was during these jumps that he damaged his back leading to a lengthy period of hospitalisation and conception of the SAS (see Davies' entry under Hanover War Cemetery, Germany, Volume III, for full details).

However, Lewes' proposed operation was not to be and at the beginning of July he and an advance party of sixty-six all ranks were sent to Tobruk to bring some relief to its besieged garrison. On arrival they found that not only would they not be reinforced as planned but that they had been sent 'either by some official oversight or else under false pretences'. The area commander intended to keep hold of them and use them at their current strength. Undeterred, Lewes led No.4 Troop in a successful attack during the night of the 17–18th on an Italian-held strong point known as 'Twin Pimples' for the loss of only one man. Periods on the perimeter facing both the Italians and Germans followed and although these included a successful prisoner-snatch Lewes commented on the news that Layforce was to be disbanded that the men 'were tired of being hawked about the perimeter like professional "pugs" at a fair.'

On his return to active duty Stirling went up to Tobruk to try and persuade Lewes to join him in the formation of L Detachment, SAS Brigade. However, Lewes would not be drawn from his task and it was not until the Commandos returned to Egypt during August, and he himself was forced into a Cairo hospital due to over-work, that Stirling finally succeeded. Lewes was thus appointed Training Officer and Second-in-Command of the fledgling unit, writing to his former colonel: 'After a period of debauchery in Alexandria and Cairo, during which time I discovered that return to one's unit in the UK was not on the cards, I finally resigned myself to serving in the Middle East for the duration, and as a result here I am, second-in-command of a detachment of parachutists – and liking it.' He subsequently earned the nickname 'The Wizard' after his experimental mixing of explosives culminated in the invention of the 'Lewes Bomb', a lightweight combination of diesel oil and plastic explosive that enabled many such devices to be carried by a single man and used to great effect against Axis aircraft. His imagination did not stop there and he designed the SAS wings. Stirling, educated at Cambridge, chose the primary SAS colour as Cambridge Blue whilst Lewes added the darker Oxford Blue, later sending a set to his father:

It is my design and I must say it looks well on khaki. It is not very well executed, but good enough to begin with. We have rather taken things into our own hands with regards to it, and have deliberately diverged from home practice first because we have trained this unit without the least assistance from home or from trained instructors. Second because we are fundamentally a unit, and not a pool or a school, and third because we are essentially operational, and wish to be differentiated from non-operational staff and instructors. My ambition now is to change our name from the present absurd title to 1st (Middle East) Parachute Battalion: after all you can't go on being a detachment all your life [written on 2 December 1941].

The wings were produced in Cairo by tailors John Jones & Co from who they could be privately purchased by any man producing an issued chit as proof of qualification (personal interview with Bob McDougall, 2007). The set seen here are one of three bought by McDougall in early 1943, by which time their execution had been refined. The recipient was entitled to wear them on his right arm until awarded 'Operational Wings' by his Commanding Officer, generally after completing three operations. They would then be transferred to the left breast and the enhanced entitlement entered in the individual's AB.64. This convention continued throughout the war in all SAS Regiments, as well as being worn by parachute trained personnel within Middle East Raiding Forces, including the LRDG. As such they are as good a symbol to represent all those commemorated within this work that can be found. Although they are now solely worn on the right arm the design has barely changed, modern wings being issued rather than purchased.

Lewes commanded 1 Troop during OPERATION SQUATTER, the first SAS raid. Planned for the night of 16–17 November 1941 on the eve of the British offensive, OPERATION CRUSADER, L Detachment was to attack airfields at Tmimi and Gazala behind enemy lines in Libya. Having dropped over a large area in gale force conditions the parties could not regroup into numbers sufficient to undertake the proposed raids. Their equipment had also been scattered and what little remained was ruined by rain. Lewes therefore led his team of nine to a pre-arranged RV with Captain 'Jake' Easonsmith's R.1 Patrol, LRDG, on the evening of the 19th (WO 218/89 – see Easonsmith's entry under Leros War Cemetery, Greece, Volume II).

Soon after SQUATTER Lewes commanded a raid on Agheila airfield, flying to Jalo on 6 December 1941 then being delivered by the LRDG's T.2 Patrol to within 20 kilometres of the objective. Having walked towards the target during daylight his patrol found no aircraft but captured thirteen Libyan soldiers. That night Lewes and a small group destroyed a ten-ton ammunition lorry and trailer as well as communication lines for 800 metres. The following night the whole party, mounted on LRDG trucks, motored down the main road and on approaching the small anchorage at Mersa Brega attacked a group of approximately twenty lorries and a large number of men standing around them at close range. Having inflicted several casualties and destroyed numerous vehicles they mined the road. Enemy vehicles in pursuit were thus destroyed whilst further communication lines were cut before the patrol returned to Cairo via Jalo.

On 26 December 1941 Lewes' patrol left Jalo once more, again being transported by T.2. Three days later they were dropped 27 kilometres short of Nofilia airfield that they attacked that night. Aircraft were found to be widely dispersed and bombs placed on the first plane went off before the second could be reached. With the alarm raised Lewes withdrew, reaching an RV with Captain Bill Fraser and the LRDG after a difficult compass march. Spotted by aircraft on the 30th the group was subjected to intense bombing and strafing from 1000hrs to 1600hrs, an artery in Lewes' knee being severed by a canon shell. He died before the bleeding could be arrested. In November 1942 Stirling, who was said to have been very angry with those that left Lewes' body behind, wrote to his mother:

> Jock could far more seriously claim to be the founder of L Det and the SAS Regt than I.
>
> … he applied and got permission to detach a section from the unit (CDOs) and to train it on the lines required to enable it to cover an operation which he himself had planned. Although this operation was never executed owing to lack of decision at the top, there was never any doubt that it would have been successful …
>
> After this operation was postponed I think three times Jock was included in a detachment of our Commando which went up to Tobruk … I have frequently heard it said that in this period Jock earned a DSO.
>
> Later ME [Middle East HQ] instructed me to go ahead and form a unit on the lines of this proposal. Inevitably the first officer whom I applied for was Jock. In fact I built the unit around him.
>
> There is no doubt that any success this unit has achieved up to the time of Jock's death and after it, was, and is, almost wholly due to Jock's work. Our training programmes and methods are, and always will be, based on syllabuses he produced for us. They must show the extent of his influence.
>
> Jock was killed while returning from an operation against Nofilia aerodrome by strafing from German fighter aircraft. He was hit high up in the leg by a canon shell which apparently cut the main artery. The truck in which he was travelling also carried the medical orderly and his equipment so that Jock had almost instant attention by a trained professional. He remained conscious and continued to fire instructions to his men almost until he died fifteen minutes later. He was buried 20 miles inland south east of Nofilia [*Jock Lewes: Co-Founder of the SAS*, by John Lewes].

Jim Almonds recalled in his diary: 'I thought of Jock, one of the bravest men I have ever met, an officer and a gentleman, lying out there in the desert barely covered with sand. No one will stop by his grave or pay homage to a brave heart that has ceased to beat – not even a stone marks the spot' (*Joy Street*).

A few weeks before his death Lewes had written a last letter to his father: 'When I can write to you of this good company I shall; but until then know that I have been happy in its midst and at its head after David, and that I am proud to share its future.' In a final telegram he spoke of being recommended for the Military Cross.

Son of Arthur and Elsie Lewes of Tudor Court, Castle Way, Hanworth, Middlesex – Brother of Elizabeth McArthur.

Age 28.

Column 53. Also commemorated at Christ Church, Oxford, and by a statue at Credenhill, the headquarters of 22 SAS near Hereford.

LIEUTENANT EOIN CHRISTOPHER McGONIGAL [97290] ROYAL ULSTER RIFLES, CAMERONIAN RIFLES, NO.11 COMMANDO AND L DETACHMENT SAS BRIGADE

Eoin McGonigal was born on 5 December 1920 in Dublin where he attended Clongowes College and Trinity College before qualifying as a solicitor. In 1938 he joined the Royal Ulster Rifles (TA) whilst living in Belfast and was commissioned in August 1939. At the outbreak of war he was posted to the RUR's infantry training centre at Ballymena before being attached to the 2nd Battalion, Cameronian Rifles, at Aberdeen in June 1940. Two months later he volunteered for No.11 (Scottish) Commando and forged a close friendship with fellow officer, Paddy Mayne. Despite being of different religious persuasion they had much in common such as rugby and law and jointly ran range packages on the Isle of Arran.

McGonigal was promoted to lieutenant in January 1941 and disembarked in Egypt that March, No.11 having been temporarily retitled C Battalion of Layforce. At the end of the April, having been

stood-down from a raid on Bardia that month, it moved to Cyprus in readiness for OPERATION EXPORTER, the campaign in Syria against the Vichy French. In the early hours of 9 June his troop, No.4, which was designated as part of Z Party under Captain George More, landed on a sandbank not far north of the Litani River and assaulted its allotted beach under machine-gun fire. Having carried out several attacks on enemy positions McGonigal's men were obliged to retire before French armoured cars mounted with two-pounder guns. Moving south along the beach they were machine-gunned whilst cutting through enemy wire near Aiteniye in the early hours of the 10th and forced to surrender. However, the French commander soon released McGonigal's party on realising he was outnumbered by advancing Australian troops.

Returning to Egypt on 6 August McGonigal volunteered for L Detachment, SAS Brigade, on the 15th and as the unit took shape was posted to 2 Section, D Group. On the night of 16–17 November he parachuted into OPERATION SQUATTER, the first SAS raid that aimed to destroy enemy aircraft at Tmimi and Gazala airfields in Libya. The jump was conducted in gale force conditions, men and equipment being widely scattered. According to the witness statements of Parachutists Jim Blakeney and Roy Davies, McGonigal, the stick commander on the fourth aircraft, died on the 18th from wounds sustained when dragged along rocky ground (see entries for both Blakeney and Davies under Hanover War Cemetery, Germany, Volume III). However, Lieutenant Charles Bonington, a fellow officer on the operation, later wrote from his POW camp that 'Lt McGonigal was killed on landing' suggesting an earlier date of death. With the assault force widely dispersed the operation was a failure.

Son of John McGonigal, KC, and Margaret McGonigal of Corrig Road, Dun Laughaire, County Dublin – Brother of Ambrose (a successful RUR and SBS officer described by a contemporary as 'determined to avenge him') and of Letty Carson.

Age 20.

Column 71.

TROOPER LESLIE ANGUS McIVER [37404] NEW ZEALAND INFANTRY, DIVISIONAL CAVALRY REGIMENT AND LRDG (T.2 PATROL)

Les McIver, variously known as 'Bluey', 'Red' or 'Mac', was born on 22 February 1914 at the family farm, Mohaka Station, not far from the shore of Hawke's Bay, New Zealand. Having helped his parents on the farm and then worked as a taxi driver he enlisted in June 1940 at the nearby town of Wairoa. He was subsequently posted to C (Hawke's Bay) Company, No.2 Infantry Training Unit (Central Training Battalion), at Trentham. His service record notes that he arrived in Egypt during January 1941 as reinforcement for the 31st Wellington Battalion, New Zealand Infantry, but that he volunteered for the Long Range Desert Group on 18 February from the 32nd Wellington Battalion. He was subsequently transferred to the Divisional Cavalry Regiment from where the majority of the New Zealand volunteers

originated. After initial training he was attached to the Welch Regiment for a month, this battalion being located at Abbassia in Cairo close to the LRDG's HQ.

Posted to T.2 Patrol McIver set out from Siwa Oasis on 7 November 1941 under Captain Anthony Hunter in support of OPERATION CRUSADER, the British offensive. Reaching the Wadi-el-Heleighima on the 10th the patrol dropped a British Intelligence Officer, Captain John Haselden, and his Arab colleague to gather information. Moving east it then split into three to carry out Road Watch duties, McIver staying with Hunter near to the Mechili–Derna road. When Lance-corporal Ray Porter failed to return from their observation point Hunter took McIver and Corporal Fred Kendall to look for him, the three being attacked by Italian troops. Although Hunter managed to evade capture his men were not so fortunate, the other patrol officer, Lord Freyberg's son Paul, later reporting: 'Cpl Kendall and Tpr McIver were last seen firing at the enemy though heavily outnumbered. There is little chance of their avoiding capture' (WO 218/89). It later transpired that Porter had also been taken prisoner.

On 8 December 1941 McIver embarked the SS *Sebastiano Venier*, also known as the *Jason* or *Jantzen*, at Benghazi bound for Italy. Unaware of her prisoner-of-war cargo a British submarine, HMS *Porpoise*, torpedoed her the following afternoon. In the ensuing mayhem 500 Commonwealth POWs died, although many more, including McIver, were saved by the German bosun who took control of the vessel and successfully beached her on the Peloponnese coast after the Italian crew had abandoned ship. The survivors were subsequently kept in dire conditions in makeshift camps throughout the winter before continuing their journey to Italy in March 1942. By that August McIver was being held at Campo PG.85 at Tuturano near Brindisi (POW number 3450), during September at Campo PG.65 at Gravina in Puglia, during January 1943 in Campo PG.57 at Gruppignano near Udine where he was taken ill, and finally from November 1943 at Stalag VIIIa south of the town of Görlitz in Lower Silesia (now Zgorzelec in Poland). Here he managed to secure work in the kitchens, his niece, Jean McIver, later writing:

Les was moved to a work camp at Ruckenwaldau, attached to Stalag VIIIa, where he worked on the railway. Unlike most other camps they were not moved out in early 1945, but continued keeping the railway maintained. One morning they were woken up before sunrise and had to leave the work camp immediately. They were taken down the railway line. A sniper, probably German, opened fire and killed the first two men. I think it is likely that a third bullet caught Les in the leg. The Russian soldiers arrived and there was a skirmish between them and the Germans. Les lay in the snow for seven hours from 5am until noon, with agonising stomach pains. Along with Pte Atkinson, he was picked up and taken to a house where he received first aid from a Russian Army girl. According to Pte Atkinson they were then moved to another house that had been converted into a field hospital in which an operation and comfortable treatment was given by a Russian Army doctor. Pte Atkinson says in his report that they were then shifted to another field hospital at Modlau [modern-day Modla in Poland]. According to medical records held in the Russian Medical War Museum they were admitted to Russian Field Hospital 104 on the 13th February that had been set up in a large home in Modlau and Les was operated on and received care from a doctor. He had splinter wounds to the right hip and the lower third of the right thigh, complicated by anaerobic septicaemia and obstruction of the ileus. At approximately 8pm on the 14th February he complained of wind in the stomach, but no one could make the Russians understand. At 10pm Pte Atkinson met a Russian orderly who could speak German, and he understood what the problem was. Leslie was given some sort of powder and at midnight (must have been earlier) he was sleeping and breathing normally. He died on the 14th February 1945 at 2340 due to heart failure. At 2am (now the 15th) Pte Atkinson was wakened by a thud, and in a state of semi-consciousness he witnessed Leslie's body being taken out of the room on a stretcher with his face covered. Pte. Atkinson tried to find out what happened to him, but all he could get from the Russians was 'Kaput', which he took to mean that he was dead. He never saw him again.

I believe Les would have been buried in the cemetery close to the hospital along with other Russian soldiers. These soldiers were reinterred in a cemetery close to the centre of what is now Boleslawiec. Les's remains are either at the original burial ground in Modla, or in one of two mass graves in this cemetery [personal correspondence, 2014].

CWGC, Polish and Russian sources record McIver's date of death as 14 February 1945 whereas his service record and British witness statements refer to the 16th. Because the area in which he was killed came under Soviet control it was not until 1952 that the New Zealand Government wrote to his mother explaining that a search for his body was impossible and that he would subsequently be commemorated on the Alamein Memorial. In 2002 Tony Page, a member of the New Zealand SAS Association, travelled to Modla where he discovered that McIver was originally buried alongside Russian casualties, under an identical headstone but without a red star, in a plot adjacent to the town's churchyard. He also ascertained that in 1950 the Soviets had concentrated all such graves into military cemeteries. As Page discovered one headstone without a red star piled up with those of the Red Army soldiers at its original location, it is thought that McIver was reinterred amongst such troops in a mass grave at the Russian Cemetery of Honour at nearby Boleslawiec (Cmentarz żołnierzy radzieckich).

Son of Murdock and Ann McIver of Mohaka, Hawke's Bay, New Zealand – Brother of Malcolm Ronald (Ron) McIver who joined up after his sibling was captured, Alan John McIver, and Murdoch Gordon (Pat) McIver – The James family of Shelley Avenue, Manor Park, London, regularly sent mail to McIver whilst he was a prisoner: 'I found out that the first information they had of Les being a POW came from the Automobile Association in Auckland, who had heard his details while listening to the Vatican Radio, 5th February 1942' (personal correspondence with Jean McIver, 2010).
Age 30.
Column 100. Also commemorated on an LRDG memorial within the New Zealand SAS camp at Papakura, on Mohaka's memorial board, within Wairoa Memorial Hall and by a plaque on a community hall in the village of Wierzbowa, south-west Poland, near to where he was fatally wounded.

Driver William **MARLOW** [T/119344] Royal Army Service Corps
and L Detachment SAS Brigade

William Marlow was born on 23 April 1914, later living in Carlisle where he worked as a driver. In October 1933 he married Annie Elizabeth Armstrong, their son James being born in April 1936. At the outbreak of war in September 1939 he enlisted into the Royal Army Service Corps, serving in France with the BEF from October until June 1940 when evacuated to the UK, most likely from Cherbourg. On his return he moved from one motor transport company to another until settling in C Section, 2 Reserve MT Company with which he embarked for the Middle East at the beginning of 1941. Arriving in Egypt two months later he served in Greece before being evacuated first to Crete and from there, presumably after the German invasion of May, back to Egypt. All details for this period, such as specific subunits, exact locations and dates are unfortunately recorded as 'unknown' in his service record.

Finding himself at a base depot Marlow volunteered for L Detachment, SAS Brigade, on 7 June 1942. Later that year he took part in Operation Bigamy, the large-scale raid on Benghazi: with the enemy alerted to their presence the SAS column was ambushed on the night of 13–14 September during its approach to town and forced to withdraw. By dawn it had split into smaller groups. Several were spotted by enemy aircraft, thus precipitating two days of repeated bombing. By the time the parties reached their RV at Wadi Ftilia on the 15th they had lost eighteen three-ton trucks and fifteen Jeeps, the RV itself being 'subjected to continuous heavy air attack by the enemy fighters and bombers, of which there were at no time during the next five hours less than 15 in the air' (WO 201/748). Marlow was killed in action during one such attack that day (see also Aspirant Joseph Guerpillon's entry under Sennecey-le-Grand SAS Brigade Memorial, France, Volume III).

Son of Mr and Mrs Marlow (née Lindon) – Husband of Annie Marlow of Capon Hill, Gelt Road,

Brampton, Cumberland – Father of James Marlow.
Age 28.
Column 76. Also commemorated within St Martin's Church, Brampton.

GUARDSMAN GEORGE HENRY **MATTHEWS** [2656632] COLDSTREAM GUARDS AND LRDG (G.2 PATROL, B SQN)

Known as 'Beppo' to his comrades, George Matthews was born on 2 August 1916 in Leicester. Having worked as a boot and shoe hand in the nearby suburb of Aylestone he enlisted into the Coldstream Guards in August 1934, joining the 3rd Battalion the following January. In 1936 he qualified as a mechanic before serving in Palestine during the Arab Revolt from that October until December. After a period of home service he disembarked in Egypt in November 1937, returning to troubled Palestine the following October. In April 1939 he was posted back to Egypt where he served with HQ Company before volunteering for the Long Range Desert Group on 6 December 1940. He and other volunteers from the 3rd Battalion had arrived at the Citadel in Cairo the previous day and along with recruits from the 2nd Battalion, Scots Guards, were formed into G Patrol that inherited the vehicles and equipment of the former W Patrol.

After a brief period of training the Guards joined the more experienced New Zealand T Patrol and set off for OPERATION AESOP in Central Libya: on 11 January 1941, having picked up Free French troops at Kayugi in Chad, the combined patrol closed on both Murzuk Fort that resisted heavily and the adjacent Italian airfield at which aircraft and a hanger were destroyed. The force then withdrew, briefly stopping after a few kilometres to bury two casualties, Sergeant 'Squib' Hewson and the French commander, Lt-Colonel Jean Colonna d'Ornano (see Hewson's entry under Tripoli War Cemetery, Libya, within this volume). On the 12th the patrols forced the surrender of Traghen and its Carabinieri outpost before going on to attack two further enemy positions at Um el-Araneb and Gatrun. Although they intended to capture Kufra Oasis en route to Cairo they were spotted by aircraft before reaching the cover of Jebel Sherif late in the morning of the 31st. Early that afternoon they were subsequently attacked by their Italian equivalent, the Compagnia Sahariana, losing trucks and Corporal Rex Beech who was killed in action (see his entry under Knightsbridge War Cemetery, Libya). When Italian aircraft joined the fight the patrols withdrew, three men being captured and the attack on Kufra being cancelled (see Lance-corporal Clarrie Roderick's entry under Bolsena War Cemetery, Italy, Volume II, for further details). T and G eventually returned to Cairo on 9 February.

In late March 1941 G Patrol set out for Barce in Libya where it split, one half undertaking a recce of enemy troop movements close to Marada Oasis, the other staying with the remainder of A Squadron. Although it is not known which half Matthews was with during this period both groups had lengthy and eventful exfiltrations to Jarabub after a major Axis advance. G Patrol lost much of its transport and what was left of the squadron was reorganised at Siwa into two patrols. The Guards were subsequently sent to watch over the Gardaba track for the latter half of April and then the approaches to Jarabub until mid May. With a British counter-offensive in full swing the patrol was ordered to rendezvous with the 11th Hussars and act as its advanced recce. However, on reaching the RV they mistook enemy armoured cars as the Hussars and were fired on before being chased from the area.

From June until August 1941 Matthews was hospitalised with a fractured fibula, returning to find that G and Y Patrols were now part of B Squadron. Having arrived at Kufra on 20 October they were reorganised into half patrols, Matthews being allocated to the newly-formed G.2. The whole of the LRDG was then concentrated at Siwa Oasis in time for Operation Crusader, the British offensive of mid November. G.2 under Lieutenant Alastair Timpson was ordered to patrol the area of Maatan el-Grara. In doing so it spotted an Italian aircraft that had been forced to land due to mechanical issues. The patrol attacked, killing two of the crew and capturing three others whilst the aircraft was destroyed and papers of intelligence value seized. In December it was allotted the area between Barce and Benghazi but due to a case of appendicitis was forced to return to Siwa. On Boxing Day Timpson led the patrol to the Hon–Misurata road where a truck was destroyed before breakdowns led to another withdrawal.

In the afternoon of 9 February 1942 G.2 left Siwa to conduct a traffic census in the area west of El Kharruba and to drop Captain John Haselden, MC, an Arabic speaking Intelligence Officer, to gather similar information in an area nearby. Moving via Baltat ez Zalagh in Libya the trucks were hidden in a wadi at Bir Embescer soon after midday on the 12th, Haselden later writing:

> It was decided that Lieut Timpson and party would observe the south road at a point near el-Cueifat and that I, accompanied by Sjt Dennis and Gdsman Matthews of the Coldstream Guards and Gdsman Wilson and Fernbank of the Scots Guards, would observe the north road near Mdener Tuati.
> The two parties left Bir Embescer on foot at 1500 hours on 13 Feb. We arrived at a point on the south road slightly west of Cuifat at first light on the 14th. Lieut [Alastair] Timpson's party was left there and my party proceeded north. We arrived at Siret Tomat at about 1400 hours [WO 201/812].

On 8 May Matthews, now a member of G.1 Patrol under the newly-promoted Captain Timpson, set out from Siwa. The intention was to monitor the coast road for traffic and attack enemy transport with delayed bombs in an area 32 kilometres to the west of 'Marble Arch', a memorial erected by the Italians near Ra's Lanuf to mark the Tripolitania/Cyrenaica border. From the outset the patrol was plagued by a series of punctures due to a faulty batch of tyres. Fortunately, some were scavenged from a derelict patrol vehicle that lay close by, although their lack of spares would have a knock-on effect. By the 13th the patrol had reached the coastal road and set about locating a suitable ambush site. The following evening the men prepared explosives, Timpson and six other ranks then taking one truck to their designated 'road-block'. This was constructed by dragging barrels across the road, the patrol commander and one other manning it whilst the others remained in cover. It was hoped that enemy vehicles would slow sufficiently for patrol members to throw time-delayed bombs into the back of them. This proved futile, mainly because vehicles hardly slowed at all. At 0200hrs Timpson decided that they would attempt the same tactic but from their chasing truck, a man being pre-positioned on their bonnet ready to throw a bomb in. Soon a lorry and trailer passed. The guardsmen pursued only to find that the lorry's towrope had broken when swerving to avoid their previous road-block. It continued leaving its trailer stranded with two Italians who mistook the patrol for Germans. Making excuses Timpson decided to find a different location for the following night. Whilst doing so they sustained a further puncture and with no serviceable spare the men were forced to leave the truck camouflaged about 5 kilometres from the road and to walk back to the patrol RV. On arrival in the early hours of 15 May Timpson sent a party to recover the truck, these returning at approximately 1100hrs. Timpson's post-operation report outlines subsequent events:

> At about 1pm, whilst we were having lunch, the sentry called out 'enemy troops'. I gave the order 'stand by your guns', and a few seconds later the enemy opened fire. They were attacking us, it seemed, from our west – from up the wadi, where dead ground came close to us. The sentry had seen a Spa [truck] come over the ridge about 200 yards away (probably following the tracks of G.1 and G.4). The enemy had immediately spotted us – probably the wireless aerial in particular, rigged up for the midday call – and had jumped off the truck and got into action. He [the sentry] thought they numbered about twenty-four. It was impossible to tell whether there were other trucks which might have halted on the far side of the ridge. Our trucks were well camouflaged with nets and tarpaulins, it was therefore about two minutes before any of our gunners opened fire from the time I gave the order. The enemy were using one and perhaps two LMGs [light machine guns], in addition to rifles …
> Guardsman Matthews was killed early in the fight. He was the first to get on his truck to man his gun, and a bullet hit him on the top of the head, removing the upper part of his skull …
> We made off SW expecting aircraft would follow us in a south-easterly direction, but saw no enemy aircraft or ground forces until we camped after covering 65 miles, at 6pm, at Long 17 59', Lat 29 59'. Guardsman Matthews was buried on the southern side of a summit of a hill here …

May 21st I would leave G.5 behind at our rendezvous, the brakes of which did not work and could not be repaired. The driver, Guardsman Waiting, Gdsm Matthews' best friend, and much shaken by his death, would remain with it, together with Pte Astell, the medical orderly [WO 218/91].

Son of George and Elizabeth Matthews (née Pearce) of Lansdowne Road, Leicester – Older brother of John and Robert.
Age 25.
Column 54.

LANCE-BOMBARDIER JOHN WILLIAM ROBERT **ROBSON** [886920] ROYAL ARTILLERY AND L DETACHMENT SAS BRIGADE

John Robson was born on 27 November 1920 and grew up in Gateshead, County Durham, where he later worked as a machine hand. In January 1939 he enlisted into the Royal Artillery at Newcastle-on-Tyne and served with various training and field regiments before being promoted to lance-bombardier in July 1940. Embarking for the Middle East in January 1942 he briefly served on Cyprus that April until returning to Egypt where he volunteered for L Detachment, SAS Brigade.

On 3 July 1942 Major David Stirling, DSO, left Kabrit with a large SAS contingent including Robson that established a forward operating base behind enemy lines at Quaret Hiremas on the northern edge of the Great Sand Sea. Robson subsequently took part in OPERATION NUMBER 12, a raid on Fuka aerodrome on the 7th:

Party consisting of Col Stirling [sic], Major Mayne, Cooper, Leigh, Storey, Robson, Lilly, Adamson, Gammel [sic – Gemmel], Downes, Shaw + O'Dowd to attack LG.68 in Blitz Buggy and three Jeeps. Arrived and parked off road at 2300hrs. Major Mayne, Adamson + Storey went in on foot. At 0100hrs party went in Buggy leading and three Jeeps in single file behind cruising around drome, under fire, strafing aircraft with Vickers K's etc. Forty-nine aircraft destroyed by bombs and strafing. Withdrew. Cooper fixed position by telegraph poles and we started off for rendezvous. At 0645hrs two CR.42s spotted us in open desert and strafed getting Buggy and one Jeep after thirty minutes. Broke off. Whole party returned in remaining jeeps to rendezvous. On return moved RV 15 miles west [see Lance-sergeant Chris O'Dowd's entry under Sangro River War Cemetery, Italy, Volume II].

Stirling realised that this tactic held potential. Fetching as many men and Jeeps as he could muster full-scale rehearsals were carried out close to the Querat Hiremas base and formations that ensured maximum firepower perfected. L Detachment subsequently entered the German airfield at Sidi Haneish on the night of 26–27 July 1942 and destroyed an estimated twenty-five aircraft as well as aircrew in a mass Jeep attack. However, a lone enemy machine gun could not be silenced, its fire killing Robson who was manning the forward guns on Lieutenant Sandy Scratchley's Jeep. Ginger Adamson, the vehicle's rear gunner, wrote that Robson was buried the next day on the return from the raid 'approximately 30 miles from Sidi Haneish' whilst Stephen Hastings, a former SAS officer, later recalled:

We got up and stood gathered around the grave while the body was lowered, sand and rock heaped upon it. There was no cross; some of the men were trying to make one from the scrub and a piece of old ration box, but it was not yet ready. We stood bare-headed, each with his own thoughts. Most of us had scarcely known this lad who had only joined us shortly before the operation. I remembered a cheery red face and a shock of black hair. There must have be someone, parents, a girl, going about their ordinary business far away at home. It would be weeks before the pathetic little message filtered back for all the pent up sadness of this desert moment to be loosed.

I looked round at the loneliness, the vague shapeless loneliness stretching for so many hundreds of forgotten miles. Probably no living thing would ever pass this grave again except perhaps the gazelle; even the map reference we recorded might well be inaccurate after our flight from the airfield [*The Drums of Memory*, by Stephen Hastings].

Whilst the CWGC state that he was the son of Simon and Margaret Robson his service papers record that the address of his father, Thomas Robson, was unknown and that although he had two brothers, Albert (elder) and Eric (younger), his next of kin was officially recorded as his aunt: Mrs A. Larkin of Victoria Road, Bensham, Gateshead, Co Durham.

Age 21.

Column 33.

LIEUTENANT RAYMOND HERBERT <u>SHORTEN</u> [163658] GENERAL LIST, NO.52 COMMANDO, MI(R), L DETACHMENT SAS BRIGADE AND 1ST SAS (A SQN)

Raymond Shorten was born to an English father and Italian mother on 17 May 1921 in Cairo where he grew up and attended The English School. Having worked as secretary to the Eastern Cigarette Company at Giza he was granted an emergency commission onto the General List in November 1940 and posted to No.52 (Middle East) Commando the following month. Disembarking at Port Sudan a few days later this boarded trains for Gedaref close to the border with both Eritrea and Abyssinia. Arriving at the front line on Christmas Eve the Commando faced Italian units largely consisting of native troops backed by superior air assets. It was subsequently involved in a number of skirmishes on the border with Abyssinia, Shorten being admitted to the 3rd Casualty Clearing Station during January 1941 with unspecified injuries. That March he returned, via the Sudanese border at Wadi Halfa, to Egypt where he was posted to D Battalion, Layforce, an amalgamation of No.50 and 52 Commandos. The following month, after an attachment to the Argyll and Sutherland Highlanders, he was absorbed into the Middle East Commando at Geneifa and joined C Squadron. A period of postings to various training centres and headquarters followed before he was attached to the Libyan Arab Force Commando in May 1942. This was in reality G(R), an integral part of GHQ Cairo that formed the Middle East sub-branch of MI(R), the War Office clandestine warfare department. He was promoted to lieutenant a few days later.

On 29 May 1942 Shorten and thirteen others were dropped behind enemy lines at Baltet Burgheis by the LRDG. The group was under the command of Major Vladimir Peniakoff who later formed Popski's Private Army:

22 May. Left Siwa lifted by LRDG patrol. Party included Major Peniakoff ['Popski' – the author of this report], Lt Chevalier, Lt Shorten, Cpl Langmaid, ten AORs [Arab other ranks], stores of explosives weapons, ammunition and food.

17 June. Set fire to petrol dump near Giovanni Berta … it held approximately 50,000 gallons of petrol … the demolition party consisted of myself, Chevalier, Shorten, and four AORs [WO 201/727].

A few days later Lieutenant Jack Crisp's T.2 Patrol, LRDG, collected the men, Peniakoff later writing, perhaps rather harshly, to the LRDG's Commanding Officer, Lt-Colonel Guy Prendergast:

> It should be borne in mind that officers unable to act independently under special conditions would be more of a liability than an asset. Thus, I am compelled to send back to Egypt, Lt Shorten, though he is plucky, tireless and willing, on account of his youthful lack of judgement and his lack of knowledge of Arabic.
>
> Shorten has shown remarkable pluck and a complete disregard for fatigue or personal discomfort … His slight knowledge of kitchen Egyptian Arabic does not help him at all with the Libyans. He has made two grave blunders, one of which nearly caused the failure of our attempt to blow up a petrol dump in Gubba and incidentally nearly put us in the bag. I can't run the risk of carrying him any longer and am sending him back to you – and G(R) [WO 201/727].

Shorten subsequently volunteered for L Detachment, SAS Brigade, on 2 July 1942. He was deployed on operations behind the lines later that month and manned the unit's patrol base at Querat Hiremas during the mass Jeep attack on Sidi Haneish airfield on the night of 26–27th. That September he took part in OPERATION BIGAMY, the large-scale Benghazi raid, later establishing a forward operating base near Howard's Cairn with Captain Jim Chambers (see Chambers' own entry under Fayid War Cemetery, Egypt). He was killed during this operation on 19 October 1942 whilst leading a group to cut railways lines near Sidi Barrani:

> A patrol of four Jeeps and eight men, including a lieutenant who had been born in Egypt, set off for a further attack in the Tobruk, El Adam area, moving off with the once again, good humoured banter from the rest of the base, when many hours later in the day, the patrol returned without the lieutenant and a very badly damaged vehicle. Speeding up the hard packed slopes of a high sand dune, the top finishing with a crest to an almost sheer drop the Jeep had plunged over the top. The passenger was flung out, then the vehicle turned over and killed the officer driver on its fall to the lower desert. Some of these dunes were very dangerous, their outlines changed almost daily, and sometimes, even with the slightest movement of air. The patrol buried the officer using some of the containers from the vehicles as liners, covering them with rocks and stones. The base was stunned by this news realising all the more now how vulnerable life could be almost daily [*The Lame One: 'Sod this for a Game of Soldiers'*, by Bill Deakins].

Joe Plater, former L Detachment, later recalled that Sergeant 'Chalky' White, the other passenger in the Jeep, had managed to throw himself clear. White was later regarded as somewhat of a jinx to officers having had six others killed in his company by the end of the war (see Captain Roy Bradford's entry under Crain Communal Cemetery, France, Volume III).

Shorten was buried in the desert at 'M/R 397056 Libya 1/500,000 Sheet 22 Caret Knud', his grave being used as an RV the following month. Signals sent by Major Paddy Mayne, DSO, state that he had buried him at this grid reference but pinpoints the location as 'Garet Khud' (WO 201/765).

Son of Alfred and Emilie Shorten of Sharia el-Cheik-Barakat, Kasr-el-Doubara, Cairo.

Age 21.

Column 86.

PRIVATE THOMAS JOHN SILLETT [5672780] SOMERSET LIGHT INFANTRY, NO.8 COMMANDO, L DETACHMENT SAS BRIGADE AND 1ST SAS (A SQN)

Known to his family as 'Vic', Sillett was born in Taunton, Somerset, on 29 November 1918 and grew up in the nearby village of Norton Fitzwarren. In April 1939, whilst working as a shirt cutter at the nearby Van Heusen factory, he joined the 5th Battalion, Somerset Light Infantry (TA), and was subsequently mobilised at the outbreak of war soon after returning from Annual Camp. Three days later he married Ivy Henderson in Taunton, the battalion being initially based locally. However, in January 1940 it moved to Salisbury Plain before briefly taking over the protection of supply dumps, airfields and vulnerable points at Cosham, Hullavington, Andover and Micheldever. That May, after a period at Bath and Weston-super-Mare, its companies were concentrated around Crowbrough in Sussex and subsequently posted guards at bridges and other key locations either side of the Kent/East Sussex border at Ightham, Peasmarsh and Rye. At the beginning of June it again moved, this time taking up defensive positions on the south coast between Cliff End and Appledore. It relocated farther east in August in response to the threat of imminent invasion.

Early in November 1940 the battalion was relieved and moved north, Sillett soon volunteering for No.8 (Guards) Commando that had recently been redesignated, albeit temporarily, as the 4th Special Service Battalion. Although his son Michael was born the following month there was little time for family life: lodged at Largs on the west coast of Scotland the Commando was put through an arduous training regime on the Isle of Arran before embarking for the Middle East at the end of January 1941. Having stopped at Durban the men arrived at Suez at the beginning of March as B Battalion, Layforce, this being a composite force of No. 7, No.8 and No.11 Commandos as well as one troop from No.3. Although intended to raid the Eastern Mediterranean No.8 was sent to Mersa Matruh towards the front line where a frustrating period of cancelled operations ensued. Layforce personnel were, in the main, subsequently absorbed into the newly-formed Middle East Commando at Geneifa that July.

Although posted as a carrier driver to the Middle East Weapons Training School in Palestine in January 1942 Sillett volunteered for L Detachment, SAS Brigade, at Kabrit that June. There is therefore a high probability that he took part in the mass Jeep attack on Sidi Haneish airfield deep within enemy-held

Libya the following month and that he was present on OPERATION BIGAMY, the large-scale raid on Benghazi of that September. Despite proving abortive, as well as costly both in men and transport, very little time could be spared to rest and re-equip: on 7 October A Squadron, of what had now expanded into 1st SAS Regiment, left Kabrit and reached Kufra Oasis in south-east Libya on the 13th. A forward operating base was established well behind the lines near Howard's Cairn roughly a week later, patrols being sent out to harass enemy lines of communication. Although Sillett is often reported as having been killed in action during one such raid, he died in a field hospital on 31 October, a Long Range Desert Group report confirming that:

> On 28th October [1942] a sick trooper from the SAS was picked up from their advanced operations base, returning with the patrol [the New Zealand T.2 Patrol under the command of

Lieutenant Reg Crammond] to Kufra. Subsequently this soldier died of Diphtheria. Full precautions have been taken by the Medical Officer to guard against infection [WO 218/91].

Sergeant Richmond, also of A Squadron, wrote to Sillett's wife within days:

It is with deep regret that I have to write to you in this tone. We of the Regt greatly sympathise with you in the loss of your husband. I am enclosing these two photos of his grave. I am sorry that I cannot tell you where he is buried but the Graves Commission will inform you later. What little consolation I can offer you is that he suffered very little. He only had a short illness and was game to the end, never complaining [see the entry for 'Richmond' under the Unknown Identity section within Volume III].

When the North African Campaign drew to a close Major Paddy Mayne, DSO, found the time to send his own condolences:

I must apologise for not having replied to your letter earlier but I have been on operations and have just lately returned to base.
    Your husband was with my squadron from June of 1942 and had proved himself an efficient, able and brave soldier. We are a special service unit which undertakes difficult and sometimes dangerous operations and your husband volunteered for these special duties.
    During September and October the squadron was living in the desert raiding the enemy lines of communication.
    Towards the end of October your husband developed a sore throat and was evacuated to the oasis of Kufra. When I returned to there I was told he died two days after admission from Diphtheria. He was buried in the Military Cemetery.
    I need not tell you how sorry we all were and I can only offer my own and my squadron's sympathies. We only accept the best type of man for our unit [courtesy of his son, Mike Sillett, 2015].

It appears that due to the highly infectious nature of diphtheria Sillett's remains were left in situ rather than be reinterred into a war cemetery.
    Only son of Thomas (a First World War veteran of the Somerset Light Infantry) and of Dorothy Sillett (née Parsons) of Station Road, Norton Fitzwarren, Taunton, Somerset – Husband of Ivy Sillett of Rectory Cottage, Norton Fitzwarren – Father of Michael Sillett.
Age 24.
Column 58. Also commemorated on Norton Fitzwarren's war memorial and within the village church.

WARRANT OFFICER CLASS II EUSTACE ARTHUR NICOL **SQUE** [2087918]
ROYAL ENGINEERS AND ROYAL ARMY ORDNANCE CORPS
ATT L DETACHMENT SAS BRIGADE

Sque, named Eustace after his parents' best man but known throughout his army life as Arthur, was born on 4 April 1913 at New Milton near Lymington in Hampshire. After schooling he worked locally as a mechanic at Cooper's Garage whilst living with his widowed mother. Moving to Southampton he took employment as the foreman at Wadham's Garage and in May 1939 joined 394 Company, 48th (Hants) Anti-Aircraft Battalion, Royal Engineers (TA). Three months later he transferred to the Royal Army Ordnance Corps and was posted to 43 Ordnance Company. Embodied at the outbreak of war and promoted to lance-corporal, he gained his second stripe in January 1940 having been posted to

the 6th Army Field Workshop. He was promoted to sergeant that March, to armament staff-sergeant in May, and to armament quarter-master-sergeant (WOII) in September. In February 1941 he reverted to armament staff-sergeant whilst with 20 Ordnance Workshop Company, embarked for the Middle East a month later, and on arrival was posted to the 4th Base Workshop in Cairo.

Sque was injured en route from Jalo to a rendezvous point in the Wadi Gamra in Libya during OPERATION BIGAMY, the September 1942 large-scale SAS raid on Benghazi. Reg Seekings, DCM, MM, later recalled:

We lost a very good chap there. He was thrown off a truck and broke his femur. He was on leave. He'd been working with this Irish major on our trucks. While we were working there, he said 'I'll have to come up with you' [on the operation]. But they wouldn't release him. So, he took leave. He said: 'They can't stop me. Can you get me on if I take leave?' I said 'Yeah, you can go where you like on leave, cant you?' 'Course I bloody can.' So he did, and got thrown off the truck – he was sleeping and they hit a bad bump – and broke his femur. Then, when the attack came, he got hit in his good leg and his bad leg. We had to leave him behind. One of the hardest things I had to do [IWM Sound Archive 18177].

Joe Plater, a former L Detachment fitter, later recalled:

One day I was riding on the top of one of the three-tonners with a corporal and I had a large toolbox with me. While passing a REME workshop near Heliopolis airport a sergeant-major joined us, not a member of the SAS but a friend of one of the officers … we were two or three days travelling most of the day and night. At one point during a night run we were only 15 miles away from a large Jerry airfield, we all had to drive nose to tail flat out. I was travelling on top of a lorry with two other chaps and had my toolbox with me. It was quite a large one. None of the drivers could see what they were travelling over. It was very bumpy and all three of us were thrown off the lorry including my toolbox which landed on top of one of the other chaps who was a sergeant-major injuring his hip. We strapped him on a stretcher and off we carried on. I was detailed to look after him, our Medical Officer attending to him later. We hadn't been spotted and carried on until daylight. We then camouflaged up for the day.

The aforementioned Medical Officer, Malcolm Pleydell, MC, later wrote using the nom de plume 'Malcolm James' that 'as he lay on the ground, shocked and in considerable pain, a cursory examination revealed he had fractured the upper part of his femur … we had anaesthetised him with the invaluable Pentothal' (*Born of the Desert*, by Malcolm James). Pleydell wrote to his future wife on 6 October 1942, soon after the events described:

I start off with a fractured Femur, which I had to carry on with us on the back of a lorry. I had to keep him well under with Morphia … We had to hurry to catch up with the others, and driving behind the lorry, it was hell to watch three legs and one stump being flung up in the air and falling back each time the lorry hit a bump so that we had to tie their legs down with a rope [Corporal James Webster's leg had been amputated after driving over a mine – see his entry below]. And the dust was thrown up and fell all over them, so they quickly became yellow, and we had to stop now and then to bath their faces and let them breath [IWM Documents.337 – Private Papers of Captain M. J. Pleydell, MC].

Although everything possible was done to make Sque comfortable the fact remained that the convoy had to move rapidly forward towards Benghazi, the operation having been planned to coincide with the British offensive at El Alamein. There was little that could be done to counteract the jolting of the suspension over rough ground. On 13 September the main force left Sque and Webster under the care of a medical orderly in a wadi whilst it went into Benghazi, Plater noting; 'I still had the injured SM [sergeant-major] with me so I covered him up in scrim netting whilst we went on this raid.' The attack, however, was aborted after the SAS column was ambushed on the approaches to the port. With the enemy forewarned it was forced to withdraw. Pleydell's account confirms that Sque was wounded again, almost certainly on the 15th, when the unit was bombed and strafed by aircraft; 'he had been shot in the leg which had already suffered a fracture' (*Born of the Desert*). Meanwhile, Plater recalled:

I stayed under the vehicle I was repairing and the rest scrambled for cover. The next wave were bombers. No good staying under the vehicle so I went as far away from the vehicle as I could before the next bombing run. We were crouched under a bush of spiky grass staying there from about 10.30am until 4.30pm not daring to move … every one of us was under cover, including the wounded … after everything had quietened down, our CO had us move back to the vehicles. I went to see how the wounded SM [sergeant-major] was. I had been caring for him throughout. Out of the six wounded the SM was the only one who had caught some of the machine-gun fire.

Due to the lack of remaining transport and the need for a rapid withdrawal to prevent further casualties, it was decided that the stretcher cases would be left behind with a medical orderly, referred to as 'Johnson' by Pleydell who wrote to his wife the following month:

When I got back to the others I found we had no room for stretcher cases as we had lost a good bit of transport. So I had to leave them with an Italian orderly who had given himself up. I offered to stay but I knew it wasn't really my job. It was a strange scene that night by the fitful light of the burning lorries and I tossing a one piastre piece and the two medical orderlies solemnly calling heads and tails. And so home again. I brought back two major wounded and all minor cases …
    I should have liked to have brought the man with the femur but there was no room for a stretcher [IWM Documents.337].

'Johnson' was instructed to wait until 0700hrs on the 16th and to take one Italian prisoner into Benghazi in a Jeep under a white flag to fetch help, whilst leaving the Italian medic with the wounded. Pleydell recalled that 'Wilkinson swore he was fit enough to travel' and that Lt-Colonel David Stirling, DSO, stayed in the area after the main party had moved on and saw:

… an Italian ambulance on its way to our rendezvous to pick up our wounded …
    I have since learned, with deep sorrow, that the British party who were left behind at Benghazi, died later as a result of their wounds. I can understand why Dawson died [Drongin – see his entry above]; the outlook for Longland was uncertain [Bailey – see his entry above]; Cox, I had expected to recover [Webster – see his entry below]; while the cause of Wilkinson's [Sque] death must remain a mystery. Finally Johnson, the medical orderly who accompanied them, also died some eighteen months later, although no reason for this is known [Born of the Desert – see the entry for 'Johnson' under the Unknown Identities section within Volume III].

Sque is officially recorded as having died of wounds at Benghazi on 19 October 1942. However a letter sent to the International Red Cross in January 1943 by the Senior British Officer at Campo PG.75 at Bari casts some doubt on whether the men were indeed picked up by the Italians:

The information on the attached sheets, listed under the headings given below, has been obtained from officers in this camp. It is hoped that this will be of value to you, and it is requested that you will be so good as to inform the various authorities concerned.
    Sque. Left badly wounded at Sidi Moies, Jebel, Cyrenaica. Buried Sidi Moies. By Capt [Arthur] Duveen when he went to look for food and water [Duveen of L Detachment had been separated from the main SAS party during the withdrawal from Benghazi]. When he returned he was told by the Arabs that *they* had died about 19/10/42 [author's italics, i.e. the unlikely implication that the whole party, consisting of Bailey, Drongin, Webster, and Sque, and perhaps 'Johnson', had all 'died' at the same time – see Drongin's entry above for a similar note contained in his service record].

Sidi Moies, which lies not far east of the Wadi Gamra, was unmanned by the Italians. Plater later recalled that the British were 'not not very welcome with any of the people in this place', the implication being that the men may have been murdered by locals. Seekings later recalled: 'He was killed. They finished him off. This is a side people don't see when they look at the glamour of SAS' (IWM Sound Archive 18177). Although posted missing in action Sque was automatically transferred to the Royal Electrical and Mechanical Engineers when it was formed on 1 October 1942 and is therefore officially recorded as such.

Son of Sidney and Jane Sque (née Baker) of Woodcock Lane, Hordle, Lymington, Hants – Younger brother of Sydney Sque of the Royal Army Service Corps.
Age 29.

Column 83. Also commemorated on New Milton's war memorial and within St Mary Magdalene Church, New Milton.

SERGEANT JAMES WALTER **WEBSTER** [6012106] ESSEX REGIMENT
AND L DETACHMENT SAS BRIGADE

James Webster was born on 25 October 1919 in Ilford, Essex. In November 1936, whilst working as a driver and mechanic, he joined the 4th Battalion, Essex Regiment (TA), and was mobilised at the outbreak of war, initially undertaking internal security duties in East London. Coming under the 54th (East Anglia) Division on 1 October the battalion soon moved to Kelvedon and Witham with companies being detached to Maldo, Hornchurch and North Weald for aerodrome defence. Webster was promoted to sergeant the following January and in April 1940 the battalion moved to Woller in Northumberland from where a detachment was posted to No.3 Independent Company for service in Norway.

Having embarked at Liverpool on 5 August 1940 the battalion arrived at Wilberforce Barracks in Freetown, Sierra Leone, on the last day of the month. Here Webster enlisted as a regular soldier on 24 March 1941, the battalion having been reinforced by the 2/5th Essex Regiment. He disembarked at Suez with the rest of the brigade in late July and moved to el-Tahag Camp until his battalion joined the 11th Indian Infantry Brigade at Maaten Baggush in August. Taking over the anti-aircraft and aerodrome defence of the Sidi Barrani landing grounds it remained on such duties until late October when it concentrated at Sidi Haneish. It was reassigned to the 5th Indian Infantry Division before moving to Alexandria at the beginning of November. On the 26th it sailed from Haifa for Famagusta, Cyprus, where it came under the 161st Indian Infantry Brigade until returning to Egypt via Haifa in March 1942.

Webster volunteered for L Detachment, SAS Brigade, on 4 June 1942, reverting to corporal in rank, but not in pay, in order to do so. He was wounded in action on 12 September on the approach to Benghazi during OPERATION BIGAMY. Jim Smith, former L Detachment who was in a Jeep behind Webster's, later recalled that Captain Bill Cumper, the unit's explosives officer, was ahead clearing a path through a minefield with a stick near the Trigh-el-Abd, 19 kilometres east of Msus:

> He [Cumper] said 'but whilst I'm doing this no man must go off the track.' And we had three-tonners and Jeeps and on the side of the road was this [abandoned] Daimler scout car. It was just as though it had come off the track, no camouflage, just army green … They [Webster, the driver, and the passenger, Lt-Commander Richard Ardley, RNR] just drove on with the Jeep to go and look at it. Bang they went. Well, they were told [personal interview, 2009].

Smith and others approached the now burning Jeep using its tyre tracks. Malcolm Pleydell, MC, the unit's former Medical Officer, later wrote under pseudonym that 'Cox, the driver,' (Webster - named changed for publication) had jumped out and run around to pull the officer out, but that as he did so he stepped on another bomb which 'exploded and shattered his leg' (*Born of the Desert*, by Malcolm James). Pleydell subsequently amputated Webster's leg whilst Smith held a blanket for shade so that the badly burnt naval officer, Ardley, could be treated: 'Webster was saying: "Take me boot off. It's crippling me." He didn't know he'd lost his leg, see. He thought his boot was tight' (personal interview, 2009).

Webster was loaded onto a truck with Ardley to join AQMS Arthur Sque. Pleydell cared for him, despite the almost unbearable, continuous jolting of the rough ground. That night at the unit's RV he noted that one of Webster's 'main interests concerned the welfare of the burned officer (who had died that night –

see his entry under Chatham Naval Memorial, United Kingdom, Volume III), but we satisfied him with our answers and told him that we had moved him further up the wadi to be with his friends' (*Born of the Desert*). Webster, however, gained strength and when the party went forward to raid Benghazi on the night of the 13th he and Sque were left under the care of an orderly in a wadi south-east of the harbour. He is officially recorded as having died of wounds at Benghazi on 16 September 1942, the day that he and three other wounded were left behind by the main force. There is, however, some suspicion that he, and the other men of this group, were murdered (see Sque's entry on previous pages for full details).

Son of Edward and Elizabeth Webster of Belfair Drive, Chadwell Heath, Romford, Essex.
Age 23.
Column 63.

EL ALAMEIN WAR CEMETERY

The cemetery is located close to where the three major battles of El Alamein took place. The first halted the advance of Rommel's Afrikakorps during July 1942. The second was a defensive victory to the south at Alam el Halfa during August and September. The third, a counter-offensive during October and November, marked the 'turning of the tide' and the beginning of Montgomery's advance to victory in North Africa.

The cemetery itself contains the graves of 7,240 members of the Commonwealth killed at all stages of the Western Desert campaigns, these having been concentrated from a wide area. Of these 815 are unidentified, the cemetery also containing 102 burials of other nationalities.

El Alamein is located 130 kilometres west of Alexandria on the main coast road to Mersa Matruh. The cemetery, set back from the road behind a ridge, is signposted and open daily 0700–1700hrs, although the visitors' book is not available after 1430hrs. GPS co-ordinates: Latitude 30.83819, Longitude 28.94707

TROOPER JAMES **LAMONT** [1237] DIVISIONAL CAVALRY REGIMENT
AND LRDG (A SQN)

James Lamont was born on 22 July 1905 in Scotland but as a young man migrated to New Zealand where he had family connections. Settling on the North Island he worked as a labourer for Thomas Borthwick & Sons in Feilding where he lived in the town's fire station. At the outbreak of war he enlisted into the Divisional Cavalry Regiment, embarking for the Middle East from Wellington in January 1940 after training at Ngaruawahia and Waiouru. As part of the first echelon of the 2nd New Zealand Expeditionary Force the regiment marched into Maadi Camp south of Cairo the following month. Further training ensued, the regiment's role being defined as motorised reconnaissance and flank protection.

That October Lamont suffered from dysentery but quickly rejoined his unit and in March 1941 embarked for Greece with the rest of the New Zealand Division as part of Lustre Force, tasked with bolstering Greek troops in defence of their homeland. When German forces attacked the following month the regiment attempted to delay them in front of the Kiwi-held Aliakmon Line using its few Bren Carriers and armoured cars. Soon forced to withdraw it was evacuated piecemeal from the mainland, Lamont's group being taken directly to Egypt where he was reported safe on 18 May.

That July Lamont attended the New Zealand Armoured Training School back at Maadi and on 12 September 1941 volunteered for the Long Range Desert Group. He was immediately attached to the 1st Battalion, Welch Regiment, for a month, more than likely to gain infantry experience. This was located in Cairo at Abbassia Barracks, the former home of the LRDG. Although it is unknown which patrol Lamont was assigned to when he returned to the Group he was almost certainly a member of A (New Zealand) Squadron.

On 24 February 1942 Lamont was admitted to No.8 South African Casualty Clearing Station when returning to Siwa Oasis from leave. He was subsequently placed on the seriously ill list on 11 March having been diagnosed as suffering with lobar pneumonia. He died on the morning of the 14th. The diary of 'Doc' Lawson, the LRDG Medical Officer, confirms that a member of the Group, who can only be Lamont, died of pneumonia at Mersa Matruh, the town where the Siwa track separated from the coastal road.

Son of John and Isabel Lamont of Low Wardneuk, Monkton, Prestwick, Ayrshire, Scotland – His brother, Matthew, was killed, aged 19, in the First World War whilst serving in the Royal Field Artillery and is buried at Englebelmer Communal Cemetery Extension on the Somme.
Age 36.
No inscription.
Grave 30.F.7. Also commemorated alongside his brother on Craigie's war memorial and on Feilding's cenotaph.

FAYID WAR CEMETERY

Opened in June 1941 to serve numerous local military hospitals this cemetery, originally known as Geneifa New War Cemetery, was in use until Commonwealth forces withdrew from Egypt. It contains 765 Commonwealth burials of the Second World War and 616 post-war military and civilian graves. In addition, there are 440 war burials of other nationalities.

Fayid is located 20 kilometres south of Ismailia on the western shore of the Great Bitter Lake, the mid point of the Suez Canal. This is the closest British cemetery to the original SAS camp at Kabrit. It lies on the south side of Fayid town, approximately 4 kilometres from its centre and on a connecting thoroughfare between the lake's shore and the main Ismailia–Suez road. Visitors are advised to use a private car or taxi. GPS co-ordinates: Latitude 30.30636, Longitude 32.32818

CAPTAIN TERENCE FREDERICK THOMAS <u>CHAMBERS</u> [IA/1013] ROYAL AIR FORCE, MAHRATTA LIGHT INFANTRY, L DETACHMENT SAS BRIGADE AND 1ST SAS (B SQN)

'Jim' or 'Jerry' Chambers, as he was known to his friends, was born on 4 April 1915 at Bishop's Hill in Somerset. As a day boy in Meynell House, King's College, Taunton, from 1929 to 1934 he was captain of swimming, company sergeant-major in the OTC and, in his final year, captain of rugby and of the school. At home his mother, a long-time member of the Red Cross, encouraged both him and his sister to qualify as members themselves and Chambers had completed three years' service within the organisation by September 1935. Having left King's he played rugby for Taunton, Salisbury and Wiltshire and excelled

at diving in which he also competed at county level.

Joining the Royal Air Force Chambers was commissioned as a flying officer in February 1936 and began to play for the RAF's own rugby team (service number 37747). By February 1939 he had been promoted to flight lieutenant but having been offered a permanent commission in the Indian Army he transferred, arriving at Bombay that November to serve as a 2nd lieutenant (*London Gazette* of India No.351 of 1940). Attached to the 10th Battalion, 5th Mahratta Light Infantry, he was put through officer training at Belgaum. In March 1940 he was posted to the 1st Battalion on the North West Frontier at Thal, joining the outposts at Kohat before being promoted to acting captain in command of a company later that month (*Kohat List* No.437 of 1940). Having attended various cavalry and armoured vehicle courses he arrived at Basra, Iraq, in May 1941. Although briefly evacuated back to India with malaria the following month he returned at the beginning of October. Qualifying in elementary Urdu in January 1942 he volunteered for L Detachment, SAS Brigade, on 26 May and was posted to Kabrit for training. Malcolm Pleydell, MC, the unit's former Medical Officer, later wrote under pseudonym that Chambers was the only man to parachute whenever he had the chance, if only to gain experience of doing so from different types of aircraft:

> He was a stocky chap and, on first impression, seemed to be incredibly talkative about India, with such terms as chota peg, and odd native expressions scattered liberally throughout his vocabulary …
>
> Jim had a face that was as honest as the day, and this was in keeping with his character for he was as sincere as they were made. I never heard him say a thing he did not mean, or ever adopt a hypocritical attitude, and that is high praise indeed [*Born of the Desert*, by Malcolm James].

Chambers was assigned the training of recruits at Kabrit and therefore missed the Sidi Haneish raid that July, Pleydell noting that this: 'must have been hard for Chambers to accept, but it was a very good thing for the unit, and the trainees were put through it in the old Jock Lewes style' (*Born of the Desert*). Chambers did however take part in Operation Bigamy, the large-scale Benghazi raid that September, and is noted in the post-operation report as having laid down covering fire so that the SAS column could withdraw when ambushed on its approach to the town (WO 201/748). Having later placed explosives on the Tobruk-Bardia

railway line 1st SAS' War Diary records that on 22 October: 'Capt Chambers' party left [from Kufra, consisting of Sergeant Philips, Sturmey and Henderson]. Nothing achieved but ran into very heavy mud and explosives were useless owing to rain. Chased by armoured patrol. Came by Wadi Elta and found Sillito who had walked with very little water and no food' (Parachutist 'Jack' Sillito was awarded the Military Medal for evading capture and walking over 160 kilometres alone towards Allied lines).

Lance-corporal W. Jones' application for Operational Wings records that Chambers led a party with Lieutenant Raymond Shorten to Howard's Cairn to establish a forward base during this period, Bill Deakins later recalling an operation to blow railway lines:

> The party under the command of Captain Jim Chambers, a 'hail fellow well met' type of person, who seemed to me as his first operation, out to show the mainly original regimental officers he had joined, he could do as well if not better than them …
>
> By now Captain Chambers, who from the time we had to plane down the sand dune leaving the Sand Sea outward bound, seemed to have lost his enthusiasm. He was suffering from very serious desert sores to his legs, which

although they can fester and spread quickly, I wondered if he had concealed the fact before starting the operation, to carry on and not be seen to be making excuses for not going. In the wadi where I had cleared the horned vipers, I saw him field dressing his legs, making a show of wrapping maps around, to be covered with bandages for, as he said, camouflage, if he needed to escape from anywhere. One could see his physical condition was poor, with pus soaking and staining his leg coverings …

On my return to our Kabrit base early in 1943 I was questioned on the whole incident by Captain Cumper, my OC, with no doubt David Lea [sic – Leigh – see his own entry under Époisses Communal Cemetery, France, Volume III] and the sergeant also having been questioned, although by this time, Captain Chambers, who had been flown out of the desert [to Cairo on 6 November 1942], was dead, having succumbed to diphtheria in his very weakened state [The Lame One: 'Sod this for a Game of Soldiers', by Bill Deakins].

Chambers had died at No.19 General Hospital at Geneifa on 4 December 1942 as result of these desert sores that were caused by small, infected cuts and abrasions commonly picked up on operations or in training (WO 218/96). Pleydell recalled that Chambers: 'Like quite a number of soldiers he hated 'going sick' and being sent to base on medical grounds. His conscience troubled him and he wondered if he was 'letting the squadron down.' (Born of the Desert). Major Paddy Mayne, DSO, his squadron commander, wrote:

Captain Chambers was suffering from desert sores. Captain Chambers had been operating in the Western Desert behind enemy lines from 23 Aug 42 to 5 Nov 42. I returned him to [the forward] base on the later date as he appeared to be run down and his desert sores, owing to lack of medical facilities, were becoming extensive. In my opinion his death was caused by the onerous and difficult conditions under which this unit operates i.e. short of water, always exposed to the sun, wind and sand and to the difficulties in evacuating sick.

During January 1943 Pleydell wrote to his wife:

I have lost a lot of friends. Poor old Jim Chambers and Raymond Shorten are dead – I think you have their photos. It's bloody awful. Jim was one of the best friends I had made, always ragging about …

There is Mrs Chambers – we use to call her son Jerry, only I dare not tell her that - I owe her at least two letters, but she is upset still at his death, that I feel writing does more harm than good. She has just sent me a Christmas card of a harvesting scene - very simple, a white horse and golden fields, and on the top she has written 'England' and on the back 'In memory of a noble son'. But if anyone made a joke about it, I would just about kill him – It's so easy to sneer and so hard to be honest and sincere [IWM Documents.337 – Private Papers of Captain M. J. Pleydell, MC].

King's College's Book of Remembrance notes: 'fearlessness, determination, generosity, warm-heartedness and a strong sense of duty were as characteristic of Chambers in his everyday activities and relationships as they were of him on the rugger field.'

The final word belongs to Chambers himself who had written in his will; 'I finish with the hope that I will not have died in vain and that Great Britain will not sink into the rut in which she was between 1925 and 1938.'

Only son of Thomas and Edyth Chambers (née Trott) of Mountway Road, Taunton, Somerset – Brother of Miss G. E. Chambers who served as an army nurse in West Africa.
Age 27.
'Who Dares Wins'. He died for England, now rests content. Fortis et Fidelis
Grave 1.C.2. Also commemorated on the King's College war memorial whilst his rugby caps, donated by his family, hang opposite the Headmaster's study.

PRIVATE JOSEPH ALOYSIUS <u>DUFFY</u> [3318385] SEAFORTH HIGHLANDERS, NO.11 COMMANDO AND L DETACHMENT SAS BRIGADE

Joe Duffy was born on 21 August 1919 in the town of Bathgate in West Lothian. Having worked as a colliery repairer, maintaining the wooden joists that support a mine, he enlisted at the beginning of December 1939 and was posted to the 306th Infantry Training Centre at Auchengate in Troon. Joining the Seaforth Highlanders in April 1940 he joined the 7th Battalion but volunteered for No.11 (Scottish) Commando four months later. This unit, having been temporarily reorganised as the 2nd Special Service Battalion, disembarked at Suez in Egypt as C Battalion, Layforce, in early March 1941.

At the end of April 1941 No.11, having been stood-to (and dropped from) a raid on Bardia earlier that month, moved to Cyprus in readiness for OPERATION EXPORTER, the campaign against the Vichy French in Syria. In the early hours of 9 June it subsequently landed close to the mouth of the Litani River in an attempt to seize bridges key to the Allied advance. Although these were destroyed by the French and No.11 suffered heavy casualties, the Commando effectively tied down Vichy troops until Australian forces arrived from the south. However, Duffy and his friend Private Ken Warburton were members of No.6 Troop that was left aboard HMS *Glengyle* due to the lack of landing craft. Arriving back in Egypt that August he volunteered for L Detachment, SAS Brigade, on 18 September.

Duffy and Warburton became the Regiment's first casualties during a parachute training accident on 16 October 1941. They were the first to jump from a Bombay aircraft that was carrying the third twelve-man stick of the day to a DZ on the east side of the Great Bitter Lake. As the first man, Warburton, made his exit the despatcher realised that his hook, used to connect the static line to the aircraft, had broken and that Warburton's parachute would not therefore deploy. The men were jumping in such quick succession that he did not have a chance to stop the second man, Duffy, but did manage to bar the exit of the remainder. In a memorandum on the origins of the Special Air Service Lt-Colonel David Stirling, DSO, stated:

> We had to devise parachute training methods from scratch. Repeated requests to Ringway produced no assistance whatsoever. Finally, after we had lost two men in our only fatal accident throughout training [*sic* – see Rawlinson's entry below and 'Wilson' under the Unknown Identity section within Volume III], I sent a final appeal to Ringway

> and they sent some training notes and general information, which arrived at the end of October after the completion of our parachute training course. Included in this information, we discovered that Ringway had had a fatal accident caused by exactly the same defect as in our case. Therefore if we had been sent the information earlier we would have undoubtedly avoided this accident [WO 201/721 – see Warburton's entry overleaf].

Son of Joseph and Mary Duffy of Paulville Road, Bathgate, West Lothian. Age 22.
In loving memory of my dear son Joseph on whose soul, sweet Jesus, have mercy. R.I.P.
Grave 1.D.16. Also commemorated on Bathgate's war memorial.

GUNNER FRANK WILLIAM **RAWLINSON** [831653] ROYAL ARTILLERY, L DETACHMENT SAS BRIGADE AND 1ST SAS

Frank Rawlinson was born on 4 January 1915 in Fulham, west London, where he later worked as a decorator. In September 1933 he enlisted into the Royal Artillery and was posted to the 1st Heavy Brigade with which he served in Hong Kong from January 1935. He was re-posted to the 15th Heavy Battery, 6th Heavy Regiment, in Ceylon in October 1937 but a year later stowed away on the SS *Strathallen* bound for Australia. On being discovered he was promptly returned to Ceylon and awarded fifty-six days detention for going AWOL. Arriving back in the UK in January 1939 he was posted to HQ Southern Ports and having completed his six-year engagement was transferred to the Army Reserve that June. Despite his earlier indiscretion his discharge papers, signed in Ceylon, stated: 'possesses all the attributes of a good, keen and intelligent soldier. Cheerful, reliable, and smart and has worked well. Honest and sober.'

Rawlinson was mobilised at the outbreak of war that September and posted to the Reserve Training Depot. In May 1940 he joined the 502nd Coastal Defence Regiment that was responsible for Torry Point Battery in Aberdeen and after three months was promoted to lance-bombardier. In September he was again promoted and began a series of postings to various coastal batteries before joining the 396th Coast Battery at London Road, Southend-on-Sea, Essex, in February 1941 and being advanced to sergeant.

Rawlinson embarked for the Middle East the same month and by November 1941 had been promoted to WOII (BSM). However, in June 1942 he reverted to the rank of gunner at his own request. Although his service record states he officially transferred to the SAS on 26 December 1942 he is known to have taken part in raids prior to this and his willingness to give up such seniority strongly suggests that this was the date that he actually joined L Detachment, SAS Brigade.

Rawlinson took part in OPERATION BIGAMY, the large-scale Benghazi raid of September 1942. He was promoted to lance-bombardier on the 21st, the day the SAS gained regimental status, and to bombardier the following day. Leaving Kabrit with A Squadron on 7 October he arrived at Kufra on the 13th. Here the squadron split into two, both parties making their way to the northern edge of the Great Sand Sea where they established a forward operating base. By the 22nd, with ammo and fuel dumps in place over a wide area, raiding parties were ready to attack enemy road and rail traffic. On 2 November the squadron's War Diary noted that Rawlinson had 'returned from a recovery job. Nothing achieved' whilst two days later he and two other men went out into the desert to try and bring back two abandoned Jeeps. They returned that night with one in tow and subsequently retrieved the other. Soon after he was a member of a small team under Lieutenant Miles MacDermott tasked with observing enemy traffic along the coastal road near Gazala. Despite running into six enemy armoured cars close to the el Adem–Hacheim track the patrol made a full log of movements before its position was overrun by advancing British troops on the 19th. On returning to Kufra on the 22nd Rawlinson reverted to the rank of gunner.

In late January 1943 Rawlinson travelled with the unit to Azzib on the Palestinian coast for training but by March was back at Kabrit, 1st SAS' War Diary recording: 'No.13 Parachute Course completed their jumps. Pct Rawlinson received head injuries from which he died on 11/03/43' (WO 218/97). Keith Killby joined 1st SAS that day, noting in his memoirs, *In Combat Unarmed*, that: 'we had arrived on an inauspicious day. One man had been killed on landing, for just as he touched down a gust of wind swept him up again and swung him onto a bulldozer that should never have been anywhere near.' The War Diary also notes that Rawlinson's funeral took place on the 13th whilst his casualty card confirms that on the 11th he was admitted to 19th General Hospital at Geneifa with concussion and that he died there of 'Cerebral Haemorrhage' the same day. Later that month No.4 Middle East Training School, which ran such parachute courses, moved from Kabrit to Ramat David in Palestine.

Son of Mr and Mrs Samuel Rawlinson (née Parrott) of Marnel Way, Hounslow, Middlesex.

Age 28.
In loving memory of Frank. At rest
Grave 5.B.2. His grave is incorrectly inscribed 'Army Air Corps' under which the SAS did not fall until 1 April 1944.

PRIVATE KENNETH **WARBURTON** [2821591] SEAFORTH HIGHLANDERS, NO.11 COMMANDO AND L DETACHMENT SAS BRIGADE

Ken Warburton was born in Salford on 9 July 1920. Having worked as a glove cutter in Manchester he enlisted into the Seaforth Highlanders in August 1939 and after attending various infantry training centres served with the 6th Battalion in France from April 1940. The following month the battalion vainly attempted to hold back the German Blitzkrieg: badly bombed it was pushed back to Zillebeke Lake, just south of Ypres, where it held the heavy responsibility of the left flank. On the 27th it was forced, by the sheer weight of the enemy, to retire and Warburton was subsequently evacuated to the UK, his service record noting that he rejoined his unit on 9 June.

That August Warburton volunteered for No.11 (Scottish) Commando, disembarking at Suez in Egypt as a member of C Battalion, Layforce, in early March 1941. At the end of April, having been stood-to (and dropped from) a raid on Bardia earlier that month, No.11 moved to Cyprus in readiness for OPERATION EXPORTER, the campaign against the Vichy French in Syria. In the early hours of 9 June the Commando subsequently landed close to the mouth of the Litani River in an attempt to seize bridges key to the Allied advance. Although these were destroyed by the French and No.11 suffered heavy casualties, it effectively tied down Vichy troops until Australian forces arrived from the south. However, Warburton had been a member of No.6 Troop that was left aboard HMS *Glengyle* due to the lack of landing craft.

At the beginning of August 1941 No.11 returned from Cyprus to Egypt and Warburton volunteered for L Detachment, SAS Brigade, alongside his friend and fellow Seaforth, Private Joe Duffy, on 18 September. The pair became the Regiment's first casualties during a parachute training accident on 16 October 1941 (see Duffy's entry on previous pages for full details).

Warburton was later described by Jimmie Storie, former L Detachment, as: 'a gifted pianist … One time we were walking through Cairo when we came across a concert hall being prepared for an evening performance. We persuaded Warburton to go and play something on the piano. What he played was just wonderful' (*Stirling's Men: The Inside History of the SAS in World War II*, by Gavin Mortimer).

Son of James and Edith Warburton (née Leetch) of Leopold Street, Weaste, Salford, Lancashire.
Age 21.
No inscription.
Grave 1.D.14.

HELIOPOLIS WAR CEMETERY

Opened in October 1941 to serve Cairo's military hospitals this cemetery contains 1,742 Commonwealth burials and eighty-three graves of other nationalities. The Heliopolis (Port Tewfik) Memorial, situated at the entrance to the cemetery, commemorates almost 4,000 men of the Indian Army who died in Egypt and Palestine during the First World War, and who have no known grave. It was moved here after the original memorial at Port Tewfik was destroyed during Israeli-Egyptian fighting of the 1970s. In addition, the Heliopolis (Aden) Memorial to more than 600 men who died defending Aden during the First World War and who have no known grave, was erected to the rear of the cemetery after the original was destroyed in 1967.

Heliopolis, a major suburb of Cairo, lies 10 kilometres to the north-east of the city centre, approximately 6 kilometres from the airport. The cemetery is situated opposite El Banat (Girls') College on Nabil-el-Wakkard Street from which access is gained. GPS co-ordinates: Latitude 30.07973, Longitude 31.32963

LIEUTENANT JAMES DOUGLAS <u>HENRY</u> [316338] SOUTHERN RHODESIAN TERRITORIAL FORCE, KING'S AFRICAN RIFLES, ROYAL ENGINEERS AND LRDG (S.2 PATROL, A SQN)

Jim Henry, sometimes known by friends as 'Wimpey' or 'Dopey', was born in Johannesburg. He was educated at Bradfield College in England, the University of Cape Town and finally at Rhodes University College where he qualified as a surveyor. For a number of years he worked for an aircraft operator in

Rhodesia and as a surveyor for both the South African and Rhodesian governments. His service record notes that, having served in the ranks of the Southern Rhodesian Territorial Force (service number M773), he was granted a Governor's Commission in the territorial 57th (Southern Rhodesia) Survey Unit at the beginning of March 1940. Drafted to East Africa a few days later he surveyed Kenya's Northern Frontier District. After a brief period with the 7th King's African Rifles he was commissioned into the 512th Survey Unit, Royal Engineers, on 1 June 1942 (*London Gazette* 14/04/44), the date that he disembarked in Egypt.

Having volunteered for the Long Range Desert Group on 2 August 1942 Henry's S.2 Patrol left Kufra Oasis on 20 November and reached Zouar in Chad on 2 December. Moving on towards Zouarke it returned to Zouar on the 5th so that Private Bert Jordan, who had suffered fatal injuries en route, could be evacuated by air (see Jordan's entry under Brookwood Memorial, United Kingdom, Volume III). Leading a French column north S.2 was the first patrol to help Général Leclerc's troops on their long march into Tunisia. Not only did they provide a vital wireless link to the Eighth Army but also, as Henry noted in his report, played a part in the fighting:

> We got within a couple of miles of the oasis when we were attacked by six fighters and two bombers with MG fire and bombs. Desert was good going so we fought back, gradually edging off towards the hills and dodging bombs during our spare moments. Saw a column of black smoke rising several miles north of us. My gunner said it was an aircraft burning though he had not actually seen the crash. Soon afterwards ground strafing ceased but bombing continued for some time … a Frenchman in the patrol said he had seen the aircraft crash and since ours were the only trucks that fired Colonel Ingold credited us with shooting it down and complimented us on the calm and organised way in which we had met the attack, saying that we had set an excellent example to the French troops [WO 201/815].

Henry was relieved by I.1 Patrol of the Indian Long Range Squadron at Sebha on 10 January 1943 prompting Leclerc to inform General Alexander: 'I end this letter by telling you how much I regret seeing the departure of Capt [*sic*] Henry's patrol. Their behaviour throughout the recent operations has been exemplary.' His words were heart-felt and on 30 January 1943 he awarded Henry the Croix de guerre (étoile en argent).

Having been retasked S.2 left Hon late in January 1943 to drop A Force agents and recce a route to Tozeur. It reached the latter having lost one truck due to a mine, delivered its passengers, and withdrew to an area near Foum Tatahouine, well inside Allied lines and not far from the Ghadames road. Here the patrol was challenged by a detachment of camel troops on 20 February, Lance-sergeant 'Cito' Calder-Potts later reporting:

> They were on the top of a knoll, and the OC patrol [Henry] went up in his Jeep to meet him. The man came up to the Jeep, and then ran back about 10 yards waving his hand. I saw two puffs of dust near him as he was running back. They then opened fire on the Jeep with one MG and two rifles … there was about thirty to forty men with fifty camels. We uncovered our guns (we had come through a storm the day before) and the only gun that worked was the 20mm Breda. After the Breda had moved them from the top of the knoll and we had moved behind cover, it was decided that the OC and Private ['Happy'] Rezin had been killed and the enemy held the advantage, so it would not pay us to continue the fight [WO 218/91].

Moving to Nalut the patrol learnt that the contact had been with Free French Algerian Mécharistes rather than the Italian colonial troops they had supposed. Whilst Rezin had been killed Henry had been brought to Nalut having been shot twice, one round touching his spine (see Rezin's entry under Medjez-el-Bab War Cemetery, Tunisia, within this volume). Calder-Potts saw the now paralysed Henry on the 22nd just before he was evacuated to Tripoli. His officer explained that he had mistaken the Algerians for Italians and fired two shots to warn the patrol. Captain Bill Kennedy Shaw, the LRDG's Intelligence Officer, later wrote: 'the reason for the incident can be attributed to the failure of Henry's W/T [wireless telegraphy – radio] set, which prevented Group HQ from warning him of the presence of these troops in his area' (WO 218/91). Meanwhile, a letter signed only as 'Evans' states:

> Jim was taken back to hospital, we used to visit him when we could. He was his cheerful self and refused to allow us to think he was more than slightly wounded. He was always saying that after a spot of leave at home he would be back with us again.
>
> When he died we mourned the loss of a great officer and a darn good friend [*Long Range Desert Group Rhodesia: The Men Speak*, by Jonathan Pittaway].

Henry died of his wounds on 26 August 1943 at No.15 (Scottish) General Hospital in Cairo. Leclerc, whose Free French troops went on to play a valuable part in the Tunisian campaign, was said to be 'terribly upset'; 'Truly he was a chic type.'

Son of James and Josine Henry of Paradise Road, Newlands, Cape Town, South Africa.
Age 38.
Deeply mourned by his parents and sister. His duty well done
Grave 5.J.8. Also commemorated on the cloistered war memorial on Main Street, Bulawayo.

SAPPER FREDERICK GEORGE MOORE [1877530] ROYAL ENGINEERS AND SBS (S SQN)

Fred Moore was born on 9 January 1922 at Tunbridge Wells in Kent. Having worked as a dairyman he enlisted into the Royal Engineers at Chatham in July 1939, training as a pioneer. He embarked for the Middle East late in September 1941 and arrived in Egypt at the beginning of December. Although wounded in action on 1 February 1942 whilst serving with 1st Armoured Division's 7th Field Squadron he recovered in time to take part in the battles of El Alamein later that year.

Having volunteered for special duties Moore was posted to Raiding Forces HQ on 21 November 1943. Joining the Special Boat Squadron (1st SAS) four days later he attended parachute course No.85 at Ramat David the following month. He was one of nine men that subsequently raided the Dodecanese island of Piscopi during early July 1944, the intention being to destroy aircraft at St Antonio aerodrome. However, the enemy was found to be too numerous and Moore's commander, Lieutenant R. Smith of HQ Patrol, M Detachment, decided to withdraw having carried out a detailed recce.

Later that month Moore was wounded in action on the island of Simi during OPERATION TENEMENT, an attempt to convince the Germans that British troops intended to hold the island. Situated along the extended lines of Axis communication it was hoped that occupying Simi would entice the enemy into battle, thereby presenting targets for Allied naval and air forces. Until recently Moore's fate after evacuation from the island was unknown to his comrades. However, in 2010 Ralph Bridger, a former Royal Marine and member of the wartime SBS, contacted the author:

Fred was a good friend. He was very friendly and likeable. He had a number of sisters. Fred was in S Detachment [later Squadron]. I was in M. I know he went on other raids in the Dodecanese …

[On 14 July 1944 on Simi during TENEMENT] there was a lot of sniper fire so Lt Bury gave me and Fred a message to give to Capt McBeth on top of the hill [Moore volunteered to accompany Bridger to ensure news that the enemy had surrendered in Simi Town reached McBeth whose men were assaulting positions in the area of the monastery – see Bob Bury's entry under Phaleron War Cemetery, Greece, Volume II]. We got pinned down by [a German] machine gun half way up the hill. There was two or three trees and we made for them and just as we reached them the sniper hit Fred in the left buttock. We had no medical kit so I took my jacket and laid it over his wound. He was by then unconscious. I made my way to the top and reported to Captain McBeth and Sgt Geary who were observing from the top of the hill. We had to wait until the gunfire died down before we got to Fred [personal correspondence, 2010].

Bridger later added:

He [McBeth] got on his pad and wrote one back saying 'Take this back to Lt Bury. We will see what we can do about Fred'. I got back down the hill after being sniped at about six times. I gave the message to Lt Bury and apparently what had happened in between there was another officer by the name of Fox who had come down and he was a good speaker of Italian and he managed to talk the Eyeties into giving up [interview with Ralph Bridger by kind permission of Colin and Lynn Smith, 2014].

Further investigation by Bridger and Bob Harris, brother of Private Henry Harris, SBS, who is commemorated on the Brookwood Memorial, found that Moore had been evacuated to Egypt and that his next of kin had been informed on 22 July that he had been wounded in action. Diagnosed with both a complicated fracture to the head of his left femur and Sciatic Palsy Moore died of his wounds in 63rd British General Hospital, Cairo, on 27 October 1944. Thanks to enquiries made by Bridger and Harris Moore took his place on the Regiment's Roll of Honour. He was mentioned in despatches 'in recognition of gallant and distinguished services in the field' (*London Gazette* 36907, 25/01/45), Bridger noting 'I think his MiD was awarded for bravery on Simi … I served with some very brave chaps and lots of them were killed or wounded (for what?)' (Personal correspondence, 2010).

Only son of Ernest and Mary Moore of Edwin Street, Gravesend, Kent – Believed to have had five sisters.
Age 21.
In memory or our dear son. Of your charity pray for the repose of his soul. R.I.P.
Grave 6.L.2.

SUEZ WAR MEMORIAL CEMETERY

This cemetery was opened in 1918 to serve military hospitals of the First World War. Graves from farther afield were subsequently concentrated here and those in the adjoining Arbain Indian Cemetery absorbed into its perimeter. During the last war the area was home to numerous camps, the cemetery now containing 513 Commonwealth burials of the First World War and 377 from the Second World War, some of which are commemorated by special memorial.

The port of Suez is located at the southern end of the Suez Canal, approximately 130 kilometres east of Central Cairo. The cemetery lies in the western suburbs, approximately 7 kilometres from the centre, and is open Saturday to Thursday 0700–1430hrs. GPS co-ordinates: Latitude 29.972474, Longitude 32.536310

CAPTAIN THOMAS **MONTGOMERIE** [62629] BLACK WATCH, NO.4 COMMANDO, 9TH QUEEN'S ROYAL LANCERS AND SPECIAL BOAT SECTION ATT L DETACHMENT SAS BRIGADE

Tom Montgomerie was born on 14 March 1914 in the parish of Williamfield at the coastal town of Irvine in Ayrshire. Having been educated at Wixenford and Eton he entered the Royal Military College Sandhurst and was commissioned into the Black Watch (Royal Highland Regiment) at the beginning of February 1934 (*London Gazette* 01/02/34). Initially posted to the 2nd Battalion he embarked for India to join the 1st during March 1936. At the end of the year he sailed from Bombay, disembarking at Port Sudan where he was cross-posted back to the 2nd Battalion in April 1937. He rejoined the 1st in Palestine at the beginning of 1938 for policing duties during the Arab Revolt but was back with the 2nd on its arrival that summer. By 1939 he was appointed Camp Commandant, 18th Infantry Brigade, and returned to the UK that July.

Montgomerie landed in France with the 1st Battalion as part of the BEF in October 1939 but a week later was posted to the regiment's infantry training centre at Perth, a period briefly interrupted by attending 165 OCTU at Dunbar. The following June he was promoted to acting captain and in January 1941 volunteered for No.1 Company, 3rd Special Service Battalion, in Troon, relinquishing a pip in order to do so. This formation was soon disbanded and split up into its original Commando units, No.1 Company reverting to its previous title of No.4 Commando later that month. On 21 February it embarked at Gourock for what it believed to be the next in a long series of training exercises. However, the following day at Scapa Flow the men were informed that they would land on the Lofoten Islands off Norway to destroy herring and cod liver oil factories, the product of which was being used in the manufacture of German explosives (OPERATION CLAYMORE). Specific training began in earnest and on 4 March Montgomerie led A Troop ashore at Svolvær on the island of Austvågøya, acting as a mobile reserve alongside E Troop. CLAYMORE resulted in the destruction of eleven fish oil factories and over 800,000 gallons of reserves, the sinking of ten enemy vessels, the capture of 215 Germans and ten Norwegian quislings, the recovery of 315 Norwegian volunteers and the capture of material vital to the breaking of the German Enigma code.

Despite this success moral amongst officers was low due to the Commando's slender deployment record since its formation. On 8 July 1941 Montgomerie therefore followed several of his comrades and moved on in search of action. He intended to rejoin the Black Watch but only got as far as No.8 Infantry Training Centre where he remained until transferring to the 9th Queen's Royal Lancers, Royal Armoured Corps, that September. He outlined his logic for doing so in a letter to the centre's Adjutant:

> My reason for applying is that in my opinion there is more chance of immediate active service in the Royal Armoured Corps than in the infantry; and that the Officer Commanding the 9th Lancers has expressed himself willing to accept me in his regiment.

Proved correct he embarked for the Middle East within a few days, arriving late in November. Two months later he was able to organise an attachment to the 2nd Battalion, Black Watch, but in April 1942 was nominally posted to the Middle East Commando having joined the Special Boat Section. This small team of canoeists, assigned to the Royal Navy submarine flotilla at Alexandria for special operations, fell under the command of 1st SAS later that year, although many of its members, including Montgomerie, were already attached.

Late in June 1942 Montgomerie, who by now had nominally transferred back to the Black Watch, coordinated OPERATION ALUITE from a rented house in the hills above Beirut. From here he allocated fellow former Royal Highland officers, Lieutenants David Sutherland and Eric Newby, as well as Lieutenant Tommy Langton, Lieutenant Michael Alexander and Sergeant Jimmy Sherwood, areas of coastline between Lattakia and Haifa to recce. The information gathered was intended for use in the event of an Axis thrust from the Caucasus through Turkey or Persia to the Mediterranean.

In August 1942 Montgomerie was joined by WO George Barnes, Corporal Gurney, Alexander and Sherwood, the latter now wearing the ribbon of the Military Medal awarded for attempting to save the life of an SBS officer (see Captain Robin Grant-Watson's entry under Knightsbridge War Cemetery, Libya, within this volume). The five landed from an MTB just behind the enemy lines on the Egyptian coast to destroy a transport dump at Daba. Despite having to move through a tented camp to reach their target charges were successfully laid and considerable damaged caused for the loss of Alexander and Gurney captured.

On his return Montgomerie collected the latest intelligence reports regarding the island of Rhodes. He was on this way to deliver these to fellow SBS members preparing for OPERATION ANGLO when he was killed in a road accident. That November officers of the newly-expanded 1st SAS Regiment held a court of inquiry, Private Henry Mullen being called as a witness:

> I had orders to collect Capt Montgomerie and Lieut (QM) Rees at Cairo and convey them to the 1st SAS Regt at

Kabrit for duty [*sic* – at that time still L Detachment, SAS Brigade]. I was driving a Jeep with the two officers … [illegible] … 97 Kilo mark at about 1600hrs on the 18th August 1942. I reduced speed to almost about 35 to 40mph to take a left hand, but owing to some sand on the road at this point I went into a skid which caused the Jeep to skid sufficiently far to strike a barrel placed on the side of the road, it being used as a road marker. The car, now out of control, ran over the embankment which was about 5 feet deep. Capt Montgomerie and myself were then thrown clear. After a while the car overturned through striking a pile of stones. This is all I remember of the accident.

Meanwhile, Rees stated:

When about 1 mile from the Kabrit turning, the right front wheel of the vehicle ran onto the side of the road, the effect of the sand pulled the vehicle still further causing it to run down the embankment and … [illegible] a distance of about 20 yards … [illegible] stone and overturned. At some time after the vehicle left the road, Capt Montgomery and the driver were thrown out. When I recovered I rendered first aid and stopped the first vehicle for further assistance. Estimated speed of vehicle was 35–40mph. The time was approximately 1545hrs. The road surface was good and visibility clear.

Montgomerie's death certificate confirms that he was 'attd. L Det SAS' and that he had been subsequently admitted to No.13 General Hospital with serious head injuries, dying of shock a few hours later without having regained consciousness. The inquiry attributed no blame. Henry Mullen was later murdered after capture during OPERATION BULBASKET (see his entry under Rom Communal Cemetery, France, Volume III).

Son of Captain The Hon. Francis Cunningham Montgomerie, formerly of the King's Own Scottish Borderers and the Life Guards, and of Alice Dudley Montgomerie of Gattonside House, Melrose, Roxburghshire – Younger brother of Henry Montgomerie who also died as a result of an accident in 1947.
Age 28.
'God is love, and he that abideth in love abideth in God, and God abideth in him'
Grave 2.B.12. Also commemorated at Eton College.

ISRAEL

The State of Israel was created in May 1948. Prior to this the land had been part of Palestine, its varied terrain and coastline making it ideal for the training purposes of those formations covered within this Roll of Honour.

At the outbreak of war large numbers of Palestinian Jews enlisted into the British Army. Although initially restricted to joining the Auxiliary Military Pioneer Corps, many subsequently became founding members of No.51 Commando and saw action along the North African coast and during the East African Campaign. Others went on to serve in the June 1941 campaign against the Vichy French in what is modern-day Lebanon (OPERATION EXPORTER). On the lifting of restrictions many joined The Buffs (Royal East Kent Regiment) whose Palestinian infantry companies were later to form the basis of the Palestine Regiment and then the Jewish Brigade. In April 1942 a handful of German-speaking Jews volunteered for the newly formed Special Interrogation Group (SIG) that fell under the command of Captain David Stirling, DSO. This supported raiding operations in the Western Desert (for further detail see entries for Private Eliahu Gottlieb and Corporal Petr Haas under Alamein Memorial, Egypt, within this volume, and for Captain Herbert Buck, MC, under Reading Crematorium, United Kingdom, Volume III).

Towards the end of the North African Campaign in early 1943 A Squadron, 1st SAS, began training in the Golan Heights in Syria, this region now forming part of Israel. After most of the Regiment's subunits were restructured as the Special Raiding Squadron (SRS) on 19 March it moved to a camp between Azzib and Nahariya, 32 kilometres north of Haifa and just south of the Syrian border. As part of the now named Raiding Forces (1st SAS Regiment) intensive back-to-basics training commenced, the culmination of which saw each man able to march back to camp from Lake Tiberias, a distance of roughly 72 kilometres over difficult, hilly terrain. In addition, men attended Major Grant-Taylor's close combat course in Jerusalem and, once the squadron was informed that it would soon make an operational amphibious landing, practiced cliff climbing on the border of Syria. Unbeknown to the men this was in preparation for OPERATION HUSKY, the invasion of Sicily that they would embark on that July.

HQ Raiding Forces (1st SAS Regiment) was also based at Azzib. From here it delivered the planning and command element of the SRS, SBS, the Greek Sacred Squadron, the Kalpaks, Holding Unit Special Forces, the Light Repair Squadron and the RF Signals Squadron. The Raiding Support Regiment, which provided heavy weapons capability to its operations, was co-located. From 8 February 1944 Raiding Forces became a formation in its own right, free of its Regimental title, and continued to oversee those associated units that remained in theatre until it was disbanded in July 1945.

Meanwhile, the SBS (1st SAS), which prior to 19 March 1943 had been D Squadron, 1st SAS, based itself close to the crusader fort of Château Pèlerin at Athlit, a few kilometres south of Haifa. Its men trained not only from the beach adjacent to their camp but also on Lake Tiberias. Despite embarking for the Dodecanese from Haifa that September alongside the LRDG the SBS continued to be based at Athlit until the last of the unit's elements transferred to Italy in mid September 1944.

March 1943 also saw the move of No.4 Middle East Training School, provider of the region's parachute instruction, from Kabrit in Egypt to Ramat David, midway between Mount Carmel and Nazareth. It was here that many of the men included in this Roll of Honour qualified for their wings.

One member of the LRDG and one of the Greek Sacred Squadron now rest within Khayat Beach War Cemetery near Haifa whilst a soldier of K Detachment, SAS Brigade, is buried at Ramleh War Cemetery near Tel Aviv.

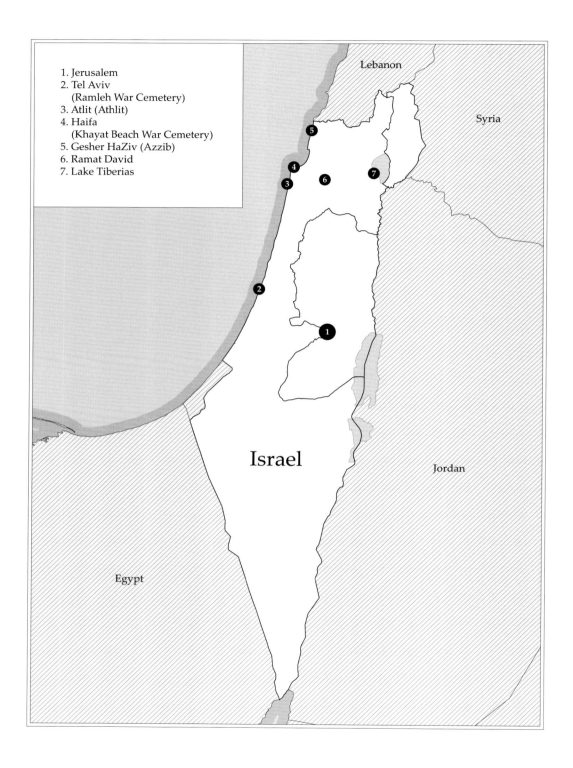

1. Jerusalem
2. Tel Aviv
   (Ramleh War Cemetery)
3. Atlit (Athlit)
4. Haifa
   (Khayat Beach War Cemetery)
5. Gesher HaZiv (Azzib)
6. Ramat David
7. Lake Tiberias

Lebanon

Syria

Israel

Jordan

Egypt

KHAYAT BEACH WAR CEMETERY

With its deep-water harbour, rail links, oil pipeline terminus and airfield, Haifa grew into a busy wartime supply hub. The cemetery, which opened in 1941, was prepared for the burial of service personnel from northern Palestine (modern-day Israel), although graves were also concentrated from the nearby Haifa (Sharon) British Civil Cemetery, from Mafrog Cemetery in former Trans-Jordan, and from Dafna Cemetery in Syria. It now contains 691 Commonwealth burials and ninety-one war graves of other nationalities. The majority of non-war burials are of soldiers who were killed during disturbances preceding the end of the British mandate in Palestine in May 1948.

The cemetery is located 5 kilometres south-west of the centre of Haifa on the east side of Route 4. Parking is available within the adjacent civil cemetery and access is twenty-four hours. GPS co-ordinates: Latitude 32.79922, Longitude 34.9618

STRATIOTIS EFSTRATIOS **LIAKATOS** [UNKNOWN S/N] ROYAL HELLENIC ARMY
ATT 1ST SAS (GREEK SACRED SQN)

On 13 March 1943 No.4 Middle East Training School (No.4 METS) moved from Kabrit, where it had provided parachute instruction for residents of the adjacent SAS camp, to Ramat David in Palestine.

It was hoped the terrain surrounding this new location would prove a more suitable training area for the next stage of the war. Although the staff had been assured that swings, jumping towers, trolley runs, slides, landing trainers and dummy fuselages had all been constructed by the Royal Engineers in advance of their arrival, this proved not to be the case. Hastily, mattresses were scavenged from the army and sand pits dug so that some form of ground training could take place. Courses eventually resumed at the end of the month but the number of those requiring instruction at the new location had increased considerably, ninety ranks qualifying as parachutists every three days in May alone. At the time courses consisted of three days ground training followed by five descents over the following three days. However, by the end of June this had been extended to two weeks which included eight days of ground training and culminated in eight jumps, two at night and two being with equipment containers. From October 1942 until this time No.4 METS had recorded 670 flying hours, resulting in 16,500 descents and even though a report at the end of June noted 'casualty figures have never been high at No.4 METS', such a workload meant injuries were inevitable (AIR 29/702).

On 12 July 1943 the War Diary of Raiding Forces (1st SAS) noted: 'One of the Greek Squadron SAS Regt killed while carrying out a parachute course at 4 METS Ramat David' (WO 218/98). Meanwhile, that day's entry within Ramat David's Operations Record Book states: 'Greek trainee killed on statichute [static line] descent. General lecture as result of accident given by OC to trainees and instructors' (AIR 29/702). There are no further details. However, despite the fact that neither log records a name, Stratiotis (Private) Efstratios Liakatos (Ευστράτιος Λιακάτος) is the only known Greek soldier within the vicinity to have died on the 12th (his headstone uses this spelling as opposed to that 'Liakatsos' of his online CWGC entry). Courses No.51, 52 and 53 were running at the time, 51 having completed the first of their descents.

A summary of the station's training program during July highlighted that the 'percentage of refusals has increased slightly, as is inevitable after a fatal accident (AIR 29/702). Airborne Forces in Palestine suffered another casualty on the 12th when Private George Burbage of the 11th Battalion, Parachute Regiment, fell to his death. He is also buried within this war cemetery. Two weeks previously, Squadron Leader Millsom, the Commanding Officer of No.4 METS, had written:

> It has occurred in the past, and will continue to occur during periods of rush training dictated by higher policy, that the standard of the finished article is reduced. During these rush periods, casualties, and, more important, refusals, definitely increase …
>
> Under conditions of pressure, our parachute packing section work 24 hours a day, and the uniformed and often quite illiterate army privates think to themselves and discuss the possibility of parachutes not being packed properly. Even officers in Parachute Battalions quite frankly state that they are not happy, and in some cases are not prepared to jump, with parachutes packed by personnel who themselves will not, or are not allowed to jump. To prove to the ordinary pupil that parachuting contains considerably less risks that are normally entailed in crossing a street in

London during rush hour, I feel that the ordinary members of this unit, as opposed to the parachute instructors, should be in a position, at the discretion of the Commanding Officer, to jump by statichute as a demonstration before the pupils, in order to maintain their morale. The casualty rate of this unit is .45% and since the beginning we have only had two fatal accidents, of which one was due to the failure of a parachute, and we have done over 20,000 descents [WO 201/2325].

Ανδρῶν γὰρ ἐπιφανῶν πᾶσα γῆ τάφος (For illustrious men have the earth world as their tomb – *Funeral Oration*, by Pericles)
Grave C.E.9.

LANCE-SERGEANT THOMAS KITCHENER <u>STIBBON</u> [6406105] ROYAL SUSSEX REGIMENT AND LRDG

Tom Stibbon was born on 19 January 1915 in the market town of Swaffham, Norfolk. In January 1940 he married Kathleen Irene Ferris at Haven Green Baptist Church in Ealing where he worked as a milkman. That June he enlisted into the Royal Sussex Regiment at Seaford, West Sussex, and was posted to 50th Battalion. Re-posted to the 10th Battalion he attended various command, physical training, and cookery courses before being promoted to lance-corporal that November. In the summer of 1941 he attended an advanced infantry assault course at the Special Training Centre at Inverailort Castle on the west coast of Scotland, passing with 86 per cent and being promoted to corporal that November. In the New Year he was attached to the East and South East Command's Wireless Transmission School.

Having embarked for the Middle East in October 1942 Stibbon arrived in Egypt at the beginning of 1943 and was posted to No.1 Infantry Training Depot before joining his regiment's 2nd Battalion later that month. Within a few days he had been confirmed as lance-sergeant and was posted to Iraq with Paiforce in March.

Stibbon volunteered for the Long Range Desert Group on 7 January 1944 and attended a parachute course at Ramat David the following month. The school's log notes that before he could make his first descent he was killed in a 'road accident' on 4 February 1944. His service record notes that there was 'negligence in that he was riding on the running board of a service vehicle' and that he was 'killed while on duty, partly to blame'. In a bizarre twist Kip Kiley, formerly of M.2 Patrol, LRDG, later recalled:

> I wonder if anybody remembers Mark. He was with the unit for only a few months but in that time he built up a reputation as someone who had rather unusual powers …
>
> One evening in our billet in Syria we persuaded Mark to give a demonstration … members of the patrol were then made to perform seemingly impossible tasks under hypnosis. For example, standing with backs and legs completely straight they were made to lean over at angles which quite defied the laws of gravity.
>
> After half an hour or so of 'conditioning' Mark declared himself ready to start the séance and selected two of the lads to assist him. Each was given a pencil and a sheet of paper and one was told to write numbers at random (or as the spirit moved him?), the other letters. Almost immediately Mark went into a trance. He started trembling and shaking. He was in communication with the spirit world.
>
> In his hand Mark had a pencil – it was about 6in. long and he held it right at the very end. The pencil moved about in a quivering sort of way and here and there, when it came into contact with the paper, it formed the rough shape of a letter of the alphabet. Meanwhile his two assistants were also writing.
>
> The séance ended after about ten minutes when Mark came out of his trance. He told us to take the sheets of paper on which his two assistants had been writing and he described how we were to de-code their scribblings. By using the numbers against the letters we unscrambled an almost word perfect message. If my memory is correct it was 'Tell them I did not suffer'. The sender's name did not appear.

> Mark gave us his piece of paper on which there was a jumble of letters. He said it would be an anagram. By shuffling the letters about we produced a name (which I can no longer recall) but we had, left over, three 'V' shaped symbols. We puzzled about this until someone – Bill Rac, I think – said 'Could it mean Sergeant?'
>
> None of us knew a sergeant of this name but a short while later a radio operator entered and said that a message had just come in from the HQ in Palestine. It read: 'Sergeant X killed today at Ramat David whilst on parachute course'. There was no possible way in which Mark could have known about this in advance.
>
> I am not a spiritualist nor do I believe that the sort of phenomenon we witnessed in Syria can happen. But it did, as some of the lads will no doubt recall [LRDG Newsletter No.25, 1969].

Son of John and Florence Stibbon (née Ong) – Husband of Kathleen Stibbon of Ludlow Road, Ealing, Middlesex.
Age 29.
I have fought a good fight, I have finished my course. I have kept the faith
Grave D.E.3. Also commemorated within St Peter and Paul's Church, Swaffham, and incorrectly as 'Stibben' on the town's war memorial.

RAMLEH WAR CEMETERY

This cemetery dates from 1917 when the 1st Australian Light Horse Brigade occupied Ramleh (now known as Ramla) on 1 November. The following month medical units were stationed here, their subsequent burials resulting in this cemetery. Further casualties were concentrated from battlefields and from the Latron, Sarona and Wilhema Military and Indian Cemeteries.

During the Second World War the cemetery was used by local Royal Air Force stations as well as by various service hospitals. It contains 3,300 Commonwealth burials of the First World War, 964 of them unidentified, and 1,168 burials from the Second World War. In addition, there are 891 war graves of other nationalities from both wars and 525 non-war burials of the inter-war and post-war eras dating up to the end of the British Mandate in Palestine in May 1948.

Ramla is located 12 kilometres south-east of the port of Jaffa near Tel Aviv, the cemetery being situated close to the junction of Routes 40 and 44. Access is Monday to Friday, 0800–1430hrs. GPS co-ordinates: Latitude 31.93018, Longitude 34.88383

Trooper Gerald Charles **KERLEY** [5727124] Dorsetshire Regiment, Royal Armoured Corps and K Detachment SAS Brigade

Gerald Kerley was born on 13 September 1919 in the parish of Hampreston near Ferndowne in Dorset. He grew up nearby on the family holding at Dairy Farm in the village of Winterborne Zelston, attending Almer School. When his parents moved to Colehill near Wimborne he finished his studies at Queen Elizabeth's Grammar School and found work locally as an apprentice mechanic at a garage at Sturminster Marshall. After the outbreak of war he enlisted into the Dorsetshire Regiment in December 1939 and was initially sent to its infantry training centre until posted to the 12th (Holding) Battalion in May 1940. The following month he was re-posted to the 50th Battalion and in July to the 2nd Battalion. During July 1941 he transferred to the Royal Armoured Corps because, according to his family, his shooting was judged too inaccurate for the infantry. Later that month he was attached to the Gloucester Technical Training Group where he qualified as a fitter before being posted to the 61st Training Regiment at Tidworth in October to continue his mechanical education.

In January 1942 Kerley embarked for the Middle East and on arrival at the beginning of March was attached to the RAC Base Depot. On 7 February 1943 he transferred to 'K Detachment SAS Brigade', this being the cover name given to the deception 'subunit' of what was, at that time, this fictional SAS formation. During this period it moved up and down the Libyan coastline erecting dummy landing craft to exhaust enemy air assets in offensive and reconnaissance actions. By March 1944 he was serving with the 46-strong detachment as an 'A1 Vehicle Mechanic'.

Kerley's date of death is officially recorded as 11 July 1944. However, his service record notes that he was admitted to No.2 General Hospital on the 3rd of the month, discharged to the SAS on the 6th, readmitted on the 8th, and died on the 12th, the cause of death being polio encephalitis.

Son of Charles and Frances Kerley (née Musselwhite) of North Leigh Road, Colehill, Wimborne, Dorset.
Age 24.
A light from our home is gone. A loving voice is stilled. 'Until the day break'
Grave 5.E.6. Also commemorated within St Mary's Church at Wimborne Zelston and on Colehill's war memorial.

LEBANON

Towards the end of the First World War the Allies broke Turkish rule in those provinces that now constitute Lebanon and Syria. The region then fell under French mandate and was collectively referred to as Syria. When France capitulated in June 1940 it was retained by Vichy forces, its proximity to the Suez Canal and vital oil pipelines proving an attractive proposition to the Axis. Enemy occupation would also sever land communications between Palestine and Iraq. The Allies, including Free French troops, therefore crossed the border from Palestine on 8 June 1941 (OPERATION EXPORTER), No.11 (Scottish) Commando being put ashore close to the mouth of the Litani River to seize bridges key to this advance in the early hours of the following morning. Many veterans of this landing would later join the fledgling L Detachment, SAS Brigade. Despite strong resistance Vichy forces surrendered the following month, the Lebanese mountains, specifically a former French Army ski school known as The Cedars, later being used by the Long Range Desert Group for training.

In January 1944 Lebanon became an independent state. Within its borders two LRDG casualties are buried, one in the capital, Beirut, and the other to the north at the port of Tripoli.

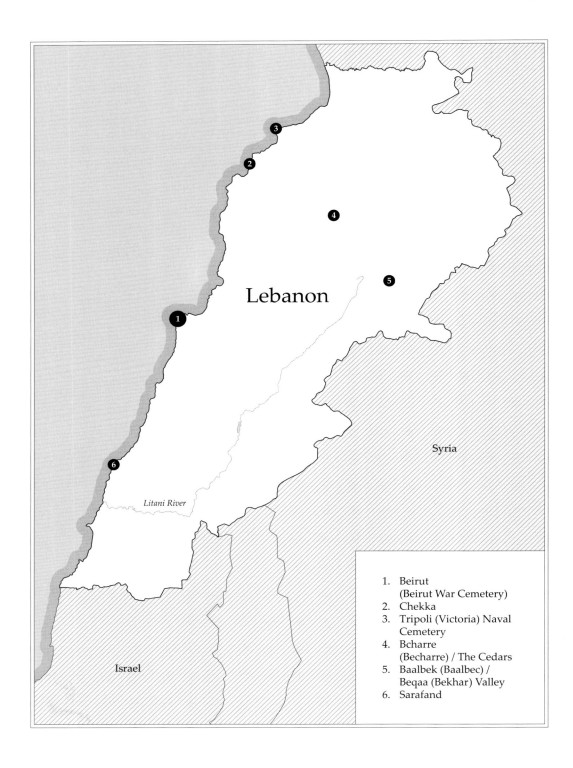

Lebanon

Litani River

Syria

Israel

1. Beirut
    (Beirut War Cemetery)
2. Chekka
3. Tripoli (Victoria) Naval
    Cemetery
4. Bcharre
    (Becharre) / The Cedars
5. Baalbek (Baalbec) /
    Beqaa (Bekhar) Valley
6. Sarafand

BEIRUT WAR CEMETERY

This cemetery was created in October 1918 when Commonwealth forces took Beirut from the Turks. Enlarged by the concentration of battlefield casualties many of the 628 First World War burials are of Indian troops, the 7th (Meerut) Division having been at the forefront of fighting in this area. The majority of the 531 Second World War casualties were incurred during the campaign against Vichy forces in modern-day Lebanon and Syria, a further 251 Indian casualties being commemorated on the Beirut Cremation Memorial.

The CWGC plot is located on the rue Jalloul in the el-Horj district, just to the west of the Forest of Pines. It is divided into two separate sections, First World War and Second World War burials being on opposite sides of the road. The latter lies on the south side between the French cemetery and the large Islamic cemetery close to the junction with avenue du 22 Novembre. It is open Monday–Friday, 0700–1430hrs. GPS co-ordinates: Latitude 33.869765, Longitude, 35.505313

LANCE-CORPORAL WILLIAM HENRY **BURTON** [318491] QUEEN'S OWN YORKSHIRE DRAGOONS AND LRDG (Y.1 PATROL, B SQN)

Known as 'Dizzy' to his comrades, William Burton was born during mid 1920 in Nottinghamshire, his family later moving to Doncaster. In November 1938 he joined the Queen's Own Yorkshire Dragoons, a territorial yeomanry regiment who's HQ Squadron was based in his hometown. At the outbreak of war the Dragoons were mobilised and moved to Louth in Lincolnshire where they were brought up to full strength. At the beginning of 1940 they crossed the Channel with their mounts and entrained for Marseille for passage to Palestine. Having disembarked at Haifa the regiment moved to the Plain of Esdraelon in modern-day Israel to guard the oil pipeline. It was whilst detailed for such duties that Burton volunteered for the Long Range Desert Group. Although his service record cannot be located a nominal roll records that he was a member of Y Patrol by the end of March 1941.

At the beginning of April 1941 British forces in Libya were in full retreat, Y Patrol, A Squadron's HQ and half of G Patrol retiring via the town of Msus where they informed Captain Pat Hore-Ruthven, liaison officer to a French Motor Company, that the enemy was hot on their heels (see Hore-Ruthven's entry under Tripoli War Cemetery, Libya, within this volume for details of his subsequent service with 1st SAS). Moving east to the area of Mechili the LRDG party was tasked by the commander of an Indian Motorised Brigade to hamper the enemy. This was done over the coming days with some success, despite the presence of enemy armoured cars. When Mechili fell to the Afrikakorps the party was lucky to escape under the cover of a sand storm before locating an enemy column on 9 April. They were subsequently attacked by both aircraft and ground forces before retiring to better cover where they finally received orders to proceed to Jarabub. When the front stabilised the re-equipped A Squadron operated from Siwa Oasis, Burton's Y Patrol setting off for Bir Raggia on 25 July. It reached this well within the Jebel Akhdar on the 27th and dropped an unknown officer and his men, most likely of G(R), the Middle East clandestine warfare department, before returning to Siwa on 2 August. On the 7th Lieutenant Jake Easonsmith led the patrol on an uneventful recce of potential landing grounds (see Easonsmith's own entry under Leros War Cemetery, Greece, Volume II).

Having refitted in Cairo Y patrol, now part of B Squadron, arrived at Kufra on 20 October 1941. Here, in further restructuring, the patrols were split into half, Burton subsequently serving in Y.2. Moving back to Siwa in early November the Group played a significant part in supporting OPERATION CRUSADER. Y.2 under Captain David Lloyd Owen was to monitor enemy movement in the area of Bir Tengeder in Libya where a number of tracks converged. It set out on the 15th. Four days later it took over the duties of Y.1 that had been strafed by RAF Beaufighters and now needed to replace their burnt-out wireless truck. At dawn on the 20th Captain David Stirling and a small party of L Detachment, SAS Brigade, arrived at the patrol's new position on foot. They were making their way to an RV with Easonsmith's R.1 Patrol having carried out the Regiment's first, and abortive, operation, the target of which had been airfields at nearby Tmimi and Gazala (OPERATION SQUATTER). This encounter between Lloyd Owen and Stirling, during which they discussed raiding tactics, is said to have formed the basis of future SAS operations. On 26 November Y.1 returned not only with a new W/T truck but also with an order to commence offensive action. Although the combined party quickly located suitable ambush sites little was achieved until the morning of the 29th when Y.2 captured a truckload of Italians on the Derna–Mechili road. One spoke English and willingly explained that he had been in the process of collecting rations for an isolated fort near el Ezzeiat. Lloyd Owen decided to attack and after a brief exchange of fire negotiations for the garrison's surrender were concluded by use of a rifle grenade. The surviving fourteen Italians were captured along with equipment and documentation. They yielded much intelligence including local dispositions and confirmation of the panic spread by SQUATTER's parachutists. Although the patrol was ordered to attack the airfield at Tmimi that night the enemy was found to be too alert after recent events.

Y.2 therefore strafed road traffic and cut telephone lines before returning to Siwa.

On 11 December 1941 Burton's patrol was allotted the Tobruk–Derna road as its next target area. However, the speed of the Eighth Army's advance meant that it was retasked, this time to attack the route between Benghazi and Agedabia. Due to increased enemy activity it was ordered to return to Siwa, arriving on the 21st. On Christmas Eve the patrol set off to recce the area south of the Jebel Nefussa, this time accompanied by the CO of the Indian Long Range Squadron and one of his soldiers who were gaining insight into the operational environment that their squadron would soon face. The round trip of 2,414 kilometres was uneventful, the patrol returning having suffered the mechanical loss of one vehicle but having gained valuable intelligence of an area never before traversed by Allied forces.

After Rommel's counterattack of January 1942 there was further restructuring, Burton moving to Y.1 Patrol with which he served until his death. After a series of recces this returned to Cairo to re-fit and recruit suitable men. In late May it set out from Siwa to drop a party of agents at Tarhuna, approximately 64 kilometres south-east of Tripoli. One of the party, an Italian national, wandered off at night in an attempt to betray the others. Caught, he was returned to Siwa before the patrol took a small group of the Libyan Arab Force under Major 'Popski' Peniakoff to the Jebel Akhdar. Having dropped them off they took over Road Watch duties between Mechili and Msus. The patrol was relieved by G.1 on 9 June and took up similar tasks along the coastal road. These were largely plagued by mechanical failures which were dealt with by the patrol fitter, Craftsman 'Snowy' Tighe (see his entry under Phaleron War Cemetery, Greece).

During the autumn of 1942 Burton's Y.1 supported OPERATION AGREEMENT, an abortive attack on Tobruk during the night of 13–14 September: having guided a large contingent of the 1st Special Service Regiment (formerly the Middle East Commando) to Ed Duda the patrol destroyed enemy transport and held the port's eastern perimeter until it was realised that the assault had failed and the commandos had been captured. Y.1 therefore retired to Kufra, which it reached after some difficulty on the 25th only for Lloyd Owen to be badly wounded in an air raid.

Returning to Road Watch duties the patrol, now under Captain E. Spicer, operated during late October 1942 and early November in the area of the Arco dei Fileni, a memorial near Ra's Lanuf erected by the Italians on the Libyan coastal road to mark the Tripolitania/Cyrenaica border and known to the British as 'Marble Arch'. After an abortive raid on the landing ground at Hon the following month the patrol left the LRDG's new base at Zella on Christmas Day to carry out a recce deep within enemy-held territory. Large numbers of Italian troops were encountered before the patrol returned to Hon on 23 January, the Group's HQ having moved up to this location shortly before.

After the end of the North African Campaign B Squadron, now commanded by the recovered Lloyd Owen, carried out strenuous training in the Lebanese mountains during the summer of 1943. Burton was killed during a vehicle exercise on 24 August 1943, Jim Patch of the same patrol later recalling:

He was killed when the Jeep he was travelling in turned over in the melting snow on the col d'Ainatre which is the pass over the Lebanon mountains between Becharre and Baalbec in the Bekhar Valley [the LRDG was based at The Cedars Ski School, located on this pass]. The Jeep was driven by 'Bob' Davies [Daniel Evan Davies] whose back was seriously injured [personal correspondence, 2011].

In December 1942, i.e. after Burton had joined the LRDG, the Queen's Own Yorkshire Dragoons was redesignated the 9th Battalion, King's Own Yorkshire Light Infantry (Yorkshire Dragoons), hence the confusion that often surrounds his parent regiment and the cap badge engraved on his headstone.

Son of Samuel and Beatrice Burton (née Gibson) of Doncaster, Yorkshire. Age 23.
His memory to me is a treasure, his loss a life long regret
Grave 3.A.1.

TRIPOLI (VICTORIA) NAVAL CEMETERY

On 22 June 1893 the Royal Navy battleship HMS Camperdown rammed and sank HMS Victoria off the coast of Tripoli during a fleet exercise. The ground occupied by this cemetery was gifted by the occupying Turks to enable the burial of 358 crewmen that were killed in the incident. In addition, the cemetery now contains the graves of eighty-seven Commonwealth service personnel, the majority of whom lost their lives during the 1941 campaign in Lebanon and Syria. There are also twelve Polish and Greek war graves and seven non-war naval burials.

The cemetery lies close to the sea on Kwas el Hamam Street in the al-Mina district, roughly 2 kilometres north-west of Tripoli's centre. GPS co-ordinates: Latitude 34.44524, Longitude 35.81532

PRIVATE NORMAN ARTHUR <u>HOLT</u> [4923972] SOUTH STAFFORDSHIRE REGIMENT AND LRDG (HEAVY SECTION, GROUP HQ)

Norman Holt was born on 24 December 1918 in Wolverhampton. Having worked as a bread salesman he enlisted into the South Staffordshire Regiment at Hereford in July 1940 and was posted to the 14th Battalion. This took up anti-invasion duties on the east coast at Acle, not far from Yarmouth in Norfolk. Promoted to lance-corporal during November 1941 he was attached to No.23 Infantry Training Centre at Worcester on Boxing Day. In January 1942 he embarked for the Middle East at Liverpool docks, arriving in Egypt that May where he was attached to No.5 Bulk Petrol Company, Royal Army Service Corps.

Posted to No.1 Infantry Training Centre he volunteered for the Long Range Desert Group within a week of arrival on 18 October. After spending a month in No.63 British General Hospital at Helmiah, Cairo, for an unknown reason at the end of 1942 he rejoined the LRDG and is noted on a 1943 nominal roll as being a member of the Heavy Section under Captain 'Skip' Arnold. The beginning of 1943 proved a busy period for this section, the LRDG War Diary noting that it:

> … increased to a total of twenty three-ton Chevrolets and six ten-ton Macks, was fully employed during this period. Its work included journeys to Cairo and Tobruk from Kufra, and forward dumping [of supplies], from Hon, nearly as far west as the Tunisian Frontier. The Section, and LRDG, had a severe loss when Arnold was killed on a land mine in Hon on January 15th after more than eighteen months valuable service with the unit [WO 218/91 – see Arnold's own entry under Tripoli War Cemetery, Libya, within this volume].

After hostilities in North Africa had ceased the LRDG was withdrawn to Cairo, later moving to Syria (modern-day Lebanon) where it carried out mountain training at The Cedars, a pre-war popular resort and French Army ski school. Holt was subsequently admitted to No.11 Mobile Casualty Clearing Station at 2230hrs on 8 September 1943. He was conscious but in a state of extreme shock having apparently fallen from a cliff. He died of his injuries in the early hours of the following day.

Son of Albert and Alice Holt (née Benton) of Walker Avenue, Low Hill, Wolverhampton.
Age 24.
'Yea though I walk through the valley of the shadow of death I will fear no evil'
Grave 3.A.7.

83

LIBYA

The strategic significance of North Africa increased significantly after Italy's June 1940 declaration of war and the collapse of France. Vastly outnumbered small British patrols were able to cross the border from Egypt and cause disproportionate amount of damage and disquiet amongst Italian forces in Cyrenaica, the eastern coastal region of Libya. One of those whose Roll of Honour entry is included in this section commanded the first of these patrols. In September the Italians advanced a short distance into Egypt where they were held in the area of Sidi Barrani. Thanks to accurate signal intelligence a Commonwealth offensive at the end of the year, OPERATION COMPASS, not only resulted in heavy enemy losses, but also captured the key Libyan port of Tobruk. In addition, large numbers of Italian troops were taken prisoner from as far west as Beda Fomm, with Major-General Richard O'Connor's Western Desert Force settling into positions at Mersa Brega.

Success was short-lived, the German Luftwaffe and Afrikakorps coming to the aid of their weaker partner. Under Generalleutnant Erwin Rommel, a counter-attack was made on 31 March 1941 and Commonwealth forces, whose supply lines were extended, were obliged to withdraw to the border of Egypt, leaving Tobruk under siege. The counter offensive that June, OPERATION BATTLEAXE, began well but when endangered by a flanking movement was forced to withdraw. In the autumn the Eighth Army was formed and took up a renewed offensive, OPERATION CRUSADER, in mid November. In its support the recently formed L Detachment, SAS Brigade, carried out its first operation, the objective being the destruction of Axis aircraft stationed at Tmimi and Gazala. Whilst strong Axis counter-attacks resulted in both the annihilation and capture of many Commonwealth units, Tobruk was eventually relieved, the front line moving farther west back to its former position at Mersa Brega.

Rommel advanced again in January 1942 and, aided by the capture of British supplies and the port of Benghazi, succeeded in pushing back Commonwealth troops to a string of defensive 'boxes' that formed a line running roughly south from Gazala through Bir Hacheim. The Afrikakorps renewed its advance late in May and after fierce fighting those forces within such boxes were overrun or withdrew, the results being that Tobruk fell and that much British armour was destroyed. The Eighth Army subsequently took up positions in the narrow gap between El Alamein and the Qattara Depression, only 262 kilometres from Cairo itself. After a series of German probing raids Lieutenant-General Bernard Montgomery, CB, DSO, took the offensive, the Second Battle of El Alamein beginning late that October. This was the 'turn of the tide', Axis forces being pushed out of Egypt and back into Libya. Pursuing them along the coast the Eighth Army had recaptured Tobruk and Benghazi by the end of November, followed by Tripoli on 23 January 1943. Within days the enemy had been pushed into Tunisia.

This then was the background to which the Long Range Desert Group and the Special Air Service operated. Although the former was originally tasked with Road Watch duties, a traffic census of Axis vehicles vital to Allied planning, both carried out aggressive, tactical action in support of long-term strategy.

The to-and-fro nature of the fighting in Libya is reflected by the casualties buried here, SAS and LRDG graves having been concentrated into three cemeteries from remote locations separated by vast distances. There are three members of the LRDG and two of the SAS buried at Benghazi War Cemetery, two members of the LRDG and three SAS at Knightsbridge War Cemetery, and eight members of the LRDG and one SAS buried in the capital at Tripoli War Cemetery.

1. Tripoli
   (Tripoli War Cemetery)
2. Nalut
3. Murzuq (Murzuk)
4. Sirte
5. Ajdabiya (Agedabia)
6. Jalu (Jalo)
7. Benghazi War Cemetery
8. Al Marj (Barce)
9. At Tamimi (Tmimi)
10. Acroma (Knightsbridge
    War Cemetery)
11. Tubruq (Tobruk)
12. al-Jaghbub (Jarabub)
13. al-Kufrah (Kufra)
14. Tunis
15. Sfax
16. Mareth
17. Cairo
18. El Salloum
    (Sollum / Halfaya Pass)
19. Siwa
20. Marsa Matruh
    (Mersa Matruh)
21. el-Alamein
22. Alexandria
23. Kabreet (Kabrit)
24. Suez
25. el-Kharga (Kharga)

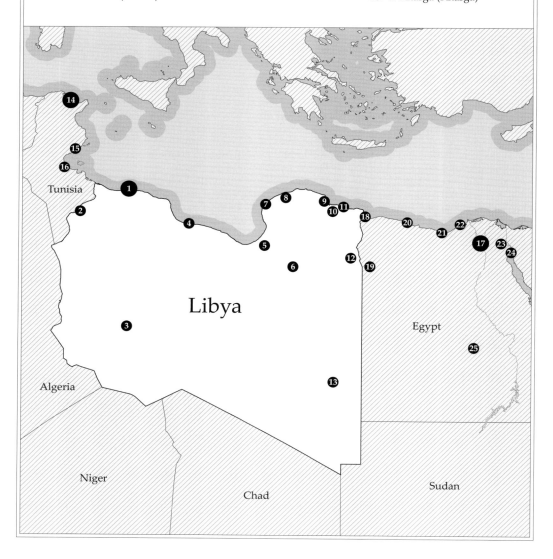

BENGHAZI WAR CEMETERY

Benghazi's port and nearby airfield at Benina were prized by both sides during the North African Campaign. As such the town was subject to small-scale raids by the Special Boat Section from as early as May 1941 whilst L Detachment, SAS Brigade, twice attempted to destroy shipping in its busy harbour during the following year.

The cemetery contains the graves of 1,214 members of the Commonwealth, 163 of which are unidentified, and twenty-five non-Commonwealth burials. Aircraftsman 1st Class William Humphries of 216 Squadron, RAF, who was killed on SQUATTER, the SAS' first operation, is buried here in grave 8.E.27. He was a member of Flight Sergeant Charlie West's crew whose Bombay aircraft, named 'Bermondsey', was shot down whilst carrying a stick of L Detachment parachutists. He is believed to have died as a result of wounds sustained in the crash (see Sergeant 'Barney' Stone's entry below for full details).

The cemetery is located 7 kilometres south-south-east of the port on the Second Ring Road, close to the children's hospital and zoo. GPS co-ordinates: Latitude 32.07696, Longitude 20.08936

CORPORAL LAURENCE CROSSLEY **ASHBY** [6296206] RHODESIAN ARMY, THE BUFFS AND LRDG (S.2 PATROL, A SQN)

Laury Ashby was born on 1 December 1919 in Southern Rhodesia. Having worked as a blacksmith he is believed to have enlisted into the Rhodesian Army at the outbreak of war, although no service record can be located. What is certain is that having disembarked in the Middle East he transferred to The Buffs (Royal East Kent Regiment) in mid May 1940 at Safad in Palestine. He was appointed lance-corporal on posting to the 1st Battalion and by the end of the year had been advanced to corporal. On 31 January 1941 he volunteered for the Long Range Desert Group and as such was an original member of S Patrol, the unofficial history of the Group noting:

> Personnel for the Southern Rhodesian Patrol had been ordered by GHQ (A Branch) to be provided from the Northumberland Fusiliers and the Argyll and Sutherland Highlanders [and presumably The Buffs], and to arrive on January 5th, but owing to reluctance on the part of the formations concerned to part with any men while they were taking part in the Battle of Sidi Barrani, the Southern Rhodesian patrol did not come into being until 31st January [WO 201/808].

During March 1941 Ashby attended an Anti-Gas Instructors Course at the Middle East Training School. That October, having carried out a successful recce of the Jalo–Agedabia area, as well as Road Watch operations on the coast, S Patrol left Kufra making a recce of Jalo Oasis itself as well as its alternate approaches. Although attacked from the air it was able to return to Kufra on the 17th with valuable intelligence and without casualties.

At the end of the month the LRDG was reorganised into 'half' patrols, Ashby serving from then on in S.2 Patrol under 2nd Lieutenant John Olivey. In November it undertook a joint recce of the Mechili–Benghazi road with R.2 Patrol. Receiving orders to take aggressive action the patrol destroyed enemy trucks along this road on the evening of the 29th causing many casualties before being withdrawn to Group HQ at Jalo. It set out again in mid December:

> The second operation [of this phase] was that by Olivey (S.2) and [2nd Lieutenant Paul] Eitzen (RA Section) against the small Italian fort at Stafia SSW of Agedabia. This attack was made on the afternoon of December 16 and after a few rounds from the 25pdr [25 Pounder - a field gun that the patrol had transported through the desert on a lorry] the garrison fled. Two MGs [machine guns] and four prisoners were taken. Three days later Olivey took a party of [eight L Detachment, SAS Brigade] parachutists [from Jalo, under the command of Captain Bill Fraser] to

> a point 9 miles from Agedabia whence they made a night attack on the LG [landing ground] there and destroyed thirty-seven aircraft, being picked up on the 22nd at a prearranged rendezvous. Unfortunately, on their return journey to Jalo [having met Brigadier Reid's E Force] the party was suddenly attacked by two RAF aircraft while halted in the Wadi el Faregh [south of Al Qayqab] and Cpl Ashby and Pte Riggs were killed [on 22 December 1941 - WO 218/90].

Olivey's own report notes that the planes 'suddenly appeared very low and machine-gunned' the patrol whilst it was awaiting Group HQ to reply to one of its signals. He also recorded that the pair were buried 'at Bir Quetn that evening'. A third man was wounded (WO 218/89).

Son of Leonard and Florence Ashby of Hillside, Bulawayo, Southern Rhodesia.
Age 22.
Through deep sorrow and his supreme sacrifice shall dawn the freedom of mankind
Joint grave 8.B.28–29. Also commemorated on the cloistered war memorial on Main Street, Bulawayo.

PRIVATE REGINALD **RIGGS** [RH/6296787] THE BUFFS
AND LRDG (S.2 PATROL, A SQN)

'Ginger' Riggs was born on 17 September 1919 in the UK, later migrating to South Africa. Having worked as a handyman he enlisted into either the South African, or more likely the Rhodesian Army, and subsequently disembarked in the Middle East. He transferred to The Buffs (Royal East Kent Regiment) at Safad in Palestine on the same day as Laury Ashby during May 1940 and was also posted to the 1st Battalion. The pair volunteered for the Long Range Desert Group on 31 January 1941 and as such were both original members of S Patrol that was formed that day.

At the end of October the LRDG was reorganised into 'half' patrols, Riggs joining S.1 Patrol under Captain 'Gus' Holliman. Setting out from Kufra on the 30th they reached the Hon–Misurata road on 6 November. Having captured a lorry and its crew the following morning it was decided to mine this route and to attack the busier coastal road. Here a recce was carried out on a roadhouse near to Tmed Hassan, this being attacked that night:

> Five of us, [Mike] Sadler, Riggs, Gus, myself and another crash down the two heavy trellis gates in the front and open up with machine and Tommy guns. Screams of terror come from every corner of the large courtyard that we have entered [Ben Doherty's account in *LRDG Rhodesia: Rhodesians in the Long Range Desert Group*, by Jonathan Pittaway and Craig Fourie].

Having returned to Siwa the patrol was tasked with planting a fake map in the area of the enemy-held Jalo Oasis. This was carefully marked with fictitious attack plans. On 9 November 1941 the patrol made sure that it was in sight of a local man at a well and prepared a meal before moving off, 'accidentally' leaving behind navigational instruments and the doctored map. This was found in the town commandant's office when overrun the following month by Allied troops during OPERATION NICETY (WO 218/89).

Riggs was killed in a blue-on-blue incident on 22 December 1941 whilst serving with S.2 Patrol. Two RAF Blenheims strafed the patrol whilst it was static in the Wadi el Faregh (see Corporal Laury Ashby's entry opposite for full details).

Son of Mrs H. M. M. Riggs of Dartmore Farm, C/O Mrs Jousse, PO Mahat.
Age 22.
No inscription.
Joint grave 8.B.28–29.

SERGEANT SIDNEY JAMES STONE [2692673] SCOTS GUARDS, NO.8 COMMANDO AND L DETACHMENT SAS BRIGADE

Known to his comrades as 'Barney', Sidney Stone was born in Gloucester although his family lived in north-west London. In the spring of 1934 he married Emmie Edmonds in Lambeth. Although his service record cannot be located he was serving as a lance-sergeant in No.8 (Guards) Commando at Largs in Scotland by November 1940. After arduous training on the Isle of Arran the Commando was temporarily reorganised as part of the 4th Special Service Battalion and disembarked at Suez in Egypt in early March 1941 as B Battalion, Layforce. The following month it was at Mersa Matruh towards the front line, although with operations continuously drawn up and then cancelled an unsettled period ensued. That May, Stone took part in the first Middle East parachute experiments, Guardsman D'Arcy's account highlighting the pioneering, and often Heath Robinson, aspects of such training:

> Having been frustrated in his plans for a seaborne operation, Lt J. S. Lewes, Welsh Guards, decided to try it by parachute. He and his party first went to RAF HQ located somewhere near Fuka. There he discussed the details with an RAF officer, who, although none of the party had jumped before, was most helpful. He showed us the parachutes we were to use. From the logbooks we saw that the last periodical examination had been omitted but Lt Lewes decided that they were OK. Next day, along with Lt Stirling and Sgt Stone who were hoping to do a job in Syria, we made a trial flight. The plane used was a Vickers 'Valencia'. We threw out a dummy made from sandbags and tent poles. The parachute opened OK but the tent poles were smashed on landing. Afterwards we tried a 10ft jump from the top of the plane and then a little parachute control.
>
> The following afternoon we flew inland in the 'Valencia' which was used to deliver mail. We reached the landing field towards dusk, landed, fitted on our parachutes, and decided to jump in the failing light. We were told to jump in pairs, Lt Lewes and his servant, Guardsman Davies, first, the RAF officer was to despatch. The instructions were to dive out as though going into water. We hooked ourselves up, circled the field, and on a signal from the RAF officer, Lt Lewes and Davies dived out. Next time round I dived out, and was surprised to see Lt Stirling pass me in the air. Lt Lewes made a perfect landing, next came Davies a little shaken. Lt Stirling injured his spine and also lost his sight for about an hour, next myself, a little shaken and a few scratches, and lastly Sgt Stone who seemed OK. Gdsm Evans was unable to jump as the pilot decided to land owing to the approaching darkness. We slept on the landing field. Next morning we jumped again, this time a stick of four, preceded by a bundle to represent a container. The previous night we had worn KD [Khaki Drill] shirts and shorts, but from experience we decided to put on pullovers. We wore no hats. We pushed the bundle out first and Gdsn Evans, myself, Davies and Lt Lewes followed as quickly as possible. The first three landed quite close to each other and doubled forward to the container but Lt Lewes in trying to avoid some oil barrels, rather badly injured his spine, Gdsn Evans also hurt his ankle. Sgt Stone jumped after us, landed OK [WO 201/785 – see entries for Lieutenant Jock Lewes under Alamein Memorial, Egypt, within this volume, and for Private Roy Davies under Hanover War Cemetery, Germany, Volume III].

Stone volunteered for L Detachment, SAS Brigade, on its formation that summer and is recorded as being a member of No.2 Troop on the unit's September nominal roll. He subsequently took part in OPERATION SQUATTER, the first SAS raid, the objective of which was to destroy Axis aircraft on the Tmimi and Gazala airfields. Boarding the fifth aircraft his stick, under Lieutenant Charles Bonington, estranged father of the famous climber, took off from Ma'atum Bagush airfield close to Mersa Matruh on the night of 16 November 1941 and headed for the target area. Here the plane was badly damaged by anti-aircraft fire and in the increasingly strong wind the crew decided to abort the parachute drop. With the petrol tanks holed the pilot, Flight Sergeant Charlie West, was forced to make an emergency landing. Successfully touching down in the desert it was found impossible to locate their position as the instruments were shot away. As dawn of the 17th approached the parachutists therefore went out to capture a prisoner, bringing back an Italian who informed them that they were 'near el-Gazala and about 45 miles from Tobruk' (WO 208/3337). West decided to take off and make for Allied lines with what little fuel remained. According to Major F. C. Thompson, Frontier Force Rifles, who accompanied the SAS as despatcher:

> Almost immediately the aircraft was fired on by a German fighter ME 109F and, after attempting evasive action, was attacked again, the navigator [sic – co-pilot] being killed and a number of parachutists seriously wounded [the co-pilot, Pilot Officer Donald Martin, RAFVR, is buried at Knightsbridge War Cemetery, Libya].
> Shortly afterwards the aircraft hit low sand-hills and crashed.

I attribute it to the skill of the pilot, and to the fine peak of training to which the men had been brought, that more -indeed all – were not killed in the crash, in which the aircraft was completely destroyed, portions of it strewing the ground for 200 yards …

Since a number of badly wounded men were pinned under the wreckage of the fuselage immediate action was taken to prevent the destruction of the wrecked fuselage by fire and efforts made to release those inside, in order that the force might be reorganised as a fighting unit.

Before this could happen the position came under fire from enemy troops …

It was soon perceived that to oppose an enemy attack or effect action likely to extricate the force was impossible and, on the enemy attacking, surrender was made to a German officer of the Luftwaffe.

This occurred at 0700hrs 16 [*sic* – 17] November 1941 [CAB 106/4].

Stone was one of those either wounded by enemy action or seriously injured in the crash. Despite treatment Berlin's centre for POW records was informed that Stone had died on the morning of 5 December 1941 at a field hospital in Derna (message dated 7 May 1942). He was originally buried at Derna (Lighthouse) Cemetery.

Husband of Emmie Stone of Kensal Rise, Middlesex – Father of one son.
Age 31.
My beloved husband. Thinking constantly of you. Loving wife and son
Grave 8.E.31.

CORPORAL GEORGE FREDERICK **YATES** [T/118510] ROYAL ARMY SERVICE CORPS AND LRDG (HEAVY SECTION, GROUP HQ)

George Yates, the son of a postman, was born on 22 January 1909 in Salford. Moving to nearby Timperley he married Lilian Haynes on Boxing Day 1934. Having worked as a travelling salesman he enlisted into the Royal Army Service Corps in October 1939 at Manchester and was posted to Aldershot that day. Although it is not known when he disembarked in the Middle East he served in the region with No.21 Troop Carrying Company and was attached to the Long Range Desert Group on 5 December 1940. A few days earlier the LRDG had moved its HQ from the Fever Hospital at Abbassia Barracks to the Citadel in Cairo and this is where Yates reported, along with other reinforcements required for expansion.

Posted as a driver to the Heavy Section within Group HQ, Yates was involved in the testing of vehicles suitable for long-range transport of stores through the desert. During April 1941 HQ and the patrols moved forward to Kufra Oasis in south-east Libya, thus extending their operational range. Yates arrived on the 18th in a party commanded by 2nd Lieutenant Dick Croucher, having topped up with fuel and water at Kharga Oasis in southern Egypt. The responsibility of Kufra's supply was initially allocated to the Sudan Command, convoys struggling 1,125 kilometres over the desert from Wadi Halfa. These were eventually followed on 18 July by elements of the Sudan Defence Force that had recently seen action during the Abyssinian Campaign and which now took over garrison duties at the oasis.

The Kufra Garrison War Diary records that at 0100hrs on 20 December 1941 Yates was 'shot dead by an anti-aircraft battery sentry having failed, through deafness, to hear the challenge' (WO 169/7288). It notes that the following day at 0830hrs 'Cpl Yates was buried 100 yards NW of the fort gate, B Coy, 1 A&SH [Argyll and Sutherland Highlanders], providing the escort' and that at 1030hrs 'a court of inquiry was held under El Kaim A.O. Powell to enquire into the circumstances of his death.' At the beginning of 1942 the RASC Records Office wrote to Yates' wife stating:

> Further to this office telegram dated 14th January informing you of the sad death of your husband, No.118510 Cpl Yates G F, due to enemy action. I have now received a report from the Middle East stating that Cpl Yates' death was not due to enemy action. He approached a gun pit, failed to reply to the sentry's challenge and was shot dead.

The 'report' referred to is a signal that states:

> Death 118510 Cpl Yates GF not (not) due enemy action deceased approached gun pit 6 LAA Bty [6th Light Anti-Aircraft Battery] Sudan Regt SDF [Sudan Defence Force] 2100hrs 19/12 failed reply sentry's challenge was shot dead opinion court of inquiry sentry justified in action taken.

Although two different dates of death are referenced this is officially recorded as 19 December 1941.

Son of Ernest and Edith Yates of Hannah Street, Longsight, Manchester – Husband of Lilian Yates of Haddon Grove, Timperley, Cheshire.
Age 32.
Always remembered. A dearly loved husband, son and brother
Grave 4.C.11.

KNIGHTSBRIDGE WAR CEMETERY, ACROMA

The cemetery is located close to the former strongpoint that was known as 'Knightsbridge'. This heavily fortified box dominated a series of key supply routes and stood guard over Eighth Army positions at Acroma, El Adem, El Duda, Gambut and Sidi Razegh. Heavy fighting took place at all of these locations with battlefield cemeteries created at each. Many were later concentrated here as well as graves from more remote locations. The cemetery now contains 3,651 Commonwealth burials, 993 of them unknown, as well as the graves of eighteen non-Commonwealth and one non-wartime military personnel.

2nd Lieutenant George Gunn, brother of 1st SAS' Medical Officer, Major Phil Gunn, MC, is buried here in grave 4.F.1. Already the holder of the MC he was killed in the action near Sidi Rezegh on 21 November 1941 and posthumously awarded the Victoria Cross (see Philip Gunn's entry under Birkenhead Landican Crematorium, United Kingdom, Volume III). Pilot Officer Donald Martin, Royal Air Force Volunteer Reserve, of 216 Squadron, is also buried here in grave 8.H.3. He was the co-pilot of Flight Sergeant Charlie West's Bombay aircraft, 'Bermondsey', which was shot down during OPERATION SQUATTER, *the first SAS raid (see Sergeant 'Barney' Stone's entry under Benghazi War Cemetery, Libya, for full details).*

The cemetery is located 25 kilometres west of Tobruk in open country south of the road from Tobruk to Tmimi. GPS co-ordinates: Latitude 32.09586, Longitude 23.71913

CORPORAL FRANCIS REX **BEECH** [1093] NELSON-MARLBOROUGH MOUNTED RIFLES, DIVISIONAL CAVALRY REGIMENT, LRP AND LRDG (T PATROL)

Rex Beech was born at the port of Picton on New Zealand's South Island on 24 July 1908. After schooling, during which he was a member of the cadets, he farmed with his family at Kenepuru Head in the Marlborough Sounds. When they moved back into Picton he worked for his father as a maritime radio engineer being a keen boxer and member of the territorial Nelson-Marlborough Mounted Rifles in his spare time. At the outbreak of war such mounted units formed the foundations of the Divisional Cavalry Regiment, into which he enlisted at Blenheim during October 1939. Promoted to corporal within two months he embarked at Wellington for the Middle East as a member of HQ Squadron the following January. Arriving at Port Tewfik, Egypt, in February 1940 he was posted to the Middle East Signals School in Palestine that May and also attended an instructor's course. A posting to the Royal Artillery Base Depot at Abbassia near Cairo followed, this barracks also housing the newly-formed Long Range Patrol (later the Long Range Desert Group) at this time. Although it is not known exactly when he volunteered for this unit he was serving as a corporal in W Patrol, LRDG, under Major 'Teddy' Mitford by the beginning of December 1940. Days later the Group was reorganised, this patrol being disbanded and its men shared between R and T Patrols. Beech moved to the latter coming under the command of Captain Pat Clayton.

T and the newly-formed and less experienced G Patrol left Cairo on 27 December 1940 for OPERATION AESOP. Having picked up a small party of Free French at Kayugi in Chad the column attacked the Italian-held fort at Murzuk, southern Libya, on 11 January 1941. During this action, which also wrecked aircraft and a hangar on the nearby airfield, Sergeant 'Squib' Hewson and the French commander, Lt-Colonel Jean Colonna d'Ornano, were killed (see Hewson's entry under Tripoli War Cemetery, Libya). On the 12th the patrols forced the surrender of Traghen and its Carabinieri fort before going on to attack two further positions at Um el-Araneb and Gatrun. Although the capture of Kufra Oasis was intended en route to Cairo the patrols were spotted by enemy aircraft and forced into the cover of Jebel Sherif late on the morning of the 31st. At 1340hrs they were attacked from the air as well as by ground forces of the Compagnia Sahariana, the Italian LRDG equivalent, which approached from the south with a 20mm canon. In the ensuing firefight two of the Italian prisoners taken at Murzuk were killed and the remaining two probably recovered by the enemy. Beech lay down covering fire from his truck, T.10 'Te Anau', so that other men could evade capture and continued to do so until he was killed in action. Nine days later a French patrol, guided by LRDG navigators, passed through the Jebel Sherif, Captain George Mercer Nairne, liaison officer to Général Leclerc, later reporting:

Corporal Beech had evidently been killed whilst firing his Vickers gun from the running board of his stationary truck. There was a considerable heap of spent cartridges beside him. His body was face downwards and one of his legs was wedged under the running board of his gutted truck, which was badly holed and had subsided on the axles. Though somewhat charred the body of Corporal Beech was easily recognisable to Kendall, Burnand and Clark. Half of one of his identity discs was recovered and has since been given to Lieutenant Kennedy Shaw by Captain Mercer Nairne.

Corporal Beech was buried with military honours and the last rites were said by the French padre. At the head of his grave is a wooden cross bearing his name and unit, and buried with him is a bottle containing paper with a similar inscription. The Italian postman from Murzuk was buried beside him towards the south with the same ceremony [WO 201/808].

This appears to have been the first clash between Allied and Axis Special Forces of the Second World

War. Although recommended for the Military Medal strict policy regarding posthumous awards meant that Beech received a Mention in Despatches (*London Gazette* 08/07/41). For some reason his date of death is officially recorded as 1 February 1941. Russell Ball, who had since been commissioned into the Divisional Cavalry, later wrote to Beech's mother:

> By this time you will have heard all about our pal Rex and the splendid deeds he performed. I have here with my own boys many fellows who are intensely proud of having been pals of Rex's and know too that no man could have answered the call more gloriously than him [Beech family collection courtesy of Brendan O'Carroll].

Son of Francis and Ethel Beech of Mairau Road, Picton, Marlborough, New Zealand.
Age 32.
No inscription.
Grave 6.J.13. Beech's remains were moved to Knightsbridge War Cemetery in April 1951. Also commemorated on war memorials at the New Zealand SAS camp at Papakura, at Blenheim, at Picton, and on the Torea Saddle at the junction of the Queen Charlotte Track and the Torea Bay-Portage road.

GUARDSMAN JOHN **EASTON** [3054349] ROYAL SCOTS, SCOTS GUARDS AND LRDG (G PATROL)

John Easton was born in the village of Dolphinton, Peebles, on 3 June 1918 and later worked on Parduvine Farm near the mining community of Rosewell, south of Edinburgh. Having joined the 7/9th (Highlanders), Royal Scots (TA), at the age of 15 he enlisted into the Scots Guards in January 1937. Posted to the 2nd Battalion he was promoted to lance-corporal that November, trained as a groom in 1938 and was subsequently re-posted to London for Sovereign duties that it appears he did not enjoy. He disembarked at Alexandria, Egypt, in November 1938 for what was hoped to be a routine tour of two years. After training at Mersa Matruh at the beginning of 1939 the battalion returned to Kasr el-Nil Barracks in Cairo where it was still garrisoned at the outbreak of war.

Easton reverted to the rank of guardsman at his own request in January 1940. With his battalion still untried in action, but fully aware of the Coldstream's participation in recent victories, Easton volunteered for the Long Range Desert Group on 6 December 1940. He and other volunteers from both the 2nd Battalion, Scots Guards, and the 3rd Battalion, Coldstream Guards, had arrived at the Citadel in Cairo the previous day and were formed into G Patrol, taking over vehicles and equipment of the former W Patrol.

At the end of the month, after a brief period of training, the Guards were led by the more experienced New Zealand T Patrol into Central Libya to attack Murzuk Fort (OPERATION AESOP). On 11 January 1941, having picked up a small group of Free French at Kayugi in Chad, the combined party closed on both the fort, that resisted heavily, and the nearby Italian airfield at which aircraft and a hangar were destroyed. The force then withdrew, briefly stopping after a few kilometres to bury two casualties, Sergeant 'Squib' Hewson and the French commander, Lt-Colonel Jean Colonna d'Ornano (see Hewson's entry under Tripoli War Cemetery, Libya). The following day they forced the surrender of Traghen but on the 31st were spotted by enemy aircraft and followed to the Jebel Sherif where they were attacked from the air and by the Italian LRDG equivalent, the Compagnia Sahariana (see also Corporal Rex Beech's entry above). Easton was aboard T.6, 'Te Aroha' of T Patrol, when wounded in the throat and the vehicle put out of action. With the remainder of the LRDG trucks having been forced to withdraw he, New Zealander Trooper 'Skin' Moore, Fitter Alfred Tighe, an Italian prisoner and Guardsman Alex Winchester took cover in the rocks above Beech's truck. After waiting until the enemy had dispersed they descended and began to walk towards Bishara, approximately 20 kilometres to the south-west. However, after spending the night in the open desert they returned to the jebel the following day and recovered a two-gallon tin of water but no food before again heading south-west. Having agreed that they should make for Allied territory rather than give themselves up the men released their prisoner and continued to walk throughout the next two days, finding only a tin of jam and some lentils that made them feel sick. On the 5th Tighe was too tired to go further (it was later reported that he had suffered a hernia) and he was left with a share of the water. On the 6th, having battled through a sandstorm, the others reached a hut at Sarra, a crow-fly distance of approximately 195 kilometres from Jebel Sherif. Here they bathed their feet in motor oil and made a fire. The following day Tighe, who had found the strength to push on, arrived at the hut but could go no farther. The others continued on towards Tekro. On the evening of the 9th a French patrol found Tighe, his first thought being to urge them to head south and pick up his companions. French planes were directed to the area and dropped food and lemonade to the men. However, the food could not be located in the fading light and the cork came out of the bottle of lemonade. Captain George Mercer Nairne, liaison officer to Général Leclerc, later reported:

10th Feb: French aeroplane again over. Second party from Camp 'S' found first Easton about 90km south of Sarra Well, next Winchester 20km further on and finally Moore was still plodding along when the trucks came up to him.

At about 7.30pm Easton died. He was buried 100 yards to the SW of Sarra Well on February 12th with military honours. The Padre read a few prayers. A fine grave was made for him and his name and unit hammered in metal on the wooden cross at his head.

Two hours before he died Easton was smiling and trying to joke, though his body was so withered up that the doctor (who did everything within the limited means at his disposal) could hardly extract a drop of blood from his veins [WO 201/808].

Although there are several such credible accounts of Easton being found shortly before he died Moore's own contradictory version was published in *Illustrated* magazine on 14 June 1941. Recalling how late in the second day they approached an Italian vehicle deciding to give themselves up, only to find it abandoned, he described their subsequent search of the vehicle:

We were about to give up when I found a water can amongst the debris of the car that had about a gallon and a half of water left in it.

I just can't describe how I felt after that discovery, but I knew it meant we still had a little longer to live. We took a condensed milk can, and in it we boiled up some of the dried tea leaves. It looked awful, and tasted worse, but oh boy, that was the finest cup of tea I've ever had.

We left the Eyetie there – he had a chance of being picked up, and we couldn't divide our water into five. I don't know how he fared, but he could have taken water from the radiator – I don't know why the four of us didn't think at once of doing that ourselves. Then the four of us set out again across the sand.

It was bitterly cold that night. None of us had more than just our shirts and shorts – so we dug a hole in the sand and lay, with our arms round each other, trying to keep warm.

We had found a field dressing that morning, so had been able to dress Easton's wound and bandage my foot … Our water we rationed out among the four of us, drinking only a mouthful or so, night and morning – but we had no food.

I remembered where, a few days ago, we had camped in the sand. Cookie had given us lentils for supper. None of us liked lentils, and we all had thrown them away – we cursed poor Cookie too.

That was at Sarra – 125 miles from where we took to the sand. I kept thinking of those lentils, and, as it was on our way south, we made for our old camp, and we got there in four days.

We were getting very weak by now. Four days with nothing but a few drops of water each day – and it was heavy going too through the sand. But we found the camp, and we found the lentils.

They had been stewed or something, and were more like thick soup when we threw them away. But they had been dried out by the sun, and were so salty we couldn't eat them. Again we scraped out the milk cans that had been thrown away.

We were very weak now, and as Alfred Tighe was in a pretty bad shape, he decided to remain at Sarra thinking there would be more chance of being picked up there than there would be farther south.

There was not much water left by now, but we divided what little there was, putting Tighe's share in an empty lentil bottle we found at the camp, and the three of us went on alone.

Later, when I saw Tighe again I learned the bottle we had put his water in had so much salt in it from the lentils, that the water was like brine and he couldn't drink it.

I lost all count of time after that. We just walked on, heading south and stopping every hour for a few minutes' rest. Each night I thought I would never live to see another day – the cold was so intense, and it was always some time before I could get my legs to work when we set out again at dawn.

Then one morning, I think it must have been the second after leaving Tighe, John Easton could not get up. Winchester and I rubbed his legs to start the circulation, and, finally, got him to his feet, but he could not stand for long – just stumbled a few paces and dropped in the sand.

He did this several times, trying all he could to keep going, but I knew, somehow, by the staring look in his eyes, that he was done. He asked for water, and I gave him half of what was left, but it was no good, and a few minutes later he died. We just buried him where he was, in the sand, and Winchester and I went on alone.

Perhaps this version of events was published to disguise the fact that there were other patrols in the area. According to Moore, Winchester dropped out soon after and the New Zealander plodded on alone. He was picked up 362 kilometres from the group's start point having lasted ten days. Winchester and Tighe had already been picked up, the latter being killed in action in 1944 (see his entry under Phaleron War Cemetery, Greece, Volume II).

Whatever the true story Easton's date of death is recorded as 12 February 1941. Whilst Moore received the Distinguished Conduct Medal, Easton was posthumously mentioned in despatches, the Commanding Officer of the Scots Guards writing to his father: 'Nothing would have given me more pleasure than to have handed this certificate of honour personally to your son, who was the essence of a good soldier, and in every way upheld the traditions of the Scots Guards' (*London Gazette* 04/07/41, Supplement 08/07/41). Easton's patrol commander, Captain Michael Crichton-Stuart, later funded a Thistle Foundation home in Craigmillar, Edinburgh, where ex-servicemen could live and work. He named this 'Easton House' and Guardsman Thomas Wann of G Patrol, who was paralysed during an operation in Libya, became a long-term resident.

Son of Adam and Bessie Easton of Monktonhall Terrace, Musselburgh, Midlothian.
Age 22.
No inscription.
Grave 8.F.21. Also commemorated on Musselburgh's war memorial fountain.

CAPTAIN ROBERT DE MERVÉ LOW **GRANT-WATSON** [56997] GENERAL LIST, SCOTS GUARDS, SPECIAL BOAT SECTION ATT L DETACHMENT SAS BRIGADE

Known as 'Robin', Grant-Watson was born on 18 January 1910 at the British Legation at Petropolis in Brazil to a British diplomat and his American wife. As such he spent his childhood in various countries including the United States, Guatemala, Denmark, Portugal, France, Germany, and Spain, although the family home was at Princes Gate, Kensington, an address made famous by the SAS in 1980 when it brought a siege at the Iranian Embassy to an end.

Having studied at Eton Grant-Watson went up to Magdalen College, Oxford, where he read Philosophy, Politics and Economics. Commissioned onto the General List (TA) he was attached to the 1st Battalion, Scots Guards, from November 1933 until mid February 1934. Despite receiving a mixed report he was commissioned into the regiment the following month. Posted initially to the 1st Battalion he qualified as an interpreter in German during January 1935 and transferred to the 2nd Battalion that April, being promoted to lieutenant in September. At the beginning of 1936 he qualified as an interpreter in French and embarked for Palestine in April, disembarking at Haifa less than two weeks later. Between May 1937 and April 1938 he was attached to MI3 at the War Office, this department being responsible for intelligence matters concerning Germany and Eastern Europe.

In November 1938 Grant-Watson disembarked at Alexandria with the 2nd Battalion assuming 'the duties of Garrison Adjutant and quartermaster Cairo area'. Soon after the outbreak of war he was sent to Syria as liaison officer with French forces. This proved a short posting and having rejoined the 2nd Battalion at Mersa Matruh at the end of 1939 he was promoted to captain on 1 September 1940 and appointed Intelligence Officer. By the time the battalion moved up to the desert to counter Rommel's first offensive in April 1941 he was serving as Brigade Intelligence Officer at HQ, 22nd Guards (Motor) Brigade, first seeing action during OPERATION BREVITY, an attempt to relieve Tobruk. That June the battalion again saw action during OPERATION BATTLEAXE, a similar attempt to ease pressure on the beleaguered garrison. Despite capturing Capuzzo and a large number of prisoners, the operation failed and the battalion was withdrawn to Cairo where it refitted for a mechanised infantry role.

Having been wounded on 19 September 1941 Grant-Watson was mentioned in despatches 'for gallant and distinguished services in the Middle East for period July-October 1941' (*London Gazette* 30/06/42). He subsequently volunteered for the Special Boat Section on 21 November. Although this unit was absorbed into the Middle East Commando the following January it appears that he was one of a number of its members first loaned, then attached to, L Detachment, SAS Brigade, for raids against Axis harbours and island airfields. He drowned in March 1942, Major Michael Kealy of the section writing to his father a month later:

I would like first of all to send you, on behalf of myself an all ranks of this unit, our very deepest sympathy in your great loss. He was an officer who was tremendously liked and respected by everyone and one whom I shall find impossible to replace.

As he may have told you, he and I shared a flat together for the last three months and can tell you that I feel I have lost not only a first rate officer but a great friend as well.

On March 26th [his date of death is officially recorded as the 27th] Robin was in Tobruk with a small party operating from MTBs [Motor Torpedo Boats] when he got a message to the effect that two German pilots had crash landed on a small island (Gazala) about 30 miles away. He immediately volunteered to take out a small party consisting of himself, Lt [Tommy] Langton, Irish Guards, and two other ranks to capture them [Sergeant Jimmy Sherwood, RASC, and Sergeant W. Dunbar, A&SH]. On arriving off the island in an MTB, they launched their canoes and started paddling towards the beach. When they got into the surf Robin's canoe was caught by a very large wave and was over-turned. Langton's canoe was cracked and Robin called out to them to try and paddle back to the MTB and that he and his sergeant would try and swim back.

Langton got back to the MTB which switched on its searchlight in an attempt to locate Robin. This unfortunately attracted low flying aircraft and had to be abandoned.

Langton then set out in the MTB's rubber boat and proceeded to search the areas as thoroughly as possible and finally landed on the mainland just inside our own lines where he contacted some South Africans and with them proceeded to search the foreshore. It was now nearly five hours since Robin and his sergeant had last been seen.

Soon afterwards a faint shout was heard from the sea, whereupon Langton again went out in the rubber boat and found the sergeant (Sherwood) almost unconscious but still supporting Robin who was by then already dead.

He got them ashore and with the help of the South Africans managed to revive the sergeant who has since recovered.

This sergeant said at one moment, when Robin must have felt his strength going, he tried to make him take his life jacket as he felt he was being a handicap [Sherwood was subsequently awarded the Military Medal and was later commissioned, serving with No.2 SBS until the end of the war].

In conclusion, I should like to quote to you the remarks of the senior naval officer, Tobruk, in his official report:- 'I deeply regret the loss of Captain Grant-Watson, a very brave officer who impressed all who met him by his willing and courageous spirit. I am sure he saw there was a sporting chance of success when nothing would stop him from trying.'

He was buried the following morning, near the scene of his very gallant attempt, by the padre of the Scots Guards. His grave now lies at Gazala point, over-looking the sea.

I can only repeat how much we all miss him and how much we sympathise with you [service record].

Son of Herbert and Anna Grant-Watson (née Low) of Princes Gate, Kensington, London – Known to have had an older brother. Age 32.

Be ye faithful unto death

Grave 10.C.18. Also commemorated at Eton College, on the war memorial at Magdalen College and by The Robin Grant-Watson Memorial Fund created in 1943 by his father, primarily to help other ranks of the Scots Guards particularly in regard to obtaining employment.

CORPORAL ALLAN **SHARMAN** [7887122] ROYAL TANK REGIMENT, L DETACHMENT SAS BRIGADE AND 1ST SAS (A SQN)

Allan Sharman was born on 3 October 1918 in Sunderland, County Durham. Having worked as a shop assistant he enlisted into the Royal Tank Corps in October 1936 and was posted to Bovington. After initial training he was re-posted to the 5th Battalion, Royal Tank Regiment, disembarking in Egypt to serve with the 6th Battalion in November 1937. When the Royal Armoured Corps was formed in April 1939 the regiment was absorbed into it, Sharman being promoted to lance-corporal. Returning to the UK on New Year's Day 1941 he was posted to the 53rd, then 59th Training Regiments at Tidworth and advanced to the rank of corporal. Returning to Egypt at the end of August he served as a lance-sergeant, then sergeant, in HQ 8th Armoured Brigade before volunteering for L Detachment, SAS Brigade, on 3 June 1942. He reverted to the rank of corporal in order to do so.

Having taken part in OPERATION BIGAMY, the large-scale September 1942 abortive raid on Benghazi, the unit returned to its base at Kabrit where it was granted regimental status and thus reorganised. The newly-formed A Squadron subsequently set out for Kufra in Libya on 7 October. Arriving on the 13th it split into two, both parties making their way separately to the northern edge of the Great Sand Sea where they established a forward operating base. By the 22nd, with ammunition and fuel dumps in place over a wide area, raiding parties were ready to disrupt enemy road and rail traffic. On the 26th Lieutenant Miles MacDermot's four-Jeep party, which included Sharman, set off for operations. It returned a week later having put four machine gun posts out of action for the loss of one vehicle. In addition, railway lines, sidings, trucks, food and water dumps, and communications had been destroyed on the Barrani–Bir line whilst the group had also strafed road traffic destroying two trucks. From the squadron War Diary it appears that Sharman was subsequently granted the rank of acting unpaid sergeant.

On Friday 13 November 1942 Lieutenant Douglas Kennedy led his three-Jeep patrol, consisting of 'Sgt Sharman, O'Reilly, Briar, Wall, Cpl McDiarmid, Tillyer', to retrieve another vehicle from the Sand Sea and to carry out operations in the area of Martuba. On the 20th the patrol was returning to the main party when Kennedy's Jeep drove over a mine. He was killed instantly, Sharman and Gunner Thomas Wall dying of wounds soon after (see Kennedy's entry under Alamein Memorial, Egypt, within this volume). 1st SAS' War Diary for this period confirms that on the 20th '2 O.Rs died in 151st Lt Fd. Amb Station resulting from mine wounds incurred in the desert' (WO 218/96 – see Wall's entry below).

Son of Allan and Nora Sharman (née Cawthorn) of St Bedes, East Holdon, Durham – Fiancée of Mildred Ireland of the Women's Auxiliary Air Force. Age 24.
No inscription.
Grave 1.D.10.

Gunner Thomas Henry WALL [1462626] Royal Artillery, L Detachment SAS Brigade and 1st SAS (A Sqn)

Thomas Wall was born on 14 October 1921 in Tooting, south London. By the age of 17 he was working as a joiner in Epsom and attested into the local 228th Battery, 57th Anti-Tank Regiment (TA), Royal Artillery, in May 1939. Having attended Annual Camp he was embodied at the outbreak of war that September and from October was posted to various anti-tank and heavy anti-aircraft units. At the end of April 1941 he embarked for the Middle East where he joined the 28th Heavy Anti-Aircraft Battery before volunteering for L Detachment, SAS Brigade, on 28 May 1942.

After Operation Bigamy, the September 1942 large-scale raid on Benghazi, the SAS returned to Kabrit. Here it was granted regimental status, Wall's newly-formed A Squadron setting out for Kufra Oasis on 7 October. Arriving on the 13th it split into two, both parties making their way to the northern edge of the Great Sand Sea where they established a forward operating base. By the 22nd, with ammunition and fuel dumps in place over a wide area, raiding parties were ready to attack enemy road and rail traffic. On the 26th Wall was a member of a four-Jeep party, under Lieutenant Miles MacDermot, which set off to do so. They returned a week later having put four machine gun posts out of action for the loss of one vehicle. In addition, railway lines, sidings, trucks, food and water dumps, and communications had been destroyed on the Barrani–Bir line whilst the group also destroyed two trucks.

On Friday 13 November 1942 Lieutenant Douglas Kennedy led his three-Jeep patrol, consisting of 'Sgt Sharman, O'Reilly, Briar, Wall, Cpl McDiarmid, Tillyer', to retrieve a vehicle from the Sand Sea and to carry out operations in the area of Martuba. On the 20th the patrol was returning to the main party when Kennedy's Jeep drove over a mine. He was killed, Corporal Allan Sharman later dying of wounds (see Kennedy's entry under Alamein Memorial, Egypt, within this volume, and Sharman's above). Until recently the exact identity of a third fatality could not be established. 1st SAS' War Diary noted that on the same day; '2 ORs [other ranks] died in 151st Lt Fd. Amb Station [Field Ambulance] resulting from mine wounds incurred in the desert' (WO 218/96). Parachutist Frederick Briar was wounded on the 20th and is believed to have been the third other rank mentioned by the Regiment's former Medical Officer, Malcolm Pleydell, MC, as having been involved in this incident: 'One officer and three men were killed outright' (sic – Born of the Desert, by Malcolm 'James', Pleydell's nom de plume). Meanwhile, Captain Bill Fraser of A Squadron had sent a note to SQMS Harold Cranford:

> I'm unable to return to Kufra - Eighth Army have given me a job.
> Will you carry on as planned. Send a party to Death Valley as soon as possible and return any salvaged vehicles by road. When you are recalled come back to Tobruk. If you pass Eighth Army HQ look in I'll probably be there.
> Captain Chambers died in hospital yesterday [of desert sores on 4 December 1942 – see his entry under Fayid War Cemetery, Egypt]. Sgt Sharman and Wall died of wounds – mine.
> W. Fraser Capt

Initial research into the only two possible candidates for 'Wall' proved inconclusive, their service records noting that they had both died of wounds, but on dates (the 17th and 19th) incompatible to those that appear on the service records of both Sharman and Kennedy (the 20th). Neither was noted as being members of the Regiment, although the possibility remained that this was simply an administrative omission – indeed the service records of many of those casualties that appear in this Roll of Honour make no mention of any such transfer. Despite his date of death being officially recorded as 19 November 1942 the recent release of grave concentration records conclusively prove that it is this Wall, Thomas Henry, whose remains were recovered at the same time as Sharman's and whose unit was noted as 'HAA Bty, SAS Bde', that died of wounds sustained on the 20th. Subsequently registered on war graves paperwork solely as '28 HAA Bty RA' he has been omitted from the SAS Roll of Honour until now.

Son of John and Rhoda Wall of Grosvenor Road, Epsom Downs, Surrey. Age 21.
The dearest son the world could hold with tender smile and heart of gold
Grave 1.K.25. Also commemorated in the Borough of Epsom and Ewell Book of Remembrance on display within the Town Hall.

TRIPOLI WAR CEMETERY

Axis forces occupied Tripoli until pushed westwards by Montgomery's Eighth Army on 23 January 1943. The arrival of numerous Commonwealth hospitals led to the creation of this cemetery, although some graves, as will be seen, were concentrated from farther afield. It contains 1,369 Commonwealth burials, 133 of them unidentified. In addition, there are nineteen non-Commonwealth burials and seven non-wartime burials.

The cemetery is located at Babgrgaresh, 2½ kilometres west of the city centre. Access is via the north side of the disused Italian Municipal Christian Cemetery just to the south of Al Jamahirriyah Street. GPS co-ordinates: Latitude 32.87955, Longitude 13.16199

CAPTAIN PHILIP <u>ARNOLD</u> [178072] FRENCH FOREIGN LEGION, GENERAL LIST AND LRDG (HEAVY SECTION, GROUP HQ)

'Skip' Arnold, as he was known to his men, was born to a Belgian father and British mother on 24 May 1912 in Paris. Here he attended the Lycée Janson de Sailly from 1920 to 1929 and the University of Paris until 1930. Having worked as an engineer on road construction he was acting superintendent of motor transport for a Saudi mining syndicate at the outbreak of war. His service record notes that by this time he was fluent in Arabic, Italian and French as well as having knowledge of Yemeni, Hegazi, Hasawi, German and Amharic.

From January to March 1940 Arnold served with the French Foreign Legion at Baalbek in Syria (modern-day Lebanon), at some point passing his corporal's examination at the Legion Training Centre (service number unknown). Perhaps due to disagreement with its Vichy leadership he registered as a member of the British Army Officer's Emergency Reserve in Egypt some time after. Despite the best efforts of the Intelligence Corps to poach him he was commissioned onto the General List during January

1941. Posted to Aden soon after he spent five months in Somaliland during the East African Campaign before returning to Egypt. Here he volunteered for the Long Range Desert Group on 4 September. Due to his language skills he initially served as its Intelligence Officer, although he took part in an offensive patrol the following month on accompanying S Patrol to ambush enemy transport on the Hon–Misurata road. By early December he had taken command of the Heavy Section, a contemporary report noting:

> Arnold with the Heavy Section reached Jalo with the first load from Kufra on January 6 [1942], accompanied by [Lieutenant Ken] Lazarus the Survey Officer who had been holding the fort at Kufra since the end of November. From Jalo the Heavy Section went off almost at once to [the] railhead for rations and fuel returning in very good time on January 18. On January 23 it left again for Matruh and Tobruk, reinforced by five Italian Lancia lorries which Arnold had salvaged at Jalo. By the time the Section had returned to Siwa on February 7 it had covered some 3,400 miles in the first five weeks of 1942 [WO 218/90].

At some point that year Arnold took photographs of Saudi Arabia, forty of them being lodged with the Central Asian Society for 'safe-keeping', although his reason for the visit is unknown. The prints, including scenes of Riyadh and Jeddah, were later donated by the society, which had changed names to the Royal Society for Asia Affairs, to The National Archives: 'The file includes a numbered typed list of the photographic subjects prepared by Lt Arnold … Also included in the file is a covering letter from Lt Arnold to the Society, and a note from the Press Censor' (RSAA/M/36).

Having been mentioned in despatches that June (*London Gazette* 26/06/42, Supplement 30/06/42) Arnold was promoted to lieutenant the following month, crossing the Qatarra Depression from Cairo to resupply Major David Stirling's L Detachment, SAS Brigade, with fuel and ammunition. In addition, his section laid a 320-kilometre string of emergency escape dumps containing food, water and basic supplies at a distance of nearly 1,600km from the nearest forward operating base. According to his Commanding Officer's account each contained 'food, water, shoes etc., for the use of any of our men, who, like T.2 Patrol in January last, might have to walk home after losing vehicles by enemy action' (WO 201/813).

Having resupplied OPERATION CARAVAN, the September 1942 LRDG raid on Barce, Arnold was promoted to acting captain that November. The beginning of 1943 proved a busy period for him and his men, the LRDG War Diary noting:

> The Heavy Section, increased to a total of twenty three-ton Chevrolets and six ten-ton Macks, was fully employed during this period. Its work included journeys to Cairo and Tobruk from Kufra, and forward dumping, from Hon, nearly as far west as the Tunisian Frontier. The Section, and LRDG, had a severe loss when Arnold was killed on a land mine in Hon [modern-day Hūn] on January 15th after more than eighteen months valuable service with the unit [WO 218/91].

Arnold had asked the section's fitter, Les Sullivan, to help him investigate abandoned Italian vehicles. Though they normally did this together Sullivan was busy fixing another patrol's vehicle so Arnold took Driver Harry Gravil in his place (personal interview with Les Sullivan, 2008 – see Gravil's entry). Both men were killed by a landmine as they drove forward and were originally buried side by side in the oasis. They were posthumously mentioned in despatches (*London Gazette* 22/06/43, Supplement 24/06/43).

Son of Mary Arnold of Manchester.
Age 30.
No inscription.
Grave 7.F.20.

Driver John Henry **GRAVIL** [T/153906] Royal Army Service Corps and LRDG (Heavy Section, Group HQ)

Known as 'Harry' to his comrades, John Gravil was born on 28 April 1915 at Thorne near Doncaster. Having worked as a lorry driver he enlisted into the Royal Army Service Corps at Grimsby in February 1940 and was posted to 78 Training Company. At the end of March he was re-posted to 52 Divisional Training Company at Boswell in Scotland where he qualified as a driver mechanic. His service record notes that on 11 June he was serving 'overseas', most likely in north-west France as part of the BEF, but was back in the UK with his unit, D Company, 530 Divisional Supply Column, by the 24th.

Late that December Gravil was posted to a holding battalion, subsequently disembarking in Egypt at the beginning of March 1941. He joined 4 Lines of Communication Company a few days later. Although temporarily re-posted to No.2 Company, Middle East Base Depot, he was back with 4 LoC Company by mid April. At the time this unit was helping supply the Long Range Desert Group for which Gravil volunteered on 8 January 1942. Posted as a driver to the Heavy Section he was promoted to lance-corporal four days later. The section, under the direction of Captain Philip Arnold, laid a series of emergency supply dumps across Libya from Jarabub to Bir Etla. These contained not only food and water but also spare footwear, the intention being to sustain LRDG evaders. In addition, it continued its primary task of bringing forward supplies so that patrols could operate effectively.

Gravil died of wounds received in a landmine explosion in Hon Oasis on 15 January 1943 (see Arnold's entry on previous pages for full details). Having been evacuated from the scene he was taken to No.1 Mobile Military Hospital where he died soon after. His father later wrote to both the War Office and the RASC Records Office: 'I deeply appreciate the enquiries you have made concerning the way my late son 153906 L.Cpl J H Gravil met his death, and as a result I have received a kind and explanatory letter from Major J. R. Easonsmith, LRDG, MEF' (see 'Jake' Easonsmith's own entry under Leros War Cemetery, Greece, Volume II). Both Gravil and Arnold were posthumously mentioned in despatches (*London Gazette* 22/06/43, Supplement 24/06/43).

Son of Fred and Maria Gravil (née Everest) of Browns Lane, Thorne, Yorkshire. Age 27.
No inscription.
Grave 7.F.19.

Gunner Ernest Joseph Hamilton **HENDERSON** [RH/1095786] Southern Rhodesia Light Battery, Royal Artillery, Royal Horse Artillery and LRDG (S.1 Patrol, A Sqn)

Known by his middle name of Joseph, Henderson was born in Armagh, now in Northern Ireland, sometime during 1911. After the sudden death of his father, three years later his mother moved to South Africa where numerous relatives, including her mother, brother, several sisters and her in-laws, were living. The young Henderson is therefore likely to have grown up in Durban, although he later moved to Salisbury in Rhodesia where he married.

Having worked as a surveyor at Rezende Gold Mine in Penhalonga Henderson enlisted into the Southern Rhodesia Light Battery in September 1940 (service number X3260). The following April he was promoted to lance-bombardier but in August reverted to the rank of gunner at his own request in order to serve abroad. Embarking from South Africa he arrived at Port Tewfik in Egypt towards the end of September 1941. Here he and many other men of the 4th Rhodesian Anti-Tank Battery were briefly absorbed as D Battery into the 'Noodles', the 102nd (Northumberland Hussars) Anti-Tank Regiment, Royal Artillery, which had incurred losses in Greece and Crete. Taking up position along the Libyan border Henderson was re-posted to the 2nd Anti-Tank Regiment that November for the duration of OPERATION CRUSADER, an attempt to recapture territory in Cyrenaica and Tripolitania and to destroy enemy armour. Heavily rebuffed Henderson rejoined the Northumberland Hussars and was wounded near Gazala in February 1942. On being discharged from hospital that April he found the unit's batteries had been broken up and that he had been posted, with many of his former D Battery colleagues, to the 4th Regiment, Royal Horse Artillery, at Sollum. By 27 May, when Rommel struck, the men were occupying a fortified position known as the 'Retma' Box that faced Bir Hacheim. Despite a spirited defence against German armour a general withdraw was ordered and the men eventually reached Alamein. Here Henderson was again admitted to hospital in July but the following month volunteered for the Long Range Desert Group.

In a relatively short period Henderson gained a strong reputation for his map-reading skills. During September 1942 he was navigator of S.1 Patrol, guiding L Detachment's X Force under Lt-Colonel David Stirling, DSO, to raid Benghazi (OPERATION BIGAMY). Three SAS parties left Kufra on the 4th, Henderson guiding the third that consisted of six officers and sixty men, even though it was not until December that he officially qualified as a navigator.

At the beginning of 1943 Henderson guided a joint force consisting of his patrol and men from Popski's Private Army to make a 'topographical recce of an area in Tunisia'. S.1 set out from Zella on 6 January and reached the Wadi Zem Zem near the modern-day village of Abugrein on the 15th. Here it dispersed amongst good cover. At 0915hrs an enemy convoy of approximately fifty vehicles was seen approaching. Although this was seen to pass the patrol came under fire at 1030hrs, Alexander Bond later recalling that they were attacked by a German armoured car and numerous other vehicles:

> Caught between two fires and unable to move our remaining undamaged vehicles in any direction, the patrol made for what meagre ground cover was available. Eric Henderson [*sic* or nickname?] was badly hit and lay where he had fallen. Just behind him, in a slight depression, Low found himself with two Cockneys and a Canadian. Low had lost the magazine of his Tommy gun and the little party were without arms of any description. And then Henderson showed the stuff he was made of. He commenced a running commentary on the movements of the enemy. Asked how he was, he said his legs were becoming paralysed. His comrades were arranging to go back to one of the trucks to obtain morphia but Henderson pointed out the hopelessness of getting across the open space. He continued to report on what he could see going on in front and said that four enemy vehicles were approaching their position. He urged his comrades to make a getaway, for he believed himself to be mortally wounded. 'They've seen me hit and fall,' he said, 'so they won't fire on me again. You chaps make a dash for it.' …
>
> A report was made that Henderson had been seen, lifted into one of the enemy's vehicles. Later his grave was found clearly marked where the Germans had given him an honourable burial. Wandering tribesmen reported that a volley had been fired over his grave and that the German officers had saluted it [*LRDG Rhodesia: Rhodesians in the Long Range Desert Group*, by Jonathan Pittaway and Craig Fourie].

LRDG Rhodesia also states:

> One of the members of Sonderkommando Dora [a special unit created to guard the Afrikakorps' southern flank], Mr Pillewizer, was a POW at Schloss Kransberg in the Taunus in Germany in 1946. When he was asked by his interrogators, some Americans and one British officer, 'Do you know where Mr Henderson is?' he asked them to bring the maps of the area between Esc Sciueref [the Jebel Sherif] and Mizda and he showed them the exact location where they had buried him with full military honours.

The circumstances of Henderson's death are perhaps best summed up by a poem found by the wife of former Popski's Private Army officer, Captain Alec Petrie, after his death:

> *In Wadi Zem Zem as we did lay*
> *There came our moment that fateful day.*
> *We heard the clang of iron treads*

A sound that every soldier dreads.
Then crashing on us like thunder's roar
Eight armoured cars came to the fore.
Guns blazing firing left and right
Oh God! It was a fearsome sight.
We must escape, our position's dire
As one by one our trucks caught fire.
The flames tore at us with searing heat.
The smoke did aid us to retreat.
Then to the scattered scrub we came
With four Jeeps only to our name.
Out on a rock with anguished cry
One of us lay there to die.
One more wounded, no hope had he
We had not the chance to set him free.
Again we had to leave the field
This was not our target in order sealed [IWM Documents.5797 – Private Papers of Captain A. G. Petrie].

Son of Joseph and Mary Henderson (née Mann) – Husband of Marion Henderson of Salisbury, Southern Rhodesia – Predeceased by a baby brother aged 11 weeks, and by a sister, Marjorie, aged 12.
Age 32.
My beloved. Deathless he passed the portal
Grave 11.G.10. Also commemorated on his mother's headstone at West Street Cemetery, Durban.

SERGEANT CYRIL DESMOND <u>HEWSON</u> [1030] AUCKLAND (EAST COAST) MOUNTED RIFLES, DIVISIONAL CAVALRY REGIMENT, LRP AND LRDG (T PATROL)

Known as 'Squib' to both family and comrades, Cyril Hewson was born on 27 January 1908 at Devonport, New Zealand, on Auckland's North Shore. Growing up at his parents' dairy farm at Puriri, south of the Coromandel Peninsula, he attended the village school from 1913 to 1921. From the age of 13 he helped on the farm but by the time he reached 20 was working on an oil barge on the Waihou River. After his family was forced to give up their holding during the Great Depression he and his older brother laboured nearby for the Lands and Survey Department, helping to drain the Hauraki Plains around the Torehape Works Camp near Ngatea where the pair was accommodated. In his spare time Hewson served for three years as a trooper in the territorial Auckland (East Coast) Mounted Rifles at Paeroa and at the outbreak of war enlisted into the Divisional Cavalry Regiment, being promoted to lance-corporal by December 1939.

In January 1940 Hewson embarked from Wellington for the Middle East as a member of the first echelon of the 2nd New Zealand Expeditionary Force. En route he was admitted to the ship's hospital with a badly bruised leg but disembarked at Port Tewfik, Egypt, in good health the following month. Having trained at Maadi Camp not far south of Cairo he volunteered for the newly-formed Long Range

Patrol on 25 July 1940 and by the beginning of December was serving as a corporal in the expanded Long Range Desert Group's T Patrol under Captain Pat Clayton. Midway through the month he was promoted to sergeant.

On 27 December 1940 T Patrol and the newly-formed, and less experienced, G Patrol left Cairo under Clayton for OPERATION AESOP. Its object was to extend the LRDG area of operations and enable Free French troops in Chad to participate in raids into Libya. To achieve this a joint force would attack numerous Italian-held oases in the Fezzan region from the south. Having collected a small party of French from Kayugi in northern Chad the patrols therefore re-crossed the border into southern Libya and closed on Murzuk Fort on 11 January 1941. Although taken by surprise its garrison put up an effective defence and during the ensuing action Hewson, aboard T.3 'Te Hai', was killed. Whilst in the process of clearing a stoppage on the truck's Vickers machine gun an incoming round bounced off the top of the radiator and pierced his heart. After two hours it was realised that the force lacked the numbers to take the fort and it withdrew, stopping a few kilometres farther on to bury Hewson and the French commander, Lt-Colonel Jean Colonna d'Ornano, who had also been killed. The two were wrapped in blankets and buried by the roadside in a single grave. Whilst Clayton read the funeral service a cross, made from the wood of a petrol case, was erected and an *Onwards* New Zealand cap badge nailed to it.

'Tony' Browne, who was awarded a Distinguished Conduct Medal for his actions at Murzuk and who went on to win a Military Cross whilst commissioned within the LRDG, later sent photos of Hewson's grave to the NZ Army Department in 1954:

> I was among the group who buried the body of Cyril Hewson on a hillside north of the oasis and a few days later the Italians moved him and others into a specially prepared little walled garden where they now lie. Within the tomb adjoining Cyril Hewson's rests Colonel Count Colonna d'Ornano who fell with him and in memory of whom one of the principal thoroughfares in Algiers has been re-named [service record].

Son of William and Laura Hewson of Sealey Street, Thames – Younger brother of Corporal William 'Snow' Hewson, New Zealand Army Service Corps, who was killed in June 1942 in a motor accident and who is buried at Aleppo War Cemetery, Syria, and of Marjorie Hewson who died the year before Squib was born – Older brother of Able Seaman Charles 'Chook' Hewson, RN, who was lost overboard north of New Zealand in June 1930 whilst serving on HMS *Dunedin*, and of Mae, Raymond (acting second-lieutenant in the Auckland (East Coast) Mounted Rifles, NZ Armoured Regiment, who did not go overseas), Nita, Frederick (known as 'Bluey', wounded in action whilst attached to the 5th Field Ambulance, NZ Medical Corps, from the Service Corps), Doris and Ernie 'Socks' Hewson (who was also attached to the 5th Field Ambulance, NZ Medical Corps, from the Service Corps and who served in Egypt and Italy).

Age 32.

No inscription.

Grave 12.B.21. Also commemorated on an LRDG memorial within the New Zealand SAS camp at Papakura and at the Auckland War Memorial Museum.

CAPTAIN THE HON. ALEXANDER HARDINGE PATRICK HORE-RUTHVEN [55987]
GENERAL LIST, RIFLE BRIGADE AND 1ST SAS (B SQN)

Known as Pat to both family and friends, Hore-Ruthven was born on 31 August 1913 in Quetta, at that time part of India, to a famous Scottish officer and Irish mother. He was educated at Hawtreys and Eton before going up to Magdalene College, Cambridge, where he was an enthusiastic member of the OTC. Although he harboured ambitions of becoming a professional jockey, he followed his father into the army. His first choice of the Scots Greys, where, importantly, he would have a horse, was thwarted and having been commissioned onto the General List (TA) as a university candidate in July 1933 he was appointed a regular commission in the 1st Battalion, Rifle Brigade (Prince Consort's Own), in 1934 (*London Gazette* 31/08/34). Serving on Malta from May 1936 he was re-posted during March 1938 to the 2nd Battalion in India where he was stationed at Meerut and Kaylana. Whilst on sick leave during January 1939 he married society beauty, Pamela Margaret Fletcher, at Westminster Abbey. She later noted in her memoirs *A Cloud of Forgetting*: 'when I first met Pat, he had been temporarily rusticated from Cambridge for biting a policeman on the nose.'

From July 1939 Hore-Ruthven served in Palestine during the final month of the Arab Revolt before being promoted to captain and moving to Egypt as a company commander in early 1940. In his preface to *The Happy Warrior*, a 1943 posthumous volume of Hore-Ruthven's own verse, fellow Greenjacket General Sir Henry Maitland Wilson, GBE, KCB, DSO, wrote: 'Pat took out the very first patrol that was ever made in the Western Desert … It was the first small beginning of those vast and successful operations that led to the liberation of North Africa.' For this first patrol into Libya Hore-Ruthven received a Mention in Despatches (*London Gazette* 01/04/41, Supplement 25/04/41) and by December was serving as a liaison officer with the Free French forces, taking part in ambushes, recces, and the relief of Tobruk. He was noted for his scruffiness and 'Jumbo' Wilson affectionately wrote; 'Tell Pat's father that his son is still the worst-dressed man in the Desert.'

During the enemy advance of April 1941 Hore-Ruthven was attached to a French motor company at Msus in Libya. Elements of A Squadron, LRDG, arrived to warn him of an imminent enemy advance and with a hostile column spotted to the south he destroyed all stores and withdrew (WO 201/809). The following month his term with the French was up and he was earmarked to join an infantry base depot. However, he engineered to stay in post a while longer, acting at the same time as personal assistant to Wilson. This took him to Iraq and Syria and gained him the offer of a majority and a further staff job from Jumbo. Feeling that he should get back to his regiment he declined and as a reward was promoted to major and given command of the 1st Battalion's I Company. Having been attached to the 64th Medium Regiment, Royal Artillery, from March until May 1942 he returned to his battalion. He was subsequently involved in fierce fighting around the Alam el-Halfa Ridge during the August and early September 1942 battles at El Alamein.

Hore-Ruthven volunteered for 1st SAS on 27 September 1942, relinquishing his acting rank of major in order to do so. Posted to B Squadron he wrote to his mother that November telling her of his transfer:

I am with a great lot of chaps indeed, all volunteers, officers and men. We do rather specialised training of a tough nature which includes parachute jumping, but that is only one side of our activities. I am now a qualified 'brolly hopper', having completed my course without accident or injury …

In addition, we do some very terrific night-marches across country. The other night I did 30 miles carrying a 40lb pack, and got through all right, though I was pretty tired at the end. The process of weeding out officers and men is quite rightly very ruthless, and I did not write and tell you about it before in case I could not make the grade. However, I made it all right and I am now a troop-leader, and if all goes well should get a squadron very soon.

My colonel is a rather remarkable chap called David Stirling, Scots Guards, who is only 26 but has already got a DSO and Bar [*sic*], and has done most awfully well [*The Joy of Youth: Letters of Patrick Hore-Ruthven*, edited by Ethel Anderson].

Hore-Ruthven wrote to his wife in similar vein:

You will see by the address that I have moved again and am now doing what I always wanted to do when it was first mooted … I am now fully qualified as a parachutist having taken very kindly to it all …

Now we are doing some very tough marching and training but I am getting very fit and seem to make it as well as anybody else … we are all volunteers and most of us have come down in rank.

At the moment I am commanding this squadron but think this is only temporary. I have no doubt that great adventures lie ahead.

I am so happy in my new 'home' with lots of friends – the most wonderful lot of men that have ever been together, I am only a captain again, but have a splendid command, the sort of thing that I have always hankered after. Vivian Street is my squadron leader and is such fun to soldier with [*A Cloud of Forgetting*, by Pamela Cooper (née Fletcher)].

B Squadron left Kabrit on 20 November 1942 tasked with moving deep behind the lines in Libya and harassing enemy traffic making its way to the front. Major Vivian Street, MC, later wrote to Hore-Ruthven's father:

We did not contact the enemy until crossing the road near Bungem, when going in a north-westerly direction. We had hoped to slip across unseen, but as we approached it about midday [*sic* – at 1630hrs on 11 December 1942] we ran into ten Italian armoured cars which were obviously waiting for us. They opened fire on us at about 1,000 yards and Pat's Jeep was hit – bursting a tyre. It was still a runner but obviously not much good to go into action with. Pat quickly realised the situation and jumped into a Jeep armed with a .5 [Browning heavy machine gun] which was close beside him. He himself manned the gun and went round the enemy's flank with four other similarly armed Jeeps. This diverted the enemy's attention, with the result that the lighter armed Jeeps managed to race across the road and into the hills. As soon as they were clear Pat followed them with the .5 Jeeps. I cannot help thinking that our successful passage of the road was largely due to Pat's presence of mind, for you can well imagine that fifty Jeeps are hardly a match for ten armoured cars, even though the latter were manned by Italians.

After this encounter we drove on all through the night and reached Faschia, which is about 100 miles south of Misurata. Here we split up, each party being allotted a sector of the road. Pat had the sector from Misurata to Torga [*The Joy of Youth*].

Hore-Ruthven subsequently led his patrol into the Wadi Henscir el-Gabu on 19 December. The following evening he took a small party to mine the road south of Gioda. Having finished doing so they came across a number of vehicles, including tanks, parked on the side of the road. Hore-Ruthven decided to attack and although his party destroyed two vehicles he was subsequently wounded, the patrol separating in the ensuing melee. In two separate, and sometimes conflicting, accounts Reg Seekings, DCM, described the events:

The night before we had found a heavy concentration of vehicles which had been too large to attack, so to-night, Captain Hore-Ruthven said, we must have a go at these. Three nights before, we had destroyed twenty trucks and mined the road about 3 miles farther down, and this had been a very successful raid and now all the Italians were on alert. Well, we found they were guarded. About 40 yards from the trucks we were challenged [*The Joy of Youth*].

I had just got into position when the sentry challenged – he was in hysterics, then the grenade went off. In the flash I was horrified to see Captain Hore-Ruthven had not waited for them [the grenades] to go off and had run right on to them. Even worse, if possible, the three men with him were running away like hell … I ran to the trucks calling the captain; he came towards me, then I could see he was very badly wounded, calling to me to get out of it … I carried him 150 to 200 yards to a sand hummock; everything they had was turned on us. It was a miracle we were not blown to pieces.

I then endeavoured to get him to crawl. He begged me to get out and save myself. He was finished. I could see he was hit very badly in the right shoulder, chest and side. He passed out, and I tried to drag him along, but could not manage … feeling terribly downhearted, I was compelled to leave him, and I had only just got clear and the firing had ceased, when I heard a shout of 'Reg, Reg', and then the firing broke out again. In the flash of the guns and tracer I could see the captain running, then suddenly he fell and the firing stopped. I ran over to him. Alas, the Italians beat me to it by a couple of yards. The wretched officer emptied his revolver into him as he lay on the ground, just sheer murder. In their excitement they failed to notice who I was, so I quickly eased away from them … in approx half an hour a large truck blew up. Captain Hore-Ruthven must have used a time pencil – it pleased me to think he had achieved his target.

Before leaving Kabrit Capt Hore-Ruthven had received a large fruit cake from his mother in Australia; his intentions were to cut it on Christmas Day, and Mac and I vowed however hungry we got that cake would not be cut until Christmas Day, silly idea perhaps, but we felt that a way of paying our last respects.

Asked by a family friend how Hore-Ruthven had been during his last days Seekings replied:

In fine form. Very cheerful and happy, and enjoying it very much. Said it was his idea of real soldiering. He had a big black beard – he had not shaved for a month, and we all laughed over it. I liked him very much. He was brave. Not many men would have rushed in like that [*The Joy of Youth*].

Hore-Ruthven's parents were notified that he was missing, known to be wounded, and believed to be a prisoner. Newspapers subsequently reported that he had died 'at an Italian Hospital in North Africa of wounds received on December 20th' [*sic*]. It was not until the Allies advanced that his grave was found, his family receiving a message from a British officer:

Passing through Misurata on my way here I discovered Patrick Hore-Ruthven had died of wounds in an Italian hospital on 24 December. He is buried Italian cemetery at Misurata Marina. I visited both hospital and cemetery. I saw [the] doctor who appears to have nursed him. I feel sure they did everything possible. He was wounded through [his] lung and died of pneumonia [*A Cloud of Forgetting*].

Meanwhile, *The Rifle Brigade Chronicle* carried his obituary:

The death of Pat Hore-Ruthven in an Italian hospital in Tripolitania on Christmas Day [*sic*], 1942, as a result of wounds received in action, deprived the regiment of a very gallant officer whose wit, loyalty, courage, and cheerful personality had endeared him to all who knew him.

Pat possessed a strange mixture of attractive traits and characteristics … a grand leader with an intense dislike for any form of administration – a brilliant wit, widely and deeply read – the possessor of a streak of wildness which served him in good stead on several occasions, the donor of what was sometimes almost quixotic loyalty to those in trouble or in difficulty – and the owner of a great sense of the ridiculous both on the appropriate and sometimes on quite the opposite kind of occasion. He may fairly be said to have belonged more to the seventeenth century than to this and would have been completely at home in the court of the Restoration.

A book of Hore-Ruthven's letters home entitled *The Joy of Youth* was published in 1950 to celebrate his life and to teach his two sons, who he never met, about their father. Perhaps most poignant of all is the poem he wrote as a schoolboy after the death of his favourite horse, seen above:

So when we both are dead
And we meet on farther shore,
We'll start together fresh my Dolly Grey.
We'll go roving, roving, roving
As we ever did before,
Unencumbered by the flesh my Dolly Grey.

Son of Brigadier-General Alexander Hore-Ruthven, 1st Earl of Gowrie, Governor of Australia, VC, PC, GCMG, CB, DSO*, who had followed his own father, a veteran of the Indian Mutiny, Crimea, Sudan and the First World War, into the Rifle Brigade, and of the Countess of Gowrie (née Pollok) – Husband of Pamela Hore-Ruthven of Calne, Wiltshire – Father of Grey and Malise. Age 29.

Deeds show (the family motto)

Grave 5.C.19. Also commemorated by the Patrick Hore-Ruthven Memorial Fountain at Government House, Canberra.

Signalman Nadir **Khan** [A/1717] Indian Signal Corps
and Indian Long Range Squadron (Signals Section) Att LRDG

The Indian Long Range Squadron (Indian Armoured Corps) was formed at Damascus in Syria during January 1942, mainly from volunteers of the 3rd Indian Motor Brigade. However, at least four British and four Indian signallers, Nadir Khan being one, were also attached and spread between its four patrols. As with other Indian units within the British Army these subunits were segregated: M (Mohamedans), S (Sikhs), J (Jhats), R (Pathans), a Heavy Section (mixed – sometimes known as Q Patrol) and the Squadron HQ. All set about training for their new duties during the early part of the year.

In July 1942 the ILRS moved to Egypt and applied to 'work with the LRDG in its correct role' (WO 218/95). As of 1 October all patrols therefore forward-mounted to Kufra Oasis in Libya and were placed under the command of the Long Range Desert Group to gain operational experience. On arrival their callsigns were changed to avoid any confusion with those of the LRDG, M becoming I.1, S becoming I.2, J becoming I.3, and R being retitled I.4.

On 16 January 1943 the LRDG's HQ moved to Hon Oasis where the whole unit, including the ILRS, was to be based. Corporal Ernie George, one of those attached from the Royal Signals, later wrote:

> Meanwhile [on 22 February 1943] my Indian operator friend Nadder [sic – Nadir] Khan had been nosing about where he shouldn't have wandered and had blown himself and his mate to pieces by setting off a mine by trip wire [sic – only Khan was killed]. Another operator Fhazal Dhad, a huge Pathan tribesman had blown off some of his fingers whilst fiddling with some fuses. So – when the rest of the squadron joined us, the CO [Major Sam McCoy] gave them a severe talking to about the dangers of wandering in suspect areas and tinkering with strange objects [*A Second World War Soldier: Before, During and After*, by Ernest George].

The ILRS War Diary confirms that on 22 February:

> Sigm Nadar [sic] Khan was killed and W/C Sadar Din severely wounded by an enemy mine while retrieving a battery from a derelict truck near the perimeter wire at Hon. Major McCoy recovered the body of Nadar Khan which was buried in the Mohd Cemetery at Hon in the evening [WO 169/14944].

Son of Khan Muhammed of Jabbi, Shahpur (now in Pakistan).
Age 24.
[God is] the much forgiving. From God we come and to God we return [translated from Arabic]
Grave 2.H.2.

Captain Francois Edward LE ROEX [74235] South African Engineer Corps Att LRDG

At the beginning of December 1942 R.1 Patrol of the Long Range Desert Group's A Squadron arrived in Benghazi where it was tasked by Eighth Army. In his forthcoming offensive Lt-General Montgomery, CB, DSO, planned to trap Axis forces by turning their inland flank whilst engaging them frontally near to the coast. R.1 was to supply ground knowledge, guide the 2nd New Zealand Division around the southern flank, carry out recces of the Wadi Tamet, the Wadi Chebir, and the Wadi Zem Zem to the enemy's rear and lastly to take 'astralfixes' within these wadis 'so as to help co-relate air photographs' (WO 218/91).

Having received his orders from Lt-General Bernard Freyberg, VC, DSO**, on 9 December, from Montgomery on the 10th, and from 51st (Highland) Division on the 11th, the patrol commander, Captain Tony Browne, DCM, who had served in the ranks from the formation of the Long Range Patrol, gathered his men for inspection by both generals. The patrol then led their fellow Kiwis and the 4th Light Armoured Brigade south from el Haseiat before turning north-westwards towards the coast, thus completing the required left hook. However, Rommel, forewarned by aerial reconnaissance, withdrew his forces consequently preventing encirclement. R.1 reached the coastal road to the west of 'Marble Arch' near Ra's Lanuf on the 16th. The following day it again led the New Zealanders around the enemy's southern flank near Nofilia, witnessing a minor tank engagement en route. Again the enemy slipped away. 2nd Lieutenant Paddy McLauchlan, who was learning the ropes from Browne, took up the narrative in his post-operation report:

> The patrol [then] moved to Nofilia to NZ Div's new location and met there Capt. Browne returned from Army, and on 22nd the recce party as set out in Strength paragraph for Task C [five officers, eleven other ranks, three Chevrolet trucks and two Jeeps], proceeded westwards [behind enemy lines]. Lt-Col Pieman of the 7th Armd Div was to supply the technical knowledge and the two S.A. [South African] Officers were to take Astralfixes as and when possible in the main wadis.
>
> The patrol arrived at El Machina LG [Landing Ground] Ref.RY5017 and unfortunately a Jeep carrying Capt. Browne and S.A Capt Le Rou [*sic* – Le Roex from 46 Survey Company] ran over a Tellermine. The injured men were brought back to 7 Armd Div B.D.S [dressing station] at Nofilia where we arrived at 0800hrs on 23rd. Capt. Le Rou died an hour after the accident. Capt. Browne was suffering from severe shock and bruises and a broken collar bone and consequently had a most unenviable trip back [Browne was awarded the Military Cross for these recces which resulted in the turning of the Agheila position].
>
> I was called to Eighth Army and briefed for Task D on 29th, Lt.Col. Pieman remained attached and a S.A. Capt. Alexander replaced the remaining S.A. Lieut [WO 218/91].

Le Roex, whose service record cannot currently be located, is officially recorded as having been killed in action on 23 December 1942.
No known next of kin details.
Age unknown.
No inscription.
Grave 12.C.26.

LANCE-CORPORAL NUI BRUCE **O'MALLEY** [16372] NELSON-MARLBOROUGH-WEST COAST REGIMENT, WELLINGTON EAST COAST MOUNTED RIFLES, DIVISIONAL CAVALRY REGIMENT AND LRDG (R.1 PATROL, A SQN)

Nui (meaning 'big' in Maori) O'Malley was born on 9 October 1910 at Havelock in Marlborough, New Zealand, where he later served for a year with the territorial Nelson-Marlborough-West Coast Regiment. Moving to the North Island he worked as a shepherd for Wairoa Flaxmills Ltd. before enlisting in January 1940. Serving locally as a corporal in the Wellington East Coast Mounted Rifles (service number 2/12/79) he married in February 1941. On transferring to the Divisional Cavalry Regiment at Burnham Camp in October 1941 he reverted to trooper but was soon promoted, first to lance-corporal and then back to corporal.

Having embarked for the Middle East in April 1941 O'Malley arrived in Egypt the following month and was posted to a composite training battalion as a lance-corporal. That September he returned to the Divisional Cavalry Regiment, this time reverting to the rank of trooper. The New Zealand Division was in action near to Sidi Rezegh in late November and having been hard-pressed by the Germans was eventually withdrawn from the line in December. Around this time O'Malley was separated from his squadron, presumably during a German advance, and was not noted as being 'safe with [his] unit' until 20 January 1942. Here he found that he had been absorbed into the New Zealand Armoured Corps that had formed on New Year's Day. He volunteered for the Long Range Desert Group on 22 February and was initially posted to A Squadron's HQ Patrol.

By June 1942 O'Malley was serving in R.1 Patrol and from late that month until 23 July was engaged on Road Watch duties to the west of Agheila on the Tripoli-Benghazi coastal road. He later became the patrol's navigator and after a spell in hospital with sandfly fever was promoted to lance-corporal at the end of October 1942. He was killed in action that November: his patrol, commanded by Captain 'Tony' Browne, DCM, had been tasked with delivering fresh stores and a relief wireless operator to agents working around Bir Tala. On the 18th it was attacked by Italian aircraft having taken cover in the banks of Wadi Tamet. All ranks attempted to fight off the planes, O'Malley receiving a fatal stomach wound whilst manning the guns (see Captain Mark Pilkington's entry overleaf for further details).

Son of James and Agnes O'Malley (née Pullman) of Piopio, New Zealand – Husband of Ethel O'Malley of Frasertown, Hawke's Bay – Father of Michael O'Malley, born soon after he left New Zealand for the last time – Brother of Louis O'Malley of Manunui, Taumarunui.
Age 32.
No inscription.
Grave 12.D.4. Also commemorated on Piopio's war memorial and on the LRDG memorial within the New Zealand SAS camp at Papakura.

Captain Mark Leslie **PILKINGTON** MC [76537] Life Guards, Arab Legion, Middle East Commando and SOE Att LRDG

Mark Pilkington was born on 12 January 1914 at Egerton Place in Knightsbridge, London, his wider family being the owners of Pilkington Glass. Having been educated at Heatherdown Preparatory School near Ascot he entered Eton in 1927 where he held the rank of sergeant in the OTC and was recommended to Oxford University by his housemaster: 'as nice a boy as you will find – trustworthy and charming with the pleasant hobby of Birds – above the average in "schoolwork" intelligence as well as generally speaking. He will be captain of my house next year'. Going up to Christ Church he was a whipper-in for Oxford University Drag Hounds whilst studying history for two years. By 1938 he was living with his wife, Susan (née Henderson), on Cheyne Walk, Chelsea, and had followed his father into the Stock Exchange. Concurrently he was the Conservative prospective candidate for East Woolwich and had been freshly commissioned into the Life Guards Supplementary Reserve. Mobilised at the outbreak of war he was posted to the Household Cavalry Training Regiment in Windsor, disembarking in Palestine with the Household Cavalry Regiment in January 1940.

In early 1941 Pilkington volunteered for service in East Africa and was subsequently promoted to acting captain on 1 March before being awarded the Military Cross:

> For conspicuous gallantry in action over a prolonged period from April 1941 to 27 November 1941.
> This officer entered Ethiopia in March 1941 in command of an operational centre composed of Ethiopians from the Sudan. He was directed against the Debra Tabor area in April. Together with other Ethiopian forces under British officers he led many harassing attacks against that place until its surrender in June 1941 [located on a hill this stronghold of 6,000 Italians had blocked the key route from Gondar to Dessie].
> Taking over a complete unit known as the Uollo Banda, consisting of 1,500 Italian-trained irregulars who volunteered to serve against the Italians after the surrender of Debra Tabor, Captain Pilkington continued to set an example of a high order in his raids and harassing attacks on the Italian lines of communication between Kulkaber and Gondar.
> With the arrival of regular troops in the Gondar area, Captain Pilkington and his Uollo Banda took part in the attacks of the Kulkaber position on the 13th and 21st November, giving particularly valuable assistance in the latter action in spite of heavy casualties to his troops. On 27th November he led his troops in the final attack on Gondar with great dash and gallantry, taking all objectives assigned to him [*London Gazette* 08/07/43, WO 373/29].

A period attached to the headquarters of the Arab Legion in Transjordan under Glubb Pasha followed. However, on 20 March 1942 Pilkington was posted to Holding Squadron, 1st Special Service Regiment (Middle East Commando), just a few days after his brother, Flying Officer Charles Leslie Pilkington, RAF, had been killed in action with his crew when returning from an operational flight over Germany. That June his father also died.

Pilkington volunteered for MO1 (SP), a cover name for the Special Operations Executive, on 1 November 1942 (HS 9/1189/2). At the time of his death he was on the strength of MO4, the Middle East branch of SOE, but attached as Liaison Officer to the Arab Legion having himself organised a month's attachment to the LRDG (service record and WO 201/815). As noted by GHQ Middle East as early as June 1942 'the role of the Arab Legion in the Syrian Desert has many points of similarity with that of the LRDG and, while the Arab Legion is of course expert in desert navigation and topography in its own part of the world, it is felt that operationally it would learn a great deal from the LRDG' (WO 201/2587). According to a signal sent to the High Commissioner of Palestine Pilkington and seven of his men travelled to the LRDG base at Kufra 'so that we may have a few of these men [of the Arab Legion] trained in the conditions of the Western Desert in case we may need them there in the future … This party would spend its time partly on patrol with LRDG and partly at Kufra under instruction in navigation etc' (WO 201/2587). On arrival it was decided that Pilkington should join Captain Tony Browne's R.1 Patrol that was tasked with delivering fresh stores and a relief wireless operator to agents working around Bir Tala in Libya. They left Kufra on 12 November, Browne taking up the narrative after a short action during which the patrol had knocked out two enemy vehicles:

> On the morning of 17/11/42 [*sic* – 18th] we arrived at a prearranged RV, where we were joined by Y.2 Patrol and the detachment of the Heavy Section. After refilling with petrol we continued north-westward, having arranged to meet

Capt Hunter with Y.2 in the Wadi Tamet (Ref RY2332). Shortly before reaching the wadi we were seen by a [Italian] Ghibli recce aircraft. There are steep cliffs on either side of Wadi Tamet, and each of my vehicles selected a cleft with bonnets facing downhill. Half an hour after our arrival a Heinkel flew over and was then joined by two Capronis which flew round in a wide circle but took no action. At about midday several CR42 Italian fighter aircraft arrived and machine-gunned our vehicles half-heartedly. All our guns were firing and none of the enemy pilots seemed disposed to make a determined attack. About 1230 all the aircraft disappeared and I took the opportunity of moving my vehicles to new positions. Within half an hour a larger number of CR42s arrived, (fourteen were counted). At least two of these disregarded our fire and low level attacks were made. During these attacks it is regretted that Capt Pilkington, Life Guards, and L/Cpl O'Malley, NZEF, patrol navigator, were mortally wounded and died within two hours. Both men were shot while firing machine guns. Pte Fogden, NZEF, was shot in the legs. The W/T and patrol commander's truck were both damaged beyond repair. At dusk, Capt Pilkington and L/Cpl O'Malley were buried in one grave on the western side of the wadi [WO 218/91].

The patrol then split, one party returning with the wounded man, the other going on to complete their task. Meanwhile the LRDG War Diary confirms: 'three officers and two Arab ORs [other ranks] from the Arab Legion were attached to LRDG for instruction for some weeks in October and November. One officer, Captain Pilkington, was killed in action on patrol with R.1, near the W. Tamet' (WO 218/91). The following month a brother officer wrote a personal tribute for *The Times*:

With his good looks and peculiar lazy charm, Captain Mark L. Pilkington, the Life Guards, passed for one of the most fortunate of men. His sense of humour and his dislike of pretension made him no friends among the pompous and aggressive. He had a queer, almost fey gentleness and fineness of character, which he covered by a vague desultory manner. Mark Pilkington was a most hardy and gallant soldier – as was recognised by all officers and men who served with him in the patriot guerilla forces in Abyssinia. During the rains of 1941 the Italian garrison of Gondar – 15,000 strong – was successfully contained by guerilla forces under the direction of a few British officers and NCOs. Mark, with two other officers of the Cavalry Division, shares the honours of numerous tough encounters in the wild mountains around Lake Tana. On one occasion Mark, at the head of his own devoted Wollo tribesmen, commanded in a twenty-eight hour action against an Italian Brigade under Colonel Torelli – the most competent of the Italian officers in Gondar. With all his gay and light-hearted face to the world, Mark Pilkington was a thoughtful and even studious fellow, who might have served his country as well in peace as he did in war. His talents were varied. His gift for languages gave him a quick facility in Amharic and Arabic. He proved to have a real gift for practical diplomacy, and won a considerable influence with the turbulent Abyssinian chieftains with whom he worked for so many months. He was a delightful companion in travel; an excellent photographer, and a keen naturalist. The daily world was a constant joy to him, as he was a source of comfort and encouragement to those who were lucky enough to share his friendship in strange and difficult days [15 December 1942].

Pilkington's fellow soldiers were not the only ones to pay tribute to him, the War Office writing to his wife at the beginning of February 1943: 'I am directed to state that the Department has been requested

to convey to you an expression of deep sympathy of His Imperial Majesty The Emperor of Ethiopia at the sad loss of your husband.' Soon after the war his mother wrote *Mark Pilkington: Some Letters 1939–42* in order to preserve his memory.

Son of Hubert and Ruth Pilkington (née Leslie) of Little Offley, Hitchen, Hertfordshire – Estranged husband of Susan Pilkington of Burr Hill Cottage, Chobham, Surrey – Father of Simon Pilkington – Brother of Flying Officer Charles Pilkington buried in Offley St Mary Magdalene's churchyard, Hertfordshire, and of two other brothers who survived the war, one as a prisoner in Germany. Age 28.
'*Day shall clasp him with strong hands, And Night shall fold him in soft wings*' (the final lines of Julian Grenfell's First World War poem *Into Battle*)
Grave 10.H.3. Also commemorated at Eton College and Christ Church, Oxford. He and his brother are named on Offley's war memorial at St Mary Magdalene's that states that he served in 'Palestine, Abyssinia, Transjordan, and with the Long Range Desert Groups [*sic*] in North Africa where he was killed'.

NEW ZEALAND

Despite disproportionate casualties during the First World War, and its small and geographically isolated population, New Zealanders enthusiastically volunteered at the outbreak of renewed hostilities. Many Kiwis felt a strong affinity for Britain that was still considered the 'mother country'. In addition to providing personnel for the Royal Air Force and Royal Navy an amalgam of pre-war regular and territorial soldiers was rapidly trained and formed into battalions, these being numbered on top of their provincial pre-war titling. The first echelon of the 2nd New Zealand Expeditionary Force subsequently sailed for the Middle East in early January 1940, successive echelons marching into camp and embarking as reinforcement throughout the war.

After training in Egypt a limited number of New Zealanders supported OPERATION COMPASS, the December 1940 thrust against the Italians in the Western Desert. However, the New Zealand Division's first full test was as part of OPERATION LUSTRE, the defence of mainland Greece against Axis troops. This proved unachievable and having been forced to withdraw to Crete in late April 1941 its commander, Major-General Bernard 'Tiny' Freyberg, VC, DSO**, took control of this strategically important island. His troops did not have long to prepare or re-equip, large numbers of German parachutists landing on 20 May and gaining a foothold despite spirited resistance.

Withdrawn to Egypt after heavy losses, the Kiwis subsequently played a key role in every major battle from OPERATION CRUSADER of November 1941 through to the end of the North African Campaign. Moving to Italy the NZ Division continued to build a fearsome reputation amongst both allies and adversaries alike and by VE-Day it was the only division still serving with Eighth Army since its formation. The courage of its men was legendary, Captain Charles Upham being the only man to win two Victoria Crosses during the Second World War, and one of only three ever to do so.

Men of the 2nd NZEF proved perfectly suited for special operations. With their rural upbringing and 'number 8 wire' mentality they were used to making do with what they had and getting the job done. The creator of the Long Range Patrol, Major Ralph Bagnold, recognised the value of such traits and the ranks of this precursor to the Long Range Desert Group were made up entirely of Kiwi volunteers. They later formed one of the Group's two squadrons.

Today the New Zealand SAS carries on the tradition set by fellow countrymen who served in the wartime Special Forces. The Royal New Zealand Returned and Services Association commemorates their contribution in much the same way as the Royal British Legion does in the United Kingdom.

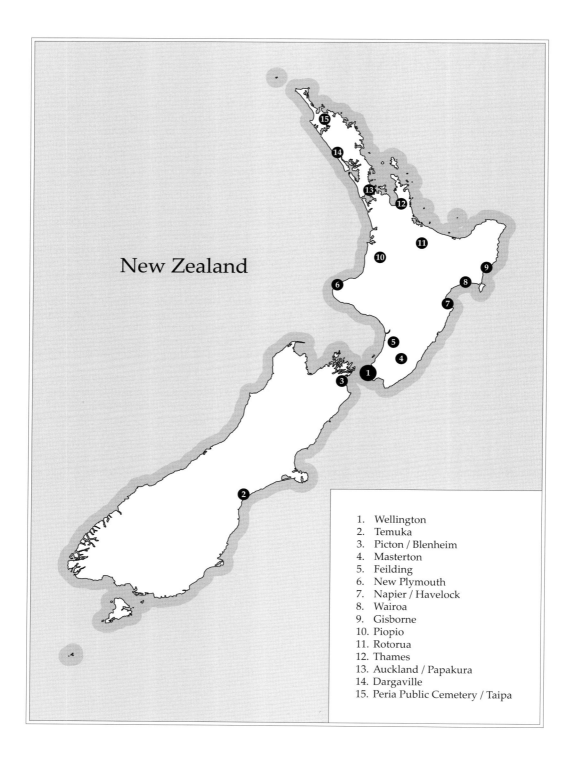

New Zealand

1. Wellington
2. Temuka
3. Picton / Blenheim
4. Masterton
5. Feilding
6. New Plymouth
7. Napier / Havelock
8. Wairoa
9. Gisborne
10. Piopio
11. Rotorua
12. Thames
13. Auckland / Papakura
14. Dargaville
15. Peria Public Cemetery / Taipa

PERIA PUBLIC CEMETERY

Peria is located approximately 12 kilometres south of Taipa and 20 kilometres east of Kaitaia in Northland Region of the North Island. The cemetery lies on Oruru Road, 400 metres south-west of the junction with Kohumaru Road and approximately 1 kilometre west of Peria Sale Yards. It contains one Commonwealth burial of the Second World War. GPS co-ordinates: Latitude -35.087878, Longitude 173.506367

TROOPER FRANCIS **RHODES** [1331] NORTH AUCKLAND MOUNTED RIFLES, DIVISIONAL CAVALRY REGIMENT, LRP AND LRDG (HEAVY SECTION, GROUP HQ)

Frank Rhodes, alternatively known to his family as Darrell, Dal or Frankie, was born on 4 April 1913 at his parents' dairy farm at Fern Flat near Peria in the province of North Auckland. Having attended the local school he qualified as a heavy goods driver as soon as he was old enough and drove rounds to pick up cream pails from nearby farms. At the same time he served for four years in the territorial North Auckland Mounted Rifles, either at Kaikohe or Whangarei, before taking employment as a bushman for the State Forests Department at Te Whaiti near Rotorua.

Rhodes enlisted into the Divisional Cavalry Regiment on 20 September 1939, soon after the outbreak of war. Entering Ngaruawahia camp near Hamilton early the following month he was amongst the first draft of men to form the 2nd New Zealand Expeditionary Force, many of whom had also been drawn from territorial regiments. Rapid basic training ensued, this being aimed largely at converting them to foot drill whilst improving marksmanship and fitness in preparation for large-scale exercises

119

at Waiouru that December. Limited to Bren Carriers and a handful of ageing armoured vehicles, the Divisional Cavalry Regiment's role was established as motorised reconnaissance and flank protection. On 4 January 1940 it entrained at Hopuhopu and was waved off by crowds at many of the stations en route to Wellington. Here the men embarked the *Rangitata* as part of the First Echelon to head for the Middle East. Arriving six weeks later, after a journey via Fremantle, Ceylon and Aden, the men disembarked at Port Tewfik in Egypt. Having boarded trains once again they finally marched into their tented camp at Maadi, south of Cairo, in mid February 1940.

Rhodes was briefly admitted to a field hospital that April but soon volunteered to become one of founding members of Major Ralph Bagnold's Long Range Patrol, the official history of the Divisional Cavalry noting that in July it:

… lost some personnel to the newly-formed Long Range Patrol. They were marched out to Abbassia in three drafts [accommodation was initially at Abbassia's Gymnasium Barracks within the Royal Artillery Base Depot with vehicles and stores being housed in Stable Lines] and by the end of the month three officers, Lieutenants Ballantyne, Sutherland and McQueen, and about fifty other ranks had gone …

There was, too, bitter disappointment, even jealousy, on the part of some men who saw others chosen for the LRP. This was not of course eased by the romantic rumours that crept out concerning the Patrol's task [*Divisional Cavalry*, by R. J. M. Loughnan].

With experience of driving on the sand that surrounded Northland dairy farms Rhodes was readily accepted into the LRP. The following month the whole unit, i.e. W, R and T Patrols, plus the 'Marmon-Herrington party' of which he was now a member, left Cairo for desert training. Rhodes' group, mounted on South African-designed six-ton, 6×6 trucks under Lieutenant Bill Kennedy Shaw, cached stores, the pre-positioning of which was vital for the LRP to operate for sufficient periods of time. Having established fuel dumps at 'Mushroom Rock' north of Baharia it continued its training programme and passed through Dalla on their way to the Great Sand Sea where further stockpiles were dropped. In September Rhodes and his comrades, temporarily commanded by Lieutenant Gus Holliman, moved additional supplies of petrol, water and food from Wadi Halfa in the Sudan to the southern end of the Gilf Kebir in south-west Egypt. His photograph collection, which he left with his sister on strict instruction not to publish the images until after his death, and which was donated by his nephew to the Auckland War Memorial Museum, records that apart from serving as a driver one of Rhodes' secondary duties was patrol cook.

In October 1940 Major-General 'Tiny' Freyberg, VC, DSO**, commander of the 2nd NZEF, demanded that all New Zealand LRP personnel return to their parent division. Agreement was reached that this was to occur gradually so that British patrols could be recruited and trained. This also enabled the process of establishing dumps to be repeated by Rhodes' team during October and November. On 11 November approval was given for the unit to expand into the Long Range Desert Group, the Marmon-Herrington party becoming the 'Heavy Section' within Group Headquarters. At the beginning of December the LRDG ceased to be a purely Kiwi formation, British personnel arriving on the 5th, the day following the unit's move from Abbassia to the Citadel in Cairo. As it was still understood that all New Zealand troops were to be returned, handover training began in earnest.

Rhodes rejoined the Divisional Cavalry Regiment in January 1941 and qualified as a driver mechanic at the beginning of March. He subsequently embarked for Greece to join Lustre Force, the regiment patrolling in front of the Aliakmon Line that was being held by the New Zealand Division. After the German invasion and subsequent collapse of this line the regiment fragmented, its elements being evacuated from the mainland piecemeal. Rhodes was reported safe on Crete on 18 May and saw action when the island was invaded by German parachutists and airlanding troops on the 20th. Having fought in rearguard actions he was subsequently evacuated, this time to Egypt where he was reported safe on 10 June. Here he attended a three-week course at the RAC School at Abbassia before another brief period in hospital resulted in a posting to the Composite Training Depot. From January to March 1942 he was attached to the 5th, then 4th, New Zealand Infantry Brigades but on 27 March rejoined the LRDG. Although it is not known which operations Rhodes subsequently took part in, this was a busy period for the Group that provided a behind-the-lines 'taxi' service for various agents and raiding parties of L Detachment, SAS Brigade, and the Middle East Commando, in addition to meeting its own Road Watch, offensive and recce objectives.

At the beginning of June 1943, with hostilities in North Africa at an end, Rhodes embarked for New Zealand, *Divisional Cavalry* noting that the names for this draft of home leave were drawn out of a hat. The *New Zealand Herald* listed those who returned 'on extended furlough' the following month, a 'Tpr F. B. Rhodes (Mangonui)' being amongst them. His service record confirms that he arrived at Wellington on 12 July for three months leave. However, he was still awaiting movement orders that October, rumour having been prevalent in Egypt that men sent home would man an armoured school that was soon to be formed. Whilst waiting he therefore returned to work for the State Forestry Department at Te Whaiti and was fatally injured on the morning of 10 November 1943. Having been admitted to Rotorua Public Hospital he died around 2300hrs that night, the *Auckland Star* reporting the following day:

> Transport organised by the Army last night and today conveyed the parents of Trooper Rhodes from Peria to Rotorua, a distance of over 500 miles, in fourteen hours. A sad aspect was that Trooper Rhodes died shortly before their arrival at Rotorua. News that he had been seriously injured was received by the Whangerei office shortly after 5 o'clock yesterday afternoon. Less that a quarter of an hour later an Army car, with two drivers, headed north for Peria, picked up the parents, Mr and Mrs A Rhodes, and returned to Whangerei. While the parents were given light refreshments at Whangerei, their luggage was transferred to another Army car, with new men at the wheel. A third car was used from Auckland, which was reached at 4am and arrived at Roturua at 8.30am.

The *New Zealand Herald* later recorded:

> An inquest was held [at Rotorua] by Mr W. L. Richards, coroner, into the death of Frank Balfour Rhodes, aged 30, who was on furlough from the Middle East, and who was fatally injured while working in the State forestry area at Te Whaiti.
> Roger Hulton, tractor driver for the State Forestry Department, who had been with [the] deceased at the time, said they had been hauling logs, [the] deceased being a breaker-out. 'I had parked my tractor on the ridge of a hill overlooking the position where Rhodes was,' said the witness. 'He was coupling a log to the main tractor rope and gave the signal that everything was in order for hauling. I moved my machine to take up the slack and commenced winching the log but owing to the excessive strain I alighted from the tractor and returned to the brow of the hill. I then heard Rhodes calling for help. I ran down to discover that he was lying under a matai log, seriously injured.'
> [The] Witness added that it appeared to him that the accident was due to the winch rope fouling an uprooted log, which was flung in deceased's direction. There appeared no doubt in his mind that the log struck Rhodes when it was hurled in the air.
> The coroner returned a verdict of accidental death [20 November 1943].

Rhodes' sister, Esther, later recalled how he was due to return home for the birth of her child but instead remained to cover another bushman who was on leave. Meanwhile, *The Bay of Plenty Beacon* reported:

> The Coroner commented that a sad feature of the case was that deceased had been on furlough after serving in the Middle East from the commencement of the campaign. He had enjoyed a few weeks' leave and then had decided to work at his previous occupation. He had indicated an industrious turn of mind and it was regrettable that he had lost his life in such extremely sad circumstances.
> Evidence of identification was given by Arthur George Rhodes of Peria, Mangonui, North Auckland, who said that his son was an experienced bushman and had been in the best of health following his return from overseas. His son had previously been employed in the State Mill at Te Whaiti, prior to joining the Army in 1939 [23 November 1943].

Although Rhodes was on extended furlough at the time of his death, which was therefore deemed as not having taken place whilst 'on active service', he was in receipt of military pay and therefore still serving, his unit being recorded on his military death certificate as 'NZ Patrols LRDG'. He was buried with military honours on 13 November 1943, his resting place being officially recorded as a war grave by the Commonwealth War Graves Commission.

Son of Arthur and Mabel (May) Rhodes of Peria, Northland – Younger brother of Bill (known as 'Boy' who also served during the Second World War and who later became a national two-man cross-cut, standing 12-inch and overhead wood cutting champion), Evangeline (known as 'Girlie') and Morna (Shirley) – Older brother of Messines (known as 'Brown' but named after the place her father was gassed in the First World War whilst serving as a sniper in the 1st Battalion, Auckland Regiment, 1st NZEF), of Esther and of Keith (who served in the Royal New Zealand Air Force in the Pacific Islands) – Fiancé of Eva Ohlson of Waiwera House, Rotorua.

Age 30.

At Rest

Grave 4.B.1. Also commemorated, alongside his brothers Bill and Keith, on the Peria District Roll of Honour plaque within Peria School.

TUNISIA

Jutting out into the Mediterranean, Tunisia was prized by the Axis for its strategic importance. Retaining their grip denied the Allies free naval passage to the Suez Canal and therefore to the East, the alternative route around the Cape tying down much shipping that might be used elsewhere. Meanwhile, the Allies intended to clear the Germans and Italians from North Africa so that it could be used it as a springboard onto mainland Europe. After landing along the Algerian and Moroccan coast in November 1942 during OPERATION TORCH, the British and American First Army advanced rapidly into western Tunisia, although a combination of strong resistance and poor weather meant it was held short of the key ports of Bizerte and Tunis.

To the east, Axis forces were chased out of Libya by the Eighth Army at the beginning of 1943, taking up a defensive line at Mareth between the Matmâta hills and the Tunisian coast. This formidable obstacle was outflanked, thanks to reconnaissance by the Long Range Desert Group, and the enemy forced back. It was harassed by British and French patrols of 1st SAS as it went. Whilst such parties provided the initial physical link with the First Army, their operations were not without casualties. One member of the LRDG now rests at Medjez-el-Bab War Cemetery, two members of 1st SAS at Sfax, and four of their comrades at Enfidaville.

Although the Eighth Army's advance was halted by resistance around Enfidaville, progress to the north had resumed and Tunis fell to the First Army on 7 May 1943. The next day Bizerte followed suit, Axis troops trapped in the 'Tunisia Tip' capitulating on the 9th. With their position now untenable, those holding Enfidaville and other pockets were forced to surrender on the 12th. The whole of North Africa was finally in Allied hands paving the way for a large-scale amphibious assault against southern Europe.

As the campaign ended the fledgling 2nd SAS, whose men had been training in Algeria, moved forward to commence operations in the Western Mediterranean. These were either diversionary, in direct support of the invasion of Sicily, or raids of local strategic importance. One man killed during such a raid is commemorated on the Medjez-el-Bab Memorial alongside a comrade posted missing during the campaign in North West Europe that was yet to come.

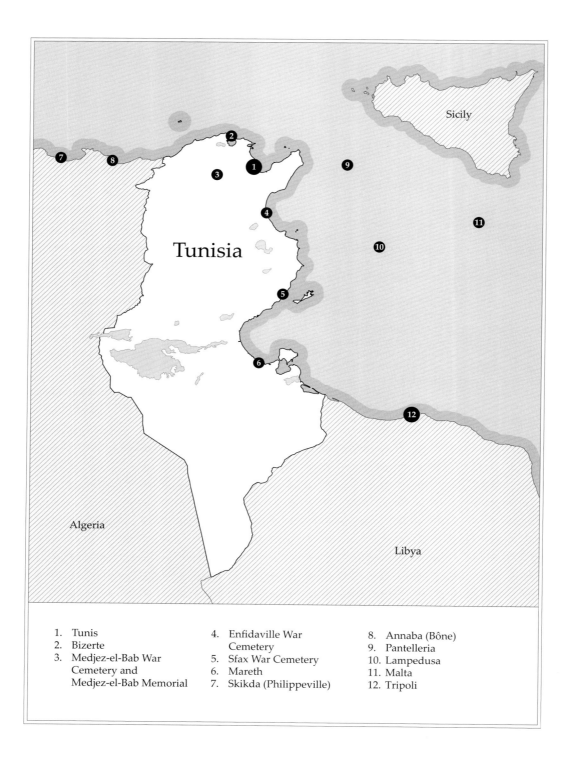

1. Tunis
2. Bizerte
3. Medjez-el-Bab War Cemetery and Medjez-el-Bab Memorial
4. Enfidaville War Cemetery
5. Sfax War Cemetery
6. Mareth
7. Skikda (Philippeville)
8. Annaba (Bône)
9. Pantelleria
10. Lampedusa
11. Malta
12. Tripoli

ENFIDAVILLE WAR CEMETERY

Eighth Army's assault on Axis strongpoints near to the village of Enfidaville began on 19 April 1943 but was fiercely resisted. However, with First Army's advance to the north moving more swiftly, the enemy's position rapidly grew untenable and it was forced to surrender on 12 May.

The majority of the 1,551 Commonwealth servicemen buried here died in the final battles in North Africa between March and May 1943, eighty-eight of their graves being unidentified.

Enfidaville is located 100 kilometres south of Tunis, not far from the A1 coastal motorway. The cemetery lies 1 kilometre west of the town on the road to Zaghouan. GPS co-ordinates: Latitude 36.13406, Longitude 10.37435

CORPORAL LESLIE JOCK **BROWN** [5437777] DUKE OF CORNWALL'S LIGHT INFANTRY, NO.8 COMMANDO, MIDDLE EAST COMMANDO AND 1ST SAS (B SQN)

Leslie Brown was born on 18 November 1916 in the parish of Princes Gate, Knightsbridge, Central London, an address that would subsequently become famous in regimental history following the 1980 Iranian Embassy siege. However, his family later moved to Penzance in Cornwall and it was here during April 1939, whilst working as a clerk for a wine and spirits merchant, that Brown joined the 4/5th Battalion, Duke of Cornwall's Light Infantry (TA). Embodied as a lance-corporal at the outbreak of war he volunteered for special service the following year and reported to No.8 (Guards) Commando at Knightsbridge Barracks, close to his place of birth, on 22 August 1940. After initial training at Burnham-on-Crouch in Essex the Commando, temporarily redesignated as the 4th Special Service Battalion,

125

completed its pre-deployment preparations in Scotland. At the end of January 1941 it subsequently embarked for the Middle East, arriving at Suez in Egypt early in March as B Battalion of Layforce, an amalgam of Commando units that was to raid the Eastern Mediterranean and along the North Africa coastline. However, having been posted to Mersa Matruh a series of abortive operations ensued with only a fraction of the Commando seeing action whilst posted to Tobruk.

With the disbandment of Layforce during the summer of 1941, Brown was posted to the Commando Depot at Geneifa, reverting to the rank of private in late August. He was promoted back to lance-corporal two months later, enjoying some rare leave in Jerusalem before being attached to the Latrun Training Centre in Palestine. Absorbed into the Middle East Commando on 20 January 1942 he served in Syria from February until April that year. He was subsequently promoted to corporal and remained with the Commando when it was retitled the 1st Special Service Regiment on 31 July. Soon after he was admitted to hospital for an unknown reason before being discharged, firstly to No.2 Convalescent Depot, and then to 178 Transit Camp from where he was posted back to his unit. He returned to Syria with the regiment in mid October, volunteering for 1st SAS a few days later on the 28th.

Brown was killed in action whilst en route to harass the enemy in southern Tunisia. His Jeep patrol was intending to cross the border from Libya when attacked on the 17th near to Nalut (see Captain Denis Murphy's entry below for full details). His date of death is officially recorded as having occurred between 15 and 18 January 1943.

Son of Leslie and Mabel Brown of Trendeal Gardens, Penzance, Cornwall.
Age 26.
No inscription.
Grave 5.C.20.

Captain Denis Luke Maurice MURPHY [IA/664] Central India Horse AND 1st SAS (B Sqn)

Denis Murphy was born in Kashmir, India, on 22 August 1916. Having been educated at Lancing College in West Sussex, where he was a member of the OTC, he entered Sandhurst in February 1935 and was commissioned into the Indian Army in August 1936. His exit report noted:

He has worked well at all times … He is a fine athlete … I consider he is intelligent and capable … He will make a good officer if he is kept up to the mark. He got a ½ Blue for Soccer, swims for the RMC [Royal Military College] and has represented the company in athletics and cross country running.

Arriving back in India that October Murphy was attached to the 1st Battalion, East Surrey Regiment, at Faizabad as a platoon commander. He finally joined his intended regiment, the Central India Horse (21st King George V's Own Horse), on 1 April 1937. Serving at the Meerut cantonment as a squadron officer he was noted as being popular with all ranks and was subsequently promoted to acting captain at the outbreak of war. Ordered to give up its mounts the CIH hurriedly engrossed itself in mechanised training, enthusiasm only being dampened by a lack of vehicles. However, on embarkation at Bombay in July 1940 the regiment's Sikh B Squadron refused to board ship after being influenced by a left-wing radical within its ranks. It was disbanded as a result whilst the remainder of the regiment, A Squadron's Punjabi Muslims and C Squadron's Jats, disembarked in Egypt the following month. Joining the 4th Indian Division they were deployed on protection duties whilst completing training, although they did see action against the Italians in December at Sidi Barrani during OPERATION COMPASS.

Murphy entered Sudan in February 1941. Advancing to Keren in Eritrea the CIH operated in a dismounted role carrying out nocturnal fighting patrols and supporting infantry with its mortar detachment. It was among the first regiments into Asmara, eventually helping to mop up Italian resistance. Murphy was subsequently mentioned in despatches for 'distinguished services in the Middle East during the period February 1941 to July 1941' (*London Gazette* 30/12/41). After a spell of sick leave Murphy attended the Middle East Tactical School in Cairo that autumn. At the beginning of 1942, having been promoted to acting major, he was posted as a squadron commander to the Indian Wing of the Middle East RAC School and Base Depot. That spring, whilst attending a 2-pounder anti-tank course at the School of Artillery, he came up with the idea of a desert Q Patrol; vehicles armed with anti-tank guns that would masquerade as innocent transport along much the same lines as First World War Q ships. It is not known whether the idea was ever adopted but having been appointed Second-in-Command of No.14 Reinforcement Camp he was posted to HQ 3rd Indian Motor Brigade that August.

Murphy volunteered for 1st SAS on 21 October 1942 and was posted to B Squadron with the rank of captain. With Axis forces being pushed out of Libya the squadron was ordered to harass the enemy in southern Tunisia. Murphy therefore led his Jeep patrol to the area west of Nalut hoping to cross the border to the north-west. Parachutist E. Robinson was captured in the incident that followed and having been released by the advancing Allies reported:

Our orders from Col Stirling were to cut roads, blow up bridges, and generally to hamper the retreat of the enemy ...
At the 15 kilo stone before Nalut (we came from Wadi Zugga) Capt Murphy left us to go on a recce. He returned and definitely stated that there were four German Infantry battalions in Nalut and that we would have to by-pass it. In doing so we got lost and went to sleep at 3am intending to find a hide-out at dawn. We found a Wadi. We had been there about three hours when we were attacked without warning by a force of Italian infantry and members of the Afrika Korps. Capt Murphy at once gave orders to start the Jeeps and make a run for it. This we were unable to do. A fight ensued which lasted about 1½ hours, at the end of which the enemy had taken five prisoners ...
I saw Sgt Senior dragging Nixon, who was unconscious from the blazing Jeep. The Jeep blew up after about 20 mins; the Sgt may, or may not, have got clear but it is doubtful if he could have done so while still dragging Nixon as he had one arm raised in surrender and was dragging Nixon with the other. I saw Hearne W. wounded in both cheeks. I padded him up [*sic* – William Hearn (no 'e'), see his entry under Sangro River War Cemetery, Italy, Volume II – not to be confused with his near-namesake A. Hearne who was captured during this action]. He dashed for another Jeep and I lost sight of him. About this time I saw Capt Murphy jump into somebody's Jeep with the intention of starting it up. After getting behind the wheel he shuddered as though hit and got out. I did not see him again [WO 218/97].

Sergeant Ted Badger and Parachutists Ronnie Guard and William Hearn were brought back through Allied lines by Arabs on 10 February. There appears to be some confusion as to the exact date of the contact, W. Ridley, the station officer of the then liberated Nalut, writing to the War Office that December:

On 12 Oct 43 I made enquiries as to what four mounds of earth and bricks were.

The result was: four English soldiers were engaged by the Italians, at Nalut about 12 Dec 42 [*sic?*]. Apparently they were in a small car, which was hit by shell fire. The shell exploded under the driver's seat, and killed all four [*sic?*]. The car is on a salvage dump, here in Nalut.

As there were no means of identification or crucifixes I reported to the CAO [Civil Administration Officer]. I was asked if I could have the bodies transferred to the cemetery. With assistance from the Muktar I did so. On each occasion, the Union Jack was placed over them. The cemetery is only a 100 yards from their burial place.

I found a bottle in each grave, with the attached papers i.e. Capt Murphy, Sjt Senior, Corp Brown, and Pte Nixon. I searched the bodies and only found a parachute [badge] on the right shoulder of the sergeant.

I have undertaken to erect a cross on each grave with names, and give them a more appropriate resting place. With your kind permission may this be sent to the proper authorities …

An attempt has been made by a Grave Registration Unit to locate these graves and concentrate them into Tripoli Cemetery, but badly rain-bogged tracks forced them to abandon the trip.

A further effort will be made when climatic conditions improve [WO 361/1075].

Meanwhile, the same file contains a letter from Gunner 'Mac' McClements of 1st SAS dated 22 December 1943: 'The above mentioned [Brown, Nixon and Senior] were killed on January 15th 1943 [*sic?*] and I was present as a prisoner when they were buried by the Germans at Nalut which is about 200 miles SW [of] Tripoli.' Unlike his men, whose deaths are officially recorded as 15–18 January 1943, Murphy's is specified officially as having occurred on the 18th.

Son of Sir Stephen and Lady Murphy, formerly of the Indian Civil Service, of Costebelle, Kyrenia, Cyprus – Brother of Mrs H. S. Waters of Bombay. Age 26.
No inscription.
Grave 5.C.18. Also commemorated on the war memorial at Lancing College.

Private Malvern NIXON [3056939] Royal Scots, No.2 Independent Company, No.11 Commando, Middle East Commando, L Detachment SAS Brigade and 1st SAS (B Sqn)

Malvern Nixon was born on 20 July 1919 in the hamlet of Lambley near Haltwhistle, Northumberland, later living across the border in Peebles where he worked as a railway porter. In May 1939 he joined the 8th Battalion, Royal Scots (TA), and was mobilised at the outbreak of war that September. Two months later he was posted to No.2 Independent Company, a forerunner of the Commandos, joining the newly-formed No.11 (Scottish) Commando the following spring. Temporarily redesignated as the 2nd Special Service Battalion soon after, this disembarked at Suez in Egypt at the beginning of March 1941 as C Battalion, Layforce. A frustrating period followed for Nixon and his comrades, the Commando being stood-to, then stood-down, from a raid on Bardia in mid April.

Although disappointed, No.11 moved to Cyprus at the end of the month in readiness for Operation Exporter, the campaign in Syria against the Vichy French. In the early hours of 9 June 1941 it subsequently landed close to the mouth of the Litani River in an attempt to seize bridges key to the Allied advance. Although these were destroyed by the French, and No.11 suffered heavy casualties, the Commando effectively tied down Vichy troops until Australian forces arrived from the south. On the battalion's return to Egypt via Cyprus Layforce was disbanded, Nixon being posted to the Middle East Commando at Geneifa near Kabrit on 20 January 1942. This was retitled the 1st Special Service Regiment on 31 July. He volunteered for L Detachment, SAS Brigade, some time before that September and would therefore have taken part in the large-scale but abortive raid on Benghazi that month (Operation Bigamy). He was posted to B Squadron when 1st SAS Regiment was formed a few days later.

Nixon was killed in action near Nalut whilst en route to harass the enemy in southern Tunisia. Although initially posted as 'missing believed wounded and prisoner of war' he was officially recorded as having been killed in action between 15 and 18 January 1943 as of the following January. Nixon's family had enquired after him throughout the intervening year, although his remains were positively identified in October 1943 (see Captain Denis Murphy's entry on previous pages for full details).

Son of Robert and Lily Nixon of Leithen Lodge, Innerleithen, Peebleshire. Age 23.
Sweet memories, dear Malvern, cling round your name. In life and death we love you just the same
Grave 5.C.21. Also commemorated on Peebles' war memorial.

Lance-Sergeant Fred **SENIOR** [2696965] Scots Guards, No.8 Commando, Middle East Commando, L Detachment SAS Brigade and 1st SAS (B Sqn)

Fred Senior, the son of a plasterer, was born on 3 March 1911 in Leeds as the eldest of three sons. Living in Glasgow, where he based himself as a travelling salesman for Mars Confectionery, he enlisted into the Scots Guards in November 1939 and was posted to Chelsea Barracks, London. The following February he married Jessie Finlayson Irvine at Cathcart in Glasgow whilst stationed at Pirbright in Surrey. Volunteering for No.8 (Guards) Commando on 7 August he was posted to 4 Troop having been promoted to lance-corporal. Initial training was at Burnham-on-Crouch, Essex, additional pre-deployment exercises taking place in Scotland after the Commando had been temporarily reorganised as part of the 4th Special Service Battalion. Embarking for the Middle East aboard HMS *Glenroy* on the last day of January 1941 it arrived at Suez, Egypt, in early March as B Battalion, Layforce. The following month the men moved to Mersa Matruh, although Senior was admitted to the 6th British General Hospital at el-Tahag Camp in June 1941 and was at Haifa in Palestine during July.

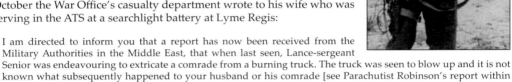

After the break-up of Layforce that summer, Senior was posted to the Middle East Commando at Geneifa. Although it is not known when he volunteered for L Detachment, SAS Brigade, at nearby Kabrit it is likely to have been sometime in mid 1942. He would therefore have taken part in the large-scale but abortive raid on Benghazi that September (OPERATION BIGAMY) and when the unit was granted regimental status a few days later he was posted to B Squadron. He was killed in action whilst en route to harass enemy supply lines in southern Tunisia (see Captain Denis Murphy's entry on previous pages for full details). That October the War Office's casualty department wrote to his wife who was serving in the ATS at a searchlight battery at Lyme Regis:

I am directed to inform you that a report has now been received from the Military Authorities in the Middle East, that when last seen, Lance-sergeant Senior was endeavouring to extricate a comrade from a burning truck. The truck was seen to blow up and it is not known what subsequently happened to your husband or his comrade [see Parachutist Robinson's report within Murphy's entry above].

The following January a further letter brought the news his wife had been dreading:

I am directed to inform you, with deep regret, that information has now been received which the Department has accepted as reliable evidence that Lance-sergeant Senior lost his life during special operations in the Western Desert. The information has been furnished by a soldier of your husband's unit who was captured at the time and was present when your husband's body was buried by the enemy after the action. It is consequently being recorded that Lance-sergeant Senior was killed in action between the 15th and 18th January, 1943 [see Gunner 'Mac' McClements' statement within Murphy's entry].

Son of Ernest and Helen ('Nellie') Senior of Sandhurst Avenue, Leeds (his father had been wounded twice, once severely, whilst serving in the trenches on the Western Front) – Husband of Jessie Senior of Langside Road, Crosshill, Glasgow – His brother, John, saw action with the Royal Navy during the D-Day landings whilst another, Ernest, was mentioned in despatches for turning round the Pasir Laba coastal battery at Singapore, thereby shelling the Japanese attack on the causeway. He was captured having been wounded and survived the war.
Age 31.
No inscription.
Grave 5.C.19.

Medjez-el-Bab War Cemetery

Medjez-el-Bab was on the front line from December 1942 until the final advance of May 1943. Nearly 3,000 Commonwealth servicemen of the Second World War are buried here or commemorated on the Medjez-el-Bab Memorial that stands within the cemetery (see separate section below). Of this number 385 burials are unidentified. In addition, the plot contains five burials of the First World War and special memorials commemorating four men whose graves are now lost.

The cemetery is located 60 kilometres west of Tunis and 6 kilometres north of the A3 motorway on the P5 towards the town of Medjez-el-Bab itself. The gates are never locked, although the visitors' book is only available during working hours. GPS co-ordinates: Latitude 36.626687, Longitude 9.57044

Private Gordon Donald REZIN [R2990810] Rhodesian Army, Argyll and Sutherland Highlanders and LRDG (S.2 Patrol, A Sqn)

Known as 'Happy' to his patrol, Gordon Rezin was born in Salisbury, Southern Rhodesia, on 16 September 1916. Educated at Prince Edward School he later joined the family business, Rezin & Taylor, as an outfitter. Although very little detail is contained in his service record he joined the Rhodesian Army in November 1939 (service number CR1929 – unknown regiment) before starting his journey to the Middle East, probably via South Africa, in April 1940. Sometime after disembarking in Egypt he transferred to the Argyll and Sutherland Highlanders (Princess Louise's) and may have seen action with them at Sidi Barrani at the end of the year. He volunteered for the Long Range Desert Group on 29 January 1941 and was posted to No.2 Patrol that had been formed from South Rhodesian units. Two days later this was reorganised into S (South Rhodesian) Patrol that incorporated more men from the Argylls as well as others from the Northumberland Fusiliers and The Buffs.

In early September 1941 S Patrol carried out a recce of the area between Jalo and Agedabia, reporting on the going for different weights of transport, the most favourable routes for any advance and 'no-go' areas before returning to Kufra. The following month it carried out two Road Watch operations before

setting out from Kufra once again, this time to recce Jalo Oasis and its approaches. Although attacked from the air the patrol was able to return on the 17th with valuable intelligence and without casualties.

At the end of October 1941 the LRDG was reorganised into 'half' patrols and it is believed that Rezin served from then on in S.2 Patrol, initially under the command of 2nd Lieutenant John Olivey. In November it undertook a joint recce of the Mechili–Benghazi road with R.2 Patrol. Having received fresh orders to take aggressive action it destroyed enemy trucks along this route on the evening of the 29th causing numerous casualties before being withdrawn to Jalo. The patrol set out again in mid December, this time taking with it the LRDG's 'RA Section'. This consisted of a sole artillery piece mounted on the rear of a truck. However, it proved sufficient to prompt an exodus of Stafia's Italian garrison after a few rounds were fired into its fort.

A few days later S.2 dropped off a raiding party from L Detachment, SAS Brigade, that subsequently destroyed thirty-seven planes on a landing ground not far from Agedabia. The patrol was mistakenly strafed by RAF aircraft on its return journey with the loss of Corporal Laurie Ashby and Private Ginger Riggs (see their entries under Benghazi War Cemetery, Libya, within this volume).

By the beginning of February 1942 both S Patrols were refitting back in Cairo, although S.2 was engaged in further Road Watch operations from the end of the month. In March it ferried another L Detachment party, this time to raid the airfields at Benina and Barce and to attack shipping in Benghazi harbour. These operations were of mixed result but proved valuable for the purpose of route recce. Two months later S.2 was to drop off a combined party of Middle East Commando and Libyan Arab Force to conduct Road Watch operations in the foothills of the Jebel Akhdar. However, a similar party, previously dropped by Y.2 Patrol, reported that the enemy was searching the area, S.2 subsequently returning to Siwa with both groups. That September it was joined by S.1 Patrol in guiding a large SAS force, consisting of three columns, to attack Benghazi during OPERATION BIGAMY. The raid was a failure, most likely due to lax security in the planning stages, the column first being ambushed on the approaches to the port and then bombed repeatedly on its withdrawal (see multiple entries under Alamein Memorial, Egypt, within this volume for full details).

Setting out from Kufra on 20 November 1942 under 2nd Lieutenant Jim Henry, S.2 reached Zouar in Chad on 2 December. Moving on towards Zouarke it returned to Zouar on the 5th so that Private Bert Jordan, who had suffered fatal injuries en route, could be evacuated by air (see Jordan's entry under Brookwood Memorial, United Kingdom, Volume III). From here S.2 subsequently led Général Leclerc's Free French column north on its advance into Tunisia.

Relieved by the Indian Long Range Squadron at Sebha, south-west Libya, in mid January 1943 the patrol was retasked; leaving Hon later that month it dropped agents of MI9's A Force before pioneering a route to Tozeur in western Tunisia. Reaching this location it withdrew to an area near Foum Tatahouine, well inside Allied lines and not far from the Ghadames road. Here, on 20 February 1943, it was challenged by a detachment of camel troops, Lance-sergeant 'Cito' Calder-Potts later recalling:

> They were on the top of a knoll, and the OC patrol [Henry] went up in his Jeep to meet him. The man came up to the Jeep, and then ran back about 10 yards waving his hand. I saw two puffs of dust near him as he was running back. They then opened fire on the Jeep with one MG and two rifles … there was about thirty to forty men with fifty camels. We uncovered our guns (we had come through a storm the day before) and the only gun that worked was the 20mm Breda. After the Breda had moved them from the top of the knoll and we had moved behind cover, it was decided that the OC and Private Rezin had been killed and the enemy held the advantage, so it would not pay us to continue the fight [WO 218/91].

Moving to Nalut the patrol learnt that the contact had been with Free French Algerian Mécharistes rather than the enemy and that whilst Henry was badly wounded Rezin had indeed been killed. The failure of the patrol's radio had prevented it from being informed that these friendly camel troops were in the area (see Henry's entry under Heliopolis War Cemetery, Egypt). Leclerc's Free French troops, which had so ably been guided by Rezin and his comrades, went on to play a valuable part in the Tunisian campaign.

Son of William and Alexanderina Rezin of Salisbury, Southern Rhodesia.
Age 26.
He died that we might live
Grave 17.A.16.

MEDJEZ-EL-BAB MEMORIAL

The memorial commemorates nearly 2,000 men of the First Army who were killed during the campaigns in Algeria and Tunisia between 8 November 1942 and 19 February 1943 as well as those of the First and Eighth Armies who died in operations in the same theatres between 20 February 1943 and 13 May 1943, all of whom have no known graves.

The memorial is located within Medjez-el-Bab War Cemetery, 60 kilometres west of Tunis and 5 kilometres west of Medjez-el-Bab on the road to Le Kef (Route P5). The gates are never locked, although the visitors' book is only available during working hours. GPS co-ordinates: Latitude 36.626687, Longitude 9.570444

GUNNER ERNEST MAXWELL **HERSTELL** [14317992] GENERAL SERVICE CORPS, ROYAL ARTILLERY, SMALL SCALE RAIDING FORCE AND 2ND SAS

Ernie Herstell was born on 9 May 1916 in the parish of St Clement, Manchester, where he married Florence Irving during January 1942. That October, whilst living at Cotham Vale in Bristol where he is believed to have been a policeman, he enlisted into the General Service Corps and was immediately posted to the Commando Training Depot at Achnacarry. During that summer and autumn the depot received large intakes of former police officers, the Commandant, Colonel Charles Vaughan, MBE, noting that 'they were the finest material that I ever had to deal with in all my soldiering' (*It Had to be Tough: The Origins and Training of the Commandos in World War II,* by James Dunning). After completing his training late that December Herstell was nominally transferred to the Royal Artillery having been posted to No.62 Commando, the cover name for the Special Operations Executive's Small Scale Raiding Force. At the time this unit was being reorganised, Herstell and a significant number of its men disembarking in North Africa in late February 1943. They subsequently formed the foundation on which 2nd SAS was raised on 13 May.

Herstell was posted missing in action during OPERATION SNAPDRAGON, a recce of the strategically important island of Pantelleria that lies in the narrows between Sicily and Tunisia. Possession of its airfield was judged essential for the forthcoming assault on Sicily. A ten-man team, led by Major Geoffrey Appleyard, DSO, MC*, was therefore inserted by rubber dinghies launched from HM Submarine *Unshaken* on the night of 28–29 May 1943 (see Appleyard's entry under Cassino Memorial, Italy, Volume II). The men were to take a prisoner and ascertain the enemy's alertness. Having scaled the sea cliff they took cover as an Italian patrol passed. Deciding to snatch a lone sentry a suitable candidate was identified and tackled to the ground. However, his muffled cries alerted a second sentry who rushed to the scene. Herstell, nearest to this new threat, ran forward to silence him despite only being armed with a rubber cosh. He was shot and with more of the enemy arriving was left by the raiding party that was forced to withdraw down the cliff face.

Herstell either died of his wounds or was murdered after capture in the early hours of 29 May 1943. His service record notes that he was reported 'missing and known to be wounded' as of that date.

Son of Frank and Florence Herstell (née Taylor) of Oswald Road, Chorlton-cum-Hardy, Manchester – Husband of Florence Herstell of Leeswood Avenue, Chorlton-cum-Hardy.
Age 27.
Face 7.

PRIVATE GERHARD **WERTHEIM** [BNA/13809492] FRENCH FOREIGN LEGION, PIONEER CORPS AND 2ND SAS (HQ SQN)

Gerhard Wertheim was a German Jew who before volunteering for 2nd SAS had served in the French Foreign Legion and 337 (Alien) Company, Pioneer Corps. The latter consisted entirely of German and Austrian nationals who had fled Nazi oppression. Once in France they had joined the Foreign Legion in order to escape French internment camps but on reaching Vichy-held North Africa were employed on tasks verging on hard labour and were treated almost as prisoners. After the Allies landed in the region during November 1942's OPERATION TORCH a process began enabling such men to volunteer for the British Army's Pioneer Corps. Although Wertheim's service record cannot be located, war crimes correspondence note that he had dental treatment at Cap Matifou near Algiers in June 1943, his service number suggesting that he had enlisted into the company approximately two months previously. It is not known when he volunteered for 2nd SAS, although jump records from No.1 PTS Ringway show that during April 1944 he attended parachute course 111A. Here he was recorded as being an 'average jumper, keen'.

Wertheim parachuted into France, close to the German border in the area west of Ingwiller, on the night of 15–16 September 1944 for OPERATION PISTOL. With heavy ground mist and no reception committee, his patrol, B.1 under Lieutenant Ron Birnie, landed in trees, two of the party being separated as a result. They regrouped the following day, the pair having been guided by the footprints of their comrades. This unavoidable laying of sign was shortly to prove the patrol's undoing. Wertheim and Birnie subsequently made contact with two woodcutters who helped them to dispose of their parachutes and locate their supply pannier, pinpointed their position and later provided information on enemy dispositions as well as some welcome beer. However, when the woodcutters failed to return later that day as promised Birnie grew suspicious and moved the patrol's lay-up point farther into the wood.

Marching north on the 17th Birnie and Wertheim went to observe train traffic on their target, the railway line running towards the front. Returning to the patrol they found that children and adults had followed their tracks, Birnie therefore sending the German-speaking Wertheim to keep them at distance whilst the group packed up. However, a German policeman was amongst the civilians and spotted them. He could not be caught and appeared to be trying to ascertain their numbers so the patrol rapidly stripped down its kit and moved off. That night, having prepared explosives, Birnie took Wertheim and Lance-corporal 'George' Davison to attack the railway line in a tunnel north of Puberg, making arrangements to rendezvous with the remainder of the group at a later date. 2nd SAS subsequently reported that: 'this party did not return to the [patrol's] RV arranged for the 21st Sept, but resupply dropped for them was received by the right recognition letter at Q669430 on 24/25th Sept' (WO 361/716). Meanwhile, PISTOL's post-operation report notes that the 'attack probably successful as it was reliably reported subsequently that all traffic stopped for four days' (WO 218/205).

'Missing Parachutists', the SAS War Crimes Investigation Team's final report, later established that Wertheim's group was: 'taken prisoner near Wingen [on 1 October] and brought to Strasbourg where they were confined in the rue du Fil prison. Here Wertheim was separated and the remainder sent to Stalags' (see Birnie's entry under Groesbeek Memorial, Netherlands, Volume III). Kriminalrat Marie Uhring, a member of the Gestapo later held in the same prison for suspected war crimes, confirmed:

> At the end of September or beginning of October 1944 I interrogated a number of English parachutists who had been captured in the Wingen area. I can remember a Lieut Birnie, and a signaller called Davison, a Frenchman called Voisin [Corporal G. Voisin of the same patrol], and a Jew who had been born in Germany, with a German name. I took Prof Gallinski as my interpreter ... he got no results.
>
> In my report I particularly emphasised that these men were prisoners of war. I pointed out that as they were wearing uniform and had 2 SAS on their shoulders they were obviously regular troops. Schneider [SS-Obersturmbannführer Wilhelm Schneider, deputy commander of the SD in Alsace] with whom I discussed this, said it was not at all clear whether SAS was a regular formation or not. I assumed that this group was not killed because Isselhorst [Dr Erich Isselhorst, commander of the SD in Alsace] and Schneider were afraid that I would split on them and tell the Red Cross [WO 309/717].

By the beginning of July 1945 the truth was beginning to unravel, the Regiment's message log noting: 'Source Armand Souchal. Wertheim reported killed Niederbuhl [a camp across the Rhine in Germany] 8 Dec. Will investigate. Do not take as conclusive yet' (WO 218/216). Roger Souchal, a member of the Maquis who had worked alongside 2nd SAS not far from PISTOL on OPERATION LOYTON, and who was known as Armand to members of the Regiment, subsequently stated:

> I left Schirmeck for the camp at Niederbuhl on the 22nd November 1944. On arrival at the camp at Niederbuhl I saw an SAS soldier in battle dress wearing a red beret, and with the letters SAS on his shoulders. He was a German Jew, and I remember his name was Wertheim. I saw him again with a party that was moved to Ottenau, at the beginning of December, where we remained three days, but after returning to Niederbuhl, Wertheim disappeared and I never saw him again [WO 311/1154].

Dr Armand Fritz, a fellow inmate assigned the role of camp doctor, took up the story:

> The day after our return [around 27 November], between 3 and 4 o'clock in the afternoon, a green truck and gendarmerie in green uniform arrived at the camp [Niederbuhl]. Two of them came in and asked for 'the two men'. Pfeifer, the Commandant of the camp, then pointed out the first parachutist whom I have described [Wertheim], and an epileptic Alsatian from Colmar or Mulhausen [a man later identified as a Mr Heckmann]. Both were taken to the truck outside the camp, were handcuffed and driven away in the direction of Rastatt [WO 311/1154].

Meanwhile, Paul Philippi, assistant to Fritz in the camp's infirmary, recalled:

> I saw the two parachutists for the first time at Ottenau at the end of November 1944. The first had black curly hair, looked Jewish, had a brown face and was about 1m75 tall. He was wearing khaki waterproof jacket, and had no head-dress. He spoke German and said that he had left Germany about ten to twelve years before, and that he had

lived in America. The second was smaller and thinner, and I do not know what happened to him.

I saw the first parachutist whom I said looked Jewish, being taken away from the camp at Niederbuhl. This occurred between the 5th and 7th of December. I think the Chief of Police of Niederbuhl or Rastatt was present at the truck, and I noticed the green uniform different to the [Wehrmacht's] feldgrau. I saw this clearly from the camp dispensary. The soldier was put in handcuffs, and a young epileptic civilian was taken at the same time. The truck left in the direction of Rastatt [WO 311/1154].

Although one investigator wrote 'suggest we defer presumption [of death] pending completion of further enqs … of German nationality, remains remote chance he turned renegade under pressure' Major 'Bill' Barkworth, the commander of the SASWCIT, noted that 'the possibility that he was not killed is extremely low' (WO 361/730). His team's 'Interim Report' simply states: 'Lieut Birnie and Pct Wertheim were left with the Gestapo at Zabern when the other member of the party [Davison] was moved to Strasbourg. Lieut Birnie and the other man [Davison] have already been reported PW by the Germans' (WO 218/209).

Wertheim's French Foreign Legion pay book, found at Niederbuhl camp, was retained as an exhibit for any subsequent war crimes trial. In view of the evidence Barkworth had already concluded that Wertheim had been killed and his body disposed of en route to the nearby Rotenfels camp as there was no record of him arriving there. Sadly the case summary simply reads:

1. No evidence after leaving Niederbuhl. 2. No statements of Baumann or Weiler and Pfeifer. Further evidence required: 1. Identity of accused 2. Wertheim employed in operation and has not returned 3. Discover grave. Captured; 5 Oct 44. Shot; After 7th Dec 44 [WO 311/1154].

Despite witness statements Wertheim's date of death is officially recorded as 2 December 1944. Both Isselhorst and Schneider were tried over separate war crimes involving members of the SAS and subsequently sentenced to death (see Black's entry under Durnbach War Cemetery, Germany, Volume III, for further details).

Son of Solomon and Selma Wertheim of Riverside Drive, New York.

Age 30.

Face 38. The reason that Wertheim is commemorated here rather than on the Groesbeek Memorial in the Netherlands is unknown although it may be because he enlisted into the British Army in this region of North Africa.

SFAX WAR CEMETERY

The port of Sfax, key to the Allied advance now that Tripoli was 480 kilometres distant, was taken on 10 April 1943. Its war cemetery contains the graves of 1,253 Second World War Commonwealth servicemen, fifty-two of whom are unidentified. The majority were killed in attacks on Axis positions at Medenine, the Mareth Line and in the Wadi Akarit during March and April as the Eighth Army fought its way north towards Tunis. The cemetery also contains one Greek soldier of the 1939–45 war and a single grave of the First World War.

Sfax is located 270 kilometres south of Tunis. The cemetery lies 2 kilometres south of the town centre near the junction of the inner ring road and the road to Gabes (the P1). The gates are never locked, although the visitors' book is only available during working hours. GPS co-ordinates: Latitude 34.71995, Longitude 10.73416

ILARCHOS GRIGÓRIOS **BOURDAKOS** [UNKNOWN S/N]
ROYAL HELLENIC ARMY ATT 1ST SAS (GREEK SACRED SQN)

By February 1943 the Greek Sacred Squadron, 1st SAS, was operating in western Libya. Having reached Ksar Rhilane in Tunisia on the 21st its Jeep patrols joined forces with Free French troops led by Général Leclerc. Although attacked in strength on 10 March, the squadron pushed forward aggressively and on 3 April was tasked to work alongside the New Zealand Division for what was to become the closing stages of the North African Campaign. Its patrols were subsequently split between the NZ Cavalry and the King's Dragoon Guards and passed through the newly opened Gabes Gap on the 8th. Grigórios Bourdakos (Γρηγόριος Μπουρδάκος) is commemorated on the Greek Sacred Regiment memorial within

Ares Park (Pedion Areos), Athens, as having been killed in action that day. Although his headstone records his rank as major, the memorial, erected by his comrades, notes it as ilarchos (captain). It is likely that he lost his life whilst harassing German forces on their northbound retreat.

Ανδρῶν γὰρ ἐπιφανῶν πᾶσα γῆ τάφος (For illustrious men have the earth world as their tomb – *Funeral Oration*, by Pericles)
Grave 14.D.19.

Corporal-of-horse Montagu **STAPLES** [304543] Royal Horse Guards, No.8 Commando, Middle East Commando and 1st SAS (C Sqn)

'Monty' Staples was born in Orpington in Kent on 26 February 1904. Having worked as a groom he enlisted into the Royal Horse Guards in October 1922. After eight years' home service he left the army to become a bus driver in Tottenham, north London, and was posted to the reserve list. His discharge papers describe him as 'a thoroughly reliable and trustworthy man', despite the fact he had been awarded 168 hours detention at Aldershot for 'drunkenness on duty i.e. Sovereign's Escort' during the summer of 1927. Finding his new life dull he joined the Palestine Police Force in October 1930, returning to the UK and to reserve service in November 1932. He soon slotted back into regimental life, winning two Household Brigade medals for athletics whilst a trooper during the following year. In January 1933 he married Lilian Maud Mechen at West Green, north London, the couple producing a son, Brian, in 1934.

Staples, now working as a milkman in Harringay, extended his commitment to the Army Reserve in October 1934 and 1938. He was mobilised two days before war was declared in September 1939, rejoining the Royal Horse Guards and being promoted to acting lance-corporal the same day. Volunteering for special service he was posted to No.8 (Guards) Commando in August 1940, this soon being temporarily reorganised as part of the 4th Special Service Battalion. Having completed arduous pre-deployment training in Scotland the men embarked for the Middle East at the end of January 1941. They arrived at Suez, Egypt, in early March as members of B Battalion, Layforce. Staples was promoted acting corporal-of-horse a few days later. A frustrating period of cancelled raids followed with only a fraction of No.8 seeing action when posted to Tobruk. Most of Layforce was subsequently disbanded that summer, Staples being posted to the Middle East Commando Depot at Geneifa and then attached to various units for brief periods, including a spell in Syria from April 1942. He volunteered for 1st SAS in Egypt on 26 September 1942 and was posted to C Squadron, although he spent much of August to October in hospital. Stopped £4 from his pay for losing his rifle at Tel-el-Kebir on 2 December 1942 the subsequent paperwork records that at the time he held the rank of sergeant.

The Regiment's War Diary notes that on 30 December 'an Advance Party of C Squn left Kabrit to take part in operations with the Squns already in the Western Desert' (WO 218/96). Staples, a member of this party, was subsequently reported missing, then killed in action, on 20 January 1943, although his wife was still writing to the Red Cross that October to ask if he had been taken prisoner. A February 1944 cable records that he was originally buried within Tatahouine Municipal Cemetery in Tunisia not far from the Libyan border and that the means of identification were from the cross and the municipal records. The circumstances of his death were unclear until Alan Angus, former 1st SAS, described his capture whilst a member of the same squadron:

We spent Christmas [1942] at the Base Depot [Kabrit], and then, after a few days collecting specially equipped Jeeps from Abbassia Barracks [in Cairo] and loading them with petrol, water, food, ammunition and explosives, we set off up the desert on 30th December …

Our party consisted of about thirty men in twelve Jeeps and three three-ton lorries; our commanding officer was a Captain Weir, and I shared a Jeep with Lieut Gutteridge. Our route took us through many of the places which had become well-known during the campaigns of the previous two years – Mersa Matruh, Sollum, Bardia, Tobruk, Gazala – and on through the Jebel Akhdar (passing through Maraua, the target of our abortive raid in June) [ME Commando's aborted attack on Maraua Fort – see Lance-bombardier Joe Fassam's entry under Sangro River War Cemetery, Italy, Volume II, for further details] till we dropped down to the coast at Tocra. We then followed the coast road round the Gulf of Sirte, via Benghazi, Agedabia, El Agheila and Marble Arch to Nofilia, where we left the road and turned inland. The grassy sand-hills near the coast soon gave way to rolling dunes in which it was a constant struggle to keep moving, especially for the heavily laden three-tonners …

The next night we came to a deep wadi (wadi Zemzem?), and had to negotiate the steep and rocky descent in darkness. At the bottom we came across some Arabs encamped with their camels. We pressed on, and on the following day reached the forward dump (Bir Guedaffia?) where we were to rendezvous with Colonel Stirling. Several men from A and B Squadrons were already there …

We stayed at the dump for three days during which Colonel Stirling arrived and plans for future operations were finalised. Our party, comprising eleven Jeeps and a three-tonner under Capt. Weir (we had lost one Jeep on a mine near El Agheila) was to operate in the area between Ben Gardane and Medenine, more than a 100 miles west of Tripoli. We set off on the 19th January, accompanied initially by various other groups including one led by Major Thesiger, who in his woolly hat and flowing robe stood out as a somewhat eccentric figure.

We travelled all through the first night in order to get across the Misda road in darkness. A day or two later we were surprised to see a column of troops approaching from the south; they turned out to be the vanguard of a Free French force being brought up from Chad by General Leclerc. Shortly after we dumped the three-tonner, its supply of fuel being exhausted, and the next day we parted company with Major Thesiger and the other groups …

By now we were close to our target area, and as we were finally stopped, parked our Jeeps in what hollows we could find, and concealed them as best we could under camouflage nets. A rum ration was issued (perhaps a mistake as things turned out), and most of us settled down to get some sleep; one of the officers, however, went off on his own and found a German truck parked at the side of a track a short distance away, with two men sleeping beside it. He took the two men prisoner and set fire to the truck. I was still awake when he returned with the two Germans, and although I wondered what on earth we could do with prisoners, I was too tired to worry about it and was soon asleep. I was wakened by the sound of rifle shots. They seemed very close …

I could not understand how we were taken so completely by surprise; I was told afterwards that there had been a constant stream of enemy traffic along the track which passed within a stone's throw of our position, and that at one time a staff car had stopped beside the burnt-out lorry. The next thing was that a convoy of trucks suddenly stopped right alongside us and disgorged a company of Italian infantry. They were on to us before the men on watch were able to give any warning …

Five or six men in our party were wounded, and one, Sgt Stapleton [sic - Staples], died of his wounds a day or so later … I am reasonably certain that Sgt Stapleton was a regular soldier from the Royal Scots Greys [*sic*], and that he had been a member of one of the Middle East Commandos (50, 51 or 52?) before ending up as I did with A Squadron, ME Commando, and then 1st SAS. I was present when the Italian doctor pronounced him dead only a day or so after we were taken prisoner – he had been wounded in the stomach …

The place where we were taken prisoner must have been a few miles south of Tatahouine – I know that the Italians were taking us by ambulance to Gabes the first place we passed through was Beni Barka.

The accompanying photograph, taken whilst Staples was a sergeant in the Middle East Commando, shows him towering above Glubb Pasha, the commander of the Arab Legion.

Son of William and Alice Staples of Prospect Cottages, Pratts Bottom, Orpington, Kent – Husband of Lilian Staples of Stanhope Gardens, Harringay, Middlesex.
Age 38.
Beloved. May God watch over our boy until we meet again
Grave 6.A.10.

The SAS and LRDG Roll of Honour 1941–47

Volume II – Utmost Devotion
Central and Eastern Mediterranean

Ex-Lance-corporal X, QGM

Published in the UK by SAS-LRDG-RoH
http://www.sas-lrdg-roh.com

First Published 2016
Second Imprint 2018

British Library Cataloguing in Publication Data
Data available

ISBN 978-1-5262-0332-8

Project managed, printed and bound by Cedar Group. UK Main Office: Unit 1 Triton Centre, Premier Way, Abbey Park Industrial Estate, Romsey, Hampshire, SO51 9DJ
Tel: 01794 525 032. Email: design@cedargroup.uk.com

Design by Ex-Lance-corporal X. Artwork and illustration by R. Chasemore and R. Farnworth

Typeset in Palatino Linotype. The text follows *New Hart's Rules – The Handbook of Style for Writers and Editors* published by Oxford University Press

Freedom is the sure possession of those alone who have the courage to defend it.
Pericles

CONTENTS

Volume II – Utmost Devotion – Central Mediterranean

FORMER YUGOSLAVIA

By the outbreak of the Second World War, Yugoslavia represented a brittle mesh of previously autonomous states. Created by the 1919 Treaty of Versailles it nurtured little sense of national identity, its myriad of loyalties being hinged on regional, cultural and religious rivalries. During the 1930s a fascist movement, the Ustaše, had risen in Croatia. Its exiled leadership, strongly supported by Mussolini, had ordered the October 1934 assassination of King Alexander of Yugoslavia in the streets of Marseille.

Geographically Yugoslavia was key to Axis designs on Greece and the Eastern Mediterranean, although Hitler failed in his February 1941 attempt to persuade its leaders to join him. However, the following month German forces entered the border nations of Bulgaria and Romania, Prince Paul and his Yugoslav government being pressured into signing the Tripartite Pact. The result was instantaneous mass protest, the overthrow of those responsible, withdrawal from the pact by the new military government and the installation of the 18-year-old King Peter. Hitler responded rapidly: German, Italian and Hungarian forces struck simultaneously against Yugoslavia and Greece on 6 April. Despite defiant resistance the Yugoslavs faced overwhelming odds and surrendered on the 17th, King Peter going into exile in London.

Whilst Croat nationalists took the opportunity to declare a separate state, a quisling Yugoslav government was put in place and two separate resistance groups began to emerge. One, a collection of Serb nationalists known as the Chetniks under General 'Draža' Mihailović, loyally supported the monarchy. The other, a manifestation of the Yugoslav Communist Party under Tito (born Josip Broz), became known, notably only after the German invasion of Russia forty-five days later, as the Partisans. Despite initial efforts to work together these two groups were embroiled in combat by the close of 1941, openly vying for post-war power. Whilst the Ustaše massacred ten of thousands of their opponents and Mihailović did his best to avoid the retributive massacre of civilians (his men even helping fascists to hunt down Partisans), Tito's movement slowly won over hearts and minds. In June 1943 Churchill redistributed British aid accordingly, by now convinced that the Partisans were more effective than their Chetnik counterpart. That September he also sent Tito a further military mission under the command of Brigadier Fitzroy Mclean, MP, assisted by Major Vivian Street, MC, Major Gordon Alston, Major Randolph Churchill, and Sergeant A. Duncan, all former members of the SAS (see details of Street's earlier rescue from an enemy submarine within WOII Dave Lambie's entry, Alamein Memorial, Egypt, Volume I).

Until the July 1943 Allied invasion of Sicily, very few aircraft were able to supply the Partisans. However, in the spring of 1944 Allied air forces carried out bombing raids in support of Tito's offensive thus inhibiting enemy troop movement. At the beginning of the summer the importance of pinning down such German formations was underlined by the D-Day landings in France and the advance of the Red Army. A large number of German troops, badly needed elsewhere, were thus tied up in Greece, Albania and southern Yugoslavia. To contain them further a joint Allied and Partisan force, including elements of the Raiding Support Regiment, occupied the Dalmatian island of Vis. With two good harbours and a 16-kilometre separation from other islands, this was held as a forward operating base through which to send supplies to the Partisans and also to launch raids up and down the coastline. In addition, the Long Range Desert Group pushed north along the Croatian coast to report enemy shipping movements so that the Royal Navy and RAF could strike against them. It also mounted small-scale offensive actions against key locations, often struggling to maintain an increasingly strained Partisan relationship. By July the LRDG, based at Rodi on the Italian coast, was drawn under Brigadier George Davy's Land Forces Adriatic and undertook recces for Special Boat Service raids in the region as well as their original tasks.

During the autumn of 1944 a joint Allied and Partisan offensive known as OPERATION RATWEEK brought about a more systematic arrest of German road and rail troop movement from Greece. OPERATION NOAH'S ARK, again supported by the RSR, prevented many more Axis troops entering Yugoslavia from its southern neighbours. Belgrade was liberated, albeit with heavy losses to both sides, on 19 October, Soviet units having crossed the Danube the previous month. In late January 1945 Partisan forces took

1

the port of Zara, the SBS operating from this base until shortly before the end of the war and the LRDG right up until that time.

Today three men of the Special Boat Service and one member of the Long Range Desert Group are buried at Belgrade War Cemetery.

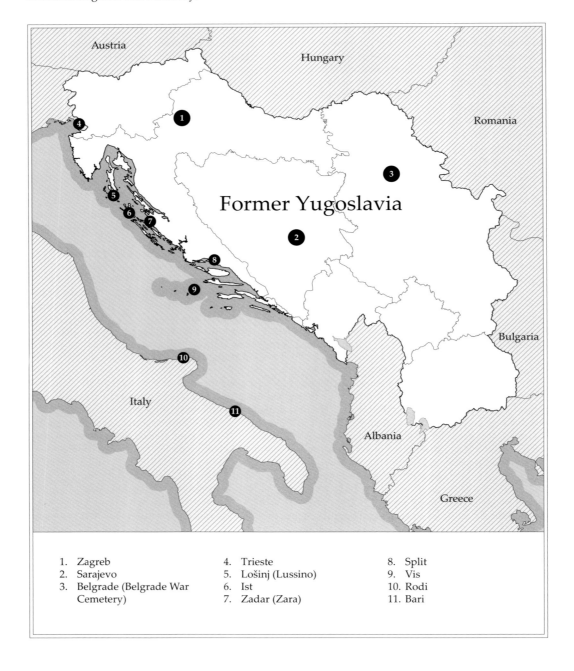

1. Zagreb	4. Trieste	8. Split
2. Sarajevo	5. Lošinj (Lussino)	9. Vis
3. Belgrade (Belgrade War Cemetery)	6. Ist	10. Rodi
	7. Zadar (Zara)	11. Bari

BELGRADE WAR CEMETERY

This cemetery contains 483 Commonwealth graves of the Second World War that were concentrated from over sixty burial sites all over Former Yugoslavia. They include those of escaped prisoners of war from Italy and Greece as well as some civilian casualties.

Captain Jack Bare of the Artists Rifles, attached Royal Welch Fusiliers and No.2 Commando, is buried in grave 9.A.6. He died of wounds received on 4 February 1944 whilst assaulting an enemy position on the Dalmatian island of Hvar during a raid mounted from Vis. He was brought back and temporarily buried on the island, No.2 Commando's War Diary noting that he was 'the first British serviceman to be interred there for a hundred and thirty years'. In 1897 his father, Captain Arnold Bare, MVO, TD, joined the Artists Rifles, a TA regiment now closely associated with the SAS. He was killed in action at Passchendaele in October 1917 whilst commanding B Company and is commemorated on the Tyne Cot Memorial.

The cemetery is located east of the city centre within the Bulbulder district. Access is gained from Baja Sekulica Street (Svecog Nikole), 5th Region. GPS co-ordinates: Latitude 44.80549, Longitude 20.49113

LANCE-CORPORAL ELLIS **HOWELLS** [3910267] SOUTH WALES BORDERERS,
NO.12 COMMANDO ATT SMALL SCALE RAIDING FORCE, NO.10 COMMANDO,
SOE AND SBS (Q PATROL, S SQN)

'Taffy' Howells was born on 18 February 1919 at Bonymaen in Swansea where he later worked as a painter and decorator, sometimes rendering coach livery. Rugby was a big part of his life and he played

for the city's team, only the outbreak of war preventing him from progressing to international level. Having enlisted into the South Wales Borderers in October 1939 he was posted to the regiment's infantry training centre and promoted to lance-corporal in February 1940. He was re-posted to the 11th Holding Battalion the following month and to the 50th Battalion at Aberystwyth in June. Although promoted to corporal within weeks, he dropped one rank that September on posting to B Company, 7th Battalion, which was based at Stanley House in Cardigan. Having broken his leg whilst playing company-level rugby he was deprived of his remaining stripe by his CO for leaving camp whilst sick.

During the autumn of 1941 Howells volunteered for special service and after completing training that November was posted to No.12 Commando at Warsash near Southampton. It is not known whether he saw action with this unit during the raid on the Lofoten Islands that December or during the recovery of members of the 2nd Battalion, Parachute Regiment, involved in the famous Bruneval Raid of February 1942 (OPERATION BITING). What is certain is that by July of that year, when the Commando was beginning to fragment, he was a member of D Troop based at Netley and the following month was again promoted to lance-corporal. On the night of the 11–12 November he took part in OPERATION FAHRENHEIT, a combined Small Scale Raiding Force and No.12 Commando raid on a cliff-top German signal station at the Pointe de Plouézec in Brittany. Although the intention was to take prisoners, surprise was lost and having killed four of the garrison, one of whom Howells himself accounted for with his Tommy gun, the party came under fire. Forced to withdraw down the cliff to their awaiting boat it was realised that one man was missing and without hesitation Howells re-scaled the face to retrieve his comrade who had become entangled in branches. The pair returned to the boat just as the assault commander was deciding whether to abandon them.

Six days later Howells was attached to No.1 Commando School at Blandford, this more than likely being the cover used for his continued attachment to the nearby SSRF. However, after cross-Channel incursions became unpopular with the intelligence community the majority of the SSRF were moved to North Africa in early 1943. Howells remained in the UK and was attached to 158 Pioneer Company and then the 551st Anti-Aircraft Battery, Royal Artillery, at Netley whilst continuing cross-Channel raids with No.12 Commando and recces under OPERATION FORFAR. That November, along with a small party of men from his unit, he was posted to the Commando Holding Unit, later coming under the umbrella of No.10 (Inter-Allied) Commando.

Based at Freshwater on the Isle of Wight, Howells' small team became known as Fynnforce after its commander, Major Ted Fynn, MC. His fellow officers were Captain Ian Smith, MC, and Lieutenant Ambrose McGonigal, MC (see the entry for Ambrose's brother, Lieutenant Eoin McGonigal of L Detachment, SAS Brigade, under Alamein Memorial, Egypt, Volume I). By the beginning of 1944 Smith, McGonigal and Howells, with nine other men, were living independently from the rest of No.10 Commando at the Louis Napoleon pub at Newhaven and tasked with the recce of French beach defences. Smith later described their training:

> One of the exercises at which we became expert was to roll an empty bean tin down the face of a quarry and then with single shots keep the tin in the air. Strangely I was the King Pin at this, followed by Cpl Howells, a splendid young man who played in the centre for Cardiff RFC [sic], and except for the war would have worn the red jersey [Private Papers of Major I. C. D. Smith, MC*, IWM 15632].

With their tasks completed the men lacked any defined role, Smith later recalling how they came to change theatre to the Adriatic:

> It also happened that Fitzroy Maclean, then a brigadier, was in London. He was in charge of the mission to help Tito's Partisans who were harassing the Germans in Yugoslavia and he wanted agents to drop into various Partisan

units. [Brigadier Bob] Laycock recommended Ambrose and myself writing that 'they are very good officers, but bloody independent'. We managed to include Sgt-major Brodison, Cpl Nash, and L/Cpl Howells in our party, and so we were inducted into the Special Operations Executive. The Official Secrets Act was signed, finger prints were taken, and we were told, on pain of something awful happening, not to breathe a word to anyone [Private Papers of Major I. C. D. Smith, MC*, IWM 15632].

Having been found suitable Howells was officially posted to SOE's Special Training Schools Holding Unit and on 3 June 1944 his small party flew with Maclean to Gibraltar, then Algiers, before arriving at Brindisi on the dawn of D-Day. Reporting to Force 399, the SOE detachment at Bari responsible for Yugoslavia, Albania and Hungary, the men settled in, Howells learning that he had been mentioned in despatches for his part in OPERATION TARBRUSH, a series of cross-Channel raids that May (*London Gazette* 03/08/44).

In August Major David Sutherland, MC*, persuaded McGonigal to transfer himself and his men to the Special Boat Service, Howell temporarily relinquishing his lance-corporal's rank in order to do so. Ivor Flavell, MM, a former SBS sergeant, recalled that he, McGonigal and ten men of Q Patrol went 'to Yugoslavia [Montenegro] to teach Partisans to shoot up convoys' during OPERATION HEALTH BAKER (sub OPERATION RATWEEK). Having landed close to the border with Albania on 28 August McGonigal's party was met by an LRDG patrol under Lieutenant John Shute that had recced the area. In consultation with Partisans the combined group split up to locate targets whose destruction would delay the withdrawal of German divisions and therefore the possibility of them joining the Italian front. Howell and his commander subsequently made a recce of Bar where they found the vehicle parks they had been informed of did not in fact exist. Various attacks on the railway line and roads were then made, although the presence of large numbers of Ustaše made daylight movement extremely difficult. However, fascists were not their only worry – whilst carrying out an ambush on 13 September the patrol was attacked by Chetnik guerrillas and forced to retire. After a plan to kidnap the German commander of Bar was frustrated by Gestapo arrests, and after their supplies were dropped in error to the enemy, the patrol hoped for pick-up but waited at their beach RV in vain. By 4 October it was in poor condition and split, McGonigal taking Captain Robert Eden (attached to Q Patrol from SOE during this period), Howells, Marines Gartland and Fenn, and Trooper Humphries to attack the railway near Limljani:

> 7 [October 1944] Attacked the train at A820455 at 1530hrs. The demolition charge laid by Capt. Eden and Mne Fenn blew a five foot gap in the track, blew the wheels off the engine and burst the boiler. Enemy casualties were nine Germans, six Italian fascists, ten Chetniks killed, four Chetnik [and] one Italian prisoner. Pte Howells killed was the only casualty we had. The train was five wagons loaded with food, flour, cement and hay, and one empty wagon at the rear. These were set on fire and all except the last one were completely burnt out. The cylinders of the engine were destroyed by a Lewes bomb.
> 8 [October] Howells buried at church [at grid] 795455 [WO 170/4012].

Flavell later recalled: 'Williams [*sic* – Howells] was hit in the head with a stray bullet from which he died. Locals said they would look after the grave but whether that occurred or not I don't know' (personal correspondence, 2009). Smith, who had been separated for a short mission to Tito's men, wrote on his return:

> Ambrose McGonigal who has also been in Jugland [Yugoslavia] where he had the great pleasure in blowing up a train, which he was told was full of Home Guard troops but it was in fact full of fearsome Bulgarians who gave him a wild chase. It was in this chase that L/Cpl Howells was killed [Private Papers of Major I. C. D. Smith, MC*, IWM 15632].

Meanwhile, Eden wrote in somewhat slight contradiction:

> One day we heard that a train loaded with supplies and ammunition would be passing … By this time our numbers were down to five but we had some Partisan support. I made up and laid the charges and crouched in the bank beside where I thought the engine would come to rest.
> Eventually I heard the sound of a train approaching, but it was moving at a low walking pace, and I could see machine guns clustered all along the roof …

The explosion took me by surprise, with the din of raised voices and hissing steam, the clatter of magazine springs as ammunition was loaded, the shots and confusion …

Then the grenades started to fly. The enemy evacuated the train and we pursued them down the railway line where they took cover in a wood at the side of the line. It was now hand-to-hand fighting and I suddenly realised that some German soldiers were shouting to each other in English! I discovered that we were fighting the English brigade of the SS. I believe it was part of the Prince Eugen or Deutschland Division. My feelings were beyond description. Here were my countrymen, fresh from burning children alive in wooden churches, dropping old people down wells for a laugh, and other disgusting crimes, fighting as mercenaries against their own country …

One of our number, a corporal who had earned the Military Medal elsewhere [sic – MiD], lay mortally wounded. We carried him down to the church. Next day, with full ceremony, the Orthodox priest held a proper funeral service, and we buried him in the churchyard. His body has been retrieved by the Graves Commission and reburied in a war cemetery [Private Papers of R. J. P. Eden, IWM 13339].

Son of Richard and Annie Howells (née Thomas) of Cefn Road, Bonymaen, Swansea.
Age 25.
'Until the trumpet shall sound', 'Nes can yr udgorn', I Cor. XV.52
Grave 2.E.2.

MARINE THOMAS **KITCHINGMAN** [PO/X105923] ROYAL MARINES
AND SBS (R PATROL, S SQN)

Tom Kitchingman was born in Leeds on 18 February 1924. Having worked as a milkman he enlisted into the Royal Marines at Exmouth reserve depot in May 1941 at the age of 17. After serving with the Portsmouth Division he joined the shore establishment HMS *Canopus* in Alexandria, Egypt, in March 1942. A short period with a similar establishment, HMS *Sphinx*, followed before serving aboard HMS *Euryalus* where, according to his service record, he 'attempted to give secret information to person not authorised to receive' and collected fourteen days in the cells for his troubles (see below for details). He volunteered for special service in late October 1943, reinforcing the Special Boat Squadron at HMS *Saunders*, the Combined Training Centre at Kabrit.

Having passed parachute course No.88 at Ramat David, Palestine, in January 1944 Kitchingman landed on the Aegean island of Mikonos on the night of 7 May. His small party, commanded by Lieutenant Keith Balsillie, was tasked with reporting on enemy shipping and set up an observation post within a monastery,

although poor weather meant that little was seen before the men were withdrawn.

Despite not officially transferring to the SBS until that December, Kitchingman took part in OPERATION RATWEEK on the Yugoslav coast during August 1944: a contemporary report notes that an LRDG patrol under Lieutenant David Skipwith was put ashore to recce targets on the night of the 18–19th (WO 204/9681). O Patrol under Captain Andy Lassen, MC*, and K Patrol under Lieutenant Jim Henshaw, both of S Squadron, subsequently left Bari in motor launches on the afternoon of the 27th. Just before midnight they landed on a beach not far from Gruda where they were met by Skipwith's men and a group of Partisans. The combined party reached their target, a railway bridge between Bar and Budva at Karasovici, at 2115hrs on the 30th after 'the civilians of Plocice had supplied food and wine'. By 2245hrs the bridge was destroyed, Lassen's own report recording that they were attacked by a mixed force of 400 Ustaše and Germans on 2 September and that: 'Lt Henshaw with 5 men defended the ridge.' Although three men, including Skipwith, were captured the remainder successfully disengaged from the enemy and returned to Italy on 6 September (see Lassen's entry under Argenta Gap War Cemetery, Italy, and Henshaw's under Cassino Memorial, Italy, both within this volume).

Kitchingman was killed in action on 9 March 1945 at Lussingrande on Lussino, an island off the coast of modern-day Croatia. The commander of R Patrol, Lieutenant Ivan Jones-Parry, described the attack on the fascist-held Villa Punta in his post-operation report:

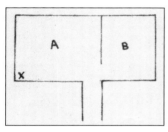

Machine gun and tripod mounted in a garden covering harbour. Mne Kitchingman found Italian hiding behind it. Killed same … Ran with Sgt McDougal and Mne Kitchingman to front door of house …

Went up to door (room A) and listened. No sound, very dark. Rushed in, paused. No movement. Went into room B. Kitchingman coming into room A covering my back, Sgt McDougal covering corridor. Kitchingman asked 'Are you alright, Sir?' 'Yes'. Burst of MG fire from room A (point X). Hit in arm and chest. Kitchingman collapsed. Bit confused in thinking. Changed magazine. Tommy gun on sling around neck so stable. Opened fire from door B into corner X, traversing along far wall and floor. Emptied magazine. Walked out into corridor. Kitchingman casualty – burst through head. Reported to Capt [Ambrose] McGonigal [see the entry for McGonigal's brother, Lieutenant Eoin McGonigal of L Detachment, SAS Brigade, under Alamein Memorial, Egypt, Volume I]. Went on to road for dressing. Lay on road until told the wounded were to move. Walked back to ML [WO 170/7529].

With numerous other casualties, and with enemy reinforcements on their way, the SBS party was forced to withdraw over a steep and rocky ridge leaving Kitchingman's body behind. Jones-Parry, although wounded in the spleen and arm, had killed the German who shot him. Given six months to live Jones-Parry recovered fully, only to be killed accidentally in 1946 whilst serving with the Allied Screening Commission on Crete.

Paul Ogden, Kitchingman's nephew, later wrote:

He was a kind hearted, very determined, intelligent and resourceful young man. His younger sisters Joan, Molly, Sheila, my mother Veronica, and Margaret, all adored him. He and his brother Harry were named after earlier generations of Kitchingmans that were once a prominent mercantile family in Leeds. A couple of anecdotes may help to illustrate Tom's personality and character. When he was 14 he had an argument with his father, Harold. He left home for two weeks surviving in the local woods with his dog, Tiny, by catching and eating rabbits.

On another occasion during the war Tom dived overboard to save a German serviceman from drowning. Unfortunately, he spent a few days in the ship's brig for this indiscretion [see above for the note in his service record].

When he was 17-years-old he enlisted as a Royal Marine in Portsmouth and subsequently served on HMS *Euryalus*, sailing to the equator and witnessing the bombardment of Tripoli. I have a photograph of Tom in Alexandria in 1943 wearing a Royal Marine cap and possess a letter dated 31/10/43, headed 'S Det SBS, 1st SAS'. In the letter Tom gives little indication of what he is doing in the SAS but adds that the work he is involved in is 'just up my street'.

In the autumn of 1944 Tom was shot in the arm on 14/11/44 and admitted to HMS *Maine*, then transferred to the *Orion* on 18 December and thence to the Royal Naval Hospital Malta on the 19th. Captain Henshaw wrote to Tom's mother in November telling her not to worry, the wound was not serious and that he was having 'a whale of a time' in hospital and everybody loved him.

Around this time Tom met a young Greek woman who had just left school and was working for an English company. I still have some of the letters she wrote to my mother and grandparents.

After the war my grandmother and two of her daughters, Joan and Molly, stayed with Lady Madeleine Lees at Lychett Manor in Dorset. Her son, James, was killed in the same action as Tom [personal correspondence, 2010 – see Lees' entry below for further details of the Lussino raid].

Son of Harold and Bridget Kitchingman (née Daly) of Rathwell Road, Halton Moor, Leeds, Yorks – Brother of Harry, Joan, Molly, Sheila, Veronica and Margaret Kitchingman.
Age 21.
Lamb of God who takest away the sins of the world. Have mercy on him R.I.P.
Grave 8.C.6.

CAPTAIN JAMES **LEES** [175078] KING'S ROYAL RIFLE CORPS
AND SBS (H PATROL, M SQN)

Known to his patrol as 'Tansy', and as Jimmy to other military colleagues, Lees was born on 3 March 1920 at Belgaum in western India where his father, a First World War veteran, was serving in the 4th Battalion, King's Royal Rifle Corps. As heir apparent to the family baronetcy Lees attended St Aubyn's prep school then Eton from May 1933 to 1938 where he boxed and rowed for the college as well as being active in the OTC. A keen horseman he was a county point-to-point champion at the age of 18. Having entered Sandhurst he was commissioned into the 2nd Battalion, KRRC, in July 1939, remaining on home duties at Tidworth when the battalion was sent to France.

In January 1941 Lees was promoted to lieutenant and that September disembarked in the Middle East. Having been advanced to captain he was wounded by a mine in June 1942 whilst leading A Company at Gazala. Although treated for blast injuries he suffered with deafness and pain in his ear for months until an operation resulted in a spell of convalescence in Jerusalem. He was, however, back in time for the Battle of El Alamein in October 1942 during which he led the company. In May 1943, having fought at the Battle of Mareth and through the advance to Tunis, he relinquished his temporary rank of major. He volunteered for the Special Boat Squadron that October, joining the unit at Athlit on the coast of what was then Palestine (modern-day Israel).

After ski training at The Cedars in Lebanon during January 1944 Lees arrived at Port Deremen on the coast of Turkey in March. As commander of H Patrol, M Detachment, he led a recce of the Aegean island of Calino in June. Once it was ascertained that the Germans were present in force his patrol extracted after a brief exchange of fire. The following month he led his men on OPERATION TENEMENT, a multi-patrol attack on the island of Simi on 14 July. It was here that the camera used to take the accompanying photo, showing a captured Nazi flag and uniform, was 'liberated'. On 29 September he, Lieutenant Hutchins and twenty-nine other ranks were landed on the coast of Albania for OPERATION GHETTO: operating near to the town of Permet they were able to harass German troop movement before a Dakota landed to extract the patrol.

By January 1945 Lees was operating from the SBS base at Monte Sant'Angelo on the Adriatic coast of Italy, moving with elements of both M and S Squadrons to Zara on the Yugoslav coast in mid February. On the night of 2 March he and Corporal Allen carried out a reconnaissance of the small village of Ćunski on the island of Lussino. Having launched a Folbot from *ML 238* they landed at Tomosina and spent three days mapping enemy positions and strengths. On his return to the forward operating base on Uljan Island Lees found that his patrol had deployed to attack the enemy-held Villa Punta at Lussingrande, information having been previously received from a fascist deserter that this man's comrades wished to surrender (WO 170/7529). However, the first attempt was aborted, Lees being mortally wounded during the subsequent follow-up raid on the island during the night of 9–10 March. The two-patrol party was fired on just after midnight as soon as it broke cover to form up for the attack, perhaps indicating that the 'deserter' had been a plant or that the enemy had been alerted by the earlier landing. In any case the party's guide reported that the guard had been increased, Ralph Bridger of Lees' patrol recalling:

When we got there it was a complete hash … as we were walking up this road [towards the Villa Punta, seen here in the photo] there was a big wall on one side and on the other [towards the sea] there was a 2ft parapet and all of a sudden there was a voice in German; 'Halt!' and a machine gun opened up. All the blokes dived down and Captain Lees hid behind the parapet and crawled up to the Villa Punta and I was right behind him. Two of the blokes jumped over on the sea side and eventually we got there and there was Lieutenant [Ambrose] McGonigal, Lieutenant Parry-Jones and Captain Lees.

Captain Lees went to the front and the two lieutenants went down the side of the building with half a dozen blokes. I went to the front with Captain Lees and it was murder. Absolute hell. Bullets flying all over the place, grenades going off, people shouting. Captain Lees said to me 'Go over there' which I did and as I went into the room someone must have thrown a hand grenade. It exploded in the room and the door hit me and I went flying and when I woke up I had blood all over me as my nose had burst.

I staggered out of the room and there were three bodies lying on the floor. Initially I couldn't hear anything because of the explosion. All of a sudden somebody said to me 'Tansy's down!' That was Captain Lees' nickname and someone else said 'Tommy Kitchingman's down' …

In the meantime the Germans had fired a Very pistol up the chimney to warn the garrison half an hour away, with lots of Germans, and so we went over to Captain Lees and he was gurgling. Someone said 'he's finished' and Tommy Kitchingman was killed outright … We had to leave Captain Lees and Tommy because we had to go [back] over the mountains [carrying the wounded] and down to the shore [for collection by the Royal Navy – interview by kind permission of Colin and Lynn Smith, 2014].

Ken Smith, another former member of Lees' patrol, recalled that he went in search of his officer on hearing that he had been wounded:

Smashing chap he was. A gentleman. A real gentleman. I couldn't speak too highly of him … as I went down [towards the villa] Lees was lying by the doorway. The only light was coming from the flames from within the house. As I approached I could see that Captain Lees was near the doorway but my officer said 'Leave him there, he's had it. Grab that prisoner'. He was only semi-conscious really with a lot of blood around him [personal interview, 2014].

With a steep climb over a rocky ridge ahead of them to reach the pick-up beach, and with one wounded man already being carried by four others on one of the villa's doors, the best hope for survival was for the badly wounded Lees to be left to the enemy for immediate medical attention and Smith reluctantly moved on.

In 1950 Lady Lees received a letter from Dr Wasmuht, a German who had served as the Medical Officer on Lussino:

> The large and trackless island was only held by us Germans in small and isolated posts far apart. We were supported by Italian Commandos. In the south of the island, about 6km from Lussingrande and halfway between it and Lussinpiccolo, there stood, on a rocky promontory, a lonely house set in a large garden. At the time the garden was in full blossom and in the house lived the Italian unit commanded by the newly-arrived Lieutenant Comotti, a lad of about 18 or 19. He was a hot blooded and enthusiastic soldier of the Fascist Militia who had had to take over a very thankless task because his predecessor had been shot in the back a few days previously when in a Partisan locality …
>
> This is what had happened. Your son, with some of Tito's followers [sic], had landed from an electric motorboat somewhere on the Lussingrande coast and had surprised the post at Villa Punta. He had then himself dashed up to the first floor and had suddenly come face to face with the Italian Comotti in one of the rooms. Both had their revolvers. At this moment the bomb that the Commandos had brought into the hall of the house exploded. The whole staircase went up, and your son and Lieutenant Comotti were on the first floor and could not get back. From the evidence we had we understood that your son and Comotti shot at each other. The Italian was severely wounded by a shot through one lung and was hors de combat. During the fight the ceiling collapsed and your son was struck on the head by a falling beam and became unconscious. Tito's Commandos climbed up from the outside – I don't know if there were Englishmen there too – and tried to rescue your son and carry them away with them, but they had to give it up as they could not manage it …
>
> All this happened in a very short space of time. A few minutes later I arrived at the unlucky spot and found the two leaders of the opposing units badly wounded and a few slightly wounded men. I could not see a trace of Tito's men. Your son's pulse was so good that I believed he would soon recover now that the commotion had died down, especially as apart from a quite slight wound on his right heel there did not appear to be any other injury. I found Comotti at death's door. He had written 'Long live Italy' on the ground beside him with his blood …
>
> Your son was perfectly peaceful, and showed no signs of pain, but he did not regain consciousness in the days that followed. About two or three days after the fight he died peacefully. He was buried with all honour in the little churchyard at Lussinpiccolo.

In 1954 Lady Lees travelled to Greece and Yugoslavia where she visited the villa before tracing Roberto Comotti to Salo on Lake Garda. She told him 'I want you to know I do not hold you responsible for what happened at Villa Punta, and I entirely forgive you and want you to become part of the family'. As her other son, Sir Tom Lees, writes: 'this had such an effect on the town that the Council made a gold medal for reconciliation and presented it to her. Comotti was still suffering from the effects of his wounds, but he had recovered sufficiently to come to Lytchett Minster Parish Church where he was asked to unveil the memorial to Jimmy which is in the church as you go in' (personal correspondence with Sir Thomas Lees, Bart. 2014). A plaque within the family plot in this churchyard records:

> Capt James Lees KRRC attached Special Boat Service eldest son of Col John Lees Bt, DSO, MC, and of Lady Lees, born 3rd March 1920 died 11th March not 18th 1945 of wounds received in action at Villa Punt, Lussine, Dalmatia. His grave by San Martini church was devotedly cared for by the people of Lussine Piccolo until in 1950 it was moved to St Nicolas Cemetery Belgrade and this vase and cross were sent home from Lussine [these are now within the family plot within the churchyard].

Lees is officially recorded as having been killed in action on 9 March 1945, the night of the raid. Bridger later wrote: 'I don't think the lads ever got over the death of Captain Lees. He was the finest officer and man I ever met in the armed forces, and we had some damn good officers in our unit. May his ride to Valhalla be a good one' (*Mars & Minerva*, December 2004). His Commanding Officer wrote that 'his vitality, personality, great bravery and leadership will long be remembered' whilst the family's local newspaper reported that 'Capt Lees was equally as popular with his tenantry of Lytchett as with his wide circle of friends.' For many years after the war SBS and SAS veterans and their families were invited to holiday at the family home.

Eldest son of Colonel Sir John Lees, DSO, MC, 3rd Bt. and of Lady Lees (née Pelly) of Post Green, Lytchett Minster, Dorsetshire – Younger brother of Katherine and older brother of Rosamund, Benita Anne, Thomas (injured whilst serving in the wartime RAF), Jane and Mary Gabriel – Nephew of Lieutenant Sir Thomas Lees, Queen's Own Dorset Yeomanry, killed in action 24/08/15 at Gallipoli and commemorated on the Helles Memorial.
Age 25.
God is love
Grave 10.C.9. Also commemorated on war memorials at Eton College and Lytchett Minster.

Signalman Kenneth SMITH GC [2328696] Royal Corps of Signals and LRDG (Signals Sqn Att Y.2 Patrol, B Sqn)

Ken Smith was born on 7 December 1920 at Market Rasen in Lincolnshire. Having worked as a labourer he enlisted into the Royal Corps of Signals in January 1939 and was posted to 50th (Northumbrian) Divisional Signals. Serving with the BEF from late January 1940 his unit withdrew from Belgium in the face of the German Blitzkrieg that May, first to Loos and then Vimy Ridge before being evacuated from Dunkirk on 29 May. With Divisional HQ established at Langton House in Blandford, Dorset, Smith settled down to life in the adjoining tented camp. The following April he embarked for the Middle East, reaching Port Tewfik at the entrance to the Suez Canal after a six-week passage via Freetown, Durban and Aden. Soon after he re-embarked for 'an unknown destination' that was soon revealed as Cyprus. However, that November the 50th Division was moved to Kirkuk in northern Iraq to counter any German move through the Caucasus.

By January 1942 the threat had abated, Smith serving in Syria until March when the 50th moved into the Western Desert and fell under command of the Eighth Army. Having improved communications within and between defensive boxes his unit kept these maintained, despite German armour, during Rommel's next offensive. Obliged to withdraw it took up positions to the rear of the Alamein Line having suffered many casualties. Promoted to lance-corporal Smith then rotated through a series of postings, twice reverting to the rank of signalman, firstly during a period in hospital and secondly by choice when he volunteered for the Long Range Desert Group on 30 November 1943. The following January he qualified for parachute pay having attended course No.88 at Ramat David. He was subsequently posted to Italy in late March 1944 and to the LRDG's Signals Squadron that June.

Having been attached to Y.2 Patrol under Captain Archie Gibson, MM, Smith was on the Yugoslav island of Vis by August 1944, his team receiving orders to establish an observation post over Mostar airfield. Landing on the mainland on the 14th a German offensive rendered the mission impossible. Ten days later the men again tried to get through to the city but heavy fighting between Partisans and Ustaše, in which they played a part, prevented this. Despite a severe shortage of food they remained in the area reporting on enemy movements until 8 October when the patrol returned to Vis. Gibson noted in his report that on 2 October he had:

> Left Turnova accompanied by Sgn Smith, K. We were fired on by a German ground force near Rilic Q700034 but managed to hide in a wooded area until dusk then continued to Brikva without further excitements. We had one tin of corned beef between us and our boots had worn right through to the socks [WO 218/92].

It appears that although granted a short period of leave members of both Y.1 and Y.2 Patrols left the Italian port of Manfredonia on 14 November to take over duties at 'Kickshaw', the LRDG detachment on the Yugoslav island of Ist. Their main task was to report on enemy shipping movement within the nearby channels. This they did, passing a predominantly quiet deployment marred only by sickness that resulted in Gibson's evacuation. Sergeant 'Tich' Cave, MM, took over and on 9 January 1945 was warned by LRDG HQ 'to be on the lookout for possible German raid' (WO 218/92). Cave subsequently reported the events of the following night:

> Sgt Cave and five men occupied a room on the first floor of a house approximately 400yds from the jetty at Ist. Another room on the ground floor was used as an office. The remainder of the ground floor was occupied by the owner, a woman and her five children.
> In a house next door three men lived in the W/T [Wireless Telegraphy] room and in a third house, approximately 200yds from ours, used by a midwife as a hospital, Sgt Jetley, Tpr Hutchinson and Pte Metcalfe were housed there. The two first named had not been well for some days.
> Nothing had transpired during the day to give us a suspicion of impending trouble. At 2115hrs I was about to retire when I heard three shots. Thinking either the *Palma* or possibly the *Kufra* [LRDG supply vessels] was coming in late I went outside and seeing nothing went to bed. A few minutes later three more shots were fired and shortly afterwards Watson of Y.2 came in and told me there was a time bomb outside the W/T room door. I at first treated the matter as a jest. Wooller went downstairs with him and Smith, CRS [Cyril], came into my room carrying his kit. I dressed immediately and taking Taylor with me, went downstairs to investigate. We had reached the bottom of the stairs when there was an explosion and we were blown off our feet. The black-out arrangements or fixtures saved everyone from injury by flying glass from the windows. When I arrived at the W/T room I encountered Buckwald carrying Wooller who had been wounded. A Partisan guard was lying on the ground. Taylor and I carried him to our room. I sent Smith, CRS, to fetch Sgt Jetley and the MO and Watson and Taylor to fetch the W/T set and ciphers. The latter were also told to find Smith, K in the meantime I rendered what first aid I could to Wooller and the Partisan. Buckwald took the woman and five children in our building to another house occupied by friends. Taylor and Watson returned with the W/T and ciphers and reported they were unable to find Smith, K. Sgt Jetley arrived with Hutchinson and Metcalfe. A guard of four (two of our men and two Partisans) was placed in the garden. Metcalfe readjusted the dressings on the two wounded men while Watson related what had happened.
> Smith, K, was in his bed. Watson and Smith, CRS, were about to retire when they heard a noise outside the door. They opened it and Watson saw what appeared to be two large bombs. He warned the others and then came and told me. On his return he saw some Partisans looking at the bombs. Picking up one he threw it outside. Smith, K, picked up the other and carried it outside. About 5 yards from the house it exploded and he was killed instantly, we decided, when we found his remains in the morning.
> Watson was badly shocked but unhurt. Sgt Jetley and I decided to telegraph Zara and ask for Navy assistance. Buckwald and I walked to the Post Office and the Partisans collected their wounded man. Taylor and Watson went in search of further bombs which might possibly have been laced about the building. Sgt Jetley and the remaining men were preparing to evacuate. The searchers found a bomb in the workhouse. I was about 300yds away when I heard them shout. Everyone immediately left the building, forgetting all about Wooller. Watson who was outside, noticed this, ran in and brought him away …
> The probability of the Partisans may have had a hand in the attack made it safer for us to be billeted in their midst. Although it was kept under the surface, there had always been a certain amount of friction between the Partisans and ourselves …
> At daylight … Buckwald and I went to see the extent of the damage … Smith, K, had been blown to bits. All we found were his legs …
> A late report from the Partisans stated ten more bombs had been found and at the north of the island a Folbot paddle, blankets and a knife [WO 218/92].

Lieutenant George Pitt arrived on the MFV *La Palma* the following day and took statements and inspected the scene before writing:

At approximately 2300hrs on 9 Jan 45 the Partisan prowler guard located two men and demanded to know who they were. Of these two men only one spoke. The Partisan guard did not ask them to prove their identity … The man who spoke said they were Partisans who had just arrived. They had not previously been on the island and consequently did not know their way about. The guard then said you cannot sleep in that house (pointing) as it is Partisan HQ. The guard then pointed out the following houses – Partisan magazine and ration dump, British magazine, British house and British radio room. On expiration of that night's duties the guard did not report that he had challenged two strange men nor did he check up and see who the new arrivals were. It was only after the night of the 10th after the first explosion that he mentioned the previous night's happenings …

On the night of the 10th Jan at 2245hrs the Partisan prowler guard on duty in the village called on two men to halt. They did not. He fired three rounds from his rifle and five from a Schmeisser. The men continued on. At 2300hrs the first bomb exploded in the British radio room …

At the time of the first explosion the Partisan officers stated that Sgn Smith found a stranger under the table in the radio room. He went through a door to fetch his Tommy gun. The stranger disappeared. Smith called out to some Partisans who were outside, four of them came at his request. He then saw the large time bomb on the table on which all the wireless sets were. He heard it ticking – they did too. He said something which they did not understand. He then pushed them aside and endeavoured to get the bomb away. He pointed as he walked that his intention was to place it behind a wall nearby. He had only gone 5 yards when it exploded. Smith was killed instantly. The four Partisans were wounded – one very seriously.

All Partisans were rounded up and a search of the island carried out. At 0600hrs two Folbot paddles, one blanket, one greatcoat and one blood stained knife were found in a small creek in the north bay. Two sheep had been killed and taken away [WO 218/92].

Smith's selfless action saved the lives of his comrades and civilians. However, due to security concerns details could not be made public in the citation that accompanied the subsequent award of his George Cross:

> The King has been graciously pleased to approve the posthumous award of the George Cross, in recognition of most conspicuous gallantry in carrying out hazardous work in a very brave manner to No. 2328696 Signalman Kenneth Smith, Royal Corps of Signals [*London Gazette* 37311, 16/10/45, Supplement 19/10/45].

An anonymous correspondent later recalled in an LRDG newsletter:

> Ken's patrol were on a shipping watch on the island, pinpointing enemy shipping for an attack by the Royal Navy or the Royal Air Force. A group of Ustashi landed unseen on the island and planted two bombs at night, one adjacent to the house where most of the patrol were billeted, the other at the house where Ken had his radio. The latter bomb was discovered by Jock Watson who roused the others and he, Cyril Smith and Ken together removed the radio equipment to a place of safety. The family whose house it was were asleep in the back room and Ken, no doubt thinking of them, went back to the house, picked up the bomb, which was ticking, and was carrying it away when it exploded, killing him and a Partisan and wounding another member of the patrol. The other bomb exploded later, destroying part of the main billet, but all personnel were out of the way by then and there was no injury.
>
> Ken was fully aware of the nature of these bombs. He knew that many contained devices to explode them if moved. His action was therefore taken in the full knowledge of the danger he exposed himself to. Ken's mother went to Buckingham Palace to receive his medal from the King. She died in 1968 and the medal was later sold [LRDG Newsletter No.21 of August 1965].

This newsletter also quoted former LRDG member, Bill Morrison:

> Ken Smith was a friend of mine. He joined us after the desert campaign and I trained him on our commercial

procedure which we always used on patrols hoping we would not be recognised as an army radio …

When Ken's patrol returned the sergeant brought in the radio and I checked it piece by piece. All signalmen had a wristwatch issued for patrol and it was known as a very attractive item and if they could lose it and persuade me it was genuinely lost and keep it themselves – well, they did very well. So, when that item did not appear I said 'Come on, what about the wristwatch?' Gil Jetley, the sergeant, said 'Wristwatch? There wasn't any wristwatch – there wasn't any wrist. We buried his boots!'

He was married [sic] and there was a collection for his widowed mother and we all gave well, but none so well as the other members of his patrol whose lives he had saved by giving his own. I have told this story so many times, in Sunday School, in Church and other places. It is the only story that matters in Christianity. The example of the cross has affected our whole way of life, even those who do not acknowledge Him. [A] few years ago from Yugoslavia they asked for a photo of Ken to put in their Museum of Heroes – in an old church. He was still remembered even in that communist, atheist land.

Smith's family were rightfully proud, their local newspaper reporting:

Last night at her tiny cottage home, the walls of which are covered with photos of her hero son and her late husband who died two years ago from the effects of gas poisoning in the First World War, Mrs Smith heard from a reporter of the award of the George Cross to her son.

'I am not surprised', she said, 'judging by the fine letters I have had from his officers and soldier pals paying tribute to his amazing gallantry without regard to his own life. It was just typical of him to do what he did.

'But we had planned such a grand welcome home for him and now I am left to struggle along with seven children – five girls and two boys.

'Ken was always very reserved about what he did, but he was a grand boy. He always wanted to go into the army from a boy and joined up for twelve years' service.

'He was never happier than when he could get his dad to talk about his experiences in the Great War, but his dad said: "My boy, when you have been through what I have you wont be so keen."

'But he went all the same, and when he came back from Dunkirk his biggest desire was to have another go at Jerry' [*Courier & Advertiser*, 20 October 1945].

Son of Bertie and Alice Smith of Five Oaks, Humby, Grantham, Lincolnshire. Age 24.
At the going down of the sun and in the morning, we will remember them
Grave 6.D.9. Also commemorated on Ropsley's war memorial, on a memorial within St Mary Magdalene Church in Old Somerby, and by a memorial dedicated to him on Ist where his photo is on display within the island's town hall. His George Cross is on display to the public at the Royal Signals Museum, Blandford.

GREECE

On 28 October 1940 the Italian Army invaded Greece from Albania. After a series of humiliating and costly defeats it was pushed back over the border by the Greeks, other Balkan countries taking heart over the damage caused to Mussolini's prestige. However, the following March it was necessary to divert over 60,000 Commonwealth servicemen from the Western Desert to counter an anticipated German attack, Hitler having been forced to bolster his weaker ally in order to secure this southern flank. His offensive came a few weeks later, Axis forces quickly driving south to seize mainland Greece. Nearly 51,000 Commonwealth personnel were evacuated, mostly to Crete where, for some, their freedom was only extended until late May when the island fell to a German airborne invasion. In the interim similar Axis parachute assaults had overwhelmed other Aegean islands of strategic importance.

For nearly two years this was how the situation remained. However, in early 1943, with the Axis all but defeated in North Africa, 1st SAS and the Long Range Desert Group returned to the Middle East. Whilst the former was largely restructured as the Special Raiding Squadron and trained for the invasion of Sicily, its D Squadron was reorganised as the Special Boat Squadron (1st SAS) and allocated the Eastern Mediterranean alongside the LRDG. Early operations such as Ten D and Albumen disrupted enemy air assets or drew attention away from the Allied invasion of Sicily, at the same time hoping to encourage Turkey to enter the war against the Axis. After Italy signed an armistice in September 1943 a number of islands held by her forces were seized before the Germans could do so. Of these the most important were Cos with its airfield and Leros with its deep-water port. The key to the Aegean, Rhodes, was not obtained despite efforts to do so. Operations subsequently sought to stimulate resistance in Greece and the Balkans and, if possible, to divert German forces from the Italian front. Enemy garrisons in the Dodecanese were to be the initial targets, the men of Raiding Forces regularly paying visits having been landed from fishing caiques of the Levant Schooner Flotilla (later the First Anglo-Hellenic Schooner Flotilla). However, despite maintaining the element of surprise conditions were far from ripe. Not unnaturally the local population was wary of surrendered Italian garrisons that had occupied their islands since before the First World War. Meanwhile, violent political instability was bubbling away just below the surface. In addition, due to the lack of Allied landing grounds in the region, air support was virtually non-existent. Those casualties listed here due to enemy bombing or parachute assault are testament to this, as were the later loss of Cos, Leros and Samos. Once the airfield on the former had been captured the fate of the other two islands was sealed.

In October 1944 the liberation of the Greek mainland, codenamed Operation Manna, was put into effect when elements of the SBS and LRDG were amongst those that landed on the Peloponnese and fought their way to Athens and beyond. With the capital liberated the stage was set for open civil war, despite British hopes that the timely arrival of the Greek Government in exile would forestall political vacuum. On one side was the communist EAM-ELAS (the National Liberation Front and its National Popular Liberation Army) that under Axis occupation had set up its own clandestine government opposed to both the King and his official government. Since the Italian surrender it had grown stronger, having acquired much of their former enemy's armament. On the other was the socialist EDES (National Republican Greek League) that had also resisted the Germans and opposed royalty but who were anti-communist. The ensuing six-week struggle was suppressed by the British, albeit temporarily, with significant difficulty and loss.

The casualties commemorated in this section are buried throughout modern Greece. Three members of the LRDG and four of the SBS are buried at Phaleron War Cemetery. Commemorated at the same location on the Athens Memorial are seven casualties of the SBS and four of the LRDG, their final resting place being unknown. On Crete four casualties of the SBS and one attached member of the Raiding Support regiment are buried at Suda Bay War Cemetery, whilst on other islands six members of the LRDG and one of the SBS lie within Leros War Cemetery, and six SBS and three LRDG within Rhodes War Cemetery.

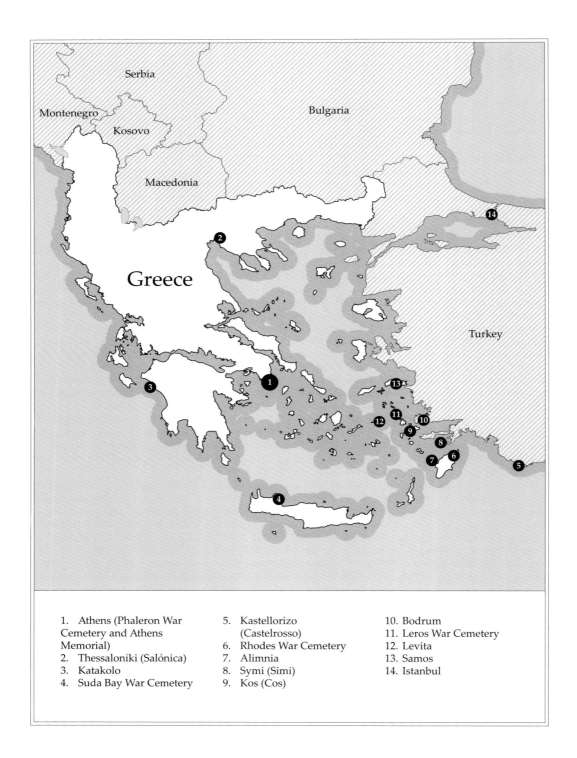

1. Athens (Phaleron War
    Cemetery and Athens
    Memorial)
2. Thessaloniki (Salónica)
3. Katakolo
4. Suda Bay War Cemetery

5. Kastellorizo
    (Castelrosso)
6. Rhodes War Cemetery
7. Alimnia
8. Symi (Simi)
9. Kos (Cos)

10. Bodrum
11. Leros War Cemetery
12. Levita
13. Samos
14. Istanbul

ATHENS MEMORIAL

This memorial commemorates nearly 3,000 members of the Commonwealth land forces who have no known grave having lost their lives during the campaigns in Greece and Crete during 1941 and 1944–45, and in the Dodecanese Islands and Former Yugoslavia from 1943–45.

The memorial is located within Phaleron War Cemetery, approximately 8 kilometres south of the city centre at the boundary between the districts of Old Phaleron and Kalamaki. Access is gained from the Athens–Vouliaghmen coast road. GPS co-ordinates: Latitude 37.91749, Longitude 23.70495

TROOPER JOHN TIMOTHY **BOWLER** [36701] NEW ZEALAND INFANTRY, DIVISIONAL CAVALRY REGIMENT AND LRDG (R.2 PATROL, A SQN)

Johnnie Bowler was born in Napier, New Zealand, on 25 September 1914 and later worked as a shepherd. Having previously served in the cadets he enlisted in October 1939 and was posted to an anti-tank company of the 32nd Battalion, New Zealand Infantry. He embarked for the Middle East at the beginning of February 1941 and on arrival in Egypt was transferred to the Divisional Cavalry Regiment's Composite Training Depot. That December he volunteered for the Long Range Desert Group and was posted to A Squadron. The following March his patrol, R.1 under Captain Jake Easonsmith, was engaged in Road Watch duties in the region of Marble Arch, a 25-metre-high monument at Ras Lanuf marking the border between Tripolitania and Cyrenaica (WO 201/812 – see Easonsmith's entry under Leros War Cemetery, Greece). His service record notes that he was also engaged on such duties between May and July but that in August 1942 he was posted back to the Composite Training Depot. Although briefly back to special duties in September, he was re-posted to the Divisional Cavalry Regiment until November when he was admitted to No.92 General Hospital with an unknown injury or illness. A month later he was discharged to the reserve depot and in January 1943 was posted to the New Zealand Armoured

Corps Training Depot from where he returned to the LRDG.

After the end of hostilities in North Africa the Group undertook Jeep and mule training in Palestine during the summer of 1943. That September the Italians surrendered and elements of both the LRDG and SBS embarked at Haifa in order to seize their former enemy's garrisons in the Dodecanese Islands before German troops could do so. Bowler subsequently landed on Leros where A and B Squadrons manned various coastal batteries.

In October 1943, HMS *Hedgehog*, a steam trawler of the Levant Schooner Flotilla, resupplied an LRDG patrol on the island of Stampalia and embarked German POWs for her return passage to Leros. After it developed engine trouble, German air reconnaissance reported that she had put into Levita for repairs and on 18 October Brandenburger parachutists mounted a successful rescue mission. Having released their comrades and captured both *Hedgehog's* British crew and Italians based at the island's small wireless station, the Brandenburgers were replaced by a Luftwaffe detachment. Back on Leros it became clear that all was not well, Brigadier 'Ben' Brittorous, DSO, MC, ordering members of the LRDG, including Bowler, to retake Levita. This mixed party, collectively known as Olforce after its commander, Captain John Olivey, MC, landed on the evening of the 23rd having been denied the time required to conduct any recces. Colonel Guy Prendergast, DSO, who had recently been appointed Second-in-Command of Raiding Forces, wrote:

> The plan for the attack on Levita was difficult to form since there was little accurate information available of enemy strength or disposition consequently it was with great misgivings that fifty men were embarked on such a foolish operation, but no appeal to the OC [Brittorous] would rescind his orders that it was vital to the Navy that the enemy garrison be liquidated. One party of twenty-five strong under Lt Kay were to land on the SW end of the island and sweep towards the centre, a second party of similar size under Lt Sutherland [Bowler included] were to land on the NE coast and carry out a similar task. The whole operation was commanded by Captain Olivey who had a small operational HQ, with W/T communication to Leros and also to Lt Sutherland's party.
>
> On the 24th October little news was heard of them until at 0900hrs a signal was received saying that both landings had been unopposed but that Sutherland's party had later met slight opposition. However, Olivey was confident that he would easily overcome the garrison. For some hours there was no further news until a signal was received stating that opposition had become considerably stronger and that he had had no news of Sutherland's party but could hear heavy firing from that direction. Olivey also reported that Cpl Bradfield had been wounded. For that time on we had no news, but throughout the afternoon we watched from Leros heavy and continuous attacks by Stukas and Ju88s [from Cos]. This was only to be expected and to undertake any operation except in the form of a 'hit and run raid' on a small island without air support was the height of folly. At dusk Lieut-Col Easonsmith left by ML to go to the prearranged RVs on Levita to collect the force whom it was hoped would have successfully completed their task. After much difficulty he contacted Capts Olivey and Lawson together with the wounded Cpl Bradfield and five ORs [other ranks]. There was no sign of the remainder of the force despite every effort to contact them, and so the unit was faced with the loss of forty-three operational and trained members of the LRDG. A further attempt the next night was made by Major Guild in an ML but he too failed to contact any more of those missing. Capt Olivey on his return could only give an account of what had happened in the SW end of the island. It appears that both landings had gone well and Capt Olivey's party by dawn had made much ground, unopposed. Soon after first light they encountered a few enemy, who were captured at once. Capt Olivey then deployed his force into two parties of eight men to attack certain high features and he kept a few men in reserve, the battle then devolved into an infantry attack against an enemy in prepared positions – a task for which our men were neither trained, armed, nor suited. They were, however, gaining ground well until the arrival of the Stukas, which with the usual German thoroughness co-operated as one with the ground forces while heartily and systematically bombing our troops. They succeeded in pinning our troops firmly to the ground while a surprise enemy counter attack from front and rear almost completely surrounded the small party. Capt Olivey with a few others broke out and lay in hiding until dusk, when he then made for the coast. It is assumed that the others were all taken prisoner but no news of Sutherland's party ever reached us although some firing on the island was reported next day. The loss of these officers and men was a bitter blow and an unnecessary one [WO 201/818].

Bowler was posted missing in action as of the 24th having volunteered to go back to the squadron's landing place with Trooper Doug Davison. Ron Hill later recalled:

> The only hope was to last out until dark and endeavour to make our way to the boat and try to rendezvous with the ML. Two troopers were sent to reconnoitre the position regarding the Folbot [folding canoe] but they did not return and did not appear later as POW. Presumably they were killed [LRDG Newsletter No.49 of 1993].

Jim Patch, captured on Levita but who later escaped with Hill whilst being transported through Yugoslavia, noted:

> All were short of food and out of water; Trooper J T Bowler volunteered to go and get some together with a runner from Gill to Sutherland. Neither of them seen again and presumed killed. It could not last very long. Soon A Squadron joined B in captivity [LRDG Newsletter No.39 of 1983].

In the same journal Hill was able to add further detail:

> About 3pm Capt Sutherland sent off a patrol of two men, accompanied by one German POW to bring water from the boats for the prisoners and to reconnoitre the situation from that point. This patrol did not return and, it is believed, was ambushed and killed. Neither man was brought in POW while we were on the island.

Bowler's fate is unknown, his date of death being officially recorded as 24 October 1943. The Germans found his pay book, if not his body itself, at the time (see Davison's entry below for further detail).

Son of John and Margaret (Madge) Bowler of Sealy Road, Napier, Hawke's Bay, New Zealand – Older brother of Dorothy Mary Roundhill of Feilding and of Margaret Bowler.
Age 29.
Face 12. Also commemorated within the Napier War Memorial Centre and on an LRDG memorial within the New Zealand SAS camp at Papakura.

TROOPER DOUGLAS ATHOL **DAVISON** [263694] NORTH AUCKLAND REGIMENT AND LRDG (R.2 PATROL, A SQN)

Doug Davison was born on 29 July 1921 at the isolated logging and sheep-farming hamlet of Aomarama-Whatoro near Dargaville on the North Island of New Zealand. Here his Australian father and New Zealand mother owned a 458-acre farm nestled amongst 60,000 acres of bush. Their four sons and four daughters, of which Davison was the second oldest, therefore had an active upbringing. Although he enlisted into the 1st Battalion, North Auckland Regiment, New Zealand Infantry Brigade, in October 1940 he was working on the land at the time. As this was a reserved occupation his service, which amongst other things consisted of Commando training, was interrupted by periods of unpaid leave during which he continued his farm duties. However, in April 1943 he joined the 9th Reinforcement Draft and embarked for the Middle East the following month. Arriving in Egypt on 11 June he was posted to the 31st Battalion, New Zealand Infantry, but volunteered for A Squadron of the Long Range Desert Group just five days later.

After Jeep and mule training in Palestine, Davison embarked at Haifa on 21 September 1943 for operations in the Dodecanese, landing on Leros as a member of R.2 Patrol the following day. Here

he and his comrades held the coastal battery on the heights of Mount Scumbardo before being included in a combined A and B Squadron party tasked to assault the enemy-held island of Levita. Encountering stiffer resistance than expected the majority were killed or captured, Davison and Trooper Johnnie Bowler, both members of Corporal James Gill's patrol, being posted missing in action (see Bowler's entry above for details of this operation). The pair had volunteered to go back to the squadron's landing place, Davison's father later summarising all known information for Bill, his other son serving abroad:

Six of them were holding a position on the extreme right of a long low range of hill country covered with huge boulders and bush, cut up with deep narrow gorges. Gill's party about a mile from main crowd (Lt Sutherland's). Having not heard from Sutherland for eight or nine hours and they could see that they were going to be cut off Doug set off to find out whether they should stay to the coast or get out whilst they could. Gill walked him from where he was getting along alright almost to objective, was sure then that he had got there as he could see Sutherland's position from where he was. Gill and party hid up for four days before giving themselves up but on meeting the others a week later found out Doug was not accounted for. Germans told Gill that they had found Johnnie Bowler dead and gave Gill pay book. Germans were all over the island but did not say anything about Doug's body. Gill thinks he must have been killed near Sutherland's camp – Cemetery with five of the boys' grave when Gill was there – thinks Germans may have found Doug's body and buried since and information not been sent out. That is his account. I asked him to give his personal opinion whether good or bad. I have written to [illegible but believed to be George Knowles] who was supposed to have last seen Doug. Well Bill it looks black but I still do not think these boys are correct. I have a forlorn hope because they are convinced he could not get off the island. But Capt Tinker wrote to me and said that two nights running motor launches went to the island and put the night in searching. If motor launches could get there without being seen other craft (Greek) may have shipped into the little harbour for other reasons close to where Doug was last seen and he might have got away. He was so good in the dark he may have even found a boat there, it's almost a certainty to have been some round that harbour and got out to sea and been picked up by Greeks. He was learning to go by the stars when he wrote to us … Mum feels the news about Doug. It has been a long awful time [Davison family collection].

The fact that Gill saw five graves is relevant. Gunner Sam Federmann and Trooper Hector Mallett are known to have died on Levita whilst Trooper Archibald Penhall died of wounds in Athens. The only other LRDG casualties were Bowler and Davison. However, the New Zealand Minister of Defence wrote to Davison's father three years later:

On making investigations, I have ascertained that a Graves Unit visited the Island of Levita in February, 1946. The burial place of one New Zealand soldier was found (see Mallett's entry under Rhodes War Cemetery, Greece) but, unfortunately, the graves of your boy and another soldier also presumed to have lost his life on Levita were not located [family collection].

The presumption is that Davison fell into a rocky crevice and was lost at sea, his date of death being officially recorded as 23 October 1943 even though Bowler's is recorded as the 24th and though both men left the main party together on this later date. Davison's sister, Jeanie, later wrote:

Doug – fit, energetic, the brightest of us all, did not come home. His life was cut short at 22 years of age, on a little island in the Dodecanese, about 70 miles off the coast of Turkey. Before going to war he had known only hard work. Earlier, in his teens he had been, along with Bill, cross-cutting kauri logs in the Mangakahia Valley. From there he went to work for a dairy farmer, getting up early to milk a big herd of cows. Finishing milking in the evening was not the complete job. In between milkings he hand-sowed fertiliser, did fencing and many other jobs …

Harking back to when we were kids! Doug was our leader. How he could catch eels with his hands! I know it's hard to believe, but he did. They weren't large eels. He would rub silt on his hands, stand quietly in a pool, with water about up to his knees til an eel came near. As quick as lightning, he would grab it and throw it as far as he could, up on the grass, for us to knock on its head [memoirs of Jeanie Margaret Subritzky].

Son of William and Elizabeth Davison of Whatoro, Auckland, New Zealand – Younger brother of Bill

Davison who served as a driver in an ammunition company – Older brother of Jeanie, George, Jack, twins Mavis and Heather, and Mearl.
Age 22.
Face 12. Also commemorated at the Auckland War Memorial Museum and as 'Davidson' at both the Kaihu Valley War Memorial Hall and the Northern Wairoa Returned and Services Association at Dargaville. In 2013 members of his family placed a plaque, engraved with his name and date of death, on Levita.

PRIVATE AUGUSTUS GEORGE EVANS MM [4976245] SHERWOOD FORESTERS AND SBS (P PATROL, S DET)

Known to his family as George, Augustus Evans was born on 20 July 1920 in London as the second of four children. Within a few years his father, a railway worker, was transferred north and the family moved to Derby where Evans attended Nottingham Road School in Chaddesden. Having worked at Ley's Malleable Castings as a mechanic he attempted to join the Royal Navy. Ruled out due to colour-blindness he enlisted into the Sherwood Foresters at the beginning of January 1939 and joined the 2nd Battalion. Having been briefly posted to Palestine with the 1st Battalion that August he was working as the Sergeants' Mess waiter in Cyprus when war was declared the following month.

Early in 1942 the battalion moved to Egypt where it converted to a motorised infantry role and moved up to the Western Desert. Evans was subsequently posted missing in action as of 20 June 1942 before being reported as a prisoner of war in Italian hands. His service record notes that he was located in Cairo having escaped, the citation for his immediate Military Medal, recommended by MI9's Middle East representative, covering the intervening period:

Pte Evans was a driver in the B Echelon of his battalion at Tobruk. His truck was destroyed by German fire. On 21/06/42, when they were told to disperse and try to escape, he went with a dozen others eastwards along the coast.

One evening they were walking along the coast when enemy sentries on a rock above spotted them and started to throw hand grenades. The Englishmen scattered. Evans went into the sea and swam across to another beach. As the enemy were on a cliff they could not get down to the same beach. Pte Grundy of the Welch Regiment did the same.

Between Bardia and Sollum Pte Evans lost Pte Grundy when they had another brush with enemy sentries.

He continued alone along the coast, travelling in the early morning or late evening until he reached the battle lines.

Here he remained for a fortnight west of Tel el Kisa under the artillery fire of the Australians. He lived on scraps of food that he could find and water from disused vehicles. One night three Arabs gave him food and water.

At the end of August he made his way through to the Australian lines, where he was able to tell them what he had seen of their artillery fire. They said his information was very valuable to them.

Pte Evans not only escaped alone, but showed the most remarkable endurance. He walked slowly on through the enemy, confident that he would arrive in the end, and finally, by remaining under Australian artillery fire in spite of great privation, was able to bring back useful information. A courageous effort [*London Gazette* 20/11/42, WO 373/62].

Local papers reported that Evans had walked 640 kilometres over a nine-week period. Most of his battalion had been captured and his subsequent postings before volunteering for the Special Boat Squadron in early 1944 are unknown. He attended parachute training at Ramat David in Palestine during February 1944 although he injured his ankle on his fifth descent on 1 March and therefore could not complete the course.

On 7 April 1944 Evans was captured during OPERATION FIREATER with the other members of what is now referred to as the 'Alimnia Patrol': having embarked *LS.24*, a caique of the Levant Schooner Flotilla (LSF), the patrol reached the island of Alimnia and went ashore to recce whilst the crew rested. German records indicate that a V-Mann, reportedly a local in their pay, had warned their command on Rhodes that British 'commandos' were in the area. As a result Kustenjager Brandenburgers (German coastal Special Forces) entered the harbour at approximately 0730hrs, capturing all but one of the crew after a brief firefight in which two Greeks were wounded. A fourth Greek crewman was ashore and remained undetected. Meanwhile, the SBS patrol heard the gunfire, a local fisherman later testifying that he was approached by a British 'corporal' who asked the crew of his vessel to help him and his comrades reach safety. Having accepted the soldier boarded and guided them to a point farther up the east coast where his four colleagues were collected. Setting sail north-easterly towards the nearest point of neutral Turkey, a German vessel fired a shot across their bows and boarded. The five SBS were subsequently found under a tarpaulin (WO 361/1089). A German version of events, written by Randolf Kugler, appeared in *Das Landungswesen in Deutschland seit 1900* (German Amphibious Operations Since 1900):

On 7 April 1944 the first operation of the Kustenjager was started as Operation Munchhausen against the islands of Calchi and Alimnia. The platoon of the Kustenjager company was on four engineer landing boats under Leutenant Glaser and on the motor boat *Malona*, escorted by boats of the 21 Submarine Chaser Flotilla. Calchi was found free of enemies but on nearing Alimnia a camouflaged motor sailing vessel of some 20ts [tons] was spotted behind Greek caikis. Five men in British uniforms jumped on the pier and Lt Glaser ordered to open the fire. Two British [*sic* – Greeks] were wounded and the rest surrendered. One of the Kustenjager had observed that one of the British [most likely Telegraphist Ronald Carpenter, RN] had thrown a bag overboard. This was recovered later and it was found that it held signal books until 15 April 44 [and Carpenter's personal diary]. Five enemies were taken prisoner [the crew]. The schooner *LS.24* was captured with 20mm AA, two MG 13.2mm, two MG 7.7mm and two radio sets. The boat met a Greek caiki on the north-east cape of Alimnia which was stopped and searched. In its hold another five British were discovered and taken prisoner. In all two British officers, five men and three Greek were taken prisoners. The schooner was taken over by the Kustenjager and named *Erika*.

Having convinced the Germans that they had forced the Greek fishermen to take them aboard, the captured patrol and LSF crew were taken to Rhodes that evening (see photo above). Here the other ranks were kept in the town gaol whilst Captain 'Bill' Blyth of the SBS and Sub-Lieutenant Allan Tuckey, Captain of *LS.24*, were separated from the group and driven to headquarters for interrogation. The next day Blyth was flown to Athens and then onto Germany, where, although a signal was received to pass him to the SD for 'execution', he remained until liberated. He died in the 1970s apparently without making any record of the events of April 1944.

The other ranks were flown to the Abwehr headquarters in Salonika on 11 April where they were interrogated 'in depth'. Notes from one such interrogation record that Evans merely stated he had joined the SBS two months before capture and that his parachute course had been in Palestine. The following day British sources were already reporting that 'German wireless claims liquidation British Commando patrol in Rhodes' (WO 201/802). On the 26th a top-secret telex was sent from the Wehrmacht's Army Group E noting: 'Further interrogation of British Alimnia Commandos without result. Request decision on whether the prisoners now to be handed over to SD' (MOD report, 1986). The reply was received from

Commander-in-Chief South East the following day; 'the prisoners are to be handed over to the SD for interrogation if they see fit and subsequent Sonderbehandlung ['special treatment'] in accordance with the Führerbefehl' (Hitler's 'Commando Order' – see Appendix 2, User's Guide, for full details).

Although their date of death was officially recorded as 7 April 1944 it is now assumed that the men were murdered by the SD in late April or early May, the precise date and location being unknown. Tuckey and three of his Greek seamen were also murdered, probably alongside the SBS men, whilst Carpenter and Coxswain Lisgaris, Royal Hellenic Navy attached to the LSF, were detained until around 4 June when they were also murdered. The discovery of Carpenter's diary with references to bases in neutral Turkey brought the 'Alimnia Patrol' to Hitler's personal attention and was probably the reason that the pair's murder was delayed. *LS.24* was later reported to have been 'taken to Cos and given to a German Naval Officer by way of compensation for the loss of his wife and children in a British air raid' (WO 218/108).

Although Lieutenant Thanos of the Greek Sacred Squadron and Sergeant Henderson of the SBS were immediately sent to the area to investigate the patrol's disappearance it appears no real consideration was given to the possibility of their murder. It was only the refusal of Tuckey's family to accept incomplete answers that led to the involvement of the Foreign Office and British war crimes investigators. Kurt Waldheim, Secretary General to the UN and President of Austria, was later alleged to have questioned the patrol, interrogation notes in the Washington National Archives bearing the initial 'W'. However, in 1986 an MOD investigation team concluded that the decision to murder the men had been taken whilst he was on leave in Austria. The SAS War Crimes Investigation Team had also looked into the case:

> It can be proved that von Harling, as Chief Intelligence Officer of OB Sued Ost gave instructions for the liquidation of the prisoners. There is also documentary evidence that Strnad and Merrem, two of his IOs [Intelligence Officers] drafted the signals for him, which he subsequently signed [Ministry of Defence report, 1986].

Major 'Bill' Barkworth, MBE, the team commander, wrote to HQ Germany in January 1949:

> Proceedings were not instituted against v Harling and the others who might be accused in this case because the case was not sufficiently far advanced by 15 August 48 to allow it to be submitted for trial before 1 Sept 48, the date by which the last war crimes cases produced by War Crimes Group were supposed to have begun [MOD report, 1986].

Further SASWCIT correspondence record that: 'von Harling refused to answer any questions at the time of his arrest though undoubtedly has the necessary information. Major Barkworth reports him to be a very unpleasant type' (MOD report, 1986). The contemporary investigation had produced no leads although it was noted:

> Capt Blyth further says that he has belief that they [the SBS patrol members] were later (about 16.4.44) at or near Mooseburg Transit Camp [in Germany]. The IRRC [International Red Cross Committee] at Geneva, in reply to an enquiry from this office as to whether they were at Mooseburg Transit Camp, state that there is no trace of them as prisoners of war [WO 361/1089].

Only son of Augustus and Ada Evans (née Salisbury) of Dorchester Avenue, Chaddesden, Derby, who were presented with his Military Medal by His Majesty the King on 26 November 1946 – His niece, Holly Kendrick, wrote: 'His mother never gave up hope of him coming home and when she was dying in 1950 she was delirious and thought he had come back' (personal correspondence, 2009).
Age 23.
Memorial Addenda. Also commemorated within St Paul's Church, Athens, and erroneously on the Alamein Memorial (Column 66).

Gunner Raymond Walter JONES MM [1469628] Royal Artillery
and SBS (P Patrol, S Det)

Ray Jones, sometimes known to his comrades as 'Jonah', was born on 6 November 1922 at Aston in Birmingham where he worked as a die caster. Having been rejected by the Royal Navy due to colour-blindness in June 1939 he saw his friend Ray Nixon, who had also been turned away, on leaving the recruitment centre. Nixon persuaded him that they should join the Royal Artillery together, both later transferring to the SBS. Jones, claiming to be two years older than he really was, found himself posted to various training regiments before embarking for the Middle East with the 105/119th Field Regiment that November. Serving in the Western Desert he was wounded in action twice, once in June 1941 and again that December, before being posted to Cyprus in April 1942. He volunteered for the Special Boat Squadron in April 1943 and subsequently reported to the unit's camp at Athlit on the Palestinian coast (personal correspondence with Jones' brother-in-law, Sid Cruxton, 2010).

Having tested coastal defences along the Syrian coastline during May, Jones deployed on Operation Albumen: tasked with destroying Axis aircraft on Crete that posed a threat to the Allied invasion fleet that was soon to pass en route to Sicily, the operational party of three officers and fourteen other ranks embarked *ML 361* at Bardia on 22 June 1943. In the early hours of the following morning they landed at Cape Kokinoxos and lay up for the day in a wadi. That evening they split up to carry out their tasks, Patrol C, which Jones was assigned to, setting off for the airfield at Kastelli Pediada. The citation that accompanied the immediate award of his Military Medal takes up the narrative:

> This man was, together with Lt A Lassen, responsible for the diversionary attack on Kastelli Pediada aerodrome in Crete, on the night 4 July 1943. Passing through formidable perimeter defences he bluffed his way past three German sentries guarding Stukas, but was fired upon and the alarm was raised. Caught in the light of flares and ground searchlights he was subjected to very heavy machine-gun and rifle fire from close range and forced to withdraw. Half an hour later he again entered the airfield in spite of the fact that all guards had been trebled and the area was being patrolled and swept by searchlights. Great difficulty was experienced in penetrating towards the target and the enemy, reinforced by men from the eastern side of the aerodrome drove him into the middle of an anti-aircraft battery where he was fired upon heavily from three sides. Ignoring this danger he placed bombs on a caterpillar tractor nearby, which was destroyed. The increasing numbers of enemy in that area finally forced him to withdraw. It was entirely due to the diversion carried out by this man that planes and petrol were destroyed on the eastern side of the airfield, since he drew off all the guards from that area. Throughout the attack and during the very arduous approach march the keenness, determination and personal disregard of danger shown by this man were of the highest order. (It is requested that details of the above operations should not be published owing to their secrecy) [*London Gazette* 36168 dated 14/09/43, WO 373/46].

Lassen and Jones became separated on their withdrawal from the airfield but made contact with each other two days later and reached the rendezvous. After a brief contact with the enemy, which resulted in the loss of one officer, all patrols were picked up by motor launch in the early hours of 12 July (see Lieutenant Ken Lamonby's entry under Suda Bay War Cemetery, Greece, for further details, and that of Major Andy Lassen, VC, MC**, under Argenta Gap War Cemetery, Italy, within this volume).

It is not known what operations Jones took part in during the second half of 1943. He was captured during Operation Fireater on 7 April 1944 and murdered on an unknown date (see Private Augustus Evans' entry above for full details). German interrogation resulted in very little, his dress being described as:

> Thick woollen khaki battledress with distinctive badge over upper left breast pocket (parachute with two wings). Lightweight uniform as weather protection. In response to the description of a cap captured on an earlier raid

(khaki-brown cap with distinctive cockade – vertical sword with wings half way down, underneath a scroll with the woven inscription – Who Dares Wins) he stated that it was part of the regular uniform [MOD report, 1986].

Son of Bertram and Beatrice Jones of Yew Tree Road, Aston, Birmingham – Younger brother of William Jones. His Military Medal was presented to his family on 3 December 1946. After the war Nixon visited Jones' mother only to be turned away and informed that if it hadn't been for him then Jones would not have lost his life (personal correspondence with Sid Cruxton, 2010).
Age 21.
Face 2. Also commemorated within St Paul's Church, Athens, and Birmingham's Book of Remembrance.

BOMBARDIER JOHN **JOUGHIN** [1472411] ROYAL ARTILLERY AND SBS (M DET)

Known to his family as Jack or Jackie, John Joughin was born on 24 July 1912 at Peel on the Isle of Man. In June 1939, whilst working as a car sales man in Herne Hill, south-east London, he joined the 36th Battery, 12th Light Anti-Aircraft Regiment (11th Battalion, London Regiment), Royal Artillery (TA), at Penton Street. Over the next two years he took trade tests to qualify as a motor mechanic, was promoted to lance-bombardier in October 1940, to bombardier in April 1941, and was appointed acting lance-sergeant that June. The following month he embarked for the Middle East serving in Iraq and Kuwait with Paiforce until the beginning of May 1943 when, having volunteered for the SAS, he was posted to M Detachment, Special Boat Squadron. Reporting for parachute course No.43 at Ramat David on the 21st he subsequently trained in the area of Athlit on the Palestinian coast in preparation for operations in the Aegean.

That September Italy signed an armistice and the SBS and LRDG rapidly embarked at Haifa to seize islands in the Dodecanese from her surrendered garrisons before German troops could do so. Having taken up residence on Samos detachments of both units were relieved by the Royal West Kent Regiment on 1 October 1943 and proceeded to the peaceful island of Calino. The hope was that this would become Raiding Forces HQ for the autumn season. However, having cleared their new billets the men awoke in the early hours of the 3rd to find German forces invading the nearby island of Cos and the following day they were ordered to fall back to Leros which was also being bombed. Rapidly requisitioning local vessels, both units set sail under the cover of darkness and disembarked at Lakki Bay before midnight. By dawn on the 5th the tired men had unloaded their jumble of stores and lay down to sleep. They were still on the dockside at 0900hrs when attacked by German aircraft. Major David Sutherland's report of SBS activities in the Dodecanese between 1 October and 1 December 1943 records that: 'Unfortunately, Capt Belcher and three ORs [other ranks], [No.]30 Commando and Sgt Joughlin SBS were killed when a bomb fell close by them.' This spelling mistake, i.e. 'Joughlin' not Joughin, meant that for many years he was not listed on any SAS Roll of Honour. No.30 Commando's post-operation report adds further detail:

In convoy with several other caiques we made the crossing to Leros without incident, arriving approximately 0200 hours on the 5th where we unloaded all stores, etc., on the dockside. The LRDG and the SBS who had been evacuated from Kalymnos [Calino] were already sleeping alongside their kit on the dockside. We also slept beside our kit and Captain Belcher informed us that we would be awakened at 0430 as there was no danger of bombing. We had just finished breakfast that morning when a reconnaissance plane came over at approximately 0530. We moved away from our kit undercover. At approximately 0615 aircraft were heard approaching. Captain Belcher shouted 'Follow me lads' and started running towards a shelter. All the men went with the exception of McDiarmid and Levy, who were looking for their Bren gun, which had been taken by mistake by a man in the SBS. McDiarmid and Levy were running to retrieve their gun and saw bombs bursting in the direction where Captain Belcher and the men had gone. They had run into a stick of bombs … The raid was severe and it was concentrated on the dockside where all the troops and stores were [WO 218/71 – see also Signalman 'Pusher' Wheeldon's entry under Leros War Cemetery, Greece].

Only son of John and Jessie Joughin (née Watterson) of Lyndale Avenue, Peel, Isle of Man.
Age 31.
Face 2. Also commemorated on his parents' headstone within Peel Cemetery, this stating that he was 'interred on the island of Leros'.

Lance-sergeant George William John MILLER MM [7914293] 3rd County of London Yeomanry, 1st SAS and SBS (P Patrol, S Det)

Known to his comrades as 'Lofty', George Miller was born on 25 May 1920 in Brixton, south London, later living a short distance away in Camberwell. Having worked as a clerk he enlisted into the Royal Armoured Corps in July 1940 and was posted to the 52nd (Heavy) Training Regiment. After serving with other training regiments at both Bovington and Catterick he spent much of the period between that October and the following July in hospital for an unknown reason. He subsequently embarked in late 1941 and joined the 3rd County of London Yeomanry (Sharpshooters) in the Middle East early in 1942. Promoted to lance-corporal that November he volunteered for 1st SAS on 21 December having relinquished his rank in order to do so.

After a spell at the Middle East Infantry Training Centre to gain further experience Miller was posted to the Special Boat Squadron the day it formed on 19 March 1943. He subsequently attended parachute course No.26 at Ramat David later that month. During May he was involved in exercises that tested defences along the Syrian coast, then training at the SBS camp at Athlit in Palestine.

In June 1943 Miller and Captain Harold Chevalier joined the Levant Schooner Flotilla's *LS.1* at Cyprus before it moored on the Turkish coast in preparation for recces of the Dodecanese Islands. Approaching that of Sirina during darkness the vessel was holed by a reef and quickly sank. All aboard reached the rocky coast and took stock, Miller and his officer exploring the island and collecting rainwater whilst the remainder fished using a sewing kit that Chevalier had about his person. Having discovered the only inhabitants were a fisherman's family living in a stone hut the men took up residence with a flock of sheep in a nearby cave. On the ninth day a Greek vessel approached, its crew landing to trade with the family. These men were half hijacked, half persuaded, to take the party to Marmaris on the Turkish coast. After passing close to Alimnia, an island later integral to Miller's fate, they took on supplies at the neutral port before reaching the LSF base at Beirut, much to the surprise of its staff who believed the vessel had been lost with all hands. Miller subsequently returned to the temporary SBS HQ at Zahle,

east of Beirut, until redeploying to the islands with S Detachment that September.

Miller was promoted to corporal on 18 November 1943 whilst on Leros. Captain 'Bill' Blyth's report on the island's subsequent battle notes: 'The patrols of Sgt Workman and Cpl Flavell carried out every task allotted to them without hesitation, although badly in need of sleep. In particular Cpl Dryden, Tpr [*sic*] Miller 293, and Tpr Laverick set examples to their keenness and cheerfulness and devotion to duty.' After the island fell Miller repeatedly returned to pick up evading soldiers, amongst them Colonel Guy Prendergast, DSO, Captain Dick Croucher, Captain Ron Tinker and four other members of the LRDG. These operations, carried out from Bodrum in neutral Turkey, were facilitated by *HSL 2542* under the command of Sub-Lieutenant Allan Tuckey, a man whose own fate would be closely tied to that of Miller's. Working mainly with Corporal Ivor Flavell in a Folbot, he towed numerous evaders to the awaiting HSL in inflatables. Having been appointed lance-sergeant in March 1944 the pair were awarded Military Medals for these actions later that month:

> For conspicuous gallantry and devotion to duty whilst engaged in evacuating British troops from Leros and in re-embarking British patrols from Mykonos and Cos.
>
> This man on the night 20th/21st November, 1943, rowed ashore one sergeant and one Greek civilian and landed them safely at a point south of Canna del Despota on the east coast of Leros in spite of heavy surf. Although he had fought with distinction throughout the battle of Leros and managed to escape after capitulation Trooper Miller immediately volunteered to assist in the evacuation. He returned to the same place on the night 21st/22nd November, 1943, and contacted and successfully embarked by rowing boat three officers and four other ranks, amongst whom was the Commanding Officer of Raiding Forces, Aegean [Prendergast]. This necessitated three separate journeys inshore in a bad sea [at a point on the east coast of Monte Tortore opposite the island of Pega]. He again returned on the night 22nd/23rd November, 1943 and together with an NCO [Flavell], landed at a pre-arranged point on the west coast of the island close to enemy defended positions. Once on shore, he patrolled about the landing place making his presence known by shouting and only finally returned to the ship when he was certain that there were no British in the area to be re-embarked. Together with the NCO he was responsible for contacting British patrols on Mykonos on the night 25th/26th November 1943 and on Cos on the night of 28th/29th November 1943. In both cases the re-embarkation was completed quickly in spite of bad weather due to the skill and determination shown by this man. Throughout this series of operations, the conduct of this man left nothing to be desired [*London Gazette* 23/03/44].

Miller was captured during OPERATION FIREATER on 7 April 1944 and murdered sometime after (see Private Augustus Evans' entry above for full details). German interrogation notes merely state; 'despite repeated questioning, refused to answer any questions of a military nature' (MOD report, 1986).

Son of Mr and Mrs G. R. Miller (née Barton) of Lewis Trust Buildings, Warner Road, Camberwell, south London, who were presented with their son's Military Medal on 29 October 1946.
Age 23.
Face 1. Also commemorated within St Paul's Church, Athens.

Private Leo Gerald <u>RICE</u> [5955044] Bedfordshire and Hertfordshire Regiment, No.7 Commando, Middle East Commando, 1st SAS and SBS (P Patrol, S Det)

'Digger' Rice, as he was known to his comrades, was born on 29 September 1920 at Maryborough in Victoria, Australia, but left home and moved to Wellbury Park, Hitchin in Hertfordshire. Having worked as a handy man he enlisted into the Bedfordshire and Hertfordshire Regiment in May 1940 at St Albans and was posted to the 70th (Home Defence) Battalion. After training he volunteered for the 3rd Special Service Battalion in December 1940, being nominally transferred to No.7 Commando when the battalion was retitled as such at the end of January 1941. Disembarking at Suez in Egypt in early March as A Battalion, Layforce, the unit carried out a largely abortive raid on Bardia along the Libyan coast on the night of 19–20 April. On their return the disgruntled men were held aboard HMS *Glengyle* until the beginning of May when they were allowed ashore at Alexandria.

Later that month A and D Battalions disembarked on Crete to help in the evacuation of Commonwealth troops after the German invasion. They subsequently formed part of the rearguard, fighting a running battle en route to the embarkation point on the south coast. Rice was one of those lucky enough to be taken off to Egypt, the majority of his comrades going into captivity. When Layforce was disbanded that July he was posted to the Middle East Commando Depot at Geneifa. This was subsequently reorganised as the 1st Special Service Regiment in mid 1942, Rice being posted to B Squadron. He volunteered for 1st SAS at nearby Kabrit on 26 September 1942 and was posted to No.1 Special Boat Section the following January, this having been absorbed into D Squadron, 1st SAS. On 19 March the Regiment was restructured, A, B and C Squadrons forming the Special Raiding Squadron (1st SAS) and D becoming the Special Boat Squadron (1st SAS).

Captain Walter Milner-Barry of the SBS recalled that he took a patrol to the island of Chios at the end of September 1943:

> The objective was a German OP of four men, which was to be wiped out and prisoners taken. No maps were available unfortunately so we had to rely on a naval chart which, of course, though strong on the coast, showed nothing of the interior, except hills as they appeared to the sailor from the sea. Left after dark [of the 28th] in an ML with a very charming captain whose name I forget, taking Sibbert and Rice, as well as Morris and my own patrol [see Private Thomas Morris' entry under Suda Bay War Cemetery, Greece] …
>
> The plan of attack was that we would go in about 8.00pm. I would have liked to make it later, but had we done so we could never have got back to the ship in time …
>
> Landed on a very rough beach with a steep ascent, after Morris and Rice had selected a suitable landing place in the Folbot, and marched on a compass bearing over very hilly country, though cultivated whenever possible and interspersed with wadis [IWM Documents.16758 – Private Papers of Captain W. J. Milner-Barry].

Having found no enemy post the patrol was extracted the following night. Rice was subsequently wounded in action on 17 November, either on Samos or on Leros, although there are no further details. He was captured during Operation Fireater on 7 April 1944 and subsequently murdered (see Private Augustus Evans' entry above for full details). German interrogation notes merely confirm that he had been in action on Samos the previous October and that he had missed several operations due to malaria (Ministry of Defence report, 1986).

Son of Leo and Monica Rice of Mentone Parade, Mentone, Victoria, Australia – Brother of Paul and Suzette.

Age 23.

Face 5. Also commemorated within St Paul's Church, Athens.

SIGNALMAN AYLMER KNOX **SPARROW** [2360566] SOUTH NOTTINGHAMSHIRE HUSSARS, ROYAL CORPS OF SIGNALS, 1ST SAS AND SBS (S DET)

'Spadge' Sparrow was born to Irish parents on 15 January 1919 in Sneinton, Nottingham. Having attended King William's College on the Isle of Man, where he was a member of the OTC from 1934 to 1936, he worked as an apprentice in the wool trade. Enlisting into the Royal Corps of Signals in July 1939 he declared his interests as reading, tennis, golf and rugby, whilst his service record notes that he had previously held a commission in the South Nottinghamshire Hussars. He subsequently served with the BEF in France as a dispatch rider from the end of January 1940 until 28 May when he was evacuated.

Arriving in Iraq in June 1942 Sparrow served with Paiforce until volunteering for 1st SAS on 2 January 1943. The following month he was noted as having arrived in the Middle East with the Regiment and was officially posted to the Special Boat Squadron on 3 August. However, he is known to have been serving with the SBS from at least April, attending parachute course No.43 at Ramat David in Palestine during May. Dick Holmes, MM, a former member of S Detachment, recalled that Sparrow 'hated the name Aylmer', hence the nickname 'Spadge' (personal correspondence, 2009).

That November the SBS fought German airborne forces on Leros before evading to various anchorages on, or not far from, the Turkish coast. Sparrow's group found itself on the island of Samos and it was here that he was killed in action on 17 November 1943:

> On a sunny afternoon we were subjected to an attack by several squadrons of Stukas who obviously had identified their target. Initially I sheltered in a slit trench some distance from the house in which we were billeted but during a short interlude I rushed into the house to retrieve my rucksack which contained some valuables and spare ammo and food that could become very useful in the near future. George Munro and Sparrow were lying on the floor. I assumed they were both sleeping. I yelled at them to get the hell out of the house, grabbed my Bergen and raced outside just as another Stuka attack started. I scrambled over a low brick wall about 20 yards away from the house and watched as the building suffered several more direct hits. When the raid was over several other members of J Patrol entered the house to collect their belongings and reported that George Munro had been killed [see Sergeant George Munro's entry under Rhodes War Cemetery, Greece] and all that remained of Sparrow was a solitary boot with a foot in it … A runner in a class of his own [he was] able to run the mile in under five minutes drunk or sober [personal correspondence with Dick Holmes, MM, 2009].

Although Sparrow is commemorated on the Athens Memorial to the missing there is a possibility, which Holmes himself believes, that Sparrow's remains were interred in the Unknown Soldier's grave next to Munro within Rhodes War Cemetery. *The Nottingham Evening Post* later reported:

> The Notts RFC [Rugby Football Club] have lost another valuable young member in Aylmer Knox Sparrow, of the

Royal Corps of Signals, who has been killed in action …

In addition to playing for Notts, he assisted the Notts Public Schoolboys, and was considered as one of the most promising youngsters Notts had in membership in their last full season [3 December 1943].

Son of Dr Henry and Mary Sparrow (née Martin) of St Stephens Lodge, Sneinton, Nottinghamshire. Age 24.
Face 4.

Corporal Johannes Daniel VAN RENSBURG [SR/598906V] Southern Rhodesia Light Battery, King's Royal Rifle Corps and LRDG (S.1 Patrol, A Sqn)

'Ginger' van Rensburg was born in the Transvaal on 9 February 1919 but by the time he joined the army was working in Salisbury, Rhodesia, as an apprentice carpenter for W. R. Siebert. Enlisting at the King George VI Barracks at the beginning of August 1941 he was initially posted to an infantry training company (service number X1357). However, a few days later he transferred to the Southern Rhodesia Light Battery that was being trained rigorously during this period (service number RH/6857925). He was promoted to lance-bombardier the following February and in August 1942 to bombardier. That October he attended a Commando course at Gwelo, qualifying with a grade 'A' and in January 1943 was appointed lance-sergeant. However, he reverted to the rank of lance-bombardier before passing through the Imperial Trans-shipment Centre at Clairwood, Durban, en route to Egypt. Here he volunteered for the Long Range Desert Group and was nominally enlisted into the King's Royal Rifle Corps with the rank of rifleman. The Group spent that summer training in Palestine, in the hills of modern-day Lebanon and on the coast of what is now Israel.

The LRDG proceeded to the Aegean theatre in September 1943, van Rensburg serving as the signaller in Captain Alan Redfern's patrol that sailed from Leros to Simi on the 24th. Redfern's post-operation report outlines how it was to assist with the island's defence:

Occupy OP at opposite end of island to SBS detachment. To ascertain position of cable from Simi to Rhodes. To observe and report on all shipping, air and other activity in vicinity of Rhodes. To endeavour to persuade an Italian to go to Rhodes to obtain information [WO 218/91 – see Redfern's own entry under Leros War Cemetery, Greece].

After completing these tasks the patrol was taken to Leros in time for the German naval and airborne assault that resulted in its fall:

Captain Olivey then immobilised one of the two remaining naval guns [at Clidi Heights] and Rflm van Rensburg the other. At 0845 [on 17 November 1943] Captain Olivey called us together and confirmed that the island had surrendered. He told us to hide out all day then make our way to an RV point where he would meet with us that night. There were fifteen of us and, after Captain Olivey failed to turn up for two nights, we agreed to split up and make our own way. Skinny Evans, van Rensburg and myself [Don Coventry] from Rhodesia, Signalman Watson who was in S.1 Patrol, and three New Zealanders, Munro, MacLeod and Ellis, were taken off six nights later by an aircraft rescue launch. Jack Rupping got off in a fishing boat seventeen days later. The rest ended up POWs [LRDG Newsletter No.49 of 1993].

On returning to Palestine van Rensburg qualified as a parachutist at No.4 Middle East Training School, Ramat David, and was promoted to lance-corporal. At the beginning of April 1944 the LRDG moved to Italy, one squadron at any time being tasked by SOE's Force 266 to work in the Adriatic in support of SBS and Partisan operations. From late June until August he was a member of small party from R.1 Patrol that subsequently carried out shipping watch from the island of Ist, he himself rowing over to the nearby island of Silba alone to collect information before returning to the squadron's Advance HQ on Dugi island (OPERATION ALLAH, WO 218/92).

On 26 September 1944 a composite patrol of eleven other ranks of Z.1 Patrol, van Rensburg from S.1 and two fitters, all under the command of Captain John Olivey, MC*, landed at Katakolo on the west coast of the Peloponnese for OPERATION TOWANBUCKET. It was tasked with Jeep-borne reconnaissance for the Special Boat Service and to assist the RAF Regiment in defensive tasks. On 1 October it transported SBS patrols to collect members of a fascist security battalion who wished to surrender, subsequently moving these men to the rear throughout the night. In the early hours of the 2nd the patrol marched them from TOWANBUCKET's forward HQ to a school hostel. Around midday the patrol was sorting through their surrendered arms when: 'one rifle accidentally went off, shooting [Acting] Sgt van Rensburg in the left breast. He died shortly before the MO [Medical Officer] arrived' (WO 218/92). He was buried the next morning by the RAF Regiment's padre in a local cemetery (grid 0664811) on the outskirts of Patras with Z.1 Patrol in attendance.

There are no known next of kin details although a D. C. van Rensburg also served in the wartime Southern Rhodesia Light Battery.

Age 25.

Face 14. It is unclear why van Rensburg's body was not recovered.

CORPORAL GEORGE WILLIAM **WALSHAW** [7956581] ROYAL ARMOURED CORPS, 1ST SAS AND SBS (S DET)

George Walshaw, the son of a clock repairer, was born on 14 September 1906 in the parish of Potternewton, Leeds, where he married Beatrice Adelene Pratten in July 1931. Having worked as an insurance clerk he enlisted into the Royal Armoured Corps in March 1942 and was posted to the 51st Training Regiment. That September he was re-posted to the 52nd Training Regiment and having sailed from Glasgow to Durban disembarked in the Middle East on New Year's Eve. After a period as a clerk he volunteered for 1st SAS on 20 January 1943 and was posted to the Special Boat Squadron on its formation two months later. He was promoted to lance-corporal the same day and to corporal in April. He continued his clerk duties within the squadron and having been requested by signal both he and his typewriter embarked at Famagusta on 23 October for Castelrosso.

Although Walshaw is officially recorded as having been killed in action on the island of Leros on 17 November 1943 Captain 'Bill' Blyth's report states that this was on the 12th, soon after German parachutists had begun to land:

In the meantime three MG 15s were withdrawn from their positions and in the process, Cpl Walshaw was sniped through the neck and died immediately …

At 1000hrs on the 15th Nov. SQMS was ordered with four men for the following tasks: 1. Locate and bury Cpl Walshaw …

This patrol at 1800 hours, with all tasks completed, returned and reported that they had buried Cpl Walshaw at MR 06114215' [Operational Report No.HQ 1].

Son of Harry and Elizabeth Walshaw of Stratford Terrace, Hunslet – Husband of Beatrice Walshaw of Seahouses, Northumberland.
Age 37.
Face 1.

Bombardier Robert Buchanan YOUNG [SR/598513V] Southern Rhodesia Light Battery Att South African Artillery and LRDG (S.2 Patrol, A Sqn)

Bob Young was born on 23 May 1923 in Glasgow, although his family later migrated to Bulawayo, Southern Rhodesia, where he worked as a clerk. At the beginning of November 1941 he enlisted into the Southern Rhodesia Light Battery and was promoted to lance-bombardier the following August. Between October and December 1942 he undertook a commando and demolitions course, probably at Gwelo under Captain Alan Redfern, from which he qualified with a grade 'A' (see Redfern's own entry under Leros War Cemetery, Greece). In January 1943 he was appointed acting bombardier and that March was attached to the 6th Field Regiment of the South African Artillery, 6th South African Armoured Division, with the rank of temporary bombardier. The bulk of the men selected to form his subunit, the 17th (Rhodesia) Field Battery, were comrades from the Light Battery. In April it embarked at Durban, arriving at Port Tewfik in Egypt at the end of the month. Accommodated at Khatatba Camp, halfway between Alexandria and Cairo, the regiment began training in earnest. However, on 6 November Young volunteered for the Long Range Desert Group and was posted to B Squadron. Having reverted to the rank of private in order to do so he qualified as a parachutist at No.4 METS, Ramat David.

In December 1943 the LRDG returned to Palestine from the Aegean and was restructured, the Rhodesians replacing the New Zealand patrols to form A Squadron. The following March Young arrived in Italy, his patrol carrying out two recces from MTBs in the area between Spille and Himara in Albania during May to July. He subsequently helped guide an attacking force of No.2 Commando, No.9 Commando and No.40 Commando, as well as C Company of the Highland Light Infantry to the coastal town of Spille on the night of 28–29 July (Operation Healing II). The objective was to create a bridgehead in order to supply Partisans, the Raiding Support Regiment providing firepower for the assaulting troops and the defence of the beachhead itself. Having sailed from the Italian port of Monopoli in the early hours of 28 July the force landed just after midnight on the 29th at a beach about a mile south of the town, the RSR establishing an initial beachhead by dawn. A naval bombardment opened up on the enemy at 0500hrs followed by the 75mm guns of the RSR and at 0600hrs the attack went in supported by the regiment's mortars. The Allied force met heavy opposition from the German defenders who had been tipped off by Albanian sympathisers, the post-operation report recording that: 'a notable feature in this fighting was the considerable assistance lent to the enemy garrison by Albanian snipers who inflicted many casualties on our troops' (WO 204/9681). At 1130hrs, with between 25 and 50 per cent of the enemy garrison still holding out, a decision was made to withdraw, one officer and ten other ranks having been killed. The post-operation report noted:

> Gnr Young led the Heavy Weapons Recce Group to a position on the left of the road, instead of the previously selected position on the right of the road. Before landing this group he had taken other people onto both these positions and had decided that a better view could be obtained from the left one. He remained with this group pointing out targets until they were mortared later in the morning [WO 218/92].

On 20 August 1944 Young's S.2 Patrol parachuted into a small DZ near Ravna Gora in northern Yugoslavia near the modern-day Croat/Slovenian border during Operation Adair. Two men landed in trees and one on a roof although this was the least of their troubles – their Bergens had been dropped 'free' and bar their sleeping bags everything within them was ruined. It was ten days before a resupply could be parachuted to the Patrol. Although tasked with reporting enemy shipping targets between Fiume and Novi for the Balkan Air Force it initially neutralised a battery that had been shelling the Partisans and blocked the Novi–Ogulin road. On 19 September Young and Sergeant Charlie Ryan set off for Kraljevica farther up the coast although their guide refused to take them close enough to see anything of use. On 9 October the patrol commander, Lieutenant Cecil Jackson, MM, was summoned to Partisan HQ and informed that he and his men must leave as they had not been granted passports by Tito. They were subsequently evacuated by air from a landing strip near the village of Zemeli on the night of the 11th (WO 218/92). During the operation Young had been promoted to temporary bombardier.

S.2, consisting of Jackson, Ryan, Corporal Dod Moyes, Young and Signalman John Whale left Bari on 24 October 1944 by motor launch and landed on the Albanian coast for Operation Concord, a recce of enemy positions in the area of Lesh in preparation for another Commando attack. It was met Major David Smiley, MC, of SOE who supplied the men with mules and a guide before returning to Italy on the ML. The patrol made its way to Lt-Colonel 'Billy' McLean's HQ at Tomak before reaching N'Darf by nightfall of the 25th. Having completed the recce the men were later joined by the rest of the LRDG detachment but pushed forward alone to recce Snjin. Negotiating marshland they reached the River Drin at 1600hrs on 1 November deciding to cross before dark using inflation aids. The river was 200 yards wide and fast flowing and despite having entered the water together the men were soon in difficulty. Jackson made it across but saw two others floundering. He managed to save Ryan but Young had disappeared and after an unsuccessful search the patrol had no choice but to continue with its tasks. On the 27th Jackson received a report that: 'an English soldier had been found and buried at 170905. I went down and identified the body as that of Pte R B Young who had been lost in the Drin River on 1st November' (WO 218/92). He later 'took a party across to 170905 to erect a cross and name plate on Pte YOUNG's grave.' Jackson was later to receive an MBE for saving Ryan although the citation shows that he had originally been recommended for the George Cross, then the George Medal.

Son of Robert and Elizabeth Young of Birchenough Street, Bulawayo, Southern Rhodesia.
Age 21.
Face 14.

Phaleron War Cemetery, Athens

This cemetery, known locally as the Alimos Allied War Cemetery, was designated as a burial ground during the Greek Civil War. Second World War graves were subsequently concentrated here from all over mainland Greece. It contains 2,028 Commonwealth burials, 596 of which are unidentified. In addition, seventy-four Indian servicemen are commemorated on the Phaleron Cremation Memorial, their remains having been cremated in accordance with their faith.

The cemetery lies 8 kilometres south of the city centre, close to the boundary between the districts of Old Phaleron and Kalamaki. The entrance is opposite the Alimos Marina on the coast road to Vouliaghmen. GPS co-ordinates: Latitude 37.916946, Longitude 23.704694

Rifleman Arthur Samuel BOTHA [RH18000046] Southern Rhodesian Reconnaissance Regiment, King's Royal Rifle Corps and LRDG (Z.1 Patrol, A Sqn)

Artie Botha was born on either 8 February or 8 March 1925. Having studied to be a farmer at Norton, Southern Rhodesia, he enlisted at the King George VI Barracks at Salisbury, presumably in 1943 on reaching the age of 18. Posted to No.2 Training Centre at Bulawayo he joined the Southern Rhodesian Reconnaissance Regiment based at Umtali and in 1944 was attached to the Southern Rhodesian Signals Depot before proceeding to the Middle East (service number X18020). On arrival he nominally enlisted into the King's Royal Rifle Corps and volunteered for the Long Range Desert Group, disembarking in Italy in late July 1944.

On 26 September Botha and ten other members of Z.1 Patrol, Corporal 'Ginger' van Rensburg from S.1 and two attached fitters, all under the command of Captain John Olivey, MC*, landed at Katakolo on the west coast of the Peloponnese for OPERATION TOWANBUCKET (see van Rensburg's entry under Athens Memorial and Corporal Alf Tighe's within this section). Tasked with Jeep-borne reconnaissance for the Special Boat Service, and to assist the RAF Regiment in defensive duties, the men were at the vanguard of the action at Patras and the Corinth Canal before entering Athens and continuing to pursue German forces northwards.

Despite being due to return to Italy political unrest meant the LRDG detachment was ordered to the Greek capital on 24 November. Here it held Iosiphoglion Orphanage, just south-west of the city centre, where a platoon of the Greek National Guard was being recruited and trained. By 5 December ELAS, the communist Greek People's Liberation Army, was engaging British troops on the streets and in the coming days the LRDG cleared road blocks and rescued isolated groups of police. On the 11th Botha drove Olivey into the city for supplies. They were meant to link with another Jeep but a report was received that the pair had been ambushed by ELAS in the area of Omonia Square and that they had been evacuated to the 97th General Hospital:

> Capt. Olivey turned up a seemingly quiet street, but, as the Jeep was being turned round, it was fired on from houses opposite, wounding Botha; Capt. Olivey was also wounded whilst assisting his driver from the Jeep. Both were evacuated to hospital. Botha died shortly after being admitted with a serious wound in the head [WO 218/92].

The following day Captain Armstrong, who had taken command of the detachment, attempted to reach the hospital but was fired on. Botha had already died of wounds, an LRDG summary noting that he was buried in the hospital grounds.

Son of Adriaan and Gorgenia Botha of Hatfield, Salisbury, Southern Rhodesia.
Age 19.
Tho lost to sight, to memory ever dear, his loving family.
Grave 17.A.4. Also commemorated on the cloistered war memorial on Main Street, Bulawayo.

LIEUTENANT ROBIN CYRIL LINDSAY **BURY** [287459] CORPS OF MILITARY POLICE, NO.7 COMMANDO, INTELLIGENCE CORPS, GENERAL LIST, SRS AND SBS (S SQN)

Commonly known as Bob, Robin Bury was born on 3 February 1918 at Marylebone in London, his father dying of wounds just before Armistice Day later that year. Having passed through Eton he went up to New College, Oxford, in October 1936 to read Modern History. The previous year his Eton housemaster had anticipated the move and forwarded the following testimonial:

He is a hard-working and intelligent boy. In December last, at the age of 16 years 10 months, he obtained the School Certificate of the Oxford and Cambridge Schools Examination Board with 7 passes with credit … In January 1935 he started to specialise in History, and in this he shows considerable promise: after one half's work in the subject he was placed 5th in the examination for the Rosebery History Prize (open to the whole school) out of 90 candidates, some of who had specialised in History for 2 years or even more. As he hopes to be a candidate for the Civil Service, he studies French and German as well as History …

Physically he is strong: he is a good boxer who has 3 times won the cup for his weight in school competitions [courtesy of New College, Oxford].

Bury became an active member of the university's OTC and after graduating in 1939 enlisted into the Corps of Military Police out the outbreak of war. After initial training he was promoted to lance-corporal and posted to France as a member of the Field Security Section within HQ II Corps (service number 7685712). The following April he was appointed lance-sergeant whilst attached to the 3rd Division's Supply Column, Royal Army Service Corps. Having withdrawn towards Dunkirk he was wounded in his left leg by a bomb splinter at La Panne on 31 May 1940. Evacuated, he recovered at Halifax Hospital before returning to the Field Security Depot at Winchester.

In August 1940 Bury volunteered for special service and was posted to B Troop, No.7 Commando, at Newmarket as a lance-corporal. After training at Girvan and on the Isle of Arran he embarked HMS *Glengyle* on 31 January 1941, No.7 having been temporarily reorganised as No.2 Company, 3rd Special Service Battalion, the previous November. Following his arrival in Egypt he took part in a largely abortive raid on Bardia that April as a member of A Battalion, Layforce. After the German invasion of Crete A and B Battalions disembarked at Suda Bay on the night of 26–27 May to help facilitate the evacuation of Commonwealth troops. They subsequently suffered heavy losses during rearguard actions whilst making their way to embarkation points on the south coast. Bury was one of those lucky enough to be evacuated from Sphakia on the 31st. Back in Egypt he transferred to the Intelligence Corps when Layforce was disbanded that summer and was posted to the 255th Field Security Section with which he served in Syria, Palestine, and Iraq. Moving to Persia as a corporal he was keenly involved in the training of the Kalpaks. These were Kurds and Armenians recruited mainly from Aleppo prison in 1942 by Special Operations Executive for operations in eastern Turkey. Forming part of Raiding Forces at Azzib they were described thus:

A small unit of Kurdish 'thugs' intended for 'stab in the back' operations or recce. Comd is Capt [Bruce] Mitford, a British offr with a knowledge of Greek and Turkish and who has great control over them. Trained to work in ones and twos, or as a single patrol [WO 201/1653].

Some of this training is known to have taken place at the School of Irregular Warfare on Mount Carmel above Haifa in Palestine, Patrick Leigh Fermor, a former SOE officer, later noting:

The Kurds were a very spectacular lot, all tall, scowling and fiercely whiskered and very soldierly with impeccable battledress and sheepskin kalpaks worn dead straight [the headgear from which the unit took its name]. In their midst was a rather shorter and slighter figure, similarly clad, but wearing spectacles and very pink cheeked compared. I said to your father [Mitford] 'That one doesn't look as fierce as the others', and he said 'No, he's an Old Etonian called Bob Bury, and a very good scholar.' This is the only glimpse of the Kalpaks. It must have been in 1942, about the middle, as shortly after I was sent off to Crete (24 June '42) [Mitford family collection].

Bury was commissioned onto the General List in mid June 1943 stating that he spoke 'French, German, Turkish, Italian, Arabic, Persian, Kurdish (slight), Polish (slight), Greek (slight)' with a knowledge of 'India (childhood), France, Germany, Italy, Switzerland, Austria, Egypt, Palestine, Syria, Iraq, Persia, Dodecanese' (*London Gazette* 16/11/43). He was immediately posted to the Special Raiding Squadron (1st SAS) and the following month attended parachute course No.54 at Ramat David. He is noted on 1st SAS orders as being involved in a debate in the unit's cinema that September:

> The motion before the house is that 'The British system of democratic government is an adequate one and is not in need of radical reform' – Proposed by Major R. V. Lea & seconded by Lt. G. R. Ward [see Gerry Ward's own entry under Langley Marish Churchyard, United Kingdom, Volume III]. Opposed by 2/Lt. R. C. L. Bury & seconded by Sgt. Neill.
> A lively discussion is anticipated and all interested are cordially invited [WO 218/107].

Bury was posted to the Special Boat Squadron on 28 October 1943, subsequently operating in the Aegean. Returning to the squadron's base at Athlit at the beginning of December he was promoted to lieutenant and had completed sniper training by the end of the month. Close combat and ski courses followed at the beginning of 1944, plus the odd small-scale operation commanding H Patrol. Ken Smith, one of its former members, later recalled:

> We got on leave down in Alex [Alexandria, Egypt]. Lovely evening and up pulls this Jeep with Bob Bury in it and he says 'Jump in lads'. So different to Marine officers [Smith's parent unit was the Royal Marines]. Now in Alex there were some wealthy French left over from when they built the Suez Canal and off we went to visit them. There was this lovely lady speaking French, then English, then French. So humbling. We were a rabble really. That evening they had an auction and Bob outbid everyone on a bottle of wine, brought it back to the table, and shared it with us. Paid a bomb for it [personal interview, 2012].

Leigh Fermor continued:

> I didn't see Bob Bury again until May 1944, when he landed from a rubber dinghy with a handful of commandos [of F Patrol, M Detachment, SBS, having embarked from Bardia for OPERATION BRICKLAYER]. It was the MTB [*sic – ML 355*] that had come to take us out with General Kriepe [the commander of the German 22nd Division who had been kidnapped on Occupied Crete by Leigh Fermor and Billy Moss]. He had been told that the Germans were hot on our tracks, as he jumped ashore with his Tommy gun at the ready, and seemed rather disappointed that the embarkation went ahead so quietly. He talked excellent German to the General when introduction took place on deck. He was a delightful chap [Mitford family collection].

In late July 1944, having raided Simi during OPERATION TENEMENT a few days earlier, Bury led F Patrol on an uneventful recce of the island of Calino. On 14 September the same team embarked at Taranto alongside Lieutenant Jim Henshaw's O Patrol for OPERATION APLOMB. They landed the following night at the small village of Avlemonas on the south-east coast of Cythera, an island off the south-east tip of the Peloponnese. Having secured this Bury left Foxforce, consisting of the SBS, RSR, LRDG and No.9 Commando, and moved north to recce the islands of Poros, Aiyina, Salamis, Ayios Georgios, Pstittalia and Fleves that all lie on the approach to Athens (WO 170/4012). He was killed on the 30th by friendly fire during one such coastal recce: the SBS caique was attacked by Royalists who were expecting an attack by ELAS, the communist Greek People's Liberation Army. The man at the helm, John McPherson, was severely wounded and Bury took over. In an effort to persuade the locals to cease-fire Bury swung his vessel towards shore shouting from the helm whilst his men took cover. Former SBS member Lionel Densham later recalled: 'At this time, with the German Army safely off Greek soil, the Greeks thought it was time to fight each other ... nationalists against communists. That, by the way, is how Lt Bury was killed, the Greeks on the armed caique who were nationalists thought we were communists (*Mars & Minerva*, March 1986). Although accounts vary as to the exact location, some stating off the coast of

Salonika, some off Volos, his remains were recovered from the island of Spetses where he is believed to have been buried close to the Poseidonian Grand Hotel.

Having been posthumously mentioned in despatches (*London Gazette* 04/01/45) a tribute in *The Times* noted: 'The war for him was a personal crusade, and measuring his merits by his own impossibly high standards, he refused for four years to take a commission while volunteering at every opportunity for the most dangerous forms of service.' It also noted he had been evacuated wounded at Dunkirk, from Crete and from Leros; 'Now, like his father in the 1914–18 war, he has been killed in action and many mourn his loss beside his mother and step-father Mrs and Lt-Col H C Cory.' Ralph Bridger, former member of H Patrol, recalled: 'After Captain Lees he was one of the finest officers I had the honour to serve under. He was a man you could talk to easily. He was very brave, very quiet.'

Son of Captain Eric Lindsay Bury, MC, of the Royal Engineers who is buried at Bristol (Canford) Cemetery, and of Dolores Bury (née Thornton) of Monewden Hall, Woodbridge, Suffolk – His mother remarried to become Mrs H. C. Cory of The Gate House, Syresham, Brackley, Northants.
Age 26.
I thank my God upon every remembrance of you
Grave 21.A.6. Also commemorated at Eton College, at Monewden by a stained glass window above the altar of St Mary's and in the south cloisters of New College, Oxford.

FUSILIER JAMES ALEXANDER **CARMICHAEL** [6980528] ROYAL INNISKILLING FUSILIERS AND SBS

Jim Carmichael was born in the parish of Drumragh in Omagh, County Tyrone, Northern Ireland. Having worked as a general labourer he enlisted into the Royal Inniskilling Fusiliers at the outbreak of war, declaring his date of birth as 14 January 1919. However, it was later discovered that he had falsified his age, probably in an effort to ensure that he served abroad. Posted to the regiment's infantry training centre he was promoted to lance-corporal that December but reverted to the rank of fusilier at his own request the following February. In May 1940 he was again promoted to lance-corporal and having been posted to the 2nd Battalion the following month rose to corporal that September.

On 6 May 1942 the battalion was landed on the Vichy-held island of Madagascar during OPERATION IRONCLAD. This denied the Japanese a potential air and naval base that would paralyse the Commonwealth convoy route to the Middle and Far East. It also ensured control of the Mozambique Channel through which such convoys passed. The Inniskillings came ashore at a bay west of Diego Suarez in the third wave and advanced east towards the port of Antsirane. Despite a fierce French defence all local resistance had collapsed by daybreak of the 7th, the British fleet entering the harbour that morning. The 13th Infantry

Brigade, of which the 2nd Battalion a part, subsequently sailed for India where Carmichael was reduced to lance-corporal in July 1942 for minor misdemeanours. Five months later, whilst serving in Iraq with Paiforce, he was deprived of his remaining stripe for another minor offence.

Leaving Iraq in March 1943 Carmichael volunteered for the Special Boat Squadron on its formation on the 19th of that month, subsequently attending parachute course No.43 at Ramat David in Palestine that May. He was a member of No.1 Patrol under Lieutenant Charles Bimrose that attempted to rescue the crew of a downed British bomber reported stranded on the island of Scarpanto: leaving Simi at dusk on 30 September 1943 the patrol relieved that of Captain Andy Lassen, MC, on Calchi before landing on Scarpanto on 1 October. Carmichael went ahead with another operator in a Folbot to guide the patrol ashore, only for Bimrose's men to find that the Germans had already captured the aircrew. After some trouble getting off the island, during which Private Henry Harris drowned, the party returned to Simi on 3 October (see Harris' entry under Brookwood Memorial, United Kingdom, Volume III, for full details of this operation).

Carmichael was killed in action on 11 October 1944. Unfortunately, no details can be found regarding the circumstances. Until any come to light all that can be said is that elements of the SBS were deployed on OPERATION MANNA, the liberation of Greece, at this time. He was originally buried at the Greek Civil Cemetery at Megara suggesting that he was a member of Major Ian Patterson's Bucketforce that had parachuted onto Araxas airfield in the Peloponnese on 23 September 1944 during OPERATION TOWANBUCKET and that was fighting its way to the Greek capital. *The Egyptian Gazette* summarised the period in which Carmichael lost his life:

> He [Patterson] crossed the Corinth Canal where a few casualties were suffered from mines and caught up with the Germans. After the Megara airfield had been captured by Patterson's two-Jeep force the Germans launched a counter attack. A few reinforcements had arrived and the RAF Regiment armoured cars were also available. Meanwhile the enemy had sent twenty-two cyclists into Megalo Pevco to retake the village. They were cut off by armoured cars and annihilated. One of Patterson's patrols set off into the hills to try to blow up the road from Piraeus to the north but the Germans drove them off [25 October 1944 – see Patterson's entry under Bari War Cemetery, Italy, within this volume for full detail of this operation].

Son of Arthur and Annie Carmichael of Ashfield Terrace, Omagh, County Tyrone, Northern Ireland – Brother of Sergeant W. Carmichael of HQ Northern Ireland.
Age 24.
At the going down of the sun and in the morning we will remember him, our son.
Grave 17.E.15. Also commemorated on a plaque within St Columba's Church, Drumragh.

PRIVATE WILLIAM OWEN **FISHWICK** [66847] ROYAL ARMY SERVICE CORPS, EAST YORKSHIRE REGIMENT AND SBS (S DET)

William Fishwick, the son of a textile designer, was born in the market town of Darwen in Lancashire on 25 August 1908. Having worked as a hairdresser he enlisted into the Royal Army Service Corps in November 1938 at Birmingham stating that he had been born in 1909. As a driver he was posted to various motor transport companies, arrived in France with No.1 Reserve Motor Transport Company to serve with the BEF at the end of October 1939, and was promoted to lance-corporal that December. After promotion to corporal the following April he was evacuated to England from an unknown location either at the end of May or during June.

Fishwick's company arrived in Egypt at the end of March 1941, his record noting that he subsequently served on mainland Greece during OPERATION LUSTRE and that after the German invasion he was evacuated to Egypt via Crete. Here he served with various motor transport companies before being admitted to hospital in October 1941 having broken his back whilst on duty. As a result he was evacuated to Cape Town, South Africa, in the spring of 1942 and was admitted to Wynberg Hospital. Discharged late that July he was posted to an infantry training centre before returning to Egypt in October to rejoin the RASC. On 3 May 1943 he transferred to the East Yorkshire Regiment and then to Raiding Forces HQ at Azzib, Palestine, on 3 July. He reverted to the rank of private at his own request the following day and volunteered for the Special Boat Squadron on 30 August having attended parachute course No.53 at Ramat David during July. Ken Smith, former SBS, later recalled: 'Fishwick? I was on the bottom bunk on this ship and the chap above me he was called Fishwick. He seemed like an old man to me. I was only in my twenties and he was in his thirties – that seemed like an old man to us!' (Personal interview, 2013).

At the end of June 1944 a joint party consisting of fifteen men of the Greek Sacred Squadron and ten men of S Detachment, SBS, landed on the island of Calino during OPERATION FIREATER. On the evening of 1 July they attacked the German garrison at Vathi Bay. Although the assault was carried out successfully, a second enemy contingent mortared the area during their withdrawal. Fishwick, Private Jackson and Sergeant John Dryden were wounded. Although Jackson managed to retire Dryden was too comatose to move and Fishwick too seriously injured. Private James Doughty, an American medic serving with the SBS, stayed with them, the three being taken in by locals and hidden. However, the two wounded men were too weak to march and it was therefore decided that the inhabitants should reveal their presence to the Germans so that they could receive life-saving treatment.

Doughty, who as the medic had been unarmed, was transferred to Rhodes for further interrogation, then to Athens and Salonika, subsequently surviving the war in a POW camp in Germany. Meanwhile, Dryden and Fishwick were taken to Leros and then to the German Air Force hospital at Piraeus near Athens on 5 July. Here blood was taken from Dryden for transfusion to his comrade but despite

treatment Fishwick died of his wounds on 7 July 1944, his death being properly recorded and reported to the British through normal channels. Although it is often reported that he died whilst under interrogation on Leros Dryden's own evidence proves otherwise. Contemporary German interrogation records note: 'Private Fishwick, personal details unknown, flown over to Athens, died there in the base hospital' (Ministry of Defence report, 1986). Dryden's wounds resulted in the amputation of a toe although, having been interrogated and kept in solitary confinement under the threat of 'execution' for a lengthy period, he managed to escape whilst being marched to Sarajevo. Making contact with Yugoslav Partisans and an Allied Military Mission he was eventually repatriated to Italy.

Son of William and Hannah Fishwick of Shear Brow, Blackburn Road, Darwen, Lancashire
Age 35.
Never selfish, nor unkind, a beautiful memory left behind. Mum and Dad
Grave 10.E.7. Also commemorated on Penwortham's war memorial.

SERGEANT FRANK CHARLES NORTON **KINGSTON** [7345605] ROYAL ARMY MEDICAL CORPS, 1ST SAS AND SBS (P PATROL, S DET)

Frank Kingston was born on 18 May 1920 in Cardiff. In July 1938, whilst working as a laboratory attendant, he joined the local 158th Field Ambulance, Royal Army Medical Corps (TA), and was called up at the outbreak of war the following year. Disembarking in France with the BEF that October he returned to the UK two days before Germany invaded the Low Countries in May 1940. Nearly two years of home duties followed before he embarked for India where he served until posted to Iraq in September 1942. He volunteered for 1st SAS on 15 February 1943 and after initial training, including parachute course No.44 at Ramat David in Palestine, was posted to the Special Boat Squadron on 6 July.

Kingston was promoted to corporal in September 1943 and took part in the defence of Leros against German parachutists that November. Moving independently from position to position, either on foot or by Jeep, he ensured that the wounded reached definitive care, Captain 'Bill' Blyth stating in his post-operation report:

> Cpl Kingston RAMC carried out his duties as medical orderly under fire with complete disregard for his own safety and worked untiringly throughout the battle attending to the wounded, and where necessary in the case of those unable to walk, carrying them single handed to medical posts [Operational Report No.HQ 1].

Kingston was subsequently promoted to sergeant on S Detachment's return to Palestine that December. By the following spring he was engaged on OPERATION FIREATER, the detachment making small raids from their temporary base at Yedi Atala on the neutral Turkish coast. On 19 April 1944 P and Z Patrols set sail for the Aegean island of Thira aboard two caiques of the Levant Schooner Flotilla. On the evening of the 21st a Greek lieutenant serving with the SBS, Stephanos Kazoulis, and Captain Andy Lassen, MC*, went ashore to gather information from a monastery near Perissa. As none was forthcoming they returned to the ship and lay up camouflaged against the satellite island of Nea Kameni during the 22nd. Here a local fisherman informed them, having been well lubricated with ouzo, that a mixed garrison of Italians and Germans was billeted on the first floor of the Bank of Athens within Thira Town. Although tasked with capturing or destroying enemy shipping there was no sign of any such vessels and the force fell back on its alternative objective of attacking opportunistic targets. That night both patrols therefore landed near Vourvoulos where, having collected further intelligence, Lassen planned three simultaneous actions. At 0045hrs on the 24th he, Kazoulis and twelve other ranks including Kingston attacked the bank as outlined in his subsequent report:

> We succeeded in getting the main force into the billet unobserved, in spite of barking dogs and sentries. The living quarters comprised twelve rooms. It was our intention to take the troops there prisoner. This idea had to be abandoned, and will have to be abandoned in similar circumstances in the future, until raiding parties are issued with good torches. Casualties were sustained during the general mix-up in the dark. Instead, the doors of the rooms [were] kicked in, a grenade thrown into the room, and two/three magazines of TSMG [Thompson Sub-Machine Gun] and Bren emptied into each room.
>
> Lt Casulli [as Kazoulis was known in the SBS] was killed almost instantaneously [believed to be by gunfire whilst stood in a doorway – see his entry within the Unknown Location section within Volume III], and Sgt Kingston seriously wounded by shots fired either from the rooms or by the sentries outside.
>
> At approx 0245hrs, and when I was satisfied that all the enemy were killed or wounded, we left the building, carrying Sgt Kingston. Shots were exchanged with stray enemy during the withdrawal. We returned to the cave [near Vourvoulos where they had rested the evening before] to find Lt Balsillie waiting for us with eight prisoners; he had completed a neat job.
>
> Sgt Kingston was fully conscious when we left the building, he himself, as a medical orderly, considered that he was not dangerously wounded. The next day [having walked a considerable distance to get away from the target area] the local doctor was called to attend to him, and on his recommendation we decided to leave him by the roadside for the Germans to pick up, as he had suddenly taken a turn for the worse. He died before this could be done. Arrangements were made with the local doctor for him to be buried with full honours. The same request was made about Lt Casulli and I have every reason to believe that this was carried out [Operation Report No.13].

Lassen had signalled *LS.11*, one of the LSF caiques that had dropped the party, to pick them up sooner than arranged in an effort to save Kingston. The raid brought about reprisals in the form of the murder of civilian hostages.

Nephew of Mr W. Kingston of Red House Crescent, Ely, Cardiff, and of Mrs C. Williams of Green Road, Langley, Oldbury, Birmingham.
Age 23.
No inscription.
Grave 23.D.14. Also commemorated, alongside Kazoulis, on Thira's war memorial.

TROOPER ARCHIBALD JOSEPH **PENHALL** [565573] NEW ZEALAND CHAPLAIN'S DEPARTMENT, HOME GUARD, WELLINGTON REGIMENT AND LRDG (A SQN)

Archibald Penhall was born to Australian parents on 14 March 1910 in Masterton on the North Island of New Zealand. By 1935 he was a Salvation Army officer working farther north in Waro but was commissioned into the Territorial Chaplain's Department as a captain in December 1936 whilst working as shepherd in the remote province of Mangamingi (Chaplain, 4th Class, service number 1164). He married in July 1939 and in August 1941 received a second commission as a lieutenant into the local Te Ngutu (Eltham) Battalion, Home Guard, where he commanded No.1 Platoon. Although he later moved with his wife and daughter to Campbell's Bay in Auckland he resigned both commissions to enlist into the infantry in July 1942.

In March 1943 Penhall was sent to 15 OCTU for pre-selection and was once again commissioned, this time into the 2nd Battalion, Wellington Regiment (City of Wellington's Own). His final report states: 'Very fair knowledge of all subjects – keeps good control when instructing – leadership and command in the field were good – recommended as a Pl. Comd' (Platoon Commander). However, within two weeks he had volunteered for service within the ranks of the 10th Reinforcement Draft, 2nd NZEF, and was posted to the Reserve of Officers Supplementary List. He subsequently embarked for the Middle East with the 32nd Battalion in July 1943 with the rank of sergeant, arriving in Egypt in August and reverting to corporal. A month later he volunteered for the Long Range Desert Group, reverting to the rank of trooper in order to serve in A Squadron.

Penhall was taken prisoner on 25 October 1943 after a stick grenade burst in his face during the failed attack on the Dodecanese island of Levita: A Squadron had been clearing a small building in the centre of the island that was being used as a German HQ. Penhall's condition deteriorated and Private Bruce Steedman, the medic, arranged for him to be handed over to the Germans under a white flag for treatment. He died of his wounds in the early hours of the 28th at the Lazarett Luftwaffe base in Athens and was buried at the British Military Cemetery at Kokinia. An unknown veteran later recalled:

> They [Penhall's party] were taken in the rear by heavy machine-gun fire from the vicinity of their landing place. The detachment was kept pinned down by this for some time but eventually they put in a counter attack and rushed the enemy positions taking a German patrol of twelve men prisoner. Trooper H L Mallett was severely wounded in this attack and died later [see Mallett's entry under Rhodes War Cemetery, Greece]. They kept pushing forward toward the ridge and secured it before daylight in the face of further small arms fire, losing Trooper A J Penhall killed [*sic*] and Trooper R G Haddow severely wounded in process [LRDG Newsletter No.39 of 1983 – see Trooper Johnnie Bowler's entry under Athens Memorial, Greece, for full details of this operation].

Son of John and Sarah Penhall (née Siddall) – Husband of Nita Katherine Penhall of Castle Street, Eltham, Taranaki, formerly of Devon Street West, New Plymouth – Father of Diana Grace Penhall.
Age 33.
No inscription.
Grave 13.B.19. Also commemorated on an LRDG memorial within the New Zealand SAS camp at Papakura.

CORPORAL ALFRED **TIGHE** MM [7615706] ROYAL ARMY ORDNANCE CORPS, ROYAL ELECTRICAL AND MECHANICAL ENGINEERS AND LRDG (LRS ATT A SQN)

Known to his comrades as 'Snowy', Alf Tighe was born in Pendlebury, Salford, on 2 August 1919. Having worked as a pipefitter he enlisted into the Royal Army Ordnance Corps in November 1939 and disembarked in Egypt the following April. Three months later he was posted to Khartoum in the Sudan and having been attached to HQ Company, 2nd West Yorkshire Regiment, volunteered for the newly-expanded Long Range Desert Group on 5 December 1940 as a fitter.

At the end of the month G Patrol was led by the more experienced New Zealand T Patrol, to which Tighe appears to have been attached, into Central Libya to attack Murzuk Fort (OPERATION AESOP). On 11 January 1941, having picked up a small party of Free French at Kayugi in Chad, the combined patrol closed on both the fort, that resisted heavily, and the Italian airfield at which aircraft and a hangar were destroyed. It then withdrew, briefly stopping after a few kilometres to bury two casualties, Sergeant 'Squib' Hewson and the French commander, Lt-Colonel Jean Colonna d'Ornano (see Hewson's entry under Tripoli War Cemetery, Libya, Volume I). The following day the patrols forced the surrender of Traghen but on the 31st were spotted by enemy aircraft and followed to the Jebel Sherif where they were attacked from the air and by the Italian LRDG equivalent, the Compagnia Sahariana. With his vehicle immobilised Tighe took cover in the rocks with Trooper 'Skin' Moore, an Italian prisoner, and Guardsmen John Easton and Alex Winchester. Corporal Rex Beech had laid down covering fire so that they could do so (see his entry under Knightsbridge War Cemetery, Libya). After waiting until the enemy had dispersed the five men descended and began to walk towards Bishara, approximately 20 kilometres to the south-west. However, after spending the night in the open desert they returned to the jebel the following day and recovered a two-gallon tin of water but no food before again heading south-west. Having agreed that they should make for Allied territory rather than give themselves up they released their prisoner and continued to walk throughout the next two days, finding only a tin of jam and some lentils that made them feel sick. On the 5th Tighe, who was suffering the effects of a previous abdominal operation, was left behind with his share of scavenged water. It was not until the others had marched onwards that he found the water too salty to drink. He reached Sarra, having covered 217 kilometres, on the seventh day just as his comrades were moving off. Too exhausted to join them he took shelter in some huts, lit a fire with a match that he found, and was picked up by a French Patrol there on the evening of the 9th. The story of this trek was reported globally, most detailed, although also most susceptible to propaganda, when related by Moore in *Illustrated* magazine on 14 June 1941 and again in the same magazine on 8 August (see Easton's entry under Knightsbridge War Cemetery, Libya, for full details). Captain George Mercer Nairne, Liaison Officer to the Free French, subsequently reported: 'Though he had been alone for four days and without water for that time and consequently in a dreadful condition of nerves and exhaustion Tighe at once thought of his three companions.' He was later flown out of Fort Lamy in Chad to Khartoum for treatment.

Having fully recovered Tighe carried out Road Watch duties with Captain David Lloyd Owen's Y.1 Patrol during July 1942 before learning that he had been mentioned in despatches (*London Gazette* 24/06/43, 1725/43). Having been nominally absorbed into the Royal Electrical and Mechanical Engineers his LRDG service was recognised by the award of an immediate Military Medal on the recommendation of its Commanding Officer, Lt-Colonel Guy Prendergast, DSO:

> In Jan 1941 Cftsn Tighe was a member of a patrol which lost some of its vehicles by enemy action south of Kufra. He, together with two other men, walked a distance of 230 miles over absolutely barren desert with virtually no food and water, until picked up by French troops. The leader of this walk, Pte Moore received an immediate DCM, while the third man died on the way [Moore is seen on the previous page with Tighe on the right]. Since this epic walk, Cftsn Tighe has been constantly on patrol. He is normally a fitter, but has frequently shown great gallantry as a gunner. For example in December 1942 during an attack on Hon landing ground, when his patrol were attempting to destroy enemy aircraft on the ground, he volunteered to accompany the small party with which the patrol commander was attempting to enter the landing ground. During the battle that ensued with the enemy defences, Cftsn Tighe manned his gun with the utmost devotion to duty and accounted for several enemy casualties. He then repaired a Jeep under intense enemy fire, thereby enabling the crew to return to the remainder of the patrol [*London Gazette* 22/07/43, WO 373/46].

Tighe undertook parachute training at Ramat David in Palestine during January 1944 before being promoted to lance-corporal in March and to corporal in May. He was subsequently attached to Z.1 Patrol from the LRDG's Light Repair Squadron, the patrol being tasked to provide Jeep-borne reconnaissance for the Special Boat Service during OPERATION TOWANBUCKET: having embarked at Bari on the Italian coast Z.1 landed at Katakolo on the Peloponnese on 26 September 1944. After fighting through Patras they chased the retreating Germans to the Corinth Canal. Here, after a rapturous welcome from the local population, the patrol continued towards Megara, leaving Tighe behind with one jeep to help a party of Royal Engineers clear mines. Two days later the patrol commander, Captain John Olivey, MC*, wrote:

> The death of Cpl Tighe was reported to me. It seemed that he had run over a mine with his Jeep, on the south bank of the Corinth Canal whilst driving an RE on duty on the 10th October. Cpl Tighe MM was buried by an SBS detachment in the British Military Cemetery, Corinth [WO 218/92].

Tighe was a popular member of the LRDG, his former CO, Lloyd Owen, later writing:

Tighe was a quiet, shy, unassuming man who was a master at his craft. I believe also that no unkind thought ever entered his mind. I certainly never heard one pass his lips in the years when I had lived close to him. His reputation in the unit stood high … that he should have been killed on a mine, so near to the end of the war and after suffering and enduring so much, was a twist of fate which was hard to understand. His death was a great loss to us all [*Providence Their Guide: The Long Range Desert Group 1940–1945*, by David Lloyd Owen].

Son of James and Martha Tighe (née Morris) of Ada Street, Pendlebury, Lancashire.
Age 25.
Without farewell you fell asleep with only memories for us to keep.
Grave 17.D.8.

LEROS WAR CEMETERY

The remains of 183 Commonwealth servicemen were concentrated here from all over the island. However, due to enemy destruction of local records fifty-eight burials are unidentified whilst the exact location within the plot of eighteen others is uncertain. These men are commemorated by special memorials.

The cemetery lies on the east side of the island on the shore of Aghia Marina Bay and is separated from the sea by the coast road. It is situated approximately 2 kilometres west of the town of Leros. GPS co-ordinates: Latitude 37.15978, Longitude 26.83746

TROOPER PETER STANISLAUS **BORROWDALE** [7939136] ROYAL TANK REGIMENT AND LRDG

On enlisting into the Royal Armoured Corps during May 1941 Peter Borrowdale stated that he had been born on 13 March 1922 in the parish of Deepdale in Preston, Lancashire, and that he had previously worked as a chemist's assistant. However, as his birth was not registered until the last quarter of 1923 his age is uncertain.

After initial training with B Squadron, 57th Training Regiment, at Warminster Borrowdale was posted to the 45th Royal Tank Regiment in December 1941 and qualified as a driver operator. In May 1942 he embarked for the Middle East, arriving at Port Tewfik at the beginning of July. Admitted to hospital that August he was posted to the 6th Royal Tank Regiment on being discharged the following month, moving to Iraq as part of Paiforce that December. After a further spell in hospital he volunteered for the Long Range Desert Group on 2 July 1943 and began training in the Lebanese mountains. That October the LRDG disembarked on the Dodecanese island of Leros and was active during its attempted defence after the German airborne and naval invasion of 12 November. Borrowdale was killed during this period although there are no known details of the circumstances. He was initially reported as having died 'of accidental wounds', this later being corrected to having been 'killed in action' on 14 November 1943. Lieutenant Peter Mold noted that on the 29th, after Leros had fallen:

I visited the ex LRDG HQ and collected odds and ends of my own kit and destroyed a number of W/T [Wireless Telegraphy – radio] sets and telephones which had been left in the Bde HQ Signals tunnel undamaged. I checked that the graves of Sgm Whitehead and Sgm Borrowdale were properly marked etc, I then returned to hospital [WO 218/91 – see Signalman Cliff Whitehead's entry under Rhodes War Cemetery, Greece].

There are no known next of kin details although his mother's maiden name was Carter – Nephew of Miss Eleanor Dugdale Carter of Fyloe Road, Preston, Lancashire.
Age officially recorded as 21.
No inscription.
Grave 1.A.11.

LIEUTENANT-COLONEL JOHN RICHARD **EASONSMITH** DSO, MC [140546] ROYAL TANK CORPS, GLOUCESTERSHIRE REGIMENT, ROYAL TANK REGIMENT AND LRDG (HQ)

Known as Jack to his family and as Jake to his comrades, Easonsmith was born on 12 April 1909 at Almondsbury in Bristol. After schooling at Mill Hill in north London he became a travelling salesman for firstly Wills and then the Emu Wine Company (now part of Thomas Hardy). At 18 he joined the 21st (Royal Gloucestershire Hussars) Armoured Car Company, Royal Tank Corps (TA), at Bristol, serving in the ranks as a driver until November 1932 (service number 7879575). In July 1935 he married Honor 'Topsy' Marsh, the couple living in a caravan whilst selling wine to public houses and hotels in the West Country.

Easonsmith enlisted into 449 Company, 4th Battalion, Gloucestershire Regiment (66th Searchlight Regiment), at Wells the day before war was declared and rose to the rank of lance-sergeant. In July 1940 he was commissioned from 102 OCTU into the 4th Battalion, Royal Tank Regiment, Royal Armoured Corps, his final report noting: 'A very good type. He's picked up AFV [Armoured Fighting Vehicle] tactics quickly and is evidently a leader. He should make an excellent officer.'

After serving with various training regiments, Easonsmith disembarked in Egypt during February 1941 and volunteered for the Long Range Desert Group that March. Although appointed Second-in-Command of Y Patrol he led the composite H Patrol from June (see Guardsman 'Hoppy' Hopton's entry under Alamein Memorial, Egypt, Volume I, for details). Having returned to Y Patrol by August he was successfully recommended for the Military Cross by his Commanding Officer, Lt-Colonel Guy Prendergast, DSO:

> During the period June 1st 1941 to July 5th 1941, this officer has led several small motorized patrols from Siwa to the Jebel el Akhdar region, to obtain information and to transport agents. These patrols have been operating 200 miles behind the enemy lines, and have been very successful in all their enterprises.
>
> They have destroyed at least twelve enemy vehicles. 2/Lieut Easonsmith has displayed daring, initiative and a high power of leadership in avoiding detection and in completing successfully the tasks allotted to him. I recommend the award of a Military Cross to this officer [*London Gazette* 30/12/41, WO 373/18].

Easonsmith was subsequently promoted paid acting captain as of 11 August 1941 and joined R.1 Patrol. In late October he was operating in the region of Ain Bu Sfia when he came across an enemy tented camp. Having observed the area and dropped some 'specially doctored boxes of Italian MG ammuntion' he decided to stage a breakdown along a nearby track with the aim of taking prisoners:

> Our little act had to be put on very hurriedly and I feel lost some of its virtue as a result. Of my crew of four, two bent over the engine, the gunner hid under a tarpaulin and I held up my hand. The leading lorry, a large SPAF, stopped so I walked up to it and opened the cab door. Although suspicious the Italians were still in doubt as to our respectability. My Tommy gun I had been attempting to hold behind my back coming across. The time to produce it had come. This I did very clumsily, standing too close to the driver and he with some guts fell down from the cab onto me and with this sudden move got the gun. We had a short hand-to-hand tussle after this but he got away and ran off. I had a fairly lucky shot with a grenade and he did not use the Tommy gun. The passenger, an officer, had in the meantime used up all his revolver ammunition and run. He was wounded or killed. Things became quite fast and furious. Fortunately none of the leading Italian trucks had an MG but quite a supply of men with rifles were appearing by now [WO 218/94].

Withdrawing rapidly the patrol returned to Siwa. The following month Easonsmith led it into Libya again, this time to pick up SAS troops after OPERATION SQUATTER, L Detachment's first operation that had targeted airfields at Tmimi and Gazala. He recovered a total of twenty-one parachutists including Captain David Stirling and Lieutenants Jock Lewes and Paddy Mayne. His actions, and those of other LRDG patrols, prompted the Regiment to revise and improve its methods (most of the recovered men are seen here, Stirling in the centre with sunglasses).

Easonsmith was appointed Second-in-Command of the LRDG in May 1942. His immediate award of the Distinguished Service Order, also recommended by Prendergast, was for leading Operation Caravan, the raid on Barce designed to cause maximum damage in synchronisation with similar raids on Benghazi (Operation Bigamy) and Tobruk (Operation Nicety):

> Maj Easonsmith commanded a LRDG Sqn which, on the night 13/14 Sep 42, destroyed twenty aircraft and damaged twelve others on Barce LG [landing ground], inflicted casualties to the garrison, and destroyed petrol dumps. Maj Easonsmith himself on one vehicle caused damage to vehicles and casualties to personnel in an attack on an MT [motor transport] park.
>
> On the return journey the Sqn was ambushed by 150 tps. By his cool leadership and example under fire Major Easonsmith brought the Sqn through the ambush with few casualties. Later, when all vehicles save two had been destroyed by fighter aircraft he dispatched the wounded by car to LG 125 whence they were flown to Cairo and himself led a walking party 70 miles across country to a RV with another LRDG patrol. The safe return of the majority of his personnel and the success of the operation can be largely attributed to Major Easonsmith's personal courage and untiring devotion to duty. (Owing to the secret nature of these operations it is requested that no publication [of this citation] be made) [*London Gazette* 26/11/42, WO 373/46].

At the beginning of January 1943 Easonsmith visited Allied Headquarters in Algiers:

> … to examine the possibility of sending part of LRDG to operate from a base in Tunisia. It was decided that this was not desirable, but Easonsmith arranged for supplies of POL [petrol, oil and lubricant] and rations to be available at Tozeur for the use of any patrols in that area. At the same time he obtained much useful information about the Tunisia–Tripolitania borderland [WO 201/815].

That summer, with hostilities in North Africa at an end, the LRDG concentrated on retraining and refitting, Easonsmith travelling:

> … to Syria [modern-day Lebanon] to find a suitable training ground, and was fortunate in being able to arrange for the unit to take over the Cedars Hotel in the Lebanon Mountains, which hitherto been used by the ME Ski School. This building is situated in perfect training country at 6,300 feet, with mountains up to 10,000 feet in the close proximity [WO 218/91].

Having been quickly deployed to the Aegean in September 1943 after the Italian armistice Easonsmith took command of the LRDG the following month and was promoted to acting lieutenant-colonel on the 26th. He was killed in action soon after on 16 November on Leros, this having been subject to German naval and airborne landings since the early hours of the 12th. Captain Charlie Saxton, who commanded T.1 Patrol, later noted:

> Other patrols were being used to mop up parachutists and to patrol and local recce work. To carry out one such task on the night of 15/16 Nov, Lt Col Easonsmith personally led a small party of men to recce the town of Leros to discover the extent of the enemy's penetration in the area. Rounding a bend in the road the CO was surprised at the head of his party by a hidden German who fired at him with a Tommy gun at very close range. The CO was killed and the remainder of the party had to withdraw [WO 218/91].

Doc Lawson, the unit's former Medical Officer, noted that having been captured when the island fell he:

> … got permission to look for Jake and went off after a heavy sick parade with Whitehead, Curle, Jenkinson, Hill, Booker, McKay and a guard. Found him in Leros on the lower road. He must have died instantly. A miserable feeling of loss and could hardly believe it. Whitehead made a cross and the owners of the house in whose vineyard we buried him promised to look after the grave [LRDG Newsletter No.35 of 1979].

Unsurprisingly, the news had a huge effect on the Group, Saxton writing:

> The death of such an outstanding officer, whose ability and cheerfulness in all conditions was an inspiration to the unit, is a blow that has taken so much from us all. He was a magnificent leader, who had done such grand work in the desert as a patrol and squadron commander, and whose experience and kindness made him the perfect Commanding Officer. This news seriously deranged the LRDG [WO 218/91].

The unit's former Intelligence Officer, Bill Kennedy Shaw, later noted that Easonsmith had been known to the Arabs as 'Batl es Sahra', 'Hero of the Desert', describing him as: 'brave, wise, with an uprightness that shamed lesser men, he was, I think, the finest man we ever had in the LRDG' (*Long Range Desert Group: The Story of its Work in Libya 1940–1943*, by W. B. Kennedy Shaw).

Son of George and Daisy Easonsmith – Husband of Honor Gertrude Easonsmith of Lower Hazel, Rudgeway, Gloucestershire – Father of Charlotte who he never met – Brother of Nancy who served in the ATS throughout the war.
Age 34.
Some corner of a foreign field that is for ever England
Grave 3.B.3. Also commemorated on Clifton RFC's war memorial as 'Eason-Smith'.

CAPTAIN DESMOND CAMPBELL **HOLT** [65566] ROYAL ARTILLERY AND SBS

Desmond Holt, the son of a textiles salesman, was born on 17 November 1915 in Didsbury, Manchester, later living at Heaton Mersey. Having attended Moor-Allerton Preparatory School he studied at Denstone College where he was a cadet sergeant in the Officer Training Corps. Whilst working as an insurance clerk he was commissioned into the 238th Battery, 60th (6th Cheshire and Shropshire) Medium Brigade, Royal Artillery (TA), at Stockport (*London Gazette* 10/07/35). Promoted to captain in March 1939 he was embodied into the 81st Anti-Aircraft Regiment late that August before embarking for Palestine with the 20th AA Battery the following January.

Holt fractured his pelvis in a road accident in December 1941 whilst serving with the 28th Heavy Anti-Aircraft Battery:

> At approx 1030hrs I was driving along a long straight stretch of the Gaza Ridge to Beersheba road. In the middle of this was a very slight bend. Here the car skidded and though I rectified this the car skidded in the opposite direction and overshot the road into the ditch. The car then completely overturned landing on top of my hips and pinning me down (the car being a Ford V8 open two seater the hood was down). No one saw this happen but luckily nearby Arabs working in the fields came and lifted the car from off me. A passing Australian car then stopped and brought me to the above hospital [1st Australian General Hospital at Gaza]. It was ascertained afterwards that there was a film of mud across the road at the particular point where I skidded. This was undoubtedly the cause of the accident.

Holt was bedridden for a month before extensive physiotherapy enabled him to walk again. After leave, and whilst still recovering, Holt was appointed as a staff officer at HQ Palestine Area. He held this post until late February 1943 when he moved to a similar appointment at the Motor Transport Branch, GHQ Middle East Forces. Although promoted acting major in May, he relinquished this rank late that August.

Holt volunteered for the Special Boat Squadron on 28 October 1943 and immediately deployed to the Aegean where he joined the unit on Leros. He was killed in action on 12 November during the defence of the island, just a few days short of his 28th birthday:

The squadron commander ordered Captain Holt and his patrol to proceed to the area of Navy House [located at the junction of the San Nicola–San Quaranta road] to engage the [German] parachutists …

On withdrawing to the pre-arranged RV at dusk Captain Holt was reported missing by his patrol sergeant and that he was last seen advancing by himself in the vicinity of Navy House engaging the parachutists …

During the same morning two officers of the Greek Squadron attached to the SBS proceeded to the area in which Capt Holt was last seen but returned by dusk, reporting that they had visited every house in that area but could not find any trace of him [Operational Report No.HQ 1].

Despite this report Holt is officially recorded as having been killed in action on the 17th, his body being recovered at a later date. WO 304, the War Office's Roll of Honour, records him as the recipient of the Distinguished Service Order and two Military Crosses. However, a note in his service record states that this is an error and it seems probable that there was confusion with Lt-Colonel Jake Easonsmith, DSO, MC, who is buried in the same location (see his entry within this section).

Son of Richard and Jessie (née Campbell) Holt of Stafford Road, Newport, Shropshire.
Age officially recorded as 28.
A beloved son and brother. Valiantly as he lived he nobly served to the end
Grave 3.C.7.

RIFLEMAN LOUIS JOHANNES NEL OELOFSE [6857918] SOUTHERN RHODESIA LIGHT BATTERY, KING'S ROYAL RIFLE CORPS AND LRDG (S.1 PATROL, B SQN)

Lou Oelofse was born on 3 July 1917 in Cape Province, South Africa, and attended school in Dordrecht before working as a grocer's assistant. In December 1940 he joined the Rhodesian Army at the King George VI Barracks at Salisbury and was promoted to lance-corporal the following May whilst on police duties within the camp (service number X321). A month later he was advanced to corporal but that October reverted to the rank of gunner on transferring to the Southern Rhodesia Light Battery. In April 1942 he was promoted to lance-bombardier and to lance-sergeant that August. Attending a Commando course at Gwelo from October until December he passed with a grade 'A' before arriving at the Imperial Forces Trans-shipment Camp at Clairwood, Durban. Having reverted to the rank of lance-bombardier he embarked for Egypt in February 1943 and arrived at Port Tewfik the following month. Here he nominally enlisted into the King's Royal Rifle Corps and immediately volunteered for the Long Range Desert Group.

Oelofse was killed in action whilst manning a small fort and its battery

of antiquated guns at Clidi Heights on Leros. Captain John Olivey, MC, the patrol commander, stated that after German troops came ashore from landing craft on 12 November 1943: 'Rfn Oelofse was killed in the trench to the east of the fort. It was now impossible to get forward to No.3 gun in the east' (WO 218/91). Don Coventry confirmed: 'Our first casualty was Rflm Oelofse, a Rhodesian, who received a direct hit from a mortar on his position in the forward trenches' (LRDG Newsletter No.49 of 1993). Despite these reports Oelofse's date of death is officially recorded as 18 November.

Son of Jan and of Anna Oelofse (née Nel) of Dordrecht, Cape Province, South Africa.
Age 26.
No inscription.
Grave 1.B.4.

Captain Alan Gardiner REDFERN MBE [291976] Rhodesian African Rifles, King's Royal Rifle Corps and LRDG (B Sqn)

Alan Redfern was born in Salisbury, Southern Rhodesia, on 8 February 1906 as the eldest of three sons. He attended Salisbury Boys' High School and was:

… never happier than at weekends and during school holidays, when he camped out in the veld. On such occasions he took very little equipment apart from a light rifle and a blanket, and would set off with no other food than mealie meal and condensed milk. He and his native companion were content to live on these and on the wild doves which they shot and cooked.

Alan passed his Matriculation examination before reaching the age of 17 years. Shortly afterwards he joined the Southern Rhodesia Civil Service, and held posts in the Native Department (later renamed Internal Affairs) in various localities, notably at Mtetengwe, near present day Beit Bridge, Zaka and Plumtree, bordering the Bechuanaland Protectorate (now Botswana). While stationed at Mtetengwe he met his wife-to-be, Opal Wilson. They were married in the South African mining town of Messina in March 1931. Alan studied, and became highly proficient in, both the main local African languages, Chishona and Sindebele. While based at Plumtree, he was appointed Assistant Native Commissioner.

With the outbreak of the Second World War, he volunteered for military service and was commissioned into the newly-formed Rhodesian African Rifles (RAR) in 1940, where his knowledge of native languages and customs was needed, as recruits came from the tribal areas. Later, when an invasion of Southern Africa by the Axis powers was considered a possibility, Capt Redfern (OC, B Coy, 1 RAR at the time) was tasked with training men [at Gwelo] as Commandos who could undertake guerrilla operations. Many men trained by Capt Redfern in irregular warfare volunteered for the LRDG and formed S.1 Patrol. Alan Redfern's successful training of Commandos earned him the MBE (awarded 01/01/43 as T/Capt Rhodesian African Rifles). He accepted this honour with the understanding that he could join the men of the LRDG, whom he had personally trained and for whom he had high regard …

His main hobby was the study of nature and wildlife. Along with his father, he turned from hunting big game animals with a rifle to photographing them in their natural environment. While on a hunting trip in 1935, Alan's father was attacked by a lion. Alan managed to kill the lion while it was on top of his father, who had been severely mauled. Alan negotiated sandy bush tracks to the nearest hospital at Livingstone, about 200 miles. Arthur Redfern survived the ordeal, and Alan promised his wife Opal that he would never shoot another lion after this – his twelfth! [Personal correspondence with his son, John Redfern, 2010].

Having disembarked in Egypt Redfern nominally transferred to the King's Royal Rifle Corps in late April 1943 (*London Gazette* 15/10/43) and subsequently took command of S.1 Patrol, Long Range Desert Group, the following month whilst it was in training at The Cedars in Lebanon (WO 218/91). After Italy signed an armistice that September the LRDG and SBS embarked for the Aegean in an effort to seize her garrisons before the Germans could do so. Soon after S.1 sailed from Leros to Simi in the Levant Schooner Flotilla's steam trawler, HMS *Hedgehog*, to recce and help in the island's defence:

S.1 Patrol under Redfern had sailed on the 24th for Simi which was already in British hands as Lapraik's detachment of SBS were there. On the 26th he came up with a WT signal and from then onwards throughout the week reported regularly. Most of the information he was sending referred to Rhodes and should be of great value to Force HQ. SBS were ferrying parties across from Simi to Rhodes and gathering much of the stuff that he sent, also small parties of Italian refugees who were escaping and telling him all that they knew. Redfern was anxious to move his patrol over to Rhodes but permission for this was not granted …

Up until Oct 5th Redfern continued to send in regular and valuable reports about the situation around Rhodes. From Oct 5th no signals were received until the morning of the eighth when it was reported that the Germans had made an unsuccessful attack on Simi. On Oct 7th a small force of about eighty Germans had been beaten off by the Garrison. The Germans only maintained a foothold on the island for ten hours. They lost sixteen killed and six captured, many were wounded, and successful Breda fire was brought bear on their departing schooner. The combined British and Italian losses were three killed and nine wounded so this little engagement had most satisfactory results [see Private Bill Morrison's entry under Rhodes War Cemetery, Greece, for further details]. On the following days enemy reprisals took the form of Stuka raids but there were no casualties to LRDG personnel. Redfern was given a free hand to direct his own affairs and to take what so ever course he thought fit. Those open to him were to remain in Simi, advance to Rhodes or to evacuate to Castel Rosso, or Leros or Cyprus …

S.1 who was at Simi with a detachment of SBS was badly bombed by Stukas and had to evacuate to Castel Rosso via Turkey on 11/10. He lost no personnel or equipment … [the SBS did, however, sustain casualties – see entries for Corporal Sidney Greaves, MM, Lance-corporal 'Mac' McKendrick and Guardsman Tommy Bishop under Rhodes War Cemetery]

Early in the morning of 22nd [October] Capt Redfern MBE arrived [at Leros] by caique from Castel Rosso. His party were very tired but in good heart. They had worked extremely well during their month's absence. Capt Redfern's main complaint was that his party was not permitted to penetrate into Rhodes …

The following additional arrangements of appointments was necessary with the unit; On Oct 23rd Capt A Redfern MBE was dressed up as a Major to enable him to take over B Squadron; this to become Acting Rank as soon as the 2i/cs appointment is approved [WO 218/91].

Soon after German amphibious and airborne forces landed on Leros: 'At approximately 1500hrs on 12th November an enemy air fleet of some thirty troop carriers came in below Clidi Heights and dropped parachutists, which resulted in cutting the island in half' (LRDG newsletter No.49 of 1993). Redfern gathered a combined LRDG and SBS quick reaction force of three officers and twenty-seven men that he held in reserve at Point 112, north of Gurna Bay, just a few hundred yards from the German drop zone. One of his officers, Captain Charlie Saxton, later reported after escaping from the island that they had attempted to deny the enemy parachutists access to their weapon containers:

LRDG and SBS got their MGs [machine guns] into action immediately and must have had some success. Range was about 800–900yds. After ten minutes we had received no orders so Major Redfern split LRDG into three parties. T.2 to stay on feature 065425. Y Patrol to approach paratroops on the north side of feature 64 (071424) [above the hamlet of Germano] and Major Redfern and T.2 to go over feature 64 and down into valley 073424. SBS were going to put MGs on top of feature 64 and south of it. Y took up posns vic.072425 and got MGs into action. T.1 [Saxton's patrol] ran into MG and mortar fire around the NE face of feature 64 …

In one close struggle Major Redfern was killed. His loss is a very sad blow to the unit and to his squadron because he was an officer of remarkably sound and able character. He was a most gallant leader who thought always of his men before himself and his cool judgement was always a clear guide to the solution of any problem … I took my medical orderly out to Major Redfern and verified my first impression that he had been killed instantly by MG burst. Germans could be heard talking in houses just below … We attempted to bury Major Redfern [on 14 November] but came under MG fire from Rachi and could not do the job [WO 218/91].

Son of Arthur and Margaret Redfern of Salisbury, Southern Rhodesia – Husband of Agnes Opal Redfern of Salisbury – Father of Margaret, born January 1934, and of John, born November 1938.
Age 37.
Rest in Peace
Grave 3.C.9. During the 1950s the primary school at Plumtree was named the Alan Redfern School in recognition of the contribution he made to his country, both in peace and war.

SIGNALMAN HAROLD ARTHUR **TODMAN** [SR/598851V] SOUTHERN RHODESIA SIGNALS (DEPOT) COMPANY, SOUTH AFRICAN CORPS OF SIGNALS AND LRDG (X.2 PATROL, B SQN)

Known to his comrades as 'Toddy', Harold Todman was born on 8 July 1918 at Meerut where his father was an officer in the Indian Army Reserve. However, he later lived with his mother in Salisbury, Rhodesia, where he worked as a telegraphist. In 1940 the Southern Rhodesia Signals (Depot) Company was raised using fifty postal and telegraph service workers, including Todman, as its foundation. It was to provide trained manpower for a variety of Commonwealth units. At the beginning of July 1943, whilst already serving in the Middle East, he transferred to the Union Defence Force of South Africa and was posted to the South African Corps of Signals. However, on the 20th he volunteered for the Long Range Desert Group and was posted to B Squadron that he joined at The Cedars Mountain Warfare School in Lebanon. He subsequently disembarked on the Dodecanese island of Leros at the beginning of October and after the German naval and airborne assault began on 12 November manned a Bren gun during an assault to retake Clidi Heights:

The Buffs were ordered to attack this ridge [Clidi], being led by one LRDG member to each section of Buffs, because we were familiar with the area. As we were advancing up this ridge we were under heavy machine-gun fire and fighter attack from the air, which aborted our attack and we withdrew. Todman, a Rhodesian, was wounded and sadly later died from his wounds [Don Coventry, LRDG Newsletter No.49 of 1993].

Captain John Olivey, MC, later stated that on 14 November 1943: 'Patrol then dividing into threes led by The Buffs to the north on to Mount Vernon where the infantry commander was killed and Rfn Todman was seriously wounded' (WO 218/91). He was subsequently reported 'missing believed POW' as of the 18th. Gordon Broderick, who joined the LRDG with Todman and who fought in the same patrol, later recalled that on the 23rd: 'He [a German guard] directed us to what had been our forward dressing station, still manned by British medics. It was here I saw Toddy for the last time. He gave me a wan smile and then died' (*Long Range Desert Group Rhodesia*, by Jonathan Pittaway).

Son of Arthur and Ella Todman of Gatooma, Southern Rhodesia – Younger brother of Stanley.
Age 25.
Til the day dawns. Missed by Mother
Special Memorial "C" 1.A.7.

SIGNALMAN HAROLD **WHEELDON** [2048644] ROYAL ENGINEERS, ROYAL CORPS OF SIGNALS AND LRDG (SIGNALS SQN ATT Y.1 PATROL, B SQN)

'Pusher' Wheeldon, as he was known to his comrades, was born in the parish of Newbold in Chesterfield on 17 April 1918. In January 1938, whilst working as a sorting clerk and telegraphist for the GPO, he joined the 358 Company, 40th (Sherwood Foresters) Anti-Aircraft Battalion, Royal Engineers (TA), at Chesterfield. He transferred to No.3 Company, North Midland Corps of Signals in March 1939 serving with them in France as part of the BEF from late March 1940 until 31 May when he was evacuated from Dunkirk. That September he married Beryl Bambrook in his home parish.

Wheeldon disembarked in Egypt in August 1941, volunteering for the Long Range Desert Group on 5 January 1942. That November he served under Captain Alastair Timpson as G.1 Patrol's signaller during Road Watch duties behind enemy lines:

> Wheeldon was always a cheering and reliable companion. He and I would work all day helping to summarise the voluminous results of the previous Road Watch party, then encode it and finally transmit it. The last phase alone would often take three or four hours. He also did much to cheer those returning tired to camp. At the start we had a tin or two of treacle and also of Nescafe. A portion of these luxuries would be the prerogative of the incoming relief, prepared by Wheeldon for our return after dawn. He never had anything but Bully beef, biscuits and water himself. Later on, that was all anyone had [*In Rommel's Backyard*, by Alastair Timpson].

Wheeldon was promoted to lance-corporal in April 1943 but reverted to the rank of signalman at his own request that August. The following month the SBS and LRDG moved into the Dodecanese, aiming to fill the void left by surrendered Italian garrisons before the Germans did so. Having embarked at Haifa the force forward-mounted to the island of Castelrosso and was issued subunit responsibilities. B Squadron moved to Leros from where four patrols, including Y.1 that Wheeldon was attached to, were landed on the island of Stampalia on the evening of 18 September. Tasked with bolstering the Italian garrison in the event of invasion and with watching for enemy shipping all patrols returned to Leros having made their reports.

On 24 September the LRDG and SBS HQs took up residence on the peaceful island of Calino where they were joined by their detachments from Samos on 1 October. The hope was that this would become Raiding Forces HQ for the autumn season. However, having cleared their new billets the men awoke in the early hours of the 3rd to find German forces invading the nearby island of Cos and the following day they were ordered to fall back to Leros that was also being bombed. Rapidly requisitioning local vessels both units set sail under the cover of darkness and disembarked at Lakki Bay before midnight. By dawn on the 5th the exhausted men had unloaded their jumble of stores. They were still on the dockside at 0900hrs when attacked by German aircraft. Whilst they took cover and returned rifle fire Wheeldon retrieved a Bren gun from a boat, set it up in the open and was subsequently fatally wounded [personal interview with Jim Patch, 2009]. The post-operation report notes:

> This was the first time that the LRDG had been seriously bombed as a whole unit and all ranks were commendably steady. Signalman Wheeldon LRDG and several SBS and [No.]30 Commandos were killed and wounded. The officer casualties included Capt Belcher, [No.]30 Commando, and Major Sutherland, SBS, wounded [WO 218/91].

An anonymous report within the same file describes the scene:

> Our next sensation was one of terrific machine-gun fire, whipped up in a fury and increased by rifle fire, until it reached a shattering crescendo, culminating in the high pitched whine, when seconds are counted before the ear splitting crash of bursting bombs. We fell on our faces and counted these seconds and suffered the din in our strange surprise to find ourselves alive, and then there was silence, a silence accentuated by the smell of cordite and the rising smell of dust which billowed up and accentuated the eerie gloom. The bombs had fallen close, and at first we had only thoughts for the others. Casualties were slight but the grim realisation of death was vile, one could be only sickened and enraged and feel a little helpless. This raid was only a taste of worse to come, but we had enough time to disperse the men and get a few light automatic weapons on the hill – and then it came again, first the noise of diving aircraft, then the piercing whistle which preceded their unnatural thunder. This time a ship was hit and our stores were knocked into indescribable chaos. Clouds of black oily smoke swirled into the sky as the other AA [anti-aircraft] guns speeded the parting raiders. We really knew not how long this went on, but we were diving for cover quite often and then emerging from a hole to see if the others were alright. Or machine-gunners stood their ground magnificently and fired unceasingly at Stukas which seemed to dive right down the barrels of the guns, but always there was that frightened silence just after the bombs had fallen and a choking dusty smell that permeated the air. How helpless we really were, but how little of this was really felt. A rather simple resignation to one's fate, which is spurned on by the horror of it all, merely leaves one oblivious to all sense of time or material considerations. At last there was a lull yet it was unreal and seemed as though balanced on an edge and seemed ready to crack again into fury at the slightest hint …
>
> The early morning scene of peaceful shipping lying along-side the quay faced with fine buildings, and cheerful faces had been transformed into a mass of wreckage heightened by burning ships and stores, and dust rising from shattered and ruined buildings. The fine streets were a mass of rubble and drooping telephone wires lying across charred and blackened craters. The piles of rations and ammunition were a mass of broken tins and exploded cartridges. Much was still burning and so were many hearts as we saw the quick destruction of so much fine equipment. We left the docks behind to sort ourselves out and see who may be missing. Casualties were light and we praised our luck [WO 218/91].

Patch, a friend of Wheeldon, later recalled:

> Pusher was the Sparks [signaller] with Y Patrol in the desert for quite some time. The first operation on which Pusher was with Y did not involve any direct action against the enemy and he remarked that this was the first patrol he had been on without having to fire his gun. Every evening he set aside a few minutes to write to his wife and kept these pieces until he returned to base and was able to send them. He was a man of immense courage and resource. In the incident which led to his death he set up his Bren gun without cover because the enemy attack was at its height and he had no time to look for suitable cover [personal correspondence, 2011].

Despite the reports above Wheeldon is officially recorded as having been killed in action on 9 October 1943. He was posthumously mentioned in despatches for his actions (*London Gazette* 13/01/44, 36327).

Son of Charles and Elsie Wheeldon (née Wood) of Chesterfield, Derbyshire – Husband of Bessie Wheeldon of Hunloke Avenue, Boythorpe, Chesterfield. Age 25.
Time changed many things but memory will always cling
Special memorial "C" 4.D.3.

RHODES WAR CEMETERY

At the end of the war in Europe the remains of seventy-eight Commonwealth servicemen, who lost their lives on this and other Dodecanese Islands, were concentrated to this cemetery. In 1957 a further sixty-five were reinterred from Cos War Cemetery that closed.

The cemetery is situated on the southern outskirts of the old town of Rhodes on the coastal road to Lindos. It lies close to the Zepheros market on the junction of Kallitheas Avenue and Akramitou, the entrance being opposite the Italian, Jewish and Turkish cemeteries. GPS co-ordinates: Latitude 36.4274, Longitude 28.22892

GUARDSMAN LANGSLOW THOMAS **BISHOP** [2616790] GRENADIER GUARDS, LRDG AND SBS (X DET)

Known variously as 'Bish' or 'Tommy', Langslow Bishop was born on 5 January 1917 in Wolverhampton. At the age of 3 his father, who had held a commission in the Wiltshire Regiment and been shell-shocked at Gallipoli, left his wife and children and migrated to Australia where he died in 1932. Bishop's mother was therefore left little option but to sign him over to the care of his uncle, Major Thomas Bishop, OBE, whilst she continued to look after her two daughters. His uncle stipulated that his offer was only open if she agreed not to contact her son from then on.

At the outbreak of war Bishop, who was working as a merchant seaman for the ship owners Everards & Sons of Greenhithe, London, returned to his hometown to enlist into his uncle's regiment, the Grenadier Guards. After depot he was posted to the Training Battalion and then in April 1940 to the newly-formed 4th Battalion. However, he served as a member of the BEF in France from 15 May 1940 with No.2 Infantry

Base Depot and was evacuated from Dunkirk at the beginning of June. On his return he joined the 1st Battalion's No.3 Company.

That August Bishop was attached to merchant shipping defence in the Port of Clyde, his service record recording a number of hospital entries including that of 20 November when his work aboard HM Trawler *Pentland Firth* resulted in him 'suffering from gunshot wounds to left foot and exhaustion'. He was nominally transferred to the newly-formed Royal Artillery's 1st Maritime Anti-Aircraft Battery at the beginning of May 1941, manning anti-aircraft guns on merchant shipping for a period of two months and being one of those commended 'for brave conduct when their ships encountered enemy ships, submarines, aircraft or mines' (*London Gazette* 18/03/41).

Although posted back to the 1st (Motorised) Battalion, Grenadier Guards, Bishop embarked for Egypt with the newly-formed 6th Battalion in early 1942. He travelled on to Palestine and Jordan before finally arriving at Quatania not far from Damascus. Departing for Egypt in order to join the Long Range Desert Group he served in G Patrol from 17 October 1942 and took part in its last operation under Lieutenant Bernard Bruce during February and March 1943. As the men moved into Tunisia he was wounded in the chest on 13 February but appears to have carried on with his duties.

With the Afrikakorps defeated and hostilities in North Africa at an end the LRDG based itself at Athlit in Palestine, Bishop transferring to the nearby Special Boat Squadron on 2 August 1943 after G Patrol had been disbanded. The following month both units were tasked to fill the void left by surrendered Italian garrisons and seize the Dodecanese Islands before German troops could do so. As such X Detachment, a composite force consisting of members of both S and M Detachments, sailed to the area, its War Diary noting that on 5 October 1943 Bishop and two others embarked at Simi bound for Turkey in order to pick up British escapees from the island of Cos. Their vessel, the *Merano*, was back at the island the following day, the three SBS presumably having returned with it (WO 201/795). On the 7th the Germans attempted an amphibious landing. X Detachment repulsed, killed or took prisoner all that came ashore for the loss of one man (see Private Bill Morrison's entry within this section for further details). Revenge came in the form of severe air attacks, Bishop and Corporal Sidney Greaves, MM, being trapped under the rubble of their HQ following a Stuka raid on 8 October 1943. Bishop, whose foot was lying across the throat of Greaves, agreed to have it amputated so that access could be made to save his friend. Amidst the wreckage in very cramped conditions, and with no more instruments other than scissors and a small wood saw, Flight Lieutenant 'Hank' Ferris, the Medical Officer of No.74 Squadron, and Private Porter 'Joe' Jarrell, an American serving as a medic with the SBS, amputated by candlelight and pulled Bishop clear. Sadly he died of shock, it also being too late for Greaves (see his entry within this section).

Whilst it is difficult to understand why Bishop's sacrifice went unrecognised Ferris was awarded a Military Cross for this and other actions on Simi. Meanwhile, Jarrell, previously rejected by the American and Greek armies as well as the French Foreign Legion due to short-sightedness and flat feet, received the George Medal, as did Sergeant Harold Whittle, also SBS and an ex-miner, for assisting him. Their citations highlight what Bishop and Greaves must have suffered:

Jarrell, acting with Sergeant Whittle, worked for 27hrs, without rest to the point almost of collapse, and with Sjt Whittle shares the credit for the two men being rescued alive. He entirely disregarded personal risk, crawling along perilous tunnels through the debris to administer morphia, feed and cheer the trapped men; the next minute working feverishly to clear the debris. Owing to the RAF doctor having an injured wrist, under the Doctor's supervision in appalling conditions, by candlelight, on his back he did most of the leg amputation necessary to release one man. His movement was restricted by the likelihood of the shored up debris falling in on himself and the trapped men [*London Gazette* 02/03/44].

Whittle supervised rescue operations, working like a man possessed himself. He worked for a period of 27hrs without rest, exposing himself to extreme risk. He continued work throughout two further raids when a bomb falling anywhere in the slightest vicinity would have brought the remnants of the building upon him. He was a source of inspiration to all workers and the credit that the two were released alive (unfortunately both died later) was almost entirely due to his direction, initiative, in making do with the crude tools at his disposal and his entire disregard of personal risk. He himself made and shored up a passage under the debris to one man [*London Gazette* 02/03/44].

The SBS War Diary noted: 'Bishop very brave ... died through shock and loss of blood ... [on 9 October] 1700hrs burial party left quay side with Cpl Greaves, Bishop and [Lance-corporal 'Mac'] McKendrick for cemetery' (WO 201/795). Captain Alan Redfern, MBE, of the LRDG summarised his own operations between 24 September and 22 October, noting:

8 Oct ... After breakfast Stuka bombing commenced, and as target was concentrated it was not pleasant. Three Ju88s [*sic* – 87s] came at first. One was shot down into the sea but the remaining two bombed us at intervals all day until sunset, when a second was clearly badly hit.

In the course of the second raid a direct hit was secured on our HQ and two men killed outright [McKendrick and Leading Aircraftsman Norman Gay] and Greaves and Bishop (ex LRDG) trapped in the wreckage.

We worked on them all day (which meant we could not escape the Stuka attacks by disappearing into the hills) and all night. Bennett did particularly good work. Bishop was cleared but caught by ankle. Amputation was only course and he did not survive the operation. Greaves was removed twenty-nine hours after the bomb hit and died as he was being lifted clear [Operation Report No.90].

According to Jarrell, Bishop, Greaves and McKendrick were buried on Simi in temporary graves, the intention being that they would later to be buried at sea as the ground was so rocky (presumably Leading Aircraftsman Norman Gay was buried alongside them – see McKendrick's entry below). However, due to the intervention of members of the Greek Sacred Squadron and of Lord Jellicoe, the bodies were reinterred at Rhodes War Cemetery on 9 December 1945.

The Derby Evening Telegraph later reported:

Guardsman Langslow Thomas Bishop (26), a nephew of Major T. H. Bishop of Bearwardcote, Etwall, has died of wounds ... An Old Derbeian, he enlisted in the Grenadier Guards at the outbreak of hostilities and was attached to the Mercantile Marine as a gunner. He had intended taking up the mercantile service as a career. While serving at sea he was twice torpedoed, and wounded in action. He was mentioned for gallantry in despatches [*sic* – received a commendation. Article published 29 October 1943].

Son of Fred and Edith Bishop (née Slang of Llandudno) – Brother of Margaret Shord (who served in the ATS) and Sonia Mirrington (of the WAAF) – Nephew of Major Thomas Bishop, OBE, of The Gables, Rangermore, Burton-on-Trent, Derby – In 1950 Sonia, who was trying to trace her brother, learnt of his death and had the distressing task of having to break the news to his mother.

Age 26.

Rest eternal grant unto him, O Lord; and let light perpetual shine upon him

Grave 4.A.5. Also commemorated on a marble plaque within Simi's cemetery.

GUNNER HERBERT FEDERMANN [PAL/8363] ROYAL ARTILLERY
AND LRDG (Y PATROL, B SQN)

Known to his friends as 'Sam', Herbert Federmann was born in Vienna on 3 May 1921 to Austrian parents. Whilst both later became Czech nationals, Federmann took Palestinian citizenship and served in the Palestinian Special Police during 1938. He subsequently enlisted into the Palestinian Battery, Royal Artillery, at Sarafand in May 1941 noting that he was a student. His service record states that he spoke good English, excellent Czech, fluent French, excellent German and good Hebrew, and that his preference for employment was liaison or interpretation work. Having served with the 14th and 178th Coastal Regiments at Haifa he was re-posted as an instructor to the Middle East Ski School at The Cedars in Lebanon in December 1942. He was promoted to lance-bombardier the following February and to bombardier in March. On return to his regimental HQ Federmann reverted to the rank of gunner and volunteered for the Long Range Desert Group on 29 May 1943. Posted to B Squadron he subsequently returned to The Cedars in the Lebanese mountains and was involved in a training accident, former squadron member Ron Hill recalling:

> A new recruit, called Federmann, was at the wheel of the Jeep with an experienced driver beside him. Another Y Patrol member and myself in the back. I was sat behind the co-driver and as Jeeps were left hand drive this was the edge or off side. All went well until we were about two thirds of the way up and approaching the snow line when a particularly vicious hairpin Federmann got into an uncontrollable slide on the scree like surface and over the Jeep went – With The Cedars a little dark patch about three thousand feet below. I have a very clear recollection of the sequence of events: Federmann scrabbled out from behind the steering wheel as the Jeep tottered on the edge and the passenger on my left calmly stepped out onto the road as the rear wheels went over. The co-driver and myself stayed put, there was no road on our side to step onto. I distinctly remembered the Jeep somersaulting as it went over the edge and the world turning full circle [IWM Documents.6911 – Private Papers of W. R. Hill].

B Squadron moved into the Aegean theatre on 12 September 1943, aiming to fill the void left by surrendered Italian garrisons before the Germans could do so. The following month HMS *Hedgehog*, a steam trawler of the Levant Schooner Flotilla, embarked German POWs from Stampalia and was returning to Leros when it developed engine trouble. Enemy air reconnaissance reported that she had put into Levita for repairs and on 18 October parachutists of a German Brandenburger company mounted a successful rescue mission, releasing their comrades and capturing both *Hedgehog's* British crew and Italians based at the island's small wireless station. The Brandenburgers were then replaced by a Luftwaffe detachment. Back on Leros it became clear that all was not well, Brigadier 'Ben' Brittorous, DSO, MC, ordering forty-seven members of the LRDG, including Federmann, to retake Levita. This party, collectively known as Olforce after its commander Captain John Olivey, MC, landed on the evening of the 23rd having been denied the time to recce enemy dispositions. Lt-Commander Frank Ramseyer, Royal Navy Liaison Officer at Raiding Forces HQ, subsequently reported:

> Information indicated that only 20–30 Germans were on Levita and LRDG considered that a force of 47 troops should be able to deal with the situation.
> The landing went according to plan, and the LRDG were landed in two parties, one in the west and one in the south of the island. The MLs [Motor Launches] withdrawing and later bombarding areas where he enemy were reported to be concentrating. After completing their part of the operation the MLs returned to Leros.
> Unfortunately the following morning the Germans contacted their air force in Cos and were able to attack LRDG units [that had occupied strategic high points] from the air before they had established themselves, and later in the day the enemy took control.
> On the night of 24/25th ML 579 with Major [Jake] Easonsmith, LRDG, returned to Levita and recovered seven of their personnel, who described the above incidents [see Easonsmith's entry under Leros War Cemetery, Greece] …
> Altogether the operation was very disappointing and proved once again the importance of air superiority, even where small forces are employed [see Trooper Johnnie Bowler's entry under Athens Memorial, Greece, for further details of this operation].

Federmann had been killed in action on the 24th. Although there has been some suggestion that he had shot himself just before capture due to his Jewish faith, Jim Patch, who was taken prisoner, later recalled:

He spoke fluent German and, during the assault on Levita, as the B Squadron party approached a building thought to be a weather station with a view to taking it and not knowing whether it was occupied by the enemy, Sam shouted to any possible garrison to surrender. The building turned out to be unoccupied. After we were captured and Sam had been killed there was no talk of his having shot himself. I do not know how the story that he had shot himself arose. I made his cross and carved his name on it [personal correspondence, 2011].

Patch had previously written that after being taken prisoner he was:

… marched down to the German HQ where [Sergeant] Harris and his patrol were being held. This HQ was in a small group of store houses in the centre of the island, Harris told me that his patrol had been attacked simultaneously from two sides by two enemy patrols each of which outnumbered his own. In the skirmish that followed Gnr Federmann had been killed before the patrol was forced to surrender [LRDG Newsletter No.39 of 1983].

A subsequent newsletter includes the following:

Bill (Jock) Fraser sadly reports the death of Boozie Gunn. He had only a short time before found his address through a mutual friend. Jock recalls how on Levita Island, during that hopeless battle, they had had to bury poor old Sam Federmann and Boozie helped to dismantle the Bren gun to be buried with him because they were out of ammo [Newsletter No.44, 1988].

Son of Viteslav Federmann of Park Road, West Kirby.
Age 22.
Unforgotten by his parents, brother, sister, and many friends in Israel
Grave 1.A.12. Although reinterred within Cos War Cemetery, Federmann's remains were moved here on 8 July 1957 when this closed.

CORPORAL SIDNEY **GREAVES** MM [1882893] ROYAL ENGINEERS, NO.7 COMMANDO, MIDDLE EAST COMMANDO, SPECIAL BOAT SECTION, 1ST SAS AND SBS (X DET)

Sidney Greaves was born in the town of Castleford, Yorkshire, on 2 November 1914. Having worked as a joiner he enlisted into the Royal Engineers at Leeds in October 1939 and was posted to the depot at Chatham. After training he initially joined 207 Field Company before being posted to 553 Company where he was employed as a carpenter and joiner. In May 1940 he married Ethel Johnson at Pontefract and having been promoted to lance-corporal the following month volunteered for No.7 Commando that October, reverting to the rank of sapper to do so. In November this was temporarily reorganised as No.2 Company, 3rd Special Service Battalion, Greaves regaining his lance-corporal's stripe a few days later.

In March 1941, Greaves' unit, having been reconstituted as No.7 Commando, arrived in Egypt and was accommodated under canvas at Sidi Bishir as A Battalion, Layforce. It is likely that he saw action during the largely abortive raid at Bardia on the Libyan coast that April. What is certain is that he was on Crete between 24 and 26 May, fighting rearguard actions so that Commonwealth troops could be evacuated.

He himself was one of those lucky enough to be taken off by the Royal Navy. After Layforce disbanded he was absorbed into the Middle East Commando on 29 January 1942 and on 1 August joined No.1 Special Boat Section. Promoted to corporal, the section was gradually absorbed into 1st SAS during the latter half of 1942. In January 1943 D Squadron was formed and those that had come from No.1 SBS posted to it. When the Regiment was restructured on 19 March this separated from the newly-formed Special Raiding Squadron under the title of the Special Boat Squadron. Basing itself at Azzib on the Palestinian coast it trained hard for forthcoming operations and in mid May tested coastal defences along the Syrian coast.

Greaves subsequently returned to the island of Crete for Operation Albumen: tasked with destroying Axis aircraft that posed a threat to the Allied invasion fleet that was soon to pass en route to Sicily, an operational party of three officers and fourteen other ranks embarked *ML 361* at Bardia on the morning of 22 June 1943. In the early hours of the following morning they landed at Cape Kokinoxos and lay up for the day in a wadi. That evening the group split to carry out its tasks, Patrol C setting off for the airfield at Kastelli Pediada. The citation that accompanied the immediate award of Greaves' Military Medal takes up the narrative:

> This NCO, with 3056933 Sjt Nicholson, J, Royal Scots, was entirely responsible for planning and carrying out the attack on Kastelli Pediada aerodrome from the east on the night 4th July 1943. In spite of considerable opposition they successfully entered the aerodrome. Although fired on by sentries on three occasions they continued with the attack and destroyed five aircraft and two petrol dumps, withdrawing only when lorry loads of reinforcements prevented further action. Throughout the duration of the operation, the conduct of this NCO was of the highest order. (It is requested that details of the above operations should not be published owing to their secrecy) [*London Gazette* 36168 of 10/09/43, 2nd Supplement 14/09/43, citation later released within WO 373/46].

Having regrouped the raiding party was picked up by motor launch after a brief contact with a German patrol that resulted in the loss of Lieutenant Ken Lamonby (see his entry under Suda Bay War Cemetery, Greece, for full details). On its return to Mersa Matruh the men rested before making their way to Cairo where they took two German prisoners to Groppi's restaurant for ice cream. This act of human decency was appreciated somewhat more by the captives than their awaiting interrogators.

After the Italian armistice of September 1943 the SBS was tasked to seize Aegean islands before Germans troops could do so. The War Diary of X Detachment, a composite force of both S and M

Detachments, subsequently records that Greaves and Corporal Pollock were both wounded in the back on 6 October 1943 when fired on at a beach whilst attempting to pick up Captain 'Stud' Stellin's patrol from Cos (WO 201/795). Having returned to Simi, Greaves was treated at the SBS HQ. However, he and Guardsman Tommy Bishop were trapped under the building on the 8th as a result of a German air raid. Although Bishop agreed to have his foot amputated so that access could be gained to Greaves, both men died of shock on being released from the rubble on the 9th:

> Sat 9 Oct 43 … Greeves [*sic*] was freed about 1400hrs. Leg badly squashed and stomach also. Shock and strain of release after twenty-seven hours buried killed him shortly after release. Had been living on nerves and morphia only …
>
> 1700[hrs] burial party left quay side with Cpl Greeves, Bishop and McKendrick for cemetery [WO 201/795 – see Lance-corporal 'Mac' McKendrick's entry below].

Son of Joshua and Dora Greaves of Carlton Avenue, Castleford, Yorkshire – Husband of Ethel Greaves of Burley-in-Wharfdale, Yorkshire (formerly of Castleford) – Father of Janet Greaves.

Age 28.
Always remembered by a dear wife and daughter
Grave 3.A.3. Also commemorated on a marble plaque within Simi's cemetery.

SERGEANT ERNEST HENRY ALBERT **HAWKES** [850546] ROYAL ARTILLERY, 1ST SAS AND SBS (M DET)

Known as 'Badge' to his comrades, Ernest Hawkes was born on 26 July 1920 at Faversham in Kent but was educated in India and Ireland as a result of his father's army career. In September 1935 he enlisted as a boy soldier at Chatham, later holding the rank of trumpeter having been posted to India himself in January 1937. After serving with the 7th Field Battery, 4th Field Regiment, Royal Artillery, Hawkes bought his discharge for £35 during February 1939 in Hyderabad, signing off at Winchester on 1 April. His final report, which described his conduct as exemplary, noted:

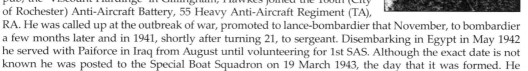

> Gunner Hawkes is an intelligent, honest, sober and trustworthy man who throughout his three and a half years service has always been well reported on by the officers he has served under. For the first three years of his service he was a trumpeter and has only recently become a gunner and as such was shaping well. He is keen on games and a good hockey player.

Two months later, whilst working as a barman, most probably at his father's pub, the 'Viscount Hardinge' in Gillingham, Hawkes joined the 166th (City of Rochester) Anti-Aircraft Battery, 55 Heavy Anti-Aircraft Regiment (TA), RA. He was called up at the outbreak of war, promoted to lance-bombardier that November, to bombardier a few months later and in 1941, shortly after turning 21, to sergeant. Disembarking in Egypt in May 1942 he served with Paiforce in Iraq from August until volunteering for 1st SAS. Although the exact date is not known he was posted to the Special Boat Squadron on 19 March 1943, the day that it was formed. He subsequently attended parachute course No.43 at Ramat David in Palestine during May.

That September Italy surrendered and the SBS and LRDG rapidly embarked at Haifa to fill the void left by her garrisons in the Dodecanese before the Germans could do so. Having taken up residence on Samos detachments of both units were relieved by the Royal West Kent Regiment on 1 October 1943 and proceeded to the peaceful island of Calino. The following day Hawkes was accidentally killed in a shooting incident.

The SBS Medical Officer of the time, Captain McIntyre, recalled Hawkes 'died after accidentally shooting himself while cleaning his revolver on Dodecanese island of Calynos [*sic*] just before Cos fell to the Germans.' This is confirmed by a signal to Raiding Forces HQ: 'Sjt Hawkes M Det died 0945hrs 2 Oct result revolver accident' (WO 201/1653). His local newspaper, *The Chatham, Rochester and Gillingham News*, carried his obituary on 29 October: 'Combining the fearless qualities of the trained soldier with the daredevilry of youth, he was ideally suited for the daring sorties that his raiding force had to undertake.'

Son of Captain Ernest and Elsie Hawkes (née Goodlan) of Gillingham, Kent. Age 23.
'Who Dares Wins'
Grave 1.B.4.

LANCE-CORPORAL ROBERT ALEXANDER McKENDRICK [7954759] ROYAL ARMOURED CORPS, 1ST SAS AND SBS (X DET)

'Mac' McKendrick was born on 11 December 1909 in Bootle, Lancashire. Although he later worked as a corn merchant in Leicester he returned to Merseyside to marry Sarah Elizabeth Irvine at St John's Church in November 1932. By the outbreak of war they had settled in Leicester, McKendrick working as an insurance agent. Enlisting into the 61st Training Regiment, Royal Armoured Corps, at Tidworth during March 1942 he was re-posted to the 52nd Training Regiment at Barnard Castle and embarked for the Middle East late that October. Having arrived in Egypt on New Year's Eve he volunteered for 1st SAS' Signal Troop on 14 January 1943 and was promoted to lance-corporal that day.

McKendrick joined the Special Boat Squadron on 28 May 1943 and embarked at Haifa for operations in the Aegean that September. He was a member of No.1 Patrol under Lieutenant Charles Bimrose that attempted to rescue a downed British bomber aircrew stranded on the island of Scarpanto: having set sail from Simi at dusk on the 30th the patrol relieved that of Captain Andy Lassen, MC, on Calchi, before landing on Scarpanto on 1 October. Finding that the Germans had already captured the aircrew they had difficulty in leaving the island, Private Henry Harris being drowned in the process (see Harris' entry under Brookwood Memorial, United Kingdom, Volume III, for full details of this operation).

Having returned to Simi on 3 October McKendrick took part in the successful defence of the island on the 7th (see Private Bill Morrison's entry below for details). Revenge came in the form of German air attack and he was subsequently killed in action alongside Leading Aircraftsman Norman Gay on the 8th. Two Stukas, which had spent the day dive-bombing, going back and forth to Rhodes to re-arm and refuel, scored a direct hit on the British HQ where the pair was based. They were originally buried on the evening of the 9th alongside two other SBS casualties, Lance-corporal Sidney Greaves and Guardsman Tommy Bishop, in a cemetery on the island. The following month McKendrick's wife received a letter from Captain Hamer of Raiding Force Signals:

> You will have heard from the War Office of the death of your husband and I hasten to write you this letter offering you my deepest sympathy. I know that words are very poor compensation in matters like this but they are at least sincere.
>
> I've known Mac for some time now as his Commanding Officer and always found him one of the best. He was a fine soldier and ever willing to go where danger threatened, never without a smile or some droll wisecrack. He is missed but not forgotten by all of us here. It is not easy to express one's feelings on these occasions, and they happen all too

frequently, but I'm certain it will be some small comfort to you to know that you are not alone in your loss. You have children too and both they and you can be undeniably proud of their father and your husband. And take it from me Mrs McKendrick that it is you and people like you who are back at home and wait that are really winning this war – you who receive the worst news and yet go on with great courage and cheerfulness – and we mere soldiers salute you with all our hearts [McKendrick family collection].

Son of Alexander and Mary McKendrick of Ibstock Road, Bootle – Husband of Sarah McKendrick of King Richard's Road, Leicester – Father of Roland, Neil, Robert and June – Younger brother of Laura, Florence and Rhoda McKendrick. Age 33.
No inscription.
Grave 3.A.2 where he is buried between Gay and Greaves. Also commemorated on a marble plaque within Simi's cemetery.

TROOPER HECTOR LAWRENCE **MALLETT** [16545] DIVISIONAL CAVALRY REGIMENT AND LRDG (A SQN)

Hector Mallett was born in New Zealand on 3 April 1914 and lived at Temuka in Canterbury. Having worked as a teamster and lorry driver he enlisted at Stratford, Taranaki, in June 1940 and was posted to the Divisional Cavalry Regiment at Burnham the following January. Having embarked for the Middle East in April 1941 he arrived in Egypt that May and was posted to various training depots, briefly being hospitalised at Maadi that December for an unknown reason. He volunteered for the Long Range Desert Group in late April 1942 and was posted to A Squadron with which he took part in desert operations. After hostilities in North Africa drew to a successful conclusion he qualified as a driver mechanic, embarking at Haifa for operations in the Dodecanese on 21 September 1943.

Olforce, which combined elements of both A and B Squadrons, was tasked with seizing the enemy-held island of Levita but was denied the time required to recce enemy dispositions. It found stiffer resistance than expected. Jim Patch, one of those subsequently captured, believes that Mallett's party ran out of ammunition, whilst an unknown correspondent in an LRDG newsletter recalled that on 24 October 1943:

> They [Mallett's party] were taken in the rear by heavy machine-gun fire from the vicinity of their landing place. The detachment was kept pinned down by this for some time but eventually they put in a counter attack and rushed the enemy positions taking a German patrol of twelve men prisoner. Trooper H L Mallett was severely wounded in this attack and [despite the efforts of the patrol's medic, Private Bruce Steedman] died later [LRDG Newsletter No.39 of 1983].

Although originally buried in the Greek Field in the centre of Levita overlooking the harbour, Mallett was reinterred in the British Military Cemetery on the island of Cos after an investigation team located his remains in February 1946. It had hoped to also find those of Troopers Johnnie Bowler and Doug Davison but was unable to do so (see Bowler's and Davison's entries under Athens Memorial, Greece, for full details of this operation).

Son of William and Cecilia Mallett of Seddon Street, Temuka, Canterbury, New Zealand – Brother of Mrs Cecilia Fawdray – Fiancée of Miss Inez Marcelline Frank of New Plymouth.
Age 29.
No inscription.
Grave 4.B.11. Although reinterred within Cos War Cemetery Mallett's remains were moved here on 8 July 1957 when this closed. Also commemorated on an LRDG memorial within the New Zealand SAS camp at Papakura and on Temuka's war memorial.

Private William **MORRISON** [2820617] Seaforth Highlanders and SBS (X Det)

Bill Morrison was born on 9 February 1918 in the village of Duffus near Elgin, Morayshire. In late 1936, whilst working as a farm servant, he joined the local 6th Battalion, Seaforth Highlanders (TA), and was embodied at the outbreak of war. He subsequently served with the battalion in France as part of the BEF from late January 1940 until 1 June when he was evacuated from Dunkirk.

After nearly two years of home duties Morrison's battalion landed on the Vichy-held island of Madagascar on 5 May 1942 during Operation Ironclad, thus denying the Japanese a potential air and naval base that would paralyse Commonwealth convoys to the Middle and Far East. The operation also ensured control of the Mozambique Channel through which such convoys passed. The Seaforths came ashore at a bay west of Diego Suarez in the second wave and advanced east towards the port of Antsirane. Although the French put up a dogged defence all resistance in the area had collapsed by daybreak on the 7th, the British fleet entering the harbour that morning. The 17th Infantry Brigade, of which the Seaforths were a part, then sailed for India where Morrison was stationed until moving to Iraq as part of Paiforce that September. Arriving in Egypt in mid April 1943 he volunteered for the Special Boat Squadron on the 27th, attending parachute course No.43 at Ramat David during May.

On 11 September 1943 a composite SBS force known as X Detachment embarked at Haifa and sailed for Castelrosso. On the 17th it landed on the Dodecanese island of Simi where it took control of defences from the recently surrendered Italian garrison. At the beginning of October it was reinforced by forty RAF ground crew who had been diverted whilst en route to Cos. The extra manpower was soon to come in use when a force of approximately forty Germans arrived from Rhodes and landed at Pedi Bay on the 7th. Whilst one of the airmen forced most of the enemy into cover using an anti-aircraft gun, Lieutenant Charles Bimrose of the SBS took No.1 Patrol to deal with a troublesome machine gun overlooking Simi Town. En route they came under contact and Morrison was killed whilst two men, including Bimrose himself, were wounded (WO 201/795).

The defenders of the island, including the Italian garrison of 150, were subsequently organised by Captain Andy Lassen, MC, and the enemy successfully routed (see Lassen's entry under Argenta Gap War Cemetery, Italy, within this volume).

Son of William and Williamina Morrison of Newtonmore, Invernesshire, later of Durraway, Forres, Morayshire.
Age 25.
In loving memory of Bill our dearest son and brother. Asleep in Jesus
Grave 4.A.4. Also commemorated on his father's headstone in Auldearn parish churchyard.

SERGEANT GEORGE **MUNRO** [3323555] HIGHLAND LIGHT INFANTRY, NO.11 COMMANDO, MIDDLE EAST COMMANDO, 1ST SAS AND SBS (S DET)

George Munro was born on 5 March 1914 at Govanhill in Glasgow. After working in a grocery store he enlisted into the Highland Light Infantry at Troon at the end of May 1940. That September, having completed training during which he was promoted to lance-corporal, he volunteered for No.11 (Scottish) Commando. He served with this during its temporary absorption into the 2nd Special Service Battalion, its reconstitution as No.11, and its subsequent arrival in the Middle East as C Battalion, Layforce, in early March 1941.

Having deployed to Cyprus as a corporal at the end of April 1941 Munro took part in the Litani River landings that June, fighting against the Vichy French in what is modern-day Lebanon (OPERATION EXPORTER). Returning to Egypt in August No.11 was absorbed into the Middle East Commando. Munro was subsequently posted to Paiforce at the beginning of September 1942 to serve in Persia and Iraq. He volunteered for 1st SAS on 20 January 1943 and was posted to D Squadron, picking up his sergeant's tapes two months later when this became the Special Boat Squadron.

Having deployed to the Aegean Munro was killed in action on the island of Samos on 17 November 1943. Dick Holmes, MM, later recalled:

> On a sunny afternoon we were subjected to an attack by several squadrons of Stukas who obviously had identified their target. Initially I sheltered in a slit trench some distance from the house in which we were billeted but during a short interlude I rushed into the house to retrieve my rucksack which contained some valuables and spare ammo and food that could become very useful in the near future. George Munro and Sparrow were lying on the floor. I assumed they were both sleeping. I yelled at them to get the hell out of the house, grabbed my Bergen and raced outside just as another Stuka attack started. I scrambled over a low brick wall about 20 yards away from the house and watched as the building suffered several more direct hits. When the raid was over several other members of J Patrol entered the house to collect their belongings and reported that George Munro had been killed and all that remained of Sparrow was a solitary boot with a foot in it … George Munro was my first patrol sergeant when I joined the SBS and he was a very popular man, who possessed a very good sense of humour. He was a great loss to the Regiment [personal correspondence, 2009].

An official report differs slightly:

It is definitely known that, at the time of the first attack, Sgt Munro was outside in the garden at the rear of the house with other personnel of the SBS. He was hit by splinters of the first bomb which dropped in the corner of the garden. His left leg was completely severed at the thigh and he was practically buried by the debris of the house, which was hit almost immediately after the first bombs had exploded. Due to the severity of the attacks it was not possible to evacuate him to hospital, but instant medical assistance was rendered by Pte J.C. Jarrell the medical orderly. Later during the time between the second and third attack he was uncovered by personnel of the SBS but he had to be left as the third attack came with increased violence and personnel who had been endeavouring to get him away had to take cover. When the attack had ceased it was found that he had died due to the extreme loss of blood and shock. During the latter part of the day he was buried by the Italians.

Munro's remains were later reinterred at this cemetery on Rhodes. Whilst 'Spadge' Sparrow is commemorated on the Athens Memorial to the missing Holmes believes that there is some likelihood that his remains were buried under the Unknown Soldier's headstone that forms the joint grave with Munro's (correspondence with Dick Holmes, 2009).

Son of John and Jeanie Munro of Ardbeg Street, Glasgow.
Age 29.
He lives for ever in our hearts. Loved and not forgotten
Joint grave 2.B.6.

SIGNALMAN CLIFFORD HENRY **WHITEHEAD** [RH2553920] RHODESIAN ARMY, ROYAL CORPS OF SIGNALS AND LRDG (S.1 PATROL, B SQN)

Cliff Whitehead was born on 11 May 1920 in Umtali, Southern Rhodesia, where he attended the local high school and worked as an apprentice storeman. He joined the Rhodesian Army in September 1940 at Salisbury (service number X862) and nominally enlisted into the Royal Corps of Signals in February 1942 having arrived in Egypt the previous month. He immediately volunteered for the Long Range Desert Group as a trained signaller. During January 1943 he took part in a joint operation by S.1 Patrol under Lieutenant Ken Lazarus, the LRDG survey officer, and Popski's Private Army 'to make a topographical recce of an area in Tunisia' (WO 218/91). Attacked in the Wadi Zem Zem by enemy armoured cars and infantry on the 15th all but one truck became bogged in and had to be abandoned, although Whitehead evaded capture (see Gunner Joseph Henderson's entry under Tripoli War Cemetery, Libya, Volume I, for full details of this incident).

Whitehead was hospitalised in July 1943 for an unknown reason before proceeding to the Aegean theatre that October. Reaching Leros he rejoined S.1 Patrol, which had just returned from Simi, but was killed in action on 15 November during the German assault on the island. Former B Squadron member, 'Toity' du Toit, later recalled:

> The bombing was aimed at HQ, and when the planes left, we all made our way to HQ separately. I then noticed that Cliff Whitehead was not with us, and so went in search of him. I found him buried in a slit trench, a bomb crater in close proximity. After seeing his boot sticking out of the ground, I dug down and eventually extracted him, but he was already dead. Cliff's body was taken to HQ where the doctor pronounced him dead and suggested we bury him. I then decided to bury him in the same slit trench that he was found in, so with Cliff lying on the

> stretcher in the open next to me, I then proceeded to dig the grave. I was busy doing this when a Stuka appeared overhead again. I ignored it and carried on with the burial. The Stuka then dived down onto us and at the last minute pulled away without strafing or bombing, circled overhead several times, waggled its wings and disappeared. I could only presume that the pilot had seen Cliff's body on the stretcher and realised that a fellow soldier was about to be buried [*Long Range Desert Group Rhodesia*, by Jonathon Pittaway].

Although reinterred within Cos War Cemetery Whitehead's remains were moved here on 8 July 1957 when this closed. However, it is not known why this occurred when a war cemetery already existed on Leros.

Son of Frederick and Florry Whitehead of East London, Cape Province, South Africa.
Age 23.
Sacred. To our dear son and brother. Ever a beautiful memory of him we loved so dear.
Buried in joint grave 1.A.4–5. The reason for this is unknown.

SUDA BAY WAR CEMETERY

Prior to the German invasion of May 1941 Suda Bay, a busy naval fuelling base, had been regarded as strategically key to the defence of Egypt. Its loss aggravated all of the Mediterranean difficulties.

This cemetery was established after the Second World War as the resting place of 1,500 Commonwealth servicemen. Their remains were reinterred from four burial grounds established by German forces, and from isolated sites and civilian cemeteries. Nearly 800 are unidentified. In addition, there are nineteen burials of the First World War that were moved from Suda Bay Consular Cemetery, seven burials of other nationalities, and thirty-seven non-war burials.

Suda Bay is on the northern coast of Crete, the cemetery being situated at the north-western corner of the bay, 5 kilometres east of Hania (or Khania) and 3 kilometres north of the Hania–Rethymnon–Heraklion road. It is well signposted from this and lies within an olive grove. GPS co-ordinates: Latitude 35.50017, Longitude 24.06028

CAPTAIN CHARLES MAURICE <u>CLYNES</u> MC [132520] ARGYLL AND SUTHERLAND HIGHLANDERS, ROYAL IRISH FUSILIERS, SPECIAL BOAT SECTION AND SBS (M SQN)

Charlie Clynes was born on 2 November 1918 at Newtonards in County Down but grew up in Glasgow where he attended Hindland Academy and worked as an engineer's correspondent. He married Dorothy Wells at Maryhill in March 1937, his son, Charles, arriving a year later. Having enlisted into the Argyll and Sutherland Highlanders Militia at Stirling on the outbreak of war he was posted to the regiment's infantry training centre before attending 165 OCTU at Dunbar (service numbers 10327886 then 2985255). Commissioned into his father's regiment, the Royal Irish Fusiliers, in May 1940 he was posted to its own infantry training centre at Ballykinlar (*London Gazette* 28/05/40, Supplement 31/05/40).

That August Clynes embarked for Malta amongst a large batch of reinforcements and joined A Company of the 2nd Battalion that had been engaged in constructing coastal defences since the outbreak of hostilities. The island had already been under aerial bombardment for two months, the Faughs forming working parties during the day and manning their defensive positions at night. By early 1943 the siege had abated, Clynes having already joined the Special Boat Section via a commando school on Manoel island within Marsamxett Harbour. Having set up camp at Tripoli in Libya he led a raid on the Kerkennah Islands off Sfax on the Tunisian coast that April, only to find that the Italian garrison had withdrawn the day before. Having returned to Malta he embarked HM Submarine *Trooper* the following month, subsequently picking up agents from the Greek island of Zante on the night of 25 May using a Folbot (Operation Entertain). A few weeks later he delivered equipment to Italian Partisans near Bari, again via Folbot from *Trooper* (Operation Tiger), before being hospitalised with severe jaundice.

Sailing for Egypt in July 1943 Clynes was posted to the Special Forces Holding Unit and soon after volunteered for the Special Boat Squadron. Having joined the unit at Athlit on the 31st he took command of 5 Section, No.2 Troop, but was soon involved in a serious accident:

> At about 2015hrs, 1 August 1943, I was a passenger in the rear of a Jeep travelling towards Haifa. The Jeep hit a wheel of a cart on the side of the road, swerved some barrels and veered off up a bank on the right side of the road, finishing up at a blockhouse. I was somersaulted out of the back of the Jeep. I finished up on the other side of the blockhouse.

Despite breaking his back Clynes soon returned to duty as a captain. That September he carried out recces of Simi and Calchi, the SBS having been tasked to seize such Dodecanese islands from recently surrendered Italian garrisons before German forces could do so. At the beginning of October he commanded three caiques of X Detachment that sailed from Simi to Cos to evacuate British troops from the Monte Dizheo area, returning to Athlit on 4 December (WO 201/795).

Having attended a parachute course at Ramat David during January 1944, Clynes undertook ski training at The Cedars in the Lebanese mountains the following month. A UK-based course on mobile flotation units followed, these being long-range boats that could be submerged while their crew operated ashore, and which resurfaced automatically at a pre-arranged time. The SBS War Diary records that he returned to Athlit on 30 June and on that 1 July he and four other ranks 'proceeded to an unknown destination.' However, by the 5th he was en route for Beirut to arrange for a navigation course. Within a few days he embarked for Simi once again, the citation for his resulting immediate Military Cross taking up the narrative:

> The above officer was commanding the west force in Operation Tenement on Symi on 13–14th July 1944. The fact that this force was in position by zero hour despite difficulties of terrain was due in no small measure to the drive and initiative displayed by Capt Clynes.
>
> The dispositions of his force for the capture of the strong enemy position at San Fanouria were excellent. On the order to attack being received he exposed himself fearlessly to accurate enemy MG fire to better to direct his forces. He himself led the final assault under heavy fire. His use of ground left our casualties ridiculously low. After the fall of the position he moved part of his force to bring fire on the Castello and ordered the destruction of all enemy installations.
>
> He displayed gallantry and leadership of the highest order in the rapidly taking of a heavily wired and mined position, the capture of which was essential to the general plan of the operation [*London Gazette* 04/01/45, WO 373/46].

In mid September 1944 Clynes was admitted to hospital in Bari having again damaged his back when falling out of a truck. However, by the beginning of October he was recruiting in Naples before returning to Palestine. Mid month he embarked to join OPERATION TOWANBUCKET during the liberation of Greece and when Bucketforce continued north to pursue the retreating Germans he was left behind 'to look after our interests in Athens.' He soon found that the SBS was to fulfil an unfamiliar and unwelcome policing role. However, having taken over the room of Captain Andy Lassen, MC*, at the Hotel Grande Bretagne, he had more pressing matters to deal with, as described by Captain Walter Milner-Barry:

> The following morning [24 October] he woke to find a stranger in his room brandishing a revolver, and emitted a loud cry which caused his assailant to miss a vital spot and shoot him in a leg. It had been subsequently discovered that the man was an outraged husband whose wife had been violated by Andy Lassen, and he thought he was shooting Andy. Fortunately Charlie had made a complete recovery now and was accompanying Andy to Crete [IWM Documents.16758 – Private Papers of Captain W. J. Milner-Barry].

Clynes, who had received a severe gunshot wound to his left calf, later stated that:

> Some time about 0630 I was awakened by a noise to find a man by my bed. He had a pistol in his hand. I jumped up in my bed and knocked his arm down. He fired and the bullet went into my left leg. We struggled and I managed to knock the pistol from his hand. He then ran from the room.

A brother officer stated that the weapon used was a Colt .45 Automatic pistol belonging to Clynes himself, and that the Corps of Military Police had investigated but discovered nothing.

The SBS detachment on Crete was to render: 'heavy support to any attack or defensive action which might take place in the near future. In addition it is believed that the presence of regular, disciplined troops in their ranks will have a heartening effect on the Partisans' (WO 170/7529). However, the situation soon degenerated into civil war, Clynes being wounded by a sniper belonging to ELAS, the communist Greek People's Liberation Army, near to Heraklion on 29 January 1945. Captain Charles Bimrose, travelling in the same Jeep, was also wounded whilst Craftsman Leslie Cornthwaite, their escorting motorcyclist, was shot dead (see his entry opposite). The SBS War Diary notes that Clynes died as a result of his wounds on 6 February and that he was buried at Heraklion Military Cemetery at Konstantinos Church on the 7th (WO 170/7529). All three men had been unarmed, an ELAS court later pronouncing the Greek gunman as insane.

Eldest son of Mrs Margaret Clynes of Havelock Street, Glasgow – His father, Charles, who had held a commission in the Royal Irish Fusiliers during the First World War was medically discharged due to wounds and died before the second war – Clynes himself had divorced in July 1944 shortly after his last leave in the UK.
Age 26.
Gone but not forgotten
Grave 16.A.20. Originally buried within St Konstantinos British Cemetery in Heraklion.

CRAFTSMAN LESLIE J. <u>CORNTHWAITE</u> [7596146] ROYAL ARMY ORDNANCE CORPS, ROYAL ELECTRICAL AND MECHANICAL ENGINEERS AND SBS (M SQN)

Leslie Cornthwaite was born on 31 March 1921 in the parish of Miles Platting, Manchester, where he later worked as a motor mechanic. Joining the Royal Army Ordnance Corps (TA) at the beginning of May 1939 he was embodied at the outbreak of war and subsequently posted to No.5 Army Field Workshop. That November he qualified as a fitter and was re-posted to 4 Anti-Aircraft Divisional Workshop Company before moving on to the 11th Divisional equivalent the following April.

In November 1941 Cornthwaite was posted to the 55th Heavy Anti-Aircraft Regimental Workshop and then to No.1 Army Ordnance Workshop until embarking for Iraq in December. After further training as a fitter whilst serving with Paiforce during the spring of 1942 he was transferred to the Royal Electrical and Mechanical Engineers on its formation on 1 October. A few days before Christmas he was re-posted to the Transportation Directorate at Tehran and soon after was attached to 155 Workshop, Royal Engineers. In August 1943 he returned to No.1 Army Ordnance Workshop and was promoted to sergeant that December, although he reverted to the rank of craftsman the following month prior to his next posting.

Cornthwaite joined III Corps' Troops Workshop in March 1944 and after further trade training moved on to 342 Infantry Troops Workshop that September. Having attended a special diesel course at the REME depot in Egypt during November he disembarked in Italy, more than likely having recently volunteered for the Special Boat Service. He joined M Squadron on Crete soon after and thus fell under the command of the newly-arrived Captain Andy Lassen, MC*. He was shot dead by a communist sniper of ELAS (the Greek People's Liberation Army) near Heraklion on 29 January 1945 whilst riding escort to the Jeep of Captains Charles Clynes, MC, and Charles Bimrose. All three were unarmed, Dave Evans, former SBS, later recalling:

> They knew I could ride a motorcycle as I used to ride a German motorcycle everywhere. Very few people had civilian driving licences in those days. On that occasion they were after a motorcycle rider. They knew he could ride a motorcycle too and they chose him. He wasn't normally a dispatch rider but was a normal member of the SBS [personal interview, 2013].

An ELAS court later pronounced the Greek gunman insane (see Clynes' entry above for further details).

Son of Fred and Annie Cornthwaite (née Dixon) of Lodge Street, Miles Platting, Manchester – Brother of Mary Cornthwaite.
Age 23.
No length of time can dim our loved one's past. For treasured memories last
Grave 16.B.1. Originally buried within St Konstantinos British Cemetery in Heraklion.

Gunner Albert Ernest KNAGGS [1140131] Royal Artillery
and Raiding Support Regiment att SBS

Albert Knaggs was born on 16 January 1922 in Hull. Having enlisted into the Royal Artillery in February 1942 he passed through the 9th Field Training Regiment and was posted to the 136th Field Regiment. An unsettled period of minor misdemeanours ensued before he embarked for the Middle East with the 173th Field Regiment in mid December 1943. Arriving on New Year's Day 1944, he was posted to the 15th Field Regiment the following month and embarked for Italy. He subsequently volunteered for the Raiding Support Regiment on 19 June 1944 and attended parachute course No.4 at Gioia del Colle on 5 August as a member of E Battery's 12 Troop.

Knaggs was killed in an air crash in the hills of the Tzumiades area of Crete on 18 December 1944 and was buried in a joint grave with fellow passenger, Private Thomas Morris of the SBS (see his entry below for full details). Both men were members of Senforce, commanded by Acting Major Andy Lassen, MC*, SBS, at the time of their deaths, half of 12 Troop having been attached to the SBS for operations against German occupational troops (see Lassen's entry under Argenta Gap War Cemetery, Italy).

Son of Ernest and Annie Knaggs of Park Grove, Princes Avenue, Hull.
Age 22.
To a beautiful life came a sudden end, he died as he lived everyone's friend
Grave 16.B.2.

Lieutenant Kenneth Butler LAMONBY [160965] Royal Artillery,
Suffolk Regiment, Special Boat Section and SBS (S Det)

Ken Lamonby was born on 24 October 1919 in Wimbledon, south-west London, but grew up in Essex. Having attended Colchester Royal Grammar School from 1927 to 1938 he worked as a solicitor's clerk. Whilst doing so he joined the local 104th (Essex Yeomanry) Regiment, Royal Horse Artillery (TA), at the beginning of May 1939. Posted to the newly-formed 147th (Essex Yeomanry) Regiment, RHA (TA), two months later he was mobilised on 1 September (service number 914850). In June 1940 his unit was redesignated the 147th Field Regiment and having been promoted to lance-bombardier the following month he was attached to the 50th Holding Battalion, Suffolk Regiment, that September. He was subsequently commissioned into the Suffolks at the end of the year from 164 OCTU at Barmouth (*London Gazette* 06/01/41).

Although Lamonby's service record is incomplete it appears he arrived in the Middle East in early September 1942 and volunteered for No.1 Special Boat Section on 23 December. This was attached to 1st SAS and officially absorbed into D Squadron the following January. This in turn became the Special

Boat Squadron on 19 March 1943, Lamonby becoming the unit's boating instructor at Athlit.

Having attended a close combat course in April 1943 Lamonby led Patrol B on OPERATION ALBUMEN: tasked with destroying Axis aircraft on Crete that posed a threat to the Allied invasion fleet that was soon to pass en route to Sicily, an operational party of three officers and fourteen other ranks embarked *HMML 361* at Bardia on 22 June 1943. In the early hours of the following morning they landed at Cape Kokinoxos and lay up for the day in a wadi. That evening Patrol C set off for the airfield at Kastelli Pediada whilst Lamonby's Patrol B marched towards its own target, the airfield at Heraklion. Finding this devoid of planes they blew up a petrol dump near the village of Peza before returning to the base party in the wadi just before midnight on 10 July. The operation's commander, Captain David Sutherland, MC, later noted:

At about 2000hrs [on the 11th] two German soldiers were observed approaching up the wadi, men from Patrols C and D scattered and lay in the rocks and Patrol B prevented any movement by the Cretans [a group of civilians who had guided the patrols and who now required evacuation]. The enemy eventually worked up to our position, were surrounded and captured without a shot being fired. Whilst the prisoners were being searched some of the Cretans saw two more Germans (the other half of the patrol) at the bottom of the wadi, and being for once in their lives more or less on equal terms started firing at them. The enemy quickly withdrew towards the sea pursued by about fifteen armed Cretans completely out of control. Whereupon a miniature engagement took place, the Germans having taken up positions with their backs to the sea. This lasted for about three-quarters of an hour, during which time a considerable number of rifle and sub machine-gun shots were exchanged together with grenades. The enemy, by skilful use of ground and cover had the better of the Cretans who were completely disorganised and had bad weapons. The wind had died down and the noise of the skirmish must have been clearly audible for a considerable distance up and down the coast. Grave consequences might easily have resulted if news of our presence had been telephoned to Pirgos since it was 2045hrs, and as a strong north wind had been blowing all day the ML might not have arrived for another six hours.

I therefore sent Lt Lamonby and four men down the wadi to stop the firing, this was ultimately done since it was getting dusk, and two Cretans were left to prevent the patrol moving along the coast. Lt Lamonby sent back the men but failed to return himself. I concluded as it was dark that he had gone straight to the beach …

There being no sign of Lt Lamonby, I sent out Lt Lassen and the rest of Patrol C with instructions to search the wadi where he was last seen shouting his name at regular intervals. He returned at 2345hrs having seen or heard no sign of this officer.

Posted missing in action Lamonby had been wounded by one of the two Germans he was stalking and later died in a hospital at Heraklion. His date of death is officially recorded as 11 July 1943.

Only son of Harold and Dora Lamonby (née Atkinson) of Victoria Road, Colchester, Essex.
Age 23.
There's some corner of a foreign field that is forever England
Grave 13.E.12. His remains were concentrated from Timbakion on 12 October 1945.

PRIVATE THOMAS G. **MORRIS** [T/79471] ROYAL ARMY SERVICE CORPS
AND SBS (M SQN)

Thomas Morris was born on 16 May 1920 in the parish of St Winifred's, Manchester. In April 1939, whilst working as a cabinet maker, he joined his local Royal Army Service Corps (TA) that formed part of the 42nd (East Lancashire) Infantry Division. Embodied at the outbreak of war he served with 503 Supply Company in France, supporting the division within the BEF from 8 April to 31 May 1940 when he was evacuated from Dunkirk.

Having completed trade training as a carpenter and joiner Morris arrived in the Middle East that November and was posted to No.7 Motor Transport Supply Depot. He was attached to XIII and XXX Corps' HQs in the Western Desert between October 1941 and July 1942, firstly with 9 Field Butchery Company and then with the Divisional Supply Column. Joining 30 General Transport Company he helped supply the Eighth Army at Alamein until volunteering for the Special Boat Squadron on 23 September 1943. He subsequently landed on the Aegean island of Chios under Captain Walter Milner-Barry at the end of the month:

The objective was a German OP of four men, which was to be wiped out and prisoners taken. No maps were available unfortunately so we had to rely on a naval chart which, of course, though strong on the coast, showed nothing of the interior, except hills as they appeared to the sailor from the sea. Left after dark [of the 28th] in an ML [Motor Launch] with a very charming captain whose name I forget, taking Sibbert and Rice, as well as Morris and my own patrol …

The plan of attack was that we would go in about 8.00pm. I would have liked to make it later, but had we done so we could never have got back to the ship in time … Landed on a very rough beach with a steep ascent, after Morris and Rice had selected a suitable landing place in the Folbot, and marched on a compass bearing over very hilly country, though cultivated whenever possible and interspersed with wadis [IWM Documents.16758 – Private Papers of Captain W. J. Milner-Barry. See Private 'Digger' Rice's entry under Athens Memorial, Greece].

On this occasion their intelligence was faulty, the patrol finding no such enemy post and being extracted the following night.

Morris undertook parachute training at Ramat David in Palestine during January 1944. Having been posted to Crete with M Squadron he was killed in an air crash in the hills of the Tzumiades area of Crete on 18 December 1944: his Baltimore aircraft of 13 Squadron exploded on hitting the ground and only small pieces of debris could be located. He was buried in a joint grave with fellow passenger, Gunner Albert Knaggs of the Raiding Support Regiment, both men being under the command of Acting Major Andy Lassen, MC*, SBS, at the time of their deaths (see Lassen's entry under Argenta Gap War Cemetery, Italy, within this volume). No traces could be found of the four aircrew. A subsequent board of inquiry concluded that the accident was due to 'unauthorised low flying' and that the 'pilot lost his head when he unwittingly pulled up into cloud, and dived into ground, coming out of cloud too steeply. Pilot was "beating up" [flying low over a] friend's house.' Milner-Barry later wrote:

News from Crete that Morris had been killed in a plane smash. Felt very bad about him, as apart from the fact that he was an exceptionally nice fellow, he was due to go back to England, and I contributed to inducing him to stay an extra month, in the hope that the whole unit would go back [IWM Documents.16758 – Private Papers of Captain W. J. Milner-Barry].

In January 1945 *The Manchester Evening News* reported:

MORRIS – Pte Thomas G. Morris (RASC), aged 23 years, dearly-beloved only son of Margaret Morris, killed while serving with the Central Mediterranean Forces (aeroplane accident) Dec 1944. May the Sacred Heart of Jesus have

mercy on his soul. Sadly missed by his loving mother. Also Thomas H. Morris, who died March 25, 1941, dearly beloved husband of Margaret. On his soul sweet Jesus have mercy – 15 Eastnor St, Old Trafford.

Age officially recorded as 25.
Saint Anthony pray for him, May he rest in peace
Grave 16.B.2. Originally buried with Knaggs within St Konstantinos British Cemetery in Heraklion.

ITALY

Italy entered the Second World War on 10 June 1940, invading neighbouring France only after the German Blitzkrieg had brought the country virtually to her knees. This was pure expansionism, Benito Mussolini's fascist state having occupied Albania under the same agenda the previous year. The urge to add to her existing colonies, namely the Dodecanese Islands, Libya, Ethiopia, Italian Somaliland and Eritrea, led to Italy's undoing. Despite some distinguished actions, most notably in East Africa where her army entered Kenya and Sudan in addition to conquering British Somaliland, almost five years of disaster were to follow: in September 1940 Italian troops invaded Egypt from Libya, their eyes firmly fixed on the Suez Canal, the key to the Mediterranean and the East. Suffering huge losses they were quickly thrown back and, although Rommel's Afrikakorps arrived to drag its weaker partner forward again through a series of victories, both were forced to capitulate in May 1943. Italy had also invaded Greece in late October 1940, this resulting in a similar defeat that was only reversed, once more, by the fighting quality of her Axis backer. Having been obliged through Italian egomania to secure his southern flank, Hitler looked on as Italy lost the last of her East African colonies in May 1941. To add to her misery the Italian Army joined the German thrust into Russia soon after, only to suffer over 40 per cent casualties when the Soviet Army turned the tide at Stalingrad.

This catalogue of errors weakened the resolve of the Italian people, the distant and romantic blur of war being violently brought into sudden focus after the July 1943 Allied invasion of Sicily (OPERATION HUSKY). Mussolini was dismissed from power, the new government under General Pietro Badoglio initiating secret negotiations for an armistice. This was signed on 3 September, Commonwealth troops having landed on the toe of Italy that day during OPERATION BAYTOWN. The Italian defection was publically announced on the 8th and in its immediate wake two further Allied landings were made; OPERATION AVALANCHE at Salerno and OPERATION SLAPSTICK at Taranto. German reaction was of equal speed and aggression: taking control of strategic points within Italy, as well as in those territories that she occupied, Italian soldiers that offered resistance were shot or deported to Germany as slave labour. Whilst Badoglio's government fled into exile, Mussolini, who had been held under arrest, was freed after a daring German glider assault on a mountain top hotel. Meanwhile, the Allied advance ground to a halt in the face of stiffening defence and poor weather, the January 1944 landings at Anzio initially only adding to the stalemate. Rome was eventually liberated on 4 June 1944, eight long months of fighting having been required to advance the 160 kilometres from the beaches of Naples. German ground forces withdrew to prepared positions and held out in the north until 2 May 1945, five days after Partisans had shot Mussolini and less than a week before the war in Europe ended.

During the Italian Campaign 1st SAS was employed as an amphibious assault force under its temporary guise of the Special Raiding Squadron. As such it was at the forefront of the HUSKY landings at Capo Murro di Porco and Augusta, the BAYTOWN landing at Bagnara on the Italian mainland, and at Termoli during OPERATION DEVON. Although these actions successfully enabled more rapid Allied advances the unfamiliar role proved costly, as will be seen. At the end of 1943 the SRS was withdrawn to the UK in preparation for D-Day operations.

2nd SAS had cut its teeth during small-scale deception raids on Italian-held Mediterranean islands. It took part in similar operations on Sicily in addition to cutting communication lines after its invasion. Landing at Taranto on the mainland as part of OPERATION SLAPSTICK its Jeep-borne squadrons harried the retreating Germans and were often the spearhead to the following army. They were first to link with the SRS and Special Service Brigade at Termoli. In addition, the Regiment carried out numerous attacks on railway lines, thus delaying the rush of German reinforcements towards the Allied bridgeheads. In conjunction with MI9's 'A' Force, amphibious and parachute operations were also mounted to rescue evading Allied POWs who had chosen escape rather than enforced shipment to Germany. The Regiment was withdrawn to the UK in early 1944 and joined the reconstituted 1st SAS in Scotland.

The LRDG also had a hand to play: although it mainly used Italy as a base for forthcoming operations in the Adriatic and Balkans, it also carried out OPERATION JUMP during June 1944, sending back intelligence on enemy traffic north of Rome before the Eighth Army's renewed offensive.

At the beginning of 1945 2nd SAS' No.3 Squadron returned to Italy. Basing itself at the Villa Sabina near Leghorn elements parachuted into the north for OPERATIONS GALIA, TOMBOLA, CANUCK and COLD COMFORT, its men working in partnership with Italian Partisans to disrupt the enemy's rear echelons, thereby diverting German troops from the front.

From August 1944 the Special Boat Service had launched operations across the Adriatic in Greece and the Balkans from its base at Monte Sant'Angelo. However, during the final month of the war some elements supported Commando landings at Comacchio by carrying out OPERATION FRY under Major Andy Lassen, MC*. He was the last member of the SBS to be killed in action, his bravery resulting in the award of a posthumous Victoria Cross.

Thirty members of the SRS, twenty-nine members of 2nd SAS, twelve members of the SBS and five members of the LRDG are commemorated or buried at fifteen different locations on mainland Italy, or on Sicily or Sardinia.

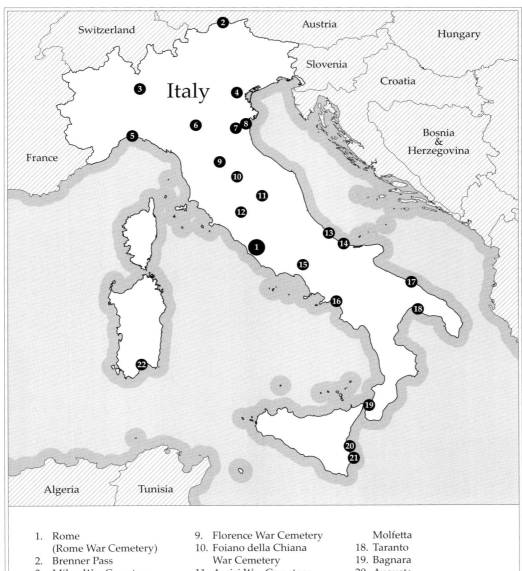

1. Rome
   (Rome War Cemetery)
2. Brenner Pass
3. Milan War Cemetery
4. Padua War Cemetery
5. Genoa (Staglieno War
   Cemetery)
6. Albinea
7. Argenta Gap War
   Cemetery
8. Comacchio
9. Florence War Cemetery
10. Foiano della Chiana
    War Cemetery
11. Assisi War Cemetery
12. Bolsena War Cemetery
13. Sangro River War
    Cemetery
14. Termoli
15. Cassino Memorial
16. Salerno War Cemetery
17. Bari War Cemetery /
    Molfetta
18. Taranto
19. Bagnara
20. Augusta
21. Syracuse War Cemetery /
    Capo Murro di Porco
22. Cagliari (San Michele)
    Communal Cemetery

ARGENTA GAP WAR CEMETERY

The most northerly German defensive line in Italy, the Gothic Line, was partly breached in the autumn of 1944. However, the Wehrmacht continued to hold the Allies until the final push through the Argenta Gap the following spring. This cemetery was initially formed by the 78th Infantry Division for battlefield burials of this offensive. Graves from farther afield were later concentrated here, amongst them casualties of the April 1945 OPERATION ROAST *landings at Comacchio that secured the right flank of the Allied advance through this area. It now contains 625 Commonwealth burials, eight of which are unidentified.*

The cemetery is located 2 kilometres north of the town of Argenta, not far from the SS16 that connects Ravenna with Ferrara. GPS co-ordinates: Latitude 44.63447, Longitude 11.83218

TROOPER ALFRED JOHN CROUCH [7952333] ROYAL ARMOURED CORPS, 1ST SAS AND SBS (S SQN)

Freddy Crouch, sometimes known by comrades as 'Crouchie', was born on 9 January 1918 at Westcliff-on-Sea in Essex. His mother Margaret (née Haley) had left her husband and six daughters to run away with Freddy's father, Alfred Crouch senior. After an elementary education in the Manor Park area of east London the young Crouch became a clerk before joining the Metropolitan Police in July 1938. During training he achieved a remarkable 99 per cent marking and was assigned to P Division as PC 409P. His

police record notes that he was a member of the athletic club and that he lived in East Dulwich before moving to Catford.

In November 1941 Crouch married Raymonde Barbara Culley at Lewisham and although he joined the Royal Armoured Corps (TA) on the last day of January 1942 the Met would not release him for full-time service until mid March. After training with the 60th then 52nd Training Regiments Crouch embarked for the Middle East at the end of October. Bored with depot life he volunteered for 1st SAS on 14 February 1943 and was posted to the Special Boat Squadron when it was raised the following month. Attached to the 11th Battalion, Parachute Regiment, he attended parachute course No.51 at Ramat David that July, his qualifying jumps being delayed for unknown medical reasons. Crouch was subsequently posted to S Detachment and taken under the wing of more experienced operators, Dick Holmes, MM, later recalling:

I went on a raid to Crete in July of that year [1943] and when I returned to Palestine, as it then was named, I was made up to corporal and put into J Troop of which Freddy was a member. We became great friends over the next couple of years.

In September 1943 about sixty of us were given the task of disarming the Italian garrisons on a number of the islands in the Eastern Aegean. Sometimes a few of us would land on an island only to find that the Germans had already taken over and awkward situations developed. At such times Freddy was always a tower of strength, with his calm demeanour and ready wit. He had a tremendous sense of humour and this often helped. The culmination of the Dodecanese Campaign was the dive-bombing we were subjected to on the island of Samos, which resulted in us being evacuated to Turkey [see entries for Sergeant George Munro under Rhodes War Cemetery, Greece, and Signalman 'Spadge' Sparrow under Athens War Memorial, Greece, within this volume for further details]. We were interned for several weeks, one of the most miserable periods of my life. On the subsequent train journey through Turkey we were unable to boil water for our tea and it was Freddy who prevailed upon the driver of the train to allow us to drain some of the water from the boiler every time we stopped. Saved our lives, I can tell you [correspondence courtesy of Crouch's niece, Shirley Joyner].

In the spring of 1944 S Detachment took over from L, Holmes noting that:

The following spring we went back to those islands, raiding from a Greek caique moored in Turkish waters [OPERATION FIREATER]. A number of times I was sent on recces to ascertain the numbers of the German garrisons and likely targets. On many of these forays Freddy was my partner and we came to have the utmost faith in one another. We often enjoyed ourselves, strange as that may seem [courtesy of Shirley Joyner].

On 21 April 1944 Crouch's patrol set out for the Aegean island of Ios. Here he, Holmes and Guardsman Roger Wright ambushed three Germans before rejoining their patrol commander, Captain 'Nobby' Clarke. Having then sailed to the island of Amorgos Clarke set about destroying the radio station, sending Crouch and his close comrades on another task:

He [Crouch] and I, with two others, Jack Cree and Al Sanders, were landed on the Island of Nisiros to bring back a German prisoner. Unfortunately, our Greek guide selected a hideout that just happened to be on the route patrolled by the Germans. We were discovered and in the ensuing action we managed to dispose of three of the enemy without any damage to ourselves. During the course of the firefight Freddy remained cool and steadied the rest of us [personal correspondence with Dick Holmes, MM, 2009].

That May Crouch accidentally shot himself in the hand whilst handling a captured weapon. The wound was not severe and he soon returned to the squadron. S Detachment was relieved by M at the beginning of June and returned to the SBS base at Athlit on the Palestinian coast after what had been a very busy period of raiding. In August 1944 the Greek Sacred Squadron took over such duties in the Aegean and the SBS, now renamed the Special Boat Service with squadrons rather than detachments, moved to Italy where it set up base at Monte Sant'Angelo on the Gargano Peninsula. Under the command of the Bari-based HQ Land Forces Adriatic it carried out operations within Yugoslavia and along the Dalmatian coast, Holmes later recalling: 'when we moved to Italy Freddy came with me on a couple of recces in Yugoslavia and we had some harrowing times. He also went with another group to Albania while I was involved in something else' (courtesy of Shirley Joyner).

In February 1945 M Squadron, and a mixed bag of others including Crouch, moved up to the front line in northern Italy. He was subsequently killed in action during OPERATION FRY at Comacchio on the night of 8–9 April 1945: Major Andy Lassen, MC*, had selected him and Corporal 'Rocky' Roberts to bolster his team (see their entries within this section). Whilst the patrol was securing the narrow causeway that runs towards the town Crouch slipped into the mud alongside and drowned. It is commonly believed that he did not struggle, as he knew that any noise would immediately attract machine-gun fire. Dave Evans, former SBS, confirmed that drowning was one of the things that Crouch had talked about being afraid of. Posted 'missing believed drowned' the Raiding Support Regiment's War Diary notes that on the afternoon of 21 April: 'OP found two English dead at south bank. Pte Crouch of SBS at 592662 and a Lieut of the Gds Bde at 595665. Both were buried on the spot that afternoon' (WO 170/4825).

'Hank' Hancock, former SBS, recalled that Crouch had premonitions of his death and used to tell him; 'I wake up at night and I see myself lying there.' He had also received a 'Dear John' from his wife before the Comacchio operation, Joyner later writing:

> I found the entry of his marriage to Raymonde and also that he had a son, John Douglas … I found that Raymonde married … a Mr George Cunningham only a few months after Freddy died. I made every effort to find her and John but with no success … I was hoping so much that John would learn about his father … I understand that Freddy was uneasy and worried leading up to the Comacchio campaign but I think he knew what was happening at home and this can't have helped his frame of mind [personal correspondence, 2009].

Holmes remains full of praise for his former comrade:

> You can be sure that however he met his end it was while doing his duty, he was that sort of man. The irony of it was that [Comacchio] was the last raid we carried out … Serving in the SBS was one of the most rewarding periods of my life and it was men like Freddy Crouch that made it so [courtesy of Shirley Joyner].

Perhaps his greatest tribute again comes from Holmes: 'The whole of S Squadron mourned his death' (personal correspondence, 2009).

Husband of Raymonde Crouch of Sportsbank Street, Catford – Father of John Douglas Crouch.
Age 27.
No inscription.
Grave 3.G.22. Also commemorated on the Comacchio Memorial on the causeway from which he had slipped and in the Metropolitan Police Book of Remembrance.

Fusilier Stanley Raymond HUGHES MM [4130995] Cheshire Regiment, King's Regiment, Royal Irish Fusiliers and SBS (M Sqn)

Known to his comrades as 'Spike', Stanley Hughes was born on 6 August 1921 in the border village of Cefn Mawr near Ruabon in Denbighshire. Having worked as a clerk he enlisted into the Cheshire Regiment in June 1940 at Liverpool and was posted to the 8th (Home Defence) Battalion before transferring to the King's Regiment three months later. Joining the 70th (Young Soldiers) Battalion he was promoted to lance-corporal that November and at the end of the year to corporal. In July 1941 he re-enlisted on a regular engagement, remaining with the 70th Battalion but reverting to the rank of private in order to do so. That October he married Hilda May in Liverpool and the following year their daughter, Janet, was born. During 1942 he qualified as a PT Instructor, specialised in anti-tank weapons, and by the time he embarked for North Africa with the 9th Battalion in May 1943 he had risen to the rank of corporal once more.

On arrival Hughes transferred to the Royal Irish Fusiliers and landed with the 1st Battalion on Sicily during the July Allied invasion (Operation Husky). Having taken part in the capture of key German hilltop defences around the village of Centuripe on the night of 2–3 August 1943 he was wounded in action whilst assaulting German positions on the northern bank of the River Salso on the 4th. A machine-gun round struck his left hand at approximately 1500hrs, although his service record notes that he carried on of his own accord until late that afternoon.

Hughes was discharged from hospital on 5 October 1943 and returned to the 1st Battalion near Termoli on the Adriatic coast. At the end of the month he saw further action at the River Trigno and at San Salvo just beyond it: on the night of the 27–28th his battalion assaulted enemy positions in the area of San Salvo's railway station but soon took casualties from mines and machine-gun fire before being forced to withdraw. Soon after Hughes was awarded an immediate Military Medal:

> At approximately 0400hrs 2 Dec 43 Cpl Hughes entered St Vito as 2i/c of a patrol led by Lt Day. The main German positions were 5 miles to the south and the town itself was strongly held by Germans. As the patrol fought their way into the town two Germans pounced on the back of a Bren gunner, these Cpl Hughes promptly killed with his Tommy gun. He then took charge of one section of the patrol and advancing boldly down the main street. He took eight German prisoners and killed three German motor cyclists. By this time the town was in an uproar and finding that Lt Day had been badly wounded by fire from armoured cars he collected the patrol and cleverly hid them in houses until the town was taken by 6 Inniks [6th Battalion, Royal Inniskilling Fusiliers] twelve hours later.
>
> It is considered that this spirited entry into the town and the havoc wrought by this NCO and his men must have seriously embarrassed the main German forces holding the river to the south. Reports from the men in the patrol prove that Cpl Hughes is a fearless and outstanding leader [*London Gazette* 23/03/44].

After a brief rest near Naples Hughes' battalion returned to the line to take part in the final stages of the Battle of Cassino. On the morning of 17 May 1944 it captured a ridge that dominates Highway 6, the road key to the Allied advance to the north. Hughes, by now a sergeant and obviously a very brave man, must have been exhausted and on 14 June he went AWOL. He surrendered to Military Police a month later and was held under close arrest until reduced to the ranks and posted to the 4th Battalion, Infantry Reinforcement Training Depot, in November. It was from here that he volunteered for the Special Boat Service, although the exact date is unknown.

Hughes was killed in action in the early hours of 9 April 1945 during Operation Fry at Comacchio during the action in which Major Andy Lassen, MC*, earned a Victoria Cross. Despite this their dates of death are officially recorded as the 8th and 9th respectively. A letter from Sergeant Ronald Waite of the same patrol notes that: 'Hughes was right behind Major Lassen and in front of me when he was hit by a storm of Spandau bullets' (*En dansk Soldat: Major Anders Lassen, VC, MC*, by Jørgen Halck – see Lassen's entry below). Donald Thompson, former SBS, recalled: 'We later found, when we went up to the village of Comacchio, that the Germans had got the carpenter to construct rough wooden coffins for the bodies of Andy and the others killed there – one of whom was Spike Hughes MM, a great chap. A rather nice gesture on the part of the enemy' (*Mars & Minerva*, December 1995). The Military Medal was presented to Hughes' family on 5 November 1946.

Son of Edward and Bertha Hughes (née Richards) – Husband of Hilda Hughes of Moscow Drive, Stoneycroft, Lancashire – Father of Janet Hughes – Brother of Hazle Hughes.
Age 23.
Greater love hath no man than this. That a man lay down his life for his friends
Grave 2.E.10. Also commemorated on the Comacchio Memorial on the causeway where he lost his life and on the Commando Memorial at the National Memorial Arboretum.

Major Anders Frederik Emil Victor Schau LASSEN VC, MC** [234907] SOE, Small Scale Raiding Force, The Buffs, General List, 1st SAS and SBS (M Sqn)

Andy Lassen was born at Mern in Denmark on 22 September 1920. Growing up in Southern Sjælland he boarded at Herlufsholm School before attending a gymnastics academy at Svendborg on the island of Fyn. In January 1939 he signed as a cabin boy for the East Asiatic Company, sailing to locations as distant as Bangkok. That May he left Denmark for the last time as an apprentice seaman aboard a tanker. After Germany invaded his homeland he organised the crew of the ship, then in the Persian Gulf, to persuade their captain to sail into the war. Arriving at Cape Town Lassen signed onto a British tanker and disembarked in the UK on Christmas Day 1940. By this time his father, an adventurer in his own right, was fighting for the Finns against the Russians.

Lassen enlisted into the British Army in January 1941 and was soon sent for by the Special Operations Executive:

M [Brigadier Colin Gubbins, DSO, MC] advised that 2379 [Lassen] is employed under the Naval Officer in Charge of the Poole base as member of the crew for ship under ISRB [the Inter-Services Research Bureau, one of SOE's many cover names]. Formerly student at the training schools. Remarks as follows: Speaks English (fluently) German (well) Norwegian and Swedish (fair). Description: Height 6', weight 11st7. Eyes blue, hair fair.

Commandant's remarks: Determined and keen. Comes of very good Danish family. Well educated. Failed on exam when studying forestry and, I think, ran away to sea. Considerable experience of hunting and shooting. Should do well as an individual or as a leader of a patrol. Might develop into a good officer later. Has missed much of the training owing to a poisoned foot (25/01/41) …

1340 [an unknown SOE instructor] reported: 2379 is the weakest character of the party. He is the black sheep of a good family, who has run away from home and become a sailor. He is keen enough on the job, but cannot stand being kept in, he would definitely not be reliable enough for special duties; he might not keep sober when on leave and he might give away secrets (11/03/41) …

The Brigadier required a man for Patrol-boat work. I recommended 2379 who is quite clever and well mannered and speaks English fairly well. He would fit into a job like that better than a regiment as his nature does not like drill and military discipline (15/04/41) [HS 9/888/2, Lassen's SOE personnel file].

Having received further training at Arisaig Lassen was therefore posted to Captain Gus March-Phillipps' Maid Honor Force and sailed to West Africa aboard the team's Brixham trawler of the same name. Finding themselves not entirely welcomed by local British forces they set about their own roaming commission, searching for secret German submarine bases and supply depots. At this time U-Boats were sinking

Allied shipping faster than it could be built. Eventually they were allotted a more specific task, OPERATION POSTMASTER, the capture of the Italian cargo liner *Duchessa d'Aosta* from the island of Fernando Po (modern-day Bioko off the coast of Cameroon). This was successfully achieved on the night of 14–15 January 1942, the German tug *Likomba* and the barge *Bibundi* also being taken in tow by the raiders. By the evening of the 21st all three prize ships were safely moored at Lagos.

Lassen briefly stayed on in the Nigerian capital but had arrived back in the UK by May 1942 when he was commissioned onto the General List. He continued to serve with March-Phillipps whose command had by now been expanded and retitled the Small Scale Raiding Force. Lassen subsequently took part in numerous cross-Channel raids: on the night of 2–3 September 1942 he was a member of a party that successfully raided Les Casquets lighthouse in the Channel Islands, taking prisoners and seizing codebooks during OPERATION DRYAD. Five nights later he was raiding the small Channel Island of Burhou during OPERATION BRANFORD in order 'to determine the suitability of the Island as a battery position for an assault on Alderney'. The post-operation report states: 'Captain Ogden-Smith, 2/Lt Lassen and six ORs [other ranks] embarked in the goatley [collapsible boat] at 0020 hours and paddled the 600 yards to Burhou island in eight minutes … 2/Lt Lassen, as cox of the landing craft, displayed excellent judgement and seamanship throughout the operation' (DEFE 2/109).

On 4 October 1942 Lassen took part in OPERATION BASALT, a raid on the small island of Sark in the Channel Islands. His team included Lieutenants Pat Dudgeon and Philip Pinckney and Major Geoffrey Appleyard, MC* (see Dudgeon's and Pinckney's entries under Florence War Cemetery, Italy, and Appleyard's under Cassino Memorial, Italy). The post-operation report notes Lassen had: 'acted very ably as bowman and the party was disembarked dryshod … 2/Lt Lassen was sent up the cliff to make a reconnaissance of the reported MG [machine gun] post on top of the Hog Back and the rest of the party followed more slowly' (DEFE 2/109). Having silently taken German prisoners from the Dixcart Hotel the party bound them and began its return journey to the embarkation point. However, before this was reached their captives attempted to escape and raise the alarm. In the ensuing effort to subdue them all but one were killed and although the raiders withdrew successfully the dead Germans were later discovered by their comrades with their hands still tied. As a result of this and two raids in Norway Hitler imposed his infamous 'Commando Order' that called for raiding parties 'to be annihilated to the last man, whether in uniform or not … whether in combat, or in flight, or after capture' (see Appendix 2 within the User's Guide for full details). It was an order that resulted in the death of many of the men included in this Roll of Honour, including Dudgeon.

Lassen was awarded the Military Cross on recommendation of Lord Mountbatten, the Chief of Combined Operations, this being approved by His Majesty the King on 7 December 1942:

> 2/Lieut Lassen has at all times shown himself to be a very gallant and determined officer who will carry out his job with a complete disregard for his personal safety. As well as, by his fine example, being an inspiring leader of his men, he is a brilliant seaman possessed of sound judgement and quick decision. He was coxswain of the landing craft on Operation Branford and effected a landing and subsequent re-embarkation on a dangerous and rocky island with considerable skill and without mishap. He took part in Operation Barricade on which he showed dash and reliability [an attack on German coastal positions a few miles south of Barfleur on the night of 14–15 August 1942]. He recently took part in the highly successful SOE Operation Postmaster in which he was the leader of that part of the boarding party that was responsible for the difficult job of making fast the tug's towing hawser to the liner's bows. Regardless of the action going on around him, Second-Lieutenant Lassen did his job quickly and coolly and showed great resource and ingenuity. Second-Lieutenant Lassen also took part in another operation, as bowman on landing, and then made a preliminary reconnaissance for a reported MG [machine gun] post. Not to be gazetted [citation released in WO 373/93].

Late that November HQ Combined Operations wrote to the Military Secretary:

It is requested that, if his recommendation is approved the name of Second-Lieutenant A Lassen may not be gazetted. He would, I understand, be the first Dane serving in the British Army to receive an award, and it might be harmful to his family in Denmark if any publicity were allowed to be given to the award. This should not however prevent him from wearing the ribbon of a decoration.

Around this time Lassen undertook a parachute course at No.1 PTS Ringway. Late that year Captain The Earl Jellicoe of 1st SAS returned to the UK for medical treatment and whilst there met Lassen at Combined Operations. He subsequently arranged for him to be posted to the Regiment that was developing its own amphibious capability. As a result the Dane and fellow SSRF officer, Pinckney, disembarked in Egypt and were attached to 1st SAS from 22 February 1943. Lassen was nominally transferred to The Buffs (Royal East Kent Regiment), this regiment's Colonel-in-Chief being the King of Denmark. He joined the Special Boat Squadron when it was raised on 19 March, initially taking command of 7 Section, No.2 Troop, S Detachment, and took part in OPERATION ALBUMEN on Crete. Tasked with destroying Axis aircraft that posed a threat to the Allied invasion fleet that was soon to pass en route to Sicily, he was subsequently awarded a Bar to his Military Cross whilst a temporary captain:

This officer was in command of a patrol which attacked Kastelli Pediada aerodrome on the night 4th July [1943]. Together with 1469628 Gnr Jones J, RA, he entered the airfield from the west, passing through formidable perimeter defences [see Jones' entry under Athens War Memorial, Greece, within this volume]. By pretending to be a German officer on rounds he bluffed his way past three sentries stationed 15 yards apart guarding Stukas. He was, however, compelled to shoot the fourth with his automatic, and in doing so raised the alarm. Caught by flares and ground search light he was subjected to very heavy machine-gun and rifle fire from close range and forced to withdraw.

Half an hour later this officer and other rank again entered the airfield, in spite of the fact that all guards had been trebled and the area was being patrolled and swept by searchlights. Great difficulty was experienced in penetrating towards the target, in the process of which a second sentry had to be shot. The enemy then rushed reinforcements from the eastern side of the aerodrome and, forming a semi circle, drove the two attackers into the middle of an anti-aircraft battery, where they were fired upon heavily from three sides. This danger was ignored and bombs were placed on a caterpillar tractor which was destroyed. The increasing numbers of enemy in that area finally forced the party to withdraw.

It was entirely due to this officer's diversion that planes and petrol were successfully destroyed on the eastern side of the airfield since he drew off all the guards from that area. Throughout the attack, and during the very arduous approach march, the keenness, determination and personal disregard of danger of this officer was of the highest order [dated 27/09/43, *London Gazette* 21/02/46].

That September Italy signed an armistice initiating a race between British and German troops to seize control of those Aegean islands that she garrisoned: a composite force, known as X Detachment, was rapidly formed, Lassen and approximately twenty-five other SBS subsequently landing on Simi. Having taken control of the Italian soldiers and organised defences he was awarded a second Bar to his Military Cross for his ensuing actions:

This officer, most of the time a sick man, displayed outstanding leadership and gallantry throughout the operations by X Det in Dodecanese, 13 Sept 43 to 18 Oct 43. The heavy repulse of the Germans from Simi on 7 Oct 43 was due in no small measure to his inspiration and leadership on the one hand, and the highest personal example on the other. He himself, crippled with a badly burnt leg and internal trouble, stalked and killed at least three Germans at close range. At that time the Italians were wavering and I attribute their recovery as due to the personal example and initiative of this officer. He continued to harass and destroy German patrols throughout the morning. In the afternoon he himself led the Italian counterattack which finally drove the Germans back to their caiques, with the loss of sixteen killed, thirty-five wounded, and seven prisoners, as against a loss on our side of one killed and one wounded [dated 15/02/44, *London Gazette* 21/02/46 – see Private Bill Morrison's entry under Rhodes War Cemetery, Greece].

Having served on Leros, Lassen was tasked to retrieve British soldiers wounded during the fighting on Samos. However, when Leros fell on 16 November 1943 the situation on Samos, which was already being bombed, became untenable, Lassen and his men being evacuated by caique to Turkey where they were briefly interned by their neutral hosts (see Private Davey Fairweather's entry under Haidar Pasha Cemetery, Turkey, within this volume for further details). Lassen's party eventually arrived back at HQ

SBS at Athlit, Palestine, on 1 December.

In early 1944 S Detachment forward-mounted to an SBS base at Yedi Atala on the neutral Turkish coast. From here its patrols conducted OPERATION FIREATER, the raiding of enemy garrisons in the Aegean. On the night of 1–2 February Lassen took half a patrol to Calchi where a 25ft motor launch, an Italian officer, five Italian other ranks and three German soldiers were captured. However, any success was short-lived Lassen being accidentally shot by one of his own men, Sergeant Sean O'Reilly. Robert Hill, a former SBS signaller, recalled the event:

> He and Paddy Reilly had gone to do a job to which Reilly had objected violently. Finally Lassen had said 'All right, if you're afraid to come I'll go myself'. Paddy still grumbling in a rich Irish brogue had given way and gone with him. On landing, as they were getting out of the dinghy Paddy's Schmeisser, a German weapon and notoriously unreliable, went off and shot Lassen in the leg. This cancelled the job and Lassen instantly accused Paddy of doing it on purpose. Paddy of course denied it. It made no difference to the friendship which existed between them and which continued until Paddy got badly wounded on the same job as that on which Lassen died getting his VC. Consequently Lassen, who refused to go back to Palestine to have his leg seen to was only able to hobble about the ship and the inactivity annoyed him.

Despite his injuries Lassen led a raid on Thira in mid April (see Lieutenant Stephanos Kazoulis' entry within the Unknown Location section within Volume III for full details). He then took over as training officer at Athlit on 5 June. However, that August the SBS moved to Bari on the east coast of Italy where his detachment, S Squadron of the now Special Boat Service, had fallen under the command of HQ Land Forces Adriatic. Settling into the nearby town of Monte Sant'Angelo Lassen and his men were soon disrupting lines of communication along the Yugoslav coast. At the end of the month he led two patrols that destroyed the main coastal railway bridge at Karasovici in Yugoslavia during OPERATION HEALTH ABLE (sub OPERATION RATWEEK). Having landed near Gruda at a beach sponsored by the LRDG's M.1 Patrol on the night of the 27th the party was guided inland and laid their charges three nights later:

> … the demolished bridge effectively blocking the road. This force at once retired into the hills to join the local Partisans but was pursued by some 400 Ustachi who attacked on the morning of 2 Sep [the Ustaše was a fascist movement, predominantly Croatian in membership]. After several hours of fighting our patrols managed to escape with a loss of three captured [two members of the LRDG and one SBS], having however killed five Ustachi and wounded many others [the party was picked up by the Royal Navy in the early hours of 6 September - WO 204/9681].

On 30 September 1944 Lassen sailed to the east coast of the Peloponnese for OPERATION APLOMB, the thrust of which was to support of Major Ian Patterson's Bucketforce that was engaged in OPERATION TOWANBUCKET to the north (see Patterson's entry under Bari War Cemetery, Italy). Having been persuaded to sail to the port of Volos, Lassen moved farther on towards Salonika, he and his small force liberating the city on requisitioned fire engines at the end of October. That month he was appointed acting major. Moving to Athens in November (where he is reputed to have parked his Jeep outside his room within the Grand Bretagne Hotel) Lassen embarked for Crete on 1 December to take command of M Squadron (see Captain Charles Clynes' entry under Suda Bay War Cemetery, Greece, within this volume for details of the mayhem Lassen left behind him in the Greek capital). Captain Walter Milner-Barry, a fellow SBS officer, wrote:

> I lunched with Andy, and drove with him to Piraeus to assist in his arrangements for departure. A terrifying drive, during which I reached, I suppose, the extremity of human terror, because I had the feeling that Andy simply didn't care if he did knock somebody down and kill him [IWM 08/138/1 Papers of Walter Milner-Barry].

Lassen was promoted to temporary major in January 1945, M Squadron and half of 12 Troop, E Battery, Raiding Suport Regiment, having been tasked with monitoring the enemy and safeguarding the Cretan population under the title of Senforce. This returned to Italy on 11 February, the SBS moving north to the front line the following month. Lassen was subsequently killed in action at Comacchio in the early hours of 9 April 1945 during OPERATION FRY whilst leading two patrols in an attack on a causeway south of the town as diversion to nearby British Landings (OPERATION ROAST). The citation that accompanied the award of Lassen's posthumous Victoria Cross gives the following particulars:

In Italy, on the night of 8th/9th April, 1945, Major Lassen was ordered to take out a [composite] patrol of one officer and seventeen other ranks to raid the north shore of Lake Comacchio.

His tasks were to cause as many casualties and as much confusion as possible, to give the impression of a major landing, and to capture prisoners. No previous reconnaissance was possible, and the party found itself on a narrow road flanked on both sides by water.

Preceded by two scouts, Major Lassen led his men along the road towards the town. They were challenged after approximately 500 yards from a position on the side of the road. An attempt to allay suspicion by answering that they were fishermen returning home failed, for when moving forward again to overpower the sentry machine-gun fire started from the position, and also from two other blockhouses to the rear.

Major Lassen himself then attacked with grenades and annihilated the first position containing four Germans and two machine guns. Ignoring the hail of bullets sweeping the road from three enemy positions, an additional one having come into action from 300 yards down the road, he raced forward to engage the second position under covering fire from the remainder of the force. Throwing in more grenades he silenced this position which was then overrun by his patrol. Two enemy were killed, two captured and two more machine guns silenced.

By this time the force had suffered casualties and its fire power was very considerably reduced. Still under a heavy cone of fire Major Lassen rallied and reorganised his force and brought his fire to bear on the third position. Moving forward himself he flung in more grenades which produced a cry of 'Kamerad'. He then went forward to within 3 or 4 yards of the position to order the enemy outside, and to take their surrender.

Whilst shouting to them to come out he was hit by a burst of Spandau fire from the left of the position and he fell mortally wounded, but even whilst falling he flung a grenade, wounding some of the occupants and enabling his patrol to dash in and capture this final position.

Major Lassen refused to be evacuated as he said it would impede the withdrawal and endanger further lives, and as ammunition was exhausted the force had to withdraw.

By his magnificent leadership and complete disregard for his personal safety, Major Lassen had, in the face of overwhelming superiority achieved his objects. Three positions were wiped out, accounting for six machine guns, killing eight and wounding others of the enemy, and two prisoners were taken. The high sense of devotion to duty and the esteem in which he was held by the men he led, added to his own magnificent courage, enabled Major Lassen to carry out all the tasks he had been given with complete success [*London Gazette* 07/09/45].

Ronald Waite, a former SBS sergeant, later recalled:

> We attacked. Major Lassen shouted orders to all of us. We were forced to take cover, but the Major didn't give any thought to his own safety. He was standing up, shooting like a man possessed, throwing hand grenades and giving us more orders … Major Lassen came back for more hand grenades and shouted to the boys, and then he fired a green flare as a signal to attack and took the front himself, once again. The last time I saw him he was lying approximately 5 yards from the machine-gun position where he'd been hit. Even then he thought to fire a red flare as a signal to retreat … Major Lassen didn't give any thought to his own safety, and it was thanks to his energy and complete lack of fear that approximately 90 per cent of his men survived the battle [*En dansk Soldat: Major Anders Lassen, VC, MC*, by Jørgen Halck].

News of his death affected every man, regardless of rank, Dave Evans later recalling: 'I was a wireless operator and so I got the message that Andy Lassen had had it. None of us could believe it. "Lassen had it? Don't give us that" Everyone was hit by it. He was invincible' (personal interview, 2015).

The attack at Comacchio was M Squadron's last operation of the war and Lassen was the last member of the SBS to be killed in action before it disbanded that August. David Sutherland, his former Commanding Officer, later noted: 'In my opinion Anders caused more damage and discomfort to the enemy during five years of war than any other man of his rank and age' (*Andy: A Portrait of the Dane Major Anders Lassen*, by Mogens Kofod-Hansen). Adrian Seligman, former officer of the Levant Schooner Flotilla, later wrote of him:

> Quiet, sensitive, poetic at times and deeply sentimental, especially about children and dogs. He took with him everywhere a miserable little woolly-coated cur he had picked up in a back street of Beirut … when not on operations, Andy was scatter brained and harum-scarum, usually penniless and, owing to his really god-like beauty and quiet devil-may-care manner, extremely attractive to women [*War in the Islands*, by Adrian Seligman].

Another former LSF officer noted: 'In the SBS – themselves a lot of hand-picked men – who savaged the Germans on every possible opportunity and with every possible weapon – he even managed to stand out.

I could praise him no higher than this' (*Dust upon the Sea*, by Walter Benyon-Tinker). However, perhaps it was Raymond Fletcher, MP, who summed up Lassen best: 'Freedom is a word that is understood in all languages. Andy Lassen was the spirit of freedom. A tragic episode in a long and bloody war prevented him from growing to his full height' (*Mars & Minerva*, Spring 1985).

Son of Kaptajn Emil Lassen and Suzanne Lassen (née Countess Raben-Levetzau) of Nyhavn, Copenhagen, Denmark, who were presented their son's VC by His Majesty the King at Buckingham Palace on 18 December 1945 – His brother, Frants Axel Lassen, also joined SOE and returned to Denmark where, despite being captured and beaten by the Gestapo, he survived the war – Two of Lassen's cousins, whose father was German, fought in the Wehrmacht on the Russian Front: one was killed whilst the other, Hauptmann Axel von dem Bussche, a holder of the Knight's Cross, was chosen to model a new set of equipment for Hitler. On being inspected he intended to initiate two grenades secreted in his overcoat pockets and grasp the Führer tightly, thus blowing them both to pieces. His plan failed when Allied bombers destroyed the train carrying the new uniforms, von dem Bussche being sent back to the Eastern Front. Despite severe wounds he survived, succeded the family baronetcy, and served in the West German Diplomatic Service.

Age 24. *Kaemp for alt. Hvad du har kaert. Do om sad et gaelder. Da er livet ej saa svaert. Doden ikke heller* (Fight for all you hold dear, die if necessary. Then life is not so hard, nor death)

Grave 2.E.11. Also commemorated by statues outside the Frihedsmuseet (The Museum of Danish Resistance) within Churchill Park in Copenhagen, at his brother's home at Holmegaard, at Lassen Farm at Herlufsholm School, at the Jæger Corps barracks at Aalborg Air Base, at the Frogman Corps base at the Torpedo Station, Kongsøre, at HQ SBS (RM Poole), at 22 SAS Hereford and at 23 SAS' barracks at Invergowrie. He is commemorated by name on the Comacchio Memorial close to where he was killed, at St Peter's Chapel in Praesto Fjord, Denmark, at the Lassen Memorial Grove within the Danish Forest, Hill of Galilee, Israel, on the Commando Memorial at the National Arboretum and on a memorial bench at Glenfinnan, close to where he was originally trained. He is also commemorated by The Anders Lassen Foundation that provides welfare for Danish military personnel and their families. His medals were displayed at the Frihedsmuseet until it was ravaged by fire in 2013. Although saved their current whereabouts is unknown.

CORPORAL EDWARD **ROBERTS** [5884746] NORTHAMPTONSHIRE REGIMENT, BEDFORDSHIRE AND HERTFORDSHIRE REGIMENT, HAMPSHIRE REGIMENT AND SBS (M SQN)

'Rocky' Roberts, also known as Eddie or Ted, was born on 11 April 1922 in the parish of St Paul's, Cheltenham, where he attended St Gregory's School. In October 1937, aged just 15, he falsified his age to join the Northamptonshire Regiment's Supplementary Reserve at Gloucester. At the time he was living with his aunt and working as a bricklayer's mate. He enlisted into the regular regiment at Northampton the following March and was posted to the 2nd Battalion. After further training he was re-posted to the 4th Battalion and in July 1940 promoted to lance-corporal.

That October Roberts transferred to the Bedfordshire and Hertfordshire Regiment and having joined the 70th (Young Soldiers) Battalion was promoted to corporal in February 1941. He volunteered for the Commandos in March 1942 having reverted to the rank of private in order to do so. After three months of training he was returned to his unit and that September was posted to the 6th Battalion, disembarking in North Africa in May 1943. The following month he transferred to the Hampshire Regiment and was posted to the 5th Battalion where he was promoted to lance-corporal once more. However, that August he lost his stripe for a minor misdemeanour whilst based at Bône in north-east Algeria.

Roberts was posted to the Middle East at the end of March 1944 and volunteered for the Special Boat Service on 9 September. By the following spring he had been promoted to corporal. Dave Evans, former SBS, confirms that Roberts' nickname 'Rocky' was a result of his boxing prowess: as his sparring partner Evans recalled having his gloves up one moment and the next being on the floor holding his chin. 'What was that? A lorry?' asked Evans. 'That was my right hook,' answered Roberts.

Having been posted to M Squadron Roberts was killed in action on the night of the 8–9 April 1945 at Comacchio during OPERATION FRY and was originally buried alongside Major Andy Lassen, MC*, and Fusilier Spike Hughes, MM (see their entries above for details). Lassen had selected him and Trooper Freddy Crouch to bolster his patrol (see Crouch's entry above).

Son of Leonard and Catherine Roberts of Brunswick Street, Cheltenham, Gloucestershire – Younger brother of Jack Roberts – Known to have had two other brothers, all three siblings having served in the forces.
Age 23.
Safe in the arms of Jesus
Grave 2.E.9. Also commemorated on the Comacchio Memorial situated on the causeway where he was killed and on Cheltenham's war memorial.

ASSISI WAR CEMETERY

The majority of burials in this cemetery date from the June–July 1944 Allied advance from Rome. These were concentrated here after the cemetery was opened that September. It now contains 945 Commonwealth graves.

The cemetery is located south of Assisi at Rivotorto, just to the north of the SS75 on Via del Sacro Tugurio. GPS co-ordinates: Latitude 43.04639, Longitude 12.60922

MAJOR EDWARD ANTONY FITZHERBERT **WIDDRINGTON** MC [63144] GENERAL LIST, ROYAL INNISKILLING DRAGOONS, TRANSJORDAN FRONTIER FORCE, QUEEN'S BAYS AND 2ND SAS

Commonly known as Tony, Edward Widdrington was born on 1 March 1914 at the garrison town of Rawalpindi, North West India, where his father was serving in the 60th Rifles. Having attended St Aubyn's at Rottingdean he was sent first to Winchester College and then to Stowe School nearer to the family home. Having gone up to Hertford College, Oxford, he was commissioned onto the General List (TA) (*London Gazette* 20/07/34). After an attachment to the 5th Inniskilling Dragoon Guards at Aldershot during the summer of 1934, during which he was noted as 'reliable, energetic and tactful' and the possessor of 'a determined character', he transferred to this regiment in October 1935. As a keen rifle shot he represented England from 1935–37 and the following winter was granted six months' leave for Great

Britain's tour of South Africa, Australia and New Zealand. His near perfect long-range score on Anzac Ranges near Sydney in February 1938 helped Team GB return with the coveted Empire Trophy.

Having served in Palestine Widdrington was posted to A Squadron, Transjordan Frontier Force, and promoted captain in December 1939. During 1941 he was mentioned in despatches, more than likely for his part in OPERATION EXPORTER, the campaign against the Vichy French in Syria (*London Gazette* 30/12/41).

On 1 March 1943 Widdrington joined the Queen's Bays (2nd Dragoon Guards) at Tmimi in Libya. The regiment left for Tripoli that day, arriving at Ben Gardane close to German positions on the Mareth Line on the 13th. He was subsequently wounded in action near el-Hamma on the 27th whilst outflanking these positions during the Eighth Army's advance into Tunisia (OPERATION PUGILIST): as the Bays rolled towards the town they were engaged by 88mm guns and four tanks, including Widdrington's, were quickly destroyed, two men being killed whilst Widdrington and four others were wounded.

Having returned to the Bays he was awarded an immediate Military Cross whilst a temporary major. The regiment's War Diary records that C Squadron's Crusaders took on entrenched German infantry, anti-tank guns and a Tiger tank whilst attempting to cut off enemy forces in the Cap Bon peninsula. The accompanying citation notes:

On 9 May 43 the leading squadron was held up by an impassable wadi which was covered by enemy HE [high explosive] and AP [armour piercing] fire. This officer volunteered to carry out a recce on foot. On topping a rise some 1,800 yards from the start he came face to face with an infantry position where he came under heavy mortar and MG [machine-gun] fire. Acting with great coolness he made his way back with full information of enemy dispositions and possible line of approach completing in all a distance of 3.5 miles on foot, all the time under heavy fire. On finding that his squadron leader had become a casualty he led the squadron forward with great dash and skill and gained the next objective. The cool manner in which he carried out his long and dangerous task displayed complete disregard for danger and the highest example to his whole squadron [*London Gazette* 17/08/43, Supplement 19/08/43].

Widdrington and his men subsequently returned to Libya where he learnt of his MC, before passing through Tunisia en route to Algiers. He volunteered for 2nd SAS soon after, joining the Regiment at their camp at Philippeville and subsequently leading an attack on Sant'Egidio airfield in Central Italy during OPERATION POMEGRANATE. This was designed to 'put out the eyes' of the Germans by destroying reconnaissance aircraft in the run up to the Anzio landings. The post-operation report, written by Lieutenant Jimmy Quentin Hughes, who was captured but subsequently escaped to reach Allied lines that March, records that the SAS party took off from Gioia del Colle in a Dakota, parachuting into a drop zone:

… east of Lake Trasimere, between 2200hrs and 2230hrs [on 12 January 1944], from a height of about 500 feet. All the party and the containers dropped within a small area and contact was made immediately …

There were however, trees, in which two parachutes caught and we had to pull these down [he later wrote in *Who Cares Who Wins* that Widdrington was one of those hung up in branches]. We were using oil drums as containers to avoid the necessity of having to bury them. I believed that we were seen from the road which was only 20 yards away [WO 218/185].

The six-man team was challenged by a sentry at Ponte della Resina on the 15th and dispersed. Unable to regain contact with their men, the two officers went onto the airfield alone:

At 2230hrs [on 19 January] we arrived at the northern boundary of the aerodrome. We encountered no barbed wire. At this end there were four Ju88s in a row. Their engines were still warm. At 2300hrs we prepared our bombs and placed them on the starboard wings of the four Ju88s. Then we continued down the east side of the aerodrome and put bombs on two Fiesler Storch co-operation planes and on a three-engined Ju52 …

By 0200hrs [on the 20th] we reached the south side of the aerodrome and were unable to find any more aircraft to attack. We sat down and began to disarm the remaining bombs. I had finished my work and was about 4 yards away from Major Widdrington when a bomb in his hands blew up, about one hour and twenty minutes after it had been set. We were using L delays and not time pencils. I was blinded and nearly completely deaf and my trousers were blown off. I managed to feel Major Widdrington's body and discovered that he had lost both hands and was badly wounded in the right leg and in the chest. I found my morphia syringe but dropped the piercing pin and as I was blind I could not find it. I made a fire of what papers and maps I could find and fired my automatic in the air to attract attention. Some German sentries arrived and later an ambulance. Major Widdrington appeared to be dead [WO 218/185].

Hughes later recalled that Widdrington: 'was a big man in every sense of the word. He was tall, with a large moustache and a natural ability to command. He inspired confidence without the slightest trace of arrogance … It was all like a cricket match to him' (*Who Cares Who Wins*, by Jimmy Quentin Hughes, MC). He also noted that twenty-nine aircraft were destroyed or damaged that night, enough to prevent the Anzio landing force being located two days later and that the Italian sergeant in charge of the guard was court martialled and shot. An explosives officer investigated the cause of the premature explosion: 'I can only suggest that after they had laid the bombs Major Widdrington carried those that he had left with the delays in his hand, or close to his body, and thus warming them up. This would reduce the timing of the delay, which, in fact, went off after one hour and twenty minutes' (WO 218/185).

Widdrington was originally buried by the Germans in a civilian cemetery at Ospedalicchio, very close to the airfield and to his current resting place. He received a posthumous Mention in Despatches for this operation. The citation, fowarded by his Commanding Officer, Lt-Colonel Brian Franks, MC, on 5 July 1944, gives an account of the Sant'Egidio attack and notes: 'Major Widdrington MC displayed throughout high courage, determination and devotion to duty' (*London Gazette* 11/01/45, WO 373/96). For further details of Hughes see Appendix 2 in the User Guide.

Son of the late Brigadier-General Bertram Widdrington, CMG, DSO, who died in early 1942, and of Mrs Widdrington of Maids Moreton House, Buckingham – Brother of Captain Francis Widdrington of the Welsh Guards. *The Times* reported that he lived at 'Newton Hall, Northumberland' at the time of his death.
Age 29.
Also served with the Transjordan Frontier Force and the Queen's Bays. 'Joye sans fin' ('Joy Without End' – the family motto)
Grave 10.C.8. Commemorated on a plaque at Newton-on-the-Moor's village hall and within St James' Church, Shilbottle.

BARI WAR CEMETERY

The Adriatic port of Bari became an important supply hub to the advancing Allied armies. Seven general hospitals were based in or around the city at various times from October 1943. Their burials were added to by casualties concentrated from all over southern Italy. The cemetery now contains 2,128 Commonwealth graves of the Second World War, 170 of which are unidentified. In addition, there are war graves of other nationalities, eighty-five First World War burials that were concentrated here from Brindisi Communal Cemetery and some non-war burials.

The cemetery is located south-east of Bari on the SP 144, an extension of the SP 135, approximately 1½ kilometres west of the junction with the SS100. GPS co-ordinates: Latitude 41.06481, Longitude 16.8947

CAPTAIN ROBERT ANTHONY <u>CASE</u> [198237] ROYAL FUSILIERS, KING'S OWN YORKSHIRE LIGHT INFANTRY, SHERWOOD FORESTERS AND SBS (HQ SQN)

Known as 'Tony' to his friends, Robert Case was born on 17 November 1921 in the village of Littleover close to Derby. Having attended Bromsgrove School in Llanwrtyd Wells, where he was a member of the OTC, he continued his education at Derby Technical College. In January 1940 he joined the Royal Fusiliers (TA) at Nottingham University and was immediately posted to the Army Reserve (service number 6466172). Called to the colours in February 1941 he transferred to the King's Own Yorkshire Light Infantry and was posted to its infantry training centre at Strensall. That July he was commissioned from 167 OCTU into his father's former regiment, the Sherwood Foresters (Nottinghamshire and Derbyshire Regiment). Posted to the 2/5th Battalion the following April he suffered the first in a series of accidents, breaking a leg and dislocating a knee after colliding with an army vehicle whilst riding a motorbike.

At the end of 1942 Case embarked for North Africa, his battalion being transported from Algiers to the front line in Tunisia early in 1943. It saw action at Sedjenane and Djebel Guerba, Case being wounded on 17 March having reinforced the hard-pressed 3rd Battalion of the Parachute Regiment that was facing fierce counter attacks at Tamera. It was five months before he had recovered sufficiently to return to the Sherwoods, although during this period he met his wife-to-be, Joy Barber of the Queen Alexandra's Imperial Military Nursing Service (Reserve). *The Derby Daily Telegraph* later reported that in September 1943 Case had taken part in the Salerno landings (OPERATION AVALANCHE) and the breakout of the Anzio bridgehead, although what regiment he was with at the time is uncertain due to lack of entries in his service record. By October he was at No.1 Infantry Replacement Training Depot where he remained until March 1944 when posted to the 13th Infantry Brigade. Three months later he was posted back to No.1 IRTD as an instructor with the rank of captain.

Case volunteered for the Special Boat Service on 16 February 1945 whilst in Italy. The unit's War Diary states that he reported for duty two days later and that on the 19th he moved to the SBS base at Monte Sant'Angelo for training (WO 170/7529). On 12 March he dislocated his right shoulder after a heavy parachute landing at No.4 Parachute Training School at Gioia del Colle and was again hospitalised.

After VE-Day on 8 May 1945 all ranks were granted leave, Case spending the 14–28th in Rome. On 21 June the SBS received news that it was to be disbanded. However, on 28 July its War Diary recorded; 'Capt Case on DI [dangerously ill] list after accident' (WO 170/7529). A statement dictated by Case from his hospital bed reads: 'at 11am on 28/07/45 the a/m officer was bathing at the Monopoli beach. He dived off the diving board and struck his head on the bottom.' In doing so Case suffered a broken neck and was paralysed from the shoulders down. Trooper Chisholm confirmed at the ensuing court of inquiry:

> On 28 July at 1100hrs I attended a recreational training parade at Monopoli bathing beach. I was sitting on a raft about 15yds from the diving board and saw Capt Case dive in. As he came up I paid little attention. He went down and came up again and I realised he was in trouble. Two men dived in to help him out. They called for a stretcher and a vehicle.

The War Diary subsequently recorded on 31 July: '1330 hours Capt Case died in 98 General Hospital' and noted the following day '1430 hours British Military Cemetery Bari Capt Case buried with full military

honours' (WO 170/7529). The court of inquiry recommended that the diving board be removed.

Son of Captain Robert and Margaret Case (née Richardson) of Irongate, Derby – Husband of Joy Case of Derwent Avenue, Allestree, Derby – Father of one daughter.
Age 23.
And life is eternal and love is immortal
Grave 9.F.10. Also commemorated on Allestree's war memorial within the grounds of St Edmund's Church.

PRIVATE WILLIAM KITCHENER HOWELL [6348751] QUEEN'S OWN ROYAL WEST KENT REGIMENT, PARACHUTE REGIMENT AND SRS (No.1 TROOP)

Bill Howell was born in Bermondsey, south-east London, on 30 September 1915, although his family later relocated to Downham near Bromley in Kent. Having worked as a shop assistant he enlisted into the Queen's Own Royal West Kent Regiment in April 1940 and joined the 4th Battalion that June. Volunteering for Airborne Forces he transferred to HQ 1st Parachute Brigade and was re-posted to the 1st Battalion, Parachute Regiment, in mid January 1942. He qualified as a parachutist the following month but returned to the Royal West Kents in August. Joining the 7th Battalion he embarked for the Middle East in late October and on arrival in Egypt was posted to No.1 Infantry Training Depot. After qualifying as a Class II Signaller in May 1943 he was posted to Raiding Forces HQ at Azzib on the Palestinian coast and volunteered for the Special Raiding Squadron (1st SAS) on 6 June.

Howell landed at Capo Murro di Porco on Sicily during the early hours of 10 July 1943 during OPERATION HUSKY, the SRS destroying coastal batteries that threatened the Allied invasion fleet. On the evening of the 12th he took part in the capture of Augusta, the seizure of this port facilitating a more rapid advance up the east coast. He was subsequently killed in action during OPERATION BAYTOWN after the SRS landed at Bagnara on the toe of mainland Italy. Squadron Sergeant-Major Rose, MM, later noted: 'Sgmn C Richards killed in action 4th Sept. Sgmn W Howell killed in action 4th Sept. Both buried at 584670 (ph265229) below the road in garden at alleyway between two houses.' Having come ashore early that morning Howell and Richards were serving as signallers within No.1 Troop, whose commander, Major Bill Fraser, was preparing breakfast: 'another bomb had landed fair and square in the middle of the space where Bill's cooking operations were taking place. Two signallers of his headquarters were killed instantly' (*SAS – Men in the Making: An Original's Account of Operations in Sicily and Italy*, by Peter Davis, MC). In September 1943 Rose wrote to Howell's mother:

Bill, as he was known to us all, came to the Squadron some time in May [*sic*] as a troop signaller. At that time we were training hard for a big operation and your son worked well and hard, soon becoming a valuable addition to the Squadron. The operation eventually turned out to be the invasion of Sicily and I know you will be proud to know that your son was one of the first men to land on the island and he went through the whole campaign acquitting himself with honours on every occasion when we were in contact with the enemy. It was during the invasion of

Italy that he met his untimely end but I can assure you, in the hope that it will bring you some small comfort, that he passed away quietly and without pain. Your great loss is shared by the entire Squadron. Bill was more than liked by the boys and many is the time have I listened and laughed at his imitations of Maurice Chevalier. Always smiling, always ready to help anyone at any time, he leaves a gap in the ranks that can never be filled. His personal effects will be forwarded to you at our very earliest convenience together with the unit badge which is inscribed 'Who Dares Wins.' I pass on to you the condolences and sympathy of his Commanding Officer, officers and other ranks in this moment of your great bereavement. We pay homage to the memory of a brave soldier and a gentleman.

Son of John and Eve Annie Howell (née House) of Downham Way, Downham Estate, Bromley, Kent – Brother of Frederick and Sidney Howell.
Age 27.
In loving memory of our dear Bill. He died that we might live
Grave 7.D.14.

LIEUTENANT PETER HAROLD <u>JACKSON</u> MC [138196] ROYAL TANK REGIMENT, 1ST NORTHAMTONSHIRE YEOMANRY ATT QUEEN'S BAYS AND 2ND SAS (D SQN)

Peter Jackson was born in Putney, south-west London, on 9 November 1920. Having attended Emanuel School in nearby Wandsworth he continued his education at a building school run by Messrs Bovis Ltd. However, in April 1939 he enlisted into the Royal Tank Regiment and was posted to the 42nd Battalion at Warlingham until attending 102 OCTU at Blackdown as a sergeant. Commissioned into the RTR the following July his final report noted: 'a Cadet of the right type with a clear head and plenty of initiative and sound sense. He should make a very good officer' (*London Gazette* 19/07/40). Having initially been posted to the 55th Training Regiment at Farnborough he transferred to the 1st Northamptonshire Yeomanry, Royal Armoured Corps, at Trowbridge in December 1940. On promotion to lieutenant he attended the Armoured Fighting Vehicle School at Bovington from May–June 1942 and embarked for Egypt the following month. Arriving that September he was posted to the Queen's Bays and was wounded in action late in October during the final Battle of El Alamein. He subsequently spent most of the remainder of 1942 in hospital, although he was briefly attached to the Middle East RAC School.

Jackson rejoined the Bays, who were in reserve at Tmimi in Libya, in mid January 1943 and went back into action that March during the Eighth Army's advance into Tunisia. As such he was a contemporary of Major Tony Widdrington who was also soon to join the Regiment (see his entry under Assisi War Cemetery, Italy). Jackson was awarded the Military Cross for assaulting German positions during OPERATION PUGILIST, the outflanking of the Mareth Line, learning of his award that May whilst stationed at Bou Arada:

On 26th March 1943 during the advance of the 1st Armoured Division of El Hamma, Lt Jackson was commanding the leading troop of Shermans of the Queen's Bays. After passing through the NZ Div final objective at about 1800hrs his troop was constantly under heavy anti-tank fire from the front and from both flanks. By the fire of his troop he destroyed many anti-tank guns that were holding up the advance and enabled a steady forward movement to be continued. Just before last light his tank was hit and disabled. He immediately got into another tank of his troop and again led an advance when it re-commenced at midnight. His tank was again hit by an 88mm at 250yds; in spite of this he continued to fight his tank and by accurate Browning fire forced the enemy to abandon the gun.

On the morning 27th during the advance in daylight both the remaining tanks of his troop were hit by heavy HE [high explosive] and caught fire. Regardless of the heavy shelling he supervised the removal of the wounded from both tanks and collected Morphia from another tank, finally shepherding both crews back to safety.

His coolness, courage and determination throughout were an example to all who saw him [*London Gazette* 28/05/43, 5th Supplement 01/06/43, WO 373/93].

Still suffering from wounds Jackson required several stints in hospital, volunteering for 2nd SAS on 30 August 1943 directly from a period of convalescence. He was taken on strength on 4 September and posted to D Squadron, later landing with the Regiment at the port of Taranto on the heel of Italy at dusk on 10 September (OPERATION SLAPSTICK). He was subsequently at the forefront of the Allied advance towards Termoli, as outlined in the post-operation report:

[15 September] Lt Jackson patrolled area Pisticci as far as Ferrandina road and reported all clear …

16th Sept Lt Jackson left at first light for area Ginosa and obtained good observation on road. Bumped German patrol near Ginosa, and scattered them with fire from Vickers gun …

[18 September] Lt Jackson's troop crossed SAS bridge and bumped a German A/Tk [anti-tank] position near Miglionico. Shot them up and then got a good position on a flank to observe Matera. Gave reports and movement of MT [motor transport] all day …

[25 September] Loss of one Jeep. Crew, Lt Jackson, L/Cpl Duifan and Pct Roache all safe after spirited attempts to salvage Jeep under intense fire. Fire was returned to the enemy by Lt Jackson's Jeep …

[28 September] Lt Jackson and SSM Mitchell's Jeep chased a German M/C [motor cycle] patrol for 5 miles, and after exciting street fighting (in which Italians were dealt with as severely as Germans) we took two German prisoners. One M/C knocked out … [see Private Jim Downey's entry under Terre-Natale Communal Cemetery, France, Volume III, for further details of this incident]

[2 October] Convoy and all traffic held up by blown bridge across swollen stream 7 miles S. of Termoli. Lt Jackson and Capt Farran [his Squadron Commander, Roy Farran, MC**] crossed on a raft, and were first to link hands with SS Bde [Special Service Brigade], including 1st SAS [Special Raiding Squadron] who had taken the town that day (1500hrs) [on the 3rd – WO 218/176].

Having taken part in the defence of Termoli Jackson was killed in a road accident on 10 November 1943 when returning to Taranto. Parachutist 'X' [name omitted for publication] of 2nd SAS stated later that day:

At a point about 10km from Taranto I observed an Italian horse and cart advancing towards me, the driver was walking alongside the cart, nearest the half of the road from Taranto traffic. At the time it was slightly raining, and the road was very greasy, and I was proceeding down a slight gradient. On nearing the horse it grew frisky, and I lightly, owing to the surface of the road, applied pressure to the foot brake. Almost at once I felt the rear beginning to slide towards the horse and cart. I immediately released the pressure from the brakes and narrowly missed hitting the horse and cart. By then the skid was carrying the Jeep towards the right hand side. I then locked the wheels the opposite way to the skid and the Jeep started to slide to the left hand side, beyond control from me, where we eventually ended up hitting a post or girder. I was thrown out of the Jeep on impact and lay dazed on the ground. The next thing I remember was a soldier helping me into another Jeep, and another soldier bending over Lt Jackson MC who was laying limp still in the Jeep. The two soldiers then carried Lt Jackson into the same Jeep and took us to the 70th General Hospital outside Taranto. On reaching the hospital the doctor looked at Lt Jackson MC who was still in the rear of the Jeep laying down, and announced after examination that he had passed away.

The signpost that the Jeep crashed into was marked 'Discesa Pericolosa' (Dangerous Descent), the court of inquiry finding that the accident was caused by the surface of the road and that no one was to blame. Jackson was initially buried at the British Military Cemetery at Taranto, Farran later writing:

His grandfather had won two Victoria Crosses and I feel sure that Peter would also have deserved one had he not been killed in a Jeep accident a month later. He loved a fight and was very hurt when I told him to withdraw … He was such a reckless, gay person that it was impossible to realise that he was dead [*Winged Dagger: Adventures on Special Service*, by Roy Farran].

Son of Harold William and Ethel Jackson (née Miles) of Erpingham Road, Putney, south-west London – Brother of Mr M. Jackson.
Age 23.
A very dearly loved son and loving brother who will live forever in our hearts
Grave 6.E.39.

LANCE-CORPORAL JOHN McGUIRE [3314921] HIGHLAND LIGHT INFANTRY, PIONEER CORPS AND 2ND SAS

John McGuire was born on 16 October 1921 in the parish of Blythswood, Glasgow. In May 1939, whilst working as an apprentice electrical engineer at D. H. Sutherland, he joined the 9th (Gordon Highlanders) Battalion, Highland Light Infantry (TA), and was embodied that August. In February 1941 he was re-posted to the 2nd Battalion, Gordon Highlanders, and soon after transferred to the 'Special Wing Pioneer Corps' where he joined No.831 Smoke Production Company. He was promoted to lance-corporal in June 1941 and to corporal at the beginning of August, but reverted to lance-corporal later that month on being 'surplus to establishment.' He applied to join Airborne Forces in June 1942 but received no response. Two months later he was posted to a new company in Ledbury where one of his NCOs noted 'small and plenty of punch'. In April 1943, whilst serving with 293 Company in Gloucester, he reverted to the rank of private at his own request and embarked for North Africa as a reinforcement. Although it is not known when he volunteered for 2nd SAS it is likely that this was soon after its formation the following month. He regained his stripe that August.

McGuire took part in OPERATION SLEEPY LAD B in Italy towards the end of 1943. Tasked with destroying enemy lines of communication on the Adriatic coast his party of five was put ashore close to the mouth of the River Musene, south of Ancona, on the night of 18 November. Led by Major Sandy Scratchley the men moved inland and took refuge at a friendly farm. The following night McGuire and Parachutist Selwyn Brown blew the railway line north of Porto Recanati, stopping an oncoming train and being shot at for their troubles. The arrival of fresh German troops restricted further attacks and when the Royal Navy failed to pick the party up from their pre-arranged beach the men found themselves stranded, with McGuire now suffering from malaria. He struggled to keep up during the march to Porto Civitanova where Scratchley hoped they might steal a boat to return to Allied territory. They arrived on 2 December just in time to watch the Navy sink the only two available motor schooners and the RAF bomb the town. Having waited for the enemy to repair one of the vessels so that they could take it from them, the intended ship set sail at night and they were forced to requisition a fishing boat. They weighed anchor on the 14th, crossing Allied lines the following evening despite being shelled by a German battery en route (see Brown's own entry under Moussey Churchyard, France, Volume III).

McGuire died of 'aspiration asphyxia' on 20 February 1944 at No.1 Mobile Military Hospital having been found unconscious in his nearby billet. A signal dated 2 May points to the probable cause: 'Mob Mil Hosp report death probably due Vagal reflex from inhalation piece chewing gum into bronchis no delay treatment.'

Son of William and Elizabeth McGuire of Ferguson Street, Glasgow.
Age 22.
A.M.D.G. (The motto of the Catholic Society of Jesus meaning 'For the greater glory of God') *Let perpetual light shine on him, O Lord. May he rest in peace. Amen*
Grave 2.D.25.

Private Benjamin Thomas McLAUGHLAN [2888636] Gordon Highlanders, 1st SAS and SRS (No.2 Troop)

Benjamin McLaughlan was born in the Lowland town of Hamilton on 19 June 1920. Having worked locally as a painter and decorator he enlisted into the 5/7th Gordon Highlanders in July 1940 at Motherwell. After home service he disembarked in the Middle East in June 1942, volunteering for the newly-constituted 1st SAS on 1 October. Posted to B Squadron he subsequently took part in operations to harass enemy lines of communication along the Libyan coast and the Axis retreat into Tunisia.

After hostilities in North Africa ceased the Regiment was withdrawn to Palestine. It briefly returned to Kabrit in Egypt where the majority of its subunits, including B Squadron, were restructured as the Special Raiding Squadron on 19 March 1943. Training for the Allied invasion of Sicily, Operation Husky, followed in both Palestine and the Gulf of Aqaba. The SRS subsequently landed at Capo Murro di Porco on 10 July, destroying coastal batteries that threatened the invasion fleet. On the evening of the 12th it captured the key port of Augusta, thus facilitating a more rapid advance up the east coast. Soon after McLaughlan applied for Operational Wings and although it is not known whether these were awarded similar cases suggest so.

The SRS next saw action at Bagnara having landed on the toe of mainland Italy in the early hours of 4 September 1943 during Operation Baytown. After periods of rest and training on the west coast and Sicily it then sailed from port to port until settling at Manfredonia on the Adriatic coast. It subsequently landed with the Special Service Brigade in the early hours of 3 October to seize the vital port of Termoli during Operation Devon. Having secured the town the force was subject to fierce counter-attacks and on the morning of the 5th Captain Tony Marsh's No.2 Troop found itself being shelled and mortared, the SRS War Diary recording that at 1400hrs that day C Section was:

> Ordered to withdraw into wood 803780 to bolster Recce Regt personnel [56th Reconnaissance Regiment]. On arrival in wood find that they [the Recces] are leaving abandoning their carriers and A/T [anti-tank] guns. Asked to man A/T guns further left, but find that they have been taken out.
>
> Advance down into valley in order to cover dead ground in front of [No.]3 Commando.
>
> 1700hrs C Sect closes in to A Sect, No.2 Tp, still in original position and whole party commences to withdraw. A Sect No.2 Tp is pinned down in culvert 900x east of bridge 796788 and is unable to get out till dark. Casualties: one killed, four wounded, several missing from both their sections [WO 218/99].

McLaughlan was wounded when this section was mortared during this final move. He died of these wounds on 12 October 1943 (see also Lance-corporal Ginger Hodgkinson's entry under Sangro River War Cemetery, Italy).

Son of William and Agnes McLaughlan of Low Waters, Hamilton, Lanarkshire.
Age 23.
He died that we might live
Grave 10.E.7. Originally buried within the British plot of Barletta Civil Cemetery.

Private Thomas Alfred <u>PARRIS</u> [6345605] Queen's Own Royal West Kent Regiment and SRS (No.2 Troop)

Thomas Parris was born at St Mary Cray in Kent on 12 July 1920. In April 1939, whilst working as a butcher, he joined the local 4th Battalion, Queen's Own Royal West Kent Regiment (TA), and was mobilised at the outbreak of war that September. He served with the BEF in France from the beginning of April 1940 until being evacuated from Dunkirk on 1 June. Having married Edna Ivy Bramble at Pontefract, Yorkshire, in April 1941 he was promoted to lance-corporal that July, although he relinquished his stripe two months later. Disembarking in the Middle East in May 1942 he was posted to No.1 Infantry Training Depot the following spring and qualified as a signaller. He volunteered for the Special Raiding Squadron (1st SAS) on 13 May 1943, joining the unit in its build-up training for Operation Husky, the Allied invasion of Sicily.

Parris subsequently landed at Capo Murro di Porco in the early hours of 10 July 1943, the SRS destroying coastal batteries that threatened the invasion fleet. On the evening of the 12th he took part in the capture of the key port of Augusta. He was subsequently killed in action at Bagnara during Operation Baytown, during which the SRS landed on the toe of mainland Italy in the early hours of 4 September. At the time he was a member of Major Harry Poat's No.2 Troop:

He [Poat] was carrying a wad of maps in his thigh pocket, and as he was giving orders out to someone, a tracer bullet passed right through his pocket, setting it on fire ... In truly characteristic fashion, Harry calmly patted out the smouldering flames with his hand and went on talking. The bullet passed right through his pocket killing a signaller [Parris] who was standing nearby [*SAS – Men in the Making: An Original's Account of Operations in Sicily and Italy*, by Peter Davis, MC].

Squadron Sergeant-Major Graham Rose, MM, noted; 'Sgmn Parris Killed in Action 4th Sept. Buried at 584670 (ph275220) above bend of the road behind corner house in garden.' The following month *The Orpington and St Mary Cray Kentish Times* reported:

Mr and Mrs T. Parris of 227, High Street, St Mary Cray, have been officially informed that their son, Pte Thomas Alfred Parris, aged 23, of The Queen's Own Royal West Kent Regiment, has been killed in action in the Central Mediterranean. In 1939 he joined the Cray Company of Territorials, of which his father had been a Colour-Sergeant, and was mobilised at the outbreak of war.

An old boy of St Mary Cray Council School, Private Parris went to France with the British Expeditionary Force and was in the evacuation of Dunkirk. In the Middle East he saw service from April 19, 1942 [*sic*], in Egypt, Tunisia and Sicily.

Before being mobilised he was in the employment of Mr Knight, butcher, of Petts Wood, for four years. His father is one of the oldest members of the Orpington and Crays branch of the British Legion, who have sent a letter of sympathy to his family.

Son of Thomas and Emily Parris (née Durling) of St Mary Cray, Kent – Husband of Edna Ivy Parris of High Street, St Mary Cray.
Age 23.
He gave his life for his comrades and in his heart he fell for his country
Grave 7.D.16. Also commemorated on Orpington's war memorial, his father being commemorated on two local war memorials to those who fought, and returned from, the First World War.

Major Ian Norman **PATTERSON** MC [69411] Royal Artillery, Scots Guards, Parachute Regiment and SBS (L Sqn)

Ian Patterson was born to a Scottish doctor and English mother on 2 April 1914 at Stratford Mansions, South Molton Street in Mayfair, Central London. He attended Harrow School from 1928 to 1933 where he was a member of Bradbys House and a cadet-under-officer in the OTC. Whilst working as an engineer he was commissioned into the Supplementary Reserve of the Royal Artillery (*London Gazette* 13/10/36) and from November 1936 until February 1937 was attached firstly to the 9th Field Brigade at Bulford, and then the 1st Training Brigade at Woolwich. At the outbreak of war he was subsequently embodied into the 9th Field Regiment and briefly went to France as reinforcement to the BEF in February 1940. However, later that month he briefly returned home, relinquishing his commission to serve in the ranks of the short-lived 5th (Special Reserve) Battalion, Scots Guards. Nicknamed 'The Snowballers' this was raised largely from officers of other regiments and was ski-trained at Chamonix with the intention of helping the Finns in their fight against the Russians. Before it could be mobilised Finland was overwhelmed and the unit disbanded.

Returning to the BEF in April 1940 Patterson served as a temporary captain in the 9th Field Regiment before being evacuated from Dunkirk. Having attended 125 OCTU at Ilkley from February to March 1941 he disembarked at Bombay, India, that September.

On 11 February 1942 Patterson volunteered for the 151st Parachute Battalion at Delhi. Moving to Khadakwasla near Poona its men were trained in amphibious landings by the Combined Operations School, a skill that Patterson would later put to good use. That October the battalion was stood-to for a move to the Middle East and for cover reasons sailed from Bombay posing as the 20th Queen's Regiment at the beginning of November. Disembarking in Egypt the unit was renamed the 156th Parachute Battalion in line with deception plans, Patterson being appointed Staff Captain. The following March Lt-Colonel Shan Hackett, DSO, MC, MBE (GSO I Raiding Forces) detailed a number of officers to form the 11th Battalion, Parachute Regiment, Patterson being appointed the unit's Second-in-Command with the rank of major (*London Gazette* 29/01/43, Supplement 02/02/43). He subsequently set about recruiting from the region's camps in order to bring the battalion up to strength.

11 Para parachuted onto the Dodecanese island of Cos on the night of 14–15 September 1943. It was met by the Special Boat Squadron and set about organising the island's defences. Two months later, on 8 November, Patterson, a pre-war skiing companion of the SBS Commanding Officer, Major The Earl Jellicoe, DSO, volunteered to take over the command of L Detachment from Tommy Langton who was returning to the UK. The squadron immediately noted his relaxed and somewhat scruffy appearance. By February 1944 he was operating back in the Aegean. On receiving reports that two German P lighters were to be put into the island of Nisiros Patterson, who much to his frustration had been sat at the SBS forward operating base in neutral Turkish waters, assembled a scratch patrol under Lieutenant Dick Harden. Landing on the island before the enemy Patterson discovered that the Germans intended to remove a party of children from an orphanage some distance from the quay. Using their luggage as a lure, and dressing in priest's attire, he posted his men around the building before inviting the enemy in. Hand-to-hand fighting ensued, the SBS capturing the survivors and rapidly making their way to positions overlooking the moored enemy vessels. They were just in time to overwhelm the enemy crews who had been alerted by a runner. Patterson was subsequently awarded an immediate Military Cross on the recommendation of Jellicoe:

> On the island of Nissero [*sic*] on 7 Mar this officer personally commanded the party which captured two enemy assault craft. This operation would not have been successful save for the careful planning of this officer, his resourceful improvisation on the spot at considerable risk to himself and the dash and disregard of personal safety which he showed in the conduct of the operation.

The assault on the boats was made possible by the accurate fire of this officer from a Bren gun although in an exposed position.

As a result of this operation two assault craft were captured, twenty-two enemy killed or taken prisoner and much equipment and arms taken.

This officer commanded the SBS detachment operating in the Aegean in Feb, Mar, and early Apr. The success of these operations was due to his initiative and to the personal inspiration he gave in leadership and in disregard to his own safety on the above occasion and in other operations in the islands of Cos, Patmos and Pserimo.

Owing to the nature of these operations it would be appreciated if this citation is not published [*London Gazette* 13/07/44, WO 373/46].

Patterson attended Anglo-Turkish negotiations in Istanbul but in July 1944 led his squadron on a joint raid with SOE's Force 133 against fuel dumps on Crete. Although security was lax amongst the locals, and the Germans therefore aware, some results were achieved, his team destroying 35–40,000 gallons of petrol and killing ten Germans at Apolstoldi. The same month he visited Syria and Jerusalem, later taking over training at Athlit, the now Special Boat Service base on the Palestinian coast. That August the unit moved to Italy, settling at Monte Sant'Angelo on the Gargano Peninsula.

When it was realised that German forces were about to pull out of Greece Patterson and L Squadron were parachuted onto Araxas airfield in the Peloponnese on 23 September 1944 during OPERATION TOWANBUCKET. From here he pursued the retreating enemy, leading a mixed force of men from the Parachute Regiment, the Raiding Support Regiment, the SBS, the Royal Engineers, the RAF Regiment and the Long Range Desert Group, along with four 75mm guns and an ambulance detachment, collectively known as Patforce or Bucketforce. *The Egyptian Gazette* of 25 October 1944 takes up the narrative:

Major Ian Patterson who commanded the force then set off for Patras. Late in the afternoon he left his men outside the town and went in, accompanied by the representative of the Swedish Red Cross, to demand the surrender of the German forces.

He told the German second-in-command that unless they surrendered by noon the next day he would attack with his entire force of parachutists. He convinced the Germans he had a strong striking force and was told they were willing to surrender after getting permission from Athens. When Athens refused permission Patterson realised he was in no place to attack positions held by 1,200 German Marines supported by a strong Greek Security Battalion. He decided to negotiate a surrender during the night without the knowledge of the Germans.

At 8pm the entire Security Battalion began to stream out. Meanwhile Patterson later learned that reinforcements had landed at Katakolon. These consisted of members of the RAF Regiment and Long Range Desert Group. The transport at Patterson's disposal was five Jeeps and two RAF Regiment armoured cars. He took them into Patras and started shooting up every German soldier and vehicle he could find. By the time the Germans had discovered that the Greek Security Battalion had pulled out, and though the big attack had started, they prepared to leave themselves. But when daylight came it was clear the British force consisted of only a handful of men raging around the streets. The enemy opened fire and things became so uncomfortable that Patterson had to withdraw to the suburbs …

Patterson had one captured Italian mortar and one mortar belonging to the RAF Regiment and with these he opened fire. The barrage from the mortars was kept up for three hours and the Germans, again thinking the big attack had started, hastily evacuated Wireless Hill. Patterson was now in a strong position. The force had grown and in addition he had captured a 1908 model 75mm gun without sights. He immediately opened fire with the captured gun on the barges in harbour which were preparing to leave with the German garrison … The following afternoon Lt Col Lord Jellicoe decided to pursue the Germans who were however stretched out over 100 square miles from Katakolon to Patras. Patterson set out with his force travelling in two Jeeps one towing the captured 75mm gun.

First contact was made at Rion 10 miles away. The Jeeps were held up by extensive demolition but were within range of the German barges and opened fire with their gun [a fellow SBS officer, Walter Milner-Barry, noted that Patterson loaded the gun himself 'ramming the shells with an iron bar']. The Germans again thought the big attack was coming and a landing craft carrying the entire German force put out into the Gulf of Corinth. The German force got away and Patterson had great difficulty in catching up again. He crossed the Corinth Canal where a few casualties were suffered from mines and caught up with the Germans. After the Megara airfield had been captured by Patterson's two Jeep force the Germans launched a counter attack. A few reinforcements had arrived and the RAF Regiment armoured cars were also available. Meanwhile the enemy had sent twenty-two cyclists into Megalo Pevco to retake the village. They were cut off by armoured cars and annihilated. One of Patterson's patrols set off into the hills to try to blow up the road from Piraeus to the north but the Germans drove them off.

It was then decided to enter Athens without waiting for the Germans to withdraw. On the night of October 11 a small party entered at Athens having travelled by rowing boat from Megara to Scaramanga and walked the rest of the way. They made for an airfield but arrived too late to save it from destruction. They then went to the power station and found that the civilian employees had the situation in hand. The small patrol then just waited in Athens. They were followed the next night by Jellicoe and Patterson with a further patrol who went to Scaramanga in caiques (Greek boats) then rode into Athens on bicycles they had captured at Megalo Pevco. The Germans were pulling out fast and this small force were bicycling into Athens along the same road. Parachutists from Magara followed the next day.

Jellicoe himself noted in his report that:

> After an exhilarating ride we entered Athens and reported to General Spiliotopoulos, the Greek Military Governor of Attica. The following day, amid scenes of genuine and delirious enthusiasm for the Allies and the British, I attended the Te Deum service for the liberation of Athens at the cathedral and Maj Patterson accepted the surrender of the Athens Security Bn. Parties and politics then ensued.

For this series of actions Patterson was mentioned in despatches (*London Gazette* 02/01/45, Supplement 04/01/45) although he wrote to his mother outlining his disappointment when the Greek Civil War broke out:

> I am desperately sorry for Greece as I love the ordinary people so very much indeed; it is infuriating to see them and their country treated in this fashion by a small communistic minority controlling an army mostly composed of thieves and vagabonds, and I do think that it represents to a great extent what we are fighting for; a freedom to think and believe what you wish without being murdered in your sleep.

Patterson was killed on 21 December 1944 when the Dakota aircraft transporting him from the Greek capital to Brindisi crashed into a hillside near Toritto, 27 kilometres south-west of Bari, on the north side of the road to Altamura. An instrument approach had been attempted in bad weather, the plane's starboard wing tip striking a tree, the ground, further trees and then a wall causing the airframe to cartwheel and catch fire. A court of inquiry assessed that visibility had in fact been good enough and that the cause of the accident 'was due to a combination of faulty navigation and airmanship.' The aircraft had been loaded with wounded and all aboard bar one, a total of four aircrew and eighteen passengers, were killed. Patterson is buried in a row of ten of these men.

Only son of Norman and Winifred Patterson (née Crockford) of Nobs Crook, Ashridge Park, Berkhamsted, Hertfordshire – Brother of Dorothea Patterson. Age 30.
Who Dares, Wins
Grave 12.A.5. Also commemorated on war memorials at Little Gaddesden and Harrow School.

MARINE REGINALD ROY <u>PHILLIPS</u> [CH/X2364] ROYAL MARINES AND SBS

Reginald Phillips was born 26 October 1919 at Smethwick in the West Midlands. Having worked locally as a capstan hand at Messrs Mansell & Booth Ltd from 1935 to 1938 he enlisted into the Royal Marines for twelve years at nearby Birmingham. His subsequent conduct whilst serving with the Plymouth, Portsmouth and Chatham Divisions was assessed as 'very good'. During December 1941 he was aboard the light cruiser HMS *Arethusa* when it led the Commando raids on the Lofoten Islands, the ship returning to Scapa Flow on New Year's Day 1942 having been damaged by air attack (OPERATION ANKLET). Phillips remained with her on convoy escort duties to Malta that June when she again suffered damage from air attack (OPERATION VIGOROUS). On the night of 12–13 August she bombarded Rhodes in support of the Pedestal convoy bound for Malta.

In October 1942 Phillips was posted to HMS *Nile*, a shore establishment at the port of Alexandria in Egypt. He served here until October 1943 when re-posted to HMS *Saunders*, the Combined Training Centre at Kabrit. Having attended parachute course No.83 at Ramat David that December he volunteered for the Special Boat Squadron on 2 May 1944. That August the unit, now retitled the Special Boat Service, moved to Monte Sant'Angelo on the east coast of Italy where it fell under the command of HQ Land Forces Adriatic.

Phillips was killed in a motorcycle accident whilst on duty. Although the SBS War Diary recorded the incident on 5 January 1945 his date of his death is officially recorded as the 4th (WO 170/7529). No further details can presently be traced.

Son of Henry and Gladys Phillips of Wellington Road, Bearwood, Smethwick, Staffordshire.
Age 25.
Darling, we miss you more as years roll by; may God be with you till we meet again.
R.I.P.
Grave 7.B.30.

GUARDSMAN MAURICE JOSEPH <u>REYNOLDS</u> [2718228] IRISH GUARDS AND 2ND SAS

Maurice Reynolds was born on 14 April 1913 in the parish of Kilcogy near Granard in what was County Cavan, Eire (now County Longford). Having worked as a grocer's assistant he followed his brother, Owen, into the Irish Guards, enlisting at Liverpool in July 1935 and serving in Egypt and Palestine from November 1936 until December 1938. During this period he was awarded a Mention in Despatches having been 'brought to the notice of the General Officer Commanding for distinguished conduct in action during operations against armed bands in Palestine in August 1938' in the course of which he was wounded on the 18th of that month (General Order 440, 1938 – *London Gazette* 25/04/39). His demobilisation certificate of July 1939 notes that his service had been exemplary: 'an exceptionally good man in every way. He is very hard working and reliable, very capable and willing.'

Having been mobilised from the Army Reserves at the outbreak of war Reynolds rejoined the 1st Battalion and served in HQ Company. He married Kathleen Hickey at Camberley that December, their son Maurice being born the following year. On 15 April 1940 the battalion landed at Harstad in Norway to help counter the German invasion. Nearly a month later its positions were taken over by Polish troops. It subsequently embarked the HMT *Chrobry* tasked with reinforcing the Scots Guards at the front line farther to the south. However, the ship was inexcusably held at anchor awaiting orders until the evening of 14 May, during which time she was lucky not to be hit in successive air attacks. Once finally under way the *Chrobry*, with its escort far behind, was followed out to sea by a German spotter plane and just after midnight bombed and set on fire. All hands were forced to abandon her with heavy losses, including the battalion's CO, both senior majors and all four company commanders. The captain of HMS *Wolverine*, the escort that came alongside and took aboard survivors, noted that this would not have been possible had it not been for 'the superb discipline of the men of the Battalion'. A few days later a new complement of officers arrived and the men dug in near Bodø. Within twenty-four hours they were exchanging fire with German infantry and after a week of holding their line were ordered to withdraw. A long march ensued before the battalion embarked for the UK, only just ahead of the pursuing enemy.

Reynolds landed in North Africa in March 1943, the battalion seeing fierce fighting the following month during the 'Battle of the Bou' at the Djebel bou Aoukaz. Having captured key German positions that dominated the Medjez plain it successfully defended against counter-attacks, thereby facilitating the advance towards Tunis.

After hostilities in North Africa concluded Reynolds volunteered for 2nd SAS alongside Captain John Gunston on 29 June 1943 (see Gunston's entry under Cassino Memorial, Italy). Having deployed to Italy that September during OPERATION SLAPSTICK Reynolds was killed in a 'battle accident' on 11 December 1943. This is believed to have taken place when cleaning enemy weapons that he and his comrades had been testing. At the time his brother, Owen, was serving with his former battalion at Taranto, the CO of the Irish Guards sending a firing party to Bari for the funeral.

Son of Mary Reynolds of Kilnaleck, County Cavan – Husband of Kathleen Reynolds of Hallowell Road, Northwood, Middlesex – Father of Maurice Reynolds – Brother of Owen and Daniel Reynolds.
Age 30.
No inscription.
Grave 14.E.35.

LANCE-CORPORAL CHARLES TEVERSON **RICHARDS** [7955348] HOME GUARD, ROYAL ARMOURED CORPS, 1ST SAS AND RAIDING FORCES SIGNALS SQN ATT SRS

Charlie Richards was born in Wrexham in Denbighshire on 23 March 1908, although by 1911 his family was living in Great Yarmouth where his father was the manager of a chemist. Having attended the local grammar school, where he was a member of the OTC from 1922 to 1926, he followed in his father's footsteps and moved to Sandown on the Isle of Wight to work as a dispenser. A few days after the outbreak of war he married Nadine Ruperta Gauntlett at Portsmouth. Having served in the Home Guard he enlisted into the Royal Armoured Corps in March 1942 and was initially posted to the 54th Tank Regiment at Perham Down and Barnard Castle before being interviewed by No.5 War Office Selection Board that September. Deemed unsuitable for a commission in the Royal Artillery he returned to his unit and was promoted to lance-corporal.

In November 1942 Richards was posted to the 52nd Training Regiment and reverted to the rank of trooper. Disembarking in Egypt the following January he volunteered for 1st SAS on 14 February 1943. When the majority of the Regiment's subunits were restructured as the Special Raiding Squadron the following month he was posted to Raiding Forces Signals Squadron and on 6 June attached to the SRS. He was promoted to lance-corporal on 1 July, just in time for OPERATION HUSKY, the Allied invasion of Sicily. The SRS subsequently landed at Capo Murro di Porco in the early hours of the 10th and destroyed coastal batteries that threatened the fleet. It went on to capture the key port of Augusta on the evening of the 12th.

Richards was killed in action during OPERATION BAYTOWN, the SRS having landed at Bagnara on the toe of mainland Italy to hasten the German withdrawal. Squadron Sergeant-Major Graham Rose, MM, recorded: 'Sgmn C Richards killed in action 4th Sept [1943]. Sgmn W Howell killed in action 4th Sept. Both buried at 584670 (ph265229) below the road in garden at alleyway between two houses.' The pair were signallers within No.1 Troop, whose commander, Major Bill Fraser, had been preparing breakfast: 'another bomb had landed fair and square in the middle of the space where Bill's cooking operations were taking place. Two signallers of his headquarters were killed instantly' (*SAS – Men in the Making: An Original's Account of Operations in Sicily and Italy*, by Peter Davis, MC).

Son of Thomas and Flora Richards of Salisbury Road, Great Yarmouth – Husband of Nadine Richards of Broadway, Sandown, Isle of Wight – Younger brother of Kathleen and older brother of Geoffrey.
Age 35.
In loving memory of a brave soldier and a gentleman
Grave 7.D.20. Also commemorated on Sandown's war memorial.

GUARDSMAN CHARLES FRANCIS **TOBIN** [2719627] IRISH GUARDS, NO.8 COMMANDO, MIDDLE EAST COMMANDO, 1ST SAS AND SRS (NO.2 TROOP)

Charlie Tobin was born on 20 October 1919 in the parish of Bawnrickard near Clonmel in County Tipperary, Eire. Having worked as a builder's labourer he enlisted into the Irish Guards at Isleworth in November 1939. Posted to the Guards Depot at Caterham he joined the 1st Battalion in February 1940 and was attached firstly to the 2nd Battalion, then to the Training Battalion. Having returned to the 2nd Battalion in June he was posted to a Special Service Battalion two months later, this being temporarily absorbed into No.4 Special Service Battalion in November. Reconstituted under its original title of No.8 (Guards) Commando he subsequently disembarked at Suez, Egypt, at the beginning of March 1941 as a member of B Battalion, Layforce. An unsettled period followed for the Commando that based itself at Mersa Matruh, it being stood-to for numerous operations that were all cancelled at the last minute. Although a detachment was sent to Tobruk Layforce was, in the main, disbanded in July 1943, Tobin being absorbed into A Squadron of the Middle East Commando at Geneifa.

Tobin subsequently took part in the aborted attack on Maraua Fort in Libya during June 1942 (see Lance-bombardier Joe Fassam's entry under Sangro River War Cemetery, Italy, for full details of this operation). Having been ordered to withdraw to Dekhaila in Egypt the unit's War Diary notes that on 27 June: 'a trap was laid for some Egyptian arms-traffickers who had approached Gdsm Tobin with a view to buying rifles. At 2200hrs three Egyptians were caught red-handed. One of them was shot and killed while trying to escape, and the other two were handed over to the FSS [Field Security Section] Amiriya.'

Tobin volunteered for 1st SAS on 15 October 1942 and was therefore involved in the closing stages of the North African Campaign. In March 1943 the majority of the Regiment's subunits were restructured as the Special Raiding Squadron and began training for OPERATION HUSKY, the Allied invasion of Sicily. Tobin subsequently landed at Capo Murro di Porco in the early hours of 10 July as a member of No.2 Troop. Having destroyed coastal batteries that threatened the invasion fleet the SRS went on to capture the key port of Augusta on the evening of the 12th.

On 4 September 1943 the SRS landed at Bagnara on the toe of mainland Italy in order to hasten the German retreat during OPERATION BAYTOWN. No.2 Troop's B Section, under the command of Lieutenant Peter Davis, advanced up one of the steep roads that climb out of the town but was fired on from dug-in concrete positions and forced into cover behind a house. Davis later noted Tobin's response:

> 'Let's have a bang at them, Sir' he continued … he fingered his EY rifle lovingly … 'Look, just let me put a couple of grenades over there with this,' he pleaded, 'I am sure I can wake them up and give them something to think about' [*SAS – Men in the Making: An Original's Account of Operations in Sicily and Italy*, by Peter Davis, MC].

Tobin subsequently volunteered to accompany Davis and Sergeant Andy Storey to recce a culvert that ran under the road 15 yards ahead of their position and that might lead to a better position from which to fight. He and Storey moved without waiting for their officer and although Storey made cover Tobin was killed by a burst of machine-gun fire that struck him in the chest. Having withdrawn under cover of darkness the men returned the following day:

> We laboriously dug a shallow grave among the vines [Squadron Sergeant-Major Graham Rose, MM, recorded the burial location as '587670 (ph215255) below only house on first terrace'] …
>
> Then after a minute of silence, during which each of us was left to his own thoughts, we sadly trooped down the hill to rejoin the rest of the regiment.
>
> I found Sgt McNinch at my side as we descended, and it came as something of a surprise to me to see this hardened and usually so cheerful soldier overcome with emotion. 'You know, Sir' he said, as though to himself, 'it's funny that

it is always the best that catch it. Charlie Tobin was the kindest-hearted man in the section – he would never say a hard word about anyone – and they have to go and kill him. And here am I, a drunken old reprobate, and am still alive.' In Tobin's pay-book had been found a pathetic will leaving various of his pals in the regiment a few shillings here and a pound or two there [*SAS – Men in the Making: An Original's Account of Operations in Sicily and Italy*, by Peter Davis, MC – see also Lance-sergeant Bill McNinch's own entry under Sangro River War Cemetery, Italy].

Son of Charles and Bridget Tobin of Thomastown, County Kilkenny, Eire. Age 23.
In memory of Charles of Thomastown Co. Kilkenny, Eire. R.I.P.
Grave 7.D.18.

BOLSENA WAR CEMETERY

After the liberation of Rome on 4 June 1944 German forces attempted to halt the Allied advance in the area immediately north of the Italian capital. During its push towards the Trasimene Line the 6th South African Armoured Division subsequently clashed with elements of the German 362nd and 365th Infantry Divisions, the 4th Parachute Division, the 3rd Panzer Grenadier Division and the 26th Panzer Division in the area to the east of Lake Bolsena. Fierce fighting, most notably at Cellano, Bagnoregio, Orvieto and Chiusi, in conjunction with the speed of the continued advance, meant that burials were scattered throughout the region.

In November 1944 this site, which had served as General Alexander's advanced HQ, was chosen as a concentration point for such graves. In addition, forty-two graves of men killed during OPERATION BRASSARD *were concentrated here from the Island of Elba during 1947. The cemetery now contains 597 Commonwealth burials, forty of which are unidentified. It is located on the east shore of Lake Bolsena on the SR2 between Rome, 104 kilometres to the south, and Siena, some 115 kilometres to the north. GPS coordinates: Latitude 42.58562, Longitude 11.99863*

LANCE-CORPORAL LAWRENCE DOUGLAS <u>RODERICK</u> [1113] DIVISIONAL CAVALRY REGIMENT, LRP AND LRDG (T.1 PATROL)

Known as Laurie to his family and as Clarrie to comrades, Lawrence Roderick was born on 19 February 1913 at Gisborne on the shore of Poverty Bay, New Zealand. Having worked as a drover at Opotiki he 'went to Australia during the Depression in the 1930s for two years and found work in a travelling circus, fighting anyone who was fooled by his stature' (he stood at 5'3" – personal correspondence with his cousin, Brian Roderick, 2015). Returning to New Zealand's South Island, where his parents had since settled, he joined his older brother, George, working as a linesman for the Marlborough Electric Power Board.

Soon after the outbreak of war Roderick enlisted into the Divisional Cavalry Regiment. An intense period of training followed before its men embarked the *Rangitata* at Wellington in January 1940, thus joining the first New Zealand convoy to head to the Middle East. After a six-week voyage via Fremantle, Ceylon and Aden the regiment arrived at Port Tewfik, Egypt, where it boarded trains to finally march into its tented camp at Maadi, south of Cairo, in mid February. Having attended a physical training course at Abbassia that April Roderick was promoted to lance-corporal. Three months later he volunteered, and was accepted from a mass of potential recruits, to become one of the founding members of the Long Range Patrol, this being expanded as the Long Range Desert Group in November 1940. By the beginning of December he was serving as a lance-corporal in W Patrol under Captain Teddy Mitford but was posted to HQ Troop of T Patrol under Captain Pat Clayton before the end of the year.

Roderick was serving as a gunner in T.1 Patrol when taken prisoner at the Jebel Sherif in South East Libya on 31 January 1941: T and G patrols were returning from OPERATION AESOP, a raid on the oasis town of Murzuk, well behind enemy lines in the south-west of the country. Located by Italian aircraft they were attacked by the Compagnia Sahariana, the Italian equivalent of the LRDG, Clayton, Roderick and Lance-corporal 'Wink' Adams being forced to surrender after machine-gun fire punctured two tyres, the radiator and the petrol tank of their truck, 'Te Rangi'. The two New Zealand other ranks became the first men from the 2nd NZEF to be captured, Clayton later writing to his sister-in-law from a POW camp:

> Roderick put twenty-two bullet holes in the plane and wounded the observer … I told Roderick and Adams to give in as the car was hit with a big bullet in the tank. They were not hurt and were excellent throughout … They [the Italians] gave Roderick trousers to replace his which were torn to ribbons in the scramble and fed us with their own officers and men respectively. The next day after a little air raid we were taken off by plane [to Benghazi], and then sent on [to Tripoli] by motorbus full of refugee women and children. We were well looked after by our Carabinieri guards, but it was a tough journey [Clayton family collection].

Clayton also wrote to Adams' mother commenting that; 'your boy and Roderick mended the tyres under constant interruption from machine guns.'

Having been transported to mainland Italy Roderick was held at Agazzano near Piacenza before being transferred to the nearby PG.41 at Montalbo in September 1942. He was moved to PG.38 at Poppi near Arezzo that November and, after either escaping or walking out of this camp at the Italian armistice of September 1943, joined Partisans of the Brigata Mameli who came to know him as 'Captain Lorenzo Rodrich'. Whilst leading them in an attack on the fascist barracks at Sasso d'Ombrone near Grosseto on 6 April 1944 he was either killed in action or murdered after capture and buried beneath bushes in the area of Monte Cucco. Lieutenant John Lion, thought to be an American, later stated:

> I, 1st Lieutenant Lion, certify that Cpl Cleary Rodrick [*sic*], a former member of the Royal Long Range Desert Patrol [*sic*] who had been captured during the Libyan Campaign, was leading a small band of Italians in work against the Germans. Rodrick tried to contact an Italian officer of another band, and had arranged the time and place of meeting.

This information was obtained by the fascists, and the New Zealander was ambushed and shot at about 9 o'clock on or about 5 April 1944 [service record].

Roderick's remains were subsequently moved to the public cemetery at Orvieto and were reinterred at Bolsena War Cemetery in May 1945. Recording his death in the official history of the Divisional Cavalry R. J. M. Loughnan noted that:

Clarry, who was in the LRDG at the time, was the regiment's first PW loss. His death exposed a sad coincidence. Somewhere near Sora, when escaped prisoners were very much on everybody's mind, Dan Tomlinson happened upon a great sheaf of messages held by a local priest. They had been written by some 1,200 prisoners whom he had helped. This priest had sorted one from 'a New Zealander' of recent date and this happened to have been written by Roderick, only a few weeks before, saying that he had received assistance and was on his way back to the Allied lines … it was tragic that he should come to his end so near to friends and freedom after long captivity [*Divisional Cavalry*, by R. J. M. Loughnan].

Son of George and Elsie Roderick (née Williams) – Younger brother of William (Bill), Ruby, George (Paddy), Ron, Noble Tasman (who served in a transport unit in wartime North Africa) and older brother of Enid Cora – Father of Michael Peter Bailey born in August 1937 to Miss Winifred Bailey of Raukokore.
Age 31.
No inscription.
Grave 3.A.3. Also commemorated on an LRDG memorial within the New Zealand SAS camp at Papakura, on Blenheim's war memorial, on the war memorial at Grosseto's Town Hall and on a plaque within the civil building in the village of Cinigiano near to where he was killed.

CAGLIARI (SAN MICHELE) COMMUNAL CEMETERY, SARDINIA

This cemetery contains those lost on OPERATION HAWTHORN, *a series of aerodrome attacks carried out by six teams of the Special Boat Squadron's L Detachment that had been forward-mounted from Palestine and attached to 2nd SAS. They were initially inserted by submarine from Algiers, much of the pre-deployment training having been conducted at 2nd SAS' base at Philippeville. This was an area notorious for malaria, many of the men subsequently suffering from vomiting and diarrhoea aboard HM Submarines* **Saracen** *and* **Severn**. *Assumed to be due to unpleasantly cramped conditions their illness was in reality the onset of the disease, the consequences of which would prove fatal on an individual and operational level.*

San Michele Cemetery is located 4 kilometres north of Cagliari on the road to Monastir. The Commonwealth plot contains sixty burials, the majority being those of airmen. Access is gained from the Piazza dei Castellani off the roundabout connecting the Via Puglia and the Via Abruzzi. GPS co-ordinates: Latitude 39.24375, Longitude 9.10118

Sergeant Duncan McKERRACHER [1520288] Royal Artillery, 1st SAS and SBS (L Det)

Duncan McKerracher was born on 19 December 1914 in the village of Mid Calder near Bathgate, West Lothian. Having worked as a baker he married at Grangemouth in June 1939 and that November enlisted into the Royal Artillery at Stirling. Posted to the 103/32nd Light Anti-Aircraft Regiment at Bainsford in Falkirk he was promoted to lance-bombardier the following March and to bombardier in October 1940. He was re-posted to the 103/26th LAA Regiment in February 1941, appointed sergeant that October and disembarked in the Middle East the following month. Annotations on his service record make it likely that between January and June 1942 he was serving alternately between Limassol on Cyprus and Spinney Wood, a small, tented camp close to the town of Ismailia within Egypt's Canal Zone.

Although it is not known exactly when McKerracher volunteered for the Regiment it seems likely that it was either late in 1942 or early the following year. What is certain is that he was posted to L Detachment, Special Boat Squadron, at the beginning of April 1943. During Operation Hawthorn he was a member of Captain John Thomson's 'Daffodil' Party that was tasked with attacking Ottani airfield on Sardinia. Embarking HM Submarine *Severn* on 28 June they surfaced on the night of 1–2 July and, alongside Lieutenant A. Duggan's 'Bluebell' team, paddled the 5 kilometres to shore. Cyril Feebery, the senior NCO present, later wrote:

> This sudden burst of activity in the fresh air left Sgt McKerrica [*sic*] and Ptes Thomas 401 and Thomas 501 [*sic* – 521] in a bad way – I jollied them along (believe that, you'll believe anything) but when we reached the beach [north of Capo Pecora on the west coast] they could hardly stand. They tried to help with the unloading while Lt Duggin [*sic* - Duggan] and I went for a scout round and Pte Noriega buried the deflated boats. 50 yards inland was a cliff about a hundred feet high. We couldn't find a path so I climbed it, taking a rope with me. It was steep but made of very soft, crumbly stuff in which it was easy to kick footholds and get a purchase. I tied the rope off round some scrubby bushes and climbed down again. We spent the next couple of hours shifting our gear from the beach to an overgrown spot about 200 yards inland from the cliff top. McKerrica and the two Privates had to be tied on and hauled up because they were all feverish by now, shivering one minute and sweating buckets the next [*Guardsman and Commando: The War Memoirs of RSM Cyril Feebery, DCM*, edited by David Feebery].

A statement by Parachutist Fred Gill, MM, of McKerracher's patrol is included in the post-operation report. He confirmed that having buried their rubber dinghies the two patrols split up as arranged, McKerracher's group moving off 500 metres before being forced to lie-up for the next two days due to Corporal Shackleton being sick. On the evening of the 3rd it set off again but by this time McKerracher was himself suffering to a far greater extent and progress was therefore slow. The following night Gill and Guardsman Bill Thomas approached a farmhouse for water and having lost their bearings did not return until dawn. Gill noted that on the night of the 5th the patrol was subsequently obliged to leave Thomas and McKerracher behind, the latter agreeing to wait three days before giving himself up so as not to jeopardise the operation. The remainder of the patrol was captured soon after and informed by an Italian officer that Thomas had died and that McKerracher was in hospital close to death (WO 218/174).

Unaware of events the SBS somewhat optimistically noted that as of 30 June McKerracher was 'regarded as missing special operations, probably safe with friendly population enemy territory'. Although the post-operation report states that he 'died in prison in Sardinia' Gill's statement confirms that he died of malaria on 9 July in a Sardinian hospital (see also Guardsman Bill Thomas' entry overleaf).

It appears that Private Louis Timparano, aka 'Tronch', an Italian American attached to the SBS from the Office of Strategic Services, deserted to the Italians two nights after the patrols landed. Hawthorn veterans suspected that he betrayed both the 'Daffodil' and 'Bluebell' parties, as well as the operation's overall objectives.

Son of Duncan and Mary McKerracher – Husband of Jane McKerracher of George Street, Grangemouth, Stirlingshire.
Age 28.
Deep in our hearts a memory is kept of one we loved and will never forget
Grave 1.A.5. Also commemorated on Grangemouth's war memorial within Zetland Park.

GUARDSMAN LEONARD **THOMAS** [2700521] SCOTS GUARDS, 1ST SAS AND SBS (L DET)

Known as 'Tommo' to his comrades, Leonard Thomas was born on 1 July 1921, later working in Warrington as an arc welder. He enlisted into the Scots Guards in January 1941 and having passed through the depot at Chelsea Barracks was posted to the Training Battalion at Pirbright. That October he was re-posted to the demolitions platoon at the School of Small Arms until returning to the Training Battalion the following February. Soon after he joined the Holding Battalion, based firstly at the Tower of London and then at Chelsea Barracks, until disembarking in Egypt that July as a much-needed reinforcement to the 2nd Battalion. Joining it at Mena just outside Cairo. He briefly undertook defensive taskings on the approaches to the capital before the battalion moved to Qatana near Damascus in Syria that September. It was here that he volunteered for 1st SAS on 15 January 1943, subsequently attending parachute course No.22 at Kabrit the following month before being posted to the Special Boat Squadron when it was raised on 19 March.

During OPERATION HAWTHORN Thomas was a member of Lieutenant A. Duggan's 'Bluebell' Party that was tasked to attack Villasidro airfield on Sardinia. Corporal Sid Dowland of the same patrol later stated that, having paddled 5 kilometres from HM Submarine *Severn*, the party came ashore on the night of 1–2 July north of Capo Pecora:

> We had a very steep climb to get off the beach and it was obvious that Thomas 521 was sick and in no condition for anything. The SSM [Squadron Sergeant-Major Cyril Feebery] went back to help him up the cliff, and he had lost his bombs and M1 Carbine without the slightest idea of where he had left them. He had a Carbine of one of the other patrol when we separated.
>
> After a short rest on the top of the cliff, the patrols separated and we marched on a bearing due east. It was about 0330hrs at this time, about an hour before dawn. Thomas could not keep up and I helped him along a short way and called Mr Duggan back and said we would find a lying up place and see if Thomas was any better the next day, if not we should have to leave him.
>
> We rested all day of the 2nd of July. Mr Duggan went on a recce and reported no signs of life at all. Thomas seemed to be OK but I developed a slight attack of malaria and was duly 'dosed up' and sweated. It got dusk about 2230hrs and we prepared to move, we were only going a short distance (5 miles) to get near water. I felt fit enough to try and

Thomas felt alright or said he did. On starting however, Thomas fell over a bush and sat down and said he could not make it. Mr Duggan then decided to leave both of us, Thomas and myself, to follow on if we got better, and to give ourselves up if we got worse. They made sure we had water etc and Mr Duggan checked over the bearing etc with me and gave instructions about burying escape money and bombs, maps, etc, if we looked like getting caught. He also told me to go over it all again with Thomas the next day as he (Thomas) was hopeless to try to explain anything to at this time.

Thomas and I lay up the next day, the 3rd of July, and he seemed well enough but would not take any quinine or anti-malarial tablets, also I continually had to caution him about drinking too much water. That night we moved to a wadi with a river and a light railway running down it, two or three kilos north of where we had been lying up. I left Thomas on the south edge of the wadi with both our packs (this would be about 8 miles on a bearing of 45 degrees from Capo Pecora about 1 to 2 kilos from the river mouth) while I took the water bottles to the river. I was feeling very sick at this time and the river was further than I had judged, so it took me nearly until dawn to get back to the vicinity where I had left Thomas and then I could not find him. I looked until 1000hrs on the morning of the 4th and shouted, but still could not find him and then I fell over and I think I was delirious for a few hours, and only drank water. After a bit of sleep that night, I found Thomas early on the morning of the 5th about 200 yards away. He asked me who I was at first, but then he recognised me and called me by name. I gave him a drink and made some tea and then put some ointment on his lips which were quite sore. He was wearing just KD trousers and PT shoes, and must have lain like that at least one day in the hot sun and through one night. I got him in the shade and made him some soup from the dehydrated mutton, also stewed him some of the dried apricots we were carrying. I also managed to get some tablets into him.

He seemed to sleep peacefully all day, but in the evening he started to pant heavily and at about 1800hrs he stopped breathing altogether. I buried him in the shelter of a bush using his sleeping bag cover as a shroud and lying his belt, revolver, compass and carbine with him. I moved on that night and kept moving in short stages until the day of the 9th of July when I was captured, outside the village of Monteechio [WO 218/174].

Dowland subsequently directed the Italians to Thomas' grave, his remains being later reinterred at their current location.

Son of John and Sarah Thomas of Wellfield Street, Warrington, Lancashire – Believed to have had a brother in the Scots Guards.
Age 20.
Beatae Memoriae
Grave 1.A.12. Also commemorated on Warrington's war memorial at Bridge Foot.

GUARDSMAN WILLIAM HENRY **THOMAS** [2621401] GRENADIER GUARDS, 1ST SAS AND SBS (L DET)

Bill Thomas was born on 13 August 1913 in Salford. Both his parents died before the war, he and his siblings continuing to live in the family home. At the outbreak of war Thomas was working as a driver for a copper tube manufacturer whilst being a volunteer member of a 'decontamination squad'. However, he enlisted into the Grenadier Guards during September 1940 in Manchester and after training

was posted to the newly-formed 6th Battalion at Chelsea Barracks. At the end of 1941 he qualified as a driver mechanic at the British School of Motoring in Fulham and was recommended for the advanced course. However, the following June he embarked for the Middle East, arriving in Egypt that August. He volunteered for 1st SAS on 19 December 1942 having been interviewed by one of the SAS 'Originals', Sergeant Dave Kershaw, MM. Attending parachute course No.21 at Kabrit the following February he was posted to the Special Boat Squadron when it was raised on 19 March 1943

During OPERATION HAWTHORN Thomas was a member of Captain John Thomson's 'Daffodil' party that was tasked to attack Ottani airfield on Sardinia. Having landed north of Capo Pecora on the night of 1–2 July 1943 he died of malaria on the 8th. Although the post-operation report states that 'Gdsm Thomas, 421 [sic], (Gren Guards) died in prison in Sardinia', it also contains the contradictory, but more reliable, statement of Parachutist Fred Gill, MM:

I was with Capt Thomson whose party landed with that of Lt Duggan. Buried everything. Both parties split up and made for their objectives which were aerodromes.

The first night we spent 500yds from the coast and laid up all day on the 2/3rd. Capt Thomson gave orders we were not moving that night (2nd) owing to Cpl Shackleton having a severe cold. We stopped at the same spot all day on the 3rd, and moved off about 1800hrs. Sgt McKerracher held us up through falling sick and we could not go far that night. Meanwhile I had given all my water to Gdsm Thomas (Gren Gds) who was feeling feverish and went without myself. On the night of the 4th Cpl Shackleton told Capt Thomson that I and Thomas had no water. There was a farm building, 800yds from where we were and I told Capt Thomson I could get water from the well, which was 800yds from the house. Capt Thomson said I could go that night for water. I took a bearing on the house and Gdsm Thomas went with me; but through being delirious he led me off my bearing, causing me to sleep out on the hill at night and to arrive at the well at dawn. I arrived back and reported having got the water and told him Thomas was following, having gone back in search of his revolver and water bottle which he lost during the night.

Cpl Shackleton told me when I arrived back that Capt Thomson had, in my absence with Thomas, given orders that the rest of the party were to use the remainder of the water to shave 'as they might as well give themselves up.'

The possible reason for this in my opinion was that Capt Thomson felt that in view of the condition of Sgt McKerracher and Thomas who, as we did not return that night with water, had possibly been captured, the whole party's whereabouts had been disclosed to the enemy.

On the night of the 5th, having already decided to leave Sgt McKerracher behind, we were obliged to leave Gdsm Thomas as well who had drunk a great deal of the water fetched the previous night, and who was still very sick. Sgt McKerracher agreed to stay behind and give himself up in three days time [WO 218/174].

Having been captured by Italian troops Gill noted that: 'the chains and the handcuffs were taken off us and we were told by the CO of that unit he had picked up two men, one dead, and one dying, who we later found out were Gdsm Thomas dead and Sgt McKerracher (then in hospital) dying' (WO 218/174).

Predeceased by his parents – Younger brother of Gladys and David Thomas of Astley Street, Pendleton, Salford, Lancashire.
Age 29.
In loving memory of my dear brother William. His duty nobly done
Grave 1.A.7.

CASSINO MEMORIAL

It was here that the Eighth Army won the Battle of Cassino, thereby opening the route towards the liberation of Rome and the final freeing of all of Italy. Unveiled by Field-Marshal Lord Alexander of Tunis in 1956 the Cassino Memorial commemorates over 4,000 members of the Commonwealth that lost their lives during the Italian Campaign but that have no known grave. It forms the centre piece of the Cassino War Cemetery that contains the graves of 4,266 service personnel killed in the same historic battles.

Overlooked by the hard-won Abbey of Monte Cassino, the memorial and war cemetery are located 139 kilometres south-east of Rome and to the south of the town centre. Access is gained from the SP76, the Via Sant'Angelo. GPS co-ordinates: Latitude 41.47763, Longitude 13.82609

MAJOR JOHN GEOFFREY <u>APPLEYARD</u> DSO, MC* [86639] ROYAL ARMY SERVICE CORPS, NO.7 COMMANDO, SOE, SMALL SCALE RAIDING FORCE AND 2ND SAS (A SQN)

Known as Geoff or 'Apple' to his comrades, Geoffrey Appleyard was born on 20 December 1916 at Bramley in Leeds. Having attended the Quaker Bootham School in York from 1930 to 1935 he went up to Caius College, Cambridge, where he was Captain of Boats from 1937 to 1938 and from where he graduated with a First in Engineering. In his spare time he was a keen downhill skier, building a strong international reputation whilst captain of the British team.

Appleyard was commissioned into the Royal Army Service Corps' Supplementary Reserve in April 1939 whilst working for the family company, Appleyard of Leeds Ltd Motor Service Works (*London*

Gazette 31/03/39). Mobilised at the outbreak of war he commanded the workshop of an ammunition park at Bulford before embarking for France as a member of the BEF four weeks later. Having withdrawn before the German Blitzkrieg the following May he befriended Captain Gus March-Phillipps of the Royal Artillery whilst sheltering from air attack in the dunes at Dunkirk. Evacuated he was subsequently mentioned in despatches:

The above officers carried out their duties under difficult conditions. They were often on duty at key points under enemy machine gun and bombing attacks for long periods. When on duty preventing French traffic entering the perimeter at a bridge over the Dunkirk canal an ugly scene was avoided by tact when a French Officer drew his revolver threatening to shoot the above officers. 2/Lt Appleyard by his fine example materially assisted in the efficient running of Corps transport under most difficult conditions under enemy fire [WO 373/16].

Although Appleyard returned to regimental duties he was soon recruited by March-Phillipps as one of his section commanders in B Troop, No.7 Commando. However, when this unit embarked for the Middle East in January 1941 Brigadier Colin Gubbins, DSO, MC, SOE's Director of Operations and Training, employed both men. Appleyard, designated as '1441', subsequently qualified as a parachutist and officially joined the Inter-Services Research Bureau, one of SOE's many cover names, late that month.

On the night of 4–5 April 1941 Appleyard collected two French servicemen from the coast of France after a failed attempt to ambush German pilots at Meucon (OPERATION SAVANNA, SOE's first parachute operation into France). With dawn approaching, and with two canoes already rendered useless by strong waves, Appleyard managed to paddle both Capitaine Georges Bergé and Adjudant Jean Forman to the awaiting HM Submarine *Tigris* in a Folbot designed for only two men. Sergent Joël Le Tac, a third member of the team, had to be left behind to continue SOE work. Appleyard was subsequently awarded the Military Cross, the citation for which cannot be located (*London Gazette* 23/05/41. Bergé was later captured on Crete whilst serving with the Free French Squadron of L Detachment, SAS Brigade – see Caporal Pierre Leostic's entry under Rosendaël Communal Cemetery, France, Volume III, for further details).

Appleyard joined W Section, SOE's West African department, at the beginning of August 1941 and set sail for Freetown, Sierra Leone. Here he received Maid Honor Force, a party under the command of March-Phillipps that had sailed their Brixham trawler of the same name from the UK. Not entirely welcomed by local British forces the men set themselves the task of searching for secret German submarine bases and supply depots, U-Boats having sunk thirty-two British ships in the area during May alone. Eventually they were allotted a more tangible objective, OPERATION POSTMASTER, which was summarised by Gubbins in his successful recommendation for Appleyard's second Military Cross:

Captain Appleyard was second-in-command in the operation for the cutting out of the Italian liner Duchessa D'Aosta and the German vessels Likomba and Bebundi at Fernando Po [an island off Cameroon now known as Bioko]. The operation took place on the night 14th–15th January, 1942.

Captain Appleyard led the party which was to blow the forward anchor chains, boarding the liner from the tug which carried his party. Owing to a slight recoil as the tug made contact with the liner in the dark, Captain Appleyard was faced with a rapidly widening gap between the steamer and the tug and he was the only member of the party to attempt the jump gaining the steamer's side over a good eight feet of water. He then dealt single-handed with the forward cables until the rest of the party came up. One of the charges failed to explode on the prearranged signal and Captain Appleyard, without waiting to see if the fuse was still burning, laid and blew another charge in little less than a minute, thus ensuring the freeing of the liner which was a matter of vital importance. These operations were performed with complete disregard of his own personal safety and the cutting-out of the liner ensured.

Captain Appleyard then assumed the position of second-in-command of the captured liner and throughout the voyage of one week displayed initiative and ability to command under circumstances of great difficulty of a very high order indeed. He is very strongly recommended for a Bar to his MC [*London Gazette* 28/07/42].

Having returned to the UK in February 1942 Appleyard was posted to Special Training School 62 at Anderson Manor, an Elizabethan house near to Blandford. This was home to No.62 Commando, the cover name for the Small Scale Raiding Force as March-Phillipps' expanded force was now named. Peter Kemp, a fellow SSRF officer and veteran of the Spanish Civil War, later recalled:

> He [March-Phillips] was fortunate in his second-in-command. Of more equable temperament but similar romantic nature, less impetuous but just as obstinate, Geoffrey Appleyard had a flair for planning and organisation together with superb skill in battle and an astonishing – unique, I thought – ability to instil confidence in the face of danger. Beneath a broad forehead his deep-set blue eyes looked out from a fresh-complexioned face with a calm steadiness matched by the low timbre of his voice. He had the stamina of a championship skier, which his extraordinary willpower put under inhuman strains [*The Thorns of Memory*, by Peter Kemp].

After numerous raids on the Channel Islands Appleyard, by now an acting major, was awarded the Distinguished Service Order on recommendation of Vice Admiral Lord Louis Mountbatten, the Chief of Combined Operations:

> Major Appleyard has taken part in five raids carried out by SSRF between the 15th August and 5th October [1942]. During all these operations he has acted as navigator to raiding craft MTB 344 and as second-in-command on the other four. The success of these operations has been largely dependent on his courage, determination and great skill in navigation. On all occasions MTB 344 has proceeded unescorted and has often passed through enemy minefields.
> On an operation at Cap Barfleur which took place on the night 14th/15th August, he went ashore with the landing party which escaped undetected after killing and wounding several Germans [OPERATION BARRICADE]. On an operation against the Casquets which took place on the night 2nd/3rd September [OPERATION DRYAD], he went ashore with the landing party [having navigated their craft to the Casquets] which returned with seven prisoners [who had been dragged from their beds wearing hair nets]. This operation was carried out with a wind force 3 rising to force 5 and the landing and re-embarkation took place from a Goatley boat on a very rocky island. It was largely due to his skill that this very difficult operation was successfully accomplished. During a raid at St Honorine on the night 12th/13th September [OPERATION AQUATINT] he remained in the landing craft owing to injuries received on the previous operation [a broken ankle sustained whilst re-embarking from DRYAD]. The landing party got into difficulties and he kept the MTB close inshore under heavy enemy fire until eventually forced to turn seawards by direct fire over open sights. He then evaded enemy patrol boats and as quickly as possible returned and scoured the coast on the chance of picking up any of the landing party. During this time he was again under fire and only one engine of the MTB was working. Only when all chances of picking up the raiding party had disappeared did he turn back and successfully navigate the MTB with one engine out of action, through enemy minefields to the home port [his Commanding Officer, March-Phillipps, had been killed]. He commanded the raid against Sark on the night 3rd/4th October and led the raiding party which spent three to four hours ashore, capturing one prisoner and killing three enemy, without any casualties of his own [OPERATION BASALT]. NOTE: The raids for operational reasons have not been announced to the press and the above citation should on no account be published [*London Gazette* 11/12/42, Supplement 15/12/42, WO 373/93].

With March-Phillipps dead Appleyard took command of the SSRF, determined to carry on the work his friend had started. He went on to lead OPERATION FAHRENHEIT, landing on the coast of Brittany from an MTB to destroy a communications station at Plouézec on the night of 11–12 November 1942.

In mid February 1943 the majority of the SSRF embarked for North Africa where they formed the foundations on which 2nd SAS was raised on 13 May. Although Gubbins ordered that Appleyard be returned to the UK to continue running the remnants of the SSRF he remained with the Regiment after a brief power struggle, double-hatting as both Operations Officer and the commander of A Squadron. His presence in theatre had been deemed vital to the success of small-scale raids planned in support of OPERATION HUSKY, the Allied invasion of Sicily. He subsequently led OPERATION SNAPDRAGON, a recce of the Mediterranean island of Pantelleria, in late May (see Gunner Ernie Herstell's entry under Medjez-el-Bab Memorial, Tunisia, Volume I, for further details). Lieutenant John Cochrane, who also served in both the SSRF and 2nd SAS, had written to his parents that March:

> My OC is a chap by the name of Major Appleyard, aged 26 with the Distinguished Service Order and the Military Cross with Bar. He's a natural born leader and I for one would follow him anywhere. Everyone has the greatest confidence in him. His rank doesn't matter a damn to him in so far as it affects his relations with the rest of us [IWM Documents.19040 – Private Papers of Lieutenant J. P. Cochrane].

Appleyard was killed in action on 13 July 1943 when his Albemarle aircraft of 296 Squadron failed to return from a parachute drop over Sicily. He had despatched Captain Philip Pinckney's 'Pink Party' during OPERATION CHESTNUT, a cipher from 'Massingham', SOE's base in Algeria, stating: 'Appleyard was not repeat was not to operate but he decided to accompany force commander's (Pinckney) aircraft and watch drop … presume therefore that aircraft was shot down or ran out of petrol on return journey' (see Pinckney's own entry under Florence War Cemetery, Italy). Meanwhile, the post-operation report notes: 'Plane failed to return to base. Unconfirmed report that wreckage and bodies of crew only found. [Appleyard] Is accordingly reported missing, believed killed. Awaiting report from 38 Wing on No. of bodies found with wrecked plane' (WO 218/175). In fact, no bodies, either of the five aircrew or of Appleyard, were found, the confusion being created by the fact that Major John Lander, the CO of the 21st Independent Parachute Company whose body was recovered from a similar crash the same day, is often reported to have been in Appleyard's aircraft. Despite being warned of the flight corridor 'friendly fire' from the invasion fleet accounted for a large percentage of Allied air losses.

Son of John and Mary Appleyard (née Northrop) of Linton-on-Wharf, Wetherby, Yorkshire – Younger brother of Margot – Older brother of Major Ernest Ian Appleyard who became a post-war international rally driver and skier, and of Jenny (Joan) Appleyard – Half-brother of John.
Age 26.
Panel 12. Also commemorated by a stained glass window within Linton-on-Wharfe's village church. This is a joint memorial with friend and fellow officer Graham Hayes, also of the SSRF, who initially evaded capture after OPERATION AQUATINT and who was murdered at Fresnes prison near Paris on the same day that Appleyard was last seen alive. They are also commemorated, along with five others, by the Linton-on-Wharfe Village Memorial Hall, within which their photos appear. In addition, Appleyard is commemorated on the war memorial within Caius College Chapel, by a memorial tree on Sark and on the OPERATION FAHRENHEIT memorial at Pointe de Bilfot.

PRIVATE LESLIE CHARLES **BENNETT** [10584880] ROYAL ARMY ORDNANCE CORPS AND 2ND SAS (C SQN)

Leslie Bennett was born on 22 September 1919 in Pontypool, Monmouthshire, where he worked as a bricklayer. Enlisting into the Royal Army Ordnance Corps during March 1942 he was posted to B Company, No.2 Training Battalion, at Hinckley where he qualified as a storeman before joining the 6th Battalion that August. Two months later he was re-posted to the Ordnance Company at 38th Infantry Brigade and that November embarked for North Africa. Although his movements during the ensuing campaign are unknown he volunteered for 2nd SAS on 21 June 1943 after hostilities in this region had been brought to a successful conclusion.

Bennett parachuted onto a DZ near Colle Futa, north-west of L'Aquila in the Abruzzo region of Central Italy, on 7 January 1944. As a member of Lieutenant Henry Parker's patrol he was tasked with attacking the Terni–Foligno railway line during OPERATION MAPLE THISTLEDOWN. This had initially been planned to disrupt enemy transport moving towards the Anzio bridgehead but was delayed by poor weather. Six patrols were instructed to exfiltrate independently on completion of their tasks. No radios were issued. Although progress was slow due to deep snow Bennett's team found a local guide, reached their objective and laid charges on the line on the night of the 13–14th. Having returned to the guide's farm at Salto del Cieco Parker instructed Partisans how to attack the same line in the months ahead before

setting out for Allied territory on the night of the 15–16th. The patrol was accompanied by a handful of former POWs who had joined it. On the 18th they met Party No.4, separating from them the following day. Reaching a point near Vallopietra on the 28th Bennett and Parachutist Monk fell ill. Due to deteriorating weather, including heavy snowfall and drifts, the party was left stranded at an abandoned house on Monte Aurore during which time the men cared for seventeen ex-POWs.

On 7 March conditions improved and the group split up to pass through the lines. Bennett, Monk and Parachutist John Claridge made their way to the small town of Collelongo where they met with Parker and an ex-POW as arranged and were sheltered by the Ranelli family. On the 20th fifty Italian fascists were seen approaching and Parker split the party into two. He moved off with Monk and the ex-POW whilst Bennett, Claridge and Flying Officer Geoffrey Pitout, a South African Spitfire pilot who had been seen to bail out, were to set off twenty-four hours later. This second party did not make it to Allied lines and the Ranelli daughter later stated that the three had stayed locally until the end of April when they planned to join a band of Partisans in the mountains. In February 1945 the 409th Field Security Section was able to outline subsequent events:

> The above [Bennett and Claridge] were arrested in company with a member of the South African Air Force named Geoffrey William Pitout on the Maiella mountains [to the east of where they were last seen by Parker] by German troops on the 6th May 1944 and brought to Sulmona Gaol on the 9th May 1944 as POW to be detained at the disposition of the German Command. They were removed by German soldiers on the following day. The prison authorities know nothing more about these men [WO 311/695].

Pitout was the only one of the three to be reported by the Germans as having been captured. Parker himself was taken prisoner but the SS officer in charge of his case had a motorcycle accident and he was fortunate to be forgotten about until liberated. Subsequently posted to the SAS War Crimes Investigation Team he reviewed all SAS cases in Italy, including that of his two missing men:

> Would be grateful if you could get someone institute [sic] enquiries into following. One Flying Officer Pitout SAAF returned UK May 1945 says captured [near the village of] Pizzone 7th May 1944 with Parachutists Bennett and Claridge of 2 SAS [having run into a German patrol]. Taken to Sulmona gaol lodged in separate cells. On 10th May 1944 taken to Italian internment camp near Sora repeat Sora where interrogation officer stated Bennett and Claridge would be shot. About 16th May 1944 all moved to Aquila repeat Aquila where Pitout saw Bennett for few minutes. Bennett said they were threatened with shooting as saboteurs but had not given information [Pitout was then sent to an airforce camp]. Claridge wearing civilian clothes. Claridge seen in prison Fort San Brocco near Verona Cemetery in June 1944 by Guardsman Mitchell 2696593 Scots Guards. If unable enquire please pass 5th Army War Crimes Section [WO 218/219].

Although Fifth Army could find no trace at the Verona prison there is some evidence that the pair were still alive that November (see Claridge's entry below). Meanwhile, Parachutist Fred Dellow of 2nd SAS stated that he 'saw a man in Camp 344 or Stalag 7a [both in Germany] who resembled L/Cpl Bennett' (WO 361/651). Despite Pitout's, Mitchell's, and Dellow's statements Bennett's date of death is officially recorded as 10 May 1944, the War Office presuming his death in October 1945. When interrogated the commandant of the former police transit cage in Bolzano stated that he was quite certain that Bennett and Claridge were never in his charge and was of the opinion that they had been killed 'whilst attempting to escape' between Verona and Bolzano (WO 311/630).

Son of Walter and Clara Bennett (née Guest) – Brother of Elsie Thomas of Lower Mill Row, Pontymoile, Pontypool, Monmouth – Known to have had a brother serving with the Central Mediterranean Force at the time that he went missing.
Age 24.
Panel 12. Also commemorated on the war memorial gates of Pontypool Park.

Sergeant Robert Thomas **BENSON** [4121828] Cheshire Regiment
and 2nd SAS (C Sqn)

Robert Benson was born on 29 January 1914 in Woolwich, south-east London, as the eldest son of thirteen children. He enlisted as a boy soldier into the Cheshire Regiment in September 1928 at Great Scotland Yard, aged just 14. Initially posted to the 2nd Battalion he joined the 1st Battalion in March 1929, serving in India where he attended a water duties course at Landi Kotal near the Khyber Pass. In 1931 he won the regiment's welterweight boxing title at Chaubattia and soon after turning 18 the following year was appointed lance-corporal. Reverting to private at his own request three months later he was promoted again in March 1936, again reverting to private after six months. In 1938 he was a member of the Cheshires' team that topped the Western India Football Association's First Division.

By the outbreak of war Benson was serving at Atbara in the Sudan where the 1st Battalion had been stationed since the end of 1938 and where he was promoted once more to lance-corporal. In October 1939 he was deprived of his stripe for an unknown offence, the battalion embarking for the UK in January 1940 and arriving home that March. Having been initially posted to the Machine Gun Training Centre Benson was posted to the 5th Battalion in Northern Ireland. In May 1940 he married Doreen Manville at Heswall in Cheshire. Promoted once more to lance-corporal the following month he was advanced to corporal that September and confirmed as lance-sergeant on 28 December. He was appointed sergeant on completing a course at the Small Arms School at Netheravon during February–March 1941 and attended XII Corps' School of Vehicle Maintenance at Otterden between April–May 1942. In April 1943 he embarked for North Africa, his son, also called Robert, being born in London four months later.

Benson volunteered for the newly-formed 2nd SAS on 1 July 1943, joining them at their base at Philippeville on the Algerian coast before qualifying for parachute pay four days later. He subsequently jumped into Sicily under Lieutenant McCorquodale on the night of 14–15 July 1943 as reinforcement for Operation Chestnut's 'Pink' Party: tasked with operating in the Randazzo area he and Parachutists Brunt and Summers cut numerous communication wires. They later discovered a camouflaged truck on which they decided to lay charges, Summers noting; 'Pte Brunt covered Sgt Benson and myself from the rear with the Tommy gun' (WO 218/98). When the driver and his two companions awoke to find the pair helping themselves to their cigarette supplies the parachutists bluffed that they were German and made off. Having cut further communication lines the three men skirted Mount Etna, living off the land and collecting information, Summers later reporting:

> We took longer to get back to our lines than we had expected. The nights were very cold. When it was too dark or we felt too tired to march any longer we used to take it in turns who would sleep 'centre man'. This was the envied place. Generally the marching had made us perspire a lot and when we woke up we felt rather cold and wet. We made a point of generally moving at first light to get warm … Daytime marching was again impossible and the nights were very black. The surrounding countryside was mostly large estates of orchards and vineyards … the

vineyards and orchards were all terraced. Every 10 yards we had to jump up or climb down about 4 yards. The terraces were made of rough lava. In the dark we all took some hard falls, Sgt Benson was hurt the most. His right leg was poisoned and very swollen. All these incidents slowed what was previously a good pace down considerably. By now we were beginning to wonder where the Allied lines were. We had marched about 80 miles by the map and almost double that distance in actual marching [WO 218/98].

The men eventually met the advancing 51st Highland Division on the night of 21 July and, having passed on everything they had learnt to the relevant Intelligence Officers, were flown from Syracuse to Tunis to rejoin the Regiment (see Bernie Brunt's entry under Florence War Cemetery, Italy).

Benson went on to command Operation Maple Driftwood's Party No.6, this being tasked with attacking the Ancona–Rimini railway line that runs along Italy's Adriatic coast. After two false starts due to poor weather his team, and that of Captain John Gunston, emplaned at Gioia del Colle on the evening of 7 January 1944 and parachuted into a DZ 13 kilometres west-north-west of Iesi late that night. It had been intended to reinforce these two parties by sea in order to destroy a railway bridge but the weather prevented this and the task was later carried out independently under Operation Baobab. Meanwhile, Benson's group failed to rendezvous with their pick-up boat 8 kilometres south-east of Fermo near Torre di Palme on the night of 25–26 January. In early February Parachutist 'Cookie' Cook of 2nd SAS, who had escaped from a POW camp after being captured in October 1943 during Operation Jonquil, was making his way south when he met Gunston in the Fermo area. The officer informed him that he intended to evacuate his party after completing a further task. It seems certain that Benson's party was with Gunston at this time as on the night of 4 February Captain Robert Matthews of the South African Corps of Signals, also in the process of evading, met Gunston who told him that 'he was leaving by sea for Allied lines with 8 parachutists, Capt Clubb, 2 NZEF, and one other man' (WO 311/695). The same report notes that 'on 7 Mar 44 Gunston's party left by boat from a point a little south of Porto San Giorgio in a 22-ft boat'. The eight SAS (Gunston's party of Pugh, Dodds and Loosemore and Benson's of Glen, Lockeridge and Evans) were reported missing with effect from that date. Due to the fact that the Regiment believed that they might still be operating behind the lines this was not done until March 1945 and their deaths not presumed until that October. Frederick Clubb, MC, was also reported missing as of this date. The identity of the remaining man is unknown although two others are commemorated on the Cassino Memorial with this date of death: Sergeant Norman Anderson and Bombardier George Worthington.

However, three members of 2nd SAS who had been taken prisoner during Operation Galia in Northern Italy later reported that on 3 January 1945 they were interrogated at the headquarters of German mountain troops:

> Again a list of the names of the SAS men was read out to us. This was a longer list and included the names of Lieut Silly [murdered on Operation Loyton – see his entry under Moyenmoutier Communal Cemetery, France, Volume III], Sgt Benson, Cpl Lawrence, Cpl Austin [murdered on Operation Loyton – see his entry under Durnbach War Cemetery, Germany, Volume III], Pct Loosemore and Cpl Phillips. We were not told whether these men were killed or were PW and we couldn't ask as we denied all knowledge of them, but we got the impression they were prisoners and that we would be meeting them when the interview was over or at some PW camp we would be going to [WO 361/651 – Gunston was also mentioned].

Major 'Bill' Barkworth, the commander of the SAS War Crimes Investigation Team, subsequently wrote to the War Office in May 1945, stating; 'It increases the possibility that these three [Benson, Loosemore and Gunston] were either at one time prisoners in German hands or that their bodies were washed up, identified and buried' (WO 361/351). Further anecdotal evidence suggested the missing men had been captured:

> During a visit to Porto San Giorgio in February 1945, Major Barkworth found an Italian civilian named Armato Campofiloni who stated that he remembered Capt Gunston's party leaving by boat. He also had a story which was not very clear that a boat-load of ex-PW had been forced to return about this time and all the occupants *except one* captured [author's italics]. He was not sure if it was the same boat [WO 311/695].

The SAS continued the search, noting in June 1945:

Very decomposed body in British battledress found San Giorgio in stream 386933 sheet 1/100,000. One man rubber raft around body. Following articles only means identification. Cigarette case and lighter hankerchief key chain 1939/45 Star Ribbon W/D compass WO Class 1 badge and 9 carrat gold ring with initials RJH. Benson's wife stated husband wore ring with initials RB. His full initials RTB. Remains buried civil cemetery 407953. DAAG endeavouring trace issue of W/D property through ordnance services [AIR 20/8844]

Although Barkworth thought it likely the remains were those of a member of the SAS, the serial number of the compass could not be matched and no further information appears to have been forthcoming. Benson was subsequently posted as missing as of 7 March 1944 and in October 1945 the War Office informed his wife that it had officially presumed that he had been killed in action that day (see also Gunston's entry below).

In a bizarre twist a man impersonating Benson surrendered himself to the 25th Field Engineer Regiment, Royal Engineers, at Maidstone on 9 January 1951. He claimed that he had deserted in late 1943 whilst serving on Malta. Following questioning by civil police he admitted that he was not Benson but refused to divulge his true name and address. As a result he was escorted to the Cheshire Regiment at Whittington Barracks in Lichfield and held under close arrest pending proof of identity. He escaped from the guardroom before further enquiries could be made and before Benson's wife could arrive to confirm that he was not the man he purported to be. Although the imposter was not traced and his physical description was different from Benson's, his initial questioning showed the man had very good knowledge of Benson's personal and service life, listing his postings with exact dates. He was also in possession of Benson's cigarette case that is now with Benson's son.

Son of Robert and Laura Benson (née Hiles) of Lynsted Gardens, Eltham, South East London – Husband of Doreen Benson of Garbutt Place, Marylebone, London, who served as a Civil Defence ambulance driver through the Blitz – Father of Robert Benson - Older brother of Kenneth and Frederick Benson. Age 30.
Panel 6.

LANCE-SERGEANT GEORGE EDWARD <u>CASS</u> [2616121] GRENADIER GUARDS, NO.8 COMMANDO, SPECIAL BOAT SECTION ATT L DETACHMENT SAS BRIGADE, 1ST SAS AND SBS (L DET)

George 'Flash' Cass was born on 1 June 1921 in Bramley, Yorkshire, where he later worked as a lathe operator at the binocular department of A. P. Kebshaw Instrument Makers. In December 1938 he falsified his age, enlisting into the Grenadier Guards a year early in order to join his friend, Ronald Wheeler, in the 2nd Battalion. After training Cass was posted to Pirbright and from September 1939 served with the BEF in France. That November his father sent his birth certificate to the Grenadiers, thus proving that he was below the age for foreign service and ensuring that Cass was sent home, even though he was by then a lance-corporal. Undeterred he volunteered for special service in August 1940 and was posted to 2 Troop, No.8 (Guards) Commando. He subsequently embarked for Egypt on the last day of January 1941, arriving at Suez early in March as a member of B Battalion, Layforce. This special service brigade was disbanded that summer, Cass volunteering for the Special Boat Section that December and being promoted to corporal in January 1942. Early that February Cass landed agents and stores on an island off Albania during OPERATION HYDRA, noting in his post-operation report:

Sailed from Alexandria with Sgt Moss [aboard HM Submarine *Thorn*]. On board were Major [Terence] Atherton, Cpl [Patrick] O'Donovan [both of SOE], two Yugoslav officers, one Yugoslav sergeant and one other. Destination proved to be the Isle of Madget off the coast of Albania. Arrived and prepared to land. One boat was completely filled with wireless, blankets, rations etc. Sgt Moss, an officer and myself were in the other boat. Rowed ashore and left [Yugoslav] officer. On return I took the loaded Folbot ashore and Sgt Moss took the sergeant ashore. Landed successfully and returned to sub.

A week later we returned to the Isle of Madget and it was decided to land the remainder of the party. Had to wait one night as sea was running too heavily for laden Folbots. Sgt Moss and Major Atherton and myself with another officer paddled ashore in Folbots. Major Atherton carried a large amount of money. Breakers on the shore damaged boats badly and I had to tow Sgt Moss and his boat back to the sub. Sgt Moss and I took Cpl O'Donovan and remainder of stores ashore. Boat damaged further. Started back to sub and boat soon filled with water. Routine patrol was then continued. Signed G Cass Cpl. Special Boat Section [both Atherton and O'Donovan were murdered by Chetnik Partisans late in April, an inquiry concluding that the motive was probably the substantial amount of money they were carrying].

Later that year much of the Special Boat Section was attached to L Detachment, SAS Brigade, Cass appearing on a C Squadron, 1st SAS, nominal roll of November 1942 as 'Cpl Gren Gds'. He officially transferred to 1st SAS on New Year's Day 1943 and was confirmed as lance-sergeant, the section having been absorbed into the Regiment. Five days later D Squadron, the precursor to the Special Boat Squadron, was formed, this being absorbed into the SBS on its formation on 19 March 1943.

Having mounted exercises along the Palestinian coastline one troop of L Detachment, SBS, was attached to 2nd SAS at Philippeville in Algeria for OPERATION HAWTHORN. Tasked with destroying aircraft on Sardinia as a feint to the imminent invasion of Sicily, Cass was a member of the 'Hyacinth' base party that was put ashore by HM Submarine *Saracen*. This was to act as a reserve and supply depot for five other SBS groups that had been allotted various target airfields. Signalman Jock Johnston of this patrol later wrote in the post-operation report:

I was a member of a base party landed in Sardinia, on the 1st of July 43 near Cape Santoni (near Villaputza). The other members of the party were Lt Cochrane, Sgt Cass, Pct Murray, Pct Killby, and Sgm Schofield. On the night of the landing we carried the supply of rations and the rubber dinghy, which we had with us, a short distance inland, and we slept near them. On the second day we buried the rations and the dinghies.

On the 6th of July, while we were lying in a wood, where we slept for two nights, we heard a number of Italian troops moving towards us, making a great deal of noise. We stayed very quiet, hoping they would be passing straight by us, but they came into the wood and discovered us, and took us prisoners [WO 218/174 – see Johnston's own entry under Groesbeek Memorial, Netherlands, Volume III].

Former Parachutist Keith Killby later recalled that after capture the Italians tried to load them onto a lorry: 'but it wouldn't start again. Serg Cass, used to handling in the desert much Italian captured material got it to go.' The men were subsequently interrogated:

KK was soon taken out and Sergeant Cass followed him in. When he came out he caused great mirth as he had told them that the code (for the wireless brought with us) had been in the only modern book we could find in English in recently liberated Algiers. It was called 'No Orchids for Miss Blandish' and was the nearest to pornography for those days [personal correspondence with Keith Killby, OBE, 2010].

The men were eventually held at Campo 59 at Servigliano in the Le Marche region of Eastern Italy. However, on 14 September 1943, just after the Italian armistice, Cass, Gunner George Jacques, Signalman H. Schofield, Corporal Shackleton and Sergeant Brack capitalised on the lack of guards and escaped. MI9's debrief of Jacques takes up the narrative:

They headed west and then south and stayed at a farm until the middle of Nov near San Martino, where they were given shelter and food. Then Source [Jacques], Sgt Cass and Sigm Schofield went on, making for Campo Basso, and by-passing big towns and traffic. They eventually reached British lines at an outpost near Gissi [WO 208/3344].

It is unclear why neither Jacques nor Schofield mentioned in their debriefs that Cass had been shot and killed by an Italian fascist on 5 November 1943. Another member of OPERATION HAWTHORN, Sid Dowland, met the pair after their escape and learnt of Cass' death:

> The two signallers [their parent unit was the Royal Corps of Signals] had been on the run with Sgt Cass … apparently the group had been apprehended by the Italian, who held them at gunpoint. George, daring as ever, had thrown his coat at the fascist and had attempted to overpower the man. But he had been shot in the process. The remainder of the group had managed to escape, but they owed their freedom to George. Sid remembered his friend's face and his defiant attitude. Cass was always the one to confront the prison guards, or to take the mickey out of them, often to his own detriment [*An Active Service: The Story of a Soldier's Life in the Grenadier Guards, SAS and SBS, 1935–58*, by Richard Dorney].

In October 1944 Major 'Bill' Barkworth of the SAS War Crimes Investigation Team forwarded a list of missing, including Cass, to the War Office stating that: 'all belong to 1 SAS Regiment. As however this party was on operational detachment to 2 SAS, we are probably in a better position to give you details than the other Regiment' (WO 361/351). Despite enquiries, Cass' remains were not located.

Son of George and Maria Cass (née Borman) of Wedderburn Drive, Woodlands, Harrogate, Yorkshire, who unsuccessfully attempted to find their son's grave in Italy during 1946 – Older brother of Allan who served in the wartime Royal Navy.

Age 23.

Panel 3. Also commemorated on Harrogate's war memorial.

Private John Henry **CLARIDGE** [2598942] Royal Corps of Signals, Army Catering Corps and 2nd SAS (C Sqn)

Known to his family as Jack, John Claridge was born on 24 December 1921 at Ilford in Essex. Having worked as a hotel chef in Baildon, Yorkshire, he enlisted into the Royal Corps of Signals during July 1941 and was posted to No.1 Company, 10th Anti-Aircraft Divisional Signals. In April 1942 he took trade training as a cook and subsequently transferred to the Army Catering Corps the following month, continuing his preparation as a chef but also keeping up his signalling duties. Having married Betty Smith at Baildon Parish Church that September he embarked for North Africa the following month, landing in Algeria during OPERATION TORCH. In February 1943 he was admitted to the 94th General Hospital for an unknown reason and having been discharged in March was initially posted to the 138th Infantry Brigade's Defence Platoon, then to the 2/5th Leicesters in April. He volunteered for 2nd SAS on 8 June 1943 but spent much of the next three months in and out of various hospitals.

Claridge parachuted into a DZ near Colle Futa, north-west of L'Aquila in the Abruzzo region of Central Italy, on 7 January 1944 under Lieutenant Henry Parker. Tasked with attacking the Terni–Foligno railway line during OPERATION MAPLE THISTLEDOWN the team's previous insertion had been delayed due to poor weather. The subsequent post-operation report states: 'L/Cpl Bennett, Pct Claridge and F/O [Flying Officer] Pitout are known to have been captured in the Maiella on the 6th May 1944. F/O Pitout has been reported as a PW but no further news of Bennett and Claridge has been received' whilst 2nd SAS' Casualty Report notes that they were 'probably moved to Germany' (WO 361/716 – see Private Leslie Bennett's entry within this section for full details of both the operation and the pair's capture).

Despite such reports the fate of the two men remains unclear. Major 'Bill' Barkworth of the SAS War

Crimes Investigation Team signalled the War Office's POW Casualty Branch in August 1945: 'Claridge was wearing civilian clothes when captured on evidence Pitout. Date seen by Mitchell [an evading POW of the Scots Guards] Verona also ties up with information available.' On the same day he added: 'Claridge and 2 others last seen by Mitchell approx 10/5/44. Claridge wore civilians one of others jumping jacket' (WO 361/351). A contemporary war crimes file notes:

> Both Mandozzi, Rodrigo, and Don Carlo Signorato have stated that they saw Claridge in the bath room at Forte San Leonardo, Verona, at the end of November or the beginning of December, 1944 …
> The Commandant of the Police Transit Cage, Bolzen (U/Stuf Titho) states that he is quite certain that these men [Claridge and Bennett] were never in his charge. When asked for his opinion, he said that he thought that they had been killed 'whilst attempting to escape' between Verona and Bolzen. There is no reason to disbelieve this witness [WO 311/630].

Meanwhile, Corporal Harry Kinder of 2nd SAS' Intelligence Section signalled Barkworth in August 1945:

> Copy of letter by Sgt Smoker to Harvey received this HQ states quote While prisoner in Transit Camp at Montova I was informed by two other prisoners (not SAS) that they had seen Claridge killed unquote letter states also it is believed that body was incarcerated for period at Civil Goal in Verona. Smoker unable to remember names of 2 prisoners.

In October 1945 Parker, by now a captain and 2nd SAS' investigating officer in Italy, wrote to his Commanding Officer, Lt-Colonel Brian Franks, DSO, MC:

> L/Cpl Bennett and Claridge. An Italian witness informed me that on the 27th of November 1944 he saw Claridge at Fort San Leonardo, Verona. He states that Claridge was imprisoned in Forte S Sophia (Verona) and had been brought to San Leonardo (which is very close) for a bath – there is no bath-house at S Sophia.
> On the other hand, I have the record book of S Sophia, kept by Feldwebel Marx, who was a methodical, accurate and reliable man (and also treated prisoners, particularly British, very well) and I can find no mention of Claridge or Bennett in the book. Apart from that there is an entry for every prisoner who was taken there with dates in and out and cell number. Personally I do not think this witness knows what he's talking about, but is anxious to please, so invents things rather than give a negative answer [WO 311/630].

Domenico Sigismondo later confirmed that he met Claridge at San Leonardo prison:

> He was accompanied by two other soldiers and to the bext of my recollection was in San Leonardo prison for about 2 months.
> Relying on my memory because of having no means whereby I can fix the exact date I saw during the month of Nov 44, Fdwl [Feldwebel] Otto Mayer place handcuffs on the man I identify as Pte Claridge whilst we were exercising in the prison yard one afternoon. After Pte Claridge had conversed with the German priest he was placed aboard a lorry and taken away [WO 310/58].

By then the War Office had already summarised the case:

> An officer of the [2nd SAS] Regt is still in Italy making enquiries, but it is improbable now that the graves of the men will be identified nor an official record of their death be discovered. We shall therefore have to presume [death] in any case. Submit we presume all forthwith at the same time informing N of K [next of kin] that enquiries are still going on to find out precise date, place, and circs of death, and if further inform is found we will write again.
> There can be no doubt that these men would have shown up by now had they been living. They were specially picked for hazardous tasks. With regard to Claridge and Bennett the man Pitout who was in jail with them at Sulmona has apparently given his statement to Major Barkworth but able to furnish little, he was a S African and was not seemingly classed as a saboteur [WO 361/351].

Investigations were inconclusive and Claridge's death was presumed to have taken place on or around 30

November 1944. This was against the wishes of his father who urged the War Office to find further details: 'We have gone through so much anxiety and suspense that we are quite prepared for anything which might be revealed in your investigations' (WO 311/630).

Son of Percy and Dorothy Claridge (née Woodward) of The Drive, Ilford, Essex – Husband of Betty Claridge of Enfield Road, Baildon, near Shipley, Yorkshire.
Age 22.
Panel 13.

GUARDSMAN ARTHUR THOMAS **DENCH** [2617852] GRENADIER GUARDS
AND 2ND SAS (HQ SQN ATT B SQN)

'Digger' Dench was born on 21 October 1909 at Eastbourne in East Sussex where his father was groundsman and part-time kennel man on a large estate, acting as whipper-in of hounds (correspondence with his sons Richard and Paul Dench, 2010). After schooling, Dench became a landscape gardener, married Marjorie Joyce Fincham at Rye in November 1939, and enlisted into the Grenadier Guards in January 1940. Posted to the 3rd Battalion he served in the UK until April 1943 when he embarked to reinforce No.3 Company, 6th Battalion, which had suffered heavy casualties during its advance into Tunisia. He volunteered for 2nd SAS on 9 September, a letter sent home confirming that he had been posted to HQ Squadron. Early the following morning the Regiment landed at Taranto on the heel of Italy, helping to hasten the German retreat (OPERATION SLAPSTICK).

Dench was killed in action on the morning of 5 October 1943 when the schooner he was guarding within Termoli harbour was destroyed in a German air raid. This vessel, the *San Vito*, had come up from Monopoli and was intended for OPERATION JONQUIL, a joint SAS and A Force operation to gather together former POWs stranded behind enemy lines and evacuate them from the Adriatic coast. Such schooners, that would be used to pick these men up under the cover of darkness, had only just arrived at the recently captured port to extend JONQUIL's range. Captain Simon Baillie later wrote to Dench's wife:

> The harbour was dive-bombed and unfortunately the boat, on which your husband was onboard while looking after some stores received a direct hit, and sank like a stone. At the time, I was behind the enemy lines on an operation, so didn't hear about it until I came back about a month later.

2nd SAS' 'Taranto to Termoli' report states: 'Remainder of Sqn arrived [at Termoli]. 4 dive bombing attacks by Focke-Wulfs on harbour during day. Caique of B Sqn struck (1 killed and 5 wounded). Shelling of town began in the evening' (WO 218/176). B Squadron's own War Diary confirms: '5th Oct four fighter-bomber attacks during day. HQ schooner hit about midday Capt Baillie's batman, Dench, killed. Two American interpreters, and 3 Italian crew wounded.' The following day the remaining schooners were forced to withdraw to Bari due to further air raids.

Son of Arthur and Kate Dench – Husband of Marjorie Dench of Bowrey Place, Bexhill-on-Sea, Sussex – Father of Paul, Richard and Margaret Dench – Known to have had four sisters.
Age 33.
Panel 3. Also commemorated on Bexhill-on-Sea's war memorial.

Sapper William <u>Dodds</u> [2135077] Royal Engineers and 2nd SAS (C Sqn)

William Dodds was born on 13 February 1919 in the coal mining community of Newtongrange, Dalkieth, just south of Edinburgh. Having worked as a coal heaver he enlisted into the Royal Engineers in December 1940 and was mustered as a miner in A Company, No.2 Training Battalion. After serving in the UK with various units of a similar nature he disembarked in North Africa in late November 1942 to join 86 Chemical Warfare Company. He subsequently volunteered for 2nd SAS at Philippeville, Algeria, on 10 July 1943.

Dodds parachuted into Italy for Operation Maple Driftwood on 7 January 1944 as a member of Captain John Gunston's Party No.5, having been tasked to attack the Urbino–Fabriano railway line. The group failed to make its sea rendezvous on the night of 25–26 January and was last seen on 7 March. Dodds was therefore presumed to have been killed in action on this date (see Gunston's entry below for full details).

During June 1945 Lt-Colonel Brian Franks, DSO, MC, the Commanding Officer of 2nd SAS, signalled the Regiment's Administration Officer, Major The Hon. John Bingham: 'Please give latest information on Dodds to Betty Crang his NOK [next of kin]. You will recall that he was reported back in error by DPW' (Department of Prisoners of War – AIR 20/8844).

Son of Mr and Mrs Robert Dodds of Reed's Drive, Newtongrange, Midlothian.
Age 25.
Panel 3. Also commemorated on Newtongrange's war memorial.

PRIVATE JOHN **EVANS** [4130239] CHESHIRE REGIMENT AND 2ND SAS (C SQN)

John Evans was born on 28 July 1917 in Edgeley, a suburb of Stockport. Having worked as a doubler at a local cotton mill he enlisted into the Cheshire Regiment in February 1940. Initially posted to the Machine Gun Battalion at Whitby Bay he embarked for the Middle East that August, arriving in Egypt the following month to serve with the 1st Battalion. In February 1941 this moved from Benghazi to Malta where it remained throughout the island's siege under aerial bombardment. It was here that Evans was interviewed and accepted by 2nd SAS during the summer of 1943, subsequently landing at Algiers on 25 August and joining the Regiment at Philippeville that day.

Evans parachuted into Italy on 7 January 1944 as a member of Sergeant Robert Benson's Party No.6, this being tasked to attack the Ancona–Rimini railway line in the Le Marche region during OPERATION MAPLE DRIFTWOOD. The group failed to make its sea rendezvous on the night of 25–26 January and was last seen on 7 March 1944. Major 'Bill' Barkworth, commander of the SAS War Crimes Investigation Team, later signalled Corporal Harry Kinder of 2nd SAS' Intelligence Section:

> Simpson is misinformed in considering Gunston's party drowned at sea Feb 44 as we have adequate evidence all seen early March 44 with Clubb [2nd Lieutenant Frederick Clubb, MC, of the 26th New Zealand Battalion, at that time an escaped POW] at Porto San Giorgio … consider also that repetition of names Gunston, Benson, Evans, Loosemore by Germans interrogating lends support theory that these four were prisoners [WO 361/351].

Further enquiries into the group's disappearance proved fruitless (see Benson's entry within this section and Gunston's entry overleaf for full details of the operation and subsequent investigation).

Son of Edward and Jane Evans of Ratcliffe Street, Stockport, Cheshire.

Age 26.

Panel 6. Also commemorated within Stockport's War Memorial Art Gallery.

SERGEANT WILLIAM OSBORNE **GLEN** [1443815] ROYAL ARTILLERY AND 2ND SAS (C SQN)

William Glen was born in the parish of Possilpark, Glasgow, on 22 August 1914. Having married Jeannie Finlay McDivitt in November 1936 their daughter, Mary, was born the following year. In February 1939 he joined the 57th Searchlight Regiment, Royal Artillery (TA), whilst working as a bus conductor and was promoted to bombardier two months later. That August a second daughter, Catherine, was born.

Mobilised at the outbreak of war Glen was posted to the 220th Searchlight Training Regiment. Joining the 513th Searchlight Battery he was promoted to sergeant in March 1941 and after a brief period with the 11th Anti-Aircraft Divisional School was appointed battery sergeant-major in May. Disembarking in North Africa in late January 1943 he volunteered for 2nd SAS on an unrecorded date that year.

Glen parachuted into Italy on 7 January 1944 as a member of Sergeant Robert Benson's Party No.6, this being tasked to attack the Ancona–Rimini railway line along Italy's Adriatic coast (OPERATION MAPLE

Driftwood). The group failed to make its sea rendezvous on the night of 25–26 January and was last seen on 7 March 1944. Glen was presumed to have been killed in action on this date (see Benson's entry within this section and Gunston's entry below for details of the operation and subsequent investigation).

Son of Dougald and Catherine Glen – Husband of Jeannie Glen, of Hillhead, Glasgow – Father of Mary and Catherine Glen.
Age 29.
Panel 2.

Captain John St George GUNSTON [124477] Royal Fusiliers, Irish Guards and 2nd SAS (C Sqn)

John Gunston was born on 17 February 1919 in Westminster, Central London. From 1932 to 1936 he was a boarder at The Grove at Harrow School where he was also a member of the OTC. Despite going up to Trinity College, Cambridge, in 1938 he interrupted his studies soon after the outbreak of war to enlist into the Royal Fusiliers (City of London Regiment) (service number 6464676). On doing so he stated that he had lived in Paris, Tours, Madrid, San Sebastian and Valencia, although he did not explain that the latter were due to him having taken part in the Spanish Civil War. As a later report notes: 'he felt very strongly politically, and, after somewhat grim experiences, was returned to this country in a state which he describes as one of starvation.' Subsequently plagued by chronic illness, Gunston remained of slight build and susceptible to infection.

A few weeks after enlistment Gunston was posted to the 161st Officer Cadet Training Unit at Sandhurst and granted an emergency commission in the Irish Guards at the end of March 1940. His final report states: 'This cadet has done very well. He has worked hard and is very keen. He has a pleasant manner and is always cheerful. He is intelligent and has shown powers of leadership.' Posted to the Training Battalion at East Grinstead he joined the 1st Battalion, his father's former battalion, that December. Although his service record notes that he spent much of the second half of 1941 and the beginning of 1942 in hospitals and convalescent homes he was back with the Training Battalion at Lingfield as a lieutenant from that May until November. He embarked for North Africa with the 1st Battalion in February 1943, arriving the following month. Having been appointed acting captain, and seen fierce fighting at the 'Battle of the Bou' at the Djebel bou Aoukaz in late April, he was admitted to hospital for an unknown reason in May. On being discharged he was posted to No.1 Infantry Reserve Training Depot. Despite the fact that he was regularly medically debilitated he volunteered for, and was accepted by, 2nd SAS on 20 June 1943, a few days after having been appointed captain.

Gunston was in command of C Squadron when it disembarked at the Italian port of Taranto on 10 September 1943 during Operation Slapstick. After a failed attempt to attack Gioia del Colle aerodrome he and eight men were taken out in Jeeps to guard the rail and road crossing between Metaponto and Pisticci whilst a special train, manned by 2nd SAS' French Squadron, ran through to liberate prisoners in a concentration camp. On the 20th his squadron was withdrawn to North Africa.

Gunston parachuted into Operation Maple Driftwood on 7 January 1944. After two false starts due to poor weather his team, and that of Sergeant Robert Benson, emplaned at Gioia del Colle that evening, dropping late that night at a DZ 13 kilometres west-north-west of Iesi, a little way inland from Italy's Adriatic coast. Gunston, in command of Party No.5, was tasked with sabotaging the Urbino–Fabriano railway line. Although it had been intended to reinforce his and Benson's parties by sea in order to destroy a railway bridge the weather prevented this, the task being later carried out independently under OPERATION BAOBAB. Meanwhile, Gunston's group failed to rendezvous with its pick-up boat 8 kilometres south-east of Fermo near Torre di Palme on the night of 25–26 January.

Early in February 1944 Parachutist 'Cookie' Cook of 2nd SAS, who had escaped from a POW camp having been captured the previous October during OPERATION JONQUIL, was making his way south when he met Gunston near Fermo. The officer told him that he intended to evacuate his party after completing a further task (WO 361/651). It seems certain that Benson's patrol was with Gunston's at this time as on the night of 4 February Captain Robert Matthews, also in the process of evading, met Gunston who told him that 'he was leaving by sea for Allied lines with 8 parachutists [*sic* – likely he and the seven other members of MAPLE DRIFTWOOD], Capt Clubb, 2 NZEF, and one other man … On 7 Mar 44 Gunston's party left by boat from a point a little south of Porto San Giorgio in a 22-ft boat' (WO 311/695). The men were never seen again. The eight SAS (Gunston's party of Pugh, Dodds and Loosemore and Benson's of Glen, Lockeridge and Evans) were reported missing with effect from that date. Due to the fact that the Regiment believed that they might still be operating behind the lines this was not done until March 1945 and their deaths not presumed until that October. Frederick Clubb, MC, was also reported missing as of this date. The identity of the remaining man is unknown although two others are commemorated on the Cassino Memorial with this date of death; Sergeant Norman Anderson and Bombardier George Worthington. The post-operation report notes:

> Admiralty weather report for the Adriatic coastline 7th March 1944 was wind strength 5–6 easterly veering south-east, moderating towards midday.
> There seems little reason to doubt the above extract [Matthews' statement]. Capt Gunston's party may either have been attacked by Allied aircraft (who were instructed to fire on craft off the enemy coast) or have been capsized some distance from the shore.
> There is also the possibility that they were forced to land again in enemy-occupied territory. In this connection it is noteworthy that a German Intelligence Officer read out the names of Capt Gunston, Sgt Benson, and Pct Loosemore, as SAS captured in Italy when interrogating three SAS prisoners in January 1945 [WO 361/897].

Major 'Bill' Barkworth, commander of the SAS War Crimes Investigation Team, wrote to the War Office in May 1945: 'It increases the possibility that these three [referring to Benson, Loosemore and Gunston] were either at one time prisoners in German hands or that their bodies were washed up, identified, and buried.' The day before Barkworth, perhaps in an effort to keep the investigation alive, had informed the War Office that: 'all the SAS were trained in seamanship and swimmers. Captain Gunston in particular was a keen yachtsman' (WO 361/351). Meanwhile, 2nd SAS reported:

> During a visit to Porto San Giorgio in February 1945, Major Barkworth found an Italian civilian named Armato Campofiloni who stated that he remembered Capt Gunston's party leaving by boat. He also had a story which was not very clear that a boat load of ex-PW had been forced to return about this time and all the occupants except one captured. He was not sure if it was the same boat. Arrangements have been made with the Allied Screening Commission for him to be fully interrogated [WO 311/695].

As time passed other theories were explored. On 24 May 1945 Barkworth signalled the welfare branch of Central Mediterranean Force: 'Have you investigated report alleged shooting 10 'American' soldiers village Montebuono A8419 repeat Montebouno A8419 April 1944? Description may refer to American equipment as carried by Gunston's party 2 SAS. Number given as 10 corresponds size Gunston's party when last seen' (WO 361/651). Another note in the same file notes; 'Unconfirmed report that Capt Gunston is with Tito's forces.' This refers to a signal received by Allied Forces HQ on 10 September 1944 stating that: 'It is reported that T/Capt St G Gunston I.G. and possibly seven others may have joined Brig Fitzroy Maclean direct from Ops. Can you ascertain and reply earliest possible.' Found to be a false lead Gunston's father was meanwhile making his own enquiries, as an unattributed newspaper clipping illustrates:

Sir Derrick Gunston, MP, today revealed the story behind a notice in *The Times* seeking information regarding Captain John St George Gunston, Irish Guards, attached Second Special Air Service Regiment, and seven paratroopers missing since March 1944. Sergeant Benson, Garbutt Place, Marylebone, was one of the party. 'My son and his men were dropped behind the enemy lines in Italy in January 1944 to do demolition work including blowing up several bridges,' Sir Derrick said. 'They completed this and were given a roaming commission. They were seen south of Ancona in March 1944. Then came the news that they had been drowned trying to get away by boat. Next, a rumour reached London that they were in a German prisoner of war camp and not allowed to communicate with anyone. Men from the camp will now have arrived in Britain and may be able to confirm this.'

At the beginning of October 1945 Captain Henry Parker, 2nd SAS' sole permanent investigative officer in Italy and himself a veteran of Operation Maple, wrote to his Commanding Officer, Lt-Colonel Brian Franks, DSO, MC:

Enough evidence has been collected to piece together the following story, although the evidence is not very reliable, so much of the story must necessarily be based on deduction.

On the night of 7–8th March 44 Captain Gunston and his party put out to sea from a point a little south of Porto San Georgio – their boat however had been laid up on the beach throughout the winter, and the seams had opened. After putting to sea the party found that the boat was not sufficiently seaworthy to get them back, so they were forced to land again.

This they did without trouble, and proceeded to work inland. It is my belief that Captain Gunston had entertained the possibility of trying to join up with either Lt Worcester or myself in the Terni area.

He and his party got as far as Montebouno – a very small village near Gurbio, were caught by the Germans (possibly 16 SS Div, who have a very unsavoury reputation) and were shot.

I have got a graves registration unit onto making a very thorough search of this area and, if any bodies are found and identified, and I am fairly confident that they will be, I can then set about identifying the Germans concerned [WO 311/630].

Three weeks later Franks wrote somewhat less optimistically to the War Office: 'Owing to the fact that we [1st and 2nd SAS Regiments] are to be disbanded by the middle of next month I shall have to recall Capt. Parker. It seems very doubtful whether in the time available he will be able to provide any more definite evidence' (WO 311/630). That month Gunston's father, now resigned to his son's fate, wrote to the War Office:

Thank you for your letter of September 26th about my son Captain J St G Gunston, Irish Guards. I am afraid that there can be no hope left, but I would be grateful if your department would inform me officially as soon as possible that his death must be presumed. Thank you very much for the trouble you have taken.

The Times subsequently reported on 10 November 1945:

Previously reported missing in Italy, March, 1944, now believed to have been shot by the Germans after capture, Captain John St George Gunston, Irish Guards, attached 2nd SAS Regiment, elder son of Sir Derrick and Lady Gunston, Petty France, Badminton, Glos. 'Quis Separabit?' [Who Will Separate Us? The motto of the Irish Guards].

Son of Major Sir Derrick Gunston Bt, MC, MP, and Lady Gunston (née St George) of Southend, Wickwar, Gloucestershire – At the time of his disappearance Gunston was engaged to a Miss E. Halama – Older brother of Richard Gunston.
Age 25.
Panel 4. Also commemorated on Harrow School's war memorial, by a stained glass window within Holy Trinity Church, Wickwar, and on the war memorial within Trinity College Chapel in Cambridge.

SERGEANT JOSEPH **HAMMOND** [5495725] HAMPSHIRE REGIMENT AND 2ND SAS

Joseph Hammond was born on 18 January 1913. Whilst working as a gardener he joined A (Machine Gun) Company, 4th Battalion, Hampshire Regiment (TA), in Winchester during February 1931. As a regular attender he was promoted to lance-corporal in February 1938 and to corporal in April 1939. He was subsequently embodied at the outbreak of war and in February 1941 appointed paid acting sergeant. Promoted to war standing sergeant that August he disembarked in Algeria with the 1/4th Battalion at the beginning of January 1943, his brigade helping to halt OPERATION OSCHSENKOPF, a German offensive, at Hunt's Gap near Ksar Mazouar, Tunisia, in late February. The following month his battalion suffered heavy losses whilst carrying out defensive patrols and in late April he either received light wounds or fell sick resulting in a fortnight's convalescence away from the front line. He volunteered for 2nd SAS on 12 June after hostilities in North Africa had ceased, qualifying as a parachutist on 26 July.

There are no known details of Hammond's fate. Although his death certificate states he died in 'North Africa', his casualty card notes that he was 'presumed killed in action at sea'. Meanwhile, his service record states that he was reported missing in 'N/Africa (Italy)' by 2nd SAS on 23 November 1943, this later being annotated to 'killed in action' on 27 October 1943. Although several operations were being carried out at this time in Italy, most notably OPERATION CANDYTUFT, an amphibious raid to cut the Ancona–Pescara railway line on the night of 27–28 October, Hammond does not appear on its nominal roll. No trace can be found of the report outlining its sub-operation, SAXIFRAGE. His service record notes that he was posted missing 'Cat C', this denoting 'those cases in which there is evidence which to some extent is helpful but which does not enable us to deal with the case other than as one of the presumption [of death] in view of the lapse of time' (WO 162/205).

Son of Arthur and Harriett Hammond of Olivers Battery, Stanmore, Winchester.
Age 30.
Panel 7. Also commemorated within the war memorial chapel at the Hospital of St Cross, Winchester.

LIEUTENANT JAMES CYRIL **HENSHAW** [233815] GRENADIER GUARDS, ROYAL ARTILLERY AND SBS (Z PATROL, M SQN)

Jim Henshaw, the son of a police sergeant, was born on 1 September 1918 at St Mary's in Chesterfield. Having attended Tapton House Secondary School from 1930 to 1934, and having been employed as an electric welder for The Chesterfield Tube Company, he enlisted into the Grenadier Guards in January 1937 (service number 2615141). Posted to the 1st Battalion he was promoted to lance-corporal that October and served in No.8 Platoon, King's Company, during the spring of 1939. At the outbreak of war he was promoted to acting corporal and soon disembarked in France to serve with the BEF. By mid October 1939 the battalion was positioned on the Belgian border billeted at Annappes. It was still there on 10 May 1940 when Germany invaded the Low Countries, thus ending the 'Phoney War'. By the following night it had moved into Belgium where it took up positions around Louvain on the 11th. Five days later the battalion was ordered to withdraw, this being the first of many moves towards Dunkirk from where its men were evacuated on 1 June. Roger Wright, former Grenadier Guards and SBS, later wrote:

> This NCO [Henshaw] was to me the perfect specimen of a man – 6'4", 14 stone, the company PTI, striker for the battalion at soccer. He competed in and won many events in the Lawson Cup and was a non-smoker, unusual in

those days. We did the Troop [Trooping the Colour] in 1939 then went to France with the BEF. Monty was Divisional Commander, our platoon sergeant was made PSM [platoon sergeant-major], and Jim made platoon sergeant. We had no officer. During the eight or nine months in France and Belgium, Jim Henshaw was an excellent platoon sergeant and made us into a very good fighting force. He continued this for another nine months after Dunkirk and the platoon came back from Dunkirk almost unscathed [*Mars & Minerva*, December 2001].

Having been promoted to war standing sergeant Henshaw married Johanna McDonnell at St Pancras Parish Church, London, in December 1940. He was subsequently posted to the Royal Artillery's 133 OCTU at Shrivenham in December 1941 and received an emergency commission into the 93rd Heavy Anti-Aircraft Regiment the following May (*London Gazette* 29/05/42). His final report notes: 'Sound, pleasant, hardworking and keen. He is thoroughly reliable and should make a very useful officer.' By this time he and his wife had moved from Chesterfield to Victoria in Central London.

Henshaw was promoted to lieutenant in November 1942 and disembarked in the Middle East the following April. Volunteering for Raiding Forces on 13 June 1944 he joined the Special Boat Squadron (1st SAS) at Athlit the next day. Wright takes up the narrative:

It was the spring [*sic*] of 1944, we were having a regatta on the beach in Palestine 'between raids', when I saw this figure ahead of me in PT [physical training] kit – it was Jim Henshaw. He informed me that he had come to join us in the SAS. Whatever other rank joined us was reduced to trooper. I was a full corporal at the time. Knowing that I was to be made sergeant next day, I said to Jim to get into my patrol and he said he certainly would. With that I was called away to collect a prize I had won. I searched the camp for him that night but failed to find him. The following morning I was marched in for promotion. Three officers sat behind the table, one of them was Captain Jim Henshaw with a big grin on his face. I waited for him outside, he came out and said 'I got in your patrol, sergeant.' We had a good laugh.

That July Henshaw attended the Close Combat Course in Jerusalem, the now renamed Special Boat Service moving to Italy at the beginning of August. He and Captain Andy Lassen, MC*, subsequently led two patrols, O and K, to blow up a railway bridge at Karasovici in Yugoslavia (OPERATION HEALTH ABLE sub OPERATION RATWEEK). A contemporary report notes that an LRDG patrol under Lieutenant David Skipwith was put ashore to recce targets on the night of 18–19 August 1944 (WO 204/9681). The SBS patrols followed on from Bari in motor launches on the afternoon of the 27th and landed on a beach near Gruda at 2359hrs where they were met by Skipwith's men and a group of Partisans. They reached the bridge at Karasovici at 2115hrs on the 30th after 'the civilians of Plocice had supplied food and wine' and by 2245 the bridge was destroyed. Lassen's own report records that they were attacked by a mixed force of 400 Ustaše and Germans on 2 September and that: 'Lt Henshaw with five men defended the ridge.' Although three men, including Skipwith, were captured the remainder of the group successfully disengaged from the enemy and returned to Italy on 6 September (see Lassen's own entry under Argenta Gap War Cemetery, Italy).

Twelve days later Henshaw's F Patrol left Brindisi for OPERATION APLOMB, a recce of islands that guarded the approaches to Athens. Wright recalled: 'we were the first into Athens, then on to Salonica. We entered the harbour in two Greek fishing boats.' Having liberated the latter mounted on requisitioned fire engines Henshaw, a German speaker, negotiated with the enemy to prevent the destruction of petrol installations to the north-west.

Henshaw completed parachute training that November, M Squadron moving to Crete around the same time. Here Z Patrol, which he now commanded, and Captain Charles Bimrose's E Patrol were tasked to provide: 'heavy support to any attack or defensive action which might take place in the near future. In addition it is believed that the presence of regular, disciplined troops in their ranks will have a heartening effect on the Partisans' (WO 170/7529).

M Squadron returned to Italy on 11 February 1945. On the 16th Henshaw's patrol was attached to S Squadron and sailed for Zara on the Yugoslav coast, which it reached the following day. Having been promoted to acting captain on 10 March, Henshaw and the combined squadron deployed from their forward-operating base on Uljan Island on the afternoon of the 18th bound for Lussin. The men landed on the island at 0245hrs the following morning to attack the bridge at Ossero. Within half an hour Henshaw had been killed in action, Wright later recalling:

> It turned out that our lads had run into a German patrol. Of the five German men, four were killed and one got away; our other patrol had three walking wounded. By now the Jerry were well alert and were soon firing heavy machine guns, one down the narrow streets we had just left. I think they were on set lines. We had just reached a small square which gave us some cover and ahead of us was a mass of barbed wire. The machine gun appeared to be on the upper floor of a house about 30 yards away. Captain Jim decided that I should have a go with the PIAT and Ginger with the Bren.
> I had never used this weapon on a building before. The first missile hit the house on the lower half. Captain Henshaw was reloading for me when he keeled over and lay inert. I stayed in my position and instructed Cole and Strachan to see to Captain Henshaw. They thought he was dead – it was black dark. Williams was in a dangerous position for the machine gun was still firing up the street. I brought him under cover and decided to pull back to our reserve patrol, taking our Captain on a door with us. He was dead. It was decided we would retire to the boats.

Ian Smith, MC, a fellow SBS officer, later wrote:

> … what became obvious was that the whole operation was unnecessary and pointless, because the swing bridge between the two islands [Lussin and Cres] spanned a channel about twenty-five feet, with firm flat abutments. So even if we had blown the bridge it would have been a simple task for the enemy engineers to have made a replacement bridge with a few girders or tree trunks. It would have taken a competent crew of sappers but a few minutes. So, one young life lost for nothing [IWM Documents.15632 – Private Papers of Major I. C. D. Smith, MC*].

The SBS War Diary notes: 'Monday 19 Mar 45. Capt Henshaw buried at sea [according to his service record this being at Scala Point], firing party provided by HMS *Colombo*' (WO 170/7529).

Son of Joseph and Florence Henshaw (née Foster) of Pond Street, Chesterfield – Husband of Jean Henshaw of Sussex Gardens, Hyde Park, London – Brother of Tristram and Richard Henshaw. Age 24. Panel 2.

BOMBARDIER JOHN **HOLMES** [842771] ROYAL ARTILLERY AND 2ND SAS (G SQN)

John Holmes was born on 2 July 1916 and resided in Leeds. Having worked as a farm hand he enlisted into the Royal Artillery in December 1934, serving for three years in a light anti-aircraft battery in the UK and Egypt before transferring to the Army Reserve. In February 1939 he married Millicent Alice Hodgkins in Bradford and was called up that June in the build up to war. Initially posted to the 5th Battery, 2nd Heavy Anti-Aircraft Regiment, he served with the BEF in France before being evacuated sometime in June 1940, most likely from Cherbourg. He was promoted to lance-bombardier that November.

From July 1941 Holmes served on Malta with the 5th Battery, 4th Heavy Anti-Aircraft Regiment, and was advanced to bombardier the following month. When the siege of the island abated he volunteered for 2nd SAS, disembarking at Algiers on 25 August 1943 and joining the Regiment at Philippeville that day. He drowned along with three others on 11 January 1944 during a training scheme off the coast of Algeria, his being the only body not recovered (see entries for Gunners Arthur Betts, Leonard Garnham, and Trevor James under Bône War Cemetery, Algeria, Volume I, for full details).

Husband of Millicent Holmes of Birstall, Leeds.
Age 27. Panel 2.

Sapper Alan **LOCKERIDGE** [1987141] Royal Engineers and 2nd SAS (C Sqn)

Alan Lockeridge was born on 9 October 1919 and grew up in Manchester. Whilst working as a carpenter and joiner he enlisted into the Royal Engineers Supplementary Reserve on 27 June 1939 and was subsequently mobilised the day that war was declared. The following month he disembarked in France with 110 Army Troops Company to serve with the BEF until being evacuated on 1 June 1940. After over two years of home service he embarked for North Africa in November 1942 and volunteered for 2nd SAS on an unknown date whilst there.

Lockeridge parachuted into Italy for Operation Maple Driftwood on 7 January 1944 as a member of Sergeant Robert Benson's Party No.6. This was tasked with sabotaging the Ancona–Rimini railway line. It failed to make its sea rendezvous on the night of 25–26 January, the men last being seen on 7 March 1944. Lockeridge was reported missing as of this date and later presumed to have been killed in action (see entries for both Benson and Gunston in this section for full details).

Son of Maria Lockeridge of Hillkirk Street, Beswick, Manchester. Age 24. Panel 3.

Private Herbert **LOOSEMORE** [4698891] King's Own Yorkshire Light Infantry, Durham Light Infantry and 2nd SAS (C Sqn)

On enlisting into the King's Own Yorkshire Light Infantry in June 1941 Herbert Loosemore stated that he had been born in Sheffield on New Year's Eve 1922 and that he had previously worked as a lorry driver's mate. However, his birth was not registered until the first quarter of 1924 and it is therefore likely that he falsified his age to join up a year early. Although initially posted to the 70th (Young Soldiers) Battalion he later joined the 6th Battalion, embarking for North Africa on 10 April 1943 as a reinforcement. On arrival he was posted to No.1 Infantry Reinforcement Training Depot and despite transferring to the 16th Battalion, Durham Light Infantry, six days later he volunteered for the newly-formed 2nd SAS on 30 May.

Loosemore parachuted into Italy for Operation Maple Driftwood on 7 January 1944 as a member of Captain John Gunston's Party No.5 that was tasked with sabotaging the Urbino–Fabriano railway line.

This missed its sea rendezvous on the night of 25–26 January, the men last being seen alive on 7 March 1944. That November the War Office wrote: 'Understood from 2 SAS Regt this man believed still to be operating and is not to be posted missing at present; also that next-of-kin has been informed of the position by 2 SAS Regt.' However, further investigation into the group's disappearance proved fruitless, all eight men of Gunston's and Sergeant Robert Benson's parties later being presumed to have been killed in action (see Gunston's entry within this section for full details).

Son of George and Ethel Loosemore (née Linacre) of Portland Street, Sheffield – Younger brother of George and Cyril Loosemore who both served in the York and Lancaster Regiment – Nephew of Arnold Loosemore, First World War recipient of both the VC and DCM.

Age officially recorded as 21.

Panel 10.

BOMBARDIER ALBERT HENRY **PUGH** [2043553] ROYAL ENGINEERS, ROYAL ARTILLERY AND 2ND SAS (C SQN)

Albert Pugh was born on 30 May 1919 at Eltham, south-east London, where his family lived on Greenvale Road. Whilst working as an electrical apprentice he joined the 34th Anti-Aircraft Battalion, Royal Engineers (TA), in June 1937. He was subsequently mobilised during September and October 1938 as a result of the Munich Crisis and again during July and August 1939 before being embodied at the outbreak of war. Qualifying as a searchlight operator that November he was promoted to lance-corporal in June 1940. When his unit was redesignated as the 34th Searchlight Regiment, Royal Artillery, two months later he was transferred to this corps with the equivalent rank of lance-bombardier. Promoted to bombardier in March 1941 he attended a searchlight instructor's course that June and was mustered as an electrical fitter in September. He embarked for North Africa the following February, volunteering for 2nd SAS on 20 September 1943.

Pugh parachuted into Italy for OPERATION MAPLE DRIFTWOOD on 7 January 1944 as a member of Captain John Gunston's Party No.5 that was tasked with sabotaging the Urbino–Fabriano railway line. This failed to make its sea rendezvous on the night of 25–26 January and was last seen on 7 March 1944, Pugh being reported missing in action, later missing presumed dead, as of this date (see Gunston's entry for full details).

Son of Rose Pugh of Eltham, south-east London, later of Hall Green, Birmingham, and Wharf Street, Leicester.

Age 25. Panel 2.

LANCE-BOMBARDIER ROBERT JOSEPH **SCHERZINGER** [1080354] ROYAL ARTILLERY AND SRS (NO.1 TROOP)

Rob Scherzinger was born on 13 February 1912 at Brixton in South London to a Swiss father and British mother. He married Doris Todd in September 1933, the couple producing a daughter, Josephine, the following year. They separated before the war whilst Scherzinger was working as a professional wrestler. On 30 September 1940 he enlisted into the Royal Artillery and was posted to the 953rd Defence Battery. The following August he arrived at RAF Ringway where he served as a gunner until disembarking in the Middle East in May 1942. At some point between then and the invasion of Sicily in July 1943 (OPERATION HUSKY) he volunteered for either L Detachment, SAS Brigade, 1st SAS or the Special Raiding Squadron.

Scherzinger was a member of C Section, No.1 Troop, by the time the SRS destroyed coastal batteries at Capo Murro di Porco on 10 July at the forefront of HUSKY. The unit subsequently captured the key port of Augusta on the evening of the 12th and the town of Bagnara on the toe of mainland Italy on 4 September (OPERATION BAYTOWN).

To prevent the enemy taking up defensive positions on the River Biferno the SRS joined No.3 Commando and No.40 (RM) Commando in launching OPERATION DEVON, the combined force landing 1½ kilometres north-west of Termoli in the early hours of 3 October 1943. Whilst the Commandos secured the port and its perimeter the SRS pushed down towards the Biferno to hold two bridges and a road junction key to the advancing 78th Division. On the evening of the 4th Scherzinger's section, under Lieutenant 'Sandy' Wilson, joined A and C Sections of No.2 Troop and moved to the west side of the port to take up positions on the Torrente Sinarca to fill a gap in the perimeter. The following day the Reconnaissance Regiment abandoned its anti-tank guns and the combined sections struggled to hold back fierce counter-attacks. However, by 1900hrs Wilson's men were back to the east of Termoli and dug in to the front of a goods yard. At 0500hrs on the 6th their positions were the target of enemy shelling, mortars and small arms fire. Again the Recce Regiment deserted their guns but by 0930 Wilson's men had taken these over and were using them to engage enemy infantry in houses to their front. Although abandoned temporarily these were reoccupied at 1000hrs and mortars deployed from their vicinity. Reg Seekings, DCM, MM, a former SRS sergeant, later recalled their effect:

> [Wilson's] section had taken over an abandoned 17-pounder anti-tank gun, positioned under a haystack. And he was having a go at these tanks [sic], but mortars got on to him and in the process they wounded just about everybody and set the haystack on fire. And there was a chap there, cant remember his name, a big freckled all-in wrestler, huge chap, a tough bugger [Scherzinger], and though he was wounded himself, he was dragging the chaps out. But before he could get Sandy out, the stack collapsed over the gun and the rest of them [sic – both of them] were burnt to a cinder [IWM Sound Archive 18177 – see Wilson's entry below].

Surprisingly, Scherzinger's gallantry went unrewarded, his entry on an SRS nominal roll being merely annotated as 'killed on 06/10/43'. Squadron Sergeant-Major Graham Rose, MM*, recorded the same date at '1000hrs at 818782 100x south of track at burnt haystack.' According to the anonymous caption found on the photograph shown here he was killed about an hour after it was taken, his date of death being officially recorded as 5 October 1943.

Son of John and Florence Scherzinger (née Collier) of Lorn Road, Brixton, South London – Former husband of Doris Scherzinger of Russell Gardens, Stangate Street, Lambeth, South London – Father of Josephine Scherzinger.

Age 31.

Panel 2.

Lieutenant Alexander Melville **WILSON** [203919] Royal Scots, King's Shropshire Light Infantry, North Staffordshire Regiment, Gordon Highlanders, L Detachment SAS Brigade, 1st SAS and SRS (No.1 Troop)

Known as 'Sandy' to his comrades, Alexander Wilson was born on 2 October 1921 in Aberdeen as the youngest of three children. He followed in his father's footsteps and boarded at Cheltenham College from 1935–39 where he was a member of the OTC. Having matriculated into the faculty of medicine at Edinburgh University he joined the Royal Scots (TA) in October 1939 (service number 3059203) and transferred to the King's Shropshire Light Infantry in November 1940. After reporting to 164 OCTU the following March he was commissioned into the North Staffordshire Regiment in September 1941 and posted to its 9th Battalion. His final report states: 'This cadet has improved considerably and I now consider that he is fit for commission to make a good Platoon Commander with more experience in command, and when he overcomes his shyness.' Due to family connections and the personal intervention of the Colonel of the Regiment, he transferred to the Gordon Highlanders that December. The following month his brother, Sub-Lieutenant John Wilson, RNVR, was posted missing in action when the Swordfish he was piloting failed to return to Malta after an attack on Italian shipping.

Although it is unknown when he arrived in the Middle East, Wilson volunteered for L Detachment, SAS Brigade, on 18 July 1942. He is therefore likely to have taken part in Operation Bigamy, the large-scale, abortive raid on Benghazi that September. Reports show that he was operating behind the lines in Libya with A Squadron, 1st SAS, at the beginning of November but that he was sent back to Kufra on doctor's orders. He later laid supply dumps westwards from Bir Zelten, ensuring that A and B Squadrons could operate close to the Libyan coast road and that C Squadron could operate near to Nalut.

From early 1943 1st SAS was training along the Palestinian and Syrian coastline, the majority of the Regiment's subunits being restructured as the Special Raiding Squadron back at Kabrit that March. Wilson attended parachute course No.32 at Ramat David in April and the Grant-Taylor revolver course in Jerusalem at the beginning of May. Having been appointed acting captain that month he spent June training in the Gulf of Aqaba. The SRS subsequently landed at Capo Murro di Porco in the early hours of 10 July and destroyed coastal batteries at the spearhead of Operation Husky, the Allied invasion of Sicily. On the evening of the 12th it captured the key port of Augusta, Wilson's self-written application for SAS Operational Wings listing his activities up to this point:

1. Lt Sadler and self recce Fort Maddelena area [near the Libyan/Egyptian border] reporting all movements by truck and air. 2. Capt Marsh and self Beurat-Gildalia road [Libya] blew up 4 x 10-ton trucks and trailers by day with ammo on board. Strafed coast road by night two trucks set on fire. Mined coast road. 3. Blew up three trucks and armoured car. 4. Sicily x 2.

The wings were awarded on 23 July, the SRS going on to capture the town of Bagnara on the Italian mainland on 4 September (OPERATION BAYTOWN).

Wilson was killed in action during OPERATION DEVON at Termoli on 6 October 1943 whilst commanding C Section, No.1 Troop. His men were manning an anti-tank gun within a haystack when mortar fire set it alight trapping the men inside. Although wounded Lance-bombardier Rob Scherzinger dragged several out before going back in to get Wilson. The stack collapsed as he did so and both were killed. Their date of death is officially recorded as the 5th (see Scherzinger's entry on previous pages for full details).

Youngest son of Walter and Helen Wilson (née Stolker) of Chipping Campden, Gloucestershire – Younger brother of Marguerite Macfie and Sub-Lieutenant John Wilson, killed in action on 30 January 1942 and commemorated on Lee-on-Solent's Fleet Air Arm Memorial.
Age 22.
Panel 11. Also commemorated on Chipping Campden's war memorial and at Cheltenham College.

FLORENCE WAR CEMETERY

Having stalled the Allies at the Trasimene Line German forces had withdrawn to Florence by late July 1944, it forming the centre of their Arno Line. However, the Eighth Army mopped up the last pockets of resistance within the city on 13 August, the cemetery being created three months later to serve military hospitals and so that burials could be concentrated to it. Post-war eighty-three graves were brought in from Arrow Route Cemetery on the Borgo San Lorenzo–Faenza road, this having proved impossible to maintain. The plot now contains 1,632 Commonwealth burials.

The cemetery is located east of the city on the north bank of the River Arno. Access is gained from the SS67, the Via Aretina, approximately 100 metres east of Girone bus terminal. GPS co-ordinates: Latitude 43.77016, Longitude 11.34284

GUNNER BERNARD OLIVER **BRUNT** [1800118] ROYAL ARTILLERY
AND 2ND SAS (A SQN)

Bernie Brunt was born on 7 August 1921 in Rotherham. Having worked as a chipper's assistant he enlisted into the Royal Artillery at Aberystwyth in May 1941 and began a succession of home service postings to various light and heavy anti-aircraft regiments. Sailing for North Africa in November 1942 he disembarked the following month and volunteered for 2nd SAS on 2 June 1943. He qualified for his wings ten days later and was subsequently posted to A Squadron.

On the night of 14–15 July 1943 Brunt parachuted into north-east Sicily in the area between Randazzo

145

and Santa Domenica. His patrol, under Lieutenant McCorquodale, was intended as reinforcement for OPERATION CHESTNUT's 'Pink' Party. On the 16th it split, Brunt, Sergeant Robert Benson and Parachutist Summers sabotaging anything they could find. Summers later noted in his report; 'Pte Brunt climbed one telephone pole and cut the telephone wires' (WO 218/98). The three later found a camouflaged truck on which they decided to lay charges, Summers reporting that 'Pte Brunt covered Sgt Benson and myself from the rear with the Tommy gun'. When the driver and his two companions awoke to find Benson and Summers helping themselves to their cigarette supply the parachutists pretended to be German whilst Brunt 'covered one of the Italians with his Tommy gun at a range of about 3 yards. This Italian did not see him and was waving his pistol in our direction.' Having cut further communication lines they skirted Mount Etna, living off the land and collecting information until eventually meeting the 51st Highland Division on the evening of 21 July. Having passed much information to the 51st's Intelligence Officers the three were flown from Syracuse to Tunis to rejoin the Regiment (see Benson's entry under Cassino Memorial, Italy).

Brunt parachuted into the area north of La Spezia in Liguria on the night of 7–8 September 1943 for OPERATION SPEEDWELL. Having regrouped the six-man team slept before dividing into pairs: Captain Pat Dudgeon and his batman, Brunt, moving off to attack the Genoa–La Spezia railway line, Sergeant 'Geordie' Foster and Corporal Jim Shortall to cut a different section of the same track, and Lance-corporal 'Tanky' Challenor and Lieutenant 'Tojo' Wedderburn tasked with disrupting the line between La Spezia and Bologna. Although the Italian armistice was announced during the evening of the 8th the latter pair was the only one to make the arranged RV seven nights later. Brunt and Dudgeon had been taken prisoner at La Cisa Pass and murdered a short distance away on 3 October 1943 (see Dudgeon's entry within this section for full details including some discrepancy over the date). Hauptmann Wolfgang Neuhaus, Staff Captain to the 65th Infantry Division, later stated:

General von Ziehlberg [the commander of the 65th Infantry Division] then disclosed to the captain [Dudgeon] that he was forced to have him shot. The captain kept his bearing when he heard of the decision, and then was taken away. The interrogation of the English soldier [Brunt] was carried out in a similar way. He did not make any statement, and also retained his poise when he heard the General's decision …

Concerning the shooting of the soldier, who was shot after the captain, Schmitt [sic - Leutnant Victor Schmit] said that he had been asked by the captain before he was shot whether an English lieutenant-colonel had been also been taken prisoner, which Schmitt denied. Schmitt, therefore, at the instance of the battalion commander of the 65th F.E.B. [Feld Ersatz Bataillon, 65th Division - a field replacement battalion] has asked the English soldier at the place of execution whether and how many other English groups had parachuted or had been landed in the area. The English soldier had replied that it did not interest him what the captain was said to have stated and he gave no further information in reply to the question. When he was asked if he had a last wish he even refused this. When Lieutenant Schmitt repeated his question as to whether he was ready to state his home address for the subsequent information of his family he answered in the negative. He was then shot too [WO 309/99].

In September 1945 the War Office wrote to 2nd SAS' Commanding Officer, Lt-Colonel Brian Franks, DSO, MC:

We are considering case of Gunner Brunt for presumption of death; a pity Schmidt [sic] who gave much regarding Captain Dudgeon said so little of the men with him. However, there cannot unhappily be any doubt that Gunner Brunt also paid with his life. As soon as we decide I will let you know [WO 361/351].

Most official records, even those of the SAS War Crimes Investigation Team, incorrectly state that Brunt and Shortall were paired on SPEEDWELL with Dudgeon and Foster as another pair (see Foster's and Shortall's entries under Staglieno War Cemetery, Italy). The Special Investigation Branch officer assigned to the case even captioned a photo of Brunt's unmarked grave, which he discovered at the site of the murder, as: 'containing the remains Sgt Forster [*sic*] … Very little clothing but that was British. Army boots, no identification discs, just a piece of broken string. Army type watch, and small Artillery badge.' These remains were, without doubt, those of Brunt. They, and those of Dudgeon, were exhumed in August 1945, both men being reinterred in Florence side by side. Although a trial followed those convicted of war crimes in connection to the murders were sentenced to just six months imprisonment.

In September 1944 the Royal Artillery records office, suspecting that Brunt was either a casualty or a deserter, had tasked Rotherham's Chief Constable's office to make discreet enquiries as to his whereabouts. The Chief Constable himself responded:

> His parents are very anxious for news regarding their son and have made numerous enquiries through the Red Cross.
>
> In February of this year a personal friend of Gunner Brunt's called to see them and handed the mother a wallet which contained personal papers and five pounds in French money. The soldier referred to is Pte Sidney Bird, a parachutist, who informed Mrs Brunt that the last time he saw her son was when he was boarding a plane in North Africa, in September 1943. Apparently, Bird was to have gone with the party but he had a temperature and was ordered to stay behind. The wallet was handed to Bird by Brunt, who asked him to hand it to his mother if he got back to England. Bird promised he would and when he arrived in this country he changed the money into English. Mrs Brunt produced the wallet to me with the money and contents intact.
>
> In the course of the interview Mrs Brunt stated that she has met two or three of his mates since they have returned to this country, but apart from this man Bird, none of them have had any news of her son.
>
> His father is a pensioner from the last war and there is another brother serving with HM Forces. The mother also states that she writes to this soldier every Friday and has had no correspondence returned, and in a letter from the Red Cross in June of this year, they informed her that he was safe and well.

Son of Bernard and Frances Brunt (née Oliver) of Victoria Street, Masbro, Rotherham, Yorkshire.

Age officially recorded as 21.

There's a face that is always with us. There's a voice we long to hear. Adieu

Grave 9.H.9. Also commemorated on a memorial close to the murder site at Cisa Pass, this having been organised by Brian Lett, QC, author of *SAS in Tuscany 1943–1945*, with full support and financial assistance from the Comune di Pontremoli.

CAPTAIN PATRICK LAURENCE **DUDGEON** MC [131676] ROYAL CORPS OF SIGNALS, SMALL SCALE RAIDING FORCE AND 2ND SAS (A SQN)

Pat Dudgeon was born on 10 July 1920 in Cairo, Egypt, his mother dying in childbirth. Educated at Oundle School in Northamptonshire from 1934 to 1939, he was head of St Anthony's House and a keen member of the OTC. Although he entered the Royal Military Academy at Woolwich he enlisted into the Royal Corps of Signals at the outbreak of war (service number 2588236). Immediately posted to 151 OCTU he was commissioned into his parent unit the following May (*London Gazette* 28/05/40). Having joined I Corps Signals he was promoted to lieutenant during November 1941 before moving to 42nd Armoured Division Signals where he was promoted to captain. After volunteering for special duties he was posted to the Special Operation Executive's HQ Special Training Schools at the beginning of May 1942. He subsequently joined STS.62, the Small Scale Raiding Force at Anderson Manor in Dorset, temporarily relinquishing one pip in order to do so.

Dudgeon was awarded the Military Cross on the recommendation of the Chief of Combined Operations, Lord Louis Mountbatten for SSRF raids on the Channel Islands:

> Lieut [*sic* – he regained his captaincy in June 1942] Dudgeon has shown himself to be a most trustworthy and reliable officer, and to be possessed of resourcefulness and determination in action. In addition to the power of leadership which he has displayed, he speaks fluent German, and proved himself invaluable on Operation Dryad [the raid on Les Casquets lighthouse on the night of 2–3 September 1942] when it was necessary to interrogate German prisoners. On this operation Lieut Dudgeon's task consisted of entering one of the buildings alone and overcoming any resistance met with; he took two prisoners in this building and whilst holding them up extracted useful information from them regarding the disposition of arms, number of men on the post and other details. He has proved at all times to be cheerful and willing and to be a brave and courageous officer. Lt Dudgeon also took part in Operation Basalt [the raid on Sark on the night of 3–4 October 1942] and as one of those trying the doors and windows of the houses entered did excellently. He was also invaluable as an interpreter [*London Gazette* 11/12/42, Supplement 15/12/42, WO 373/93].

During BASALT Dudgeon's group raided the Dixcart Hotel and took five German prisoners whose hands they tied. Starting back towards their boat the captives attempted to raise the alarm, some breaking free. Dudgeon accidentally killed one in an effort to silence him: Hitting him with the barrel of his pistol and not the butt he shot the man in the head. Another prisoner was killed in the ensuing scuffle, one left wounded, and one escaped, the SSRF party withdrawing rapidly with the remaining man. When daylight broke the German garrison discovered their men bound as if murdered after capture, Hitler ordering the manacling of Commando prisoners and issuing his infamous 'Commando Order'. This was the death warrant of many of those listed within this Roll of Honour, including Dudgeon (see Appendix 2 within the User's Guide for full details).

The majority of the SSRF embarked for North Africa in February 1943, its men forming the foundation on which 2nd SAS was raised on 13 May. At the end of the month Dudgeon led a party on OPERATION MARIGOLD: he and seven of his men embarked HM Submarine *Safari* on the 26th alongside a small team from Z Special Boat Section. The latter dropped 'a suitably marked notebook' for deception purposes at a defended beach on the east coast of Sardinia, the whole party then going ashore at Porto Gonone to simulate a recce in force and to try and capture a prisoner. Owing to out-of-date aerial photography not showing an emplacement, and the fact that a member of the party dropped his Tommy gun, surprise was lost and the team withdrew under heavy fire, one of them being taken prisoner (DEFE 2/357 – see Sergeant 'Ginger' Milne's entry under Brookwood Memorial, United Kingdom, Volume III, for details).

Dudgeon took part in OPERATION CHESTNUT, parachuting into Sicily on 12 July 1943 as a member of the ten-man 'Brig' party. His report describes the actual drop: 'the only casualty was myself. I strained my right knee on landing, which developed synovites, and was some hindrance at time to movement' (WO 218/175). Despite this injury, and being only able to locate three men and no equipment containers, his party cut telegraph cables before making contact with the advancing Allies eleven days later.

On the night of 7–8 September 1943 Dudgeon parachuted into a DZ 11 kilometres south-west of Borgo Val di Taro in the Emilia-Romagna region of northern Italy for OPERATION SPEEDWELL. Timed to coincide with the Italian armistice, subsequently announced on the evening of the 8th, his team was tasked with disrupting rail links north of La Spezia, thereby preventing German reinforcement of the south of the country. Having regrouped on the DZ the men slept nearby, collected their containers at first light and spent the day in preparation. They then divided into three pairs: Dudgeon and his batman, Parachutist Bernie Brunt (see Brunt's entry on previous pages), Sergeant 'Geordie' Foster and Corporal Jim Shortall (see their entries under Staglieno War Cemetery, Italy), and Lieutenant 'Tojo' Wedderburn and Lance-corporal 'Tanky' Challenor. Moving off, Brunt and Dudgeon were later given shelter near Barbarasco Tresana by Pietro Massimo Petricioli, a peasant farmer who had already provided food and a roof for Wedderburn and Challenor, and who later stated:

> He [Dudgeon] stayed about six days, and during that time he seemed to be constantly watching German troop movements and he continually questioned me as to their numbers and identities. At about 2030 on a day which I believe to be the 24th September 1943 [sic?], the captain and the soldier left. Before leaving, he spoke to me and told me that his intention was to reach the main Sarzana-Parma road, and take a German car, even if it meant killing in its theft. He also said that he did not intend to wear any uniform other than his own, as this meant an added danger of being shot in the event of capture.

Having left his address with Petricioli, Dudgeon set off. He and Brunt were caught a few hours later at La Cisa Pass, Brian Lett, QC, stating in *The SAS in Tuscany 1943–45* that this was on the night of 30 September–1 October. The pair appears to have ambushed a car near Pontremoli wounding two German signallers, one of whom managed to raise the alarm. They were subsequently captured at a road-block at Cisa Pass, a war crimes team later noting:

> The [German] platoon stopped it, asked for their papers, and Captain Dudgeon with some speed of mind replied in German apparently that he had left his paybook at Italian Headquarters, and he was on his way to get it. Unfortunately for him, however, the sentry who was stopped him was brighter than most sentries usually are, and he noticed that there were bullet marks on the car [WO 235/525].

Leutnant Albert Rasshoffer of the field replacement battalion stationed at the pass later stated:

> When I went to the battalion orderly room shortly before 1500 hours 2nd Lt Schmitt [sic - Leutnant Victor Schmit] also appeared at the same time, and told me that he was going to the prisoners in order to inform them that they were to prepare for execution. When I came out of the battalion office again the captain was just being taken out onto the road so that he could be escorted to the place of execution which was about 400m away from the guard room. 2nd Lt Schmitt had told me that the English soldier, who was with the captain, was only taken to the place of execution after the captain had been shot. When the captain saw me go out of the battalion orderly room onto the road he turned round and asked me whether he would be shot from behind. I replied that he would be taken to the execution place and accompanied him to the next bend of the road from which the place could be seen. There he already saw that the execution squad was waiting for him. There I left the captain and returned to the quarters …
>
> Towards 5 o'clock in the afternoon, when I happened to meet him [Schmit], he told me the following: the captain had been asked at the place of execution for his last wish, whereupon he had asked to be allowed to kneel down to pray, which he did. He then rose and stood at the post [WO 309/99].

Rasshoffer also recalled: 'I remember that the captain and his companion were wearing coloured berets, on the front of which was a badge of two wings, and earth coloured battledress.' Former comrade Challenor later wrote:

> Group Two had a splendid commander in Capt Dudgeon. Just 23, a sturdy six-footer, he is remembered as something of a Captain Bligh character. Very positive in manner …
>
> He was nicknamed Toomai, after the elephant in Kipling's Sabu story. He was, in fact, built on that massive scale

and would charge through the undergrowth like an enraged bull. We loved him …

A German doctor in the group which killed Capt Dudgeon and Pct Brunt wrote to Capt Dudgeon's father after the war and spoke of both men's bravery and bearing at the time of their execution [*Mars & Minerva*, Spring 1982].

The correspondence referred to was written during May 1945 by former Leutnant Victor Schmit, a Luxemburger who was being held in prison for having served in the Wehrmacht:

By this letter I fulfil my word pledged to the bravest of English officers I met in all my life. This officer is your son, Captain Dudgeon, who fell for his country in Italy on October 3rd 1943. Before he died I had to promise him to give you information about the circumstances and the spot where he was buried.

I was at that time a platoon commander in the 65th Infantry Division of the Germans. My unit lay in the Passo della Cisa about 30 miles west of Parma on the road Parma-La Spezia.

About 0100 o'clock a.m. I was awakened by my men who told me they had captured two English soldiers driving in the direction of Parma, their clothes smeared with blood, in their bags they had about 40lbs of explosives. I went down and found in the guard room two English soldiers, one of them a captain. When I asked who they were they gave me their military cards. I reported to the Coy Comdr and later to the Division. The Divisional Officer on duty told me that half an hour ago a German Sgt and a Private driving towards La Spezia had been shot both and the car stolen.

This having happened several hundred miles behind the lines and the two soldiers carrying explosives they had to be treated as Freischarler [saboteurs] and would probably be shot.

The battalion commander who had arrived in the meantime tried to get out of your son anything about his purposes, where he was coming from etc etc, I being the interpreter. When the German insisted your son asked me to translate 'if you were my prisoner should you betray your country talking about your mission?'

Upon this my captain told him that probably he had to be shot by an existing order of the Führer. Captain Dudgeon took the news, answering something like this: 'All right I'll die for my country.'

When my captain had withdrawn I sat beside your son on the straw and we were speaking together all night long. He told me he knew little of Germany, that he had been during his holidays to Switzerland etc.

In the morning the Divisional Commander, General von Ziehlberg, informed the Bn [battalion] that he would come and see the English captain before he was to be shot. I told him (your son) that the German officers were scandalised that an enemy who had behaved in so brilliant a manner had to be shot but were mightless against an order of the Führer. To me the behaviour of the young officer of 23 years old had made such an impression that I couldn't help telling him when we were alone 'your country may be proud of you. If you were not my enemy I should ask you to be my friend.' Captain Dudgeon gave me his hand saying 'I thank you for telling me that.'

The interview with the General was quite resultless. At the end of it (all German officers were present) the General told me to translate to your son the following sentence: 'Sagan sie ihm dass ich vor Seined Haltung alle Achtung habe. Er wird, mit seinen Kameraden in einer Stunde erschossen' (Tell him that I have every respect for his bearing. He will, with his comrade, be shot in an hour).

Your son saluted militarily and left the General. He asked me to stay with him until it would be over. He gave me your address asking me to inform you. I gave him my word upon this. He asked for a protestant priest. Before he died he asked to die with free hands and open eyes. He knelt down for a short while praying with his hands in front of his face.

Then he got up and died like a hero. I was not allowed to give you notice of your son's death by way of the Red Cross as the enemy was to have no information whatever regarding the efficiency of the parachutists. So I had to wait and keep the address hidden up to now.

The grave of Captain Dudgeon is 200 metres south-west of the chapel on the Passo della Cisa going in the direction of La Spezia, 100 metres behind the last of the buildings.

I am yours sincerely,

Victor Schmit c/o Veuve Schmidt-Zoller, Hostert, pris de Luxembourg [TS 26/538].

Schmit escaped from prison the following year but was traced to Brussels in 1948 and subsequently corroborated his statement. From the available evidence the War Office ascertained that Dudgeon and Brunt were murdered some time between 1 and 3 October 1943, although it did not presume their deaths until September 1945. Sergeant John Baxendale of the Special Investigation Branch discovered that Dudgeon had been buried face down, that he was still in uniform despite his killers' claims, and identified his remains by his ID discs:

The photographs were taken and arranged at my request by my interpreter Luigi Lodi-Focardi, to disprove any German accusation at subsequent War Crimes Trials, that the Capt and Sergt [*sic*] were dressed in German uniform.

They also tear into shreds the post war wailings of the German officers of the unit concerned in the shooting. They are supposed to have held the Capt in high regard, paid tribute to his bravery, then dumped his body face down in his grave.

The remains of Dudgeon and Brunt were exhumed in August 1945 and reinterred in Florence War Cemetery side by side. Von Ziehlberg lost an arm in late November 1943 whilst fighting the British at the River Sangro. He went on to command the 28th Jäger Division on the Russian Front where he was promoted to generalleutnant and awarded the Knight's Cross. After the July 1944 plot to assassinate Hitler he was ordered to arrest his Staff Officer who had obtained the explosives used in the attempt. When von Ziehlberg gave him the option of committing suicide instead this man deserted to the Russians. Von Ziehlberg was initially charged with negligence but returned to his division. However, he was summoned to Berlin that October, put on trial and subsequently put in front of a firing squad on 2 February 1945. Those later convicted of war crimes in connection to the SAS murders were sentenced to just six months' imprisonment. Dudgeon was posthumously mentioned in despatches (*London Gazette* 28/08/45, Supplement 30/08/45).

Son of Lt-Colonel Christopher Robson Dudgeon, OBE, MC, of the RAMC, and of Alice Mary Dudgeon (née Pumphrey) of Headley, Hampshire. Age 23.
Captured at La Cisa after many special missions by sea and air. He was shot next morning. Perfecit
Grave 9.H.8. Also commemorated by Oundle School's Dudgeon Venture Award that is presented to pupils who undertake travel related adventure projects, on Headley's war memorial, on the Commando Memorial at the National Memorial Arboretum, and on a memorial close to where he and Brunt were murdered below Cisa Pass. This was organised by Brian Lett, QC, author of *SAS in Tuscany 1943–1945*, with full support and financial assistance from the Comune di Pontremoli.

CAPTAIN PHILIP HUGH PINCKNEY [100670] ROYAL ARTILLERY, SCOTS GUARDS, NO.12 COMMANDO, SMALL SCALE RAIDING FORCE, SBS AND 2ND SAS (A SQN)

Philip Pinckney was born on 7 April 1915 at Hidden Cottage near Hungerford in Berkshire as the fourth of six children. Educated at St Neot's Preparatory School and then Eton, he went up to Trinity College, Cambridge, in 1934. Having decided against further study he spent a year in London as a tea broker in his father's business before travelling in 1937 to India and Tibet where he devoted much of his time hunting. Returning to the London end of the business he visited Iceland before joining the 396th (Berkshire Yeomanry) Field Battery, Royal Artillery (TA), in August 1939 (service number 927551).

At the outbreak of war Pinckney was commissioned into the 145th Field Regiment (Berkshire Yeomanry) (*London Gazette* 03/10/39) but returned to the ranks the following February to serve with the 5th (Special Reserve) Battalion, Scots Guards, carrying out ski training in Chamonix. When this unit's proposed expedition to assist the Finns fight against the Russians was cancelled the battalion was disbanded, Pinckney being appointed Staff Captain (Traffic) at HQ British Troops in Ireland. Within days he had volunteered for No.12 Commando that was being raised in Northern Ireland. As a section commander in E Troop he put his men through a rigorous training regime before leading them on a Commando

course at Achnacarry. The reputation of his troop grew, as did that of his penchant for realistic training, a fact graphically illustrated whilst on an exercise the following April when Pinckney, now commanding E Troop, received a bayonet wound in his right arm. A note in his file states: 'Ref bayonet wound of 2/Lt Pinckney on Salisbury Race Course. The injury was inflicted by a sentry in the course of night operations against the Rifle Brigade and Home Guard … It occurred in the darkness and the sentry in question being in ignorance that an operation was being carried out.'

In July 1941 E Troop moved to Bursledon on the River Hamble in preparation for OPERATION CHESS, a recce of German coastal defences at Ambleteuse, south-west of Calais. On the night of the 27–28th Pinckney and his men subsequently crossed the Channel in an LCA (Landing Craft Assault) and went ashore to collect samples of German wire. When discovered the craft began taking accurate fire and Pinckney therefore assaulted the machine-gun position responsible so that an effective evacuation could be made. On the return trip he attended to the raid's only casualty, Commander Sir Geoffrey Congreve, DSO, who had sustained wounds that proved fatal. Back at home, mindful that each of his men had shared equal risk, he recommended that all of them be mentioned in despatches. None was awarded for what had proved to be a successful raid.

Having been promoted to captain in November 1941 Pinckney took part in OPERATION ANKLET, the December raid on the German-occupied Lofoten Islands off Norway. This was a new concept for the men of No.12 Commando who were used to operating in small groups. The whole unit had moved to Scapa Flow in preparation and crossed the North Sea in convoy. Pinckney's party subsequently landed on the island of Moskenesoy early on Boxing Day, spending two days destroying inter-island communications and installations, occupying the towns of Reine and Moskenes, and capturing the surprised German garrison and Norwegian Quislings. However, Pinckney was not at all happy leaving the local population to their fate and on the way back to the UK he threw a propaganda film taken of the raid, which showed their reaction to the Commando withdrawal, overboard. For this he was tried by a general court martial, found guilty, and was reprimanded. During the same period he was informed that his brother David (known as Colin), a Battle of Britain pilot, had been killed in action in the Far East.

Soon after returning to the UK Pinckney and his men were posted to Churston Manor near Brixham to support operations mounted by SOE's Small Scale Raiding Force. Lord Louis Mountbatten, Chief of Combined Operations, visited No.12 Commando in February 1942, later sending his thanks: 'In fact I was most impressed by Pinckney's troop. I hope that he was none the worse for being completely frozen up during the proceedings, and thought of him when you were regaling me with hot coffee!' (WO 218/41).

That June Pinckney hatched a plan with RAF test pilot Jeffrey Quill, whom he had met whilst at Bursledon, to capture one of the new FW190 German fighters that were taking their toll on Allied aircraft and about which little was known. Codenamed OPERATION AIRTHIEF, Pinckney suggested that the pair should paddle ashore from an MTB, make their way to one of the numerous Luftwaffe aerodromes in France, enter at first light whilst the aircraft engines were being run for inspection, kill the ground staff, and ensure Quill took off in the stolen fighter before Pinckney escaped on foot, presumably via Spain. The operation was cancelled when a German pilot landed an FW at RAF Pembrey in South Wales in error, having become disorientated during air-to-air combat. Quill later noted that Pinckney was 'outraged' at this turn of events (*Spitfire: A Test Pilot's Story*, by Jeffrey Quill, OBE, AFC, FRAeS).

On the night of 3–4 October 1942 Pinckney and four of his troop joined seven officers and men of the SSRF, including Major Geoffrey Appleyard, MC*, Captain Pat Dudgeon, and 2nd Lieutenant Andy Lassen, on OPERATION BASALT, a raid on the Channel island of Sark: having arrived off the island by MTB and rowed ashore the party quietly took five German prisoners from their billet at the Dixcart Hotel. After binding their hands they set off back to their awaiting boat. Pinckney's prisoner somehow broke free and ran back towards the hotel where other Germans were sleeping, shouting at the top of his voice. Pinckney shot him and in the ensuing panic another prisoner was killed, one escaped, and one left wounded, the party making a hasty withdrawal with their sole remaining charge. When the dead Germans were subsequently found bound and shot Hitler ordered that such raiders would be 'destroyed to the last man' (the 'Commando Order' - see Appendix 2 within the User's Guide for full details and entries for Appleyard, Dudgeon and Lassen under Cassino Memorial, Italy, this section and Argenta Gap War Cemetery, Italy, respectively).

In January 1943 Pinckney was permanently attached to No.62 Commando, the cover name for the Small Scale Raiding Force. However, the following month he and Lassen flew from the UK to 1st SAS in Egypt, the Regiment's War Diary noting that Pinckney was attached to the unit at Kabrit on 8 March and posted to the Special Boat Squadron on its formation on the 19th. Here he took command of No.3 Troop, receiving submarine training at Beirut during May before attending parachute course No.42 at Ramat David alongside men of the 11th Battalion, Parachute Regiment, later that month.

Posted to Philippeville in Algeria Pinckney soon rejoined fellow members of the SSRF in becoming founder members of 2nd SAS on 13 May 1943. On the night of 12–13 July he subsequently parachuted into Sicily for OPERATION CHESTNUT, his Albemarle aircraft then crashing with the loss of his squadron commander and friend, Appleyard. Pinckney's party, although dropped from only 400 feet onto rough, volcanic ground and a considerable distance from their intended DZ, cut telegraph wires and attacked railway lines before making contact with the advancing Allies. The post-operation report states: 'It is noteworthy that Captain Pinckney, who, alone of the officers landed in Sicily, had been able to benefit from previous training, was conspicuous in being able to collect the highest percentage of men and containers … Captain Pinckney was about to sabotage some enemy guns when the arrival of American troops caused them to withdraw' (WO 218/175). Having linked with US forces on the 28th he spent some time conducting recces in advance of them.

Pinckney was next tasked with disrupting rail movements north of Florence during OPERATION SPEEDWELL. Commanding Group 1 he and his men parachuted into a DZ south of Castiglione dei Pepoli and east of Lake Brasimone at 2315hrs on 7 September 1943. Dropped from approximately 7,000ft in strong winds the stick was widely dispersed, Corporal Pete Tomasso later stating that Pinckney landed 300 yards from him but out of sight around a hill. As per standard operating procedure he waited to be joined by his officer who did not appear. Lieutenant Tony Greville-Bell's post-operation report states: 'all appeared except Capt Pinckney, who was heard on the ground (by Cpl Tomasso), but failed to contact with No.2' (WO 218/177). The patrol waited for him without result, a truckload of Italian soldiers arriving to search the area the following morning. The result of this sweep remains unknown and Pinckney was later posted missing in action. A subsequent signal states:

Local source states he [Pinckney] dropped in vicinity Baigno [a village west of the lake but not far from the actual DZ] 7 Sept 43 shot same day by number of Carabiniers [sic – Carabinieri]. Buried in Baigno map ref 665093 sheet 98/111. Body dressed in American overalls and shorts. Reburied BE [British Empire] Military Cemetery Florence 22 Feb 45 [AIR 20/8844].

However, Captain Henry Parker of the SAS War Crimes Investigation Team noted in July 1946:

A body was later discovered at Bagni [sic – Baigno] which was later identified as that of Capt Pinckney. The body was clothed in overalls and two fighting knives were found in the pockets. It is alleged that the body had been shot in the back. In view of this it seems unlikely that Capt Pinckney was shot after surrendering … S/Com Topham informed Capt Parker in Sept 1945 that the case had been completely investigated by the FSS [Field Security Section] attached to 6 SA Arm Div [6th South African Armoured Division] who were in possession of all affidavits necessary. Attempts have been made to obtain these, but no answer has been received from the FSS Sect in question.

Despite this 2nd SAS' Casualty Report states: 'Cook [Parachutist 'Cookie' Cook of 2nd SAS who, having been captured in October 1943 during OPERATION JONQUIL, had escaped from a POW camp and was making his way towards Allied lines] met an Italian [Partisan] band [at] Lucieguano [sic – Lucignano] who said that a Capt Pinkie who belonged to "Special Service" had been with them until April or May [1944]' (WO 361/651). This report also notes that Cook had met the band at Monte San Savino, north of Perugia. Given the distance of the latter from where Pinckney's remains were found this is either incorrect or he was captured and taken back to the area of his drop zone to be murdered.

Pinckney had been concealing a back injury he sustained on OPERATION CHESTNUT, Sergeant Horace Stokes later stating:

> He jumped first and I second. I heard his old familiar bellow and saw him vanish through the aperture and I followed hard on his heels. It was a nice night and I could see everyone clearly – just before we landed I swung out of line and started to drift away and the captain yelled to me: 'Watch your drift, Stokes, watch your drift.' I hollered back: 'OK, sir.' I then saw him half wave his arm in acknowledgement. That's the last I saw of him as my drift continued, and a few seconds later I landed smack into a house in an Eyetie village. We all got together except for the captain, and against orders spent an hour and a half looking for him … There is no doubt at all in my mind that his back gave way when he landed [*Your Uncles*, by Roger and Anne Gresham-Cooke].

In June 1945 Pinckney's father wrote to Major Bill Kennedy Shaw, OBE, at SAS Brigade HQ:

> My informant, Sergeant Robinson, also told me that Philip cracked the base of his spine on his previous expedition when he landed in Sicily, and that he had given Sergeant Stokes a bottle of freezing mixture with which to treat him if he damaged it again. However, after waiting the prescribed time, Stokes and Robinson had to proceed on their job, and as we know now, Philip's grave was found in the civilian cemetery at Baigno under date 7th September, 1943 [the date subsequently recorded by the CWGC – WO 218/219].

Perhaps his character was best summarised by Quill:

> Philip was a man of rare and timeless character. One might have encountered him accompanying Drake's raid on the Spanish treasure trains in Panama, or steering a fireship amongst the Armada anchored off Calais, or with Shackleton on his epic open-boat journey from Antarctica to South Georgia. Equally he was in no way out of place in the Ritz bar; he was a man for all seasons … his exploits became a sort of legend wherever he went … Such men as Philip Pinckney appear from time to time in all ages, and seem set aside a little from their fellow men whether in peace or war [*Spitfire: A Test Pilot's Story*, by Jeffrey Quill].

Son of John Pinckney, CBE (awarded in 1920 for his contributions to the War Trade Intelligence Department during the First World War) and of Winifred Pinckney (née Hill) of Hungerford, Berkshire – Younger brother of Winifred, Elizabeth and Rosalie – Older brother of Diana and Flight Lieutenant David John Colin Pinckney, DFC, of No.67 Squadron, RAF (killed in action on 23 January 1942 and commemorated on the Singapore Memorial).
Age 28.
In proud and loving memory of a splendid life
Grave 2.E.17. Also commemorated on Hungerford's war memorial, at St Neot's Preparatory School, at Eton College, within St Peter's Church at Charlton St Peter and at Trinity College, Cambridge.

FOIANO DELLA CHIANA WAR CEMETERY

The majority of those buried here lost their lives in early July 1944 whilst facing fierce German resistance in the Chiana valley. Originally created by the British 4th Infantry Division further casualties were concentrated to this cemetery at a later date. It now contains 256 Commonwealth burials.

Foiano della Chiana lies 31 kilometres south of Arezzo in Eastern Tuscany. The cemetery is located north-east of the town in the direction of Arezzo, amongst fields on the Via del Porto. GPS co-ordinates: Latitude 43.26207, Longitude 11.82183

LIEUTENANT SIMON DENIS ST LEDGER <u>FLEMING</u> [166084] ROYAL ARTILLERY AND LRDG (M.2 PATROL, B SQN)

Simon Fleming was born on 6 January 1921 at Bangor Castle, the family home in Northern Ireland. Attending St Andrew's School in East Grinstead from 1928 to 1934 he went on to Harrow where he was in Rendalls House until 1939. Although he graduated from the Royal Military Academy, Woolwich, that summer he enlisted into the Royal Artillery in October at the Honourable Artillery Company barracks at Finsbury (service number 939488). During March 1940 he was posted to the 5th Field Training Regiment at Dover and four months later sent to 122 OCTU at Larkhill. He was subsequently appointed an emergency commission the following January and posted to the 27th Field Regiment at Melton Mowbray.

Embarking for the Middle East in December 1941 Fleming joined the RA Base Depot at the beginning of February 1942 before being posted to the 1st Regiment, Royal Horse Artillery. This joined the 4th Armoured Brigade and moved into Libya in late March. After Rommel's offensive it withdrew across the

border in June and took up positions on the Alamein Line. Fleming was subsequently wounded in his left thigh by a shell splinter on 16 July and after two months' convalescence, and having been promoted to lieutenant, he rejoined the RHA. That December the regiment moved into Palestine and in January 1943 Fleming's Commanding Officer recommended him for a regular commission: 'he has seen a year's service with the regiment in the Western Desert and done very well. Qualified at entrance exam to RMA Woolwich before the war. Strongly recommended. Well above the average.'

Fleming volunteered for the Long Range Desert Group that August, joining the unit at Azzib on the Palestinian coast on the 7th. Appointed commander of B Squadron's M.2 Patrol, he attended a parachute course the following March, almost certainly at Gioia del Colle in Italy. He subsequently deployed on OPERATION JUMP on 13 June 1944 having been tasked with reporting enemy traffic north of Rome before the Eighth Army's renewed offensive. Corporal Jim Swanson reported on his return through the lines:

At approx 0400hrs on 13 June 44 M.2 Patrol jumped from the A/Craft. Lt Fleming & L/Cpl Parry Jones going first and second Keeley, Locke, Murray, Kiley, Savage and myself. It was a very clear night and I could see nine or ten parachutes open in the air. The bulk of the patrol landed just in and around a cornfield. I landed about 200 yards from them. I walked in the general direction of the patrol and met Kiley. I asked if he had seen any of the others, he replied 'no'. We followed a track for about 50 yards and came on Keeley, Locke and Savage. They said that Murray & Parry Jones had gone to look for Lt Fleming. At that moment Murray & Parry Jones arrived back and said that they had seen no sign of Lt Fleming. They also reported that they had heard shots in the direction of where Lt Fleming had landed.

We found the wireless hamper quite close and I ordered Locke & Keeley to start unpacking. Savage was left with the parachutes about 20 yards away; Murray & Parry Jones went off again to see if they could locate Lt Fleming and the rest of the kit. Kiley and myself also went to search for Lt Fleming. We had been looking around for about two minutes when we met Murray & Parry Jones again. They had found one of the packs. Lt Fleming had previously arranged with us that we should stay where we dropped and then we would close in on him. I think he must have heard the shots and I am unable to say whether he was able to keep to his original plan.

I decided that as we had very little darkness left we had better unpack the kit and hope that Lt Fleming would turn up. We moved off to the kit and we heard people moving ahead. We crouched down and listened and someone called 'Hey Johnnie come here' in a foreign accent. We kept still and tried to spot them but could only hear them. Then I saw that there were quite a few people ahead of us (about four or five). They were 20 yards away. I ordered the others to get back to the W/T set and operators who were in a line of olive trees. We then moved off as quietly as possible but the corn caused a lot of 'rustle'. As soon as we moved they opened fire and Parry Jones dropped down. I did not see what happened to Kiley & Murray. The firing was only in the general direction of us and I am certain they could not see us.

The moon was still just up and it was an ideal night for the drop. Parry Jones and I then moved again but this brought another burst over our heads and Parry Jones dropped down again. I kept on moving until I got to the line of olive trees and took cover. I looked back for Parry Jones … I went down to the left to try and contact the signallers but the people who had got Parry Jones [captured him] were between me and the trees where the signallers had been left [WO 218/92].

B Squadron's in-house investigation later concluded:

On night 12th 13th June M.2 Patrol LRDG jumped by parachute behind enemy lines in the area of Pienza …

Shortly after landing the Germans opened up with light automatic fire and the patrol was forced to scatter. Lieut Fleming was never seen by any members of the patrol after he jumped from the plane …

On 2nd February 1945 the following [members of M.2] proceeded to the Pienza area … to try and find out if they knew anything of the fate of Lieut Fleming or Rfn Savage.

On 3rd February 1945 the party arrived at S.Quirico 0488 where they contacted the Carabinieri, who were on duty during the German occupation.

From Carabinieri records it was established that in the early hours of 13th June 44 a number of parachutists had landed near a German HQ a few miles from S.Quirico. One of these parachutists had been captured and one had been killed later in the day [Rifleman Bob Savage – see his entry overleaf]. Four days later (17 June 44) the body of another parachutist was found in a wheat field. This man's parachute had failed to open and the body had been badly smashed on hitting the ground. The Italians buried both bodies about 200yds from each other, in the area Abbadia 030893.

The party visited the area where the parachutists had dropped and the local farmer gave an identical account to that given by the Carabinieri. The farmer of Abbadia farm had himself buried the parachutist whose parachute had failed to open complete with parachute and harness.

The party visited the graves of the two parachutists and Sgt Swanson, Cpl Keeley and Rfn Kiley all recognised the area as being the identical place where they were dropped on 13th June 44.

David Lloyd Owen, former Commanding Officer of the LRDG, later wrote:

It was not for some time that we learnt of Simon Fleming's death. He was never seen alive again after Bob Maxwell had despatched him from the plane. His parachute failed to open. Simon had joined us soon after the fiasco of Leros. I was very fond of him, because he had great charm and a glorious sense of humour. He was essentially straight and open. He also had an impertinent disregard for authority, but was wise enough to know it was important to keep just on the right side of it. Outwardly he had a light-hearted and carefree attitude to life, but this façade hid a wisdom and intelligence unusual in one so young. We could ill afford to lose such a fine officer [*Providence Their Guide: The Long Range Desert Group 1940–45*].

The Times reported Fleming as missing, presumed killed in action, stating he was the only son of Major and The Hon. Mrs Harold Fleming (née Bingham), of Barton Manor, Great Barton, Bury St Edmonds:

Educated at Harrow he was a school monitor, Captain of his House at both cricket and football, and was awarded his 'flannels' in the Eton v Harrow match the year that war was declared. At the outbreak of war he enlisted in the Royal Artillery, and, having volunteered for the Middle East, served with the Eighth Army in North Africa, where he was wounded in July 1942. Back again he took part in the advance from El Alamein, and in 1943 was seconded to the Long Range Desert Group, with which he was killed in action while on special operations … as his corporal wrote, 'a grand chap, a good skipper, and a gentleman'.

Age 23.
No inscription.
Grave 1.G.1. Also commemorated within Great Barton Church, within Bangor Parish Church (St Comgall's), on Harrow School's war memorial and by Alexander Christie's 1946 portrait seen here.

RIFLEMAN ROBERT WILLIAM SAVAGE [6855058] KING'S ROYAL RIFLE CORPS
AND LRDG (M.2 PATROL, B SQN)

Bob Savage was born on 6 September 1920 at St Johns, Lancashire, later living at Kirkdale in Liverpool. He enlisted into the King's Royal Rifle Corps in August 1941 and was posted to the Rifle Depot at Winchester. By November 1942 he was serving with the 1st Motor Training Battalion but was re-posted to the 10th Battalion before disembarking in the Middle East in September 1943. Having volunteered for special duties he joined the Raiding Forces Holding Unit at the end of January 1944 and was taken on strength by the Long Range Desert Group on 22 March.

Savage's death is often attributed to a parachute malfunction during OPERATION JUMP south-east of Siena. However, Kip Kiley, former member of M.2 Patrol, later recalled:

The thirteenth of any month is a date on which it is unwise to tempt the fates. For M.2, caught up in a war, there was no choice.

In June 1944 four patrols of B Squadron were to be dropped behind the lines in Italy. Their two-fold objective was to create havoc and to feed back information to Eighth Army HQ.

The eight members of M.2, Simon Fleming (Skipper), Sgt Swanson, Cpl (Thumper) Murray, Mick Keeley, Parry Jones, Taffy Lock, Bob Savage and I boarded a DC [Dakota] at Salerno [Gaudo airfield]. Our destination was a point some 30 miles south of Siena.

Over Anzio one engine caught fire and we had to turn back. It was July 12th and the drop was put back twenty-four hours. All of us had a sense of foreboding about the postponement and although we tried to keep it to ourselves Bob Savage voiced the general view when he said 'this could mean serious trouble' …

The following night we took off again and had an uneventful flight. As we approached the dropping zone we took up 'Action Stations' and when the green light glowed we jumped.

We jumped – but we were 54 kilometres off target and came down right in the centre of the HQ of the German 1st Parachute Division. They were waiting for us and opened fire. Skipper Fleming was killed instantly [*sic* – see his entry within this section for details]. The rest of us managed to form up but we were unable to get to our equipment which was dropped separately.

The Germans sent dogs in to flush us out and Bob Savage – poor Bob who had feared the worst – shot one of the dogs and was himself then killed [LRDG Newsletter No.25 of 1969].

Savage was posted missing in action, later confirmed as killed in action, as of that day, 13 June 1944.

Son of Robert and Mary Savage of Lambeth Road, Kirkdale, Liverpool. Age 24.
Treasured memories of our son Bob. In our hearts always near. Mam and Dad
Grave 1.G.2.

MILAN WAR CEMETERY

On 24 April 1945 the Committee for National Liberation in Northern Italy ordered a general uprising, the city of Milan being liberated by local Partisans the following day. The American IV Corps reached it on 2 May, the same day that German forces in Italy surrendered. Thankfully there were few casualties in this closing scene of the Italian Campaign and the majority of the 417 Commonwealth burials found here, twenty-seven of which are unidentified, are of prisoners of war or airmen concentrated from the surrounding area after the end of hostilities. In addition, there are six war graves of foreign nationals.

The cemetery lies 7 kilometres west of the city centre, just north of the SS1 towards Novara. The entrance is located on the Via Cascina Bellaria, the plot being bordered by the Parco di Trenno. GPS co-ordinates: Latitude 45.48499, Longitude 9.10346

CORPORAL STANLEY **BOLDEN** MM [3316568] HIGHLAND LIGHT INFANTRY, CAMERON HIGHLANDERS, NO.12 COMMANDO, NO.6 COMMANDO AND 2ND SAS (3 SQN)

Known as 'Sammy' to his comrades, Stanley Bolden was born on 27 June 1920 at Eastwood in the Giffnock suburb of Glasgow. Having worked as a timber foreman and been a member of Glasgow University's OTC from 1937 to 1939 he enlisted into the Highland Light Infantry at the outbreak of war. Two weeks later he transferred to the Cameron Highlanders and was posted to the regiment's infantry training centre. Volunteering for special service he joined D Troop, No.12 Commando, at Netley near

Southampton on 3 March 1941. He was subsequently awarded the Military Medal on recommendation of Brigadier Bob Laycock for his actions during OPERATION CARTOON, an attack on a pyrite mine on the Norwegian island of Stord south of Bergen. A mixed force of No.12 Commando and the Norwegian Troop of No.10 (Inter-Allied) Commando put the mine out of action for a year, the men withdrawing in MTBs having also sunk shipping and captured prisoners and documents. Eight sailors and two Commandos, Bolden being one, were wounded and one man killed. The citation that accompanied his award notes:

> L/Cpl Bolden was with a detachment of the Special Service Brigade which landed at Sagvaag, Norway on the night of 23rd/24th January 1943.
>   Before the actual landing took place, L/Cpl Bolden was wounded in the side, but although in pain, he continued and carried out his duties ably and well. He personally led a party which cut the communications and was later in charge of a road block on the Savaav-Fitjar road. Throughout the operation he showed the good leadership and determination upon which a small raid of this nature depends for its success [*London Gazette* 23/03/43].

Having married Sergeant Andre Margaret Chapman of the ATS in Newton Mearns that April he was invested with the medal on 18 May. He transferred to No.6 Commando that October but was deprived of his lance-sergeant's appointment the following March for a minor offence. Six days later he was posted to No.9 Infantry Training Centre at Aberdeen as a corporal.

  Bolden volunteered to become a parachutist on 24 May 1944 and was posted to the Airborne Forces depot for training. From here he attended parachute course 121 at No.1 PTS Ringway during June and was noted as an: 'outstanding performer, keen and confident. Very good NCO. Morale A1.' He subsequently volunteered for 2nd SAS on 7 August from the Airborne Forces Holding Unit, reverting to the rank of private in order to do so. A few days later he was reappointed lance-corporal and after D-Day took part in OPERATION RUPERT in north-east France, Jack Paley, a fellow patrol member, later recalling:

> [We] came in on a resupply drop on 25th August [1944]. Some of the stick I remember! Lt Arnold, Sgt Guscott, Patterson, Drew, Fack, Paley, Cpl Sam Bolden MM. Our stick lost contact with Major Rooney's main party mainly because of heavy German activity. Also Lt Arnold was not present for a few days trying to locate Major Rooney. Consequently, with Sgt Guscott in command, we operated with what supplies that had dropped along with the local Maquis. Our stay was soon overrun by the American Army. At that time Lt Arnold had our stick work with the Americans. A Jeep was used for reconnaissance. Taking turns three would go out with the Jeep – patrol reconnoitring … I first met him [Bolden] while in Scotland training along with others. He certainly was a tough egg! [Personal correspondence, 2009 – see Sergeant Sid Guscott's entry within this section and that of Parachutist Eddy Drew under Choloy War Cemetery, France, Volume III].

The patrol returned to the UK via Arromanches on 10 September, Bolden being sent on an escape and evasion exercise in the New Forest with Guscott and Lieutenant Alex Robertson. He was promoted to corporal in November and by the end of the year had completed ski training in Scotland.

  By early January 1945 the whole of No.3 Squadron had been deployed to the Italy. Bolden subsequently parachuted into a DZ near Case Balocchi in the Emilia-Romagna region of Northern Italy on 9 March as a member of No.1 Stick to reinforce OPERATION TOMBOLA. The squadron commander, Major Roy Farran, DSO, MC**, then set about training and equipping a Partisan battalion consisting of Russian deserters from the Wehrmacht, communist Garibaldis, and a right-wing faction known as the Green Flame Brigade. On the night of 26–27 March the combined force attacked two villas at Albinea that housed the headquarters of the German 51 Mountain Corps. As Farran noted in his post-operation report insufficient time was allowed for those attacking the General's billet, the Villa Rossi, to reach their objective. By the time Bolden's party did so in the early hours of the 27th the alarm had been given, the area lit up, and the guards stood-to:

> The British ran through machine-gun fire, through the main gate, and killed the four sentries. The front door was

open. After fierce fighting the ground floor was taken but the Germans resisted furiously from the upper floors, firing and throwing grenades down a spiral staircase. Capt M. Lees [Mike Lees – an SOE officer] led one attack up the stairs which was repulsed with heavy casualties [WO 218/215].

Bolden was killed in action during this assault. Church records note that his body, and those of Riccomini and Guscott who had been killed soon after in the same attack, was delivered by the Germans to Albinea's priest that morning and buried in the north-east corner of the cemetery. The three were joined by Parachutist 'Robert Bruce' after he was killed in action the following month (see his entry below). Archives show that all four were exhumed and moved to Milan War Cemetery on 14 February 1946.

Son of Thomas and Annie Bolden of Eastwood Avenue, Giffnock, Renfrewshire – Husband of Andre Bolden of Havant, Hampshire.
Age 24.
Leaving him to sleep in trust till the resurrection day
Grave 5.A.6. Also commemorated on Giffnock's war memorial and on a plaque at the Villa Rossi, Albinea.

PRIVATE 'ROBERT BRUCE' – REAL NAME JUSTO BALERDI [ME/13041866] SPANISH FOREIGN LEGION, QUEEN'S ROYAL REGIMENT, NO.50 COMMANDO, PIONEER CORPS AND 2ND SAS (3 SQN)

Nicknamed 'Jose' by his comrades, Justo Balerdi was born on 25 July 1920 in Sestao, near the Port of Bilbao in northern Spain. Having worked as a telephonist he joined the Spanish Foreign Legion. However, this right-wing formation was not to his liking and he is believed to have fought on the Republican side during the Spanish Civil War, most likely taking refuge in France after Franco's victory. What is certain is that he enlisted into the British Army on 13 October 1940 at Fayid in Egypt. Although he joined the 2nd Battalion (Spanish Volunteers), Queen's Royal Regiment, he was immediately posted to No.50 (Middle East) Commando. A month later he was promoted to lance-corporal, embarking for Crete as a member of D Battalion, Layforce, late that November. He served there until March 1941, thus missing the German invasion and subsequent withdrawal during which many of his comrades were captured or killed.

Back in Egypt Layforce was disbanded, Balerdi being posted to the Middle East Commando Depot at Geneifa and relinquishing his lance-corporal's rank for a period of two months. For administrative reasons he nominally rejoined

161

the Queen's Royal Regiment as a corporal that October (service number 6100552) and transferred to the Pioneer Corps in January 1942 at Fayid (service number ME/13808212), all the while remaining with the Middle East Commando. He was still with this unit when it was retitled as the 1st Special Service Regiment in May 1942 but was posted to the Pioneer Corps Base Depot that October and spent much of the latter part of the year in hospital.

During August 1943 Balerdi was posted to Algeria where he joined 337 (Alien) Company before volunteering for 2nd SAS on 16 December. After the Regiment returned to the UK in March 1944 he qualified as a parachutist having attended course 111A at No.1 PTS Ringway in early April. 'John Coleman', one of a handful of Spaniards recruited into 2nd SAS, recalled that they were then summoned to the unit's cookhouse and asked if they wanted to change their names so as not to identify them as Spanish Republicans if captured. Balerdi chose the pseudonym 'Robert Bruce', whilst his friend Rafael Ramos chose 'Francis Drake'. All the names, except the latter, were approved by the War Office and Balerdi's service number therefore changed on the 29th of that month. 2nd SAS' nominal roll of that summer records him as being employed as a signaller. Ramos stuck to his given name rather than lower his standards.

In the early hours of 5 August 1944 Balerdi parachuted into a DZ near to Bailly-le-Franc in the Aube département of Northern France as a member of OPERATION RUPERT's replacement recce group (see multiple entries of the original party under Graffigny-Chemin Communal Cemetery, France, Volume III). The eight-man team, under the command of Lieutenant Duggie Laws, sponsored the DZ for two reinforcement sticks that dropped on the night of the 12–13th. On the 15th the party was in action and went on to receive further reinforcement drops and to organise Maquis attacks, Balerdi serving as Major 'Micky' Rooney's signaller when the latter moved north to recce the Argonne region on the 24th. Despite the radio set being put out of service during the Jeep journey when a member of the Maquis sat on it another was borrowed and the group was soon back in touch with SAS Headquarters. On the 29th it met the advancing Americans and went on to recce crossings of the rivers Meuse and Moselle for them, in the process shooting up a troop train, until withdrawing on 10 September. Balerdi is listed under his real name in the post-operation report.

By the beginning of January 1945 the whole of No.3 Squadron, in which Balerdi served within HQ Stick, had deployed to Italy. He subsequently parachuted into a DZ near Asta in the Emilia-Romagna region of northern Italy on 4 March as a member of Major Roy Farran's advance party for OPERATION TOMBOLA. During the drop his kit bag broke away smashing his carbine on impact. On the night of 26–27th he took part in the attack on the German 51 Mountain Corps HQ at Albinea (see Corporal Sammy Bolden's entry for details). He was killed in action on the night of 20–21 April 1945 near Torre Maino when two Jeeps attacked a German position, Farran later writing:

Tysoe [Lieutenant 'Ticker' Tysoe], who commanded the two Jeeps I lost in the plains, launched his daring attack from Torre Maino. He led his two Jeeps, guns blazing with tracer bullets, against a German supply dump protected by an anti-aircraft battery. His attack was successful but Bruce, one of our Spaniards, was struck in the head by a flying bullet and killed instantly. Tysoe destroyed a large truck and ammunition trailer and exploded a quantity of anti-aircraft shells. A German truck and many prisoners were taken. One of our Jeeps was damaged [*Winged Dagger: Adventures on Special Service*, by Roy Farran].

Balerdi's service record variously describes him as the son, then nephew, of Candida Balerdi of Tangiers, Morocco. Ramos, often reported to be his sibling, although more likely his best friend, was awarded the Military Medal for his actions during TOMBOLA and Farran wrote that he had approached him asking for leave to bury his 'brother'. Farran also noted that they had fought in the Spanish Civil War together and that they could both speak Italian. Lieutenant David Eyton-Jones, an officer on the operation, later recalled that he recovered Balerdi's remains from a field where local villagers had buried them in a shallow grave wrapped in a tarpaulin: 'his face was still locked in grim determination with eyes open and teeth bared' (personal interview, 2012). Eyton-Jones reinterred Balerdi next to the operation's other casualties, Corporal Sammy Bolden, MM, Lieutenant Jimmy Riccomini, MBE, MC, and Sergeant Sid Guscott in the north-east corner of the cemetery at Albinea recalling that the priest was very nervous as the Germans were still in control of the area. An Italian stonemason erected marble crosses above the graves, Church archives recording that all four were exhumed and moved to their present location in mid February 1946.

Age 24.

No inscription.

Grave 5.A.3.

SERGEANT SIDNEY ELLIOTT <u>GUSCOTT</u> [5627376] DEVONSHIRE REGIMENT AND 2ND SAS (3 SQN)

Known as Sid or 'Gus' to his comrades, Sidney Guscott was born on 10 April 1920 at Pennymoor near Tiverton in Devon. Although his father was a wheelwright his parents owned the village general store, his mother keeping this open at all hours. Having attended Bagdon School in Puddington, then Witheridge Senior School, he was employed as a chauffeur at Tidecombe House, marrying Doreen Mary Hartnell, whom he had met at a dance, in December 1938. The couple were keen ballroom dancers and won many competitions, only the outbreak of war preventing them from turning professional (personal interview with Ken Guscott, 2014).

Guscott enlisted into the Devonshire Regiment in June 1940 and after training was posted to the 12th Battalion, this being responsible for beach defences along the south Devon coastline. Promoted to lance-corporal that November his daughter, Pauline, was born the following month. Having qualified as a sniper in 1941 the battalion moved to coastal defence duties on the Isle of Wight in September 1942, his son, Ken, being born the following March.

During the summer of 1943 Guscott's battalion was designated as a glider-borne unit within 6th Airlanding Brigade, 6th Airborne Division, and relocated to Bulford in Wiltshire to retrain. Having been promoted to corporal he volunteered for 2nd SAS on 22 March 1944, attending parachute course 111A the following month at No.1 PTS Ringway. Here he was noted as being 'a good performer, cheerful and hardworking'. Advanced to sergeant in July he jumped into north-east France for OPERATION RUPERT the following month, tasked with disrupting enemy lines of communication east of the River Marne. However, the operation was mounted too late, its area being swiftly reached by the advancing Allies. Jack Paley of the same patrol recalled:

> [We] came in on a resupply drop on 25th August [1944]. Some of the stick I remember! Lt Arnold, Sgt Guscott, Patterson, Drew, Fack, Paley, Cpl Sam Bolden MM. Our stick lost contact with Major Rooney's main party mainly because of heavy German activity. Also Lt Arnold was not present for a few days trying to locate Major Rooney. Consequently, with Sgt Guscott in command, we operated with what supplies that had dropped along with the local Maquis. Our stay was soon over-run by the American Army …
>
> It was not long after that incident that Lt Arnold decided we make our way to the coast to Arromanches and back to England [they arrived in the UK on 9 September. Personal correspondence, 2009 – see Drew's entry under Choloy War Cemetery, France, Volume III, and Bolden's within this section].

Training for future operations continued, Guscott taking part in escape and evasion exercises in the New Forest with Bolden and Lieutenant Alex Robertson before moving to Scotland for ski training at the end of the year.

By the beginning of January 1945 the whole of No.3 Squadron had deployed to the Italy, Guscott, a sergeant in HQ Stick, commanding Operation Brake II that was summarised by the Regiment thus:

A party of three other ranks under Sergeant Guscott, infiltrated through the lines with WT [Wireless Transmission] set on 31 January, 1945 for reconnaissance work a little to the west of [Operation] Galia. Valuable information obtained of enemy locations and movements. Party is expected to infiltrate back shortly.

After twelve days the team, consisting of Guscott, Parachutist Rafael Ramos (an Italian-speaking Spaniard serving in 2nd SAS), Private Jock Simpson (a No.1 Special Force radio operator) and 'Tullio' (a rogue Partisan), reached the Rossano valley where it made contact with the Galia party on 11 February. Although tasked 'to speed up information from Galia area and render assistance on [Galia's] way home' new orders were received from HQ the following morning. The men were now to remain in the area and receive a reinforcement party. In the event this was not forthcoming and Guscott and Ramos subsequently marched eastwards over mountainous, occupied territory to join Major Roy Farran's Operation Tombola south of Reggio Emilia on 17 March.

Guscott died of wounds in the early hours of 27 March 1945 following an assault on the Villa Rossi, the German 51 Mountain Corps commander's residence in Albinea. Farran, the squadron commander, later wrote:

Alarm was given by a hooter on the roof and all the lights were switched on. The British [Lieutenant Jimmy Riccomini, Guscott and eight others including Lance-corporal Sammy Bolden, MM] ran through machine-gun fire, through the main gate, and killed the four sentries. The front door was open. After fierce fighting the ground floor was taken but the Germans resisted furiously from the upper floors, firing and throwing grenades down a spiral staircase [WO 218/215].

Guscott and Riccomini attempted to fight their way up the stairs. When his officer was killed Guscott dragged his body down and charged back up only to be mortally wounded (see Riccomini's entry opposite). Farran later wrote to Guscott's parents:

I had a great regard for Sergt. Guscott who was the best sergeant in my Squadron, and would have been a Sergt. Major after the operation … We formed a guerrilla battalion of Russians, Italians and British and I wanted a good NCO to act as RSM so I ordered Sergt. Guscott to join me in our area south of Reggio. He walked across the mountains and covered 60 miles in three days in awful country. He organised all the equipping and training of this battalion, which eventually played a big part in smashing the Germans in Italy … He was a fine, brave boy, and I know he is in good company. One day, when I am considered good enough, I hope to see him in the place to which only the best soldiers go.

Lieutenant-Colonel Brian Franks, DSO, MC, the Commanding Officer of 2nd SAS, also wrote to Guscott's parents:

Sergt. Guscott did a magnificent job, and was at all times in action an inspiration to all ranks with him. It is wretched that he should have been killed such a short time before the cessation of hostilities, but I can assure you that his death was not in vain, as the detachment of this Regiment played a big part towards bringing about the final surrender of the German armies in Italy.

Church records note that the Germans delivered the bodies of Guscott, Riccomini and Bolden to Albinea's priest that morning. They were buried without delay in the north-east corner of the cemetery and joined by Parachutist 'Robert Bruce' after he was killed in action the following month. All four were exhumed and moved to their current location in mid February 1946.

Son of Frederick and Molly Guscott (née Elliott) of Cruwys Morchard – Husband of Doreen Guscott of Rices Buildings, St Peters Street, Tiverton – Father of Pauline and Ken Guscott – Younger brother of Colonel Jack Guscott

of the Royal Army Ordnance Corps (served in WWII and later wounded in Korea) and of Corporal Fred Guscott of the Royal Air Force Volunteer Reserve (later a councillor at Exeter).
Age 24.
No inscription.
Grave 6.A.7. Also commemorated on a plaque at the Villa Rossi in Albinea, on Cruwys Morchard's war memorial plaque, on his parents' grave and on Tiverton's Royal British Legion wall of remembrance.

LIEUTENANT JAMES ARTHUR RICCOMINI MBE, MC [137803] ROYAL ARMY SERVICE CORPS, SCOTS GUARDS, SOE AND 2ND SAS (3 SQN)

Jimmy Riccomini was born on 4 July 1917 in the parish of St John's, Leeds, as the eldest of five sons. When his family moved south from Nottingham he remained behind to finish his schooling at Henry Mellish Grammar School, Highbury Vale. Around the age of 18 he joined the family at Maidstone in Kent and, having attended Medway Technical College at Gillingham, found employment as a civil engineer at the Ministry of Transport. Whilst in post he joined the 507 Ammunition Company, Royal Army Service Corps (TA), at Maidstone in April 1939 (service number T/77437). He was subsequently mobilised at the end of August with war on the horizon. At the outbreak of hostilities the following month he married Joyce Mary Rule whilst a corporal, soon after being appointed lance-sergeant and posted to No.2 Depot Battalion at Bulford.

On 13 February 1940 Riccomini volunteered for 'The Snowballers', the 5th (Special Reserve) Battalion, Scots Guards, which had been formed to assist the Finns in their fight against the Russians. He relinquished his rank and became a guardsman in order to do so. After a period in France ski training with the 199th Battalion of the Chasseurs Alpins at Chamonix, Finland signed the Moscow Peace Treaty and the battalion disbanded, Riccomini arriving back at Bulford on 30 March. A month later he reported to the RASC's Officer Producing Centre at Ramsgate and although his course was interrupted by ten days service with the BEF in France that May he was soon commissioned (*London Gazette* 22/06/40).

Having been posted to No.5 (Special) Lines of Communication (Railhead) Company in Gloucester, Riccomini disembarked in Palestine where he served until moving to Habbaniyah in Iraq that October. Arriving in Egypt on Christmas Day 1940 he was captured in Libya in June 1941 whilst on a recce as Liaison Officer to the Polish Army Service Corps. He attempted escape a number of times and as a result was imprisoned at PG.5 at Gavi, the infamous 'bad boys' camp often referred to as the Italian equivalent of Colditz. His wife's complaints about his treatment there prompted questions being raised in Parliament.

After the Italian armistice of September 1943 the Germans emptied Gavi and Riccomini again attempted escape by hiding with other officers under floorboards. He recorded this event, and others of the period from 13 September to 13 December 1943, in his diary; 'I personally had never needed a smoke so badly in my life.' The citation that accompanied the award of his subsequent MBE takes up the narrative:

Lieut Riccomini was captured at Halfaya Pass on 16 Jun 41 and was imprisoned in Camp 5 at the time of the Italian armistice.

This camp was taken over by the Germans on 9 Sep 43 and the main body moved to Germany on 13 Sep 43. With several other officers, Lieut Riccomini hid in the camp while the move took place, but was discovered three days later and moved by bus to Mantova. On the evening of 18 Sep 43, he and sixteen other officers were locked in a cattle truck for transportation to Germany. Immediately the train started they began to cut a hole in the back of the truck; this was completed in about three hours and they drew lots as to who should jump first. Lieut Riccomini and another officer jumped from the moving train just north of Roverto [sic – Rovereto] at about 0430hrs on 19 Sep 43 and walked south-east making for Yugoslavia. A week later they joined a Partisan band led by an Italian ex officer.

Lieut Riccomini and his companion remained with this band until Jan 44, helping to organise resistance, getting together dumps of ammunition, and obtaining intelligence reports. The band was broken up by Germans, and these officers then organised a route to Switzerland by which they themselves and several other ex-P/W in the area crossed the Swiss border on 11 Jan 44 [*London Gazette* 01/03/45, WO 373/63].

Riccomini and Lieutenant 'Pete' Peterson of the Australian Imperial Force, the other officer mentioned in the citation, had obtained false identity papers but were eventually betrayed. However, although the family that sheltered them was questioned carefully, their possessions confiscated and house ransacked, they said nothing and were released, the officers remaining at liberty as a result. Riccomini noted in his own journal:

> From that time on, our operations started. First we did small jobs like the shooting of an obnoxious fascist official here, followed by the removal of a proved spy from a village 20 or 30 kilometres away. We operated over a wide area, moving quickly, striking suddenly, and instantly disappearing, in a way that we could not be connected with any particular village or district.
>
> We had our own doctors who could be trusted to look after our wounded, and it was essential that, should any of the band be killed, the bodies be removed before they could be identified.

The group went on to destroy a railway bridge over a river near a village Riccomini recorded as Cavello. Research pinpoints this as Carollo, south-east of Thiene: wearing fascist uniforms the men travelled by train from Schio before marching to the village magazine on what is now the Thiene airstrip, this presumably holding stock used for local quarries. Here they helped themselves to the necessary explosives before incapacitating the guards at the bridge and setting their charges. Warned by La Lena, the daughter of their benefactors, that a troop train had arrived at the nearby station Riccomini waited until this was crossing and threw himself to the ground, trying to shelter the girl as he blew the bridge from only a short distance away:

> There was an almighty explosion, a whooping crescendo of sound, followed by a screaming of metal and indescribable splintering crashes. The world was flooded with scarlet followed by a pall of thick blackness. The ground shook, and I had the absurd notion that we were being shelled. Jenkinson [a Royal Engineer former POW] pulled me to my feet; I was deaf and stupid. We started to run [towards awaiting getaway vehicles] and my hearing returned. There were agonised screams, a babble of voices and movement of feet on the ballast of the tracks.
>
> We stumbled, sobbing for breath over the fields, on to the road and back towards the town. Somewhere behind us and to our right came the crack of rifles and the rattle of automatic weapons. At the crossroads were two trucks, engines revving …

At some point during the action La Lena had been fatally wounded. She bled to death in Riccomini's arms during the return journey without having said anything or without him realising in his shocked condition. Seven other Partisans were killed in the attack, Riccomini and Peterson eventually making their way over into neutral Switzerland at the beginning of 1944.

Riccomini was subsequently recruited by the Special Operations Executive as 'an agent in the field' and allotted the designation '24267'. He crossed into France on

26 August 1944, joining the Haute Savoie Maquis at Aiguebelle near Grenoble in order to recce positions of the 90th Panzer Grenadier Division in the Isere Valley. Having liaised with the US Seventh Army's artillery, resulting in the shelling of these troops, and advised the Maquis how to defend against counter attacks, he re-crossed into Switzerland on 20 September. His SOE personnel file states: 'Lieuts Riccomini and Easton [who later also joined No.3 Squadron, 2nd SAS] arrived in Allied lines in France on 26 Sep 44 and should be S.O.S w.e.f. [struck off strength with effect from] that date. It is understood that they have been repatriated to UK' (HS 9/1252/5). On returning to England on 9 October Riccomini noted in his report:

> Although disappointed with the outcome of this mission, I would welcome an opportunity of further work of this nature. I spent four months trying to organise Partisan groups of Italians in the hills of Venezia, with Lt H A Peterson, AIF, from September 1943 to January 1944. I speak and write both German and Italian, though not sufficiently well to be taken for a native in either language. May I also request an interview with Lt Col William Stirling, SAS. I was with his brother Lt Col David Stirling in PG.5 Gavi, Italy, and was recommended by him for appointment to the SAS Regiment.

Although granted a period of indefinite sick leave to recover from his efforts Riccomini was now keen to pursue a permanent career in the army and volunteered for 2nd SAS on 18 December on a month's probation. The Regiment was so eager to have him that it claimed that he had served with them in North Africa before capture in order to increase the likelihood of his posting. The following day he flew to Italy with elements of No.3 Squadron on the proviso that if taken prisoner again he would pose as the fictitious 'Lieutenant Richard Hood'.

On the afternoon of 27 December 1944 Riccomini parachuted into the Rossano valley of northern Tuscany for OPERATION GALIA. Chris Leng of SOE, who accompanied the party, later wrote:

> As there was some doubt as to whether the reception would be in enemy hands, Jim [Riccomini], a wireless operator, and myself were dropped ahead of the rest, with a Verey Light pistol … This was Jim's first parachute descent and it must have taken a lot of courage to make a first jump an operational one [he was caught up in a tree on landing near Peretola] … During this period I met Jim from time to time, always a happy experience – as nothing ever got him down and his great sense of humour was a real tonic in hard times. Living in a rough shelter in what is now called a ski resort, on a diet of maize flour in the middle of winter can be called hard times.

Riccomini was awarded an immediate Military Cross as a result of this operation. The citation, written by his commander, Captain Bob Walker-Brown, MBE, states:

> This officer dropped behind enemy lines by parachute on the 27th Dec 44 as 2nd i/c of an SAS troop. On the 11th Jan 45 he was commanding a detachment which ambushed a German column on the Genoa-Spezia road near Boona del Pignone. One lorry was completely destroyed and a staff car was riddled with machine-gun fire. Thirty casualties in killed and wounded were inflicted on the Germans. The success of this operation was entirely due to this officer's personal skill and courage. He directed the fire attack on the column in full view of the enemy, completely ignoring fire returned by them. On the 19th Jan 45 he again ambushed two vehicles on the road Pontremoli-Spezia as they were crossing a bridge at point 742363, sheet 95, Italy 1/100,000. One truck was destroyed and a number of casualties were inflicted on the Germans. When 10,000 enemy troops were conducting a 'rostrellimento' [a sweep] against the SAS contingent on several occasions it was entirely this officer's skill and personal courage which prevented the enemy from capturing or killing personnel under his command. Despite a badly poisoned foot, in Arctic conditions of gales, sleet and snow, he made his way through deep snow drifts with his men, never failing to carry out any task allotted to him.
>
> Throughout the operations lasting from 27 December 44 to 20 February 45 he was a personal source of inspiration and encouragement to his men. His conduct could not have been excelled in any way being far above the normal call of duty [*London Gazette* 01/03/45, WO 373/13].

The men subsequently walked from the Rossano valley back to Allied lines, which they crossed on 20 February 1945. Despite being entitled to rest Riccomini volunteered to be parachuted into OPERATION TOMBOLA on 10 March. He was killed in action in the early hours of the 27th whilst assaulting the Villa Rossi, the residence of the German 51 Mountain Corps commander in Albinea. Major Roy Farran, DSO, MC**, wrote in the post-operation report: 'Riccomini killed four sentries through the iron railing with his Tommy gun and then rushed the door … After fierce fighting the ground floor was taken but the Germans resisted furiously from the upper floors, firing and throwing grenades down a spiral staircase' (WO 218/215). Riccomini was killed whilst fighting his way up this staircase. Farran described him thus: 'perhaps the most outstanding officer of the Troop … I required him again for his knowledge of Italian, good interpreters being rare. He received the news with something akin to delight' (*Winged Dagger: Adventures on Special Service*, by Roy Farran). Meanwhile, Walker-Brown wrote to Riccomini's wife that May:

> I am most sad to have to tell you that Ricci was killed in action in Italy on the 27th March 1945. 'Ricci' as we called him, died a rare and gallant death at the head of his men during one of the most dangerous and effective attacks ever undertaken by this Regiment against the enemy. Ricci was a very great friend of mine having both been POW and as an officer was the best in the Squadron. The men would have done anything for him [Riccomini family collection].

Church records state that on the morning of the 27th the Germans delivered the bodies of Riccomini, Corporal Sammy Bolden, MM, and Sergeant Sid Guscott to the priest at Albinea. They were buried without delay in the north-east corner of the cemetery and were joined by Parachutist 'Robert Bruce' when he was killed in action the following month. All four were exhumed and moved to their current location in February 1946 (see Bruce's entry within this section).

Son of James (a First World War veteran of the 28th (County of London) Battalion, London Regiment (Artists Rifles), and Royal Engineers) and Kate Riccomini (née Lunn) of Bower Mount Road, Maidstone, Kent – Husband of Joyce Riccomini of Knowle Road, Maidstone, who was presented his medals by His Majesty King George VI in July 1946 – Older brother of Robert, Geoffrey, Lieutenant Desmond Riccomini, RIASC (killed in a Dakota crash on 30 April 1946 and buried at Rawalpindi War Cemetery), and of Basil Riccomini who served with the Royal Tank Regiment before transferring to the Glider Pilot Regiment and serving in Korea. He later migrated to the USA attaining the rank of colonel in the US Air Force.
Age 27.
Bitter and brief would I have my end. It were better that way, Lord
Grave 5.A.4. Also commemorated on a plaque at the Villa Rossi in Albinea.

PADUA WAR CEMETERY

This cemetery contains 517 Commonwealth burials of the Second World War, thirty-two of them being unidentified. In addition, there are four non-Commonwealth graves and one non-war burial.

The cemetery is located 4 kilometres west of Padua on Via della Biscia, near the junction of the SS11 and the SR47. GPS co-ordinates: Latitude 45.42165, Longitude 11.83996

CORPORAL JOSEPH PATRICK <u>CROWLEY</u> [3710217] KING'S OWN ROYAL REGIMENT, NO.12 COMMANDO ATT SMALL SCALE RAIDING FORCE, NO.6 COMMANDO AND 2ND SAS (3 SQN)

Known to his comrades as Joe or Dave, Joseph Crowley was born to Irish parents on 15 January 1918 in the parish of Mount Carmel, Salford. After his mother died he enlisted into the King's Own Royal Regiment in June 1932 at the age of 14 and was initially posted to the 2nd Battalion with the rank of boy. A year later he was re-posted to the 1st Battalion serving with them in Egypt and India, his conduct report describing him as: 'a very good instrumentalist who has been registered for Neller Hall [the Army School of Music in west London]. A very clean and intelligent boy, who has nice manners and takes pride in himself.' He was subsequently appointed bandsman soon after turning 18.

The outbreak of war found Crowley still serving in India, although he returned to the UK at the beginning of 1940. Having married Emily May Lynch at St Peter's Church in Lancaster in February 1941 he was posted to his regiment's infantry training centre as a lance-corporal. Late that month he volunteered for special service and having attended the Special Training Centre at Lochailort was posted to 4 Troop, No.12 Commando, which often carried out cross-Channel raids in support of SOE's Small Scale Raiding Force. On Boxing Day he took part in OPERATION ANKLET, a joint British and Norwegian raid on the Lofoten Islands designed to divert the enemy's attention from OPERATION ARCHERY that was being mounted concurrently at Vaagso. ANKLET's force of 300 withdrew after two days having, without loss, occupied three towns, rounded up numerous Germans and Quislings, and destroyed and captured equipment, including an Enigma machine.

The following January Crowley's first son, David, was born. Although based at Dunoon on the Firth of Clyde during March he was at Blandford in Dorset by November supporting No.62 Commando, the cover name for the SSRF that was billeted at the nearby Anderson Manor. He subsequently took part in OPERATION FAHRENHEIT, his ten-man combined force raiding a cliff-top German signals station at the Pointe de Plouézec in Brittany on the night of the 11–12 November. Although the intention was to take prisoners surprise was lost, the party being forced to withdraw down the cliff face to their awaiting boat having come under heavy fire, despite killing four of the enemy.

At the end of April 1943 Crowley attended parachute training at No.1 PTS Ringway where he made nine descents to qualify for his wings. That autumn he was appointed lance-corporal and in October, as No.12 Commando was disbanding, he was posted to No.6 Commando at Hove, spending a few days at Ringway for further parachute training. In April 1944, two months after his second son, Geoffrey, was born, he was promoted to corporal and on 6 June landed on Sword Beach on the dawn of D-Day: having taken Ouistreham the Commando reached Major John Howard's D Company, Oxford and Buckinghamshire Light Infantry, which had captured what is now known as Pegasus Bridge over the Caen Canal. It then mounted a joint attack with the 9th Parachute Battalion on the village of La Plein before digging in and settling into defensive duties. Crowley was wounded during fierce fighting on the 12th when a phosphorous shell burst close to his face. This left him with burns to his hands and with photophobia. Evacuated to the UK he was admitted to St Richard's Hospital in Chichester and on discharge was posted to the Commando Holding Unit.

Having briefly returned to No.6 Commando Crowley was posted to 2nd SAS at Colchester at the beginning of November for a course. He transferred to the Regiment later that month. Jack Paley, a former comrade, later recalled that Crowley, who had joined No.3 Squadron's HQ Stick as a corporal, was a talented boxer. By the beginning of January 1945 both men had deployed to Italy along with the rest of the squadron.

Crowley was taken prisoner during OPERATION COLD COMFORT, an attempt to block the route to the Brenner Pass by initiating a landslide near Ceraino. Some accounts note that he was wounded when captured. SS-Oberscharführer Albert Storz, one of those later accused of his murder, stated Crowley had been 'examined repeatedly at our headquarters.' He was shot alongside Major Ross Littlejohn, MC, and 2nd Lieutenant Charles Parker, USAAF, at Bolzano on 19 March 1945 (see Littlejohn's entry opposite for full details and discrepancy over dates).

An unattributed newspaper clipping states that on 15 January 1946 Storz, SS-Sturmbannführer August Schiffer and SS-Sturmführer Heinz Andergassen were sentenced to death for the murder of Littlejohn and Crowley: 'An American officer who gave evidence said he was in a cell in which the previous prisoner, a British corporal, had scratched his name and regiment and the word "tortured" on the wall, with a date' (WO 208/4670). The three Germans were hanged at Livorno that July.

Son of William Joseph Crowley of Ashton Street, Manchester – Husband of Emily Crowley of Southdean Road, Liverpool – Father of David and Geoffrey Crowley – Younger brother of William and Christopher Crowley.
Age 27.
Very much loved and sadly missed. At rest
Grave 3.F.5.

Major Ross Robertson **LITTLEJOHN** MC [197229] Royal Fusiliers, Black Watch, No.12 Commando att Small Scale Raiding Force, No.6 Commando, No.4 Commando, No.2 Commando and 2nd SAS (3 Sqn)

Ross Littlejohn was born to British parents in Melbourne, Australia, on 1 October 1921. He was educated locally at Scotch College between 1928 and 1930 and 1931 and 1933, and at Rose Hill Preparatory School at Banstead, Surrey, in the intervening year and again from 1934 to 1935. Having attended Uppingham School between 1935 and 1940, where he was a member of the OTC, he went up to New College, Oxford. In March 1941, whilst staying with his mother in Dunfermline, he enlisted into the Royal Fusiliers but as a university student was immediately transferred to the Army Reserve (service number 6477330). However, ten days later he was embodied and posted to 164 OCTU at Barmouth where he received excellent reports before being commissioned into the Black Watch (The Royal Highland Regiment) that July.

Posted to the 7th Battalion Littlejohn volunteered for special service in November 1941, subsequently joining 4 Troop, No.12 Commando, which often supported SOE's Small Scale Raiding Force in cross-Channel operations. The Black Watch attempted to poach him back during January 1943 but the commander of the Special Service Brigade intervened making short thrift of their claims. Littlejohn may have been one of those involved in Operation Cartoon later that month when fifty-three members of No.12 and ten members of No.10 Commando destroyed a pyrite mine on the Norwegian island of Stord. What is certain is that he continued to serve with the Commando until its disbandment in October 1943 when he was briefly posted as an instructor to the School of Infantry's Night Fighting Wing. Having joined No.6 Commando *The Times* reported his marriage on 20 December at Dunfermline Abbey to Section Officer Honora Edgeworth Butler of the Women's Auxiliary Air Force.

On 31 January 1944 Littlejohn was promoted to captain and transferred to No.4 Commando, moving with them to Bexhill at the end of February. The following month the whole Commando took part in amphibious exercises, firstly on the Dorset coast and then in the Moray Firth. At the end of May it moved to Southampton where it was sealed within Camp 18 for detailed briefing of its D-Day role. Littlejohn subsequently landed in the first wave on Sword Beach in the early hours of 6 June, taking part in the capture of Ouistreham that day. After a period of intense fighting that saw casualties within No.4 rise to an estimated 50% by D+4, a policy of night fighting patrols was instigated. Littlejohn was recommended for the DSO, although awarded a Military Cross, after one such venture:

Lt Littlejohn went out at 1430hrs 19 June by way of La Grande Ferme du Buisson with the idea of crossing the enemy lines along the Longuemare-Gonneville Rd …

At about 1930 hours 20 June, Lt Littlejohn decided to try and work his way between two of the posts and they crawled forward to the road, reaching it about 2130hrs. On raising his head to observe, Lt Littlejohn found himself looking straight down the muzzle of an enemy rifle. It had been decided that in the event of surprise being lost, grenades would be thrown and the party would separate and make a dash for it.

The enemy was apparently more surprised than Littlejohn. At any rate his reactions were slower. Lt Littlejohn threw a grenade into the pit and dashed back, making for the cover of the gully, but was shot and badly wounded in the leg on the way. Sgt Thompson reached the shelter of a bomb crater in the open field.

Lt Littlejohn reached the gully however, and though wounded remained there observing, intending to make another attempt to penetrate further south, but was too badly injured to do so.

A search party about an hour later of about 10 men came out from enemy lines. One fired at Lt Littlejohn from 2 yards range and missed him. Littlejohn unable to move shammed 'dead'.

The search party stripped him of his pistol and amn [ammunition] but made no attempt to search him for maps or papers.

They checked that he was 'dead' by turning him over with a kick and prodded him in the face with a bayonet. Littlejohn still made no move in spite of great pain, and eventually the Germans moved off leaving him for 'dead'.

Sgt Thompson is presumed to be a prisoner as Lt Littlejohn heard the Germans who were searching him say 'der einer ist gefangen der anderer ist tot' ['one is a prisoner the other is dead'].

Lt Littlejohn still had not the strength to move and about forty minutes later a second looting party came out, who dragged him out of the gully into the open ground on the east of the stream where they removed his boots, compass, his watch and field glasses, but again did not take his papers or his map. Lt Littlejohn still made no move and pretended to be 'dead'.

By darkness Lt Littlejohn mustered sufficient strength to move, and in spite of his wounded leg, crawled back over 2,000 yards to No.47 Commando's lines, where he was picked up in an exhausted condition at 0530hrs 21 June 44 [WO 373/48, *London Gazette* 29/08/44, Supplement 31/08/44].

Littlejohn, left with a close-range entry wound in his left buttock and large exit wound in his left femoral triangle, made a surprisingly rapid recovery. Less than three months later he was telling a medical board that he was 'quite well and can walk 22 miles over the hills without difficulty'. He was reclassified as 'A' Category fit as a result. Writing to 2nd SAS' CO, Lt-Colonel Brian Franks, DSO, MC, the Regiment's Administration Officer, Major The Hon. John Bingham, noted: 'Littlejohn (MC) who was with Mickey [Rooney] in a Commando has come to us. I should say he's very good indeed.' Having volunteered for 2nd SAS whilst at the Commando Holding Camp at Wrexham Littlejohn would have been called to the Regiment sooner had Franks not been deployed on OPERATION LOYTON at the time. As it was, Littlejohn was posted to No.3 Squadron on 24 November 1944, taking part in winter survival training near Loch Rannoch. 2nd SAS' Medical Officer, Captain Joe Patterson, later recalled: 'I remember Ross as a rather serious lad whose quiet modesty and obvious resolution marked him as a most exceptional young officer'. By early January 1945 the whole of No.3 Squadron had been redeployed to Italy, Littlejohn going with them as a troop commander. One of his men, 'Charlie' Radford, later recalled:

We were all impressed by his quiet, self-deprecating, yet confident manner and his easy sense of humour. Though not more than 5'8" in height, he looked strong and fit: on one of his cheeks was a noticeable scar … the group of us who were detailed for the forthcoming Operation Cold Comfort felt no qualms about his leadership when he informed us that he would be commanding it.

Having volunteered for future operations in the Far East, Littlejohn was promoted to major just before parachuting into COLD COMFORT. This was an attempt to block the road towards the Brenner Pass, the main supply route, and likely line of retreat, of German forces. A railway engineer had suggested this might be achieved by blowing an outcrop of rock and inititiating a landslide near Ceraino. Littlejohn and his advance party, consisting of Corporal 'Dave' Crowley, Corporal Clarke and 'Conti', an Italian guide on loan from Special Forces, were therefore dropped at Monte Pau near Trento on the night of 13-14 February 1945. Here they met SOE British Liaison Officers Major John Wilkinson, Captain John Orr-Ewing and Captain Chris Woods, the party eventually reaching Wilkinson's HQ at Laghi after three nights travel. From the 22nd the area was subject to a 'rastrellamento', a German sweep, seemingly due to the recent frequency of drops highlighting the presence of an SOE Mission. Despite this, at 0300hrs on the 25th, Littlejohn and his team, accompanied by Partisans, set off from the village of Posina towards Pasubio, that night's DZ for the main SAS party. Reports from that moment onwards vary, although it appears that they encountered an enemy patrol and were perhaps separated. On the 3rd one of the men sent a final message recommending that the 'main party should not be dropped as conditions for operating for the present were too difficult, both on account of the extreme cold, and strong enemy guards on supply routes and the party's location being compromised' (WO 205/93). It was too late as ten members of the reinforcement team had been parachuted into the area, more than 20 kilometres away from the DZ, on the night of 25–26 February. Partisans subsequently reported that Littlejohn's group had run into a ski patrol, variously described as being made up of Germans or White Russians, at Rifugio Lancia on top of Monte Pasubio on 7 March and that Littlejohn and Crowley, 'last seen engaging the enemy at a distance of 30 yards near Griso', had been captured. Whilst Clarke and Conti were able to escape Wilkinson received information that two British soldiers wearing red berets were seen at the SS headquarters at Rovereto (WO 311/350).

Littlejohn and Crowley were transferred to Gries Concentration Camp on the southern outskirts of Bolzano where they were seen by Corporal 'Stretch' Silsby, a captured member of an American OSS

Operational Group. Silsby was subsequently informed by the local SD and Gestapo commander, SS-Sturmbannführer August Schiffer, that the pair had been removed to a 'jumper's camp' in Germany. In fact, they had been sent to the local German HQ, the Corpo d'Armata, where according to SS-Sturmführer Heinz Andergassen Littlejohn had undergone 'thorough interrogation' in the 'machine room', the basement below Schiffer's office. According to Andergassen Littlejohn was questioned in the presence of himself, Schiffer, SS-Oberscharführer Albert Storz, possibly SS-Hauptscharführer Josef Placke, and two females - Schiffer's secretary, Christa Roy, and an interpreter, Dr Marianne Schifferegger:

> Littlejohn, since the stricter interrogation system was not sufficient to make him talk, was then tied and an iron bar passed through his elbow and knee junctures and then suspended to a stepladder. Schiffer called this procedure the "Schaukel" [the 'see-saw'] …
> I remember that Littlejohn as an officer was asked to order his NCO Josef [*sic*] David Crowley to drop his silence and talk [TS 26/418].

Meanwhile, Storz stated:

> He was not whipped, since Littlejohn, after preparations were made, declared himself ready to make a statement. I remember that Crowley was brought from his cell into the machinery room, where Littlejohn released him from his oath of secrecy and authorised him to speak out as he was doing. Littlejohn in this conversation however signified to Crowley that he should not talk too much. The attending interpreter Dr Schifferegger or Josef Placke immediately caught this remark and brought it to Schiffer's attention.
> It is not known whether Littlejohn was thoroughly interrogated a second time [TS 26/418].

Roy later stated: 'I remember Captain Littlejohn in the beginning showed himself very obstinate and took the view he was a soldier of an enemy unit, and therefore should merely be taken prisoner and put in a POW camp' (*The Brenner Assignment*, by Patrick K. O'Donnell).

Littlejohn and Crowley, along with 2nd Lieutenant Charles Parker, a pilot of the 489th Bomb Squadron, United States Army Air Force, who had been shot down two days before, were reportedly murdered on 19 March 1945 at Bolzano. According to Storz's statement the three were being taken away that evening for 'execution … in such a manner that the impression would be created that the three were shot while attempting to escape' when the car had a puncture (TS 26/418). The three prisoners, 'acting curiously wanted to make sure that we had a flat tyre', were induced to leave the vehicle and walk down a side street where they were shot by machine pistol and then given a coup de grâce. They were reportedly buried in the Cemetery of the Resurrection in Bolzano that day.

However, a month later, on 19 April, i.e. a month after the murders, the International Red Cross in Geneva cabled the War Office stating:

> Informed by Swiss Consular Representative, Milano, following recently seen as POW. German hands at Merano. All wishing NOK [next of kin] be informed. 1. Capt R R Littlejohn 197229 2nd SAS Regiment NOK Mrs Littlejohn 11 Abbey Park Place Dunfermline Scotland. 2. Corporal I D [*sic*] Crowley 3710217 2nd SAS Regiment NOK Mrs Crowley 43 Southgreen Road [*sic*] Liverpool 14 [IRCC ref SB 4849 – WO 311/630]

2nd SAS' Intelligence Section interpreted this as the men having been seen at Merano on 19 April and passed the news to the next of kin on the 30th. The two men had told the Swiss Representative that they had been 'shot down' on 25 February. Given the detailed statements volunteered by those accused this could easily be put down to inaccuracy of dates were it not for a Reuters report, filed from Italy by their correspondent Robert Allen, and published in *The Manchester Evening News* that May, which also casts doubt on the accepted version of events:

> Captured Allied paratroopers thrashed by Nazis says British Governess – Miss May Taylor of Sheffield over twenty years governess to Italian family just returned from six months concentration camp near Bolzano relates that more than once during her stay members British American special service prisoned after jumping from plane were brought to camp prison where SS men beat them cruelly with cudgels crowbars inflicting severe injuries in vain attempt extort information. Miss Taylor also says two British soldiers liberated with her *April 29th* [author's italics] taken by Red Cross to recuperate at Merano were billeted in private house were ordered by German officer to uphold hands then shot cold blood. German officer later executed by Partisans – Reuter [WO 311/630].

There is no other known case of British soldiers being murdered during this period in Northern Italy. Whatever the truth that July Major 'Bill' Barkworth of the SAS War Crimes Investigation Team signalled the War Office; 'OSS report in addition to German already held whose name is Plucke [*sic* – Placke] hold Albert Store [*sic* – Storz] who confesses having shot Littlejohn and Crowley'. Andergassen, Storz, and Schiffer, all of whom escaped to Innsbruck at the end of the war, were captured and tried in Naples. Despite pleading not guilty and claiming that they had merely followed orders, and despite appeals to Pope Pius XII, the three were hanged by the Americans at Livorno in July 1946 for the murder of Littlejohn, Crowley, Parker and his crew, as well as the murder of Captain Roderick Hall of the OSS. Schifferegger and Roy appear to have escaped punishment. Placke, who had considerable success in penetrating SOE circuits in France, and who appears to have been concerned in the murder of Parachutist Fred Puttick in the Vosges, also seems to have walked free (see Puttick's entry under Groesbeek Memorial, Netherlands, Volume III).

Son of Charles and Edith Littlejohn (née Robertson) of Abbey Park Place, Dunfermline, Fife – Husband of Honora Littlejohn of Eton, Buckinghamshire. Age 23.
I had not loved thee dear, so much. Loved I not honour more.
Grave 3.F.7. Also commemorated on the Commando Memorial at the National Memorial Arboretum – Jack Paley of Littlejohn's troop named one of his sons 'Ross' in honour of him.

ROME WAR CEMETERY

In the early hours of 22 January 1944 the Allies landed behind the German Gustav Line at Anzio during OPERATION SHINGLE. *However, initial surprise was not exploited and it was the hard-fought breakthrough at Cassino on 18 May that effectively opened the way towards Rome. Five days later 150,000 Allied troops that had been trapped within the Anzio beachhead finally broke out and turned north. Nonetheless rearguard actions meant that the Germans were able to ensure the withdrawal of virtually all of their forces before the city fell on the evening of 4 June. Despite being the first Axis capital to be captured the victory was largely overshadowed by the D-Day landings thirty-six hours later. The Commonwealth cemetery was created soon after, the majority of the 426 burials being of the occupying garrison, although a small number were concentrated here from the surrounding area.*

The cemetery is located alongside the Aurelian Wall of ancient Rome, close to the Piramide Metro Station, and on the Via Nicola Zabaglia 50, Monte Testaccio. It is open Monday to Friday but can be accessed out of hours by ringing the telephone number on the gate. GPS co-ordinates: Latitude 41.87502, Longitude 12.477238

PRIVATE DAVID LAING **SINGERS** [2756763] BLACK WATCH
AND LRDG (X.2 PATROL, B SQN)

Dave Singers was born on 17 April 1919 in Dundee, his family living within the city at the North Lodge of the fourteenth-century Invergowrie House. Having worked for a cardboard-box manufacturer he enlisted into the Black Watch (Royal Highland Regiment) at the outbreak of war and was posted to the Holding Battalion. He disembarked in France on 16 April 1940 and joined No.1 Infantry Base Depot at Rouen. On 3 June he was posted to the 4th Battalion, although it is unknown whether due to heavy fighting he ever reached it before, as his service record notes, being evacuated, most likely from Cherbourg, in mid June. That July he arrived on Gibraltar after his troopship, the *Athlone Castle*, had been subjected to aerial and submarine attack en route. Promoted to lance-corporal in July 1942 he served on the Rock until the battalion returned to the UK at the beginning of May 1943. The following January he embarked for North Africa, relinquishing his stripe to join a reinforcement draft. He subsequently volunteered for the Long Range Desert Group on 12 July and was deployed to Italy.

Singers died of an injury sustained during training, Russell Weir, of the same squadron later recalling:

As far as my memory goes back Dave Singers and George Ross (both from the Black Watch Regt) were in a party of us who attended the School of Mountain Warfare at M. Terminilo just north of Riete (north of Rome) [from 20 February 1945]. The day Dave was injured we were on a map reading exercise (in the snow), some of us were issued with ice-axes and others were given ski-poles in case we fell on the slopes. Dave, unfortunately, had a ski-pole and when he fell on a steep slope he struck a tree and suffered a broken rib. He was taken to hospital in Rome [104th General Hospital] and died two or three days later [on 28 February]. I visited his grave shortly after. From what I was told the broken rib had punctured his spleen and he bled internally [personal correspondence, 2009].

The course had been in preparation for proposed operations behind enemy lines in northern Italy and southern Austria. A pathologist's report submitted to the subsequent court of inquiry attributed the cause of Singer's death to: 'post operative Peritonitis due to Staphylococcus aureus. Source of the infection remains obscure.' As his personal effects included a 100-Kuna banknote there is a strong possibility that he had been deployed on B Squadron's operations along the Dalmatian coast during late 1944 and early 1945.

Son of David and Margaret Laing Singers of North Lodge, Invergowrie House, Dundee.
Age 24.
Worthy of everlasting remembrance
Grave 2.D.5. Also commemorated on Dundee City Council's online roll of honour.

SALERNO WAR CEMETERY

After the successful invasion of Sicily three Allied divisions landed on the beaches of Salerno on 9 September 1943 during OPERATION AVALANCHE. *The landings were planned to coincide with those on the toe of Italy a few days earlier (*OPERATION BAYTOWN*), and those of the British 1st Airborne Division at Taranto that day (*OPERATION SLAPSTICK*). Despite fierce German counter-attacks, during which evacuation was considered, the advancing British Eighth Army broke through to the Salerno bridgehead on the 17th. The combined force then marched on Naples.*

The cemetery was created in November 1943, the majority of the 1,846 Commonwealth burials being from the initial landings and bridgehead battles, although graves were later concentrated from all over south-west Italy. There are 107 unidentified burials and one special memorial to a casualty of the First World War, whose grave in a local civil cemetery was lost.

The cemetery is located 14 kilometres south of Salerno on the Pontecagnano-Battipaglia road (the SS18) opposite Pontecagnano Airport. GPS co-ordinates: Latitude 40.62508, Longitude 14.92202

LANCE-BOMBARDIER JOHN HENRY BALL [5186123] GLOUCESTERSHIRE REGIMENT, ROYAL ENGINEERS, ROYAL ARTILLERY, 1ST SAS AND SRS (NO.1 TROOP)

John Ball joined the 5th Battalion, Gloucestershire Regiment (TA), in July 1939 at Thornbury whilst working as a labourer. On doing so he stated that he had been born on 25 January 1922 at Westbury-on-Trym in Bristol. However, his birth was not registered until exactly a year after this date and the authorities later realised that he had falsified his age in order to join up early. Embodied into the 7th Battalion that August, he transferred to the Royal Engineers in February 1940 and was posted to the 37th Anti-Aircraft Battery. A month later this was redesignated the 37th Tyne Electrical Engineers Searchlight Regiment, Royal Artillery, and he was therefore transferred to that corps with the rank of gunner. Having been appointed lance-bombardier with the 123rd Battery of the newly-designated 37th Light Anti-Aircraft Regiment he embarked for the Middle East late in August 1941.

There is no record of when Ball volunteered for the Regiment but he was with the Special Raiding Squadron during OPERATION HUSKY, the Allied invasion of Sicily. As such he took part in the destruction of coastal batteries that threatened the invasion fleet at Capo Murro di Porco on 10 July 1943 and in the capture of the port of Augusta on the evening of the 12th. He was recommended for Operational Wings by Captain 'Sandy' Wilson, commander of C Section, No.1 Troop, these being granted on 23 July (see Wilson's entry under Cassino Memorial, Italy). This indicates that he had previously taken part in operations in North Africa as a member of 1st SAS.

At 0445hrs on 4 September 1943 forward elements of the SRS landed at Bagnara on the toe of mainland Italy during OPERATION BAYTOWN. Ball's section occupied the northern beach without opposition and went to ground in a wadi before moving up through the town alongside B Section. The men soon encountered heavy machine-gun and mortar fire, two signallers being killed (see entries for Lance-corporal Charlie Richards and Private Bill Howell under Bari War Cemetery, Italy). Several men, including Ball, were wounded. He died of these wounds at 189 Forward Ambulance the following day.

Son of Ernest and Ethel Ball (née Pimm) of Eastfield Road, Northwick, Gloucestershire.
Age 20.
Happy and smiling always content, loved and respected wherever he went
Grave 6.C.26. Also commemorated on Pilning's war memorial.

SANGRO RIVER WAR CEMETERY

By the end of October 1943 the River Sangro formed the eastern end of the Gustav Line. This series of German strongpoints, including those dominating the key junction with Highway 6 at Cassino, stretched across Italy to contest the Allied advance. Although the Eighth Army breached the Sangro sector in late November it was not until Cassino fell the following May that the advance to Rome could resume.

The cemetery, laid out as an amphitheatre, contains 2,617 Commonwealth burials that overlook the former battlefield from which they were concentrated. In addition, the Sangro River Cremation Memorial commemorates more than 500 men and officers of the Indian forces whose remains were cremated in accordance to their faith.

Sergeant Alexander Westwater, an original member of L Detachment, SAS Brigade, is buried here amongst former comrades: Having been captured in Libya during OPERATION SQUATTER, *the SAS' first raid of November 1941, he was awarded the Distinguished Conduct Medal for no less than six escapes from camps in Italy. On his return to Allied lines in early November 1943 he rejoined the SAS, which at the time had been restructured as the Special Raiding Squadron, but was soon recruited by A Force, the cover name for MI9. This organisation facilitated the extraction of POWs from behind enemy lines, Westwater being killed aboard one of their pick-up vessels in an explosion whilst taking on petrol off Termiti Island (see grave 10.C.33).*

The cemetery is located in the Contrada Sentinelle, 2 kilometres from the Marina and 7 kilometres south-east of the train station of Torino di Sangro. GPS co-ordinates: Latitude 42.21912, Longitude 14.5365

PRIVATE GEORGE **CASSIDY** [6028881] ESSEX REGIMENT, 1ST SPECIAL SERVICE BATTALION, QUEEN'S OWN ROYAL WEST KENT REGIMENT, 1ST SAS AND SRS (No.1 TROOP)

Georgie Cassidy was born on 23 April 1920 in the parish of Cortober, Carrick-on-Shannon in County Leitrim, Eire. Having worked as a plasterer he enlisted into the Essex Regiment in late August 1940 at Omagh and was posted to its infantry training centre at Warley in Essex. That December he volunteered for the 1st Special Service Battalion that he joined at Derwent Lodge, Dartmouth. This was later reorganised as No.1 and No.2 Commandos, Cassidy being absorbed into the latter at the beginning of March 1941. However, five months later he was posted back to the Essex Regiment and joined the 2nd Battalion.

Cassidy transferred to the Queen's Own Royal West Kent Regiment in May 1942 and that month embarked with the 4th Battalion for the Middle East. Here he volunteered for 1st SAS on 16 October and after taking part in the last of its desert operations was with the Regiment the following March when the majority of its subunits were restructured as the Special Raiding Squadron. His recommendation for Operational Wings records that as a parachutist of A Section, No.1 Troop, SRS, he subsequently landed on Sicily at the forefront of OPERATION HUSKY, his troop being responsible for the destruction of a coastal battery that threatened the invasion fleet before helping to clear other such positions. Having re-embarked the *Ulster Monarch* at Syracuse the SRS was put ashore at Augusta on the evening of the 12th. The capture of this key port enabled a more rapid advance up the east coast, Cassidy's wings being granted on the 23rd. The SRS went on to see fierce fighting after landing at Bagnara on the toe of mainland Italy on 4 September (OPERATION BAYTOWN), and, after a period of rest and training, subsequently sailed from port to port around to the Adriatic coast.

To prevent the enemy taking up defensive positions on the River Biferno the SRS joined with a Special Service Brigade consisting of No.3 Commando and No.40 (RM) Commando in launching OPERATION DEVON. The combined force came ashore 1½ kilometres north-west of Termoli in the early hours of 3 October 1943, the Commandos securing the port and its perimeter. Concurrently the SRS pushed down towards the Biferno to hold two bridges and a road junction key to the advancing 78th Division. Although Lieutenant John Tonkin's B Section was captured at the vanguard to this advance (see Lance-bombardier Joe Fassam's entry for details) other sections successfully ambushed enemy vehicles before securing their areas of responsibility.

After linking with British infantry that evening the SRS was relieved and found billets in the Seminario Vescovile, a priest's college in the centre of town. The following day No.2 Troop and C Section of No.1 Troop were deployed to fill a gap in the bridgehead's perimeter, German counter-attacks being stronger than expected. On the 5th these increased and the remainder of No.1 Troop was therefore ordered to prepare for action and mount trucks awaiting them on an adjoining street, the Via Regina Margherita di Savoia. Having done so Lieutenant Johnny Wiseman and his men were about to be driven to their new positions when a runner from their Commanding Officer, Major Paddy Mayne, DSO, arrived. Wiseman got out to receive him a second before a shell landed on his truck, the runner and the majority of the troop being killed. Most of the remainder were wounded, Cassidy dying in Termoli's hospital

later that day. He was originally buried within the hospital grounds whilst those killed outright were buried by their comrades that evening, across the low wall from the destroyed truck in the south-east corner of the Seminario's garden (the wall has since been removed and the garden opened up as a square to serve as a public car park). Their remains were reinterred at their current location in May 1944. Two local children and their mother who had laundered the men's clothes were also killed in the same incident. A German observation post is said to have later been discovered in a tower overlooking the truck's position, although Wiseman believed that it was 'one lucky shell. They couldn't have aimed it at us' (IWM Sound Archive 20337).

Son of Patrick and Bridget Cassidy of Cortober, Carrick-on-Shannon, County Leitrim, Eire.
Age 23.
'Georgie' Short was your life, Dear, may Jesus in his mercy grant you eternal rest
Grave 11.A.15.

LANCE-BOMBARDIER CLARENCE **CRISP** [884074] ROYAL ARTILLERY AND SRS (NO.1 TROOP)

Having worked as a screen hand Clarence Crisp enlisted into the Royal Artillery in June 1938 stating that he had been born on 8 April 1920 at Pontefract in Yorkshire. However, it later transpired that his birth had not been registered until the last quarter of 1921 and that he had falsified his age to join up early. After training he was posted to the 14/4th Medium Regiment, serving as part of the BEF in France until being evacuated on 28 May 1940. He embarked for the Middle East in December 1941 and was posted to Cyprus the following April. Having returned to Egypt just before Christmas 1942 he volunteered for the either 1st SAS before March 1943, or the Special Raiding Squadron after that date. Although the exact date is unknown he was involved in a road traffic accident in May 1943 whilst a member of B Subsection, No.2 Section, A Troop, SRS, as outlined by Lance-corporal R. Gladwell:

> On the 11th May 1943 at about 1030 hours Pct Crisp, C. 884074 was proceeding on duty with me to Jerusalem when a civilian lorry struck our WD 15cwt. Pct Crisp was sitting in the back of the truck on the floor with his back towards the front of the truck. After the accident I found Pct Crisp lying at the side of the road with a bad cut above the left eye and he was in a state of semi-consciousness and at the same time complaining about his back.

Crisp was discharged from hospital eighteen days later and promoted to lance-bombardier on 10 July, the day that he landed at Capo Murro di Porco at the forefront of the Allied invasion of Sicily (OPERATION HUSKY). That morning the SRS destroyed coastal batteries that threatened the invasion fleet, No.1 Troop being at the vanguard of this action. On the evening of the 12th the unit captured the key port of Augusta, thereby enabling a more rapid advance up the east coast. It then landed on the toe of mainland Italy on 4

September, seeing fierce fighting in the assault on Bagnara during OPERATION BAYTOWN.

Having landed at Termoli in the early hours of 3 October 1943 during OPERATION DEVON, Crisp was killed in action on the 5th when a shell hit the truck he was sitting in (see Private George Cassidy's entry within this section for full details).

Son of John and Amy Waller of Dickinson Terrace, Featherstone, Pontefract, Yorkshire.
Age 22.
We loved him too dearly to ever forget. His loving Mother and Father
Grave 10.C.1.

PRIVATE SYDNEY DAVISON [4627437] DUKE OF WELLINGTON'S REGIMENT, DURHAM LIGHT INFANTRY AND SRS (No.1 TROOP)

Despite it being often reported, due to his stature and youthful looks, that 'Titch' Davison lied to join up early his birth certificate confirms that he was born in Bradford on 25 May 1923, the date that he gave on enlistment. He did so in April 1942 having worked as a dairyman and was initially posted to No.4 Infantry Training Centre, Duke of Wellington's Regiment (West Riding). That July he qualified as a driver mechanic and was posted to the 10th Battalion, before embarking for the Middle East in late December within a reinforcement draft. On arrival the following month he transferred to the Durham Light Infantry and seems to have been held in a depot until volunteering for the Special Raiding Squadron the day it was formed, 19 March 1943. Soon after the unit began training for what was to become OPERATION HUSKY, the Allied invasion of Sicily, Reg Seekings, DCM, MM, later recalling:

> We were at Maharia and Dempsey was commander XXX Corps I think, and he came along to give us a pep talk …
> Then he saw little Titch. He was little. He said 'Who is that man?'
> I said 'Davison, Sir.'
> 'How old is he?'
> 'I don't know, 14 or 15 I suppose.'
> He said 'That's what I would reckon, I'd like to talk to him.'
> 'OK, Davison? The General would like to speak to you.' So the General said: 'How old are you?'
> '21, Sir.'
> He said 'No, no, your real age.'
> '21, Sir.'
> 'No, no, no, I'm not going to do anything to you, I just out of curiosity want to know your proper age.'

'21, Sir and if you don't fucking like it, you can fucking stuff it!' I thought 'Oh, Christ, we've had it now.'
Dempsey just laughed and said: 'This is a bad thing to say, but I wish we had two to three divisions like him.
Keep an eye on him Sah Major' [IWM Sound Archive 18177].

Davison subsequently landed at Capo Murro di Porco on 10 July 1943, No.1 Troop quickly clearing a coastal battery that threatened the invasion fleet with the other SRS troops in support. On the evening of the 12th the unit captured the port of Augusta, thus enabling a more rapid Allied advance up the east coast. On 4 September the men assaulted Bagnara on the toe of mainland Italy during OPERATION BAYTOWN, seeing fierce fighting before sailing from port to port around southern Italy towards their next operation. This was to be codenamed DEVON, a landing in conjunction with No.3 Commando and No.40 (RM) Commando to capture the port of Termoli on the Adriatic coast. Having come ashore in the early hours of 3 October Davison was killed in action when a shell hit the truck he was sitting in on the 5th (see Private George Cassidy's entry within this section for full details).

Son of Fred and Jessie Davison (née Llewellyn) of Lumb Lane, Bradford, Yorkshire – His two older brothers predeceased him: Craftsman Herbert Davison, Royal Electrical and Mechanical Engineers attached to the 13th (Honourable Artillery Company) Regiment, Royal Horse Artillery, died in April 1943 and is buried at Shipley (Nab Wood) Cemetery, whilst Driver Ernest Davison of 18 Water Tank Company, Royal Army Service Corps, was killed in January 1943 and is commemorated on the Brookwood Memorial. Age 20.
At the going down of the sun and in the morning we will remember him
Grave 10.C.35.

PRIVATE ALLAN **DUNCAN** [2759014] BLACK WATCH, 1ST SAS
AND SRS (NO.1 TROOP)

Allan Duncan was born on 18 September 1919 in Dundee, enlisting into the Black Watch (The Royal Highland Regiment) in January 1940 and being posted to the Holding Battalion. Although it was intended to send him to France this was cancelled towards the end of May when it was clear that the BEF was to be evacuated. He was therefore re-posted to the 5th Battalion where he found it hard to settle. In June 1942 he embarked for the Middle East and by mid September was at a training depot from where he volunteered for 1st SAS on 18 October.

It is not known which desert operations Duncan was involved in but as a member of No.1 Troop, Special Raiding Squadron, he took part in the destruction of enemy coastal batteries at Capo Murro di Porco on 10 July 1943 at the forefront of the invasion of Sicily. This was followed by the capture of the port of Augusta on the evening of the 12th. On 4 September his troop saw fierce fighting during the capture of Bagnara on the toe of mainland Italy during OPERATION BAYTOWN.

Duncan was killed in action on 5 October 1943 at Termoli when a shell hit the truck he was sitting in during OPERATION DEVON (see Private George Cassidy's entry within this section for full details).

Son of Joseph and Margaret Duncan of Alloway Terrace, Linlathen, Dundee.
Age 24.
Ever remembered
Grave 10.C.42.

LANCE-BOMBARDIER JOSEPH WILLIAM <u>FASSAM</u> [874242] ROYAL ARTILLERY, No.8 COMMANDO, MIDDLE EAST COMMANDO, 1ST SAS AND SRS (No.3 TROOP)

Joe Fassam was born on 9 October 1919 in Plymouth where, whilst working as a butcher, he joined the local 164th Heavy Battery, Devonshire Heavy Brigade, Royal Artillery (TA), in November 1937. Embodied at the outbreak of war he volunteered for No.8 (Guards) Commando in July 1940, this later being temporarily reorganised as the 4th Special Service Battalion. After pre-deployment training he disembarked at Suez, Egypt, early the following March as a member of B Battalion, Layforce. A frustrating period of cancelled raids followed for this special service brigade and it was disbanded that summer, Fassam being briefly posted to a coastal battery at the beginning of 1942. He soon rejoined the remnants of Layforce, which had been brought together as the Middle East Commando, and was posted to A Squadron.

Early that June Fassam took part in a recce of Maraua Fort behind enemy lines in Libya. On the 10th the party was detected by a spotter plane and on the 14th the force, now on its way to assault the fort, was attacked from the air. Left with just one vehicle the Commandos withdrew. After only 8 kilometres the vehicle struck a boulder in the dark and had to be abandoned after the steering was found to have been wrecked. The party therefore set off on foot for their forward operating base, Fassam becoming separated from the main group during the night. He was recovered by the Long Range Desert Group's Y.1 Patrol, which located the remainder of the men the following morning. As they were in greater need Fassam was left with a jerry can of water and instructions of how to make his way back to base (WO 218/160). What he thought of this arrangement is not recorded.

By the end of June 1942 A Squadron was holding defensive positions at Dekhaila close to Alexandria. Although Fassam's service record does not confirm when he volunteered for the Regiment it is believed that this was on 26 September 1942 and that he was involved in 1st SAS' last operations of the desert war. What is certain is that he took part in OPERATION HUSKY, the Allied invasion of Sicily, as a member of A Section, No.3 Troop, Special Raiding Squadron. As such he landed at Capo Murro di Porco in the early hours of 10 July 1943 to destroy Italian coastal batteries, and at Augusta on the 12th to capture this key port. He was awarded Operational Wings soon after, going on to see fierce fighting during the SRS landings at Bagnara on the toe of mainland Italy on 4 September (Operation Baytown).

Fassam was killed in action on 3 October 1943 during Operation Devon, the capture of Termoli by a combined force consisting of the SRS, No.3 Commando and No.40 (RM) Commando. Having landed 1½ kilometres north-west of the port his section, under Lieutenant John Tonkin, was tasked with securing the area of the River Biferno to the south. The post-operation report notes: 'No.3 troop advance across country towards Termoli-Campomarino road with No.1 Troop behind and slightly north. 0530hrs B Sect (Lt Tonkin) capture three Germans walking up wadi at bridge 828765, but section sniper ambushed and captured.' Tonkin himself later recalled:

It was another sudden job with little information and no maps. We were warned to take care as our own troops might well be there before us. In fact the German 1st Parachute Division were there in strength. I was detailed to spearhead the thrust south to the Biferno River asap. Penetrated too deep, too fast and by daylight was hopelessly cut off. No sign of own troops (they didn't arrive until some days later). Ran out of ammo – was captured – very degrading [*SAS Operation Bulbasket: Behind the Lines in Occupied France, 1944*, by Paul McCue].

That December Bombardier Russell Jessiman wrote to Fassam's father:

Dear Mr Fassam,

It is with deepest regret I am writing this letter but I know you will want to know what happened when Joe met his death. I was with him at the time as we were both in the same section. Our job was north of Termoli and we made a landing in German lines on the night of October 3rd [*sic* – the early hours of the 3rd]. Our objective was approx 8 miles inland over very rough country occupied by the enemy. We had been marching approximately to 4 'o' clock in the morning of the 4th [*sic* – 0530 on the 3rd] when we had a fight, we overpowered the enemy and were going on our way when we met very stiff opposition from the enemy. We had a pretty rough time of it as we were outnumbered and the Germans had field guns which they were firing at us.

Our officers decided to outflank the enemy and if possible bypass them. Our luck began to desert us for when we retreated we got into a wadi surrounded on all sides by the road (we did not know it at the time but we were in the middle of the German parachutists' lines). It was just breaking daylight then and the Huns were firing mortars and machine guns at us. No way could we get out of the wadi unobserved or out of his range. He gradually closed in on us and we had the order to try and break out of the other end of the wadi. This we tried to do but Joe tried to get up the side of the wadi when a burst of machine-gun fire caught him in the chest. It was instantaneous. He did not suffer any pain and passed away before any of us could reach him. Nearly all of us lads were taken prisoner. I happened to be lucky enough to escape [he and Lance-corporal Sid Payne lay low amongst the scrub]. Later that day we took his body south of Termoli and buried him at the cross roads. One of the boys placed a wreath of flowers beside the cross. The padre Capt Hunt was there and he gave the service. Each day before we left one of us attended to the grave and when we left Termoli it was arranged that the grave would be kept in order.

Mr Fassam I was not Joe's closest friend. His friend Chris McAvoy, who was section sergeant, is now a prisoner  of war. I knew Joe very well. Liked by all, officers, NCOs and men admired him for his courage and cheery ways. On and off parade he was known as 'one of the best'. I've often overheard remarks passed about him as Joe Fassam a great guy. Believe me Mr Fassam everyone thought the world of him. I've known him for a long time. We left home together, he being in the 8th Commando, myself in the 7th. After the Commando got bust up we amalgamated together as one Commando under the name of ME Commando. We were both together there and joined the SAS together [Jessiman joined on 26 September 1942]. During all the time I've never known anyone who did not like and admire Joe.

Mr Fassam on behalf of his comrades I want you to know you have our sincerest sympathy. One of the lads has Joe's photographs which he is forwarding on to you and also writing. If I can be of any assistance to you in any way I will be only too pleased to help in any way I can.

Yours sincerely,

Russell Jessiman [See Jessiman's own entry under Rom Communal Cemetery, France, Volume III].

Son of Charles and Margaret Fassam of Steeple, Langford, Salisbury, Wiltshire.

Age 23.
He fought, that we might all be safe and free. We mourn his loss in Italy
Grave 10.C.7.

SERGEANT JOHN SUMMERS **FINLAY** [1436147] ROYAL ARTILLERY, L DETACHMENT SAS BRIGADE, 1ST SAS AND SRS (NO.1 TROOP)

Known to his family as Iain and to his comrades as 'Jock', John Finlay was born on 6 February 1918 in Glasgow. As a lad he was a keen member of The Boys Brigade and after schooling took a junior post within the Accident Department of the Edinburgh Assurance Company. The following year, 1938, he joined the 231st (City of Glasgow) Anti-Aircraft Battery, Royal Artillery (TA), and was mobilised in August 1939. Disembarking in Egypt in October 1940 he volunteered for L Detachment, SAS Brigade, on 26 June 1942, taking part in OPERATION BIGAMY, that September's large-scale, abortive raid on Benghazi. He was promoted to lance-bombardier a week later when the SAS was granted regimental status and to bombardier the following month.

During October 1942 Finlay was a member of Lieutenant Edward MacDonald's party that left Howard's Cairn in Jeeps to blow 400 metres of the railway line south of Mersa Matruh. MacDonald, who had been awarded a DCM as a sergeant, wrote in his post-operation report: 'No incidents. On our return we met Major Mayne at the entrance to the Sand Sea, where he told us that the offensive at El Alamein had begun. Thus it was likely that the blown railway was of more hindrance to us than the enemy!' Early the following year elements of 1st SAS, including Finlay, moved to Palestine where he briefly served at Raiding Forces HQ at Azzib. He rejoined the Regiment, by then restructured as the Special Raiding Squadron, in time for preparations for the Sicily and Italy campaigns.

Finlay had been appointed lance-sergeant on 19 March 1943, the day the SRS was formed. He was recommended for Operational Wings on the 23rd of that month whilst a member of A Troop, 2 Section, B Subsection. His application outlines his activities up to this time: 'Sept 1942 Benghazi mass attack, Oct 1942 Sidi Aziz LG [landing ground] and cut railway [he left Kufra in MacDonald's A Squadron party and returned on 30 October having placed charges that blew the line], Nov 1942 Piccadilly cutting railway'

(his group left base on 3 November 1942 in three Jeeps under MacDonald and returned on the 11th).

Finlay attended parachute course No.42 at Ramat David during May 1943. He was promoted to sergeant on 10 July, the day the SRS destroyed key coastal batteries at Capo Murro di Porco at the forefront the invasion of Sicily (OPERATION HUSKY). Two days later it captured the port of Augusta, thus enabling a more rapid Allied advance up the east coast. Finlay's Operational Wings were granted on the 23rd. He went on to take part in the landings at Bagnara on the toe of mainland Italy on 4 September during OPERATION BAYTOWN.

Having sailed from port to port around Southern Italy Finlay was killed in action during OPERATION DEVON at Termoli when a shell hit the truck he was sitting in on 5 October 1943 (see Private George Cassidy's entry within this section for full details). Reg Seekings, DCM, MM, later recalled:

I was wondering where Jock was. He was another sergeant, absolute first class, Jock Finlay. Very clever man, studying to be an auctioneer, he'd practically passed all his exams, engaged to be married. There were big bushes of mock orange in this garden, and as I hacked that away, there was Jock. His face was unmarked, a grin on it – it had been so sudden all of this you see – a perfect bust. But that was all we could find of him, just his head. Not a mark on it [*The Originals: The Secret History of the Birth of the SAS*, by Gordon Stevens].

Only son of Robert and Margaret Finlay of Paisley Road, West Glasgow.
Age 25.
And from the ground there blossoms red life that shall endless be
Grave 10.C.37.

Corporal Charles Martin **GRANT** [T/88783] Royal Army Service Corps, 1st SAS and SRS (No.1 Troop)

Charles Grant was born on 4 July 1918 and grew up in Liverpool. Having worked as a clerk he enlisted into the Royal Army Service Corps at the outbreak of war. Less than three weeks later he arrived in France as a driver in 1st Armoured Division's supply column. Shortages of both men and equipment meant that the division was effectively put out of action just five days after the German invasion of the Low Countries began, Grant being evacuated to the UK at the beginning of June 1940.

After disembarking in the Middle East in early 1941 Grant served with the RASC Section of the 25th Light Anti-Aircraft Regiment, Royal Artillery. That May he was posted to HQ RASC in Cairo with which he served until volunteering for 1st SAS on 23 October 1942. Unfortunately, there is no record of which operations he took part in during this final phase of the desert war. However, he had been promoted to lance-corporal by the time that the Regiment took part in the Allied invasion of Sicily under the temporary guise of the Special Raiding Squadron. After destroying coastal batteries at Capo Murro di Porco on 10 July 1943 and helping to capture the key port of Augusta two days later, he was admitted to hospital for an unknown reason late on the 29th. He was discharged on 3 August in time for Operation Baytown, during which the SRS saw fierce fighting after a landing at Bagnara on the toe of mainland Italy on 4 September.

Grant died of wounds in hospital at Termoli on 5 October 1943 during Operation Devon, a shell having hit his truck that day (see Private George Cassidy's entry within this section for full details). Reg Seekings, DCM, MM, later recalled the aftermath:

One, Sgt Patterson [*sic* – believed by process of elimination to be Lance-sergeant 'Jocky' Henderson], was hanging upside down with all his chest blown open – I could see his lungs and heart beating – and his Tommy gun was on his chest. He said 'Reg, take that gun off, its hurting me.' Seemed calm and collected. I got him down, and he got his arm and pulled it off and said 'It's a bad one this time.' I said 'You'll be alright, we'll get you to hospital.' I knew we wouldn't [*sic*]. He wanted some water. I stepped across a mass of pulp and a voice said: 'Sgt, can you get me a drink please, I'm thirsty.' It was Cpl Grant. His face was pulp, I couldn't recognise him, only his voice. He was the other one that took his arm and dropped it to one side, again the heart and lungs were visible. One lived an hour and a quarter, the other an hour and a half. They were good lads [IWM Sound Archive 18177].

Grant was originally buried within the grounds of Termoli's hospital, Ginger Adamson, former SRS, later writing: 'I hope he will be traced as he was one of the unit's characters and his death upset me very much.'

Son of Charles William and Lillian Grant of Prescot Road, Aughton, Lancashire.
Age 22.
'Stand Fast – Craigellachie' (the war cry of the Grant Clan)
Grave 10.C.6.

Private Edgar **GRIMSTER** [3661499] South Lancashire Regiment, Gordon Highlanders, 1st SAS and SRS (No.1 Troop)

Edgar Grimster was born on 5 June 1920 at West Ham in east London. Having worked as a laundry man he enlisted into the South Lancashire Regiment (The Prince of Wales Volunteers) on 26 July 1940. Posted to the 8th Battalion he trained as a personnel carrier specialist the following year. In order to serve overseas he transferred to the 5/7th Gordon Highlanders during May 1942, embarking for Egypt the following month. He volunteered for 1st SAS on 1 October whilst at an infantry base depot and although it is not known which desert operations he took part in he was with the Regiment when it was restructured as the Special Raiding Squadron on 19 March 1943. Over the following three months the unit trained rigorously both on sea and land in readiness for Operation Husky, the Allied invasion of Sicily.

As a member of No.1 Troop Grimster was at the forefront of Husky, landing at Capo Murro di Porco in the early hours of 10 July 1943 to destroy coastal batteries that threatened the invasion fleet. Two days later, on the evening of the 12th, the SRS landed at Augusta and captured the port, thus enabling a more rapid Allied advance up the east coast. He was wounded in action at Bagnara during Operation Baytown, the landings on the toe of mainland Italy, on 4 September, but returned to his troop in time for Operation Devon at Termoli. It was here that he was killed in action on 5 October 1943 when a shell hit the truck he was sitting in (see Private George Cassidy's entry for full details). His father was informed by letter from his section commander rather than via the War Office and this, combined with the fact that he had received word that his son had been wounded only a month before but no news of his discharge, led to some initial doubt over the reporting.

Son of Frank and Edith Grimster (née Strickland) of Wellesley Road, Leytonstone, Essex.
Age 23.
No inscription.
Grave 10.C.2.

PRIVATE WILLIAM HERBERT HEARN [5625251] DEVONSHIRE REGIMENT, NO.3 COMMANDO, NO.8 COMMANDO, MIDDLE EAST COMMANDO, 1ST SAS AND SRS (NO.1 TROOP)

William Hearn was born at Teddington in Middlesex on 21 November 1916, later living on Winstead Street in Battersea, south-west London. Having worked as a stationery packer he enlisted into the Devonshire Regiment during March 1940. After training he volunteered for special service and was subsequently posted to A Troop, No.3 Commando. That November this was temporarily absorbed into the 4th Special Service Battalion, Hearn disembarking at Suez, Egypt, the following March as a member of B Battalion, Layforce. On 5 July he 'embarked for an unknown destination', he and approximately sixty other members of the battalion, having now reverted to its original title of No.8 (Guards) Commando, being landed at the besieged port of Tobruk in Libya. Here he took part in a successful raid on the Italian-held 'Twin Pimples' feature on the night of the 17–18th. Returning to Egypt on 25 August the detachment found Layforce had been disbanded, Hearn being posted to various depots as a member of the newly-formed Middle East Commando.

In May 1942 Hearn was admitted to hospital for an unknown reason and discharged to a convalescent depot two months later. That September the Middle East Commando was reorganised as 1st Special Service Regiment although he soon volunteered for 1st SAS on 28 October. Having joined B Squadron Hearn was posted 'missing in Libya' as of 18 January 1943. He had been wounded in action the day before when his patrol, commanded by Captain Denis Murphy and en route to harass enemy supply lines in Tunisia, was surprised in a wadi west of Nalut. Although one of three patrol members to evade capture, five of his comrades were taken prisoner whilst Murphy and three others were killed. Sergeant Ted Badger reported the incident:

> Captain Murphy ran from Jeep to Jeep endeavouring to get the crews organised and the Jeeps started ... Sergt Badger himself was able to start his engine, and while it was warming up, opened fire with a Vickers K MG [machine gun] at the enemy, who by this time were firing from both sides of the wadi. One other Jeep was firing, but another was burning.
> After he had fired three magazines Sergt Badger's machine gun jammed and he decided to try and get his Jeep out of the wadi to the north, shouting to Pte A. Hearne (DCLI) [sic] who had been slightly wounded, and Pte R. Guard (Liverpool Scottish) to come with him [see Private Ronnie Guard's entry under Rom Communal Cemetery, France, Volume III]. In spite of getting ditched soon after they started they contrived to get away, noticing that all fire had ceased in the wadi, and reached a point about 6 miles to the south-east at about 1530hrs. There they waited until

0830hrs next day (18th) but no one else turned up. Sergt Badger adds that at the moment of leaving the wadi they saw Capt Murphy unhurt and trying to start a Jeep, Pte Hearn DCLI (it is not clear whether Pte Hearne escaped or not) [Hearne should not to be confused with Hearn – both were members of the patrol, the former being captured], Pte M. Nixon (Royal Scots) wounded, Pte E. Robinson RASC under cover, and Pte L. Buxton RA running for cover [WO 218/97].

Arabs brought Badger, Guard and Hearn to Allied lines on 10 February and he was therefore with the Regiment when the majority of its subunits were restructured as the Special Raiding Squadron on 19 March 1943. Its men began amphibious training for OPERATION HUSKY, the Allied invasion of Sicily. Hearn subsequently landed at Capo Murro di Porco in the early hours of 10 July, No.1 Troop destroying a coastal battery that threatened the invasion fleet before moving on to help clear others. Two days later the SRS captured the key port of Augusta, thus enabling a more rapid advance up the east coast. On 4 September it landed at Bagnara on the toe of mainland Italy where it saw fierce fighting during OPERATION BAYTOWN.

Hearn was killed in action on 5 October 1943 during OPERATION DEVON at Termoli when a shell hit the truck he was sitting in (see Private George Cassidy's entry within this section for full details).

Son of Frank Hearn of Fulwell Road, Teddington, Middlesex.
Age 26.
No inscription.
Grave 10.C.36.

LANCE-SERGEANT JOHN BROWN **HENDERSON** [2695776] SCOTS GUARDS, L DETACHMENT SAS BRIGADE, 1ST SAS AND SRS (NO.1 TROOP)

'Jocky' Henderson was born on 13 May 1919 in Glasgow where he worked for carpet manufacturers, Messrs J. Templeton & Co. In January 1938 he enlisted into the Scots Guards and was posted to the 2nd Battalion that November when it embarked for Egypt. The outbreak of war found him at Mersa Matruh near the Egyptian/Libyan border where the battalion had been deployed two weeks previously. In March 1940, having sat out the desert 'Phoney War', it was relieved and returned to garrison duties in Cairo. Henderson took the opportunity to qualify as a bricklayer during what was a frustrating period for the battalion that was too stretched with guard duties to train for the inevitable action ahead. It remained in Cairo until January 1941 when it moved to the Canal Zone on air defence duties. As of March it joined the 3rd Battalion, Coldstream Guards, in forming the 22nd Guards Brigade and proper training finally commenced in the area of Kabrit. Almost immediately the Afrikakorps launched an offensive and the brigade was moved into the line just to the west of Sidi Barrani, although that July Henderson was back in Cairo where he qualified as a mason. Having taken part in OPERATION CRUSADER, the British counter-offensive that November, the battalion was either in action or at the front line until April 1942 when it was granted three weeks' rest at Buq Buq.

Henderson volunteered for L Detachment, SAS Brigade, on 3 May 1942 and was promoted to corporal on 21 September, the day that the unit was granted regimental status as 1st SAS. His self-written application for Operational Wings is the best surviving record of his activities:

> Fuka series [of airfield raids, July 1942] – was driver to Capt Fraser's [A Squadron] party. Stayed outside of the drome. Daba – was with French [the Free French Squadron of L Detachment, SAS Brigade], got strafed officer mortally wounded, turned back [July 1942, see Lieutenant Robin Gurdon's entry under Alamein Memorial, Egypt, Volume I]. Sidi Haneish – was on Sgt Lilly's Jeep on big strafing job [July 1942]. Benghazi – was on party that took the fort [Fort Benito, an Italian wireless stronghold on an escarpment overlooking the approaches to the town during OPERATION BIGAMY, September 1942]. Capt Bailey i/c [see Chris Bailey's entry under Alamein Memorial, Egypt]. Howards Cairn – went with Mr Shorten. Got turned back. Job not finished [October 1942, see Lieutenant Raymond Shorten's entry under Alamein Memorial, Egypt]. Mr Chambers' party got chased with armoured cars, got bogged. Job not finished [October 1942, see Captain Jim Chambers' entry under Fayid War Cemetery, Egypt]. Bir Zelten – Mr MacDonald's party. Stayed with Jeeps, first job partly blew up road at Beurat. Mined road near Beurat. Strafed trucks south Sirte. Took prisoners.

Lieutenant Edward McDonald, DCM, strongly recommended Henderson for 'coolness and courage throughout the attack on 21/12/42' during the last of the actions mentioned above: McDonald's five-man party had reached its operational area near Wadi Mruh, close to Beurat and approximately 13 kilometres from the main road, on the 15th. Recces were carried out and Beurat's wireless mast and water towers blown up on the morning of the 17th. Having laid low whilst the enemy searched for them McDonald led his team to Tamet airfield only to find it empty. On the 20th they mined the Tmed Hasan-Bel Zidin track having heard armour. The mines subsequently went off, although the results remained unknown. In the morning the party headed due east, reaching the Wadi Tamet at midday. Finding itself facing three German armoured cars sat on the opposite crest only 500 metres away McDonald hoped to bluff it out. When the enemy sent up a white flare he replied with a similar recognition signal and one armoured car drove towards them. Waiting until it was below them in difficult ground the patrol opened fire before heading south, rapidly outrunning their pursuers. Later that day they attacked a small convoy, killing eleven men and taking prisoners from a Panzer unit. They reached Eighth Army lines on the 22nd.

From 19 March 1943 the Regiment began amphibious training having been temporarily restructured as the Special Raiding Squadron. Henderson subsequently landed at Capo Murro di Porco on 10 July at the forefront of OPERATION HUSKY, the Allied invasion of Sicily. As a lance-sergeant in No.1 Troop he was instrumental in the destruction of a coastal battery that threatened the invasion fleet. Two days later the SRS captured the key port of Augusta, thereby enabling a more rapid advance up the east coast. On 4 September the unit saw fierce fighting after landing at Bagnara on the toe of mainland Italy during OPERATION BAYTOWN.

Henderson died of wounds at Termoli on 5 October 1943 during OPERATION DEVON after a shell hit the truck which he and his troop were sitting in (see Private George Cassidy's entry within this section for full details). Reg Seekings, DCM, MM, a staff-sergeant at the time, later recalled:

> One, Sgt Patterson [sic – by process of elimination this is believed to be a description of Henderson], was hanging upside down with all his chest blown open – I could see his lungs and heart beating – and his Tommy gun was on his chest. He said 'Reg, take that gun off, its hurting me.' Seemed calm and collected. I got him down, and he got his arm and pulled it off and said 'It's a bad one this time.' I said 'You'll be alright, we'll get you to hospital.' I knew we wouldn't. He wanted some water. I stepped across a mass of pulp and a voice said: 'Sgt, can you get me a drink please, I'm thirsty.' It was Cpl Grant. His face was pulp, I couldn't recognise him, only his voice. He was the other one that too his arm and dropped it to one side, again the heart and lungs were visible. One lived an hour and a quarter, the other an hour and a half. They were good lads [*The Originals: The Secret History of the Birth of the SAS*, by Gordon Stevens].

Although the post-operation report states that Henderson was buried within the grounds of Termoli's hospital his service record notes that he was originally buried in Termoli's 'square facing Elementary School on 6.10.43'. This is believed to be the gardens that once adjoined the priest's college at the scene of the incident.

Son of Hugh and Jane Henderson of Shettleston Road, Glasgow – Brother of James, Hugh and Peter Henderson, and of Mrs A. Aitchison.
Age 24.
To live in the hearts you left behind is not to die. Good-night, John
Grave 10.C.5.

LANCE-BOMBARDIER JOHN OWEN **HODGKINSON** [843285] ROYAL ARTILLERY, NO.5 COMMANDO, 1ST SAS AND SRS (NO.2 TROOP)

'Ginger' Hodgkinson was born on 23 August 1919 in Liverpool but grew up in Hull where he attended Southcoates Lane School and developed into a nationally known junior footballer. In January 1935, aged 15, he enlisted into the Royal Artillery and by the beginning of the following year held the rank of trumpeter within a field regiment. At the end of his boy service in August 1937 he was mustered as a gunner and having been promoted to lance-bombardier in May 1939, was serving with the 19th Field Regiment at the outbreak of war. Two days later he disembarked in France as a member of the BEF's 1st Division Artillery. Promoted to bombardier that day he was evacuated to the UK on 1 June 1940.

In February 1941 Hodgkinson was posted to the 5th Special Service Battalion, this being reorganised as No.5 Commando the following month and initially basing itself at Barrhead before settling at Falmouth. That August he was re-posted to the Royal Artillery depot from where he joined 140th Field Regiment four weeks later. In October he was posted to the 1st Reserve Field Regiment and reverted to the rank of gunner on his own request, although after only a few days he was promoted lance-bombardier once more. Within a month he held the rank of lance-sergeant and by the end of the year was serving in the Middle East. In July 1942 he was either wounded or taken ill and on discharge from hospital found himself at the Royal Artillery Base Depot. It was from here that he volunteered for 1st SAS on 24 February 1943, reverting to the rank of gunner in order to do so.

On 19 March 1943 the majority of the Regiment's subunits were restructured as the Special Raiding Squadron and began rigorous training in preparation for OPERATION HUSKY, the Allied invasion of Sicily. As a member of No.2 Troop Hodgkinson landed at Capo Murro di Porco in the early hours of 10 July at the forefront of this operation, the SRS destroying coastal batteries that threatened the invasion fleet. Two days later it captured the key port of Augusta, thereby enabling a more rapid advance up the east coast. He was promoted to lance-bombardier on 5 September, the day after fierce fighting during the capture of Bagnara on the Italian mainland (OPERATION BAYTOWN).

Hodgkinson is often reported to have been killed in the truck-shelling incident at Termoli during OPERATION DEVON. However, although he was buried alongside those that lost their lives in this incident in the gardens of the Seminario Vescovile, Sid Payne, of the same troop, later recalled that Hodgkinson had joined C Section under Lieutenant Derrick Harrison just as it was mortared and that he was mortally wounded in the back by shrapnel (personnel interview, 2009). The SRS War Diary records that at 1400hrs on 5 October 1943 C Section, No.2 Troop, was:

> Ordered to withdraw into wood 803780 to bolster Recce Regt personnel. On arrival in wood find that they [the Reconnaissance Regiment] are leaving abandoning their carriers and A/T [anti tank] guns. [C Section] Asked to man A/T guns further left, but find that they have been taken out.
> Advance down into valley in order to cover dead ground in front of [No.]3 Commando.
> 1700hrs C Sect closes in to A Sect, No.2 Tp, still in original position and whole party commences to withdraw. A Sect No.2 Tp is pinned down in culvert 900x east of bridge 796788 and is unable to get out till dark. Casualties: one killed, four wounded, several missing from both their sections [WO 218/99].

Son of John and Mary Hodgkinson of Meadowbank Road, Hull.
Age 24.
Greater love hath no man than this. He laid down his life for his country
Grave 10.C.44.

PRIVATE WILLIAM MUIR McALPIN [3058778] ROYAL SCOTS, GLASGOW HIGHLANDERS, GORDON HIGHLANDERS, 1ST SAS AND SRS (NO.1 TROOP)

William McAlpin was born on 26 September 1918 at Abbeyhill in Central Edinburgh where he worked as a bartender. After the outbreak of war he enlisted into the Royal Scots in October 1939 and was posted to the regiment's infantry training centre. He transferred to the 2nd Battalion, Glasgow Highlanders, in June 1940 and after home service transferred again, this time to the 5/7th Battalion, Gordon Highlanders, in May 1942. He disembarked in Egypt the following month. Having served in the Eighth Army he volunteered for 1st SAS on 1 October, John Noble, former SAS, later recalling:

> This other fellow and myself, a guy called McAlpin, we'd been co-driving this truck, and we didn't know it but we were being RTU'd because the guy that had been in charge of us, a Swedish officer [Lieutenant H. Leljevahl], and he was saying: 'Dump these two bums.' And Rhodes was speaking to me on the way back and said: 'Well, we're not going to send you back.' That was the first I knew about it. For a young fellow in the SAS to be RTU'd

was the end of the world. Wrecked a truck. I suppose that's what we'd done. Anyway, Rhodes said: 'We're going to keep you.' Oh great. So the two of us stayed and subsequently the next stage was back from the desert to Kabrit and then from there to Ski School [IWM Sound Archive transcript 18175].

McAlpin is noted in 1st SAS' War Diary as being posted from B Squadron to A Squadron on 23 January 1943. That March the majority of the Regiment's subunits were restructured as the Special Raiding Squadron and began training for what was to be OPERATION HUSKY, the Allied invasion of Sicily. As a member of No.2 Troop McAlpin subsequently landed at Capo Murro di Porco on 10 July, the SRS assaulting coastal batteries that threatened the invasion fleet. Having re-embarked the *Ulster Monarch* it captured the key port of Augusta on the evening of the 12th, thereby enabling a more rapid advance up the east coast. On 4 September it landed on the toe of mainland Italy, seeing fierce fighting at Bagnara during OPERATION BAYTOWN.

After rest and training the SRS sailed from port to port around to the Adriatic coast and landed at Termoli in the early hours of 3 October 1943 for Operation Devon. It was here that McAlpin was killed in action on the 5th when a shell hit the truck he was sitting in (see Private George Cassidy's entry within this section for full details).

Son of William and Henrietta McAlpin of Edina Place, Edinburgh.
Age 25.
No inscription.
Grave 10.C.45.

LANCE-CORPORAL JOHN McDONALD [4128862] CHESHIRE REGIMENT,
ROYAL NORTHUMBERLAND FUSILIERS, L DETACHMENT SAS BRIGADE,
1ST SAS AND SRS (NO.3 TROOP)

John McDonald was born in the summer of 1921. Although his service record lacks detail it is known that during May 1939, whilst working in a tannery, he joined the 4/5th Battalion, Cheshire Regiment (TA). Mobilised at the outbreak of war he transferred to the 1st Battalion, Royal Northumberland Fusiliers, in February 1942. He subsequently served in the Middle East until volunteering for L Detachment, SAS Brigade, sometime before that September when McDonald took part in OPERATION BIGAMY, the large-scale but abortive raid on Benghazi.

Having returned to Kabrit, where the SAS was granted regimental status, the newly-formed A Squadron set out on 7 October 1942 for Kufra Oasis. Arriving on the 13th it split into two, both parties making their way to the northern edge of the Great Sand Sea where they established a forward operating base. By the 22nd, with ammo and fuel dumps now cached over a wide area, raiding parties were ready to attack enemy road and rail traffic. McDonald was a member of Captain 'Sandy' Scratchley's three-Jeep patrol that set out on 2 November and made a successful recce of the area near Landing Ground 105 at el Daba.

On 19 March 1943 the majority of the Regiment's subunits were restructured as the Special Raiding Squadron. The following month its War Diary noted that McDonald was 'detained by MPs' (military policemen) with Parachutists Perry and Cave in Haifa on the Palestinian coast where the squadron was training. Having subsequently taken part in the landings on Sicily during OPERATION HUSKY he was recommended for Operational Wings whilst a member of B Section, 3 Troop, for: 'Benghazi, Sirte, Tripoli, Sicily.' These were granted on 23 July 1943, McDonald seeing fierce fighting during the capture of Bagnara on the toe of mainland Italy on 4 September (OPERATION BAYTOWN).

Having landed at Termoli in the early hours of 3 October 1943 McDonald was killed in action on the 5th when a shell hit the truck he was sitting in during OPERATION DEVON (see Private George Cassidy's entry within this section for full details).

Son of James and Minnie McDonald (née Preece) of Dover Street, Runcorn, Cheshire.
Age 22.
Utterly unselfish. And so to the end
Grave 10.C.38.

DRIVER ALEXANDER NEIL McKINNON [3129833] ROYAL SCOTS FUSILIERS, ROYAL ARMY SERVICE CORPS, LRDG, ROYAL CORPS OF SIGNALS, RAIDING FORCES SIGNALS SQN ATT LRDG

Alexander McKinnon was born on 23 November 1912 in Ayr where he later worked as a lorry driver. Having married in September 1931 his first son, Alexander, was born early in 1932, followed by a second, Henry, in December 1933. In April 1936, three months after his third son William was born, he joined the local 4/5th Battalion, Royal Scots Fusiliers (TA). Sadly William died that October and McKinnon was given permission to remain at home rather than attend Annual Camp. Mobilised in August 1939 he was embodied at the outbreak of war the following month.

In June 1940 McKinnon was appointed acting lance-corporal and on the 12th disembarked at Brest in north-west France to serve with the BEF. Transported by train the battalion took up positions close to Fresnay, 200 kilometres south-west of Paris. Typical of this period its War Diary notes that 'information regarding the enemy was vague and conflicting … the [French] Liaison Officer attached to the unit stated that the enemy had surrounded Paris on three sides and penetrated to a considerable extent on the coast.' On the 15th, with the Germans having entered the capital the previous day, the battalion was ordered to withdraw to Cherbourg using its own limited transport. On the 17th the men embarked, having driven all vehicles that could not be loaded into the harbour. From the 18th the battalion was billeted in the colleges of Cambridge University and in surrounding private houses. However, it was still not safe, the city being bombed the following day. Further attacks necessitated a move to nearby Pampisford Park where orders were received to form part of Cambridge's defence in the event of invasion. The following month McKinnon lost his stripe as a result of a minor misdemeanour, September bringing better tidings when his wife gave birth to twins, David and Margaret. He transferred to the Royal Army Service Corps in June 1941 and was posted to 172 Company, 30th Armoured Brigade, where he qualified as a driver mechanic that November.

Having been re-posted to 10 Tank Transporter Company McKinnon disembarked in the Middle East in September 1942. The following month he joined 24 Tank Transporter Company and was hospitalised, for an unknown reason, on 10 December. On being discharged he reported to 15 Tank Transporter Company but volunteered for the Long Range Desert Group on 17 September 1943. Less than a month later he was either wounded in action in the Aegean or injured in an accident. On discharge from hospital he was posted to Raiding Forces Signals Squadron supporting the LRDG, transferring the same day to the Royal Corps of Signals, more than likely for administrative reasons.

Moving to Italy at the end of March 1944 McKinnon was based at the Raiding Forces Signals camp on the hill overlooking RFHQ at the small fishing town of Rodi. He was killed in a traffic accident on 8 May whilst driving a 15cwt truck the short distance down this hill to go into town with other members of the unit. Fred McKinnon, not related but another member of the Signals Squadron, recalled that there was no other vehicle involved and that Captain 'Doc' Parsons, the LRDG's Medical Officer, attended the scene. The ensuing court of inquiry found that McKinnon was not to blame.

Husband of Margaret McKinnon of Clare Road, Levenshulme, Manchester – Father of Alexander, Henry, William, David and Margaret McKinnon.
Age 31.
No inscription.
Grave 2.D.16.

LANCE-SERGEANT WILLIAM MATTHEW McNINCH MM [327865] CAVALRY OF THE LINE, NO.11 COMMANDO, MIDDLE EAST COMMANDO, 1ST SAS AND SRS (NO.2 TROOP)

Bill McNinch, sometimes known as 'Willie' or 'Mac', was born on 19 June 1912 at Port Glasgow in Renfrewshire where he later worked as a bank clerk for a wine and spirits merchant. A month after the outbreak of war he enlisted into the Cavalry of the Line stating that he had previously been a member of the OTC. Posted to the 3rd (Heavy) Cavalry Training Regiment he volunteered for No.11 (Scottish) Commando in August 1940 and was promoted to lance-corporal a few days later. This Commando was temporarily absorbed into 2nd Special Service Battalion that November, McNinch being promoted to corporal at the same time. It subsequently disembarked at Suez, Egypt, in early March 1941 under the interim title of C Battalion, Layforce.

At the end of April, having been stood-to (and dropped from) a raid on Bardia earlier that month, No.11 Commando moved to Cyprus in readiness for OPERATION EXPORTER, the campaign against the Vichy French in Syria. At 0420hrs on 9 June 1941 McNinch's No.4 Troop landed alongside No.10 Troop north of the mouth of the Litani River and engaged enemy machine-gun positions. Despite capturing numerous prisoners and a battery of French guns the combined party found itself in an ever-precarious position, especially as both its wireless sets had been rendered useless coming ashore. Although it carried out further attacks, the enemy managed to inflict several casualties and to release its own men by nightfall. Whilst withdrawing the two troops separated and in the early hours of the 10th No.4 began moving south along the beach where it became caught up in wire at Ainteniye. It was machine-gunned at short range and with one officer and four men killed, plus three wounded, there was no option but to surrender. Treated well the party was released a few hours later when the French commander realised he could not hold out against advancing armoured vehicles and Australian infantry.

Later that year Layforce was disbanded, its remnants, including McNinch, being gathered at the Commando Depot at Geneifa. The following January he was posted to the newly-named Middle East Commando, this being redesignated the 1st Special Service Regiment in May 1942. That September he was promoted to sergeant and in December was posted to the Special Forces Holding Unit. On 6 January 1943 he volunteered for 1st SAS, reverting to corporal in order to do so, but was confirmed as lance-sergeant on 19 March when the majority of the Regiment's subunits were restructured as the Special Raiding Squadron. Posted to B Section, No.2 Troop, he was attached to the 10th Battalion, Parachute Regiment, to attend parachute course No.42 at Ramat David during May.

In the early hours of 10 July 1943 the SRS landed at Capo Murro di Porco at the forefront of OPERATION HUSKY, the Allied invasion of Sicily. Having overrun coastal batteries that threatened the invasion fleet the men re-embarked the *Ulster Monarch* at Syracuse the following day and were put ashore at Augusta farther up the east coast on the evening of the 12th. The capture of this key port enabled a more rapid advance towards the Strait of Messina.

On 4 September 1943 the SRS crossed this obstacle and landed on the toe of mainland Italy to capture Bagnara during OPERATION BAYTOWN. It was as a result of this action that McNinch was awarded an immediate Military Medal, the citation for which states:

On the morning of 4th September 1943 Sgt McNinch's sub section moved up the road leading northwards from Bagnara and although under mortar and machine-gun fire got to within 200 yards of the enemy who were in concealed positions. Sgt McNinch controlling his sub section with great coolness.

Later the enemy brought up another machine gun which completely overlooked the sub section's position. In spite of this Sgt McNinch gave very valuable help in observing the enemy and locating his position and although every movement bought down enemy fire he continued to move forward encouraging his sub section and controlling the fire of his Bren with great effect.

Later when the Bren gunner was wounded he dressed his wounds regardless of the heavy enemy fire.

When for a time his sub section were completely pinned to the ground he continued to encourage his men and take steps for their safety moving about regardless of his own safety.

Throughout he was a very fine example of coolness and efficiency in action [*London Gazette* 13/01/44, WO 373/4].

McNinch landed at Termoli in the early hours of 3 October 1943 during OPERATION DEVON. He was killed in action when a shell hit the truck he was sitting in on the 5th (see Private George Cassidy's entry within this section for full details). Sid Payne, a fellow troop member, later recalled that McNinch was a comic who 'had a nice line in monologues' and who had volunteered to drive No.1 Troop up to the front (personal interview, 2008). Lieutenant Peter Davis, McNinch's section commander, later wrote: 'to their delight, my lads found that the driver of one of the lorries was McNinch who, because of a bad foot, had been left out of the battle ...' (*SAS – Men in the Making: An Original's Account of Operations in Sicily and Italy*, by Peter Davis, MC). His friends clambered aboard only to be moved to another truck and be replaced by Johnny Wiseman's section. Seconds later the shell landed on that in which McNinch was sat. Reg Seekings, DCM, MM, recalled the aftermath:

> Then I went to the cab of the truck and saw McNinch still sitting there. I said: 'Christ Mac, what the hell's wrong with you? Come on, get out and give us a hand. Don't sit there grinning like a bloody Cheshire cat.' I thought his nerves had gone. He didn't move, still grinning. I was mad by this time and I yanked the door open. Dead as a door nail. There wasn't a mark on him. Just sitting there with a big smile on his face [*The Originals: The Secret History of the Birth of the SAS*, by Gordon Stevens].

After Guardsman Charlie Tobin had been killed at Bagnara, McNinch, who had helped bury him, had said to Davis: 'You know, Sir' he said, as though to himself, 'it's funny that it is always the best that catch it. Charlie Tobin was the kindest-hearted man in the section – he would never say a hard word about anyone – and they have to go and kill him. And here am I, a drunken old reprobate, and am still alive' [see Tobin's entry under Bari War Cemetery, Italy] ... 'Worshiped by the men, he [McNinch] was the humourist of the section ... none could get more out of the men than he ... I recalled his words at Bagnara, and the strange philosophy he had expounded on the occasion of Tobin's death' (*SAS – Men in the Making: An Original's Account of Operations in Sicily and Italy*, by Peter Davis, MC).

Son of James and Elizabeth McNinch of St Gabriels, Barrs Brac, Port Glasgow, Renfrewshire – His Military Medal was presented to his mother in December 1945.

Age 31.

Where Willie McNinch sleeps in peace until the dawn. 1939–1943

Grave 10.C.39. Also commemorated on Port Glasgow's war memorial.

LANCE-SERGEANT CHRISTOPHER O'DOWD MM [2719054] IRISH GUARDS, NO.8 COMMANDO, MIDDLE EAST COMMANDO, L DETACHMENT SAS BRIGADE, 1ST SAS AND SRS (NO.1 TROOP)

Chris O'Dowd, sometimes known to his comrades as 'Christy' or 'Paddy', was born on 6 September 1920 at a farm in Cahernabruck, Shrule, near the west coast of Ireland. As the ninth of twelve children he attended Gortjordan National School and took a job as a shop assistant before running away to join his brother in London where he worked as a barman. On enlisting into the Irish Guards in May 1939 he stated that he had been born in Galway on 12 August 1920. After passing through the brigade depot he spent a brief period with the Training Battalion before being posted to the 2nd Battalion that October.

In April 1940 O'Dowd was re-posted to the 1st Battalion and subsequently landed at Harstad in Norway on the 15th. Nearly a month later the battalion positions were taken over by Polish troops, the men embarking HMT *Chrobry* to reinforce the Scots Guards at the front line to the south. However, the vessel was held at anchor awaiting orders until the evening, during which time it was located and lucky not to be hit by successive German air attacks. Once finally under steam the *Chrobry*, with its escort far behind, was followed out to sea by an enemy spotter plane and, just after midnight on 15 May, was bombed and set on fire. All hands were forced to abandon her, the Commanding Officer, both senior majors and all four company commanders having been killed. Despite this loss of leadership the Captain of HMS *Wolverine*, the escort that came alongside and took survivors aboard, noted that this would not have been possible had it not been for 'the superb discipline of the men of the Battalion'. A few days later a new complement of officers arrived and the men dug in near Bodø. Within twenty-four hours they were exchanging fire with German infantry and after a week of resistance were ordered to withdraw. A long march followed, before the battalion embarked only just ahead of the pursuing enemy.

On his return to the UK O'Dowd volunteered for No.8 (Guards) Commando, this being temporarily reorganised as the 4th Special Service Battalion that November. He subsequently disembarked at Suez in Egypt in early March 1941 as a member of B Battalion, Layforce. An unsettled period followed. The Commando, which had based itself at Mersa Matruh, was put on standby for numerous operations, all of which were cancelled at the last minute. Although a detachment was sent to Tobruk, Layforce was, in the main, disbanded that July and O'Dowd posted to the Commando Depot at Geneifa. In November the remnants of Layforce based there were reorganised as the Middle East Commando and it is believed that O'Dowd volunteered for L Detachment, SAS Brigade, during May 1942. He was appointed acting lance-corporal that September and before the end of the year had been awarded Operational Wings for those raids outlined in his self-written application:

Went on the first job to Fuka airdrome with Major Mayne's party [a combined force of LRDG and L Detachment assembled at Qaret Tartura on the northern edge of the Great Sand Sea on 6 July, their objective being to destroy enemy aircraft as prelude to a forthcoming British offensive. On the night of 7–8 July 1942 Lieutenant Robin Gurdon's G.2 Patrol, LRDG, dropped an SAS party for what was to be an abortive attack on one of the three Fuka landing grounds. However, that same night Mayne led a party onto the airfield at nearby Bagush, thirty-seven aircraft being destroyed and it is likely that this is the raid that O'Dowd refers to. After mining a nearby road Gurdon picked up the Fuka parties reuniting them with the Bagush raiders at their lay-up point at Qaret Tartura. On the 8th the base was moved west to Bir el Quseir, although the landing grounds in the area of Fuka remained the principal targets]. Then went to El Kaba but had to turn back because Lt Gurdon got killed when we were strafed [Gurdon was killed on the 12th whilst taking a party consisting of men mainly from L Detachment's French Squadron, but it seems including at least O'Dowd and Henderson, to attack a landing field at El Daba - see Gurdon's entry under Alamein Memorial, Egypt, Volume I, and Lance-sergeant 'Jocky' Henderson's within this section].

Went to Fuka again [in fact prior to Gurdon's death on the night of 11–12 July, between fifteen and twenty aircraft being destroyed and sentries attacked with grenades]. Was on the Benghazi job from the Sand Sea [the large-scale, but abortive, OPERATION BIGAMY launched on the night of 13–14 September 1942].

Went with Major Mayne to Fuka but had to turn back. On the way back we shot up Italian convoy.

Went with Capt Marsh and blew up the line at Barrani.

Went with Capt McDermot [on an A Squadron Jeep operation – O'Dowd left Kufra on 27 October 1942 to replace Parachutist Reg Wortley who had set out with the group the day before and who had been sent back injured – see Wortley's entry under Bayeux Memorial, France, Volume III] strafed MT [motor transport] on the Barrani-Matruh road. Blew up the line and destroyed four machine-gun posts south of Barrani.

O'Dowd returned from this last job on 3 November 1942, his party, of what was now A Squadron of the recently created 1st SAS, having lost one Jeep. Three days later he went back out again under Lieutenant Douglas Kennedy (see Kennedy's entry under Alamein Memorial, Egypt). On the 9th he again left the forward operating base, this time under Major Paddy Mayne, DSO, returning to Kufra Oasis on the 24th. He was subsequently awarded the Military Medal, the citation for which gives further detail of his raids:

> Cpl O'Dowd has taken part in five successful operations with the 1st SAS Regiment. In all these operations he has shown consistent bravery and steadiness.
> At Fuka aerodrome on the 8th July 1942 he assisted to destroy thirty enemy aircraft. While engaged on a raid at Benghazi on 14th September 1942 he was in the last vehicle to leave covering the withdrawal by accurate and sustained machine-gun fire which drew the defenders fire from the main withdrawing party.
> On 23rd October 1942 he was the senior NCO of the raiding party which attacked an enemy convoy driving from Siwa to Mersa Matruh assisting in destroying four Lancias.
> On 26th October 1942 he assisted in blowing up the railway lines west of Mersa Matruh.
> On 1st November 1942 he was the senior NCO in a party of six which strafed traffic at Sidi Harrani and then attacked a railway siding capturing eighteen prisoners, four machine guns, blowing up the railway line, and destroying wireless equipment [*London Gazette* 14/10/43, WO 373/26].

As the North African Campaign drew to a close the majority of 1st SAS' subunits were restructured as the Special Raiding Squadron, O'Dowd being appointed lance-sergeant within Major Bill Fraser's No.1 Troop. He attended ski training at The Cedars in the Lebanon between pre-deployment exercises in the run up to the Allied invasion of Sicily (OPERATION HUSKY). He subsequently landed at Capo Murro di Porco in the early hours of 10 July, his troop successfully destroying a coastal battery that threatened the invasion fleet before helping to neutralise others. Two days later he took part in the capture of Augusta, thereby enabling a more rapid advance up the east coast and on 4 September saw fierce fighting at Bagnara during OPERATION BAYTOWN, the assault on the toe of mainland Italy.

O'Dowd went ashore at Termoli in the early hours of 3 October 1943 during OPERATION DEVON. He was killed in action on the 5th when a shell hit the truck he was sitting in (see Private George Cassidy's entry within this section for full details).

Son of James and Sarah O'Dowd of Badgerfort, Shrule, County Galway, Irish Republic – Brother of Martin O'Dowd (who was presented his Military Medal by His Majesty the King on 20 February 1945) and of Angela. Age 23.

Lord have mercy on our darling son Chrissy. His fond parents

Grave 10.C.4. Also commemorated on Castlebar's war memorial.

Private Emrys POCOCK [5437461] Duke of Cornwall's Light Infantry, King's Own Royal Regiment and SRS (No.3 Troop)

Emrys Pocock was born in the coal-mining town of Abertillery in Monmouthshire. Although his exact date of birth is unclear it is known that he attended Gelli Crug School. In April 1938, having worked alongside his father, a WWI veteran, at Cwmtillery Colliery, he enlisted into the Duke of Cornwall's Light Infantry at the Central London Recruiting Depot at Scotland Yard. Posted to the 2nd Battalion he was promoted to lance-corporal that November, although he reverted to the rank of private at his own request during March 1939. He was re-posted to the 1st Battalion in India that July and at the outbreak of war was stationed in Lahore. Having attended an animal transport course during February 1940 he was reappointed lance-corporal two months later.

In November 1941 Pocock's battalion boarded the troopship HMT *Lancashire* at Karachi, disembarking at Basra in Iraq to join the 10th Indian Brigade on garrison duties. By mid December it was stationed at Hindiya before moving to Habbaniya in February and to Taji near Baghdad on 1 April 1942. With Russian victories making the threat of Axis invasion less likely, and with the campaign in North Africa escalating, the battalion left Baghdad on 17 May. Moving overland via Haifa in Palestine it reached Ismailia in Egypt on the 24th and Alexandria two days later. On the 28th it moved up to Mersa Matruh and crossed the Libyan border to arrive at Tobruk five days later. With Rommel's offensive in full swing the battalion was rushed towards the Knightsbridge Box south of Gazala. Totally unprepared, both in terms of equipment and experience, it was overrun by the 15th Panzer Division at Bir el Harmat on 5 June. Virtually destroyed it was subsequently disbanded, Pocock, one of the few who escaped capture, being withdrawn first to Palestine and then Cyprus.

Returning to North Africa in late August 1942 Pocock was transferred to the 1st Battalion, King's Own Royal Regiment. He was trained as a driver mechanic before volunteering for 1st SAS on 19 March 1943, the day the majority if its subunits were restructured as the Special Raiding Squadron. Having carried out amphibious exercises along the Palestinian coastline and within the Gulf of Aqaba he landed as a member of A Section, No.3 Troop, during the Allied invasion of Sicily that July (Operation Husky). His recommendation for Operational Wings confirms that he took part in the destruction of coastal batteries at Capo Murro di Porco on 10 July and the capture of the key port of Augusta two days later.

Pocock was next in action on 4 September 1943, landing at Bagnara on the toe of mainland Italy during Operation Baytown. This bridged the Strait of Messina and hastened the enemy withdrawal from Calabria. After a period of rest and training the SRS then moved by sea round to Termoli where it saw fierce fighting during Operation Devon: having come ashore 1½ kilometres north of the port in the early hours of 3 October Pocock was killed in action on the 5th when a shell struck a parked lorry within which members of Lieutenant Johnny Wiseman's No.1 Troop were sitting. Wiseman later recalled that he had just got out to speak to a messenger sent by his Commanding Officer, Major Paddy Mayne, DSO, when the shell landed. Although Wiseman survived the messenger was killed. There is a strong possibility that Pocock, who was a member of another troop, was that messenger (see Private George Cassidy's entry within this section for full details of this incident).

Son of George and Ruth Pocock (née James) of Somerset Street, Abertillery, Monmouthshire – Older brother of Henry (Harry), who served post-war in the Royal Engineers, and of Rhys Pocock.

Age officially recorded as 26 – although Pocock declared his date of birth as 16 January 1920 on enlistment, his birth was registered in the first quarter of 1918.

Hearts that loved you never forget. In memory you are with us yet. Mam, Dad and brothers

Grave 10.C.3. Also commemorated on Abertillery's war memorial and on a plaque found within the town museum from the now demolished Gelli Crug Primary School.

GUNNER SIMON ARON **SILIFANTS** [1462315] ROYAL ARTILLERY, 1ST SAS AND SRS (NO.1 TROOP)

Simon Silifants was born on 22 January 1920 in Clitheroe, Lancashire, to a Dutch father and British mother. In May 1939, whilst working in the fur trade, he joined 156th (East Lancashire) Battery, 52nd Light Anti-Aircraft Regiment, Royal Artillery (TA), at Darwen. The following month he was posted to the headquarters of 168th Battery, 56th LAA Regiment, but two weeks after the outbreak of war arrived in France to serve with his parent unit as part of the BEF. This defended the I Corps area during its withdrawal through Tournai and Bailleul towards Dunkirk, from where it was evacuated with 102 enemy aircraft to its credit.

Silifants embarked for the Middle East in August 1940. Having arrived in Egypt his battery was posted to Crete, its Bofor guns being spread over a wide area of responsibility, between Heraklion and Maleme, in time for the May 1941 German airborne invasion. Silifants was one of the lucky few to be evacuated from the island, although during his passage to Egypt on the night of 30–31 May he received treatment for a hand injury aboard HMAS *Perth*. Many of his regiment had been captured and having been discharged from the 64th Australian General Hospital, Silifants found that his battery had been disbanded. Although his service record gives no clues it is therefore likely that he was absorbed into one of the regiment's surviving batteries or posted to a depot.

The date that Silifants volunteered for 1st SAS is not known but during the spring of 1943, whilst a lance-corporal in A Section, No.1 Troop, Special Raiding Squadron, he was recommended for Operational Wings. His self-written application records that he took part in 1st SAS' last desert operations: 'Mined road at [illegible] with Major Fraser and Greeks [the Greek Sacred Squadron, part of Raiding Forces]. Captured Mark IV tank and strafing'.

Silifants landed at Capo Murro di Porco in the early hours of 10 July 1943 at the forefront of OPERATION HUSKY, the Allied invasion of Sicily. His troop was responsible for the assault and destruction of a coastal battery that threatened the invasion fleet. Having completed this task it helped clear other such positions before re-embarking the *Ulster Monarch*. On the evening of the 12th the unit captured the key port of

Augusta, thereby enabling a more rapid British advance up the east coast. Silifants was subsequently granted his Operational Wings on 23 July before going on to take part in the capture of Bagnara on 4 September during the assault on the toe of mainland Italy (OPERATION BAYTOWN).

Silifants landed at Termoli on the Adriatic coast in the early hours of 3 October during OPERATION DEVON. Having helped capture the town he was killed in action on the 5th when a shell hit the truck he was sitting in (see Private George Cassidy's entry within this section for full details).

Son of William and Rose Silifants of Castle View, Clitheroe, Lancashire.

Age 23.

No inscription.

Grave 10.C.40. Also commemorated on Clitheroe's war memorial.

Sapper Alexander Grant <u>SKINNER</u> MM [1883722] Royal Engineers, L Detachment SAS Brigade, 1st SAS and SRS (No.1 Troop)

Alex Skinner, sometimes known to his comrades as 'Blondie' or 'Jesus', was born on 18 May 1920 in Newcastle-on-Tyne. Moving to Temple Road in Cricklewood, north-west London, he found work as a railway clerk. In May 1940 he enlisted into the Royal Engineers where his previous trade was put to use as a company clerk. He was posted to the 16th, then the 14th, Railway Battalions at the end of the year and embarked for the Middle East in January 1941. On arrival he was posted to GHQ Middle East where he joined the section responsible for transportation of troops on both railway systems and through ports. The following month he was assigned to the Assistant Director of Operations in Sudan in a similar role and in October returned to Egypt where he was posted to Movement Control of the Suez Canal.

In December 1941 Skinner was re-posted to Eighth Army's Movement Control pool but within a few days had volunteered for L Detachment, SAS Brigade. Jim Smith, a friend who joined the Regiment at the same time, recalled that they spent their Christmas leave together at Alexandria before starting intensive training. The photograph seen here shows Skinner on the left and Smith on the right on Alexandria's beach. Smith also remembered that Skinner, whose biblical nickname was due to the beard he grew behind the lines, took part in Operation Bigamy, the large-scale September 1942 raid on Benghazi (personal interview, 2010). For some reason Skinner's service record states that he was not officially taken on strength until 22 October 1942.

As desert operations drew to a close the majority of the Regiment's subunits were restructured as the Special Raiding Squadron and began training for the Allied invasion of Sicily (Operation Husky). Reg

Seekings, DCM, MM, a former sergeant in No.1 Troop, recalled that during the SRS landings at Capo Murro di Porco he and his men assaulted a coastal battery that threatened the invasion fleet:

Our mortars got cracking and set fire to one of the barracks, which were burning. Then I got my chaps together, and it must have been one of the few bayonet charges of the war ... We took the command post and the only casualty we had was a chap named Skinner, tall blond bloke. One of them [an S-Mine] exploded on his leg [*The Originals: The Secret History of the Birth of the SAS*, by Gordon Stevens].

Skinner was subsequently awarded an immediate Military Medal on 20 August 1943 on the recommendation of his Commanding Officer, Major Paddy Mayne, DSO:

Pct Skinner was wounded by shrapnel in the leg and hip during the first hour of fighting on Cape Murro di Porco on 10th July 1943.

Nevertheless he took his full share in the advance and continued to fight throughout the action which lasted seventeen hours and covered over 24 miles. During the attack on the farmhouse Marsa Alacona he himself stalked and killed three enemy snipers.

On hearing that another operation was to take place shortly he did not visit the unit Medical Officer but had his wounds dressed privately. He went into action again with the squadron on 13th July [sic – the evening of the 12th] at Augusta. Only after this operation were his wounds discovered and he was then admitted to hospital [*London Gazette* 36217, 19/10/43, Supplement 21/10/43].

It is not known whether Skinner was discharged in time to take part in the 4 September SRS assault of Bagnara on mainland Italy (OPERATION BAYTOWN), but he certainly landed with the unit at Termoli in the early hours of 3 October 1943 during OPERATION DEVON. He was killed in action on the 5th when a shell hit the truck he was sitting in (see Private George Cassidy's entry within this section for full details).

Son of Samuel and Elsie Skinner (née Grant) of Dalkeith Road, Ilford, Essex – His younger brother, Dennis, died after falling from his Moscow apartment in June 1983. A British coroner later returned a verdict of unlawful killing amidst allegations of KGB involvement.
Age 23.
Proud and loving memories of our dear son at rest. Age shall not weary him
Grave X.C.34.

GUNNER WILLIAM **STEWART-JOHNSON** [1609969] ROYAL ARTILLERY, L DETACHMENT SAS BRIGADE, 1ST SAS AND SRS (NO.1 TROOP)

William Stewart-Johnson was born in the Gateshead suburb of Wardley on 18 July 1921. Having worked as a miner he enlisted into the Royal Artillery in January 1941 although, due to his reserved occupation, he was immediately posted to the Army Reserve. However, the following month he was embodied and posted to the 208th Light Anti-Aircraft Regiment. After a period of training he joined the 87th Heavy Anti-Aircraft Regiment that May and embarked for Iraq two months later.

Stewart-Johnson volunteered for L Detachment, SAS Brigade, on 31 May 1942. He went on to serve behind the lines in the Western Desert, most notably during OPERATION BIGAMY, the large-scale September 1942 raid on Benghazi. The following March the majority of 1st SAS' subunits were restructured as the Special Raiding Squadron and began rigorous training on the Palestinian coast. Stewart-Johnson supplemented this by attending parachute course No.42 at Ramat David in May, his service record noting that he was slightly injured whilst doing so.

As a member of No.1 Troop Stewart-Johnson was at the forefront of OPERATION HUSKY, the Allied invasion of Sicily, landing at Capo Murro di Porco in the early hours of 10 July 1943 to assault a coastal battery that threatened the invasion fleet. Two days later the SRS captured the key port of Augusta, thus enabling a more rapid British advance up the east coast towards the Strait of Messina. He was subsequently recommended for Operational Wings for: 'Benghazi, Sirte Rd, Tripoli, Sicily', these no doubt being awarded later that month.

On 4 September the SRS saw fierce fighting when assaulting Bagnara on the toe of mainland Italy during OPERATION BAYTOWN. Sailing from port to port it then landed behind the lines at Termoli on the Adriatic coast in the early hours of 3 October 1943 (OPERATION DEVON), Stewart-Johnson being killed in action when a shell hit the truck he was sitting in on the 5th (see Private George Cassidy's entry within this section for full details).

Son of William and Eliza Stewart-Johnson of Lingley Gardens, Wardley, County Durham.
Age 22.
Dearly loved we will meet again
Grave X.C.43.

STAGLIENO CEMETERY, GENOA

During the final year of the First World War Commonwealth troops fought on the Italian Front, Genoa being home to various military hospitals. The Commonwealth War Graves plot, split over three terraces on the edge of a large civilian cemetery, contains 230 burials of this war as well as 122 of that which followed. Amongst the latter is the joint grave of Corporal William Oldershaw and Driver James Cox, both air despatchers of the Royal Army Service Corps (grave 3.A.6–7). They and an American aircrew were killed when their C-47 Dakota crashed at La Dolce on 30 December 1944 whilst resupplying 2nd SAS' OPERATION GALIA.

The cemetery is located 5 kilometres north-east of Genoa at Staglieno on the north bank of the River Bisagno. Access is gained from the western end of the cemetery, signposted San Antonio. Having continued past the main entrance and civil monuments one must walk through a second set of gates and take the steps on the right. Access to the war graves plots is solely via these steep stairs, the SAS graves being at the top level. GPS co-ordinates: Latitude 44.42829, Longitude 8.95115

SERGEANT WILLIAM JOHNSTONE FOSTER [829582] ROYAL ARTILLERY, NO.3 COMMANDO, NO.14 COMMANDO, SMALL SCALE RAIDING FORCE AND 2ND SAS (A SQN)

Bill Foster, sometimes known as 'Geordie', was born on 27 July 1915 at Ellenborough, a suburb of the coastal town of Maryport in Cumbria. Whilst working as a labourer in Workington he joined the 204th Field Battery, Royal Artillery (TA), and in October 1933 enlisted into the regular army. In January 1937 he was posted to India, not returning to the UK until March 1939 when he was also promoted to lance-bombardier. In April 1940 he disembarked in France with the 58th Field Regiment and was evacuated, most likely from Cherbourg, on 15 June.

The following month Foster volunteered for the newly-formed No.3 Commando and joined F Troop as a bombardier. After a brief period attached to the Commando Training School he took part in OPERATION ARCHERY, a raid on the islands of Vaagso and Maaloy off Norway. On a tactical level the objectives were the destruction of fish oil factories whose product was used in the manufacture of munitions, the sinking of enemy shipping, and the capture of suspected Quislings. Strategically it was hoped the raid would force the German High Command to commit increased manpower to the occupation of Norway. After a naval and air bombardment the Commandos landed on the morning of 27 December 1941 to the daunting prospect of urban fighting. Resistance was stiff but eventually the objectives were achieved before the men re-embarked in the early afternoon. Valuable experience of tri-service amphibious operations had been gained, casualties being twenty killed in action and a further fifty-seven, including Foster, wounded.

By the following March Foster had been appointed lance-sergeant and was based at Largs with 4 Troop. On 18 August 1942 he embarked at Newhaven for what was to be the disastrous OPERATION JUBILEE, the raid on Dieppe. No.3 Commando was tasked, under the codename OPERATION FLODDEN, with neutralising the German coastal battery at Berneval on the eastern flank of the main beach assault. Foster returned to Weymouth the next day and it is not known if he was one of the few members of his unit to make it ashore.

In February 1943 Foster arrived in North Africa as a member of No.14 Commando, quickly being posted on the 16th of that month to No.62 Commando, the cover name for SOE's Small Scale Raiding Force. On 13 May he was 'interposted' to 2nd SAS, the SSRF having been used as the foundation on which the Regiment was raised that day. Qualifying as a parachutist in June, he may have taken part in OPERATION CHESTNUT the following month as a member of Captain Philip Pinckney's Pink Party. Having parachuted onto Sicily on the night of 12–13 July this group cut telegraph wires before making contact with the advancing Allies. The post-operation report notes that a 'Sgt Foster' operated against the Messina-Palermo road, the same man later leading similar attacks on the Gangi-Palermo road before meeting the advancing American Army. He then guided US forces to retrieve three sick patrol members who had been left behind enemy lines (see Pinckney's own entry under Florence War Cemetery, Italy).

What is certain is that on the night of 7–8 September 1943 Foster parachuted into a DZ 11 kilometres south-west of Borgo Val di Taro in the Emilia-Romagna region of northern Italy for OPERATION SPEEDWELL. He and Corporal Jim Shortall were detailed to blow sections of the railway line between Genoa and La Spezia. Having separated from the rest of the party in order to go about these tasks the pair disappeared. Posted as missing from 17 September 1943, a German transmission of the 23rd picks up the narrative:

> On the 20.9.43, 2km NW of La Spezia, two British parachutists, officer James Shortall and W.O. William Foster, were captured and pretended to be Italians. Armed and equipped: two pistols with ammunition, two different types of explosive charges, detonators, various types of fuses and tools.
>
> Interrogation showed clearly that they were of an airborne saboteur-troop. Information regarding day and place of

landing, orders, name of their unit, was refused; alleged that their orders had not yet been carried out. In compliance with the special order for such cases the saboteurs were shot [WO 311/350].

A summary of the case, written in November 1945, concluded that:

On 20 Sep 43 the above named soldiers (Forster [*sic*] and Shortall) were captured by a German patrol in the vicinity of La Spezia. They were escorted to Ponzano Magra and placed in the custody of the Carabinieri. On 21 Sep 43, about 1245hrs, two or three motor cycles and vehicles containing German soldiers arrived at the Carabinieri Station and took away the soldiers to the Torrente Belaso, where they were tied to a tree and shot by a firing squad under command of Captain Sommer.

The victims were buried at the spot, and on 16 Oct 45 the bodies were exhumed by the New Zealand GRU [Graves Registration Unit] and reinterred at the British Empire Military Cemetery at Genoa.

Whilst in the custody of the Carabinieri, Cpl Shortall wrote his name on a piece of paper which is produced as Exhibit A.

Enquiries reveal that the victims, both members of A Squadron 2 SAS Regiment, were dropped by parachute in the area about 8 Sep 43.

Responsibility for the shooting seems to rest with two men as under: General Feuerstein, who apparently gave the order, Captain Sommer, who commanded the firing squad [WO 311/350].

Michele Machi, a local man collecting brushwood with his family had witnessed the murders:

Six German soldiers arrived carrying picks and shovels. They commenced to dig what appeared to be a grave. A few minutes after they had finished digging I saw two groups of German soldiers approaching, and as they drew near I saw that each group comprised of one English soldier and twelve German soldiers … The group halted near the grave.

Whilst several German soldiers stood guard, one of the English soldiers was tied to a nearby tree. Twelve of the Germans lined up a short distance from the tree, and on an order given by the German commander, raised their rifles and fired. I then saw the German commander walk to the tree and fire a shot from his pistol into the body of the English soldier.

Two or three German soldiers then cut down the body and left it lying on the ground. The remaining English soldier was then tied to the same tree and shot in exactly the same manner.

Both bodies were thrown into the grave, one on top of the other, and the Germans went away leaving behind two soldiers who filled in the grave. These two German soldiers then covered the grave with grass and leaves and a few minutes later they left.

In company of my son I went to the spot where I had seen the bodies buried and placed upon the grave a small wooden cross [WO 311/350].

Unteroffizier Fitz Bost, the senior rank in the firing squad, later gave his version of events:

The taller of the prisoners [Shortall] was then taken to the tree, and tied to the tree by two Military Policemen. They then tried to blindfold him. This, however, the prisoner refused. He then went on talking after he was already tied. Captain Sommer asked Interpreter Grether: 'What does he want?' The latter replied: 'He is asking for the priest.' Captain Sommer answered: 'We have no time for that.' I can remember this episode with certainty …

When the rifles were brought up to the aim awaiting the order to fire, the prisoner at the tree suddenly turned a little to the side. The order to fire was stopped, and two military policemen blindfolded the prisoner. So far as I can remember, Captain Sommer also went up to him at the tree.

The Lieutenant of the punishment platoon then gave the order to fire. The prisoner collapsed. The Lieutenant of the punishment platoon went to the tree, undid the cords and gave the man, who had been shot, the coup de grace in the head with a pistol.

The man who had been shot was laid a little to one side and the second prisoner was then led up to the tree. I do not know for certain whether he was already blindfolded when he was tied to the tree.

When the second prisoner was tied up, the Lieutenant of the punishment platoon gave the order to fire. This prisoner also collapsed at once. The Lieutenant of the punishment platoon again went up to the tree, undid the cords and gave him the coup de grace in the same way as he did to the man who had been shot first [WO 309/99].

The Grave Registration Unit reported:

The grave was located [on 16 October 1945] in the Torrente Belaso near the village, and was covered with grass and leaves. This was removed and work commenced. The first body was discovered. Buried some 3 feet down, it was face uppermost … An examination revealed that the clothing was part of a pair of overalls. The boots were brown, size 10, and were half-soled, with rubber soles and heals. The shirt was of a khaki heron-boned type. On the body was found a GS watch No GS Mk 2 A84758, a pipe, one round tin of 50 cigarettes (HD & Wills) and part of a handkerchief. Very few teeth remained in the jawbone.

The second body was then uncovered. It was in the same grave buried some 6″ below that of the first body, and the legs were well spread apart. The hair appeared to be dark brown, and the teeth were in good condition. There were a few missing but this could be accounted for by the length of time the body had been buried. The boots were identical to those of the first body but were of a smaller size (approx 7 or 8) …

In the grave we found two leather bands of the type that is worn on some issue types of berets. There was also part of a red identity disc, partly rotted, which when cleaned and examined under a magnifying glass revealed the following letters and numbers: POTT 8464231 [Shortall's service number, see his entry below – WO 311/350].

The SIB investigator, Sergeant Nunn, noted that: 'although it has not been possible to establish positive identification of Sgt Forster [*sic*], there is little doubt about it' (WO 311/350). Despite the evidence his date of death is officially recorded as 30 September 1943. Of the seven brought to trial in connection with the murders only two, Oberstleutnant Klaus von dem Knesebeck, Operations Officer to von Ziehlberg, and Hauptmann Hans Sommer, were found guilty. They received sentences of just six months imprisonment.

Son of John and Rose Foster (née Johnston) of Corporation Road, Workington, Cumberland – Known to have had an elder brother who served in the Royal Army Service Corps.
Age 28.
He gave his life that we may live with memories ever dear
Joint grave 1.C.31. Also commemorated alongside Shortall on a memorial behind the disused ceramic factory to the east of Ponzano Magra. This was organised by Brian Lett, QC, author of *The SAS in Tuscany 1943–45*, with full support and financial assistance from the Comune di Santo Stefano di Magra.

CORPORAL JAMES PATRICK **SHORTALL** [6464231] ROYAL FUSILIERS, NO.8 COMMANDO, NO.3 COMMANDO, SMALL SCALE RAIDING FORCE AND 2ND SAS (A SQN)

Jim Shortall was born on Armistice Day 1918 in Dublin, Eire, later living in north-west London. Having worked as a clerk he enlisted into the Royal Fusiliers (City of London Regiment) at the outbreak of war and was promoted to lance-corporal a month later whilst at an infantry training centre. Having volunteered for special service he was posted to No.8 (Guards) Commando as a corporal in October 1940 but by March 1941 had been re-posted to No.3 Commando at Weymouth. That October he was reduced to the rank of fusilier for a minor misdemeanour. Unfortunately, his service record gives no clue as to whether he took part in the Vaagso raid of December 1941 (OPERATION ARCHERY), nor the Dieppe raid of August 1942 (OPERATION JUBILEE). What is certain is that he married Isabella McLeod Milton in May 1942 at Brodick on the Isle of Arran, the couple later producing a daughter, Eileen. He was promoted to lance-corporal that December and to corporal the following February. Having arrived at Gibraltar in March 1943 the unit disembarked in North Africa in April. Here Shortall was posted to No.62 Commando, the cover name for SOE's Small Scale Raiding Force that formed the foundation on which 2nd SAS was raised on 13 May. As a founding member of the Regiment he attended its first parachute course held at No.1 Airborne Division Parachute Training Centre during early June.

On the night of 7–8 September 1943 Shortall jumped into a DZ 11 kilometres south-west of Borgo Val di Taro in the Emilia-Romagna region of northern Italy. He and Sergeant 'Geordie' Foster were detailed to blow sections of the Genoa–La Spezia railway line as part of OPERATION SPEEDWELL. Separating from the rest of the party they were captured on the 20th and murdered the following day (see Foster's entry within this section for full details).

A signal sent to Berlin on the 25th stated: 'Please find enclosed an open report of the Gen.Kdo. 51 Geb.A.K dated 23.9.43 concerning the extermination of a sabotage troop composed of the British parachutists Officer James Shortall and W.O William Foster, in Italy.' The local Carabinieri chief at Ponzano Magra later told investigators:

> About 2345hrs I retired to bed, but fifteen minutes later I heard the German soldiers return [to the Carabinieri post] and take away with them one of the English soldiers. Two German policemen remained in my office on guard. Every hour from midnight until early morning, the Germans kept taking away the English soldiers separately for interrogation …
>
> I did not see the English soldiers again but I heard later that they had been executed in the Belaso Canale …
>
> During the time that the two English soldiers were in my barracks, one of them wrote his name in pencil on a piece of red envelope. This piece of envelope I have handed to Sgt Nunn, 78 Section SIB, and is shown as Exhibit A [see below].
>
> I describe this English soldier as being about 6′ in height, 24–25 years of age, very dark complexion, black hair, robust build, healthy teeth, dark brown eyes, normal nose, wearing khaki overalls, black boots, brown beret with a blue insignia which resembled a ships anchor.
>
> The other soldier did not have the opportunity of leaving me his name, but I can describe him as being about 26–27 years of age, 5′-5′2″ in height, black hair, dark complexion, thin in the face, dark brown eyes, large curved nose. Both soldiers were dressed in a similar manner [WO 311/350].

Obergefreiter Dieter Schmitt, a clerk at the 65th Infantry Division's headquarters, later stated:

> Sonderführer Grether [Dr Emil Grether, the division's interpreter] and I drove to the local Italian police station late in the evening. The first one was English [Foster], the second one was Irish [Shortall]. So far as I remember the name of one of them was Foster. I do not know their ranks. I remember one of them was tall and slender, a dark type, while the second was smaller and looked stocky. Sonderführer Grether ordered the Englishmen to be searched for weapons and their kit to be searched by the Military Police who were present. When the attempt was made to question them, the two Englishmen were very reticent and stated only what was absolutely necessary. After that they were taken to an empty villa …
>
> Sonderführer Grether attempted to carry out an interrogation of the prisoners in my presence in the villa. They refused to make any statement except their personal particulars. They did not state anything either concerning the time and means of landing [WO 309/99].

Despite evidence to the contrary Shortall's date of death is officially recorded as 30 September 1943.

Husband of Isabella Shortall of Oakbank, Brodick, Isle of Arran, Scotland – Father of Eileen Shortall.
Age 24.
No inscription.
Joint grave 1.C.31. Also commemorated alongside Foster on a memorial behind the disused ceramic

factory to the east of Ponzano Magra. This was organised by Brian Lett, QC, author of *The SAS in Tuscany 1943–45*, with full support and financial assistance from the Comune di Santo Stefano di Magra.

SYRACUSE WAR CEMETERY, SICILY

In the early hours of 10 July 1943 Allied forces landed by air and sea on Sicily during OPERATION HUSKY. *The majority of those buried here died during these landings or in the course of follow-up operations in the early stages of the Allied advance. Most prevalent are members of the 1st Parachute Brigade that landed in the area of Primasole Bridge to the west of Syracuse. The cemetery contains one First World War burial and 1,059 of the second, 134 of which are unidentified.*

Located alongside the communal cemetery, 3 kilometres west of Syracuse on the north side of the SS124. GPS co-ordinates: Latitude 37.0747, Longitude 15.25795

CORPORAL JOHN WILLIAM **BENTLEY** [7521867] ROYAL ARMY MEDICAL CORPS
ATT SRS (NO.2 TROOP)

John Bentley was born on 9 August 1916 in the parish of St Thomas in Stockport. Having worked as a thread doubler he enlisted into the Royal Army Medical Corps in December 1939 and on leaving 1st Depot Training Establishment at Cookham was posted to a military hospital in Oxford. In May 1941 he was appointed lance-corporal and three months later promoted to corporal. He was re-posted to the 210th Field Ambulance in April 1942, moving on to No.66 General Hospital in Leeds the following month. Having disembarked in the Middle East late that summer this hospital was located at Mussayib in Palestine, Bentley joining No.12 General Hospital at Sarafand that November. After a brief period working at No.3 Convalescent Depot he volunteered for Raiding Forces on 23 May 1943 and was attached to No.2 Troop, Special Raiding Squadron.

In the early hours of 10 July the SRS landed at Capo Murro di Porco at the spearhead of OPERATION HUSKY, the Allied the invasion of Sicily. It destroyed coastal batteries that threatened the invasion fleet before re-embarking the troopship *Ulster Monarch* on the 12th. That evening this steamed up the east

coast and entered the enemy-held harbour of Augusta where the SRS took to landing craft. They were within 300 yards of the shore when the first shell exploded amongst their escorting Motor Gun Boats, Joe Schofield, MBE, later writing:

The quiet evening was now filled with the noise of battle as the cruiser [HMS *Norfolk*] now entered through the boom with all guns blazing. The MGBs were all firing at previously noted pillboxes. The pillboxes covered the beach on which we had to land and our LCAs were approaching it fast. The LCAs now came under intensive machine-gun fire from the front and sides. A quick glance over the side and we could see the cruiser, MGBs and the *Ulster Monarch* were pumping fire into the foreshore and beach defences with everything they had. One pillbox was blasted off the face of the earth, a MGB ran into the beach to silence another at point blank range. Twin Vickers machine guns on the front of the LCAs were belching ammunition at the beaches ahead and the houses behind. It was a good landing, we simply flew across the beach and into the streets beyond. We dashed for the houses and doorways. Two medical orderlies were killed ['Operations by the Special Raiding Squadron in Sicily and Italy 1943', Joe Schofield's unpublished account].

Bentley was mortally wounded by machine-gun fire whilst disembarking from a landing craft. He was buried 'at 086486 100 yards inland' in a joint grave with the other medic, Private George Shaw (see his entry within this section). Sid Payne, former SRS, recalled wading towards the shore and the man next to him being killed outright. This was Shaw. Payne pulled his body over a rock and carried on. When he reached the beach he saw Captain Phil Gunn, the unit's Medical Officer, treating one of the other orderlies who had been wounded. As Payne watched, the man, who can only have been Bentley, died, Gunn throwing down a bandage in frustration whilst shaking his head (personal interview, 2008 – see Gunn's own entry under Birkenhead Landican Crematorium, United Kingdom, Volume III).

For some reason the service records of both Shaw and Bentley incorrectly state that they were killed on the 13th rather than the evening of the 12th. Their headstones therefore also carry the same error.

Son of John and Sarah Bentley (née Kidd) of Shawcross Street, Stockport, Cheshire.
Age 26.
Greater love hath no man than this. That a man lay down his life for his friends
Grave 6.G.14.

BOMBARDIER GEOFFREY <u>CATON</u> [1455205] ROYAL ARTILLERY, NO.11 COMMANDO, MIDDLE EAST COMMANDO, L DETACHMENT SAS BRIGADE, 1ST SAS AND SRS (NO.1 TROOP)

Geoff Caton was born in the parish of St Paul's in Widnes, Lancashire, on 14 November 1920. In April 1939, whilst working as a wood machinist, he joined 432 Company, 61st Searchlight Regiment, Royal Artillery (TA), and was embodied at the outbreak of war that September. Volunteering for special service in August 1940 he was posted to No.11 (Scottish) Commando and disembarked at Suez in Egypt the following March as a member of C Battalion, Layforce. Caton subsequently took part in the Litani River landings in Syria that June, fighting against the Vichy French in what is modern-day Lebanon (OPERATION EXPORTER). Although his intervening postings are absent from his service record it is highly likely that he was absorbed into the Middle East Commando before volunteering for L Detachment, SAS Brigade, in June 1942. His subsequent self-written application for Operational Wings outlined his operational activity in the Western Desert:

> Set out for the Fuka series of Ops [raids on airfields, July 1942] but returned due to truck breaking down.
>   Benghazi operation [OPERATION BIGAMY, September 1942] – front gunner in Jeep in the late Capt Chambers' party [see Captain Jim Chambers' entry under Fayid War Cemetery, Egypt, Volume I].
>   Howards Cairn – went out from Sand Sea with Capt Marsh to Sidi Barrani, mined the road and blew railway line.
>   Bir Zelten – again went with Capt Marsh's [A Squadron, 1st SAS] party around Beurat, Bkungen, Jebelakia. Went out five times twice being unsuccessful. 1). Set out for coastal road returned owing to trouble with Jeeps stuck in slit trenches etc [in November 1942 Caton, whilst on a three-Jeep patrol under Lieutenant Tony Marsh, was thrown clear of his vehicle when it was driven into a trench. Although uninjured the Jeep's tires had to be temporarily repaired using Elastoplast]. 2). Captured and destroyed four (ten-ton) lorries and trailers loaded with arms and ammunition (& Italians). 3). Went out to mine road but chased by armoured cars. 4). Strafed vehicles moving along coast road. 5). Mined a secondary road, laid booby traps, and also mined a parking area for vehicles which was in use very near to the coast road.

In March 1943 the majority of 1st SAS' subunits were restructured as the Special Raiding Squadron and began training for OPERATION HUSKY, the Allied invasion of Sicily. The SRS subsequently landed at Capo Murro di Porco at the forefront of this operation in the early hours of 10 July 1943, Caton's No.1 Troop under Lieutenant Johnny Wiseman being tasked with assaulting a coastal battery that threatened the invasion fleet. Having done so the men moved inland to deal with further enemy positions. During the ensuing action Caton went forward to take the surrender of an Italian gun emplacement that was showing a white flag. He was hit around the groin by a burst of machine-gun fire and died of his wounds soon after. His local newspaper reported his death under the heading 'Killed in Sicily – Widnes Parachutist':

> Information has been received that Corporal Geoffrey Caton, SAS, has been killed in action in Sicily, bringing to a close a brilliant and successful career. He was 22 years of age, the son of Mr and Mrs Thomas Caton, 37 Stewards Avenue and formerly of Eleanor Street. He was an old boy of Simms Cross and the Central schools. After leaving the latter he was apprentice woodworking machinist at Messrs. Evans Timber Works, and attended Manchester University for trade tuition. He excelled in all kinds of sport, boxing being his favourite. His boxing was developed in his father's club under Tommy Burns, his clubmates being Jack Stanner and Bert Chambers. He won a silver cup in the championships at Manchester.
>   In February 1939 Sergt. Caton joined the Widnes Territorials (South Lancs Regiment) [sic]. His adventurous spirit was not satisfied with home service, however, and volunteered for transfer to the Commandos when they were first formed. He served overseas with the late Lt.-Colonel Keyes, VC, and in the Syrian campaign was wounded in the raid on Litani River, along with the only two Widnes pals, Dick Myler and Tommy Carter. He spent six weeks in hospital in Jerusalem, and on being discharged, volunteered for service with the Special Raiding Squadron. He was in the vanguard of all the major engagements in Cyprus, Crete, Tunisia and Egypt, many of the exploits being at

present a military secret. He successfully passed the ski-ing course on Mount Lebanon, and was awarded parachute wings for special operations. He was in the first 200 paratroops who made the bridgehead in the first landing in Sicily, and an officer, Lieut. J.M. Wiseman, writing to the bereaved parents, gives an account of Corporal Caton's gallant death. He writes:

'It is with very real and personal regret that I have to offer you my sympathy on the death in action of your son, Geoffrey. Your son was one of my subsection leaders, and I had great admiration both for his personal courage and abilities as a leader. He took part in the first landing on European soil and was one of those who made the original bridgehead through which our armies are advancing. He fought extremely well all day, until an unexpected burst of fire caught him. We did all we could to make him comfortable, and he suffered his wounds bravely, before passing peacefully away. He is buried on Cape Murro di Porco, about 8 miles south-east of Syracuse. Believe me, I feel his loss very much, and I offer you my very, very sincere sympathy.'

His pal, Sergt. William M. McNinch has written the following to his mother in Glasgow who has forwarded it on to Mr and Mrs Caton: 'I'm sorry to say I have lost my best friend in this lot. We've been together now for three years, and have been the greatest of friends, and I'll miss him more than I can say' [see McNinch's own entry under Sangro River War Cemetery, Italy].

Mr Pat Sinnott writes: 'With the deepest regret I saw the sad news in the Weekly News, and offer my deepest sympathy to Geoffrey's mother, father and family in their great sorrow. In the hey-day of Jack Stanner, young Geoff Caton was one of his chief sparring partners. Only a boy in those days, he was my favourite boy boxer. I feel as if I have lost a son. I liked Geoffrey not only as a promising boxer, but because his manners and conduct in the ring and out, were exemplary.'

Geoffrey's eldest brother, Thomas, is serving overseas as meteorologist with the Fleet Air Arm; his younger brother, Ronald, is in the Royal Navy; and his sister, Joan, is a Nurse [*Weekly News*, 13 August 1943].

That October the same newspaper published the following under the heading 'Parachutist Praised – Officer's Tribute':

Mr and Mrs Thomas Caton, 37 Stewards Avenue, Widnes, have received another letter from overseas paying further tribute to the heroism of their son, Corporal Geoffrey Caton, who was killed in Sicily in August this year. The letter is from Squadron Sergt. Major G. Rose, MM, who is in the Special Raiding Squadron of the Special Air Service Regiment, CMF, and is as follows:

'Sincerely hoping that I shall not cause any further sorrow, I take this opportunity of offering you my deepest sympathy in your recent bereavement caused by the death in action of your son Geoffrey. As his squadron sergeant-major, I feel it is my duty to write and tell you of his activities in the unit, of how he met his death, and how he is missed by all his comrades.

Geoff, as he was known to us all, joined us in June, 1942, he completed his parachute course shortly afterwards and then played a great part in the unit's activities in the Western Desert. Our operations consisted solely of sabotage work behind the enemy lines, and your son played a [illegible] and noble part in many of them, which resulted in his being promoted to corporal. These operations are too numerous to mention here, but at a later date you will hear of them, and you son's name will be coupled with many of them. For the part he played, his Commanding Officer awarded him Operational Wings, an honour unique in the British Army, and one which only members of this unit can obtain, namely that of wearing his parachute wings on his left breast.

On the 10th July, 1943, this squadron took part in the invasion of Sicily, and it was during this operation that Geoff met his untimely end. He was in the thick of the battle and won praise from all sides for his coolness and courage. I was the last person to speak to him before he died and we buried him beneath an olive tree, the squadron paying silent homage while the padre read the last rites. I knew Geoff very well, and I felt his passing very keenly. He leaves a gap in our ranks which can never be filled. I shall forward his wings to you along with his badge, on which is inscribed "Who Dares Wins."

I pass on to you the condolences and sympathy of the whole of the squadron in this hour of your great bereavement. We salute the memory of a great and gallant soldier' [29 October 1943].

Albert Youngman, former SRS, later recalled that the wounded Caton had been taken inside a building where the padre and the Commanding Officer, Major Paddy Mayne, DSO, stayed with him until he died: 'I clearly remember that Paddy held his hand to the end and Geoff said to him "I'm ever so sorry to be such a nuisance, sir"' (personal interview, 2011). Rose later recorded that Caton was originally buried 'at farm [Marsa] Alacona 165263 on left side of lane leading to farm 50x from latter'.

Son of Thomas and Ellen Caton (née Ellis) of Stewards Avenue, Widnes, Lancashire – Younger brother of Tom and older brother of Ronald, Joan, Alecia, Harry and Irene Caton.

Age 22.
'Our Geoff.' Dearly loved and remembered by Dad, Mam, Margaret and all at home
Grave 2.F.13. Also commemorated on the cenotaph at Victoria Park, Widnes.

PRIVATE GEORGE **SHAW** [7344428] ROYAL ARMY MEDICAL CORPS
ATT 1ST SAS AND SRS

George Shaw was born on 27 February 1918 in the parish of St Augustine in Derby where he worked for Rolls Royce and then as a conductor for the Trent Motor Traction Company. In May 1936, whilst employed as a bobbin storeman and living in the Derby suburb of Spondon, he joined the 187th Field Ambulance, Royal Army Medical Corps (TA). Mobilised at the outbreak of war, he was promoted to lance-corporal in February 1940 and having been posted to the 185th Field Ambulance was advanced to corporal two months later. That June he married Margaret Hobson at the Methodist Chapel at Gainford, their daughter, also Margaret, being born in November 1941. Having reverted to private on posting to the 3rd Light Field Ambulance that month he regained a stripe in December and embarked for the Middle East in May 1942. Although without a unit on arrival he joined the 150th Light Field Ambulance at the end of the year and again reverted to the rank of private. He volunteered for 1st SAS on 5 March 1943 from a reinforcement depot, two weeks before the majority of the Regiment's subunits were restructured as the Special Raiding Squadron.

Shaw subsequently landed at the forefront of OPERATION HUSKY, the Allied invasion of Sicily, on 10 July 1943. The SRS destroyed coastal batteries that threatened the invasion fleet before being tasked with capturing the key port of Augusta on the east coast, along which Lt-General Miles Dempsey's XIII Corps was advancing. Shaw was killed in action during this assault on the evening of 12 July whilst coming ashore from landing craft on the east side of the port's peninsula. He was buried not far away 'at 086486 100x inland' in a joint grave with Corporal John Bentley [see his entry within this section]. Alf Dignum, a former squadron member, later recalled:

> Landing at Augusta we were unable to get close to the shore and had a bit of swimming to do under very heavy fire [from Italian machine-gun positions across the bay]. When I got to shore on the beach I'm afraid the RAMC lad was laying across a dead trooper and was also dead. I had no time to stop as we were under heavy fire and also had a job to do …

In between work he [Shaw] did all he could to help the local population with their medical problems … I liked the way that he concerned himself with the locals and their problems …

I can assure you that the poor lad died at Augusta in the afternoon between 4/5. I well remember reading the forces' newspaper issued in the following week remarking that it was the (first) daylight landing of the war [personal correspondence, 2010].

Son of Mr and Mrs Thomas Shaw of Derby – Husband of Margaret Shaw of Arch House, Gainford, County Durham – Father of Betty and Margaret Shaw.

Age 23.

No inscription.

Grave 6.G.13. Also commemorated on the war memorial within St Mary's churchyard, Gainford.

SWITZERLAND

Even before the war, refugees began crossing into Switzerland to escape Nazi oppression. After the outbreak of hostilities it developed into a neutral island within Occupied Europe, the crossing of its border forming the aspiration of political, racial and religious asylum seekers. Having escaped from camps in Germany and Italy, Allied prisoners of war, eager to be repatriated, joined those refugees, as did men evading capture during operations. Amongst them were numerous members of the SAS, SBS and LRDG: Lieutenant Jimmy Riccomini of 2nd SAS (see his entry under Milan War Cemetery, Italy, within this volume) and Troopers Jim Blakeney and Roy Davies of 1st SAS (both now buried at Hanover War Cemetery, Germany, Volume III), who later redeployed on operations, were but three. The one man we commemorate in Switzerland sadly did not survive internment.

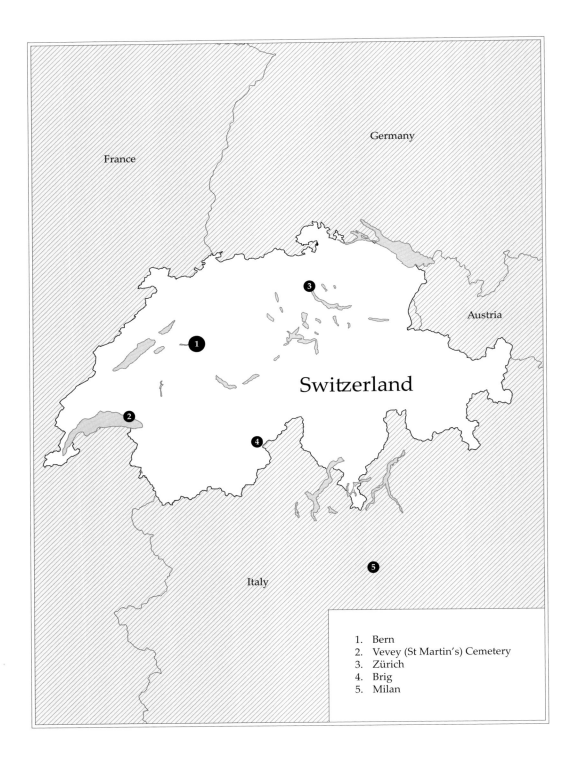

1. Bern
2. Vevey (St Martin's) Cemetery
3. Zürich
4. Brig
5. Milan

VEVEY (ST MARTIN'S) CEMETERY

Despite measures to repatriate interned Allied servicemen, their numbers in Switzerland increased rapidly, especially after the Italian armistice of September 1943 when many took the opportunity to walk out of their POW camps and attempt the hazardous border crossing before German guards took over. Thus the Commonwealth graves within this plot are those of either escaped prisoners of war or of airmen who crashed in Switzerland.

Vevey is located on the north-east shore of Lake Geneva. The cemetery lies to the east of, and above, the main railway station, its entrance being on the chemin du Point-du-Jour. The Commonwealth war graves form part of Plot 53 that is roughly in the centre of the cemetery. GPS co-ordinates: Latitude 46.46315, Longitude 6.84824

GUARDSMAN CYRIL SIDNEY MALCOLM RICHARDSON [2657262] COLDSTREAM GUARDS AND LRDG (G.1 PATROL, B SQN)

Known as 'Lofty' to his comrades, Cyril Richardson was born on 30 September 1917 in Sussex. Having worked as a butcher, he enlisted into the Coldstream Guards at Guildford in January 1936 hoping to gain experience before joining the police. After basic training at Caterham, he was posted to the 3rd Battalion and embarked for Egypt in November 1937. Here he carried out policing duties until October 1938 when the battalion took up a similar role in Palestine, Richardson serving with No.3 Company. In April 1939 he arrived back in Egypt where he and his comrades expected to be relieved by the 2nd Battalion later that year and thus return to the UK.

The outbreak of war meant this was not to be, and the 3rd moved up to the Western Desert in July 1940 and converted to motorised infantry. Patrolling the frontier with Libya, its task was to report any Italian advance rather than to offer outright resistance. That September the enemy crossed the border on a narrow front close to the coast, Richardson's battalion carrying out a successful five-day rearguard action back to prepared positions at Buq Buq until ordered to withdraw to Mersa Matruh. In December General Sir Archibald Wavell, MC, launched a counter-attack against the numerically superior enemy, the 3rd Battalion's assault on the coastal sector playing a key diversionary role (OPERATION COMPASS).

In January 1941, the Coldstream was withdrawn to the Nile Delta where it joined the 2nd Battalion, Scots Guards, in forming the 22nd Guards Brigade. Time away from the front line was short-lived. Rommel launched his own offensive that April which precipitated a move back to the Libyan border. Here the battalion saw hand-to-hand fighting on the 15th during a night raid on a German stronghold above Sollum. The following month it defended Halfaya Pass against a Panzer counter-offensive until ordered to withdraw.

A period of training in the area of Daba followed, Richardson volunteering for the Long Range Desert Group before the end of July 1941 and being posted to G Patrol. Having served in the army for over five years he welcomed the change, writing to his brother:

> At last I am with a unit which is interesting and exciting, in fact just what I have always wanted. Yes, George at last I can say I like the job the army has now given me to do, and I hope it will last a long time. You will hear all about us and our work after the war and I am willing to gamble it will make very interesting reading [Richardson family collection].

That October the now reorganised G.1 Patrol under Captain Tony Hay left Cairo passing through Kharga, Kufra and Siwa en route for Road Watch duty along the Libyan coast. After patrolling the area of Bir-ben-Gania, it was ordered to join G.2 at Maaten el-Grara and attack enemy traffic on the Benghazi–Agedabia road. On its way it was bombed by a German Ju-87 and Richardson noted in his diary: 'I got a few shots off at him before the gun mounting broke and my Vickers [machine gun] went flying over the side of the truck.' Arriving at the wrong RV the patrol was ordered to attack the coast road on the night of 28 November 1941 without G.2, which was, in any case, having mechanical issues. It soon located a target:

> After going for about 5 or 6 miles down the road passing odd lorries we saw our prey. It was a house on the side of the road with lorries parked all around it. I think it was a kind of ordnance yard or petrol filling station. By this time it was just about dark and as each lorry of ours pulled off the road they let fly with everything they had got into this house and the parked lorries [Richardson's personal diary, from the family collection].

Lying-up in nearby hills until the following afternoon, the patrol returned to the road and ambushed a fuel tanker that night. Subsequently ordered back to Siwa, it arrived on 3 December to find new orders from Eighth Army to 'act with the utmost vigour offensively against any enemy targets or communications within reach.' Accordingly, having been allotted its previous operational area between Benghazi and Agedabia, the patrol set out again on the 10th, reaching its former hideout near Beda Fomm on morning of 14th. Here it was joined by Y.2 Patrol, and plans to attack local targets were drawn up. Having destroyed a staff car south of Magren on the evening of the 15th, G.1 drove all night towards Agedabia:

> There was a force of Indians and South African armoured cars expected to reach the place we were making for on the 17th [sic – 16 December 1941 during OPERATION CRUSADER] with the intention of taking Adgadabia [sic] and doing a pincer movement to cut off the retreating Jerry. So, when about 8 o'clock the following morning we almost run into some SAF [South African Forces] trucks everyone was quite sure that we had run into our own force …

Everyone was feeling sleepy and hungry and were not as careful as we should have been. The officer [Hay] drove forward and disappeared [to recce ahead] over a rise in the ground [personal diary].

Whilst out of sight, Hay and his sergeant, Nolan, were captured, and the enemy returned in their vehicle as a ruse to seize the remainder of the patrol:

Everyone was walking around their trucks trying to keep warm when all the fun started, although I did not think it was fun at the time. MGs [machine guns] opened up from about four places and I made, along with the other two members of the truck, one big dive for the rear wheel … it was useless to climb into the back of the truck for the lead was flying in all directions. The three of us made ourselves as small as possible behind the rear wheel and spent a very uncomfortable two or three minutes while the supposed Indians peppered our truck. A section of them came out to collect us, or I suppose they thought to bury us. But we were more than lucky that day for none of us, up to that moment, had been hit. They came up shouting in their guttural language, one of them with a nasty looking Hotchkiss gun so, seeing as we were definitely at their mercy, we stood up to give ourselves up [personal diary].

Although six men managed to get away with two vehicles, twelve men, including Hay, Nolan and Richardson, were captured. Posted missing in action the following day, Richardson was interrogated by the Italians at Agedabia and imprisoned at Benghazi, Barce then Cyrene before being returned to Benghazi. From here he was transported by boat, first to Tripoli and then to the Italian port of Naples on 29 December. After a month in a tented transit camp at Capua he was sent to PG.59 at Servigliano until late February 1943 when he was transferred to PG.53 at Sforzacosta. In mid May he and Sergeant 'Tam' Pratt, also of G.1 Patrol, were posted to Camp 133 that supplied POW labourers to farms in the Novara region south of Lake Maggiore. That June he wrote to his brother once more:

Myself I cannot grumble. In the month I have been working on this farm I have regained my former fitness and am tanned off nice and brown even if I still am a bit thin. But I honestly say I am feeling 100% better working. Something to occupy my mind, we are out all day and have Sunday off. Of course I am not permitted to say much except we are doing farm work. But I am happy at last after being caged up for eighteen months so that should make mum and you all happy to know …
Italy is really a wonderfully interesting country. I would like to visit it after the war [family collection].

However, a few days after the Italian armistice of September 1943 Richardson wrote in his diary: 'Our position is delicate. There are dozens of Itie soldiers moving around the countryside. Jerry is shooting all their soldiers who are not fascists. So, I suppose that is what will happen to us if he gets us. I would like to let mum and them know for now we are safe.' On the 18th he noted: 'if things get too hot for us here we will try to get to Switzerland. That will mean getting interned but that is better than a POW I think.' The following day his mind was made up for him: 'The old farmer had us at his house today. Told us we had to go. Gave us some fresh clothes, 50 lira each. So, tomorrow I think we will hit the trail for Switzerland. He gave us a map marked out best route.' On the 20th he noted in his diary:

The weather today was lovely and clear but a bitter freezing wind blowing. We moved off with the guide at 7am. We climbed steadily for about four hours. My hands were about frozen but we was [sic] happy of the thought of at last making the border … Plenty of snow knocking about on top made our progress slow and dangerous. On reaching the top we looked down into Switzerland.

However, Richardson became too exhausted to continue, and he and Pratt were forced to drop back into Italy briefly before crossing over the border at a later date. On Thursday 30 September 1943 he was able to write as a free man from Brig inside neutral Switzerland: 'Well, my birthday today. 26 years old.'
However, escape did not bring relief. On 2 October he penned: 'I have got my usual cold in the head and sore lips. The Medical Officer told me to go sick. He gave me some ointment for my lips and some stuff to clear my head. Our new billets are very disappointing. Overcrowded, no blankets just straw. The meal tonight just soup and a little bread.' The following day he wrote: 'But roll on the end of the war. I am getting tired of all this messing around. I would like to go home again.'
Unfortunately this was not to be and on 12 October 1943 Richardson made the last entry into his diary: 'Weather dull. Am feeling half dead today with a cold in the head, sore throat. Still, there is

no wonder everyone's got a cold. We are peeled [*sic*] in like sardines and colds soon spread.' At the back of the diary there is a note entered in different handwriting:

> Nine days later Richardson died [of pneumonia on 21 October 1943 at Krankenasyl Hospital in Wald, Zurich]. In the Autumn of 1984 Tam returned to the Swiss Cemetery where he had been laid to rest. The headstone had long gone and all that remains is the simple statement 'Cyril Richardson 25th Oct 43' found in the register.

Richardson, who had originally been buried with full military honours at Zurich Wald Cemetery, had been reinterred at his current resting place in April 1965, a service of remembrance having been held at the Guards' Chapel in early November 1943.

Son of William and Kate Richardson (née Denman) of Horsham, Sussex – Younger brother of George of a reserved occupation and the Home Guard, of Bert who served in the Royal Electrical and Mechanical Engineers in Iraq, and of Nellie – Older brother of Eva Richardson.
Age 26.
Gone but not forgotten by those he loved the best
Grave 82A. Also commemorated on Horsham's war memorial.

TURKEY

After the sweeping German Blitzkrieg of 1940 Turkey, anxious not to be drawn into the widening conflict, announced its 'non-belligerency'. However, Hitler's 1941 occupation of Yugoslavia and Greece appeared to signal a forthcoming Nazi invasion or forced alliance, either of which would threaten Middle Eastern oil reserves and the Suez Canal. Despite this, Turkey maintained her stance, even whilst pressured by the Axis grip on the Aegean islands. The see-saw nature of the campaign waged over these islands, some of which lie literally within swimming distance of the Turkish coast, saw both sides using her waters to moor their vessels, either overtly or covertly. A blind eye was even turned when British Raiding Forces, serviced by Motor Torpedo Boats and fishing caiques of the Royal Navy's Levant Schooner Flotilla, set up a forward operating base near Bodrum. The Turks, however, continued to walk a fine tightrope between the warring nations and if the Axis appeared to have the upper hand SBS and LRDG patrols often found themselves temporarily interned by local authorities.

Although Turkey ceased to supply war materials to Germany in April 1944 she was keen to retain a strong military capability to guard against post-war Soviet expansionism and remained equidistant from both sides. It was not until February 1945, during the final stages of hostilities, that she declared war on Germany and Japan.

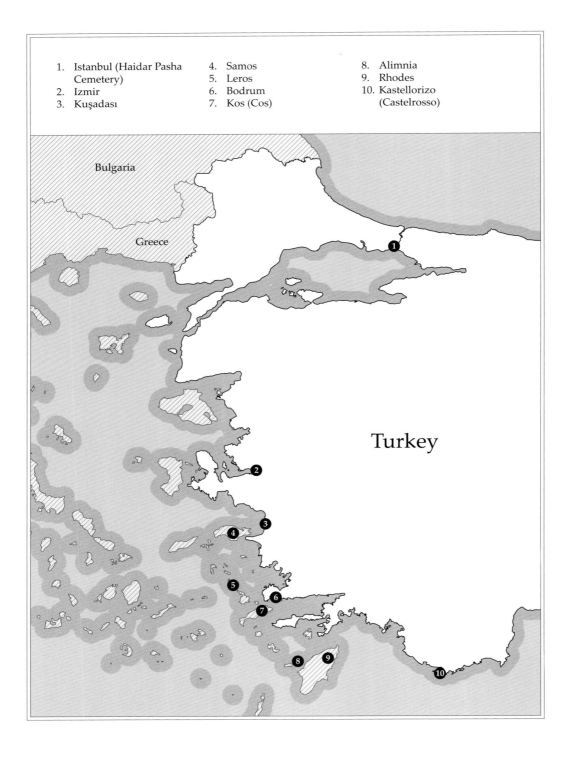

1. Istanbul (Haidar Pasha Cemetery)
2. Izmir
3. Kuşadası
4. Samos
5. Leros
6. Bodrum
7. Kos (Cos)
8. Alimnia
9. Rhodes
10. Kastellorizo (Castelrosso)

Bulgaria

Greece

Turkey

HAIDAR PASHA CEMETERY

In 1855 the Turkish Government gave the ground occupied by this cemetery to the British as the resting place for approximately 6,000 troops of the Crimean War. The majority of them died as a result of a cholera epidemic in Istanbul. Their ranks were joined by British civilian burials as well as Commonwealth prisoners of war buried by the Turks during the First World War. When the city was occupied after the November 1918 armistice, further burials were made, some from No.82 General Hospital and others being graves concentrated from smaller cemeteries. Turkey's neutrality during the Second World War Turkey meant that those Commonwealth servicemen buried here from 1939 to 1945 were mainly prisoners of war who died whilst attempting to escape and whose bodies were washed up on the Turkish coast.

The war graves plot contains 407 Commonwealth burials of the First World War, sixty of which are unidentified, and thirty-nine of the Second World War (fourteen unidentified). Due to the risk of earthquake, the graves are marked by stone plinths rather than by the usual headstones. It also contains the Haidar Pasha Cremation Memorial that commemorates 122 soldiers of the Indian Army who died in the years 1919–20 and who were originally commemorated at Mashiak and Osmanieh cemeteries. In addition, the Haidar Pasha Memorial commemorates more than thirty servicemen of the First World War who were killed fighting in south Russia, Georgia and Azerbaijan, and in post-armistice operations in Russia and Transcaucasia, and whose graves are unknown. An Addenda panel commemorates over 170 Commonwealth casualties who were buried in cemeteries in this region whose graves can no longer be maintained.

Haidar Pasha is a suburb of Istanbul on the Asiatic side of the Bosphorus. The cemetery is located adjacent to the Neafa Military Hospital, access being gained via a large path to the right-hand side as you face the hospital gates. Opening hours are 0800–2100hrs. GPS co-ordinates: Latitude 40.99981, Longitude 29.02005

Private David Calder **FAIRWEATHER** [2763524] Black Watch, No.11 Commando, Middle East Commando, Special Boat Section and SBS (S Det)

Davey Fairweather was born on 17 November 1919 at Larbet in Falkirk where he grew up as a keen scout in the 2nd Torwood Group. Having worked as a house painter he enlisted into the Black Watch (Royal Highland Regiment) in July 1940 and was promoted to lance-corporal the following month whilst at an infantry training centre. That November he reverted to the rank of private having volunteered for No.11 (Scottish) Commando that disembarked at Suez, Egypt, in early March 1941 as C Battalion of Layforce, an amalgamation of similar units that was intended for raiding operations in the eastern Mediterranean.

At the end of April, having been stood-to (and dropped from) a raid on Bardia earlier that month, No.11 Commando moved to Cyprus in readiness for Operation Exporter, the campaign in Syria against the Vichy French. In the early hours of 9 June it subsequently landed close to the mouth of the Litani River in an attempt to seize bridges key to the Allied advance. Although these were destroyed by the French and No.11 suffered heavy casualties, the Commando effectively tied down Vichy troops until advancing Australians arrived from the south.

Back in Egypt, Layforce was disbanded, Fairweather and many of his No.11 comrades being posted to the Middle East Commando at Geneifa near Kabrit. He volunteered for No.1 Special Boat Section on New Year's Day 1943, this unit being attached to 1st SAS at the time and officially absorbed into the Special Boat Squadron (1st SAS) when this was raised on 19 March 1943.

Fairweather was a member of an S Detachment party under Captain Andy Lassen, MC, that landed on the Aegean island of Samos on 13 September 1943. According to Captain Walter Milner-Barry of the SBS this was 'to anticipate a possible fascist coup against the pro-Badoglio governor of the island'. Although reinforced by the Greek Sacred Squadron, the fall of Leros left the Samos garrison in a precarious position. Faced with the prospect of another British-held island being overrun and the resulting loss of face, not least to the Turks who had assisted in Samos' supply, a decision was made to evacuate. Casualties resulting from heavy Luftwaffe air raids expedited matters (see entries for Sergeant George Munro and Signalman 'Spadge' Sparrow under Rhodes War Cemetery, Greece, within this volume). On the night of 21 November the men therefore embarked at Port Vathy, packing onto caique fishing vessels of the Levant Schooner Flotilla. Having crossed to Kuşadası on the Turkish coast, Fairweather was accidentally shot late that night whilst still aboard, Lance-bombardier Cunnington of the SBS stating at the ensuing inquiry:

> Pte Fairweather was shot and critically wounded onboard ship on the 21st November 1943 at Kurddisi [*sic*], Turkey. A Greek signaller withdrew my revolver from my pocket as I turned from him and fired into a crowd of men who were standing quite near. Amongst them was Pte Fairweather D, and the bullet entered the left side of his head and passed through, coming out through the right side of his head. I could see that he had been critically wounded, and that his condition was very serious. Pte Jarrell, the medical orderly, rendered what assistance could be given medically and Pte Fairweather was evacuated to the sick-bay ashore. I, to the best of my knowledge, thought I had emptied my revolver the previous night, but I cannot swear to this. Pte Fairweather was moved to hospital [court of inquiry, Samakh, 21 February 1944].

The medic, Private Porter 'Joe' Jarrell, an American who was awarded the George Medal whilst serving with the SBS, stated:

> The death of Pte Fairweather D occurred at 0430 hours 22/11/43 as a result of severe head wounds received the previous day from an accidental shooting. The morning after the evacuation of Samos two of the evacuating caiques were lying side by side in a neutral port, one carrying SBS personnel, the other of the Greek Squadron. Pte Fairweather boarded the Greek Squadron caique to get a cup of tea. As he was doing this a Greek soldier of the

Sacred Squadron was examining a .45 revolver and accidentally caused its discharge. The bullet from this revolver struck Pte Fairweather in the back of the head, slightly to the left-hand side. The force of the discharge being at very close range splintered fragments of the bones of the skull and tore small arteries of the brain. Pte Fairweather was given immediate medical attention by an orderly and was sent ashore accompanied by a Greek medical officer and rushed to a nearby hospital. The nature of the wound was of such severity that two doctors agreed there was almost no hope of saving Pte Fairweather's life. Pte Fairweather remained in a coma with his right side paralysed from the wounding of the nerves in the brain and at 0430 hours, the following morning 22/11/43, he was dead [court of inquiry – see Guardsman 'Tommy' Bishops' entry under Rhodes War Cemetery, Greece, for full details of Jarrell's George Medal action].

Private 'X' of the Greek Sacred Squadron [name redacted for publication] stated: 'I was playing with the revolver, turning it round by the trigger guard as it hung from my finger. I turned it round perhaps four times, and the fourth, without realising how, it went off.'

Fairweather was buried at Smyrna on the 24th, Dick Holmes, MM, a former member of S Detachment, later recalling:

After several abortive attempts to evacuate a number of Italian soldiers to Turkey we were ordered to board a small Greek boat that would transport us [from Samos] across the narrow strait to the mainland. Completely pissed off from the ridiculous attempts to help a large number of Italians escape to Turkey several of us had taken refuge in the hold of the boat and as we sat on the ballast we heard a shot fired. A head peered over the edge of the hatch and informed us that Davey Fairweather had been killed by a stray bullet from the pistol of one of the Greeks who were on board. The body was taken ashore and buried on the beach, as we thought. Only later did we discover that that was not so.

From a distance of sixty-five years our lack of action appears unforgivable but in late November 1943 many of us had been on active service in the Middle East for nearly three years and had been exposed to death in many varied forms – decapitation, burned alive by flaming petrol, bullet wounds of various degrees of severity, bodies missing parts, drowning – you name it!!! We had come to the conclusion the best way of dealing with it was to ignore it. That's what we did …

[Davey was] an excellent footballer and ballroom dancer with great ability [personal correspondence, 2009].

Son of John and Lena Fairweather of Rae Street, Stenhousemuir, Stirlingshire.
Age 24.
Dearly beloved son of J. and L. Fairweather. Larbert, Scotland
Row B, grave 12. Also commemorated on 2nd Torwood (Forth Region) Scout Group's war memorial at Torwoodhead, Torwood.

THE SAS AND LRDG ROLL OF HONOUR 1941–47

VOLUME III – 'WE WERE GOOD MEN'
North West Europe

EX-LANCE-CORPORAL X, QGM

Published in the UK by SAS-LRDG-RoH
http://www.sas-lrdg-roh.com

First Published 2016
Second Imprint 2018

British Library Cataloguing in Publication Data
Data available

ISBN 978-1-5262-0332-8

Project managed, printed and bound by Cedar Group. UK Main Office: Unit 1 Triton Centre, Premier Way, Abbey Park Industrial Estate, Romsey, Hampshire, SO51 9DJ
Tel: 01794 525 032. Email: design@cedargroup.uk.com

Design by Ex-Lance-corporal X. Artwork and illustration by R. Chasemore and R. Farnworth

Typeset in Palatino Linotype. The text follows *New Hart's Rules – The Handbook of Style for Writers and Editors* published by Oxford University Press

Freedom is the sure possession of those alone who have the courage to defend it.
Pericles

CONTENTS

Volume III – 'We Were Good Men' – North West Europe

BELGIUM

As dawn broke on 10 May 1940 German forces advanced into Holland and Belgium. Both countries had chosen to remain neutral, placing all their hopes in Nazi good faith and respect for treaties. The British Expeditionary Force (BEF) had, therefore, until this moment, been forced to wait in France unable to prepare adequate defences. Although now rushed forward into Belgium, the Germans had been granted the space required to capture positions key to their lightening drive. The BEF was thus soon being pushed back and with evacuation underway Belgium was forced to surrender in the early hours of 28 May. Over the following days fishing vessels brought off small groups of Belgian soldiers, these later forming the army-in-exile. One of its units developed into the Belgian Independent Parachute Company. In early 1944 this was absorbed into the SAS Brigade, within which it was more commonly known as 5th (Belgian) SAS. After the Allied landings in Normandy that June, its patrols mounted numerous operations behind German lines in France. Those involved in OPERATION NOAH became the first Allied troops into Belgium when they crossed the frontier to assist local Resistance networks. With friendly forces advancing into their homeland soon after, further patrols were dropped into Belgium during OPERATIONS BRUTUS, BERGBANG and CALIBAN.

As 1st SAS' operations in France drew to a close at the end of September 1944 its men drove to newly-liberated Brussels where they refitted for future deployment. Jeep patrols from C Squadron subsequently crossed the border into Holland in order to arrest known Nazis and pick up Allied agents. Whilst elements of their Belgian counterpart were parachuted into Holland for OPERATIONS GOBBO/PORTIA, REGAN/FABIAN and FRISE, the remainder of what was now officially named 5th (Belgian) SAS provided forward reconnaissance during OPERATION REGENT, helping to counter that winter's German offensive in the Ardennes.

Two members of 1st SAS are buried in Belgium; one at Brussels Town Cemetery and the other at Leopoldsburg War Cemetery.

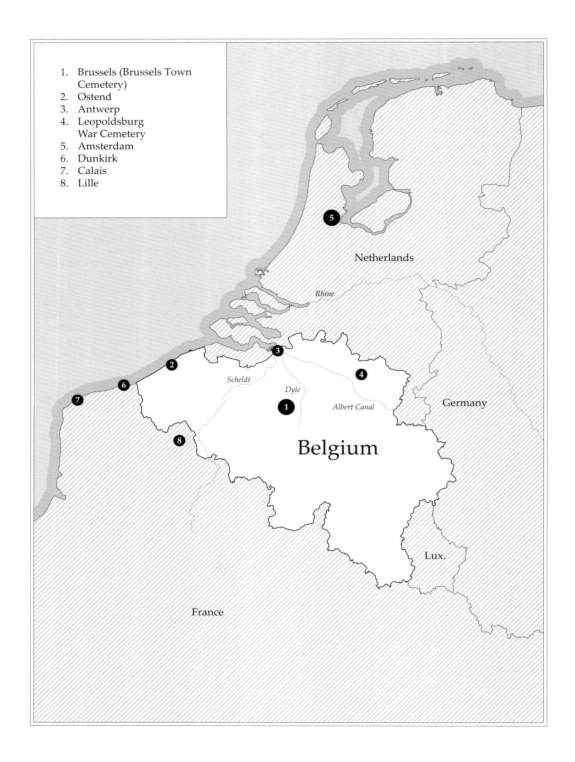

1. Brussels (Brussels Town Cemetery)
2. Ostend
3. Antwerp
4. Leopoldsburg War Cemetery
5. Amsterdam
6. Dunkirk
7. Calais
8. Lille

Netherlands

Rhine

Scheldt

Dyle

Albert Canal

Germany

Belgium

Lux.

France

Brussels Town Cemetery

All but four of the First World War burials found here are of Commonwealth prisoners of war whose remains were brought back from Germany in 1919. The majority of the 587 Second World War casualties lost their lives whilst manning lines of communication after the liberation of Brussels in September 1944. Others were killed covering the BEF's withdrawal to Dunkirk in 1940 or during bombing missions over Germany or Belgium itself. The cemetery also contains thirty-five non-Commonwealth, and five peacetime, service burials.

The Commonwealth war cemetery is located within the Cimetière de Bruxelles in the Evere district north-east of the city centre. The entrance lies on the junction of avenue Cicéron and the avenue du Cimetière de Bruxelles. On entering the main gates walk straight ahead and straight over the roundabout, the cemetery being on the left at the end. Open Tuesday to Sunday 0830–1630hrs, no admittance after 1600. GPS co-ordinates: Latitude 50.86437, Longitude 4.41732

Major Robert Marie Emanuel MÉLOT MC [163579] Belgian Army, Belgian Air Force, General List, Druze Legion, Middle East Commmando, MI(R), SOE, L Detachment SAS Brigade, SRS and 1st SAS

Bob Mélot was born on 19 September 1895 at Ixelles, a suburb of Brussels. As a student at the outbreak of the First World War he enlisted into the Belgian infantry in November 1914. He was subsequently promoted to caporal in September 1916, wounded in 1917 and promoted to sergent in September 1918 (service number 62662). The following month he joined 4th Squadron, Belgian Air Force, having qualified as a pilot and was appointed Adjutant in a reserve squadron after the war. Having been awarded a Croix de guerre in 1921 he resigned in December 1930 and migrated to Egypt. Here he and other expats made numerous pioneering journeys to explore the desert by motorcar, a period only interrupted when he became a forestry manager for the Belgo-Canadian Pulp and Paper Company at Shawinigan Falls in Canada.

By the outbreak of the Second World War Mélot was running the family import business in Egypt and fluent in a number of languages including Arabic. Although it had been over twenty years since he fired a shot in anger he applied to join Belgian forces in the Congo. Refused due to his age, he offered his services to the British who noted his potential in October 1940 and registered him on the Army Officers' Emergency Reserve. Appointed an emergency commission onto the General List the following January (*London Gazette* 04/02/41) he was posted to No.102 Military Mission, the Libyan Arab Force. Two months later he was advanced to captain, although he increasingly found his unit's role, consisting mainly of guard duties, too sedate. He therefore transferred to the newly-formed Druze Legion, one of the last cavalry units ever raised in war and, despite the fact he could not ride a horse, briefly commanded its mounted 4th Squadron. The explorer, and soon-to-be fellow SAS officer, Wilfred Thesiger, was one of his contemporaries.

Mélot volunteered for special service in July 1941. That September he was subsequently posted to G(R), an integral part of GHQ Cairo that formed the Middle East sub-branch of MI(R), the War Office's clandestine warfare department. Training in unarmed combat and explosives at the Middle East Commando's Holding Squadron followed, as did numerous information-gathering operations behind enemy lines alongside volunteers from the exiled Libyan community: in November 1941 he and a companion were taken by T.2 Patrol, Long Range Desert Group, to the Jebel Akhdar in Libya to receive returning members of Operation Flipper, No.11 Commando's failed attempt to kill Rommel. Late the following February Mélot accompanied Captain Gus Holliman's S.1 Patrol, LRDG, on a Road Watch operation near to the village of Lamluda in the same area. Due to flash floods, the clutches of two trucks were damaged and later burnt out, the party having to return to Siwa on the two remaining vehicles.

Officially joining GHQ Middle East for intelligence duties on 1 April 1942, Mélot was awarded an immediate Military Cross for his work of this period:

From 18 Feb to 10 Mar; from 5 May to 4 Jun [Operation Humourist, a joint (G)R and Inter-Services Liaison Department (MI6), intelligence gathering mission south-east of Benghazi with Lieutenant Segal, WO 201/727 – see Gurdon's entry under Alamein Memorial, Egypt, Volume I, for further details]; from 8 Jul to 29 Jul. This officer has made three sorties behind enemy lines and has stayed a total of seventy-four days in enemy country. He has passed some extremely useful information by W/T [wireless telegraphy]. He has shown great energy and initiative and a complete disregard for his personal safety. He has often found himself short of rations and has lived in great discomfort, but in spite of this has always carried out his mission.

In view of the secret nature of this officer's task details should not be published [recommended 02/10/42, *London Gazette* 26/11/42, WO 373/46 – Operation No.7, an attempted raid on Benghazi, for which he was attached to L Detachment, SAS Brigade, from 15 to 31 March 1942 and transported by S Patrol, LRDG, is omitted from the citation].

Mélot was posted to the SAS in late August 1942 'for the purpose of undertaking an operation', this being

OPERATION BIGAMY, the large-scale Benghazi raid of the following month. From veterans' statements, and from original photographs stamped accordingly, it appears that he did so whilst posing as a Belgian war correspondent. However, he also took an active part in the fighting. The LRDG post-operation report notes that 'on the evening of 10 Sep Capt Melot went as far as the escarpment [ahead of the main force] and sent his Arab agent into Benghazi for the latest information' (WO 201/815). Mélot and Captain Chris Bailey were subsequently wounded in action on 13 September whilst neutralising Fort Benito, an Italian outpost on this escarpment that overlooked the town's approaches and whose wireless might provide warning of that night's raid. One of their men, unaware that Mélot was inside, threw a grenade in through the window (see Bailey's entry under Alamein Memorial, Egypt, Volume I). With subsequent wounds to his stomach, thighs and legs the Medical Officer wanted to leave Mélot to be treated by the Italians but he insisted, despite a broken femur that guaranteed an unpleasant return journey, that he be included in the main party's withdrawal. His insistence saved his life as those that were left behind later died under suspicious circumstances (see Corporal Anthony Drongin's entry under Alamein Memorial, Egypt, for full details). After initial treatment in Cairo he was moved near to his wife at Alexandria and discharged to his own home at the end of November. That month he was officially taken on strength of MO1(SP), one of the many cover names for SOE (HS 9/1017/8). On recovery in January 1943 he joined the SAS permanently as a captain and when the majority of the Regiment's subunits were reorganised as the Special Raiding Squadron two months later he was the natural choice for Intelligence Officer. However, this did not prevent him taking an active part in both training and operations as Peter Davis later noted:

> [Mélot] was one of the most perfect gentlemen I have ever met … The men worshipped him and would make every effort to abide by his wishes and not let him down … he was more capable of enduring hardship and pain than most of us and was more than able to do anything the regiment did [*SAS – Men in the Making: An Original's Account of Operations in Sicily and Italy*, by Peter Davis, MC].

That July the SRS was at the forefront of the Allied invasion of Sicily (OPERATION HUSKY). Despite the fact that Mélot initially stayed in Palestine at Raiding Forces HQ he had rejoined the squadron by mid August and was presumably involved in the landings at Bagnara on the toe of mainland Italy on 4 September (OPERATION BAYTOWN).

To prevent the enemy taking up defensive positions on the River Biferno the SRS and units of a Special Service Brigade (No.3 Commando and No.40 (RM) Commando) launched OPERATION DEVON on the Adriatic coast: the combined force came ashore from landing craft 1½ kilometres north-west of the port of Termoli in the early hours of 3 October, the Commandos securing the town and its perimeter whilst the SRS pushed down towards the Biferno. Moving with No.1 Troop, Mélot was wounded in action once more; shot through the shoulder at approximately 0615hrs he initially refused to be evacuated or treated as a 'lying case'. After minimal treatment away from the line he signed his own discharge papers and rejoined the unit the following morning.

With the Regiment required for the forthcoming liberation of France Mélot was granted leave in Egypt, attended parachute course No. 85 at Ramat David in Palestine that December, and travelled to the UK early in 1944. He was promoted to major at the end of April whilst the SAS Brigade was training in Scotland and later parachuted into the Nièvre département of Central France for OPERATION HOUNDSWORTH. Major Bill Fraser, MC, A Squadron's commander, subsequently reported: 'July 29th [1944] Major Mélot arrived with two Jeeps. Both Jeeps pranged' (WO 218/192). When HOUNDSWORTH was due to be expanded by the addition of C Squadron under OPERATION KIPLING, Mélot made contact with the local Maquis and identified a suitable DZ at Les Placeaux on the edge of the Forêt de Merryvaux west of Auxerre. Here he received Captain Derrick Harrison and five men of KIPLING's advance party. He then set about teaching the Maquis how to use the weapons that this group had brought in, found alternate camp locations, and received further supplies, Jeeps, and the remainder of the squadron.

With the operation at an end and the Germans in full retreat, Mélot made his way north to Belgium with C Squadron following on. It was here, at Ronquières south of Brussels, that he was killed in a Jeep accident on the evening of 28 October 1944. The date is often recorded incorrectly, including on his headstone, as 1 November. Captain David Barnby of C Squadron stated at the subsequent court of inquiry:

The Jeep, driven by Maj Mélot, was returning from a reconnaissance from a small arms range. The road was wet and muddy and narrow. The Jeep slid off the road so that the left side wheels were running in a shallow drainage channel on the left edge of the road. It ran along thus for about 10 yards, then regained the road, but after a further 5 yards it slipped back into the ditch again. It then ran along for a further [illegible] yards, where it hit a culvert, which caused the Jeep to round, and come to rest, throwing the driver out. As the Major was thrown out it appears that he hit his head on the [armoured] plate.

The court concluded that 'his death was caused by Jeep accident due to the bad condition of the road' and that Mélot was not to blame. David Danger, who served with him in North Africa, Italy, and on OPERATION HOUNDSWORTH later recalled that Mélot was a 'fearless driver, and one needed to have courage as a passenger'. Missed by all ranks the Commanding Officer of 1st SAS, Lt-Colonel Paddy Mayne, DSO*, wrote to Mélot's wife:

> I find it impossible to tell you how sorry I am about Bob's death. We find it hard to realise that we will not see him again, there is no officer or man in the unit who could have been spared less … Our Regiment has suffered a very grievous loss: Bob was respected and liked by everyone in the unit and I myself have lost a very good friend and a person whose advice and council meant very much to me … your husband was one of the finest persons I have ever known.

Mélot was buried with full military honours in Brussels War Cemetery on 3 November 1944 and was posthumously mentioned in despatches for his work in France (*London Gazette* 10/05/45).

Son of Albert and Lucile Mélot – Husband of Suzanne Mélot of Knoke, Belgium, and of rue Sidi Metwalli, Alexandria, Egypt - Father of at least one child – Brother of Henri Mélot.
Age 49.
No inscription.
Grave X.18.30.

LEOPOLDSBURG WAR CEMETERY

A small proportion of those buried here were killed during the BEF's 1940 defence of Belgium. To these were added the graves of aircrew, men who died in a nearby military hospital during the latter part of 1944 and those since concentrated from surrounding areas. The cemetery now holds 767 burials of the Second World War, sixteen of which are unidentified, as well as a number of Polish and Dutch graves.

Leopoldsburg, also known as Bourg-Leopold, is located 58 kilometres north-east of Leuven on the N73. The cemetery lies 1 kilometre south-east of the town's rail station on Koning Leopold II Laan. GPS co-ordinates: Latitude 51.11271, Longitude 5.26833

LANCE-CORPORAL ARTHUR <u>ROGERSON</u> [2932601] QUEEN'S OWN CAMERON HIGHLANDERS, 1ST SAS, SRS AND 1ST SAS (C SQN)

Known as 'Darky' to his comrades, Arthur Rogerson was born on 9 October 1918 at Toxteth Park in Liverpool. Having worked as a labourer he enlisted into the 1st Battalion, Liverpool Scottish, Queen's Own Cameron Highlanders, in October 1939. The following spring he attended a pioneer course run by the 55th Division and disembarked in Egypt at the beginning of September 1942. Posted to the 2nd Battalion, the majority of which had been captured at Tobruk earlier in the year, he volunteered for 1st SAS on 17 October.

Rogerson was posted to Raiding Forces HQ on 19 March 1943, the day that the majority of the Regiment's subunits were reorganised as the Special Raiding Squadron. However, he was back with the SRS by the time it landed at Capo Murro di Porco on 10 July at the forefront of the Allied invasion

7

of Sicily (OPERATION HUSKY). Recommended for Operational Wings for this amphibious assault and operations previously carried out in the Western Desert, he subsequently took part in the landings at Augusta on the evening of 12 July and at Bagnara on the toe of mainland Italy on 4 September (OPERATION BAYTOWN). After then seeing fierce fighting around Termoli the following month during OPERATION DEVON he arrived back in the UK at the beginning of January 1944 (see Major Bob Mélot's entry under Brussels Town Cemetery, Belgium, for details of DEVON).

Rogerson and half of C Squadron emplaned at RAF Broadwell on 28 August 1944, landing at Orléans in north-central France for OPERATION KIPLING. Here the men were met by Major Harry Poat, MC, who led their Jeep column through enemy lines to the rest of the squadron at the Forêt de Merryvaux west of Auxerre. Finding that Kipling was not to be reinforced as originally planned, the squadron set about disrupting enemy lines of communication as an extension of OPERATION HOUNDSWORTH to the south. With German forces in retreat their work soon drew to a close and the squadron motored north to Brussels in Belgium to refit for future operations. Whilst here Rogerson was promoted to lance-corporal on 1 October.

Rogerson's service record notes that on 14 November 1944 he was: 'admitted dead to 3rd Field Dressing Station RAMC (overseas) – Road accident circumstances N.Y.K.' (not yet known). C Squadron's commander, Major Tony Marsh, DSO, signalled his CO, Lt-Colonel Paddy Mayne, DSO*: 'L/Cpl Rogerson killed. Jeep accident November 14. Details follow.' Unfortunately, none appear to have been recorded although it is known that he was originally buried at nearby Wijchmaal and reinterred here on 12 April 1946.

Son of A. J. and E. M. Rogerson (née Cropper) of Ackers Hall Avenue, Liverpool.
Age 26.
For us his precious life he gave. Rest, dear son, rest and sleep
Grave 1.D.16.

FRANCE

The SAS Brigade was allotted vital tasks during the 1944 liberation of France. These began with OPERATION TITANIC in direct support of the Allied landings in Normandy: just after midnight on D-Day six men of 1st SAS dropped alongside dummy parachutists and pyrotechnics in the area south of Carentan, thus diverting attention from nearby American landings. An hour later two officers of 1st SAS parachuted into central France as the advance party of OPERATION BULBASKET, the first of many such operations tasked with hindering the movement of German troops and armour towards the Allied beachhead. Concurrently French troops of 4th SAS landed in Brittany to arm, train and bolster local Resistance and also prevent German reinforcements moving towards Normandy. In the days and months that followed parties from the British 1st and 2nd SAS Regiments, the French 3rd and 4th Regiments, and the Belgian Independent Parachute Company (later 5th SAS), all supported by F Squadron of GHQ Liaison Regiment (Phantom), were designated strategic areas in which to carry out further operations. Relatively small numbers of men were able to ensure the continuous disruption of enemy lines of communication, provide a steady stream of intelligence and targets for Allied air strikes, stiffen the Maquis, and later that summer harass the enemy's withdrawal towards his own border.

Although what was achieved saved innumerable lives, the cost was high. There are more wartime SAS casualties commemorated in France than in any other country. Sixty-six men of 1st SAS, thirty men of 2nd SAS, four men attached from F Squadron, GHQ Liaison Regiment (Phantom), one member of the RAF attached to 1st SAS, two members of the French SAS regiments attached to their British counterparts, and ten men of the Free French Squadron of L Detachment, SAS Brigade, are commemorated in twenty-six locations.

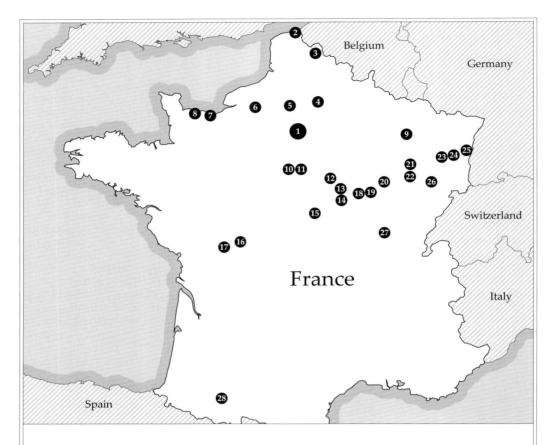

1. Paris (Batignolles Cemetery and Clichy Northern Cemetery)
2. Dunkirk (Rosendaël Cemetery)
3. Lille
4. Dreslincourt Communal Cemetery
5. Beauvais (Marissel French National Cemetery)
6. Rouen (Saint-Sever Cemetery Extension)
7. Ranville War Cemetery
8. Bayeux War Cemetery and Bayeux Memorial
9. Choloy War Cemetery
10. Chilleurs-aux-Bois Communal Cemetery
11. Chambon-la-Forêt Communal Cemetery
12. Les Ormes Communal Cemetery
13. Crain Communal Cemetery
14. Tannay Communal Cemetery
15. Villequiers Communal Cemetery
16. Verrières Communal Cemetery
17. Rom Communal Cemetery
18. Époisses Communal Cemetery
19. Villaines-les-Prévôtes Communal Cemetery
20. Recey-sur-Ource Communal Cemetery
21. Graffigny-Chemin Communal Cemetery
22. Varennes-sur-Amance (Terre-Natale Communal Cemetery)
23. Moyenmoutier Communal Cemetery
24. Moussey Churchyard
25. Strasbourg
26. Velorcey Communal Cemetery
27. Sennecey-le-Grand SAS Brigade Memorial
28. Ossun Communal Cemetery

BATIGNOLLES CEMETERY

The Cimetière Parisiens des Batignolles is located in the Épinettes district of Paris, in the north-eastern quarter of the 17ᵉ arrondissement. The entrance lies at the junction of avenue du Cimetières des Batignolles and rue Saint-Just. GPS co-ordinates: Latitude 48.896511, Longitude 2.313661

ASPIRANT ANDRÉ LOUIS ARTHUR **ZIRNHELD** [UNKNOWN S/N] DÉFENSE CONTRE AVIONS, 24ᴱ RÉGIMENT D'INFANTERIE COLONIALE, 1ᴱᴿ BATAILLON D'INFANTERIE DE MARINE, 1ᴱᴿ COMPAGNIE DE CHASSEURS PARACHUTISTES
ATT L DETACHMENT SAS BRIGADE (FRENCH SQN)

André Zirnheld was born in Paris on 7 March 1913 to an Alsatian family that had moved to the city during the Franco Prussian war of 1870. His father died when he was 9, and after secondary schooling at Saint-Jean de Passy he read Philosophy at the Sorbonne. In 1937 he was appointed Professor of Philosophy at the Lycée Carnot in Tunis, accepting a similar appointment at the French Mission to Tartus in Syria during October 1938.

At the outbreak of the war Zirnheld was assigned to an anti-aircraft battery in Lebanon. However, after the June 1940 armistice he crossed over into Palestine and joined the Free French 24ᵉ Régiment d'infanterie coloniale, subsequently being convicted of desertion by the Vichy French Army. Having seen action against the Italians at Sidi Barrani in September 1940 as a sergeant in the 1ᵉʳ Bataillon d'infanterie de marine he was posted to Cairo the following January as Deputy Director of Propaganda. Quickly requesting a transfer he attended officer cadet training in

Brazzeville that June, passing out with the rank of aspirant. In February 1942 he volunteered for the 1er Compagnie de chasseurs parachutistes and was one of those subsequently incorporated into L Detachment, SAS Brigade, as the French Squadron.

Zirnheld commanded a five-man team on OPERATION TEN C: having flown from Kabrit to Siwa Oasis on 5 June 1942 his party was transported by the LRDG behind the lines to the area of Berka aerodrome in Libya. They attacked on the night of the 13–14th, destroying eleven planes and killing seventeen of the enemy. Captain David Stirling, DSO, recommended Zirnheld for the Military Cross for this raid, although it was not awarded.

Realising that the enemy were wise to his tactics in attacking such airfields, Stirling decided that a change was required: fetching as many men and Jeeps as he could muster, full-scale rehearsals were carried out near to the unit's temporary base behind enemy lines at Querat Hiremas. Formations that ensured maximum firepower were developed, L Detachment subsequently entering the German airfield at Sidi Haneish on the night of 26–27 July 1942 and destroying an estimated twenty-five aircraft as well as aircrew in a mass Jeep attack. 1st SAS' War Diary notes that during the withdrawal, 'one detachment of Free French was discovered and its commander, 2nd Lieut Zirnheld, was killed'. His vehicle had suffered a puncture and although another under Aspirant François Martin stopped to help they were caught in the open by four Stuka aircraft. Zirnheld was soon wounded in the shoulder and stomach and died approximately thirteen hours later. He was buried nearby below a cross constructed of two Credit Union boards inscribed: 'Andre Zirnheld Aspirant, died for France July 27, 1942.' Martin, who was later murdered by the Germans in Brittany during OPERATION SAMWEST, found the following prayer, written by Zirnheld in Tunis during April 1938, in his effects. It has since become the prayer for all French parachutists and translates thus:

I'm asking You God, to give me what You have left.
Give me those things that others never ask of You.
I don't ask You for rest, or tranquility. Not that of the spirit, the body, or the mind.
I don't ask You for wealth, or success, or even health.
All those things are asked of You so much Lord, that you can't have any left to give.
Give me instead Lord what You have left.
Give me what others don't want. I want uncertainty and doubt. I want torment and battle.
And I ask that You give them to me now and forever Lord, so I can be sure to always have them, because I won't always have the strength to ask again.
But give me also the courage, the energy and the spirit to face them.
I ask You these things Lord, because I can't ask them of myself.

Zirnheld was awarded a posthumous Croix de guerre avec palme on 6 March 1947 for his overall achievements, a second being awarded on 11 April 1947 specifically for the Berka raid which he is noted as having carried out with 'remarkable aggression' and 'effectively contributing to the rear disorganisation of the enemy during a particularly crucial time for the 8th Army'. He was awarded the Médaille de la Résistance on 3 August 1946, the Médaille militaire on 22 October 1947 and made Compagnon de la Libération on 23 November 1949.

Age 29. Zirnheld's remains were reinterred firstly to a military cemetery at Mersa Matruh and then, on 29 March 1952, to the Cimetière Parisiens des Batignolles. He is also commemorated within Notre-Dame d'Auteuil Church, within Sainte-Jeanne de Chantal Church, on the Mémorial National des Scouts Morts pour la France in Liévin, and by a French Army promotion badge named after him (see previous page).

BAYEUX WAR CEMETERY

This is the largest Commonwealth cemetery of the Second World War located in France, the majority of the casualties having lost their lives during the Normandy Campaign from 6 June 1944 until the end of that August. It contains 4,144 burials of which 338 are unidentified. In addition, there are 505 war graves of other nationalities, the majority being German.

Bayeux is located 24 kilometres north-west of Caen within the Calvados département of Basse-Normandie. The cemetery lies south-west of the centre on the rue de Sir Fabian Ware, the city by-pass. GPS co-ordinates: Latitude 49.27412, Longitude -0.71399

PRIVATE THOMAS NORMAN <u>BINTLEY</u> [11052369] ROYAL ARTILLERY, ARMY AIR CORPS AND 2ND SAS (C SQN)

Thomas Bintley was born on 2 February 1915 in Liverpool. After attending Granton Road School in Anfield he worked at the Dunlop Rubber Company at Walton, marrying Ellen Green in January 1938 at Brougham Terrace Registry Office. Their son, Tony, was born a few days after the outbreak of the war. Due to air raids Bintley's family was evacuated to Chorley near Bridgnorth, Shropshire, in early 1940, although due to his reserved occupation, key to the war effort, he himself remained in Liverpool. In April 1941 he enlisted into the 233rd Searchlight Training Regiment, Royal Artillery, and the following month was posted to the 241st Light Anti-Aircraft Battery, 78th LAA Regiment. He was promoted to lance-bombardier in February 1942 but reverted to gunner at his own request a month later. That July he was

re-posted to the 386th Battery, 36th LAA Regiment, and embarked for North Africa in January 1943 where he served with the 29th LAA Regiment.

Bintley's award of the Italy Star indicates that he served on Sicily or mainland Italy at some point between July 1943 and mid October when he was posted to an infantry reserve training depot. Almost immediately he was admitted to hospital for a brief period before returning to the UK at the beginning of 1944. Having volunteered for Airborne Forces he was posted to Hardwick Hall, the Airborne Forces Depot near Chesterfield, and attended parachute course 104 at No.1 PTS Ringway. Here he was noted as 'quiet, moody, confident'. Posted to the Airborne Forces Holding Unit he officially transferred to the Army Air Corps on 4 April 1944, volunteering for 2nd SAS on 26 May.

Bintley was killed in action on 20 August 1944 during OPERATION TRUEFORM. He had been dropped into Normandy on the night of 17–18 August as a member of TRUEFORM-3, a party of six British SAS and four men of the Belgian Independent Parachute Company under Sergeant Percy Thorpe (see Thorpe's entry within this volume under Becklingen War Cemetery, Germany). Tasked with destroying petrol supplies, harassing the enemy, and reporting on movement, they were dropped blind (that is, without an arranged reception committee) 18 kilometres north-north-west of their actual DZ near Louviers. The post-operation report notes 'no half hour to go and no lights given', hence the inaccuracy of the drop. Bintley was separated from the others during the descent and subsequently made contact with the TRUEFORM-1 party under Captain Dick Holland, MC. Father Sanquer, a local priest, later recalled:

> I was advised on 18 Aug 44 that a British Army parachutist was in a farm at approximately 12 kilometres from my home, near Amfreville-la-Campagne. I immediately went there with a horse-drawn cart and having dressed him in civilian clothes I took him back to Saint Eloy-de-Fourques [Saint-Éloi-de-Fourques] where there was a British unit, commanded by Capt Holland. Since it was late when we arrived at Saint-Eloy-de-Fourques and that there were Germans in the district I thought it wise not to hand him over to Captain Holland before the next day and he spent the night in a farm. This parachutist was called Bintley.
> I took him the next day to the wood where Captain Holland was [WO 311/904].

Sanquer also noted that Bintley had damaged his foot on landing, although it is clear that he continued to operate. 2nd SAS' Casualty Report quotes Holland:

> This man was last seen by me on Sunday Aug 20, when he and another [Parachutist Harold Erlis] set out to lay tyre bursters on the road near Brionne [Holland variously recorded the date as the 20th or 19th]. On the way they went to a farm which was occupied by Germans, with the idea of placing some incendiaries in the German trucks. They ran into four Germans lying under a hedge who gave themselves up. Sixteen more Germans then gave themselves up and while dealing with these shooting started. According to the Maquis, Bintley was hit in the head and died almost at once (while Erlis was taken prisoner having presumably stayed behind to look after Bintley). I have only the word of the Maquis for these details, but it seems certain, because the Maquis held a large memorial service for Bintley on Sunday Aug 27th. Bintley's remains are in the care of the Cure of St Eloi de Fourques, near Brionne [WO 361/716].

However, the statement of Joseph Bardel, a local farm worker, portrays a slightly different version of events:

> On Sunday 20 Aug 1944, around three o'clock in the afternoon a German came into the wood near the farm which I occupy and found a group of parachutists. A fight began. There were at that moment three Englishmen. One Englishman was captured. A quarter of an hour later another Englishman was killed … While they were interrogating the British prisoner [Erlis] they took us to dig a grave in order to bury the Englishman who had been killed, but not on the spot where he is now since they had put him on a pile of rubbish, 50 centimetres below the surface …
> After eight days I took the body of the Englishman. I put it in a coffin and buried it at the edge of the wood [WO 311/904].

Whatever the case, Sergent-chef Alphonse Marais, who was present during the skirmish at the spot known as Le Buhot, later stated:

> This soldier [Bintley] was dressed in a pair of British Army trousers and wore boots and a shirt which had been part of his equipment. His other clothes were civilian clothes.
>   At the time he was killed by a bullet that passed under his jaw (right side) and come out through his skull (left side), this parachutist carried maps and personal objects of no importance. He was armed with an American Colt automatic pistol 13mm (?) lent by one of his comrades, since he had lost his weapons in landing [WO 311/904].

Although officially recorded as 20 August 1944, Bintley's date of death does not align with that of Erlis, the 19th (see Erlis' entry under Saint-Sever Cemetery Extension, France, for further details of the discrepancy in date). Bintley's daughter, Keizah, was born the following January, his wife returning to Liverpool from Bridgnorth to find their house had been bombed.

Predeceased by his parents, John (Henry) and Elizabeth Bintley of Anfield, Liverpool – Husband of Ellen Bintley of Teulon Street, Anfield – Father of Tony and Keizah Bintley.
Age 29.
No inscription.
Grave 28.G.3. Reinterred here in January 1948.

PRIVATE JAMES KENNETH **WILKINSON** [1442014] ROYAL ARTILLERY
AND 2ND SAS (A SQN)

James Wilkinson was born on 9 March 1920 at West Derby in Liverpool. Whilst working as a clerk, he joined the 177th Heavy Battery, Royal Artillery (TA), in February 1939. Called up on 24 August he served at Aberdeen with the 502nd, 243rd and 501st Coast Regiments, before being posted to No.3 Battery, 1st Heavy Regiment, as a lance-bombardier in December 1942. During the spring of 1943 Wilkinson was involved in a string of misdemeanours resulting in a period of detention. Having appealed, stressing that he was eager to fight overseas, his sentence was suspended by the commander of 80th Division so that he could embark with the 195th Field Regiment.

Arriving in North Africa on Christmas Day 1943 he served in Italy before volunteering for 2nd SAS on 22 February 1944. He returned to the UK on 16 March and the following month attended parachute course 111A at No.1 PTS Ringway, his instructor noting: 'made rapid improvement on actual descents. GT [ground training] fair'. He had obviously fitted into the Regiment without difficulty and that August the Adjutant, Major Denny Reynolds, wrote: 'the above mentioned soldier [Wilkinson] has worked well and has not incurred any entry on his conduct sheet since suspension of his sentence on 10 December, 1943. It is therefore recommended that the sentence remain in suspension for a further two months' (see Reynolds' own entry within this volume under Durnbach War Cemetery, Germany).

Wilkinson deployed to Normandy under Lieutenant John Dick during Operation Defoe. Although tasked with providing intelligence directly to Second Army, the team's arrival was unexpected. The officer in command, Captain 'Bunny' MacGibbon-Lewis, therefore sent out small groups to gain battle experience, Dick's team being attached to the South Staffordshire Regiment and then their relief, the Highland Light Infantry. On 3 August they were conducting a foot patrol in Monceaux when:

> … crossing from one building to another they heard an explosion and saw two men lying in the street behind them, one dead [*sic* – Wilkinson fatally wounded] and one dying with head injuries [*sic*]. Obviously caught by a booby trap. On looking around they found the place to be sewn with S Mines and booby traps. They withdrew with the bodies [*sic* – the post-operation report, WO 361/725, confirms that the operation incurred '1 x KIA, 1 x WIA'].

An SAS signals log contains a message sent by the Defoe team on 4 August: 'one casualty 1442014 Pte Wilkinson in General Hospital. May not live.' The following day MacGibbon-Lewis wrote; 'Wilkinson is not dead as I write, but he has not regained consciousness and has no chance.' His prognosis was correct and Wilkinson succumbed to his wounds later that day, 5 August 1944.

Son of Albert and Elsie Wilkinson (née Ellis) of Bowley Road, Stoneycroft, Liverpool.
Age 24.
Duty Nobly Done
Grave 2.K.23. Also commemorated within Stoneycroft Methodist Church.

BAYEUX MEMORIAL

Most of those listed below were posted missing in action after their aircraft, Stirling LJ850 of 620 Squadron, 38 Group, failed to return to the UK. OPERATION HOUNDSWORTH's report notes: 'on the night of 17/18 June three Stirlings took off with reinforcements for A Squadron but were unable to find the DZ [at Les Valottes west of Dijon] owing to thick cloud. Unfortunately one aircraft with Lt Cairns and his party failed to return' (WO 361/732). Captained by Pilot Officer Robert Crane of the Royal Australian Air Force, the Stirling had taken off from Fairford at 2320hrs on the 17th. A radio fix placed it outbound over the Channel at 0050hrs on the 18th, the aircraft disappearing thereafter. Crane, and five other aircrew also lost, including Sergeant Philip Wilding the RAF despatcher, are commemorated on the Runnymede Memorial. Unlike their SAS passengers their dates of death are correctly recorded as 18 June 1944. At the time of going to print there is some speculation as to whether wreckage recenty located in Normandy is that of LJ850.

Bayeux, liberated on D-Day+1, became a key headquarters for both British forces and Charles de Gaulle's government. The Bayeux Memorial commemorates over 1,800 men of the Commonwealth who died in the period between the Normandy landings on 6 June 1944 and 29 August, and who have no known grave. It was unveiled by the Duke of Gloucester on 5 June 1955, its main inscription 'Nos a Gulielmo Victi Victoris Patriam Liberavimus' meaning 'We, once conquered by William, have now set free the Conqueror's native land.'

The memorial is located opposite the Bayeux War Cemetery on the rue de Sir Fabian Ware, the city's ring road that was built by British soldiers. GPS co-ordinates: Latitude 49.27412, Longitude -0.71399

PRIVATE JAMES FLEMING SPIERS **ARBUCKLE** [2985863] ARGYLL AND SUTHERLAND HIGHLANDERS, SRS AND 1ST SAS (A SQN)

James Arbuckle was born on 29 December 1918 at Kirkliston in West Lothian. He enlisted into the Argyll and Sutherland Highlanders (Princess Louise's) in October 1939 and was posted to the 11th Battalion. The following April he married Alice Steel in Edinburgh, their daughter, Janet, being born at Polmont during August 1942.

In March 1943 Arbuckle embarked for the Middle East where he was posted to Raiding Forces HQ. He volunteered to serve with HQ Troop, Special Raiding Squadron (1st SAS), on 29 June 1943, just in time for OPERATION HUSKY, the invasion of Sicily. Having landed at Capo Murro di Porco on 10 July the SRS destroyed coastal batteries that threatened the invasion fleet. Two days later it captured the port of Augusta after another amphibious assault, thus enabling a more rapid advance up the east coast. On 4 September it was put ashore once more, this time on the toe of mainland Italy to take the town of Bagnara during OPERATION BAYTOWN. Arbuckle's troop was at the forefront of these actions and went on to see fierce fighting in the defence of Termoli during OPERATION DEVON that October. He returned to the UK with the Regiment in mid March 1944, was posted to A Squadron of the reinstated 1st SAS, and undertook parachute training at No.1 PTS at Ringway.

Arbuckle was reported missing in action during OPERATION HOUNDSWORTH when his aircraft disappeared in the early hours of 18 June 1944. His date of death is officially recorded as the 17th although the last known position of the Stirling was logged the following morning (see Lieutenant Les Cairns' entry within this section for full details).

Son of Robert and Janet Arbuckle of Almondside, Kirkliston, West Lothian – Husband of Alice Arbuckle of Kirk Entry, Old Polmont, Falkirk, Stirlingshire – Father of Janet Arbuckle.
Age 25.
Panel 18, column 2.

PRIVATE JOHN SEYMOUR **BOWEN** [899930] ROYAL ARTILLERY, 1ST SAS, SRS AND 1ST SAS (A SQN)

John Bowen was born on 21 February 1920 in the village of Madeley near Crewe, Staffordshire, but later lived in north London. In April 1939, whilst working as a shop assistant, he joined the 358th Battery, 90th Field Regiment, Royal Artillery (TA), and was embodied at the outbreak of war. Promoted to lance-bombardier in March 1941 he reverted to the rank of gunner at his own request the following February.

Having embarked for the Middle East with the 74th Field Regiment in late May 1942 Bowen was posted to the 65th Anti-Tank Regiment that September. He volunteered for 1st SAS on 24 February 1943 and was therefore present when it was reorganised as the Special Raiding Squadron the following month. As a member of No.1 Troop he landed at the spearhead of OPERATION HUSKY, the invasion of Sicily on 10 July, helping to destroy coastal batteries at Capo Murro di Porco that threatened the Allied fleet. Two days later the SRS was put ashore again, this time capturing the port of Augusta thus facilitating the advance up the east coast. On 4 September it landed at Bagnara during OPERATION BAYTOWN, hastening the German retreat from the toe of Italy. Having captured the Adriatic port of Termoli on 3 October during OPERATION DEVON Bowen's troop was sitting in a truck two days later when it was hit by a shell.

Wounded, he was eventually discharged from hospital on 18 November (see multiple entries under Sangro River War Cemetery, Italy, Volume II, for full details of this incident).

Bowen arrived back in the UK the following January. Having been posted to A Squadron of the now reinstated 1st SAS he undertook parachute training at No.1 PTS at Ringway during February. He was reported missing in action during OPERATION HOUNDSWORTH after his aircraft disappeared in the early hours of 18 June 1944. His date of death is officially recorded as the 17th although the last known position of the Stirling was logged the following morning (see Lieutenant Les Cairns' entry for full details).

Son of Ernest and Kate Bowen (née Seymour) of Merfield Road, Solihull, Warwickshire.
Age 22.
Panel 18, column 2.

LANCE-CORPORAL HAROLD **BROOK** [2615070] GRENADIER GUARDS, No.8 COMMANDO, MIDDLE EAST COMMANDO, 1ST SAS, SRS AND 1ST SAS (A SQN)

'Ginger' Brook was born on 15 July 1918 in Rochdale. Having worked in the Lancaster silk trade he enlisted into the Grenadier Guards in November 1936 to serve alongside a friend who had already signed up. Posted to the 3rd Battalion his service record describes him as 'a good, quiet, hardworking man who does his work well'.

After the declaration of war Brook's battalion left Barossa Barracks in Aldershot and disembarked in France on 20 September 1939 as part of the BEF. All three Grenadier battalions manned defences along the Franco-Belgian border north-east of Arras, the 3rd digging positions around the villages of Genech and Bachy. When the German offensive began on 10 May 1940 it left its billets at Normain and advanced into Belgium. Having reached Huldenberg the men laboured at defensive positions only to find that their line had been outflanked and that they were to retire. During the subsequent withdrawal to the River Escaut (Scheldt), Brook was wounded by a bomb splinter on the 19th and admitted to 159 Field Ambulance the following day. He was evacuated to the UK on the 25th.

Having recovered at an Epsom hospital Brook volunteered for special service and subsequently joined 2 Troop, No.8 (Guards) Commando, on 6 August 1940. After being temporarily reorganised as the 4th Special Service Battalion and undertaking arduous build-up training on the west coast of Scotland, the Commando disembarked at Suez, Egypt, in early March 1941 as B Battalion of Layforce. The following month the men were at Mersa Matruh towards the front line, although with operations drawn up and then cancelled an unsettled period ensued. After Layforce disbanded Brook joined the Middle East Commando on 20 January 1942, serving in Syria before volunteering for 1st SAS on 26 September. As such he is likely to have taken part in the Regiment's last desert operations.

In March 1943, with Axis forces in North Africa close to defeat, the Regiment was reorganised, the majority of its squadrons forming the Special Raiding Squadron. Carrying out intensive training near Azzib in Palestine during May, and in the Gulf of Aqaba in June, it subsequently landed at the forefront of OPERATION HUSKY, the Allied invasion of Sicily, on 10 July. Having neutralised coastal gun positions at Capo Murro di Porco the SRS captured the port of Augusta two days later. Moving to the mainland they landed at Bagnara on 4 September during OPERATION BAYTOWN before helping to capture the port of Termoli on the Adriatic coast during fierce fighting the following month (OPERATION DEVON). Brook was promoted to lance-corporal on 6 November and in January 1944 returned to the UK with the rest of the squadron where it was reorganised with regimental status as 1st SAS once more.

Brook was posted as missing in action during OPERATION HOUNDSWORTH after his aircraft disappeared. His date of death is officially recorded as 17 June 1944 although the last known position of the Stirling was logged on the 18th (see Lieutenant Les Cairns' entry opposite for full details).

Son of Mrs Jane Brook of Lancaster Road, Torrisholme, Morecambe, Lancashire.

Age 23.

Panel 18, column 2. Also commemorated on Morecambe's war memorial.

Corporal William **BRYSON** [2880083] GORDON HIGHLANDERS, ROYAL SCOTS GREYS, ROYAL ARMY VETERINARY CORPS, MIDDLE EAST COMMANDO, 1ST SAS, SRS AND 1ST SAS (A SQN)

Known as Barney, Bryson was born on 10 April 1921 in the parish of St Nicholas in central Aberdeen. In April 1938, whilst working as a labourer, he joined the 4th Battalion, Gordon Highlanders (TA), enlisting into the Royal Scots Greys in August 1939 just before the outbreak of war. Initially posted to the 3rd Cavalry Training Regiment he embarked for Palestine in September 1940 where he joined No.3 Remount Squadron. Transferring to the Royal Army Veterinary Corps the following April, he volunteered for the Middle East Commando on 23 March 1942, and was promoted to lance-corporal two months later. By the beginning of that November he had qualified as a parachutist and was serving with 1st SAS, being promoted to corporal later that month.

With the Regiment reorganised as the Special Raiding Squadron, Bryson took part in the invasion of Sicily, codenamed OPERATION HUSKY, as a member of A Section, No.1 Troop. After landing at Capo Murro di Porco to destroy coastal batteries on 10 July 1943 the SRS was put ashore again two days later to capture the port of Augusta, Bryson being awarded Operational Wings on the 23rd. He was subsequently wounded in action during OPERATION BAYTOWN after the SRS landed at Bagnara on 4 September in order to hasten the German withdrawal from the toe of mainland Italy.

At the beginning of January 1944 the squadron returned to the UK where it was reorganised with regimental status as 1st SAS once more. Bryson was posted as missing in action during OPERATION HOUNDSWORTH after his aircraft disappeared. His date of death is officially recorded as 17 June 1944 although the last known position of the Stirling was logged on the 18th (see Lieutenant Les Cairns' entry opposite for full details).

Son of Patrick Bryson of Littlejohn Street, Aberdeen.

Age 23.

Panel 18, column 2.

Lieutenant Leslie George **CAIRNS** [164967] Royal Artillery, Army Air Corps and 1st SAS (A Sqn)

Les Cairns was born on 4 April 1920 in Stirling. His father, a solicitor and actuary for the Stirling Savings Bank, died when he was 16. After attending Newstead School in Doune he read History at Edinburgh University where he was a member of the OTC. It was during this period that he fell in love with his future wife, Irene Young, carrying out a constant correspondence with her until his death.

On the outbreak of war Cairns volunteered, only to be told that the army was not taking recruits below the age of 20. Eventually, in May 1940, he was sent to a Royal Artillery training regiment at Harrogate where he volunteered for special duties the following month. However, after attending the Royal Artillery's 125 OCTU at Ilkley he was commissioned that December and posted to the 152nd Field Regiment (Ayrshire Yeomanry) at Ferryden, Montrose (*London Gazette* 28/01/41). The following November the regiment moved to Epping in Essex and in May 1942 Cairns embarked for the Middle East. Arriving in Egypt late that June he was posted to the 11th Field Regiment, taking part in the Battle of El Alamein and eventual advance into Tunisia from where he wrote:

The past year has been the most peculiar and the most testing in my life. There were many hours of boredom and discouragement, even more of physical discomfort – the flies, the corpses stinking in the sun, dysentery too, and hours of mental agony and nervous strain – those horrible Stukas last summer in Egypt. And sometimes there was the excitement of a good fight. Perhaps you think that the 'lust of battle' doesn't exist nowadays; believe me, it does, and its an odd experience [*Enigma Variations*, by Irene Young].

In June 1943 Cairns was posted to the 137/166th Newfoundland Regiment (RA) in Tunis before being re-posted to an infantry reinforcement training depot that September. Embarking for the UK the following month he transferred to the Army Air Corps in November: 'I've often wondered if I'd ever actually have to write this … I have transferred to the Parachute Regiment' (*Enigma Variations*). After training at Hardwick Hall he attended a parachute course at No.1 PTS Ringway and was awarded his wings two days before Christmas 1943. He and Irene married a week later, Cairns being posted to the Airborne Forces Holding Unit from where he volunteered for 1st SAS on 11 February 1944.

Cairns was posted as missing in action after the aircraft carrying his stick for a parachute drop into Operation Houndsworth in the Morvan region of France disappeared on the night of 17–18 June 1944. A subsequent report enquired as to the circumstances of the loss:

Stories given by parachutists who returned suggest that there was dense cloud that night, that other aircraft returned without dropping their parachutists, but the lost machine was last seen staggering home with engine trouble. Is there anything (e.g. wireless messages) to support this? If so, was the machine well over the sea when last heard of on the return journey [WO 361/732].

None of the reports could be verified and although efforts were made to locate the missing aircraft no trace could be found. During 1947 the RAF Missing Research and Enquiry Service resumed extensive searches of the Morvan without result. In 1989 his wife wrote *Enigma Variations* in which she stated:

Transcendent in this book is my desire to carve out some modest memorial to one who has no real memorial. Leslie Cairns's short adult life was a counterpoint of love and war. I had the honour to be the object of that love. If I am accused of unblushing candour in quoting extensively from intimate correspondence, my justification must be that the man himself is his best biographer, and that his letters interpret his character and its development – from something little more than a schoolboy to that of a seasoned officer in the Special Forces – far more truly than could any words of mine …

His nature was deep but uncomplicated, genuine, passionate yet balanced; he had keen intelligence and was dubbed as 'effortlessly bright'. Interested in innumerable subjects, he fell short, I think, of the truly scholarly. *People* were of primary importance to him, and he had a quick perception of and delight in the quirks and oddities of human behaviour. He had a lively humour – humour, perhaps, rather than wit – sweet to medium-dry; a portion of wit, too, was his, but he had not lived long enough for it to be sharpened by disillusionment. Friends observed that whenever he entered a room everyone's spirits rose …

He was too happy, too buoyant, too loving of life. He had a sort of 'fatality' about him.

On 10 July 1944 Lt-Colonel Paddy Mayne, DSO*, Commanding Officer of 1st SAS, wrote to Irene:

I imagine by now you have received official notification that Leslie is missing. We are all terribly sorry and worried about this, as we don't know what has happened. On the 17th day of June he left by plane with his section to join his squadron commander in France. The plane did not return and we have not been able to find out what happened. The plane might have been forced down by fighters or other enemy action, or had to land for some other reason, and we don't know whether the men were able to get away all right or not. Leslie had a very good lot of men in his section, some of them had been with us for a long time. If they got out of the plane, they will probably be hiding now and trying to make their way back. I am terribly sorry this should have happened and I sincerely hope that we hear from them. I needn't tell you how well we all like your husband.

Enquiries in national newspaper placed by Cairns' family proved fruitless. Then, in October 1945, the following arrived:

With reference to War Office letter of 3rd March 1945 regarding your husband Lieutenant L G Cairns, Army Air Corps, I am directed to inform you that in view of the length of time which has elapsed since Lieutenant Cairns was reported missing, during which no news of him has been received from any source, the Department has reluctantly, and with deep regret, reached the conclusion that he lost his life. It is consequently being officially recorded that Lieutenant L G Cairns, Army Air Corps, is presumed to have been killed in action on the 17th of June 1944. I am to convey to you an expression of the sincere sympathy of the Army Council.

The actual date of death of Cairns and his men is contentious. From 620 Squadron's Operations Record Book LJ850 is known to have taken off at 2330hrs on the 17th carrying Cairns' stick, and to have sent its last transmission at 0050hrs on the 18th. Whereas the missing aircrew were eventually posted as having been killed in action on the 18th Cairns' party are all officially recorded as having lost their lives on the 17th.

Son of George and Agnes Cairns of Grange Terrace, Edinburgh – Husband of Irene Jessie Cairns of Thirlestane Road, Edinburgh.

Age 24.

Panel 18, column 2. Also commemorated on his father's gravestone within Snowden Cemetery, Stirling.

Private William John CREANEY [7019654] Royal Ulster Rifles,
Parachute Regiment and 1st SAS (A Sqn)

William Creaney was born on 6 March 1922 at Shankill in Belfast to an English father and Irish mother. Having worked bottling mineral water he enlisted into the Young Soldiers' Company, 6th (Home Defence) Battalion, Royal Ulster Rifles, during August 1940 and was posted to their infantry training centre at Ballymena. Joining the 70th (Young Soldiers) Battalion that September he was subsequently posted to the defence platoon of the 1st (Airborne) Battalion in October 1942 and was attached to HQ 1st

Parachute Brigade.

Almost immediately Creaney's platoon embarked at Greenock, finding out once at sea that the brigade's destination was North Africa. On 15 February 1943 he was transferred, as one of a large batch of reinforcements, to the 1st Battalion, Parachute Regiment, which had suffered heavy casualties during fierce fighting in Tunisia. The battalion continued to see such action within the Bou Arada sector before being relieved the following month. Having taken up positions at the base of the Djebel Bel the parachute brigade successfully defended against heavy attacks before the 1st Battalion captured enemy positions on a prominent position known as Bowler Hat (Sidi Bou Delaa). On the night of 27–28 March they struck once again, capturing a large formation of Italian troops forward of this position.

During May, right at the end of the North African Campaign, Creaney was either taken ill or wounded, rejoining his unit in June. It is likely that he took part in the battalion's drop on Primasole Bridge on Sicily during July and, although his service record notes that he was briefly admitted to No.71 General Hospital at Sousse that September, it is also believed that he served on mainland Italy before embarking for the UK that November. Arriving home the following month he volunteered for 1st SAS on 16 March 1944.

Creaney was posted as missing in action during OPERATION HOUNDSWORTH after his aircraft disappeared. His date of death is officially recorded as 17 June 1944 although the last known position of the Stirling was logged on the 18th (see Lieutenant Les Cairns' entry within this section for full details).

Son of Mr and Mrs William Creaney of Coolfin Street, Belfast.

Age 22.

Panel 18, column 2.

SERGEANT FRANK WILFED DUNKLEY [7889452] 1ST NORTHAMPTONSHIRE YEOMANRY, PARACHUTE REGIMENT AND 1ST SAS (A SQN)

Frank Dunkley was born on 11 April 1921 in the village of Roade, Northamptonshire. In April 1938, whilst working as a fitter, he joined the 25th Armoured Car Company (Northampton Yeomanry), Royal Tank Corps (TA). Having been posted to HQ Squadron he was embodied at the outbreak of war, was absorbed into the Royal Armoured Corps ten days later, and by July 1942 was serving with B Squadron, 1st Northamptonshire Yeomanry, as a driver and mechanic. During this period he sought the advice of a plastic surgeon who advised him to wait until after the war before addressing the facial scars he had been left with following a motorcycle accident.

Dunkley was promoted to lance-corporal in October 1942 and to corporal that December, before volunteering for Airborne Forces on 11 May 1943. Attending a parachute course two weeks later at No.1 PTS Ringway he was noted as a 'good leader [and] efficient worker'. On disembarking in North Africa he was posted to the 3rd Battalion, Parachute Regiment, which had returned from operations in Sicily that July. He subsequently landed with the battalion at Taranto on mainland Italy on 11 September and was promoted to sergeant a few days later. In December the battalion returned to the UK and on 14 March 1944 Dunkley volunteered for 1st SAS, relinquishing one stripe in order to do so, although he was soon promoted back to sergeant.

Dunkley parachuted into OPERATION GAIN at a DZ 2 kilometres west of Pithiviers in the Centre-Val de Loire département of Loiret, northern France, on the night of 13–14 June 1944. Tasked with disrupting rail traffic the party, led by Lieutenant Cecil Riding, spent the next twelve days cutting lines between

Malesherbes-La Chapelle La Reine, Malesherbes-Puiseau, and Fontainebleau-Lemours. Riding then moved his men to the main GAIN base at the Forêt d'Orléans before resuming operations under the command of Major Ian Fenwick. Although forced to move location, Fenwick returned to the Forêt d'Orléans on 7 August to collect a radio and codebook that had been left behind, his Jeep crew shooting up two German trucks loaded with troops on the return journey. Fenwick was driving, Corporal William Duffy manning the front guns and Dunkley those at the rear. Lance-corporal Albert Menginou, attached from 4th SAS, sat on one side of him and Aspirant Pierre Hebert, an officer of the local Maquis, perched on the other. Duffy later stated that at approximately 1330hrs (other accounts record the time as approximately 1700hrs), they ran into an ambush at Chambon-la-Forêt, Fenwick being killed instantly (see his entry under Chambon-la-Forêt Communal Cemetery, France). Hebert and Menginou were also killed (see Menginou's entry under Ossun Communal Cemetery, France). The wounded Duffy was taken prisoner, later escaping from hospital dressed as a German officer to report:

> When I regained consciousness, I was laid on the grass first and I had been bandaged on my head, hand and knee. There was actually a bandage on my leg at the time and Sergeant Dunkley was stood just behind me. He came forward and spoke a few words, and from what I could see, his hands were bound together, handcuffed …
> I remember him speaking a few words to me and the Germans marched him away [TS 26/853].

Dunkley was never seen again and is assumed to have been murdered, date and place unknown. However, there is a possibility that his was the unidentified body found on 29 August 1944, close to where the remains of Privates John Ion and Les Packman had been discovered, that was buried alongside them within Chilleurs-aux-Bois Communal Cemetery on the 8th. The testimony of Duffy, who positively identified Dunkley's clothing and facial scars, certainly suggests so (see the Unknown Soldier's entry under Chilleurs-aux-Bois Communal Cemetery, France, for further details).

Son of Benjamin and Lilian Dunkley of Council House, Hyde Road, Roade, Northhamptonshire.
Age 22.
Panel 18, column 2. Also commemorated on the Roade Village War Memorial.

PRIVATE DONALD MAURICE GALE [5726852] DORSETSHIRE REGIMENT, No.7 COMMANDO, MIDDLE EAST COMMANDO, 1ST SAS, SRS AND 1ST SAS (A SQN)

Donald Gale was born in the village of Powerstock near Bridport in Dorset on 25 July 1919. He joined the 4th Battalion, Dorsetshire Regiment (TA), at Wimborne in May 1939 and was embodied at the outbreak of war that September. Posted to the 5th Battalion he married Lily Louretta Watton at Blandford the following May. Having volunteered for special service he was posted to E Troop, No.7 Commando, at Girvan, this temporarily forming part of the 3rd Special Service Battalion later that year. After disembarking at Suez, Egypt, in early March 1941 as a member of A Battalion, Layforce, his unit carried out a largely abortive raid on Bardia along the Libyan coast on the night of 19–20 April, the majority of the targets having been wrongly identified by intelligence. On their return the disgruntled men were held aboard HMS *Glengyle* until the beginning of May when they were allowed ashore at Alexandria.

On the night of 26–27 May 1941 A and B Battalions landed at Suda Bay on Crete to help evacuate Commonwealth troops after the German airborne invasion. They formed part of the rearguard that fought a running battle on the march across the mountains to embarkation points on the south coast.

Despite being wounded in his left leg Gale was one of the lucky few to be taken off to Egypt on the 31st, the majority of his Commando comrades going into captivity. Having been discharged from hospital late in June he was posted to the Middle East Commando Depot at Geneifa near to Kabrit.

Although it is unknown when Gale volunteered for the SAS, he learnt that he had become a father that autumn before qualifying as a parachutist on 25 February 1943 at Kabrit as a member of 1st SAS. He was therefore with the Regiment when it was reorganised as the Special Raiding Squadron the following month. Subsequently landing at Capo Murro di Porco on 10 July the SRS destroyed Italian coastal batteries at the spearhead of OPERATION HUSKY, the invasion of Sicily. It landed at Augusta two days later, securing the port after initial stiff resistance. He was admitted to a casualty clearing station on 16 August although it is not recorded whether he was back with the SRS for their landings at Bagnara on 4 September during OPERATION BAYTOWN, or at Termoli the following month during OPERATION DEVON.

Having returned to the UK at the beginning of 1944 the SRS was reconstituted as 1st SAS, Gale qualifying as a shoemaker in May. He was posted missing in action during OPERATION HOUNDSWORTH after his aircraft disappeared. His date of death is officially recorded as 17 June 1944 although the last known position of the Stirling was logged on the 18th (see Lieutenant Les Cairns' entry within this section for full details).

Son of Wallace and Ellen Gale (née Boyt) of Hemsworth near Witchampton in Dorset – Husband of Lily Gale of Verwood, Dorset, formerly of Pilley near Lymington, Hants – Father of Shirley Gale.
Age 24.
Panel 18. Also commemorated on a memorial plaque within Witchampton Church and on Boldre's war memorial within the New Forest.

PRIVATE WALLACE ALBERT **HALL** [5337039] ROYAL BERKSHIRE REGIMENT, 21ST INDEPENDENT PARACHUTE COMPANY AND 2ND SAS

Wally Hall, who was known to his comrades as 'Red' or 'Ginger', was born on 29 April 1923 in Shoreditch, east London. After his parents divorced he grew up with his grandmother in nearby Haggerston, his aunt and uncle helping to raise him. His father, also Wallace Albert, had been a First World War dispatch rider and something of a local hero and it appears that Hall was keen to emulate him. During July 1938 he subsequently falsified his date of birth to join the 5th (Hackney) Battalion, Royal Berkshire Regiment (TA), aged just 15, giving his trade as 'van guard'.

Having been embodied at the outbreak of war Hall was serving with the 70th (Young Soldier) Battalion by October 1940. In June 1941 he was promoted to lance-corporal although his stripe was taken away from him in November for a minor misdemeanour. On 4 April 1943 he transferred to the Army Air Corps and later that month attended parachute course 61 at No.1 PTS Ringway where his instructor noted 'consistently good. Fine type.' He disembarked in North Africa a month later with the 21st Independent Parachute Company and was disappointed to find the campaign over. During the invasion of Sicily that July only a select few members of the company were deployed, the morale of those left behind, including Hall's, being lowered considerably. That September he therefore transferred back to the Royal Berkshire Regiment. However, on 24 February 1944, whilst still in North Africa, Hall volunteered for 2nd SAS, embarking for the UK at the beginning of March. Having requalified as a parachutist he took part in pre-D-Day build-up training, telling his girlfriend: 'they will never get me. I'm a lucky redhead.'

Hall parachuted into the Vosges département of eastern France for OPERATION LOYTON on the night of

12–13 August 1944 at a DZ near the village of Le Mont. Parachutist 'Dusty' Crossfield, a fellow member of Captain Henry Druce's recce group, wrote: 'Ginger had damaged his knee [on landing] so it was a slow march to cover the 9 miles [from the DZ] to the first camp.' This location in the hills above Moussey was betrayed by the wife of one of the Maquis and German troops closed in. Druce's post-operation report states that on the 17th he left a rear party that included Hall under the command of 'Captain Goodfellow', the pseudonym of Frenchman Robert de Lesseps, to cover the main group's withdrawal. Druce later noted that: 'Capt. Goodfellow's party had tried to move south over the watershed which at the time was controlled by the enemy. At V472840 on the 18th August they ran into a German party, Pct Hall was killed [sic] and the remainder, less Sjt Lodge who became separated on the way north to Allarmont, made their way by Pierre Percee to the Sciere La Jus' (WO 361/721 – see Sergeant Robert Lodge's entry under Moussey Churchyard, France). During the contact, which is variously recorded as having taken place on the 17th or the 18th, Crossfield went over to check on Hall whom he found to have been shot twice in the chest and who told him to leave him. 2nd SAS' Casualty Report quotes Crossfield: 'Later I heard that he was buried in the valley south of Allarmont together with three others believed to be the crew of a plane, piloted by a Canadian P/O who escaped and joined us' (WO 361/716). However, this was not the case, the Canadian pilot officer who was also with this rear party, Lew Fiddick, later recalling:

> I do remember us looking for Hall who had gone down but never did find him. We assumed he was captured …
>
> After about an hour of hiking [from the Maquis camp], shots rang out from just in front of us and bullets began zipping past us. We had been ambushed … We all simultaneously hit the ground and began to return their fire …
>
> I looked behind me to see a depression in the ground and as there was a lull in the firing I made a run for it and then jumped into the hole where I landed right on top of one of our group members … There were two others in the hole, which meant one member was still out there [Hall]. The Captain ['Goodfellow'] then said for sure this missing fellow had been hit and had likely been picked up by the Germans. We cautiously came out of our hole and scouted the area for our companion but to no avail … so we decided to continue on our mission [personal correspondence, 2012].

'Missing Parachutists', the SAS War Crimes Investigation Team's final report, confirms that Hall was captured. The team's commander, Major 'Bill' Barkworth, later stated that this was by a Wehrmacht unit, and that Hall was taken to Schirmeck Concentration Camp where he was interrogated (WO 235/554). It is believed that he was murdered between this location and Natzweiler-Struthof Concentration Camp where it is thought that his body was cremated. A sworn statement given by SS-Obersturmbannführer Wilhelm Schneider, SD Deputy Commander of Alsace and one of those later accused of being concerned in the deaths of SAS men, recalls the events at Schirmeck:

> Seymour [the signaller from SOE's Jedburgh Team Jacob who had been captured whilst working alongside the SAS] had been brought in in the morning and another English prisoner who wore the same uniform as Seymour arrived some hours later. He looked younger than Seymour and looked stronger and more athletic. He had short blond hair [sic] and a healthy fresh complexion. He was placed at the entrance of the camp [Schirmeck], like Seymour, but about 6 metres away from him. I can remember the name Hall clearly from this period, but I cannot state with certainty that it applied to this man [TS 26/644].

A further statement by Schneider confirms that Hall was at Schirmeck: 'one of the prisoners (Seymour) was moved to a prisoner of war camp whilst the two others (Hull [sic] and Davis) as I learned later on were killed … at any rate those that fetched them were people from the Struthof' (WO 309/224). At trial he clarified his previous statements:

> [A] few days later for some reason I went to [a] Camp and Law conference with [SS-Hauptsturmführer Karl] Buck [Commandant of Schirmeck] and the car was outside (Van Police number). Beside it was a man called 'Kurt Giegling'. I spoke to him 'we've just finished off the Englishman with that …'. I asked how it was done. 'We were taking him to Natzweiler. On the way we stopped, walked him to slope of small hill and there he was shot.' I abhorred this

shooting because it was Davis … [*sic* – WO 235/559]

> After the body of Davis had been found 35 kilometres further away I am bound to believe that it was not Davis, but Hall [WO 235/554].

Further investigation ascertained that Emil Vierling, a Wachtmeister at Schirmeck, was also implicated in the murder and noted that: 'Capt BJW Stonehouse [Brian Stonehouse, MBE, a former SOE officer who had been imprisoned at Natzweiler-Struthof] evidence to be obtained in the form of an affidavit to the effect that he reorganises [*sic*] Hall's photo as the body he saw' (WO 311/84). This evidence was later summarised thus:

> In August 1944, [Stonehouse] was taken down to outside the crematorium by another prisoner to see a naked dead body which he was told was that of a 'British Airman shot while trying to escape'. The body was brought up to the camp in an SS car, and dumped outside the crematorium. It lay outside a whole day and Stonehouse did a sketch of it which he subsequently lost. But he described it as 'Strongly built, short, typical young English face, fair hair, small nose, fresh complexion, blue eyes' [WO 311/701].

Stonehouse himself later stated that:

> It was the body of a well built young man who appeared to be in his early twenties with a blood soaked bandage round his head and a bullet wound or wounds in his body. As far as I can honestly remember the wound was either in the side of the chest. I took a closer look at his face, removing the bandage round his head. I could then see that his hair was lightish but discoloured by dirt and possibly blood. It was also wavy. The hair line and whole features of the face correspond with the photograph shown to me as that of Parachutist Hall [WO 208/4670 – Stonehouse, a professional fashion illustrator by profession, had a keen eye for facial features].

Asked whether he recognised Hall a worker at Natzweiler's crematorium, Franz Berg, stated that:

> The photograph shown to me marked as Hall is of a face familiar to me, though during my thirteen years in prison I have seen many faces, and during my time at Natzweiler I burnt between five and seven thousand bodies, so it is understandable that I can not place him exactly. The average number of bodies that I remember burning per month was about 500 [WO 235/172A].

Meanwhile, Barkworth gave the following evidence at trial:

> Parachutist Hall was separated from the small party under Captain Goodfellow in the area of Le Jardin David above Moussey on the 17th August 1944. He was taken to Schirmeck camp and from there was transferred to Struthof/Natzweiler Concentration Camp and his dead body was subsequently seen there. I verily believe that Hall was taken prisoner [*sic* – interrogated and murdered] by members of Kommando Schoner under the direction of Dr Isselhorst [WO 235/559].

SS-Standartenführer Dr Erich Isselhorst, Commander of the SD in Alsace, was subsequently sentenced to death in 1946. On 12 April 1947 Barkworth questioned him over further war crimes. At the end of their session Barkworth informed him that he would no longer be required at trials and Isselhorst must have deduced that either he was to be transferred to the French authorities, or that his sentence was soon to be promulgated. On his return journey to prison the truck slowed and Isselhorst jumped over the tailboard to mingle with a crowd, thus preventing his escort from shooting. Although pursued he escaped, albeit it only temporarily: he was recaptured on the 27th and handed over to the French that day. The following month they passed their own death sentence upon him, executing him in Strasbourg in February 1948. Schneider was also sentenced to death and hanged. Meanwhile, SS-Hauptscharführer Kurt Giegling was brought to trial over the murder of Sergeant Frederic Habgood, RAFVR, for which he received the death sentence. He was handed over to the French who in turn sentenced him to ten years hard labour regarding separate charges before his original sentence was commuted to imprisonment. Vierling, an Alsatian and therefore French national, was also located. Although French authorities blocked Barkworth's efforts to obtain him for trial they were, in theory, compelled under international extradition treaty to try him themselves. Whether a case was subsequently built against him is unknown. Hall's date of death is officially recorded as 18 August 1944.

Son of Wallace Hall of Lawrence Road, Upton Park, London.
Age officially recorded as 23.
Panel 18, column 2.

PRIVATE GEORGE MALGWYN **HAYES** [6085839] QUEEN'S ROYAL REGIMENT, WELCH REGIMENT AND 1ST SAS (A SQN)

George Hayes was born on 25 August 1916 in Glamorgan but later lived in Surrey. His army number is from a batch allocated to the Queen's Royal Regiment and it is believed that he joined one of its Territorial battalions whilst working as a labourer. In April 1935 he enlisted into the Welch Regiment at Guildford and was posted to its depot for training. That September he joined the 1st Battalion and was promoted to lance-corporal in March 1936, although he reverted to the rank of private three months later at his own request. In January 1938 he was re-posted to the 2nd Battalion to serve in India.

Hayes was still on the subcontinent at the outbreak of war, going up and down in rank again during 1940 before arriving back in the UK in February 1941. He volunteered for 1st SAS in early 1944 and was posted missing in action during OPERATION HOUNDSWORTH after his aircraft disappeared. His date of death is officially recorded as 17 June 1944 although the last known position of the Stirling was logged on the 18th (see Lieutenant Les Cairns' entry within this section for full details).

Son of George and Lizzie Hayes (née Lewis) of Addison Road, Guildford, Surrey.
Age 28.
Panel 18, column 2. Also commemorated within St John the Baptist Church in the centre of Cardiff and on the Charlotteville War Memorial, Guildford.

PRIVATE GEORGE DALTON **LAW** [3603627] BORDER REGIMENT, 1ST SAS, SRS AND 1ST SAS (A SQN)

George Law was born on 3 December 1921 at Lower Broughton in Salford. Having worked as a general labourer he enlisted into the Border Regiment in June 1940 and was subsequently stationed with the 8th (Home Defence) Battalion at Kendal in the Lake District. Although re-posted to the 70th (Young Soldiers) Battalion that October he was, like many of his regiment, transferred to the Royal Armoured Corps during February 1942 and was initially sent to the 61st Training Regiment. The Borderers continued to wear their cap badge but on an RAC beret whilst converting to their new role, Law soon joining the 52nd Training Regiment before disembarking in the Middle East as a reinforcement on New Year's Eve.

Law volunteered for 1st SAS on 14 February 1943 and was therefore with the Regiment when it was reorganised as the Special Raiding Squadron for the forthcoming invasion of Sicily. He subsequently landed at Capo Murro di Porco on 10 July at the spearhead of OPERATION HUSKY to destroy coastal batteries that threatened the Allied fleet. Two days later the SRS captured the port of Augusta after a further landing, thus enabling a more rapid British advance up the Sicilian east coast. It went on to assault Bagnara on the toe of mainland Italy on 4 September (OPERATION BAYTOWN). Having seen fierce fighting during the capture and defence of Termoli in early October (OPERATION DEVON) the SRS was withdrawn and returned to the UK at the beginning of January 1944 where it was redesignated 1st SAS.

Law undertook parachute training with other members of A Squadron at No.1 PTS at Ringway during February 1944. He was posted missing in action during OPERATION HOUNDSWORTH after his aircraft disappeared. His date of death is officially recorded as 17 June 1944 although the last known position of the aircraft was logged on the 18th (see Lieutenant Les Cairns' entry within this section for full details).

Son of Arthur and Annie Law (née Beardall) of Warwick Street, Lower Broughton, Salford, Lancashire. Age 22.

Panel 18, column 2.

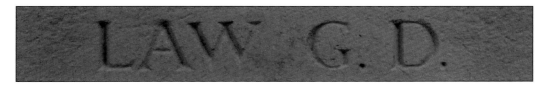

CORPORAL WILLIAM **LEADBETTER** [921086] ROYAL ARTILLERY, L DETACHMENT SAS BRIGADE, 1ST SAS, SRS AND 1ST SAS (A SQN)

'Watson' Leadbetter, as he was known, was born on 7 June 1921 in the St Leonard's district of Edinburgh. In May 1939, whilst working as a seedsman, he joined the local 312th Battery, 78th Field Regiment, Royal Artillery (TA). Embodied at the outbreak of war he was re-posted to the 77th Anti-Aircraft Regiment and promoted to lance-bombardier during May 1941. He embarked for the Middle East the following month and volunteered for L Detachment, SAS Brigade, on 28 May 1942. He is sometimes confused with H. Leadbeater who took part in OPERATION SQUATTER, the first SAS raid of November 1941. He did, however, take part in OPERATION BIGAMY, the large-scale September 1942 raid on Benghazi, as well as numerous other operations behind enemy lines in Libya.

In January 1943, with Axis forces in North Africa all but defeated, the Regiment moved to Azzib on the Palestinian coast for training. It briefly returned to Kabrit in Egypt where it was reorganised as the Special Raiding Squadron and Special Boat Squadron that March. Leadbetter attended parachute course No.42 at Ramat David in Palestine during May. Having been promoted to lance-corporal on 7 July he landed with C Section, No.1 Troop, SRS, at Capo Murro di Porco three days later at the spearhead of OPERATION HUSKY, the Allied invasion of Sicily. His troop was instrumental in the destruction of coastal batteries that threatened the fleet before helping to capture the port of Augusta on the evening of the 12th. He was subsequently recommended for Operational Wings by his troop commander, Captain 'Sandy' Wilson, who noted that Leadbetter had been involved in:

1. Benghazi raid 13/09/42. 2. Placed explosives on Tobruk-Bardia railway. 3. Established forward base. 4. Jeep Op from Bir Zelten to mine coast road east of Cirte Oct 1942 under Lt Wiseman. 5. Sicily x 2 both under Capt Wilson [see Wilson's own entry under Cassino Memorial, Italy, Volume II].

The wings were granted on 23 July, Leadbetter going on to take part in fierce fighting at both Bagnara on the Italian mainland on 4 September during OPERATION BAYTOWN, and during the capture and defence of Termoli the following month during OPERATION DEVON. He returned to the UK with the rest of the unit at the beginning of January 1944 with the rank of corporal.

Leadbetter was posted missing in action during OPERATION HOUNDSWORTH after his aircraft disappeared. His date of death is officially recorded as 17 June 1944 although the last known position of the aircraft was logged on the 18th (see Lieutenant Les Cairns' entry within this section for full details).

Son of William and Jeanine Leadbetter of Stow, Midlothian, formerly of St Leonards Lane, Edinburgh. Age 21.

Panel 18, column 2.

PRIVATE DOMINIC McBRIDE [14643720] GENERAL SERVICE CORPS, ROYAL WARWICKSHIRE REGIMENT AND 1ST SAS (A SQN)

Dominic McBride was born on 9 June 1919 in the town of Lifford in County Donegal, Eire. In June 1943, having worked as a pneumatic tool operator, he enlisted into the General Service Corps, giving his address as Cranford Post Cottage. Posted to No.12 Primary Training Centre he transferred to the Royal Warwickshire Regiment that August and volunteered for 1st SAS on 13 January 1944. Six days later he attended parachute course 99 at No.1 PTS Ringway where, having earned his wings, he was assessed as a 'good worker, confident, average parachutist'.

McBride was posted missing in action during OPERATION HOUNDSWORTH after his aircraft disappeared. His date of death is officially recorded as 17 June 1944 although the last known position of the aircraft was logged on the 18th (see Lieutenant Les Cairns' entry within this section for full details).

Son of John and Mary McBride of Letterkenny, County Donegal. Age 25.

Panel 18, column 2.

Private Charles MacFARLANE [215922] Royal Army Service Corps, SRS and 1st SAS (A Sqn)

Charles MacFarlane was born on 11 September 1909 in Clackmannanshire but later lived in nearby Dunbartonshire in the Lowlands. He married at Helensburgh in August 1932 with three sons being born over the next five years. Having worked as a garden labourer he enlisted into the Royal Army Service Corps in March 1941 and after a period in a training battalion was posted to 141 Company. He subsequently disembarked in the Middle East the following January where he served with 6 Bulk Petrol Company until arriving in Italy in late August 1943. He later volunteered for HQ Troop, Special Raiding Squadron, his service papers unfortunately recording the transfer as having taken place on Boxing Day, the day the SRS weighed anchor at Algiers to return to the UK. Although it is likely that he had been serving with the unit prior to this date it is impossible to say whether he saw action. Regardless at the beginning of January 1944 he disembarked in the UK with the rest of the unit (where it was redesignated 1st SAS) and the following month attended parachute training at No.1 PTS Ringway.

MacFarlane was posted missing in action during Operation Houndsworth after his aircraft disappeared. His date of death is officially recorded as 17 June 1944 although the last known position of the aircraft was logged on the 18th (see Lieutenant Les Cairns' entry within this section for full details).

Son of Charles and Lillian MacFarlane – Husband of Margaret MacFarlane of Cryers Hill, High Wycombe, Buckinghamshire – Father of Alexander, Edward and Charles MacFarlane.
Age 34.
Panel 18, column 2. Also commemorated on Balfron's war memorial, Stirlingshire.

Sergeant Ronald MILLER [1578003] Royal Artillery, L Detachment SAS Brigade, 1st SAS, SRS and 1st SAS (A Sqn)

'Dusty' Miller, as he was predictably known, was born on 24 March 1920 at Penygroes in north Wales. His father's work as a supermarket manager saw the family moving to Bridgend where Miller attended the local grammar school. In June 1940 he graduated with a First in Geography from Aberystwyth University where he was a member of the OTC. He enlisted into the Royal Artillery the following month and was initially posted to No.2 Coastal Defence Training Battery. He subsequently joined the 207th Coastal Battery and was promoted to lance-bombardier that September. Disembarking in the Middle East in November he was promoted to bombardier the following January, only to revert to the rank of gunner at his own request a month later.

Miller was promoted back to lance-bombardier in March 1941 and although he was officially posted to 1st SAS on 26 September 1942 he is known to have taken part in Operation Bigamy, the large-scale L Detachment raid on Benghazi earlier that month. In January 1943 he was training at Azzib and was briefly posted to the Special Boat Squadron from 19 March when the Regiment was restructured. However, having attended parachute course No.42 at Ramat David in Palestine that May he was with the Special Raiding Squadron during Operation Husky, the invasion of Sicily, that July. He was subsequently awarded Operational Wings on the 23rd of that month for his actions at Benghazi, Siwa and for both the SRS landings on Sicily. Having seen fierce fighting on the Italian mainland at Bagnara on 4 September during Operation Baytown, and during the capture and defence of Termoli the following month during

OPERATION DEVON, he embarked for the UK on Boxing Day. Arriving home in early January 1944 he was promoted first to bombardier and then sergeant that same month, the unit having regained regimental status as 1st SAS.

Miller was posted missing in action during OPERATION HOUNDSWORTH after his aircraft disappeared. His date of death is officially recorded as 17 June 1944 although the last known position of the Stirling was logged on the 18th (see Lieutenant Les Cairns' entry within this section for full details). Bridgend Grammar School's website notes: 'He is remembered as a quiet and reserved man, blessed with great intelligence and determination. He was a talented musician, but also one of the fine rugby forwards the school was fortunate to have in the years just before 1939.'

Son of Mr and Mrs Jesse Miller of Bonham Avenue, Bridgend.

Age 24.

Panel 18, column 2.

PRIVATE JOSEPH OGG [11006397] HOME GUARD, ROYAL ARTILLERY, GENERAL SERVICE CORPS, AUXILIARY UNITS AND 1ST SAS (B SQN)

Joe Ogg was born on 20 December 1922 in the hamlet of Enzie near Portgordon in Banffshire and was one of eleven children who grew up in nearby Elgin. Having attended Alves Primary School he joined the local Home Guard at the outbreak of war. Whilst working at Lachlan Wells Farm, he joined the Royal Artillery (TA) and was posted to the Coastal Artillery Training Centre. A year later he was embodied into the General Service Corps and posted to No.26 Primary Training Centre. At the end of May 1943 he transferred back to the Royal Artillery and, after various postings to medium regiments, served as a member of the Alves Patrol of the Auxiliary Units as a corporal (WO 199/3388). On 1 February 1944, with the threat of German invasion greatly diminished, he volunteered, alongside many fellow Auxiliaries, for 1st SAS, relinquishing his rank in order to do so. He subsequently attended parachute course 105 at No.1 PTS Ringway the following month and was noted as 'keen and intelligent'.

Ogg, Corporal John Kinnivane and Troopers Sam Pascoe and George Biffin, were parachuted blind (that is, without an arranged reception committee) into the Deux-Sèvres département of western France for OPERATION BULBASKET. Jumping on the night of 10–11 June 1944 they were tasked with cutting the Niort–Parthenay railway line. An inauspicious start saw Kinnivane, Pascoe and Ogg landing in the main square of Airvault where they were fired on by Germans before becoming separated. Biffin, landing a short distance away, was captured. Ogg later rejoined Kinnivane and Pascoe, the three arriving at the SAS camp in the Forêt de Verrières on the 28th. On 2 July the operation's commander, Captain John Tonkin realised that the camp had been compromised and moved his party to another location. However, on finding that there was no water supply at the new camp the men were forced to return to Verrières in the early hours of the 3rd. Tonkin later noted in his post-operation report that the following morning they were:

… surrounded and heavily attacked by 400 to 500 SS troops with mortars and artillery at 0700 hours. I gave the order to disperse immediately and meet at a prearranged RV … Very few of the men dispersed … thirty-one men, three of them wounded, and Lieut Crisp, also wounded, were believed POW. Enemy casualties were twenty killed and several wounded [WO 219/2389 – see Lieutenant Richard Crisp's entry under Rom Communal Cemetery, France, for further details].

Ogg was one of those wounded, suffering injuries to his knee and tibia before being taken prisoner. Although initially taken to the Hotel Dieu Hospital at Poitiers he was collected by the Germans on the 8th and murdered, most likely by a lethal injection administered by Hauptmann Dr Georg Hesterberg. A letter from Supreme Headquarters Allied Expeditionary Force records that:

On the morning of 8 July 1944 a party of FFI [French Resistance] raided the hospital and took away two FFI patriots. That same afternoon the Germans removed the three British patients [Corporal Reggie Williams, Ogg and Pascoe], telling the hospital authorities that if the British soldiers were left there, they might be rescued next. Evidence shows that Ogg and Pascoe were still definitely hospital cases and should not have been moved. They were taken from the hospital on stretchers. The hospital authorities believe they were then conveyed in an ambulance, probably to Tours. There is however no evidence of what happened to them after they left the Hotel Dieu [WO 218/219].

Correspondence from the Judge Advocate General's office dated 1947 confirms that the three men 'were transferred to the Feldkommandantur Prison. It is believed that the misunderstanding about their transfer to the German Military Hospital at Tours arose through an error (afterwards admitted) on the part of Koestlin [Köstlin], one of the accused in this case' (WO 311/79). This file notes that Dr Tonshoff, the Feldkommandantur's Medical Officer, had stated:

… that he saw these three wounded men in the prison of Pierre Levee but that he was informed that their medical treatment was a matter for the Corps Headquarters. Tonshoff goes on to say that he heard in conversation later, that one of them had died as a result of his wounds, a sequel which in Tonshoff's opinion would not have occurred had the man received proper surgical treatment.

The file concludes that 'it is known that they died in this prison, either through unattended wounds as a result of neglect on the part of their captors or more probably that they were killed by lethal injection administered by Hesterberg on the orders of Gallenkamp'. Ogg's date of death is officially recorded as the 8 July 1944 although there is some evidence that he was seen by Hesterberg sometime around the 13th by which time his wounds were gangrenous. His body was disposed of secretly.

The 'Poitiers Case' was put before a Military Court at Wuppertal in March 1947, the Prosecutor summarising thus:

The facts are complicated. In the last three days certain facts have been proved. Köstlin gave the order for the killing of the wounded. Schönig passed it on. Hesterberg acknowledged it but denies carrying it out. The condition of the wounded varied. They all died the same day. The bodies of the dead were secretly removed and their burial place has never become known [WO 311/724].

Curt Gallenkamp, the General who had commanded the German LXXX Corps, was sentenced to death shortly after failing to take his own life. His sentence was later commuted to life imprisonment. He was released in 1952 and died in 1958. Hesterberg was also sentenced to hang although he walked free when this was quashed by the Commander-in-Chief Germany, Lord Sholto Douglas. Oberst Herbert Köstlin, Gallenkamp's Chief-of-Staff who had ordered Hesterberg to administer the injections, was sentenced to life imprisonment although in 1952 he too was released. Hauptmann Dr Erich Schönig, Intelligence Officer of LXXX Corps who admitted passing on the order, received a five-year sentence.

Son of George and Annie Ogg of Spynie, Elgin, Morayshire – Brother of Peter, Jimmy, George (Dod), William, Cathy Peterkin, Jesse (Janet), Nan Wilson, Betty McDonald, Nell and Andrew.
Age 21.
Panel 18, column 2. Also commemorated on the Saint-Sauvant Forest Memorial and on war memorials at both Elgin and Alves.

Private James O'REILLY [1602722] Irish Artillery Corps, Royal Artillery, L Detachment SAS Brigade, 1st SAS, SRS and 1st SAS (A Sqn)

James O'Reilly was born on 25 June 1914 in the city of Waterford, Eire. Having spent eight years in the Irish Artillery Corps Reserve (service number 71052) whilst working as a greengrocer, he enlisted into the 24th Anti-Aircraft Training Regiment, Royal Artillery, during July 1940. Disembarking in the Middle East at the beginning of January 1941 he was posted to the 231st Battery, 74th Heavy Anti-Aircraft Regiment, two months later. Re-posted to the 230th Battery in February 1942 he volunteered for L Detachment, SAS Brigade, on 19 June, seeing action on various desert operations that year.

At the beginning of 1943 1st SAS, as L Detachment had been expanded into the previous September, began training at Azzib but returned to Kabrit in Egypt in March. Here O'Reilly was promoted to lance-bombardier when the unit was reorganised as the Special Raiding Squadron on the 19th. He subsequently took part in the SRS landings at the spearhead of Operation Husky, the Allied invasion of Sicily, at Capo Murro di Porco on 10 July and two days later at Augusta where he was wounded in action. His application for Operational Wings at the end of the month summarised his career with the Regiment until that time:

> Passed Parachute Training Course 4 METS [No.4 Middle East Training School, Kabrit]. Operations: Fuka – Sidi Anish with T Patrol LRDG [the mass Jeep attack on Sidi Haneish airfield on the night of 26–27 July 1942]. Benghazi – Col Stirling's Party [Operation Bigamy of September 1942]. Sand Sea 1 operation at El Daba. 1 operation at Charing Cross (Capt Fraser). Sidi Barrani with Lt Kennedy [during November 1942 – see Lieutenant Douglas Kennedy's entry under Alamein Memorial, Egypt, Volume I].

O'Reilly returned to the UK in early 1944 and was posted to A Squadron of the newly redesignated 1st SAS before being deprived of his lance-bombardier's stripe for a minor misdemeanour that March. He was posted missing in action during Operation Houndsworth after his aircraft disappeared. His date of death is officially recorded as 17 June 1944 although the last known position of the aircraft was logged on the 18th (see Lieutenant Les Cairns' entry within this section for full details).

Foster son of Michael and Ellen Reher of Ballygunner, County Waterford.
Age officially recorded as 21, although according to his enlistment details he was aged 29.
Panel 18, column 2.

PRIVATE HENRY JAMES **PASCOE** [5729548] DORSETSHIRE REGIMENT, AUXILIARY UNITS AND 1ST SAS (B SQN)

Known to all as 'Sam', Henry Pascoe was born on 22 February 1916 in the small town of Wellington in Somerset where he later worked as an apprentice radio electrician and circular saw operator whilst playing club-level rugby. Enlisting into the Dorsetshire Regiment in mid March 1940 he was posted the regiment's infantry training centre before attending the 5th Emergency Cook's Course from August until October. However, on 24 November he was posted to the Auxiliary Units and nominally attached to 3rd Division Signals at Blandford. The Auxiliaries, whose covert role was to form the basis of an underground resistance army in the event of German invasion, trained realistically with these duties in mind; during November 1941 Pascoe was kept in hospital for nine days suffering cuts and bruising to his left eye having been struck with a revolver during a self-defence lesson.

In early 1944 Pascoe was one of the many Auxiliaries recruited into 1st SAS: marched to the Curzon cinema in Mayfair they were addressed by the CO, Lt-Colonel Paddy Mayne, DSO*, who invited them to volunteer. Those that did were then interviewed, Pascoe being accepted and as a result attached to the Airborne Forces Holding Unit on 13 February. Officially joining the Regiment two days later he attended parachute course 105 at No.1 PTS Ringway the following month where his instructor recorded 'very keen hard worker, became average performer'.

Pascoe was dropped blind (that is, without an arranged reception committee) into the Deux-Sèvres département of western France for OPERATION BULBASKET on the night of 10–11 June 1944. His group, under the command of Corporal John Kinnivane and also consisting of Troopers Joe Ogg and George Biffin, was tasked with attacking the Niort–Saumur railway. An inauspicious start saw Kinnivane, Pascoe and Ogg landing in the main square of Airvault and becoming separated when fired on by Germans. Biffin, who led the stick from the aircraft, landed a short distance away and was captured but survived the war against the odds. Pascoe's nephew states that his uncle and Biffin had tossed a coin to see who would jump first, this act of chance sealing the deviation in their fates. Pascoe later rejoined Kinnivane and Ogg, the three arriving at the SAS camp in the Forêt de Verrières on the 28th. When German troops attacked this location on the morning of 3 July he was wounded in the back by a mortar splinter and taken prisoner. Lieutenant Peter Weaver, who managed to evade the encircling enemy by crawling through a cornfield, reported that a small party attempted to follow him a few minutes later and 'were stopped by shells, where Tpr Pascoe was badly wounded'.

Although local evidence given at the subsequent inquiry suggested that Pascoe had been beaten with rifle butts immediately after capture, the French medic that attended to him stated that there were no other injuries apart from the wound to his back. Taken to the Hotel Dieu Hospital at Poitiers, he received treatment until taken away by the Germans and murdered, most likely by lethal injection administered by Hauptmann Dr Georg Hesterberg. Although his date of death is officially recorded as the 8th there is some evidence that he was seen by Hesterberg on, or around, the 13th by which time his wound was infected through lack of care. His body was disposed of secretly (see Private Joe Ogg's entry for further details of the ensuing war crimes case). SHAEF's Special Investigation Branch later noted:

> The enclosed envelope, containing the sum of one thousand (1,000), blood stained, French Francs, and an unknown substance wrapped in heavy paper, was received by a Special Investigation Officer of this Headquarters from the Director of the Hotel Dieu Hospital at Poitiers, France, a M Boulet, who states this money, (5) 100 franc notes and (1) 500 franc note, had been given to him on 8 July 1944, by a British soldier named Pascoe, on the day that Pascoe was discharged from the hospital and taken away under a German guard. Further investigation revealed the following: Hotel Dieu, Poitiers, was supervised by the Gestapo but staff remained civilian during the German occupation. Record sheets of the Hospital show: Pascoe, Henry James. Born 22 February 1916 at Welllington, Somerset, England. Admitted 3 July 1944, discharged 8 July 1944. Fractured vertebrae, wounds, case 193. Bruises lumbar region.

This file, WO 218/219, also contains an inquiry from MI9, the intelligence directorate concerned with escape and evasion, asking whether 'the 1,000 French francs represent an escape aid or the personal property of the soldier'. 1st SAS replied: 'I think it may be safely assumed that the 1000 francs were operational money issued to Tpr Pascoe and as such should be retained by War Office F Branch.'

Son of Edith Maud Pascoe of Mantle Street, Wellington, Somerset.

Age 26.

Panel 18, column 2. Also commemorated on the Saint-Sauvant Forest Memorial.

Private John Kenneth ROGERS [1835335] Royal Artillery, 1st SAS, SRS, SBS Att 2nd SAS and 1st SAS (A Sqn)

'Buck' Rogers, as he was predictably known, was born on 24 May 1922 in Doncaster. Having worked as a telegraph lad he enlisted into the Royal Artillery in August 1941 and was posted to the 286th Battery, 91st Heavy Anti-Aircraft Regiment, at Grimsby. He arrived in the Middle East the following May and volunteered for 1st SAS on 21 December 1942.

Having attended parachute course No.22 at No.4 Middle East Training School, Kabrit, during February 1943 Rogers was with the Regiment when it was reorganised as the Special Raiding Squadron and the Special Boat Squadron the following month. Soon after he was posted to L Detachment, SBS, and attached to 2nd SAS at Philippeville in Algeria for Operation Hawthorn, a series of airfield raids on Sardinia. As a member of the 'Periwinkle' group under Captain John Verney he was to be inserted on to the island from HM Submarine *Severn* and attack Capoterra aerodrome. In the event, after embarking at Algiers on 28 June, many of the raiders began to experience malarial symptons, this having been contracted whilst at 2nd SAS' camp. *Severn* landed two parties before her air compressor developed a defect and the patrols led by Verney and Captain Edward Imbert-Terry were forced to return to Algiers. They left again, this time by Halifax bomber, on the night of 7–8 July and were parachuted into the area west of Ottana village at 2300hrs. Having been designated a new target Verney and Imbert-Terry's combined team, which included Rogers, managed to penetrate the defences at Ottana airfield in the early hours of 10 July, the group laying-up in a bush to observe the positions of aircraft. The following night they left their Bergens to collect later and split up to lay their charges. The party then moved south-east cross-country in two groups, fully aware that the enemy would be scouring the area for them. The going was extremely rough and owing to the slow pace Verney, Rogers and Lance-sergeant John Scott took to the roads, buying food from the village of Crani where they told the inhabitants that they were Germans whose truck had broken down. Scott later wrote:

> That night, passing through another village, we met two young Italians who offered us some wine. They led us to the police station where several Carabinieri turned out. Everything looked bad. Then the Marshal came with some soldiers. Capt Verney spoke in German to the Marshal who could not understand. Then Capt Verney tried French, the Marshal understood, so Capt Verney told him he was a German officer who had a bet with his Colonel he could march so many miles that night, and if they thought they would stop him they were wrong, and off we went leaving them not able to make up their minds. Again south of Villanova we ran into Italians soldiers on the road and Capt Verney told then we were Germans from Villanova, as we knew Germans were there, and once again we got away.
>
> South of Tertenia two civilians we passed did not seem to believe us when we told then we were Germans, and must have sent word to the Carabinieri in Tertenia, and showed them where we were. When we heard the Carabinieri we dropped our packs, made up a hill, and hid in a bush, the only cover. We could hear them but not

see them. It was a very low bush and we had to lie down in order not to be seen. By this time it was 0500hrs and dawn was breaking. The first Carabinieri saw us [Scott states on 15 July, Rogers on the 18th] and the rest about five, and several civilians rushed over, and before we could move or get up they had us all well covered … We were then taken as prisoners to Tertenia [WO 218/174].

Scott added that he and Rogers were put into a civil gaol where they were interrogated two days later. Rogers himself later noted that his own interrogator had previously been a scrap-metal merchant in Scarborough and that: 'the next morning I was taken to the aerodrome we had attacked. I saw four planes lying burnt out. The German station commandant asked me how we had managed to pass the sentries onto the airfield. I told him that the sentries must have been asleep. He did not seem pleased' (WO 218/174). After a week the men were sent to a POW camp at Villagrande where they learnt that Private Louis Timparano, aka 'Tronch', an Italian American member of the Office of Strategic Services who had been attached to the operation, had deserted two nights after landing and told his captors everything. All teams that had deployed on HAWTHORN were subsequently captured. A fortnight later they were taken to Fort Maddalena on the island of La Maddalena, just off the north coast of Sardinia, before being shipped to the Italian mainland. Here the other ranks were put into PG.59 at Servigliano near the Adriatic coast, Rogers having somewhat optimistically been posted, as of 30 June 1943, as 'missing on special operations probably safe with friendly population in enemy territory'.

After the Italian armistice that September the Senior British Officer in the camp ordered his men not to escape. Rogers and his friend Sergeant Charles Stallings, an American serving in the Green Howards, thought otherwise. They managed to get over the wall but failed to penetrate the perimeter wire. However, a few nights later Rogers and eighteen other members of the SBS, plus Stallings, managed to escape despite being fired on by the Italian guards. The next morning they split into smaller groups, Scott taking Parachutists 'Jock' Johnston (see his entry under Groesbeek Memorial, Netherlands, within this volume), Neil McMillan and Rogers along with Stallings. They later divided again, Rogers and Stallings moving on as a pair and contacting a team from 2nd SAS' French Squadron under Captain 'Raymond Lee' (real name Raymond Couraud) at Cugnoli. This had been tasked to round up escaped POWs from behind the lines (OPERATION JONQUIL). Taken to a coastal RV at Francavilla on the night of 9–10 October 1943 Rogers and Stallings were reunited with Scott's party, although the scheduled Royal Navy pick-up vessel did not materialise. Moving back into the hills Stallings decided to move on alone whilst Lee, Scott, Johnston, McMillan and Rogers reached Allied lines at Termoli in a fishing boat two weeks later. Scott returned with elements of 2nd SAS to look for other evading POWs the following night, as did Rogers the night after: as he landed behind the lines his boat turned over and he and his party were obliged to wait five days before being taken off with the remainder of the French Squadron. He finally rejoined 1st SAS on his return to the UK in January 1944.

Rogers was posted missing in action during OPERATION HOUNDSWORTH after his aircraft disappeared. His date of death is officially recorded as 17 June 1944 although the last known position of the aircraft was logged on the 18th (see Lieutenant Les Cairns' entry within this section for full details).

Son of Vere and Myfanwy Rogers (née Jones) of Arksey Lane, Bentley, Doncaster, Yorkshire.
Age 22.
Panel 18, column 2.

CORPORAL JOHN REGINALD BERNARD **WILLIAMS** [2066732] ROYAL ENGINEERS, ROYAL ARTILLERY, ARMY AIR CORPS AND 1ST SAS (B SQN)

Reggie Williams was born on 26 April 1921 in Kidderminster, Worcestershire, his family later moving to Morden in Surrey. In December 1938, whilst working as a clerk, he joined the 31st (City of London) Anti-Aircraft Battalion, Royal Engineers (TA), at Sutton. He was mobilised in July 1939, his unit being redesignated as the 31st Searchlight Regiment, Royal Artillery, in August 1940. As a result he was transferred to that corps.

In February 1942 he was posted to the 123rd Light Anti-Aircraft Regiment and was promoted to lance-bombardier and then bombardier that November. He transferred to the Army Air Corps on 22 December 1943 and the following month attended parachute course 99 at No.1 PTS Ringway where his instructor noted; 'hard worker, good morale, average performance, good NCO'. Posted to the Airborne Forces Holding Unit he volunteered for 1st SAS on 6 February 1944. Joe Schofield, MBE, a fellow member of B Squadron, later recalled that, although a corporal on paper, Williams served as a trooper in the Regiment (personal correspondence, 2011).

Williams parachuted into a DZ north of Bouesse in the Indre département of central France for OPERATION BULBASKET on the night of 7–8 June 1944. His nine-man party, under Lieutenant 'Twm' Stephens, was met by their commander, Captain John Tonkin, who had jumped into the area with Lieutenant Richard Crisp in the early hours of the 6th (see Stephens' entry under Verrières Communal Cemetery, France, and Crisp's under Rom Communal Cemetery, France). The following day the group was transported westwards by truck, a decision then being made to concentrate farther west in order to attack the railway line north and south of Poitiers.

Williams was wounded in action on 3 July 1944 when the SAS camp within the Forêt de Verrières was attacked by German troops. Having been captured he was taken to the Hotel Dieu Hospital at Poitiers where he was assessed to have been wounded in the back and to have sustained a haemothorax. He and Privates Sam Pascoe and Joe Ogg were removed from the hospital by the Germans on the 8th and murdered, most likely by a lethal injection administered by Hauptmann Dr Georg Hesterberg. Although his date of death is officially recorded as the 8th there is some evidence that he was seen by Hesterberg sometime around the 13th and that his wounds were infected through neglect. His body was disposed of secretly. A memo within an SAS war crimes file notes:

> On November 21st, 1944, [i.e. over four months after his death] the parents of Corporal Williams received a message from their son through the 'Service Social d'Aide au Emigrants' of the International Red Cross.
>
> The message was addressed from rue de l'Hotel-Dieu, Poitiers, Vienne, France, and said: 'Keep smiling. Do not worry too much about me. Give my love to every one. Write to the above address. All my love, John' [WO 311/702].

His parents replied but the following January received a letter from the Regional Director of the French Ministry of Information at Poitiers misinforming them that the Germans had moved their son, along with Ogg and Pascoe, 'on July 8th, to the German Military Hospital at Tours'. It was November 1945 before the three were presumed to have been killed (see Ogg's entry for details of the ensuing war crimes case). Williams' mother and father spent many years in correspondence with the authorities trying to establish what happened to their son. Sadly both passed away without any answers. Repeated efforts by former members of B Squadron, most notably those of Schofield, were equally unsuccessful.

Son of Thomas and Kate Williams (née Jones) of Kingsbridge Road, Stonecot Hill, Morden, Surrey – Brother of Thomas and Queenie (Kate) Williams.
Age 23.
Panel 18, column 2. Also commemorated on the Saint-Sauvant Forest Memorial.

WILLIAMS J. R. B.

SERGEANT REGINALD JOSIAH **WORTLEY** [4863732] LEICESTERSHIRE REGIMENT, WEST YORKSHIRE REGIMENT, 1ST SAS, SRS AND 1ST SAS (A SQN)

Reg Wortley was born on 9 March 1920 in the village of Shepshed in Leicestershire and enlisted into his county regiment in June 1940. After training he was posted to the 8th Battalion where he served in No.7 Platoon, A Company, and was promoted to lance-corporal. He was granted agricultural leave in the autumn of 1941 but embarked for the Middle East on his return. Transferring to the 2nd Battalion, West Yorkshire Regiment, as a private in April 1942 he took part in the defence of Tobruk. In early June the battalion was moved up to the front to close gaps in the front line but its supporting armour was soon outgunned by the 15th Panzer Division and two of the battalion's companies were quickly overrun. What was left withdrew and reorganised at Sidi Razegh only to suffer further heavy losses during fighting at Ruweisat Ridge during July and August. It was relieved in early September 1942, Wortley and his comrades being withdrawn to Mena near the Pyramids. He volunteered for the SAS on the 21st, the day that it was granted regimental status. On 26 October, after minimal training, he set out from Kufra in a Jeep patrol of A Squadron under Lieutenant Miles MacDermot but was somehow injured and returned to Kufra the next day having been replaced by Lance-corporal Chris O'Dowd (see O'Dowd's entry under Sangro River War Cemetery, Italy, Volume II).

Wortley was promoted to lance-corporal on 19 March 1943, the day the Regiment was reorganised as the Special Boat Squadron and the Special Raiding Squadron. As a member of C Section, No.1 Troop, of the SRS he landed at Capo Murro di Porco at the forefront of OPERATION HUSKY, the Allied invasion of Sicily, on 10 July. His troop was instrumental in the destruction of coastal batteries that threatened the invasion fleet. Two days later the SRS landed at Augusta, capturing this key port on the east coast to enable a more rapid Allied advance. On 4 September he was shot in his left calf during OPERATION BAYTOWN, the SRS landings at Bagnara on the toe of mainland Italy. Whilst recuperating he was recommended for Operational Wings by Captain 'Sandy' Wilson and promoted to corporal that November (see Wilson's own entry under Cassino Memorial, Italy). Embarking for the UK on Boxing Day he was promoted to sergeant on arrival on 7 January 1944.

Wortley was posted missing in action during OPERATION HOUNDSWORTH after his aircraft disappeared. His date of death is officially recorded as 17 June 1944 although the last known position of the aircraft was logged on the 18th (see Lieutenant Les Cairns' entry within this section for full details).

Son of Edwin and Elizabeth Wortley (née Fox) of Loughborough Road, Shepshed, Leicestershire. Age 24.

Panel 18, column 2. Also commemorated on Shepshed's war memorial.

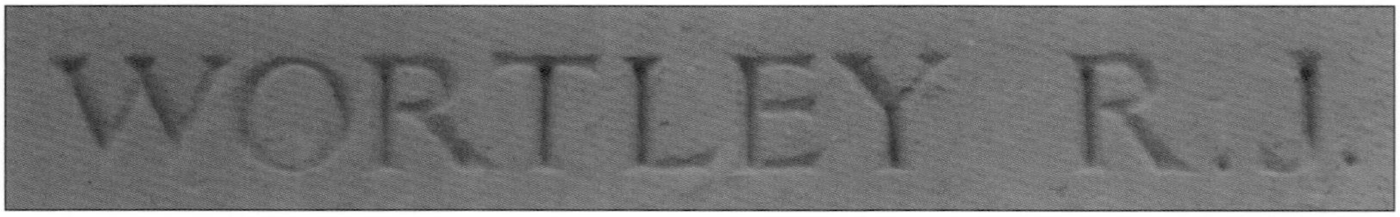
WORTLEY R.J.

CHAMBON-LA-FORÊT COMMUNAL CEMETERY

The village of Chambon-la-Forêt is located 34 kilometres north-east of Orléans in the Loiret département of central France. The cemetery, which contains one Commonwealth burial, lies east of the village on the route du Péage. GPS co-ordinates: Latitude 48.05993, Longitude 2.29952

Major Ian FENWICK [70468] Leicestershire Yeomanry, Royal Artillery, King's Royal Rifle Corps, Auxiliary Units, SOE, Army Air Corps and 1st SAS (D Sqn)

Ian Fenwick, known to his family as 'Johnnie', was born on 11 August 1910 at Norton Grange in Malmesbury, Wiltshire. His parents moved regularly until they settled at Market Overton in Rutland. Fenwick was initially educated at The Grange School in Crowborough, East Sussex, and then followed in his father's footsteps to Winchester College, where he excelled at drawing and was a member of the 1st XI Cricket Team in 1929. At Pembroke College, Cambridge, he read architecture before taking a clerk's position with Shell. Discontented with that, Fenwick then travelled to Berlin where he studied art, socialised with the expatriate community, and became an Honorary Attaché at the British Embassy. On his return to the UK he continued his studies spending nine months at Leicester Art School developing his talents.

Having become a professional cartoonist, Fenwick regularly sold work to *Punch*, *The Tatler*, *Razzle*, *Men Only* and *The Strand*. In February 1937 he was commissioned into the Leicester Yeomanry (TA), later producing *I'm Telling You*, a cartoon guide to winter sports, at which he also excelled. The following year

his father died and in November 1938 Fenwick sailed to New York aboard the *Normandie*, travelling throughout the United States and mixing with stars such as Gracie Fields, Cary Grant, Marlene Dietrich, and Ernest Hemingway.

Embodied at the outbreak of war Fenwick was with the Leicester Yeomanry in February 1940 when it was redesignated the 153rd Field Regiment, Royal Artillery, and was therefore transferred to that corps. However, his portfolio records that he visited Gallipoli, Istanbul and Ankara in Turkey between February and May of that year whilst working for *The Sunday Dispatch*. On his return Fenwick wrote to the War Office: 'On Saturday I returned from a three month trip from Turkey and the Balkans … and am anxious to join up again now. I should very much like to join the KRRC (60R) especially as my father Captain C H Fenwick, was in it.'

As a result Fenwick transferred to the 1st (Motor Transport) Battalion, King's Royal Rifle Corps, in June 1940, but that November was attached to the Special Operations Executive and appointed Intelligence Officer for the Somerset Auxiliary Units based at Monmouth Street in Bridgewater. This secret movement was trained for guerrilla warfare in the event of German invasion and by late 1941 Fenwick, now a captain, was responsible for forty-four Auxiliary patrols consisting of 287 men under nine group commanders, with fifty underground hideouts and an additional four under construction.

Fenwick's mother died in July 1942 and that September he officially joined SOE as an acting major, reporting to Room 98 at Horse Guards, the Headquarters of SOE's Special Training Schools. The following month he attended a parachute course at No.1 PTS Ringway and at the beginning of November was appointed Commandant of No.4 STS at Winterfold near Cranleigh in Surrey. It was whilst there, assessing potential agents, that he heard his half-brother had been killed in action in the Middle East.

Fenwick transferred back to the 1st Battalion, KRRC, at Strensall, in June 1943 and was posted to the Airborne Forces Depot at Hardwick Hall in Chesterfield the following month. In October he completed a parachute refresher course after a period in the medical centre with an injured leg. During his convalescence he contributed many cartoons to the mess of the PTS. A fellow student noted:

> His composure was noteworthy … he is an enormous man of slightly horsey mien. His height [6'4"] is naturally no help in dropping through the hole, or landing on the ground. It is very difficult for him to roll up into a cosy human ball as prescribed …
>
> He was great man for disappearing. We didn't really feel that he was involved to the same degree as other people. His air of detachment placed him in a little world of his own …
>
> We came in for a good deal of criticism from the Battle School instructors, who said that we were not properly under cover, and wouldn't accept Major Fenwick's heated rejoinder that neither were the enemy forces which he himself, let alone the rest of us, had already annihilated [*An Apple for the Sergeant*, by Anthony Cotterell].

Fenwick is believed to have volunteered for 1st SAS in January or early February 1944, soon after the Regiment had returned from Italy. After taking command of D Squadron, he devoted his energy to preparing his men for the coming liberation of Occupied Europe.

On the night of 13–14 June 1944 the aircraft that was to drop Fenwick's party into France 'managed to remove the end of its wing while taxiing out of its bay and decided not to go' ('Summary of 1st SAS activities up to 19/07/44'). Three nights later, on the 16–17th, after a further delay due to the weather, his party took off from RAF Fairford and parachuted into a DZ south of Pithiviers in the Loiret département of central France for Operation Gain.

From their base in the Forêt d'Orléans Fenwick's men immediately got down to work, blowing the tracks in several places to cut the railways lines. Other elements of the squadron had been dropped into the area and after completing similar tasks these gathered at Fenwick's HQ Section. Jeeps were subsequently dropped to enable a wider area of operations. Although further attacks on the railway and rolling stock were carried out, mobile firepower made strikes against German road transport possible. The squadron destroyed trucks and fuel lorries before its base was attacked and the men forced to disperse.

On 7 August Fenwick returned to the Forêt d'Orléans to collect a radio and codebook that had been left behind by another section. On the way back his group shot up two German trucks loaded with troops. Fenwick was driving, Corporal William Duffy manned the front guns and Sergeant Frank Dunkley manned those at the rear. Lance-corporal Albert Menginou, attached from 4th SAS, was sitting on one side of Dunkley, whilst Aspirant Pierre Hebert, an officer of the local Maquis, sat on the other. Duffy later stated that at approximately 1330hrs (other accounts record the time as nearer 1700hrs), they ran into an ambush at Chambon-la-Forêt and Fenwick was killed instantly:

> The last thing I can remember quite clearly is that I looked down at the speedometer of the car and we were doing just 60 miles an hour. At that moment Major Fenwick fell across the wheel. I felt the blood, which I found later was his, coming from his face because it felt just like water sprinkling on my face, and he flopped at the same moment. He fell across the wheel; from then on I lost consciousness, I was hit [TS 26/853].

The wounded Duffy was taken prisoner, later escaping from hospital dressed as a German officer, whilst Hebert and Menginou were killed in action (see Menginou's entry under Ossun Communal Cemetery, France). Dunkley was captured and never seen again (see Dunkley's entry under Bayeux Memorial and that of an 'Unknown Soldier' under Chilleurs-aux-Bois Communal Cemetery, France, for full details). Antoine Krouchelnitsky, a member of the local Maquis whose house was being used by Fenwick as a temporary HQ, noted that he had come to visit him around 1500hrs on the 7th:

> My wife and I begged him [Fenwick] not to go [back to the compromised forest camp]. He answered it was his duty to go since he had to find his radio as well as his documents. Around 1700hrs, as he was coming out of the forest he saw two German trucks and attacked them with the machine guns on his Jeep. The Germans then opened fire and Major Fenwick was killed on the spot by a shot from an anti-tank gun. Parachutist Menginou tried to escape but was killed himself by machine-gun fire about 50 yards further. Their bodies were picked up that same night and taken to the village hall at Chambon-la-Forêt. They were buried at the village cemetery the next day in presence of M. Louis Trembleau [the mayor]. On 29 Aug the Nancray resistance movement held a ceremony at the cemetery in honour of these two glorious soldiers in the presence of American troops [TS 26/853].

A book of Fenwick's cartoons, *Enter Trubshaw*, was published soon after his death. The actor David Niven, a childhood friend, wrote the preface and Lt-Colonel Ian Collins, of Collins the publishers and SAS Staff Officer at HQ Airborne Forces, noted in the foreword:

> Ian's infectious cheerfulness, wit and ability were an inspiration to his men and to the whole regiment.
>
> On one occasion, when he and a small patrol had successfully attacked a troop and ammunition train at night, chasing it in Jeeps which had been parachuted to his base, and firing on the train until it had been successfully burnt out, he ended his report with this short epigram, 'We are happy in our work' [*Enter Trubshaw*, by Ian Fenwick]

A few weeks before his death Fenwick had written to his sister, Angela: 'By the way should anything occur, such as my finger getting scratched, or my nose broken, you, as my next of kin, will be notified, and in time can send on the glad news' (van Straubenzee family collection). On 19 August she received this exact notification from the War Office and *The Times* published this tribute a few days later:

> Although we officers and men of the SAS (with whom he was serving when he was killed) had not known him very long, we had quickly come to regard him as an excellent companion and a fine leader. While he was with us our days were enlivened by his wit and infectious cheerfulness, as were the walls of our billets by his amusing topical sketches. He died in action well behind enemy lines but not before he had caused the enemy a great deal of damage and trouble, and contributed no mean share towards their present defeat [26 August 1944].

Collins wrote to Angela in September 1944: 'I cannot emphasise sufficiently how much we all felt Ian's loss. I met him first in January and had seen him a lot since then … We all thought the world of Ian and his loss is quite irreplaceable' (family collection). Squadron Sergeant-Major Jim Almonds, MM*, had written the previous month:

> I was the sergeant-major under your brother's command in France. He was a gallant officer and a gentleman dearly loved by all members of his Squadron. The French people in the area admired him greatly and his death was a blow to all …
> The graves of your brother and the two men who died with him are in the top right hand corner of the cemetery, well kept and covered with flowers. A simple inscription on the Major's grave read 'A Comrade' [family collection].

The former Padre of 1st SAS, The Reverend Fraser McLuskey, MC, later wrote:

> Ian's death in a German ambush in France robbed us of a brilliant Squadron Commander and the country of a very gifted artist …
> Ian had only worked in the area for a few weeks, but already his name had become a byword. His short command was as skilful as it was courageous. Tributes have been paid to him elsewhere, both as an artist and as a man. No Squadron Commander was more beloved or admired by his men [*Parachute Padre*, by J. Fraser McLuskey, MC].

Brigadier 'Rory' McLeod, Commander of SAS Troops, noted in the foreword to the Gain post-operation report: 'this operation proved extremely successful … I attribute this very largely to the daring, energy and initiative of the late Major Fenwick, whom I would certainly have recommended for a decoration had he survived.' Instead he received a posthumous Mention in Despatches (*London Gazette* 10/05/45).

Son of Captain Charles and Winifred Fenwick of Market Overton, Oakham – Brother of Angela van Straubenzee – Half-brother of Lilian (known as 'Pinkie'), Audrey Blewitt, and of Major Charles Fenwick who was killed in action on 2 November 1942 whilst serving with the Warwickshire Yeomanry, RAC, and buried at Heliopolis War Cemetery in Egypt – Fiancé of Margaret Dundas of Melville Castle, Midlothian, who Fenwick had met at a YMCA canteen whilst on a parachuting course.
Age 33.
No inscription.
Grave D.1. Also commemorated within Boxted Parish Church and as J Fenwick on a memorial close to the spot where he was killed at Chambon-la-Forêt. The village square is named 'Place 7th Aout 1944' in commemoration of Fenwick and the two Frenchmen who lost their lives alongside him. Today Fenwick's cartoons are proudly displayed within the Special Forces Club.

CHILLEURS-AUX-BOIS COMMUNAL CEMETERY

This cemetery contains three Commonwealth burials of the Second World War, one of which is unidentified. Chilleurs-aux-Bois is located 26 kilometres north-east of Orléans in the Loiret département of central France. The cemetery lies on the rue du Vivier to the north of the village, 400 metres off the N152. GPS co-ordinates: Latitude 48.07403, Longitude 2.1281

PRIVATE JOHN **ION** [3325519] HIGHLAND LIGHT INFANTRY AND 1ST SAS (D SQN)

John Ion was born on 6 April 1915 at Kirkbampton near Carlisle and by the outbreak of war was married to a divorced midwife named Madeleine Gill (née Elwell). Having worked as a builder's labourer he enlisted into the Highland Light Infantry at Manchester during June 1940 and two days later was posted to the 50th Battalion. It was here that he served as clerk and driver to Lieutenant Cecil Riding with whom he would later join the Regiment. In October 1942 he qualified as a storeman at HQ 137th Armoured Brigade and was promoted to lance-corporal on 24 February 1944. However, the following day he volunteered for 1st SAS, reverting to the rank of private in order to do so. At the beginning of March he attended parachute course 105 at No.1 PTS Ringway where he was found to be a 'keen pupil, shaky at start but jumped quite well'.

Ion dropped into OPERATION GAIN 2 kilometres west of Pithiviers in the Loiret département of central France on the night of 13–14 June 1944. His group, commanded by Riding, was tasked with cutting railway lines in the area. Having spent the next twelve days doing just that, Riding's stick joined the remainder of D Squadron at the Forêt d'Orléans. Jeeps were then dropped enabling patrols also to attack German road transport, Ion serving as Riding's driver. After the squadron commander, Major Ian Fenwick, was killed in action, Riding took command and set up a series of Road Watch patrols so that information could be sent back to the UK. Vic Long, a lance-sergeant of the same party, later stated:

> On Sunday 12th August 1944 I was detailed with Trooper Morton to go on listening patrol.
> That night at 10.30pm we left the base in a Jeep with Trooper Ion driving it. I was to go and relieve Captain C.J. Riding, MC. We met Captain Riding about a mile from the main Orléans–Pithiviers road. I told Trooper Ion that he was to meet us there the following morning at 8.30am. Then Trooper Morton and myself proceeded to the main Orléans–Pithiviers road.
> At 8am on Monday 13th August 1944 I left the main Orléans–Pithiviers road and made my way back to where we were to meet the Jeep. I arrived there at 8.25am and I was waiting for the Jeep to come when I heard machine-gun fire coming from the direction that the Jeep should have been coming. I got my binoculars and had a look up the road. All I could see was a cloud of dust. When the dust cleared away I saw the Jeep in the middle of the road but I could not see anybody in it. Where the ambush took place was about 500 yards from me.
> A few seconds later there were shots that sounded like rifle or .45 automatic, which lasted for about ten minutes.
> As the country was wood it was very hard to see so I went about 200 yards closer to have a better look and see if Ion and Packman had got away and were trying to make their way to us, but we could not see them. Where the ambush took place the wood had been cut down.
> At 9am about twenty Germans came out of the side of the road and pushed the Jeep into the ditch and then went back to their places and fired on the Jeep …
> As I could not see Troopers Ion or Packman and it had been two hours since they had been ambushed I thought they were captured so we started to make our way back to the base [WO 311/74].

Meanwhile, Trooper Morton stated: 'I saw the Jeep containing Tpr Ion and Sig Packman attacked by a German AFV [Armoured Fighting Vehicle] and driven into the hedge. I was three quarters of a mile away and could not see very clearly the men in it.'

Ion and Packman were taken to the Château de Chamerolles at Chilleurs-aux-Bois. Although they were kept handcuffed, the French owner saw Ion laughing and joking with his captors. Due to the Allied advance the Germans were forced to leave the area on the 15th, the château's caretaker, Monsieur Jesse-Curely, making a horrific discovery a few days later:

> … the bodies of three men, two of them dressed in British paratroop battle dress. Two of these bodies have since been identified beyond any reasonable doubt as those of Packman and Ion and the third as the body of a Spaniard who lived in the neighbourhood. The paratroopers had been shot at the base of the skull from the rear and had received blows in the face from a blunt instrument which resulted in fractured jaws and noses and the loss of teeth [TS 26/343].

Statements of Squadron Sergeant-Major Jim Almonds, MM*, provide further detail:

> I personally heard from the caretaker and his wife of the Chateau at Chilleurs-aux-Bois [Château de Chamerolles] that they saw two men held prisoner in the courtyard of the Chateau who answered to the description of the A/M [aforementioned] soldiers in height, colouring and clothing.
> The same caretaker found two bodies by the roadside in a decomposed state four days later. He informed the Gendarmerie of the village who collected the bodies and interred them in the village cemetery …
> We inspected the area (of the Chateau) and found tracks leading down to the river and to a small bridge over the river. It appeared as if our men had been shot on this bridge and their bodies flung into nearby bushes. Four days had elapsed before their bodies had been discovered by the French who buried them in the cemetery at Chilleurs-aux-Bois. When we inspected the area we found hair which I can identify as that of Tpr Ion. We also found their hands [sic – a post-mortem concluded that the skin of the men's hands had deteriorated due to contact with the river] …
> One of the gendarmes gave to Capt Riding in my presence the following articles which he said he had taken from the two corpses: One signet ring from off the body of one man, two lucky charm rings from the pocket of the same man, one green fountain pen, one British Army whistle. I recognise the signet ring as the property of Trooper Ion, as it had his initials on it. I also recognise the two lucky charm rings as being his property. I know Signalman Packman was possessed of a green fountain pen and a British Army whistle. I saw a tuft of blond, curly hair on the ground where the bodies had lain – it exactly corresponded to that of Trooper Ion.

A paper written in April 1945 by Major Bill Kennedy Shaw, the SAS Brigade's Intelligence Officer, states:

A report, of more than 100 foolscap pages, has been received here from SHAEF court of inquiry into the shootings of 1 SAS PW at Chilleurs-aux-Bois in August 1944.

Briefly the findings of the court are: -

(a) That Tprs Packman and Ion were murdered by German tps near Chilleurs-aux-Bois between 13 and 15 August, 1944.

(b) That the German who murdered them came [either] from the 1st and 2nd Bns of the 1010 Mot. Regt [sic – known as 1010 Security Regiment] commanded respectively by Rittmeister Marschler and Hauptman Kubale.

(c) That there is no evidence of the fate of Sgt Dunkley who remains unaccounted for. It has not been possible to prove that the third body found dressed in British uniform was in fact his.

The court made certain recommendations for tracing the Germans responsible and for obtaining further evidence, and also that;

'1 SAS Regt be requested to continue their efforts to identify the body of the third man dressed in parachutist uniform' (i.e. the one at first believed to be that of Sgt Dunkley).

Meanwhile Captain Mike Sadler, MC, MM, Intelligence Officer of 1st SAS, investigated the case and noted:

Everyone appeared to be commanded by an Oberleutnant with glasses and a scar from the left corner of his mouth. He ordered the shooting of various people, his sentences being carried out by a staff-sergeant in a field grey uniform. Both these men had a sign 'SD' on the left cuff (Sicherheitsdienst).

In 1945 Ion's wife wrote to 1st SAS:

I am appealing to you as a last measure for your help in the recovery of my husband's personal belongings which I am unable to obtain despite all my enquiries to various War Depts who ignore my letters.

My husband was executed by the Germans at Villeurs-aux-Bois [sic] France on the night of August 14th 1944 with a co-paratrooper named Packman.

Capt Riding of D Squadron received from the Gendarmes the articles found on his body which included two gold rings and a small wallet. These he personally informed me he handed over to the authorities here in England, and I was also told by the Padre, Rev Fraser McCluskie [sic], that they were here and would be immediately despatched to me after the atrocity had been investigated.

This was brought up in Parliament in April and yet I am unable to get these things returned. One of the rings was bought by me on our wedding day and bears inside an inscription to that effect. I feel sure that you will understand that this ring will be my greatest treasure, and I also feel confident you will do your best to help me to regain the articles. I fully understand that these things take time but I'm sure that thirteen months is ample time considering the articles have been here since October.

The rings and wallet were eventually returned to his wife in September 1946.

Although members of the 1010 Security Regiment were extradited to London from the American Zone

in Germany it is not believed that any trial was held. Ion's date of death is officially recorded as 16 August 1944.

Husband of Madeline Ion of Gillford Crescent, Harraby, Carlisle.
Age 29.
No inscription.
Grave 2. The unidentified murdered Spaniard is buried to the right of Ion.

PRIVATE LESLIE HERBERT WILLIAM **PACKMAN** [6285463] THE BUFFS, ROYAL CORPS OF SIGNALS, SRS AND 1ST SAS (D SQN)

Les Packman was born on 27 March 1914 at Whitstable in Kent where he worked as a labourer prior to joining the Queen's Own Buffs. This regiment's newsletter later reported:

Leslie entered into The Buffs in February 1933 [enlisted 15 February 1933 at Canterbury] where he was posted to Amherst Squad. He played cricket for the Depot and after a posting to the 2nd Battalion in August 1933 he played football for them [and was an officer's servant in S Company]. He then went to the 1st Battalion, at that time in Lucknow in India. In 1939 Leslie rejoined 2 Buffs in the UK and went with them to France [having married Alice Muriel Watson in January 1940]. He gained promotion to L/Sgt in February 1942. With the Battalion in the Middle East in 1942 he saw action at Alam Halfa and later Alamein [as a sergeant, reduced to the rank of private for a minor misdemeanour that December]. He was a member of C Company.

In March 1944 he reverted to Private [sic] and joined 1st Special Air Service Regt, Army Air Corps, and became Trooper Packman. Leslie parachuted into France in August 1944 [sic – in the early hours of 18 June] to aid the Resistance in the area around Chilleurs-aux-Bois, living in the woods with Resistance members. On August 13th in Operation Gain he and a colleague were instructed by their CO, Colonel Paddy Mayne, to operate on the Orléans–Pithiers road. Whilst on this operation they were captured by the Gestapo and taken to Chateau Chamerolles where they suffered terrible torture. They were taken to the woods after two days of suffering and were shot. The bodies were left where they lay. When it was safe to do so the bodies were taken by a villager and buried in the local cemetery after removal of items that would later identify them. They were both in their thirties at the time of death [sic].

Memorials to them were erected, one in the woods and one in the cemetery. Every year on August 13th the villagers stop and hold a commemorative service in Chilleurs. The graves are looked after by the village and flowers regularly put upon them. Both men are considered heroes. Les, because of his height and long legs was known in the Battalion as 'Legs'. He left a widow and a daughter who he never saw. As a footnote to this our Regimental Secretary at the time of the amalgamations and in response to a newspaper article, wrote to the Mayor of Chilleurs thanking the village for their efforts in caring for the graves of the two men. The reply is … 'We heard about Sgt Packman's great merit with real emotion. We all consider him a hero. This man, like his comrade in arms, sacrificed his youth and his valourous engaging cost him his life. Consequently, it is a modest thanks to let them share in the tribute we pay to our compatriots who were shot down by the Germans in August 1944. We also perpetuate their memory all the year long at the time of the religious feasts, putting flowers on their graves as we do for other deceased. Thanks to M.Legivre, who is now 80 years old, Sgt Packman and his comrade have now a proper sepulchre. This man left aside the danger in order to bury them with dignity. By the way M.Legivre was personally thanked by members of Sgt Packman's family who regularly come over to attend the commemorative ceremonies' [December 1996 edition].

Packman had joined the Special Raiding Squadron (1st SAS) on 21 May 1943 and was promoted to lance-corporal on 20 September, i.e. after the unit's landings on Sicily (OPERATION HUSKY) and the Italian mainland at Bagnara (OPERATION BAYTOWN). He relinquished his rank at his own request on 25 October having fought during the capture and defence of Termoli (OPERATION DEVON) and in late November was admitted to a general hospital for an unknown reason.

On return to the UK Packman attended parachute course 111A at No.1 PTS Ringway in April 1944, his report noting his 'good performance when under supervision'. He was taken prisoner during OPERATION GAIN and murdered on 16 August 1944 (see Private John Ion's entry on previous pages for full details). His body was found with a fountain pen and pocketbook that he used when assisting in signalling duties. Inside the latter he had tucked his Africa Star medal ribbon and several good luck charms.

Son of Bertha Packman (née Care) of Westmeads, Whitstable, Kent – Husband of Alice Packman of Park Lane, Cottingham, near Hull – Father of June Patricia Packman born in June 1941.
Age 30.
No inscription.
Grave 3. Also commemorated on Whitstable's war memorial.

UNKNOWN SOLDIER

This is possibly the grave of Sergeant Frank Wilfred Dunkley who was taken prisoner during OPERATION GAIN. The Intelligence Officer of 1st SAS, Captain Mike Sadler, MC, MM, investigated the shooting of Ion and Packman, also noting that:

> … on Tuesday, 29 August 1944, M. Jesse-Curely discovered a fourth body [near the Château of Chamerolles]. The local doctor thought that the man had been killed about 13/14 August. As far as could be ascertained he was 1 metre 75 centimetres tall, dark brown curly hair, he was wearing battledress with parachute trousers, brown shoes, grey socks, blue underpants. This was found in the long grass under some bushes in a field adjoining his vegetable garden, on the far or north side of the highway running past the Chateau. This body was also in the uniform of a British paratrooper, and so resembled in appearance and dress the description of given of Sjt Dunkley that it was originally thought to have been his body. However the evidence of F/Lt Morgan, the dental officer, given after making an examination and comparison of the teeth found in this body with Sjt Dunkley's dental treatment card, seems to rule out the possibility of this identification …
>
> This unidentified body was also concealed in the long grass, under the branches of trees, and bore bullet wounds in the back of the head and crushed facial bones. The body was found about 100 metres from the road, along which M. Jesse-Curely said the Germans had parked a very large number of vehicles during the time they were at the Chateau.
>
> Sjt Duffy in his testimony describes Sjt Dunkley as being about 25 years old, 5'7" in height, stocky and well built, his face scarred as a consequence of a motor cycle accident, and as having dark brown, bushy, curly hair. On the day he was captured he had borrowed a pair of trousers and was wearing under them a pair of blue PT trunks. He also wore an issue khaki shirt and a warm greyish coloured long, wool pullover. On his feet he wore brown canvas gym shoes and grey wool socks.
>
> The pathologist reports that this unidentified body was that of a man approximately 5'7" or 5'8", wearing khaki parachutist trousers, blue PT trunks, an issue khaki shirt and a bluish-grey wool shirt, having a collar and breast pocket. On the feet he wore brown brogue type low shoes and black lyle socks. The body wore no other identifying marks except for an old healed fracture of the left humerus [TS 26/853].

Meanwhile, a further file underlines that: 'During the whole period of activity of the paratroopers in the Forest, their only casualties not accounted for were the two men above mentioned, Troopers Packman and Ion, and a third, Sergeant Dunkley' (TS 26/343). However, Major Bill Kennedy Shaw, the SAS Brigade's Intelligence Officer, filed a report on atrocities involving members of the Regiment in late April 1945:

> There is no evidence of the fate of Sgt Dunkley who remains unaccounted for. It has not been possible to prove that the third body found dressed in British uniform was in fact his. The court made recommendations for tracing the Germans responsible and for obtaining further evidence, and also that 1 SAS be requested to continue their efforts to identify the body of the third man dressed in parachutists uniform i.e. the one at first believed to be that of Sgt Dunkley.

Owing to the missing lower jaw and damage caused to the upper teeth, the pathologist could not positively identify this body as Dunkley. A dental expert testified that it was impossible for it to be so and the Court of Inquiry therefore followed suit. Dunkley's identity discs were found in the pocket of Ion's trousers although evidence suggests that these may have been left with Ion before Dunkley left their forest camp. However, as stated there were no other members of the SAS, or any other British Airborne unit, left unaccounted for in this area and the fact remains that this is grave contains either Dunkley or an unknown member of the Maquis who had been captured wearing parachute trousers (see Dunkley's full entry under Bayeux Memorial, France).
Grave 1.

CHOLOY WAR CEMETERY

This cemetery was created for the concentration of isolated burials, and of those from communal cemeteries and church graveyards, from all over north-east France where regular maintenance was not possible. As such the majority of the graves are of airmen. The cemetery contains one Commonwealth burial of the First World War and 461 of the 1939–45 war, of which twenty-three are unidentified. In addition, there are seven non-Commonwealth and 334 non-war burials.

Choloy is located 28 kilometres west of Nancy in the Meurthe-et-Moselle département of Lorraine. The cemetery lies 5 kilometres west of Toul on the north side of the D11B, next to the barracks and the French War Cemetery. GPS co-ordinates: Latitude 48.66669, Longitude 5.85094

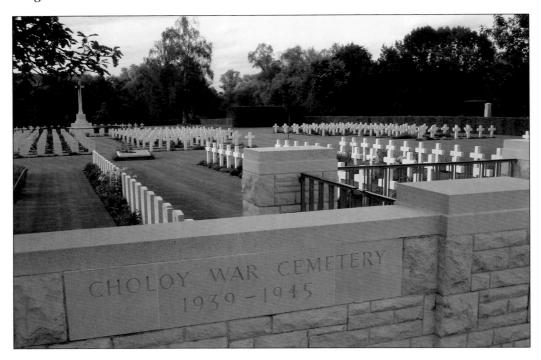

PRIVATE EDWARD **DREW** [4105406] HEREFORDSHIRE REGIMENT, No.2 INDEPENDENT COMPANY AND 2ND SAS (3 SQN)

Known to his comrades as 'Eddy', and to his family as 'Bill', Edward Drew was born on 26 September 1919 at Kington in Herefordshire. In May 1939, whilst working as a lorry driver for local grain and seed merchant, Passey Nott & Co, he joined the Herefordshire Regiment (TA). At the outbreak of war he was embodied into the 1st Battalion just days after it returned from Annual Camp at Weston-Super-Mare,

the battalion subsequently moving to Tenby in Pembrokeshire. The following April he was posted, along with fellow members of the 53rd (Welsh) Division, to the newly formed No.2 Independent Company, one of the small formations of shock troops that later expanded into the first Commandos.

In early May 1940 No.2 and four other Independent Companies formed Scissorforce under Colonel Colin Gubbins, MC. Under OPERATION AVONMOUTH they were tasked with preventing German forces moving north from Trondheim in Norway. On 14 May 1940 Drew's company subsequently landed at the key port of Bodø, far north of the Arctic Circle, where it formed a rear base. As the enemy rapidly approached No.2 joined Norwegian troops, No.3 Independent Company and the Irish Guards in defending the hamlet of Pothus. On the 25th they were attacked by both air and ground forces but held their positions. However, having taken casualties they were outflanked on the 26th and forced to withdraw the following day. Informed that the British Army was to evacuate Norway, and with bridges to their rear blown, survival hinged on a hasty cross-country speed march. Knowing that those that fell behind would be left to the enemy the company arrived, without loss, at Rognan from where it continued its withdrawal to the now burning Bodø for embarkation. Landing firstly on the Lofoten Islands the company then returned to Scotland from where it had originally sailed in early June.

When the Independent Companies were reorganised that November, Drew was posted back to the 1st Battalion, Herefordshire Regiment, which was now in Northern Ireland. He was promoted to lance-corporal in March 1941 and to corporal that July, although he reverted to private at his own request in October 1942 when back in England. He was promoted to lance-corporal once again in January 1943 and embarked for North Africa as an infantry replacement later that month. On arrival he suffered bouts of malaria and by August, having been in and out of hospital, he found himself at No.1 Infantry Reinforcement Training Depot. It was from here that he volunteered for 2nd SAS on 2 September, relinquishing his stripe in order to do so. Two months later he was again promoted to lance-corporal and having served in Italy arrived back in the UK in mid March 1944. In December he was again forced to give up his rank having been hospitalised with a further attack of malaria.

On the night of 25 August 1944 Drew parachuted into a DZ south-west of Saint-Dizier in the Haute-Marne département of north-east France for OPERATION RUPERT. The initial recce party had been lost in a plane crash on the night of 23–24 July (see multiple entries under Graffigny-Chemin Communal Cemetery, France) and a replacement team was inserted on 4–5 August. This sponsored reinforcement drops including Drew's on the 25th. Jack Paley, a member of Drew's patrol, later recalled:

> Some of the stick I remember! Lt [Bertie] Arnold, Sgt Guscott, Patterson, Drew, Fack, Paley, Cpl Sam Bolden MM. Our stick lost contact with Major Rooney's main party mainly because of heavy German activity. Also Lt Arnold was not present for a few days trying to locate Major Rooney. Consequently, with Sgt Guscott in command, we operated with what supplies that had dropped along with the local Maquis. Our stay was soon over-run by the American Army [personal correspondence, 2009 – see entries for Guscott and Bolden under Milan War Cemetery, Italy, Volume II].

Tasked with attacking lines of communication in the area east of the River Marne the operation was mounted too late to be of use, mainly due to 'the reluctance of 38 Group [RAF] to fly to the area' and 'opposition of Special Forces [SOE] to having uniformed troops in the area' (WO 218/199). Further delay was caused by poor weather and broken equipment.

After the patrol had been overrun by the Allied advance Arnold's stick worked ahead of American troops. It was whilst carrying out these duties that Drew was killed in action near the River Meuse on 4 September 1944. Arnold later wrote: 'on the way back at U737062, at 1950hrs we were ambushed by Germans with Schmeissers at 20 yards range. Drew was killed' (WO 361/716). Paley, a friend of Drew, recalled that:

At that time Lt Arnold had our stick work with the Americans. A Jeep was used for reconnaissance. Taking turns three would go out with the Jeep – patrol reconnoitring. It was at this stage Edward Drew was operating driving the Jeep.

When that party came under fire the Jeep went over, Eddy being killed. Lt Arnold and Pat Patterson made a run for it. Fortunately they got away [personal correspondence, 2009].

Son of Arthur and Mary Drew (née Harris) of Sunset Cottage, Kington, Herefordshire – Older brother of Raymond (who served in the Pioneer Corps), Robert, Vincent (who served in the Royal Army Service Corps), Peter (who served in the Black Watch), John (who served in the Fleet Air Arm) and of Norman Drew.

Age 24.

Just a short farewell until we meet again. We will meet again you and I

Grave 4.B.10. Originally buried within Sexey-aux-Forges Communal Cemetery and reinterred here on 6 July 1950. Also commemorated on Kington's war memorial.

Private William Charles HOLLAND [7021035] Royal Ulster Rifles, No.3 Commando, No.14 Commando, Small Scale Raiding Force and 2nd SAS (C Sqn)

Bill Holland was born on 10 September 1922, although little is known of his family life. Having worked as a milkman he enlisted into the Royal Ulster Rifles (London Irish) in February 1941 at Acton, stating that he lived with his father in Battersea. After posting to the 70th (Young Soldiers) Battalion he volunteered for special service and reported to the Commando Depot in October 1942. A month later he joined No.3 Commando although he was re-posted to No.14 Commando at the beginning of February 1943. Twelve days later he disembarked in North Africa and on 1 April was posted to No.62 Commando, the cover name for SOE's Small Scale Raiding Force that formed the foundation on which 2nd SAS was raised on 13 May.

Posted to D Squadron, Holland took part in Operation Candytuft, an attack on enemy railway lines on the east coast of Italy: four parties, under the command of Captain Roy Farran, MC*, landed near the mouth of the River Tronto from an MTB on the night of 27–28 October 1943, despite observing a German submarine anchored just 500 yards away. Tasked with derailing rolling stock the parties made their way inland independently. Holland's group, consisting of Sergeant B. Rawes and Parachutists Mick Malcolm and Bill Rudd, failed to RV with the other teams as planned but later destroyed the line in six places, mined a road and blew down telegraph lines before meeting Farran and their comrades on 2 November. The whole group was picked up by MTB in the early hours of the following day (see Rudd's entry under Villaines-les-Prévôtes Communal Cemetery, France).

Holland returned to the UK in March 1944 only to be hospitalised with malaria. However, he recovered sufficiently to attend parachute course 111A at No.1 PTS Ringway the following month, his instructor noting that he was 'enthusiastic and cheerful' and that his 'performance has been good'.

On 19 August 1944 Holland and other members of his squadron were flown to Rennes with their Jeeps under the command of the now Major Farran, MC**. This party (OPERATION WALLACE) drove through German lines to link with that of OPERATION HARDY that had parachuted near to 1st SAS' HOUNDSWORTH base at the end of July. During this move Holland served as the rear gunner to Lance-sergeant Harry Vickers and had his first taste of combat during the Villaines-les-Prévôtes contact of the 23rd. He was killed in action a week later on the 30th during the battle for Châtillon-sur-Seine. Vickers and his crew were tasked with holding one of the entry points to the town whilst the attack on the German HQ went in at first light. Whilst doing so a German convoy appeared and, having let the enemy vehicles advance to close range, they engaged. Vickers, who was awarded the Distinguished Conduct Medal as a result of this action, later stated:

> At approx 30/31 Aug, I took up a position on the Chatillon-Montbard road, with a Jeep on the river bridge. Shortly afterwards five German vehicles and one DR [Dispatch Rider] approached the bridge towards Chatillon, whereupon we opened fire with the Vickers and Bren, burning all the vehicles, killing the majority of the men who were in the burnt up vehicles, several escaped from the rear vehicle and in the ensuing engagement Pct Holland was killed.

Charlie Radford, also of C Squadron, added further detail recalling that during the attack a Frenchman had beckoned to him:

> We ran to his house and he waved us into the living room. On the floor was lying the body of Bill Holland who had been shot through the stomach and was dying. Captain [sic] Mackie and myself knelt down beside him and tried to listen to what Bill was saying: He had been ambushed by the Germans and shot before he could retaliate. We told the Frenchman to hide the body from the Germans.

The then Lieutenant Jim Mackie's post-action report tied both accounts together:

> I sent Sjt Vickers' Jeep to cover the Montbard road as that seemed the most likely line of approach. He took up position on the cross roads side of the bridge … as the [German] trucks appeared on the bridge down a straight piece of road, it was obvious that the Germans had no idea we were there. Sjt Vickers opened up at 30 yards … Pct Holland had been killed early in the encounter by a series of shots from the right of the road. I left him in a French house and he was later buried by civilians in Chatillon cemetery. I managed to extract his papers of identification before I left [WO 361/720].

It was later reported that the discovery of Holland's body prevented the Germans from executing civilian hostages for what they imagined had been a Maquis attack.

Although he had stated that he lived with his father on enlistment, Holland is believed to have been a Barnardo's Boy. Freddie Oakes, one of his comrades, later wrote to the children's charity:

During SAS operations in France our fatalities were buried in local French cemeteries. After the war the Commonwealth War Graves Commission planned to transfer the remains to War Cemeteries but, without exception, the local French people made it clear that they wanted our men to remain where they were and, with the agreement of the next-of-kin, this was agreed to by the CWGC. However in Bill's case, we understand that in the absence of a next-of-kin consent, his remains were transferred to the Choloy War Cemetery. For the townspeople the matter did not end there so they constructed this fine memorial in tribute to his sacrifice [see details of the memorial below].

Son of Mr Holland of Henley Street, Battersea, south-west London. His mother's maiden name was Bowen.

Age 21.
No inscription.
Grave 3.F.1. Also commemorated by a memorial sponsored by the people of Châtillon-sur-Seine on the bridge near to where he was killed.

SERGEANT KITCHENER STEVEN **ROBERTSON** [3061376] ROYAL SCOTS, AUXILIARY UNITS AND 1ST SAS (C SQN)

Stevie Robertson, as he was known to his comrades, was born on 31 August 1914 in Kirkcaldy and was a resident of Dundee. Having worked as a shop assistant for Menzies & Sons he enlisted into the Royal Scots in May 1940, marrying Eleanor McAulay the following month. Initially posted to an infantry training centre he was promoted to lance-corporal and in April 1941 was re-posted to HQ Auxiliary Units in the Forfar area. He was advanced to corporal that November, picked up his third stripe in April 1942, and remained with the Auxiliaries until volunteering for the SAS. Although initially posted to what was being conceived as the new British formation, 3rd SAS, on 1 February 1944 he was re-posted to 1st SAS on 1 April when its establishment was cancelled (the designation was taken by one of two French SAS regiments). Robertson subsequently attended parachute course 105 at No.1 PTS Ringway where his instructor noted 'hard worker, good pupil' and that he 'became [a] good parachutist'.

Robertson and half of C Squadron (forty men) emplaned at RAF Broadwell on 28 August 1944 and landed at Orléans in northern France.

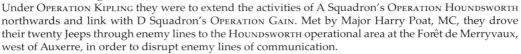

Under OPERATION KIPLING they were to extend the activities of A Squadron's OPERATION HOUNDSWORTH northwards and link with D Squadron's OPERATION GAIN. Met by Major Harry Poat, MC, they drove their twenty Jeeps through enemy lines to the HOUNDSWORTH operational area at the Forêt de Merryvaux, west of Auxerre, in order to disrupt enemy lines of communication.

Although the exact circumstances of Robertson's death are not known, the signal log for this operation notes that Captain Peter Davis received a message on the morning of 17 September 'to instruct Sgt Robertson to return immediately with Jeep'. The following day the log records 'Sgt Robertson of C

Squadron killed in a Jeep accident whilst on patrol.' A further signal from KIPLING notes: 'Robertson died 17 Sep. Buried in cemetery at St Benindazy due east Nevers' (WO 218/206 – he was originally buried within the Benoist d'Azy family tomb in Saint-Benin-d'Azy Communal Cemetery).

Youngest son of the late Llewellyn and Janet Robertson of Nairn – Husband of Eleanor Robertson of Alexander Street, Dundee – Twin brother of Able Seaman Don Robertson who was killed in action whilst serving with the Merchant Navy early in the war, and brother of Louis Robertson of Dundee. Age 30.
No inscription.
Grave 1A.C.14. Also commemorated on Nairn's war memorial alongside his twin.

Clichy Northern Cemetery

This cemetery contains the graves of forty-two soldiers and 184 airmen of the Commonwealth. Captain Joe Radice, codenamed 'Peso' of SOE's JEDBURGH TEAM BUNNY, who died of wounds whilst operating alongside 2nd SAS' OPERATION WALLACE, is buried here. His headstone incorrectly states that he was a member of the Regiment.

Clichy is a commune in the north-western suburbs of Paris. The cemetery lies between the Town Hall and the River Seine on the rue Général Rouget, the Commonwealth plot being located in the southern corner. GPS co-ordinates: Latitude 48.90876, Longitude 2.31308

PRIVATE 'STANLEY HENDERSON' – REAL NAME STANISLAS APOSTOLIDES
[14416545] MARINE NATIONALE, ROYAL NAVY, GENERAL SERVICE CORPS,
21ST INDEPENDENT PARACHUTE COMPANY AND 2ND SAS (G SQN)

Stanislas Apostolides was born on 1 December 1916 at Marseille in the south of France. Serving with the French Navy (Marine nationale) it is believed that he was aboard the destroyer *Triomphant* when she was seized in July 1940 by the British at Plymouth as part of OPERATION CATAPULT. The appropriation of such vessels, which might have returned to France on Vichy orders, prevented their potential use by the Axis. Given the option to be repatriated to French territory Apostolides instead transferred to the Royal Navy in August. He subsequently served as a leading steward on various vessels including HMS *Fidelity*, a freighter of the French mercantile marine that had been converted firstly as a Q ship, and then

as an SIS/SOE blockade runner that landed and picked up agents and escaped Allied personnel on the French coast. The officers and crew were French but had been forced by their captain to assume Scottish or Irish names in order to pass themselves off as French Canadians if captured. Apostolides thus became 'Stanley Henderson' (service number P/LX25403).

Fidelity was not a happy ship. Officers and crew alike were apparently terrified of their Captain, Claude Péri (alias 'Jack Langlais'), whose ferocity, in the form of verbal and physical abuse plus the odd pistol shot, was continuously aimed at the nearest of them. It was perhaps because of this that, after meeting a member of the 21st Independent Parachute Company in a Portsmouth pub, Henderson enlisted into the General Service Corps in December 1942 and was immediately posted to his new drinking partner's company. He may also have transferred because *Fidelity* was soon to sail for the Far East and he wished to stay in Europe, or perhaps he was one of two men that were on leave when she weighed anchor. In any case it was a reprieve, albeit only temporary, as all hands were lost when the *Fidelity* was sunk later that month.

Despite his transfer it was not until mid May 1943, after training and leave, that Henderson eventually joined the 21st at Larkhill. Three days previously he had married Phyllis Morgan at Fulham Registry Office and just a week later the company embarked at Liverpool for North Africa. He seems to have found transition to army life a difficult experience, serving short periods of detention for minor offences before and after arriving at Oran in Algeria. Although fighting had ceased in North Africa the unit moved into Tunisia during the third week of June having carried out arduous training. Whilst billeted amongst olive groves at M'Saken Henderson became the unit's first active service casualty: 'Frenchy Henderson sustained a nasty bite from a scorpion in his sleeping bag. His whole arm swelled to twice its normal size and turned an ugly black-blue. It was thought he might lose the limb, but, happily, this cheerful, tough, swarthy Corsican was returned to the company some time later, complete in all his parts' (*First In!* by Ron Kent – note that this, and other publications, state that Henderson was originally from Corsica although he may have told his comrades this to protect his family in the event of capture).

Having recovered by the end of July Henderson found himself temporarily posted to No.1 Infantry Reinforcement Training Depot before rejoining his company. The latter landed at Taranto on mainland Italy on 10 September 1943 soon settling into patrolling and forming the Jeep-borne spearhead towards the port of Bari, Foggia, and then on to San Severo and Apricena. Withdrawing to Gioia and then Taranto the majority of the company embarked for the UK arriving at the end of the year. However, although Henderson's service record officially records him as joining the SAS on 1

April 1944 it is believed that he volunteered for 2nd SAS either in Italy or during the 21st's return journey via Algeria as he disembarked in the UK during March 1944. His wife had sadly died on 21 February whilst he was still abroad.

Henderson parachuted into a DZ close to Bailly-le-Franc in the Aube département of northern France in the early hours of 5 August 1944 as a member of OPERATION RUPERT's replacement recce group (see multiple entries of the original recce party under Graffigny-Chemin Communal Cemetery, France). His eight-man team, under the command of Lieutenant Duggie Laws, sponsored the DZ for two reinforcement sticks dropped on the night of the 12–13th. The patrol then made a reconnaissance of St

Dizier aerodrome before contacting a Maquis group. Whilst with them they were attacked and forced to withdraw, later receiving further reinforcement drops. RUPERT's post-operation report records that Henderson was one of four men that ambushed a German staff car on 30 August killing both occupants. The following day the patrol contacted the advancing Americans. A subsequent message sent by Laws states: '16 Sept 1944 2050hrs 161400hrs from RUPERT 503 Henderson injured evacuated one zero one hospital' (101st American Evacuation Hospital) whilst his service record notes: 'Died result of accident in battle [16 September 1944] Diag ruptured spleen, pulmonary edema [sic], Lt ventricular failure.' No further details can be traced.

Son of Antoine Apostolides of boulevard du Petit-Nice, Grotte Rolland, Madrague de Montredon, Marseille, France – His next of kin was officially registered as his brother-in-law, Richard Morgan of Onslow Road, Richmond, Surrey, who had always believed him to be French Canadian.
Age 27.
No inscription.
Grave 16.10.7. Originally buried within a temporary American cemetery at Champigneul-Champagne and reinterred here on 3 May 1945. Also commemorated on the Place Engalière war memorial near to Grotte Rolland.

LANCE-CORPORAL HOWARD **LUTTON** [7013186] ROYAL ULSTER RIFLES
AND 1ST SAS (D SQN)

On enlisting into the Royal Ulster Rifles in February 1937 Howard Lutton stated that he was born on 5 January 1919 in County Armagh (Northern Ireland from May 1921), and that he had previously worked as a moulder. However, birth records show that a Howard Irwin Lutton was born at Lurgan, near to where he gave his next of kin address, in early 1920 and it is therefore likely that he falsified his age in order to join the army a year early. After training he was posted to the regiment's 2nd Battalion, serving in Palestine from January 1938 thus experiencing the tail end of the Arab Revolt. In April 1939 he was re-posted to the 1st Battalion and was garrisoned on the North West Frontier of India until July 1940.

Returning to the UK Lutton found home service challenging and spent periods in detention as a result of minor offences before returning to the 1st Battalion in May 1941. That December this converted to an airlanding role and moved from Hereford, where it had been held for anti-invasion duties, to Newbury in Berkshire. Glider training ensued and the airborne maroon beret issued. Having volunteered for the SAS, Lutton attended parachute course 108 at No.1 PTS Ringway in March 1944. Completing his jumps he was assessed as 'a good average performer – has worked hard' and officially transferred to 1st SAS on 1 April.

Lutton parachuted into a DZ at La Ferté-Alais near Fontainebleau, south-east of Paris, in the early hours of 5 July for OPERATION GAIN. The DZ had been compromised and he was subsequently wounded and taken prisoner (see Captain Pat Garstin's entry under Marissel French National Cemetery, Beauvais, France, for full details). He died of his wounds on 6 July 1944 at the Pitié-Salpêtrière Hospital in Paris and was originally buried at Pantin Communal Cemetery.

Son of Mr C. Lutton of Margaret Street, Portadown, Northern Ireland.
Age officially recorded as 25.
No inscription.
Grave 16.16.14. Also commemorated on Portadown's war memorial.

LIEUTENANT MICHELE ARTHUR KENNEDY PINCI [284101] BEDFORDSHIRE AND HERTFORDSHIRE REGIMENT, ROYAL ARMY ORDNANCE CORPS, ROYAL ARTILLERY, SOE AND 2ND SAS (C SQN)

Mike Pinci was born on 13 June 1923 at Pangbourne in Sussex to an Italian Count and Australian mother. Having attended Lambsrook Preparatory and Sherbourne School in Dorset, where he was a member of the OTC from 1937 to 1939, he took an aircraft fitter's apprenticeship at de Havilland's. Here he was responsible for the inspection of high-precision components, studying for an aeronautical engineering degree in his spare time. On enlisting into the Bedfordshire and Hertfordshire Regiment at St Albans in December 1941 he was therefore deemed, with true army logic, ideally suited to operate a Bren gun (service number 5961093). Although posted to the 71st Battalion he transferred to the Royal Army Ordnance Corps in September 1942, serving as a driver in No.4 Company, 27th Battalion. Here he suffered a severe crush injury to his hand that came close to ending his military service.

Having passed a War Office Officer Selection Board at Aldershot Pinci was sent to the 148th Training Brigade at Wrotham prior to posting to 125 (Royal Artillery) OCTU at Ilkley in March 1943. Here he was interviewed by an SOE officer who found he had 'certain qualifications which may render him suitable for special employment at this headquarters after training'. Commissioned into the Royal Artillery that June he was posted to the 78th Anti-Tank Regiment at Bognor Regis, his final course report noting: 'should make a quick, tough young leader. Manner now quite confident in a quiet way.'

Less than three months later, on 5 November 1943, Pinci joined 'MO1 (SP)', one of the many cover names for SOE, and reported to Room 238 at the Hotel Victoria in London for employment as an 'agent in the field'. Security checks found that although his parents were living in Occupied France, and that their house had been taken over as a German HQ, they were not considered a threat. He was therefore cleared to begin training. However, although his course reports note his courage and determination, and that he was 'consumed with a passionate zeal for his work, almost to the point of fanaticism', his overall temperament was found to be unsuitable for F Section. As a result he was briefly passed to Special

Training School 51 where, although he completed JEDBURGH training, he was again deemed incompatible with the role. Fearing that he might not see any action he asked to be posted to an Airborne unit and subsequently reported to HQ 2nd SAS at Doonfoot Camp south of Ayr. Posted to C Squadron at nearby Fairfield Camp, Monkton, he was officially transferred to the Regiment on 6 April 1944.

Pinci parachuted into a DZ near Aignay-le-Duc in the Côte-d'Or département of eastern France with six men on the night of 23–24 August 1944 (OPERATION HARDY). Tasked with disrupting enemy lines of communication the men were absorbed into Major Roy Farran's OPERATION WALLACE, subsequently ambushing a petrol wagon on the 27th during an assault on the German garrison at Châtillon-sur-Seine and supporting a Maquis attack on Nod-sur-Seine on the 29th.

When WALLACE closed down, OPERATION ROBEY began, this being tasked with continuing activity in the area of its forerunners. A post-operation report, which encapsulates all three operations, states: 'When Capt Hibbert's Jeep squadron had moved out Lieuts Pinci, Walker-Brown, Taylor and Kerr, together with 19 ORs [other ranks] were left to operate in the Plateau de Langres area under command of Lieut Pinci' (WO 218/197). It also records that Pinci left Auberive on the afternoon of the 11th in a civilian car without recognition markings that was subsequently attacked by Allied aircraft. Monsieur E. Pouztale, a member of the local Maquis, later summarised Pinci's activities in France:

> Lt Michael Pinci of the SAS was dropped by parachute in the area of Aignay-le-Duc at the beginning of the month of August 1944 [sic].
>
> Henceforward he collaborated with his group of parachutists in the sabotage and offensive operations of the Maquis organisations of Burgundy under the command of Colonel Claude. He worked with the greatest success to co-ordinate the activities of the British with those of the FFI [Forces Françaises de l'Intérieur – the Resistance] taking part himself with the greatest vigour in several ambushes and coups de mains.
>
> The area of the Langres plateau became at the beginning of September 1944, as the result of the general development of operations, an extremely important zone militarily. Lt Pinci concentrated his efforts on strengthening the offensive power of his group and of the Maquis forces with which he collaborated by improving their armament.
>
> It was for this purpose that he went to Troyes and then to the neighbourhood of Paris on 7 September accompanied by Capt Peter Heskell of the British Army who was charged with liaison between the Maquis in those areas and the Allied army. He had meetings with several people, notably Generals Chaban and de Joinville. As the result of these meetings, he believed that he had obtained an allocation of twenty Jeeps armed with machine guns.
>
> On the morning of Saturday, 9 September 1944, Lt Pinci left Paris. He had agreed to take me with him to permit me to rejoin the Maquis of Burgundy to whom I belong, and from that moment I was constantly with him.
>
> We arrived at Châtillon-sur-Seine. The town had been evacuated that same morning by the German Garrison, which was composed of about 500 men in a convoy of 100 trucks. This town was occupied by a certain number of FFI groups.
>
> The German convoy remained a menace having been stopped 5kms from Châtillon on the road to Langres by the group France of Recey twenty-two men strong. Faced with this situation and the fact that there were a few American motorised troops in the neighbourhood, Lt Pinci immediately got into touch with his officers and induced them to modify their plan of action in order to assist in the protection of the town. He was only partially successful but sufficiently so in holding up the entire convoy during the whole night of 9–10 September in spite of the enemy's efforts to cut a way through.
>
> The convoy was attacked on the morning of Monday 11 September (partly with the direction of Lt Pinci) by various forces of the FFI to whom he had brought the assistance of various groups of the Corps France of Auberive where he had his Headquarters.
>
> Realising the impossibility of obtaining a decision with the forces at his disposal, Lt Pinci went with me and Colonel Claude, who commands the Maquis forces in the Burgundy area to Gen Leclerc's HQ about 50kms north of Châtillon.
>
> As the result of the report made to him General Leclerc agreed to send a group of tanks and armoured cars to participate in the action.
>
> The attack took place on Monday morning after the Germans had made several attempts to cut their way out during the night, some of these were menacing and Lt Pinci took part personally in the actions to repel them.
>
> In the morning nearly all the Germans were made prisoners and the remainder gave themselves up in small groups on the following days. The number of prisoners made was about 500 including the Colonel and a Lt-Colonel. The whole convoy of about 100 trucks and lorries were taken.
>
> Having returned to Auberive towards midday to make dispositions, Lt Pinci was on his way to Châtillon to take part in the distribution of the captured vehicles and to ask for the allocation of a certain number of them to the Corps France of Auberive and to the group of English parachutists, when his vehicle was attacked by planes. I was myself

in the vehicle he was driving, in which there was also Col Michel, commanding FFI in the department of Haute Marne, and a driver. We were followed by a car manned by three English parachutists.

Our little convoy was attacked when moving at great speed just outside the little village of Recey by two fighter planes with Allied tricolour markings, before we were aware of their presence.

The bursts of shells straddled the vehicle. We thought at first that we were under machine-gun fire from an ambush. As Lt Pinci braked to prepare to fight, a third burst struck his car, covering it with hits, he himself was struck in the head and killed on the spot.

His death interrupted an action which had [been] particularly useful and efficacious.

He has constantly given proof of the greatest military ability. He knew how to effect a co-operation often difficult between FFI and the regular elements of the Allied army [WO 218/193].

The suggestion is that with only one vehicle displaying the white star Allied recognition markings, the pilot believed that he was attacking a German car chasing a Maquis vehicle. Pinci was originally buried within Auberive's communal cemetery. In an interview with the Imperial War Museum Bob Walker-Brown stated:

Mike Pinci then had the splendid idea of making more use of the air forces so we sent a signal back asking for air cover on the RN74 just south of Langres every morning at first light when there was usually some German movement. Pinci, who spoke fluent French, managed to commandeer a French civilian car which had some petrol, and he drove it onto the RN74 at the very point where he'd called an air strike on – he wanted to see the fun and unfortunately he was the first victim. He was immediately taken out by two low flying Thunderbolts and killed. So, after burying him in a French churchyard [Auberive Communal Cemetery] I took over the troop [IWM Sound Archive 20604].

Son of Count Mario Pinci, Director of French Mining Industries, and of the Countess Pinci (née Gwendoline Kennedy) of rue la Fontaine, Paris – Grandson of Mrs Kennedy of Crichel near Wimborne in Dorset.
Age 21.
When can their glory fade?
Grave 16.13.13. Also commemorated on the Auberive Maquis Memorial.

CRAIN COMMUNAL CEMETERY

Crain is located 34 kilometres south of Auxerre and 2 kilometres east of Coulanges-sur-Yonne in the Yonne département of Bourgogne. The cemetery lies on the D39 towards Mailly-le-Château. GPS co-ordinates: Latitude 47.530405, Longitude 3.560886

CAPTAIN LAURENCE ROY **BRADFORD** [124886] DEVONSHIRE REGIMENT, AUXILIARY UNITS AND 1ST SAS (A SQN)

Roy Bradford, as he was commonly known, was born on 27 July 1916 in the town of Barnstaple, north Devon, where he attended grammar school. In April 1939, whilst working as an architect and surveyor's chief assistant, he joined the 6th Battalion, Devonshire Regiment (TA), and was serving as a lance-corporal in the mortar platoon when embodied at the outbreak of war (service number 5620500). Having attended 167 OCTU at Aldershot he was commissioned into his parent regiment in March 1940 and was posted to its infantry training centre in Exeter. Here he met Joan Gilbert who he married the following April before rejoining the 6th Battalion at Battle in Sussex. He was promoted to lieutenant that September and in June 1942 was posted to HQ Auxiliary Units. Having been appointed Scout Officer at Tottington Manor near Small Dole in West Sussex his daughter Faith was born that August.

 In July 1943 Bradford was promoted to captain and appointed Intelligence Officer of the Auxiliaries in Devon and Cornwall. After the threat of German invasion had abated, and with the role of the Auxiliaries thus redundant, he volunteered for the SAS. He joined it on 8 February 1944, the day he qualified as a parachutist. Although initially due to report to 3rd SAS this proposed British Regiment did not come

to fruition (the designation was taken by one of two French SAS regiments) and he was taken on strength of 1st SAS on the 24th of that month.

Bradford dropped into OPERATION HOUNDSWORTH with A Squadron's main party on 22 June 1944 at a DZ at Les Vellottes, 8 kilometres north of Ouroux-en-Morvan in the Nièvre département of central France. The men were collected by the local Resistance in buses and taken to the camp of the Maquis Bernard. At dusk the next day Bradford's 3 Troop was again transported by bus to join another camp at Vieux Dun. Sergeant Jeff DuVivier's post-operation report states: 'The worst difficulty arose when Capt Bradford and some seventeen other men who had been allotted an area some 40 miles from our static base, had only one Jeep in which to transport both personnel and supplies' (WO 218/192). The troop operated effectively despite the limitation and it was over this camp that a US Liberator and an RAF Halifax collided in mid air, Bradford's troop recovering the bodies of the American crew and collecting the personal effects of the British crew.

At 0800hrs on 20 July Bradford's Jeep was moving via side roads to the Forêt des Dames to RV with DuVivier's party. Its crew found itself face to face with a German officer and NCO. Not realising that they were British, the Germans tried to wave them down. The front gunner, Sergeant 'Chalky' White, DCM, MM, replied with a burst from his twin Vickers, the Jeep moving forward past a line of seven parked trucks whose occupants, who had been preparing breakfast on either side of the road, were now fully alerted. Craftsman Andy Devine, the fitter and rear gunner, was killed by machine-gun fire and Bradford, who was seated in the front between Sergeant 'Maggie' McGinn and White, was wounded in the left arm. With Devine slumped over the rear guns the incoming fire remained unopposed. In addition, the Jeep's top speed had been reduced to 30mph due to damage caused by small arms. As they passed the last vehicle Bradford was killed, Jacques Morvillier, an interpreter from the Maquis Jean, had his elbow shattered and White was wounded in the leg, left hand and shoulder. Just out of sight to the enemy the Jeep engine died and McGinn was able to help the two wounded men to safety.

The Germans recovered several documents from the abandoned Jeep, although these were later retrieved when another convoy was attacked by the SAS. White was regarded as somewhat of a jinx to officers having had six others killed in his company during previous operations.

The Reverend Fraser McLuskey, MC, 1st SAS' former Padre, later wrote:

Roy Bradford's death cast a shadow over the whole squadron. Like Leslie Cairns, lost in the missing plane, he was one of the finest officers and finest men in the unit. A man of strong Christian character, his influence was felt wherever he went. The men of his own troop, and his friends in the regiment will not easily forget him. My last memory of him is at the Communion service we shared together on the hillside near his camp a few days before he left. It was the preparation he would have wished for what lay ahead [*Parachute Padre*, by J. Fraser McLuskey, MC – see Cairns' entry under Bayeux Memorial, France].

Son of Charles and Mabel Bradford (née Palmer) of Castle Street, Barnstable, Devon – Older brother of Geoffrey Bradford who he recruited into the Auxiliaries – Husband of Joan Bradford of Barnstaple.
Age 28.
At the going down of the sun and in the morning we will remember him
Grave 3.T.1. Also commemorated with Devine by a memorial on the rue de 20 Juillet where the action took place, 1 kilometre from their graves.

Craftsman William Henry DEVINE [5337350] Royal Berkshire Regiment, Royal Army Ordnance Corps, Royal Electrical and Mechanical Engineers and 1st SAS (A Sqn)

Andy Devine, as he was known to his comrades, was born in Holborn, central London, on 19 April 1920 and later lived in Stoke Newington. In May 1939, whilst a steel worker, he joined the 5th (Hackney) Battalion, Royal Berkshire Regiment (TA), and was embodied for service with the 7th (Stoke Newington) Battalion late that August, just before the outbreak of war. In April 1940 he passed a cook's course, completing training in water hygiene during the spring of 1941. That June he married Edith Dinning at Durham and later in the summer was attached to HQ 54th (East Anglia) Infantry Division before attending a fitter's course. On qualifying he transferred to the Royal Army Ordnance Corps and in mid November 1942 transferred to the newly formed Royal Electrical and Mechanical Engineers.

Devine volunteered for 1st SAS on 18 February 1944 and attended parachute course 114A that May at No.1 PTS Ringway. Here his instructor found him 'a very good performer' who 'worked hard' and was 'always cheerful'. Dropped into France for Operation Houndsworth on 11 July 1944 he was killed in action on 20 July (see Captain Roy Bradford's entry on previous pages for full details). The Reverend Fraser McLuskey, MC, the Regiment's former Padre, later wrote: 'Devine worked like a Trojan from the moment he arrived, overhauling our much-abused Jeeps, and improvising as only a very clever craftsman can … We all felt Devine's loss. He was a born comedian as well as a first-class fitter, and everybody liked him' (*Parachute Padre*, by J. Fraser McLuskey, MC).

Son of Mrs L. Devine (née Ward) of Oldfield Road, Stoke Newington – Husband of Edith Devine of Lodge Hill, Gillings Gate, Durham.
Age 24.
No inscription.
Grave 3.T.2. Also commemorated with Bradford by a memorial on the rue de 20 Juillet where the action took place, 1 kilometre from their graves.

DRESLINCOURT COMMUNAL CEMETERY

Dreslincourt is located in the Somme département of Picardie, west of the D1032 and north of the neighbouring community of Ribécourt-Dreslincourt. The cemetery lies on the rue de Cinq Piliers at the northern boundary of the village. GPS co-ordinates: Latitude 49.531974, Longitude 2.922870

LANCE-CORPORAL ROGER ACHILLE <u>FANEN</u> [41272] 3ᴱ BATAILLON D'INFANTERIE DE L'AIR, 3ᴱ RÉGIMENT DE CHASSEURS PARACHUTISTES (3RD SAS) ATT 2ND SAS

Roger Fanen was born on 22 July 1921 in the village of Dreslincourt. Although details of his early service life are unknown it appears that he joined the 3ᴱ Bataillon d'infanterie de l'air at Rouiba in Algeria during October 1943, this unit disembarking in the UK that November. The following April it was reorganised as the 3ᴱ Régiment de chasseurs parachutistes, more commonly known within the SAS Brigade that it had joined as 3rd (French) SAS. By August 1944 he was attached to F Squadron, 2nd SAS, this being formed of an eclectic mix of mainly foreign nationals known within the Regiment as the 'Funnies'.

In the early hours of 4 August 1944 Fanen parachuted into the area of the Forêt de la Guerche, south-east of Rennes in Brittany, as a member of Capitaine Jacques Lazon's Party IV for OPERATION DUNHILL. The stick, made up exclusively from 2nd SAS' F Squadron, was dropped blind, that is without an organised reception committee. It was tasked with harassing retreating enemy forces on the roads between Châteaubriant, Segre and La Guerche. Lazon's noted in the post-operation report that: 'Felger, Fanen, and Centolle, slipped their kit bags in mid-air and the contents were destroyed on falling to the ground'. In this way 'One Tommy gun, two Sten guns, and a wireless ceased to be useable' (WO 361/726). Landing 34 kilometres north of their intended DZ, the group was overrun by the advancing Allies the following day. Incorporating itself into the US 42nd Cavalry Squadron the patrol became this unit's reconnaissance element and it was during this period that Fanen was killed in action. 2nd SAS' Casualty Report quotes Lazon: 'L/Cpl Fanen was killed on 17th Aug at 0600hrs near Blain during an engagement between patrols' (WO 361/716).

Son of Louis Adolphe Marie and Angèle Lucie Marthe Moutard.
Also commemorated on the French SAS memorial at Plumelec, on Dreslincourt's war memorial, and by the rue Roger Fanen leading into the village.
Age 23.

ÉPOISSES COMMUNAL CEMETERY

The village of Époisses is located 70 kilometres north-west of Dijon in the Côte-d'Or département of Bourgogne. The cemetery lies on the east side of town on the rue de Semur (D954). GPS co-ordinates: Latitude 47.50929, Longitude 4.1752

LIEUTENANT DAVID BLAIR **LEIGH** [336518] YORK AND LANCASTER REGIMENT, GREEN HOWARDS, L DETACHMENT SAS BRIGADE, 1ST SAS ATT 2ND SAS, GENERAL LIST AND 2ND SAS (C SQN)

David Leigh was born in Shanghai on 8 November 1917 to an English father and Australian mother. Having attended the King Edward VI School at Bury St Edmunds he enlisted into the York and Lancaster Regiment at Crownhill in April 1940 (service number 4751938). On doing so he declared his address as Warwick Street, London, that he was an 'air ministry auditor' and that he could speak, read and write 'fair' French. Posted to the regiment's infantry training centre he transferred to the 4th Battalion, Green Howards, in June. The following April this embarked for the Middle East, arriving at Port Tewfik on the Suez Canal two months later. Although initially stationed at Fuka it took up garrison duties on Cyprus from August until November. Moving to Palestine then back to Egypt it crossed the Libyan frontier in January 1942, just in time to withdraw to Tengeder then Bir Hacheim in front of Rommel's offensive. Although Leigh had reached the rank of corporal by this time he relinquished his stripes on volunteering for L Detachment, SAS Brigade, on 7 April. His natural ability ensured reduction in rank was only a temporary measure and within five months he had regained both stripes.

Having left Kabrit on 3 July 1942 Leigh and a large SAS group under Major David Stirling, DSO, established a base at Quaret Hiremas on the northern edge of the Great Sand Sea. He subsequently took part in OPERATION NUMBER 12, a raid on Fuka aerodrome on the 7th:

Party consisting of Col Stirling [*sic*], Major Mayne, Cooper, Leigh, Storey, Robson, Lilly, Adamson, Gammel, Downes, Shaw & O'Dowd to attack LG.68 in Blitz Buggy and three jeeps. Arrived and parked off road at 2300hrs. Major Mayne, Adamson & Storey went in on foot. At 0100hrs party went in Buggy leading and three jeeps in single file behind cruising around drome, under fire, strafing aircraft with Vickers K's etc. Forty-nine aircraft destroyed by bombs and strafing. Withdrew. Cooper fixed position by telegraph poles and we started off for rendezvous. At 0645hrs two CR42s spotted us in open desert and strafed getting Buggy and one jeep after thirty minutes. Broke off. Whole party returned in remaining jeeps to rendezvous. On return moved RV 15 miles west ['1st SAS Bde L Detachment Operations' – see entries for Lance-bombardier John Robson under Alamein Memorial, Egypt, Volume I, and Lance-sergeant Chris O'Dowd, MM, under Sangro River War Cemetery, Italy, Volume II].

That September Leigh took part in OPERATION BIGAMY, a large-scale raid on Benghazi. On the approach to the port the SAS convoy was ambushed, Reg Seekings later recalling:

My driver was a chap called David Lee [*sic*]. His father was Superintendent of Police in Shanghai. Born and bred out there he was. A gentleman. Beautiful cultured accent. Errol Flynn wasn't a patch on him. Davie would not show any fear. He must have experienced fear, he was an intelligent man, but he wouldn't show it. Never back down to a German, air attack, or anything, he would not take cover. I said to Davie: 'Take the wheel, I'll take the guns, lets get the convoy turned back.' His guns were still firing like hell. They [the enemy] were masked behind blankets. You couldn't see them properly. I said 'Davie, turn round for Christ's sake! I didn't say attack.' He said 'Don't get a flap on, I'm turning round' and drove right up into the area where the guns were, reversed and drove back [*The Originals: The Secret History of the Birth of the SAS*, by Gordon Stevens].

The following month Leigh was a member of Captain Bill Fraser's A Squadron party that left Kufra on 14 October and blew the railway line east of Fuka before returning on the 25th. He was returned to Kufra under doctor's orders on 11 November. Later that month, having attended an LRDG course in navigation, Leigh guided a group of forty Jeeps, under the command of Major Paddy Mayne, DSO, to establish a dump at Bir Zeltan, covering the 700-kilometre trip in thirty-six hours. The report asks; 'Is this a record?'

Bill Deakins later wrote that Leigh also acted as navigator during an operation under Captain Jim Chambers to mine railway lines and that on their return to their Sand Sea base in early 1943: 'David Lea [*sic*] was very ill. He had slept near me at night and I wonder if he had a touch of diphtheria or similar, for at times he would be almost choking. I would lie and listen, wondering whether he would recover' (*The Lame One: 'Sod this for a Game of Soldiers'*, by Bill Deakins). Luckily a change of environment followed, George Daniels recalling: 'Major Barlow and myself and Sergeants Dave Leigh and Dave Kershaw, of the original SAS, were ordered to recruit and train 2nd SAS Regiment recruits, then being raised at Philippeville in Algeria, North Africa' (*Daggers Drawn: Second World War Heroes of the SAS and SBS*, by Mike Morgan). Leigh's service record states this was officially with effect from 1 July 1943 although it is believed that Leigh took part in OPERATION SNAPDRAGON, a recce of Pantelleria, in late May during which his party had to make a fighting withdrawal down a sea cliff (see Gunner Ernie Herstell's entry under Medjez-el-Bab Memorial, Tunisia, Volume I, for further details of this operation).

Although it is unknown whether Leigh served on mainland Italy he embarked for the UK at the end of January 1944 and was commissioned onto the General List (*London Gazette* 27/08/45). Posted to 2nd SAS on 7 February 1944 he married Ethel Cormack Stewart on 1 June at Prestwick and was promoted to war substantive lieutenant on 7 August.

On 19 August 1944 Leigh and fellow members of C Squadron were flown to Rennes with their Jeeps under the command of Major Roy Farran, MC**. This party (OPERATION WALLACE) drove through German lines to link with OPERATION HARDY that had parachuted near to 1st SAS' HOUNDSWORTH base at the end of July. Leigh is described in the post-operation report as 'an officer of considerable experience of operations of this nature' (WO 218/197). On the 22nd Farran split his column into three parties, placing Leigh in charge of the third group of six Jeeps. The report continues: 'When Lieut Leigh's party approached Villaines [Villaines-les-Prévôtes on 23 August] fierce fighting broke out. Lieut Leigh was seriously wounded and Lieut Gurney took over command. He engaged the enemy to prevent them from outflanking the party to the rear and ordered the Jeeps to be turned round' (see Lieutenant Hugh Gurney's entry under Velorcey Communal Cemetery, France). One of Gurney's men, 'Tanky' Challenor, later wrote 'Lieutenant Leigh was shot in the head and dragged clear of the Jeep by two of the crew while his driver, Corporal McEachon [*sic* – McEachan, see his entry under Villaines-les-Prévôtes, France], continued to fire the Vickers over the steering wheel' (*Tanky Challenor: SAS and the Met*, by Draper and Challenor).

Lieutenant Alex Robertson and Parachutist Cyril Griffiths, who was one of those that carried Leigh away from the contact, placed him in a Jeep and were guided to Époisses by Henri Bourgoin where the latter knew of a good Maquis doctor. On arrival Bourgoin asked at the baker's where the lady of the house, Francoise Bethaut, insisted that they bring Leigh in and that he be laid on her bed. Two doctors, Monsieurs Abraham and Boudin, arrived soon after but Leigh died a minute later having never recovered consciousness. Robertson, knowing that it would cause trouble for the inhabitants to be found with the body of a British soldier, suggested he take Leigh back towards Villaines and bury him himself in a temporary grave, or that he leave him to be buried by the Germans. The French, however, would not hear of this and the four of them organised his funeral to which half the town turned out, sentries having been placed to warn of any German approach (personal interview with Alex Robertson, 2013). Leigh's best man, Captain Ian Miller, delivered news of his death to his wife.

Leigh's parents had died pre-war – His wife, Ethel (Estelle) Leigh of Ayr Road, Prestwick, later presented a lectern to the church at Époisses in gratitude for the manner in which the villagers had maintained her husband's grave. She never remarried and in 2011 her ashes were interred in the same plot – Leigh's brother Tom, an Australian serving in the RAF, was murdered after taking part in 'The Great Escape' from Stalag Luft III. His Halifax had been shot down during August 1941, his date of death being recorded as 31 March 1944. He is buried in Poznan Old Garrison Cemetery in Poland. Estelle learnt of Tom's murder on the day of her engagement party and waited until it had finished before telling Leigh. Tom's next of kin are officially recorded as 'David and Constance Emily Carena Leigh [sister] of Sydney, New South Wales, Australia.'

Age 26.

No inscription.

GRAFFIGNY-CHEMIN COMMUNAL CEMETERY

Those members of G Squadron, 2nd SAS, buried here took off from RAF Fairford as the recce group for OPERATION RUPERT. *They were killed, along with four aircrew of 190 Squadron and their despatcher, when their Stirling aircraft crashed into the hill behind the village of Graffigny-Chemin in the early hours of 23 July 1944. The previous night the same group, less Parachutist James Simpson, had attempted to drop but was forced to return to the UK as no lights were shown on the DZ near the Forêt du Der west of St Dizier.*

Parachutist Rex Boreham and the aircraft's Canadian navigator, Joe Vinet, survived the crash and were taken prisoner. Vinet later wrote a book entitled '02.13' – the precise time of impact, his watch stopping at that moment. Fellow crew member, Flight Sergeant Paul Bell, evaded capture and returned to the UK but was later killed when his Stirling was shot down, coincidentally whilst on a practice parachute drop of SAS containers in Essex (see Captain George Slater's entry under Brookwood Military Cemetery, United Kingdom, within this volume for full details).

2nd SAS' Casualty Report notes that the local population pretended to bury more bodies than they had found in order to forestall any German search for survivors: 'The rest of the personnel in the aircraft were buried in a grave in the wood at the scene of the crash by the French in the village of Graffigny. The grave was kept well with memorials and a wooden railing around it. It had been kept decorated with flowers much to the annoyance of the Germans … who placed MGs [machine guns] at all the entrances to the cemetery' (WO 361/716). The remains were reinterred from La Montagne to Graffigny-Chemin Communal Cemetery during May 1946.

The village is located 38 kilometres north-east of Chaumont, and 5 kilometres south of Bourmont, in the Haute-Marne département of Champagne-Ardenne. The cemetery lies in the centre of town on the avenue du Général-Leclerc. GPS co-ordinates: Latitude 48.17025, Longitude 5.6362

To visit the crash site and its memorial, take the road from the cemetery towards Bourmont. After 1½ kilometres take the footpath into the woods on the left, following the 'Stele Avion' signs. Behind the memorial there are thirteen trees representing each of those killed in the crash.

Pilot Officer Frank **COPLAND** [161569] Royal Air Force Volunteer Reserve att SAS (Brigade HQ)

Frank Copland was born on 18 February 1915 at Bradford in Yorkshire where he married Mary Robinson in 1936. He enlisted into the Royal Air Force Volunteer Reserve on 12 September 1940 and was trained at Padgate. In July 1942 he was posted to No.1 Parachute Training Centre, RAF Ringway, near Manchester as a flight sergeant instructor and alternated between duties there and the Airborne Forces Depot at Hardwick Hall near Chesterfield. Having attended a commissioning course at Cosford in November 1943 he returned to Ringway, now No.1 PTS, as a pilot officer and was attached to the SAS Brigade. Group Captain Maurice Newnham, OBE, DFC, confirmed in his history of the formation of British Airborne forces that:

> The attachment of PTS instructors to the regular Airborne Divisions was proving so valuable that the commander of the Special Air Service troops asked for similar assistance for his units. Although they could be ill-spared, Flight Lieutenant Leo Norriss, Pilot Officer Frank Copland and Sergeant H T Thompson were accordingly sent to Scotland … this small attachment commenced an association between the School and the SAS which developed into a remarkably friendly and efficient combination of forces …
>
> Finally when they set flight for the locality where they were to be dropped a PTS instructor would be in the aircraft with them to ensure that the parachuting equipment was in perfect order, to help them with their kitbags and other equipment, to tend their sickness and, by the confidence engendered by his presence, give them a good send-off upon their perilous adventures. After the men had jumped the instructor would despatch panniers and containers of additional equipment to the 'reception committees' that were usually waiting at the selected localities … it was inevitable that misfortune should sometimes overtake such perilous missions, and Sergeant Phil Wilding was the first of the Ringway men to lose his life in such circumstances [unlike Copland it can not be established whether Wilding was officially attached to the SAS Brigade – see his entry under the Unconfirmed section within Volume III]. A week or two later Frank Copland was killed when his aircraft crashed into the side of a deep valley [*sic*] while the pilot was trying to find the dropping area under conditions of bad visibility [*Prelude to Glory: The Story of the Creation of Britain's Parachute Army*, by Group Captain Maurice Newnham, OBE, DFC].

1st SAS was keen to reiterate the close relationship between its men and their despatchers:

> Those known to us best of all were our Despatchers – those men who shout 'Go!' in such a way that one just 'Goes!' These Despatchers did a tour of operations consisting of fifteen trips before being grounded. Ask any officer or man in the Regiment what he thinks of these fellows, and the answer will always be 'smashing blokes'. They won the admiration of everyone … some were called upon to make the supreme sacrifice.

Chris Nelson, Operation Rupert researcher and resident of the area, writes:

A contact in Bourmont who visited the crash site on the morning of the crash told me that one of the aircraft's occupants was hanging from a tree under a partially developed canopy – my guess is that he was P/Officer Copland who as the despatcher would have been 'hooked up' thus allowing his parachute to develop when thrown clear from the aircraft at impact [personal correspondence, 2012].

An unknown newspaper cutting paid tribute to Copland:

Pilot Officer Frank Copland who was reported missing on September 1st, is now known to have been killed on active service. He was 29. His widow and little girl of six live in Valeway Avenue, Anchorsholme. A native of Bradford, he was the younger son of Mr and Mrs F Copland but never saw his father, who was killed in the last war [L/Cpl Frank Copland of the West Yorkshire Regiment, killed in action 20/09/14 and commemorated on La Ferte-sous-Jouarre Memorial]. Educated at Hanson High School, Bradford, and Loughborough College, he was a teacher [of woodwork and metalwork] at Poulton when he joined up. P/O Copland had lived in Anchorsholme for seven years, and attended St Andrew's Church, Cleveleys. He was in the RAF for four years. Last year, as senior sergeant paratroop instructor, he was presented by his unit with a cup for proficiency.

A further cutting states: 'Copland – Previously reported missing on air operations in July last, now reported killed in action. Pilot Officer Frank Copland, RAF (Parachute Training School), attached 1st SAS Regt.'

Son of Frank and Gertrude Copland (née Hare) – Husband of Mary Copland of Cleveleys, Lancashire – Father of David (who predeceased him by three months), of Carolyn and of Paul who was born three months after his death. Age 29.
Beloved husband of Mary. Adored Daddy of Carolyn & Paul. Cleveleys, Lancashire
Collective graves 12–22.

Private Leonard William CURTIS [6025725] Essex Regiment, No.3 Commando, Small Scale Raiding Force and 2nd SAS (G Sqn)

Len Curtis was born in Walthamstow, East London, on 9 May 1922. Having worked as a clerk he enlisted into the Essex Regiment at Whipps Cross in June 1940. Initially posted to the 7th (Home Defence) Battalion he joined the 70th (Young Soldiers) Battalion that September and at the beginning of October, having volunteered for special service, reported to the Commando Depot in Scotland. The following month he joined No.3 Commando, embarking for North Africa in April 1943. On arrival he was re-posted to No.62 Commando on 5 May, this being the cover name for SOE's Small Scale Raiding Force. This unit formed the foundation on which 2nd SAS was raised just a few days later on the 13th, Curtis qualifying as a parachutist on the 18th.

On the evening of 7 September 1943 Curtis took off from Kairouan in Tunisia for Operation Speedwell. At 2315hrs his seven-man team parachuted into a DZ near Castiglione dei Pepoli in the Emilia-Romagna region of northern Italy. On landing the stick commander, Captain Philip Pinckney, could not be located and having laid-up the next day the party split into two groups (see Pinckney's entry under Florence War Cemetery, Italy, Volume II). Curtis and Sergeants 'Robbie' Robinson and 'Stokey' Stokes marched by night to the Bologna–Prato railway line that they blew up in a tunnel near Vernio on the 14th. Exhausted by their night-time efforts and lack of food, the three started to take larger risks en route to Allied lines. They began buying supplies and travelling in daylight before joining a group of Italian soldiers who were hiding in the hills from their former comrades, the Germans. Soon after they separated from all but two of the Italians, considering them 'useless'. One of this pair suggested that they might take the train south and the three British therefore changed into civilian clothes, buried their equipment and main weapons, and on the 24th caught a train from Crespino del Lamone to Faenza where they changed for Rimini. Due to German checks the men, now less suitably attired to brave the elements, started out on foot in the direction of the Allies. Taking to the hills they

accepted lifts and offers of shelter whenever they could, posing as escaped prisoners of war. However, on 7 October Stokes could no longer go on and was left at a farmhouse near Fabriano suffering from a rupture sustained in the initial drop a month before. Reluctantly Robinson and Curtis continued, finally contacting Canadian forces at Frosilone on 30 October, fifty-four days after parachuting behind the lines.

Having rejoined 2nd SAS Curtis disembarked in the UK on 16 March 1944 and was killed in action on 23 July (see this section's introduction for full details).

Son of Bertie and Sarah Curtis (née Saunders) of Century Road, Walthamstow, east London.
Age 22.
Gone from us but not forgotten. Never shall thy memory fade
Collective graves 12–22.

LIEUTENANT IAN MAXWELL **GRANT** [180710] KING'S REGIMENT, MANCHESTER REGIMENT, GORDON HIGHLANDERS, No.6 COMMANDO AND 2ND SAS (G SQN)

Ian Grant was born in Crosby north of Liverpool on 13 July 1920, although his family later moved to Oxten in Birkenhead. Here he attended a local school before Wrekin College in Shropshire where he was a member of the OTC as well as a keen boxer, swimmer, long-distance runner and rugby player. His headmaster noted in his final year: 'a splendid term and I endorse all his House report. He has many fine qualities for which I admire him. He has plenty of grit and he should make a success of his chosen career.

All good luck to him and thanks to him for his help.'

Having worked as an assistant manager at Woolworths, Grant enlisted into the King's Regiment in October 1939 (service number 3773639). He transferred to the Manchester Regiment the following July, serving at the Machine Gun Training Centre (MGTC) at Ashton-under-Lyne before reporting to 170 (MG) OCTU at Droitwich that September. Subsequently commissioned into the Gordon Highlanders in April 1941 he joined 342nd MGTC at New Barracks, Gosport. Short periods with the 7th Battalion, Wiltshire Regiment, the MGTC Royal Northumberland Fusiliers, the 70th Battalion, Royal Warwickshire Regiment, No.2 Driver Training Battalion, RASC, and at No.11 and 48 Infantry Training Companies followed. During the late summer of 1941 he attended a junior leaders course and in October 1942 was promoted to lieutenant.

Grant was plagued by illness throughout his service resulting in numerous periods within military hospitals and in front of medical boards. In late March 1943 he was posted to the Commando Depot at Achnacarry and a month later was unlucky enough to be admitted to Fort William's military hospital suffering from multiple wounds caused by an explosion during 2-inch mortar training. He had recovered by May and joined No.6 Commando but was again posted sick undergoing tuberculosis-related surgery that December. Determined to do his bit his doctor noted in January 1944: 'Convalescent and improving. Can find no primary focus. As this infection followed trauma I hope it is ended. In view of the particular nature of the case and his eagerness to continue serving in the Forces I recommend that he be placed in Category B. He appeals for reconsideration.'

Having been found fit for active duty Grant was posted to No.9 Infantry Training Centre in Aberdeen. Whilst here he was interviewed by officers of 2nd SAS, subsequently joining the Regiment on 6 May 1944 and attending parachute course 120 at No.1 PTS Ringway the following month. He was killed in action on 23 July 1944, his remains being identified by his moustache and distinctive climbing boots (see this section's introduction for full details).

Youngest son of Lt-Colonel John Leslie Grant, MC, of the King's Own Scottish Borderers, and of Ida Grant (née Murdoch) of Cearns Road, Oxten, Birkenhead, Cheshire.
Age 24.
Beloved 2nd son of Leslie and Ida Grant
Collective graves 12–22. Also commemorated within the chapel of Wrekin College.

Signalman Wilfred LEACH [2580970] Royal Corps of Signals, 2nd SAS and GHQ Liaison Regiment Att SAS

Wilf Leach was born on 10 November 1921 at Stranton in West Hartlepool as the eleventh child and seventh son of twelve children. In April 1939, whilst working as a factory hand at Igranic Electrical Company in Bedford, he joined the local H Signals Section, Royal Corps of Signals (TA), his father signing his papers as he was under 18. In his youth he had been an amateur radio enthusiast and he was therefore well suited in his role of signalman attached to the 54th (East Anglian) Division. Embodied at the outbreak of war he was posted to K Section, No.3 Company, 46th Division Signals, late that year. In January 1943 he disembarked in North Africa where he was promoted to lance-corporal in April.

Leach volunteered for the newly-formed 2nd SAS on 12 June 1943, reverting to the rank of signalman in order to do so. He saw action in Italy before returning to the UK in March 1944. After a month's leave he suffered a bout of malaria and on 23 June transferred to F Squadron, GHQ Liaison Regiment (Phantom Signals), which was attached to the SAS Brigade.

Leach was killed in action on 23 July 1944 in the crash described within this section's introduction. 2nd SAS' Casualty Report states: 'The Germans however, have reported that a man called Leach (no number given) was taken PW on 23 July (the morning of the crash), they give no place of capture' (WO 361/716). This report was later disproved, Leach's remains having been buried by local inhabitants at the same time as the others.

Son of Robert and Mary Leach (née Sowerby) of Collie Road, Bedford – Brother of Rachel, Bob (who served in MEF), Bill, Joe (Royal Navy), Albert (who served in the army) and Eric (Royal Navy).
Age 22.
He died that we might live
Collective graves 12–22.

Sergeant Douglas Hays McKAY [319314] 16th/5th Lancers and 2nd SAS (G Sqn)

Douglas McKay was born on 20 December 1917 in the small town of Seaham Harbour on the Durham coast, his family later moving to Scunthorpe in Lincolnshire. Having worked in the steel industry he enlisted into the 16th/5th Lancers in June 1936. Disembarking in India in October 1937 he served at Peshawar and Ahmednagar with D Squadron, was promoted to lance-corporal in March 1938, and to corporal the day before arriving back in the UK in January 1940. A typical annual reports reads: 'a sturdy reliable man … plenty of common sense. Can be thoroughly trusted to carry out any task set him'.

McKay reverted to the rank of trooper at his own request in May 1940, was promoted once again to lance-corporal that November, to corporal the following January, and confirmed as lance-sergeant in September 1941. He married Elizabeth Gilroy at Gateshead in March 1942 and disembarked in Algiers that November during OPERATION TORCH, the British and American landings that secured the Vichy French-held North African coastline. Having fought at Bou Arada in January 1943 and at Kasserine the following month McKay was promoted to sergeant on 1 March. The regiment then swapped its Valentine tanks for Shermans and after rapid retraining again saw action in April, breaking through the heavily defended Fondouk Pass that was key to the Allied advance. On the 24th McKay was wounded in action at el Kourzia but returned to the Lancers a month later and was involved in the battles around Tunis during the final stages of the North African Campaign. The 16th/5th was subsequently withdrawn to Philippeville on the Algerian coast and it was here that he volunteered for 2nd SAS on 6 July 1943.

McKay took part in operations in Italy before disembarking in the UK in March 1944. He was killed in action on 23 July (see this section's introduction for full details).

Son of Robert and Elena McKay (née Hays) of Ravendale Street, Scunthorpe – Husband of Elizabeth McKay of Albert Street, Gateshead, County Durham – Younger brother of Robert McKay.
Age 26.
No inscription.
Collective graves 12–22.

PRIVATE JAMES WILLIAM BEATTIE **REILLY** [2758399] BLACK WATCH, ROYAL SCOTS AND 2ND SAS (G SQN)

James Reilly was born on 27 November 1918 in Dundee where he attended Stobswell Central School and was employed as a jute worker. In November 1939 he enlisted into the Black Watch (The Royal Highland Regiment) and was initially posted to the 7th Battalion. Having attended an infantry training centre during May 1941 he was re-posted to the 9th Battalion. He married Elizabeth Storey Porter at Stonehaven in November 1942, disembarking on Gibraltar the following April. Here he was promoted to lance-corporal and transferred to the 30th Battalion, Royal Scots, in May. His son, also James William Beattie, was born that August.

Having volunteered for 2nd SAS Reilly disembarked in Algiers on 4 December 1943, joining the Regiment at Philippeville that day. A few days after returning to the UK in March 1944 the Commanding Officer, Lt-Colonel Brian Franks, MC, deprived him of his stripe for a minor misdemeanour. Soon after, he attended parachute course 128A at No.1 PTS Ringway where his instructor noted: 'very good jumper, diligent & conscientious, controlled nerves well'.

From the image seen here, taken from a G Squadron group photograph, it appears that Reilly had regained acting rank by the time he was killed in action on 23 July 1944 (see this section's introduction for full details). According to RAF Fairford's Watchkeeper's Log Reilly was one of the despatchers for the operation on which he was killed. His body was identified by the ring he wore, 2nd SAS' Casualty Report noting that: 'the ring was made from a coin bearing the effigy of King George VI, Chinese inscriptions, and the word Hong Kong' (WO 361/716).

Son of James and Annie Reilly (later O'Brien) of Hepburn Street, Dundee – Husband of Elizabeth Reilly of Brickfield Road, Stonehaven, Kincardshire – Father of James Reilly – A younger brother is known to have served in the wartime Highland Light Infantry.
Age 25.
Ever Remembered
Collective graves 12–22.

PRIVATE JAMES **SIMPSON** [6977054] ROYAL INNISKILLING FUSILIERS, ARMY AIR CORPS, AND 2ND SAS (HQ SQN ATT G SQN)

Jim Simpson was born on 17 March 1914 in the parish of Glendermott on the outskirts of Londonderry. Having worked as a labourer he enlisted into the Royal Inniskilling Fusiliers in April 1932 under the alias of 'James Hunter'. Posted to the 1st Battalion he served at Shanghai in China from October 1934 until January 1936 when the battalion was redeployed to Malaya. Having arrived back in the UK he took a vocational course in metal polishing and was discharged to the Army Reserve in May 1939. His exit report noted: 'has had five years experience as a regimental signaller where he obtained an elementary knowledge of cable work. Honest and sober.' Moving to Slough he soon found employment but was called up late that August.

In mid September 1939 Simpson disembarked at Cherbourg with the 2nd Battalion as part of GHQ's reserve. The German invasion of the Low Countries the following May found the battalion training far to the rear and it was subsequently marched forward and then transported to Halle in Belgium on 15–16 May. Here the men dug defensive positions on the banks of the Brussels–Charleroi Canal. After several defensive actions the battalion withdrew to the Ypres–Comines Canal and then towards Dunkirk from where the survivors, including Simpson, were evacuated on 31 May 1940.

In February 1941 Simpson admitted that he had joined the army under a pseudonym and that May was therefore able to marry Eleanor Isabella Maitland at Slough under his real name. No reason for the pretence was recorded. Posted to India he went on to serve in Iraq from August 1942 until March 1943 when his battalion moved to the Middle East. On 10 July it landed at Cassibile near Syracuse, fighting its way up the east coast of Sicily during OPERATION HUSKY. Simpson was shot in the hand at Solarino or at the Simeto Bridgehead at the end of August and was evacuated to the 96th General Hospital at Guelma in Algeria. He returned to the UK either during December 1943 or January 1944 and volunteered for Airborne Forces. Relinquishing his rank he attended parachute course 104 at No.1 PTS Ringway at the end of February and was noted as 'intelligent and keen'. He was subsequently posted to the Airborne Forces Holding Unit but spent the end of April and beginning of May in hospital suffering with malaria before volunteering for 2nd SAS on the 26th of that month.

Simpson is officially recorded as having been killed in action on 23 July 1944, although Berlin reported on 28 September that he had been captured and that he died as a prisoner of war. It has not been able to confirm this although it seems unlikely (see this section's introduction for full details of the crash).

Son of George and Margaret Simpson of Alfred Street, Waterside, Londonderry – Husband of Eleanor Simpson of Parker Street, Byker, Newcastle-on-Tyne.
Age 30.
No inscription.
Collective graves 12–22.

CAPTAIN FELIX JOHN STEWART **SYMES** [172271] IRISH GUARDS, SUFFOLK REGIMENT, EAST SURREY REGIMENT, ROYAL HAMPSHIRE REGIMENT AND 2ND SAS (G SQN)

John Symes, as he was more commonly known, was born in Genoa, Italy, on 29 January 1918. Having attended the Oratory Prep near Reading, he studied at Downside School from September 1931 and was a member of the OTC. Going up to Pembroke College, Cambridge, he read History with a view to following his father into the Diplomatic Service. However, at the outbreak of war he enlisted into the Irish Guards and was posted to the depot at Caterham (service number 2719354). He was discharged a month later 'his service being no longer required with a view to proceeding to an Officers Cadet Training Unit (University)'. Re-enlisting into the Suffolk Regiment reserves the following day (service number 5829570), he transferred to the East Surrey Regiment in May 1940 and was posted to their infantry training centre at Kingston. Having reported to 166 OCTU at Colchester that October he was granted an emergency commission into the Hampshire Regiment, in which his father had served, on 15 February 1941. His service record notes that he spoke fluent French and had knowledge

of France, Italy, North Africa, Sudan, Greece, Austria and Switzerland. On applying for a regular commission in September 1942 his Commanding Officer wrote: 'strongly recommended. A very keen, reliable, officer. I should be very glad to have him in my Regiment as a Regular Officer after the war.'

Symes disembarked in Algiers in November 1942 during OPERATION TORCH, the Allied landings along the Vichy-held North African coast. A few days later the 2nd Battalion, of which he was a member, moved to Tebourba just 32 kilometres short of Tunis, the Tunisian capital. However, on the 30th it was heavily shelled and on 1 December was outflanked by German troops. It took three days of hand-to-hand fighting just to facilitate an organised withdrawal. Finding that there was no one to fall back on, and that it was completely cut off, the battalion broke into small parties and attempted to walk back through the lines. Many were captured, less than a third reforming at Medjez-el-Bab. The battalion was subsequently withdrawn from the line, Symes having been appointed Adjutant by the time he volunteered for 2nd SAS in June 1943.

Taking command of G Squadron with the rank of major, Symes was instrumental in 2nd SAS' landings at Taranto on the Italian mainland on 10 September 1943. The following month he commanded part of OPERATION JONQUIL, endeavouring to rescue escaped prisoners from behind enemy lines in conjunction with MI9's A Force. The post-operation report notes that: 'a party under command of Major Symes, with a total strength of eight, was landed on the night of 15/16th of October at Punta del Moro. This area was by now filling up with German troops, and movement and concealment were alike difficult' (WO 218/181). Despite the difficulties his team shepherded 120 ex-prisoners to an evacuation point, although this and subsequent attempts to get them away were frustrated either by the Germans or by the Royal Navy failing to pick the men up. The report concludes that: 'Major Symes with thirteen men embarked in this [a small boat bought for 10,000 Lire] within 50 yards of a German sentry and returned to Termoli on the 6th of November.' His own post-operation report states:

> There was considerable chaos at first, as there was not sufficient room in the boat to work the oars, but eventually order was restored. The sail was hoisted, and we set off at good speed. Unfortunately the wind dropped at midnight, and we rowed the rest of the way, but the tedium was alleviated by first seeing a submarine, which we later heard was German, and was duly sunk the next day by the navy, and later by a magnificent 'Monty' barrage, as we were passing the lines …
>
> Major A J Scratchley had previously arrived, and taken over command of the detachment, leaving me in charge of SAS troops working for A Force. He now took over this command as well [WO 218/181].

Symes willingly reverted to the rank of captain to take charge of training, remaining in Italy until December 1943 and receiving a Mention in Despatches for his work there (*London Gazette* 24/08/44). Having organised numerous exercises at 2nd SAS' base at Philippeville in Algeria (see numerous entries under Bône War Cemetery, Algeria, Volume I) he eventually returned to the UK in mid March 1944 and was killed in action on 23 July (see this section's introduction for full details).

Son of Lt-Colonel Sir George Stewart Symes, GBE, KCMC, DSO, Governor General of the Sudan, and of Lady Symes (née Brown) of Chelsea, London – Brother of Barbara Crichton-Stuart.
Age 27.
Pro Regie et Pro Patria R.I.P.
Collective graves 12–22. Also commemorated on Pembroke College's war memorial.

SIGNALMAN LACHLAN **TAYLOR** [2385791] ROYAL CORPS OF SIGNALS, 2ND SAS AND GHQ LIAISON REGIMENT ATT SAS

'Lachie' Taylor, as he was known, was born on 8 March 1923 at Killean-Kilkenzie near Campbeltown in Argyll. His family farmed sheep at High Crubesdale Farm close to Muasdale, a remote hamlet on the Kintyre peninsula where he grew up with his brother and two sisters. As the holding was not big enough to support all the children, Taylor worked as a bus conductor in Campbeltown to supplement family income.

He enlisted into the Royal Corps of Signals in February 1942 and was posted to 46th Division Signals with which he disembarked in North Africa the following January. As such he was a contemporary of Signalman Wilfie Leach, both men volunteering for 2nd SAS on 12 June 1943 (see Leach's entry above). Taylor was awarded the Italy Star and must, therefore, have taken part in operations on the Italian mainland or Mediterranean islands with 2nd SAS before returning to the UK in March 1944. That May he was serving in the SAS Brigade Signals Section but was attached to 2nd SAS. He transferred to F Squadron of GHQ Liaison Regiment (Phantom) on 23 June whilst attending parachute course 121 at No.1 PTS Ringway. Here he was noted as being 'cheerful, reliable, average performer'.

Taylor was killed in action on 23 July 1944 having been recommended for promotion to lance-corporal two days previously (see this section's introduction for full details). The following month his father wrote to the Royal Corps of Signals Records Office:

My son 2385791 Sigmn Taylor L was posted as missing on July 22nd. He was I believe a member of the 2nd Special Air Service Regt, which is I understand a Parachute Regt. I know how difficult it will be to trace a man under these circumstances. I wonder however if any information as to where and how he became 'missing' could be obtained or if there are any of his comrades with whom it would be possible to communicate.

Son of John and Isabella Taylor of High Crubesdale, Tarbet, Argyllshire – 2nd SAS recorded him as a lance-corporal and his next of kin as: 'Father, Council Cottage, Gretton, Nr Winchcombe, Cheltenham.'
Age 21.
Too dearly loved to be forgotten
Collective graves 12–22.

Les Ormes Communal Cemetery

Les Ormes is located 24 kilometres west-north-west of Auxerre and 19 kilometres south-south-west of Joigny in the Yonne département of Bourgogne. The cemetery lies to the north of the village on the D14 towards Aillant-sur-Tholon. GPS co-ordinates: Latitude 47.854035, Longitude 3.270589

Lance-corporal James HALL [900883] Royal Artillery, L Detachment SAS Brigade, SRS and 1st SAS (C Sqn)

Known as 'Curly' or 'Jimmy', James Hall was born on 16 May 1922 in Newcastle-on-Tyne where he joined the 286th Field Regiment, Royal Artillery (TA), in April 1939. Giving his occupation as 'engineer' it appears that he joined aged 16 whilst claiming to be a year older. Having been called up that August he served in various heavy anti-aircraft regiments at home and in Iraq before volunteering for L Detachment, SAS Brigade, on 31 May 1942. As such he is likely to have taken part in the unit's July mass Jeep attack on Sidi Haneish airfield during the night of 26–27 July, and in the large-scale raid on Benghazi that September (Operation Bigamy). Late in October he was a member of Lieutenant Harry Poat's A Squadron party that left Kufra with two Jeeps. Having established that their target, Gazala airfield, was not in use the men destroyed roadside communications. The following month he and Lieutenant Miles MacDermott carried out Road Watch duties, monitoring coastal traffic before returning to Kufra.

In January 1943 Hall moved with the rest of his squadron to Azzib on the Palestinian coast for training. When the Regiment was reorganised as the Special Raiding Squadron that March he was promoted to lance-corporal and attended parachute course No.42 at No.4 Middle East Training School, Ramat

David, in May. Having landed at Capo Murro di Porco on 10 July at the spearhead of OPERATION HUSKY, the Allied invasion of Sicily, he was wounded in action during the capture of Augusta on the evening of the 12th. Sustaining a gunshot wound to his right thigh he was admitted to No.45 General Hospital on Malta where his records were later amended to read 'accidental injury'. By November he was back with 2 Troop in Italy, his Operational Wings having been granted on 23 July.

Hall embarked for the UK on Boxing Day 1943. After a period of training in Scotland with C Squadron of the reconstituted 1st SAS he was parachuted into France in the early hours of 14 August 1944 for OPERATION KIPLING. The object was to 'recce and extend the [Operation] Houndsworth area of operations further north and link up with the [Operation] Gain area' (WO 218/192). Hall and four other men under Captain Derrick Harrison formed an advance party received by Major Bob Mélot, MC, on a field at Les Placeaux on the edge of the Forêt de Merryvaux west of Auxerre. Having been reinforced by two other sticks a pair of Jeeps was also dropped on the night of 18–19th.

Hall was killed in action on the afternoon of 23 August 1944: The two Jeeps were on their way to contact the Maquis at Aillant-sur-Tholon. On arrival at Les Ormes the patrol found several houses alight and could hear gunfire. Driving Harrison's Jeep into the village, Hall's crew, and that of the other Jeep, attacked around 250 members of the SS who were in the process of murdering local men. Whilst the majority of the local hostages were able to make their escape, the enemy, who suffered between fifty and sixty casualties, returned fire. Harrison later wrote:

> Even as I fired I shouted at Hall to reverse. The Jeep jerked to a halt about 30 yards from the church. The Germans who had escaped the first fury of our assault were now returning our fire. I turned to see why Hall had not got the Jeep moving back. He lay slumped over the wheel.
>
> Back in camp I broke the news that Hall was dead. It was hard news to tell. He had been with me ever since I joined the SAS, always bright, cheery and philosophical [*These Men are Dangerous*, by Derrick Harrison].

Soldat Marcel Friedmann, a Frenchman attached to 1st SAS from 4th SAS, was awarded a Medaille militaire for retrieving Hall's body under fire (see Friedmann's own entry under the Unknown Location section within this volume for details of his award). Although the inhabitants of Les Ormes only had one coffin they laid Hall's body in it with two dead hostages on either side of him, his SAS comrades attending the funeral in the village a few days later.

Son of James and Winifred Hall of Monkchester Road, Newcastle upon Tyne.
Age 22.
Ever remembered by Leo, Rupert, Patricia and Aunts Bridget and Winifred. RIP

Marissel French National Cemetery

The five members of D Squadron, 1st SAS, buried here were captured in the early hours of 5 July 1944 during Operation Gain. *They were subsequently murdered on 9 August having endured weeks of interrogation (see Captain Pat Garstin's entry within this section for details). A memorial to them stands close to the scene of the crime, south-east of Noailles and Beauvais itself, on the junction of the D137 and D44 (GPS co-ordinates Latitude 49.32367, Longitude 2.22115).*

This French military cemetery, known locally as the Cimetière Militaire Marissel de Beauvais, was created in 1922, the area having been home to First World War hospitals. Nineteen Commonwealth burials were concentrated here from several small cemeteries and were later joined by 158 burials of the 1939–45 war, four of which are unidentified.

Beauvais is located approximately 65 kilometres north of Paris in the Oise département of Picardie. The cemetery lies on the east side of the rue d'Amiens (D1001), just north of the city centre. GPS co-ordinates: Latitude 49.44188, Longitude 2.09107

Private Thomas James **BARKER** [6986237] Home Guard, Royal Inniskilling Fusiliers, Royal Ulster Rifles and 1st SAS (D Sqn)

'Tot' Barker, as he was known to his family, was born on 16 July 1923 in the parish of Derryloran in Cookstown, County Tyrone, Northern Ireland. Working as a grocer's assistant he joined the Home Guard in May 1940, enlisting into the Royal Inniskilling Fusiliers at Omagh in June 1942. Having joined

the 70th (Young Soldiers) Battalion he was posted to No.25 Infantry Training Centre at the end of the month. That November he transferred to the Royal Ulster Rifles and was posted to the 70th Battalion. He joined the 1st (Airborne) Battalion, part of the 6th Airlanding Brigade, in July 1943 and volunteered for 1st SAS on 14 March 1944. Five days later he attended parachute course No.108 at No.1 PTS Ringway where his instructor noted; 'average all round performer – always cheerful'.

Barker parachuted into OPERATION GAIN on the night of the 4–5 July and was captured on landing:

> When Lieut [Johnny] Wiehe [the stick's second-in-command] was on the ground he noticed that the layout of the ground was not as he expected, and he thought that it was the wrong DZ. However, he contacted one of Capt Garstin's men, Tpr Barker. They had landed close to the edge of a wood and they saw two vague shapes moving in the wood. They drew their pistols and approached. When they were only a few yards from the figures, they were shot at. Barker fell wounded. Lieut Wiehe was wounded once in the left shoulder and twice in the abdomen, losing the power of his legs [WO 309/1400].

Both men were subsequently captured and taken, along with Captain Pat Garstin, MC, and Lance-corporal Howard Lutton, to the Pitié-Salpêtrière Hospital in Paris for basic treatment. Approximately five weeks later Barker and Garstin rejoined the remainder of the stick that was being held at a hotel converted into a prison on the place des États-Unis. They were subsequently murdered in a wood near Beauvais on 9 August 1944 (see Garstin's entry below for full details of their capture and subsequent fate).

Son of John and Florence Barker of Oldtown Street, Cookstown, County Tyrone – Brother of Evelyn and Louis.
Age 20.
Until the day breaks and the shadows flee away
Collective graves 326–329.

CAPTAIN PATRICK BANNISTER <u>GARSTIN</u> MC [95531] ROYAL ULSTER RIFLES, PARACHUTE REGIMENT AND 1ST SAS (D SQN)

Pat Garstin was born on 17 July 1919 in Bombay, India, attending Herne Bay College where he was a member of the OTC from 1934 to 1937. He enlisted into the Royal Ulster Rifles in July 1939 at Parkhurst on the Isle of Wight and that October disembarked in France to serve with the 2nd Battalion as part of the BEF. Seeing action in Belgium as one of A Company's platoon commanders, he suffered deafness from a bomb blast and was awarded the Military Cross, believed to be for his actions countering German infantry attacks at Louvain on 15–17 May 1940. Although presented with the medal ribbon by Major-General Bernard Montgomery, DSO, at Tourcoing on 26 May it appears his citation was not officially retained (*London Gazette* 09/07/40, Supplement 11/07/40). Evacuated from Dunkirk on 1 June he received a bomb splinter in his left forearm whilst being taken off the beaches by HMS *Skipjack*. This minesweeper was bombed as it made its way to the open sea and sank rapidly. Most of those aboard were lost, Garstin apparently escaping through a porthole.

Having been invested at Buckingham Palace that September Garstin disembarked in East Africa three months later and was attached to C Company, 1st Battalion, Northern Rhodesia Regiment. In January 1941 he was admitted to hospital in Nairobi with acute appendicitis and was granted two months sick leave. However, only a few days later he joined the divisional recce unit and by mid February, having been promoted to lieutenant (*London Gazette* 01/01/41), he was back with C Company and fought through the Somaliland campaign. That June, after again suffering from abdominal spasms, a medical board recommended that he return to England for 'treatment and final disposal'. He subsequently disembarked in the UK in August and was posted to No.25 Infantry Training Centre at Omagh. However, ill health did not deter him and having volunteered for Airborne Forces he was posted to the 4th (Wessex) Battalion, Parachute Regiment, in January 1942. He qualified as a parachutist that March having attended course 9 at No.1 PTS Ringway.

Although part of Garstin's colon was removed, resulting in a lengthy period of convalescence, he was posted to HQ 1st Parachute Brigade at the end of August 1942. That October he was re-posted to No.1 Airborne Forces Holding Unit, probably as an instructor, and married Susan Nicola Beresford-Jones in the latter part of the year. Briefly attached to 297 Squadron, RAF, he rejoined the 4th Battalion and embarked for North Africa in April 1943. Here he was promoted to captain that June and the following month was discharged from the 70th General Hospital at Sousse either having been injured or suffering from further illness. He was re-posted to the 6th (Welsh) Battalion, Parachute Regiment, for two months before being admitted to the 95th General Hospital at Beni Aknoun for reasons unknown. When discharged he flew from Algiers to the UK where he volunteered for 1st SAS on 15 February 1944 from the Airborne Forces Holding Unit.

On the night of 13–14 June 1944 the aircrew carrying Garstin and his eleven-man stick failed to find their DZ in France, and therefore turned for home. En route the plane ran into flak, one engine being damaged and having to be shut down. As a result its pilot jettisoned the stick's equipment containers into the Channel and was compelled to make a forced landing having crossed the south coast. No one was hurt and in the early hours of 5 July the same party parachuted into a DZ near La Ferté-Alais, south of Paris, tasked with cutting railway lines during OPERATION GAIN. They fell straight into the hands of the Germans who expected to intercept stores intended for the Maquis, having discovered that night's recognition signal either through a radio playback deception or the interrogation of a Resistant. Major Harry Poat, MC, Second-in-Command to 1st SAS and one of those later investigating the case, stated at the subsequent court of inquiry:

> When they landed they were met by a civilian who was hailed with 'Vive la France', and Captain Garstin was taken away to the side. They stuck a pistol, in his back and twisted his arm and said: 'Bring your men over here', which he refused to do. So he heard the German say; 'Right; we will shoot this officer anyway.' Apparently Captain Garstin made a break for it, shouting to the rest to try and make a break for it. He was very close to the Germans and they put a burst of Schmeisser into him; he was wounded in the neck and arm, and in the shoulder underneath the arm. Before they did this they had torn his decorations off and his badges of rank. They said he was a terrorist and not a soldier [TS 26/855].

A firefight broke out and the enemy, a mixed force of Gestapo and French traitors, subsequently captured nine members of the patrol, four of them having been wounded. Lance-corporal Howard Lutton died of his wounds at the Pitié-Salpêtrière Hospital the following day (see his entry under Clichy Northern Cemetery, France) whilst Lieutenant Johnny Wiehe was later liberated, suffering with serious wounds from which he would never fully recover. The remaining three stick members evaded capture and eventually returned through Allied lines.

The five uninjured men were held for five weeks in a Parisian hotel on the place des États-Unis that had been converted into a temporary prison, their hands bound in front of them twenty-four hours a day. Here they were 'forcibly interrogated', without result, by SS-Sturmbannführer Hans Kieffer, head of the Gestapo at the infamous avenue Foch. The Germans appear to have believed that they were the forerunners of a large airborne assault. Meanwhile, SAS Brigade HQ presumed that everything had gone according to plan: 'On the night of 4/5 July Capt Garstin, Lt Wiehe and ten men dropped to a friendly reception in the north of D Squadron area. As they were operational parties with supplies but no W/T transmitter they may not be heard of for some time' (Summary of 1st SAS activities up to 19/07/44).

The men were eventually joined by the wounded Garstin and Private Tot Barker. Corporal Serge Vaculik, a member of the French 4th SAS attached to 1st SAS recalled for *The Daily Telegraph* that 'about a week after [other accounts state five weeks later] our officer arrived from hospital. He had five wounds, two in his neck and three in his back, and could hardly walk.' Vaculik later wrote that Garstin had told him:

> The swine didn't attend to me in hospital; just questioned me and questioned me, twisting my arms. My wounds are open and festering. They treated me as though I were a spy; cut off my ribbons and my shoulder straps. If I don't get away and you should happen to, then let my wife know, will you, old man? You know the address [*Air Commando*, by Serge Vaculik].

On the evening of 8 August Kieffer ordered the group to change into civilian clothing and to board a truck. They were told that they were being taken to the border of neutral Switzerland where their clean uniforms would be returned and where they would be exchanged for captured German agents. It was not until two of these men reached the UK that the truth was learnt. One of them was Vaculik whose joint report with Corporal 'Ginge' Jones notes:

> At 1am on 9th August we were taken by lorry north of Paris to a wood near Beauvais and to the east of Noailles.
> At about 0600 we were ordered out of the lorry and taken up a narrow path to a clearing in the wood. Cpl Vaculik asked if we were to be shot and received a reply to that effect.
> We were lined up in the following order (from left to right) Jones, Garstin, Vaculik, Varey, Barker, Walker (or Walker, Barker), Young.
> Facing us were two officers of the Gestapo with Sten guns at the 'ready' and who read out the sentence, a sergeant of the Gestapo who interpreted and a Gestapo agent in civilian clothes:
> The sentence was 'for having wished to work in collaboration with the French terrorists and thus endanger the security of the German army you are condemned to the penalty of death and will be shot.'
> On hearing the word 'shot' we all made a spring for the woods. Corporal Vaculik managed to get clear followed by the Gestapo, firing as they ran. Cpl Jones tripped and fell and the Gestapo ran past him, probably taking him for dead [WO 309/1400].

Vaculik's official statement adds further detail:

> At the moment that Captain Garstin said the word 'shot', and seeing that no true aim was being levelled at me at the moment, I threw off my handcuffs [he had previously managed to pick them with the spring from his watch] and ran as hard as I could, slightly towards the firing party but away off to the right. I covered a few yards but fell down. At that moment I heard firing and realised that the shooting party had opened fire. I leapt to my feet at once and started to run as fast as I could. I heard further shots and realised that they were shooting at me …
> After I had been [in hiding] with the butcher's cousin for about a week, I was told that the leader of the Resistance in an adjoining village had been caring for a British soldier; from his description I realised it was probably Jones. I investigated and found it was Jones. He told me that when the Germans had opened fire, he had fallen on his face and pretended to be dead. He had not got up. He told me that he had seen the rest of our party lying dead. He had made off and, in due course, had contacted the Resistance [WO 309/660].

Jones later reported: 'Capt Garstin was in a very weak state at the time of the shooting and I had to help him out of the lorry. He was unable to run and could only just walk' (WO 309/1400). SS-Obersturmführer Otto Ilgenfritz, one of those later accused of the murders, admitted:

> Uneasiness became noticeable amongst the prisoners and before the interpreter was finished with his translation some of them in middle and on the left tried to escape. A moment before one of the prisoners had spoken a few words to the other, but I could not pick out or could not understand their meaning. On their trying to escape we made use of our weapons immediately …
>
> While three prisoners remained dead on the spot others who tried to break away to the left collapsed dead after a few meters while two prisoners succeeded in breaking through our midst and reaching the edge of the wood …
>
> As I was searching the wood further, suddenly one of the prisoners stood up behind a pile of wood, and despite my calling to him, tried to continue his flight. I made use of my weapon at a distance of 30–40 meters and inflicted mortal injuries on him as he was escaping. I went back to the place I had started from and reported what had happened to Dr Schmid. He came to meet me half way and told me that during the search one of the dead men [Jones] had disappeared in a way which could not be accounted for [WO 311/76].

SS-Hauptscharführer Karl Haug, one of those subsequently convicted by a war crimes tribunal, dryly confirmed that having murdered the other men they realised that Vaculik and Jones were missing; 'searching and swearing now began on a grand scale'. A local Luftwaffe unit was press-ganged to help comb the woods, the Gestapo also tasking their airforce colleagues to bury the bodies. They did so in an orchard at the nearby Château Parisis Fontaines three days later.

After the area had been liberated Jones led Captain Mike Sadler, MC, MM, Intelligence Officer of 1st SAS, to this site, the latter's subsequent report noting:

> There were five bodies, all dressed in civilian clothes, and all showing obvious signs of having been handcuffed. One of the bodies was undoubtedly that of Captain Garstin.
>
> There was also a camouflage scarf or veil in the grave. They were [re-] buried in the cemetery of Marissel at Beauvais, Captain Garstin in grave 325 and the others, whom I did not know well enough to identify even if it had been possible, in graves numbered 326–329 [WO 309/659].

Vaculik and Jones' testimony led to several of those responsible for this and other murders being captured by Major 'Bill' Barkworth's SAS War Crimes Investigation Team. The 'Noailles Case' was subsequently heard before a Military Court at Wuppertal on 7–14 March 1947. SS-Standartenführer Dr Helmut Knochen, the Head of the SD in Paris, had been reduced to the ranks after the fall of the French capital. He survived combat duty and was subsequently brought before the court. Found guilty he was sentenced to death and handed back to the French for a separate trial concerning the deportation of Jews. His sentence was commuted and the French released him in 1962. He died a free man in 2003. Kieffer, who was discovered to be working as a cook in an officers' mess at Garmisch, received the death sentence and was hanged in June 1947. He had been responsible for the interrogation, and sending to concentration camps, of many SOE agents in addition to murders of other SAS men (see entries within this volume for Major Denny Reynolds and Captain Andy Whately-Smith under Durnbach War Cemetery, Germany, and Parachutist Fred Puttick under Groesbeek Memorial, Netherlands). SS-Hauptsturmführer Richard Schnur, who had led the firing squad and read Garstin's men their death sentence, was found guilty and hanged in June 1947. Haug unsuccessfully appealed against his own death sentence, claiming that he had allowed Vaculik and Jones to escape, purposely not shooting at them. Meanwhile, Ilgenfritz was sentenced to fifteen years imprisonment. At the trial it was alleged that in 1945 he made several attempts to save a drowning British soldier at Budelsdorf and that his conduct had been commended by a court of inquiry. SS-Oberscharführer Fritz Hildeman received five years for his part in the murders whilst SS-Hauptscharführer Dr Julius Schmidt, also cited, was believed to have been killed in action before the end of the war and SS-Unterscharführer Alfred von Kapri (also known as Meressy), was 'understood to have been murdered and thrown into the Tegernsee in April or May 1945' (WO 311/78).

During the 1960s the French authorities proposed to award posthumous Croix de guerres to all five victims. The British government intervened stating that its policy was not to accept foreign honours more than five years after the relevant events.

Son of Captain Richard Hart Garstin, CBE, RIN, killed in action on 27/10/42 when SS *Stentor* was sunk by U-509 (commemorated on Liverpool Naval Memorial), and of Mary Amelia Garstin of Tankerton, Kent – Husband of Susan Garstin of Marine Parade, Tankerton – Father of Patrick Garstin born three days before his father was shot – Older brother of John, who served in the RAF, and of Roy who served in the Merchant Navy.
Age 25.
The lord is my shepherd. He maketh me to lie down in green pastures
Grave 325. Also commemorated on the All Saints Church war memorial in Whitstable.

Sergeant Thomas **VAREY** [811752] Royal Artillery, Queen's Own Cameron Highlanders, Auxiliary Units and 1st SAS (D Sqn)

Thomas Varey was born on 21 July 1914 in the parish of St Martin's, York. Whilst working as a printer's compositor he joined the 213th Medium Battery, Royal Artillery (TA), rising from the rank of boy to bombardier from April 1931 to 1936 (service number 2938101). By the outbreak of war he had also joined the Auxiliary Fire Service serving with the serial number 213. He enlisted into the Queen's Own Cameron Highlanders in June 1940 and was soon appointed lance-corporal. That December he was posted to 'HQ, Auxiliary Units Scout Section' at Coleshill House in Wiltshire. Such sections trained secret civilian Auxiliary patrols that had been formed to resist any German occupation, whilst preparing for the same tasks themselves. Varey was promoted to corporal in December 1941 and to sergeant in April 1943. As the threat of invasion abated the Auxiliaries began to be stood-down and he, like many of his comrades, volunteered for 1st SAS on 1 February 1944.

Varey parachuted into Operation Gain on the night of 4–5 July 1944 and was immediately taken prisoner. Corporal Serge Vaculik, a survivor of this stick, stated at a court of inquiry that he had administered morphine to Varey after capture. However, Varey was not taken to hospital in Paris with the other wounded. The men were murdered in a wood near Beauvais on 9 August 1944 (see Captain Pat Garstin's entry above for full details).

Son of Alfred and Annie Varey (née Knowles) of Thorpe Street, Scarcroft Road, York – Believed to have had three siblings.
Age 32.
His brother Harry, Sergeant RAF died 17/12/44 age 24. Reunited (Sergeant Harry Varey of 49 Squadron, Royal Air Force Volunteer Reserve, who is commemorated on panel 239 of the Runnymede Memorial).
Collective graves 326–329.

Private Joseph **WALKER** [7019954] Royal Ulster Rifles and 1st SAS (D Sqn)

Joe Walker was born on 18 August 1922 in County Down, Northern Ireland, where he later worked as a farm labourer. He enlisted into the Royal Ulster Rifles in Belfast in September 1940 and, after training with the 6th (Home Defence) Battalion, was posted to the 70th (Young Soldiers) Battalion. Although his spirited character led to periods of detention for minor offences he was posted to the 1st Battalion in March 1943, this forming a key component of the 6th Airlanding Brigade from that May. He volunteered for 1st SAS on 15 March 1944 and four days later attended parachute course number 108 at No.1 PTS Ringway where his instructor noted; 'cheery disposition – worked hard – average jumper'.

Walker parachuted into Operation Gain on the night of the 4–5 July 1944 and immediately captured. He was murdered in a wood near Beauvais on 9 August after weeks of interrogation (see Captain Pat Garstin's entry within this section for full details). An unidentified newspaper clipping states that his parents went to visit his grave in France:

… where they will receive the Croix de guerre which the French Government has posthumously awarded their son. Joseph Walker joined the Royal Ulster Rifles at the age of 17, was transferred to the Airborne Division and later volunteered for the Special Air Service …

Today, almost twenty years after, the Mayor of Barthecourt, backed by the French Government, has decided to erect a small memorial to those who died during the mission and it will be at the unveiling of this memorial on September 27 that Mr and Mrs Walker are to receive one of France's highest military honours.

It is unknown whether the medal was, as the text suggests, presented in spite of the British government's refusal to accept awards to the five victims.

Son of Mr and Mrs Isaac Walker of Castlevue Park, Moira, County Down – His parents had already lost one son, Guardsman Isaac Lilly Walker, also aged 21, who was killed on 28/04/43 in Tunisia whilst fighting with the Irish Guards and who is buried at Massicault War Cemetery in Tunisia.
Age 21.
No inscription.
Collective graves 326–329. Both sons are commemorated on Moira's war memorial.

PRIVATE WILLIAM PEARSON <u>YOUNG</u> [7018947] ROYAL ULSTER RIFLES AND 1ST SAS (D SQN)

Billy Young was born in the village of Caddy near Randalstown, County Antrim, on 2 January 1921, this county being one of six that formed Northern Ireland that May. Having worked as a dairyman he enlisted into the Royal Ulster Rifles on 18 July 1940 and was posted to the 7th Battalion. In November 1942 he was re-posted to 1st Battalion that was absorbed into the 6th Airlanding Brigade the following May. He volunteered for 1st SAS on 15 March 1944, the same day as fellow Ulsterman Private Joe Walker (see his entry opposite), and attended parachute course 109 at No.1 PTS Ringway later that month.

Young dropped into OPERATION GAIN on the night of the 4–5 July 1944 and was immediately captured. He was murdered in a wood near Beauvais on 9 August following weeks of interrogation (see Captain Pat Garstin's entry within this section for full details).

Son of William Young of Kemmel Hill Park, Randalstown, County Antrim – A contemporary newspaper cutting states: 'News of the murders first reached England through a letter from a chaplain [Captain The Reverend Fraser McLuskey, Padre of 1st SAS] who had written to the parents of Trooper William P. Young of Randalstown, Co Antrim, informing them their son was one of the victims.'

Age 22.

No inscription.

Collective graves 326–329.

MOUSSEY CHURCHYARD

Christopher Sykes, a former Intelligence Officer of 2nd SAS, wrote in **Mars & Minerva**, *the journal of the SAS Regimental Association:*

> *After the war, it was decided, at the suggestion of the parish priest, the Abbé Gassman, to make a little SAS cemetery at Moussey in the graveyard by the church. In the late summer of 1945 the whole Moussey population, and that of the villages adjoining, came to the funeral of our ten ...*
>
> *A few years after this, the Imperial War Graves Commission noted that the SAS cemetery at Moussey was an irregularity, and they moved for reinterment in one of their official places of burial. Their policy is very reasonable: With the passage of years memories become dim, and unless graves are assembled in official cemeteries worthy upkeep cannot be guaranteed. These arguments were not well received, however, in Moussey; indeed they were bitterly and even violently and threateningly resented. These were <u>their</u> English graves, the people said, and had they not earned the right to keep them if they wished? The parish priest warned the authorities that a reinterment might cause lasting ill-feeling and even unedifying scenes. The Commission wisely acquiesced, and, in consideration of the extraordinary circumstances, they registered the graveyard of Moussey as an official war cemetery [December 1961 edition].*

The village of Moussey is situated 51 kilometres north-east of Épinal and 16 kilometres north-east of Saint-Dié-des-Vosges in the Vosges département of Lorraine. The church is located on the main thoroughfare, the D49. GPS co-ordinates: Latitude 48.42522, Longitude 7.01698

Signalman Peter **BANNERMAN** [2369000] Royal Corps of Signals and GHQ Liaison Regiment Att SAS

Known as 'Patti' to both family and friends, Peter Bannerman was born on 15 February 1921 at the small fishing village of Gourdon in Kincardineshire. Having worked in his father's butcher shop, 'Bannermans' at nearby Inverbervie, he enlisted into the Royal Corps of Signals in April 1941. Posted to 3rd Depot Signals he joined the 3rd Operator's Training Battalion a month later. On completion of trade courses he was re-posted to the 3rd Holding Battalion and ten days later, on 27 October, he volunteered for GHQ Liaison Regiment (Phantom). As a member of F Squadron, which was attached to the SAS Brigade, he attended parachute course 108 at No.1 PTS Ringway during March 1944, his report noting 'parachuting average but cheerful and unhesitating'.

In the early hours of 3 August 1944 Bannerman jumped into the area west of Grand-Fougeray in the Ille-et-Vilaine département of Brittany, north-west France. His team, Party I of Operation Dunhill under Captain Tony Greville-Bell, was tasked with reporting enemy movement and sponsoring reinforcement drops. Contact was made with the advancing Americans the same day thus nullifying their primary objective. However, after receiving Party II the combined group, in co-operation with US forces, fought small actions at the villages of Messac and Lohéac over the coming days. Greville-Bell then drove to Le Mans where he contacted Major Airey Neave of IS9 who took the party under his wing for an operation: using requisitioned local transport, including a fire engine, the group drove through enemy lines to rescue '137 Allied airman who had been shot down and been hiding in a wood near Forêt de Fréteval [MI9's Operation Sherwood]. The party returned to the UK on 20 Aug 44' (WO 218/199).

Bannerman was not at home long. He parachuted into a DZ near Veney in the Vosges département of eastern France in the early hours of 1 September 1944 as a member of one of two Phantom patrols assigned to Operation Loyton. Having carried out their signalling duties he, Lieutenant Peter Johnson and Signalman 'Jock' Johnston stayed behind to close down the operation. Bannerman was subsequently killed in action on 20 October whilst the three were exfiltrating to Allied lines: believing that they had arrived in the American sector they sat down to rest. A German patrol was watching and opened fire, killing Bannerman instantly, wounding Johnston who was later murdered (see his entry within this volume under Groesbeek Memorial, Netherlands), and also wounding Johnson who was able to escape. There was initial confusion as to whose body was recovered from the scene of the action, it being incorrectly identified as Johnston's. Major 'Bill' Barkworth of the SASWCIT later wrote: 'The misapprehension dates back to an error on the part of Capt. Sykes who claimed to identify the body of a Phantom man as that of Johnston. This was in fact that of Bannerman. This identification was unfortunately accepted by Casualty Branch.'

According to WO 361/716, a report on missing members of the SAS, Bannerman's remains were 'found by villagers of Menarmont at [grid reference] 193815. Lt Johnson saw body in Feb, believes it to be Bannerman. Incident took place at edge of wood [grid] 1883 between Domptail V.1784 and Meuarmont V.1932'. The file also notes that Bannerman was buried at 'Fontenoy-La-Joute … The grave has an Army cross erected over it with the inscription *An Unknown Soldier*.' 'Chippy' Wood, a fellow Phantom signaller attached to the SAS, later wrote:

Long ago memory, a conversation with John Hislop [former Phantom officer and veteran of Loyton]. I remember him saying that they had exhumed the body of Sig Bannerman and had identified him by his boots. Where this was done I have no knowledge or why. They had also recovered his personal radio receiver. But I seem to have gathered that it was near the village where he was shot and not at Moussey where he is buried.

Bannerman's remains were later moved to their current location.

Only child of George and Isabella Bannerman of Bridge End, Cowgate, Inverbervie, Kincardineshire.
Age 23.

Thy will be done
Grave 4. Also commemorated on Inverbervie's war memorial at Bervie Parish Church, on his parents' grave, and within the Phantom Memorial Garden at the National Memorial Arboretum, Alrewas. This was organised and constructed by former Phantom sergeant, Len Owens, MM, and his family.

PRIVATE SELWYN PERCIVAL **BROWN** [315950] 17TH/21ST LANCERS, 9TH QUEEN'S ROYAL LANCERS, 17TH/21ST LANCERS AND 2ND SAS (2 SQN)

Selwyn Brown was born on 8 December 1907 in the village of Greens Norton near Towcester in Northamptonshire. Having worked as a general labourer he enlisted into the Corps of Lancers of the Line in August 1926 and was posted to the 17th/21st Lancers. In January 1929 he transferred to the 9th Queen's Royal Lancers, subsequently serving in India and being promoted to lance-corporal in 1930. Reverting to the rank of trooper at his own request in November 1931 he returned to the UK soon after and, having married Jane Armstrong in Edinburgh the following April, was discharged to the Army Reserve in August 1932. His conduct sheet records: 'hardworking, honest, sober, and trustworthy. Has been employed as an officer's servant and is thoroughly reliable.' His sons, Frank and William, were born in 1935 at Salisbury and 1937 at Andover respectively.

In August 1938 Brown re-engaged at Tidworth in order to complete twenty-one years' service, rejoining the 9th Lancers who had swapped their horses for light tanks two years previously. The regiment was absorbed into the Royal Armoured Corps on its formation in April 1939 and posted soon after to the 2nd Light Armoured Brigade. However, shortly before it was sent to France with the BEF, Brown was re-posted to the 4th Cavalry Training Regiment before returning to the 17th/21st Lancers, now also a mechanised regiment, in November 1940.

Having disembarked in Algeria in late November 1942 the 17th/21st, equipped with Valentine and Crusader tanks, advanced into Tunisia. It saw action at Bou Arada the following January before being rapidly reduced in strength during fierce fighting at Kasserine in February; outgunned and with only light armour the regiment was left with just twelve tanks. It was subsequently withdrawn and refitted with more suitable M4 Shermans. Having rapidly retrained it was back in the front line for the Battle of Fondouk where its tanks were ordered to take the pass at any cost. Thirty-two tanks were put out of action before its sister regiment, the 16th/5th Lancers, carried the day. Having fought at el Kourzia Brown's regiment was involved in the liberation of Tunis that brought hostilities in North Africa to a close.

Although it is unknown exactly when Brown volunteered for 2nd SAS he took part in OPERATION SLEEPY LAD B in Italy late in 1943: tasked with destroying enemy lines of communication on the Adriatic coast his party of five was put ashore close to the mouth of the River Musene, south of Ancona, on the night of 18 November. Led by Major Sandy Scratchley the men moved inland and took refuge at a friendly farm. The following night Brown and Corporal John McGuire blew the railway line north of Porto Recanati, stopping an oncoming train and being shot at for their troubles. The arrival of fresh German troops restricted further attacks and when the Royal Navy failed to pick the party up from its pre-arranged RV the men found themselves stranded with McGuire now suffering from malaria. He was forced to struggle during the march to Porto Civitanova where Scratchley hoped to steal a boat and return to Allied lines. They arrived on 2 December just in time to watch the Navy sink the only two available motor schooners and the RAF bomb the town. Having waited for the enemy to repair one of the

92

vessels so that they could take it from them the ship sailed one night and they were forced to requisition a fishing boat. They subsequently weighed anchor on the 14th, arriving in Allied territory the following evening despite having been shelled by a German shore battery en route (see McGuire's entry under Bari War Cemetery, Italy, Volume II).

Having returned to the UK the following March, Brown was parachuted into a small clearing above the village of Moussey in the Vosges département of eastern France on the night of 21–22 September 1944. He was one of fourteen men that dropped with three Jeeps under the command of Captain 'Bunny' McGibbon-Lewis as reinforcement for OPERATION LOYTON. Having served as McGibbon-Lewis' Jeep front gunner the operation drew to a close and Brown became separated from the party with which he was exfiltrating towards Allied lines. He was captured around 7 October, 2nd SAS' Casualty Report quoting Parachutist Mason and Craftsman Hopkins:

> We were told the Americans were at Azerailles V230882, but when we got to within 300 yards of the village we were machine-gunned and mortared and once again had to run for cover. In doing so we lost Brown, he ran to our right. After lying in cover for a short time we heard voices on our right and we felt sure that we heard some English spoken, that is why we think Brown was taken prisoner. There was nothing we could do because the place was full of Germans. Date: - 7 Oct 44 [WO 361/716].

Michel Wojnarowski, a local doctor from Senones, outlined the circumstances of Brown's capture:

> At that moment he [SS-Oberscharführer Max Eckert of Kommando Wenger who used the pseudonyms 'Max Kessler' and 'Matu Kester'] said 'We still have a score to settle with the Canadian [sic] camp which is around Moussey.' Eight days later, when he came back to see me, he told me the following story. He was with his friends in a Jeep which had been captured from the parachutists and he was wearing a camouflage hood. On the road from Senones to Petit Raon he saw a Canadian soldier who made a sign and who was made prisoner, since he had believed that they were Englishmen. This man was, according to him, the camp cook [Brown carried out such duties in addition to his normal tasks]. He had been put up by two or three French people from the Moussey district [WO 219/5069].

Lieutenant Jim Silly and Parachutist Donald Lewis soon joined Brown in captivity, the three being taken to Schirmeck Concentration Camp where they are believed to have been kept in the women's cells. SS-Hauptsturmführer Karl Buck later stated at his trial:

> I can remember an official from the Gestapo at Saales who brought three parachutist prisoners to the camp of Schirmeck. He told me that I would be only required to hold them for a short period and that they would be collected again. They were wearing uniform similar to that which is shown to me as battle dress. I can not remember their names, but the photographs shown to me as Brown and Lewis awake recollections in my mind. After a period which I estimate as a day, they were collected on the orders of Dr Ernst by one of his subordinates … So far as I can remember, these three men were taken away in a private car. I never saw these men again [WO 235/557].

Although Brown's date of death is officially recorded as 7–16 October 1944 a subsequent court of inquiry, held in Moussey on 20 March 1945, summarised the case as follows:

> At 1300 hours, on 16th October, 1944, some twelve to fifteen members of the German Sicherheitsdienst or Gestapo, in uniform and armed, and led by two senior non-commissioned officers, approached the Joseph Quirin house at Le Harcholet, near Moussey, Vosges, from the wooded slopes to the north-east. They approached in two or three small parties and congregated in one group in front of the Joseph Quirin house, which had been burned by a party of Germans previously to this date and of which only a small wooden outhouse about 10′ by 6′ remained intact.
>
> The Germans brought with them three prisoners. These were: i). 315950 Private Brown S. ii). 14410725 Private Lewis D, both of 2nd Special Air Service Regt, British Army, and iii). An unidentified Frenchman, believed to be a member of the Maquis and a native of Moyenmoutier.
>
> Privates Brown and Lewis were in normal British battledress, one wearing a peaked cap and the other a red beret and one of them had his hands tied together. Both were known to have been participants in the operations described … The Frenchman was mainly in civilian clothes, but was probably wearing in part a form of battledress.
>
> On arrival at the Joseph Quirin house sentries were posted round the house by the Germans, who then took the three prisoners into the ruins of the house, where they appeared to be carrying on some form of interrogation of the prisoners for a few minutes. The two senior NCOs then went, with some of their men, to an adjacent house occupied by witness Martin, whence they obtained some straw which was carried to and placed in, the outhouse beside the

ruins of the Joseph Quirin house, into which outhouse the prisoners were then marched. Immediately afterwards the straw was seen to have been lighted and to be burning. A further amount of straw was then obtained by the Germans from the house occupied by the witness Lyautey, which was taken back to the outhouse and added to the fire. Immediately afterwards, two bursts of fire from machine carbines were heard, which appeared to the witness Lyautey to be fired by one or both of the German Senior NCOs standing inside the doorway of the outhouse. A minute or two later three distinct shots, described as rifle shots were heard by this witness, similarly believed to be fired by the NCOs who then emerged from the outhouse.

The fire in the outhouse was thereafter fed by members of the German party with odd wood from the immediate vicinity and with a further amount of straw obtained from the house of the witness Lyautey, who states that during this period he saw by the light of the fire what he believed to be the dead bodies of the prisoners swinging from a rafter inside the outhouse. Lyautey further states that he was expressly warned by one of the German Senior NCOs, who was fetching the second lot of straw from his house, that he would suffer punishment if he said a word of what was then going on at the Quirin house or took any subsequent action. The witness Martin also states that she was told by the German NCOs to stay in the house and not come out, so that she was not an eye-witness after the prisoners had been taken from the ruins into the outhouse.

The witness Lyautey was an eye-witness of the whole of the proceedings as above recounted, until such time as the second load of straw from his barn was added to the fire and he saw what he took to be dead bodies hanging from the rafters in the outhouse. Throughout this time he states that the prisoners, who were unarmed, gave no sign of resistance to the Germans or any attempt to escape from them.

At approximately 1400 hours the German party departed leaving a guard at the [illegible] house, a burned-out house, some 90 yards away on the hillside to the north-east, which guard remained there until Thursday 19 October 1944 presumably to see that nobody should approach the ruins of the Joseph Quirin house.

At about 1500 hours the witness Lyautey passed the Joseph Quirin house and saw a dead body lying face upwards on a manure heap about 15 feet to the north of the burned-out outhouse.

At about 1100 hours on Thursday 19 October 1944, after the departure of the aforementioned guard from the [illegible] house, the witness Lyautey covered the body on the manure heap with a barrowful of potato waste and with the charred wood from the burned-out house and out-house. He similarly covered two other dead bodies which he found in the ruins of the outhouse on Friday 20 October 1944.

The bodies, thus covered, remained undisturbed by human [illegible], though subject to the attentions of animals, until partly uncovered by Lyautey, in company with US Army Personnel about 25 November 1944 when they were not otherwise disturbed.

On or about 1 December 1944 the three dead bodies, which were still protected by the charred wood put over them by the witness Lyautey on 19–20 October 1944, and by snow, and which had also now been covered by Tricolour flags, were completely uncovered by the witness Captain [Christopher] Sykes, of 2nd Special Air Service Regiment, who had himself been engaged in the operations by the Regiment, previously referred to in paragraphs 4 and 6 herein, and who is regimental Intelligence Officer, had been detailed by Commander SAS Troops to carry out investigations in the Vosges and in regard to missing personnel of his Regiment.

The bodies were then thoroughly examined on the spot by Captain Sykes, an officer with considerable battle experience, with a view to finding means of identification and also with a view to ascertaining the likely cause of death [WO 219/5069 and summarised in WO 311/72].

Lyautey stated at this court of inquiry that, in order to frighten the men who were suspended by their arms, a small fire had been started in the outhouse before they were shot and that the flames only grew large after this. The murders were attributed to the Kommando Wenger who had murdered Sergeant Michael Fitzpatrick, Lance-corporal Jack Elliott and Parachutist John Conway in the same manner the previous month (see their entries within this section). Witness statements suggest that the Kommando's senior ranks demanded coffee that they sat down to drink whilst watching their men gathering straw. They left the scene laughing (WO 218/209). Untersturmführer Gerhard Preil, one of those accused of being concerned in the murders, later confessed:

About the middle of October 1944 Hstuf Wenger gave orders to me and to the competent official Schneider, to take a number of prisoners away from Étival in a gasogene vehicle and to shoot them on the way. Hstuf Wenger wished that the English officer [Silly] should be present with Schneider at the execution, so that Schneider should have easier work at subsequent interrogations and might be able to obtain better statements …

On the lorry there were besides those entrusted with the task and the members of the Wachkompanie, the following prisoners who had been kept in Étival: - one young French civilian, two Englishmen in uniform [Brown and Lewis] and one English officer. The above-mentioned officer was wearing an English uniform, a peaked cap and glasses. In March 1946, I recognised him when I was shown a picture by Major Barkworth which was marked 'Lieutenant

Silly'. I particularly noticed him on account of his dark complexion and dark hair. The two other Englishmen in uniform were of medium height and wore berets of which I cannot now remember the colour exactly. The fourth was a French civilian of small build.

Before we left Hstuf Wenger gave further instructions that if possible we should leave no traces of the execution. We then drove through La Petite-Raon in the direction of Belval and on account of the falling off of the performance of the lorry, we had to leave it in the wood and continued on foot with the prisoners to a point in the hill slope above the house which had already been burned down. We had marched through the wood in the direction of Moussey Le Harcholet for about twenty–thirty minutes according to my estimate …

We left this farmhouse and walked down to the above-mentioned second ruin and ordered the three prisoners to go into the wooden shed and sit down. Meanwhile Schneider went with the English officer to one side in the direction of the house of the old couple. Since we had been instructed to remove all traces as far as possible, several bundles of straw were brought along subsequently.

In the wooden shed the three prisoners had to sit on a rafter but Schneider stayed with the English officer a little way off the house, while I with three or four members of the Wachkompanie remained standing before the door of the wooden shed. The prisoners were sitting with their back to the entrance of the wooden shed.

In accordance with my order to fire, the NCOs of the Wachkompanie discharged their machine pistols in the direction of the prisoners. (According to my memory there were three NCOs of which one was Unterscharführer Gimbel). Two machine pistols did not work and only the third fired.

The fire extended and burned down the shed, but as the corpses therein were not consumed, some hand grenades were thrown into the shed, but as some charred remains of bodies still showed within the ashes, Gimbel threw an egg grenade in the direction of these remains. The explosion did not occur immediately and I went back to the farm-house to explain to the inhabitants that it would not be advisable to go to the house during the next hour since, a hand grenade had not exploded. After we left the farm-house, we made for, with members of the Wachkompanie towards the house of the old couple in order to return to the lorry. On the way we heard the explosion go off behind us.

After this we went back with the English officer to the truck and drove back to Étival via Moussey [see Silly's entry under Moyenmoutier Communal Cemetery, France]. Schneider and I reported to Wenger that the order had been carried out [WO 309/359].

As soon as German troops withdrew from the area the remains were brought to the attention of the Allies. Sykes later stated that he had initially identified Brown by an identity disc in one pocket, also remarking that his hands had been tied behind his back:

Immediately after this examination by Captain Sykes, the three bodies were buried by the Cure of Saulcy in the parish churchyard at Saulcy, whence they were exhumed on or about 3 December 1944, by Captain Sykes and an unnamed doctor from Senones in order to seek further definitive evidence of identification. At this exhumation an identity disc was found embedded in the flesh of body No.1 and reading '315950, C.E, S Brown'. The bodies were then reinterred at the same spot and then duly marked as containing the bodies of 'Brown, an unknown Frenchman, and one other British soldier' [WO 219/5069].

This file also notes that due to the lack of any evidence of ropes at the scene of the crime 'the implied assumption that death may have been partly due to hanging is rejected.' Hauptsturmführer Erich Wenger, the commander of the Kommando responsible, later referred to Brown as 'one further [SAS prisoner] who had been an officer's soldier servant and who had had to do with horses in his civilian profession' (WO 311/87). Meanwhile, a local forester, Albert Freine, confirmed at the subsequent hearing that: 'Eight days later [on 3 December] Captain Sykes came back and the bodies were exhumed. Around the neck of one he found a serial number and that is how he discovered that this man was his batman in England' (WO 219/5069). The remains were later interred at their present location.

Members of the Kommando Wenger were also concerned in the murders of Parachutist Fred Puttick ('Belval Case' – see his entry within this volume under Groesbeek Memorial, Netherlands), of Signalman 'Jock' Johnston ('Etival Case' – see his entry under Groesbeek Memorial, Netherlands), Lieutenant Jim Silly ('Moyenmoutier Case' – see his entry under Moyenmoutier Communal Cemetery, France) and Sergeant Michael Fitzpatrick, Lance-corporal Jack Elliott and Parachutist John Conway ('Pexonne Case' – see their entries in this section).

The SAS War Crimes Investigation Team implicated Preil, SS-Hauptscharführer Arnold Schneider and Unterscharführer Wilhelm Gimbel in the 'Harcholet Case' although no trial appears to have ever taken place. Wenger himself appears to have assumed an alias in a prison camp after his interrogation and to have subsequently been released in error. In 1950 he joined the West German Federal Government under a false name but four years later resumed his identity and joined the country's intelligence service. He died as a retired officer in 1978.

Son of Frank and Martha Brown of Greens Norton near Towcester, Northamptonshire – Husband of Jane Brown of Lochend Drive, Edinburgh – Father of Frank and William Brown.
Age 36.
No inscription.
Grave 10. Also commemorated on a memorial above Harcholet at the spot where he was murdered.

LIEUTENANT GEOFFREY CHARLES CASTELLAIN [177329] CAVALRY OF THE LINE, ESSEX REGIMENT, 16TH/5TH LANCERS AND 2ND SAS (2 SQN)

Geoffrey Castellain was born on 19 February 1920 at Bagshot, Surrey, into a family of cotton brokers that lived near Gloucester Road Tube Station in London. Having attended Westminster School from September 1933 he went up to Christ Church, Oxford, in 1938 where he read Greek and Latin Classics. Shortly after the outbreak of war he enlisted into the Cavalry of the Line at Lincoln's Inn and was transferred to the Army Reserve. Called to the colours in July 1940 he was transferred to the Essex Regiment and posted to their infantry training depot at Warley before being attached to the 13th/18th Hussars that October (service number 327435). The following month he attended 102 OCTU at Blackdown and was granted an emergency commission into the 16th/5th Lancers during March 1941 (*London Gazette* 28/03/41). At the time he stated that he spoke fluent French and Greek and that he had knowledge of Italy and France.

Posted to No.7 Light Tank Troop Castellain was attached to the 70th (Young Soldiers) Battalion, Welch Regiment, in April 1942 before being re-posted to HQ 6th Armoured Division that September. It is likely that he landed at Algiers during late November seeing action at Bou Arada in January 1943, at Kasserine the following month, at Fondouk Pass and El Kourzia in April, and taking part in the fall of Tunis and final battles of the North African Campaign in May.

Having volunteered for 2nd SAS in June 1943 Castellain fractured his back during parachute training in August and was admitted to No.99 British General Hospital at Rivet near the airfield at Blida:

This officer was doing his third jump on his first parachute course. His parachute opened in the normal way after he had jumped. The wind was slight but gusty. Just before reaching the ground Lt Castellain was caught by a gust which resulted in his landing on a backward swing. He landed on his back. It was an accident and is no way the fault of the officer concerned [service record].

Still in plaster Castellain was invalided home. Disembarking in the UK that October he was nominally posted to the 51st Training Regiment, attending regular medical boards to assess his fitness for duty. The following March, having been passed A1 fit, he returned to 2nd SAS at Doonfoot Camp, Alloway in Ayrshire. When the SAS Brigade moved to Fairford Transit Camp that June he was appointed Camp Security Officer although made time for parachute course 121 at No.1 PTS Ringway later that month. Here his instructor noted; 'cheerful hard worker … enjoyed a good course'.

Castellain commanded OPERATION PISTOL's B.2 Patrol that parachuted into the area of Sarreguemines in the Moselles département of eastern France close to the German border on the night of 15–16 September 1944. On the DZ, Parachutist Christopher Ashe was found to be missing (see his entry within this volume under Durnbach War Cemetery, Germany). All PISTOL groups were dropped at pre-arranged locations but without reception or organised contact with the local populace. They had specific sabotage tasks to carry out before exfiltration and Castellain and his four remaining men blew the main Enchenberg–Lemberg railway line before making their way cross-country to reach OPERATION LOYTON's base party on the 1st or 2nd of October.

Castellain was wounded by a German patrol on the Bertrichamps–Raon L'Étape road on 12 October 1944. He died of these wounds shortly after, his grave being 'discovered and identified at V 315809' (WO 218/209). His family was informed the following January: 'his grave has been located and it was clearly marked with his name and date of his death'. *The Times* had already reported him as missing: 'Officially reported as missing in Western Europe, Oct 1944, Lieut Geoffrey Castellain, 16th/5th Lancers, att Army Air Corps. Any news gratefully received by his mother, Mrs E F Castellain, The Gate House, Fritham, near Lyndhurst, Hants.'

Only son of Ernest and Annie Castellain (née James) later of Hill Deverill, Wiltshire – Known to have had one sister.
Age 24.
He gave his life for his friends
Grave 7. Also commemorated at Westminster School and Christ Church, Oxford.

Private John Joseph CONWAY [14567132] General Service Corps, Royal Artillery, Royal Berkshire Regiment, Oxfordshire and Buckinghamshire Light Infantry and 2nd SAS (2 Sqn)

John Conway was born in the parish of St Pauls, Cardiff, on 4 February 1925. He enlisted into the General Service Corps in March 1943, transferring to the Royal Artillery the following month to serve in the 4th Light Anti-Aircraft Regiment. That October he transferred again, this time to the Royal Berkshire Regiment that posted him to 17 Infantry Training Centre. In February 1944 he transferred to the Oxfordshire and Buckinghamshire Light Infantry joining the 2nd Battalion. This formed part of the 6th Airlanding Brigade and at the time was carrying out glider training for operations in Europe. However, Conway volunteered for 2nd SAS on 13 March and subsequently attended parachute course 111A at No.1 PTS Ringway the following month. Here his instructor noted him to be 'a good performer, cheerful, keen and confident'.

Conway was captured during Operation Loyton on 16 September 1944 and murdered at Pexonne on the 19th (see Lance-corporal Jack Elliott's entry for full details).

Son of Mrs Catherine Conway (née Warnock) of North William Street, Adamsdown, Cardiff.
Age 19.
No inscription.
Grave 1. Also commemorated on Pexonne's war memorial.

Sergeant Gerald Donovan DAVIS [6898743] Queen Victoria Rifles, Royal Armoured Corps and GHQ Liaison Regiment Att SAS

Gerry Davis was born on 20 April 1918 at Maidenhead in Berkshire where he worked as a railway clerk. At the beginning of May 1939 he joined the 2nd Battalion, Queen Victoria Rifles, a London TA unit affiliated to the King's Royal Rifle Corps. Embodied for service as a result of the German–Soviet Pact late that August he was employed guarding London's docks until February 1940 when posted to No.10 Military Mission. This newly formed unit, later known as GHQ Liaison Regiment (Phantom), was based at Willems Barracks in Aldershot, the majority of its motorcycle troop recruited thus, *en bloc*, from the

'Queen Vics' who were trained riders. They soon earned the respect of their regular colleagues, the majority of whom had been recruited from the Royal Tank Regiment.

Landing at Le Harve on 19 February 1940 Davis' troop joined the now-named 'Hopkinson British Military Mission' as part of the BEF and settled into the frantic training of the 'Phoney War' at Valenciennes near the Belgian border. After the German invasion of the Low Countries that May the unit made a fighting withdrawal to the beaches of La Panne at Dunkirk, the last of its members being taken off on 31 May.

On its return, Phantom, at this time referred to as GHQ Reconnaissance Detachment, based itself at Ryton House in Lechlade, Gloucestershire. Promoted to lance-corporal that December Davis was advanced to corporal the following March. During 1942 he was attached to the Commando Training Centre at Inverary, to the 2nd Canadian Division, and to a Special Service Brigade. Confirmed as lance-sergeant in October 1943 he nominally transferred to the Royal Armoured Corps the following March but remained with Phantom as a sergeant. Later that month he completed parachute course 108 at No.1 PTS, Ringway, his instructor noting: 'set good example, excellent jumper – morale high'. When Phantom's F Squadron was attached to the SAS Brigade at the end of February 1944 he was the obvious choice as one of the patrol sergeants.

On the night of 12–13 August 1944 Davis parachuted into a DZ near the village of Le Mont in the Vosges département of eastern France as a member of Captain Henry Druce's recce party for OPERATION LOYTON. Tasked with establishing the region's suitability for operations, and with securing a base and DZ for any reinforcements, the team settled at a Maquis camp in the nearby hills north of Moussey. This was betrayed, the party being forced to move on 17 August. In the process Davis was separated from Captain John Hislop's group whilst hiding from a German patrol near Vexaincourt. One of the Maquis with them raised his head and was spotted. Coming under fire the group scattered and three days later, on the 20th, Davis asked for food at the farm of Monsieur le Grand and then from the parish priest at St Jean-le-Saulcy, this being close to the DZ at which he had been inserted. He was refused by both, the priest, Abbé Colin, subsequently reporting to the nearby headquarters of the SD's Kommando Schoner at the Château de Belval. Whilst he was there a truck left the château and returned with the Davis. It would seem that he was taken to Schirmeck Concentration Camp that day. Here he was interrogated and:

> … made to strip in the passageway of the cells while his clothes were searched … These were given back to him, and he was taken away the same afternoon. Obstubaf Schneider remembers interrogating a prisoner whom he remembers as Davis by name and appearance. He states that he would answer no questions. He was collected by Gehrum and Schoner for further interrogation after an argument concerning his disposal [WO 309/230].

SS-Hauptsturmführer Julius Gehrum, the Head of Counter Espionage and Sabotage in Alsace, later stated that his commander, SS-Standartenführer Dr Erich Isselhorst, had told him that Davis 'must be made to talk' (WO 235/559). Attempts to do so were unsuccessful, SS-Obersturmbannführer Wilhelm Schneider, deputy to Isselhorst and one of those subsequently tried for war crimes, later stating:

> I got this prisoner to write his name for me. He wrote in block capitals DAVIS. He was tall and well built. He would not tell me where his home was, but said he was a railway clerk before the war. He refused to say where he was born. I told him he would be treated a Maquisard for being with them, in accordance with the instructions we had received. He replied; 'my country right or wrong, I am a soldier and I have to do my duty'. I told him he had to prove to me he was a soldier, for he had no pay book or identity discs which he could show me. At last he produced some pennies from his pocket as proof he had come from England. He would answer no military questions. I admired his attitude which was in great contrast to that of Seymour [Sergeant Ken Seymour, a JEDBURGH radio operator captured the same day]. I was so impressed by his soldierly bearing, and his impassivity when told he would be shot as a Maquisard, that I made representations to Isselhorst, that this soldier should be treated as a POW and set to an appropriate camp [WO 309/717].

Isselhorst later confirmed at trial:

> Schneider did tell me something about one of the members of the parachutists having behaved very bravely, and I believe he did ask if something could not be done for this man. I believe I have already testified in the witness box

that this man was another reason why I phoned Muller [his superior], but then after the clear decision of Muller, my explanation came, and therefore the action which had to be taken was the same for all SAS who were captured at that time, because it was proved that they were collaborating with the Maquis [WO 235/555].

Schneider also stated that Davis' pay book, which showed that he was from Maidenhead, had been recovered from the Maquis camp, as had two large bags of mail which were found hanging in a tree. Two letters were addressed to Davis and were passed to him during interrogation (WO 235/559). Gerhardt Callies, another of Isselhorst's interrogators, claimed at trial to have taken much the same line:

I then told him he had been taken prisoner in connection with the Maquis and if he could not prove that he was a British soldier he would be treated like a Maquis and thereupon he again gave no answer. I then asked him whether he knew how he would be treated as a Maquis; thereupon he didn't answer. I then gave him ten minutes to consider, and told him that I did not have so much time that I could talk for hours on end with him. Davis then smoked a cigarette and said to himself: 'I would not like to be hanged'. When the ten minutes was over I asked him whether he was ready to answer my questions, and Davis then said: 'No, I will not give any answer'. I then called the guard and had Davis returned to his cell [WO 235/555].

Meanwhile, Davis had been posted missing in action, there being no news of him until his remains were discovered the following year:

I [Antoine Verdier], a gendarme of Moussey accompanied by gendarme Lachambre went with Armand Gerard who claimed to have found a body in the woods, to a spot two hours march north-east of Moussey in the woods, which is called Le Calvaire [it later transpired that a local forester, Albert Freine, had made the discovery on 1 April 1945]. The body was covered by a light layer of earth …
   The body was dressed in the remains of khaki trousers, with a pleated pocket on the right thigh, and had a pair of socks in grey wool on which was marked H&M LDT 1944 'Warnorm' trade mark …
   The body was taken to Moussey and buried in a cemetery there [WO 309/230].

Freine himself stated that the remains were found 'buried in the woods' between 'Jardin David and the Calvaire', this being the area of the betrayed camp. They were identified as those of Davis and buried at Moussey on 4 April. Schneider's subsequent statement gave the first indication of who had been responsible:

While I was at Strassburg [sic] I wondered what had happened to these three prisoners, and in particular to Davis. Shortly afterwards when I next had occasion to visit Schirmeck I asked Buck what had happened to the prisoner. He replied that the matter was settled. I then asked Kurt Buck's [sic – Dr Karl Buck's] driver [SS-Hauptscharführer Kurt Giegling] for details, he showed me the closed truck standing in the camp and told me that 'the Englishman' had been shot on the way up to the camp at Natzweiler. He told me that the truck had stopped, and that the prisoner had been made to walk up the hill before being shot, I assume from behind. The photograph marked Sjt Davis is, I believe to be able to say with certainty that of the English prisoner who came last of the three to Schirmeck, and who wrote his name as Davis. The address of one of his letters was from Maidenhead [WO 309/717].

Although it appears this particular statement by Schneider may well refer to Parachutist Wally Hall, others suggest that Davis was murdered in the same manner. It is therefore believed that Davis was taken back to the area of the Maquis camp in an attempt to force him to reveal the whereabouts of his comrades, and that he was murdered when he refused to do so. His date of death is officially recorded as 20 August 1944, the day that he was captured.

Abbé Colin, who had fetched the SD, later stated that he thought that Davis might have been a German plant to trap him and that, in any case, he had been ordered to the German HQ that morning. However, SS-Unterscharführer Peter Liedloff, another of those later accused of being concerned in the killing, stated that:

I never saw any English prisoners at Château Belval, nor heard that any had been taken, until the end of September when I saw Schoner again in Strasbourg. I asked him if any prisoners had been taken from the English of whom we had heard, and he said only one, and that he would not have been able to capture him if the priest of the next village to Belval had not come and given information [WO 309/230].

Several local inhabitants, who had come to attend Mass, were witness to Davis' capture, identifying him by his distinctive peaked mountain cap (WO 309/230). Another file notes that: 'there is no evidence to charge any individual of murder. More of Kdo Schoner should be interrogated … Abbé Colin to be added to list of accused' (WO 311/84).

Len Owens, MM, a fellow Phantom sergeant on LOYTON, later recalled:

> I knew Gerry. We used to go drinking together and he was a funny lad – he had a cleft pallet and he used to talk in a strange way. Oh, I drank many a pint with Gerry. In fact, I remember one incident in Richmond where we were in some pub or other and there was singing going on and the funniest thing I've ever heard was Gerry Davis singing. But he was a hell of a good lad. He was my opposite number – he was the NCO in charge of Johnny Hislop's wireless patrol and I was the NCO in charge of Peter Johnson's … I did receive a phone call from a fellow in Maidenhead who said 'I am the Headmaster of Maidenhead School and we remember Gerald Davis well. He was part of our cricket team' [personal interview, 2010].

Hislop wrote of him in *Anything but a Soldier*:

> Davis was a veteran of Phantom, having come to the Regiment from the QVRs like many early members. He was a tall, lean, athletically built young man, intelligent, responsible and absolutely reliable. He had a somewhat cynical outlook on life, possibly on account of an impediment in his speech, but was a man of sterling character and an excellent soldier …
>
> Davis had a strong, independent nature and was not overawed by anyone … He was hard-working, conscientious and never became flurried; his subordinates liked but respected him.

Isselhorst received the death sentence from both British and French courts. He was executed by the latter in 1948 (see Private Wally Hall's entry under Bayeux Memorial for further details). Schneider, who referred to Davis in court as a 'specially brave and upright man', was also sentenced to death and hanged. Giegling was brought to trial over the murder of Sergeant Frederic Habgood, RAFVR, and received the death sentence. He was handed over to the French who in turn sentenced him to ten years hard labour regarding separate charges before his original sentence was commuted to imprisonment. It is not known whether Abbé Colin was ever charged, although as a French citizen it seems unlikely.

Son of Mr and Mrs George Davis (née Deadman) of Furze Platt Road, Maidenhead, Berkshire.
Age 26.
Loyal unto death
Grave 6. Also commemorated within the Phantom Memorial Garden at the National Memorial Arboretum, Alrewas, which was organised and constructed by Owens and his family.

LANCE-CORPORAL JOHN HERBERT ELLIOTT [4200829] ROYAL WELCH FUSILIERS, KING'S OWN ROYAL REGIMENT AND 2ND SAS (2 SQN)

Jack Elliott, as he was known, was born to Irish parents on 15 July 1919 in Collyhurst, Manchester, and later lived in the spa town of Buxton in Derbyshire. According to his family he was a vehement communist from an early age and served in the International Brigade during the Spanish Civil War. To get there he had attempted to travel to Paris to join under his real name but had incurred the interest of MI5 and was subsequently banned from leaving the country. Obtaining documents under the name of 'Jack' Elliott he succeeded in reaching the French capital and then Spain, his family referring to him as 'Uncle Jack' from then on. MI5 records confirm that he applied for a passport in 1936, that he made an attempt to reach mainland Europe in 1937, that managed to do so on 13 February 1938, that on arriving in Paris he was rejected for service, but that he subsequently left for Spain in any case. After that there is no known information except that the Security Service believed that he had been killed in May 1938 (KV 5/112/5). However, elsewhere in the same file a 'John Elliot' from Manchester is reported as having been taken prisoner that July.

Although it is unknown when Elliott returned to the UK he enlisted into the Royal Welch Fusiliers in April 1940 and was posted to A Company, 311th Infantry Training Centre. That June he transferred to the King's Own Royal Regiment and, having joined D Company of the 8th (Pioneer) Battalion, disembarked on Malta in July 1941. Having been garrisoned here throughout the island's siege as a lance-corporal he volunteered for 2nd SAS. He subsequently arrived at Algiers on 23 August 1943 and joined the Regiment at Philippeville later that day. After intensive training he returned to the UK with his squadron the following March.

On 7 September 1944 Elliott parachuted into a DZ near Pexonne in the Vosges département of eastern France to reinforce OPERATION LOYTON. He was separated from the rest of the stick along with Sergeant Michael Fitzpatrick and Parachutist John Conway and broke his thigh on landing, perhaps from falling into the surrounding trees. The three men took shelter at a quarry within a wood adjoining the farm of La Fosse at Pexonne. Madame Secile da Silva, a local witness in the subsequent war crimes case, later stated:

> Of the three photographs now shown to me I recognise one as a wounded man I have seen who had curly red hair. I know the name of another one as being Patrick [*sic* – Fitzpatrick]. My son was a member of the Resistance movement and I know that the three men shown in the photographs were three English parachutists. On Wednesday 13th September 1944 at about 1400 hours I went with my son to some woods. We found there a red-haired parachutist who was lying in some moss sheltered with pine branches and two other prisoners of war [*sic*]. My son identified himself to them as being a member of the Resistance and he had undertaken to bring back the wounded man to my house so that he could be looked after. For that purpose we took with us a little cart on which to transport him back. I stood at the edge of the road to see if there were any Germans about. I heard my son tell them, 'I will bring your friend into the village. My mother will look after him with the help of the doctor. As for you two, I will come and get you in the late evening at sunset and will take you to the Maquis command post at La Scierie La Jus.'
>
> The owner of the wood was Lucien Jaco [*sic* - Jacquot] who was the owner of La Fosse Farm near to it, and he was there with my son at the time. M. Jaco would not let the parachutists go. Thereafter my son kept these prisoners supplied for three days and they stayed in the wood hidden there [WO 311/72].

Robert Husson, the village doctor, confirmed:

> On Wednesday 13 September I went to La Fosse Farm and was taken by M. Jaco into a little wood near the farm by the road. We found three Englishmen including one who was stretched out on a parachute. They were wearing British uniform, and there was one sergeant. (The witness was shown photographs of the three parachutists Elliott, Fitzpatrick and Conway which he recognised as the men which he saw). They told me their names as being

Fitzpatrick, Conway and Elliott. I was not able to give much treatment because I had not much equipment at hand but made a splint for the wounded man [WO 311/72].

The local Maquis leader later told a court of inquiry that: 'The two men who were not wounded, Fitzgerald and Conway, did not want to leave their wounded friend. The other one could not be transported. That was on the Friday, the last day on which I saw them.' The three were captured on the afternoon of the 16th having been betrayed by Genevieve Demetz, one of two local sisters, who fetched the SD's Kommando Wenger. She allegedly denounced the owners of the farm because the Maquis had cut her hair for fraternising with Germans (WO 219/5067). Local inhabitants reported that she and her sister, Yvette, had subsequently escaped from the local Resistance movement when it was attacked by the Germans on 4 September at Viombois. Madame da Silva continued:

> At the end of three days someone [Demetz] went into the woods to pick some fruit and she found these men lying down and reported them to the Germans. M. Jaco then moved them into the garden of La Fosse Farm. The last time my son saw them was at about 2300 hours on Friday 15th September 1944. On Saturday 16 Sep 44 my husband went to join the American tanks and he returned on the Sunday. On his way to join the Americans he had gone to the woods to get them out but apparently did not do so.
> On Saturday 16 September 1944 I was in my house when I saw some members of the German Gestapo. They passed my house about 3 or 4 in the afternoon. There were two cars which had come from La Fosse Farm after burning it down. In the first there were five officers and one driver. In the second there were a number of German soldiers standing up with machine carbines. There were also three of the British parachutists I had seen in the woods. The wounded man was half lying down in the truck. At the time they passed I was at the fountain. I noticed that the British prisoners were dressed in khaki and were bare headed. I knew then that they had been made prisoner [WO 311/72].

Having shot the farm owners, Madame Delphine Jacquot and her son Lucien, the Germans set fire to the property before taking the three SAS to the Kommando Wenger's house at La Neuveville for interrogation. Two of them, Fitzpatrick and Conway, were brought back to the farm on the 19th and shot, their bodies being burnt in the apiary (WO 311/72). Fragments of German hand grenades found at the scene, and explosions heard by villagers, suggested that there was a concerted effort to destroy the bodies not only by fire. Madame da Silva recalled the events of this later date:

> On Tuesday 19 September 1944 I again saw the truck but was not near enough to see who was in it except that I did notice that there were helmeted Germans. There were again two vehicles and they were the same ones that I had seen on the 16th. When I saw them on the 19th it was about 1600 hours and it went in the direction of La Fosse Farm. According to rumours I heard between the 16th and 19th the prisoners were taken to Raon. On this date there was another fire at La Fosse Farm. I cannot see La Fosse Farm from my place but I have been told that the Germans stopped at La Fosse Farm. I know that for the second time La Fosse was burning. I saw the smoke. There was a girl riding in the car who was dressed like a German soldier. Her name is Jenevieve [sic] Demetz who worked for the Germans.
> My son had the names of the British Parachutists and I know that the wounded man was named Elliott. Another one was named Patrick [WO 311/72].

A further witness stated that he had seen Germans returning from La Fosse with a large bouquet on the front of their vehicle and realised that the Kommando had picked flowers having murdered the parachutists.

Although it has been reported that all three SAS were killed together it appears that, whilst his comrades were murdered at La Fosse, Elliott suffered a different fate:

> [SS-Hauptscharführer] Ferdinand Daberger [a member of the Kommando Wenger] subsequently shot the wounded Elliott whilst he was dozing on a couch in the unit's quarters. The body was afterwards wrapped in a blanket and taken to the nearby woods for burial … The body of Pct Elliott is said to have been buried near the road leading from Raon l'Etape to Neufmaisons and, if found, will be examined when final statements are taken from Da Silva and Simon in the near future [WO 235/556 and WO 235/559].

Major 'Bill' Barkworth, the commander of the SAS War Crimes Investigation Team, related the full story:

During the conversation with a former member of Kommando Wenger I have since learned that the 3rd member of this party was shot on his way back from interrogation and was placed in the luggage compartment of the car of the commander of that particular detachment as a joke so that when he opened the luggage compartment of his car the body would fall out. I understand the joke was successful [WO 235/554].

The remains of Fitzpatrick and Conway were recovered by Barkworth and Captain Christopher Sykes at the beginning of December 1944 and placed in one coffin in the military cemetery at Badonvilliers. Presumably Elliott's were recovered later, the three men being then reinterred at their present location.

Members of the Kommando Wenger were also concerned in the murders of Parachutists Selwyn Brown and Donald Lewis at Le Harcholet ('Harcholet Case' – see their entries in this section), Lieutenant Jim Silly ('Moyenmoutier Case' – see his entry under Moyenmoutier Communal Cemetery, France), Signalman 'Jock' Johnston ('Etival Case' – see his entry within this volume under Groesbeek Memorial, Netherlands), and Parachutist Fred Puttick ('Belval Case' – see his entry under Groesbeek Memorial).

In March 1945 a court of inquiry was held into the 'Pexonne Case' in the town hall, close to where the murders took place. It implicated SS-Hauptscharführer Ferdinand Daberger and Henri Przebilisky as those that carried out the actual shootings. The former had proved so violent that Hauptsturmführer Erich Wenger, the Kommando's leader, had subsequently banished him from his unit. The latter, a Pole, was said to have been shot by the Germans at Saint-Dié for looting French houses. Other members of the Kommando were cited as being concerned in the killings: SS-Oberscharführer Max Eckert (who used the pseudonyms 'Max Kessler' and 'Matu Kester' and who had been implicated in the 'Noailles Case' in which five members of 1st SAS were murdered), SS-Untersturmführer Hans Schumann, SS-Oberscharführer Erich Wild, and Frenchmen René Louvrier and Bobby van Houtte (who deserted the Kommando in November 1944 but was captured by the Americans in Austria). Hauptscharführer Willi Hess and Unterscharführers Wilhelm Gimbel, Zerves, Bettendorf, Maurer and Markie, all members of an associated Wachkompanie, were also cited in this and other SAS cases.

Despite the best efforts of the SASWCIT no trial appears to have taken place, perhaps because insufficient numbers of those implicated were traced to ensure solid convictions. SS-Hauptsturmführer Richard Schnur, who had interrogated the three men, had previously led the firing squad concerned in the 'Noailles Case' and was found guilty at this trial. He was hanged in June 1947 (see five entries under Marissel French National Cemetery, France). After his interrogation Wenger appears to have assumed an alias in a prison camp and to have been subsequently released in error. In 1950 he joined the West German Federal Government under a false name. Four years later resumed his identity and joined the country's intelligence service. He died as a retired officer in 1978.

Son of William and Mary Elliott (née McArley) – Brother of William, Francis, James and Arthur Elliott.
Age 27.
No inscription.
Grave 3. Also commemorated on Pexonne's war memorial.

SERGEANT MICHAEL BENEDICT **FITZPATRICK** MM [321375] ROYAL NAVY VOLUNTEER RESERVE, 12TH ROYAL LANCERS, ROYAL TANK REGIMENT, No.3 COMMANDO, SMALL SCALE RAIDING FORCE AND 2ND SAS (2 SQN)

Michael Fitzpatrick was born to a British father and Irish mother on 26 October 1916 in the parish of St Michael's, Tipperary, Eire. Having worked as a machinist he enlisted into the 12th Royal Lancers (Prince of Wales's) in August 1938 at Birmingham stating that he had previously served in the Royal Navy Volunteer Reserve aboard HMS *Eaglet* at Shetland Docks (service number MD/X 2165). Based at Tidworth he was transferred to the newly formed 52nd Royal Tank Regiment, Royal Armoured Corps, in April 1939. Having been promoted to lance-corporal that June he volunteered for No.3 Commando at the beginning of July 1940 and is likely to have taken part in OPERATION AMBASSADOR, an unsuccessful raid on Guernsey on the night of the 14–15th of that month. Later in the year this unit was absorbed into the 4th Special Service Battalion but was reconstituted as No.3 Commando in March 1941, Fitzpatrick being promoted to corporal two months later.

Fitzpatrick took part in two raids on Norway planned to arrest enemy production of fish oil that was being used to manufacture explosives: on 4 March 1941 No.3 Commando was landed with other special service troops on the Lofoten Islands for OPERATION CLAYMORE where the relevant factories, 18,000 tons of shipping, and 800,000 gallons of oil and glycerine were destroyed. Over 200 Germans were captured, as was an important set of rotor wheels for an Enigma cipher machine. Fitzpatrick also took part in OPERATION ARCHERY, a similar raid on the islands of Vaagso and Maaloy on 27 December 1941. As a member of No.6 Troop under Captain Peter Young he was tasked with destroying German gun positions. The citation that accompanied the award of his subsequent Military Medal reads:

> Almost immediately after landing at Vaagso [*sic* – Maaloy] in S Norway, Cpl Fitzpatrick was acting as leading scout to his section. The advance was held up by a wire obstacle covered by heavy enemy fire. Cpl Fitzpatrick without hesitation moved forward alone and cut a gap through the wire, thus allowing the advance to continue without loss of time. The moment was somewhat critical as a hold up in the early stages might have had serious delaying affects on the operation as a whole. Cpl Fitzpatrick's coolness and presence of mind quite definitely prevented any such delays occurring [WO 373/93, *London Gazette* 03/04/42].

Later that day Fitzpatrick, still at the forefront of the action, was shot in the chest and on the force's return to the UK was taken aboard HMS *Isle of Jersey*, a hospital ship within Scapa Flow. Despite a further spell in Oldmill Emergency Hospital in Aberdeen he was invested with his MM on 19 May 1942, four days after having been confirmed as lance-sergeant.

That August No.3 Commando was landed to the east of Dieppe to destroy enemy gun positions during OPERATION JUBILEE, the ill-fated and large-scale amphibious assault on the town itself. Fitzpatrick's part in this raid is unknown but Young's troop was the only one to successfully attract the fire of their objective away from the main Allied forces and to withdraw successfully.

Fitzpatrick arrived on Gibraltar at the beginning of March 1943 and disembarked in Algiers the following month. In early May he was posted to No.62 Commando, the cover name for SOE's Small Scale Raiding Force, and was therefore one of the original members of 2nd SAS, the SSRF forming the foundation on which the Regiment was raised on the 13th of the month. Less than two weeks later he took part in OPERATION MARIGOLD during which members of 2nd SAS, and those of Z Special Boat Section attached to it, were inserted by HM Submarine *Safari* to snatch a prisoner from a guardhouse on Sardinia's east coast. It was hoped that the raid would reinforce the deception created by the now famous OPERATION MINCEMEAT, i.e. that the Allies planned to land on Sardinia rather than Sicily. 'Tanky' Challenor, who also deployed on this operation, later wrote: 'I was comforted to find I was in the same section as Sergeant Fitzpatrick, a tough professional soldier whose air of coolness impressed me considerably' (*Tanky Challenor: SAS and the Met*, by Draper and Challenor). Having embarked in Algiers harbour on the 26th the twelve-man party landed at 0155hrs on 1 June after some difficulty due to submerged rocks. Moving only a little way inland one of the men dropped his Tommy gun, the raiders being subsequently engaged by small arms and illuminated by enemy flares. They were therefore forced to make a silent, but hasty, withdrawal to the submarine, Fitzpatrick leading one section and Captain Patrick Dudgeon, MC, the other. Sergeant Loasby of Z SBS was captured (see Dudgeon's entry under Florence War Cemetery, Italy, Volume II).

Having been promoted to sergeant, Fitzpatrick took part in OPERATION SASSOON on the Italian mainland under Captain 'Loopy' Cameron. Their party sailed from Termoli on the night of 15–16 December 1943 to collect Allied evaders from behind enemy lines. They came ashore in two dinghies at the mouth of the Chienti River and quickly assembled former POWs, but repeated efforts to have them picked up failed. Eventually, on the seventh attempt, the team and POWs were taken off by the Royal Navy on the night of 20 January 1944. Fitzpatrick returned to the UK with the rest of the Regiment that March.

On the night of 6–7 September 1944 Fitzpatrick parachuted into the Vosges département of eastern France for OPERATION LOYTON. He was captured on the 16th at La Fosse near Pexonne (see Lance-corporal Jack Elliott's entry above for full details). On the 19th he and Parachutist John Conway were brought back to the same location and murdered:

> The party [the Kommando Wenger] then divided into two groups. The larger group consisting of Schumann, Daberger, Prczebilisky and most of the others, took Sgt Fitzpatrick to the apiary which still remained standing in the grounds of the destroyed farm house. Wild, Wegener, as well as one or two from the Wachkompanie took Conway in the direction of his previous hiding place in order to see whether any arms, ammunition or food had been left there. It was while on their way back from the thicket in question to the truck which lay interposed between them and the house that Wild heard (according to his evidence) a shot. They remained standing where they were. Shortly afterwards Daberger walked across and took Conway with him saying: 'Now I want this one.' Again on the evidence of Wild, Daberger took Conway in the direction of the apiary and shortly afterwards there was another shot. Wild says that he heard the actual shooting was carried out by Daberger and Prczebilisky.
>
> Wild himself gives an honest impression and it is not considered that he has withheld any information known to him or that he has misrepresented any facts [WO 309/359].

A Dental Officer later suggested that a certain tooth fracture in Fitzpatrick's lower jawbone was caused by 'extraordinary violence' (WO 219/5067). Captain Christopher Sykes, who had himself been deployed on LOYTON, was one of those to investigate the crime scene: 'The articles, namely eyes, zip fasteners

and buckles were identified definitely as part of a parachutist's harness. The remains after investigation were buried in one grave in the Badon Villers [*sic* – Badonvillers] cemetery. The grave was marked with the names of Sergeant Fitzpatrick, Private Conway and Private Elliott' (WO 311/72). The last had in fact been murdered separately and it was the remains of Fitzpatrick and Conway that were buried by the French in one coffin within the military section of Badonvillers cemetery before being reinterred at their current resting place (see Elliott's entry within this section for details of the ensuing war crimes trial).

Son of Catherine Fitzpatrick of Great Howard Street, Liverpool.
Age 27.
No inscription.
Grave 2. Also commemorated on Pexonne's war memorial and on the Commando Memorial at the National Memorial Arboretum.

CORPORAL 'GEORGE <u>KING</u>' – REAL NAME BORIS <u>KASPEROVITCH</u> [BNA/13301351]
PIONEER CORPS AND 2ND SAS (1 SQN)

Known to his comrades as 'Gasper', Boris Kasperovitch was a Russian national born on 24 July 1911. He is believed to have enlisted into 362 Company, Pioneer Corps, at Maison-Carrée in Algiers on 29 July 1943, taking the alias 'George King'. Despite this he appears on a 2nd SAS nominal roll from the summer of 1944 as 'Kasperovitch 1 Sqn', whilst his assumed name is variously recorded elsewhere as 'Boris King' or 'G King'. As his service record cannot be located under any permutation of these names, or of his service number, it is impossible to trace his military career and exact identity.

What is certain is that Kasperovitch parachuted into a small clearing above the village of Moussey in the Vosges département of eastern France on the night of 19–20 September 1944. He and five others were dropped along with two Jeeps as reinforcement to OPERATION LOYTON. Two nights later three more Jeeps were dropped and as the Commanding Officer, Lt-Colonel Brian Franks, MC, had been informed that the advancing Americans would arrive imminently the men were divided into crews for mobile operations, Kasperovitch serving as one of Captain Henry Druce's gunners. The latter recalled how the pair, along with Sergeant 'Jock' Hay as the other gunner, had been out for twenty-four hours looking for food (see Hay's entry within this volume under Durnbach War Cemetery, Germany). On their way back to camp from shooting up German troops at village bathhouses they scavenged a large cheese:

I asked a woman as we came into the village [of Moussey] from the south. I said; 'are there any Germans here?' 'No', she said, 'there are no Germans in the village.' So we then drove in and then just by the monument and the school were on the right hand side, damn it if there weren't a whole twenty Germans on parade standing by the monument …

It was a huge thing. Now where the hell do you put a huge cheese like that? I was very proud of myself so we put it on the bonnet of the Jeep and indeed when we got through to this group in the centre of Moussey we were shooting through this cheese so it really looked like a Swiss cheese at the end of it. It was holier than thou …

That was the only time my gun worked. Kasperovitch was on the right hand side and he shot the sentry by the two posts of the school. There was a sentry who more or less saluted us as we went in, you know, he didn't realise. He certainly didn't take any action and Gasper thought it was time he died and he turned his two guns on him and shot him there …

We then went up with the Jeep on that road straight through I guess 5 miles up the road before we stopped and then we came back because Brian [Franks] and the main group were still very close to the village of Moussey at the time and we came back and it was then that Gasper was shot [IWM Sound Archive 18033].

Kasperovitch was accidentally killed on 26 September 1944 when, on returning from the aforementioned patrol, he dismounted to approach the SAS camp on foot. Len Owens, MM, a former Phantom signaller on the same operation, later recalled:

I remember him. He was a lad who didn't speak a lot but he could speak English and we understood he was Russian. He was said to be an expert on explosives. One night he had been out on patrol and on the way back he was approaching the camp through the undergrowth and the two sentries who were on duty that night, a fella called … wish I could remember … Anyway he was on patrol guarding the approaches to camp with another SAS chap … Anyway they heard this rustling in the bushes as somebody was approaching so they challenged him for the password and all they got back was a flood of foreign language. This was attested by the SAS fellow who said 'yes this is what happened.' So, they said to him; 'come out there with your hands up, lets see who you are' and all they got was a flood of Russian. And still he came on through the bushes.

I think that this lad [name omitted for publication] might have waited slightly but what he did was he shouted 'what is the password?' And he still got this foreign so he fired he said as a warning but unfortunately he hit him and killed him … he was the one that fired the shot and killed Boris Kasperovitch. There was a sort of inquiry held and the SAS bloke said 'well this is exactly what he did' … But he was a nice fella Boris Kasperovitch [personal interview, 2010].

There are no known next of kin details. Age 33. No inscription. Grave 8.

Private Donald LEWIS [14410725] General Service Corps, Middlesex Regiment, Parachute Regiment and 2nd SAS (2 Sqn)

Donald Lewis was born on 23 November 1924 in Barnet, Middlesex, as one of four sisters and five brothers. All of the boys were trophy-winning junior boxers. His father, a Great War veteran who had encouraged them, later saw action against the Japanese whilst serving with the RAF in the Far East.

Having worked as a sheet metal worker Lewis enlisted into the General Service Corps at Edgware, London, during November 1942. The following March his brother George, a sergeant flight engineer in the RAF, was shot down over Holland, the entire crew of his Lancaster being killed in action. After a period at No.76 Primary Training Wing at Chester Lewis transferred to the Middlesex Regiment in November 1943. Three months later he was posted from the 70th (Young Soldiers) Battalion to the 8th Battalion and in April 1944 was re-posted to No.26 Signals Training Centre, transferring to the Army Air Corps a few days later. He attended parachute course 114 at No.1 PTS Ringway at the beginning of May, the log of which records that his parent unit was 6th Airborne Signals. He was subsequently posted to the Airborne Forces Holding Unit from where he volunteered for 2nd SAS on 11 July.

Lewis parachuted into a DZ near Veney in the Vosges département of eastern France in the early hours of 1 September 1944 as a member of Lieutenant 'Karl' Marx's reinforcement stick for Operation Loyton. On the 9th this group ambushed a lorry on the road at La Chapelotte before making contact with the main party on the 14th. At the end of the operation Lewis and Lieutenant Jim Silly became separated from Lt-Colonel Brian Franks' group whilst exfiltrating towards Allied lines (see Silly's entry under Moyenmoutier Communal Cemetery, France). 'Missing Parachutists', the SAS War Crimes Investigation Team's final report, states 'Lt Silly and Pct Lewis were made prisoner near the crossing of the River Meurthe', whilst Corporal Ian Larley noted:

> While coming through the lines with Lieut Silly, Herbert and Lewis on 11 Oct 44, the party was ambushed and we were surrounded. We scattered to cover and Herbert was wounded. He and I reached a thicket where I bandaged him up, and we moved about in the wood avoiding the enemy who were searching the area for two–three hours afterwards. The party was armed with three Colts [semi-automatic side arms] and I heard no firing from them after scattering. Lewis had a Colt which he handed to Lt Silly. The last point at which I saw Lt Silly and Lewis was at approx V 211811 north of Bazien [WO 361/716].

Lewis and Silly were reunited with Parachutist Selwyn Brown, who had been captured a few days earlier, and taken to Schirmeck Concentration Camp. Kept in the women's cells until 16 October the three were brought back to Le Harcholet where Lewis and Brown were murdered alongside an unknown Resistance fighter (see Brown's entry for full details). Captain Christopher Sykes of 2nd SAS later investigated the crime scene: 'near by, and apparently having fallen from the body, were a boxing medal and a badge of the Middlesex Regiment, British Army (WO 219/506). Parachutist Reg Lynn, a friend of Lewis, testified that the latter wore his Middlesex Regiment and Parachute Regiment cap badges on his belt and that the boxing medal was also his. Sykes recorded: 'it is worth noting that the house where this atrocity took place was next to the empty house where Lewis had sheltered up to the 3rd October 1944'.

Son of Charles and Lily Lewis of Southgate Road, Potters Bar, Middlesex – Younger brother of Charles (who served in the Home Guard and Fire Brigade), twins Albert (who served in the RAF) and George (who is buried within Hardenberg Protestant Cemetery, Netherlands) – Older brother of Stanley, Eileen, Lily, Grace and Doris (who served in the WAAF).
Age 18.
A brave lad died that others could live

Grave 9. Also commemorated on a memorial above Harcholet at the site of his murder and on the Prisoner of War Garden of Remembrance Memorial in Potters Bar.

SERGEANT 'ROBERT LODGE' DCM – REAL NAME RUDOLF FRIEDLANDER [5550151]
AUXILIARY MILITARY PIONEER CORPS, ROYAL ARMY ORDNANCE CORPS, ROYAL ELECTRICAL AND MECHANICAL ENGINEERS, HAMPSHIRE REGIMENT, SMALL SCALE RAIDING FORCE AND 2ND SAS (2 SQN)

Rudi Friedlander was a German, non-practising Jew born in Munich on 15 August 1908. Although he studied Law and Economics, graduating with a PhD in the latter, he retrained as a carpenter in Holland in 1934 before taking up the same line of work in the UK the following year. However, by the time he enlisted into 137 Company, Auxiliary Military Pioneer Corps, in April 1940 he was working as a concrete joiner (service number 13801992). He transferred to the Royal Army Ordnance Corps in August 1941, a move that sparked the interest of SOE that allotted him the designation '8728' and earmarked him for potential future employment. Having been transferred to the Royal Electrical and Mechanical Engineers on its formation in October 1942 he volunteered for special duties, his SOE personnel file noting '8728 was engaged at STS 62 [No.62 Commando, the cover name for SOE's Small Scale Raiding Force] as Other Rank' (HS 9/544/10). Nominally transferring to the Hampshire Regiment he arrived in North Africa with the SSRF in February 1943 and on 5 March chose a new identity, 'Robert Lodge', taking his fiancée's surname. His service number was changed as a result.

On 13 May 1943 the SSRF formed the foundation on which 2nd SAS was raised, Friedlander thus being one of the original members of this Regiment. His first mission was OPERATION SPIDER, a raid on an island off Bône along the Algerian coast. He also took part in abortive raids on Bizerte, Pantelleria and Lampedusa before being parachuted into a DZ near Capizzi on Sicily on the night of 12–13 July 1943 for OPERATION CHESTNUT. As a member of the 'Brig' party, named after its commander Captain Roy Bridgman-Evans, he was tasked with destroying enemy communications. However, the party was split during the drop and he was captured with four others the next morning, Bridgman-Evans later stating:

Owing to an electrical fault our containers were not dropped with us. We therefore had no arms. We were also dropped in the wrong place, so were observed coming down by the Italians and rounded up … that evening (13 Jul) my men and

I were chained together and taken to Nicosia where we spent the remainder of the night. On 14 Jul we were taken by truck to Randazzo and kept in the local police station until 0200hrs (15 Jul) when we were interrogated and condemned to death [WO 208/3316].

After rough treatment the men were transported to the Italian mainland. However, on the night of the 22–23rd Friedlander, Private Alan Sharman of the 21st Independent Parachute Company, Parachutist Mason, and Bridgeman-Evans managed to escape, the latter noting: 'we were challenged on one occasion by a sentry guarding a railway bridge. Sgt Lodge spoke to him in German and we got away with it' (WO 208/3316). Sharman's post-operation report confirms this bluff was solely 'thanks to the Sergeant's excellent German', later describing the group's noisy attempt to return to Sicily in a rowing boat that attracted the attention of local sentries:

A machine gun also opened fire but it was being fired at random. I estimate that there were some eight to ten men firing at us and the boat was shot repeatedly, so much that it became waterlogged and it was obviously sinking, so we dropped into the sea using the boat for cover, discussed the situation, and decided that we had no choice but to surrender [WO 218/175].

However, Friedlander escaped a second time, on this occasion walking the length of the Apennines to reach Allied lines on 23 December 1943. Flown to the UK he was hospitalised before rejoining 2nd SAS on 9 May 1944, later receiving a Mention in Despatches for his escape (*London Gazette* 15/06/44).

On the night of 12–13 August 1944 Friedlander parachuted into at a DZ near Le Mont in the Vosges département of eastern France as a member of Captain Henry Druce's recce party for OPERATION LOYTON. When the Maquis camp in which this group was staying was betrayed on the 17th, the men split into smaller parties to move to another base. Friedlander's group, under the command of 'Captain Goodfellow', the pseudonym of French agent Robert de Lessops, remained to cover the withdrawal before moving themselves. Heading south they found the area thick with German troops and the following day, the 18th, were engaged by an enemy patrol. The citation that accompanied the subsequent award of Freidlander's Distinguished Conduct Medal outlines subsequent events:

On 19th [*sic* – 18th] August (1944) Sgt Lodge found himself with a party of four surrounded by a large force of the enemy who gradually closed in on them. In the face of intense automatic and small arms fire, Sgt Lodge stood up and fired a Bren magazine at the enemy at a range of about 30 yards. This allowed the rest of the detachment to escape to temporary safety and inflicted a considerable number of casualties on the enemy. Later the same day the same situation arose and Sgt Lodge repeated the same courageous act. Finally the small party was extricated with only one casualty [see Parachutist Wally Hall's entry under Bayeux Memorial, France]. Both on this occasion and on past operations, which once included an escape from an enemy POW camp, this NCO has continually shown complete disregard for his personal safety, a fine offensive spirit and gifts of leadership much above the average. His work on every occasion has been in the highest tradition of the British Army [*London Gazette* 19/03/45].

Friedlander was last seen 'whilst running towards the village of Allarmont V465873' (2nd SAS' Casualty Report) 'near Le Jardin David above Moussey' (WO 311/84). A war crimes investigation team later established that the Germans, who had told Cure Pere Gassman that Friedlander had committed suicide rather than be captured, had brought his body to Moussey on 20 August where he was buried the following day. The Cure's brother, Abbé Gassman, found a wound in the head and bayonet wounds to the stomach. Their official finding was that Friedlander had been 'murdered by Germans near Moussey on or about 18/08/44' whilst Lt-Colonel Brian Franks, MC, the Commanding Officer of 2nd SAS, concluded; 'Sjt Lodge's case is a clear one in which he was bayonetted after capture and later shot.' Perhaps trying to cover his tracks SS-Hauptsturmführer Julius Gehrum, the Gestapo's Head of Counter Espionage and Counter Sabotage in Alsace, stated during the ensuing war crimes hearing: 'I do remember having heard from a member of the Wehrmacht, that a third Englishman [not Davis or Seymour] had shot himself, just below the edge of the wood, in the same area where the others were taken prisoner, as far as I know' (WO 309/717). The investigation team subsequently:

… proceeded to Offenburg to follow up statement given by innkeeper Arnould of Moussey, leading to the possible identity of a German soldier, who came to the inn of Madam Arnould and mentioned that he had killed an allied pilot

(Lodge). That soldier stated that he had been given five days leave for doing it. He is believed to be a member of a cycle unit stationed in Offenburg and operating in the Moussey area [WO 309/1626].

Meanwhile, a further report notes:

The presence of bayonet wounds are confirmed by Claude Pierre and [Charles] Laleve, the two civilians mentioned [who had been forced by the Germans to bring the body by cart to the cemetery at Moussey].

There is no evidence available that Sjt Lodge was held prisoner, and the only indications of the circumstances under which he was killed would be found in a pathologist's report … Abbe Gassman states that the Germans spoke of the suicide of the English soldier, and Julius Gehrum repeats the story.

It is however, hard to reconcile the theory of suicide with bayonet wounds in the stomach. Sjt Lodge carried a Bren gun and a Colt.45, so it should be easy to determine whether the wound in the head could have been inflicted by the latter weapon [WO 311/84].

However, the pathologist's report appears inconclusive:

The hands were loosely tied in front of the body by a piece of woven cord, looped over the battledress blouse cuffs …

On the right side of the head, immediately above and slightly in front of the root of the zygoma, there was an entrance hole 1.2 cm in diameter [0.45" equates to 11.4mm] with ragged oval area of loss of bone behind it, and small radiating fractures …

There was no positive evidence of injury to the abdomen, but decomposition rendered examination difficult … death was due to a bullet fired through the skull from the side, that there was no positive evidence of other injuries [WO 309/230].

Despite the body being found with hands tied, a crime could not be proved and no further action was taken. Major 'Bill' Barkworth, commander of the SAS War Crimes Investigation Team, signalled Franks:

Understand 21 AG [21st Army Group's] War Crimes Investigation [Team] began Lodge case but packed up because witness would not answer. Have found him and will obtain statement. Consider essential our war crimes people take these cases seriously as can find no indication anything done on other crimes discovered last year [WO 218/216].

Meanwhile, Abbé Gassman concluded:

When the body was brought to Moussey on the 20th of August which I am able to recognise was that of Sgt Lodge, and to which I have already referred, I noticed that in addition to a large wound in the head, there were also bayonet wounds in the stomach. When, in the summer of 1945, and English pathologist examined this body, he told me that there were no bayonet wounds. The body was completely decomposed when seen by the English pathologist, and I think he must have been a stupid man, because it must have been impossible then to have said definitely that there were no bayonet wounds [WO 311/84].

Despite this a note in the same file dated February 1946 records that: 'Major B [Barkworth] considers that there is a strong possibility of suicide as Lodge was a Jew (real name Friedlander) who had been taken PW before in Italy and escaped. He swore never to be taken again.' The action points in this file include; 'Major B to ask Lt Kuschener US pathologist to examine the body for traces of bayonet wounds.' It is not known whether this was done and, if so, what the result was.

Son of Dr Max and Bella Friedlaender of Vale Close, Strawberry Vale, Twickenham, Middlesex – Fiancé of Miss Win Lodge of Oldbury Hospital, near Tring, Hertfordshire (his SOE file records his next of kin address as 'c/o Mr H Lodge, Albion Road, Pitstone, Nr Leighton Buzzard, Beds').
Age 36.
Our sacrifice will not be futile if the survivors have learnt the lessons of this disastrous war (written by Friedlander in a letter to his father)
Grave 5.

Moyenmoutier Communal Cemetery

Moyenmoutier is located 17 kilometres north-east of Saint-Dié-des-Vosges in the Vosges département of Lorraine. The cemetery lies south of the town on the D424 Saint-Dié-des-Vosges to Lunéville road. GPS co-ordinates: Latitude 48.37621, Longitude 6.91288

Lieutenant James Lovitt SILLY [304006] Home Guard, Royal Artillery and 2nd SAS (2 Sqn)

Jim Silly was born on 30 January 1924 in the town of Berkhamsted, Hertfordshire. He attended Highgate Junior School from 1932 to 1933, King's School in Chester from 1933–34, and Berkhampstead School, where he was a member of the OTC, from 1934 to 1941. He went on to study Medicine at Guy's Hospital followed by a spell at Aberdeen University. Whilst living in Tunbridge Wells he joined the local 22nd Kent Battalion, Home Guard, before enlisting into the Royal Artillery at Maidstone in April 1942 (service number 1116934). Mobilised that December he was posted to the 25th Medium and Heavy Training Regiment and then to the 148th Training Brigade at Aberdeen. Having attended 123 OCTU at Wrotham, where he was described as 'painstaking and cheerful', he was appointed an emergency commission on New Year's Day 1944 and posted to the 53rd (Worcester Yeomanry) Airlanding Light Regiment at Bulford. Only one of the regiment's batteries was deployed for D-Day and six days later, on 12 June, Silly volunteered for 2nd SAS.

The following month, having been promoted to lieutenant, Silly deployed to France on Operation Defoe. Flown over to the Normandy beachhead on 19 July the Defoe group found itself without any real role, its commander, Captain 'Bunny' McGibbon-Lewis, therefore sending Silly's section to the Royals to carry out reconnaissance forward of their line (Operation Podo). En route their vehicle was put out of action by an 88mm shell and two of his men wounded. The remainder briefly operated with

the Royal Warwickshire Regiment that had evacuated the patrol's casualties until eventually recovering their vehicle and joining the Royals. Having taken part in several minor contacts alongside this unit's armoured cars Silly's party was withdrawn and returned to the UK in late August.

A month later, on the night of 21–22 September 1944, Silly and thirteen other men parachuted into a small clearing above the village of Moussey in the Vosges département of eastern France. Dropped with three Jeeps to reinforce OPERATION LOYTON they spent a considerable amount of time retrieving one of the vehicles from dense woodland. Over the following fortnight Silly made use of homemade plastic explosive mines, destroying two enemy staff cars and a three-ton German truck before being captured whilst exfiltrating towards Allied lines. Having crossed the River Meurthe he and three men were taken in by a forest guard, René Folcher, and given shelter in the loft of his lodge at La Bourgonce. They then moved north-west, Corporal Ian Larley later outlining what followed:

While coming through the lines with Lieut Silly, Herbert and Lewis on 11 Oct 44, the party was ambushed and we were surrounded. We scattered to cover and Herbert was wounded [Parachutist Herbert was one of those previously wounded on OPERATION PODO]. He and I reached a thicket where I bandaged him up, and we moved about in the wood avoiding the enemy who were searching the area for two–three hours afterwards. The party was armed with three Colts [semi-automatic side arms] and I heard no firing from them after scattering. Lewis had a Colt which he handed to Lt Silly. The last point at which I saw Lt Silly and Lewis was at approx V 211811 north of Bazien [WO 361/716].

Silly was subsequently identified as having being held at Schirmeck Concentration Camp. Mademoiselle Hertenberger, a secretary at the camp, was definite that Silly was one of three English prisoners who were kept in the women's cells, the other two being without doubt Parachutists Selwyn Brown and Donald Lewis:

I can remember with certainty about the middle of October to have seen a soldier dressed in khaki standing one afternoon outside the Kommandantur [HQ] of the camp. There were two or three others dressed in khaki with him and a number of French. I am prepared to state that this man in khaki to whom I have referred was certainly the same as the one whose photograph has been shown to me marked Lieutenant Silly. I remember distinctly his dark black hair and glasses [WO 309/233].

The SAS War Crimes Investigation Team's 'Interim Report' contains a statement made by Victor Launay of Harcholet who positively identified Silly as being at his house immediately before Brown and Lewis were murdered on 16 October (WO 218/209). He recognised a photograph of Silly during cross-examination: 'Yes, he was handcuffed and he had a peak cap … Yes, he wore glasses. I gave him an apple and he put it to his mouth while holding both wrists together. That is when I saw him handcuffed' (WO 219/5069). At a subsequent court of inquiry Launay declared that he had recognised Silly from a previous meeting, identifying him by his glasses, peaked cap and rank, and noted that Silly, along with an unknown Frenchman and one other parachutist were interrogated inside the ruins of the Quirin house. Crucially he stated that the fire was lit in the outhouse before the men were led into it and that Silly was then substituted for another parachutist (see Brown's entry under Moussey Churchyard, France, for full details of this case).

SS-Oberscharführer Horst Gaede, a driver with the Kommando Ernst, confirmed that Silly was with two others: 'I saw with Kommando Wenger three parachutists among whom, as far as I remember, also was Lieutenant Silly. I heard on that occasion that these three parachutists had been ambushed by the Wehrmacht while swimming across a river' (WO 311/87). Whilst attempting to cover his tracks Hauptsturmführer Erich Wenger, the Kommando's leader, later highlighted his true intent: 'Should it be asserted that in one case I ordered two men to be shot before the eyes of the lieutenant in order to induce him to make statements, I can only declare that I did not give such an order. As a soldier I should never

113

have done so and from the criminological point of view this would have been absurd' (WO 311/87). One of his men, Untersturmführer Gerhard Preil, was in little doubt:

> About the middle of October 1944 Hstuf Wenger gave orders to me and to the competent official Schneider, to take a number of prisoners away from Étival in a gasogene vehicle and to shoot them on the way. Hstuf Wenger wished that the English officer should be present with Schneider at the execution, so that Schneider should have easier work at subsequent interrogations and might be able to obtain better statements …
>
> On the lorry there were besides those entrusted with the task and the members of the Wachkompanie, the following prisoners who had been kept in Étival: - one young French civilian, two Englishmen in uniform and one English officer. The above-mentioned officer was wearing an English uniform, a peaked cap and glasses. In March 1946, I recognised him when I was shown a picture by Major Barkworth which was marked 'Lieutenant Silly'. I particularly noticed him on account of his dark complexion and dark hair. The two other Englishmen in uniform were of medium height and wore berets of which I cannot now remember the colour exactly. The fourth was a French civilian of small build.
>
> Before we left Hstuf Wenger gave further instructions that if possible we should leave no traces of the execution. We then drove through La Petite-Raon in the direction of Belval and on account of the falling off of the performance of the lorry, we had to leave it in the wood and continued on foot with the prisoners to a point in the hill slope above the house which had already been burned down. We had marched through the wood in the direction of Moussey Le Harcholet for about twenty–thirty minutes according to my estimate …
>
> We left this farmhouse and walked down to the above-mentioned second ruin and ordered the three prisoners to go into the wooden shed and sit down. Meanwhile Schneider went with the English officer to one side in the direction of the house of the old couple. Since we had been instructed to remove all traces as far as possible, several bundles of straw were brought along subsequently.
>
> In the wooden shed the three prisoners had to sit on a rafter but Schneider stayed with the English officer a little way off the house, while I with three or four members of the Wachkompanie remained standing before the door of the wooden shed. The prisoners were sitting with their back to the entrance of the wooden shed.
>
> In accordance with my order to fire, the NCOs of the Wachkompanie discharged their machine pistols in the direction of the prisoners. (According to my memory there were three NCOs of which one was Unterscharführer Gimbel). Two machine pistols did not work and only the third fired.
>
> The fire extended and burned down the shed, but as the corpses therein were not consumed, some hand grenades were thrown into the shed, but as some charred remains of bodies still showed within the ashes, Gimbel threw an egg grenade in the direction of these remains. The explosion did not occur immediately and I went back to the farm-house to explain to the inhabitants that it would not be advisable to go to the house during the next hour since, a hand grenade had not exploded. After we left the farm-house, we made for, with members of the Wachkompanie towards the house of the old couple in order to return to the lorry. On the way we heard the explosion go off behind us. After this we went back with the English officer to the truck and drove back to Étival via Moussey. Schneider and I reported to Wenger that the order had been carried out [WO 309/359].

However, at least one file partly refutes Preil's statement that Silly was witness to the actual murders:

> The last part of the journey was made on foot through the woods. Silly was questioned by Schneider as to where SAS men had sheltered in the area of the small village of Le Harcholet and pointed out a wood shed attached to a ruined house. Schneider and one man of the Wachkompanie then took Silly back along the same track through the woods towards the lorry, while the others proceeded with preparations for the execution. This departure of Schneider with Silly is borne out by the evidence of the French civilian witnesses who observed a prisoner being led up the hill before the execution was begun [WO 309/359].

Whatever the case Silly, no doubt aware of the fate of his comrades, was taken back to the Kommando Wenger's requisitioned schoolhouse at Étival where he was seen by a local man, Maurice Simon of Clairfontaine:

> I and my father were arrested by the Gestapo on the 19th October 1944, taken to their house at Étival, and I was placed in the cellar. Here I saw some other French prisoners and an English parachutist lieutenant who told me that he had been arrested some ten or fifteen days before in the Bois de la Chipotte. He said he had no illusions about what was going to happen to him, and asked me to keep his name and address. He wrote this on a piece of newspaper which I hid in the ventilator of the cellar. I can remember that his name was Silly, and that part of his address was Greenway. I left the same day, towards evening, for St Die and then Schirmeck. I last saw Silly in the cells with six Frenchmen, also prisoners [WO 311/87].

Yvette Demetz, one of two traitorous French sisters associated with the Kommando, alluded to Silly's fate:

> During the time Kommando Wenger was at Étival in October 1944, I took food to an English prisoner in the cellar. He had dark hair and wore glasses. I can state with certainty that he is the same as the one whose photograph marked Lieut Silly, which has been shown to me. I remember that he was taken away in a lorry with some Frenchmen [WO 311/87].

SS-Oberscharführer Erich Wild, one of Wenger's men, took up the narrative:

> When we arrived at the house behind the saw mill [at Saint-Prayel] the prisoners were lying shot before a pile of wood and Gimbel and the remaining men of the Wachkompanie were about to carry the dead bodies into the house. I could not see who fired the shots, but I heard from Gimbel himself that he as well as two other men of the Wachkompanie had shot the prisoners simultaneously with machine pistols.
> The corpses were then burnt in the sawmill by the Wachkompanie. As I heard later on, the ruins of the sawmill were finally blown up by the Wachkompanie with hand grenades on the following day, but I cannot state who told me this [WO 311/87].

That December the French discovered a number of badly burnt bodies under the charred remains of the Barodet forest house. A local GP, Dr Thomassin, to who Simon had given the retrieved piece of newspaper with Silly's address, was called to identify the remains. These were so badly burnt he was unable to determine the cause of death. He did, however, recover a pair of steel rimmed glasses and a spectacle case, both thought to have belonged to Silly, that he forwarded to the French authorities (WO 309/2243 and WO 311/87). Silly's remains, and those of the murdered Resistance fighters, were buried in a communal grave:

> The burial took place at Moyenmoutier on Monday 11th December 1944 in the presence of the FFI of Moyenmoutier [Forces Françaises de l'Intérieur – the Resistance]. M. Gaston Gerard, the deputy Mayor, spoke of the heroic and hidden patriotism of the poor martyrs. Two coffins were sufficient for so many victims. In sum, six men, perhaps more [later believed to be eleven members of the Resistance, nine of which were forest guards, and Silly], guilty of having loved their country more than their lives, more than their loved ones, were martyred by the Germans, doubtless shot, covered with some corrosive liquid, then burnt and finally left under a heap of rubbish without burial [WO 311/87].

One of those murdered alongside Silly was René Folcher who had sheltered him and his men just before capture. Another was later identified as Head of Water and Forestry of Saint-Benoît-la-Chipotte, Paul Gerard, who had given his bicycle to a member of the Regiment making his way towards Allied lines.

In August 1945 the War Office wrote to Lt-Colonel Brian Franks, DSO, MC, the Commanding Officer of 2nd SAS: 'As regards Lt Silly; we have accepted the grave as his and are recording him as "killed in action on or shortly after 22nd October 1944". We are also informing next of kin that available evidence shows that he was shot after capture.' That July Silly's mother, having already been informed that he was missing believed captured, had received a letter from Franks who broke the news that her son's remains had been found and outlined his final days:

> It was an uncomfortable life; the weather was very cold and we were not often able to sleep under a roof. I shall never forget your son's cheerfulness under these conditions and how much more than anyone else he refused to let the hardness of the life lower his spirits or diminish his eagerness for battle. He went out on several raiding parties and acquitted himself gallantly.
> Towards mid-October our position in the Vosges was no longer tenable, mainly because all the parachute grounds were occupied by the Germans and we had no means of obtaining supplies, so I decided that we must cross over to the American Seventh Army lines. This was not very easy, as the German line was fairly closely held. A lot depended on luck … I sent one of my officers to the Vosges after the liberation in order to find out what had become of him. He discovered that James had been brought back to Moussey in order to identify a French farmer who had helped him. I am proud to say that although he was threatened he said nothing to compromise his benefactor. That was what I would have expected of him, but I know how hard it can be to maintain strength of mind when one is so helpless …
> I cannot express to you how shocked I am at the tragedy which has befallen you, and robbed us of one of our most courageous young men. James will always be remembered in this Regiment as an example of what a young officer should be in action, thoughtful for his men and the leader in bravery.

Simon later wrote to Mrs Silly from France describing how her son had:

> … assured me that the Germans were going to shoot him and it was then that he asked me to take your address which he wrote on a piece of newspaper and which I hid in the ventilator of the cellar where we were imprisoned …
> I am happy to tell you that your son contemplated his sad end with calmness and great courage. You can be proud of him. He was a brave soldier and I have nothing but admiration for him.

Members of the Kommando Wenger were also concerned in the murders of Signalman 'Jock' Johnston ('Etival Case' – see his entry within this volume under Groesbeek Memorial, Netherlands), of Parachutist Frederick Puttick ('Belval Case' – see his entry under Groesbeek Memorial), of Parachutists Selwyn Brown and Donald Lewis ('Harcholet Case' – see their entries under Moussey Churchyard, France), and of Sergeant Michael Fitzpatrick, Lance-corporal Jack Elliott and Parachutist John Conway ('Pexonne Case' – see their entries under Moussey Churchyard).

Investigations concluded that those implicated in Silly's murder ('Moyenmoutier Case') were SS-Untersturmführer Gerhard Preil, SS-Oberscharführer Erich Wild, SS-Hauptscharführer Arnold Schneider, SS-Sturmscharführer Ferdinand Halla, SS-Sturmscharführer Franz Rosenbaum (believed to have been killed fighting in Berlin during the last days of the Reich), Hauptscharführer Willi Hess, Unterscharführers Wilhelm Gimbel, Zerves and Bettendorf, and Frenchmen Rene Louvrier and Bobby van Houtte. It seems that insufficient numbers were traced to ensure solid convictions. Wenger, who led the Kommando, appears to have assumed an alias in a prison camp after his interrogation and to have subsequently been released in error. In 1950 he joined the West German Federal Government under a false name but four years later resumed his identity and joined the country's intelligence service. He died as a retired officer in 1978.

Son of Benjamin and Frances Silly (née Lovitt) of Greenway, Berkhamsted, Hertfordshire – His father, an Australian by birth and RAF Air Commodore who had won an MC and DFC in the First World War serving with the Royal Artillery and Royal Flying Corps, died, aged 50, during December 1943 in a Japanese POW camp on Formosa. He is buried at Sai Wan War Cemetery, Hong Kong.
Age 20.
Splendid you passed, O valiant heart, into the light that shall never fade
Also commemorated on the Moyenmoutier Resistance Memorial at Saint-Prayel (that confuses his mother's address given, incorrectly recording his middle name as 'Grenwley'), at the Barodet Scierie Memorial at Saint-Prayel, on Berkhamsted's war memorial, and within the Phantom Memorial Garden, National Memorial Arboretum, Alrewas.

OSSUN COMMUNAL CEMETERY

Ossun is located 11 kilometres south-west of Tarbes in the Hautes-Pyrénées département of south-west France. The cemetery lies to the east of the village on the junction of rue Georges Guynemer and Impasse Sarthou. GPS co-ordinates: Latitude 41.181909, Longitude -0.022624

LANCE-CORPORAL ALBERT ÉDOUARD <u>MENGINOU</u> [35766] ARMÉE DE L'AIR, AND 2ᴱ RÉGIMENT DE CHASSEURS PARACHUTISTES (4TH SAS) ATT 1ST SAS (D SQN)

Albert Menginou was born on 4 February 1915 in the shadow of the Pyrenees at Ossun in southern France, his mother dying three years later. Having served as a pre-war regular in the air force at Pau he fought against the German invasion of May 1940 before returning to his hometown after his country's surrender. Two years later, on 1 May 1942, he set off for Spain intending to reach Gibraltar to join the Free French. Remarking in his journal that his sole purpose was 'to do his duty' he passed through Andorra and reported to the British Embassy in Madrid where he was hidden for three months in a safe house. In August he set off for Lisbon but was arrested at Badajoz just short of the Portuguese border. Jailed for a month he claimed that he was a British citizen and as a result was interned at the infamous camp at Miranda del Oro from late September until late May 1943 when he was released under the alias of 'Monin'. Arriving in the UK he joined the Forces françaises libres (FFL) in London that June, qualified as a parachutist at Ringway during July, and joined the 2ᵉ Régiment de chasseurs parachutistes at the beginning of 1944. This was known within the SAS Brigade that it joined as 4th (French) SAS. He was subsequently posted to 1st SAS as an interpreter that April.

Menginou parachuted into OPERATION GAIN in the early hours of 17 June 1944 as a member of Major Ian Fenwick's party. He was killed in action at Chambon-la-Forêt on 7 August when Fenwick's Jeep was ambushed (see Fenwick's entry under Chambon-la-Forêt Communal Cemetery, France, for full details). Bernard Bertrand, a member of the local Maquis, stated at the ensuing court of inquiry that:

> Just before he [Fenwick] left a few members of the FFI [the Resistance], who were also hiding in the same spot, begged Major Fenwick and those that wanted to go along with him, not to go to Chambon-la-Forêt since there were many SS in the village. Major Fenwick and his men decided to go nevertheless. At the entrance to the village the Boches opened fire on the Jeep and the major was instantly killed. At that moment Parachutist [sic] Menginou attempted to escape but he was also killed with machine-gun fire. The bodies were picked up that same night and taken to the village hall. Two days later they were buried by the Mayor of Chambon-la-Forêt, Monsieur Louis Trembleau, in the cemetery in presence of two or three thousand people in honour of Major Fenwick and of Parachutist Menginou [TS 26/853].

Captain Cecil Riding, who subsequently took command of GAIN, reported that: 'We were fortunate to visit the graves of Major Fenwick, Lance-corporal Menginou, Troopers Packman and Ion, and the graves were well cared for. The local photographer is arranging to have them photographed and when conditions permit they will be sent to the Regiment' (see entries for Privates Les Packman and John Ion under Chilleurs-aux-Bois Communal Cemetery, France). Menginou's remains were later reinterred into his family plot at their current location.

Son of Francois and Maria Menginou (née Baget) of Ossun – Brother of Édouard Menginou-Bouette.
Age 29.
When walking towards the centre of the cemetery from the Impasse Sarthou entrance the Menginou family grave is found on the left after approximately 50 metres. Also commemorated on the SAS Brigade Memorial at Sennecey-le-Grand and on a memorial in Chambon-la-Forêt near to where he was killed. This refers to him as 'le parachutiste francais Menginou A du 1st SAS' whilst Sergeant Bill Duffy, who was captured in the ambush, referred to him as 'L/Cpl Menginou (attached to D Squadron from 4th French Parachute Battalion).' Also commemorated by a road named after him at Ossun.

RANVILLE WAR CEMETERY

Ranville was the first village to be liberated in France, shortly after the bridge over the Caen Canal had been captured intact in the early hours of 6 June 1944. During these opening moments of D-Day troops of the British 6th Airborne Division landed in the surrounding area, either by parachute or glider. The war cemetery and the adjoining churchyard are the final resting place to many casualties of this period.

The churchyard, which was used for burials during the fighting, contains forty-seven Commonwealth graves, one of which is unidentified. After the war the site was extended, in the form of the war cemetery, to concentrate graves from local battlefields. This now contains 2,235 Commonwealth burials, of which ninety-seven are unidentified. In addition there are 330 German graves and a handful of other nationalities.

Ranville is located approximately 10 kilometres north-east of Caen in the Calvados département of Basse-Normandie. The cemetery lies on the rue des Airbornes next to Ranville Church. GPS co-ordinates: Latitude 49.23113, Longitude -0.25776

Lieutenant Joseph Maurice ROUSSEAU [Unknown S/N] Régiment Montmagny, Régiment de la Chaudiére, 1st Canadian Parachute Battalion and 2nd SAS (A Sqn)

Joseph Maurice Rousseau was born in Montreal on 16 February 1919 as one of twelve sons and two daughters. His family was well known in its hometown of Montmagny near Quebec City and it was here that he attended The College and served in the ranks of the reserve Régiment Montmagny. He entered the Royal Military College in Kingston in 1938, graduating alongside his younger brother, Joseph Philippe, in 1940. Both joined the Régiment de la Chaudière that December. The following February he was promoted to lieutenant and in July 1941 embarked for the UK. Arriving in Scotland he was granted a short period of leave before being attached to London District for anti-aircraft training. Throughout 1942 he attended further courses and in March 1943 was posted to No.6 Canadian Infantry Reinforcement Unit as an instructor.

In August 1943 Rousseau married Agnes Hornby at Preston, was promoted to acting captain, and posted, again as an instructor, to the Régiment de la Chaudière's training company. That November he transferred to the 1st Canadian Parachute Battalion, reverting to the rank of lieutenant in order to do so. He qualified as a parachutist at No.1 PTS Ringway on Christmas Eve and was posted to the battalion's training company in February 1944. His younger brother, Joseph Philippe, who had soon followed him into the battalion, subsequently took command of his old platoon but was killed in action on D-Day+1. Joseph Maurice subsequently volunteered for 2nd SAS on 5 September 1944 in the hope of seeing action. He did not have to wait long being given command of an independent operation to the north of Operation Loyton in eastern France within a few days. His party was parachuted blind (that is, without an arranged reception committee) into a DZ near Réchicourt-le-Château, east of the Forêt de Réchicourt, from only 300 feet on the night of 9–10 September. The patrol was truly international consisting of two Britons, one German, six French, and Rousseau the Canadian, all serving within 2nd SAS. Their objective was to disrupt traffic on the Nancy–Saarburg railway line and the Luneville–Blamont–Saarburg road. Although the stick was separated on the drop, and the railway found to have already been blown by the Germans, the men regrouped and fought alongside the advancing US 2nd Cavalry Regiment. On 20 September, during one such action, Rousseau and Lance-corporal Paul Galmard, 3rd (French) SAS attached to 2nd SAS, became separated from the remainder of the patrol, Lance-corporal Marcel Maziere recalling:

> The Germans began to arrive in strength. Lieut Rousseau decided to make for the wood of Igney. As we entered it at Q325046 there was a shot, and Centelle fell. The Lieutenant and Galmard went to the right and I to the left. It was the last time that I saw them. I returned to the village of Igney and hid with some civilians. Three days later they told me that Lieut Rousseau had been taken prisoner the same day and shot at Avricourt, Q315061, and that Galmard had been shot at Foulcrey, Q352048. The night after he was wounded, Centelle reached a farm where he was looked after [WO 361/716].

Whilst it later became apparent that Galmard had evaded capture it seems likely that Rousseau died of his wounds, the SAS War Crimes Investigation Team's 'Interim Report' concluding:

> According to Monsieur Verdanal of Igney and other sources, he [Rousseau] was severely wounded in the skirmish at Igney, subsequently died, and was buried at the German cemetery at Avricourt [according to CWGC records

this was Igney Communal Cemetery]. There is a grave in that place marked 'Canadian Officer', and the keeper of the cemetery states that the officer concerned was buried about the middle of September. A member of Monsieur Verdanal's family stated that the Germans had indicated the grave of Lieut Rousseau in this manner [WO 218/209].

Son of Lacasse and Gabrielle Rousseau of Montreal, Province of Quebec – Husband of Agnes Rousseau of Montreal.
Age 25.
Ne a Montreal Canada. Epoux d'Agnes Hornby. Mort a Igney Meurthe-et-Moselle
Grave V.A.G.7. Joseph Maurice was reinterred next to his brother, Joseph Philippe, on 11 December 1945. They are seen together at the beginning of this entry whilst at Down Ampney transit camp before D-Day, Joseph Maurice being on right. He is also commemorated on Igney's war memorial.

RECEY-SUR-OURCE COMMUNAL CEMETERY

Recey-sur-Ource is located 52 kilometres north-north-west of Dijon in the Côte-d'Or département of Bourgogne. The cemetery lies west of the village on the road to Leuglay. GPS co-ordinates: Latitude 47.78193, Longitude 4.85634

PRIVATE JOACHIM **KALKSTEIN** [BNA/13809220] FRENCH FOREIGN LEGION, PIONEER CORPS AND 2ND SAS (C SQN)

Jo Kalkstein was by nationality a Polish Jew, yet born in Berlin on 21 July 1920 to a Polish father and German mother. Whilst the family ran a shoe shop, Jo secured a welding apprenticeship, although with the rise of Nazi anti-Semitism life was about to change dramatically. By 1937 he had already escaped, briefly passing through England where he had stayed with a cousin on the Abramowicz side of the family. Joining his sister in Palestine that year he had attested into the Palestinian Police in 1938 after a brief association with Betar, a revisionist Zionist youth movement that aimed at securing a Jewish state. However, after the outbreak of war he disembarked at Agde near Marseille in late 1939, enlisting into the exiled Czech Army that November under the alias 'Samuel Stern'. Having aged himself by a year he stated he had been born at Kezmorak in Slovakia. Despite the fact that he spoke no Czech, nor possessed any relevant documentation, it was five days before he was discovered and handed over to the French authorities. He enlisted into the French Foreign Legion with five other Jews the same day, displaced men often doing so to escape French internment camps. However, on reaching Vichy-held North Africa they were employed on tasks verging on hard labour and were treated almost as prisoners.

After Operation Torch, the November 1942 Allied landings in the region, a process was established that enabled ex-Legionnaires to volunteer for the British Army's Pioneer Corps. HS 3/50, an SOE report outlining the possibility of recruiting displaced persons in North Africa, noted that in late January 1943 Kalkstein was at Berroughia Internment Camp in Algeria: 'This is a small camp principally for either ex-Foreign Legion personnel who have no country to return to and who are maintained free and kept under slight surveillance, or sick prisoners from other camps.' The report earmarked Kalkstein for possible recruitment, noting: 'Age 22. 1yr in special police in Palestine. Czech Legion [*sic*] Soldat 2me Cl. Electrician. Speaks German like a native. Fair French.'

Kalkstein subsequently enlisted into 337 (Alien) Company, Pioneer Corps, at Hussein Dey, Algiers, in February 1943. He spent much of the last quarter of the year in military hospitals, in particular with a knee injury, and is believed to have volunteered for 2nd SAS soon after being discharged on 10 January 1944. His service record states the transfer took place officially on 28 March 1944 having returned to the UK with the Regiment a few days before. During pre-deployment training at the beginning of June he broke his troublesome patella but recovered quickly, 2nd SAS recording him at this time under his pseudonym '13809220 Pct Garcon J'.

Kalkstein was killed in action on 27 August 1944 when his parachute failed to open on jumping into the Burgundy region of eastern France for Operation Hardy. His former squadron commander, Roy Farran, DSO, MC**, later wrote:

> An extra plane was running in to drop two more drivers – Corporal ['Knocker'] West and Kalkstein, a little Polish Jew who had been with me on several operations. It was a dark night and although we could only see one parachute in the air, we were not particularly worried at first. I heard a loud thud on the ground and presumed that one of their leg bags had broken away [Kalkstein was carrying a heavy load of explosive]. When West came up to report that Kalkstein had jumped before him, I became a little anxious. We shouted his name all over the field but there was no reply. When dawn came they found his body under the trees. Acid had eaten through his static line in the Halifax and his parachute was not pulled out of the envelope. His little figure was lying, almost undamaged, as if he were asleep on his arms under the trees. How we cursed the inefficient maintenance of some 'penguin' in England who had committed murder by rank idleness [*Winged Dagger: Adventures on Special Service*, by Roy Farran].

The post-operation report confirms: 'Kalkstein's static line broke, it gave the appearance of having been rotted by acid' (WO 219/2401). He was buried the next day 'with 500 people in attendance', William 'Joe' Cunningham of 2nd SAS later recalling:

> This man pestered the CO almost every day: 'Sir, I came not to wear the red headdress, which may please the eye, but, to parachute and fight against the Germans who have caused me to leave my home and country. I am a Jew and I have a score to settle. May I go today?' [Courtesy of William Oakes].

Son of Maximillian and Selma Kalkstein whose daughter later wrote that they had been: 'thrown out of Germany and lived in Russia in terrible conditions. My father died in Russia of pneumonia and my mother emmigrated to Israel in 1947' – Younger brother of Ursel of Hazorea Kibbutz, Israel, where their mother died, and twin of Norbert who settled in New Zealand.
Age 24.
In memory of our brother, born in Berlin 21st July 1920, Ursel and Norbert
Grave 1.9. Farran added: 'Kalkstein was buried with full military honours in the tiny churchyard [on the night of 28 August 1944], but I have since wondered whether the Jewish faith would be quite in agreement with the ceremony' (*Winged Dagger*). In the 1990s William Oakes, the son of Freddie Oakes of 2nd SAS, with the help of the Jewish Telegraph successfully contacted Kalkstein's sister and drafted a letter for her to request that the CWGC change his headstone for one engraved with the Star of David. The CWGC acted very quickly to do so, a dedication ceremony being held in 1999.

ROM COMMUNAL CEMETERY

Those members of B Squadron, 1st SAS, buried here were captured on 3 July 1944 during OPERATION BULBASKET. *That morning their camp within the Forêt de Verrières was attacked by a composite force, the main element of which came from the 17th SS Panzergrenadier Division. The thirty SAS prisoners were subsequently murdered on 7 July in the Bois de Guron within the Forêt de Saint-Sauvant by the recce squadron of the 158th Division.*

On 17 December 1944 local hunters discovered three mass graves whilst investigating an area in which they believed wild boar had been rooting. The BULBASKET *men were duly exhumed and initial autopsies conducted in situ. Their remains were placed in coffins and taken to nearby Rom where they lay in state in the Mairie until reinterred in the village cemetery on the 23rd. Lieutenant Lincoln Bundy, a Mustang pilot of 486th Squadron, 352nd Fighter Group, United States Army Air Force, was also buried here. He had been shot down and was making his way to Spain when captured and murdered alongside the SAS. Their forest graves are now signposted and marked by stones, just to the rear of the Saint-Sauvant Memorial that commemorates the men.*

A memorial stone within the cemetery honours Corporal 'Reggie' Williams and Parachutists Joe Ogg and Sam Pascoe who were wounded in the attack on the Verrières Camp and subsequently taken prisoner. Treated at a hospital in Poitiers they were reportedly given lethal injections by Hauptmann Dr Georg Hesterberg and have no known graves (see their entries under Bayeux War Memorial, France, for full details).

Rom is located 44 kilometres east of Niort and 5 kilometres west of Couhé-Verac in the Deux-Sèvres département of Poitou-Charentes. The cemetery lies 200 metres south of the village on the rue des Martyrs de Guron. GPS co-ordinates: Latitude 46.29089, Longitude 0.11468

PRIVATE EDWARD YOUNG **ADAMSON** [4399392] GREEN HOWARDS, EAST YORKSHIRE REGIMENT AND 1ST SAS (B SQN)

Eddie Adamson was born on 6 April 1922 in the village of Choppington, Northumberland. Enlisting into the Green Howards in January 1942 he was posted to its Cleethorpes training centre before joining the 11th Battalion. He disembarked in the Middle East in March 1943 as part of a reinforcement draft and was subsequently transferred to the East Yorkshire Regiment soon after. His service record notes that he volunteered for the Special Raiding Squadron (1st SAS) on 29 August 1943 whilst it was on Sicily and it therefore seems likely that he had previously landed near Avola with the 5th Battalion, East Yorkshires, on 10 July during OPERATION HUSKY. This saw fierce fighting against German paratroops before becoming the first British battalion to enter Messina.

Adamson, a trained signaller, landed at Bagnara on the toe of mainland Italy on 4 September 1943 during OPERATION BAYTOWN. Having captured the town after fierce fighting, the SRS sailed from port to port around to the Adriatic, eventually landing behind enemy lines at Termoli in the early hours of 3 October. Here it pushed down towards the River Biferno to hold two bridges and a road junction that were key to the advancing 78th Division. Although soon relieved, casualties were high (see multiple entries under Sangro River War Cemetery, Italy, Volume II).

The SRS returned to the UK at the beginning of January 1944 and was reconstituted as 1st SAS. That May Adamson attended parachute course 114A at No.1 PTS Ringway where his instructor noted: 'jumped well. Willing worker, morale high.' On qualifying he sent his girlfriend, Jean Dalglish of Darvel where the Regiment was based, a set of sweetheart wings. The couple shared the same unusual middle name, Adamson giving Dalglish the photo seen here that had been taken in Molfetta, Italy. She later recalled that when the SAS Brigade moved to holding camps in southern England prior to D-Day she waved him off for the last time at Darvel train station (personal interview, 2010).

Adamson parachuted into central France in the early hours of 8 June 1944 for OPERATION BULBASKET as a member of a nine-man stick under the command of Lieutenant 'Twm' Stephens (see his entry under Verrières Communal Cemetery, France). Landing on a DZ north of Bouesse in the Indre département the men were met by their commander Captain John Tonkin, who had jumped into the area on the 6th.

The following day Adamson's party was transported westwards by truck, a decision then being made to concentrate still farther west in order to attack the railway line north and south of Poitiers.

Adamson was captured on 3 July 1944 when the BULBASKET camp within the Forêt de Verrières was attacked. He was subsequently murdered in the Bois de Guron within the Forêt de Saint-Sauvant on the 7th (see Lieutenant Richard Crisp's entry within this section for full details).

Only son of Stephen and Margaret Adamson (née Robertson) of South Parade, Choppington, Northumberland.
Age 22.
In memory there is no death
Row 1, graves 1–16. Also commemorated on the Saint-Sauvant Forest Memorial, on war memorials at Scotland Gate and Guide Post in the Choppington area, and within St Paul's Church in Choppington itself.

Corporal William Watt ALLAN MM [2031580] Royal Engineers, Royal Army Medical Corps Att SRS and 1st SAS (HQ Sqn)

Bill Allan was born in early 1916 at Heaton in Newcastle upon Tyne as the third of four children whose mother died in 1928. Having worked for the Post Office he moved to Elstree in Hertfordshire to drive lorries. Whilst there he joined the Royal Engineers (TA) in September 1933, adding two years to his age to do so. He transferred to join his brother in the regular Royal Army Medical Corps later that year. By January 1936 he was serving in Egypt with the 4th Field Ambulance, his sibling stationed close by. At the outbreak of war he was with No.7 Casualty Clearing Station, being promoted to lance-corporal in December 1941 and to corporal the following May. He returned to London some time during the second half of 1942, marrying Rose Reading whilst there. Shortly after returning overseas her family was bombed out and moved down to Dover.

By March 1943 Allan had returned to No.7 Casualty Clearing Station and was serving in Iraq as a member of Paiforce. Soon after he volunteered for the Special Raiding Squadron (1st SAS). Just after the war *The People* reported that he had fought in North Africa and Sicily, being wounded in Italy. The SRS War Diary confirms that a 'Pct Allan' was wounded on 10 July 1943 during the assault on the second gun emplacement at Capo Murro di Porco at the forefront of the invasion of Sicily (Operation Husky). It also notes that 'Cpl Allen [*sic*] RAMC' was wounded on 5 October at Termoli when a shell hit one of the unit's trucks (see multiple entries under Sangro River War Cemetery, Italy, Volume II, for details of this incident). Having been hospitalised he returned to the SRS at the beginning of December.

On its return to the UK in January 1944 the SRS was reconstituted as 1st SAS, Allan being posted to HQ Squadron and attending parachute course 105 at No.1 PTS Ringway during March. Here his instructor noted: 'jumped well, morale good, is very keen'. Attached to B Squadron, he subsequently parachuted into a DZ near the farm of Primo la Coupe, close to la Font d'Usson and south of Poitiers in western France, on the night of 17–18 June 1944. Dropped to a reception party along with Sergeant Bob Heavens, Parachutists Henry Mullen and David Gray, and four Jeeps, the group made contact with the enemy on leaving the area. In the rush to do so a Jeep overturned, crushing Trooper A. O'Neill's hand. Having made their escape Allan decided that to save O'Neill's arm he would have to amputate the two middle fingers and did so using scissors whilst others held the hand behind O'Neill's head so he could not watch. A cigarette was his only anaesthetic. Although Allan kept him under strict observation he was not happy with the result and men were sent to fetch a doctor who subsequently took O'Neill into care (see entries for Heavens, Mullen and Gray within this section).

Allan, clearly wearing a Red Cross armband, treated wounded during and after the attack on the SAS camp within the Forêt de Verrières on 3 July. Having been taken prisoner he was murdered in the Bois de Guron within the Forêt de Saint-Sauvant on the 7th (see Lieutenant Richard Crisp's entry for full details). Before being shot he is believed to have tried to reason with the Germans, unsuccessfully, over the fate of Lieutenant Lincoln Bundy, a downed USAAF pilot, who had also been captured whilst sheltering with the SAS party. Allan's Military Medal was recommended by Captain John Tonkin, the commander of Bulbasket, who, along with the operation's other survivors, was evacuated to the UK before the fate of those captured was confirmed. Although it has not proved possible to trace the citation, contemporary newspaper clippings suggest the medal was awarded primarily for his care of O'Neill (No.37466, *London Gazette* 12/02/46, Supplement 14/02/46). Writing to Allan's sister, O'Neill himself

described how 'for forty-eight hours he never left my side except to make tea for me, and changed dressing after dressing every thirty minutes'. His wife and 2-year-old daughter received the medal from the King at Buckingham Palace on 3 December 1946, *The People* confirming:

> Without any surgical instruments Bill amputated three [*sic*] fingers, then for two days stayed beside the wounded man, changing dressings every thirty minutes, making tea, finding a joke, offering hope. He didn't have time to sleep or eat.

Allan's remains were identified by his issued discs.

Son of John and Annie Allan (née Watt) – Husband of Rose Allan of Buckland Avenue, Dover – Father of Ann Allan born in January 1945 – Brother of Barbara, John and Margaret.
Age 29.
No inscription.
Row 2, grave 29. Also commemorated on the Saint-Sauvant Forest Memorial.

Private Alan George <u>Ashley</u> [5729859] Dorsetshire Regiment, Auxiliary Units and 1st SAS (B Sqn)

Alan Ashley was born at Balby in Doncaster on 25 January 1920. His brother, Philip, later noted that he was 'one of a close family of four children – two sisters, one two years older and the other a year younger, and myself, eight years younger' (personal correspondence, 2010). In 1928 the family moved to Weston-super-Mare, Somerset, and on leaving Weston Grammar School, Ashley trained in London as a Sainsbury's butcher. He was subsequently employed in Bath by the high-class store Cater, Stoffel and Forte, at the same time playing rugby for the Old Westonians. He enlisted into the Dorsetshire Regiment in April 1940 and after attending its infantry training centre was posted to the Auxiliary Units at Blandford that November. He is believed to have been assigned to the Scout Section and undertook a course at the Home Guard Demonstration School the following month.

Posted to the 4th Battalion, Dorsetshire Regiment, in April 1943 Ashley was appointed acting lance-corporal that July and attended a section commander's course at the 43rd Division Battle School during January 1944. He subsequently volunteered for 1st SAS and was taken on strength on 1 February 1944 having reverted to the rank of private and qualified as a parachutist that day. His brother later wrote:

When they [the Auxiliaries] were disbanded they all went to the Curzon cinema in London, where they were addressed by Paddy Mayne [the Regiment's Commanding Officer] who invited them, being fully trained in explosives and sabotage, to volunteer to join the SAS – subject to interview. My information is that they were all accepted in February 1944 [personal correspondence, 2010].

That summer Ashley was deployed on OPERATION BULBASKET as a member of Lieutenant Peter Weaver's stick. On the night of 10–11 June 1944 they parachuted blind (that is, without an arranged reception committee) 16 kilometres south of their intended DZ in the Vienne département of western France. The aircraft had already dropped Corporal John Kinnivane's party inaccurately, and despite two of the men dropping into trees, Weaver, Corporal Jim Rideout and Parachutists Sid Ryland and Ashley soon found their bearings. They made their way to the Parthenay railway line, set charges and derailed a train on the morning of the 14th, Weaver himself later reporting: 'At 1000hrs Tpr Ryland and myself heard a train in the distance followed by an explosion, after which we heard no more trains that day.' Having stretched their twenty-four hour ration packs to last four days, the party made contact with locals who supplied them with food whilst en route to the main group. Reports vary, but the stick arrived at the SAS camp within the Forêt de Verrières some time between 24 and 28 June.

Ashley was captured on 3 July when this camp was attacked. He was subsequently murdered in the Bois de Guron within the Forêt de Saint-Sauvant on the 7th (see Lieutenant Richard Crisp's entry for full details). His brother recalled: 'Alan was 24 and unmarried when executed. I well remember one evening when Padre McLuskey came to our house to comfort the family. Only my mother and I were at home at the time' (personal correspondence, 2010). In May 1945 Ashley's father wrote to the War Office:

I thank you for your letter dated 2nd May [1945], addressed to my wife regarding our son. Although we have felt we should not see him again the news that he was killed after capture, in plain words, he was murdered, has stunned us more than I can express.

At the time of his capture I am sure he would have been wearing a Rolex Oyster chrome wristlet watch, the number of this, on the inside is 126438-278. My reason for giving you this is because I sincerely hope the German who did murder him may have come into our hands, after committing his crime have taken this watch so that now it may be in our possession as his property. If so, I trust this may possibly bring him due punishment.

Please accept our deep appreciation for your expression of sympathy [WO 361/718].

Son of Harold and Margaret Ashley (née Jones) of Locking Moor Road, Weston-super-Mare, Somerset – Brother of Dorothy Ashley who at the time of his death was serving as a corporal in the ATS with an anti-aircraft battery, and of Philip Ashley.
Age 24.
Your memory abides in the hearts of those whose gain, was knowing you
Row 1, graves 1–26. Also commemorated on the Saint-Sauvant Forest Memorial and the war memorial within Grove Park, Weston-super-Mare. 'Alan's name is also on our parents' grave in Weston Cemetery. In the National Trust grounds of Coleshill House, Wiltshire, where Alan attended a training course for the Auxiliary Units, there is an oak tree planted in his memory' (correspondence with Philip Ashley, 2010).

PRIVATE JAMES **ASPIN** [10602266] RECONNAISSANCE CORPS, HIGHLAND LIGHT INFANTRY AND 1ST SAS (B SQN)

'Blondie' or 'Jimmy' Aspin, as he was known, was born on 13 December 1922 in Blackburn. He enlisted into the Reconnaissance Corps in January 1942 and was immediately attached to the King's Own Scottish Borderers' No.10 Infantry Training Depot. Two weeks later he was posted to the depot's HQ Company, transferring the following month to the 13th Battalion, Highland Light Infantry. He volunteered for 1st SAS on 25 February 1944 and a few days later commenced parachute course 105 at No.1 PTS Ringway where his instructor noted that he 'did not hesitate'.

Aspin parachuted into the Vienne département of western France in the early hours of 12 June 1944 as a member of OPERATION BULBASKET's main reinforcement group. He was captured during on 3 July when the SAS camp within the Forêt de Verrières was attacked and was subsequently murdered in the Bois de Guron within the Forêt de Saint-Sauvant on the 7th (see Lieutenant Richard Crisp's entry).

Son of Margaret Aspin of Withers Street, Blackburn, Lancashire – Brother of Alice and Jack Aspin.

Age 21.

We were not there to hear your last faint sigh or whisper, 'Dearest son goodbye'

Row 1, graves 1–26. Also commemorated on the Saint-Sauvant Forest Memorial. A small plaque left at the grave is inscribed 'Loving thoughts quietly kept of someone we love and will never forget. From your loving family in England.'

LANCE-CORPORAL JAMES HENRY MALCOLM **BAKER** [2615455] GRENADIER GUARDS, No.8 COMMANDO, MIDDLE EAST COMMANDO, L DETACHMENT SAS BRIGADE, 1ST SAS, SRS AND 1ST SAS (B SQN)

'Lofty' Baker, as he was known to his comrades, was born on 15 June 1919 in the parish of St Paul's, Weston-super-Mare. Whilst living with his adoptive parents, the Baxters, in Powder House Lane at Shirehampton, he attended Portway School. Having worked as a farm mechanic he enlisted into the Grenadier Guards in September 1937 and was posted to the 1st Battalion. For reasons unknown he did so under the alias of 'Robert James Henry Baxter' but was forced to declare his true identity at Westminster Court in March 1939, serving under his real name from then on.

After the outbreak of war the 7th Guards Brigade disembarked at Cherbourg at the end of September 1939. Having concentrated around Tennie and Bernay, the 1st Battalion settled down to digging in around the

village of Annappes on the Franco-Belgian border. That December Baker went back to the UK to join the Training Battalion and did not return to France until 2 May 1940. On the 10th the German Blitzkrieg began and the 1st Battalion moved forward to Louvain. Here an attack was beaten off on the night of the 14–15th, although with the British line being outflanked the battalion was obliged to retire. Although repositioned at Wattrelos to defend canal bridges and crossroads a further withdrawal was ordered, this time to Dunkirk. Bombed and shelled en route the Grenadiers took up a key position on the defensive perimeter at Furnes before being taken off from La Panne on 1 June.

Baker was hospitalised in Bath during July 1940 but on 25 August volunteered for No.8 (Guards) Commando and was posted to No.2 Troop. After arduous build-up training in Scotland the Commando embarked for the Middle East on 31 January 1941. It arrived at Suez in Egypt at the beginning of March as B Battalion of Layforce. The following month the men were at Mersa Matruh towards the front line although, with operations drawn up and then cancelled, an unsettled period ensued.

Baker was one of the original members of the SAS. His service record states that he was posted to the 'Commando Training Centre' at Kabrit on 29 August 1941, the day after L Detachment, SAS Brigade, was officially raised. In mid January 1942 he was a member of a party under Captain David Stirling that was transported by G.1 Patrol, LRDG, from Jalo in Libya across the Wadi Tamet and that, having entered the Great Sand Sea, then made for enemy-held Beurat. Here the men split into three groups, entering the town to destroy eighteen petrol bowsers, four food dumps and a wireless mast. Two nights later Stirling decided to attack again, this time blowing up a ten-ton trailer on the coastal road. Although ambushed on its return journey, the party arrived at Jalo without casualties and flew back to Kabrit.

Having been AWOL for three days that February, Baker was returned to his unit, which by this time had been absorbed into the Middle East Commando, and was later posted to the 181st Infantry Transit Camp. He was allowed to rejoin what was now 1st SAS on 15 October 1942 and was promoted to lance-corporal the following May when the Regiment, restructured as the Special Raiding Squadron, was in training at Azzib for the invasion of Sicily.

On 10 July 1943 Baker landed as a member of C Section, No.3 Troop, at the forefront of OPERATION HUSKY, the Allied invasion of Sicily. Having destroyed coastal batteries at Capo Murro di Porco that day the SRS captured the port of Augusta on the 12th. Baker was subsequently 'regranted permission' to wear Operational Wings, his self-written application having listed his major achievements: 'Ageilia, M'Brega, C Squad, Porco, Augusta.' The SRS next saw action at Bagnara on the Italian mainland on 4 September during OPERATION BAYTOWN and the following month took part in the capture and defence of Termoli (OPERATION DEVON). At the beginning of 1944 it returned to the UK where it was reconstituted as 1st SAS, Baker being posted to B Squadron.

Having parachuted into France for OPERATION BULBASKET, Baker was captured on 3 July 1944 when the SAS camp within the Forêt de Verrières was attacked. He was subsequently murdered in the Bois de Guron within the Forêt de Saint-Sauvant on the 7th (see Lieutenant Richard Crisp's entry for full details).

Adopted son of William and Alice Baxter of Totterdown Road, Weston-super-Mare, Somerset.
Age 22.
Given back to God 'Thy will be done' Mother
Row 1, graves 1–26. Also commemorated on the Saint-Sauvant Forest Memorial and on the war memorial within Grove Park, Weston-super-Mare (arranged by Philip Ashley, brother of Baker's comrade Alan Ashley, who noticed his name had been omitted).

Corporal Kenneth **BATEMAN** [5572359] Wiltshire Regiment, No.7 Commando, Middle East Commando, 1st SAS, SRS and 1st SAS (B Sqn)

Ken Bateman was born on 12 October 1919 at Swinton in Salford. Having worked assembling safety lamps he enlisted into the Wiltshire Regiment (Duke of Edinburgh's) in January 1940 and was posted to the 4th Battalion. At the beginning of August he volunteered for E Troop, No.7 Commando, at Girvan, this being temporarily redesignated No.2 Company, 3rd Special Service Battalion, soon after. Disembarking at Suez in Egypt in early March 1941 as A Battalion, Layforce, the Commando carried out a largely abortive raid on Bardia on the Libyan coast on the night of 19–20 April. On their return the men were held aboard HMS *Glengyle* until the beginning of May when they were allowed ashore, somewhat disgruntled, at Alexandria.

On the night of 26–27 May 1941 A and B Battalions disembarked at Suda Bay on Crete to help evacuate Commonwealth troops after the German invasion. They subsequently formed part of the rearguard, fighting a running battle over the mountains en route to the embarkation point at Sphakia on the south coast. Bateman was one of the lucky few to be evacuated to Egypt on the 31st, the majority of his comrades going into captivity. When Layforce was disbanded that July he was posted to the Middle East Commando Depot at Geneifa near to Kabrit. In April 1942 he moved to Syria, the Commando being reorganised as the 1st Special Service Regiment later that year.

Bateman returned to Egypt in December 1942 and this is likely to be when he volunteered for 1st SAS. He was promoted to lance-corporal in March 1943 when the Regiment was reorganised as the Special Raiding Squadron. His recommendation for Operational Wings as a lance-corporal of B Section, 3 Troop, records that he had been deployed on operations in the Western Desert as well as the July 1943 landings at Capo Murro di Porco and Augusta at the forefront of Operation Husky, the Allied invasion of Sicily. The SRS went on to see fierce fighting at Bagnara on mainland Italy on 4 September during Operation Baytown before sailing from port to port around to the Adriatic. Here, along with No.3 Commando and No.40 (RM) Commando, it launched Operation Devon, which aimed to prevent the enemy taking up defensive positions on the River Biferno: the combined force came ashore from landing craft 1½ kilometres north-west of the port of Termoli in the early hours of 3 October, the Commandos securing the town and its perimeter whilst the SRS pushed down towards the Biferno to hold two bridges and a road junction for the advancing 78th Division. Despite heavy casualties the town was held until relieved.

Bateman was promoted to corporal the day he returned to the UK in early January 1944. He was posted to B Squadron of the reconstituted 1st SAS with which he attended parachute training at No.1 PTS Ringway the following month.

On the night of 11–12 June 1944 Bateman, Sergeant Dougie Eccles and Captain John Sadoine of Phantom were parachuted blind, that is without an organised reception committee, 32 kilometres from their intended DZ in the Vienne département of western France for Operation Bulbasket. Two nights later they blew up a locomotive engine and railway points, repeating the latter on the night of the 15–16th.

Bateman and Eccles were captured after blowing a further set of points at St Benoit during the night of the 28–29th, Hauptmann Dr Erich Schönig, Intelligence Officer of the German 80 Corps, later stating:

At the beginning of July 1944 I was awakened one morning by an explosion which took place quite close to the HQ of the AK [Arbeitskommando – a work camp or working party]. About one hour later I was informed by telephone that two Englishmen who obviously carried out the blasting, had been taken prisoner by the guard. The two prisoners were then brought before me. As myself do not speak English, the prisoners were questioned by my interpreter, Sonderführer Dr Honigschmid (Judge of Local Court, Vienna). The prisoners wore overalls which did not necessarily give rise to the belief that they belonged to a military formation. They did not wear any badges disclosing their ranks, or any other insignia. When seen by me they wore no hats. The prisoners identified themselves as members of the British Army by showing their pay books. The interrogation revealed nothing. Although the prisoners admitted to having carried out the blowing-up of the railway line, they refused to make any further statements, also with regard to the unit to which they belonged: they referred to the Geneva Convention. According to my memory, one of them may have been a sergeant, and the other a private [*sic*]. We did not insist on questioning them any further, and I had them taken to the Military Prison in Poitiers, as we had no prisoner of war camp. I reported immediately the arrest of the two men to the Chief of Staff Col Koestlin and to General Gallenkamp ... The SD requested permission to interrogate the two prisoners. This was granted by Col Koestlin, as from a further interrogation by us no military results could be expected. Next day I learned, upon enquiry by telephone, that the interrogation by the SD had not produced any results either, and that the two prisoners had been taken by the SD to the SD office [at] Tours.

After about two or three days I was called up by the SD Poitiers and I was informed that the two prisoners had been brought back from Tours to the SD office at Poitiers. They were again lodged in the army prison at Poitiers [WO 309/1550].

Either Bateman or Eccles began to trickle feed information in the belief that, as per standard operating procedures, the main party would have moved location after their capture had been reported. This was not the case, Schönig later stating:

Hoffman called, he told me that it had been found out that these two belonged to a group of parachutists who were encamped in a wood near Poitiers. There was a group of about twenty to thirty-five men who were in touch with the Maquis.

The SD was interested in capturing this group and requested military reinforcements. This was promised by Col Koestlin. The SD sent a French confidential agent (V-Mann) to the vicinity of the camp in order to find out whether the camp was still used. This was the case. Consequently, the action against the camp was decided upon and carried out [on 3 July 1944 - WO 309/1550].

Those captured at the SAS camp within the Forêt de Verrières were reunited with Bateman and Eccles at the Poitiers prison, the whole group being subsequently murdered in the Bois de Guron within the Forêt de Saint-Sauvant on 7 July (see Lieutenant Richard Crisp's entry within this section for full details).

Foster son of Charles and Jane Seddon of Swinton Hall Road, Swinton, Lancashire – His father, H. Bateman, is known to have been living at Thorpe in Norwich during 1946, whilst his mother's maiden name was Greenhalgh. Age 24.

This day dawns with sad regret for one we loved and will never forget

Row 1, graves 1–26. Also commemorated on the Saint-Sauvant Forest Memorial.

PRIVATE MICHAEL JOSEPH **BROPHY** [6353031] QUEEN'S OWN ROYAL WEST KENT REGIMENT, 1ST SAS, SRS AND 1ST SAS (B SQN)

Michael Brophy was born at Tullamore in Offaly, Eire, on 7 July 1922. By the time he enlisted into the Royal West Kent Regiment in October 1940 he was living in Anerley, south-east London, where he worked as a barber. Known as Mick or Mike to his comrades, but as Joe to his family, he carried a pair of clippers in his kit to cut his fellow soldiers' hair.

Having been initially posted to the 70th (Young Soldiers) Battalion at Croydon he married Audrey Joyce Fry at All Saints Church at Langton Green near Tunbridge Wells in June 1942. Later that year he was admitted to military hospital with pneumonia from which he recovered slowly until posted to the

7th Battalion in November. Embarking for the Middle East just before Christmas he was posted to No.1 Infantry Training Depot on arrival and volunteered for 1st SAS on 18 February 1943. When the Regiment was restructured as the Special Raiding Squadron he was posted to C Section, 3 Troop. He subsequently took part in the destruction of coastal batteries at Capo Murro di Porco on 10 July and the capture of the port of Augusta on the 12th during OPERATION HUSKY, the Allied invasion of Sicily. For these actions he was awarded Operational Wings before taking part in OPERATION BAYTOWN, the SRS landings at Bagnara on mainland Italy on 4 September, and in the capture and defence of Termoli the following month during OPERATION DEVON. Joe Schofield, MBE, former 3 Troop, later recalled that Brophy stood out as physically very fit.

At the beginning of January 1944 Brophy returned to the UK where the unit was reconstituted as 1st SAS. Posted to B Squadron he undertook parachute training at No.1 PTS at Ringway the following month. After intensive preparation in Scotland the Regiment was moved into holding camps in southern England, Brophy parachuting into a DZ south-east of Poitiers in the Vienne département of western France on the night of 11–12 June for OPERATION BULBASKET. He was captured on 3 July when the SAS camp within the Forêt de Verrières was attacked and subsequently murdered at the Bois de Guron within the Forêt de Saint-Sauvant on his 22nd birthday, 7 July 1944 (see Lieutenant Richard Crisp's entry within this section for full details). Posted missing in action, the Brophy family later received a letter from Sergeant Johnny Holmes, one of the survivors of the operation:

I am in receipt of your letter Mrs Brophy requesting information regarding your husband. I deeply sympathise with you in your trouble and would really like to help you, but the fact of the matter is that there is no information available as yet I regret to say. We are doing our best to trace him and when we find out anything we will most assuredly let you know, meanwhile be of good heart. We miss Mike here too. He has many friends amongst us, so we hope he turns up safe and sound one of these days [Brophy family collection].

Meanwhile, Holmes also wrote to the War Office stating that he had seen Brophy on the morning of the attack:

As we were making our way through the wood [away from the German attack] we [Holmes and Trooper Tommy Cummings] were joined by Cpl Long, Tpr Spooner and Tpr Brophy. I then told them to split up. Cpl Long and Trooper Spooner left together. I saw them try to cross a track. Shots were exchanged as we were leaving. I did not see any more. Tpr Brophy was with me going through the wood in single file. After we had gone 100 yards I looked back and he was not to be seen [see entries for Corporal Les Long and Trooper Tony Spooner within this section].

In late March 1945 the War Office wrote to Brophy's wife stating: 'I am directed to inform you, with deep regret, that a report has been received from the Military Authorities which establishes that your husband, formerly reported missing believed prisoner of war on the 4th July 1944, was killed in action on the 7th July, his grave having been found and identified.' Writing to Brophy's mother Sergeant Sam Smith, another of BULBASKET's survivors, stated: 'I was with Mick when he joined the Regt. He was in my troop in Sicily, Italy. He was a great kid Mrs Brophy' (family collection).

At the subsequent court of inquiry Captain John Tonkin, MC, the operation's commander, stated that he had identified Brophy's remains not only by the initials on his ring but 'more conclusively by a photograph found in his pocket with him and his wife whom I know'.

Son of Mr Patrick Brophy – Husband of Audrey Brophy who later emigrated to Canada.
Age officially recorded as 22 (see below).
No inscription.
Row 2, grave 30. Also commemorated on the Saint-Sauvant Forest Memorial and on the grave of his parents-in-law within Speldhurst churchyard. The inscription records his age as 25, whereas his service record shows that he as 22 at the time of his death. Neither age matches the one he gave on his wedding certificate.

PRIVATE GORDON HUBERT FRANK **BUDDEN** [7958191] AUXILIARY UNITS, ROYAL ARMOURED CORPS, GENERAL SERVICE CORPS AND 1ST SAS (B SQN)

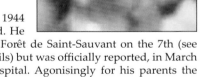

Gordon Budden was born on 12 February 1923 at Wimborne in Dorset and attended nearby Crichel School. He enlisted into the 57th Training Regiment, Royal Armoured Corps, in April 1942 at Warminster, Wiltshire, but was posted to the Army Reserve 'for an indefinite period to take up employment of national importance'. A nominal roll for the Auxiliary Units reveals that he had been a member of this covert organisation since that February, his RAC enlistment being for administrative reasons. However, in March 1943 he transferred to the General Service Corps and was posted to No.26 Primary Training Centre remaining as a reserve. Two months later he was embodied into the RAC and rejoined the 57th Training Regiment, volunteering for 1st SAS on 7 January 1944 when the Regiment returned to the UK from Italy. He attended parachute course 105 at No.1 PTS Ringway that March, being noted as an 'average parachutist' but a 'keen, hard worker'.

Budden was captured during OPERATION BULBASKET on 3 July 1944 when the SAS camp within the Forêt de Verrières was attacked. He was subsequently murdered in the Bois de Guron within the Forêt de Saint-Sauvant on the 7th (see Lieutenant Richard Crisp's entry within this section for full details) but was officially reported, in March 1945, as having been found alive at No.8 Canadian Field Hospital. Agonisingly for his parents the notification was corrected soon after.

Son of Mr and Mrs Sidney Budden (née Mitchell) of Manswood Common, Witchampton, Wimborne, Dorset.
Age 21.
No inscription.
Row 1, graves 1–26. Also commemorated on Witchampton's war memorial and on the Saint-Sauvant Forest Memorial.

CORPORAL REGINALD <u>CHICK</u> [7895914] 2ND NORTHAMPTONSHIRE YEOMANRY, 1ST SAS, SRS AND 1ST SAS (B SQN)

Reg Chick was born on 7 June 1921 in the industrial town of Tredegar in Monmouthshire, his family later moving first to south-west London and then Kettering near to where relatives were employed at Corby Steelworks. Whilst working as a shoemaker he joined the 2nd Northamptonshire Yeomanry, Royal Armoured Corps (TA), in May 1939 and was embodied as a member of C Squadron at the outbreak of war. The following summer he was posted to the 53rd Training Regiment at Tidworth as a member of the GHQ Escort Detachment until returning to the 2nd Northamptonshire Yeomanry in March 1941. Disembarking in Egypt in July 1942 as a reinforcement he was posted to 152 Leave and Transit Camp the following month and from there volunteered for either L Detachment, SAS Brigade, before 21 September or 1st SAS after this date. By November he was serving within C Squadron's Signals Section and would therefore have been behind the lines harassing Axis troops on their retreat through Tunisia during the final stages of the North African Campaign.

Withdrawn to Palestine to train, the Regiment briefly returned to Kabrit where the majority of its subunits were reorganised as the Special Raiding Squadron on 19 March 1943. Thereafter it continued its preparations for OPERATION HUSKY, the Allied invasion of Sicily. Having been promoted to lance-corporal at this time Chick was advanced to acting corporal on 1 July, a few days before the squadron landed at the forefront of HUSKY. After successfully destroying coastal batteries at Capo Murro di Porco in the early hours of the 10th, the SRS captured the key port of Augusta two days later. On 4 September its men landed at Bagnara during OPERATION BAYTOWN, capturing the town, gaining a valuable beachhead, and hastening the Axis retreat from the toe of mainland Italy. After a period of rest and raining the squadron then sailed around to the Adriatic port of Termoli, Chick (by now confirmed as corporal) seeing fierce fighting during the capture of the town and defence of its approaches alongside the Special Service Brigade (OPERATION DEVON).

Returning to the UK at the beginning of January 1944 Chick was posted to HQ Squadron of the reconstituted 1st SAS. He attended parachute course 114A at No.1 PTS Ringway that May, his instructor noting that he was 'keen and enthusiastic' and that his 'parachuting [was] above average'.

Chick was serving with B Squadron at time of OPERATION BULBASKET and parachuted into a DZ north

of Bouesse in the Indre département of central France in the early hours of 8 June 1944. Although he jumped with Lieutenant 'Twm' Stephens' main recce party, he served as Captain John Tonkin's wireless operator with the callsign 'Sabu 4' (see Stephens' entry under Verrières Communal Cemetery, France). Captured on 3 July during the attack on the SAS camp within the Forêt de Verrières, he was subsequently murdered in the Bois de Guron within the Forêt de Saint-Sauvant on the 7th (see Lieutenant Richard Crisp's entry overleaf for full details). His remains were identified by his signet ring bearing the initials 'RC'.

Youngest son of Ernest and Evelyn Chick (née Tomkins) of Stamford Road, Kettering, Northamptonshire – Younger brother of Robert, John, Bettina, Evelyn and Arthur Chick.
Age 23.
He gave his life that we may live in peace for evermore
Row 1, graves 1–26. Also commemorated on the Saint-Sauvant Forest Memorial and on Kettering's war memorial.

Private George Oliver <u>Cogger</u> [5729670] Dorsetshire Regiment, Auxiliary Units and 1st SAS (B Sqn)

George Cogger was born on 13 December 1919 in East Dulwich, south-east London. Having worked as an auditor's clerk he enlisted into the Dorsetshire Regiment in March 1940 and was posted to its infantry training centre that day. He was subsequently re-posted to the Dorset Scout Section of the Auxiliary Units in June. These sections helped train secret civilian Auxiliary patrols that had been formed to resist any German occupation, whilst preparing for the same tasks themselves. In between such duties Cogger found time to marry Gladys Edna Nunn at Camberwell in December 1942.

After the threat of German invasion abated the role of the Auxiliaries became redundant. Cogger, like many of this underground army, volunteered for 1st SAS on 1 February 1944. He subsequently parachuted into a DZ north of Bouesse in the Indre département of central France for Operation Bulbasket on the night of 7–8 June 1944. His nine-man party, under Lieutenant 'Twm' Stephens, was met by their commander, Captain John Tonkin, who had jumped into the area with Lieutenant Richard Crisp in the early hours of the 6th (see Stephens' entry under Verrières Communal Cemetery, France). The following day the group was transported westwards by truck, a decision then being made to concentrate their efforts farther west and attack the railway line north and south of Poitiers. He was subsequently taken prisoner during the attack on the SAS camp within the Forêt de Verrières on 3 July and murdered in the Bois de Guron within the Forêt de Saint-Sauvant on the 7th (see Lieutenant Richard Crisp's entry below for full details).

Son of Mr and Mrs Oliver Cogger of Casino Avenue, Herne Hill, London – Husband of Gladys Cogger of Lordship Lane, East Dulwich.
Age 24.
No inscription.
Row 1, graves 1–26. Also commemorated on the Saint-Sauvant Forest Memorial.

LIEUTENANT RICHARD **CRISP** [303259] GENERAL SERVICE CORPS, NORTH IRISH HORSE AND 1ST SAS (B SQN)

Richard Crisp was born on 13 October 1923 in Salisbury, Wiltshire, where he attended Bishop Wordsworth School until 1939. As well as being a member of the OTC he was a budding actor, winning a scholarship at the Old Vic Dramatic School that year at the age of 16. Despite having been evacuated from London due to the Blitz he contemplated registering as a conscientious objector, especially as he had hosted three German exchange students shortly before the war. However: 'The evil of Hitler and the Nazis was, he resolved, an evil greater than war itself' (*SAS Operation Bulbasket: Behind the Lines in Occupied France, 1944,* by Paul McCue). Having been called up to the General Service Corps at Bodmin in July 1942 (service number 14224286) he transferred to the Royal Armoured Corps and joined the 61st Training Regiment where he accepted the chance of an emergency commission. At the time he stated he had a fair knowledge of French, an 'operatic knowledge' of German and Italian, and that as well as being an actor he was a theatre photographer, electrician and physical training instructor. His Commanding Officer reported: 'Crisp is doing very well indeed in training. He appears rather lacking in confidence and "dash", and would benefit from further experience, but he possesses considerable personal courage.'

Crisp was commissioned into the North Irish Horse, RAC, from 100 (Sandhurst) OCTU on 19 December 1943 (*London Gazette* 18/01/44). His final report noted: 'this cadet has shown very good progress. No previous experience but by hard work has reached a standard above the average, especially his practical work and driving. Quiet and very reliable.' Another member of staff remarked: 'serious minded, hard working and shows initiative as a commander. A good instructor and should train an efficient and reliable Troop.' Although posted to the 54th Training Regiment he volunteered for the SAS on 16 February 1944, writing to his parents: 'I've got a darn sight better chance of coming through alive now anyway. Tanks had their day long ago. I feel very proud to be in this Regiment.' Although initially earmarked for what was planned as a third British SAS unit he was taken on strength by B Squadron, 1st SAS, and attended parachute course 105 at No.1 PTS Ringway the following month. Here his instructor noted: 'a good leader and parachutist, keen and intelligent'.

Crisp parachuted into a DZ 30 kilometres south-west of Châteauroux in the Indre département of central France for OPERATION BULBASKET in the early hours of D-Day, 6 June 1944. He, along with the operation's commander, Captain John Tonkin, and SOE's JEDBURGH Team HUGH, formed the advance recce group. On the 12th he laid mines on roads south of Poitiers to disrupt enemy convoys, Tonkin later writing: 'Lt Crisp seems now to have been the usual leader of convoy harassing parties. I must have thought he had quite a gift for it!' He was advanced to lieutenant on 19 June and cut a railway line and points the following night.

On 2 July Tonkin realised that their camp within the Forêt de Verrières had been compromised and moved his party to another wood. However, on finding that there was no water supply at the new location the men were forced to return to Verrières in the early hours of the 3rd. Tonkin later noted in his post-operation report that they were:

> … surrounded and heavily attacked by 400 to 500 SS troops with mortars and artillery at 0700 hours. I gave the order to disperse immediately and meet at a prearranged RV … Very few of the men dispersed … thirty-one men, three of them wounded, and Lieut Crisp, also wounded, were believed POW. Enemy casualties were twenty killed and several wounded [WO 219/2389].

Crisp had been wounded in the thigh whilst trying to evade capture and was taken prisoner. He was subsequently murdered in the Bois de Guron within the Forêt de Saint-Sauvant on the 7th. According to those accused, a German officer explained to Crisp what was about to happen and he relayed the news to the men. Hauptmann Dr Erich Schönig, Intelligence Officer of 80 Corps, claimed that the 'execution was accomplished militarily and with dignity' and that the men 'stood in a line' and 'linked arms'. Other German reports claimed that the men had chosen to throw their watches, photographs and other personal effects to the firing squad for safe-keeping, Schönig later stating that after the men had been shot he ordered their identity discs be collected so as 'to transmit them to the competent English military authorities via the International Red Cross, in order to notify next of kin' (WO 309/1550). The subsequent exhumation of the men's remains exposed the truth: all but one of the men had been laid in the graves on their sides, most of them arranged with their uppermost arm resting over the man in front. According to Albert Charron, one of those in attendance, the last man was:

> … lying on his back with his legs spread over the length of the others. He had fallen over the others. I assumed something which of course I did not put in the report, since it is merely assumption, that the ninth man [of the last group to be murdered] had placed his comrades in the grave and had been killed just as he finished working [TS 26/861].

Crisp's remains were identified by his name inscribed within his battle dress blouse. On 5 July a BBC monitoring station had translated a German broadcast that included the news that 'in central France, a British sabotage party, 43-men strong, which was dropped by parachute, was liquidated' (WO 311/79). Meanwhile, any claim that those responsible thought that it had been a legal execution was further refuted by the fact that the graves had been carefully concealed with moss, planted over with small bushes, and the surrounding earth raked using brushwood.

The 'Poitiers Case' was put before a Military Court at Wuppertal in March 1947. General Curt Gallenkamp, who had commanded 80 Corps and ordered that the murders be carried out, was sentenced to death shortly after failing to take his own life. His sentence was later commuted to life imprisonment although he was released in 1952 and died in 1958. Hauptmann Dr Georg Hesterberg, who had administered lethal injections to three of those captured, was also sentenced to hang, although he walked free after the Commander-in-Chief of Germany, Lord Sholto Douglas, quashed this. Oberst Herbert Köstlin, Gallenkamp's Chief-of-Staff who had ordered Hesterberg to do so, was sentenced to life imprisonment. He was also released in 1952. Schönig, who had passed the order on, received five years. Oberleutnant Vogt, a pre-war clergyman who had commanded the firing squad, had been killed before the end of hostilities.

Son of Richard and Honor Crisp (née Walker) of Lytchett Matravers, Dorset – Brother of George, Sydney and Iris.
Age 20.
Richard
Row 2, grave 27. Also commemorated on the Saint-Sauvant Forest Memorial, at St Laurence Church, Downton near Salisbury, and on his parents' headstone at Lytchett Matravers in Dorset.

Private Leslie Ronald <u>EADES</u> [14542517] General Service Corps, Royal Artillery, Army Air Corps and 1st SAS (B Sqn)

Leslie Eades was born on 26 January 1922 at Digbeth in Birmingham. Having worked as a machine engineer he enlisted into the General Service Corps in February 1942 and was posted to No.1 Primary Training Centre. In April 1943 he transferred to the Royal Artillery, rotating through various light anti-aircraft regiments before transferring once again, this time to the Army Air Corps. Having volunteered as a parachutist on 22 December 1943 he was posted to the Airborne Forces Depot at Hardwick Hall near Chesterfield and attended parachute course 99 the following month at No.1 PTS Ringway. Here his instructor noted 'morale good, reliable, average jumper'. Qualifying for his wings he was re-posted to the Airborne Forces Holding Unit until volunteering for 1st SAS on 24 February 1944.

Having been parachuted into Operation Bulbasket sometime between 10 and 12 June 1944, Eades was taken prisoner during the attack on the SAS camp within the Forêt de Verrières on 3 July. He was subsequently murdered in the Bois de Guron within the Forêt de Saint-Sauvant on the 7th (see Lieutenant Richard Crisp's entry for full details).

Son of Mr and Mrs Frederick Eades (née Overs) of Garwood Road, South Yardley, Birmingham – Brother of Fred, Edna, Irene and Wilfred Eades.
Age 22.
No inscription.
Row 1, graves 1–26. Also commemorated on the Saint-Sauvant Forest Memorial.

Sergeant Douglas <u>ECCLES</u> [2735399] Welsh Guards, No.8 Commando, 1st SAS, SRS and 1st SAS (B Sqn)

Dougie Eccles was born in late 1919 in Lancaster where he was educated at the Boys National School before finding employment in the office of Messrs Williamson and Sons Ltd. His service record cannot be located but it is known that he joined No.8 (Guards) Commando from the Welsh Guards and therefore would have disembarked at Suez in Egypt at the beginning of March 1941 as part of B Battalion of Layforce. At some point after this disbanded he volunteered for 1st SAS and was posted to C Squadron, the Regiment being reorganised as the Special Raiding Squadron on 19 March 1943.

By the time the SRS landed on Sicily, Eccles was serving as a lance-sergeant in C Section, No.3 Troop,

alongside Sergeant Joe Schofield. Having destroyed coastal batteries at the forefront of the Allied invasion at Capo Murro di Porco on 10 July 1943 the SRS captured the port of Augusta on the 12th, Schofield later recalling:

> 3 Troop, the leading troop, entered the main street and Sergeant 'Dougie' Eccles went down wounded in the thigh …
>
> Eccles, Schofield, Sillitto were inseparable chums in the SAS … Eccles joined 6 Troop, 8 (Guards) Commando, when I did after Dunkirk and we stayed together through the next five years. At Augusta he was wounded by my side during the initial landing [personal correspondence, 2009].

Having recovered, Eccles returned to the Regiment that November and was recommended for Operational Wings before disembarking in the UK at the beginning of 1944. He was parachuted into the OPERATION BULBASKET area with Captain John Sadoine of GHQ Liaison Regiment (Phantom) and Corporal Ken Bateman in the early hours of 12 June. On the night of the 13–14th he placed charges on a locomotive engine at Le Dorat Station and blew up railway points with Bateman, repeating this action two nights later. The pair were captured after blowing further points at St Benoit on the night of the 28–29th. Both were interrogated but said nothing for forty-eight hours as trained (see Bateman's entry above for further details). They were then handed over to the SD and either Bateman or Eccles eventually began to trickle feed details of the SAS camp, probably in the belief that their comrades would have moved location after their capture became known as per standard operating procedures. This was not the case and those captured during an attack on the SAS camp within the Forêt de Verrières on 3 July joined Eccles and Bateman in Poitiers prison. They were all murdered in the Bois de Guron within the Forêt de Saint-Sauvant on the 7th (see Lieutenant Richard Crisp's entry for full details). Sadoine later reported:

> Sgt Eccles, 1 SAS, is to be very highly recommended in the initiative he showed in organising search parties and himself going out in civilian clothes with the local Maquis chief to look for us [after being separated during their drop]. He was also responsible for getting the eight men and containers collected and hidden away [WO 219/2389].

Meanwhile, BULBASKET's commander, Captain John Tonkin, later wrote:

> Sgt Eccles was first rate (an old Western Desert and Sicily/Italy veteran) and Captain Sadoine's comments on him and what he did are accurate. What he does not mention is that, with it all, Eccles, not knowing where I was, or able to speak French, twice attacked Lot 1 on 15/6 and 18/6.

Son of Mrs J. Eccles (née Farrer) of Coniston Road, Lancaster – Known to have had a younger brother serving with the Royal Engineers in Italy.
Age 24.
In the perfect love of Jesus he is safe for evermore
Row 1, graves 1–26. Also commemorated on Lancaster Civic War Memorial and the Saint-Sauvant Forest Memorial.

Corporal James Chisholm Wilson <u>GOVAN</u> MM [3057065] Royal Scots, Royal Army Service Corps, No.8 Commando, Middle East Commando, 1st SAS, SRS and 1st SAS (B Sqn)

James Govan was born on 18 October 1913 in the town of Bellshill in North Lanarkshire, later living in Midlothian. In January 1939, whilst working as a miner, he joined the Royal Scots (TA) in Edinburgh and was posted to the 52nd Search Light Regiment, Royal Artillery. Early that August he was mobilised for service with the Royal Army Service Corps and in late February 1940 disembarked in France where he served with No.1 Works Motor Transport Company. Although he was awarded the Military Medal at Dunkirk it has not been possible to trace his citation (*London Gazette* 20/12/40).

Having been evacuated, Govan was posted to 931 General Transport Company at Tewkesbury. That November he volunteered for the 4th Special Service Battalion, this reverting to its original designation of No.8 (Guards) Commando the following February, shortly before it disembarked at Suez in Egypt as B Battalion of Layforce. Although No.8 was at Mersa Matruh later that month, the constant last-minute cancellation of operations ensured that an unsettled period ensued. Govan was admitted to hospital before the end of April and once again in October for unknown reasons.

After Layforce disbanded Govan was posted to the Middle East Commando at Geneifa near Kabrit in late January 1942, volunteering for 1st SAS on 26 September. He was promoted to lance-corporal in March 1943, the majority of the Regiment's subunits being reorganised as the Special Raiding Squadron at this time. As a member of B Section, 3 Troop, he was at the forefront of Operation Husky, the July Allied invasion of Sicily, and of Operation Baytown, the September landings on the Italian mainland. He was subsequently recommended for Operational Wings for 'Desert, Murro de Porco and Augusta'. Disembarking in the UK on Boxing Day he was posted to B Squadron of the reconstituted 1st SAS with which he undertook parachute training at No.1 PTS Ringway during February 1944. That April he married Mary Milroy Reed in Edinburgh and was promoted to corporal, eventually being presented his Military Medal by the King on 2 May at an investiture to a large group of SAS.

Govan parachuted into France for Operation Bulbasket sometime between 10 and 12 June 1944. On 3 July the SAS camp within the Forêt de Verrières was attacked, Sergeant Johnny Holmes, one of the few survivors, later stating:

> At the time of the attack I was asleep. I awoke and received the order to disperse. Owing to the close and accurate fire of the enemy we were almost pinned down. Tpr Cummings and myself ran through the wood to a point 200 to 300 yards from the camp. There we found we were surrounded so we hid until darkness fell when we discovered that the enemy had gone. We heard MG fire and mortar fire until 1200 hours in occasional bursts and nothing after that but during the morning we heard trucks moving along the tracks. I heard Cpl Govan shouting. On the following day I met a Frenchman who reported that he had seen a number of my men being taken in German trucks through the village of Verrières.

Govan was captured and subsequently murdered in the Bois de Guron within the Forêt de Saint-Sauvant on 7 July 1944 (see Lieutenant Richard Crisp's entry within this section for full details).

Son of John and Elizabeth Govan (née Wilson) of Musselburgh – Husband of Mary Govan of Edinburgh.
Age 30.

In gratitude for a devoted husband. His name liveth for evermore. Mary
Row 1, graves 1–26. Also commemorated on the Saint-Sauvant Forest Memorial and on Musselburgh's War Memorial Fountain.

Private David GRAY [320068] Royal Scots Greys, Raiding Support Regiment and 1st SAS (B Sqn)

David Gray was born in the town of Coatbridge near Glasgow on 8 December 1918 as the second of four brothers. Having worked as a cinema operator he enlisted into the Royal Scots Greys in March 1938. A year later he disembarked in Palestine, carrying on with policing duties in the region after the outbreak of war. In the course of such duties the regiment made its last charge on horseback whilst quelling Arab rioters in February 1940 and was mechanised soon after.

Although transferred to the Royal Armoured Corps in April 1941, the Scots Greys were used as mechanised infantry during Operation Exporter, the campaign against the Vichy French in what is modern-day Lebanon. Re-equipped with tanks it went into action for the first time as an armoured regiment in July 1942, making a successful counter-attack against Rommel's 21st Panzer Division. An auspicious run began with the Greys mounting successive charges against enemy armour and artillery alike, despite the fact that they were equipped with a mixed bag of failing mounts. After hostilities in North Africa drew to a close, Gray was posted to Palestine HQ, later seeing service on Sicily or mainland Italy. He subsequently volunteered for the newly formed Raiding Support Regiment on 5 November 1943, this unit being in training at Azzib back on the Palestinian coast. Under the Python scheme that repatriated those who had served abroad for four years he embarked for the UK at the beginning of February 1944 and arrived later that month. Initially posted to the RAC Depot he volunteered for 1st SAS on 27 April and was recorded as being a trained driver.

Gray parachuted into a DZ near the farm of Primo la Coupe close to la Font d'Usson, south of Poitiers in western France, on the night of 17–18 June 1944. He was dropped to a reception party along with Sergeant Bob Heavens, Corporal Bill Allan and Parachutist Henry Mullen (as well as four Jeeps), the group making contact with the enemy on leaving the area (see entries for the other members of this stick within this section). He was captured on 3 July when the Bulbasket camp within the Forêt de Verrières was attacked, and was subsequently murdered in the Bois de Guron within the Forêt de Saint-Sauvant on the 7th (see Lieutenant Richard Crisp's entry for full details).

Son of David and Jeanie Gray of School Street, Whiffley, Coatbridge, Lanarkshire – Younger brother of William and older brother of Joseph and John.
Age 25.
At the going down of the sun and in the morning I shall remember him
Row 1, graves 1–26. Also commemorated on the Saint-Sauvant Forest Memorial.

Private Ronald GUARD [2929492] Queen's Own Cameron Highlanders, No.7 Commando, Middle East Commando, 1st SAS, SRS and 1st SAS (B Sqn)

Ronnie Guard was born on 13 November 1919 in the parish of Kirkdale, Liverpool. Whilst working as a paper merchant and labourer he joined the Queen's Own Cameron Highlanders (TA) in July 1937 and was immediately posted to the 10th (Liverpool Scottish) Battalion, King's Regiment. As his birth was not registered until late 1920 there is a possibility that he falsified his age in order to join the reserves a year early. Having been embodied into the 1st Battalion (Liverpool Scottish) at the outbreak of war he volunteered for No.7 Commando at Girvan, this unit temporarily forming part of the 3rd Special Service Battalion in late 1940. Disembarking at Suez, Egypt, in early March 1941 as A Battalion, Layforce, the Commando carried out a largely abortive raid on Bardia on the Libyan coast on the night of 19–20 April. On their return the men were held aboard HMS *Glengyle* until the beginning of May when they were allowed ashore, somewhat disgruntled, at Alexandria.

Later that month A and B Battalions disembarked at Suda Bay on Crete to help evacuate Commonwealth troops after the German invasion. They subsequently formed part of the rearguard, fighting a running battle over the mountains en route to the embarkation point at Sphakia on the south coast. Guard was one of the fortunate few to be taken off to Egypt, the majority of his comrades going into captivity. When Layforce was disbanded that July he was posted to the Middle East Commando Depot at Geneifa near to Kabrit.

Having been struck by malaria at the beginning of 1942 Guard volunteered for 1st SAS that October and was posted to B Squadron. On 17 January 1943 he was a member of Captain Denis Murphy's patrol that was attacked near Nalut in western Libya. Although posted missing the following day, he managed to evade capture and had rejoined the Regiment by 20 February (see numerous entries under Enfidaville War Cemetery, Tunisia, Volume I, for full details). A short period attached to Raiding Forces HQ followed, before he returned to what was now the Special Raiding Squadron (1st SAS). As a member of C Section, No.3 Troop, he took part in the invasion of Sicily (Operation Husky), destroying coastal batteries at Capo Murro di Porco on 10 July and helping to capture the port of Augusta two days later. Having been awarded Operational Wings he took part in Operation Baytown, landing at Bagnara on 4 September to hasten the German retreat from the toe of mainland Italy. Moving round to the Adriatic coast the SRS went on to see fierce fighting during the capture and defence of Termoli the following month (Operation Devon) before disembarking in the UK in January 1944.

On the night of 10–11 June 1944 Guard was a member of Sergeant Johnny Holmes' stick that parachuted into France blind (that is, without an arranged reception committee) at a DZ 30 kilometres to the north of Châtellerault for Operation Bulbasket. Tasked with cutting the Poitiers–Tours railway line, Tommy Cummings, a fellow member of the patrol, later described their approach:

> Once we had completed a fairly hard march of about 12 miles, we came across our intended target. Sgt Holmes sent me forward 30 yards or so and Tpr E Richardson the same distance in the opposite direction. We were acting as his protection as he laid the charges which I think was a thirty minute delay. We heard a voice call out in German (who's there or something like that). We withdrew away from the immediate area and came upon a lane with hedges down both sides. Rather than be caught with nowhere to escape if ambushed here two of the blokes found a field gate (Ronnie Guard?/Ernie Richardson). They were first through it followed by me and then Holmes. Johnny slipped or tripped but ended up on his back, with the Bergan weight he was carrying, he twisted his ankle. Ronnie and Ernie walked on unaware of the situation behind them. We lost them as I helped Johnny up and helped carry some of the weight off his back. They actually found a safe house and were in the attic of a farm house. Next day, I think, by chance we met a farmer who told us he had two men in his house who were English, and we were all reunited again [correspondence between former B Squadron members Joe Schofield, MBE, and Tommy Cummings, 2010].

Guard was captured on 3 July 1944 when the SAS camp within the Forêt de Verrières was attacked and was subsequently murdered in the Bois de Guron within the Forêt de Saint-Sauvant on the 7th (see Lieutenant Richard Crisp's entry within this section for full details).

Son of Mary Guard (née Ray) of Adams Grove, Kirkdale, Liverpool.
Age officially recorded as 24.
No inscription.
Row 1, graves 1–26. Also commemorated on the Saint-Sauvant Forest Memorial.

SERGEANT ROBERT ERIC **HEAVENS** [820065] ROYAL ARTILLERY, NO.7 COMMANDO, L DETACHMENT SAS BRIGADE, 1ST SAS, SRS AND 1ST SAS (B SQN)

Bob Heavens was born on 30 July 1912 in Swindon where he later found employment at the Great Western Railway locomotive works. In May 1932, whilst living with his parents at Prospect Hill, he joined the 220th (Wiltshire) Battery, 55th (Wessex) Field Brigade, Royal Artillery (TA). After serving a four-year engagement he was discharged and married Rose Dowdeswell in September 1936 at Wroughton Parish Church, later becoming the father of three. He rejoined the TA, this time the 217th (Wiltshire) Field Battery, in April 1939 and was embodied at the outbreak of war that September.

Although initially posted to the 112th Field Regiment Heavens was attached to the 21st Medium and Heavy Regiment. In August 1940 he volunteered for No.7 Commando at Girvan and was promoted to lance-bombardier that November when it was temporarily redesignated No.2 Company, 3rd Special Service Battalion. On 31 January 1941 he was promoted to bombardier, disembarking at Suez in Egypt in early March as a member of A Battalion, Layforce.

On the night of 19–20 April 1941 the battalion carried out a largely abortive raid on Bardia on the Libyan coast. Having re-embarked, the men were held aboard HMS *Glengyle* until the beginning of May when they were allowed ashore, somewhat disgruntled, at Alexandria. They were soon back in action, A and B Battalions disembarking at Suda Bay on Crete on the night of 26–27 May to help evacuate Commonwealth troops after the German invasion. They subsequently formed part of the rearguard, fighting a running battle over the mountains en route to the embarkation point on the south coast. Heavens was one of the lucky few to be taken off to Egypt on the 31st, the majority of his comrades going into captivity.

After Layforce was disbanded Heavens volunteered for the fledgling L Detachment, SAS Brigade, on 5 August 1941 and as such was one of its original members. He was confirmed as lance-sergeant just after OPERATION BIGAMY, the large-scale September 1942 raid on Benghazi, and promoted to sergeant the following March when the majority of the Regiment's subunits had been reorganised as the Special Raiding Squadron. That May No.2 Troop's commander submitted a memo stating that Heavens had completed four operations and five parachute jumps but not yet received his Operational Wings. These were subsequently awarded after Heavens had forwarded an application to his CO, Major Paddy Mayne, DSO:

My first operation took place during the Fuka series when I was a member of the party that raided the landing ground at Sidi Haneish [the 26–27 July 1942 mass Jeep attack]. My next was the Benghazi raid [BIGAMY, September 1942]. After this I was one of the party, who, under Capt Chambers and Lieut Shorten, proceeded from Kufra to Howards Cairn to make a forward base [see entries for these officers under Fayid War Cemetery, Egypt, and Alamein Memorial, Egypt, Volume I, respectively]. I subsequently made this journey on three later occasions and one run from the Sand Sea base forward to make another small dump for returning operatives. I was also at the Bir Zelten base, from where I was a member of the party reconnoitring a path through the Sand Sea to the first dump. I made this run twice afterwards and was also in charge of the party sent out to try and locate Cpl Morris and Pct Carroll when we were lucky enough to find three other members of B Squadron.

By the time the SRS landed at the forefront of OPERATION HUSKY, the Allied invasion of Sicily, Heavens was serving in No.3 Troop. He saw action during the destruction of Italian coastal batteries at Capo Murro di Porco on 10 July and during the capture of the port of Augusta two days later. On 4 September he landed at Bagnara on the Italian mainland during OPERATION BAYTOWN and the following month took part in the capture and fierce defence of Termoli during OPERATION DEVON. He returned to the UK in January 1944 and was mentioned in despatches for operations either in North Africa or in Italy (*London Gazette* 13/01/44, No.36327).

Heavens parachuted into a DZ near the farm of Primo la Coupe close to la Font d'Usson, south of Poitiers in western France, on the night of 17–18 June 1944. He was dropped alongside Corporal Bill Allan, Parachutists Henry Mullen and David Gray (and four Jeeps) to a reception party, the group making contact with the enemy on leaving the area (see entries for other members of this stick within this section). He was captured on 3 July when the SAS camp within the Forêt de Verrières was attacked and was subsequently murdered in the Bois de Guron within the Forêt de Saint-Sauvant on the 7th (see Lieutenant Richard Crisp's entry above for full details). Heavens' family believe that he was an instructor at the time that BULBASKET was planned but volunteered to take the place of someone absent.

Son of Charles and Tryphose Heavens (née Fry) – Husband of Rose Heavens of Rolleston Street, Swindon, Wiltshire – Father of John, who died in 1947 aged 9, and of Robert and Cilla.
Age 31.
Gone from us o dearly loved one. To thy master's home above
Row 1, graves 1–26. Also commemorated on the Saint-Sauvant Forest Memorial.

Private Harry HILL [6298443] Royal Army Service Corps, The Buffs, SRS and 1st SAS (B Sqn)

Known to friends as 'Busty' or 'Ginty', Harry Hill was born on 27 July 1914 in Wrexham, Denbighshire, to a Welsh father and English mother. He married Dorothy Lilian Harris in May 1939 at Eltham in south-east London, the couple producing a son, Peter, in July 1940. Having worked as a wood machinist, he enlisted into The Buffs (Royal East Kent Regiment) in Canterbury during September 1941, stating that he had briefly served in the Royal Army Service Corps in 1934.

After home service, during which time Hill boxed for the army, he disembarked in the Middle East in May 1942. His service record notes that he was wounded accidentally in December and that having recovered he was posted to a reinforcement camp from where he volunteered for the Special Raiding Squadron (1st SAS) on 21 May 1943. He was subsequently wounded in action on 10 July whilst serving as a signaller in No.3 Troop during Operation Husky, the Allied invasion of Sicily. Having landed at Capo Murro de Porco Joe Schofield, MBE, later recalled that the squadron moved towards their secondary objectives: 'with 3 Troop on the left flank, advanced across country and came under fire. The leading section met opposition in an orchard and Pct "Ginty" Hill went down with a bullet clean through his neck' (personal correspondence, 2010). Although it is unknown when Hill was discharged from hospital it was in time to return to UK at the beginning of January 1944 when the Regiment was reconstituted as 1st SAS. Posted to B Squadron he attended a course at STS.54, SOE's signals school at Fawley Court in Henley-on-Thames, during February. He also attended parachute course 111A at No.1 PTS Ringway that April, his instructor noting that he was 'above average in performance, cheerful and confident'.

Hill parachuted into a DZ north of Bouesse in the Indre département of central France for Operation Bulbasket on the night of 7–8 June 1944. His nine-man party, under Lieutenant 'Twm' Stephens, was met by their commander, Captain John Tonkin, who had jumped into the area with Lieutenant Richard Crisp in the early hours of the 6th (see Stephens' entry under Verrières Communal Cemetery, France). The following day the group was transported westwards by truck, a decision then being made to concentrate farther west in order to attack the railway line north and south of Poitiers.

Hill was captured on 3 July when the SAS camp within the Forêt de Verrières was attacked and was subsequently murdered in the Bois de Guron within the Forêt de Saint-Sauvant on the 7th (see Lieutenant Richard Crisp's entry for full details). Hill's niece, Joan Ellison, recalled:

We tried all sorts of ways to find out what had happened. Then came the news (as the Allies advanced) that three graves had been found … soon after the Padre saw my aunt (whom Busty called Plum) and gave us all the terrible news. That sadness is still with me as I saw my aunt go through hell as well as losing a very good uncle. Uncle Harry was quiet, well spoken and well mannered – I think he was born in Liverpool – he had a slight Liverpudlian accent. He was absolutely 'sealed' as regards his job (his lips were sealed). He had a brother also in the army (contracted T.B.) in North Africa and died soon after Uncle Harry [personal correspondence, 2009].

Ellison also recalled that Hill had told her that when he was serving in North Africa he hadn't liked the thought of killing people but that he had been lying next to a comrade firing and when the shooting stopped he thought his friend was asleep, shook him and turned him over, only to see that his face had been shot off. 'After that he wanted to have a crack at the Germans' (personal interview, 2010).

Husband of Dorothy Hill of Creighton Road, Eltham, south-east London – Father of Peter Hill.
Age 29.
No inscription.
Row 1, graves 1–26. Also commemorated on the Saint-Sauvant Forest Memorial.

LANCE-SERGEANT JOHN RUSSELL JESSIMAN [1468628] ROYAL ARTILLERY, No.7 COMMANDO, MIDDLE EAST COMMANDO, 1ST SAS, SRS AND 1ST SAS (B SQN)

Russell Jessiman, as he was commonly known, was born on 30 July 1920 at Maryhill in Glasgow. Whilst working in the city as a photographer, he joined the 216th Battery, 54th Anti-Tank Regiment, Royal Artillery (TA), in May 1939. Embodied into the 64th Anti-Tank Regiment at the outbreak of war he was immediately appointed lance-sergeant, although two months later he reverted to the rank of gunner. Promoted to lance-bombardier at the end of the year he volunteered for No.7 Commando, based at Girvan, in August 1940. This was temporarily redesignated as No.2 Company, 3rd Special Service Battalion, but disembarked at Suez in Egypt in early March 1941 as A Battalion of Layforce. It carried out a largely abortive raid on Bardia along the Libyan coast on the night of 19–20 April, the men being then held aboard HMS *Glengyle* until the beginning of May when they were allowed ashore, somewhat disgruntled, at Alexandria.

On the night of 26–27 May 1941 A and B Battalions disembarked at Suda Bay on Crete to help evacuate Commonwealth troops after the German invasion. They subsequently formed part of the rearguard, fighting a running battle over the mountains en route to the embarkation point on the south coast. Jessiman was one of those lucky enough to be taken off to Egypt on the 31st, the majority of his comrades going into captivity. When Layforce disbanded that July he was absorbed into the Middle East Commando at Geneifa near to Kabrit as a bombardier from where he volunteered for the newly constituted 1st SAS on 26 September 1942.

Jessiman attended parachute course No.22 at Kabrit during February 1943, the majority of the Regiment's subunits being restructured as the Special Raiding Squadron the following month. Having taken part in the invasion of Sicily he was recommended for Operational Wings whilst a corporal of A Section, No.3 Troop, for 'Desert, Murro de Porco and Augusta'. The SRS subsequently landed at Bagnara on the toe of mainland Italy on 4 September during OPERATION BAYTOWN before taking part in the capture and defence of Termoli during OPERATION DEVON. Jessiman's service during this period is probably best summarised by his own hand – that December he wrote to the father of his friend, Joe Fassam:

Dear Mr Fassam,
It is with deepest regret I am writing this letter but I know you will want to know what happened when Joe met his death. I was with him at the time as we were both in the same section. Our job was north of Termoli and we made a landing in German lines on the night of October 3rd [*sic* – before dawn on the 3rd]. Our objective was approx 8 miles inland over very rough country occupied by the enemy. We had been marching approximately to 4 o'clock in the morning of the 4th [*sic* – 0530hrs on the 3rd] when we had a fight, we overpowered the enemy and were going on our way when we met very stiff opposition from the enemy. We had a pretty rough time of it as we were outnumbered and the Germans had field guns which they were firing at us.
Our officers decided to outflank the enemy and if possible bypass them. Our luck began to desert us for when we retreated we got into a wadi surrounded on all sides by the road (we did not know it at the time but we were in the middle of the German parachutists lines). It was just breaking daylight then and the Huns were firing mortars and machine guns at us. No way could we get out of the wadi unobserved or out of his range. He gradually closed in on us and we had the order to try and break out of the other end of the wadi. This we tried to do but Joe tried to get up the side of the wadi when a burst of machine-gun fire caught him in the chest. It was instantaneous. He did not suffer any pain and passed away before any of us could reach him. Nearly all of us lads were taken prisoner.

I happened to be lucky enough to escape [he and Lance-corporal Sid Payne lay low amongst the scrub until the Germans moved on] …

We left home together, he being in the 8th Commando, myself in the 7th. After the Commando got bust up we amalgamated together as one commando under the name of ME Commando. We were both together there and joined the SAS together …

Yours sincerely,

Russell Jessiman [see Fassam's entry under Sangro River War Cemetery, Italy, Volume II].

Jessiman arrived back in the UK with the rank of lance-sergeant at the beginning of January 1944, marrying Tess O'Malley in Glasgow on the 25th. He parachuted into France for OPERATION BULBASKET in the early hours of 12 June 1944 as the NCO in charge of eleven men. His and another stick dropped near to an advancing German convoy at the same time, BULBASKET's commander, Captain John Tonkin, later recalling:

Suddenly the sky was full of multi-coloured lights – green, blue, white and red – three to a container!! … What was sure was that they presented a grave danger to us for, almost immediately, all the German convoy lights went out, they stopped, and we could no longer hear their engines.

We moved very fast. I did not need to give any orders! Men were smashing the bulbs everywhere … We collected everything and got to blazes out of it. When we were at a reasonably safe distance, an abusive Sgt Jessiman told me it was the latest idea [*SAS Operation Bulbasket: Behind the Lines in Occupied France, 1944*, by Paul McCue].

During the night of 22–23 June Jessiman led a team that cut railway lines in two places south-west of Éguzon. Two days later he mined the N10 road south of Vivonne. He was captured on 3 July when the SAS camp within the Forêt de Verrières was attacked and was subsequently murdered in the Bois de Guron within the Forêt de Saint-Sauvant on the 7th. His remains were later identified by his signet ring bearing the initials 'JRJ' (see Lieutenant Richard Crisp's entry within this section for full details).

Son of George Jessiman of Croftend Avenue, Glasgow – Husband of Tess Jessiman of Sinclair Drive, Glasgow.

Age 23.

No inscription.

Row 1, graves 1–26. Also commemorated on the Saint-Sauvant Forest Memorial.

Corporal John **KINNIVANE** [6094156] Queen's Royal Regiment, No.8 Commando, Middle East Commando, 1st SAS, SRS and 1st SAS (B Sqn)

John Kinnivane was born on 1 August 1917 in Limerick, Eire. Having worked as a barman he enlisted into the Queen's Royal Regiment in January 1940 and was posted to the 2/6th Battalion. That October he volunteered for No.8 (Guards) Commando, this being temporarily reorganised into the 4th Special Service Battalion before disembarking at Suez in Egypt in early March 1941 as B Battalion, Layforce. When this disbanded he was posted to the Middle East Commando at Geneifa and volunteered for the SAS from there. Although his service record does not specify exactly when this was, it is likely to have been in late September 1942 when the SAS was granted regimental status and its ranks reinforced by men primarily from the nearby Middle East Commando Depot.

In March 1943 the majority of 1st SAS's subunits were reorganised as the Special Raiding Squadron, Kinnivane being posted to B Section, 3 Troop. He was awarded Operational Wings after Operation Husky, the invasion of Sicily, having landed at Capo Murro di Porco, where the SRS destroyed coastal batteries on 10 July, and again at the key port of Augusta that it secured two days later. He subsequently fought at Bagnara on mainland Italy on 4 September (Operation Baytown), and during the capture and fierce defence of Termoli the following month (Operation Devon) being promoted to lance-corporal. Returning to the UK at the beginning of January 1944 he was posted to B Squadron of the reconstituted 1st SAS. Having qualified as a parachutist at No.1 PTS at Ringway during February, he was promoted to corporal that April.

Kinnivane was dropped blind (that is, without an arranged reception committee) into the Deux-Sèvres département of western France on the night of 10–11 June 1944 for Operation Bulbasket. His group, consisting of Troopers Joe Ogg, Sam Pascoe and George Biffin, was tasked with attacking the Niort–Saumur railway. An inauspicious start saw Kinnivane, Pascoe and Ogg landing in the main square of Airvault where they were fired on by Germans before becoming separated. Biffin, who had led the stick from the aircraft, landed a short distance away and was captured. Unable to carry out their task, the remaining three re-established contact and arrived at the SAS camp within the Forêt de Verrières on 28 June.

Kinnivane was captured on 3 July when this camp was attacked and he was subsequently murdered in the Bois de Guron within the Forêt de Saint-Sauvant on the 7th (see Lieutenant Richard Crisp's entry within this section for full details).

Son of Mrs Mary Kinnivane of Catherine Street, Limerick, Eire.
Age 26.
No inscription.
Row 1, graves 1–26. Also commemorated on the Saint-Sauvant Forest Memorial.

Private Donald Macphail **LIVINGSTONE** [3324838] Argyll and Sutherland Highlanders, Auxiliary Units and 1st SAS (B Sqn)

Donald Livingstone was born on 14 October 1914 at Port Ellen on the Isle of Islay as the second eldest of thirteen children. Having worked as a baker at Curries, a small shop in his hometown, and then as a postman, he enlisted into the Argyll and Sutherland Highlanders in August 1940 at Auchengate, Troon. In April 1941 he was re-posted to HQ Auxiliary Units at Coleshill House, near Highworth in Wiltshire. When it was clear that the threat of German invasion had abated, and that the stay-behind role of the Auxiliaries was therefore redundant, Livingstone was one of many who volunteered for 1st SAS. It is likely that he did so in early February 1944, although this was not entered on his service record until 1 April. Attending parachute course 116A at No.1 PTS Ringway his instructor noted: 'jumped well. Normal reactions. Landings were good.'

Livingstone parachuted into France for Operation Bulbasket sometime between 10 and 12 June 1944. He was captured on 3 July when the SAS camp within the Forêt de Verrières was attacked and subsequently murdered in the Bois de Guron within the Forêt de Saint-Sauvant on the 7th (see Lieutenant Richard Crisp's entry for full details). His remains were one of the few confirmed by identity discs.

According to his nephews Peter Hart and Arthur Holyoake: 'at least five of his brothers served in various regiments so the odds that at least one would not return was very high. This was by far the greatest number of siblings from Islay who saw action at the same time ... Donald's mother and father had a croft (a fenced area of land, small and arable). It was Donald's mother who mostly attended to the croft, the milking of one cow and the feeding of several hens. After one early summer morning visit she returned to the family home in a state of anxiety. Family members enquired as to what the problem was and his mother explained that she had seen a soldier with a long coat and hat walking slowly down the line of the fence. She shouted at him and rattled the bucket she was carrying but the soldier never responded and drifted down the side of the field and faded into the distance! With six sons at war this event concerned her immensely and the sad news was delivered some months later that Donald's body had been discovered and that he was executed in the early morning in France. Was this apparition of the solider at the croft her son Donald? ... Donald knew the dangers of his last mission and the last member of our family he spoke to was my Great Aunt Margaret who he visited in Glasgow. She told me that Donald sat in her kitchen and was very concerned about going on the mission, saying that he would never return. When he left my aunt's she told us that there had been a towel hanging over the chair he was sitting on and that the towel was scorched – who knows! When she asked why he joined he told her that some of his friends were joining so in the war years friends stuck together' [personal correspondence, 2015].

Son of David and Catherine Livingstone (née MacPhail) of Port Ellen, Isle of Islay, Argyll – Brother of Lily, Flora, Margaret, Annie, Ian, Dougie, Islay, Duncan, Archie, William, David and Malcolm Livingstone.
Age 29.
Peace sleeping resting at last life's weary trials and suffering past
Row 2, grave 28. Also commemorated on the Saint-Sauvant Forest Memorial and on Port Ellen's war memorial.

CORPORAL LESLIE CHARLES <u>LONG</u> [6019123] ESSEX REGIMENT, ROYAL NORFOLK REGIMENT, AUXILIARY UNITS AND 1ST SAS (B SQN)

Les Long was born on 4 March 1918 in Tottenham, north London. In January 1940 he enlisted into the Essex Regiment stating that at the time he was living at Forest Gate in east London. Initially posted to the 302nd Infantry Training Centre he was soon appointed lance-corporal, marrying Lylie Eileen Martin in East Ham that May. The following month he transferred to the 2nd Battalion, Royal Norfolk Regiment, and that November was posted to the Norfolk Scout Section of the Auxiliary Units, serving alongside Private 'Chalky' White in the Wroxham Scout Patrol based at Beech House (see White's entry within this section). After Long had been promoted to corporal in July 1941, his son, Melvyn, was born in Norwich the following month. Although attached to the 902nd Defence Battery, Royal Artillery, for three months from October 1941, Long remained with the Auxiliaries until volunteering for 1st SAS, more than likely during February 1944. Attending parachute course 105 at No.1 PTS Ringway in March he was noted as being an 'attentive and hard worker' as well as a 'consistently good jumper'.

Long parachuted into a DZ north of Bouesse in the Indre département of central France for OPERATION BULBASKET on the night of 7–8 June 1944. His nine-man party under Lieutenant 'Twm' Stephens was met by their commander, Captain John Tonkin, who had jumped into the area with Lieutenant Richard Crisp in the early hours of the 6th (see Stephens' entry under Verrières Communal Cemetery, France). The following day the group was transported westwards by truck, a decision then being made to concentrate farther west in order to attack the railway line north and south of Poitiers.

Long was captured on 3 July when the SAS camp within the Forêt de Verrières was attacked, and he was subsequently murdered in the Bois de Guron within the Forêt de Saint-Sauvant on the 7th (see Lieutenant Richard Crisp's entry within this section for full details). Sergeant Johnny Holmes, one of the few survivors of the operation, later wrote to the War Office stating that he had seen Long whilst evading capture:

As we [Holmes and Trooper Tommy Cummings] were making our way through the wood we were joined by Cpl Long, Tpr Spooner and Tpr Brophy. I then told them to split up. Cpl Long and Trooper Spooner left together. I saw them try to cross a track. Shots were exchanged as we were leaving. I did not see any more [see entries for Brophy and Spooner in this section].

Son of Charles and Harriet Long (née Fisher) – Husband of Lylie Long of Rosedale Road, Forest Gate, east London – Father of Melvyn Long.
Age 26.
No inscription.
Row 1, graves 1–26. Also commemorated on the Saint-Sauvant Forest Memorial.

PRIVATE ALEXANDER McLEOD [2822451] SEAFORTH HIGHLANDERS, No.6 INDEPENDENT COMPANY, No.11 COMMANDO, MIDDLE EAST COMMANDO, SPECIAL BOAT SECTION, SRS AND 1ST SAS (B SQN)

Alexander McLeod was born on 10 June 1918 in the town of Wick on the north-eastern tip of the British Isles. In April 1939, whilst working as a labourer, he joined the local 4/5th Battalion, Seaforth Highlanders (TA), and was embodied at the outbreak of war that September. Although initially posted to the 5th Battalion in May 1940 he was re-posted to No.6 Independent Company, one of ten such companies intended for guerrilla-style operations that later formed the foundations on which the first Commando units were raised. When such companies were disbanded after the Norwegian Campaign the men were dispersed, McLeod being posted to the 2nd Special Service Battalion (later No.11 Scottish Commando) in November 1940 and embarking for the Middle East on 31 January 1941.

No.11, temporarily reorganised as C Battalion of Layforce, disembarked at Suez in Egypt at the beginning of March 1941 and was stood-to, then stood-down, from a raid on Bardia in mid April. Although disappointed, the men moved to Cyprus at the end of the month in readiness for OPERATION EXPORTER. This was to secure Syria, including what is modern-day Lebanon, from the Vichy French. In the early hours of 9 June No.11 subsequently landed close to the mouth of the Litani River in an attempt to seize bridges key to the Allied advance. Although these were destroyed by the French and the Commando suffered heavy casualties, it effectively tied down Vichy troops until advancing Australian forces arrived from the south.

On returning to Egypt Layforce was disbanded and McLeod was posted to the Middle East Commando Depot at Geneifa. In April 1943 he was re-posted to the Special Boat Section, having qualified as a parachutist that February at No.4 Middle East Training School, Kabrit. He appears to have volunteered for the Special Raiding Squadron on 28 October 1943, joining as a battlefield replacement in Italy. The SRS subsequently returned to the UK at the beginning of January 1944 and was reconstituted as 1st SAS.

Posted to B Squadron, McLeod undertook refresher parachute training at No.1 PTS at Ringway during February 1944. He dropped into France for OPERATION BULBASKET sometime between 10 and 12 June and was captured on 3 July when the SAS camp within the Forêt de Verrières was attacked. He was subsequently murdered in the Bois de Guron within the Forêt de Saint-Sauvant on the 7th (see Lieutenant Richard Crisp's entry within this section for full details). His remains were identified by his tattoos, BULBASKET's former commander, Captain John Tonkin, MC, noting at the court of inquiry that 'he was the only man with heavily tattooed arms'.

Son of Mr and Mrs Alexander McLeod of Grant Street, Wick, Caithness.
Age 26.
No inscription.
Row 1, graves 1–26. Also commemorated on the Saint-Sauvant Forest Memorial.

Private Henry MULLEN [2935098] Queen's Own Cameron Highlanders, L Detachment SAS Brigade, 1st SAS, SRS and 1st SAS (B Sqn)

Henry Mullen was born on 7 July 1915 at Eastwood on the outskirts of Glasgow. Having worked as a painter's labourer he enlisted into the Queen's Own Cameron Highlanders at Inverness in April 1940 and was posted to the regiment's infantry training centre. Here he was promoted to lance-corporal the following month and to corporal that November. In March 1941 he disembarked in the Middle East where he was posted to the 2nd Battalion. His service record states that he was 'wounded and evacuated 15/16.6.41' this being during Operation Battleaxe, an attempt to push the enemy from eastern Libya. His battalion was to clear Sollum and Halfaya Pass, exploiting any success whilst two further attacks thrust towards the besieged port of Tobruk. Rommel had other ideas. Tipped off by radio intercept, his forces were ready and Mullen's battalion was beaten back, its tank support having been depleted by mines and anti-tank guns. Mullen was subsequently posted as 'missing believed POW' as of 15 June, the first day of the attack. However, within a few days he had been located and was soon convalescing in hospital. He reverted to the rank of private at his own request on the first day of September.

Mullen was taken on the strength of L Detachment, SAS Brigade, on 24 April 1942 having reported for parachute training at Kabrit four days earlier. That summer, on his 26th birthday, he infiltrated Fuka aerodrome, far behind German lines, entering the site twice with Major Paddy Mayne, DSO, to place explosives on fourteen planes before being challenged. The two threw grenades and set charges on four further airframes before returning to the main party. This group then drove their Jeeps onto the runway destroying yet more aircraft. During the withdrawal the party was caught in the open by enemy fighters and their bogus German staff car, nicknamed the 'Blitz Buggy', was destroyed. Admitted to hospital that August after a Jeep accident, Mullen was unable to rejoin the Regiment until late October when he was promoted to lance-corporal (see Captain Tom Montgomerie's entry under Suez War Memorial Cemetery, Egypt, Volume I, for full details). Early in 1943 the Regiment was moved to the coast of Palestine (modern-day Israel) where it undertook arduous training. It briefly returned to Kabrit where the majority of the Regiment's subunits were restructured as the Special Raiding Squadron on 19 March before mounting amphibious exercises in the Gulf of Aqaba.

The SRS was at the forefront of Operation Husky, the July 1943 Allied invasion of Sicily, Mullen landing at Capo Murro di Porco on the 10th to destroy coastal batteries that threatened the fleet. Two days later the SRS captured the port of Augusta, thus enabling a more rapid advance up the east coast. Having subsequently been awarded Operational Wings, Mullen landed at Bagnara on the toe of mainland Italy on 4 September during Operation Baytown, and was later wounded in action during Operation Devon at Termoli on 5 October when a shell landed on an SRS truck (see numerous casualties under Sangro River War Cemetery, Italy, Volume II, for full details). He was released from hospital in mid November, returning to the UK in mid March 1944.

Mullen parachuted into a DZ near the farm of Primo la Coupe, close to la Font d'Usson and south of Poitiers in western France, on the night of 17–18 June 1944. He was dropped along with Sergeant Bob Heavens, Corporal Bill Allan, Parachutist David Gray and four Jeeps to a reception party, the group making contact with the enemy on leaving the area (see entries for the remainder of this stick within this section). Two days before, when the Regiment was locked down at 'The Cage', RAF Fairford, he had been deprived of his lance-corporal's stripe for a minor offence. Captured on 3 July 1944 when the SAS camp within the Forêt de Verrières was attacked he was subsequently murdered on his 29th birthday in the Bois de Guron within the Forêt de Saint-Sauvant on the 7th (see Lieutenant Richard Crisp's entry within this section for full details). Bulbasket's commander, Captain John Tonkin, later identified his remains by the embroidered boxing shorts that he always wore.

Son of Mrs Catherine Mullen of Lawmoor Street, Glasgow – Brother of Helen Mullen and of Willie Mullen of Rosendale Road, Pollokshaws, Glasgow, who also served with the Cameron Highlanders.
Age 29.
No inscription.
Row 1, graves 1–26. Also commemorated on the Saint-Sauvant Forest Memorial.

PRIVATE DONALD **PHILLIPS** [5498990] HAMPSHIRE REGIMENT, No.7 COMMANDO, MIDDLE EAST COMMANDO, L DETACHMENT SAS BRIGADE, 1ST SAS, SRS AND 1ST SAS (B SQN)

Donald Phillips was born on 1 September 1920 at Milford-on-Sea in Hampshire. In June 1937, whilst working as a mechanic, he joined D Company of the 5/7th Battalion, Hampshire Regiment (TA), at Lymington and was appointed the rank of boy. Having been called up in August 1939, and embodied two days before war was declared, he volunteered for special service the following October. He was subsequently posted to No.7 Commando based at Girvan on the west coast of Scotland. Redesignated No.2 Company, 3rd Special Service Battalion, this unit weighed anchor at the beginning of 1941 and, having stopped in South Africa and Aden, disembarked at Suez in Egypt as A Battalion of Layforce, in early March.

Returning from a largely abortive raid on Bardia along the Libyan coast on the night of 19–20 April 1941 the battalion was held aboard HMS *Glengyle* until the beginning of May when the men were allowed ashore, somewhat disgruntled, at Alexandria. On the night of 26–27 May A and B Battalions subsequently disembarked at Suda Bay on Crete to help evacuate Commonwealth troops after the German invasion. They formed part of the rearguard, fighting a running battle over the mountains en route to the embarkation point on the south coast. Phillips was one of those lucky enough to be taken off to Egypt on the 31st, the majority of his comrades going into captivity.

After Layforce disbanded that July Phillips was posted to the Middle East Commando Depot at Geneifa near to Kabrit. A short period attached to North Africa HQ followed before he moved to Latrun Training Centre in Palestine that August. In October he was posted to No.321 POW camp, probably as a temporary guard. In January 1942 he rejoined the Middle East Commando, moving a month later to Syria, then to Iraq and Transjordan before returning to Egypt in April. He volunteered for L Detachment, SAS Brigade, on 15 September 1942, a few days before it was granted regimental status.

The majority of 1st SAS' subunits were restructured as the Special Raiding Squadron on 19 March 1943, Phillips landing at the forefront of OPERATION HUSKY, the invasion of Sicily, when it assaulted coastal batteries at Capo Murro di Porco on 10 July. Two days later it captured the port of Augusta, subsequently landing at Bagnara on the toe of the mainland Italy on 4 September during Operation Baytown. Having sailed round to the Adriatic it saw fierce fighting during the capture and defence of Termoli the following month (Operation Devon).

At the beginning of January 1944 Phillips arrived back in the UK where the Regiment was once again reconstituted as 1st SAS. He parachuted into France for Operation Bulbasket sometime between 10 and 12 June 1944 and was captured on 3 July when the SAS camp within the Forêt de Verrières was attacked. He was subsequently murdered in the Bois de Guron within the Forêt de Saint-Sauvant on the 7th (see Lieutenant Richard Crisp's entry within this section for full details).

Son of Albert and Martha Phillips (née Wheeler) of Stanley Terrace, Keyhaven Road, Milford-on-Sea, Hampshire – Brother of Ronald Phillips.
Age 23.
He gave his life for us. We shall always remember him
Row 1, graves 1–26. Also commemorated on the Saint-Sauvant Forest Memorial.

Private William Ernest Liddell **RICHARDSON** [92635]
Royal Army Service Corps and 1st SAS (B Sqn)

Ernie Richardson, as he was most commonly known to both friends and family, was born on 19 December 1917 in the mining village of Cowdenbeath in Fifeshire. Having worked as a motor mechanic, he enlisted into the Royal Army Service Corps on 15 September 1939 and was posted to No.1 Training Company. Joining 3 GHQ Company in late December 1940 he arrived in France the following month as part of the BEF. Unfortunately his movements are unknown until he was evacuated to the UK when he was initially posted to 23 Motor Coach Company before joining 264 Company. In April 1941 he was re-posted to GHQ Auxiliary Units as an attached driver, and having joined HQ 45th Division in March 1943 he volunteered for 1st SAS on 1 February 1944. The following month he attended parachute course 105 at No.1 PTS Ringway, his instructor noting that he was 'keen and reliable, worked hard throughout, average jumper'.

During Operation Bulbasket Richardson was a member of Sergeant Johnny Holmes' stick that parachuted into France blind (that is, without an arranged reception committee) at a DZ 30 kilometres to the north of Châtellerault on the night of 10–11 June 1944. Tasked with cutting the Poitiers–Tours railway line Tommy Cummings, a fellow member of the patrol, later described their approach:

> Once we had completed a fairly hard march of about 12 miles, we came across our intended target. Sgt Holmes sent me forward 30 yards or so and Tpr E Richardson the same distance in the opposite direction. We were acting as his protection as he laid the charges which I think was a thirty minute delay. We heard a voice call out in German (who's there or something like that). We withdrew away from the immediate area and came upon a lane with hedges down both sides. Rather than be caught with nowhere to escape if ambushed here two of the blokes found a field gate (Ronnie Guard?/Ernie Richardson). They were first through it followed by me and then Holmes. Johnny slipped or tripped but ended up on his back, with the Bergan weight he was carrying, he twisted his ankle. Ronnie and Ernie

walked on unaware of the situation behind them. We lost them as I helped Johnny up and helped carry some of the weight off his back. They actually found a safe house and were in the attic of a farm house. Next day, I think, by chance we met a farmer who told us he had two men in his house who were English, and we were all reunited again [correspondence between former B Squadron members Joe Schofield, MBE, and Tommy Cummings, 2010].

Richardson was captured on 3 July 1944 when the SAS camp within the Forêt de Verrières was attacked. He was subsequently murdered in the Bois de Guron within the Forêt de Saint-Sauvant on the 7th (see Lieutenant Richard Crisp's entry within this section for full details).

Son of William and Anne Richardson of Foulford Street, Cowdenbeath, Fifeshire.
Age 26.
Sadly missed
Row 1, graves 1–26. Also commemorated on Cowdenbeath's war memorial and on the Saint-Sauvant Forest Memorial.

Private Sidney Jack **RYLAND** [5729976] Dorsetshire Regiment, Auxiliary Units and 1st SAS (B Sqn)

Sid Ryland (occasionally known by his middle name Jack) was born on 11 January 1915 in the village of Painswick in Gloucestershire. Having worked as a grocer's assistant and van driver he enlisted into the Dorsetshire Regiment in April 1940. After training he was posted to the Dorset Scout Section of the Auxiliary Units based at Blandford. Here he served alongside Corporal Jim Rideout, Privates Sam Pascoe, Alan Ashley, George Biffin and George Cogger, and Lieutenant Peter Weaver, all of whom later took part in Operation Bulbasket (see entries for Ashley and Cogger above, and for Pascoe under Bayeux Memorial, France). With the threat of German invasion greatly diminished, and the guerilla role of the Auxiliaries therefore redundant, they volunteered for 1st SAS on 1 February 1944. Ryland subsequently attended parachute course 105 at No.1 PTS Ringway the following month, his instructor noting that he was 'quiet and intelligent' and a 'good all round performer'.

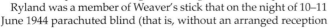

Ryland was a member of Weaver's stick that on the night of 10–11 June 1944 parachuted blind (that is, without an arranged reception committee) into the Deux-Sèvres département of western France for Operation Bulbasket. Landing 16 kilometres south of the intended DZ, it was tasked to attack railway lines. The aircraft had already dropped Corporal John Kinnivane's party inaccurately. Despite half of Ryland's stick dropping into trees, the party of four (Weaver, Rideout, Parachutists Ryland and Ashley) found their bearings, made their way to the Parthenay line, set charges, and derailed a train on the morning of the 14th. Weaver himself later reported: 'At 1000hrs Tpr Ryland and myself heard a train in the distance followed by an explosion, after which we heard no more trains that day.' Having stretched their twenty-four-hour ration packs to last four days the party made contact with locals who supplied them whilst en route to the main SAS group. Reports vary, but they reached the main party's camp within the Forêt de Verrières some time between 24 and 28 June.

Ryland was captured on 3 July when the camp was attacked. He was subsequently murdered in the Bois de Guron within the Forêt de Saint-Sauvant on the 7th (see Lieutenant Richard Crisp's entry within this section for full details).

Son of Sidney and Margaret Ryland (née Scrivens) of The Swan Inn, Minchinhampton, Gloucestershire.
Age 29.
Golden memories silently kept we who loved him will never forget
Row 1, graves 1–26. Also commemorated on Painswick's war memorial and on the Saint-Sauvant Forest Memorial.

PRIVATE ERIC GEORGE **SIMMONS** [124047] ROYAL ARMY SERVICE CORPS, AUXILIARY UNITS, ROYAL ARMY ORDNANCE CORPS AND 1ST SAS (B SQN)

Eric Simmons was born on 23 April 1918 in Sydenham, south-east London. He enlisted into the Royal Army Service Corps in December 1939 and was posted to No.7 Training Centre before rotating though various RASC companies as a driver during 1940. That December he married Rose Ada Dawson in Catford and the following April was posted to HQ Auxiliary Units at Coleshill House near Highworth in Wiltshire. He transferred to the Royal Army Ordnance Corps three months later, although it is likely that he remained with the Auxiliaries having done so. During 1943 he was posted to several different transport and light anti-aircraft companies, volunteering for 1st SAS on 1 February 1944. The following month he attended parachute course 105 at No.1 PTS Ringway alongside many other Auxiliary recruits.

Simmons parachuted into France for OPERATION BULBASKET sometime between 10 and 12 June 1944. He was captured on 3 July when the SAS camp within the Forêt de Verrières was attacked and was subsequently murdered in the Bois de Guron within the Forêt de Saint-Sauvant on the 7th (see Lieutenant Richard Crisp's entry for full details). His remains were identified by the initials 'E.S' on his ring; it is therefore unclear why his is not one of the definite graves within this row.

Husband of Rose Simmons of Knaphill Way, Bellingham, south-east London – Father of Ronald Simmons (born May 1942).
Age 26.
No inscription.
Row 1, graves 1–26. Also commemorated on the Saint-Sauvant Forest Memorial.

PRIVATE ANTHONY JOHN **SPOONER** [6216295] MIDDLESEX REGIMENT, PARACHUTE REGIMENT AND 1ST SAS (B SQN)

Tony Spooner, or Bill as he preferred to be known, was born on 1 December 1923 in Middlesex. Although he passed his 11-plus exams for grammar school his family were unable to afford the incidental costs of sending him and he therefore attended the local secondary school in Waltham Abbey. On leaving he found employment as a cost clerk for Jessop & Gough Solicitors before enlisting into the Middlesex Regiment in October 1941, increasing his age by three months in order to do so. Initially posted to the 70th (Young Soldiers) Battalion he was promoted to lance-corporal in May 1942 and was advanced to corporal two months later. Having volunteered for Airborne Forces he attended parachute course 75 at No.1 PTS Ringway during July 1943 and was noted as 'reliable, fearless, a good jumper'. However, although posted to the 9th (Eastern and Home Counties) Battalion, Parachute Regiment, the change was unsettling and after various misdemeanours he was reduced to the rank of private on the authority of the commander of 3rd Parachute Brigade. He volunteered for 1st SAS on 16 March 1944 and was posted to B Squadron.

Spooner parachuted into France for OPERATION BULBASKET sometime between 10 and 12 June 1944. He was captured on 3 July when the SAS camp within the Forêt de Verrières was attacked, Sergeant Johnny Holmes, one of the few survivors, later stating that he had seen Spooner whilst the group attempted to break contact with the enemy:

> As we [Holmes and Trooper Tommy Cummings] were making our way through the wood we were joined by Cpl Long, Tpr Spooner and Tpr Brophy. I then told them to split up. Cpl Long and Trooper Spooner left together. I saw them try to cross a track. Shots were exchanged as we were leaving. I did not see any more [see entries for both Brophy and Long above].

Having been captured, Spooner and his comrades were murdered in the Bois de Guron within the Forêt de Saint-Sauvant on 7 July 1944 (see Lieutenant Richard Crisp's entry within this section for full details). The War Office notified his family the following June:

> I am directed to state that your son was one of a party which was surrounded by a superior force of the enemy. It is deeply regretted that nothing was heard of them until certain graves were found which upon careful investigation must be presumed to be those of your son and his comrades … The circumstances of your son's death are still under investigation but it is my painful duty to tell you that the available evidence suggests that they were shot by the enemy after capture.

Son of John (known as Harry and who, having also falsified his age to join up early during the First World War, named his son 'Tony' after the horse that was shot from beneath him whilst serving in the RHA) and of Henrietta Spooner (née Wade) of Lea Road, Waltham Abbey, Essex – Older brother to Irene and Peter Spooner.
Age 20.
Golden memories silently kept of a dear one we loved and will never forget
Row 1, graves 1–26. Also commemorated on the Saint-Sauvant Forest Memorial and on Waltham Abbey's war memorial.

PRIVATE VICTOR OWEN **WHITE** [6011364] ESSEX REGIMENT, ROYAL NORFOLK REGIMENT, AUXILIARY UNITS AND 1ST SAS (B SQN)

'Chalky' White was born in West Ham, east London, on 16 October 1918, later living in nearby Stratford. In March 1935, whilst working as a labourer, he joined the local 6th Battalion, Essex Regiment (TA). Just over a year later White and a friend from the same unit joined the regular Royal Norfolk Regiment (service number 5772180), both being posted to the 2nd Battalion. Neither had left the Essex Regiment. They were disciplined when the truth came to light and in September 1937 the 18-year-old White deserted whilst serving on Gibraltar. His company commander noted dryly 'up to the time of his disappearance into Spain he had the makings of a good soldier'. Whether his motive was to see action during the neighbouring Spanish Civil War is unknown.

White surrendered to civil police in the UK in January 1941 and having been convicted by court martial forfeited all former service. That June he was posted to the Norfolk Scout Section of the Auxiliary Units. Although briefly attached to the 902nd Defence Battery, Royal Artillery, at the end of the year he served alongside Corporal Les Long in the Wroxham Scout Patrol based at Beech House (see Long's entry within this section). In May 1943 he transferred, probably only nominally, to the 1st Battalion, Royal Norfolks, but volunteered for 1st SAS on 1 February 1944. The following month he attended parachute course 105 at No.1 PTS Ringway, his instructor noting 'after a shaky start improved to become good jumper'. That May he returned to Stratford to marry Gladys Cornell.

White parachuted into a DZ north of Bouesse in the Indre département of central France for OPERATION BULBASKET on the night of 7–8 June 1944. His nine-man party, under Lieutenant 'Twm' Stephens, was met by their commander, Captain John Tonkin, who had jumped into the area with Lieutenant Richard Crisp in the early hours of the 6th. The following day they were transported westwards by truck, a decision then being made to concentrate farther west in order to attack the railway line north and south of Poitiers.

White was captured on 3 July 1944 when the SAS camp within the Forêt de Verrières was attacked, and he was subsequently murdered in the Bois de Guron within the Forêt de Saint-Sauvant on the 7th (see Lieutenant Richard Crisp's entry within this section for full details).

Husband of Gladys White of Rooley Moor Road, Lanehead, Rochdale, Lancashire – Brother of Frank White of Leytonstone.
Age 26.
No inscription.
Row 1, graves 1–26. Also commemorated on the Saint-Sauvant Forest Memorial.

ROSENDAËL CEMETERY

Rosendaël is a suburb of Dunkirk in the Nord département of Nord-Pas-de-Calais. The cemetery entrance lies on the rue de Téteghem near to the junction with quai des Maraichers. GPS co-ordinates: Latitude 51.04060, Longitude 2.42531

CAPORAL PIERRE **LEOSTIC** [53356] 1ᴱᴿ COMPAGNIE DE CHASSEURS PARACHUTISTES AND L DETACHMENT SAS BRIGADE (FRENCH SQN)

Pierre Leostic was born on 24 December 1924 at Rosendaël in Dunkirk as the only son of five children. His family moved to Brittany as refugees from the German Blitzkrieg and in June 1940, aged just 15, Leostic sailed from Brest for England leaving his mother the following note: 'My Dear Mother, I beg you do not blame me, my blood boils in my veins. My dream is to carry a gun and use it. I took one hundred francs and my identity card. Oh, God! I want to be French, even French, French forever!' Arriving in the UK he was sent to a Free French school in Wales from where he 'escaped', 'lost' his ID card, and joined de Gaulle's forces. At 6'1" he easily passed himself off as an 18-year-old. Posted to the 1ᵉʳ Compagnie d'infanterie de l'air in January 1941 he attended parachute course at No.1 PTS Ringway that April and trained at Exbury from May. Having embarked on the SS *Cameronia* at Greenock in late July 1941 he arrived at Suez, Egypt, the company then moving, via Haifa, to Beirut in Lebanon. Training in Syria followed, as did a change of name, the company being titled 1ᵉʳ Compagnie de chasseurs parachutistes from mid October. At the beginning of January 1942 this was absorbed into L Detachment, SAS Brigade, at Kabrit as the Free French Squadron and thus fell under the command of Captain David Stirling.

Leostic subsequently took part in OPERATION TEN D, a raid on Crete's Heraklion airfield timed to coincide with similar attacks to alleviate pressure on a Malta-bound convoy. Led by Capitaine Georges Bergé and Captain Earl George Jellicoe his small team, totalling six, was landed to the east of the target from the *Triton*, a Greek submarine, in the early hours of 11 June 1942. Despite numerous delays, the rocky terrain and their heavy loads, they arrived near the airfield's perimeter on the night of the 12–13th. Although challenged they conducted a recce before withdrawing. The following night, as they were lying prone cutting their way through the wire, they were approached by an enemy patrol. Thanks to the quick thinking, and loud snoring, of one of Leostic's colleagues, the men managed to pass themselves off as drunken locals before destroying one spotter aircraft and an estimated twenty-three bombers. On the 17th, having slowly withdrawn towards the south coast, they sadly received word that a large number of Cretan hostages had been shot in reprisal for the raid. Two days later Jellicoe and his Greek guide went ahead to arrange the team's evacuation but on returning that evening found that the Frenchmen had been surrounded and captured, Leostic having been killed in action:

> Some young local peasants from the neighbouring village arrived in a great state of agitation, and from what was said and the signs used, I [Jellicoe] was led to understand that Commandant Bergé had been betrayed and attacked by a party of Germans. After a resistance in which one of his party was killed [Leostic], he had surrendered and been led off.

Files of the German 164th Infantry Division's Intelligence Section on Crete were later captured, the following extract being amongst them:

> In the night 8/9.5 at the airdrome of Kastelli and on 13/14.6 at Heraklion airdrome serious sabotage was caused to airplanes. Those at Kastelli could be discovered in time but at Heraklion thirteen planes received heavy damage. The culprits are obviously enemy sabotage commandos landed during the period under review and they must have received shelter from the civilian population. As a reprisal fifty hostages were shot in Heraklion on 14.6.42.
> On the 19th of June the sabotage Commando which was active at the Heraklion airdromes has been rendered harmless. This band consisted of 'De Gaulles' and one man was shot and three taken prisoner [WO 201/772].

Bergé's own report, written after he had been liberated from Colditz, states:

> At nearly 8pm I gave the order to pack our equipment in preparation for our last move. Ten minutes later, when we were about to hit the road, two columns of Germans, each with twenty men, appeared in the east and the west. From that moment the four of us realised the game was almost up. We tried to escape to the south but met a third column coming up through the bushes at the entrance of the ravine. I decided to engage, despite the number of attackers hoping to make it to last light and then take advantage of the night to escape. The Germans, at a respectable distance, open fire. Three machine guns concentrate their fire on us four French crouching behind the bushes. Grenades launched by rifle exploded around us. As we only carried machine guns effective up to 100 yards we did not fire and retained our ammunition. A German officer who ventured too close was killed immediately. This first response cools the ardour of the attackers. Leostic, eager for a fight, jumped about 20 yards ahead to get into a better firing position. As soon as he opened fire he received a burst of machine-gun fire from a position hidden 50 yards to his left. He fell mortally wounded, got up again still insulting the advancing Germans, and fell again finished by a final burst.

The Red Cross informed Leostic's parents of his death during October 1943, his mother receiving the Greek Croix de guerre in 1946 when his remains were brought from Crete to be reinterred within Rosendaël Cemetery.

Son of Gabriel Leostic, Chief of Customs, and of Lucie Leostic (née Duriez) – Brother of Marguerite, Thérèse, Yvonne and Geneviève.
Age 17.
Section O, row 2. Also commemorated in Brest, Dunkirk and Heraklion which each has a road named after him. A small container of earth, brought back from Crete by his comrade Jack Sibard, is encased in glass on his grave.

SAINT-SEVER CEMETERY EXTENSION, ROUEN

During the First World War Rouen was home to 3rd Echelon GHQ as well as large supply depots of various Commonwealth units. Numerous service hospitals were also located in, or near to, Rouen and the dead were brought to the city's cemetery. Eventually an extension was created and this now contains 8,348 Commonwealth burials of the First World War. There are also 328 burials of the Second World War, mainly prisoners of war that died in captivity. Eighteen are unidentified.

Rouen is located in the Seine-Maritime département of Haute-Normandie. The cemetery lies off the N138 (signposted Elbeuf) on the rue Stanislas de Jardin within the commune of Petit-Quevilly. GPS co-ordinates: Latitude 49.41035, Longitude 1.06698

DRIVER HAROLD **ERLIS** [1901238] ROYAL WARWICKSHIRE REGIMENT, ROYAL ENGINEERS AND 2ND SAS (C SQN)

Harold Erlis was born in the parish of St Paul's, Liverpool, on 14 May 1919. Whilst working as a capstan lathe operator he joined the 7th Battalion, Royal Warwickshire Regiment (TA), at Coventry in May 1939 (service number 5111880). According to his record he failed to report for mobilisation at the outbreak of war that September and was declared a deserter on the 26th of that month. However, in December he enlisted into the Royal Engineers and was posted to C Company, 1st Motor Transport Depot, as a driver. After re-posting to M Company he disembarked in France at the beginning of April 1940 as part of the BEF. He was subsequently evacuated from Dunkirk on 31 May.

Once home Erlis was posted as a driver to the Royal Warwickshire Regiment's infantry training depot where his previous service with the regiment escaped detection. In November 1942, whilst serving with the 53rd Division, he married Eileen Naughalty at St Celopas in Toxteth. A year later he volunteered to become a parachutist, attending course No.92 at No.1 PTS Ringway. Initially posted to 177 Workshop and Park Company he was attached to the Airborne Forces Development Centre at Boscombe Down airfield in April 1944, although he had in fact been working there since prior to his parachute course. Having recovered from an injury sustained playing football against the RAF he volunteered for 2nd SAS on 12 May.

Erlis parachuted into France for OPERATION TRUEFORM as a member of the TRUEFORM-1 party on the night of 16–17 August 1944. Tasked with destroying petrol supplies, harassing the enemy, and reporting on movement, his team was dropped blind (that is, without an arranged reception committee) just south of Saint-Paul-de-Fourques in the Eure département of Haute-Normandie. 2nd SAS' Casualty Report quotes Captain Dick Holland, MC, commander of the operation:

> This man was last seen by me on Aug 20 when he and another set out to lay tyre bursters on the road near Brionne. On the way they went to a farm which was occupied by Germans, with the idea of placing some incendiaries in the German trucks. They ran into four Germans lying under a hedge who gave themselves up, then twelve more surrendered and while dealing with these, shooting started. According to the Maquis, Bintley was hit in the head and died almost at once, while Erlis was taken prisoner having presumably stayed behind to look after Bintley [WO 361/716 – see Parachutist Thomas Bintley's entry under Bayeux War Cemetery, France].

Holland added a little more detail in the post-operation report: 'Bintley was unfortunately hit in the head, and presumably Erlis who was his friend was obliged to look after him and was taken prisoner' (WO 218/199). The reported date of the event varies, Holland stating that it took place on the 20th, the subsequent war crimes file recording Erlis' date of death as the 19th, whilst Bintley's date of death is officially recorded as the 20th. The confusion appears to have risen after the date originally recorded, 'on or shortly after 19.8.44', was edited to the 19th only.

Sergent-chef Alphonse Marais, who was present during the engagement, took up the narrative:

> Pte Erlis was captured at the same time I was … The SS took him along with me to a stable which was in a disgustingly filthy state. We were severely beaten with fists and rifle butts. Erlis carried an American automatic carbine and a Colt automatic. He had all his equipment, both as regards clothing and as regards material (maps, compasses, etc etc). As they had taken Bintley's arms and equipment the Boches, who were furious, took away those of Erlis. These facts took place in the presence of the farmer and of one of his employees, who are from a farm next to the spot where Bintley is buried. Pte Erlis was taken away by the Germans, who were beating him all the while, to a destination unknown to me … The German SS were part of the 'Adolf Hitler' 'Hermann Goering' and 'Das Reich' Divisions. There were also Belgian Waffen SS whom I heard speaking German [WO 311/394].

Erlis was subsequently reported missing in action believed POW. However: 'on 29 October 1944 the body of Pct Erlis was found in a dyke with his hands tied securely at his sides without head cover or boots. It is thought that Pct Erlis was brutally murdered after interrogation' (WO 311/904). Holland later confirmed:

> Pte Erlis was found buried at Yvette-sur-Seine having been washed up from the Seine over two months after capture. His body was too decomposed when washed up to see if there had been any violence. The farmer where Erlis was captured stated that the Germans tried to make him tell where the rest of our party were in hiding but he refused to speak. The farmer says he was ill-treated. He was seen four days later very carefully guarded still only ¼ mile from our hide. I could find no trace of him after that, until he was washed up [WO 311/904].

The file also contains a note from the casualty department dated December 1944:

> There is no doubt as to identity as the 'rubbing' from the identity disc makes the name and Army No. quite clear. Death has been officially recorded: - Killed in action on or shortly after 19.8.44 and next-of-kin was informed accordingly on 7.12.44. Next-of-kin subsequently called here and she was informed that her husband's body was found by a Frenchman and buried, but we were not at liberty to disclose the place yet [WO 311/904].

The Frenchman, Albert Piette, stated:

On the date of 29 Oct 44 I, the undersigned Piette, game keeper at Yville sur Seine, assisted by Genet, Bernard Leclere, Gervais to bring a young Allied soldier dressed in maroon leather, either a motor-cyclist or an airman with his hands tied behind his back and bound with the belt of his clothes, without shoes. The medallion (identity disc) in the box was round his neck – the first letter defaced: GIS H. CE. 190-1238. The silver medallion of St Therese. These were handed to M. Le Comte de Malatie, Mayor of Yville s/Seine on 31 Oct 44. Buried in the courtyard of M. Barbey near to the lake [WO 311/904].

The ensuing war crimes case was summarised as follows:

Pct Bintley and Pct Erlis were involved in a clash with German soldiers on the 19 August at St Paul de Fourques, Q948910. According to the Cure of St Eloi de Forques, Q942941, Bintley was killed and Erlis taken prisoner of war.

The body of Erlis was subsequently found at Yville sur Seine, M034113, 12 miles away. His hands were tied with his belt. The position of Yville sur Seine suggest that the enemy were about to attempt the crossing of the Seine and did not wish to be encumbered with prisoners … [the bridges over the Seine had been bombed by the Allies]

Comte de Malarite, Mayor of Yville sur Seine, stated that someone had informed him of the presence of a body, an allied soldier, in the dyke at the Trou Buquet, and he had ordered M. Piette to recover it and inter it …

The grave of 1901238 Spr Erlis H, was located as well as the place where the body was discovered. There was a rough cross erected, and the details given in the statement of M. Piette is roughly engraved on a strip of tin. A helmet, Br type, hangs on the cross, but it was explained by M. Piette that it did not belong to the soldier buried there [WO 311/904].

In January 1945 the Special Investigation Bureau noted the slim likelihood of anyone being convicted:

He [Erlis] is buried near the ferry ramp, map reference 02951315 on sheet 8E/6, Duclair, 1:50,000 [near Clos Saint-Paul]. The name of the German unit who killed Bintley and took Erlis prisoner is not yet known except that they were SS of various units. The field post number is not known. The name of the German unit which bound Erlis is not known, though they were probably SS. No wounds were noted on the body by those who found him, but they stated that they had not examined it closely. The body lies in the grave, tied in the same manner in which it was found …

There seems no possibility of identifying unit or individual perpetrators, unless something turns up in POW's statements. I think 51 Div are unlikely to be able to help, as Germans were so mixed up. No further action, unless something else turns up which ties in [WO 311/904].

The SIB wrote to the Under Secretary of State two months later:

1. A Special Investigating Officer from this headquarters conducted a preliminary investigation into the alleged murder of 1901238 Spr Erlis, H. 2. Evidence exists to show that Erlis was a PW but eyewitnesses of his death, place, time and perpetrators are missing. 3. It is, therefore, NOT proposed to take further action by this headquarters on this case [WO 311/904].

As late as 1948 some authorities still believed that Erlis was at large as a deserter, the plain clothes section of Liverpool Police reporting that: 'information has now been received from the Civil Police, Liverpool, that as the result of visit to 24, Essex Street, it was ascertained from Mrs Erlis (Elsie), wife of Harold Erlis, that the latter was killed in action in 1944'. That November an inquiry noted that Erlis had been:

Found to have improperly enlisted into the Corps of Royal Engineers on a TA (D of E) engagement as No 1907238 Sapper H Erlis, and to be killed in action in North West Europe on or about 19 Aug 44. No disciplinary action taken in respect of improper enlistment and absence but pay withheld for the period from 01/09/39 to 15/12/39.

Son of William and Florence Erlis (née Appleton) of Essex Street, Liverpool – Husband of Eileen ('Elsie') Erlis of Ruby Street, Liverpool.
Age 25.
No inscription.
Block S, Grave 1.I.12.

SENNECEY-LE-GRAND
SAS BRIGADE MEMORIAL

At dawn on 4 September 1944 Jeeps of 3rd (French) SAS, under the command of Capitaine Guy de Combaud Roquebrune, formed up at this spot during OPERATION NEWTON. The four vehicles drove into Sennecey-le-Grand, concentrating all their firepower on an enemy column that was parked along the main road. Finding their planned escape route blocked they were forced to U-turn and make the return pass through the now alerted enemy. The majority of the SAS were subsequently killed, including de Combaud Roquebrune, the Germans subsequently shooting hostages that they used as human shields whilst withdrawing from the town. This was liberated by French tanks later that day.

The memorial originally commemorated wartime Free French parachutists. It was designed by Jean Melinand, himself a former member of 3rd SAS, and inaugurated in the presence of Sir David Stirling, DSO, OBE, on 4 September 1992. The following year Stirling suggested that, in order to reflect the diverse nationalities of those that made up the wartime SAS Brigade, it should become the memorial to all those members of the Special Air Service who had lost their lives during the Second World War. On 4 September 1994 bronze plaques listing their names were therefore mounted around its base, further names being added at a 2002 ceremony.

Sennecey-le-Grand is located in the département of Saône-et-Loire in Bourgogne. The memorial stands at the hamlet of Ruffey 2 kilometres south-west of the town on the D332 towards Montceaux-Ragny. GPS co-ordinates: Latitude 46.632117, Longitude 4.855924

SERGENT AIMÉ FRANÇOIS **GILLET** [52192] 6ᴱ BATAILLON DE CHASSEURS ALPINS, 1ᴱᴿ COMPAGNIE DE CHASSEURS PARACHUTISTES AND L DETACHMENT SAS BRIGADE (FRENCH SQN)

Aimé Gillet, sometimes recorded as Herve-Francois, was born on 20 May 1915 at Chazey-Bons in the Ain département of eastern France. Having fought against the German invasion of Norway with the 6ᵉ Bataillon de chasseurs alpins from April to June 1940 he was evacuated to the UK. He joined the Forces françaises libres (FFL) in London that July and was posted to the 1ᵉʳ Compagnie d'infanterie de l'air. After marrying in Manchester during March 1941 he qualified as a parachutist at nearby Ringway the following month (Brevet No.436). Following further training at Exbury on the south coast between mid May and mid July he embarked for the Middle East from Greenock on the SS *Cameronia*. Having arrived at Suez in Egypt the company moved, via Haifa, to Beirut in Lebanon. It was retitled 1ᵉʳ Compagnie de chasseurs parachutistes from mid October after completing its training in Syria. At the beginning of January 1942 it was absorbed into L Detachment, SAS Brigade, at Kabrit as the Free French Squadron and thus fell under the command of Captain David Stirling.

That June Gillet was behind enemy lines in Libya as one of a party of 'prisoners' that was being escorted by members of the Special Interrogation Group, German-speaking Jews also attached to the SAS who were tasked with infiltrating Axis camps. The 'prisoners', all fellow Free French parachutists, planned to destroy aircraft, one section peeling off to attack Martuba airfield whilst Gillet's party continued towards the Derna aerodrome. Their driver, Bruckner, one of two German pre-war French Foreign Legionnaires captured at Tobruk the previous November, who had allegedly extracted information from fellow German POWs, stopped their truck, complaining firstly of engine trouble and then of a flat tyre. Claiming that he had lost the universal key to the tool chest he went to fetch a spare from a nearby German post. The vehicle was surrounded minutes later, the enemy demanding that the party descend with their hands in the air. As they did so a fight ensued and the men scattered. All were later captured bar lieutenant Augustin Jordan, the French commander who, having reported seeing the truck explode, believed that Corporal Petr Haas of the SIG had seen that he was trapped and had flung a grenade into a pile of ammunition in the back (see Haas' entry under Alamein Memorial, Egypt, Volume I). The interrogation report of Leutnant Friedrich Koener, a Luftwaffe fighter pilot shot down the following month, appears to confirm this:

P/W Koener states that on the night of 12th/13th June he was encamped at Martuba. The Germans have been aware for some time that a group of English saboteurs, who would carry out raids on German aerodromes in Cyrenaica dressed in German uniform, was being organised by an English Colonel.

As a result a state of alarm had been ordered as from sundown on all aerodromes. P/W had heard that on the night of 12th/13th June a German lorry stopped in front of the Aerodrome Command Offices on Derna aerodrome, the driver got out, saluted the CO, and stated that he was a German soldier acting as driver of a German lorry containing a party of heavily armed English [*sic*] troops in German uniform with explosive charges to destroy a/c. The CO was rather suspicious at first, but the driver pressed him to organise as many men as possible with all speed and as heavily armed as possible to disarm the raiding party. The lorry was immediately surrounded and the occupants forced to get out. A few seconds later after the last one had got out there was an explosion inside the lorry and it was completely destroyed. A melee developed and it was believed that all the raiders had been shot. However, on the following morning a wounded man presented himself at Derna hospital saying he was a wounded German soldier needing treatment. For some reason the doctor became suspicious and on examination it turned out that he was not a German soldier but a Jew from Palestine [see Private Eliahu Gottlieb's entry under Alamein Memorial, Egypt, Volume I].

The driver [Bruckner] is said to have been awarded the German Cross in silver.

[Another] P/W, who was encamped at Derna on the night of 12th/13th June, stated that a warning was issued in advance that a British raiding party would appear to carry out sabotage on the aerodrome that night. The party would consist of British troops in German uniform, driving in a German truck [WO 201/727].

Having been taken prisoner, Gillet was lost at sea following an attack on the Italian troopship *Nino Bixio* on 17 August 1942. She was torpedoed twice by the British submarine HMS *Turbulent*, her captain being unaware that she was carrying 3,000 Allied prisoners of war between Libya and Sicily. One torpedo exploded in the prisoners' hold, killing many. Badly damaged, the ship was taken in tow by one of its escorting destroyers and limped to Navarino in southern Greece. Here those dead that could be found were buried, a total of 300 having been killed.

The *Journal Officiel de la Republique Francaise* later announced that Gillet had been posthumously awarded the Ordre de l'armée aérienne, noting that:

GILLET (Herve-Francois), Sergeant of 2nd RCP; a conscientious and devoted NCO. Joining the original Free French Forces and then the first company of parachutists, he took part in June 1942 in a raid on the German airfield of Derna. Finding himself in an impossible situation he was taken prisoner on 13/06/42. He disappeared in the sea on 17/08/42 after the torpedoing of the Italian ship *Nino Bixio* [26 February 1946].

Age 27.

ASPIRANT JOSEPH GERMAIN <u>GUERPILLON</u> [164] 1ᴇʀ COMPAGNIE DE CHASSEURS PARACHUTISTES AND L DETACHMENT SAS BRIGADE (FRENCH SQN)

Joseph Guerpillon was born on 4 January 1916 at Tarare in the Rhône département of eastern France. On graduating he took a post as a high school teacher in Kabul, Afghanistan, but by late December 1941 had made his way, via Peshawar, to Bombay where he embarked for Beirut. Here he joined the Free French 1ᴇʳ Compagnie de chasseurs parachutistes in February 1942 (formerly the 1ᴇʳ Compagnie d'infanterie de l'air). This had been absorbed into L Detachment, SAS Brigade, as the Free French Squadron the previous month and as such came under the overall command of Captain David Stirling. However, having attended the officers' school in Damascus, Syria, it was not until May that Guerpillon joined his new comrades at Kabrit.

That September Guerpillon took part in OPERATION BIGAMY, a large-scale raid on Benghazi. On the night of 12–13th the SAS column, which had driven on a circuitous route through the desert from Cairo, was ambushed on the approaches to the port and forced to abandon its objective. Guerpillon was wounded in this initial action. Located by enemy aircraft, the vehicles were bombed continuously during their withdrawal, Guerpillon receiving several shrapnel wounds during the afternoon of the 15th near to Birace Gagui, approximately 70 kilometres east-south-east of Benghazi, when attacked by Italian bombers. He died of his wounds that evening and, according to correspondence within his file, was buried 'in the middle of a large wadi' at '20° 46'-24" longitude East; 31° 51'-26" latitude Nord (1/500 000 Benghazi map) … with several [sic] English killed by the same bombs' [see Driver William Marlow's entry under Alamein Memorial, Egypt, Volume I]. In 1953 his family was invited by the French Government to visit his grave in Libya. However, on arrival it could not be located, his file also noting that 'the coordinates were obtained from the map not fixed by the stars'.

Son of Jean and Jeanne Guerpillon (née Sylvestre) of Écully, a suburb of Lyon – Younger brother of Jean Hugues Guerpillon who served in Indochina prior to the war and in a colonial infantry regiment after the outbreak of hostilities – Older brother of Pierre, Anotoinette, Jean Emmanuel and Marie Guerpillon. Age 26.

Also commemorated, alongside two of his uncles who were killed in the First World War, on the war memorial within the communal cemetery at Nuelles in the Rhône département.

SOLDAT/CAPORAL HENRI LÉON DENIS JAMES [52276] 1ER COMPAGNIE DE CHASSEURS PARACHUTISTES AND L DETACHMENT SAS BRIGADE (FRENCH SQN)

Henri James was born on 6 December 1920 at Argentan in the Orne département of north-west France. He joined the Forces françaises libres (FFL) in London on 1 July 1940 and was posted to the 1er Compagnie d'infanterie de l'air. As a former professional jockey he was small in stature but strong and known as someone who gave his all in training. He was also an amateur astronomer and held in esteem for his accurate navigational skills. He qualified as a parachutist at No.1 PTS Ringway on 10 April 1941 and, following further training at Exbury on the south coast between mid May and mid July, embarked for the Middle East from Greenock on the SS *Cameronia*. After arrival at Suez in Egypt the company moved, via Haifa, to Beirut in Lebanon and was retitled as 1er Compagnie de chasseurs parachutistes from mid October after completing its training in Syria. At the beginning of January 1942 it was absorbed into L Detachment, SAS Brigade, at Kabrit as the Free French Squadron and thus fell under the command of Captain David Stirling.

James was captured during the raid on Derna airfield after a German member of the Special Interrogation Group betrayed his group. He was lost at sea after an attack on the Italian troopship *Nino Bixio* on 17 August 1942 (see Sergent Aimé Gillet's entry above for full details of both events). James' rank at the time of his death is variously reported as soldat and caporal.
Age 21.

Chasseur Isidore **JOUANNY** [52281] 1ER C<small>OMPAGNIE DE CHASSEURS PARACHUTISTES</small> AND L D<small>ETACHMENT</small> SAS B<small>RIGADE</small> (F<small>RENCH</small> S<small>QN</small>)

Isidore Jouanny was born on 27 September 1920 at Saint-Malo in Bretagne, north-west France. Having escaped or been evacuated to the UK he joined the Forces françaises libres (FFL) in London on 1 July 1940 and was posted to the 1er Compagnie d'infanterie de l'air. He qualified for his parachute wings at No.1 PTS Ringway on 10 April 1941 (Brevet No.443) and following further training at Exbury on the south coast between mid May and mid July embarked for the Middle East from Greenock on the SS *Cameronia*. After arrival at Suez in Egypt the company moved, via Haifa, to Beirut in Lebanon and was retitled as 1er Compagnie de chasseurs parachutistes from mid October after completing its training in Syria. At the beginning of January 1942 it was absorbed into L Detachment, SAS Brigade, at Kabrit as the Free French Squadron and thus fell under the command of Captain David Stirling.

Jouanny was captured during the raid on Derna airfield after a German member of the Special Interrogation Group betrayed his group. He was lost at sea after an attack on the Italian troopship *Nino Bixio* on 17 August 1942 (see Sergent Aimé Gillet's entry within this section for full details of both events). Age 21.

Also commemorated on Ille-et-Vilaine's war memorial, St Malo, and by the rue Isidore Jouanny within this city.

S<small>OLDAT</small> E<small>MILE</small> **LOGEAIS** [52317] B<small>ATAILLON DE CHASSEURS DE</small> C<small>AMBERLEY,</small> 1ER C<small>OMPAGNIE DE CHASSEURS PARACHUTISTES</small> AND L D<small>ETACHMENT</small> SAS B<small>RIGADE</small> (F<small>RENCH</small> S<small>QN</small>)

Emile Logeais was born on 11 November 1923 at the port of Brest in the Finistère département of Bretagne, north-west France. He escaped to the UK in June 1940 and joined the Forces françaises libres (FFL) the following month. Posted to the Bataillon de chasseurs de Camberley, this unit was disbanded that December and Logeais joined the 1er Compagnie d'infanterie de l'air. He was subsequently awarded his parachute wings at No.1 PTS Ringway in April 1941 (Brevet No.456). Following further training at Exbury on the south coast between mid May and mid July he embarked for the Middle East from

Greenock on the SS *Cameronia*. After arrival at Suez in Egypt the company moved, via Haifa, to Beirut in Lebanon and was retitled as 1ᵉʳ Compagnie de chasseurs parachutistes from mid October after completing its training in Syria. At the beginning of January 1942 it was absorbed into L Detachment, SAS Brigade, at Kabrit as the Free French Squadron and thus fell under the command of Captain David Stirling.

Logeais was captured during the raid on Derna airfield after a German member of the Special Interrogation Group betrayed his group. He was lost at sea following an attack on the Italian troopship *Nino Bixio* on 17 August 1942 (see Sergent Aimé Gillet's entry within this section for full details of both events).

Age 19.

Caporal Georges **ROYER** [52117] 1ᴱᴿ Compagnie de chasseurs parachutistes and L Detachment SAS Brigade (French Sqn)

Georges Royer was born on 25 July 1920 at Saint-Brieuc in Bretagne, north-west France, and attended the Le Braz lycée. Along with his brother Jean (see his entry opposite) he boarded the schooner *Le Manou* at Paimpol and sailed across the English Channel with eighty other students. Arriving in London in July 1940 the brothers rallied to the Forces françaises libres (FFL) and were posted to the 1ᵉʳ Compagnie d'infanterie de l'air, Georges qualifying as a parachutist at No.1 PTS Ringway (Brevet No.412). Following further training at Exbury on the south coast between mid May and mid July he embarked for the Middle East from Greenock on the SS *Cameronia*, arriving at Suez in Egypt. From here the company moved, via Haifa, to Beirut in Lebanon and was retitled as 1ᵉʳ Compagnie de chasseurs parachutistes from mid October after completing its training in Syria. At the beginning of January 1942 it was absorbed into L Detachment, SAS Brigade, at Kabrit as the Free French Squadron and thus fell under the command of Captain David Stirling.

Both Royer brothers were captured during the raid on Derna airfield after a German member of the Special Interrogation Group betrayed their group. They were lost at sea following an attack on the Italian troopship *Nino Bixio* on 17 August 1942 (see Sergent Aimé Gillet's entry within this section for full details of both events).

Son of Charles Royer, veteran of both wars and Resistant – Older brother of Michel Royer who having joined the Resistance evaded to the UK and took part in the liberation of France with the Forces françaises de l'intérieur (FFI – the Resistance), and of Jean Royer.

Age 22.
Also commemorated by the rue des Frères Royer in Saint-Brieuc.

Soldat/Caporal Jean **ROYER** [53533] 1er Compagnie de chasseurs parachutistes and L Detachment SAS Brigade (French Sqn)

Jean Royer was born on 25 October 1922 or 1923 at Saint-Brieuc in Bretagne, north-west France, and attended Saint-Charles school. Having reached England with his brother Georges (see his entry opposite) he rallied to the FFL in London in July 1940, the pair being posted to the 1er Compagnie d'infanterie de l'air. He subsequently qualified as a parachutist at No.1 PTS Ringway (Brevet No.413). Following further training at Exbury on the south coast between mid May and mid July he embarked for the Middle East from Greenock on the SS *Cameronia*, arriving at Suez in Egypt. From here the company moved, via Haifa, to Beirut in Lebanon and was retitled as 1er Compagnie de chasseurs parachutistes from mid October after completing its training in Syria. At the beginning of January 1942 it was absorbed into L Detachment, SAS Brigade, at Kabrit as the Free French Squadron and thus fell under the command of Captain David Stirling.

Both Royer brothers were captured during the raid on Derna airfield after a German member of the Special Interrogation Group betrayed their group. They were lost at sea following an attack on the Italian troopship *Nino Bixio* on 17 August 1942 (see Sergent Aimé Gillet's entry within this section for full details of both events). Royer's rank at the time of his death is variously reported as soldat and caporal.

Son of Charles Royer, veteran of both wars and Resistant – Older brother of Michel Royer who having joined the Resistance evaded to the UK and took part in the liberation of France with the FFI – Younger brother of Georges Royer.

Aged 18 or 19.
Also commemorated by the rue des Frères Royer in Saint-Brieuc.

CAPORAL-CHEF JEAN-PAUL JULES **TOURNERET** [53631] 1ER COMPAGNIE DE CHASSEURS PARACHUTISTES AND L DETACHMENT SAS BRIGADE (FRENCH SQN)

Jean Tourneret was born on 9 March 1921 at Saint-Nazaire in the Loire-Atlantique département of western France. He joined the FFL on 28 August 1940 and, having been posted to the 1er Compagnie d'infanterie de l'air, qualified as a parachutist at No.1 PTS Ringway on 10 April 1941 (Brevet No.471). Following further training at Exbury on the south coast between mid May and mid July he embarked for the Middle East from Greenock on the SS *Cameronia*, arriving at Suez in Egypt. From here the company moved, via Haifa, to Beirut in Lebanon and was retitled 1er Compagnie de chasseurs parachutistes from mid October after completing its training in Syria. At the beginning of January 1942 it was absorbed into L Detachment, SAS Brigade, at Kabrit as the Free French Squadron and thus fell under the command of Captain David Stirling.

Tourneret was captured during the raid on Derna airfield after a German member of the Special Interrogation Group betrayed his group. He was lost at sea following an attack on the Italian troopship *Nino Bixio* on 17 August 1942 (see Sergent Aimé Gillet's entry within this section for full details of both events). The *Journal Officiel de la Republique Francaise* later announced that Tourneret had posthumously been awarded the Ordre de l'armée aérienne also noting that:

TOURNERET (Jean-Paul), Corporal-chef of 2nd RCP: A young energetic rank full of go, destined to be an excellent section commander and eventual junior officer. Joining the original Free French Forces and then the first company of parachutists, he took part in June 1942 in a raid on the German airfield of Martuba [near Derna] acting as group leader, taking on the functions normally reserved for an officer, and carrying out his mission under very difficult conditions. Finding himself in an impossible situation he was taken prisoner on 13/06/42. He disappeared in the sea on 17/08/42 after the torpedoing of the Italian ship *Nino Bixio* [26 February 1946].

Age 21.

Tannay Communal Cemetery

Tannay is located north-east of Nevers and 12 kilometres south-east of Clemecy in the Nièvre département of Bourgogne. The cemetery lies on the north side of village on a small by-road off the D185. GPS co-ordinates: Latitude 47.37157, Longitude 3.59084

Lieutenant Peter Holland GODDARD [124418] Royal Tank Corps, Royal Armoured Corps, Army Air Corps and 1st SAS (C Sqn)

'Monty' Goddard, as he was known in his squadron, was born on 10 November 1913 in St John's Wood in north-west London. He grew up both at Queen's Club Gardens in west London and at Wareham in Dorset, attending Oundle School, where he served in the OTC, from 1924 to 1931. He took articles with F. Rowland & Co. Chartered Accountants of Moorgate from January 1932 to 1937 where he was an income tax clerk before qualifying as a chartered accountant himself. Having married Bettine Elaine List in April 1938 at Trentham in Stoke-on-Trent he joined the 22nd Battalion (Westminster Dragoons), Royal Tank Corps (TA) that October (service number 7889569).

Having been transferred to the Royal Armoured Corps on its formation in April 1939 Goddard was called up the day before war was declared and sent to 102 OCTU from where he was commissioned on 9 March 1940. After a short spell as Assistant Technical Adjutant of the 57th Training Regiment at Warminster he was posted to the 1st East Riding Yeomanry and served with the RAC Base Depot in France from the end of April 1940 until being evacuated back to England soon after.

Having returned to his former position at the 57th Training Regiment, Goddard was re-posted at the beginning of October 1940 to the 58th Training Regiment at Bovington, Dorset, where he served in the same role as a captain. In March 1943 his application to transfer to the Royal Electrical and Mechanical Engineers, despite an excellent recommendation from his Commanding Officer, was rejected and

he therefore volunteered to become a parachutist: posted to the Airborne Forces Depot at Hardwick on 18 August, he attended parachute course 82 at No.1 PTS Ringway the following month. Here his instructor noted that he was 'very popular, keen, good leadership, jumped well'. He relinquished the rank of temporary captain on 15 February 1944, more than likely the same day that he volunteered for 1st SAS.

On 28 August 1944 Goddard and half of C Squadron were flown by Dakota from RAF Broadwell to Orléans where they were met by Captain Derrick Harrison. The latter had jumped into Occupied France two weeks earlier, commanding the advance party to OPERATION KIPLING. Harrison now led them through the lines to join A Squadron and the other half of C at OPERATION HOUNDSWORTH's base in the Morvan, the idea being for the enlarged KIPLING party to extend HOUNDSWORTH's area of operations northwards.

Goddard was killed in action near Tannay after going to collect a Jeep trailer that had been left behind the previous day. He and Squadron Sergeant-Major Bob Lilley, MM, came across some Maquis preparing an ambush and agreed to supplement the available firepower with their own Vickers machine guns. After going forward to recce the road Goddard returned, removed one gun from its Jeep mount, and began to stalk a mobile 36mm quick-firer that he had spotted. He walked steadily down the road towards it with the Vickers levelled before opening fire and killing the surprised crew. A second quick-firer opened up on him and he was hit running back to the Jeeps. There was no sign of the Maquis at this time, Major Tony Marsh's post-operation report noting:

> On 1 Sep [1944], Lt Goddard went back along the route to Kipling, to recover a trailer that had been damaged on the way down. He ran into a German column at Tannay, where, in conjunction with the local Maquis, who eventually left him to fend for himself, he destroyed one 36-mm mobile quick firer, and wiped out the crew before being killed himself by a burst of cannon-fire from a second gun which he was about to attack.
>
> Throughout the action Lt Goddard showed abnormal courage, knocking out the quick-firer with a Vickers K gun fired from the hip [WO 218/115].

That night Marsh had signalled 'Lt Goddard missing believed killed in a brush with the Hun.' It was ten days before he was able to send another signal confirming the fact and that Goddard had been buried at Tannay. In early 1947 Georges Roger, whose son Jean Roger had been killed close to the incident, traced Goddard's wife, his letter informing her that her husband had been mentioned in French despatches and awarded the 'French War Cross for his gallantry'. Included was the Mention itself, written by the Resistance Commander of the Nievre département:

> Lt Goddard of the British Expeditionary Forces came as a Liaison Officer to Chateauvert camp with two Jeeps and machine guns, did not hesitate to place himself at the disposal of the French Major to help in relieving the Chateau, and met with a glorious death during the counter-attack.

Roger also wrote to the British Council in Paris:

> My son, Guy, who was in command of the group of FFI [the Resistance] at the time, has given me the following account which perhaps may enable you to trace Lieutenant Goddard's [sic] unit and eventually his family:
> 'Lieutenant Goddart arrived from the camp of English parachutists at Chaleaux (or Chalot), Nievre, on Saturday, September 2, 1944. He was in command of two Jeeps, with three men. He intended to go to Auxerre in order to take possession of some rolling stock.
> He came to Tannay at 11.00am. Jean who was serving as interpreter invited him to have lunch with us and we had a merry meal. About 2.00pm I got a telephone message informing me that a German column was heading towards our camp at Chateauvert, a few miles from Clamecy.
> Lt Goddart readily accepted to accompany us. When the Germans attacked the Chateau after encircling it, Lt Goddart and his men very valiantly supported us with their machine guns. But the Germans were more numerous

and better armed. While Jean was shot through the head near the Chateau, Lt Goddart fell on the road below, about 4.00pm. He was machine-gunned through the body.

Although stronger than we were, the Germans broke off the engagement and we could bring Goddart's body back to Tannay at 9.00[pm].

The next day and the following night, while the district was still infested with German troops, the two coffins covered with the national flags, hastily pieced together by the population and bedecked with flowers, were guarded outside the Town Hall by the Veterans from World War 1. After a religious service in Tannay Church on Monday September 4, they were laid side by side in the cemetery.'

I will add that by my advice Guy had the two bodies placed in leaden shells a few days after the burial so that it will be easier to transfer them when the time comes.

Despite these conflicting statements Goddard's death of death is officially recorded as 3 September 1944. Roger later wrote to Mrs Goddard; 'however painful these details, I trust you will like to hear that your husband did not lose his life among unfeeling strangers'.

Late in 1947, the French sent the War Office a Croix de guerre with Silver Star for Goddard's wife 'for the conspicuous services rendered by Lieut. Goddard for the Liberation of France'. These were returned without reaching her along with a letter stating: 'My authorities regret that His Majesty's approval cannot be obtained for the acceptance of posthumous awards and as a result the citation and insignia in respect of LT P.H. Goddard are returned to you.'

Son of Sydney and Elizabeth Goddard (née Wormald) – Husband of Bettine Goddard of Selsey, Sussex – Known to have been the father of three.
Age 29.
God be in my heart and in my thinking. God be at my end and at my departing.
Buried 30 metres from the entrance towards the far wall.

TERRE-NATALE COMMUNAL CEMETERY, VARENNES-SUR-AMANCE

Varennes-sur-Amance is located south-east of Chaumont and 12 kilometres south-west of Bourbonne-les-Bains in the Haute-Marne département of Champagne-Ardenne. The cemetery lies on the north side of the village on the rue du Cimetière. GPS co-ordinates: Latitude 47.89894, Longitude 5.62719

PRIVATE JAMES **DOWNEY** [2940028] QUEEN'S OWN CAMERON HIGHLANDERS, ROYAL ARMY SERVICE CORPS AND 2ND SAS (C SQN)

Jim Downey was born on 10 April 1920 in the family home at Parr in St Helens, Lancashire. He subsequently attended Parr Flat Junior School in the same street before Rivington Road School. Passionate about football he played for Bethel Mission Church whilst apprenticed to Critchleys, a local plumbing firm. In February 1942 he enlisted into the 2nd Battalion (Liverpool Scottish), Queen's Own Cameron Highlanders, and qualified as a coppersmith at Burnley that August. Having transferred to the Royal Army Service Corps at the end of the month he disembarked in North Africa in February 1943 to serve with No.1 General Base Depot. He was attached to HQ 2nd SAS that June, volunteering to join the Regiment the following month.

Landing at Taranto on the heel of southern Italy on 10 September 1943, Downey operated with D Squadron as a member of Lieutenant Peter Jackson's Jeep patrol (see Jackson's entry under Bari War Cemetery, Italy, Volume II). On the 18th it destroyed a German anti-tank position near Miglionico before

being withdrawn to Taranto to refit the following day. Moving north once more the squadron saw fighting near Melfi, Stornarella, Ascoli and Castelnuova. It also met some resistance at San Severo, as described by the squadron's former commander, Roy Farran, DSO, MC**: 'after a scuffle in which a little chap called Downie [sic] (who was afterwards killed in France) had to knock out a big fascist on the stairs, they captured four prisoners' (*Winged Dagger: Adventures on Special Service*, by Roy Farran). On 2 October the squadron reached Termoli where it linked with the Special Service Brigade and Special Raiding Squadron (1st SAS) that landed in the early hours of the following morning. The combined force secured the port and saw fierce fighting in its defence.

Downey's squadron returned to the UK in March 1944 having passed through North Africa where he met his brother, Reg. At home, training for the forthcoming liberation of Europe began, during which Downey injured his leg whilst parachuting. However, he subsequently jumped into a DZ in the Côte-d'Or département of eastern France on the night of 8–9 August for OPERATION HARDY. His stick commander, Lieutenant Jamie Robertson, noted in the post-operation report that during an ambush on German transport on the 21st Downey 'silenced' an enemy machine-gun position with his Jeep's Vickers. Robertson went on to record that 'Pct Downey was accidentally killed on this afternoon [11 September 1944] and was buried at Varennes-sur-Amance, J460272, two days later' (WO 219/2401). 2nd SAS' Casualty Report also quotes Robertson:

> The twin Vickers had been laid in the back of the Jeep and Downey was leaning against them when [name omitted for publication] lifted the magazine off one. The action could not have been completely cocked and must have been resting on the base of the next round as the gun went off and shot Downey through the stomach. He lived for an hour after the accident and there could have been no possible chance of saving him, as the bullet sprayed out inside him, destroying his intestines and left lung. Downey's funeral was held at Varennes the following day. Date: - 11 Sep 44 [WO 361/720 and WO 361/651].

Downey was taken to a local property and a doctor summoned. Nothing, however, could be done and he died in the arms of Madame Lepoan, the lady of the house. His body was subsequently brought to Varennes-sur-Amance where, with members of the Maquis standing guard, several members of his patrol attended the funeral despite the fact that there were Germans in close proximity. Robertson later wrote to Downey's mother:

> He was in my troop during the whole of our action in France, and the least I can say is how very proud I was to have a man like him under my command.
>
> He was killed by an accidental shot just before the commencement of a battle, and I wanted to inform you that he passed away very shortly after the shot was fired, suffering very little pain. An old lady in a little cottage by the village of Daumemont looked after him extremely well and without her aid we could not have made him comfortable.
>
> The whole squadron was present at his funeral, a full military one, which was made possible by the magnificent efforts displayed by the local French Resistance hospital.
>
> It took place in the town of Varennes, south of Bonbonne and he was buried in the beautiful little cemetery there. I am sending you his wings, cap badge and Africa Star, as he carried no other personal belongings of importance with him.
>
> He was a real tonic to my men, and never ceased to remain cheerful throughout the campaign. I may say that he had done extremely well, with several good actions to his credit, and was an invaluable member to have in the circumstances under which we were fighting.
>
> I am sending with me the sympathies of his nearest comrades and those of the remainder of the squadron in your great loss. Again sympathies in the loss of a grand character and conscientious, hard working, soldier [Downey family collection].

His brother Harry was part of a family group that travelled to France in 1947 to pay their respects:

He had a reputation as something of a daredevil and never turned down a challenge. I never saw him without a smile on his face and to me he was the perfect big brother - a hero and someone to live up to. Sadly he did not survive to marry his sweetheart, Hetty. They seemed so happy together.

A childhood memory - I would imagine this goes back to 1939 at the latest. That Christmas I was alone in the living room with just the light from the fire. I was listening on the 'wireless' to a broadcast of Peter Pan. Everyone else was partying in the front room. There's a point in the story where every child who believes in fairies should clap, and of course, I did. Jim was watching me. When I turned and saw him he just smiled and went. It would have been so easy for him to have teased me or told the others. He didn't [personal correspondence, 2014].

Son of Reginald (a St Helens Pals veteran of the First World War) and Maria Downey (née Statter) of Cambridge Road, St Helens, Lancashire – Brother of Reginald (who served in the Royal Artillery in North Africa and Italy), Nellie and Harry Downey.

Age 24.

No inscription.

Grave L.27. Also commemorated on the Varennes-sur-Amance Maquis Memorial near to Plesnoy, on a small memorial outside the cottage where he was fatally wounded on the Bourbonne-Chaumont road (D417), and within St Helens Parish Church.

VELORCEY COMMUNAL CEMETERY

Velorcey is located 20 kilometres north of Vesoul and 10 kilometres west of Luxeuil-les-Bains in the Haute-Saône département of Franche-Comté. The cemetery lies behind the church on the north side of the village, 150 metres downhill from the D6 and the Grande Rue T-junction, where the action described below took place. GPS co-ordinates: Latitude 47.78019, Longitude 6.25068

LIEUTENANT HUGH CHRISTOPHER **GURNEY** [102724] ROYAL NORFOLK REGIMENT, 8TH INDEPENDENT COMPANY, NO.7 COMMANDO, LIBYAN ARAB FORCE, DRUZE REGIMENT, PARACHUTE REGIMENT AND 2ND SAS (C SQN)

Hugh Gurney was born at Courtfield Gardens in Kensington, west London, on 7 December 1917. He was brought up at the family home, Northrepps Hall, just outside Cromer on the Norfolk coast, his parents having relocated there in 1926. After Aldeburgh Lodge prep school, he moved to Charterhouse in 1934 where he was a member of the OTC. Music played a large part in family life as his mother was an accomplished classical pianist, and in 1937 Gurney won a place at the Royal School of Music, where he remained for a year. He was then awarded a music scholarship to Wadham College, Oxford, where he decided to read History. He rowed in the Wadham boat and was a keen member of the Cavalry Squadron, his music skills proving a useful source of income earned for playing the organ at society weddings in London.

181

Gurney's studies were cut short by the mounting hostilities and he was commissioned into the local 5th Battalion, Royal Norfolk Regiment (TA), the day before war was declared. When the Independent Companies, the forerunners of the Commandos, were being formed he was attached to the 1st Cambridgeshire Regiment and posted to the 8th Independent Company as Liaison Officer to the 3rd Independent Division that was stood-to for deployment to Norway. During the second half of 1940 he was trained at Lochailort and posted to No.7 Commando at Felixstowe, where he taught demolitions and map reading, occasionally returning home to lecture his father's Home Guard unit. His letters reflect not only his hopes for the future ('I shall then [after continuing his BA in History], I hope, be all set for my Theological course when I go up [to Oxford] after the war'), but also his enthusiasm for his new life:

> I am so very much enjoying my time down here at Felixstowe; and the work, though hard with rather long hours, is just what I like. For instance, I have lately been doing a lot of lecturing to the troop (on subjects I learnt at Lochailort Castle) – and I think with most encouraging results, as they come up afterwards and demand individual tuition.
>   The physical side is strenuous – but I find I can keep at it as long as anybody, which is encouraging. I enjoy the boxing, and had a Battle Royal with my troop commander yesterday. We were both very bruised this morning – but I think he was mostly! [Gurney family collection].

By October 1940 No.7 was based at Girvan on the west coast of Scotland and was temporarily redesignated No.2 Company, 3rd Special Service Battalion, that November. Embarking for the Middle East on HMS *Glengyle* on 1 February 1941, Gurney made use of his subsequent shore leaves in South Africa and Aden before disembarking in Egypt as a member of A Battalion, Layforce, the following month. Promoted to lieutenant, he took part in April's amphibious raid on Bardia along the Libyan coast, which resulted in the destruction of an Italian supply dump and coastal artillery battery, later writing to his mother:

> You know I can't tell you anything now – except just to tell you that my section was particularly complimented for its behaviour in an awkward situation – (also that I'm very proud of them!). It was terrific fun, despite bad moments … although when one is very busy one has little else to think of – fortunately [family collection].

On 1 June 1941 he wrote again, this time to his father:

> I can now tell you I am back from Crete [where the Commando lost many men in a rearguard action against the Germans]. We were sent over but there was little we could do. I had a small scratch in Suda and came back on a warship; the doctor on board was absolutely marvellous: he operated on me (it was only a slight scratch on the leg) under appalling conditions. We were going flat out and zig-zagging all the time, and all our guns were going, so you can imagine how the whole place was shaking about, and lurching, from side to side. He did marvellously.
>   We had an exciting time, and our chaps did terribly well – but obviously it was an impossible situation … even though it wasn't our job it was a great experience, and has given us all a lot of confidence for the future [family collection].

Having recuperated from what was a rather more serious wound than he let on, Gurney was posted to C Troop at the Commando Depot at Geneifa where the survivors of No.7 Commando awaited their fate. Writing to his father on the 17th:

> Great news: I can now tell you I have got the job which I have been working for these last few days! I volunteered and was chosen from quite a large crowd (mostly consisting of the remnants of my old unit); so I feel quite pleased about it.
>   Briefly what happened was this: after Crete it was decided that the very few remaining from my unit should split up, and they were sent back to their regiments. I have no regiment here to go back to, so as soon as I was well again I started looking for a good job. Then this came along, and finally I was accepted. It should be very interesting and good fun [family collection].

The new job Gurney wrote of was a company commander's post in the 2nd Battalion, Libyan Arab Force, British Military Mission 102, which he filled from mid August 1941:

We are a force raised entirely of Libyan Arabs (or 'patriots'), led by British officers. What we are going to do is obvious, and we are hoping for great things soon. We are composed of various Libyan tribes, (above all the Senoussi tribe, who under Turkish officers gave us some hot moments in the last war). They are an amazingly tough bunch of desert tribesmen and fanatically keen to get a bit of their own back. It should be an interesting job. Now I am busy learning Arabic; we have to speak it of course and also write it a bit, which isn't actually quite as difficult as it sounds.

I think it will be a great opportunity too, to see how another section of the community lives – and should be terrific fun. It may be a lonely life, after what I have done; we shall be on our own a lot, and in lonely places (I am going to have a camel you will be pleased to hear!) [family collection].

Gurney continued to travel as much as possible during his leave and to seek out any musical relaxation, making a special trip to Bethlehem that September where he was able to play the organ in the church, before moving on to Beirut and Damascus. Promoted to captain in October 1941, his Arabic went from strength to strength as he found himself the sole Briton in his remote company. In mid November he was appointed Adjutant of the 3rd Battalion, and Christmas and the New Year found him close to the front line around Benghazi in Libya:

Our men have been absolutely first rate. I do feel very proud to have been with them at the moment. I am still very happy in this job as Adjutant of the Bn. Of all the Bns ours is said to be the best – I suppose that is why we have been put the most forward [family collection].

Overtaken by Rommel's sudden advance, Gurney and a small group of men were forced to make their way back to British lines on foot, having laid-up in a marsh to avoid German patrols. Writing from Shepherd's Hotel in Cairo he recalled:

That night we set out. It was grand to walk again as we were very cold and wet, and stiff from not being able to move. We had a few tins of bully with us, and some wild tomatoes we found by the sea were excellent.

We felt amazingly alone as we walked hour after hour along by the sea, through the dunes, a full moon and a fresh wind behind us helped us a little – and we felt determined to put up a good show … We had no map – no compass – we knew nothing definitely – we had food for about four days – generally speaking the outlook (as we thought it) could not be called 'bright'. Still, having been in some funny situations previously in this war I was convinced this was but another such incident, and that we must be all right.

It was here that I began to realise what an enormous value my knowledge of Arabic, though limited as it was, was going to be to us … little did we know we were to spend another eleven days hiding, walking, dodging, behind Rommel's lines before we were to see an English face again.

It is curious, looking back, what things most occupied one's mind during this long march: I thought of the great times I had had – at home, Oxford, London, and alternatively (our minds kept inevitably moving in this direction) I imagined myself consuming a large meal at Shepherd's, or the 'Turf' back in Cairo!

We pushed on and by the evening we found some little patches of a kind of camel-grass and which, according to the Libyans, was supposed to be eatable. We picked some and ate it. It was utterly tasteless, but one got some sort of satisfaction out of chewing something. I collected quite a lot and stuffed the pockets of my battledress with some [family collection].

After 515 kilometres the men were spotted by a patrol of South African armoured cars; 'I can hardly tell you a definite reaction set in which took a little time, fully to recover from.' By late February 1942 he was back in Cairo.

Having passed his Arabic exams Gurney took command of the 4th Battalion at Mersa Matruh. Pushed back once again he was headhunted for the newly formed Druze Regiment:

I got a sort of promotion of sorts, acting unpaid local (etc, etc) 'Kaid' or Major, and wear a crown instead of my three pips. At any rate quite a step up! We also wear a Druze Arab head-dress, a 'Kafire', a hazam, and riding boots and breeches.

So we all look like something out of a film! I'll send you a photograph some day! [family collection - Gurney is seen on the previous page with a camel whistle stick presented to him by his men. He later used it to regroup his parachute sticks].

Posted to Syria that August, Gurney flourished and by mid October 1942 was Second-in-Command of the camel regiment, organising patrols along the borders of Palestine, Transjordan and Iraq. However, by late March 1943, with the war in the region nearing an end, Gurney was becoming restless and wrote to his family:

> Happy as I am with these people, I can't help feel occasionally – I should say quite often really – that I could be, and perhaps should be, doing something now rather nearer to the scene of action. I have had an admirable rest from the desert which I feel I deserved; I have seen this regiment transformed from a howling mob of savages into a respectable, disciplined, operational army; I am easily the youngest here, but feel I've had no small share in it. There would of course be many difficulties in getting back to my old 'Commando' unit, but I don't think they would be insurmountable. I am thinking it over carefully [family collection].

Gurney subsequently transferred to the 11th Battalion, Parachute Regiment, that June and began parachute training at Ramat David in Palestine where it was stationed. Although he damaged his leg on his first jump he ignored the RAF Medical Officer's advice to back-troop and qualified for his wings at the end of the month. In addition to taking responsibility for communications, he was appointed Second-in-Command of A Company, training with them in his former patrol areas on the Transjordan/Iraq border. A Druze Regiment acquaintance lent him a camel on account of his parachuting injury and he was able to continue his rounds mounted.

On 13 September 1943 A Company, reinforced by platoons from B and C, took off from Ramat David and landed on Cyprus where:

> … we learnt that we were going to drop that night on the Italian Dodecanese Island of Cos in order firstly to boost up the Italian garrison there, (they had only just signed the armistice and were presumably somewhat in the dark – as indeed they were!), and secondly to organise, with them, the defence of the island against the Germans – who were not so very far away, in Rhodes. We were to be entirely on our own having once been dropped, so would have to fend for ourselves entirely. Altogether a very nice little job for a first kick-off [family collection].

Late that October, whilst waiting to attend a mountain warfare course in the Lebanon, Gurney outlined details of the operation in a letter to his mother:

> I, standing by the door [of the plane], could recognise everything perfectly from the photographs we had been shown. It was really very satisfying. I glanced at my watch, and saw that we were exactly dead to the minute. Not a bad achievement after three or four odd hours flying! Those last minutes always seem the longest … of course they are seconds really … but I remember it seemed longer than ever as we stood there tensed, my Sgt Major and the men behind me. I glanced round to see if they were all all right – and at that moment the red light went on … and then the green, and I flung myself out into cold space. The men piled out after me – ('You couldn't see daylight between them Sir!' as the WO [Warrant Officer] told me afterwards) – and in a few seconds I had added another country to my 'list'!
>
> My first impression after touching down (I made rather a hard landing – in a ditch!) was of picking myself up and finding myself confronted by a crowd of rather bewildered looking and immaculately dressed Italian officers. Soon there were cries of 'Inglesi! Inglesi!' and the Italian officers started to clap and say 'Bravo! Bravo!' I felt like I had just done a rather clever turn at a circus! Quite the most extraordinary reception a conquering army, I should imagine, has ever had! [family collection].

Having landed in the early hours of the 14th on a DZ marked out by the SBS near the port of Cos, Gurney's company was transported to Antimachia aerodrome, arriving just before dawn. Although pounded by the Luftwaffe the men were able not only to help organise the defence of the island but also to clear unexploded bombs. On the 24th they were withdrawn to Cyprus, then Ramat David, leaving Cos in the hands of the Durham Light Infantry and the RAF Regiment. Although stood-to the following month when German parachutists made their own assault on the island, the battalion's planned operation to jump onto Leros was cancelled and it embarked at Port Said on 18 December. Passing through the Straits of Gibraltar Gurney noted 'I sometimes wonder if I shall ever see Egypt, Palestine, and Syria again.'

Having spent Christmas and New Year at sea 11 Para settled near Leicester, all ranks being granted a very welcome month-long disembarkation leave soon after.

In mid May 1944 Gurney damaged his knee in a Jeep accident whilst on exercise in Northumberland and was hospitalised at Hexham. Medically downgraded he was granted sick leave at home before being posted to a holding unit late that June. From here he initially applied for operational work in the Far East before writing to the Adjutant of the Airborne Forces Depot:

> In view of the fact that I have been deemed A1 (fit for parachute duty) and have no chance of returning to my unit (where I am told that my place has been taken) I hereby wish to submit my application for posting to a special unit (such as that known as MO4 [a cover name for SOE] which existed in the Middle East). I have had parachute operational experience – am well acquainted with the Eastern Mediterranean – have a working knowledge of Arabic and Greek – have previously worked with foreign troops. I would also add I am very keen to be in an operational theatre at the earliest possible opportunity.

Having volunteered for 2nd SAS on 18 July 1944 this opportunity was soon to arise, Gurney later writing to his father:

> Here are my first impressions of my new work: First of all, I say unhesitingly that this is a very good job – a very good job indeed … which, at this stage of the war, holds some very great possibilities, and which, at the very least, should be quite good fun.
>
> When I first applied some weeks ago at the War House – and later when I saw Col Franks, and was finally accepted into the SAS – they told me that if I wanted to keep my rank they would offer me the job of Staff Capt in their HQ at Rickmansworth (Moor Park) – but if on the other hand I required something of a more active nature they could offer me that of 'stick commander' (i.e. aircraft commander) with my own dozen or so men, but that would mean I should have to start at the bottom [in C Squadron], as it were, with my war substantive rank of Lieut. I have given these two alternatives quite a lot of thought, and finally decided on the latter. I feel that having been a Captain for nearly three years (of which a considerable period was spent as an acting Major) and having done quite a lot of things compared with many, I can now well afford to choose a job merely because I like it – without any regard for rank or pay [family collection].

On 19 August C Squadron, under Major Roy Farran, MC**, took off from RAF Brize Norton in twenty Dakotas, each of which carried a jeep. Landing at Rennes the squadron drove through the American lines south of Paris, covering hundreds of kilometres into enemy territory and collecting valuable intelligence as they went (OPERATION WALLACE). On the evening of the 22nd Farran split the party into three groups, Gurney coming under the command of Lieutenant David Leigh. Setting off at thirty-minute intervals they regrouped that night at a priory converted into a farm at the Fôret de St Jean. Here Gurney again wrote to his father:

> This is a most terribly interesting experience – for we are covering an odd hundred kilos or so per day, and sleeping in little villages and farms by night. All the people are absolutely delightful – and we are receiving a terrific welcome wherever we go.
>
> I'm writing this by candlelight, sitting in a large loft. In a few hours we shall be away again. So think of us dashing along through the highways and byways of France [family collection].

Setting off at intervals once again Gurney's patrol, the last to leave, was separated from the main party when it was ambushed at Villaines-les-Prévôtes. The post-operation report states:

> When Lieut Leigh's party approached Villaines fierce fighting broke out. Lieut Leigh was seriously wounded and Lieut Gurney took over command. He engaged the enemy to prevent them from outflanking the party to the rear and ordered the Jeeps to be turned round. One Jeep was hit in the gearbox and had to be destroyed. Lieut Gurney's party retired half a mile down the road by which [time] they had come and met Capt Lee, Lieut Lord John Manners, Pct Rushbrook, Pct O'Callaghan, and Cpl Clark (who was from Major Farran's party), all on foot. Pct McEachan, who had been wounded, was found to be dead by this time so his body was left behind. This party then came under

the command of Capt Lee and moved off through two large streams and arrived at Jeux-les-Bard, N442834. From there Lieut Leigh was taken to a Maquis hospital [*sic*] at Epoisses, where he died soon after arrival [WO 218/197 – see Signalman Ronald McEachan's entry under Villaines-les-Prévôtes Communal Cemetery, France, and Leigh's entry under Epoisses Communal Cemetery, France].

Although all three parties had been briefed to make their way to the OPERATION HARDY base near Chatillon, Captain Raymond Couraud, attached from the Regiment's French Squadron under the alias 'Raymond Lee', directed his group to 1st SAS' HOUNDSWORTH base near Avallon. Running into trouble en route, the Jeeps were saved largely due to the presence of mind of Gurney and Sergeant Pete Tomasso. Although expecting to be resupplied through 1st SAS' DZs before rejoining their squadron, Lee ordered the men to return to the UK.

Having briefly met his mother in London, Gurney and a small number of his men were subsequently parachuted back to OPERATION WALLACE during the night of 6–7 September, immediately seeing action against a large German force that was attacking the DZ. In the following days Gurney was constantly engaged against the enemy and on the night of 11–12 September his patrol destroyed a staff car, killing five senior officers including a general.

Gurney was killed in action the following evening, 12 September 1944, whilst withdrawing from a successful ambush on German transport in the small village of Velorcey. Lieutenant Jim Mackie, a fellow officer on WALLACE, wrote:

> Lieut Gurney's troop held up an ammunition truck, but L/Cpl [Tanky] Challenor and Pct [Will] Fyfe were injured in the eye and the shoulder respectively as a result of the explosion from the truck. Lieut Gurney's Jeep was so close to the burning truck that they had to evacuate it, and while Lieut Gurney was running down the road to the other Jeep he was shot in the back and fell to the ground. He died shortly afterwards and his papers were removed by the Germans. The Germans allowed the villagers to bury him in their village cemetery [WO 361/651].

Challenor later stated: 'Lieutenant Gurney, with no thought for his own safety, ran back to help me, and as he did so was hit by a hail of fire' (*Tanky Challenor: SAS and the Met*, by Draper and Challenor). A message sent the following day confirmed: 'Gurney killed Velorcey 9316. Germans refused burial dying American terrorist but civilians buried today' (WO 218/206). He was subsequently mentioned in despatches (*London Gazette* 09/08/45).

Alex Roberston, a fellow officer on OPERATION WALLACE, later recalled that Gurney was: 'a lovely man. Very quiet and a beautiful pianist. We found a deserted farmhouse with a piano in it. With Germans 2

or 3 miles away and he sat there playing Bach. I was very sorry to hear he'd been killed' (personal interview, 2013).

Second son of Major Christopher Gurney (Royal Engineers during the First World War and commander of the North Norfolk Home Guard during the Second) and of Dorothy Gurney (née Ruggles-Brise) of Northrepps Hall, Cromer, Norfolk – Younger brother of Joseph (who served in the Welsh Guards in North Africa and Italy) – Older brother of Pamela (a Voluntary Aid Detachment nurse) and of Anthony (who was wounded in Burma whilst serving with the Royal Norfolks).

Age 26.

No inscription.

Also commemorated on memorials outside, and by plaques within, churches at both Velorcey and Northrepps, and at Wadham College, Oxford.

VERRIÈRES COMMUNAL CEMETERY

Verrières is located 26 kilometres south-east of Poitiers in the Vienne département of Poitou-Charentes. The cemetery lies to the west of the village on the south side of the D13 towards Gençay. GPS co-ordinates: Latitude 46.41177, Longitude 0.58871

LIEUTENANT TOMOS W. MANSEL **STEPHENS** [95606] SOUTH WALES BORDERERS AND 1ST SAS (A SQN)

Known as 'Twm' due to his initials, Tomos Stephens was born in London on 31 May 1920 but grew up in the village of Llanstephan in Carmarthenshire. Having attended St Paul's School he entered Sandhurst from where he was commissioned into the South Wales Borderers in July 1939. By the outbreak of hostilities that September he was stationed in India at Landi Kotal near the Khyber Pass, on what was then the North West Frontier. He later moved to Cawnpore attending a Vickers machine gun course at Saugor in September 1940, a junior commander's course at Poona during January and February 1941, and a gas course at Pachmarhi in May. That November he disembarked in Iraq.

In April 1942 Stephens arrived in Palestine where he attended a PT course at Sarafand the following month. By June he was serving in Libya with the 1st Battalion that had formed a defensive box at Bel Hamed, roughly 32 kilometres south of Tobruk. On the morning of the 16th enemy infantry began to probe its positions but the Borderers were able to hold their ground until the following evening when ordered to pull back to Sollum. The men therefore retired to their trucks, roughly 16 kilometres to the east, which they reached at 0330hrs on the 18th. An hour later the leading vehicles found that they had been cut off by Panzers and in an effort to escape, the battalion lost over five hundred officers and men, Stephens being one of those captured. Shipped to northern Italy he was held at Campo 49 at Fontanellato but on 9 September 1943, the day after the Italian armistice was announced, all 500 officers and eighty other ranks left the camp and moved south in parties of 100. Stephens and two other officers soon split from their group, although he alone avoided capture in a village near Arrezo after coming across two fascists in a bar. Soon after he met two further British officers and together they reached Allied lines at Palmoli on 3 November (WO 208/5402).

Whilst undergoing standard ex-POW medical and psychiatric evaluations in North Africa, Stephens met Captain John Tonkin who had been captured at Termoli that October whilst serving in the Special Raiding Squadron (see Lance-bombardier Joe Fassam's entry under Sangro River War Cemetery, Italy, Volume II, for further details). After his return to the UK that December Stephens attended an officer reception unit at Selsdon Park Hotel in Purley at the beginning of February 1944:

A very interesting young Regular Officer whose next job in the army merits careful attention.

He was only a prisoner for fifteen months and has suffered in no way. His escape from PG.49 and his 500 mile trek, including re-capture and re-escape, is ample evidence of guts, initiative and endurance.

He has a genuine and deep-seated hatred of the enemy as anyone I know.

He is small, but well made and obviously strong. He is apt to stammer and at moments such as interviews with a senior officer the stammer can be bad, but not very bad. I have watched him, however, in the Mess and am certain that he is correct in saying that he has trained himself so to conquer his stammer that except on occasions such as interviews it never now worries him at all. I think that the self-discipline he has exerted in this connection has had a great effect on his character which for a young man of his age appears to be a fine one and very fully formed. He is alive with the spirit of initiative. A real fighter.

In the above opinion I am supported by the views of Major Bion, Psychiatrist. Airborne Commando work appeals to him as indeed does any other form of Commando work. Employment under Combined Operations – especially where the numbers engaged are small indeed – is the height of his desire.

Although initially posted to 21 Infantry Training Centre at Brecon in south Wales Stephens remembered Tonkin's accounts of SAS operations and volunteered for the Regiment himself. He joined in mid February 1944, attending parachute course 105 at No.1 PTS Ringway the following month. Here his instructor noted 'good morale – very good performer, keen'.

Stephens parachuted into a DZ north of Bouesse in the Indre département of central France for OPERATION BULBASKET on the night of 7–8 June 1944. His nine-man party was met by their commander, his former acquaintance Tonkin, who had jumped into the area with Lieutenant Richard Crisp in the early hours of the 6th. The following day the party was transported westwards by truck, a decision then being made to concentrate farther west in order to attack the railway line north and south of Poitiers. As he spoke some French Stephens was sent by Tonkin, on bicycle wearing civilian clothes, to confirm the locations of petrol-carrying trains at Châtellerault. These were later destroyed by the RAF. Having blown up a road and rail bridge south-east of Montmorillon on 11 June, and cut the railway north of St Cyr on the night of the 20th– 21st, he rejoined the main SAS party at its camp within the Forêt de Verrières on 1 July.

Stephens was wounded during the German attack on this camp on the 3rd (see Lieutenant Richard Crisp's entry under Rom Communal Cemetery, France, for further detail). Evidence given at the subsequent inquiry suggests that whilst attempting to evade capture he was shot in the thigh, either whilst crossing, or near to, the Verrières–Dienne road, and that he was discovered crawling away through a wheat field, dragged back to the edge of the forest, propped against a tree and hit repeatedly in the head by rifle butts before being shot. However, an autopsy found that although he had been shot in the head all the fractures radiated from the entry and exit wounds:

> The Court is forced to the conclusion on the evidence that there is no foundation for the story of the clubbing of Lt Stephens. The autopsy found no injuries to the skull which could not have been due to bullet wounds …
>
> From the result of the autopsy, it would appear that the leg wound was a flesh wound only; but it would also appear to have bled considerably … that Lt Stephens had been dragged from the wheat field into the wood and there despatched [TS 26/861].

What is certain is that having found his body local villagers marked the spot by driving empty casings into the tree against which he was propped. The same day Tonkin identified his remains, removing Stephens' SAS insignia and attaching them to a cross erected over his grave the following day. For some reason his date of death was officially recorded as 4 July 1944. It is said that Stephens believed the pipe he carried on operations brought him good luck as it had kept his father safe during the First World War. He was posthumously mentioned in despatches (*London Gazette* 22/03/45).

Son of Mr and Mrs T. B. Stephens (née Rees) who at the time of their son's death were resident of Woodberry Down in north London – Brother of Peter Stephens.

Age 24.

Interred in the tomb of the Mancier and Montjon families. Also commemorated on La Couarde Forest Memorial behind and to the right of which a cairn marks the spot where he was murdered, at the Llanstephan Memorial Hall, and on a plaque within Moriah Chapelyard in the same village.

VILLAINES-LES-PRÉVÔTES COMMUNAL CEMETERY

On 22 August 1944 C Squadron, 2nd SAS, that was moving well behind the lines during OPERATION WALLACE, *was split into three Jeep patrols by its commander, Major Roy Farran, MC**. The following evening all three patrols clashed with a company of Germans as they entered the village of Villaines-les-Prévôtes, a local woman having innocently informed the leading Jeeps that it was clear of the enemy. As this patrol approached the church it engaged a large group of troops through a set of metal gates with its mounted Vickers machine guns. During the ensuing fight the first two Jeeps crashed into a wall and had to be abandoned, Parachutist Bill Rudd being killed.*

Owing to the lack of inter-patrol communications, warning could not be given to those following on. The second party under Farran therefore ran into an ambush just outside the village but inflicted heavy casualties before retiring. When the third patrol arrived from the same direction Lieutenant David Leigh was mortally wounded, as was Signalman Ronald McEachan (see their entries under Époisses Communal Cemetery, France, and opposite respectively).

Damage can still be seen to the metal gates mentioned whilst the sump and bell housing of one of the destroyed Jeeps are used as flowerpots on the steps of the village church.

Villaines-les-Prévôtes is located 62 kilometres north-west of Dijon in the Côte-d'Or département of Bourgogne. The cemetery lies close to the church at the top of the rue de la Cure. GPS co-ordinates: Latitude 47.5552, Longitude 4.3058

Signalman Ronald George McEACHAN [2327605] Royal Corps of Signals, 2nd SAS, SAS Brigade Signals Section Att 2nd SAS

Ronald McEachan was born in the parish of St Cuthbert's, Edinburgh, on 19 June 1919, later living in Hampshire. Having worked as a gardener at Burnham Beeches Golf Club in Buckinghamshire he enlisted into the Royal Corps of Signals in June 1938 at Aldershot. On completing training in January 1939 he was described as: 'an excellent tradesman. Is hard working, keen, and shows intelligence in his work. Clean and smart.' He was subsequently posted to the 1st Anti-Aircraft Brigade as a signaller and served with the BEF in France from the outbreak of war until being evacuated on 1 June 1940. By the spring of 1941 he was serving in the signals section of the 4th Heavy Anti-Aircraft Regiment, Royal Artillery, his marriage certificate of that June recording that he had moved to the 67th HAA Regiment, RA Signals Section. Promoted to lance-corporal in November he reverted to the rank of signalman at the beginning of February 1942. Late that year he disembarked in North Africa and after hostilities in the region drew to a successful conclusion he was posted to a reinforcement depot. Having fallen ill during the summer of 1943 he returned to the depot in September from where he volunteered for 2nd SAS on 1 October.

Despite recurring sickness McEachan served in Italy, fighting from Taranto to Termoli, most probably with D Squadron, before arriving back in the UK in April 1944. Here he was posted to the SAS Brigade Signals Section and attached to 2nd SAS. He was briefly posted to F Squadron, GHQ Liaison Regiment (Phantom), on 23 June whilst attending parachute course 121 at No.1 PTS Ringway. Here his instructor noted that he was both cheerful and confident.

On 15 August 1944 McEachan was posted back to the SAS Brigade Signals Section and attached to C Squadron, 2nd SAS, for Operation Wallace. Having been flown to Rennes with their Jeeps on 19 August the squadron drove through the German lines on the 21st. The following day it was split into three patrols, McEachan being killed in action on the 23rd after the third patrol to approach Villaines-les-Prévôtes was ambushed by German troops on the outskirts of the village. Tanky Challenor, a member of the same patrol, later wrote:

> Almost immediately Lieutenant Leigh was shot in the head and dragged clear of the Jeep by two of the crew while his driver, Corporal McEachon [*sic*], continued to fire the Vickers over the steering wheel ... I looked round and saw that McEachon was sprawled across the Jeep with blood pumping from a wound in his throat. I waited for a pause in the firing, then sprinted across to his Jeep, slung him on my back and carried him to my own vehicle. My tunic was soaked with his blood ...
>
> As we drove off like bats out of hell, 'Will' Fyffe leaned across and told me that McEachon was dead. We drove on until we found a ditch by a mill that was a huge blaze of wild flowers, and there we laid him gently on the ground, removed his pay book and dog-tag, hoping that the Maquis would find him and give him a decent burial. Although Jerry was in hot pursuit we paused long enough for Lieutenant Gurney to offer up a simple prayer while the rest of us stood heads bowed with our berets in our hands. When we moved off I was too choked to speak, McEachon had been such a close friend [*Tanky Challenor: SAS and the Met*, by Draper and Challenor].

Parachutist Roche confirmed: 'McEachan was brought out, but after travelling 50/60 yards he died, whereupon he was left in the ditch beside the road, after an examination by Lieut Gurney to make sure he was dead' (WO 361/651). Captain Dick Holland, MC, later visited the area to search for missing men: 'an unknown SAS soldier was buried next to him [Rudd]. The local people gave me his ring from which he is identified as Sig McEachan already reported killed' (WO 218/219). Meanwhile, the village mayor stated: 'the two soldiers were placed in a coffin and buried by the Catholic priest. The whole population attended the funeral and covered the coffin with flowers. We propose to make an enclosure round their tomb' (WO 361/716).

Husband of Edith McEachan of Grove Road, South Woodford, east London – In a bizarre twist, McEachan's wallet was returned to his wife in 1948 after a major of the 4th Independent Airborne Forces Signals Squadron wrote to the Royal Corps of Signals Records Office:

Please find enclosed one wallet containing personal effects of the a/m soldier. It was picked up by me on a Naval LST [Landing Ship, Tank] during the Java landings of October 1945 and has just come to light in a recent kit 'rummage'. Could it please be forwarded to the person concerned as it may be of sentimental value.

Age 25.
No inscription.

PRIVATE LEONARD CHARLES RUDD [5727877] DORSETSHIRE REGIMENT, ROYAL ARMY SERVICE CORPS AND 2ND SAS (C SQN)

Bill Rudd, as he was known, was born on 19 April 1919 at Christchurch in Hampshire, his family later moving to Weymouth, Dorset, where he was educated at St John's School. Having worked as a joiner he enlisted into the Dorsetshire Regiment in November 1939 and after training he joined the 5th Battalion at Dover. Promoted to lance-corporal in January 1941 he attended a motor mechanic's course at Southampton later that year. Transferring to the Royal Army Service Corps in March 1942 he was initially posted to B Company, No.2 Holding Battalion, at Paisley with the trade of fitter and rank of private. Having then served briefly with No.1 Holding Battalion at Woking he was posted to VIII Corps Troops Ammunition Company that June, to No.1 RASC Mobilisation Centre at Morley twelve days later, and to 73 General Transport Company the following month. That autumn he was re-posted to No.3 Mobilisation Centre at Weybridge before moving to the 138th Infantry Brigade at Guildford.

Rudd disembarked in North Africa with the 519th Infantry Brigade in January 1943 and, after a period in hospital, was posted back to the 138th Infantry Brigade from where he volunteered for 2nd SAS on 9 June. Initially joining HQ Squadron he took part in OPERATION CANDYTUFT, an attack on enemy railway lines along Italy's Adriatic coast: four parties, under the command of Captain Roy Farran, MC*, landed near the mouth of the River Tronto from an MTB on the night of 27–28 October 1943, despite observing a German submarine anchored just 500 yards away. Tasked with derailing rolling stock the parties made their way inland independently. Rudd's group, consisting of Sergeant Rawes and Parachutists Mick Malcolm and Bill Holland, failed to rendezvous with the other teams as planned but later destroyed the line in six places, mined a road, and blew down telegraph lines before joining Farran and the other men on 2 November. The whole group was picked up by MTB in the early hours of the following day (see Holland's entry under Choloy War Cemetery, France).

Rudd returned to the UK in March 1944 and was deployed on OPERATION WALLACE that August. Having driven through the German lines C Squadron split into three parties, Rudd being a member of the leading two-Jeep patrol under Captain 'Raymond Lee', alias of Raymond Couraud. On 23 August it entered the village of Villaines-les-Prévôtes, which the men had been told was clear of the enemy. This was not the case and both Jeeps engaged a large force of Germans, Lance-corporal Stanley Walsh later stating:

> Pct Rudd was driving the Jeep, on the 23rd Aug, it crashed into the wall in the Cul de Sac at Villaines les Prevotes N484859. I knew nothing about him, until the Germans produced his AB.64 Part II [Service and Pay Book], at Villaines, when I was taken prisoner with Lieut Dodds, who also knew nothing about Pct Rudd. We were told that Rudd had been wounded in his arm, and that he died from having his head crushed between the wall and the Jeep, he died instantly. Whether this was the truth I do not know, as the Germans told me that Major Farran was dead, which was untrue [WO 361/720].

The following year Captain Dick Holland, MC, who had been tasked with locating missing men, wrote in his 'Report on Visit to France 10–20 Mar 45'; 'Pte Rudd was found buried at Villaines N482859 and can thus be reported killed instead of missing.' Meanwhile, an unknown newspaper cutting reported that:

> Early in July [1944] he came home for a week-end leave and his parents had not seen him or heard from him since. They believe he was in the fighting in Belgium [*sic*]. When Parachutist Rudd was called up with his age group he had nearly completed his five years apprenticeship as a joiner with Messrs Betts and Co, Weymouth, Ltd, for whom his father is secretary. An older brother is a flight sergeant in the RAF and his younger brother is working in an aircraft factory.

Son of Philip and Elsie Rudd (née London) of Roman Road, Radipole, Dorset. Age 25.
To us that loved and lost you your memory will never grow old
Also commemorated on Weymouth's war memorial.

VILLEQUIERS COMMUNAL CEMETERY

The village of Villequiers is located 30 kilometres east of Bourges and 3 kilometres east of Baugy in the Cher département of central France. The cemetery lies to the north of the village on the D72. GPS co-ordinates: Latitude 47.07333, Longitude 2.80425

CORPORAL JOHN JAMES HAMILTON **WILKINSON** [2100690] ROYAL ENGINEERS, ROYAL ARTILLERY, PARACHUTE REGIMENT AND 1ST SAS (A SQN)

John Wilkinson was born on 7 July 1919 in the town of Berkhamstead in Hertfordshire, but resided in Middlesex. At the outbreak of war he enlisted into the 345/36th Middlesex Anti-Aircraft Battalion, Royal Engineers, at Edgware, his attestation forms stating that he had been a member of the City of London University OTC for two years and that he had been employed as an actor. In August 1940 his unit was redesignated as the 36th Searchlight Regiment, Royal Artillery, and he was therefore transferred to this corps. The following July he was promoted to lance-bombardier and advanced to bombardier two months later. Having transferred to the Airborne Forces Depot School at Hardwick he attended parachute course 71 at No.1 PTS Ringway during July 1943. Here his instructor found him an 'average performer' but an 'intelligent pupil', Wilkinson being posted to the 9th (Eastern and Home Counties) Battalion, Parachute Regiment, that September. At the end of January 1944 he was re-posted to HQ Platoon, 3rd Parachute Brigade, from where he volunteered for 1st SAS on 17 February.

In the early hours of 15 August 1944 Wilkinson parachuted into a DZ at La Chaumotte Farm near the Forêt d'Yvoy in the Cher département of central France. As a member of Lieutenant Gordon Davidson's stick he was tasked with cutting enemy lines of communication during OPERATION HAGGARD in the area between Gien, Bourges and Nevers. He was killed in action on 26 August whilst disengaging from enemy tracked 20mm guns during a joint attack with the Maquis and French SAS. This saw the destruction of two canal bridges adjacent to the Bourges–Nevers road.

His comrades had no idea that he was an aspiring actor and poet, Davidson later noting:

> A tall, youngish, rather academic-looking man who, it transpired, was an actor who had recently worked at Stratford. I am not sure how he came to the unit, but he was a good reliable man …
>
> In one engagement, the hail of Schmeisser fire was so intense that it claimed an inevitable victim and my Corporal (the actor) was shot in the head beside me. Taken to a Maquis 'hospital', he was given every attention, but lack of supplies meant that he could not be saved [*War Diary 1939–1945*].

Just before he left for France Wilkinson had written this last poem and posted it to his mother:

Be still and cease to wail and mourn the dead,
For in the ignorant darkness round our lives
We scarce can tell the joys on which they fed,
This sudden death that life to them revives.

But what of life or death or mortal things?
Such words are flecks of cloud across the sun,
And then removed, behold the light it brings
To men whose joys have hardly yet begun.

The heroes of that fleeting moment know
That they are one with all eternity.
Exalted they no tear-lined faces show,
Not those who join that great fraternity.

Have we but tears to show for those whose youth
Outstretched the stars and grasped eternal truth?
[Courtesy of the late Joe Schofield, MBE, who served alongside Wilkinson in B Squadron]

Son of Percy and Olive Wilkinson (née Hamilton) of Hampton, Middlesex – Davidson returned Wilkinson's personal effects, consisting of his 'watch, pocket book and Shakespeare which he loved so much he took with him', to his mother who was later presented with her son's posthumous Croix de guerre (avec palme).
Age 25.
Plot CP, row 1, grave 267. Also commemorated on the Berry Maquis Memorial.

GERMANY

At the beginning of 1945 Germany was still not willing to surrender, despite facing imminent defeat of her Ardennes counter-offensive and invasion from two fronts. Having lost nearly all of the territory gained between 1939 and 1942 she remained determined to contest every inch of home soil. The young, the elderly and the sick were all mobilised to do so. Left with no other choice the Allies prepared for the final push, and for the casualties that would inevitably follow.

To the west the US First Army captured intact the Ludendorff railroad bridge at Remagen on 7 March, subsequently establishing a bridgehead over the Rhine. Farther north, the British 6th and US 17th Airborne Divisions landed across the Rhine by parachute and glider near Wesel on the morning of the 24th (Operation Varsity). Their foothold secured British crossings that had begun the previous day and provided a key platform for the battle ahead. The British Second Army under Lt-General Sir Miles Dempsey, DSO, MC, subsequently advanced through Osnabrück towards the key ports of Bremen, Hamburg and Kiel, which it captured in early May. At its vanguard was a Jeep column known as Frankforce after its commander, Lt-Colonel Brian Franks, DSO, MC, that combined elements of both 1st and 2nd SAS (Operation Archway). En route it was responsible for the liberation of Bergen-Belsen Concentration Camp.

Meanwhile, the Canadian First Army under General Harry Crerar, DSO, advanced north-east to clear Holland. Its progress was assisted by members of 2nd SAS dropped behind enemy lines during Operation Keystone, by the Jeep-borne element of this operation that led the way, and by both 3rd and 4th (French) SAS regiments that had also parachuted behind the lines farther north in the area between Groningen and Coevorden (Operation Amherst). Whilst the Army's left flank was protected by 5th (Belgian) SAS (Operation Larkswood), Crerar also thrust east into Germany towards Oldenburg and Wilhelmshaven, with 1st SAS' Jeeps initially leading the way during Operation Howard.

Germany surrendered unconditionally on 7 May 1945, this being officially ratified two days later in Berlin. Soon after both British SAS regiments were withdrawn to the UK. They refitted before being airlifted to Norway for occupational duties (Operation Apostle).

The SAS casualties incurred in this final chapter of the European war are testament not only to the ferocity of the German defence but also to the fanaticism that justified the conflict in which they lost their lives. Ten members of 1st SAS lie buried in German soil within three war cemeteries, one of which also contains the grave of a member of the LRDG, whilst twenty-four members of 2nd SAS are buried in a further three war cemeteries.

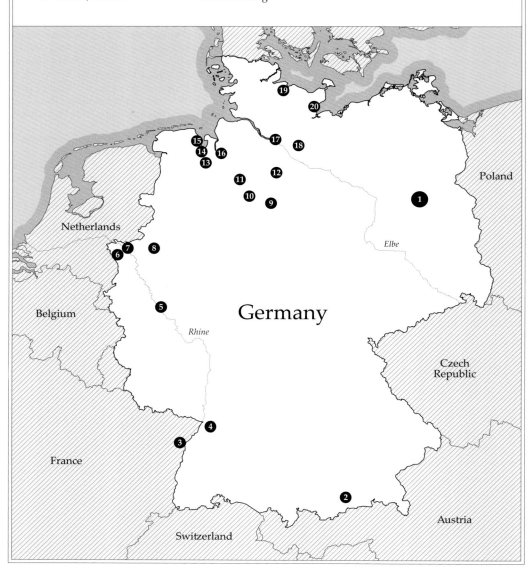

1. Berlin
2. Durnbach War Cemetery
3. Strasbourg
4. Gaggenau
5. Remagen
6. Reichswald Forest
   War Cemetery
7. Wesel / Bislich
8. Östrich
9. Hanover War Cemetery
10. Schneeren
11. Nienburg
12. Becklingen War
    Cemetery
13. Sage War Cemetery
14. Oldenburg
15. Wilhelmshaven
16. Bremen
17. Hamburg War Cemetery
18. Lütau
19. Kiel
20. Neustadt

Poland

Netherlands

Elbe

Belgium

Rhine

Germany

Czech
Republic

France

Austria

Switzerland

BECKLINGEN WAR CEMETERY

This cemetery overlooks Lüneburg Heath where Field Marshal Sir Bernard Montgomery, KCB, DSO, accepted the unconditional surrender of German forces in Holland, north-west Germany and Denmark on 4 May 1945. Burials were concentrated here from both isolated sites and former prisoner of war camps, the plot now containing 2,374 Commonwealth graves, ninety-seven of which are unidentified. In addition, there are twenty-seven non-Commonwealth burials.

The cemetery is located on the B3, 85 kilometres north of Hannover and 5 kilometres north of Becklingen village. GPS co-ordinates: Latitude 52.89028, Longitude 9.91667

SERGEANT PERCY ROY THORPE MM [6844525] KING'S ROYAL RIFLE CORPS AND 2ND SAS (3 SQN)

In November 1930 Percy Thorpe enlisted into the King's Royal Rifle Corps, refusing any other regiment in order to serve alongside his brother Frank. At the time he stated that he had been born in Brixton on 1 December 1911 and that he resided in south-west London where he worked as a carpenter. As his birth was not registered until the early part of 1913 it seems likely that he falsified his age to join up early. Posted to India in November 1931, he qualified as a theatre medical orderly at Calcutta and as the regimental chiropodist. At the end of his service with the Colours he attended a resettlement course in salesmanship in Rangoon before arriving back in the UK in March 1938. Here, having completed his full term, he was posted to the Army Reserve, his exit report noting: 'A smart intelligent and hardworking Rifleman. Was employed in BMH [British Military Hospital] Rangoon where he did very well. Has done a vocational training course of Grocery Salesmanship. Has a pleasant manner.'

Thorpe was briefly mobilised during the summer of 1939 and was embodied on 1 September, the day after he married Dorothy Mabel Shadgett, a stage contortionist, at Wandsworth and two days before war was declared. On the 10th he disembarked in France with No.12 Water Labour Company, 1st Battalion, KRRC, as a member of the BEF, although that December he returned to the UK. Posted to the 2nd Battalion, Queen Victoria Rifles, he immediately joined HQ Company, this Territorial battalion being a holding unit for both regular and TA personnel. He was promoted to lance-corporal in May 1940 and having been advanced to corporal that August qualified as a Physical Training Instructor during the autumn. In May 1941 his son, also Percy Roy, was born.

After a spell as an instructor at the 1st Motor Training Battalion, KRRC, Thorpe was posted to the Northern Command Weapon Training School where, according to his report, he was a 'very good, but unenthusiastic' infantry weapons instructor. In November 1943 he joined the 10th Battalion (The Rangers) but after failing a medical for the Glider Pilot Regiment volunteered for 2nd SAS on 24 April 1944. The following month he attended parachute course 114A at No.1 PTS Ringway where he was noted as being 'a good all round performer – morale high – example to men'.

Thorpe was parachuted into the Eure département of Haute-Normandie, France, during OPERATION TRUEFORM on the night of 17–18 August 1944 as commander of Party 3. Consisting of six men from 2nd SAS and four from the Belgian Independent Parachute Company, this was dropped from 700 feet at 0200hrs in the area of Saint-Amand-des-Haute-Terre, 18 kilometres north-north-west of the intended drop zone. The drop was blind (that is, without an arranged reception committee), hence the inaccuracy, Thorpe himself later noting:

> Flak was encountered shortly before reaching the DZ which we approached from the north … There was no warning of the drop and the first that I knew was the noise of No.1's static line running out … We searched the area for the two missing men, Fowler and Bintley, but were unable to find them [WO 361/719 – see Parachutist Thomas Bintley's entry under Bayeux War Cemetery, France, and that of Driver Harold Erlis under Saint-Sever Cemetery Extension, France, both within this volume].

Thorpe's party, tasked with harassing the retreating enemy, operated to the west of Louviers until 24 August by which time it had destroyed German billets, vehicles and tanks, and captured assorted transport and sixty of the enemy. Before returning to the UK on 28 August his team also passed important local information to the advancing Americans.

On the night of 19–20 September 1944 Thorpe and five others parachuted, along with three Jeeps, into a small clearing above the village of Moussey in the Vosges département of eastern France as reinforcements for OPERATION LOYTON. Visibility was very poor and other aircraft in the formation turned back without dropping their loads (see Parachutist Fred Ireland's entry within this volume under Twickenham Cemetery, United Kingdom). Two nights later, having been briefed by his CO, Lt-Colonel Brian Franks, MC, Thorpe set off to lay charges on railway lines to the south. On Franks' recommendation he was subsequently awarded an immediate Military Medal:

> Sgt Thorpe was dropped by parachute in the Eastern Vosges on 21/22 Sep [sic] with other reinforcements. With a party of five ORs [other ranks] he was ordered to destroy the rly [railway] line between St Die and Saales which was being continually used by the enemy and as a secondary task any tpt [transport] on the neighbouring roads. Sgt Thorpe made his way to the objective through an area which was highly populated with the enemy. In spite of finding the railway strongly guarded at the point chosen he personally placed the charges on the line. They were heard to detonate four hours later when a train was heard on the line. Turning his attention to the roads, four mines were laid on one night all of which went off – four were laid in another area which again detonated and local inhabitants reported that five vehs [vehicles] had been destroyed or damaged.
>
> Later having rejoined the main base on the 29 Sept four Jeeps which were concealed were found and attacked by approx a Coy [company] of the enemy. Sgt Thorpe with one other man succeeded in preventing the capture of the Jeeps, remaining with them and firing the MGs [machine guns] continually for over an hour. The enemy temporarily withdrew in the face of Sgt Thorpe's fire. When joined by others from the main base this NCO succeeded in extricating the Jeeps and taking them to a place of safety.
>
> On this and other ops Sgt Thorpe has shown himself to possess the highest courage coupled with gifts of leadership and determination. His actions deserve the highest praise [London Gazette 22/03/45].

At the close of Loyton Thorpe crossed through the lines and late that November returned to the UK. Here he attended a Jeep course at Dom School in Keswick at the beginning of January 1945. He was subsequently deployed on Operation Archway in Germany where he was killed in action on 19 April 1945 on the approach to the River Elbe. A signal sent to SAS Brigade HQ that day states: 'Killed Sgt Thorpe. Slightly wounded Capt Laws. Send address next of kin Thorpe and inform 60th' (the KRRC). On 21 April Major The Hon. John Bingham, the Administration Officer at 2nd SAS' HQ, wrote to Franks: 'We are all very unhappy about Sgt Thorpe – I wrote to the 60th about him.' Franks replied: 'Sgt Thorpe killed by sniper at village of Grosthondorf 12 miles NNE of Velzen date not known believed 20 Apr [sic]. Buried same day same village' (AIR 20/8844). He later wrote: 'Sergeant Thorpe, of the 60th, who was also with me in France, was most unfortunately killed by a sniper in Germany. He was a most courageous NCO and I have never seen any officer or man who was cooler in action than he was. Added to this he was a tremendous thruster and his loss was very keenly felt by us all.'

Son of Mr and Mrs Thorpe (née Valler) of Margate Road, Brixton, south London – Husband of Dorothy Thorpe of Kings Avenue, Clapham Park, south-west London – Father of Percy Thorpe – Brother of Frank Thorpe. Age officially recorded as 33.

No inscription. For some reason Thorpe's Military Medal is not engraved on his headstone.

Grave 2.J.5.

DURNBACH WAR CEMETERY

Although located in what was the post-war American zone this site was chosen due to the large number of Commonwealth aircraft shot down over this area of southern Germany and within Austria. The remainder of those commemorated here were prisoners of war who were murdered after capture, killed whilst escaping, or who died on forced marches from their camps. The cemetery contains 2,934 Commonwealth burials, ninety-three of them unidentified. In addition, one grave (3.C.22) contains the ashes of an unknown number of unidentified casualties from Flossenburg Concentration Camp whilst another contains the remains of six unidentified British airmen (4.A.21). The Durnbach Cremation Memorial, located in the Indian Section, commemorates twenty-three servicemen of India who died whilst prisoners of war.

Those members of 2nd SAS buried here, of all whom were serving on OPERATIONS LOYTON *or* PISTOL, *were either murdered as members of Lieutenant Desmond Black's stick near Saint-Dié in France, as members of Sergeant Jock Hay's stick at La Grande Fosse in France, or at Gaggenau in Germany. Regardless, all were concentrated to a cemetery at the latter location before being reinterred here on 9 July 1948. Captain Victor Gough of SOE's* JEDBURGH *Team* JACOB, *dropped with 2nd SAS' recce group on a mission tandem to* LOYTON, *was murdered with those at Gaggenau and is buried alongside them in grave 3.K.22.*

The cemetery is located 15 kilometres east of Bad Tolz and 3 kilometres north-east of the village of Durnbach on the B307 Bad Tolz-Miesbach road. GPS co-ordinates: Latitude 47.77834, Longitude 11.73354

Private Christopher ASHE [847426] Royal Artillery and 2nd SAS (2 Sqn)

The archives of Schirmeck Concentration Camp record Christopher Ashe's date of birth as 1 June 1917, his place of birth as 'Ballinceborbey' in Eire and his occupations as agricultural worker then regular soldier from 1935. Although the date of birth is correct he was born at Ballinabarney in County Wicklow where he worked as a kitchen porter. Enlisting into the Royal Artillery in June 1935 in London he served in the UK with various field regiments until the end of October 1940 when he embarked for Malta. Having served with the 12th Field Regiment throughout the island's siege he volunteered for 2nd SAS and landed in Algiers on 25 August 1943 to commence training at Philippeville. He returned to the UK in mid March 1944 with the rest of the Regiment.

Ashe parachuted into the Bas-Rhin département of eastern France for Operation Pistol on the night of the 15–16 September 1944 as a member of Lieutenant Geoffrey Castellain's B.2 Patrol. This was tasked with disrupting lines of communication in the Saargemuend area (see Castellain's entry within this volume under Moussey Churchyard, France). Ashe, who jumped last, was separated from the rest of the stick and is believed to have landed in, or to the east of, the wood south of Fromuhl village. 'Missing Parachutists', the SAS War Crimes Investigation Team's final report, notes:

> Pct Ashe, whose stick landed in a fir wood near Hinsburg, was unable to contact his commander, and was captured alone on the 23rd September, south of Bitsch. Brought to Strasbourg and lodged in the rue du Fil prison. Here, after interrogation, he was separated and sent to Schirmeck on the 27th September. Ashe retained his uniform and surprisingly was allowed medicine and special diet for the stomach trouble from which he was suffering. He grew a beard and remained in the cells until the evacuation of Schirmeck [WO 218/222].

Ashe was subsequently murdered at Gaggenau on 25 November 1944 alongside other members of 2nd SAS that had been captured on Operation Loyton (see Lieutenant David Dill's entry within this section for full details). Apart from Parachutist Gerhard Wertheim, a German Jew, all other men captured on Operation Pistol were treated as prisoners of war (see Wertheim's entry under Medjez-el-Bab Memorial, Tunisia, Volume I). Ashe may have been murdered because he was discovered alone, maybe in a farmhouse, therefore giving his captors the impression, or excuse, that he had been co-operating with the Maquis.

After the remains of the men were discovered in the spring of 1945 the SAS War Crimes Investigation Team signalled Brigade HQ asking for details of any distinguishing features. They received the following reply:

Ashe much tattooed. Left upper arm naked woman right arm cross with scroll. Quote 'In Memory of Father' unquote. Also Maltese cross Malta GC [George Cross] bird on each hand. Noticeable scar on back of one hand [WO 218/216].

However, his remains were identified by a combination of dental records, height and the blue Umbro swimming trunks that Corporal Harry Kinder of 2nd SAS reported that Ashe wore on operations.

Whilst the CWGC states he was the son of Patrick and Catherine Ashe of Folkestone it is known that during 1944 his mother was a resident of Sandfield Villas, Guildford, Surrey. His attestation papers confirm that she had previously lived in Ballinabarney, County Wicklow.

Age 27.

R.I.P.

Grave 3.K.12.

PRIVATE FREDERICK LEONARD **AUSTIN** [6287803] THE BUFFS AND 2ND SAS (2 SQN)

Known to his comrades as 'Bunny', Fred Austin was born on 29 October 1919 close to the River Thames in the village of Cliffe, north Kent. In April 1939, whilst working as a paper maker, he joined the Territorial 4/5th Battalion, The Buffs (Royal East Kent Regiment), at Sittingbourne and was embodied at the outbreak of war. He subsequently disembarked in France with the 4th Battalion that November. The following May he was posted to No.2 Infantry Base Depot and was evacuated to the UK via Cherbourg after the attempted defence of Le Havre. Disembarking on Malta that October he served throughout the island's siege until moving to North Africa in mid June 1943. Here he volunteered for 2nd SAS on the 20th. He subsequently either raided Italian-held islands in the Mediterranean or fought on Sicily or the mainland, as he was later awarded the Italy Star. He arrived back in the UK with the rest of the Regiment in March 1944.

Promoted to acting lance-corporal, Austin parachuted into the Vosges département of eastern France for OPERATION LOYTON in the early hours of 1 September 1944 as a member of Lieutenant 'Karl' Marx's stick. Having served as rear gunner in Lieutenant David Dill's Jeep he was with Sergeant Jock Hay's party when captured on 7 October and was murdered at La Grande Fosse on 15 October (see Hay's entry for full details). SS-Scharführer Hans Hubner, a member of the Kommando Ernst stationed at Saales and one of those later accused of the killings, stated: 'Of the eight prisoners I can state with certainty that I recognise three of those in the lorry from the photographs shown to me marked Neville [*sic*], Church and Austin' (WO 309/661). For some reason his date of death is officially recorded as 16 October 1944, only three of the seven men murdered alongside him being correctly recorded as the 15th.

Three members of 2nd SAS, taken prisoner during OPERATION GALIA in northern Italy, all recalled that on 3 January 1945 they were interrogated at the headquarters of German mountain troops:

> Again a list of the names of the SAS men was read out to us. This was a longer list and included the names of Lieut Silly, Sgt Benson, Cpl Lawrence, Cpl Austin, Pct Loosemore and Cpl Phillips. We were not told whether these men were killed or were PW and we couldn't ask as we denied all knowledge of them, but we got the impression they were prisoners and that we would be meeting them when the interview was over or at some PW camp we would be going to [WO 361/651].

Son of Mr and Mrs R. Austin (née Cheeseman) of Coldharbour Lane, Kemsley Village, Sittingbourne, Kent.
Age 24.
No inscription.
Grave 3.K.7. Also commemorated on the Stele de Prayé Memorial above Moussey and by a tree on Central Avenue, Sittingbourne.

Private James William Robert **BENNETT** [14219880] Home Guard, General Service Corps, Seaforth Highlanders, Highland Regiment, Parachute Regiment and 2nd SAS (2 Sqn)

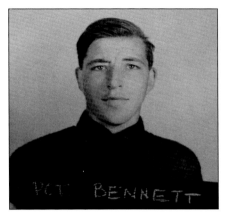

Jimmy Bennett was born on 19 July 1924 in east London and resided in Middlesex. Whilst working as a lorry driver's mate he served in the Gramophone Company of the Middlesex Regiment's Home Guard before enlisting into the General Service Corps at Acton in July 1942. His embodiment was deferred until the beginning of September when, having declared his intention of serving with a Highland regiment, he was posted to No.61 Platoon of the Seaforth Highlanders at Fort George near Inverness. He officially transferred to the Seaforths in October 1942 and a month later transferred again to the Highland Regiment. Although posted to the 1st Battalion he transferred again in July 1943, this time to the Army Air Corps and, having attended parachute course 76 at No.1 PTS Ringway, joined the 8th (Midland Counties) Battalion, Parachute Regiment, two months later.

Bennett volunteered for 2nd SAS on 8 April 1944 and parachuted into the Vosges département of eastern France for Operation Loyton in the early hours of 1 September as a member of Lt-Colonel Brian Franks' stick. Two men from Lieutenant 'Karl' Marx's party found him on 10 September whilst searching for food: 'he had been left by himself in a house at V403831' (3 kilometres south of Pierre-Percée), stated Marx in his post-operation report. Bennett had been positioned there, the main party's RV, in the hope that he might spot Sergeant Michael Fitzpatrick's party that had been separated from the remainder of its stick when parachuting into the area on the night of 6–7 September (see Fitzpatrick's entry within this volume under Moussey Churchyard, France). Bennett subsequently stayed with Marx's group until it made contact with the main SAS base two days later. He then served as front gunner in Major Peter Power's Jeep.

Bennett was with Sergeant Jock Hay's rear party when captured on 7 October and was murdered at La Grande Fosse on the 15th (see Hay's entry within this section for full details). The exhumation of his remains, identified through dental records, indicated that he was shot third from last out of the group of eight. For some reason his date of death is officially recorded as 16 October 1944 although that of three of the seven men murdered alongside him is correctly recorded as the 15th.

Son of James and Elizabeth Bennett (née Duffin) of Gledwood Avenue, Hayes, Middlesex.
Age 20.
He left us many memories and a sorrow too great to be told
Grave 3.K.4. Also commemorated on the Stele de Prayé Memorial above Moussey.

Lieutenant James Desmond BLACK [262193] Home Guard, Royal Scots, Lowland Regiment, Argyll and Sutherland Highlanders and 2nd SAS (2 Sqn)

Known as Desmond to both family and friends, Black was born on 21 November 1923 at Didsbury in Manchester. After a period of five years at Port Said, Egypt, where he attended a private school, his family settled at Tongland in Kirkcudbrightshire. Here he continued his education at Kirkcudbright Academy and Dollar Academy where he was a member of the OTC from 1937 to 1940. At the outbreak of the war he had also joined the local Home Guard and, being the owner of a motorcycle, became its dispatch rider. Knowing that he would be called up he worked on a farm to get fit and in November 1941 joined the 70th (Young Soldiers) Battalion, Royal Scots, at Dumfries (service number 3066367). Transferring to the 1st Battalion, Lowland Regiment, the following February he was attached as a lance-corporal to the 6th Battalion, King's Own Scottish Borderers, for pre-OCTU training late that April. After a period with the 10th Infantry Training Centre at Berwick he was sent to Wrotham in Kent for further instruction and then on to 161 OCTU at Aldershot in October 1942. He was subsequently commissioned into the 11th Battalion, Argyll and Sutherland Highlanders, his father's former regiment, at the beginning of February 1943 and from April was attached to the Royal Scots, also one of his father's regiments, for garrison duty on Gibraltar.

Having been interviewed on the Rock by Major Potter Miller-Mundy of 2nd SAS, Black sailed to Algiers and took a truck to Philippeville where he joined the Regiment on 15 December 1943. After parachute training west of Algiers he returned to the UK the following March where he was stationed in Ayrshire. During the subsequent build-up training for D-Day operations he often brought his troop back to the family home where excursions to the local pub sometimes resulted in minor trouble. On one such occasion they stole the local policeman's car (personal interview with his brother, Donald Black, 2012).

Black parachuted into Operation Loyton in the Vosges département of eastern France on the night of 6–7 September 1944 as a member of Major Denny Reynolds' reinforcement party. There is some confusion as to how his stick subsequently became separated from the main SAS group: 'Missing Parachutists', the SAS War Crimes Investigation Team's final report, states that this occurred during the crossing of the Plaine valley on the 10th whilst other documents, such as 2nd SAS' Casualty Report, state that it was separated after an attack on Lt-Colonel Brian Franks' base east of Pierre-Percée the following day. The report of Lance-corporal Joseph Zandarco, a Frenchman serving in 2 Squadron, 2nd SAS, appears to confirm the latter theory:

> We were attacked on 9 Jun [sic – September] by the Germans, who had learned of our presence through a French family in a nearby farmhouse. The daughter was enceinte [a French euphemism for pregnant] by a German and the son was a Milicien. We had contacted them in order to get food. They lived at Pierre Percee, south-east of Badonviller.
> The Germans fired on us from all sides before they were nearby. Major Reynolds, in charge of our party, was wounded and later disappeared into the woods. Lt Black was also wounded. We dispersed and ran for it [WO 208/3351 – see Reynolds' entry below].

However, Franks, the CO, stated that having crossed the valley he tasked Black with ambushing enemy troops on 11 September. Whatever the case Black's party was seen by Madame Yorg at her house in Les Collins where the men brewed tea before moving to the house adjoining the La Turbine sawmill east of Pierre-Percée on the valley floor. Here they found Sergeant Frank Terry-Hall, Corporal Thomas Ivison and Parachutist Jack Crosier who had been separated from Lieutenant 'Karl' Marx on the 9th (see Terry-Hall's entry within this section for full details). It was probably this latter party's use of a French guide, Gaston Mathieu, which resulted in the whole group's betrayal to the Sicherheitsdienst

(SD, the intelligence arm of the SS) at Raon-l'Étape. Quite how bad Black's wound was at this stage is unknown and although it is often reported that it was in the ensuing action on the 15th, during which he and the others were captured, that he was wounded in the leg, Zandarco's statement suggests that he had previously ignored his wound and carried on with his tasks. Paul Chavane, a French agent of the Gestapo, later outlined the events of the 15th:

I took part in this action myself as a chauffeur. We left from St Die to arrive at the house at nightfall. All together there were twelve vehicles. I remained as a guard for these vehicles. Four agents were sent up to the farm [sic – sawmill] to see if the parachutists were still there, and practically immediately the engagement began.

Fire was opened from two sides. The wife of the farmer [Maria Thirion] was killed during this engagement. During a pause in the fire the farm was encircled and the parachutists taken prisoner. The owner of the farm [Leon Marchal] was killed by a shot from the revolver of the German officer who commanded the action.

The parachutist prisoners were placed in my green lorry and were taken to La Creche at Raon l'Etape [an outpost of the SD's Kommando Ernst]. Here they were interrogated and searched. We found compasses, and silk maps which were taken from them. Interrogation was carried out by one called Manuel, the civil agent of Berger, and who had been wounded in the hand during the course of the engagement.

Manuel, born in Tiflis, was of Yugoslav nationality, and had been employed at the American Embassy in Paris before the war.

After their interrogation the parachutists were taken to a house which may have been the Hotel des Vosges at Raon l'Etape. Here they remained for the rest of the night [WO 309/703].

'Missing Parachutists' states the group was forced to march from La Creche towards Badonviller but that shortly after crossing the bridge over the Plaine river a truck was fetched, progress being slow as the wounded Black needed to be carried. The group was driven to a house at Badonviller occupied by the Kommando Pullmer and then on to Schirmeck Concentration Camp where it arrived on the 16th at around 2000hrs. The men remained one or two nights in the cells, Black having his wound dressed by Dr Stoll, the camp doctor. A gaiter, bearing Black's name, was kept by a camp stretcher-bearer and this was later used as evidence at the ensuing war crimes tribunal. Dr Hans Ernst, leader of the Kommando Ernst at Saint-Dié, is said to have exhibited extreme anger with his subordinate that he had forwarded the prisoners to Schirmeck without keeping them for 'unit disposal'. He persisted until the men were retrieved by truck the following Sunday at about 0900hrs (WO 218/222).

Although Chavane later recalled a somewhat different version of events from La Creche, his statement provided initial clues as to the group's fate:

The next day between 10 and 12 'o' clock in the morning, I took these parachutists in my lorry to St Die … when we arrived there the parachutists were taken to the hospital at Foucharupt, where they were put in cells.

They were interrogated there the same day by Stuscha Schossig. These parachutists were wearing khaki uniforms, with red berets and SAS on the shoulder. They did not remain in the hospital at Foucharupt but were taken to another barrack and placed in the cells of the military prison of this barracks.

Three or four days after they were interrogated their uniforms were distributed to Bruckle's agents at the Chateau des Allouette at St Die. I remember one agent called Josef Helandez who was wearing English uniform a few days afterwards.

Three or four days after the engagement I saw these parachutists again in the barracks prison. They had all been dressed in old civilian clothes; only the Lieutenant still had his uniform.

Between the 20th and 25th of September [the 20th] in the morning at roll call, Hscha. Griem detailed about ten men to form an execution squad. I can remember the name of Machatschek, the armourer, of Jacques Vasseur and Walter Jantzen. So far as I remember Vasseur was the only Frenchman. I believe that he now lives in Freiburg under a false name.

The same morning that Griem had given this order the men detailed went to the prison to fetch the parachutists in a truck. They left about 10 o'clock and came back about midday. I can remember that there were three Germans who could not eat their midday meal.

I imagine that the execution took place in the neighbourhood of St Die, but cannot give the exact place as I never heard Vasseur or another speak of it.

Shortly afterwards I left to join the Sonderkommando Berger, which was then at the Villa Matty at Hohwald. I remember that Berger told me that during the same period, that is between 15th and 20th of September, he had killed a number of parachutists in the region of between Schirmeck and Abreschviller [WO 309/703].

SS-Hauptscharführer Walter Jantzen, a member of the Kommando Ernst later accused of the killings, gave a more precise account and more plausible location for where the men met their fate:

A French agent employed by Berger, whose name was Manuel had discovered that there were some English soldiers in the area between the [col du] Donon and Raon l'Etape …

Manuel and another agent of Berger went on alone to the house [on the 15th]. They came back to say that instead of the three soldiers they had expected there were now eight. Ustuf Wentzel decided to attack the house which was surrounded according to his orders. After an exchange of fire Manuel called on the English to surrender. After a time the answer came back 'OK'. The prisoners were accordingly brought out one by one and disarmed …

The following day I again saw the eight English prisoners who had been handed to the Wehrmacht at Raon l'Etape. The Lieutenant, who had been wounded in the leg, had received treatment. The bullet had been removed, and the leg set in a splint …

First we drove to the barracks to fetch the English prisoners from the cells [on the 20th]. They were brought out, and loaded onto the lorry. They were still wearing uniform. It is possible that some had their hands bound. Once the prisoners were loaded we drove off in the following order: one passenger car, the lorry carrying the prisoners, and another passenger car. I think that I was in the last car. We drove off from St Die [Saint-Dié] in the direction, so far as I can remember of Raon l'Etape. After a trip of half or three quarters of an hour, our convoy turned into a valley and followed a track for a short distance. We then halted.

Guards were then placed about the area to keep civilians from observing what was about to occur. Other guards were placed round the lorry to prevent the prisoners from escaping. Among these were Holm and I. I learnt afterwards that the grave higher up on the hillside had already been prepared.

I cannot remember with certainty whether the English prisoners were told that they were going to be shot before the first one was made to get down from the lorry. This first prisoner was made to take his uniform jacket and trousers off before he was taken up the hillside. At no time while I was observing this prisoner did he make any attempt to escape or to disobey the orders given to him. I heard a shot from higher up in the wood. In the same way all the other prisoners were made to take off their uniform, and were taken up singly into the wood where they were shot.

The last prisoner to be shot was the Lieutenant whose name I gave as 'Block' and who I am able to recognise from the photograph shown to me marked Lieutenant Black. As he was wounded, he had to be carried to the place of execution by some men. I cannot recall at this moment whether or not I was one of those who carried him. In all eight English prisoners were shot on this day. I never noticed any of them try to escape or to make any movement which might be misconstrued as an attempt to do so.

I went up to the grave at the end and helped to shovel the earth in [WO 309/233].

SS-Hauptscharführer Josef Pilz, another of those later accused of the killings, also described Black's murder:

As this was the last prisoner, and there were no more left who could have tried to escape, my task as a sentry was over, and so I walked up the hill after this group carrying the last prisoner. When we came to the grave, either Wetzel or Oppelt said that the splint should be taken off the prisoner's leg. He was laid on the ground for this purpose. I am not sure if I heard the prisoner groan as the splint was taken off. When I looked back again I saw Machatschek and Oppelt throw the body into the grave.

I helped to fill in the grave and noticed that the dead bodies still had shirts on. The uniform of the dead soldiers was taken back with us in the lorry to the barracks at St Die.

About two days later Jantzen gave me a number of pieces of maps, photographs of girls and note books to be burnt. I assumed that these had been taken from the dead soldiers. I carried out this order and burnt them all. Later on the same day Jantzen gave me a number of religious medallions on chains, and medals and buttons to take away and bury [WO 309/661].

SS-Oberscharführer Horst Gaede, also of the Kommando Ernst, later stated:

One of the last prisoners who was taken up said 'I am soldier'. This gave me a pang because I understood the men only too well. They were completely right and it was also their right to be treated as prisoners of war as is laid down by the Geneva Convention. I was forced to think involuntarily of comrades who had been wounded and had fallen into the hands of the Russians, by whom they had been shot …

The wounded Lieutenant Black, was to my knowledge, shot by Machatschek [WO 235/176].

In May 1946 the remains of the eight SAS were exhumed in the vicinity of Les Moitresses west of Saint-Dié and post-mortems carried out. The pathologist, Major Mant of the RAMC, later reported:

Contents of pockets: Left hand breast pocket; letter addressed to Lt J D Black, 2nd SAS, APO, containing one letter and 1,500 Fcs French in 50 Fc notes in series and one rifle bullet, fired. Clutched in right hand was small portion of crepe paper similar to that composing German paper bandage. One escape saw found in seam of shirt front, broken in two pieces [WO 235/176].

Black's one-time cipher pad was later found at the Gestapo headquarters on the rue d'Alsace in Strasbourg.

The 'St Die Case' was brought to trial before a British Military Court at Wuppertal, Germany, between 22 and 25 May 1946. Walter Jantzen, Herbert Griem, Otto Wetzel, Richard Albrecht, Otto Holm, August Geiger, Horst Gaede, Karl Golckel, Josef Pilz and Ludwig Koch, all members of the Kommando Ernst, were found guilty of being 'concerned in the killing' of the eight SAS. Griem and Wetzel were sentenced to death and executed that September. Although the Deputy Judge Advocate General considered Jantzen's death sentence 'unreasonable' he was also executed around the same time, presumably for involvement in additional war crimes other than the murder of Sergeant Jock Hay's stick for which he received a custodial sentence. The remainder were sentenced to various terms of imprisonment ranging from three to thirteen years. Four of them had already received prison sentences for involvement in the murder of Hay's stick (see his entry within this section for full details). Those incarcerated were subsequently released for reasons of 'good conduct', 'pre-trial custody' or 'Christmas clemency'.

Ernst himself escaped from American custody to East Germany, only to be sent to a gulag in 1947 by the Russian authorities. He was released in 1956 as part of an amnesty and received compensation. Although sentenced to death three times in absentia for crimes including the mass deportation to concentration camps of citizens of Moussey, the French rulings were not recognised by West Germany. He subsequently practised law until 1977 when persistent pressure from Nazi hunters Serge and Beate Klarsfield resulted in denial of his right to do so. By the time a case was ready in 1981 he was allegedly in too poor a state of health to stand trial. He died a free man in 1991.

Senior German officers implicated in all of the war crimes cases found in this section were tried at Wuppertal between 17 June and 11 July 1946: SS-Obergruppenführer Karl Oberg (Gestapo chief for France), SS-Standartenführer Dr Erich Isselhorst (SD commander in Alsace), and SS-Obersturmbannführer Wilhelm Schneider (deputy to Isselhorst) were sentenced to death. Oberg eventually walked free whilst his two subordinates were hanged. Sturmbannführer Gustav Schlierbach (Gestapo chief in Strasbourg) was sentenced to ten years imprisonment and Generalleutnant Willy Seegers (Commander-in-Chief of the Wehrmacht in Alsace) was sentenced to three.

Son of Major John Black and Mai Black (née Cowley) of Ellerslie, Tongland, Kirkcudbright – Brother of Donald Black.
Age 20.
No inscription.
Grave 3.K.13. Also commemorated on Ringford's war memorial near Tongland – A plaque originally mounted within Tongland Parish Church bearing Black's name is now housed in Ringford Village Hall.

Private Reginald Stanley CHURCH [2938122] Queen's Own Cameron Highlanders and 2nd SAS (3 Sqn)

Reg Church was born on 20 April 1920 in Lambeth, south London, later living in nearby West Norwood. Having played cricket professionally he enlisted into the Queen's Own Cameron Highlanders at the beginning of July 1940 and was posted to the 7th Battalion. Although he attended 169 OCTU the following April he was posted to an infantry training centre as a private in mid July and two weeks later re-posted to HQ 110th Forces. In April 1942 he joined HQ First Army as a lance-corporal and, having married Gwendoline Violet Dorothy Andrew that October, embarked for Operation Torch, the landings in North Africa as a corporal. His son, Raymond Stanley, was born the following year.

In July 1943, with fighting in North Africa over, Church was posted to HQ Fifteenth Army. Having been re-posted to an infantry replacement training depot he volunteered for 2nd SAS on 9 October and was confirmed as lance-sergeant the following month. As he was awarded the Italy Star it can be assumed that he went on to serve with the Regiment on the Italian mainland. Deprived of one stripe for an unknown offence in February 1944 he returned to the UK the following month where he lost his remaining tape for a minor misdemeanour in June. At the beginning of August he attended parachute course 127A at No.1 PTS Ringway where his instructor noted 'though very nervous controls it well – hard working, average'.

On the night of 21–22 September 1944 three Jeeps and fourteen men, including Church, were parachuted into a small clearing above the village of Moussey in the Vosges département of eastern France as reinforcements for Operation Loyton. Over the following days Church served as rear gunner on Lieutenant Lord John Manners' Jeep. On 2 October, with the operation now drawing to a close, Lt-Colonel Brian Franks, MC, sent him, along with Sergeant Pat Nevill and Parachutist Peter McGovern, to recce the road to the col du Hantz (see Nevill's and McGovern's entries within this section). The three were captured that day by members of the Kommando Ernst under Leutenant Taufel, probably in the area of La Petite-Raon (WO 235/554). Taken to the Kommando's HQ at the Maison Barthlemy in Saales they were interrogated and kept with other SAS prisoners in the basement.

Church was murdered at La Grande Fosse on 15 October 1944 (see Sergeant Jock Hay's entry within this section for full details). 'Missing Parachutists' states that his remains, identified by dental records, were found at the bottom of the grave and he was therefore presumably the first to be shot. SS-Unterscharführer Georg Zahringer, one of those later accused of the killings and who drove the truck to the scene of the crime, stated:

Schossig, who spoke English, told him [Church] to take his clothes off. This the prisoner did. He was then taken, held by the arms by Wottke and Gaede, into the wood. Practically immediately I heard a shot. The remaining English prisoners on the truck did not say anything, but remained silent. This went on from one prisoner to another [WO 309/233].

Son of Mr and Mrs Church (née Faller) of St Denis Road, West Norwood, south-east London – Husband of Gwendoline Church of Gipsy Road, West Norwood.
Age 24. No inscription.
Grave 3.K.21. Also commemorated on the Stele de Prayé Memorial above Moussey.

PRIVATE JACK STANLEY **CROSIER** [14402126] HOME GUARD, GENERAL SERVICE CORPS, ESSEX REGIMENT, OXFORDSHIRE AND BUCKINGHAMSHIRE LIGHT INFANTRY AND 2ND SAS (2 SQN)

Jack Crosier was born on 13 September 1923 at Chelmsford in Essex where, along with his brothers Leslie and Dennis, he was brought up as the adoptive son of his maternal grandparents. In August 1941, whilst working as a plane grinder, he joined the 6th Essex Battalion, Home Guard, serving with them until called up into the General Service Corps a year later. Although his embodiment was deferred he joined No.51 Primary Training Wing at Warley in mid September 1942 and transferred to the 70th (Young Soldiers) Battalion, Essex Regiment, the following month. In November he was posted to the regiment's infantry training centre and joined the 2nd Battalion soon after. He transferred to the 2nd Battalion, Oxfordshire and Buckinghamshire Light Infantry, which operated in a glider-borne airlanding role as part of the 6th Airborne Division, in June 1943. However, the battalion was not used for the invasion of Sicily that summer and Crosier volunteered for 2nd SAS on 13 March 1944, attending parachute course 111A at No.1 PTS Ringway the following month. Here his instructor noted him as 'an average performer, will make a good paratroop'.

Crosier parachuted into the Vosges département of eastern France for OPERATION LOYTON in the early hours of 1 September 1944 as a member of Lieutenant 'Karl' Marx's stick (see Sergeant Frank Terry-Hall's and Lieutenant Desmond Black's entries in this section for subsequent activity). He, Terry-Hall, and Corporal Thomas Ivison, were separated from their comrades on the 9th whilst being pursued near La Chapelotte. They were captured, just after Crosier's 21st birthday, on 15 September at the sawmill at La Turbine alongside Black's stick. He was next seen with this officer by a local, Georges Noble:

> In September 1944 I remember seeing a party of captured parachutists at Raon L'Etape. These included one who was wounded and unable to walk [Black], and another whom I am able with certainty to recognise from a photograph shown to me marked Crosier. He was wearing a red beret. This party was confined in the building known as La Creche, but did not stay long [WO 309/233].

Crosier was subsequently murdered near Saint-Dié on 20 September 1944 (see Black's entry for full details).

Son of Ivy Crosier and grandson of Mary Crosier of Upper Bridge Road, Chelmsford, Essex – His brother, Leslie, was killed in Italy on 10 January 1944 whilst serving with the Essex Regiment and is buried, under the surname Crozier, at Sangro River War Cemetery – His remaining brother, Dennis, also served with the Essex Regiment.
Age 21.
God's greatest gift. Remembrance. Treasured memories of my dear grandson Jack
Grave 3.K.16.

LIEUTENANT DAVID GORDON <u>DILL</u> [265704] HOME GUARD, KING'S ROYAL RIFLE CORPS AND 2ND SAS (2 SQN)

Known as 'Diddy' to his family, David Dill was born on 1 February 1924 at Overton in Hampshire. He was educated at St Alban's Preparatory School then Radley College in Abingdon where he was a member of the OTC from 1938 to 1941, his parents having divorced in 1936. He was also a keen sportsman, being a member of his school rugby, hockey, squash and boxing teams. Concurrently he served as a dispatch rider in the 5th Battalion, Sussex Home Guard, from 1940 and as soon as his schooling finished in May 1942 he enlisted into the King's Royal Rifle Corps at Winchester (service number 6857668). Posted to the 70th (Young Soldiers) Battalion he was promoted to lance-corporal two months later and, after a period of preparatory training attached to the 4th Royal Berkshire Regiment, attended 170 (Motor Battalion) OCTU that October. On completing an officer candidate questionnaire he noted that his ambition was 'to join the army … I would not like office life', adding that he intended to stay in the army after the war. Asked his views on foreign service he wrote: 'I should personally very much like to go abroad as I should rather fight in another country than seeing the devastation of war over this country.'

Dill was commissioned into the KRRC at the beginning of March 1943 (*London Gazette* 09/04/43). His final report noted: 'Strongly recommended. This officer is keen, alert and popular with all the makings of a good officer. He has regimental connections and comes of a military family.' Having joined the 10th Battalion at Strensall he volunteered for special service in November. Interviewed and found suitable he was posted to the Commando Depot at Achnacarry the following month. He subsequently volunteered for 2nd SAS on 22 April 1944 and attended parachute course No.114A at No.1 PTS Ringway in May, his instructor noting: 'keen hard worker, popular with men – jumped well'.

Dill parachuted into the Vosges département of eastern France on the night of 12–13 August 1944 as a member of Captain Henry Druce's recce group for OPERATION LOYTON. He soon built a strong reputation and at the close of the operation he volunteered to command a rear party. This was tasked by Lt-Colonel Brian Franks, MC, with waiting for Sergeant Pat Nevill's patrol that was operating near the col du Hantz (see Sergeant Jock Hay's and Nevill's entries within this section). In addition, Dill was to make contact with 2nd SAS' missing Second-in-Command, former fellow KRRC officer Major Denny Reynolds, and 'to kill a German before he left in order to make it appear that we were still operating in the Moussey area' (see Reynolds' entry below). He was going about these duties when captured on 7 October. Roger Souchal, a young member of the Maquis who was captured whilst working with Dill, stated:

I was taken prisoner on Saturday the 7th October 1944 at the Cote des Chenes near Moussey with the following SAS – Lieut Dill, Jimmy [Bennett], Robinson, Sgt Hay, and two others. I had been with the SAS party since August, and with this particular group since the beginning of October, so it is not surprising that I knew them by name. I can state with certainty that the photographs marked Lieut Dill, Pct Bennett (Jimmy), Sgt Hay, of those SAS men taken prisoner at the same time as me.

We were taken prisoner at the end of an engagement which lasted about an hour. The officer in charge of the detachment shook Lieut Dill by the hand and said 'You are my prisoner; you are a soldier and so am I.' They told us also that they were from an SS Panzer unit which had come from Brest.

About 5 o'clock in the afternoon we were taken to Le Harcholet and placed in a room in the factory of M. Gerard. Here during interrogation I also saw Jacqueline Weber and Millelire, an Italian, both of whom I had seen before with the Maquis.

On the following Monday morning Lieut Dill, Jacqueline Weber and Rossi Millelire were taken away. I, and the remaining five English were taken to Saales where we were placed in a cell, in the Maison Barthlemy. Here we joined Lieut Dill and Rossi Millelire, but Jacqueline Weber was not there [Jacqueline Weber, a supposed French agent, was implicated in the betrayal of the party. She was certainly later convicted of collaboration by the French authorities. Millelire, said to have been a British agent, is believed to have been shot].

In the cell already were Capt Gough [Victor Gough of SOE's JEDBURGH Team JACOB], Sgt Neville [*sic* – Nevill] whose name I remember well, and two others whose names I do not remember, but whom I am able to recognise from the photographs with certainty as Pct Church and Pct McGovern [WO 309/661].

At the ensuing war crimes trial Souchal described the group's capture in further detail:

I was taken prisoner with the five men whose photographs I have just seen [Robinson, Bennett, Hay, Weaver and Austin], and with Lt Dill …We were in the [forest] camp. Col Franks left us on Friday night, and on Saturday morning at 8 o'clock German lorries arrived and German soldiers jumped out and surrounded the camp. As I was on guard I saw them, and as I also knew the mountains well we escaped. We hid in a cave, but, as the whole mountain was surrounded by the Germans, we were taken prisoner at 2.16 exactly in the afternoon …
The Germans took our weapons, all the rations that we had, and led us to the factory Gerard at Le Harcholet. We stayed until Monday night without anything to eat [WO 235/174].

A fellow prisoner, Monsieur Lyaytey of Le Harcholet, identified Dill's group at the Maison Barthlemy, the HQ of the Kommando Ernst at Saales, Souchal later noting:

Before our departure for Schirmeck on the 20th October [*sic* – 22/23rd], Dill, Gough and I were beaten. I saw the marks on Gough's back where he had been beaten, and when Dill and I were taken to another house in Saales, where Dill was beaten, I saw marks on his face and back when he came back. They had asked him where the English colonel was; he came back crying, but he had not told them [WO 309/661].

'Missing Parachutists', the SAS War Crimes Investigation Team's final report, confirms that when the SAS NCOs and other ranks were taken from Saales on the 15th to be shot, Dill, Souchal and Gough were retained until the 22nd or 23rd when they were sent to Schirmeck Concentration Camp to join other captured members of the Regiment. The same day (22nd) Franks, by now back in the UK, had written to Dill's stepfather, Lt-Colonel Oliver Thynne of SOE and Special Forces HQ:

I am writing to you about David whom I'm afraid is not yet back and it is no good pretending that I am not worried that he has failed to arrive. I last saw him on the 7th October when I left him at our old base near the village of Moussey. He was with a party of five soldiers who were all extremely good. I had arranged a rendezvous with him but had to leave before I could keep it. He had a wireless receiver with him and I broadcast to him telling him to rejoin the American lines. So far, it appears that he has failed to do so. David was absolutely first class throughout the operation. There was no job he was not prepared to tackle and was always cool, calm and collected under the most trying and difficult circumstances. He was also extremely competent and had the best party of men of any I had with me. I personally think that there is every chance of his turning up in the near future.

It was not to be, Souchal noting:

On arrival at Schirmeck Dill and Gough were taken to the cells, I was placed in the barracks. I saw them once or twice again at Schirmeck with an older officer with a bald head who wore a crown on his shoulder [Reynolds], when they went to wash [WO 309/661].

At the beginning of November Dill, Reynolds and Captain 'Andy' Whately-Smith, 2nd SAS' Adjutant, were returned to the Kommando Ernst at Saales for further violent interrogation. They were back at Schirmeck by the 6th when they were seen by a neutral official. Correspondence from this American Red Cross representative noted:

I'm sending you a list of names of American and British prisoners of war held by the Gestapo at the Concentration Camp of Schirmeck-la-Broque in Alsace. I was able to talk with them and promised to advise their families … These officers were living on 6 November, 1944 [WO 311/270].

Dill's name is on this list. According to Jeanne Hertenberger, the camp Registrar, his group was moved to Rotenfels Detention Camp in Germany when Schirmeck was evacuated ahead of the advancing Allies on 22 November. Dill is said to have given up his straw mattress to a female prisoner at this new location and to have refused to salute German officers. Wachtmeister Walter Willing, a guard at Rotenfels, stated at the subsequent war crimes trial:

Towards the end of November I remember Zimmermann calling a parade of the nine American [*sic*] prisoners of war. He gave orders through a runner from the camp office to the chief of the barracks that these nine men were to be sent away about noon. At that time I had to go into the store room in the camp building and Zimmermann saw me and he admonished me for not having the prisoners ready, and as I turned to the door I saw that the prisoners were lining themselves up with their possessions in their hands. When Zimmermann saw that they carried their belongings he yelled at me 'Why these bundles?' I replied 'Why not, if these men are to be sent to another place naturally they will need their possessions.' He then bent down to my ear and told me in his Swabian dialect 'Don't you know that they are going to be shot?' I remonstrated with him and said would it not be better to send these men to another camp. He gave each prisoner a small piece of paper and told them to write down their names which he fastened to each man's package. While this was going on Wuensch [Wünsch] came up and I asked him 'Why are they going to kill all these prisoners, after all they are prisoners of war, we could send them to another camp.' Robert Wuensch replied 'Blah – blah – blah, prisoners of war! They were with the partisans and they have to be shot today' … It was common knowledge amongst the prisoners that these British and American prisoners of war were killed on the 25th November 1944. In fact, I remember Leutnant Mussberger telling Wuensch one day that Neuschwanger did the German Reich a great favour in killing these British and American prisoners of war [WO 311/270].

Erwin Martzolf, a fellow inmate, concurred with this version of events:

Whilst at Rotenfels camp I became acquainted with six British prisoners and four American prisoners. These prisoners of war told me that they had come from Schirmeck camp. I think that they arrived at the camp at Rotenfels in November 1944 … In particular I remember having spoken to Major Reynolds, Capt Gough and Lieut Dill. They were all cheerful and maintained a good morale. They did not imagine that they were going to be shot …

On the 25th or 26th [25th] of November 1944 in the afternoon between 2 and 3 o'clock I was in Barrack 3 of the camp of Rotenfels. All the English and American prisoners of war were in this barrack. I was talking to Capt Gough when suddenly all English and Americans had to get up and leave the barrack. They had to take their kit with them. I asked Capt Gough where they were going and he said he thought they were going to a Stalag.

I shook hands with all of the ten prisoners of war before they came out of the barracks, and went out into the courtyard. I saw them lined up near the gate, and I heard Zimmermann who was acting as Commandant for Wuensch say 'No packages, leave your packages here.' I realised that there was to be a murder because I also saw some Russian prisoners with shovels near the truck which was waiting at the entrance of the camp, and I also saw Neuschwanger, Ullrich, Ostertag and Dinkel armed with machine pistols [according to a fellow prisoner, Maurice Lesoil, the Russians were former members of the Wehrmacht who had committed crimes in France, including the murder of their own officers]. These four Germans got into the truck after the ten prisoners of war had been made to jump up into it. I saw the truck leave the camp. I never saw these English or American prisoners of war again.

The same day it was general knowledge in the camp that the ten prisoners of war had been killed …

Neuschwanger, Ullrich, Ostertag and Dinkel carried out the executions, according to what Willing told me. Willing also said that these men were always impatient for another chance to kill somebody [WO 311/270].

Dill's party was driven a short distance and murdered within Erlichwald, a wood above the Mercedes Benz factory in Gaggenau. Oberwachtmeister Heinrich Neuschwanger, known as 'Stuka' due to his habit of jumping up and stomping on prisoners that he had beaten to the ground, admitted at his trial:

We turned right along the track for a distance of about 75 metres and then stopped.

Ostertag asked me how many prisoners we should do at a time. I suggested three, so he gave the order for the first three to jump down …

The first three were civilians. I remember that as we were marching them down the track one of them took a photograph out of his pocket and looked at it. We turned into the wood for a distance of 20 to 30 metres until we came to the bomb crater …

On a signal from Ostertag who was walking in the middle, we each fired at the prisoner in front of us [WO 311/270].

One of the three, Abbé Claude, the priest of Raon-l'Étape, attempted to escape:

My pistol however had a stoppage and the prisoner in front of me ran away through the wood. After he had covered a distance of about 60 metres he was stopped by a shot from either Niebel or Korb, and killed as he lay wounded on the ground by another shot through the head …

We then took most of the clothes off the bodies. The clothes were removed on the express orders of Wuensch in order to make the bodies unrecognisable.

We then went to the truck and fetched another three prisoners …

I think that everyone in the police party took either some clothing or shoes back with them. I know Ostertag had a ring and a gold pocket watch. I had a pair of black boots and Dinkel had a leather case with a zip fastener containing travel necessaries …

Somebody told me that an identity disc was lying on the ground. I then noticed a metal disc on a chain; I took this and threw it away in the woods. I was influenced by the thought that this might help to make the bodies unidentifiable [WO 311/270].

Wachtmeister Karl Dinkel, one of the guards present who claimed that he took no part in the killings, later stated at his trial:

I noticed Neuschwanger had been drinking, and immediately I thought that something was going to happen. I had heard that he was brutal and I had also been told that when he drank things happened. I had also heard that he had shot a number of people at Schirmeck …

When the remaining prisoners in the truck heard the first shots I noticed that the man in black clothes, whom I took to be a priest, gave them his blessing, and they knelt down in the truck, and prayed in a language similar to that which I have heard since with this English unit [WO 311/270 – three of the victims were members of the clergy].

On 13 May 1945 the remains of the five murdered SAS, four American servicemen and seventeen civilians were recovered from two bomb craters and reinterred 'with special honours and in the presence of a large proportion of the population' a short distance away at Gaggenau's Waldfriedhof civil cemetery. Surprisingly, Major 'Bill' Barkworth, head of the SASWCIT, was only informed of the discovery by chance. He arrived on the scene a month later, signalling Franks:

Have had all crosses painted with name, Regt and date of death. All graves well cared for with flowers … in view probability removal of all bodies French, American and English from Gaggenau cemetery later date suggestion made French erection memorial near place of execution. Have said consider good idea but must consult you both for principle and details …

Suggest text German, French and English followed list of names victims on copper plate recessed large rough hewn granite block resting stepped base and surmounted cross. German text to include warning future generation. Would like your opinion [WO 218/216].

Franks replied:

Agree principle. Consider wording should be on following lines, quote; This memorial is erected in memory of officers and men of Second SAS Regt who were murdered by the Germans in Gaggenau camp after capture contrary to all accepted rules of warfare. Unquote. Consider no warning necessary. Both actual memorial and wording should be kept as simple as possible. Your excellent work much appreciated and difficulties fully realised. Awaiting your full report with great interest. Essential all Germans responsible brought to trial [WO 218/216].

In August 1947 a memorial was unveiled at one of the craters during a ceremony organised by the French. No SAS representatives were invited to attend or even had knowledge that such a ceremony was to take place.

Dill's remains had been identified by his jump smock, a serial numbered wrist watch issued to him, his badges of rank, a broken elbow sustained playing rugby in 1939 and by dental records. *The Times* subsequently reported:

After months of anxiety the many friends of Lieutenant David Gordon Dill, the King's Royal Rifle Corps, have learnt with horror that he was shot in a German camp [*sic*] some time ago. At Radley it was clear to those who knew him well that he would make a great soldier … his many friends will mourn his loss and get inspiration from his short life. He will indeed be sadly missed.

Dill was posthumously mentioned in despatches for OPERATION LOYTON (*London Gazette* 10/05/45) whilst the War Office accepted his Croix de guerre (étoile en argent) from General Juin on 10 February 1945.

The 'Gaggenau Case' was brought to trial before a British Military Court at Wuppertal, Germany, between 6 and 10 May 1946. Whilst counsel argued that those accused had merely been following orders, and that the defendants believed that what they were doing was legal, the prosecution submitted that the attempted obliteration of all traces of the crime negated any contention of this being so. Surprisingly, sentencing was lenient: SS-Untersturmführer Robert Wünsch, SS-Sturmscharführer Zimmerman, and Police Wachtmeisters Willi Dinkel, Helmut Korb, and Xavier Vetter, were sentenced to terms of imprisonment ranging from two to ten years. Korb was later questioned in connection with the 'Poitiers Case' concerning the murder of members of 1st SAS during OPERATION BULBASKET (see multiple entries within this volume under Rom Communal Cemetery, France). Although Oberwachtmeister Joseph Muth was acquitted, he was later sentenced to seven years imprisonment for hanging a captured RAF pilot at Natzweiler-Struthof Concentration Camp.

SS-Hauptsturmführer Karl Buck (Camp Commandant of both Schirmeck and Rotenfels, who admitted ordering Wünsch to carry out the murders), Police Oberleutnant Karl Nussberger, Police Oberwachtmeister Heinrich 'Stuka' Neuschwanger, and Police Wachtmeisters Bernhard Ullrich and Erwin Ostertag, were all sentenced to death. Having been tried by the French in absentia for separate war crimes Wünsch received the same sentence. In the autumn of 1948 the British death sentences were commuted to life imprisonment. For Ullrich it was too late, the French having tried and executed him the year before for other war crimes. Buck, Nussberger, Ostertag and Neuschwanger, who had also been sentenced to death by the French in 1947, had their sentences commuted to hard labour. They appear to have been released from British custody at Werl in 1955.

Son of Major Richard Dill, MC, and of Mary Dill (née Morris) of Panters, South Stoke, Oxfordshire – Older brother of June Dill – Step-brother of Sheridan Thynne. Dill's family visited the LOYTON area in 1947, although they kept the truth of his interrogation from his mother, leaving her to believe that he had been shot immediately after capture.
Age 20.
He who would valiant be
Grave 3.K.10. Also commemorated on a plaque within Findon Parish Church, Sussex, and another within St Andrews Church in South Stoke: 'In proud and ever loving memory of David Gordon Dill, Croix de Guerre, Lieutenant 60th Rifles and 2nd SAS Regiment. Born February 1st 1924, killed behind enemy lines in Germany Nov 25th 1944 aged 20.'

PRIVATE JAMES FREDERICK **DOWLING** [T/5346560] ROYAL BERKSHIRE REGIMENT, ROYAL ARMY SERVICE CORPS, PARACHUTE REGIMENT AND 2ND SAS (2 SQN)

James Dowling was born at Small Heath in Birmingham on 14 October 1922. A removal man, he enlisted into the Royal Berkshire Regiment in June 1940, increasing his age by a year in order to boost his chances of serving overseas. Posted to the 8th (Home Defence) Battalion at Oxford he qualified as a joiner at Hackney Technical Institute during April 1941. He was subsequently taking a trade course in wood turning when he suffered a recurrent attack of impetigo and was hospitalised until mid January 1942. On discharge he joined the 70th (Young Soldiers) Battalion but that March transferred to the Royal Army Service Corps and was posted to the 8th Training Battalion.

Late in April 1942 Dowling was declared a deserter and sentenced to twelve months detention, having been detained by civil police in Birmingham that June. In December he wrote a plea from his cell:

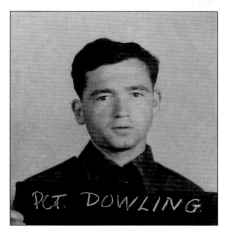

Dear Sir,

I volunteered to join a Parachute Battalion about a fortnight before going absent and also passed an examination by the Medical Officer. I was waiting to be transferred to a training battalion when I received two very grave telegrams concerning the health of [my] father who was lying seriously ill in Selly Oak Hospital, Birmingham. I did not receive complete satisfaction from my Coy [Company] Commander regarding Compassionate Leave. After waiting 48hrs without any results whatsoever I decided to take the matter into my own hands. However, this has since proved to be my downfall with the result that I am now serving a sentence of twelve months detention. This sentence however will be expired on March the 1st 1943 and it is my earnest desire that I be posted to a Paratroop Battalion directly I am released. I have had much time during the passed [sic] few months to think this over and I really and truly feel that I will be able to settle down and soldier as a Paratroop.

Sir, I sincerely hope that this application is given your full consideration and meets with your ultimate approval.

As a result of this appeal Dowling returned to duty with the 1st Holding Battalion from 1 March 1943. In April, after a further period in hospital, he joined 104 Divisional Transport Company as a driver. He subsequently transferred to the Army Air Corps, attending parachute course 94 during December 1943 at No.1 PTS Ringway. Here his instructor noted him as a 'quiet and nervous man, satisfactory parachutist'. After instruction at the Airborne Forces Depot he was posted to the 156th Battalion, Parachute Regiment, in January 1944. He volunteered for 2nd SAS on 19 March, although during June and July he was back in hospital having suffered a gunshot wound to his lower left leg during training.

Dowling parachuted into the Vosges département of eastern France on the night of 6–7 September 1944 as a member of Major Denny Reynolds' reinforcement group to OPERATION LOYTON. It is likely to have been the first time that he touched foreign soil. Soon after he was with Lieutenant Desmond Black's party that became separated from the main force during a German attack on its base camp and was subsequently taken prisoner on the 15th. The eight captured men were murdered near Saint-Dié on 20 September 1944 (see Black's entry within this section for full details). Had he been granted compassionate leave in 1942 Dowling's path might well have been different. His AB.64 (Service and Pay Book) was found at the Gestapo headquarters in Strasbourg. It records that he was eventually granted special compassionate leave in order to care for his father during July 1944 whilst serving with 2nd SAS.

Son of George and Laura Dowling (née Corbett) of Millhouse Road, South Yardley, Birmingham.
Age officially recorded as 22.
No inscription.
Grave 3.K.18.

PRIVATE MAURICE ARTHUR **GRIFFIN** [873123] ROYAL ARTILLERY, ARMY AIR CORPS AND 2ND SAS (2 SQN)

The Registrar at Schirmeck Concentration Camp recorded Maurice Griffin's date of birth as 23 April 1921, his place of birth as London and that he had formerly worked in a Bristol aircraft factory. He was born in West Ham, although he falsified his date of birth to join up a year early, his service record dating it as 23 April 1920. His record also notes that in September 1937, whilst working as a fitter's mate, he joined the Royal Artillery (TA) at Bristol, his unit being redesignated as the 236/76th Heavy Anti-Aircraft Regiment at the beginning of 1939. Mobilised late that August, he was put back onto Class 'A' Army Reserve in August 1940 'for an indefinite period for employment as Aircraft Fitter'. He was therefore not recalled to the Colours until April 1943 when he joined the 102nd Anti-Aircraft Brigade. Transferring to the Army Air Corps on 29 March 1944 he attended parachute course 113 at No.1 PTS Ringway the following month. Here his instructor noted 'average, nervous but jumps well'. Having been posted to the Airborne Forces Holding Unit he volunteered for 2nd SAS on 11 July.

Griffin parachuted into the Vosges département of eastern France for OPERATION LOYTON in the early hours of 1 September 1944 as a member of Lieutenant 'Karl' Marx's stick. Regimental activity soon provoked enemy retaliation and the main SAS group was forced to abandon its camp near Pierre-Percée and move south-east towards the area of Moussey where conditions appeared quieter. A rendezvous for this move on foot was given at Lac de la Maix and 'Missing Parachutists', the SAS War Crimes Investigation Team's final report, concluded that Griffin, who had lost his way soon after setting off, arrived at the RV before the agreed time and was captured alone on the 10th. The report also states that Griffin was taken to Schirmeck Concentration Camp the following day where he was given a glass of Schnapps in the camp office and made to exchange his uniform (WO 218/222). Major 'Bill' Barkworth, commander of the SASWCIT, later noted: 'Subsequently I spoke to Mlle Hertenberger one of the secretaries at Schirmeck camp. She recognised Griffin from a photograph which I showed her as having been brought to that camp as a prisoner.'

Marx's post-operation report differs on dates, stating that Griffin was left behind at the Pierre-Percée base camp on 7 September as he was 'medically unfit' and that he (Marx) received 'local information that one SAS man was taken prisoner yesterday [on the 11th]. I suspect it was Pct Griffin.' Meanwhile, 2nd SAS' Casualty Report quotes Parachutist Salthouse's description of 11 September that again differs in the location that Griffin disappeared:

> After about half an hour we halted at a pt V388829 on the road to see if the colonel [Lt-Colonel Brian Franks, MC] with the remainder of the party were following. When the party came into view I saw Pct Griffin coming towards us. He was only about 80 yards away but it was the last I saw of him, as we were moving forward again. He was carrying his kit and appeared to be perfectly OK. We made our way across the main Celles-sur-Plaines – Raon L'Etape road at V372800 and up into the woods towards V420805. When the whole party arrived Pct Griffin was found to be missing [WO 361/897].

Whatever the case in April 1945 the War Office wrote to the Intelligence Troop of 2nd SAS stating: 'we have an unofficial report from a reliable source (via MI9) that "Morris Arthur Griffen a British parachutist was captured near Strasbourg 11/9/44." This is presumably date of capture as man is presumably "Maurice Arthur Griffin" 873123 mssg ex Longton [sic – LOYTON] 11–12/9/44' (WO 361/651). What is certain is that Griffin was held in the cells at Schirmeck until his uniform was returned and then transferred on his own to Strasbourg on 27 October. The Germans perhaps placed more emphasis on his interrogation as, like Private Christopher Ashe, he was captured alone and therefore suspected of co-operating with the Maquis (see Ashe's entry within this section).

Griffin was reunited with other SAS prisoners at Rotenfels Camp in Germany and murdered alongside them at Gaggenau on 25 November 1944 (see Lieutenant David Dill's entry for full details). His remains were identified by dental records and by a photograph taken from his body and passed to the Red Cross by Victor Sokiloutov, one of the Russian prisoners forced to conceal the crime (WO 218/216).

Son of William Maurice and Nellie Griffin (née Winter) of Sylvan Way, Sea Mills, Bristol.
Age 23.
At the setting of the sun and in the morning we will remember you
Grave 3.K.1.

SERGEANT RALPH **HAY** [845212] ROYAL ARTILLERY AND 2ND SAS (2 SQN)

'Jock' Hay was born on 14 January 1919 in the coastal town of Burghead in Morayshire. Having worked at a garden nursery he enlisted into the Royal Artillery in March 1935 at Elgin, falsifying his date of birth to do so. Much of his army paperwork subsequently records that he was born in 1917. Promoted to lance-bombardier in January 1938, he arrived on Malta in April 1939, initially serving with the 26th Anti-Tank Regiment. He was promoted to bombardier in February 1940, posted to the 13th Mobile Coast Defence Regiment in July of that year, and transferred to the Field Branch on his unit's redesignation to 17th Defence Regiment the following February. He was advanced to sergeant during July 1942.

Having served throughout the island's siege, Hay volunteered for 2nd SAS and joined the Regiment at Philippeville in Algeria. Moving to Italy he served in Lieutenant Jimmy Quentin Hughes' troop, the latter recalling that: 'Ralph Hay was a charming Scots boy, easy going, placid and entirely dependable under any circumstances' (*Who Cares Who Wins*, by Jimmy Quentin Hughes, MC). He returned to the UK with the rest of the Regiment in mid March 1944 and was soon immersed in build-up training for the liberation of North West Europe. His nephew, Don Hay, later wrote:

[An] aunt told me that he and some of his mates parachuted down next to his parents' property as a kind of prank and to surprise his parents and their neighbours. I gather this happened while they were training in Scotland. His parents and the surrounding small crofters got a terrible fright as they thought they were Germans invading … My uncle, George Hay (Ralph's older brother), was in the Canadian Army in WWII. He was stationed in North Africa at one time and his regiment was fascinated by a group who were parachuting not far from where they were based. Some time later on leave in London George caught up with his young brother, Ralph, who, by coincidence was also on leave. The conversation at some stage turned to these parachutists and it turned out that it was Ralph's SAS group doing their training drops [personal correspondence, 2012].

During the night of 12–13 August 1944 Hay parachuted into a DZ near Le Mont in the Vosges département of eastern France for OPERATION LOYTON. At the last minute Captain Henry Druce had stood in for another officer and taken command of the recce team. Considering Hay, his own stick sergeant, 'a very fine man', he had specifically asked his CO, Lt-Colonel Brian Franks, MC, if he could take him along. After reinforcements and Jeeps were dropped Hay served as Franks' Jeep gunner and when the main SAS group exfiltrated to Allied lines he stayed behind in a small rear party to await Sergeant Pat Nevill's group that was on patrol near the col du Hantz (see Lieutenant David Dill's and Nevill's entries within this section). Roger Souchal, a Maquis interpreter attached to the Regiment, also remained with the party and later stated that on 7 October they were surrounded by troops from an SS Panzer unit. After a battle that raged for an hour they were forced to surrender owing to lack of ammunition and were taken to the factory of Monsieur Gerard at nearby Le Harcholet. Here they were interrogated with an Italian, Rossi Millelire, and a French woman, Jacqueline Weber, who were said to have been captured in the area. The SAS War Crimes Investigation Team's final report, 'Missing Parachutists', suggests that one, or both, of this pair betrayed the group, although this cannot be confirmed (see Dill's entry for further details).

On the evening of the 9th the men were taken by truck via La Petite-Raon to Saales and handed over to the Kommando Ernst at the Maison Barthlemy. This Kommando had already murdered Lieutenant Desmond Black's stick near Saint-Dié (see Black's entry within this section for details). Here they joined Captain Victor Gough of JEDBURGH Team JACOB, Sergeant Pat Nevill and Parachutists Reg Church and Peter McGovern, in a large basement cell. Souchal recalled that Hay was beaten:

> All the English except Capt Gough and Lieut Dill were taken away [from the Maison Barthlemy] on a Sunday morning, the 15th October. They were in uniform. A total of eight were taken away, that is Sgt Neville [sic- Nevill], and his two soldiers whom I recognise from the photographs as Church and McGovern, Sgt Hay, Jimmy [Bennett], [Lance-corporal George] Robinson and the two whom I recognise from the photographs as [Parachutist Edwin] Weaver and [Parachutist Fred] Austin. Weaver always said 'Fucking Germans' whenever they came in. A small German had come in and read out the names of those he wished to take away. They went out saying that they were going to a prisoner of war camp. I never saw them again.
>
> One of the Germans spoke good English and French and resembled Mussolini. I would be able to recognise him if he were shown to me. During the time before the departure of these eight English soldiers, I saw him strike Sgt Hay four times in the face, but none of the remainder of the other soldiers were, so far as I know, beaten or struck. Only Neville and Hay were interrogated [WO 309/661].

The eight SAS were driven to a spot west of the hamlet of La Grande Fosse, the exact location having been relocated, after 70 years, during the course of this research. A similar forest junction at the col de Prayé, 17 kilometres to the north-east as the crow flies, was incorrectly identified as the murder site in the 1980s and a memorial subsequently erected there, its inscription erroneously recording it as the scene of the crime. At the actual spot the men were shot one by one in front of a ready dug grave, SS-Unterscharführer Georg Zahringer, one of those members of the Kommando Ernst later accused of the killings, stating at the subsequent war crimes tribunal:

> Oppelt ordered me to open the back of the truck and the first prisoner was made to get down. They were all hand-cuffed, and I released him. Schossig, who spoke English, told him to take his clothes off. This the prisoner did. He was then taken, held by the arms by Wuttke and Gaede, into the wood. They went into the wood to my right as I was facing the back of the truck. Wuttke was carrying a Walther pistol, and Gaede also had a weapon with him. Practically immediately I heard a shot. The remaining English prisoners in the truck did not say anything, but remained silent. The next prisoner was made to jump down and undress like the other and was taken away to the same place, by, so far as I can remember, by Oppelt and Dietrich. Again I heard a shot. This went from one prisoner to another until it was the turn of the last [WO 309/233 - see Weaver's entry for further details].

Whilst the clothes of the murdered men were brought back to Saales to be burnt at the Maison Barthlemy Dr Hans Ernst, leader of the Kommando responsible, attempted to cover his tracks by signalling his superiors that eight parachutists had been 'shot whilst trying to escape' during the journey from Saales to Schirmeck.

The bodies were exhumed on 6 November 1945, Hay's remains being identified by dental records and exhumed second, thereby indicating that he was shot second to last. The American coroner reported 'there was a loose four inch strip of adhesive which encircled the body', presumably a bandage indicating that Hay had been wounded or tortured. Heinrich Klein, Ernst's personal driver and one of those later accused of the killings, admitted at trial:

> About seven [*sic*] prisoners were then brought from the house and placed in the lorry. These prisoners were English and were wearing uniform similar to that shown to me as battledress. One of them had been injured and had to be lifted on to the truck. As he was lifted, his shirt came out of his trousers and I saw that he had adhesive plaster round his stomach. I heard him groan as he was lifted [WO 309/661].

Hay was posted missing as of 11 October 1944, his family being informed of this on the 30th. It was not until August 1945 that he was presumed to have been killed in action, the War Office having accepted his Croix de guerre (étoile en argent) from General Juin in February. The citation for this reads: 'Parachuted into France in August 1944. Completely surrounded by far superior in numbers of enemy, he succeeded thanks to his courage and sang-froid to inflict severe losses on the enemy.' In addition, he was posthumously mentioned in despatches for his actions during OPERATION LOYTON (*London Gazette* 08/05/45, supplement 37072 10/05/45). For some reason his date of death is officially recorded as 16 October 1944 although that of three of the seven men murdered alongside him is correctly recorded as the 15th. Lew Fiddick, a downed Royal Canadian Air Force pilot who had evaded capture and joined up with the main SAS party, recalled:

> My relationship with Sgt Jock Hay came about as a result of Col. Brian Franks asking me if I would like to take part in some of their operations. I said yes I would, but remember I'm not a highly trained soldier like your men. He then assigned Sgt Hay to instruct me and to take me on some of his missions. Jock and I became good friends over the weeks and I think I had convinced him to come out to Canada after the war. Unfortunately, he didn't make it [personal correspondence, 2012].

'La Grande Fosse Case' was brought to trial before a British Military Court at Wuppertal, Germany, between 15 and 21 May 1946. Hans Hubner, August Geiger, Heinrich Klein, Walter Jantzen, Georg Zahringer, Horst Gaede, Karl Golckel and Ludwig Koch, all members of the Kommando Ernst, were found guilty of being 'concerned in the killing' of the eight SAS. They were sentenced to various terms

of imprisonment ranging from two to ten years. Some were handed additional sentences a few days later for involvement in the murder of Lieutenant Desmond Black's stick (see his entry within this section for full details). Major Alastair Mant, the pathologist attached to the War Crimes Investigation Unit, wrote in disbelief to the War Crimes Section of the Judge Advocate General's Branch:

> I expect you have seen the result of La Grande Fosse Case. My God! What sentences. If cold-blooded killing is going to be treated as common assault, the sooner the court is comprised wholly of lawyers or SAS, the better! ... I cannot imagine what they were thinking of. It was certainly not for want of drumming into their heads that the accused were lying [WO 309/474].

The more lengthy prison sentences were reduced in the early 1950s. Ernst died a free man in 1991.

Son of Ralph and Jessie Hay of Ivy Cottage, Miltonduff, Morayshire – Younger brother of Gladys (who served in the wartime British Army),

Anne (wartime Royal Navy), George (wartime Canadian Army), William (wartime Royal Australian Air Force) and Agnes – Older brother to Cathie.
Age 25.
To the memory of our son and brother. In silence we remember you dear
Grave 3.K.8. Also commemorated on the Stele de Prayé Memorial above Moussey and Miltonduff's war memorial.

CORPORAL THOMAS IVISON [T/73377] ROYAL ARMY SERVICE CORPS
AND 2ND SAS (2 SQN)

Thomas Ivison was born in Durham on 24 November 1912. Whilst working as a driver he joined the Royal Army Service Corps Supplementary Reserve in February 1939 and was mobilised at the outbreak of war. He was initially posted to 4 Company. However, two days later he was re-posted to 27 Company and sent to France with II Corps Petrol Park as a member of the BEF. Having moved into Belgium after the German Blitzkrieg began, the corps was pushed back to Dunkirk, Ivison being evacuated to the UK on 30 May 1940. Posted to No.2 London Division Petrol Company he went on to serve with numerous tank brigades before embarking for North Africa in January 1943. Here he volunteered for 2nd SAS on 10 June and was promoted to corporal two months later. His medal card reflects that, despite several periods of ill health, he served with the Regiment in Italy before returning to the UK in mid March 1944.

In the early hours of 1 September 1944 Ivison parachuted into a DZ near Veney in the Vosges département of eastern France as a member of Lieutenant 'Karl' Marx's stick during OPERATION LOYTON. On the 9th he, Sergeant Frank Terry-Hall and Parachutist Jack Crosier were separated from their comrades whilst being pursued by German troops near La Chapelotte (see Terry-Hall's entry for details). The three men subsequently found refuge at the La Turbine sawmill and it was here that they were captured, alongside Lieutenant Desmond Black's stick, on the 15th. The group was imprisoned at Schirmeck Concentration Camp before being murdered near Saint-Dié on 20 September 1944 (see Black's entry within this section for full details).

Son of James Ivison of Bells Ville, Gilesgate Moor, Durham.
Age 31.
No inscription.
Grave 3.K.15. Also commemorated on war memorial plaques within Durham Johnston School and Durham City Workmen's Club.

PRIVATE LEONARD EDWIN CHARLES <u>LLOYD</u> [2063834] ROYAL ENGINEERS, ROYAL ARTILLERY, PARACHUTE REGIMENT AND 2ND SAS (2 SQN)

Len Lloyd was born on 5 November 1920 in Sydenham, south-east London. Whilst working locally as a greaser he joined the Royal Engineers (TA) at Dulwich in October 1938. He was mobilised late in August 1939, shortly before war was declared. The following summer his unit was redesignated as the 35th Search Light Regiment, Royal Artillery, and he was therefore transferred to the RA. Although promoted to lance-bombardier in August 1943, he reverted to the rank of gunner on transfer to the Army Air Corps that September and subsequently attended parachute course 88 at No.1 PTS Ringway the following month. Here his instructor noted 'reliable, slow start but progressed well'. Posted to the Airborne Forces Depot, he joined the 8th (Midland Counties) Battalion, Parachute Regiment, at the beginning of November, volunteering for 2nd SAS on 8 April 1944.

Lloyd had remained in Britain throughout the war and perhaps his first time on foreign soil was when he parachuted into the Vosges département of eastern France. Dropping on the night of 6–7 September 1944 he was a member of Major Denny Reynolds' reinforcement party for OPERATION LOYTON. A few days later he was with Lieutenant Desmond Black's group that became separated during a German attack on the SAS camp and was captured with Black's party on the 15th. He was murdered near Saint-Dié on the 20th (see Black's entry within this section for full details).

Son of Charles and Mildred Lloyd (née Allen) of Hayfield Road, St Mary Cray, Kent.
Age 23.
Deep in our hearts his memory is kept. He was loved to dearly for us ever to forget
Grave 3.K.19. Also commemorated on Orpington's war memorial.

PRIVATE PETER <u>McGOVERN</u> [900715] ROYAL ARTILLERY, NO.11 COMMANDO, ARMY AIR CORPS AND 2ND SAS (3 SQN)

Peter McGovern was born on 16 September 1921 in the seaside town of Leven, Fife. In April 1939, whilst a 17-year-old miner, he joined the local 302nd Field Battery, Royal Artillery (TA), and was called up to serve with the 85th Anti-Aircraft Regiment at the outbreak of war that September. A period with 64th AA Regiment followed before he volunteered for No.11 (Scottish) Commando in August 1940. That December he transferred back to the Royal Artillery and was posted to the 268/64th Heavy Anti-Aircraft Regiment. He was soon promoted to lance-bombardier whilst serving with the 506th HAA Battery. In December 1942 he married Gladys Shaw, a lance-corporal in the Auxiliary Territorial Service and sister of Sergeant David Shaw of the SAS.

In October 1943 McGovern was deprived of his rank whilst serving with 149th Heavy Anti-Aircraft

Regiment 'for disobeying camp Standing Orders'. He transferred to the Army Air Corps on 8 March 1944 and was initially posted to the Airborne Forces Depot at Hardwick Hall, Chesterfield. Attending parachute course 110 at No.1 PTS Ringway the following month, he was noted as being 'keen and conscientious, slightly above average'. He was subsequently posted to No.1 Airborne Forces Holding Unit before volunteering for 2nd SAS on 26 May.

McGovern's daughter, Judith, was born on 15 September 1944, but was seriously ill. Although granted immediate compassionate leave he was recalled to parachute into the Vosges département of eastern France for OPERATION LOYTON on the night of the 21st–22nd. Although a member of Captain 'Bunny' McGibbon-Lewis' stick, he served as Lieutenant Lord John Manners' Jeep front gunner early in the operation. On 2 October Lt-Colonel Brian Franks, MC, sent him, with Sergeant Pat Nevill and Parachutist Reg Church, to recce the road to the col du Hantz. They were captured that day by members of the Kommando Ernst under Leutenant Taufel, probably in the area of La Petite-Raon (WO 235/554). Taken to the Maison Barthlemy, the Kommando's HQ at Saales, they were interrogated before being murdered at La Grande Fosse on 15 October 1944 (see Sergeant Jock Hay's entry within this section for full details).

McGovern's remains, identified by his dental records, were exhumed fifth, indicating that he had been the fourth man of the eight SAS to be shot. The American coroner wrote: 'the position of the wound suggests that the victim was shot while kneeling, or had been made to stand in the ditch at a level lower than his executor' (WO 309/661). Shaw was given compassionate leave to break the news to his sister. Judith, the daughter that McGovern had barely known, died that same month.

Son of Mr and Mrs McGovern of Leven, Fife – Husband of Gladys McGovern of Cheltenham Street, Tong Road, Armley, Leeds – Father of Judith McGovern – Brother of Mary McGovern.
Age 23.
No inscription.
Grave 3.K.11. Also commemorated on the Stele de Prayé Memorial above Moussey.

Sergeant Walter Henry Edgar <u>Nevill</u> [2938162] Cameron Highlanders, Parachute Regiment and 2nd SAS (2 Sqn)

Pat Nevill, as he was known, was born on 6 September 1913 at Plaistow, east London, and later lived nearby in Stratford where he worked as a coffin maker. In December 1937 he married Beatrice Baker, and their first child, Patricia Ann, was born a year later. He enlisted into the Cameron Highlanders in July 1940 and was posted to the 7th Battalion. By that November he was serving within HQ Company, passing a trade test as a carpenter in January 1941. In August 1942, having been promoted to lance-corporal in March, he transferred to the 5th (Scottish) Battalion, Parachute Regiment, which had primarily been formed from the Camerons earlier that year. Promoted to corporal, he attended parachute course 26 at No.1 PTS Ringway the following month.

Nevill disembarked in North Africa in April 1943, two months after his second daughter, Francis Margaret, was born at Mountain Ash in South Wales. After hostilities in Tunisia ceased, the 2nd Parachute Brigade, of which the 5th Battalion formed a part, was tasked with capturing the port of Augusta on Sicily. However, this operation was first postponed, then cancelled on 11 July, Augusta falling to the Special Raiding Squadron (1st SAS) on the evening of the 12th. Nevill's brigade subsequently embarked at Bizerte and landed at the port of Taranto in southern Italy on the evening of 9 September (Operation Slapstick). He was promoted to sergeant soon after. When the 1st Airborne Division was withdrawn to the UK in November the 2nd Parachute Brigade took over its positions in the area of Bari and Barletta before moving into the line north of the River Sangro the following month. Here Nevill was wounded on 12 December and evacuated suffering from concussion. Back with his battalion four days later, he and his men remained at the front line in atrocious winter conditions until moving into reserve in mid February 1944. The photograph seen here was sent to Nevill's daughter by Bernard Woodward who noted in a covering letter that her father, his wartime platoon sergeant, had saved his life in Italy. During this period the 5th Battalion mounted small-scale operations behind enemy lines, in support of those carried out by 2nd SAS under Operation Jonquil, to locate and evacuate escaped Commonwealth POWs. Although the battalion remained in Italy before moving to Greece, Nevill embarked for the UK at the beginning of March 1944, probably because he had volunteered for 2nd SAS. He was certainly posted to the Regiment on the first day of April soon after his arrival in the UK. He subsequently served on Operation Defoe and

its sub Operation Swan in Normandy under Captain 'Bunny' MacGibbon-Lewis between 18 July and 23 August 1944, his patrol providing tactical intelligence to Second Army's Main HQ.

Nevill parachuted into the Vosges département of eastern France for Operation Loyton on the night of 21–22 September 1944 as a member of MacGibbon-Lewis' stick. Initially he served as the latter's Jeep rear gunner and is mentioned in Major Peter Power's report as taking part in a successful ambush on German transport between Celles-sur-Plaine and Allarmont on 23 September. On 2 October, as the operation was drawing to a close, Lt-Colonel Brian Franks, MC, sent him, with Parachutists Reg Church and Peter McGovern, to recce the road to the col du Hantz. It is believed that the three were captured that day by members of the Kommando Ernst under Leutenant Taufel, probably in the area of La Petite-Raon (WO 235/554). Taken to the Kommando's HQ at the Maison Barthlemy in Saales, SS-Unterscharführer August Geiger, one of those later accused of the men's murders, stated: 'I was present at the interrogation of one of these English soldiers who was a sergeant. I believe his name to have been Neville' (sic).

He and seven others were subsequently murdered at La Grande Fosse on 15 October 1944 (see Hay's entry within this section for full details). His remains, identified by dental records, were exhumed sixth, indicating that he was the third man to be shot of the group of eight.

Son of Henry and Mary Nevill (née Thurnell) – Husband of Beatrice Nevill of Navigation Villas, Misken, Mountain Ash, Glamorgan, formerly of Hayday Road, Canning Town, East London, and of Romford Road, Forest Gate, east London – Father of Pat and Francis (Margaret) Nevill – Brother of Mrs M. Rose and of Mrs P. Cahill.
Age 31.
Ever remembered by wife Beat and children Pat and Margaret. Also by Dad and Mum
Grave 3.K.9. Also commemorated on the Stele de Prayé Memorial above Moussey.

Major Denis Bingham REYNOLDS [130586] Yorkshire Hussars, Royal Fusiliers, King's Royal Rifle Corps and 2nd SAS (HQ Sqn)

Known to all as 'Denny', Denis Reynolds was born to Irish parents on 21 September 1909 in Cirencester, later living at Corndean Hall, a large household nestled amongst woods close to the Cotswold town of Winchcombe, Gloucestershire. He attended Felsted School in Essex where he was a keen member of the OTC from 1924 to 1927. The outbreak of war found him working as a private secretary to Earl Fitzwilliam at Wentworth Woodhouse in Yorkshire having previously been a racing manager at Malton where he had owned and bred steeplechasers, riding many winners himself. He enlisted into the Yorkshire Hussars in mid September 1939 at Westminster, London, and was transferred to the Army Reserve the following day (service number 327294). When called up that November he joined the Royal Fusiliers but was commissioned into the King's Royal Rifle Corps in May 1940 after attending 161 OCTU at Sandhurst (*London Gazette* 17/05/40). His final report notes: 'The way in which he has worked, his general behaviour, conscientiousness, and ability make him outstanding. He has any amount of character and grit, is cheery with it all, and will make an excellent officer. Grade A.'

Having been posted to the 1st Motor Training Battalion at Chiseldon Camp near Swindon, Reynolds was promoted to captain in January 1941 and appointed Adjutant. Here he was the subject of cartoons drawn by fellow KRRC officer Ian Fenwick. The caption of that seen opposite notes:

A firm but fair Adjt, who kept 1 MTB together, he had been a pre WWII amateur steeplechaser, and hence was unfit through multiple injuries. Later he was passed fit, learnt to parachute and joined the SAS … He was a charming shooting companion at Strensall (snipe and partridges) and a perfect team worker with Col Campbell [see Fenwick's entry within this volume under Chambon-la-Forêt Communal Cemetery, France].

Reynolds was promoted to major in February 1943. He volunteered for the SAS that December, being attached 'pending posting to No.3 SAS Rgt, to No.1 French Para Bn', presumably as a liaison officer. However, when the proposed third British SAS Regiment did not materialise, he joined 2nd SAS at the beginning of April 1944 and was appointed Second-in-Command that June. He subsequently parachuted into the Vosges département of eastern France for Operation Loyton during the night of 6–7 September with fourteen other men. Len Owens, MM, a Phantom signaller already deployed on the operation, later recalled:

Major Reynolds was the one who the signal came through that he was going to drop with his parachuting dog

Hey, slowly for Anna Sake, Reynolds!

[called 'Tinker' as pictured opposite], and Colonel Franks [the CO, Lt-Colonel Brian Franks, MC] said 'We don't want a bloody dog here.' So Peter Bannerman and I had about a mile and half to run up the mountain, get out the set, and it was the only time that we deviated from standard practice that you never sent messages from the area of the camp. You always used to move off 5 or 6 miles in another direction. But we couldn't do anything else but code the message up with a priority on it and send it back to England who would then have to transmit it to the squadron to ask them to contact the aircraft to ask them under no circumstances to drop a dog. But we didn't know whether that had happened or not but of course a dog didn't drop so they must have got through … evidently he took this dog with him wherever he went and he had taught it to parachute so he decided that when he was coming in he was going to put it in … Franks nearly went berserk [personal interview, 2010 – see Bannerman's entry under Moussey Churchyard, France].

On landing near Neufmaisons, Reynolds was guided to the SAS base at Xapénamoulin near Pierre-Percée. Franks subsequently recorded in his post-operation report that he sent Reynolds and his Adjutant, Captain 'Andy' Whately-Smith, to look for a new camp location on the morning of the 9th as the current area was being swept by German troops. Two hours later Franks' camp was attacked, the main group being forced to move with the loss of their stores. Lance-corporal Joseph Zandarco, a Frenchman serving in 2 Squadron, 2nd SAS, gave a slightly different version of events on his return to Allied lines:

> We were attacked on 9 Jun [*sic* – September] by the Germans, who had learned of our presence through a French family in a nearby farmhouse. The daughter was enceinte [a French euphemism for pregnant] by a German and the son was a Milicien. We had contacted them in order to get food. They lived at Pierre Percee, south-east of Badonvillers. The Germans fired on us from all sides before they were nearby. Major Reynolds, in charge of our party, was wounded and later disappeared into the woods. Lt Black was also wounded. We dispersed and ran for it [WO 208/3351].

Whatever the case, Reynolds and Whately-Smith were separated from the main group, 'Missing Parachutists' (the SAS War Crimes Investigation Team's final report) noting that, despite repeated broadcasts of a revised RV contact could not be re-established with the pair. It concludes: 'Maj Reynolds, who had been wounded in the hand and the head during an ambush against German transport, remained at Pierre Percee with Capt Whately-Smith hidden by [the] Le Rollands' (WO 218/222). According to her own diary Myrhiam Le Rolland, an experienced nurse, was fetched to attend to the pair by a Monsieur Michel, on the afternoon of the 10th. Michel was harbouring the men at his house at Xapénamoulin. Myrhiam diagnosed Reynolds' forearm as fractured, with gangrene already present. She considered amputation whilst continuing to make daily visits over the next three days, during which time the men slept in a log cabin. They were seen in the woods by a woman liable to talk and Myrhiam and her husband Freddy therefore moved them closer to Pierre-Percée and hid them in a small and dank 1914 shelter carved out of the Roches d'Orthomont on the wooded hill above their house. The Le Rollands looked after them as best they could from 6 September until 30 October at great personal risk, mindful that German troops were billeted in their property.

Once Reynolds had regained strength the pair attacked German transport before returning to their cave. They attempted to cross through the lines near Senones but were forced to return. According to Madame Le Rolland they then managed, by means of a messenger, to receive instructions from Franks to stay hidden until called upon. 'Missing Parachutists' continues:

> On the 30th October, a Mme Le Blanc [*sic* – Leblanc] of Raon L'Etape offered to show these two officers a safe way, avoiding German posts, to reach Raon L'Etape which was then almost in the front line [the Le Rollands stated that

Leblanc was sent, with weapons and civilian clothing, by a Marie Renault with whom Reynolds and Whately-Smith had sheltered during their previous attempt to cross the lines].

After some discussion, Mme Le Blanc is said to have succeeded in persuading them that the safest way was by the main road 'because all the Germans were in the woods, and she had come by the road without seeing a German soldier' [the men were given a rendezvous at 1800hrs that evening at the La Cense de Coeur, a large house on the outskirts of Raon-L'Etape]. They took the main road and both were captured outside the Wehrmacht unit HQ La Trouche, on the afternoon of 30th October [WO 218/222].

The report notes that 'to determine whether Madame Blanc was treacherous or merely stupid would require an investigation to itself' although Corporal Kubiskie later reported that she had given him considerable help and that he believed that she had been shot by the Germans after being caught at La Trouche. Whatever the case, German troops arrived at the Le Rolland house soon after, completely ransacking and setting fire to it. Both the Le Rollands were beaten, Freddy being taken to Cirey-sur-Plaine for interrogation. Here he was confronted with Reynolds, Whately-Smith and Leblanc who initially admitted to Freddy that she had denounced him under pressure. The four were taken to the Kommando Pullmer's outpost at Allarmont and separated. Rudolf Krause, who was present at the interrogation of both men at Cirey, later stated:

> On the 31st October or 1st November 44, two officers of the British Army were brought to the German police post at Cirey as prisoners. A little later I was asked to act as interpreter for the interrogation of these officers. The interrogator in charge of this affair was Breuer, St Hauptscharführer (Oberfeldwebel of the SFP).
>
> Before we started with the interrogation Breuer told me that these two officers belonged to the 2nd SAS Battalion of the British Army/Air Force, which had been parachuted in the Vosges mountains about six weeks earlier, but had been almost completely taken prisoners in the meantime.
>
> As one could see that the officers had had a rather hard time in past weeks I asked for the permission to let them refresh themselves and Breuer gave me a free hand to talk with them and to give them everything I thought necessary. I took them into my own room, gave them necessities to wash and refresh themselves, and had a good breakfast brought to them, including wine and cigarettes.
>
> Afterwards we talked together about things in general and the officers, a major and a captain, told me the story of their hard life they had had during the last six weeks, whilst they were hidden in the Vosges forest in the south of Cirey. They had been parachuted with their group of men at the beginning or middle of the month of September. Whilst looking for a better suited camping place their men had been attacked by a group of German soldiers and taken prisoners. On their return they had also been shot at and the major was wounded on his left hand, but they hid themselves before they were taken prisoners. With all their personal belongings taken away they then led a rather hard life in the forest helped now and then by the French population. In the meantime the American troops had advanced up to the fringe of the Vosges Mountains and the two officers intended to cross the front line to join the Allied troops. On the way to the front line they had been taken prisoner by a patrol of the German Army. As they had hidden their uniforms under civilian overcoats the two officers were suspected to be spies and therefore handed over to the nearest police post, which was an outpost of the German police at Cirey.
>
> During the following two days, whilst these officers were interrogated Breuer had a rather detailed report of the capture and declarations of the other men and officers of the same group (2nd SAS Battalion). They were treated in every way possible as officers by Breuer and myself. They had their meals with us and we walked several times in the park to give them fresh air and a little exercise.
>
> The chief of our police station at Cirey, SS-Sturmbahnführer Barnek, told Breuer that he regarded the two officers as spies as they had been taken prisoners clad in civilian overcoats and that he intended them to be shot. As result of our interrogations and personal talks with them Breuer and myself were convinced that both men were really officers, though administration officers of the British Army and ought to be treated as such.
>
> We opposed the opinions of Barnek and sent a wireless report of the affair to the competent police headquarters at Frankfurt a/m of the SS-Obersturmbahnführer Kieffer who had been Chief of Section IV Espionage and Terrorism in Paris [Hans Kieffer, later hanged for ordering the murders of members of 1st SAS engaged on OPERATION GAIN – see multiple entries within this volume under Marissel French National Cemetery, France]. As a result of this wireless report Kieffer came to Cirey two days later in his car, and took the two British officers with him [to Schirmeck] after he had talked things over with Breuer and Barnek. Breuer told me afterwards (I was not present at the interview of Kieffer with Barnek and Breuer) that he was very pleased with this result, as the officers would now be brought to a camp for prisoners of war (Oberursel?) [a town in Germany] and that Kieffer had taken personal charge of this affair. He was convinced that we had by our opposition saved the two officers from being shot as spies.
>
> With regards to the persons concerned I can give these descriptions – The British major was a man of about 1.65 to 1.70m with reddish hair, fair complexion, and his left hand severely wounded but practically healed. He had been as

far as I remember the officer in charge of the provisionment of the 2nd SAS Battalion and had a Scottish name: - Mac Douglas or something similar? [*sic*]

The British captain was at least 1.80m, dark hair, darker complexion (both had long beards as a result of their life in the forest). He spoke a little French and German, and had also some administration post with the 2nd SAS Battalion. His name if I remember it correctly was Whately-Smith …

I may remark that both British officers were very pleased with the treatment accorded to them by Breuer and myself, and both hoped to see us after the war. What became of them after they were taken by Kieffer in his car I have no idea [WO 309/539].

There was to be no POW status. Taken by Kieffer to Schirmeck Concentration Camp on 4 November, Reynolds and Whately-Smith were placed in cells alongside that of Lieutenant David Dill (see Dill's entry above). The three officers were then collected for interrogation by SS-Sturmscharführer Schossig and subsequently ill-treated at the Maison Barthlemy, the HQ of the Kommando Ernst in Saales. Abbé Hett, a fellow prisoner, stated that Reynolds had been hung up by his hands and beaten so severely that bones became visible. He subsequently told Hett that he would not have thought it possible for the body to withstand such pain without death occurring. Soon afterwards, the three officers were returned to Schirmeck along with Captain Victor Gough of SOE's JEDBURGH Team JACOB, who had also been beaten after his capture on 3 October. An American Red Cross representative later noted:

I'm sending you a list of names of American and British prisoners of war held by the Gestapo at the Concentration Camp of Schirmeck-la-Broque in Alsace. I was able to talk with them and promised to advise their families … These officers were living on 6 November, 1944 [WO 311/270].

Reynolds' name is on this list. However, he and the other prisoners were subsequently transferred to Rotenfels Camp in Germany and murdered in a wood near Gaggenau on 25 November 1944 (see Dill's entry within this section for full details). Having disappeared, Franks contacted Major 'Bill' Barkworth, commander of the SASWCIT, asking: 'have you any more clues Denny etc? Write Col Thynne Dill's stepfather if you have any clue.' Barkworth's team replied: 'bodies of Denny and Andy identified. He is now examining remaining bodies'. Barkworth himself reported:

In Grave 3, row III [by this time the remains had been reinterred at Gaggenau's Waldfriedhof civil cemetery] I found a body wearing an American pattern shirt with a British Army face-veil around the neck. Sergeant Rhodes, a member of my party, found two identity discs in this grave which he showed to me. The identity disclosed the following lettering: REYNOLDS BD CE and a number commencing with the numerals 130. There appeared to be some additional numbers but I could not decipher them. The identity discs were standard British Army pattern. The US Pattern shirt was similar to those issued to members of my regiment. Madame Chalopin [a French Army nurse assisting in the case] also gave me a shoulder strap bearing the insignia of a crown as worn by a major in the British Army, also a black button bearing the insignia of the King's Royal Rifle Corps which was Major Reynolds' parent unit. She said she had found it on the clothes of one of the bodies but could not remember from which body she had taken it. I have seen Major Reynolds wearing similar badges [WO 311/270].

German forces, which had attacked SAS men deployed on OPERATION PISTOL between 14 and 18 September 1944 at nearby Autrepierre, retreated, leaving behind a parachute smock with 'D.B Reynolds' inscribed on the collar. This is thought to have come into their possession after the capture of the SAS camp near Pierre-Percée on the 9th.

Franks later wrote: 'everyone in the SAS Regiment who knew Denny has a sense of personal loss. He was the best 2nd in Command anybody could possibly wish for and he was a great friend and it is difficult to say how much I miss him.' Meanwhile, Reynolds' former KRRC Commanding Officer, Lt-Colonel Campbell, wrote: 'Denis will be remembered with deep affection by the hundreds of officers and thousands of riflemen who came under his care and were infected with his cheerfulness; and by the Regiment whose traditions he served so well up to his final sacrifice in the liberation of France' (*The King's Royal Rifle Corps Chronicle*, 1945).

Referring to the interrogation that Reynolds, Whately-Smith, Gough and Dill suffered at Saales, Barkworth signalled: 'Beater was [Sigmund] Weber whom I arrested ten days ago'. Weber was handed over to the French in connection with other war crimes and sentenced to seven years hard labour.

Son of Sylvanis and Mabel Reynolds – Brother of Sylvia Nicholas of Whitehouse Road, Newport, Monmouthshire, of Lt-Commander Sylvanus Brian John Reynolds, MBE, DSC, of Grosvenor Street, London, who died whilst on active service on 12/05/45 and who is commemorated on the Plymouth Naval Memorial (served as B. Bingham), and of Rosamond Reynolds of Oaklands Park, Tolleshunt Knights, Maldon, Essex.
Age 35.
No inscription.
Grave 3.K.5. Also commemorated on Pierre-Percée's war memorial.

LANCE-CORPORAL GEORGE **ROBINSON** [884882] ROYAL ARTILLERY
AND 2ND SAS (2 SQN)

George Robinson was born in the parish of St Marks in Armagh on 18 June 1920. Having worked as a driver he enlisted into the Royal Artillery during September 1938 and after training was posted to the 26th Anti-Tank Regiment. In April 1939 he was sent with this unit, now redesignated as a mobile coastal defence regiment, to Malta. He remained on the island throughout its siege, extending his service to remain with the Colours for twelve years before volunteering for 2nd SAS. Arriving in Algiers on 25 August 1943 he joined the Regiment at Philippeville that day and commenced training. Two 'Robinsons' were serving within 2nd SAS at this time and although at least one was deployed to Italy it appears from his medal card that this was not George. He returned to the UK with the rest of the Regiment in March 1944.

Robinson parachuted into the Vosges département of eastern France for OPERATION LOYTON during the night of 27–28 August 1944 as a member of Major Peter Power's stick. This was dropped without its equipment containers into a DZ 13 kilometres east-south-east of where the pilot thought he was. The error caused confusion amongst members of the Maquis, who had lit the drop zone in expectation of the arrival of SOE's JEDBURGH Team ALASTAIR. This team was dropped onto the same DZ shortly after the SAS landed. Realising that his party was far from its operational area, Power decided they would move towards it. On the 29th they made contact with another JEDBURGH group, this time Team ARCHIBALD, and whilst deciding what action to take they passed bombing targets to the RAF. As a result an SS HQ at Vincey was attacked and some 400 Germans were killed. A 3-million-litre petrol dump at Nomexy was also destroyed. The SAS eventually borrowed bicycles and all ten cycled through the countryside to the River Meurthe and into the LOYTON area. Hoping to blow up a railway line en route, they split up with Power, Robinson and Parachutists Edwin Weaver and Marchand crossing the river on 10 September. Despite conflicting instructions from London, a Maquis guide located the four and took Robinson to the main SAS party. He returned late on the 17th and guided the remainder of the patrol to Lt-Colonel Brian Franks' camp the following day.

Robinson subsequently served in Power's Jeep as rear gunner and was noted by him as having killed at least one German on 23 September when ambushing German transport between Celles-sur-Plaine and Allarmont. At the end of the operation Robinson was a member of Sergeant Jock Hay's rear party which was captured on 7 October and murdered at La Grande Fosse on the 15th (see Hay's entry for full details). His was the fourth body exhumed, suggesting that he was shot fifth out of the eight men. His remains were identified by dental records. For some reason his date of death is officially recorded as 16 October 1944, although that of three of the those murdered alongside him is correctly recorded as the 15th.

Son of Mary Robinson of Bridge Street, Portadown, County Armagh, Northern Ireland – Younger brother of Hugh Robinson and older brother of Albert Robinson – Fiancé of Miss B. McGovern of the Women's Land Army Hostel, Old Dailly, Girvan, Ayrshire.
Age 24.
No inscription.
Grave 3.K.3. Also commemorated on the Stele de Prayé Memorial above Moussey and on Portadown's war memorial.

PRIVATE JAMES **SALTER** [4200942] ROYAL WELCH FUSILIERS, KING'S OWN ROYAL REGIMENT AND 2ND SAS (2 SQN)

James Salter was born in Salford on 15 July 1915. Having worked as a case maker he enlisted into the Royal Welch Fusiliers in April 1940 and was posted to A Company at the 311th Infantry Training Centre. Transferring to the King's Own Royal Regiment that June, he served with the 8th Battalion on Malta from July 1941 until 24 August 1943 when he volunteered for 2nd SAS. As such he was a contemporary of Corporal Harry Winder (see his entry within this section), the pair disembarking at Algiers and joining the Regiment at Philippeville where they commenced training. They returned to the UK with the majority of 2nd SAS in mid March 1944.

On the night of 6–7 September 1944 Salter parachuted into the Vosges département of eastern France for OPERATION LOYTON as a member of Major Denny Reynolds' stick. He was with Lieutenant Desmond Black's group that became separated from the main SAS party during a German attack on its camp soon afterwards and was posted missing as of the 11th. The group was captured at La Turbine sawmill on the 15th, their presence having been betrayed. They were murdered near Saint-Dié on the 20th (see Black's entry within this section for full details).

Son of Ernest and Emma Salter (née Scragg) of Belmont Avenue, Pendleton, Salford, Lancashire – Older brother of Ernest.
Age 29.
No inscription.
Grave 3.K.20.

SERGEANT FRANK ERNEST <u>TERRY-HALL</u> [4122304] CHESHIRE REGIMENT, THE BUFFS AND 2ND SAS (2 SQN)

Frank Terry-Hall was born in East Ham, London, on 16 August 1910. Having worked as an actor he enlisted into the Cheshire Regiment in November 1929 at Liverpool. Posted to the 1st Battalion in India, where he arrived almost exactly a year later, he was promoted to lance-corporal in July 1933 but had reverted to the rank of private at his own request by December. He was promoted to lance-corporal again in April 1937 and having disembarked in Sudan late in November 1938 was advanced to corporal in March 1939. That August he joined the 2nd Battalion in the UK and was promoted to sergeant the following month at the outbreak of war. After a period at the Machine Gun Training Centre he transferred to the 10th Battalion, The Buffs (Royal East Kent Regiment), in July 1940 and was promoted to Company quarter-master-sergeant in April 1941. Late in February 1942 he married Margaret Christopher at St Paul's Church in Wood Green, north London, and disembarked in Algeria that November during OPERATION TORCH, the Allied landings in North Africa. With just days remaining of this campaign he volunteered for 2nd SAS on 13 May 1943, reverting to the rank of colour-sergeant in order to do so. He reverted to sergeant that October and arrived back in the UK the following March having served with the Regiment in Italy, more than likely having been part of B Squadron's advance into Calabria.

In the early hours of 1 September 1944 Terry-Hall parachuted into the Vosges département of eastern France for OPERATION LOYTON as a member of Lieutenant 'Karl' Marx's stick. The latter's report states that on 8 September he and Terry-Hall carried out a recce of local roads hoping to find ambush sites. On the 9th a suitable location was found, the stick ambushing a truck on the col de la Chapelotte that day. During the subsequent withdrawal the men were engaged by the enemy and Marx ordered the party into the hills:

Evidently Sjt Terry-Hall, Cpl Iveson [*sic* – Ivison] and Crozier [*sic* – Crosier] could not have heard me as they started to run straight along the track. I halted the remainder 300 yards up the hill and made them lie down in the bushes. In the distance we saw Germans with dogs running after Sjt Terry-Hall, Cpl Iveson and Crozier [WO 361/721].

The three evaders found refuge at the house adjoining La Turbine sawmill where they were joined Lieutenant Desmond Black's party that had become separated from the main SAS group. A French informer, who had seen the first three men at the mill, fetched an SD detachment and the combined SAS party was captured after an exchange of fire on the 15th (see Black's entry within this section for details). The SAS War Crimes Investigation Team's 'Interim Report' indicates the possibility that Terry-Hall initially evaded capture:

On 15/09/44 the party was surprised and seven out of the total eight captured. The escapee seems, on the weight of the evidence, to have been Sjt Terry Hall who is identified by Monsieur Dedat of Moussey and an official of the Mairie of La Petite-Raon as a 2nd SAS PW captured near Monsieur Dedat's house in the latter half of September. This is not certain as Sjt Terry Hall is also identified at Allarmont. The error, however, may be one of date not of person.

Whether Terry-Hall was captured with Black's group on the 15th or joined them later, the men were all imprisoned at Schirmeck Concentration Camp and murdered near Saint-Dié on the 20th (see Black's entry for full details). Terry-Hall's remains were later identified by dental records and by the word 'Terry', presumably his nickname, tattooed on his left forearm (WO 235/176).

Son of Frank and Jessie Terry-Hall of Old Ford Road, Bow, east London – Husband of Margaret Terry-Hall of Lymington Avenue, Wood Green, Middlesex.
Age 34.
To live in the hearts of those you loved is not to die
Grave 3.K.14.

Private Edwin Thomas **WEAVER** [1060893] Royal Artillery and 2nd SAS (2 Sqn)

Edwin Weaver was born in the parish of St Johns near Shrewsbury where his father was a serving police officer. In February 1925 he enlisted into the Royal Artillery, volunteering his date of birth as 9 December 1906. However, as his birth was not registered until early 1908 it seems likely that he falsified his age to join up early. Enlisting in Birmingham for a period of six years, he gave his civilian trade as machinist. Much of his pre-war service was spent in India, where he was promoted to lance-bombardier and served with various artillery regiments as a signaller and range-taker. During 1931 he was hospitalised at Rawalpindi with his first attack of malaria. Later that year he completed his engagement and returned to the UK to be transferred to the Army Reserve list on which he remained until 1937. His final report commended him as: 'A clean, smart, young NCO. Is honest, sober, reliable and hard working. Above the average in intelligence.' Following in his father's footsteps he initially joined Staffordshire police,

marrying May Goodfellow in October 1934. He later found employment as a milkman.

Weaver was mobilised in June 1939 and posted as a lance-bombardier to 128th Battery before being promoted to bombardier the following month. By August he was back on the reserve list but was mobilised once again at Sandown racecourse that October, this time as a lance-bombardier in the 143rd Field Regiment. By May 1940 he had been promoted back to bombardier and served in Iceland as a mechanic from October 1940 until mid April 1942. Returning to the UK, he reverted at his own request to the rank of gunner. Having been posted to the 70th (West Riding) Field Regiment he disembarked in North Africa just before Christmas 1942, subsequently taking part in the fighting in Tunisia. He volunteered for 2nd SAS on 9 June 1943 but was admitted to hospital with a further bout of malaria soon after.

Weaver led a small party on OPERATION JONQUIL during October 1943 having been tasked to locate and evacuate escaped POWs along the east coast of Italy. The post-operation report notes that his group concentrated its efforts on the 'Monte Giorgio area, working in a north-west and south-westerly direction' whilst Parachutist 'Poochy' Maybury, a member of this party, later stated:

> On leaving Capt Power on 10th Oct, Pct Weaver, Pct Bogey and myself went on a roving commission to look for escaped POWs and had orders to return to SSM Marshall on the 22nd of October. We contacted quite a few POWs on the bed of the River Mennechia, and having completed our patrol, we reported back to SSM Marshall as arranged [WO 218/181].

In mid March 1944 Weaver returned to the UK with the remainder of the Regiment, spending much of that summer in hospital with another attack of malaria. Having recovered, he parachuted into the Vosges département of eastern France for OPERATION LOYTON during the night of 27–28 August as a member of Major Peter Power's stick. Dropped far from the operational area this group eventually joined the main SAS party using borrowed bicycles (see Robinson's entry within this section for details). Weaver initially served as wireless operator on Power's Jeep but towards the end of the operation was a member of Sergeant Jock Hay's rear party. This was captured on 7 October, the men being subsequently murdered at La Grande Fosse on 15 October 1944 (see Hay's entry within this section for full details).

Weaver's remains were the first to be exhumed, proving that he was the last to be shot. He is reported as telling his murderers that they were killing better men than themselves and that they would be brought

to justice. SS-Unterscharführer Georg Zahringer, who drove the men to the site of their murder, later stated:

> Schossig, who spoke English, told him [Parachutist Reg Church] to take is clothes off. This the prisoner did. He was then taken, held by the arms by Wuttke and Gaede, into the wood. Practically immediately I heard a shot. The remaining English prisoners on the truck did not say anything, but remained silent. This went from one prisoner to another until it was the turn of the last. Just before he was taken away, he said something to Schossig, in English. I asked Schossig what he had said, and he told me that the Englishman had said, 'We were good men.' I followed this last prisoner and saw how he was made to stand near the edge of an open grave which contained the naked dead bodies of his comrades, which from his position he was able to see. He was not trembling. He was shot through the back of the head by Wuttke, and fell on to the bodies of the others [WO 309/233].

For some reason Weaver's date of death is officially recorded as 16 October 1944, although that of three of the seven men murdered alongside him is correctly recorded as the 15th.

Son of Edwin and Annie Weaver of Finger Post Farm, Forden, near Welshpool, Montgomery – Husband of May Weaver of Clinton Road, Shirley, Birmingham, who served in the ARP – Older brother of Florence and Stanley Weaver.
Age officially recorded as 37.
No inscription.
Grave 3.K.6. Also commemorated on the war memorial at St James Church, Shirley, Solihull, and on the Stele de Prayé Memorial above Moussey.

Major Anthony Robert <u>WHATELY-SMITH</u> [113612] Somerset Light Infantry, Dorsetshire Regiment, East Surrey Regiment and 2nd SAS (HQ Sqn)

Known as 'Andy' to both friends and family, Anthony Whately-Smith was born on 22 May 1915 at Worthing in East Sussex. He began his education at Hordle House prep school that his father had founded and subsequently steered as headmaster. Going on to Sherborne School, Dorset, he became head of his house as well as a keen sportsman, actor and member of the OTC, although this period was marred by the death of his mother. On leaving school, he found employment with the Vacuum Oil Company and sailed to the USA for training in January 1937. At the outbreak of war he enlisted into the Somerset Light Infantry in Bristol (service number 5675013), going on to attend 164 OCTU at Goujerat Barracks in Colchester later that month. His final report correctly predicted that he would 'make a first class officer'. He was commissioned into the 5th Battalion, Dorsetshire Regiment, in January 1940 before marrying Mary Hodgkinson at Beaulieu at the beginning of March.

As a captain Whately-Smith served as the Intelligence Officer of 130th Infantry Brigade from November 1941, as GSO III (Training) at GHQ Home Forces from April 1942, and entered staff college soon after. He also attended the first Combined Operations Staff Officers Course during June 1943 at HMS *Brontosaurus*, the Combined Training Centre at Castle Toward near Dunoon in Argyll. Having been attached to HQ 165th Infantry Brigade as Brigade Major from June 1943, he was appointed GSO II (Instructor) at the School of Military Intelligence at Matlock at the beginning of February 1944. A brief period with the 2nd Battalion, East Surrey Regiment, followed, although he was interviewed on 4 July by the 'Commander of the SAS Regiment' at the War Office. Accepted, he joined the Regiment as a captain four days later. He was officially posted to 2nd SAS on 28 July, serving as Adjutant from the beginning of August.

In the early hours of 1 September 1944 Whately-Smith parachuted into the Vosges département of eastern France for Operation Loyton as a member of Lt-Colonel Brian Franks' reinforcement party. Having moved away from the DZ near Veney, Whately-Smith picked a new drop zone close to Neufmaisons for the arrival of Major Denny Reynolds, who landed on the night of 6–7th. On the morning of the 9th, Franks sent these two officers to locate a new main base, as their present camp near Pierre-Percée was threatened by German troops sweeping the surrounding area. Two hours later Franks' camp was attacked and the main party forced to move with the loss of its stores. Despite repeatedly broadcasting a new RV to the pair, contact could not be established and they were captured on 30 October at La Trouche near Raon-l'Étape (see Reynolds' entry within this section for full details of their intervening activity). Initially taken to Schirmeck Concentration Camp, Whately-Smith, Reynolds and Lieutenant David Dill were interrogated at the Maison Barthlemy, the Kommando Ernst's HQ in Saales, on 5 November before being returned. An American Red Cross representative saw the men at Schirmeck the following day:

I'm sending you a list of names of American and British prisoners of war held by the Gestapo at the Concentration Camp of Schirmeck-la-Broque in Alsace. I was able to talk with them and promised to advise their families ... These officers were living on 6 November, 1944 [WO 311/270].

Whately-Smith's name is on this list. When Schirmeck was evacuated before the advancing Allies on 22 November the SAS prisoners were moved to Rotenfels Camp in Germany. They were murdered in Erlichwald, a wood behind the Mercedes Benz factory at Gaggenau on 25 November 1944 (see Dill's entry within this section for details). Maurice Lesoil, a fellow prisoner, later wrote to Whately-Smith's father:

As I believe I have told you, Smith [sic] thought he would be transferred to a camp for the Allied forces near Baden-Baden but Major Reynolds had expressed his fears and a horrifying foreboding of what was to happen only a few hundred yards from the camp. Andy left us happily, expressing his hopes about seeing us again soon, free at last. He jokingly said he would arrange for a tour of London in his campaign uniform which the SS had marked with white phosphorescent bands on the knees, chest and with a cross on the back.
We tried to share his optimism while the brutes chose the two or three Frenchmen who were being interviewed by those who had condemned them to death with their characteristic duplicity and cowardice. But deep down we were worried for we had heard that the Germans had asked for a group of volunteers who would be rewarded in extra food – a pot of 'wasser' soup and a packet of cigarettes [letter dated January 1958, Whately-Smith family collection].

The remains of those murdered were exhumed and reinterred on 13 May 1945 'with special honours and in the presence of a large proportion of the population' at Gaggenau's Waldfriedhof civil cemetery. Major 'Bill' Barkworth, commander of the SAS War Crimes Investigation Team, later reported:

In Grave 5, row II, I found a body which was wearing a British airborne pattern string vest and also two British identity discs. The identity discs bore the name of Second-Lieutenant A R Whately-Smith C E. They were of standard British Army pattern. I knew Lieutenant Whately-Smith and saw him last on the night of the 31st August 1944 at Fairford Airdrome when he entered a plane proceeding on a parachute operation in the area of the Vosges [WO 311/270].

In June 1945 Franks wrote to Whately-Smith's father: 'I offer you my deepest sympathy and that of the whole Regiment in this appalling tragedy. Andy was not only one of the ablest, but one of the most popular officers we ever had. We will not forget him.' Soon after the Chairman of the Vacuum Oil Company wrote to *The Times*:

As Chairman of the Company by which he was employed I would like to pay tribute to his memory. Andy volunteered for the task through which he met his death. After a parachute drop behind enemy lines, he was eventually captured by the Germans. On at least two occasions he scorned opportunities to escape, because to do so would have meant leaving his wounded brother officer [Reynolds] and a brave Frenchwoman who had befriended them [Myrhiam Le Rolland]. His body, and that of his friend, has lately been identified in a Concentration Camp [sic], and so a young life

of the greatest promise is closed. Andy's service was of the highest order. He was loved by all who were privileged to know him. He will be sadly missed but never forgotten.
There have been so many of these tragedies, that to single out one case for special thought is impossible. I think the greatest tribute we can pay to Andy is to look upon his as symbolic of a devotion to duty and utter disregard of personal safety shown by so many thousands of our young men [family collection].

Son of the Reverend Ernest Whately-Smith, MC, MA, and the late Dorothy Whately-Smith (née Calkin) of Hordle House, Milford-on-Sea, Hampshire – Husband of Mary Whately-Smith of Twynham House, Lymington, Hampshire. After the war his wife, an American citizen, returned to the United States, remarried, and died soon afterwards – Brother of Majors Peter and John Whately-Smith, both mentioned in despatches whilst serving in the 43rd (Wessex) Division.
Age 29.
Of Hordle House Milford-on-Sea, Hampshire
Grave 3.K.2. Also commemorated on Pierre-Percée's war memorial and within Walhampton School's chapel.

Corporal Harry **WINDER** [3460628] Lancashire Fusiliers, King's Own Royal Regiment, Royal Army Ordnance Corps and 2nd SAS (2 Sqn)

Harry Winder was born in Lancaster on 21 June 1914. Having worked in the print department of a linoleum works he enlisted into the Lancashire Fusiliers in mid August 1940 and was posted to the 310th Infantry Training Centre. He transferred to the King's Own Royal Regiment that October, attended a cook's course at the end of the year and transferred to the Royal Army Ordnance Corps the following March. Having reverted back to the KORR in late April 1941 he was posted to the 8th Battalion in June and served on Malta throughout the island's siege. During this period he was promoted to lance-corporal. Volunteering for 2nd SAS he disembarked in Algiers on 24 August 1943, the day he was advanced to corporal, and joined the Regiment at Philippeville. As such he was a contemporary of Parachutist James Salter, whose fate he was to share. Having served with 2nd SAS in Italy, more than likely as part of B Squadron's thrust into Calabria,

Winder arrived back in the UK in mid March 1944. That July he married Elizabeth Findlay in Glasgow.

On the night of 6–7 September 1944 Winder parachuted into the Vosges département of eastern France for OPERATION LOYTON as a member of Major Denny Reynolds' reinforcement party. He was separated from the main SAS group soon afterwards whilst moving across the Plaine valley and was captured at La Turbine sawmill with Lieutenant Desmond Black's stick on the 15th. Officially posted missing as of the 11th, witnesses recalled seeing him at Schirmeck Concentration Camp looking after the wounded Black amongst other members of the stick.

Winder was murdered near Saint-Dié on 20 September 1944 (see Black's entry within this section for full details). A subsequent post-mortem identified his remains by his signet ring (WO 235/176).

Son of Mrs Bessie Winder (née Phillipson) of Alfred Street, Lancaster, Lancs – His father, Thomas, had passed away before the start of the war – Husband of Elizabeth Winder of Hillhead Avenue, Kilmarnock, Ayrshire.
Age 30.
No inscription.
Grave 3.K.17. Also commemorated on Lancaster Civic War Memorial.

HAMBURG CEMETERY

Over 300 Allied servicemen were buried here during the First World War, the remains of more being concentrated from over 120 burial sites all over Germany during the inter-war period. The total number of First World War graves now stands at 708. The cemetery also contains 1,466 Commonwealth burials of the Second World War, 378 post-war burials and fourteen of other nationalities.

The war cemetery is located within Hamburg's Ohlsdorf Cemetery (Friedhof Ohlsdorf), the world's largest non-military cemetery. Three Commonwealth War Graves Commission plots lie approximately 3 kilometres from the main entrance and are clearly signposted. GPS co-ordinates: Latitude 53.61975, Longitude 10.03544

PRIVATE ROBERT CHARLES THOMAS **BOXALL** [11268761] ROYAL ARTILLERY AND 2ND SAS (1 SQN)

Bob Boxall was born on 5 April 1922 in Fulham, west London. He enlisted into the Royal Artillery in September 1941 and was initially posted to the 209th Heavy Anti-Aircraft Training Regiment before being re-posted to the 139th HAA Regiment that December. After reporting to the RA depot at Woolwich in November 1942, he embarked for North Africa as a reinforcement for OPERATION TORCH at the end of the month. Here he found himself without a unit and although it is not certain when he volunteered for 2nd SAS (owing to to contradictory entries in his service record), it is likely that the date was 13 August 1943. What is certain is that he served in Italy from September until returning to the UK in March 1944 when he was officially posted to the Regiment.

After the D-Day landings of June 1944 Boxall was a member of Major Roy Farran's Jeep-borne squadron that infiltrated German lines during OPERATION WALLACE. The squadron was ambushed in the village of Villaines-Les-Prévôtes on 23 August and Boxall, Lance-corporal 'Tanky' Challenor and the French-speaking Parachutist Gosselin, a native of Jersey, found themselves left behind when their patrol withdrew. Hiding overnight in the outskirts of the village they retrieved Challenor's abandoned Jeep and trailer the following morning and set off to locate their comrades, Gosselin asking directions en route. They were feted, mistakenly, as the forerunners of the liberating Allies at the nearby village of L'Isle-sur-Serein. Well fed, somewhat worse for wear, and now laden with wine and flowers, they eventually came across other survivors of the ambush under the command of Captain 'Raymond Lee' (real name Raymond Couraud). This group made its way to 1st SAS' OPERATION HOUNDSWORTH base and returned to the UK, intending to rejoin the rest of the squadron at a later date. WALLACE came to an end before they were required.

In the spring of 1945 Boxall deployed on OPERATION ARCHWAY which was to provide short-range reconnaissance for the advancing Allies in Germany. Elements of both 1st and 2nd SAS, operating in Jeeps, came together on the Allied side of the Elbe under the title of Frankforce. On 29 April 1945 Boxall was the driver of the third Jeep in a line waiting to cross this river, Wallace Rennie-Roberts of the same troop later recalling:

We were queued up on the bank of the Elbe waiting to load onto Buffalos [tracked amphibious vehicles] and we were being strafed and bombed. They [the Germans] dropped a bomb that landed just behind my Jeep and it killed Bob Boxall who was in the Jeep behind, and badly injured the Canadian officer who was with him [Captain R. A. Smith]. The third bloke on that Jeep [Parachutist Ron Dance] survived … It's funny how blast can affect people in close proximity differently – some get killed and some don't. Boxall was killed outright and the medics took him away [to be initially buried at Lauenberg – personal interview, 2013].

Boxall and Dance had planned a joint marriage after the war to a pair of friends: Boxall's bride-to-be never married.

Son of Mrs Ellen Boxall (née Hankin) of Darlan Road, Fulham, south-west London.
Age 23.
No inscription.
Grave 1A.A.10.

CAPTAIN ALFRED DAYRELL **MORRIS** [157339] GORDON HIGHLANDERS, GENERAL LIST, ARMY CATERING CORPS AND 2ND SAS

Dayrell Morris, as he was commonly known, was born on 12 February 1914 in Edinburgh and lived at Dochart House in Killin, Perthshire. Having attended Edinburgh Academy and Liverpool College he was employed by LMS Hotel Services, working in various kitchens in the UK from 1932 to 1933. Eighteen months of employment at Harzburg, at the Bristol Hotel in Berlin and at Langenbach's in Worms followed, during which time he learned German. Returning to Britain he took a post in the LMS Control Office at the Adelphi Hotel in Liverpool. During 1936 he worked as a waiter at the Palace Hotel at Lausanne in Switzerland, returning to work in the UK at Claridges, the Berkeley Hotel and as the assistant reception manager at The Savoy.

Morris joined the Territorial D Company, 2nd Battalion, The London Scottish (Gordon Highlanders), during April 1939 (service number 2882703). He was promoted to lance-corporal on mobilisation at the outbreak of war that September and advanced to corporal three months later. During February 1940 he completed courses in drill and administration, marrying Myna Wilson Moffat in Kensington the following month. That May he attended a course at the School of Small Arms at Hythe in Kent and was promoted to sergeant in August. After a period at the Army School of Cookery, Aldershot, he was commissioned onto the General List that December (*London Gazette* 03/01/41, Supplement 06/01/41). A brief attachment to the Royal Dutch Army as Messing Officer followed, before being posted as Assistant Catering Advisor to the North Wales Area at the end of January 1941. He transferred to the newly-formed Army Catering Corps that March and was promoted to captain in July, having been appointed Catering Administrator to HQ 6th Armoured Division. He disembarked in Algeria with this formation during OPERATION TORCH, the November 1942 Allied landings along the North African coast.

Morris volunteered for 2nd SAS on 8 June 1943 and later that month attended a parachute course run by the Inter-Services Signals Unit 6, a cover name for Massingham, SOE's base near Algiers. After the invasion of Italy he operated with C Squadron as the spearhead of the advance from Taranto to Termoli during the final months of 1943, arriving back in the UK with the rest of the Regiment in mid March 1944.

Despite the efforts of the Army Catering Corps to reclaim him, Morris was deployed on the initial phase of OPERATION HARDY between Troyes and Dijon in France. His party of five men and one Jeep (that 'fell without parachutes and became unrecognisable') dropped into the area during the night of 26–27 July 1944. The men made contact with 1st SAS' HOUNDSWORTH camp and having been joined by Captain Grant Hibbert and two other ranks, located their own DZ for resupply and reinforcement. Their main party, tasked under OPERATION WALLACE, subsequently infiltrated German lines by Jeep and met with Morris' HARDY team. The whole group then fell under the command of Major Roy Farran, MC**, successfully harassing enemy lines of communication. Morris, Farran and Hibbert recced the town of Châtillon-sur-Seine and during the squadron's attack of 30 August his own party was tasked with mortaring the German HQ. After 'placing 48 bombs on target' they took up a position on the Chaumont road:

> … where he [Morris] destroyed a large German truck loaded with ammunition and hand grenades and piled high with troops. It had stopped, and an enormous officer had climbed out and made a critical survey of the party, before fire was opened. The German vehicle caught fire immediately and the troops came under withering fire while attempting to take cover. It is estimated that thirty were killed. The truck subsequently exploded. Lieut. Morris's Jeep was hit in the radiator and had to be towed home [WO 219/2401].

When Farran reorganised the squadron into three groups, Morris fell under the command of Hibbert: on 4 September they broke into a German petrol depot at Foulain, stealing 1,000 gallons that they loaded onto trucks provided by the Maquis whilst under fire. When they ran out of space they opened the taps and set delayed Lewes bombs on the remaining stock; 'the resulting explosion and fire were magnificent and were observed by the Americans far to the north' (WO 218/192). On the 6th, Morris' troop, which had lost contact with the rest of the group, encountered German soldiers near Heuilley-Le-Grand. Ordered not to engage the enemy whilst en route to a new base, Morris withdrew rapidly. In doing so his Jeep turned over, trapping him underneath. Parachutist Ken Webber, who had been thrown clear, lifted the Jeep (no mean feat) and extracted Morris under fire. He then took the Vickers machine gun and engaged the enemy by firing from the hip even though to do so meant badly burning his hand. Meanwhile, the Jeep was righted, enabling the troop to proceed. Webber was awarded the Military Medal as a result. Having been overrun by the advancing Americans, the patrol returned to the UK on 26 September.

Morris spent nearly two weeks in North West Europe during March 1945 and despite returning to the UK was redeployed to Germany on 16 April for Operation Archway. Although he appears as 'Capt AD Morris MC' on that operation's nominal roll there is no *London Gazette* of such an award. Joining elements of both 1st and 2nd SAS on the Allied side of the River Elbe, he was killed in action just south of Lütau on 29 April 1945, soon after crossing the river. Wallace Rennie-Roberts of his troop recalled the events leading up to his commander's death:

> Dayrell's Jeep loaded into the Buffalo [just after Parachutist Bob Boxall had been killed, see his entry within this section] and I followed him in. Dayrell's driver was Corporal Tom Moody.
> The river as I remember at this point was about 200–250 yards wide, with sandy banks about 50 yards wide bordered by bushes and trees, good cover for enemy infantry. There was a small road about slightly left of our centre as we headed across. The Buffalos were quite slow, and Dayrell summoned me up to go forward and talk to him. There were two MG42s [German machine guns] on each corner of the little road and these were hammering away and hitting the front of the Buffalo making an enormous noise. Dayrell said: 'I will wait until I think they are changing their belts, and I will signal the bosun to drop the ramp, and when he does I will drop down the ramp and go to the left and take out the gun on the left. You will take the gun on the right, and then we will rake the grass and bushes behind.' This was exactly what we did, obliterating the two MGs with our Vickers fire. Dayrell then turned his Jeep left, and I turned mine to the right. We ran slowly along the sand to subdue fire from the hedges for about 20 or 30 yards, and then reversed back to the road. Dayrell then went up the road for about 40 yards, and I did likewise. We then put fire down into the grass and hedges from the rear to give cover for the next Buffalo to unload the next two Jeeps.
> When they were safely out and firing, Dayrell turned and went up the road about 400 –500 yards, and I followed about 150 yards behind. We were taking light fire from some houses on our left, and some intermittent fire from Hitler Youth from the fields on our right. The firing from Dayrell's Jeep died down, and the officer who was on my Vickers said, 'we will have to sit here and give cover and stop those Hitler Youth from getting behind Dayrell' to which I said, 'I will position the Jeep to give us a better field of fire.' I drove forward another 20 yards, and backed the Jeep into a field on our right, so that the officer on my Vickers could give fire to the houses across the road, and my rear gunner could cover the fields at our rear. Arthur [Huntbach, the rear gunner] was still in a part concussed state [from being bombed prior to the crossing], and I had to keep prompting him where to put his fire down.
> During this time there was intermittent fire from Dayrell's Jeep, and eventually it died away, and I was told by Moody that Dayrell got off the Jeep to take the surrender of some Hitler Youth. He didn't take his Thompson [sub-machine gun], and did not take his .45 [Colt semi-automatic pistol] from its holster, but walked towards the Hitler Youth. Apparently, although these Hitler Youth had already thrown down their arms, one of them bent down, picked up a weapon and shot Dayrell, who dropped down out of sight. Tom's rear gunner them gave a quick squirt off the Vickers, and most of them ran away or got killed. The rear gunner then went to look for Dayrell but could not find him. The theory is that he crawled away into the undergrowth. He was found the next day by British infantry … I also knew, that as Dayrell's rear gunner had told me that he had been hit by half a magazine fired at close range from a Schmeisser, there was little chance of Dayrell being alive. We got back to HQ and were told; 'It's over fellas.' In my opinion, for what it is worth, I think that Dayrell should have got a posthumous DSO for the way he conducted that river crossing, but the fact that the war was finished, everybody seemed pleased to forget about it all [personal correspondence, 2009].

Rennie-Roberts later added:

> I think we were probably getting a bit blasé as the war was all but over … The chappie who was his driver [Moody, who was later awarded a Military Medal] was very concerned that Dayrell had been killed and not been backed up. He took a commission in the parachute infantry and it was still on his conscious so he committed suicide …
> Dayrell was a very good chap, very practical and knew what it was all about: he could assess the situation quickly, analyse it, and do something about it. He was a very good, sensible, planner [personal interview, 2013].

SAS Brigade HQ signalled ARCHWAY 'everyone here distressed at Dayrell's death'. Morris was subsequently mentioned in despatches (*London Gazette* 06/11/45, Supplement 08/11/45). Although the War Office forwarded a nomination for the Croix de guerre to General Koenig on 2 October 1945 it is not known whether this was awarded.

Son of Alfred and Emma Morris of Edinburgh – Husband of Mina Morris of Mardmont Road, Edinburgh – Known to have had at least one sister.
Age 31.
No inscription.
Grave 2.H.6. Also commemorated on Killin's war memorial.

HANOVER WAR CEMETERY

This cemetery contains 2,407 burials of the Second World War that were concentrated from numerous locations including prisoner of war camps. Sixty are unidentified. In addition, there are thirty-nine non-war burials and ten of other nationalities. Hanover Military Cemetery, a post-war plot containing over 3,000 burials, is adjacent to the war cemetery.

The cemetery is located 8 kilometres west of Hannover's central railway station in the suburb of Limmer on Harenberger Meile (the K251). GPS co-ordinates: Latitude 52.37716, Longitude 9.65229

PRIVATE JAMES VENNEY **BLAKENEY** [2660354] COLDSTREAM GUARDS, NO.8 COMMANDO, L DETACHMENT SAS BRIGADE AND 1ST SAS (A SQN)

Jim Blakeney was born on 11 December 1919 in Grimsby, the eldest of four children. Although often reported to have been a trawlerman, he worked for one of the ice companies at the docks where he loaded blocks onto lorries and fishing vessels. Enlisting into the Coldstream Guards at the beginning of March 1940, he was posted to the brigade depot at Caterham in Surrey. Five months later he volunteered for No.8 (Guards) Commando, this soon being temporarily reorganised as part of the 4th Special Service Battalion. Embarking for the Middle East on the last day of January 1941 he became one of those known in the Regiment as the 'Tobruk Four' (Blakeney, Bob Lilley, Pat Riley and Jim Almonds) having snatched prisoners from the Tobruk perimeter whilst under the command of Lieutenant Jock Lewes (see Lewes' entry under Alamein Memorial, Egypt, Volume I, for further details). The five men were subsequently

recruited by Captain David Stirling for his fledgling unit, Blakeney joining L Detachment, SAS Brigade, on 4 September.

Blakeney was captured on 17 November 1941 during OPERATION SQUATTER, the first SAS raid, after L Detachment parachuted behind enemy lines during a gale to attack airfields at Tmimi and Gazala in Libya. A report written after his subsequent escape and return to the UK notes:

After landing he [Blakeney] lay up until dawn and found himself along with other members of his party, including Lieutenant MacGoneagle [*sic*], who was badly injured and died later [see Lieutenant Eoin McGonigal's entry under Alamein Memorial, Egypt] …

This party, which endeavoured to make for LRDG RV, got lost, and so made their way to the coast and were picked up by an Italian guard at Tmimi airfield as per the report of Tpr Davies, prior to arriving on the Italian mainland. After staying for ten days at Bari PW Camp, the party was moved to a PW Camp (No.52) near Genoa [at Chiavari]. Tpr Blakeney stayed at Camp 52 until June 1943, when he was moved to a small PW Camp near to Pomaro, where he was employed until the Italian armistice. He then made his escape to Switzerland. The trip to the frontier took nineteen days, after missing several German patrols.

After crossing the frontier, Tprs Robertson and Blakeney and six others from British units were picked up by Swiss sentries in September 1943 [his service record states 25 October 1943], and stayed in Switzerland until being repatriated in October, 1944 [his service record states 14 November 1944]. He then returned to UK via Algiers [see Trooper Roy Davies' entry within this section for further details].

Although initially posted to the 161st Recce Regiment, RAC, 1st SAS' Commanding Officer, Lt-Colonel Paddy Mayne, DSO*, was keen to have Blakeney back and as a result he was briefly sent to the Airborne Forces Depot in Chesterfield before rejoining the Regiment on 4 January 1945. Posted to A Squadron he was deployed to Germany that March for OPERATION ARCHWAY as a member of a combined 1st and 2nd SAS contingent known as Frankforce. This was tasked with short-range Jeep reconnaissance ahead of the Allied advance. Having crossed the Rhine at Bislich on the 25th, Captain Ian Wellsted's reserve troop, of which Blakeney was a member, took the lead on the 28th. Reaching the village of Östrich they met three British tanks and a scout car and after a quick exchange the group decided to continue their advance together. After only 50 yards they were ambushed, the scout car being knocked out and Trooper Vince Andrews being fatally wounded (see his entry under Reichswald Forest War Cemetery, Germany). Having cleared the area with considerable difficulty, the troop resumed its progress, fighting through numerous smaller contacts over the coming days.

On 8 April Wellsted's men were settled back in their reserve role when called forward to support armoured cars of the Inns of Court Regiment. Passing through the village of Schneeren the Jeeps took to woodland tracks, heading north before reaching the junction with the Neustadt–Nienburg road. Here they met two scout cars and one armoured car of the Inns of Court, the combined force setting off towards Nienburg. After only a short distance the enemy, who had allowed the armoured vehicles to pass unmolested, ambushed the Jeeps from the cover of the bordering treeline. A sharp engagement ensued, during which one man was killed, the Jeeps being forced to withdraw and concentrate at the junction with the track from Schneeren (see Trooper John Glyde's entry within this section). Here it soon became clear that their line of retreat was blocked, infantry attacking from all sides whilst two German armoured cars and a troop carrier advanced from the south. Wellsted later recalled:

Suddenly I saw the armoured cars. There were two big ones and they were coming head on up the track towards the leading Jeep, which was [Lieutenant] Dennis Wainman's [christened 'Just Married' and adorned with a bridal veil and baby's dummy]. They appeared to be firing. Dennis was gallantly firing back …

Meanwhile on the Schneerren lane the unequal contest had played itself out. Dennis Wainman, with Alec Hay and Tpr Blakeney had fired back with their twin Vickers against the 20mm cannon and heavy armour of German six-wheelers, until the enemy were so close that they were throwing hand-grenades from their turrets; until the prisoner still held by the crew was dead; until Blakeney fell mortally wounded; until the riddled Jeep was shot from under them. And then it was that Alec Hay and Dennis escaped into the woods to rejoin in their own time the forces on the cross-roads.

Withdrawing under heavy fire the men were forced to leave some of the wounded behind, Major Harry Poat, MC, later noting:

> I then went and asked for tanks to clear the wood in an attempt to reach Ferguson and Blakeney who had been overrun and captured. This was promised and the time was about 3pm … On approaching the woods we met a Polish POW who told us he had just seen approximately 80/100 SS at Crossroads B [the track/road junction where they had been attacked], five AFVs [Armoured Fighting Vehicles] and two British wounded being quite well looked after. It was not until about 7pm that the tanks arrived, but the Jerry had gone. We however recovered the bodies of Blakeney and Glyde, and had a burial service next day [WO 218/119].

Poat, who commanded Archway's 1st SAS detachment, wrote to the Regimental Adjutant four days later: 'Tpr Blakeney killed. Shot through stomach and head.'

Son of James and Ada Blakeney (née Venney) of Grimsby Road, Cleethorpes, Lincolnshire – Brother of Nancy, Jack and Joan Blakeney.
Age 25.
Deep in our hearts a memory is left of one we loved and will never forget
Grave 15.B.2. Also commemorated on his parents' headstone in Cleethorpes.

Private Samuel COOPER [3974769] Welch Regiment, Parachute Regiment and 1st SAS (B Sqn)

Sammy Cooper was born on 27 January 1923 at Crewe in Cheshire. Having worked as an apprentice metal worker he enlisted into the Welch Regiment in mid February 1941, joining the 70th (Home Defence) Battalion at Manor House, Sandy in Bedfordshire. He transferred to the Army Air Corps in March 1943 and was posted to the Airborne Forces Depot before attending parachute course 59 at No.1 PTS Ringway.

Disembarking in North Africa in May 1941, Cooper spent a brief period at an infantry replacement training depot before joining the depleted 2nd Battalion, the Parachute Regiment, in June. The following month this unit was tasked with holding the southern approaches to Primosole Bridge on the east coast of Sicily during Operation Husky: dropped on the night of 13–14 July over a wide area, and without most of their equipment containers, only a fraction of the men collected at the battalion RV to take up defensive positions by first light. Although the 1st Battalion had successfully captured the bridge, the 3rd Battalion was so scattered that its task of holding the northern approaches proved impossible. At 0600hrs Cooper's 2nd Battalion was attacked by German paratroops and required naval gunfire to hold its positions. Radio contact with the advancing Allies was lost four hours later and the remnants of the 1st and 3rd Battalions were forced to withdraw to the south side of the bridge in the early evening.

Overnight they were obliged to retire once again, this time to the 2nd Battalion that, although hard-pressed by the enemy, had held its own. The first British tanks had arrived from the south that evening, with more arriving the following morning, supported by infantry. By the 19th the brigade's survivors had been withdrawn to Tunisia.

Although the reasons are unknown, Cooper was admitted to the 97th British General Hospital at Birine, Algeria, at the beginning of August and transferred to the 104th British General Hospital at Philippeville until the end of September. Having returned to his battalion, which was now advancing north from Taranto up the east coast of Italy, the 1st Airborne Division was recalled to the UK at the end of November. Once home he volunteered for 1st SAS on 12 March 1944.

After D-Day Cooper took part in B Squadron's OPERATION HAGGARD around Bourges in the Cher département of central France: parachuting into a DZ near Villequiers on the night of 18–19 August 1944, the squadron carried out a series of ambushes and cut the Vierzon–Orléans railway line. In addition, it blew two canal bridges on the night of the 25–26th during a joint attack with elements of both the 3rd (French) SAS and the Maquis for the loss of one man (see Corporal John Wilkinson's entry within this volume under Villequiers Communal Cemetery, France). The Bourges–Nevers line was then cut and fuel dropped, this being given to a Jeep column of 4th (French) SAS before the elements of 3rd SAS moved off for OPERATION MOSES. Cooper's party was withdrawn to refit at Briare on 9 September and, having driven north to Belgium, B Squadron eventually returned to the UK on 5 March 1945.

The following month Cooper deployed once more to North West Europe during OPERATION HOWARD: B and C Squadrons left Tilbury on the morning of 6 April, the combined force disembarking at Ostend the following day. Pushing forward to its operational area, it was tasked as the spearhead to the 4th Canadian Armoured Division on its advance towards Wilhelmshaven. The topography ahead was boggy, criss-crossed with dykes and canals, with its numerous culverts and bridges having been prepared for demolition by the enemy. It was not, therefore, anywhere near ideal for Jeep operations. However, the two squadrons advanced along parallel roads, making contact with each other at pre-arranged RVs. B Squadron was ambushed on the 10th, Major Dick Bond and his driver, Trooper Michael Lewis, being killed and several others wounded (see entries for Bond and Lewis under Sage War Cemetery, Germany). Lt-Colonel Paddy Mayne, DSO**, personally restored the situation (winning his fourth DSO in the process) and subsequently directed operations. Deciding that the enemy was stronger than first thought,

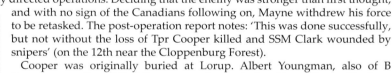

and with no sign of the Canadians following on, Mayne withdrew his force to be retasked. The post-operation report notes: 'This was done successfully, but not without the loss of Tpr Cooper killed and SSM Clark wounded by snipers' (on the 12th near the Cloppenburg Forest).

Cooper was originally buried at Lorup. Albert Youngman, also of B Squadron, confirmed that Cooper was shot in the head by a Werewolf sniper, a member of the German Resistance movement, and that Nobby Clarke, the Squadron Sergeant-Major whose Jeep Cooper had been driving, was wounded at the same time [personal interview, 2011].

Son of George and Emily Cooper (née Robinson) of Brownedge, Brereton, near Sandbach, Cheshire – Brother of Harold Cooper.
Age 22.
Time heals our griefs but memories take their place
Grave 10.A.4. Also commemorated on Brereton Heath's war memorial.

Private Roy David **DAVIES** [2734997] Welsh Guards, No.8 Commando, L Detachment SAS Brigade and 1st SAS (A Sqn)

Roy Davies was born on 24 February 1915 in Plymouth but later lived in Birkenhead on the Wirral where he married Elizabeth May Glover in September 1937. As an unemployed general labourer he enlisted into the Welsh Guards in October 1939. Unfortunately, it was not recorded in which battalion he served and it is therefore impossible to say whether he saw action with the BEF in France. What is certain is that having volunteered for special service he was posted to 5 Troop, No.8 (Guards) Commando, in August 1940 and embarked for Egypt at the end of January 1941.

That May, whilst serving as batman to Lieutenant Jock Lewes, Davies took part in the first parachuting experiments to be carried out in the Middle East. Guardsman D'Arcy's account highlights the pioneering, and often Heath Robinson, aspects of such training:

> Having been frustrated in his plans for a seaborne operation, Lt J. S. Lewes, Welsh Guards, decided to try it by parachute. He and his party first went to RAF HQ located somewhere near Fuka. There he discussed the details with an RAF officer, who, although none of the party had jumped before, was most helpful. He showed us the parachutes we were to use. From the logbooks we saw that the last periodical examination had been omitted but Lt Lewes decided that they were OK. Next day, along with Lt Stirling and Sgt Stone who were hoping to do a job in Syria, we made a trial flight. The plane used was a Vickers 'Valencia'. We threw out a dummy made from sandbags and tent poles. The parachute opened OK but the tent poles were smashed on landing. Afterwards we tried a 10ft jump from the top of the plane and then a little parachute control.
>
> The following afternoon we flew inland in the 'Valencia' which was used to deliver mail. We reached the landing field towards dusk, landed, fitted on our parachutes and decided to jump in the failing light. We were told to jump in pairs, Lt Lewes and his servant, Guardsman Davies first, the RAF officer was to despatch. The instructions were to dive out as though going into water. We hooked ourselves up, circled the field, and on a signal from the RAF officer, Lt Lewes and Davies dived out. Next time round I dived out and was surprised to see Lt Stirling pass me in the air. Lt Lewes made a perfect landing, next came Davies a little shaken. Lt Stirling injured his spine and also lost his sight for about an hour, next myself, a little shaken and a few scratches, and lastly Sgt Stone who seemed OK. Gdsm Evans was unable to jump as the pilot decided to land owing to the approaching darkness. We slept on the landing field. Next morning we jumped again, this time a stick of four, preceded by a bundle to represent a container. The previous night we had worn KD [Khaki Drill] shirts and shorts, but from experience we decided to put on pullovers. We wore no hats. We pushed the bundle out first and Gdsn Evans, myself Davies and Lt Lewes followed as quickly as possible. The first three landed quite close to each other and doubled forward to the container but Lt Lewes in trying to avoid some oil barrels, rather badly injured his spine, Gdsn Evans also hurt his ankle. Sgt Stone jumped after us, landed OK [WO 201/785].

David Stirling's subsequent period of hospitalisation led to his conception of the Special Air Service, Davies becoming one of his original volunteers for L Detachment, SAS Brigade. He subsequently parachuted behind the lines in Libya during a heavy storm on the night of 16–17 November 1941 for Operation Squatter. This, the first raid mounted by the SAS, targeted enemy aircraft on the landing grounds at Tmimi and Gazala and was timed to coincide with the British offensive, Operation Crusader. As a member of No.2 Section of Lieutenant Eoin McGonigal's D Group, Davies was present when McGonigal and Lance-corporal Sidney Hildreth died of injuries sustained in this drop (see their entries under Alamein Memorial, Egypt, Volume I). He was subsequently captured south-west of Tobruk on the 23rd whilst walking towards an LRDG rendezvous on the coast, probably with Parachutist Jim Blakeney (see his entry within this section). Taken to Derna for interrogation, he was moved to a local prison, then to Benghazi, transported aboard an Italian cruiser to Taranto in Italy, and finally to a POW camp in Bari. Admitted to hospital with gunshot wounds to his arm, he was moved to another hospital in Piacenza in late December, although it is not known whether he received these wounds on Squatter or during an attempted escape. Having been discharged in March 1942 he was held in POW camps No.52 at Chiavari, No.59 at Servigliano (from where a tunnel he was working on was discovered) and No.146 at Mortara where he worked on a farming detail. A report based on Davies' own statement notes:

> On June 8th [sic – September 8th] he escaped and made his way south hoping to get away by boat but found it was not possible so he travelled by train north to Como and made his way to the Swiss frontier and crossed near Horia.

He crossed the frontier on 26th of October, 1943, and was taken to a British camp, Negerstein. He was in Switzerland until his repatriation in October, 1944, when he returned to UK via Algiers [WO 208/4247].

His own report states that his party: 'remained at 6 Rio del Fiori, until 23-10-43. Went to farm whose owner arranged for our journey to Switzerland, also arranged for guide who took us via Milan, Como, and crossed the frontier near Chiasso' (WO 208/4247).

At home Davies rejoined 1st SAS and was posted to A Squadron. Lt-Colonel Paddy Mayne, DSO*, the Regiment's Commanding Officer, was keen to have him back, as with Blakeney. He was deployed to Germany for OPERATION ARCHWAY in March 1945 as a member of a combined force of 1st and 2nd SAS tasked to provide short-range Jeep reconnaissance for the British advance. His troop, under the command of Captain Ian Wellsted, was ambushed on 8 April 1945 north of the village of Schneeren on the Neustadt–Nienburg road. Finding themselves surrounded they were attacked from the south by German armoured cars and infantry. Blakeney was mortally wounded in the first Jeep, quickly followed by Davies in the third, the latter taking cover beneath his vehicle. Wellsted attempted to rescue him, later recalling:

> As I passed [Sergeant] Tom Rennie's Jeep, lying derelict by the roadside, I heard Davies groaning beneath it. I lay down beside him and he asked for Morphine. He was obviously badly hit and I pulled out my first aid kit and extracting the Morphine vial injected the soothing liquid into his wrist.
>
> He begged me to bring up a Jeep and get him out, but not appreciating the dangers of the difficulty, I promised we'd do all we could for him.
>
> 'Don't worry Backhouse', I said. 'We'll soon have you out of there.' Davies smiled, 'Even at a moment like this you can't get my name right, can you, Sir?'

Wellsted soon became a casualty himself and was dragged, badly wounded, back to his troop. Although warned of the danger, Troopers Dougie Ferguson and Lofty Jemson, DCM, moved forward to extract Davies. Caught in heavy fire, Ferguson was himself wounded and captured, Jemson being forced to return alone. Eventually the troop withdrew, begrudgingly leaving Troopers Glyde, Blakeney, Ferguson and Davies behind. Major Harry Poat, MC, who commanded ARCHWAY's 1st SAS detachment, later wrote to the Regimental Adjutant:

> I then went and asked for tanks to clear the wood in an attempt to reach Ferguson and Blakeney [Ferguson and Davies] who had been overrun and captured. This was promised and the time was about 3pm … On approaching the woods we met a Polish POW who told us he had just seen approximately 80/100 SS at Crossroads B [the crossroads where the action had occurred], five AFVs [Armoured Fighting Vehicles] and two British wounded being quite well looked after. It was not until about 7pm that the tanks arrived, but the Jerry had gone. We however recovered the bodies of Blakeney and Glyde, and had a burial service the next day. Later when the town of Nienburg fell we

reached the hospital and found the body of Davies in a coffin. He was buried with the other two. Nienburg was the SS HQ: We guessed they were taken there, and it was there we received the news about Ferguson [WO 218/119 – see Ferguson's entry within this volume under Groesbeek Memorial, Netherlands, for further detail].

Although it is unclear exactly when Davies died he is officially recorded as having been killed in action on 8 April 1945.

Son of Mr and Mrs Davies (née Huxham) – Husband of Elizabeth May Davies of Wilmer Road, Birkenhead.
Age 30.
At the going down of the sun and in the morning we will remember him
Grave 15.B.1.

Sergeant Edwin John <u>DOBSON</u> [12958] Nelson and Marlborough Mounted Rifles, Divisional Cavalry Regiment and LRDG (R.2 Patrol, A Sqn)

Ted Dobson was born on 15 August 1910 in Blenheim on the South Island of New Zealand. Whilst working under his older brother, Bruce, the head shepherd at Molesworth Station near to the Ure River, he served for five years in the Territorial Nelson and Marlborough Mounted Rifles. After the outbreak of war he enlisted at Wellington in May 1940, attending a signals course at Trentham during June. Promoted to lance-corporal the following month having followed Bruce into the Divisional Cavalry Regiment at Burnham, he disembarked in Egypt that December and reverted to the rank of trooper during a brief period at a composite training depot. On rejoining the Divisional Cavalry he was sent to Greece in March 1941 as part of Operation Lustre, a bid to counter the forthcoming German invasion. When this assault fell, Commonwealth and Greek forces were quickly overrun, the Dobson brothers, like hundreds of others, being evacuated to Egypt where they were reported safe during mid May. Here Ted attended a course in armoured vehicle fighting at the Royal Armoured Corps School before being promoted to lance-corporal once again that October.

Following repeated periods in military hospitals suffering from amoebic dysentery, Dobson volunteered for the Long Range Desert Group on 19 July 1942, reverting to the rank of trooper in order to serve alongside Bruce in A Squadron. His own patrol, R.2 under Lieutenant John Talbot, was soon tasked with watching the northern approaches to Jalo Oasis in Libya but on 19 September was caught in the open and bombed and strafed by enemy aircraft. Dobson and six others were wounded and treated at No.1 NZ General Hospital, Kufra. He was presently joined by Bruce, soon to be awarded the Military Medal for his actions on Operation Caravan, a raid on the Italian-held airfield and town of Barce, during which he immobilised a tank with a grenade and was wounded. The brothers were discharged at the beginning of October. According to Bruce's daughter, Marjiee Dobson, the: 'Dobson boys were renowned for their, shall we say, "colourful" language in the thick of battle and were very loyal to their fellow soldiers … Ted and my father were particularly close (both being somewhat the "larrikins" of the family)' (personal correspondence, 2014).

In June 1943, with hostilities in North Africa at an end, Bruce returned to New Zealand on furlough and was later medically discharged. Another brother, David, had arrived in the region that January and had already been wounded during March whilst fighting with the infantry in Tunisia. Meanwhile Ted was promoted once again to lance-corporal and attended a mountain warfare course at The Cedars in Lebanon during July. David joined the squadron on being discharged from a field ambulance in August. The following month Ted was advanced to sergeant, the brothers subsequently deploying on operations in the Dodecanese. By the beginning of October they were on Leros.

Later that month, HMS *Hedgehog*, a trawler of the Levant Schooner Flotilla, resupplied an LRDG patrol on the island of Stampalia and embarked German POWs for her return passage to Leros. Developing engine trouble, German air reconnaissance noted that she had put into the small island of Levita for repairs and on 18 October Brandenburger parachutists subsequently mounted a rescue mission. Having released their comrades and captured both *Hedgehog's* British crew and Italians based at the island's wireless station, the Brandenburgers were replaced by a Luftwaffe detachment. Back on Leros it became clear that all was not well, Brigadier 'Ben' Brittorous, DSO, MC, ordering members of the LRDG, including Dobson, to retake Levita. This party, collectively known as Olforce after its commander Captain John Olivey, MC, landed on the evening of the 23rd, having been denied the opportunity to recce enemy dispositions. Lt-Commander Frank Ramseyer, Royal Navy Liaison Officer to Raiding Forces, subsequently reported:

Information indicated that only 20–30 Germans were on Levita and LRDG considered that a force of 47 troops should be able to deal with the situation.

The landing went according to plan and the LRDG were landed in two parties, one in the west and one in the south of the island. The MLs [motor launches] withdrawing and later bombarding areas where the enemy were reported to be concentrating. After completing their part of the operation the MLs returned to Leros.

Unfortunately the following morning the Germans contacted their air force in Cos and were able to attack LRDG units [that had occupied strategic high points] from the air before they had established themselves, and later in the day the enemy took control.

On the night of 24/25th ML 579 with Major Easonsmith, LRDG, [see his entry under Leros War Cemetery, Greece, Volume II] returned to Levita and recovered seven of their personnel, who described the above incidents …

Altogether the operation was very disappointing and proved once again the importance of air superiority, even where small forces are employed.

Dobson was captured during this operation on the 25th, LRDG Newsletter No.39 of 1983 noting: 'In the centre was Sergeant E J Dobson with the solitary Bren gun, a Tommy gun and the bulk of the men with rifles.' He was subsequently taken to Germany and held as POW number 35876 at Stalag VIIIb at Lamsdorf. Towards the end of January 1945 he and his fellow inmates were forced to march west, away from the advancing Russian Army, through appalling weather conditions. Albert Badman, a fellow New Zealand prisoner, later stated that he:

> … saw the said deceased [Dobson] from time to time during the march. He was suffering from dysentery. For the last fortnight of the march towards the end of the month of March, 1945, we were walking together most of the time …
>
> About the end of March, 1945, we reached a place called Duderstadt, which was a sort of clearing station. Soon after my arrival I was removed to the building that served as a hospital and was joined there by said deceased on the 5th day of April, 1945 …
>
> The said deceased was placed next to me on the ground and in the morning of the 6th day of April, 1945, he was found to be dead.

Dobson's remains were moved from Duderstadt Cemetery to their current location on 30 May 1947.

Predeceased by his parents Henry and Emily Dobson (née Cawte) of Blenheim, Marlborough, New Zealand – Younger brother of Thomas (Bruce) Dobson of Seddon who, according to his daughter, 'learned of Ted's death and never (I believe) completely got over it' (personal correspondence, 2014) – Older brother of Bob Dobson of Oamaru, Lucy Dobson of Blenheim and of David Dobson of Napier who was discharged, having fought through the Italian Campaign. Another younger brother, Flight Sergeant Peter Dobson, RNZAF, a navigator of 75 (NZ) Squadron, RAF, was killed in an explosion in September 1943 whilst attempting to rescue the crew of a crashed Stirling bomber. He is buried at Cambridge City Cemetery in the UK and was posthumously mentioned in despatches.
Age 34.
No inscription.
Grave 9.A.12. Also commemorated on the LRDG memorial within the New Zealand SAS camp at Papakura, on his parents' headstone at Omaka No.3 Lawn Cemetery, Blenheim, and on Blenheim's war memorial.

PRIVATE TIMOTHY JOSEPH **FIELD** [1525892] ROYAL ARTILLERY, ARMY AIR CORPS AND 1ST SAS (A SQN)

Joe Field was born on 26 October 1919 to Irish parents who had recently moved to Islington, north London, from Cork. In January 1937 his father, who had lost the use of an arm during the First World War, died of pneumonia brought on by exposure to gas attacks. His younger sister, Ellen, also succumbed to a lung-related illness a few months later.

Field, an apprentice printer and keen ballroom dancer and accordion player, enlisted into the Royal Artillery in February 1940. Posted to the 51st Anti-Tank Training Regiment, he qualified as a fire control operator before joining the 158th Battery, 53rd Anti-Aircraft Regiment. He served with this battery in the BEF at Juvincourt near Rheims from May 1940 until his evacuation from St Nazaire the following month. Posted to the Anti-Aircraft School at Manorbier in Pembrokeshire, he joined the 5th Heavy Anti-Aircraft Training & Practice Camp in April 1942. That August he was re-posted to the 121st HAA Regiment and awarded eight days detention during September 1943 for being AWOL whilst his mother was ill. She died at the beginning of November.

Having been briefly posted to the 198th HAA Regiment during March 1944, Field joined the 86th HAA Regiment the same month. He qualified as a parachutist on 4 April, transferred to the Army Air Corps eight days later and was posted to the Airborne Forces Holding Unit late the following month. Although he volunteered for 2nd SAS on 11 July he was taken on strength by 1st SAS the next day.

Field served in North West Europe with the Regiment from 13 to 25 September 1944 and although it is not certain on which operation, it is likely it was to reinforce HOUNDSWORTH that had suffered casualties. He deployed for OPERATION ARCHWAY in Germany on 18 March 1945. Having crossed the Rhine on the 25th elements of 1st and 2nd SAS, collectively known as Frankforce, were tasked with providing short-range Jeep reconnaissance for the British advance. Field was killed in action on 8 April whilst doing so, the post-operation report stating that M Troop's eleven Jeeps, under the command of Major John Tonkin, MC, were:

> … detailed to assist a troop of The Inns of Court [Regiment] on flank reconnaissance. At m.r. [map reference] 015335 the leading Dingo [scout car] received a near miss from a Panzerfaust [a German hand-held, anti-tank weapon] which forced it and the following vehicle into a ditch, their crews baling out. The two leading sections under command of Lieut [Pat] Riley [DCM] and Lieut [J. P.] Jenson immediately went forward under heavy and accurate

> sniping fire from well camouflaged positions on the edge of the wood, m.r. 012339, and some gorse on the left flank. They neutralised several enemy positions and enabled the remaining armoured cars to evacuate the crews of the two Dingos. The troop then deployed across the fields to the edge of the wood which was swept with Vickers and .5 [machine-gun fire]. Two groups of enemy positions and several snipers hidden in the tops of trees were knocked out. By this time the tanks had come up and the troop moved back to the road and continued with a new troop of The Inns of Court which had come up to replace the first. While the Jeeps were held up by a traffic jam of tanks the rear gunner of Lieut Jensen's Jeep, Tpr Field, was killed by a sniper [WO 218/199].

Son of Thomas and Mary Field (née Santry) of Noel Road, Islington, north London – Younger brother of twins Maureen and Denis (who died at a young age before Joe was born) – Predeceased by his younger sister, Ellen Field – Fiancé of Saby (surname unknown) of Chelmsford.

Age 25.

No inscription.

Grave 16.A.8. Originally buried at Rehburg and reinterred here on 8 November 1946.

Private John James <u>Glyde</u> [3963198] Welch Regiment, Auxiliary Units and 1st SAS (A Sqn)

'Taffy' Glyde was born on 30 December 1919 in the village of Norton Bridge near Pontypridd, south Wales. During May 1939, whilst working as a factory hand, he followed his brother Emlyn into the local 5th (Glamorgan) Battalion, Welch Regiment (TA). Called up at the outbreak of war that September, he was posted to HQ Auxiliary Units in January 1942. Three months later he married Joan Allen, with his brother, who was serving with the 1st Battalion, Parachute Regiment, acting as a witness. That November Emlyn was killed in action in Tunisia by an enemy aircraft and is now buried at Beja War Cemetery. The following April Glyde was nominally posted to the 4th Battalion, Welch Regiment, his son, John Edward, being born three months later. Re-posted to the 21st Infantry Training Centre in November 1943, he volunteered for 1st SAS on 1 February 1944 when the anti-invasion role of the Auxiliaries was deemed no longer necessary. He subsequently attended parachute course 105 at No.1 PTS Ringway the following month, his instructor noting that he was 'parachuting well up to standard' with 'plenty of confidence'.

Shortly after D-Day Glyde took part in Operation Houndsworth, jumping into a DZ at Les Vellottes in the Morvan region of central France on the night of 21–22 June 1944. His stick, under the command of Captain Roy Bradford, was initially taken to the Bois de Montsauche to join the Maquis Bernard before being transported in buses to the operation's other DZ and camp at Vieux Dun (see Bradford's entry within this volume under Crain Community Cemetery, France). On 10 July Glyde, with Lieutenant 'Cocky' Trower and ten others, joined Captain John Wiseman's camp at Rolle, 19 kilometres south-west of Dijon. The party subsequently cut the Dijon–Paris and Dijon–Beaune railway lines on numerous occasions, derailing two trains in the process. On the 23rd they moved 5 kilometres closer to Dijon to join a group of Maquis at Urcy. However, the combined party was attacked by the Milice, German-backed Vichy French paramilitaries, at the end of the month and broke contact whilst their enemies mistakenly fought each other. Having returned to their previous camp they blew the line again, destroying a gasogene wood factory at Malain and derailing another train on the night of 18 August. Moving to the north of Dijon the party concentrated on arming and training a more competent Maquis in the Bois de Martiere, as well as two other local groups. They returned to the main Houndsworth party on the 31st, the operation now drawing to a close. Wiseman's men, including Glyde, subsequently drove through the lines in civilian vehicles and were flown to the UK from Orléans on 6 September.

Glyde was deployed to Germany on 18 March 1945 for Operation Archway, tasked with providing short-range reconnaissance to the Allied advance as a member of Captain Ian Wellsted's reserve troop. He was killed in action on 8 April north of Schneeren (see Trooper Jim Blakeney's entry above for details up until this point). Having turned off a track onto the road towards Nienburg the troop was ambushed,  Wellsted later recalling its withdrawal:

> But one Jeep did not move. It rested where it had been hit, a thin column of smoke still curling up from its wreckage. As we went by, I could see Glyde the gunner, one of my original section that I had had when I first joined the SAS. He was sprawled on his face in a grotesque attitude, and beneath his head the dark blood had puddled and was beginning to run down into the gutter. With a tragic irony his favourite expression crossed my mind, 'Another Redskin bit the dust!', and now the bloody tarmac pressed against his mouth.

After a protracted engagement, which resulted in the deaths of Troopers Jim Blakeney, Roy Davies and Dougie Ferguson, the SAS Jeeps finally broke contact. Major Harry Poat, MC, the commander of the 1st SAS column, returned to the scene of the action that evening and recovered the bodies of Glyde and Blakeney (see Ferguson's entry within this volume under Groesbeek Memorial, Netherlands). Writing to the Regimental Adjutant four days later Poat noted: 'Tpr Glyde killed. German Bazooka landed about 2 yards from his Jeep. His head nearly blown off' (WO 218/119).

Son of Mr and Mrs Glyde (née Durbin) – Husband of Joan Glyde of Park View, Abercynon, Pontypridd, south Wales – Father of John Glyde – Older brother of Emlyn, Joan and Robert Glyde.
Age 25.
No inscription.
Grave 15.B.3. Also commemorated, alongside Emlyn, on Pontypridd's war memorial.

REICHSWALD FOREST WAR CEMETERY

This is the largest Commonwealth cemetery within Germany. Many of those buried here took part in OPERATION VARSITY, *the airborne assault to 'jump the Rhine' on 24 March 1945. After the war, graves were concentrated from all over western Germany, the cemetery now containing 7,595 Commonwealth burials, 176 of which are unidentified. In addition, there are seventy-eight war graves of other nationalities.*

The cemetery is located 4 kilometres from the German/Dutch border and 5 kilometres south-west of Kleve on Grunewaldstraße (the L484). GPS co-ordinates: Latitude 51.74094, Longitude 6.08179

PRIVATE VINCENT **ANDREWS** [14526586] GENERAL SERVICE CORPS, ROYAL ARMY ORDNANCE CORPS, ARMY AIR CORPS AND 1ST SAS (A SQN)

Vince Andrews was born on 14 July 1924 at Pontypridd, south Wales, but later lived at Hillingdon in Middlesex where he worked as an HGV driver. He enlisted into the General Service Corps in February 1943 and was briefly posted to No.23 Primary Training Centre. The following month he transferred to the Royal Army Ordnance Corps and was re-posted to Knutsford. That July he arrived at Tatton Park, this being used by Airborne Forces as a DZ. Although later posted away, he transferred to the Army Air Corps on 19 April 1944 and after a period at the Airborne Forces Depot at Hardwick Hall near Chesterfield he attended parachute course 117 at No.1 PTS, Ringway. Here his instructor noticed that he was 'nervous of previous knee injury – made him inclined to be hesitant'. Despite this, Andrews qualified and was posted to the Airborne Forces Holding Unit in June.

Although he volunteered for 2nd SAS on 11 July 1944, Andrews was posted to 1st SAS the following day. He subsequently took part in OPERATION HOUNDSWORTH, parachuting into a DZ near Montsauche in the Morvan region of central France on the night of 26–27 August under the command of SSM

Cyril Feebery, DCM. Tasked with assisting A Squadron and the Maquis Bernard in harassing enemy lines of communication, the Regiment's more seasoned veterans were sceptical of such inexperienced reinforcements. Feebery was therefore given free rein to take Andrews and the rest of the newcomers and cause as much trouble as possible. The group soon became known as 'Feebery's Marauders', frequently ambushing German troops, before returning to the UK the following month at the end of the operation.

Having embarked for Europe on 19 March 1945, Andrews took part in OPERATION ARCHWAY as a member of C Troop of Frankforce, a combined 1st and 2nd SAS contingent tasked with providing short-range Jeep reconnaissance for the British advance. Crossing the Rhine at Bislich near Wesel on 25 March, his troop reached the village of Östrich on the 28th. Here they met three British tanks and a scout car and after a quick exchange it was decided to continue the advance together. After only 50 yards an anti-tank weapon knocked out the scout car. This initiated an ambush during which Andrews was fatally wounded in the neck and lung. Captain Ian Wellsted, the troop commander, later recalled:

> Grundy, Red's [Lieutenant 'Red' Hunter] rear gunner had been shot in the body and was in considerable pain. Andrews, the front gunner, was grey in the face and bleeding badly from a nasty wound in the throat. I did what I could to cheer them up and reported to Major Poat who had now come forward. The ambulance came up close behind him and the wounded were got away.

Although evacuated to the 24th Field Dressing Station, Andrews died of his wounds on 31 March 1945. Originally buried at Dreveneck he was reinterred here on 30 April 1947 and posthumously awarded a Commander-in-Chief's Certificate for Gallantry (21AG GROS 96 1422, dated 20 July 1945).

Son of Harry and Beatrice Andrews (née March) of Pield Heath Avenue, Hillingdon, Middlesex.
Age 20.
We miss you because we love you; to us you were dearer than gold
Grave 34.D.2.

Sage War Cemetery

The majority of the servicemen buried here were aircrew lost during bombing raids over northern Germany, their graves having been concentrated from surrounding areas since the end of the war. The cemetery contains 948 Commonwealth burials of which 158 are unidentified. In addition, there are twenty-three non-Commonwealth graves.

Sage is located 22 kilometres south of Oldenburg, the cemetery being situated 1 kilometre south of the village. GPS co-ordinates: Latitude 52.93685, Longitude 8.20857

Major Charles Frederick Gordon **Bond** [50968] Wiltshire Regiment, Auxiliary Units and 1st SAS (B Sqn)

Known to his friends as Dick, Charles Bond was born on 26 July 1911 in Dublin where his father was serving with the 2nd Battalion, Wiltshire Regiment (Duke of Edinburgh's). Four years later his father was killed in action in France, his mother remarrying and moving the family from Bude, Cornwall, to Forest Row in East Sussex. Bond's early life was spent here until taking up residence with his uncle at Whorridge Farm near Cullompton in Devon. Having been educated at Harrow from 1925 to 1930 as a member of Druries House, he entered the Royal Military College Sandhurst and was commissioned into his father's regiment during January 1932 (*London Gazette* 29/01/32). Initially posted to the 2nd Battalion at Crownhill, he was re-posted to the 1st and embarked for Singapore in February 1933 to serve in Malaya and India. In January 1935 he married Evelyn Hinchcliff at Instow, the couple honeymooning in Scotland. Two years later he relinquished his regular commission and returned permanently to the UK to farm at Cullompton whilst holding the rank of lieutenant in a reserve of officers.

Bond was mobilised at the outbreak of war and, after a period as Adjutant to the St Nazaire garrison, served with D Company, 2nd Battalion, as a member of the BEF. He was promoted to captain during this period and twice mentioned in despatches, having seen action at Rœux and almost continuously

during the Wiltshires' withdrawal to Dunkirk (*London Gazettes* 26/07/40 and 20/12/40). He was evacuated on 1 June 1940, a month after his son, Alec Charles, was born, and posted as Adjutant to the regiment's infantry training centre at Devizes.

From September 1941 to August 1942 Bond served as Intelligence Officer to the Sussex Auxiliary Units. His daughter, Robin, was born during this period. From his Headquarters at Totting Manor, Small Dole, near Steyning, he was responsible for a secret network of volunteers formed as Britain's resistance army in the event of invasion. On his appointment there were twenty-one Auxiliary patrols in the county, consisting of 134 men with twenty-eight secret underground hideouts and an additional one being built. Promoted to major, he served as GSO II (Instructor) at HQ Auxiliary Units, probably at the Special Duties Section HQ at Hannington Hall near Coleshill, until late January 1944 when he was appointed GSO I with the acting rank of lieutenant-colonel.

With the threat of invasion abated the Auxiliary Units were disbanded soon after and Bond, like many other Auxiliaries, volunteered for the SAS. He subsequently attended parachute course 119 at No.1 PTS Ringway during June, officially joining 1st SAS on 26 July 1944, shortly after his second son, Colin, was born.

Bond, now a major in C Squadron, flew with his men to Rennes in France on 19 August 1944 for OPERATION KIPLING. They were met by their Commanding Officer, Lt-Colonel Paddy Mayne, DSO*, and tasked with recceing the area north of A Squadron's OPERATION HOUNDSWORTH to extend towards D Squadron's OPERATION GAIN. Due to a lack of fuel they were not able to complete all the tasks allotted to them, but caused considerable damage to the enemy. The squadron eventually reached Brussels to refit at the beginning of October.

In February 1945 Bond took command of B Squadron for OPERATION HOWARD in Germany, B and C Squadrons leaving Tilbury on the morning of 6 April and disembarking at Ostend the following day. Pushing forward to their operational area they formed the spearhead to the 4th Canadian Armoured Division's advance towards Wilhelmshaven. The topography ahead was boggy, criss-crossed with dykes and canals, and its numerous culverts and bridges had been prepared for demolition by the enemy. It was not, therefore, anywhere near ideal for Jeep operations. However, the two squadrons advanced along parallel roads, making contact with each other at pre-arranged RVs.

B Squadron was ambushed on 10 April 1945, men from the lead Jeep being wounded. Having crawled along a roadside ditch to get to his men, Bond lifted his head and was killed by a sniper. Trooper Michael Lewis, his driver, was subsequently killed whilst trying to reach him. Roy Close, a former fellow officer, recalled hearing firing ahead, the report on the intercom that the first Jeep had been ambushed, that Sergeant Joe Schofield had been wounded, and then a few minutes later that Bond had been killed. He saw Mayne, in a 'cold rage', on his way to 'sort things out', earning his fourth DSO in the process of clearing the enemy (personal interview, 2009).

Bond and Lewis were originally buried close to Börgerwald (map reference 846857), Len Owens MM, a Phantom signaller attached to the SAS, later recalling:

> They [Bond and Lewis] were brought back. I was involved in this. We dug a shallow grave at the roadside and they were wrapped in blankets and they were put in there. Paddy Mayne said a few words and somebody found a couple of branches and made them into a cross, bound it together and put it at the head, and then we withdrew into the forest because it was obviously too dangerous for Jeeps to go down there [personal interview, 2010 – see Lewis' entry within this section].

On announcing Bond's death on 2 May 1945 *The Western Morning News* noted:

> He had represented Devon in the South West Counties Golf Championships, tied for the Army Championship in 1930, and before the war was on the committee of the Royal North Devon Golf Club.
> In the spring of 1939 he and his wife, who was formerly Miss Evelyn Hinchliff, of Instow, became joint Masters of the east side of the county of the Stevenstone Hunt. His widow and three children live at Cullompton.

Son of Major Charles and Dorothy Bond (née Pembroke, of The Plottage, Forest Row, East Sussex) – Husband of Evelyn Hinchliff Bond of The Old Rectory, Kilve, Bridgwater, Somerset.

Age 33.

No inscription.

Grave 6.A.11. Also commemorated on war memorials at Cullompton and Harrow School.

Lance-sergeant Alexander DAVIDSON [2886121] Gordon Highlanders, No.11 Commando, Middle East Commando, SRS and 1st SAS (C Sqn)

Known as 'Sandy' to his comrades, Alex Davidson was born on 18 June 1915 at Rosemount in Aberdeen, where, having worked as a railway caster, he enlisted into the Gordon Highlanders in May 1940. That August he volunteered for No.11 (Scottish) Commando, noting in his diary that he embarked on HMS *Glengyle* on the last day of January 1941 and called at Freetown and Cape Town before arriving at Geneifa, Egypt, in mid March. Landing as C Battalion of Layforce, a composite of No.s 7, 8, 11, 50 and 52 Commandos, No.11 sailed for Bardia on the Libyan coast on 18 April in support of what turned out to be an unremarkable raid. Davidson himself referred to it as the 'Bardia Stunt'. Returning to Egypt, the Commando travelled to Palestine, then Cyprus and back to Egypt again. On 6 June it boarded HMS *Glengyle* once again, this time bound for the Syrian coast for Operation Exporter, the campaign against Vichy French forces. Davidson's 8 Troop eventually landed north of the mouth of the Litani River in the early hours of the 9th. As it is unknown which section he was a member

of, little detail of his actions can be ascertained, although the Commando, which incurred heavy losses, successfully tied down the enemy, thus enabling a rapid Australian advance from the south.

Having arrived back in Egypt via Haifa and Cyprus, No.11 was billeted at No.2 Transit Camp at Amriya, spending a brief period in the Western Desert. On 10 November Davidson embarked HM Submarine *Talisman* at Alexandria which deployed to the coast of Libya the following day. Although his diary merely notes that this was for the 'Cerene [Cyrene] Stunt or Rommel job (Libya) 14th & 15th Nov 1941' this refers to Operation Flipper, a landing followed by an attempt to kill or capture Rommel close to his Beda Littoria HQ, timed to coincide with the Allied push, Operation Crusader. Only eight men got ashore from *Talisman* due to high seas and although a detachment did land from a second submarine, HMS *Torbay*, the raid was unsuccessful. That night Rommel was in Athens on his return route from two weeks leave in Rome and all but two of the men who made it ashore were killed or captured. Davidson was one of those unable to land and returned to Egypt.

In January 1942 No.11 Commando was absorbed into the Middle East Commando at Geneifa (later

1st Special Service Regiment), Davidson subsequently taking part in desert patrols behind enemy lines: arriving at the oasis town of Jarabub on 19 March he noted that his party had covered 344 miles (553 kilometres) since leaving Mersa Matruh on the 13th. It was the beginning of April before they were resupplied at Siwa. Setting out again the following day, this time under the guidance of the LRDG's R Patrol, Davidson and his comrades reconnoitred the wadis south of Benghazi before returning to Jarabub and taking a close look at the approaches to Jalo. Evacuated for treatment of an unknown nature on 12 June, he found himself back at Commando Base Depot HQ at Mersa Matruh before taking the train towards Amriya. This was 'bombed and strafed for 5hrs between Mersa & El Daba on the night of the 24th & 25th'. He rejoined C Squadron near Alexandria soon after and 'took up positions to fight as rearguard & against paratroops on Alex' until relieved by Australian troops. Hospitalised for most of July, he was posted to Palestine then Syria that August. The following month he carried out a recce of the Aleppo and Hama region noting: 'Incident while on recce, picked up as German Paratroops on the morning of 22nd Sept 1942 & taken into Dijisur where everything was cleared up.'

Having been admitted with an eye problem to No.3 British General Hospital at Sidon in October 1942, Davidson rejoined his unit at Chekka before volunteering for 1st SAS. He reported to its base at Kabrit in Egypt on 21 December. After a short period of leave in Cairo he began parachute training on 12 January 1943, making four daylight and one night descent from a Lockheed Hudson before qualifying on the 25th. His initial training, consisting of driving courses and mock attacks on airfields, was interrupted by the reorganisation of 1st SAS as the Special Raiding Squadron and he soon found himself a lance-corporal in B Section, No.2 Troop, training in Palestine. Returning to Egypt on 6 June the unit carried out amphibious exercises in the Gulf of Aqaba before embarking the *Ulster Monarch* on 5 July for OPERATION HUSKY, the invasion of Sicily. His diary describes the SRS landing at Capo Murro di Porco in the early hours of the 10th and its assault on the port of Augusta two days later:

> Destroyed four coastal defence guns … during the same day we carried on towards Syracuse clearing up about 18 square miles and destroying an ack ack battery of six guns …
> The same night (12th July) we went in and took the town of Augusta, landing in daylight at 8.30pm. We handed the town over to the 14th Brigade in the morning after having a pretty tough time for a few hours during the night.

Peter Davis, Davidson's former section officer, recalled that on 4 September they were pinned down during OPERATION BAYTOWN at Bagnara on the toe of mainland Italy. With one of their comrades already dead Davidson had tried to shift his cramped legs: The moment he had stretched out his leg a bullet had made a neat little hole through his drill trousers' (*SAS – Men in the Making: An Original's Account of Operations in Sicily and Italy*, by Peter Davis, MC – see Guardsman Charlie Tobin's entry under Bari War Cemetery, Italy, Volume II, for further details of this incident). Modestly Davidson's own diary merely states: 'Stiff resistance from Jerry. Raid lasted 30hrs. Own section pinned for 11hrs … award Operational Wings on 10th Sept 1943.' Hopping from port to port the SRS next saw action at Termoli the following month after which Davidson concluded 'heavy casualties but job successful' (see multiple entries within Volume II under Sangro River War Cemetery, Italy, for details).

Having completed operations in Italy the SRS embarked for Britain in November 1943 stopping at Bizerte, 2nd SAS' camp at Philippeville and Algiers where Davidson spent a day with his brother Bill who was serving with the RAMC. On Christmas Day the unit embarked once more, weighed anchor on Boxing Day, and arrived in the UK on 5 January 1944. After a month's leave he reported to the reconstituted 1st SAS at Darvel in Scotland, undertaking 'intensive training and doing day and night jumps from the Albemarle'. He was promoted to corporal on 27 April, noting a few weeks later:

> Married 8th June at Brinchburgh Old Parish Church to the sweetest girl in the world [Elsie Williams, a widowed WAAF that he had met in Edinburgh] … left Darvel on the 17th June for Fairford Glo England [the pre-D-Day Gloucestershire holding camp known as 'The Cage'] arriving on the 18th June … left Blighty for France on 28th August 1944 by Dakota and landed same day at Orleans [with C Squadron]. From there carried on to Ouzouer-sur-Loire 50 miles east-south-east of Orleans.

Davidson's Jeep-borne squadron infiltrated enemy lines and made its way to the area south of Avallon where it was to join the advance elements of OPERATION KIPLING. Arriving in A Squadron's HOUNDSWORTH operational area on the 29th, it moved to its own camp on 5 September, Davidson noting: 'Camp more or less surrounded by Boche on 7th Sept but managed to get away.' Over the following month the men took up where their sister squadron had left off, working in small groups to continuously harass the enemy's lines of communication. On 2 October, with the Germans in full retreat, and with Davidson having been confirmed as lance-sergeant the day before, the squadron travelled by Jeep to Brussels. Here his patrol was responsible for crossing into Occupied Holland to detain key collaborators. The following three months were intermittently spent on such incursions, one of which saw elements of the squadron infiltrate to within a mile of the German border. Davidson's daughter, Maureen, was born on 9 January, his patrol pushing into Germany the following day. After a period at Antwerp 'for defence of town & districts, average of 60 fly bombs – V1 & V2 – per day' the squadron embarked at Ostend on 6 March, arriving at Tilbury the following morning. Briefly settling into the Regiment's new camp at Hylands House near Chelmsford, Davidson was granted four weeks leave. His diary stops here.

Alec 'Boy' Borrie, a member of Davidson's patrol, later recalled that this leave was cut short by telegrams sent to all squadron members. Davidson returned three days later and, according to Borrie, told his officer, Lieutenant Roy Close: 'I didn't know whether to come back for this one or not. I don't fancy it' (personal interview, 2010). Borrie later wrote:

> A few days later, having checked the Jeeps and guns we were on our way [to Germany for OPERATION HOWARD]. I had a new partner this time, Sergeant Alexander (Sandy) Davidson from Aberdeen who had been in the SAS from its early days in the North African desert. He had not long been married and had a very young baby daughter, and he was not happy about going into action again so soon after the baby was born.
>
> One morning the handbrake of the Jeep jammed on and started smoking, and while Chris [Tilling] and I were chopping it free Sandy started complaining that it was wrong to expect married men to take part in the actual fighting. Soon after this [on 14 April 1945] the squadron lost the leading Jeep when it ran over a mine buried in the gravel road. It was only a small mine and no one was badly hurt. [There was a] road to the right also gravel with a set of tyre tracks running to a farmhouse about half a mile away. Roy Close told me to drive to the farm and see if the road carried on past it. I started off and about half way Sandy said we should be driving in the tyre tracks that were already there. I did this and after about 25yds there was a mighty flash and the Jeep rose in the air. The next thing I knew I was sitting in the field at the side of the road in perfect peace and quiet not realising that the blast had made me deaf. My hearing soon came back and I saw smoke rising from a hole in the road and what was left of the Jeep. Sandy was the worst hurt mostly in the legs … when we arrived at the casualty clearing station they took Sandy to one side and covered him with a blanket and told us he had died most probably from shock [Alec Borrie's private memoirs 'The Life So Far of Alexander Campbell Borrie'].

Borrie and Trooper Freddy Caldwell, who had been seated in rear, were both wounded in the blast, Davidson being buried at Meppen Hospital Cemetery. After his parents had been informed his father made the journey from Scotland to London to personally tell Elsie.

Son of Alexander and Jemima Davidson of Dunbar Street, Old Aberdeen – Husband of Elsie Davidson of Courtnell Street, Bayswater, London – Father of Maureen Davidson – Older brother of Bill Davidson.
Age 29.
His work done his cross laid down; Christ has given him his glorious crown
Grave 6.E.6. Reinterred here on 19 August 1947.

Private Thomas Henry <u>Kent</u> [14293591] General Service Corps, Parachute Regiment and 1st SAS (B Sqn)

Tom Kent was born on 2 January 1912 at Kilburn in north London, growing up a short distance away in Edgware. Having worked as a carpenter and joiner he enlisted into the General Service Corps at the beginning of October 1942 and was posted to No.15 Primary Training Centre in York. In March 1943, whilst serving with No.1 Training Battalion, his corps was redesignated the Royal Army Service Corps, although he transferred to the Army Air Corps as a driver that June. The following month he attended parachute course 71 at No.1 PTS Ringway, his report stating 'very good performance – good control – asset in every stick'.

Embarking for North Africa in August 1943, Kent joined the 2nd Battalion, Parachute Regiment, which had incurred heavy casualties during recent operations in Sicily. The 1st Parachute Brigade, of which the 2nd Battalion was a part, subsequently landed at the port of Taranto in southern Italy in September (Operation Slapstick) and was used in an infantry role in the advance northwards. Withdrawn from the line near Foggia the battalion returned to the UK that December, Kent volunteering for 1st SAS on 8 March 1944.

On the night of 10–11 August 1944 Kent parachuted into a DZ west of the Forêt d'Ivoy in the Cher département of central France as a member of Operation Haggard's seven-man advance party. Met by members of SOE's Ventriloquist circuit they conducted a recce of the area before being reinforced by the main party four nights later, and by the remainder of the squadron on the night of 18–19th. Having established a base north of Bourges, B Squadron carried out a series of ambushes on local roads as well as sabotage operations against railway lines. By the time the operation closed on 9 September they had destroyed nearly forty vehicles, killed or wounded over 230 enemy personnel and cut the railway four times. Kent's party subsequently withdrew to Briare to refit before travelling by Jeep to Brussels. He eventually returned to the UK for leave at the beginning of March 1945.

On 6 April 1945 B and C Squadrons left Tilbury, disembarking at Ostend the following day for Operation Howard (see Major Dick Bond's entry for full details). Kent was killed in action on the 29th having stepped on a mine near Westerscheps. That morning Brigadier Mike Calvert, DSO*, the Commander of SAS Troops, had signalled 1st SAS' Commanding Officer, Lt-Colonel Paddy Mayne, DSO**: 'Have sent personal signal CGC CDN Army [Canadian General Commanding, Canadian Army] stating you consider that owing tightness of front, mines and canals you cannot operate efficiently without heavy casualties and that I agree' (AIR 20/8843). That afternoon Mayne signalled back: 'This Sqn now formed into two Inf platoons. Advanced

1 mile today one man killed by mine. Men remarkably cheerful considering all their disappointments in role and country chosen for them.' However, a few hours later he signalled Major Harry Poat, MC, 1st SAS' commander on Operation Archway in a slightly less upbeat tone: 'Tony's Sqn [Major Tony Marsh, DSO, who led both B and C Squadrons during the latter part of the operation] now plodding along through bog and rain on their feet. Tpr Kent killed by a mine. Nobody very happy.' Poat himself had previously signalled: 'This country absolutely bloody to work in. The battle is turning into a slogging match and ourselves into mine detectors' (AIR 20/8843).

Son of Mr and Mrs J. W. Kent (née Walker) of Handel Way, Edgware, Middlesex. Age 33.

No inscription.

Grave 2.C.14. Originally buried 'north-west of Oster-Scheps' until reinterred here on 14 May 1947.

PRIVATE 'MICHAEL LEWIS' – REAL NAME MAX LEWINSOHN [13051348]
PIONEER CORPS, ROYAL ARMOURED CORPS AND 1ST SAS (B SQN)

Max Lewinsohn, a German Jew, was born on 28 April 1921 at Karlsbard in Czechoslovakia, his family being the owners of a glove factory in Johanngeorgenstadt on the German side of the border. Escaping the Nazis, he came to England and settled in Brixton, south London, enlisting into the Pioneer Corps in November 1941 under his real name. He registered his trade as glove cutter (service number 13807050). Posted to No.3 Training Centre at Ilfracombe, home of those pioneer companies formed of foreign 'Aliens', he later changed his name to Michael Lewis and therefore also his service number. In July 1943 he transferred to the Royal Armoured Corps and was posted to the 55th Training Regiment but volunteered for 1st SAS on 2 April 1944. He attended parachute course 111A at No.1 PTS Ringway a few days later, his instructor noting 'performance has been good, quiet but reliable'.

Lewis married Lotte Jelinek, a Czech WAAF, on 26 June 1944 in Cirencester before parachuting into the Cher département of central France on the night of 24–25 August to reinforce B Squadron's OPERATION HAGGARD. By the time it withdrew to refit at Briare on 9 September the squadron had caused considerable damage to the retreating Germans for the loss of one man (see Corporal John Wilkinson's entry within this volume under Villequiers Communal Cemetery, France). The squadron moved to Brussels, and it was not until March 1945 that Lewis' squadron returned to the UK for leave.

The following month B Squadron deployed to Germany for OPERATION HOWARD, Lewis being killed in action on 10 April 1945 whilst serving as Major Dick Bond's Jeep gunner during the advance towards Oldenburg (see Bond's entry within this section for full details). Accounts vary as to the exact circumstances of his death, some men recalling that Lewis was killed whilst trying to reach Bond who had been shot by a sniper, and some noting this was whilst trying to avoid the same fate. According to Len Owens, MM, a Phantom signaller attached to the SAS:

> Major Bond raised his head up to see what was going on and a sniper shot him. Driver Lewis was also in the ditch but there was a big pipe in the middle and he tried to crawl back, and when he got over the top of the pipe, the sniper got him as well [personal interview, 2010].

Son of Ludwig and Fanny Lewinsohn (née Klein) who perished in the concentration camp system along with their daughter (a memorial stone was unveiled in their home town in July 2015) – Husband of Lotte Lewis of Battersea, south London.
Age 23.
Rest in peace
Grave 6.A.12. Lewinsohn was originally buried alongside Bond close to the village of Börgerwald.

NETHERLANDS

The Netherlands, or Holland in contemporary parlance, had intended to remain neutral but was invaded, without pretext or warning, by German forces in the early hours of 10 May 1940. Under their occupation 185,000 civilians perished, the majority being Jews deported to camps, although during the winter of 1944 many died from hunger and disease in the northern-most region that remained under Nazi control.

The SAS contribution to liberation was varied in nature. During OPERATION MARKET GARDEN, the September 1944 airborne and land assault towards the Rhine, a four-man patrol from the 5th (Belgian) SAS parachuted into the Arnhem area to work with the Dutch Resistance (OPERATION REGAN/FABIAN). Led by 'Captain Fabian King', a pseudonym for Lieutenant Gilbert Sadi-Kirschen, it established a hide beneath a chicken coop, its wireless link to the United Kingdom providing a supply of strategic intelligence. It subsequently proved vital to those evading members of 1st Airborne Division making their way down escape lines. Concurrently a five-man patrol of the same company, under the command of Lieutenant Emile Debefve, had been dropped in the area of Kloosterhaar in Drenthe to report on enemy movements (OPERATION PORTIA/GOBBO). The following month a small team under Adjudant Groenewout parachuted into the north of the country near Leeuwarden in order to train local Resistance (OPERATION FRISE). All three patrols remained in position, effectively carrying out their tasks until overrun by the Allies in March and April 1945.

A handful of SAS had volunteered to reinforce their previous airborne units for the Arnhem landings, or to despatch supplies to the remnants of 1st Airborne Division surrounded at Oosterbeek. One such man, Driver Stanley Huggins, is commemorated within this section.

Meanwhile, as OPERATION KIPLING in France had drawn to a close, 1st SAS' C Squadron drove to Brussels at the beginning of October 1944. Here it carried out an extensive refit before moving to Venlo in newly-liberated southern Holland for field security operations. Its Jeep-borne patrols were tasked with infiltrating enemy lines into Germany to capture known Nazis and retrieve Allied agents for debriefing.

In April 1945 nearly 700 Frenchmen of 3rd and 4th SAS were dropped over north-east Holland during OPERATION AMHERST. This not only prevented German troops taking up defensive positions but also secured bridges key to the advance of the Canadian First Army. The men, accompanied by 'Ruperts' (dummy parachutists), were dropped in small parties to create maximum havoc and to encourage the enemy to believe that their numbers were greater. They carried this out with typical élan, perhaps best summarised by the Commander of SAS Troops, Brigadier 'Mike' Calvert, DSO:

> The following incident gives a very clear insight into the character of these French Bns, their initiative, offensive spirit, courage and lack of security: the morning before the operation started six French privates of the Bns were in hospital in Paris, with injuries or sickness. Within six hours of having heard, unofficially in Paris that morning, that the operation was to take place the following night, they were at Earls Colne [an English airfield used for AMHERST]. They received no official assistance in their journey. They dropped that night. No one in the French Bns considers this incident anything out of the ordinary [WO 106/4459].

As these men were parachuting into Holland, B and C Squadrons of 1st SAS began OPERATION HOWARD. Fresh from UK leave, they had disembarked at Ostend and driven their Jeeps forward into southern Holland. Here B Squadron temporarily took over a section of the front line whilst plans were drawn up for the forthcoming operation. Despite facing German parachutists, and the topography being largely criss-crossed with dykes and canals, thus restricting Jeeps to roads, both squadrons were able to penetrate the lines into Germany at the vanguard of the 4th Canadian Armoured Division's advance. Its left flank was protected by Jeep-borne elements of 5th (Belgian) SAS that had only recently been expanded to regimental status (OPERATION LARKSWOOD).

2nd SAS was simultaneously carrying out OPERATION KEYSTONE: parachuting into an area east of Amsterdam, a small party was able to cut key lines of communication and harass German troops, thereby lowering enemy morale considerably. Having been joined by a Jeep column that had fought its way from

Arnhem, the combined SAS group withdrew to be redeployed on Operation Archway in Germany.

Eight men are commemorated in the Netherlands – the names of one member of 1st SAS, two of 2nd SAS, one of Brigade HQ and one man attached from GHQ Liaison Regiment (Phantom) are inscribed on the Groesbeek Memorial. Two members of 2nd SAS are buried at Jankerbos War Cemetery, the final resting place of one of their comrades being Putten General Cemetery.

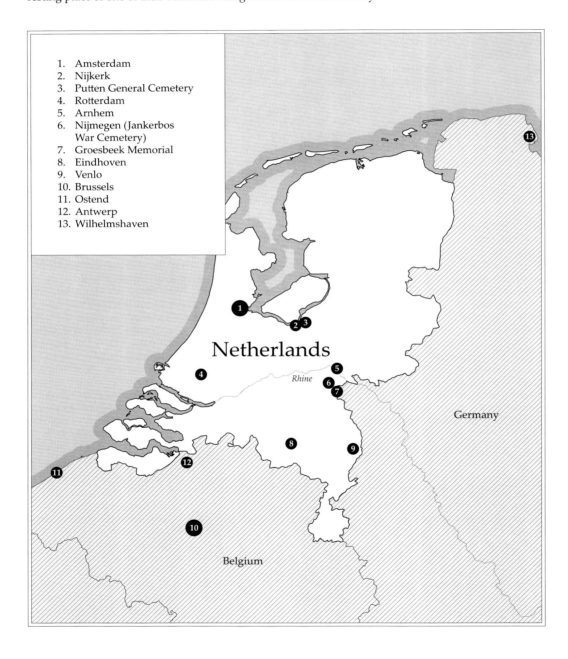

1. Amsterdam
2. Nijkerk
3. Putten General Cemetery
4. Rotterdam
5. Arnhem
6. Nijmegen (Jankerbos War Cemetery)
7. Groesbeek Memorial
8. Eindhoven
9. Venlo
10. Brussels
11. Ostend
12. Antwerp
13. Wilhelmshaven

GROESBEEK MEMORIAL

The Groesbeek Memorial commemorates more than 1,000 members of the Commonwealth who were killed during the campaign in North West Europe between the crossing of the Seine in August 1944 and the end of the war in Europe, and whose graves are not known.

Groesbeek lies 10 kilometres south-east of Nijmegen. The memorial is located within Groesbeek Canadian War Cemetery on Zevenheuvelenweg, 3 kilometres north of the village and 1½ kilometres east of Nijmeegsebaan (the main road to Nijmegen). GPS co-ordinates: Latitude 51.79815, Longitude 5.9313

LIEUTENANT RONALD JACK **BIRNIE** [237921] ROYAL SCOTS, BLACK WATCH AND 2ND SAS (2 SQN)

Ron Birnie was born on 27 December 1922 in Dundee. Educated at Morgan Academy and College of Art from 1927 to 1938 he was a keen hockey player, regularly appearing for Dundee Wanderers whilst employed as a journalist and shorthand writer by John Leng & Co newspaper publishers. Having joined St Andrew's University OTC in October 1940 he enlisted into the Royal Scots at the beginning of December 1941 and was posted to the 2nd Battalion (service number 3066452). The following month he reported to 164 OCTU at Barmouth and was subsequently commissioned into the Black Watch (Royal Highland Regiment) (*London Gazette* 28/07/42). His course report noted; 'keen and has good powers of leadership and his boxing proves him to have plenty of the offensive spirit'.

Posted to D Company of the 10th (Training and Reinforcement) Battalion, Birnie received a shrapnel wound to his left leg during mortar field firing in October 1942. Fluent in both German and French he was interviewed by MI8 (Signals Intelligence) and found suitable to specialise in German codes

and ciphers. However, having embarked for the Middle East late that December he was promoted to lieutenant the following month and posted to the 5th Battalion in early April 1943, just in time for its advance from Libya into Tunisia. Although the battalion officially saw their last action of the North African Campaign at Sfax on 9 April he was wounded on the 23rd and on recovery volunteered for 2nd SAS at Philippeville, Algeria, on 30 September 1943. After training he returned to the UK in mid March 1944 and was recommended for a regular commission that August whilst attending a Lysander Landing Course.

During OPERATION PISTOL Birnie commanded B.1 Patrol. This parachuted into eastern France in the area west of Ingwiller, close to the German border, just before midnight on 15 September 1944. Although his aircrew had failed to find the DZ due to ground mist, Birnie decided to jump 'blind'. The stick landed in trees and despite the fact that two men were briefly separated they regrouped the following day, having been guided by the patrol's footprints. This unavoidable laying of sign was shortly to prove fatal. Taking Parachutist Gerhard Wertheim, a German national, to confirm their position, Birnie made contact with two woodcutters who, in addition to helping them dispose of the party's parachutes and locate its supply pannier, later provided information on enemy dispositions and some welcome beer. However, when they failed to return later that day as promised Birnie grew suspicious and moved the patrol's lay-up point farther into the wood.

Marching north on the 17th Birnie and Wertheim reconnoitred their target, the railway line running towards the front. Returning to the patrol they found that children and civilians had followed their tracks. Birnie therefore sent Wertheim to engage them in conversation and keep them at distance whilst the group packed up. However, a German policeman was with the civilians and appeared to be trying to ascertain their numbers. He could not be caught so the patrol rapidly stripped down its kit and moved. Having formed a plan and prepared explosives Birnie then took Wertheim and Lance-corporal 'George' Davison to attack the railway tunnel north of Puberg that night, making arrangements to rendezvous with the remainder of the group at a later date. 2nd SAS' casualty report states that: 'This party did not return to the RV arranged for the 21st Sept, but resupply dropped for them was received by the right recognition letter at Q669430 on 24/25th Sept' (WO 361/716). The post-operation report simply notes: 'Lieut Birnie – B1. 17 Sep. Intended to lay charges in tunnel. Attack probably successful as it was reliably reported subsequently that all traffic stopped for four days' (WO 218/205).

'Missing Parachutists', the SAS War Crimes Investigation Team's final report, records that the men were 'taken prisoner near Wingen'. According to officials implicated in war crimes that occurred during neighbouring SAS operation, LOYTON, the three were captured on 1 October and initially interrogated by Kommando Zinhof before being confined in the rue du Fil prison at Strasbourg (WO 235/555). 'Missing Parachutists' continues; 'here Wertheim was separated [and murdered – see his entry under Medjez-el-Bab Memorial, Tunisia, Volume I] and the remainder sent to Stalags' (WO 218/222). Kriminalrat Marie Uhring, a member of the Gestapo later held in the same prison awaiting trial for war crimes, confirmed:

> At the end of September or beginning of October 1944 I interrogated a number of English parachutists, who had been captured in the Wingen area. I can remember a Lieut Birnie, and a signaller called Davison, a Frenchman called Voisin [Corporal G. Voisin of the same patrol], and a Jew who had been born in Germany, with a German name. I took Prof Gallinski as my interpreter … he got no results.
>
> I assumed this group was not killed because Isselhorst and Schneider [SD Commander of Alsace and his deputy respectively] were afraid that I would split on them and tell the Red Cross [WO 311/1154].

On 17 November 1944 the Red Cross reported that Birnie was being held at Stalag XIII-D. This had been built on the former Nazi rally grounds at Langwasser, Nuremberg, Birnie being killed when Allied aircraft bombed the area on 23 December 1944. His remains were not recovered.

Only son of Alexander and Bessie Birnie of East Haddon Road, Dundee – Fiancé of Maria Douglas of Irvine Road, Kilmarnock.

Age 21.
Panel 9. Also commemorated within St Mary's parish church, Dundee.

BIRNIE · R. J.

PRIVATE DOUGLAS **FERGUSON** MM [3311851] HIGHLAND LIGHT INFANTRY, SRS AND 1ST SAS (A SQN)

Dougie Ferguson was born on 5 March 1918 in the Parkhead area of Glasgow where, having worked as a miner, he enlisted into the Highland Light Infantry in December 1936. Posted to A Company, 2nd Battalion, he disembarked in India in late March 1938, serving here until posted to Palestine that November for the tail end of the Arab Revolt. Arriving in Egypt a year later his battalion moved to the Sudan in December 1940 and onwards into Eritrea where it was instrumental in the Italian rout from the Keru Gorge in January 1941. Despite heavy losses at the Battle of Keren on 15 March, when it became pinned down by machine-gun fire during an assault on two overlooked features, the battalion was back in action ten days later during the closing stages of the East African Campaign.

Although Ferguson's battalion was withdrawn to Cyprus, it was in the Western Desert by early June 1942 when it suffered further heavy casualties at Bir el Hamat in Libya. He volunteered for 1st SAS on 11 October and took part in the last of its North African operations. On 19 March 1943 the majority of the Regiment's subunits were temporarily reorganised as the Special Raiding Squadron, Ferguson seeing action during the invasion of Sicily and mainland Italy (OPERATIONS HUSKY and BAYTOWN). He was wounded in action on 5 October 1943, most likely in the truck-shelling incident at Termoli (OPERATION DEVON – see multiple entries under Sangro River War Cemetery, Italy, Volume II, for full details). Having recovered, he arrived back in the United Kingdom with the rest of the Regiment (now re-established as 1st SAS) at the beginning of January 1944, subsequently training in Scotland for future operations.

Soon after D-Day Ferguson took part in OPERATION HOUNDSWORTH, parachuting into a DZ at Les Vellottes in the Morvan region of central France on the night of 21–22 June 1944. His stick, under the command of Captain Roy Bradford, was initially taken to the Bois de Montsauche to join the Maquis Bernard before being transported in buses to the operation's other DZ and camp at Vieux Dun (see Bradford's entry within this volume under Crain Communal Cemetery, France). On 10 July Ferguson, Lieutenant 'Cocky' Trower and ten others joined Captain John Wiseman's camp at Rolle, 19 kilometres south-west of Dijon. The party subsequently cut the Dijon–Paris and Dijon–Beaune railway lines on numerous occasions, derailing two trains in the process. On the 23rd it moved 5 kilometres closer to Dijon to join a group of Maquis at Urcy. However, eight days later the combined party was attacked by Milice and broke contact whilst their enemies mistakenly fought each other. Having returned to its previous camp Ferguson's group blew the line again, destroyed a gasogene wood factory at Malain and derailed another train on the night of the 18th. Moving north of Dijon on 15 August it concentrated on arming and training a more competent Maquis in the Bois de Martiere as well as two other local groups before returning to the main HOUNDSWORTH force on the 31st.

With the operation now drawing to a close most of HOUNDSWORTH's men drove through the lines and flew back to the UK. However, Ferguson was one of those left to operate with C Squadron that had deployed on OPERATION KIPLING to extend HOUNDSWORTH's area of operations northwards. The operation ended soon after Ferguson's arrival, C being ordered first to Cosne on 23 September and then to Brussels in order to refit. The men arrived here on 5 October and Ferguson sailed for the UK on 26 October. He returned to Europe in March 1945 for OPERATION ARCHWAY, serving as batman to Major Harry Poat, MC, the commander of 1st SAS' Jeep column. This was tasked with providing short-range reconnaissance for the British Second Army's advance through Germany. Ferguson was awarded the Military Medal for attempting to rescue a wounded comrade during this operation (*London Gazette* 11/04/46). Although it appears that his citation has not been retained, various accounts and correspondence give insight to his actions: on 8 April 1945, having made its way to the Neustadt–Nienburg road north of the village of Schneeren, Captain Ian Wellsted's troop met two scout cars and an armoured car of the Inns of Court Regiment. Moving forward together, the vehicles drove into a well-laid ambush that struck the rear of the column. Having lost one Jeep and Trooper 'Taffy' Glyde, the SAS withdrew to the crossroads where they had joined the road, Poat bringing Squadron HQ forward to join them. The combined force was subsequently engaged from the south by armoured cars. Lieutenant Dennis Wainman's crew did its best to hold these off, although Trooper Jim Blakeney was mortally wounded and Corporal Alec Hay and Wainman were forced to abandon their Jeep and seek cover in the woods (see entries for Glyde and Blakeney within this volume under Hanover War Cemetery, Germany). The German armoured cars then turned their attention to the Jeeps next in line, severely wounding Trooper Roy Davies who crawled under his vehicle whilst his crew withdrew. Although Wellsted was able to get far enough forward to administer morphine to Davies, he himself was wounded twice and was forced to crawl back towards the crossroads. He later recalled:

Dixie [Trooper Deane] dragged me safely behind the cover of Cocky's Bren [Lieutenant Tony Trower] and he was exhausted. From there Lofty Jemson picked me up and dragged me on to the cross-roads itself. He left me close beside [Lieutenant] Mike McNaught's Jeep.

I told them about the German forces moving up on us from Schneeren and about Davies. Jemson and Ferguson, Major Poat's batman, set off to bring him in. I shouted that it was hopeless, he was right underneath the Jeep, and there were Germans all around. Nevertheless they carried on. Later Jemson came back alone. Ferguson had been badly wounded and the fire so heavy that Jemson could not even extract his friend, let alone reach Davies.

Although Ferguson's service record states that he died of his wounds, Poat wrote to the regimental Adjutant four days later:

Tpr Ferguson wounded and taken prisoner, at first believed killed but later heard of in a German hospital not yet in our hands, and wounded in the shoulder. Reported to be in good spirits. As you know he is my batman, and it is a great loss and a blow to me to have lost him. I hope to get him back when we overrun his hospital. He did a very brave thing, dashing forward to reach a wounded man when two attempts had already failed. I am putting him in for a gong [WO 218/119].

Later in the same letter Poat continues where Wellsted's own narrative left off:

I then went and asked for tanks to clear the wood in an attempt to reach Ferguson and Blakeney who had been overrun and captured [more likely Ferguson and Davies – see the latter's entry under Hanover War Cemetery, Germany]. This was promised and the time was about 3pm …

On approaching the woods we met a Polish POW who told us he had just seen approximately 80/100 SS at Crossroads B [the crossroads where the action occurred], five AFVs [Armoured Fighting Vehicles] and two British wounded being quite well looked after. It was not until about 7pm that the tanks arrived, but the Jerry had gone. We however recovered the bodies of Blakeney and Glyde, and had a burial service next day. Later when the town of Nienburg fell, we reached the hospital and found the body of Davies in a coffin. He was then buried with the other two. Nienburg was the SS HQ, we guessed they were taken there, and it was here that we received the news about Ferguson [WO 218/119].

A subsequent SAS war crimes file contains a memo stating:

The Padre of 1 SAS Regiment [Captain, The Revd Fraser McLuskey, MC] entered Nienburg with leading troops 10 April, where it was believed Ferguson had been taken and found that Ferguson had been in hospital, alive and well, and had been evacuated a few hours previously, together with other British wounded POW. The nurse, to whom the Padre spoke, believed they had gone to Rothenburg, but subsequent investigations were made in Rothenburg in vain [WO 311/702].

Confusing the case further the Red Cross recorded Ferguson as a prisoner at Stalag IV-B at Mühlberg on the Elbe (POW number 266509) and this fact, combined with his subsequent disappearance, suggest that he was murdered in line with Hitler's 'Commando Order' (see Appendix 2 within the User's Guide for full details). Major Hugh Verney, MC, formerly of ARCHWAY's Force HQ, signalled Poat in late July implying some sort of investigation was being considered; 'ask McCluskey for details hospital at Nienburg and nurse who remembered seeing Ferguson'. No paperwork regarding any such investigation has come to light.

Although his fate remains unclear Ferguson is officially recorded as having been killed in action on 8 April 1945, the date he was last seen alive.

Son of John and Margaret Ferguson of Palace Street, Parkhead, Glasgow – Brother of John and Thomas Ferguson.

Age 27.

Panel 9.

DRIVER STANLEY ARTHUR **HUGGINS** [T/152874] ROYAL ARMY SERVICE CORPS AND SAS (BRIGADE HQ)

Stan Huggins was born on 7 September 1916 in Hackney, north-east London, and married Violet Lilian Smith in May 1938. The following March their son, Michael, was born at Rochford in Essex. Having worked as a driver in Rayleigh, Huggins enlisted into the Royal Army Service Corps in mid January 1940 at Southend-on-Sea. Initially posted to the Essex Regiment's Infantry Training Centre at Warley, he was re-posted to 222 Company, RASC, at the beginning of March, to 537 Company in April 1941, to HQ 165th Infantry Brigade that December, to 539 Company in June 1943 and finally to 250 (Airborne) Light Composite Company in March 1944. This supported the 1st Airborne Division both on land and in the air, its parachute-trained personnel holding a secondary role as their brigade's defence platoon. With such a suitable background he was posted to HQ SAS on 28 May, serving as a member of BRASCO, the brigade's RASC section tasked with resupply, specifically the packing of containers and their delivery to airfields for dropping to operations.

Huggins appears as a 'BRASCO Batman/Driver' on a field return for HQ SAS Troops dated 23 September 1944: the man responsible for this entry was unaware that he had already been killed in action. There is, however, some confusion as to the circumstances of his death. In the past it has been assumed that he was posted missing in action, having volunteered as a despatcher for resupply drops over Arnhem (as other members of the Regiment had) but his aircraft failed to return. David Feebery, son of Cyril Feebery, DCM, the former SSM of HQ 1st SAS, quoted his father as confirming the use of some SAS over Arnhem in *Guardsman and Commando*. However, the late Jan Hey stated in his *Roll of Honour: Battle of Arnhem September 1944* that: 'Dvr Huggins was one of ten members of 93 Coy [93 (Airborne) Composite Company] who came in by glider (on 18 September 1944 possibly from Fairford under the command of Major Tucker). It is most probable that he was killed in the Oosterbeek defensive positions.' Hey also listed him as being attached to 250 (Airborne) Light Composite Company, his former unit, although this company's file dealing with its missing, WO 361/646, makes no mention of him. Neither does 93 Company's War Diary of this period (WO 171/2378). Despite this, his service record confirms that he emplaned on 18 September 1944 and it is therefore likely that, having volunteered, he was loaned back to an RASC company from HQ SAS for the duration of the Arnhem battle. His date of death is officially recorded as 21 September 1944.

Husband of Violet Huggins of Richmond, Virginia, USA – Father of Michael Huggins.
Age 28.
Panel 9.

SIGNALMAN GEORGE GOURLAY JOHNSTON [2583876] ROYAL CORPS OF SIGNALS, 1ST SAS AND GHQ LIAISON REGIMENT ATT SAS

'Jock' Johnston was born on 20 May 1916 in Kirkcaldy, Fife, where he attended the town's high school. Having read Mercantile Law at Edinburgh University he took a chartered accountant's apprenticeship with Anderson & Menzies in 1934, joining the 51st Highland Division Signals, Royal Corps of Signals (TA), in April 1939. Briefly called up for service that August he was embodied at the outbreak of war and posted to 9th Division Signals where he was appointed lance-corporal two days later. Promoted to corporal the following May he was re-posted to the 1st Operators Training Battalion during February 1941 and that June reverted to the rank of signalman at his own request on posting to the 1st Holding Unit.

Johnston embarked for the Middle East with No.3 Company, XIII Corps, in late July 1941, passing through Halifax in August before disembarking in Egypt that November. The following month he was posted to No.3 Lines of Communication Signals and then briefly to GHQ Troops before volunteering for 1st SAS' Signals Troop on 8 February 1943. He was subsequently attached, along with members of the Special Boat Squadron's L Detachment, to 2nd SAS at Philippeville in Algeria for OPERATION HAWTHORN. Tasked with destroying aircraft in Sardinia as a feint for the imminent invasion of Sicily, Johnston was assigned to this operation's 'Hyacinth' party. This was put ashore by HM Submarine *Saracen* to act as a reserve and supply depot for five other SBS patrols that had been allotted various airfields as targets. Johnston himself later wrote in the post-operation report:

> I was a member of a base party landed in Sardinia, on the 1st of July 43 near Cape Santoni (near Villaputza). The other members of the party were Lt Cochrane, Sgt Cass, Pct Murray, Pct Killby, and Sgm Schofield [see the entry for Lance-sergeant George Cass under Cassino Memorial, Italy, Volume II]. On the night of the landing we carried the supply of rations and the rubber dinghy, which we had with us, a short distance inland, and we slept near them. On the second day we buried the rations and the dinghies.

On the 6th of July, while we were lying in a wood, where we slept for two nights, we heard a number of Italian troops moving towards us, making a great deal of noise. We stayed very quiet, hoping they would be passing straight by us, but they came into the wood and discovered us, and took us prisoners [WO 218/174].

The group was kept in solitary confinement for two weeks, during which time it learnt that Private Louis Timparano (aka 'Tronch'), an Italian American attached to the operation from the Office of Strategic Services, had deserted two nights after landing. Armed with the knowledge he passed, the Italians interrogated the captured men who were subsequently moved through a chain of prisons on the mainland.

After the Italian armistice of September 1943 the men realised that the Germans intended taking control of their camp and subsequently broke out as described by Parachutist Neil McMillan:

The night [14 September] we left Servigliano [Campo PG.59] as I recall was not an organised escape as such. More a question of over or through the wire the best way you could, and we were fired at but fortunately over our heads. I found myself in company with John Scott, George Johnstone [sic], a signaller, a Sgt Stallings of the Green Howards, and Rogers (boyish looking very young) of the SBS [see the entry for Private 'Buck' Rogers within this volume under Bayeux Memorial, France]. After a few days we split up and Scott, Johnstone and I carried on, and the other two went in a different direction.

The three of us stayed together right through, and, as I had malaria quite badly, it slowed our progress, but they would not leave me behind.

The story of the fishing boat is quite interesting. We eventually were joined by a 2nd SAS patrol under Lt MacGregor who were sent in to round up POWs and try to get them evacuated [Operation Jonquil]. As I remember, and according to my official report, we headed towards Ortona to be picked up, presumably by Navy MTBs [Motor Torpedo Boats]. However, due to battle conditions arising at the time we started heading south.

In the meantime we were back in action ambushing German convoys etc. The decision by Lt MacGregor was that we head for the coast near Pescara and try to arrange some kind of transportation by sea. An old fishing boat and a fairly old (to us young people) very brave Italian fisherman agreed to try and get us around Pescara and as far south as necessary. It turned out that Termoli had been taken by Special Raiding Forces [sic – the Special Raiding Squadron (1st SAS)] under Col Mayne the day before we arrived in Termoli harbour around midnight. It was a very touchy situation as we were challenged by the navy patrol boats who were most unsure of who we were. However, we were allowed to land [on around 25 October] to be met by the SAS badged members.

I was interrogated by an SAS Intelligence Officer (possibly Major Barlow?) as we were the first SBS Sardinian group to be heard from.

Having arrived back in the UK during February 1944 Johnston was given refresher trade training. He also applied for an emergency commission in the infantry, for which he was recommended, but instead joined F Squadron, GHQ Liaison Regiment (Phantom), that was attached to the SAS Brigade. As a result he attended parachute course 125 at No.1 PTS Ringway that July, his instructor recording; 'above average … parachuted well'.

Johnston jumped into the Vosges département of eastern France for Operation Loyton on the night of the 12–13 August 1944. He was attached to 2nd SAS' recce group under Captain Henry Druce as a member of Captain John Hislop's Phantom patrol. He is often reported to have died of wounds on 20 October at Fontenoy-la-Joute, whilst the memorial plaque in Moussey Churchyard incorrectly states he was killed on the 11th. However, the facts are thus: Johnston, Lieutenant Peter Johnson, and Signalman Peter Bannerman, having stayed behind to close the operation, were making their way to Allied lines, only stopping to rest once they believed they had crossed into the American sector. A German patrol was watching and opened fire, instantly killing Bannerman, shooting and capturing Johnston, and wounding their officer who was able to escape (see Bannerman's entry under Moussey Churchyard, France).

After the area was liberated an investigation was launched, during which there was initial confusion over whose remains were recovered at the scene. However, Major 'Bill' Barkworth of the SAS War Crimes Investigation Team later ascertained: 'The misapprehension dates back to an error on the part of Capt. Sykes who claimed to identify the body of a Phantom man as that of Johnston. This was in fact that of Bannerman. This identification was unfortunately accepted by Casualty Branch' (WO 311/724). After lengthy inquiries Barkworth's team eventually came to the following conclusion:

On a date not yet determined but during the month of October 1944 a fourth prisoner was handed over to Kommando Wenger by the Wehrmacht. This was Sgm Johnstone [*sic*] GHQ Recce Regt att 2 SAS. It had previously been assumed that this was Pct Puttick, but Puttick is now known to have met his fate at the hands of Kommando Ernst (Case 13 Belval) [*sic* – later amended to have also been murdered by Kommando Wenger, see Fred Puttick's entry opposite]. Johnstone had been shot through the lung and when brought to Kommando Wenger by a party of the Feldgendarmerie, had pinned on his uniform the diagnosis card which accompanies a wounded man from a field dressing station. The callousness of the responsible Wehrmacht officer concerned is hard to comprehend and it is suggested that if a German army doctor willingly allowed this transfer that he cannot be said to be altogether blameless in the matter.

Johnstone was too weak to answer more than a few questions. Hauptsturmführer Wenger asserts that he had the interrogation abandoned and gave orders that the man should be shot as soon as possible in order to put him out of his misery. Untersturmführer Preil was entrusted with this task.

Gerhard Preil later confessed:

In the month of October 1944, while Kommando Wenger was stationed in Etival, a wounded English prisoner in uniform was brought to the unit by a NCO or an officer of the Wehrmacht.

From conversations and on account of the wounded label which was on the prisoner's chest, I assumed that he had come from a hospital.

He was about 30 years old, of slim build, fair hair and had shoulder badges on his arm with the SAS sign. He was placed in the guard room and I assumed he was interrogated by Hauptscharführer Schneider. I cannot say how long he remained with the unit but he stayed for at least one night. Since the prisoner who had a bullet wound in the chest seemed to be worse and since Wenger was afraid that he would not survive a further interrogation, he gave orders to [Untersturmführer] Muench and me to do away with this man.

Late in the evening Muench and I with two men of the Wachkompanie, who were Unterscharführer Gimbel and Unterscharführer Zerves and the above-mentioned prisoner, set off in a vehicle in the direction of Etival-Clairfontaine/St Die. When we came to the spot where the River Meurthe flowed in a bend near the road, we stopped. Then Muench and I went over the meadow to the head of the river. After this I came back to the vehicle and turned it round. Meanwhile, the prisoner was taken by Muench and the two men of the Wachkompanie across the meadow and was shot by Muench. He was then 'stuck' in a sack which we had brought with us and thrown into the river. I was, however, not present, since I remained on purpose with my vehicle in order to make a noise with the engine to deaden the noise of the shot.

When we reported completion of the task, Wenger asked if a stone had been put in the sack, to which I answered, 'yes, I believe so.' I said this to him because I did not wish to annoy Wenger and wished to avoid unpleasant outbursts of rage [WO 311/88].

After his arrest Hauptsturmführer Erich Wenger, the Kommando's leader, retorted:

The description given by Preil in the case of the execution of the last SAS man to be handed over to me by the Wehrmacht and who was wounded in the lung is paradoxical. I did not order the speedy execution of this man because he certainly would no longer survive a second interrogation, but because the man was very weak and already was spitting blood mixed with air. I was sorry for him and asked Schneider to carry through the interrogation as quickly and briefly as possible in order not to cause the man unnecessary suffering. The execution carried out afterwards was ordered by me solely for the purpose of releasing the man as soon as possible from his pain since according to the order there was in fact no possibility for me to take him to a hospital. Besides it was certain that the man had not come from a hospital but, but directly from a military unit which was also proved by the card for wounded (soldiers) which he carried with him.

I believe that I remember that Preil returned from the action rather quickly and reported the execution of the order. When I expressed my astonishment at the rapidity with which he had acted, he explained to me that the man had been shot, placed in a sack and sunk in a river which was at that time in flood. Already at that time I disliked his methods very much. When I asked him the obligatory question whether he had remembered the Kommandobefehl [Hitler's 'Commando Order'] imposed upon him the duty to have the dead body disposed of without trace and whether in fulfilment of this part of the order he had weighed it with a stone, Preil informed me that this had been done [WO 311/87].

Johnston's remains were never recovered. John Hislop, a Phantom officer who served on Loyton, later recalled: 'Johnston was another really good man. A Scot, he was quiet, efficient and dependable, slow in speech and solemn by nature, with a cool, clear brain. He was a first-class wireless operator and no situation disrupted his methodical and competent work' (*Anything but a Soldier*, by John Hislop).

Members of the Kommando Wenger were found to have also been concerned in the murders of Parachutist Fred Puttick ('Belval Case' – see his entry below), of Lieutenant Jim Silly ('Moyenmoutier Case' – see his entry within this volume under Moyenmoutier Communal Cemetery, France), of Parachutists Selwyn Brown and Donald Lewis ('Harcholet Case' - see their entries under Moussey Churchyard, France), and of Sergeant Michael Fitzpatrick, Lance-corporal Jack Elliott and Parachutist John Conway ('Pexonne Case' – see their entries also under Moussey Churchyard).

Investigations into Johnston's murder ('Etival Case') concluded that those concerned were Unterscharführers Wilhelm Gimbel and Zerves, and Untersturmführers Gottlieb Muench (Münch) and Gerhard Preil. Despite the latter's interrogation no trial seems to have taken place. Meanwhile, Wenger appears to have assumed an alias in a prison camp after his own interrogation and was therefore subsequently released. In 1950 he joined the West German Federal Government under a false name but four years later resumed his identity and joined the country's intelligence service. He died as a retired officer in 1978.

Johnston's date of death is officially recorded as 20 October 1944. His service record notes: 'repatriated PofW ex Italy. Arrd UK 21/02/44. Not to be sent o'seas before 20/08/44' - he had signed a waver to jump into France a week before this date.

Son of Adam and Georgine Johnston (née Gourlay) of Balwearie Road, Kirkcaldy, Fife.
Age 28.
Panel 2. Also commemorated at the Phantom Memorial Garden within the National Memorial Arboretum at Alrewas, this having been organised and constructed by former Phantom signaller, Len Owens, MM, and his family.

Private Frederick Arthur PUTTICK [6201328] Middlesex Regiment, Royal Berkshire Regiment and 2nd SAS

Fred Puttick was born on 7 August 1915 at Petworth in Sussex, although little is known about his early life. In August 1933 he joined the 8th Battalion, Middlesex Regiment (TA), whilst working as a slater and tiler at Uxbridge. He recorded his next of kin merely as 'Aunt Nell' without volunteering an address, the unit's Medical Officer noting that he was 'under weight but likely good enough'. In April 1936, whilst living in Reading, he enlisted into the regular Royal Berkshire Regiment (Princess Charlotte of Wales's), supplying no further next of kin details other than that both his parents were English. After initial training he was posted to the 1st Battalion and then to the 2nd on 20 September 1937, embarking for India the same day. According to his service record he was appointed drummer in March 1940 but from 1942 suffered an extended illness that resulted in his repatriation in February 1944 whilst the battalion was carrying out security duties at Attur, south of Bangalore. Disembarking in the UK the following month Puttick was posted to No.17 Infantry Training Centre and volunteered for 2nd SAS on 7 August. A week later he attended parachute course 129A at No.1 PTS Ringway where his instructor noted: 'average parachutist, cheerful and confident'.

Puttick jumped into the Vosges département of eastern France for Operation Loyton on the night of 21–22 September 1944 as a member of Captain 'Bunny' McGibbon-Lewis' group. When the Commanding Officer, Lt-Colonel Brian Franks, MC, decided to close the operation small teams were despatched independently to reach Allied lines. Puttick went missing during this period, 2nd SAS' Casualty Report

stating: 'Puttick lost contact with others of his party while they were being pursued by the Germans during their exfiltration through the lines. Location: near Moussey, V470810. Date: 5 Oct 44' (WO 361/897).

'Missing Parachutists', the SAS War Crimes Investigation Team's final report, states: 'listed as missing. He must have been taken prisoner as he was seen at Etival under guard of the Kommando Wenger' (WO 235/555). This refers to the testimony of Geneviève Demetz, one of two teenage sisters employed by this Kommando and concerned in the murder of other members of the LOYTON party (see Lance-corporal Jack Elliott's entry within this volume under Moussey Churchyard, France, for full details). Demetz claimed: 'I can state with certainty that an English prisoner who had a red beret, with fair hair, is the same as the one whose photograph marked Puttick, which has been shown to me. This English prisoner was in the cellar of the Kommando Wenger at Etival' (WO 309/232). Major 'Bill' Barkworth, the commander of the SASWCIT, subsequently wrote:

In this connection the evidence of Louis Perdon, a French Milice member of Kommando Wenger, is interesting, for he mentions the confinement at Etival and removal thence of an English prisoner who he says did not wear glasses. Lieut Silly, the only other English prisoner known to have been at Etival, did wear glasses and was seen wearing them there. He states further that this prisoner was taken away by a man whose name he remembers phonetically as Placke of the Group Kieffer and states that cans of petrol were placed in the car containing this prisoner, 'as the driver said he had a long journey to make and would need them'; (it is unnecessary to call attention to the fact that Kommando Wenger invariably burnt the bodies of their victims). Perdon, who is also implicated in the Pexonne case, gives a dishonest impression, and while probability remains that by his reference to the Group Kieffer he is trying to draw a red herring across the trail, it should not be forgotten that Group Kieffer was that entrusted by BDS France [Befehlshaber Der Sicherheits Polizei Und Der Sicherheitsdienst, Head of the Gestapo in France] with the task of tracking down English agents [WO 309/232].

Unfortunately, Puttick's fate remains unclear and has often been confused with that of Signalman 'Jock' Johnston. On the basis of Demetz's statement the suspicion remains that having been murdered his body was burnt at Barodet. Three of those accused of the murders of Parachutists Selwyn Brown and Donald Lewis ('Harcholet Case') were also accused of being 'concerned' in Puttick's killing 'in the neighbourhood of Etival' (see entries for Brown and Lewis within this volume under Moussey Churchyard, France). Members of the Kommando Wenger were also concerned in the killings of Johnston ('Etival Case' – see his entry above), Lieutenant Jim Silly ('Moyenmoutier Case' – see his entry under Moyenmoutier Communal Cemetery, France) and Sergeant Michael Fitzpatrick, Lance-corporal Jack Elliott and Parachutist John Conway ('Pexonne Case' – see their entries also under Moussey Churchyard).

Due to lack of evidence SS-Hauptscharführer Josef Placke, who had been successful in infiltrating SOE circuits and making use of radio 'playbacks', appears to have walked free. He was also believed to have been concerned in the murders of Major Ross Littlejohn, MC, and Corporal Dave Crowley in Italy (see their entries under Padua War Cemetery, Italy, Volume II). His commander, SS-Sturmbannführer Hans Kieffer, former head of the Gestapo at the infamous avenue Foch, was not so fortunate and received the death sentence for his part in the murders of five men of 1st SAS ('Noailles Case' - see Captain Pat Garstin's entry under Marissel National Cemetery, France). He was hanged in June 1947. Details of Hauptsturmführer Erich Wenger, chief of the Kommando responsible for Puttick's murder, can be found in Johnston's entry within this section.

Puttick's omission of next of kin details on enlistment meant that by August 1945, when he was officially presumed to have been 'killed in action on or shortly after 05/10/44', all efforts to trace relatives had proved unsuccessful. However, due to the release of the 1939 Register it is now known that Puttick married Marjorie L. I. Revitt in Horsham, Sussex, during the first quarter of 1939 seemingly whilst on leave from India. By the time the Register was collated later that year a third individual, likely to be a child (although details remain closed under the 100 year rule), was living at the address associated with the couple in Hayes Lane, Slinfold, Horsham. Through the use of genealogy search engines it seems likely that they had produced a daughter named June. From the lack of post-war correspondence within his file it appears likely that Puttick was estranged from his wife and that neither she nor their child were made aware of his fate. In addition, it is now possible to ascertain that Puttick's parents were Frederick G. Puttick and Lilian (Leaney) Bone who married in Petworth in 1913, his Aunt Nellie therefore being Nellie Johnson, one of Leaney's six siblings). Efforts to trace the fate of Puttick's parents have been inconclusive although the only death notice that can be found for a 'Frederick G. Puttick' is that of a private soldier of the Middlesex Regiment who was posted missing in action on 14 April 1917 and who is now commemorated on the Arras Memorial. Puttick's mother appears to have died in 1939, perhaps after an illness that resulted in a period of compassionate leave from India.

Age 29.

Panel 9. Not commemorated on Horsham's war memorial although this does record his cousin, Flying Officer Alexander Victor Bone of 49 Squadron, RAF, the pilot of a Lancaster that was shot down over Germany on 17 April 1943. Although he and his crew were officially commemorated on the Runnymede Memorial the aircraft was located near Laumersheim, Germany, in 2010 and excavated two years later. Their remains are now buried in a communal grave at Durnbach War Cemetery.

JANKERBOS WAR CEMETERY

Nijmegen, located only a short distance away, was the front line between 17 September 1944 and February 1945, this cemetery being created during this period by No.3 Casualty Clearing Station in a wooded area known as Jonkers Bosch. It contains the graves of 1,629 members of the Commonwealth (ninety-nine of them unidentified) and thirteen graves of other nationalities. One of the latter is that of Lieutenant Denis Devignez of the 5th (Belgian) SAS who died of wounds on 17 April 1945, his troop having been shelled at Beerta two days previously during OPERATION LARKSWOOD *(grave 5.A.6.).*

The cemetery is located 4 kilometres south-west of Nijmegen on the Burgmeester Daleslaan, close to the junction with the S100. GPS co-ordinates: Latitude 51.822420, Latitude 5.830480

SAPPER ALFRED RONALD EDWARDS [2000885] ROYAL ENGINEERS AND 2ND SAS (1 SQN)

Ron Edwards was born on 29 September 1917 in Swansea. Having worked as a shop assistant he enlisted into the Royal Engineers in February 1940 giving his trade as blacksmith. Qualifying as a military blacksmith, Edwards was posted to the 2nd, then 3rd (Cheshire), Field Squadron and disembarked in Egypt in mid November where he served with the 4th Field Squadron. From May 1941 this formed part of the 7th Armoured Division and saw action at Sidi Razegh during OPERATION

CRUSADER of that November, at Gazala during April 1942 and at the Battle of Alamein that October.

Having taken part in the advance into Tunisia in February and March 1943, Edwards volunteered for Airborne Forces and was posted to the newly-formed 4th Parachute Squadron, RE, at Moascar in Egypt at the beginning of April. After extensive training with other airborne units the squadron disembarked at Tripoli and moved into Tunisia where it carried out training exercises and demonstrations. At the beginning of September its various subunits were concentrated at the port of Bizerte, the squadron disembarking at Taranto on the heel of Italy with the 1st Airborne Division on the 9th (OPERATION SLAPSTICK). Here the men were employed on infantry and engineering tasks, such as clearing mines and repairing bridges, before returning to the United Kingdom via Algiers in the New Year. Settling into the village of Glaston in Rutland, the squadron undertook refresher parachute training at No.1 PTS Ringway during March.

Edwards volunteered for 2nd SAS on 27 April 1944. He subsequently parachuted into the Zabern Gap area in the Bas-Rhin département of eastern France on the night of 15–16 September 1944 during OPERATION PISTOL. His patrol, C.1 under Captain Maurice Scott, was scattered on landing, Scott breaking his ankle badly. Having regrouped, the men lay up whilst deciding how they should proceed, now that their commander was barely mobile. On the 19th, after a recce of the area had been carried out, Scott decided to divide his resources. Edwards and two others stayed with him to blow up the railway line to the north of Benestroff. This proved impossible, the post-operation report noting:

> Capt Scott's broken ankle made progress for this party extremely slow and in this condition it was a considerable feat for him to have covered upwards of 50 miles in three weeks. After two unsuccessful attempts to traverse the enemy lines the party was surprised by a German search party [on 7 October 1944]. Capt Scott, hampered by his injury, ordered his party to withdraw without him. He was wounded and taken PW [WO 218/205].

Edwards and the remainder of the team retired to the house of a local man who had previously helped them, sheltering there until the area was liberated by the US 4th Armoured Division on 12 November. Having been debriefed by American officers the group returned to the UK on the 19th.

Edwards parachuted into Occupied Holland for OPERATION KEYSTONE on 11 April 1945 in a stick of seventeen men tasked to harass enemy lines of communication. He was killed in action on the 18th by shellfire, Captain Dick Holland, MC, later reporting: 'at 2300hrs we were shelled. Pct Edwards who was on sentry duty was killed by the first shell' (WO 218/199). John Wardley, a fellow officer deployed on this operation, recalled that a Dutchman had been sent through the lines with a marked map showing both enemy and SAS positions and he believes that this was either misinterpreted by friendly forces or by the Dutchman, or that the map had been marked incorrectly (personal interview, 2012). Canadian artillery, believed by Wardley to be self-propelled, subsequently shelled the farm complex in which the stick was sheltering, Edwards being killed whilst on sentry duty outside. A message sent from KEYSTONE confirms: 'Edwards killed by own shell last night' (AIR 20/8843). The operation closed the following day when Holland's party was joined by its Jeep-borne element at the vanguard of the advancing Canadian First Army.

A further signal from Squadron HQ to OPERATION ARCHWAY notes: 'Holland states Edwards showed courage and initiative on KEYSTONE by laying charge in area thick with enemy returning at great risk to find what had happened when charge failed to detonate. Subsequently killed'. This refers to 15 April when Edwards and three others had laid charges on the Putten–Nijkerk railway line. Holland's post-operation report also notes that on the 16th Edwards had taken part in an ambush on German cyclists on the Putten–Nijkerk road, whilst a final signal states: 'Personal for Franks [CO of 2nd SAS]. Recommendation for C-in-C [Commander-in-Chief's] certificate to be passed by you before 5 May for Spr Edwards and L/Cpl Dowell through [illegible] under which operating'. It is not known whether this commendation was ever awarded. His family received a telegram informing them of his death during a VE-Day street party.

In 1947, Mr and Mrs Schrijver, a couple local to Jankerbos, wrote to the Edwards family:

> I think you will be very surprised to receive a letter from an unknown Dutch family, but I'll tell you the reason as we have adopted the grave of Edwards A R Spr …
>
> It's my task to take care of the grave, because our Allied soldiers have done so much for us.

Son of Maurice and Catherine Edwards of Whitcomb Street, Aberdare, Glamorgan – Older brother of Victor, David, Iris and Evelyn.
Age 30.
Peace, perfect peace. 'I found in him a resting place, and he has made me glad'
Grave 14.E.6.

PRIVATE MARTINE EDWARD TYSON [7955160] ROYAL AIR FORCE, ROYAL ARMOURED CORPS AND 2ND SAS (1 SQN)

Martine Tyson was born on 7 June 1922 in Ambleside but grew up across the Lake District at St Bees on the Cumbrian coast. Having attended St Bees School from 1935 to 1939, where he was a lance-corporal in the OTC, he enlisted into the Royal Air Force in July 1940 (service number 1104389). Although he quickly obtained the rank of sergeant and attended an officer training unit he was discharged in mid January 1942 having been deemed as 'not likely to become an efficient Air Obs' (Observer – service record). At the beginning of March he therefore enlisted into the Royal Armoured Corps at Kendal and was posted to the 56th Training Regiment at Catterick where he was also recommended as an officer candidate. However, the interviewing board thought otherwise and on 14 January 1944 he joined the 6th Airborne Armoured Reconnaissance Regiment, attending parachute course 103 at No.1 PTS Ringway the following month. Here his instructor noted that he was a 'good performer after initial nervousness'. Whether he subsequently landed by glider at Ranville on the evening of D-Day with his regiment is unknown, owing to minimal entries in his service record. What is certain is that he volunteered for 2nd SAS on 2 October 1944 and was posted to No.1 Squadron.

Tyson parachuted into Occupied Holland, approximately 40 kilometres east of Amsterdam and 5 kilometres east of Nijkerk, on the night of 11–12 April 1945 as a member of Lieutenant John Wardley's stick. The operation, KEYSTONE, was commanded by Captain Dick Holland, MC, and was tasked with 'disorganising the enemy in that area immediately south of the Ijsselmeer' (WO 218/199). Holland's and Wardley's sticks were received by a three-man recce team and were to be followed firstly by reinforcements dropped with Jeeps, and then by a Jeep force moving through the lines under Major Henry Druce, DSO. However, poor weather conditions prevented the dropping of vehicles or men and Captain Holland therefore set about attacking roads and railways lines, the post-operation report noting that Tyson, Wardley and Lieutenant P. Stuart had 'opened fire on a goods train on this line at Z486067 [the Nijkerk–Putten line] previous to SM [Sergeant-Major] Ellis's attack' earlier on the 15th (WO 218/199).

Holland noted in the same report that 'after they [a patrol] had returned [during the afternoon of the 16th] Pct Tyson was accidentally killed by one of our party while weapons were being cleaned'. Wardley later recalled that whilst he was out on patrol the remainder of the group stayed in a barn and someone, he believed a signaller, accidentally shot Tyson whilst cleaning his carbine (personal interview, 2012).

Son of Edward and Marie de Gracia Tyson (née Lopez-Saavedra) of Bank Chambers, Ambleside, Westmorland – His father served as a major in the Border Regiment during the Second World War.
Age 22.
Dulce et decorum est pro patria mori
Grave 14.E.7. Also commemorated on Ambleside's war memorial and within St Mary's Church.

PUTTEN GENERAL CEMETERY

This community cemetery contains four Commonwealth graves of the Second World War, three being of Royal Canadian Air Force personnel.

Putten is located 19 kilometres north-east of Amersfoort, not far from the A28 motorway towards Zwolle. The cemetery lies a short distance south-west of the town centre, the entrance being on Engweg. GPS co-ordinates: Latitude 52.25791, Longitude 5.60356

SAPPER JOHN WATSON **KEEBLE** [14624570] GENERAL SERVICE CORPS, ROYAL ENGINEERS AND 2ND SAS (1 SQN)

Known as 'Jack' to his friends, John Keeble was born in the fishing village of Crail, Fifeshire, to an English father and Scottish mother. Having worked as a scooper driver at Pickering in Yorkshire he enlisted into the General Service Corps in June 1943, registering his date of birth as 27 October 1923. Posted to No.10 Primary Training Centre he transferred to the Royal Engineers that November and joined the 3rd Training Battalion, although he immediately attended parachute course 92 at No.1 PTS Ringway. A month later he was re-posted to the Airborne Forces Development Centre, an establishment at Amesbury Abbey tasked with improving and testing parachute and glider equipment. It was from here that he volunteered for 2nd SAS on 12 May 1944.

Keeble parachuted into the Bas-Rhin département of eastern France on the night of 15–16 September 1944 for OPERATION PISTOL. As a member of Sergeant Edward Williams' A.2 Patrol he jumped from the same aircraft as A.1, both patrols landing amongst enemy tanks and infantry. In the ensuing confusion

A.2 was split. Keeble and four others managed to find each other in the dark and, having been challenged whilst trying to find their commander, they lay up in a wood hoping he might join them. The following afternoon a group of SS searched the area using dogs and the men were forced to abandon their Bergens and to hide in a water-filled ditch. Although the Germans came within a few feet of them, they were not detected. That evening they set off in a south-easterly direction, leaving their packs as one of their number, Parachutist E. Haeberle, a German national, had overheard the SS saying that they would lie in wait for the patrol to retrieve their Bergens. Without explosives, any attack on their objective, the railway line in the area of Benestroff, was impossible. Living off their emergency rations in poor weather, they therefore started towards the advancing Allies. Helped along their way by farmers they eventually made contact with the 4th American Armoured Division on the 22nd. Ten days later the men were back in the UK.

Keeble returned to North West Europe (location unknown) on 26 November until returning to the UK on 13 February 1945. He emplaned for OPERATION KEYSTONE on 11 April, parachuting into Occupied Holland, approximately 40 kilometres east of Amsterdam and 5 kilometres east of Nijkerk, that night. Tasked with disrupting enemy movement, small parties under the overall command of Captain Dick Holland, MC, were sent to lay charges on railway lines and to ambush roads ahead of the advancing Canadian Army.

Holland's post-operation report states that on the night of 14 April 1945, 'SM [Sergeant-Major] Ellis's party, which had accompanied us to the [Putten-Voorthuizen] road, went to operate in the area Z5806 but ran into a group of suspicious characters at Z540036 and after a short exchange of fire retired. We learnt later that it was a [Dutch] Resistance party which should not have been in the area' (WO 218/199). Although no mention is made of casualties, Holland later wrote that the following day he returned to the same road and 'on the way I found Pct Keeble unconscious at Z5436 where SM Ellis had had an exchange of fire with a Resistance party. I told a Dutch civilian to report it and heard later that he was taken by the Germans and died on the way to hospital' (WO 218/199). However, a message from KEYSTONE sent on 15 April, the day Keeble was found, appears to contradict this: 'One casualty Keebles [sic] bad head injury … Keebles left at Napier [the DZ that Holland's team had jumped into, approximately 1,200 metres from where Keeble was wounded] tell Canadians' (WO 218/216). He is recorded as having died of wounds that day.

Son of Percy and Grace Keeble of Kirkmay Road, Crail, Fife – Known to have had two sisters as well as those brothers listed below.

Age officially recorded as 23 although his family believe that he was 20 years old when killed.

He gave the greatest gift of all. The gift of his unfinished life

Plot B, row 1, grave 51. Also commemorated on the Crail War Memorial alongside his brothers Sergeant Walter Keeble of 178 Squadron, RAF, killed in action on 22 March 1945 and buried at Klagenfurt War Cemetery, and Ordinary Seaman Owen Mortimer Keeble, known as 'Morty', of the SS *Almeda Star* that was sunk by U-96 with the loss of all 360 hands on 17 January 1941, and who is commemorated on Chatham Naval Memorial.

UNITED KINGDOM

Having served in Italy under the temporary title of the Special Raiding Squadron, the men of 1st SAS returned to the UK in January 1944. Here they were re-established with regimental status under Lt-Colonel 'Paddy' Mayne, DSO*. Training began in the Lowlands, the SAS Brigade, first proposed at the end of 1943, being officially established on 8 February 1944 under Brigadier 'Rory' McLeod as part of HQ Airborne Troops, 21st Army Group. A French demi-brigade was integrated under Lt-Colonel Norbert Durand and based at Auchinleck Camp, this consisting of the 3e and 4e Bataillons d'infanterie de l'air (BIA) which were also in Scotland. The former, under Capitaine Pierre Château-Jobert, alias 'Yves Conan', became the 3e Régiment de chasseurs parachutistes (RCP) on 1 April. The latter, under the distinctive, one-armed Commandant Pierre Bourgoin became 2e RCP at the same time. Irrespective of their uprated status they were known to all nationalities within the brigade as 3rd and 4th (French) SAS respectively.

In line with expansion a brigade command structure was put in place: Brigade HQ and 20 Liaison HQ, a link with the French units supervised by Major Oswald Carey-Elwes, were both located at Sorn Castle in Mauchline, East Ayrshire, close to 1st SAS in Darvel. On 10 March F Squadron, GHQ Liaison Regiment, under Major Hon. Jakie Astor, also joined the brigade in which it was more simply referred to as 'SAS Phantom'. It based itself at nearby Auchinleck House, instructing the brigade's signallers whilst training hard alongside operational teams it would soon support behind enemy lines. A week later 2nd SAS, under Lt-Colonel Bill Stirling, brother of the Regiment's founder, joined the brigade from locations in Italy and North Africa. Owing to lack of numbers it was re-formed as a battalion until 1 April when it expanded to regimental strength once more. It was initially lodged at Doonfoot Camp in Alloway before moving to Fairfield Camp in the village of Monkton adjacent to Prestwick Airfield. The Belgian Independent Parachute Company also arrived under Capitaine Eddy Blondeel and, having based itself at Loudoun Camp in Galston, began training as 5th (Belgian) SAS. The idea of a 6th (American) SAS was even mooted (WO 171/369), Bill Stirling having already expressed an interest in adding one or two Canadian squadrons to his Regiment (WO 204/1950).

Volunteers for what had been planned as a third British SAS were absorbed into either 1st or 2nd SAS. Thereafter reinforcements were mainly recruited from the Airborne Forces Holding Unit and the Auxiliary Units that had been trained in sabotage and guerrilla activities to counter potential German invasion. Planning and training for the forthcoming liberation of France ensued. Regardless of background the majority of newcomers qualified for their wings or attended refresher courses at No.1 Parachute Training School, RAF Ringway, the modern-day Manchester Airport. On 1 April 1944 all SAS personnel were transferred to the Army Air Corps so as to ease administrative and supply issues as well as ensuring air assets. For veterans of numerous campaigns it was not a happy marriage, not least as it meant swapping their distinctive sand-coloured berets for the maroon of Airborne Forces.

In late May 1944 men from 1st and 4th SAS who were earmarked for D-Day operations were locked down in 'The Cage', a transit camp at Fairford. This was close to HQ 38 Group, RAF, at Netheravon and its airfields in Gloucestershire, Oxfordshire and Dorset. Operational briefings were held in camp and the men forbidden from leaving. Station 1090, the brigade supply dump and packing centre, was co-located accordingly. By late August 3rd (French) SAS and 5th (Belgian) SAS had also moved to Fairford, Brigade HQ (in effect now 'Rear HQ') and 20 Liaison HQ settling at Oare House near Pewsey in Wiltshire and Tactical HQ at HQ Airborne Troops, Moor Park near Rickmansworth in Hertfordshire. Those not deployed from 2nd SAS, which was now commanded by Lt-Colonel Brian Franks, MC, were encamped at Park House in the Wiltshire village of Shipton Bellinger whilst those members of 1st SAS still in the UK moved to Nettlebed near Henley-on-Thames, Oxfordshire, in September (WO 218/114).

In mid October 1944 38 Group, RAF, relocated to Essex thereby extending its operational range over Occupied Europe. The brigade followed suit within days, HQ moving to Sloe House at Halstead near Braintree, Station 1090 to Mushroom Farm ('Penny Pot') at nearby Wethersfield, 2nd SAS to Wivenhoe

Park near Colchester (now the University of Essex) and Phantom co-locating with the SAS Signals Section at Dynes Hall in Halstead. They were joined on 11 November when 1st SAS moved from Nettlebed to Hylands House near Chelmsford. Meanwhile, 5th (Belgian) SAS moved from Fairford to Brussels via Station 1090 whilst the two French SAS units settled in France. 20 Liaison HQ went with them, forward-mounting to Épernay in the Champagne-Ardenne region (WO 218/114).

After VE-Day and their return from occupational duties in Norway both British SAS regiments were stood-down, disbandment commencing on 5 October 1945, with the last of those not employed with the SAS War Crimes Investigation Team leaving camp on 30 November. In July 1947 a London Territorial unit, the Artists Rifles, was revived in an SAS role, initially as the 21st Battalion, Special Air Service Regiment (Artists Rifles) (TA), and soon after as 21st SAS Regiment (Artists), TA. Numerous veterans of the wartime brigade signed up to serve under the command of Franks. One of its squadrons was deployed to Malaya during the Emergency, this subunit being absorbed into the Malayan Scouts in 1950 under 'Mike' Calvert, the last wartime SAS Brigade Commander. The following year the Scouts formed the nucleus of a new regular unit, 22nd Special Air Service Regiment. Followed in 1959 by a further Territorial Regiment, 23rd SAS, these three units continue to uphold both the traditions and ethos of their wartime forefathers, a fact evident not only by the demands made upon them but sadly also through their own Roll of Honour.

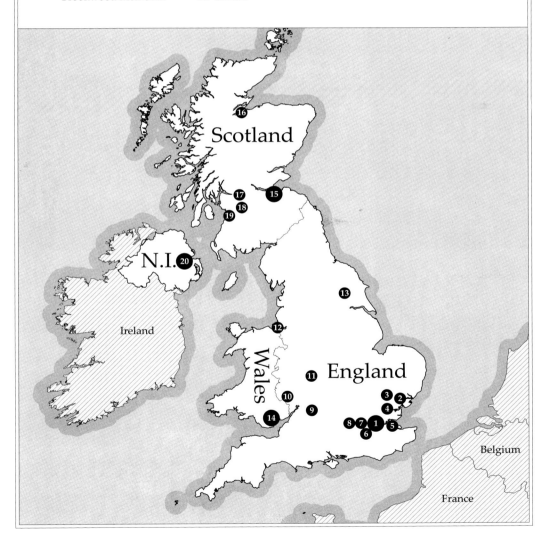

1. London (Barking Rippleside Cemetery and Twickenham Cemetery)
2. Colchester
3. Wethersfield
4. Chelmsford
5. Chatham Naval Memorial
6. Brookwood Cemetery and Brookwood Memorial
7. Langley Marish (Saint Mary) Churchyard
8. Reading Crematorium
9. Fairford
10. Hereford
11. Birmingham Municipal Crematorium
12. Birkenhead (Landican) Crematorium
13. Fulford Cemetery
14. Cardiff
15. Edinburgh
16. Inverness (Tomnahurich) Cemetery
17. Glasgow
18. Darvel
19. Prestwick
20. Belfast

BARKING (RIPPLESIDE) CEMETERY

This large civilian cemetery contains the graves of 212 Commonwealth service personnel of the First and Second World Wars. It is located on Ripple Road (A123), just north of the A13 in Barking, Essex. Opening times are Monday–Friday 1000–1600hrs and Saturday–Sunday 1000–1530hrs. GPS co-ordinates: Latitude 51.53515, Longitude 0.10386

RIFLEMAN CHARLES JOHN RIEDEL **BATEMAN** [6853044] KING'S ROYAL RIFLE CORPS AND GHQ LIAISON REGIMENT (PHANTOM) ATT SAS

Known to his comrades as 'Fan', Charles Bateman was born on 18 December 1913 at Howard Road in Barking. His father died of tuberculosis just four years later, followed by his mother when he was aged just 9. The six young children were subsequently split up, Bateman and his brothers being placed into the care of Barnardo's and his two sisters going to live with an aunt. He and one brother, Len, were later fostered by Mrs Flanders of Stapleford Abbots. Leaving school at 13 he was employed in the gardens of Aldenham House, Elstree, its owner taking a keen interest in Bateman's development. Four years later this man found Bateman a more challenging post in charge of the fruit and plant houses of Lord Hastings' Melton Constable Park. Moving on later that year the Head Gardener wrote his reference:

> I have always found him very industrious and reliable, a man who combines a keen interest with an excellent knowledge of his profession, and has justified every confidence placed in him. His personal character is excellent, strictly sober, honest, well mannered, and of good appearance.
>
> He leaves here, much to my regret, through reduction of staff, and I would welcome any opportunity of assisting his future progression.

Having found various positions Bateman settled in June 1933 as an under-gardener at Pettitts Hall, Chigwell. It was here that he met his future wife, the family nanny, Annie Kate Austin. His closest brother, Len, a steward in the Merchant Navy, was tragically killed in 1937 when he fell into the hold of his ship. In November 1938 Bateman took a gardener's post for London County Council at the Northern Outfall Works at Beckton in East Ham, he and Annie marrying at Plaistow's parish church the following March.

Bateman enlisted into the King's Royal Rifle Corps in October 1940 and was posted to the Rifle Depot (Motor Battalions) at Winchester before joining the 1st Battalion. He was re-posted to GHQ Liaison Regiment (Phantom) on 16 February 1941 and attended a storekeeping and accounting course at Nottingham in October of the following year. Two months later his daughter, Jill, was born in Barking. Having joined F Squadron that was attached to the SAS Brigade, he attended parachute course 108 at No.1 PTS Ringway during March 1944 and was noted as a 'fearless jumper – good team man – most enthusiastic'.

Assigned to Lieutenant Peter Johnsen's patrol, Bateman trained alongside the SAS in preparation for post-D-Day operations. Len Owens, a fellow patrol member later awarded the Military Medal for his work behind enemy lines, recalled:

Fan was our driver mechanic and he was due to go with us on [Operation] Dunhill [on the night of 2–3 August 1944]. However, before he could get on the aircraft, the aircraft was declared full. Representations produced no result so Fan was regrettably left behind in England.

He returned to the SAS to a place called Juniper Hill [the SAS Brigade Tactical HQ at Rickmansworth, Hertfordshire] and whilst he was there he was shown a weapon … But there was no ammunition and Fan, being the lad he was, managed to find some British ammunition that he thought fitted. And he put it in the gun and pulled the trigger, and tragedy, the whole gun exploded into pieces and several of these became imbedded in his chest. I was told later that one of the last things that he said was 'I've killed myself.' We were devastated at the news and when we returned to England we went as a group to see Mrs Bateman to ask if we could help in any way but she said she was managing. And we then went to see his grave in London.

He was a lad who was very popular, very efficient in what he did, and a sad loss, not only to us but to the SAS. We learned later that Major Jakie Astor, OC of [F Squadron] Phantom, had given Mrs Bateman a quite large sum of money to tide her over until she got herself sorted out.

Fan was the best scrounger and poacher I have ever known and, if anything was required by the patrol for their comfort, Fan would find it. And so he was the one that coined the motto for the patrol 'any fool can be uncomfortable' [personal interview, 2010].

Bateman died of his injuries on 11 August 1944, Astor writing to the KRRC: 'The death was due to the explosion of a .22 rifle which Rfn. Bateman was handling. The rifle exploded and pieces entered his chest. He immediately lost consciousness and died a few minutes later. He was not on military duty but was within military precincts (i.e. in camp).' Major Harold Light, an officer of Phantom's Training and Holding Unit at Richmond Park, wrote to Bateman's wife on 6 September:

While firing a rifle there was an explosion and pieces of the weapon were driven into your husband's chest and head … on the face of it there must have been some flaw in the weapon or the round fired must have been a faulty one … I think you are right in saying that you cannot believe your husband was negligent. He was a very good chap indeed and I never knew him fail in his duty [Bateman family collection].

A few days later Captain John Fitzwilliam, Phantom's Welfare Officer, also wrote:

I don't know the rifle in question but our armourer tells me that it isn't uncommon for the barrel to burst when the rifle hasn't been used for some time and hasn't been pulled through and cleaned. I have only knowledge of a barrel to burst when there has been a piece of twig restricting it (which got there while crawling through a thicket) …

You know the saying 'bad workmen blame their tools', well there is no question of your husband being a bad workman; he obviously trusted that rifle to be all right and it wasn't.

There is no suggestion of foul play. You want of course to know of what your husband was thinking as he stalked along (perhaps a rabbit?). He did not go with Lt Johnsen's patrol the night before because there was not room for him in the plane; but he was to have gone the next day … I think your husband knew that he would join the others the next day in France; we know he was keen to do this …

You cannot believe it ends here, your great love for him; it must go on to something else somewhere. You must feel he is watching over you and baby [family collection].

A subsequent court of inquiry recorded death by misadventure, finding that no blame could be attached to Bateman. Such was the concern of Lt-Colonel Howard, MC, his former employer at Pettitts Hall, that he re-employed Annie and petitioned to find out more about Bateman's death.

Son of Benjamin and Emily Bateman (née Riedel) – Husband of Annie Bateman of Ilchester Road, Dagenham, Essex – Father of Jill Doris Bateman – Brother of Ethel, Winifred, Benjamin (who also served in the army), Stanley (killed in action on 03/03/45 in Burma whilst serving as a corporal in the Royal Scots Fusiliers, now buried at Taukkyan War Cemetery) and of Leonard (died 1937).
Age 31.
Oh for the touch of a vanished hand and the sound of a voice that is still
Section H, grave 1686, located along the northern of edge of the cemetery.

BIRKENHEAD (LANDICAN) CREMATORIUM

Thirty-eight service men and women were cremated here during the Second World War. Their names are inscribed on a wall of Portland stone facing the Cross of Sacrifice in the Commonwealth War Graves plot. This is situated on the western edge of Landican Cemetery that surrounds the crematorium and contains the graves of thirty-five Commonwealth personnel, ninety-three others being found amongst the civilian burials of the cemetery.

Access to the cemetery is gained from Arrowe Park Road, Landican. GPS co-ordinates: Latitude 53.36548, Longitude -3.08571

Major Philip McLean GUNN MC [128655] Royal Army Medical Corps, 1st SAS AND SAS (Brigade HQ)

Phil Gunn was born on 20 September 1915 at Neston in the Wirral, Cheshire. He and three brothers were educated at nearby Mostyn House School before boarding at Sedburgh School where they were known as 'the Gunn Battery'. Phil Gunn left in 1933 and went up to Edinburgh University where he followed in his father's footsteps and read Medicine. Graduating in 1939 he took up residence at The Royal Infirmary, Salford, before moving to the Royal Hospital for Sick Children in Edinburgh. He was commissioned into the Royal Army Medical Corps in April 1940 (*London Gazette* 16/07/40, Supplement 19/07/40). A few days later he was attached to the 4th Anti-Aircraft Division, Chester, for duty with the 67th Search Light Regiment.

Although it is not known when Gunn disembarked in the Middle East he was promoted to captain in 1941 and served alongside the 9th Battalion, Rifle Brigade (Tower Hamlets Rifles). His eldest brother,

2nd Lieutenant George Ward Gunn, MC, a chartered accountant before the war, was killed in action on 21 November 1941 at Sidi Rezegh in Libya. He was posthumously awarded the Victoria Cross for continuing to man the last remaining anti-tank gun of his command when attacked by sixty Panzers.

Having seen action at Gazala during the summer of 1942, Phil Gunn joined 1st SAS at Kabrit on 16 November 1942, Malcolm Pleydell, the unit's Medical Officer at that time, noting; 'Philip Gunn perhaps the best MO I have met, and who I got to join the SAS as a second doctor' (IWM Documents.337 – Private Papers of Captain M. J. Pleydell, MC). Taking over from Pleydell ten days later, he was soon involved in operations, 1st SAS' War Diary recording that he 'returned from Western Desert 01/03/43' (WO 218/97).

When the majority of the Regiment's subunits were restructured as the Special Raiding Squadron, Gunn continued as the MO and was at the forefront of the landings on Sicily and mainland Italy during the summer and autumn of 1943. In the course of fierce fighting he gained the respect of officers and men alike, his award of an immediate Military Cross being announced to his comrades on 17 November 1943:

After the landing of the Special Raiding Squadron at Bagnara on 4th Sept '43 [OPERATION BAYTOWN] the unit came under machine-gun and mortar fire from the high ground overlooking the town, suffering several casualties. Captain Gunn, the Medical Officer attached, showed great bravery in going forward and attending to the wounded under the heavy and consistent fire which swept the streets. Later one of our patrols had five men wounded as they were advancing to attack the enemy positions and became pinned down under severe enemy fire. On hearing what had happened, Captain Gunn again went forward regardless of his own safety and although unable then to evacuate the wounded, dressed and bandaged them under heavy fire. On all operations Captain Gunn displays the same fine courage and disregard for his own safety [*London Gazette* 25/01/44, Supplement 27/01/44].

Peter Davis, a former SRS officer, recalled the scene at Termoli after a shell hit a truck crowded with SRS men engaged on OPERATION DEVON:

Phil Gunn worked methodically and calmly ... without a glance at the dead he concentrated on the living, arranging for their evacuation ... Shaken as we were, we could not fail to admire his splendid coolness, as he worked patiently and without fluster to mend broken bodies and torn flesh [*SAS – Men in the Making: An Original's Account of Operations in Sicily and Italy*, by Peter Davis, MC].

Returning to the UK, Gunn was promoted to major during early 1944 and supported the SAS Brigade in its build up for post-D-Day operations in France as its Deputy Assistant Director of Medical Services. Fraser McLuskey, MC, padre of the reconstituted 1st SAS, later noted:

Just as I was about to step into the plane [to parachute into OPERATION HOUNDSWORTH on 22 June 1944] I remember Phil Gunn, the Brigade MO, stepped forward to shake hands. Phil had been at Edinburgh University with me and had done great things with the 1st in North Africa, Sicily and Italy. No unit MO was ever more beloved [*Parachute Padre*, by J. Fraser McLuskey, MC].

Gunn was never far from the forefront of operations, the Commanding Officer of 1st SAS, Lt-Colonel Paddy Mayne, DSO*, subsequently signalling that the MO had arrived at the HOUNDSWORTH base in the Morvan region of France on 15 September 1944. An hour later Mayne received a furious reply from Brigadier Rory McLeod, the SAS Brigade Commander:

You reported arrival Gunn. When [Major Harry] Poat [MC] asked whether Gunn could visit SAS first I agreed on specific conditions that visit was brief and that he did NOT visit Houndsworth. My orders were final AND definite on this point. Order Gunn to return to England forthwith and provide necessary transport for him to reach an airfield from which he can get home ACK [acknowledge].

With no reply after five days McLeod signalled once more; 'expedite Phil Gunn return'. Mayne responded 'have apprehended Gunn', the MO eventually returning to the UK and brigade duties on the 22nd.

Gunn was killed in road traffic accident near Colchester on 9 December 1944. Major 'Freddy' Caldwell, MC, a close friend and fellow SAS officer, was driving him in a Ford V8 Utility Truck from Sloe House near Halstead in Essex to Mushroom Farm at Wethersfield, both SAS Brigade locations. Caldwell subsequently stated at the ensuing court of inquiry:

> I drove to Sloe House, Halstead. I got there about 6.45pm and left about 10pm. This was Saturday, 9th December. I left in the same vehicle. I was driving and with me was Major Gunn and Lady Rendlesham. It is a right hand drive. Major Gunn and Lady Rendlesham were sitting in the back of the car.
>
> It was dark, I had side lights and head lights on. The lights were fairly good. There was a slight haze at the time. I know the road very well. I was returning from Sloe House, Halstead, towards Wethersfield. I am not sure I saw any traffic on the road. There was not much in any case. I was travelling between 30 and 35 miles an hour. There was not much talking. When I came round Braintree Road Corner at Sible Hedingham the car seemed to go out of control. The next thing I knew was that the car was upside down. I got out of the door. When I got out I saw Major Gunn lying on the road 4 or 5 yards from the car. I think he was dead then. I found a lot of telephone wires round the car and there was a lot of twisted wire in the road. I think that was the cause of me losing control. I am sure I did not pull down the wires because the wire was before I reached the pole I hit.
>
> I had attended a party and I was perfectly sober at the time of the accident. I had four drinks of champagne. It was a military party.

The inquiry found that Caldwell was not to blame and was 'of the opinion that the accident was caused by telephone wires down on the road striking the windscreen and becoming entangled with the car causing the driver temporarily to lose control.' A local policeman testified the Caldwell was sober and that in his opinion the wires were already down. The doctor who attended the scene stated that Gunn had died from shock following haemorrhaging from a severe wound at the back of the head with a skull fracture: 'He was 8 to 10 yards from the car. I was told he walked from the car after getting out of it. This is a possible thing to have happened.' Neither Caldwell nor Rendlesham was injured.

Mayne later wrote in tribute of Gunn:

> While in the desert he carried all his medical supplies in his Jeep and was at all times cut off from any hope of resupply. For three months he remained behind the enemy's lines, and as the enemy retreated he retreated behind them, his Jeep always at the beck and call of many of the small parties working behind the enemy's lines. In the invasion of Sicily he was with the first wave of the landing, and in all took part in four sea landings behind the enemy's lines. On these attacks he and his orderly were compelled to carry all their supplies on their backs. At Bagnara, on the west coast of Italy, Maj Gunn gained his MC. After landing in the early hours he established an RAP [Regimental Aid Post], which became as the day went on a particular target of the enemy. Throughout the whole day he carried on a ceaseless medical service under a continuous barrage of mortar fire. There are many patients who would wish to thank him for his work that day. In the Regiment his popularity, both among the men and officers, was founded not only on his cheerful and courageous conduct under all conditions but on the admiration which one could not but feel for his great talents both as a doctor and a soldier. He has two surviving brothers one serving in Italy [with the Royal Artillery] and the other in Burma [as a Medical Officer in the Chindits and later SOE's Force 136]. His eldest brother, Lt Ward Gunn, VC, MC was killed at Sidi Rezegh with the RHA [and is buried at Knightsbridge War Cemetery, Libya – *The Times*, 16/01/45].

Son of George Gunn, MBE, MD, FRCSE, and of Grace Gunn of Neston, Wirral, Cheshire – One of four brothers.

Age 29.

Also commemorated alongside his brother, George Gunn, VC, MC, on a plaque within Muggleswick parish church.

BIRMINGHAM MUNICIPAL CREMATORIUM

Birmingham was home to numerous military hospitals during both wars, Birmingham Lodge Hill Cemetery, within which the crematorium is located, containing 498 burials of the First World War and 125 of that which followed. Although a small number of the latter are enclosed in a plot within Section 2E the majority are spread out amongst the civilian headstones.

Birmingham Municipal Crematorium, within which a bronze plaque commemorates those servicemen whose remains were cremated here, is located at the centre of the cemetery. Access is gained from Weoley Park Road, Selly Oak. GPS co-ordinates: Latitude 52.44006, Longitude -1.95988

Private John William <u>GOSLING</u> [5613661] Devonshire Regiment and 1st SAS

John Gosling, the son of a car body manufacturer, was born on 19 October 1905 at Sparkbrook in Birmingham. Having earned his living as a professional bodybuilder he enlisted into the Devonshire Regiment in February 1924. After home service he was stationed with the 1st Battalion in Shanghai from January–September 1927, on Malta until October 1929 and in India until December 1931. He then left full-time service and was released to the Army Reserve.

At the outbreak of war Gosling was mobilised at Exeter and posted to the Devonshires' regimental depot. The following March he was promoted to lance-corporal whilst at an infantry training centre and in June 1940 was posted to the 50th Holding Battalion. Here he was promoted to corporal before being posted to the 12th Battalion that October. Promoted to sergeant in January 1941, he reverted to the rank of private at his own request in April and joined HQ Company a few days later.

Gosling was twice admitted to hospital for unknown reasons during May 1943 and on being discharged the following month was posted to No.3 Infantry Depot. He was attached to the 11th Battalion at Weymouth in July and posted to this battalion that September. After a further period with No.3 Infantry Depot he volunteered for the SAS on 15 December 1943, attending a 'Cadre Course' at Cupar, Fife, whilst waiting for the Regiment to return from Italy. After further training he was temporarily attached to 20 Liaison HQ, which provided the link to the French SAS units, going on to qualify as a parachutist on 1 March 1944. He finally joined 1st SAS on 28 April.

The following year Gosling took part in Operation Archway as a member of a composite squadron that arrived with its Jeeps at Ostend on 20 March 1945. This then made its way, via Holland, into Germany. On the 25th Gosling's B Echelon, commanded by Captain George White, MM, crossed the Rhine at Bislich in Buffalo amphibious vehicles. His squadron and one from 2nd SAS combined to create Frankforce, named after its commander, the CO of 2nd SAS, Lt-Colonel Brian Franks, DSO, MC. This formed the spearhead of the British Army's advance towards Kiel that it reached on 3 May, Frankforce returning to the UK a week later.

Gosling subsequently arrived in Norway on 15 May 1945 for Operation Apostle, occupational duties for which the SAS Brigade was attached to the 1st Airborne Division. Taken ill, he was flown to the UK on 3 June 1945 and admitted to Colchester Military Hospital on 11 August, presumably when his condition became serious. He was transferred to St Thomas' Hospital late that month, to Horton Emergency Hospital in Epsom a few days later, to University College Hospital Middlesex at the end of September, back to Epsom in November and eventually to Barnsley Hall EMS Hospital, Bromsgrove, towards the end of January 1946. He died on the morning of 12 April 1946 of lung cancer and neurofibronata, nervous system tumours caused by gene mutation, that together brought on cardiac arrest.

Son of John and Clarissa Gosling of Allenscroft Road, King's Heath, Birmingham – Younger brother of George and older brother of Amy and Marjorie Gosling.

Age 39.

Commemorated on a bronze plaque within the crematorium chapel.

BROOKWOOD MILITARY CEMETERY

During the First World War a section of Brookwood Cemetery (The London Necropolis) was set aside for the burial of servicemen and women of the Commonwealth and the United States of America who died in the London area. Work was started on what is now the Commonwealth War Graves Commission cemetery in 1919. During the Second World War this section was extended and plots of various other nationalities created. These are adjacent to the large American Military Cemetery.

Brookwood is the largest war cemetery in the United Kingdom, containing 1,601 Commonwealth burials of the First World War and 3,476 of the second. In addition, there are 786 war graves of other nationalities that are cared for by the Commission as well as adjacent plots dedicated to the Royal Hospital, Chelsea, and to members of the nursing services.

Brookwood is located 48 kilometres south-west of Central London. The main entrance to the cemetery is on the A324, close to the village of Pirbright. GPS co-ordinates: Latitude 51.30022, Longitude -0.64212

Captain George Frederick SLATER [67935] South Staffordshire Regiment, Royal Warwickshire Regiment, Parachute Regiment and SAS (Brigade HQ)

George Slater was born on 11 July 1912 in Port Elizabeth, South Africa, to British parents. The family later lived at Elland in Yorkshire, although it appears they moved to Birmingham where he attended Aston Commercial School from 1925 to 1928. Remaining in the area he found employment as a rep in the motor trade and from June 1936 held a commission in the 5th Battalion, South Staffordshire Regiment (TA). However, in June 1939 his Commanding Officer asked him to resign his commission due to personality clashes. Under the impression that his resignation had been accepted Slater applied for another commission a year later, only to be told that his application could go no further. He later ascertained that his resignation papers had been lost and, as a result, having married Mary Hannah Crowther at the end of June 1940, he enlisted into the ranks of the Royal Warwickshire Regiment on 1 July. He subsequently served in the 50th and 14th Battalion until January 1942 during which time he 'carried out the duties of Section Commander satisfactorily (including periods on beach defence work)' (service number 5120101).

After attending 164 OCTU Slater was commissioned into the 13th Battalion in June 1942 (*London Gazette* 19/06/42) but was immediately attached to the 100th Anti-Tank Regiment, Royal Artillery, to become proficient in the use of 2-pounder guns. Having applied to become a parachutist he was posted to the Airborne Forces Depot and transferred to the 8th (Midland Counties) Battalion, Parachute Regiment, on 6 November. He attended parachute course 46 at No.1 PTS Ringway during January 1943 and from June to October was attached to HQ 3rd Parachute Brigade. During this period he was admitted to hospital for twelve days following a training exercise: a member of the Belgian Independent Parachute Company (later designated as 5th SAS), who was acting as enemy, threw a grenade at Slater, who sustained multiple wounds to his legs.

Slater was appointed Air Liaison Officer (GSO III) to the newly-formed SAS Brigade on 18 February 1944, the date of his promotion to captain. As such he was based at Sorn Castle in Ayrshire but in regular liaison with all SAS Regiments, the brigade's RASC section, with Special Forces HQ in London and of course with the RAF. That August, after most of the brigade had moved south for D-Day operations, its HQ was re-established at Oare House near Pewsey, Wiltshire, so that it could work effectively with the RAF's 38 Group based at Netheravon. When, in October, this relocated to Essex to increase its range into Occupied Europe the SAS Brigade went with it, its HQ setting up within Sloe House near Chelmsford. The brigade 'dump', Station 1090, where parachute containers were prepared, was within an easy drive at Mushroom Farm, Wethersfield. Slater's duties included employing his language skills whilst acting as Conducting Officer to French and Belgian SAS sticks prior to take-off, briefing the aircrews as to the latest ground situation according to those parties already deployed, liaising with SAS HQ when the Regiment's sorties were cancelled so that those in the field could be informed in good time, and helping to debrief crews so that lessons learnt could be fed back (AIR 20/8823).

On the night of 20 March 1945 Slater successfully supervised a parachute descent to test a new type of DZ light. However, whilst on its approach to land at RAF Great Dunmow his aircraft was shot down, 620 Squadron's log recording:

> At night one aircraft [Stirling LK116 A] carried out a container drop at Great Sampford but on return to base was attacked and shot down in flames by an intruder aircraft. The Flight Engineer succeeded in escaping by parachute, but S/Ldr G. O. S. Whitty, DFC, Officer Commanding A Flight, and the remainder of his crew and one passenger were killed.

The aircraft crashed into a bight of a small river roughly 400 metres from the airfield. Although the aircraft was still on fire, men from the squadron were able to gain access to the fuselage and recover bodies. Dennis Williams later wrote in *Stirlings in Action with the Airborne Forces*:

> There was just one survivor from the crew of Stirling LK116, the Flight Engineer, Flt Sgt Cramp, who baled out and was taken to the Saracen's Head public house in Great Dunmow after his ordeal.
> Tony Cramp, 620 Squadron, recalled: 'The night we were shot down we had an army Airborne officer with us on an exercise to check some new DZ lights at a small airfield not far away. It was a bright moonlit night, and

when we got back to Dunmow we were warned of an intruder in the area. The runway lights were out and almost immediately we were attacked from underneath. All our lights went out, the batteries were hit and with a port engine on fire, we were only at about 800 feet when we got the order to bale out. Normally as a crew we never wore parachute harnesses on local flying, but as I was cold I had put my harness on just after take-off, so I was the first to go out. I landed in a field not far from the road out of Dunmow and got a lift from a passing motorist who took me to a pub from where I was picked up by transport from the station. After this I did no more ops …'.

The loss of Stirling LK116 must have seemed doubly ironic when the list of casualties became known, for among them were two survivors of previous crashes that involved fatalities. Capt George Slater had been flying as a passenger in the 196 Squadron aircraft, LK126 N, which had been destroyed at Shepherd's Grove a month earlier, after being attacked by an intruder. LK116's Canadian air gunner, WO Paul Bell, had been on board LJ882 when it crashed in France on 23 July 1944, while taking part in an SAS operation with 190 Squadron [Operation Rupert]. The sole evader from LJ882's crew, he returned to 190 Squadron in October 1944, and was posted to 620 Squadron in January 1945 [see multiple entries within this volume under Graffigny-Chemin Communal Cemetery, France, for full details].

Son of George Frederick Slater, MBE, and of Hannah Slater of Great Barr, Birmingham – Husband of Mary Slater of South Parade, Elland, Yorkshire. Age 32.
For your tomorrow he gave his today
23.E.13. Buried alongside two of the five aircrew also killed in the incident – Bell was laid to rest nearby in the Canadian section of the cemetery.

BROOKWOOD MEMORIAL

The Brookwood Memorial commemorates 3,500 men and women of Commonwealth land forces who died during the Second World War and have no known grave. Their circumstances of death mean that they could not appropriately be commemorated on any of the specific campaign memorials in various theatres of the war. Some were posted missing during the 1940 Norway campaign or on various raids into Occupied Europe. Others were agents who died or were killed during missions within enemy-held territory. Some died at sea or on air operations. The memorial, similar in design to that at Ploegsteert near Ypres, was unveiled by Her Majesty the Queen in October 1958.

Private Theodore Schurch of the Royal Army Service Corps, who as a stool pigeon in Axis POW camps gained information from captured members of the SAS and LRDG, is commemorated on panel 17, column 3. He was arrested in Italy in 1945 and found guilty of desertion and nine counts of treachery as an enemy agent for both the Italians and Germans. He was hanged at Pentonville in January 1946.

Brookwood is located 48 kilometres south-west of Central London. Access to Brookwood Military Cemetery is from the A324, close to the village of Pirbright. The memorial stands within the grounds of the cemetery near to this entrance. GPS co-ordinates: Latitude 51.30022, Longitude -0.64212

Private Henry **HARRIS** [5570084] Wiltshire Regiment
and SBS (X.1 Patrol, X Det)

'Harry' Harris, as he was known to his patrol, was born into a Romany family at Winchester on 3 March 1919 as the eldest of seven brothers and seven sisters. Although the extended family traditionally based itself around the Kent and Sussex area, his father decided to settle on the Isle of Wight where he set up as a scrap-metal merchant. Harris therefore attended Oakfield Boys School in Ryde where, despite being a spirited youngster, he excelled in all forms of sport, notably swimming for which he won awards. As the senior child he left school early, taking an apprenticeship with a local brick manufacturer. In October 1938, perhaps hoping for better prospects and quality of life, he enlisted into the Wiltshire Regiment (Duke of Edinburgh's).

Soon after the outbreak of war, Harris disembarked at Cherbourg with the 2nd Battalion as part of the 13th Infantry Brigade whose HQ he was posted to. Settling into the monotony of guard duties during the 'Phoney War', he was deprived of pay on several occasions for misdemeanours such as being absent without leave, failing to have his vehicle ready and for having beer in his billet. However, after the German Blitzkrieg began the battalion was kept busy, fighting numerous actions before withdrawing to Dunkirk. Harris' party was evacuated in a small fishing vessel in the early hours of 1 June 1940. Reaching Ramsgate, the men were put on a train and accommodated at Kinmel Camp near Rhyl, North Wales, until the battalion was eventually concentrated once more.

Harris embarked for overseas service in 1942 and, having passed through Cape Town, took part in the third wave of landings on the Vichy-held island of Madagascar on 6 May during Operation Ironclad. This denied the Japanese a potential air and naval base that would paralyse the Commonwealth convoy route to the Middle and Far East. It also ensured the control of the Mozambique Channel through which such convoys passed. The Wiltshires came ashore at a bay west of Diego Suarez alongside the rest of the brigade and advanced east towards the port of Antsirane. Although the French defended fiercely, all resistance in the area had collapsed by daybreak on the 7th, the British fleet entering the harbour that morning. The brigade subsequently sailed for India, docking at Bombay at the end of the month for service at Ahmednagar. It re-embarked at the end of August and arrived a few days later at Basra, Iraq, before moving to Persia (modern-day Iran).

On 8 February 1943, whilst based at Qum south of Tehran, Harris volunteered for 1st SAS. Having qualified as a parachutist on 12 April, most likely at Ramat David in Palestine, he was posted to the newly-formed Special Boat Squadron the same day. He 'proceeded on a course of instruction att 11th Bn Para Regt' on 20 May, the SBS spending most of that summer training along the Palestinian and Syrian coastline.

On 11 September 1943, three days after the Italian armistice had been announced, X Detachment, SBS, a composite of men from both M and S Detachments, embarked at Haifa for the Aegean. Here it hoped to seize control of strategically located islands from Italian garrisons before German troops did so. Harris subsequently lost his life on 2 October 1943 whilst operating on the Dodecanese island of Scarpanto. His patrol, X.1 that was led by a relatively new officer, Lieutenant Charles Bimrose, had been tasked to:

> Bring back four members of the crew of a British bomber which had come down in the sea near to the village of Diafani in Scarpanto. The airmen, according to intelligence, were to be found in a house in the village.
> The patrol numbering one officer and nine other ranks left Simi at dusk on the 30th Sep with instructions to proceed to Calchi, relieve Capt Lassen's patrol, stay at Calchi until dusk on 1st Oct and proceed to Scarpanto that night [WO 218/98].

With the relief of Lassen's patrol complete on 1 October two members of Bimrose's party fell sick: 'Sgt [Ronald] Waite and Fus [Les] Stevenson complained of a temperature and internal pains. The civilian doctor on the island gave his opinion that it was due to food poisoning and it was decided to push on' (WO 218/98). Making for Scarpanto by caique at dusk the weather turned and 'the sick men had to be lashed to the hatch cover' (WO 218/98). According to Bimrose's post-operation report the patrol, less Waite and Stevenson, reached the shore and walked into Diafani only to find the Germans had captured the aircrew the previous day:

> As dawn was approaching [on the 2nd], and the land route back to the landing beach was both circuitous and hilly, it was decided to take a rowing boat from the village and to row north across Diafani Bay back to the beach. A boat which was floating in the water was selected and, accompanied by one Italian prisoner, the party set off. A stiff off-shore wind sprang up when the boat was about 300yds out and the water became very choppy. Then it was found that the seams of the boat which were before above the surface of the water leaked badly. Orders were given for the boat to make for the shore, but owing to the surplus weight of the water, the rowlocks broke. These were repaired but broke again, and finally the boat sank. The crew commenced to swim for the shore and Pte Harris, after swimming about 50yds, said he could go no further. Before immediate assistance could be given to him, he sank and approx 20secs later when he was brought to the surface, was found to be in an unconscious condition. He was taken back to the boat, which had turned turtle and placed on the keel, the force of the wind then blew the boat over again and it sank again. This time it was impossible to recover the body. The remainder of the crew after resting, swam to the shore and made their way back to the landing beach … The courage and fortitude shown by Sgt Waite and Fus Stevenson deserves to be mentioned as it was afterwards found they were both suffering from malaria [WO 218/98].

As Harris was a strong swimmer the possibility exists that he was himself weak from malaria. However, his demise remains unclear: after the war Waite visited Harris' family who report that in addition to confirming that several of the men were suffering with the disease, Waite also stated, in contradiction to Bimrose's report, that once in the water the patrol had come under fire. He related that Harris, who was swimming alongside the vessel, was subsequently wounded twice and that being weak with malaria he (Waite) was unable able to hold onto Harris, a well-built man, over the side. Waite, who was subsequently wounded at Comacchio in April 1945, was noted by fellow SBS member, Doug Wright, MM, as 'a brilliant sergeant' and was host to the Harris family on numerous subsequent occasions. Not long after Harris' death he had written to them:

> I feel it was my duty to write you, as Harry was with me when it happened. The circumstances of his death and where he was *buried* [author's italics] I am afraid I cannot disclose, but, can assure you he died nobly as he would have wished.
> His death is a great blow to all of us here, and in addition to losing a great soldier, he was a great pal to us.
> The boys send to you both, their deepest sympathy, and can understand your feelings …
> One day when I do at last return to England I shall come over and give you all the particulars but, until I am able, I am afraid all I could do is write to you.
> I sincerely hope that this letter will be of some comfort, and at least better than the official notice. Would you like to correspond? [Harris family collection].

For some reason Harris' date of death is officially recorded as 1 October 1943.

Son of Henry and Sarah Harris of Southfield Gardens, Swanmore, Ryde, Isle of Wight – Older brother of Linda (served with the NAAFI in the UK and Germany), Joe (served with the Royal Hampshire Regiment in Palestine, Greece, North Africa, Sicily and Italy where he was wounded in action in 1944), John (wounded in action in January 1945 whilst serving with the Cameron Highlanders in North West Europe), George (served in the North Atlantic and North Sea aboard Royal Navy minesweepers), Jemima (who served in the ATS in the UK), Lilly, Rebecca, Alice, Kathleen, Robert (served in post-war Egypt with the Royal Artillery), Caroline, Sidney (served with the Royal Hampshire Regiment in post-war Malaya), and Anthony (served post-war with the Royal Artillery in the UK).

Age 24.

Panel 13, column 2. Also commemorated on the Borough of Ryde War Memorial at the Town Hall, at The Rifles (Berkshire and Wiltshire) Museum and within The Church of St Michael and All Angels, Swanmore.

Gunner Bert Conrad JORDAN [851004] Royal Artillery
and LRDG (S.2 Patrol, A Sqn)

Bert Jordan was born in Maidstone, Kent, to an English father and Scottish mother and appears to have later been fostered by a couple in Glasgow. Having worked as a vehicle mechanic he enlisted into the Royal Artillery in October 1935, stating that he was born on 20 March 1917. However, as his birth was not registered until a year later it is likely that he falsified his age to join up early. After serving in the UK with the 5/2nd Field Regiment he embarked for India in November 1937 and was posted to the 1st Field Regiment with which he qualified as a signaller. At the outbreak of war his unit moved to the Middle East and served in the Western Desert. Jordan was subsequently posted to the 5th Army Observer Battery before volunteering for the Long Range Desert Group on 6 February 1941. Having initially served first as a gunner/signaller in H Section (Royal Artillery) he joined S.2 Patrol as its signaller.

S.2 was the first LRDG patrol selected to work in conjunction with Général Leclerc's Free French forces on their march towards Tunisia. Its commander, Lieutenant Jim Henry, noted that on 28 November 1942:

> S.12 (Breda Truck) developed a bad skid on treacherous surface [on the way from Zouarke to Zouar in Chad to meet the French] and, in avoiding a palm tree, hit another tree. Damaged radiator, wing and bent chassis. Signalman Jordan, who was on the truck, was taken to hospital. Enquired into accident, i.e., interviewed driver, passengers (including Jordan) and examined the scene of the accident. Finding – Car [truck] travelling at about 15mph. Crash not due to carelessness, driver not to blame, and Jordan's injuries due to his own action of jumping from the truck in the wrong direction. He (Jordan) mentioned this is his statement, at the time exonerating the driver from all responsibility and blame. Medical diagnosis on Jordan 'Badly sprained ankle and badly bruised – absolute rest for ten days before resuming duty.'
> … 5 Dec 42 … Received news that S.12 was on its way up, and that Jordan was found to have a fractured pelvis.
> … 10 Dec 42 … Received the news that Jordan was being flown to Fort Lamy [Chad] where hospital facilities were greater.
> … 17 Dec 42 … At 0800hrs received signal from Captain Adams, Liaison Officer at Fort Lamy, that Jordan had died on 13th December [1942], and had been buried at Fort Lamy [WO 218/91 – it is not known why Jordan's remains were not concentrated into a Commonwealth War Cemetery. Henry himself died of wounds received in a separate incident – see his entry under Heliopolis War Cemetery, Egypt, Volume I].

The following month Glasgow's *Evening Times* carried this announcement:

Jordan – Died in Middle East in December. Gunner Bert Jordan Thomson, 24 years. Dearly beloved son of Mr & Mrs John Thomson 449 St Vincent Street, Glasgow C3 (late of 49 Blythswood Street). At the going down of the sun and in the morning we shall remember him [6 January 1943].

Son of Bert Jordan of Coulman Street, Gillingham, Kent – His mother's maiden name was Broakens – His legal guardians were the Thomsons of Glasgow.
Age officially recorded as 25.
Panel 3, column 2.

Guardsman Harry **MALLORY** MM [2658325] Coldstream Guards
and 2nd SAS

Harry Mallory was born on 23 March 1920 in St Hilda's, the industrial hub of Middlesbrough, where he worked as a driver until enlisting into the Coldstream Guards in April 1938. Shortly after the outbreak of war Mallory's 2nd Battalion took up positions south of Lille close to the Belgian border as part of the BEF. Here the men were kept busy throughout 'the Phoney War', building defences in an attempt to extend the Maginot Line northwards. When Germany invaded the Low Countries in May 1940 the battalion was forced to withdraw to the River Scheldt where it doggedly fought off attempted enemy crossings on the 21st. Fighting was fierce and casualties high, the citation that accompanied the subsequent award of Mallory's Military Medal stating:

> On Tuesday 21st May 1940, at Pecq on the Scheldt Gdsm Mallory showed exceptional coolness and courage when driving his carrier on a reconnaissance to the bridge. It was at the height of the bombardment. Having arrived at the bridge a further reconnaissance had to be made along the canal to gain touch with the flank company. This was executed under intense machine-gun and rifle fire. Had it not been for his coolness the mission must have failed [*London Gazette* 09/11/40, Supplement 11/07/40, WO 373/15].

To avoid being outflanked both the 1st and 2nd Battalions withdrew and formed part of Dunkirk's defensive perimeter, the 2nd holding ground at Hondschoote approximately 10 kilometres south of the beaches. It was one of the last units to retire and was evacuated to the UK on 2 June having suffered heavy losses. Mallory received his decoration from His Majesty the King on 22 March 1941.

After training in Scotland the 2nd Battalion disembarked at Algiers in late November 1942 as part of the First Army's drive towards Tunis. Soon transported into action it took up positions around Medjez-el-Bab railway station in Tunisia and on the night of 22–23 December seized the German strongpoint of Longstop Hill as part of a wider offensive. However, reinforcements could not hold the feature without the battalion's help and on Christmas Eve fresh attacks had to be put in to bolster their hold. These were only carried with heavy losses. On Christmas morning the Germans counterattacked and when ammunition ran out the battalion was forced to retire, having suffered further casualties. Mallory was 'brought to notice for act of Gallantry' during this action and subsequently awarded a commendation by the Commander-in-Chief of First Army (First Army Routine Order No.152d/1/4/43).

Although the battalion remained in the Medjez area for the following three months it was subsequently put into reserve and used to plug defensive gaps that appeared up and down the line. Late in April 1943 it was involved in the thrust towards Tunis from the south-west, Mallory receiving a gunshot wound to his left arm on the 26th. Having been discharged from hospital he volunteered for 2nd SAS on 9 June, Fred Rhodes, later recalling how this came about:

> Well, I was in the Coldstream Guards. We'd been in the frontline, and the regiment was pulled out for a rest period. I saw the notice that went up in the rest camp, that Captain Barkworth was requesting people to apply for a special unit, a special regiment. One didn't think about what it was, or what work it would do. One of my pals, Harry Mallory, decided to go and have a look at what this SAS was, and on the way down we met a chap who we knew very well called Bill Stribley. He'd been in the Coldstream Guards. We said to him: 'Oh, we've not seen you for a long time, where are you now?'
>
> 'Oh,' he says, 'I'm the chauffeur to the Commanding Officer of 2 SAS.'
>
> 'Oh,' we said, 'that's where we're going, we're going down to have a look.'
>
> He said; 'I'll come back with you then.'
>
> So we went, and he went into the tent where Barkworth was doing the interviews, and he said: 'You two have got to go in now.'
>
> So we went in and were interviewed by Barkworth, and after a lot of questions that really delved into your background – you know, looking for stability, physical fitness, reliability etc. No one questioned your ability to be a good soldier etc. From that Barkworth then said: 'I have decided you two will be accepted.'
>
> We were given twenty-four hours to pack our gear. We said: 'What about approval from our own CO?'
>
> He said: 'That will be acquired, but you'll be moving up with us within twenty-four hours.' So we were picked up the following day and transported down to Philippeville in North Africa. That's when our training started, to become fully qualified members of 2 SAS [IWM Sound Archive 18176].

Unfortunately, it is not known whether Mallory went on to serve in Italy, although his service record does not note any entitlement to the Italy Star. The exact circumstances his death are unclear, his record merely stating that on 11 March 1944, whilst en route to the UK, he 'died as a result of an accident at sea' and that he was 'buried at sea at 0810hrs' the following day.

Son of Lorenzo and Ann Mallory (née Hull) of Ayresome Street, Middlesbrough, Yorkshire.
Age 23.
Panel 8, column 2.

SERGEANT ALEXANDER MILNE [2878140] GORDON HIGHLANDERS, NO.6 COMMANDO AND Z SPECIAL BOAT SECTION ATT 2ND SAS

'Ginger' Milne was born on 24 November 1918 in the parish of St Giles, Edinburgh, but was brought up by his grandfather, John Milne, at Towiemore Distillery Cottages in the remote village of Botriphnie near Keith, Banffshire. In November 1936, whilst working for the distillery, he joined the 6th Battalion, Gordon Highlanders (TA). Having then worked as a nurse at Ladysbridge Mental Hospital at Banff he was embodied at the outbreak of the war, serving with the BEF in France from January 1940 until 31 May when evacuated from Dunkirk. That July he volunteered for special service and was posted to No.6 Commando, this temporarily forming part of the 5th Special Service Battalion from November. His mother, Mrs M. Ewing of Aberdeen, died the following March. By mid July 1941 he was serving as a lance-corporal in No.6's 101 Troop, this providing a folding canoe capability for small-scale raids. On 26 April 1942 he joined No.2 Special Boat Section at Hillhead, 101 probably having been absorbed by the section on this date.

Milne was aboard HMS *Hartland* during the Allied landings in Vichy-held North Africa (OPERATION TORCH). To prevent the French Navy at Oran sabotaging key installations two Royal Navy cutters, the *Hartland* and HMS *Waleny*, rammed the port's boom in the early hours of 8 November 1942. They were loaded with US Rangers who were to storm ashore (OPERATION RESERVIST) whilst Milne and his canoe partner used experimental miniature torpedoes to prevent Vichy ships leaving the harbour. However, before any such action could be taken both cutters were fired upon and set alight. They blew up with heavy loss of life, Milne and his SBS colleagues taking to an emergency float with some Americans before being machine-gunned in the water. The survivors were taken prisoner until released by US forces. Ordered to return to the UK, the SBS party boarded the troopship, *Ettrick*, only to be torpedoed the next morning and towed to Gibraltar.

Having reached the UK Milne was promoted to sergeant at the beginning of December 1942. The following March a subunit, Z Special Boat Section, was formed for attachment to the 8th Submarine Flotilla at HMS *Maidstone* in Algiers. Although omitted from the first Z draft, Milne had returned to North Africa by 13 May 1943, the date that 2nd SAS was raised. This took on numerous scheduled operations from its predecessor, the Small Scale Raiding Force, most of which were to be inserted by submarine. The attachment of Z Special Boat Section and of a troop from L Detachment, Special Boat Squadron, was therefore the logical step to bolster the Regiment's new recruits with amphibious experience.

Milne and Sergeant Archibald Sinclair were subsequently posted missing in action after OPERATION BUTTERCUP, a raid to destroy a radar station on Lampedusa. This, the largest of the three Pelagie Islands, lies strategically between North Africa and Sicily. The combined SAS and SBS raiding party had embarked three Motor Torpedo Boats at Tabarka harbour in Tunisia and forward-mounted to Malta. It reached a point 3 kilometres off Lampedusa at 2330hrs on the night of 6–7 June 1943. Five minutes later flares were observed. Despite this, two pairs, Milne and Sinclair, and Lieutenant 'Sally' Lunn and Parachutist J. Watt, went ahead in Folbots, setting off at 2350hrs to recce alternate landing points. Once inshore they split, one pair searching one way and the remaining pair paddling the other. Meanwhile, the main group had cross-decked to small landing craft and at 0055hrs had approached the area covered by Milne and Archibald. They 'found landing too difficult' and therefore attempted to do so at the other beach:

> When 20 yards from shore they were fired on from either flank by automatic weapons, probably one light and one heavy MG [machine gun].
>
> Fire was returned from twin Vickers K [machine gun] mounted on each craft. Fire from the two MG positions was silenced by the accurate shooting of SSM Kershaw.
>
> By this time at least four MGs, also two mortars, both approximately at sea level, had opened up. Some MGs were firing from behind blankets or other cover, as no flash could be observed. The Force Commander [Captain Roy Bridgeman-Evans] then gave the order to withdraw.
>
> As the force drew away, more automatic weapons opened up, as from the direction of the OP [observation post] at Cap Ponente the force was engaged by a 37mm A/Tk [anti-tank] gun firing many parachute flares …
>
> The force while withdrawing was engaged by up to twenty MGs and at least four mortars. Fire was kept up in all directions for at least one hour.
>
> The dual purpose batteries opened up with accuracy on the MTBs just after the FBEs [Folding Boat Equipment – the small landing craft] had been taken on board.
>
> The Force Commander considers that fire was controlled by RDF [Radio Direction Finding – radar] and that the original alarm was given by RDF locations of MTBs …
>
> One Folbot failed to return to MTBs, who had to move off at once under accurate shelling. Every step has been taken to pick up the missing Folbotists who may have: a) holed their craft on rocks and been forced ashore, b) missed the MTBs and made for Sousse, c) become casualties inshore [WO 204/1950].

Milne and Sinclair, the pair that failed to return, were subsequently posted 'missing presumed killed'. The following day a vice admiral on Malta signalled the Mediterranean Commander-in-Chief:

> Operation Buttercup unsuccessful. MTBs approach apparently not detected but intense mortar and small arms fire opened on assault craft as they were about to land.
>
> Attack abandoned. During withdrawal MTBs were illuminated by searchlights and engaged with fair accuracy by two 4-inch batteries.
>
> Two MTBs returned to Malta and two were detached to search for two soldiers missing in Folbot (My 070416 refers) [unfortunately this signal is missing from this file].
>
> Otherwise no casualties military or naval and no damage to MTBs. Consider repetition of operation unlikely to meet with success [WO 204/1949].

On 9 June the late night final of *The Manchester Evening News* reported:

> 2 MISSING IN 'INVASION' OF LAMPEDUSA! Malta today told the truth about the 'invasion' of Lampedusa. The landing which the Axis waxed so loudly about and claimed to be a serious invasion attempt was merely a coast reconnaissance by our light forces! The Vice Admiral at Malta issued the following communiqué: 'Our light surface forces carried out coast reconnaissance of the island of Lampedusa on June 6 and 7. They suffered no damage or casualties, and only two of the landing party did not return.' – AP.

It was not until January 1945 that the War Office finally presumed that Milne and Sinclair had been killed in action. Despite the timings outlined in the post-operation report, their deaths are presumed to have occurred on 6 June 1943 (see Sinclair's entry within this section).

Nephew of Catherine Robertson of Towiemore Cottages, Botriphnie, Keith, Banffshire.
Age 26.
Panel 14, column 2. Also commemorated on Botriphnie's war memorial.

SERGEANT ARCHIBALD ROY MCGREGOR **SINCLAIR** [3326187] HIGHLAND LIGHT INFANTRY, NO.11 COMMANDO, MIDDLE EAST COMMANDO, SPECIAL BOAT SECTION ATT L DETACHMENT SAS BRIGADE AND SBS (L DET) ATT 2ND SAS

Archibald Sinclair was born in the Edinburgh suburb of Gorgie on 26 March 1915, where he grew up and married. He and his wife, Jane, had two daughters. Having worked as a butcher he enlisted into the Highland Light Infantry in late July 1940 and was posted to the regiment's infantry training centre. He volunteered for No.11 (Scottish) Commando that September, this being temporarily absorbed into the 2nd Special Service Battalion soon after. Having disembarked at Suez, Egypt, as C Battalion of Layforce in early March 1941 Sinclair and his comrades were stood-to (and dropped from) a raid on Bardia in April. At the end of the month, the Commando moved to Cyprus in readiness for OPERATION EXPORTER, the campaign against the Vichy French in Syria. Whilst on the island, Sinclair was promoted to corporal. In the early hours of 9 June, No.11 Commando subsequently landed close to the mouth of the Litani River on the Syrian coast in an attempt to seize locations key to the Allied advance. Although it is not known what specific role Sinclair played, the landings created an effective diversion for Australian troops advancing from the south.

On returning to Egypt Layforce was disbanded and at the beginning of 1942 Sinclair was posted to the Middle East Commando at Geneifa, close to Kabrit. Soon afterwards, he joined the Special Boat Section, a small body of swimmer-canoeists trained for raiding and the drop-off and pick-up of agents. He was subsequently attached to L Detachment, SAS Brigade, for a raid on Benghazi harbour, the unit War Diary stating:

> On 24th March [1942] a party consisting of Maj Stirling [*sic* – at this time captain], Cpl Cooper, Cpl Seekings of the SAS, Capt Elliot [*sic* - Allott] and Cpl Sinclair of the SBS, with Lt Alston as interpreter, left Wadi bu Maun in the Blitz Wagon [a utility truck disguised as a German vehicle]. They made their way to the Benghazi–El Abier road but finding the journey more difficult than expected had to postpone the raid to the following night. On the 25th they hit the road at 2300 hours, drove down towards Benghazi to Regina where they tried without success to cut the telephone wires.
>
> Passing Benina and Lete [both Axis airfields] without trouble they drove straight to Benghazi harbour, the few people they passed taking no notice of them. The Blitz Wagon had just been parked in a side street when a man put his head out of a window to enquire about all the noise. Cpl Cooper soon convinced the aggrieved man that everything was alright by the simple expedient of flourishing his Tommy gun beneath the man's nose. The window shut and there were no more interruptions. The party then moved on along the sea front, where for two hours, in total darkness, the SBS crew struggled in vain to assemble the ancient Folbot. Without this most expected piece of bad luck the raid would have had every chance of succeeding as the harbour was full of shipping. One big ship was particularly close.

Sinclair was promoted to sergeant in August 1942, the Special Boat Section falling under the command of Stirling later that year. As such Sinclair appears on an early 1943 list of personnel attached to 1st SAS as '3306187 Cpl Sinclair A, Special Boat Section'. However, on 19 March the Special Boat Squadron (1st SAS) was formed and Sinclair absorbed into one of its subunits, this also being known L Detachment after its commander, Lieutenant Tommy Langton, MC. His troop was subsequently loaned to the Small Scale Raiding Force that formed the foundation on which 2nd SAS was raised on 13 May 1943. He was posted 'missing presumed killed' after OPERATION BUTTERCUP on the night of 6–7 June 1943 (see Sergeant 'Ginger' Milne's entry within this section for full details). Unfortunately, Sinclair's wife was misinformed that he had been posted missing in early April and she therefore wrote to the War Office stating that her husband had met her brother, Gunner G. White of an anti-aircraft battery stationed on Malta, on the 3rd and 4th of June. She also noted that her husband had received a payment on Malta on the 5th. The Infantry Records Office in Perth replied late that month:

> I thank you for your letter of 27th June 1943 enclosing the airgraph and letter from your husband from which it would appear that he is safe and well. As no official word to this effect has been received to date I am retaining the airgraph and letter at present.

Soon after this office rectified its earlier mistake:

> I regret to inform you that in reply to my cable to the Middle East, information has been received that your husband was reported missing on June 6th, and not on April 6th, as reported in error on a previous cable. I am afraid, therefore, that your letter and airgraph which I return herewith were written prior to his being reported missing.

In September 1944 his wife wrote to the War Office again: 'As it is now nearly sixteen months since my husband (Sgt A. R. Sinclair 3326187 HLI) went missing I wonder if you could give me any further news of him for I feel I am at a standstill and the suspense is really terrible.' It was not until the following January that his death was officially presumed to have taken place on 6 June 1943, despite the timings outlined in Milne's entry above that suggest he was alive at 0030hrs on the 7th.

Son of Mr and Mrs Henry Sinclair – Husband of Jean Sinclair of Tranent, East Lothian – Father of Williamena and Margaret Sinclair.

Age 28.

Panel 14, column 1.

CHATHAM NAVAL MEMORIAL

After the First World War the Admiralty recommended that the three main ports in Great Britain – Chatham, Portsmouth and Plymouth – should be home to identical memorials commemorating those members of the Royal Navy who had no known grave. As a result the Chatham Naval Memorial was unveiled in April 1924 by the Prince of Wales to commemorate 8,517 such sailors. After the Second World War each of these obelisks, which serve as markers for shipping, was extended to commemorate the naval missing of that war. The panels at Chatham were subsequently unveiled by Prince Philip, Duke of Edinburgh, in 1952 to commemorate a further 10,098 seamen.

Chatham overlooks the River Medway, close to the north Kent coast. The naval memorial is located above the town, south of Brompton Barracks at the western end of King's Bastion. As a result of vandalism public access is limited to the period between 0830 and 1700hrs. GPS co-ordinates: Latitude 51.384, Longitude 0.53245

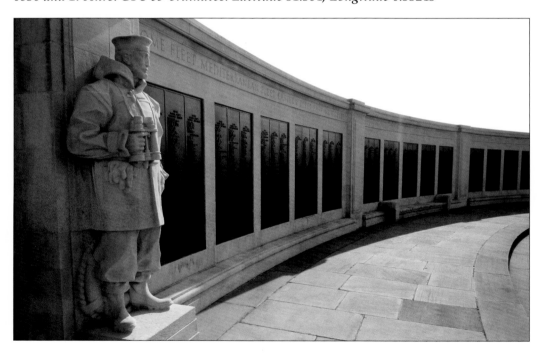

LIEUTENANT-COMMANDER RICHARD ARTHUR BLYTH <u>ARDLEY</u> [2970]
ROYAL NAVAL RESERVE ATT L DETACHMENT SAS BRIGADE

Richard Ardley was born on 29 April 1906 in Brentwood, Essex, and trained as a naval cadet aboard HMS *Conway* from 1921 to 1922. As soon as he was old enough he signed on as a merchant seaman, serving as 3rd Mate aboard the *Zingara*. He was commissioned into the Royal Naval Reserve as a sub-lieutenant in August 1929 and after a period of onshore training at HMS *Vivid* was posted to the battlecruiser HMS *Renown*. That November he was appointed 3rd Officer aboard the Royal Research Ship *Discovery II*, weighing anchor at St Katherine's Dock near Tower Bridge the following month bound for the Antarctic (see below). Here the crew carried out studies into the whaling industry. Between further arduous voyages Ardley continued his training on the minesweeper HMS *Pangbourne* and back aboard *Vivid* and HMS *Fitzroy*. He was subsequently appointed 2nd Officer in July 1930.

Ardley married Margaret Phoebe Daniell in March 1932. That August he was promoted to lieutenant and used his off-duty periods aboard *Discovery II* to write *The Birds of the South Orkney Islands* (*Discovery Reports*, Volume XII), and *The Royal Research Ship Discovery II and her Equipment* (*Discovery Reports*, Volume XIII 1936). This was achieved in not only cramped conditions but also in an often stressful environment: in May 1933 the ship's captain suffered a complete nervous breakdown and was lost overboard a few days before docking in London. After a further trip to the Falkland Islands Ardley was awarded the Polar Medal (Bronze), and Ardley Island, located in the South Shetlands, was later named after him (*London Gazette* 03/10/41, Supplement 07/10/41).

In October 1933 Ardley was appointed Port Officer and Assistant Collector of Customs in Palestine. Three years later he officially retired but opted to remain as the Port Officer and Pilot at Haifa. Here he specialised in Hydrography, subsequently writing *Harbour Pilotage and the Handling and Mooring of Ships*, the foreword of which notes:

> The author of this volume, Mr Ardley, is well equipped for his task; he is one of the younger school of seamen, combining both deep-sea experience and years of pilotage practice with a scientific habit of mind … After the 'Conway' [a training establishment] and several years at sea he served in RRS *Discovery II* in south latitudes for four years learning at first hand the fundamentals of his profession in those stormy waters. During the last eight years Mr Ardley has been a Port Officer and Pilot in the Port of Haifa handling day by day into and out of the constricted and often congested waters of this harbour a multiplicity of ships varying from 30,000-ton passenger liners to coastal tramps of a few hundred tons, but compromising principally those 'backbones' of the Mercantile Navy, the cargo liners and tramps of two to five thousand tons. That is the school in which Mr Ardley has gained the knowledge he imparts in the following pages.

Holding a reserved occupation, Ardley was exempt from mobilisation at outbreak of war but was eventually called up as a lieutenant in August 1941. Although initially posted to HMS *Nile*, a shore base at Alexandria, he was soon earmarked for special service and by January 1942 was serving as the King's Harbourmaster of Tobruk where he was described as: 'a thorough seaman and navigator, and an experienced officer. Has good power of command, combined with tactful and pleasant manner. Has good knowledge of Service customs and procedure' (service record). Posted to HMS *Stag* at Port Said that July, he was tasked 'for duty with Naval Officer in Charge Palestinian Ports' and was promoted to acting lieutenant-commander the following month. It appears he then fell out of favour; ordered to take a burning tanker out of Tobruk harbour and scuttle it he instead put out the fire and sailed it to Alexandria. It was here, whilst between postings, that he befriended David Stirling who, having failed in attempts to attack Benghazi harbour, realised that Ardley might be of use on future operations. Ardley was subsequently attached to L Detachment, SAS Brigade, taking part in OPERATION BIGAMY, the large-scale raid on Benghazi. The orders for this highlight the role he was to play:

> Force X [L Detachment] will close on the harbour area and block the exits.
> Rubber boat parties [attached from the Special Boat Section] will then proceed to sink all shipping in the harbour with the exception of one selected ship. This ship will be boarded and moved with the assistance of the RN Detachment and sunk in the entrance of the inner harbour.
> It may be necessary to hold another ship in reserve in case the blocking operation by the first is unsuccessful [WO 201/815].

Brian Dillon, a former L Detachment officer, later confirmed:

> The plan was to raid Benghazi, to sink whatever shipping there was with the exception of one which the harbour master [Ardley] was responsible for moving with an Arab tug or something to sink in the harbour mouth as a block ship, and one other ship to be got out in order that if we couldn't get out by road that we would use this vessel to evacuate down the coast [IWM Sound Archive 23787].

However, it was not to be. Ardley died of wounds on the night of 12–13 September 1942 during the approach to this operation. Jim Smith, former L Detachment, recalled that on the 12th Captain Bill Cumper, the unit's explosive expert, was ahead using a stick to clear a path through a minefield near the Trigh el-Abd track, east of Msus. He gave instructions for the column of Jeeps and three-tonners to follow in his trail and not to deviate from it. Corporal James Webster, who was driving the Jeep in front of Smith's with Ardley as passenger, veered off the track towards an abandoned Daimler scout car. He drove over a mine that the enemy had laid around the wreck, the Jeep bursting into flames. Smith and others approached using their tyre tracks to render assistance. Captain Malcolm Pleydell, the Medical Officer, amputated Webster's leg whilst Smith held a blanket for shade over Ardley. Badly burned with his skin peeling off, Ardley asked for Smith's revolver. He gave him morphine instead and later recalled: 'I thought he did a very brave thing there, wanting to do himself away to save the operation' (personal interview, 2010). Years later 'Busty' Cooper confirmed:

> I was about 20 yards to the right of it when it went off, and what a bang it was. The Jeep went up in flames. One of our sergeants jumped out of his Jeep and ran towards the Jeep that had struck the bomb. We pulled out the naval officer. He had been sitting on the petrol tank underneath his seat.
> The poor chap was all alight. He was rolled in the sand to put the flames out …
> One or two of us shielded him from the sun, which was hot, with our shirts. The NCO who was driving was pulled clear of his Jeep, but he had half of his leg blown off. I can picture him, even now, writhing about screaming.
> The Medical Officer of our unit was powerless to do anything. I would say the nearest hospital would be a couple of hundred miles away. The naval officer, who was still conscious, said to my captain 'Bill, put a bullet through here' lifting his hand to his head.
> Bill [Cumper] said: 'I can't do it. I would be had for murder.'
> 'Go on!' he said, but Bill said 'No.'
> He died after an hour or so [sic – later that night at the party's RV] and we buried him [on the morning of the 13th]. I wonder now if the spot was found where we buried him. He was a naval engineer.

Brian Scott-Garrett, another naval officer on the operation who was leading a party of attached ratings, later recalled:

> We got onto a flattened area that was strewn with wrecked vehicles and things and it was in fact where Wavell had had a battle about a year or so before. It was a battle ground, a battlefield, and absolutely covered with vehicles, tanks and things, and whilst driving along in my Jeep suddenly there was an explosion and I think it was more or less on the track I'd driven along but behind me a Jeep had blown up.
> What had happened was that it had gone over what was called a Thermos Mine. They were mines looking like a thermos flask which had been dropped, and it had blown up and oddly enough there was an RNR officer in it. He

wasn't part of our party but he was an RNR lieutenant [*sic*] who actually had been the harbour master at Haifa and I don't quite know why he was on our party to be quite honest. Whether it was because our target was Benghazi and his knowledge might have been useful I don't know. Anyway, he was blown up and the corporal driver with him was also injured as well, and the Jeep was on fire. Well, they got them out and people were all shouting 'be careful' because the bombs were everywhere you see. You suddenly realised they were lying all around you. Very, very dangerous, virtually a minefield.

Anyway, we got out, we got these two loaded onto a three-tonner and got them away and then we had a doctor with us. He treated them. And eventually he had to amputate this corporal's leg, which was rather horrible, and he then died [see Webster's entry under Alamein Memorial, Egypt, Volume I] and the RNR lieutenant, who I'd had quite a chat with before. He was a really nice chap. He told me about his family and everything and it was awfully sort of sad. He didn't seem too bad but he'd suffered a lot of burns and apparently the effect was delayed and he died and the next day we had the very unpleasant task of burying them [*sic* – only Ardley who was buried on the morning of the 13th, Webster being left behind on the 15th with three other wounded] and I always remember this because the ground was so hard and stony we couldn't dig a grave properly and it took us ages and ages and ages to dig this grave. Eventually it was hardly any depth. We just laid in the body and then piled the stones over the top and then we had a short service and that was the end of that. That was the only sort of casualty we had on the way. It did rather dampen our spirits a bit but it was really of course our own fault for fiddling around going through a minefield without taking more precautions [IWM Sound Archive 16741].

Although the SAS column was guided towards Benghazi by the LRDG, Ardley's service record incorrectly states that he was 'killed in Combined Operations with the Long Range Desert Group in Sept. 1942.' Despite a report of his death being made, and photographs of his grave taken, its exact location remains unknown.

Son of Arthur and Annie Ardley – Husband of Margaret Ardley of St Clare Road, Colchester, Essex – Father of Piers, Susan and Mark Ardley – Brother of Doris (known as Jane), Dick and Dennis (a Territorial with the Essex Regiment who was captured prior to Alamein).

Age 36.

Panel 84. Also commemorated on Lexden's war memorial and within the chapel at Chatham Dockyard.

FULFORD CEMETERY

Fulford Cemetery contains 104 burials of the First World War and 115 of that which followed. Whilst some of these form a war graves plot, others are scattered amongst the civilian headstones. In addition, the cemetery holds fifteen war graves of non-Commonwealth personnel.

The cemetery is located on Fordlands Road, Fulford, York, North Yorkshire, YO19 4QG, 4 kilometres south of York city centre and just north of the junction of the A64 and the A19. GPS co-ordinates: Latitude 53.93045, Longitude -1.06836

SERGEANT WILLIAM EDWARD <u>KENDALL</u> [402039] ROYAL SCOTS GREYS, 17TH/21ST LANCERS, 16TH/5TH QUEEN'S ROYAL LANCERS, NO.7 COMMANDO, L DETACHMENT SAS BRIGADE AND 1ST SAS

William Kendall was born on 6 October 1913 in the parish of St Clements in York. Aged just 14 he joined the Corps of Cavalry of the Line on 25 April 1928 and was posted to the Royal Scots Greys in Edinburgh with the rank of boy. Here he gained numerous certificates of education and in 1935 trained as a farrier. In October of the following year he took up this new trade on joining the 17th/21st Lancers in India. He was cross-posted to the 16th/5th Queen's Royal Lancers in May 1938 with which he continued his farrier training. When the Royal Armoured Corps was formed in 1939 this regiment was absorbed into it, Kendall returning to the UK in January 1940 where he was posted to the 4th Cavalry Training Regiment.

In August 1940 Kendall volunteered for special duties and joined the newly-formed No.7 Commando at Felixstowe. The following month he was promoted to lance-corporal and by the end of the year was on pre-deployment training in Scotland. Temporarily redesignated as 3rd Special Service Battalion, the Commando disembarked at Suez, Egypt, in early March 1941 as A Battalion of Layforce. It subsequently

310

carried out a largely abortive raid on Bardia along the Libyan coast on the night of 19–20 April, the majority of the targets having been incorrectly identified by intelligence. On their return to Egypt the men were held aboard HMS *Glengyle* until the beginning of May when they were allowed ashore, somewhat disgruntled, at Alexandria.

On the night of 26–27 May 1941 A and B Battalions disembarked at Suda Bay on Crete to help evacuate Commonwealth troops following the German airborne invasion. They subsequently formed part of the rearguard, fighting a constant running battle over the mountains en route to the embarkation point on the south coast. Kendall was one of those lucky enough to be taken off to Egypt on the 31st, the majority of his comrades going into captivity.

Most elements of Layforce were disbanded in late July 1941. Kendall volunteered for L Detachment, SAS Brigade, soon after. He was taken prisoner that November during OPERATION SQUATTER, the Regiment's first raid. His section, led by Lieutenant Paddy Mayne, was to attack an airfield at Tmimi in Libya and was parachuted into the area on the night of the 16–17th. Due to a storm, this and other parties were separated from their equipment containers and incurred heavy casualties during the drop. The operation was therefore aborted, some men, including Kendall, having been captured.

Kendall was taken to Italy. The citation for his subsequent Mention in Despatches reads:

> Kendall was captured on 20 Nov 41 near Tmimi while assisting a wounded man. His places of imprisonment [in Italy] were:- Capua, Servigliano, and Macerata (Camp 53).
>
> On the night of 15/16 Sep 43 he escaped from Macerata, but was recaptured four days later and sent to Monturano (Camp 70). By climbing over a wall and avoiding German sentries he escaped again on 23 Sep 43. After remaining in the locality for three months, through meeting an A Force officer, he attempted to cross the lines, but had to return via Chieti to Monturano.
>
> Again he was put in touch with A Force representatives, and was successfully evacuated by sea, arriving in British hands on 25 May 1944 [*London Gazette* 03/08/44, WO 373/95].

Kendall was repatriated to the UK on 5 July 1944. Although initially posted to the 59th Training Regiment, RAC, he rejoined 1st SAS on 25 October and was promoted to corporal six days later. In March 1945 he deployed on OPERATION ARCHWAY, the Jeep thrust into Germany during which he was a member of HQ Troop. Tasked as personal protection for his squadron commander, Major Harry Poat, MC, Kendall was appointed acting sergeant in April, the same month that his mother died. It is not known whether he was involved in occupation duties in Norway at the end of the war (OPERATION APOSTLE).

Kendall was promoted to war-standing sergeant on 19 October 1945 but was posted to the Y List, i.e. having been sick for twenty-one days, on 1 November. The Regiment disbanded a few days later, Kendall being released to 'Class Z Army Reserve', i.e. demobilised to the reserve list, in February 1946 whilst still in hospital. His service record notes that he died of kidney disease at County Hospital, York, on 3 May 1947 without having been discharged or transferred to another regiment. His graves registration report notes 'RAC att 1st SAS Regt AAC'.

Son of Richard and Agnes Kendall (née Simpson) of River Street, Bishopthorpe Road, York – Brother of Richard and Henry Kendall.
Age 33.
Plot 3, 73b, this being his mother's grave on which he is named and over which it is believed his ashes were scattered.

INVERNESS (TOMNAHURICH) CEMETERY

Local legend has it that Tomnahurich Hill, meaning 'the Hill of the Yews', is the seat of the Fairy Queen. Opened as a cemetery in 1863, graves were first laid out on the summit and slopes of the hill, a glacial esker, but soon spread to the surrounding area. The hill is surmounted by a war memorial to those killed in the First World War whilst the wider plot contains the graves of 162 Commonwealth service personnel.

The cemetery is located on Glenurquhart Road, 1½ kilometres south of the city centre. Opening Hours: October until March, Monday–Saturday 0800–1700hrs, Sunday 1000–1600hrs; April until September, Monday–Saturday 0800–1900hrs and Sunday 1000–1600hrs. GPS co-ordinates: Latitude 57.47035, Longitude -4.24369

PRIVATE DONALD CAMERON **CURRIE** [1450058] ROYAL ARTILLERY, SOUTH LANCASHIRE REGIMENT, ARMY AIR CORPS AND 2ND SAS

Donald Currie was born on 28 December 1919 in Inverness where he grew up as a keen member of The Boy's Brigade. In March 1939, whilst working as a radiator welder and metalworker for Craigmile & Sons, he joined the local 297th Anti-Aircraft Battery, Royal Artillery (TA). He was subsequently embodied at the outbreak of the war and posted to the 210th Heavy Anti-Aircraft Training Regiment in January 1940. Here he served as a limber gunner until qualifying as a cook. At the end of the year he was re-posted to the 389th Battery, 111th HAA Regiment, with which he served as a fitter and was promoted to lance-bombardier in February 1941.

Currie transferred to the South Lancashire Regiment with the rank of private in October 1943 and was posted to R Company, No.19 Infantry Training Centre. Here his report noted: 'Has interest in mechanical things and should do quite well. Keen and brighter than is indicated from his mortar test result.' He was recommended for future 'Carrier Crew or Mortar Dets or Driver i/c.' Currie, however, had other ideas and soon volunteered for Airborne Forces. In March 1944 he reported to its depot at Hardwick in Chesterfield and transferred to the Army Air Corps the same day. Attending parachute course 109 at No.1 PTS Ringway later that month he was noted by his instructor as having 'worked hard, showed good control, jumped well'. He subsequently volunteered for 2nd SAS on 26 May from the Airborne Forces Holding Unit.

Currie's service record notes that he served in North West Europe between 6 June and 22 July 1944. As 2nd SAS did not mount any operations until 19 July it is unknown whether the entry was made in error, or whether Currie was attached to another Airborne formation for the D-Day landings in Normandy.

At just after midnight on 23 July 1944, potentially only a few hours after he had returned to the UK, Currie was pronounced dead on arrival at 186 General Hospital, Fairford in Gloucestershire. At a subsequent court of inquiry a fellow parachutist stated:

On July 22, 1944, I left Fairford Camp at approx 1800hrs in company with Pct Currie D C. We went to Lechlade in a vehicle arriving at approx 1845hrs. We walked about the village until 2005hrs when we went into The Swan Hotel and had drinks until closing time at 2200hrs. When we left the Hotel we saw a car about 50yds from the Hotel and we decided to take it. I got into the driver's seat and Pct Currie D C sat beside me and I drove towards Fairford. After 2¾ miles we stopped at a turning in order to check that we were on the right road. We started again and proceeded towards Camp. After going about 500yds Pct Currie D C mentioned to me that there was a car coming towards us which appeared to be in the centre of the road. My speed was between 40 and 45mph. I pulled over sharply to the left hand side of the road and lost control of the vehicle. It skidded to the right hand side of the road and turned over onto its left hand side. Pct Currie was no longer beside me in the passenger seat when the car had come to a standstill and I heard him calling for help from somewhere underneath the car. The next thing I remember is a woman and a girl coming up and asking if we wanted any help. She opened the door and window and helped me out and I tried to lift the car up to release Pct Currie D C. I could not see Pct Currie D C. After that I became unconscious and remember nothing more until I came to in hospital at 0300hrs the following day.

Sergeant Maurice Pilton of 4th (French) SAS stated:

I left Lechlade at about 10pm to return on foot to Fairford. About 50 yards on the Fairford side of the turning to Whelford a car coming from Lechlade passed me in the middle of the road. I turned to signal it to stop as I wanted a lift back to camp. In the short time I saw the car I thought the wheels were wobbling. This might have been due to faulty adjustment of the wheels or due to the driver. On turning round I saw that the car had left the road and gone into the hedge. There was no other vehicle on the road at the time of the accident. The car continued along the side of the hedge with one wheel in the ditch. The driver was trying to get it back on the road but could not and the car eventually hit a bump and turned over. I thought I saw the door opening before the car turned over but it was too dark for me to see if anyone was trying to get out. I went to the scene of the accident and found the two ladies already there. I went to the driver who was very shaken. Then some people came and they lifted up the car. When they lifted the car I saw a man lying under it with his legs crossed.

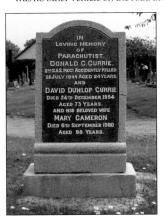

Although the court found that the men were not drunk it also found that both were to blame: 'in that they both stole the car. Pct 'X' [name redacted for publication] was to blame for the actual accident as he was driving.' This man went on to serve with distinction on operations behind enemy lines in Italy.

Son of David and Mary Currie of Muirtown Street, Inverness.
Age 24.
Section 8, class 4, grave 20. Also commemorated on the Old High Church war memorial in Inverness.

LANGLEY MARISH (ST MARY) CHURCHYARD

St Mary's churchyard, which contains twenty-one burials of Commonwealth service personnel, is located at the junction of St Mary's Road and Langley Road in Langley, Slough. GPS co-ordinates: Latitude 51.50569, Longitude -0.55399

LIEUTENANT GEORGE RICHARD **WARD** [282309] SCOTS GUARDS, NO.8 COMMANDO, L DETACHMENT SAS BRIGADE, 1ST SAS, GENERAL LIST, SRS AND 1ST SAS (HQ SQN)

Known to his comrades as 'Gerry' or 'Daddy', George Ward was born in Rotherham on 27 August 1905 and grew up Sheffield. Although very little of his service record survives he enlisted into the Scots Guards in September 1927 and by November 1940 was serving as a sergeant in No.8 (Guards) Commando at Largs in Scotland (service number 2692384). This disembarked at Suez, Egypt, in early March 1941 as B Battalion of Layforce. A frustrating period ensued for the Commando, raids being planned and then cancelled at the last minute. In the summer of 1941, as Layforce was being disbanded, Ward became one of the original members of L Detachment, SAS Brigade, and was appointed Company Quarter-Master-Sergeant. Johnny Cooper, a fellow 'Original', later wrote:

> On arrival by lorry at Kabrit we were puzzled to find that there were only two medium-sized marquees and three 180lb tents piled in the middle of the strip of bare desert allocated to us. No camp, none of the usual facilities, not even a flagpole. Across the road to the north was the RAF aerodrome and a mile or so further down was the canal control station on Kabrit point. Our lorry stopped outside one of the marquees and out strode the portly figure of CQMS Gerry Ward, who was eventually to become our Quartermaster. He ordered us to collect picks and

shovels and to start digging holes already marked for tentage … after a light meal the CQMS told us that that night we were to carry out the first SAS raid to obtain the necessary equipment to complete the camp [*One of the Originals: The Story of a Founder Member of the SAS*, by Johnny Cooper].

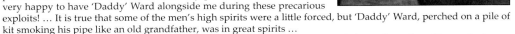

Sir Carol Mather, MC, a former L Detachment officer, described Ward just before OPERATION BIGAMY, the September 1942 large-scale raid on Benghazi:

My party was to consist of Quartermaster-sergeant 'Daddy' Ward (this was his first operation, his real job being 'Q' at base), together with three men. Our job was to travel with the main party as far as the dockside. Not waiting for the 'fusillade', we would cut off on foot making for the submarine cable to Italy (of which we presumably had some knowledge). Having destroyed this, our team of five was to attack an Italian barracks in the eastern suburb, and finally to capture the adjacent stadium and car park, which was to be used as an assembly point for our return. I was very happy to have 'Daddy' Ward alongside me during these precarious exploits! … It is true that some of the men's high spirits were a little forced, but 'Daddy' Ward, perched on a pile of kit smoking his pipe like an old grandfather, was in great spirits …

I had a flashback to Kabrit. Ward's QM stores were run on the lines of a Yorkshire village shop. You pushed open the door, which pulled a string, which rang a bell. Inside there was a counter over which you could be supplied with anything from an Arab headdress to a pound of gelignite. Despite his forebodings about our onward journey, he was an invaluable man on whom I could absolutely depend …

An uncompromising Englishman with a northern bluntness and common sense. I could always rely on him for good advice when I needed it [*When the Grass Stops Growing: A Wartime Memoir*, by Carol Mather].

The raid was unsuccessful. Even so L Detachment was granted regimental status as 1st SAS and Ward promoted to WO2 (RQMS). He was commissioned as a lieutenant (QM) onto the General List on 1 May 1943 (*London Gazette* 23/07/43). At the end of that month he rejoined the Regiment, the majority of its subunits having been reorganised as the Special Raiding Squadron. Although he helped prepare this for the invasion of Sicily and Italy, he was forced to remain at Raiding Forces HQ at Azzib and spent much of September in hospital for an unknown reason.

At the beginning of 1944 Ward returned to the UK where the Regiment was reconstituted as 1st SAS and began training in Scotland for D-Day operations. He is often recorded as having suffered a fatal heart attack on 15 April 1944 but Cooper later recalled; 'we had Gerry Ward, the Quartermaster. He committed suicide later' (IWM sound archive 18046/7). It is believed that Ward did so due to the break-up of his marriage.

Pat Riley, one of L Detachment's 'Originals', later wrote of Ward: 'CQMS Scots Guards, was instrumental in "winning" many items that were not obtainable through the normal channels. He organised raids on many neighbouring units in the area to equip the Kabrit camp – first-class chap' (*Mars & Minerva*, Autumn 1984).

Son of Noah and Blanche Ward – Husband of Alice Ethel Ward of Slough. Age 38.

The charmed circle broken, a dear face missed every day. One less at home, one more in heaven

Row 6, grave 29, this being located towards the south-east corner of the churchyard.

READING CREMATORIUM

The war graves plot is situated on the southern edge of Reading (Henley Road) Cemetery that surrounds the crematorium itself. Within the plot a screen wall commemorates thirty Commonwealth servicemen and women of the Second World War whose remains were cremated here. In addition, 118 other such personnel are buried here or within the wider cemetery, two Polish servicemen also being buried in the CWGC plot.

The entrance to the cemetery is at the end of All Hallows Road, just to the north of Henley Road (A4155). GPS co-ordinates: Latitude 51.47547, Longitude -0.95511

CAPTAIN HERBERT CECIL **BUCK** MC [IA/1117] GENERAL LIST, 1ST PUNJAB REGIMENT, (G)R (SIG), SOE (SIG, MIDDLE EAST COMMANDO) ATT L DETACHMENT SAS BRIGADE

Herbert Buck was the only son of Lt-Colonel Cecil Henry Buck of the Indian Army. He was born in India through a second marriage on 12 December 1916 but spent much of his childhood in Germany. Having boarded at Pennell House, Eastbourne College, he went up to St Peter's Hall, Oxford. Here he briefly read French and German before switching to PPE. Outside of his studies he was a keen member of the University Fencing team, the 'Assassins', representing in the sabre during a trip to the University of Bonn at the end of 1936. He was also a member of Oxford's Jujitsu team as well as the Officer Training Corps.

After graduating Buck was attached to the 2nd Battalion, North Staffordshire Regiment, at Soberton for two weeks in August 1938 whilst holding a university candidate commission on the General List (TA) (*London Gazette* 02/08/38). Ten days with the 1st Battalion, Royal Irish Fusiliers, followed straight after. That November he disembarked in India and was attached to the 2nd Battalion, Worcestershire Regiment, at Sialkot until March 1939, its Commanding Officer noting:

> This officer has a university degree, is a linguist, and is intellectually above the average. So far, he has not developed military qualities and can hardly be described as a potential cavalry officer, which he intends to be. Of average physique and a thinker rather than a doer. If he is to be a good officer in the Indian Army he will have to change his character in many ways. This report is not adverse.

Evidently the report was adverse, as Buck soon joined the 5th Battalion, 1st Punjabi Regiment, i.e. the infantry. Although briefly posted to the 1st Battalion, Worcestershire Regiment, at Rawalpindi he was back with the Punjabis by the beginning of 1940. By January 1941 he was serving as an instructor at the regiment's training school, using his free time to qualify as a German interpreter. Early the following year the Punjabis disembarked in the Middle East and at the beginning of February 1942 the 3rd Battalion's B and D Companies, under the now Captain Buck, were in Libya dug in astride the Derna by-pass to repulse the advancing Afrikakorps. Although supported by a troop of 25-pounders and another of anti-tank guns, the Germans bluffed their way through the Punjabi lines using a captured British tank. Within fifteen minutes Buck's position was overrun, he and the majority of his men being captured. The narrative is best taken up by the citation that accompanied the award his immediate Military Cross:

> Captain Buck was captured south of Derna on 2.2.42 and consistently tried in vain during the first forty-eight hours to escape with some of his men before he was separated from them.
>
> On 4.2.42 he planned to escape from Barce with a sergeant, but was moved to Benghazi. They arrived at 1700 hours and by 2000 hours were ready again, but the necessarily hasty reconnaissance caused them to mistake a sentry box for an extra sentry and they postponed the attempt till next day. Unfortunately everyone was being moved to Tripoli, so Captain Buck feigned sickness and avoided the move. That evening, the 5th February, Lt McKee was brought in and they decided to escape together.
>
> The P/W camp had been used for interning Italian civilians. After a further quick reconnaissance they chose the most feasible of two excellent escape plans. They slipped into an enemy shed with a window blown in overlooking the wire, and, having timed the sentry's beat, escaped through the wire in two to three minutes.
>
> They worked their way through the hills and crossed the Barce plain on the night of the 11th February to a position on the main road in the wooded hilly country west of Tecnis.
>
> Here they waited until a suitable vehicle came by – a Ford 15cwt truck. Capt Buck, who speaks German, in a waterproof, leather jerkin and a cap resembling a German cap, stopped the driver, saw he was alone, so asked him for his pass in German and where he was going, then held him up with a spanner held to look like a revolver. Lt McKee came up with a rifle and they bound and gagged the driver and left him behind a bush. They decided to go via the desert driving through Lamluda where there had been a petrol point. While scouting for petrol at Lamluda they were seen but escaped into the scrub followed by pistol shots although they lost their lorry.
>
> They wandered about on foot from 12.2.42 till 20.2.42 and were joined by two officers of the Norfolk Yeomanry, a sergeant and four ORs [other ranks] of the Welch Regiment, and a flight sergeant of the RAF.
>
> On 20.2.42 they arrived on the main Derna-Tmimi road about 3 miles west of Umm Er Rzem and 400 yards east of a German camp. After careful reconnaissance of the German troops in the district, with a German rifle over his shoulder, a British great-coat and jerkin and his 'German' cap, Capt Buck stopped first a large staff car, but considered it unsuitable for his purpose, then at 2000 hours a German lorry. He asked the driver how many people he had (to ascertain if there were troops in the back). He replied two (they were seated in front) so Capt Buck said 'Hande hoch', the cue for Lt McKee and another to come up on either side with pistols. While a third drove the truck down the road to where the remainder of the party were waiting and checked its petrol, oil and water, Capt Buck and McKee gagged the two Germans. They then climbed into the front of the lorry, wearing the Germans' caps.
>
> Within five minutes they were on their way and, after driving by devious routes, reached the British lines 8 miles west of Acroma at dawn February 21st.
>
> Captain Buck's escape is remarkable as an example of gallant, consistent and ingenious efforts to get away in spite of tremendous odds, supported by some extra-ordinary quick thinking. He showed unselfishness in not escaping

immediately after capture, but preferring to wait and help others. His powers of leadership in this direction were amply displayed when he afterwards led his little band of escapers back so gallantly to British territory. His courage, skill and initiative was mainly responsible for the escape of three other officers and six ORs [*London Gazette* 23/04/42, WO 373/19, recommended by Lt-Colonel Dudley Clarke, Middle East representative for MI9].

This series of events gave Buck the idea of a German-speaking subunit of the Middle East Commando, No.51 (Middle East) Commando's War Diary recording that on 17 March 1942 at Burg el Arab 'Buck selects German speaking personnel with view to certain work' (WO 218/159). On the 20th his team detached itself from the Commando, a contemporary memo to GHQ's Deputy Director of Operations from G(R), the Middle East sub-branch of MI(R), the War Office's clandestine warfare department, noting:

> It is intended that this subunit should be used for infiltration behind the German lines in the Western Desert under Eighth Army. The strength of the Special Group would be approximately that of a platoon. The personnel, a proportion of which has already been selected, are fluent German linguists. They are mainly Palestinians of German origin. Many of them have had war experience with 51 Commando. They will frequently be dressed in German uniform and will operate under the command of a British Officer who has already proved himself to be an expert in the German language. It is suggested that, if successful, the unit could be expanded …
> It is proposed to give them the cover name of 'Special Interrogation Group' [WO 201/732].

The men were separated from British units and drilled as a German platoon. In November 2000 *The Times* interviewed Ariyeh Shai, a SIG veteran who recalled how Buck had explained that a Jew caught masquerading as a soldier of the Master Race was finished: 'Captain Buck had warned that our lives would depend on our ability to wear disguises faultlessly, to learn to perfection the slang prevalent among the soldiers of the Afrika Corps and to drill in accordance with all the German methods.' Buck had told them: 'If your true identity is found out, there is no hope for you' (*Times 2*, 17 November 2000).

In April 1942 Buck was absorbed into MO4, one of the many cover names for the Special Operations Executive (SOE), although he remained in command of SIG. The unit's first mission, carried out in June 1942, was to escort a party of 'prisoners', in reality fifteen Free French parachutists attached to L Detachment, SAS Brigade, to attack airfields at Derna and Martuba. Initially guided to the target area by New Zealanders of the Long Range Desert Group's R.1 Patrol, Buck and eleven members of SIG pushed on in two separate parties. The Derna party was betrayed with only one of its number, lieutenant Augustin Jordan, avoiding death or capture (for full details see entries for Private Eliahu Gottlieb and Corporal Petr Haas under Alamein Memorial, Egypt, Volume I). Buck believed his Martuba party destroyed 15–20 aircraft. Although the men were seen and fired upon by a spotter plane during their withdrawal they 'apparently satisfied it by displaying a German flag' (WO 218/91). Having later lost all its trucks bar one, the party reached its rendezvous with the LRDG at dawn on the 16th, returning to Siwa three days later.

Buck led a party of his men during OPERATION AGREEMENT, an attack on Tobruk harbour designed to disrupt Rommel's supply chain and destroy his fuel reserves. Lieutenant Tommy Langton's report confirms the party 'included a detachment of SIG (Capt Buck)' and that it proceeded to Tobruk via Kufra from Cairo in seven three-ton lorries on 22 August 1942: 'The intention was to drive into Tobruk in three of the three-ton lorries disguised as British prisoners of war with a guard made up of the SIG party in German uniform (increased in numbers by Lt MacDonald, Lt Harrison, and myself)' (WO 201/751). On the evening of 13 September the party infiltrated the town and split into two groups to carry out their tasks. Unfortunately, reinforcements were not landed once the harbour had been captured and it wasn't long before the party itself was taken prisoner, Buck falling into enemy hands for a second time on the 14th. Private Leo Hillman, one of the few members of SIG to escape, and who was awarded the Military Medal to which he later added an MC whilst commissioned in SOE, recalled that: 'Pte Roer was wounded. Capt Buck went to help him. He carried Pte Roer into the Wadi' (WO 201/751). Meanwhile, Buck's SOE personnel file, HS 9/231/9, consists of just a single memo that confirms that he was posted missing at this time. His obituary, which appeared in *The Camberley News* during December 1945, takes up the narrative:

Captain Buck was in the desert two days before he was recaptured. He was taken to Italy by submarine where he again escaped [he was imprisoned in PG 35 (Certosa di Padula Monastery) near Potenza from January-August 1943 and at Bologna until October 1943]. Once more he was recaptured and sent by train to Germany. During the journey he cut a hole in the side [*sic* – floor] of the cattle truck and again escaped [near Bolzano, remaining at liberty for three days]. By this time he had gained the title of 'Escapee' and was locked in solitary confinement for fourteen days.

Buck had attempted to escape at Strasbourg by hiding under a drain-cleaning vehicle dressed as a Frenchman. According to his mother's statement filed alongside his MI9 liberation questionnaire, Buck subsequently: 'tried to contact a German coal merchant, who he had been told, would help him. He was however, recaptured'. Solitary confinement followed before being imprisoned at Oflag Va in Heilbronn from November to December 1943 and Oflag VIIIf at Mährisch-Trübau until his transfer to Oflag LXXIX near Brunswick in July 1944. He had kept up correspondence with the Vice-Master of St Peter's who later recorded:

As a prisoner of war in Germany he [Buck] not only introduced into his Oflag fencing and highland dancing, but conducted a class in Indian mysticism and wrote a thesis on a metaphysical subject which he has since worked up into a serious attempt to reconcile Indian mysticism with Western philosophy [courtesy of The Master, Fellows and Scholars of the College of St Peter le Bailey in the University of Oxford].

As *The Camberley News* reported Buck's endeavours did not stop with the liberation of his camp:

He, with others, volunteered to stay in Brunswick after the liberation and help with the superhuman task of controlling the riotous displaced persons. He was leader of the band … Captain Buck first set about organising French and Polish prisoners of war as armed guards. This was essential. Order was the most needed thing in confusion. In his district he had to control at least 1,500,000 people of all classes and nationalities. His tact, sympathy and understanding of 'the other fellow' enabled him to work wonders. He brought the electricity and water systems into efficient working order, and took over the feeding in the Town Hall. He also commandeered a complete German field ambulance crew and set them about the task of repairing the injured and comforting the sick. Probably the most remarkable of his feats was the uniting of Russians, Poles, Czechs, Germans, Italians and French prisoners into an efficient welfare staff. He supervised the transit of 5,000 Russian and French prisoners each day, and still controlled the other masses who would have to stay in his district [December 1945].

On his return to the UK Buck was earmarked by Major Roy Farran, DSO, MC*: 'Every effort must be made to get this officer for SAS Bde, preferably for 2 SAS.' Buck's own correspondence with the unit, all dated 31 July 1945, recorded that he was keen to go with them to India if required: 'At the moment I am being handled by the India office (Secretary, Military Dept) as a normal Indian Army casualty. It should, however, make my detachment from regimental duties easier if it be pointed out that I have not been released from special service.' At the time preparations were being made for the Regiment to support SOE's Force 136 in the Far East. Whether his proposed transfer was actioned before his death is unknown. However, his last unit, SIG, was under the command of L Detachment SAS at the time of his capture and he therefore warrants inclusion within this Roll of Honour.

Buck was killed in an air crash on the morning of 22 November 1945 at White's Farm near Broadway Pound in Somerset. This was just two weeks after he married his childhood sweetheart at St Peter's Church, Yateley, and just before the last members of the Regiment were posted to other units on disbandment. He was en route to India aboard a Liberator that had taken off from RAF Merryfield:

A/C crashed into hillside 900' high, 4.5 miles from A/F [airfield] soon after TO [take-off].
Pilot failed to maintain a straight course whilst climbing in cloud after TO made a turn to port & struck high ground. Had been briefed to climb to 1500' before turning.
Flight should not have been authorised as the pilot was not sufficiently trained and had not been checked by CO or Flt Commander [RAF Aircraft Accident Card].

All those aboard, five aircrew and twenty-two army passengers, were killed, the squadron log noting:

Local residents were first to arrive on the scene, quickly followed by Station and squadron personnel. The aircraft was found in flames and all occupants dead except the pilot who, however, died before he could be taken to hospital.

Judging from the debris the impact must have been tremendous and it is some consolation, poor though it may be, that the deaths were instantaneous. The aircraft was a complete write-off [53 Squadron's Operations Record Book, November 1945].

Two days later *The Somerset County Gazette* reported:

Apparently it did not obtain sufficient height to clear the hillside (which rises to 930 feet), struck a tree, caught fire and burned out in a field not far from Castle-Neroche, belonging to Mr J. Gent of Castle Farm, Buckland St Mary.

Buck's death certificate states his death was due to 'War Operations', his Mention in Despatches, presumably awarded for his activities as a prisoner, being published in the *London Gazette* on 23 January 1947.

Son of Lt-Colonel Cecil Henry Buck and of Eleanor May Buck of Oakhurst, Yateley, Camberley, Hampshire – Husband of Celia Buck (née Wardle) of Yateley who served in the WRNS – Buck's father is known to have dedicated his unpublished memoirs to his son.

Age 28.

Panel 1. Also commemorated on Yateley's war memorial, on a memorial stone to the victims of Liberator KH126 on Hare Lane near White's Farm, within Eastbourne College's Memorial Building and on a tablet in St Peter's College chapel.

TWICKENHAM CEMETERY

Twickenham Cemetery, which contains the graves of 126 Commonwealth service men and women, is located south of Whitton Station at the junction of Percy Road and Hospital Bridge Road. GPS co-ordinates: Latitude 51.44675, Longitude -0.36585

PRIVATE RICHARD FREDERICK **IRELAND** [1775005] ROYAL ARTILLERY, ARMY AIR CORPS AND 2ND SAS (3 SQN)

Known as Fred to his friends, Richard Ireland was born on 10 November 1913 at Twickenham in Middlesex where he attended Trafalgar School. In December 1936, whilst working as a plumber for a local company called Snells, he married his neighbour and teenage sweetheart, Nellie Winifred Smith, at Ealing Registry Office. By the outbreak of war they had produced two sons, Tony and Denis.

In late February 1941 Ireland enlisted into the Royal Artillery and was posted to the 216th Searchlight Training Regiment at Kinmel Park near Rhyl in north Wales. Three months later he was re-posted to the 16th Light Anti-Aircraft Regiment in the west Kent area. When this unit began preparations to move to Iraq that autumn he was posted to the 17th LAA Regiment. Embarking for North Africa in mid October 1942 he landed on the Algerian coastline with the First Army the following month during OPERATION TORCH. The regiment subsequently moved to Bône in December where it protected the docks. By the beginning of February 1943 it had crossed into Tunisia and was stationed at Souk-el-Arba airfield near modern-day Jendouba. The end of the North African Campaign that May found the regiment at Cap Bon and by July it was protecting Allied Headquarters. Although it is unknown when Ireland moved

to the Italian mainland he subsequently joined the 1st (Rough Riders) Airlanding Light Anti-Aircraft Battery near Campobasso in October 1943 and it was here that he became close friends with fellow gunner, Ernest 'Spud' Taylor.

The Rough Riders returned to the UK at the beginning of 1944. On 8 March, with the battery having left the 1st Airborne Division, Ireland and Taylor transferred to the Army Air Corps. They attended parachute course 110 at No.1 PTS Ringway the following month. Here Ireland's instructors noted: 'good worker, cheerful, parachuting average'. Posted to the Airborne Forces Holding Unit he and Taylor volunteered for 2nd SAS on 26 May, both joining No.3 Squadron. They deployed on their first operation together, Robin Fletcher, a former officer of 2nd SAS, later recalling:

> In September 1944 [the night of 19–20th] the plan was to drop six Jeeps into [Operation] Loyton in the Vosges mountains of Eastern France …
>
> The Halifax squadron [298 Squadron, RAF] was, I understand, based at Middle Wallop but our aircraft took off from Tarrant Rushton. We had a Jeep already fixed underneath which I was told had come from what we called the 'Brigade Dump' – centralised supply for SAS Brigade [more formerly known as Station 1090, at that time located at Williamstrip Park near the village of Hatherop north of Fairford, Gloucestershire]. We – that is to say myself and Parachutists Taylor and Ireland – had only our own personal kit in rucksacks (inverted leg bags). The despatcher was from the RAF. The pilot flew up and down trying to find the Loyton DZ [above the village of Moussey] but eventually gave up [having spent some time looking for the ground signal] and turned for home [personal correspondence, 2009].

The crew found Tarrant Rushton closed by fog and were redirected to RAF Harwell south of Oxford. En route the flight engineer admitted that he had not kept an accurate log of fuel consumption and that, due to not having dropped its load, he thought the aircraft was near empty. It was therefore diverted once again, this time heading towards Middle Wallop, Fletcher taking up the narrative:

> Trying to get into Middle Wallop (having dropped the Jeep on Salisbury Plain) I think the aircraft stalled, dropped to the ground and broke up. Ireland was killed [*sic* – see below], as was at least one of the RAF crew [Sergeant Geoffrey O'Keefe RAFVR, the wireless operator, commemorated on Panel 9 at Camberwell (Honor Oak) Crematorium], but Taylor and I got away with it.
>
> I understand that Ireland's body was taken up to London for burial almost immediately by a party commanded by Lieutenant Tom Shaughnessy of 3 Squadron [personal correspondence, 2009 – Fletcher was in fact seriously injured when thrown clear and hit by one of the engines. On recovery he supported SAS operations in Italy as No.3 Squadron's Air Transport Officer].

Initially Ireland was reported as 'slightly injured during flying battle' and his wife called to the hospital where he was being treated. He died of his injuries the following day, 21 September 1944. Both the Flight Control Officer at Harwell and the Flight Engineer were found to be at fault, a subsequent RAF inquiry noting that at 0300hrs on the 20th the Halifax:

> … undershot airfield when pilot attempting to make belly landing due believed fuel shortage in fog conditions. Pilot L'ed [levelled] off at the top of fog layer (thinking it to be 10' thick) and immediately hit ground.
>
> Pilot should have ordered troops to jump + should have jettisoned Jeep earlier – should have called on W/T + informed base of impending fuel shortage – when diverted by R/T [radio] over own base should have proceeded immediately + should have continued instead of circling calling Darky [a radio service that gave bearings and positions to lost aircraft]: F/Engn did not keep concise fuel usage record + informed pilot only 15mins fuel left over base when actually 115 gallons recovered from crashed aircraft.
>
> Belly touchdown made in attempting belly landing resulting in undershot. 38 Group recalled A/C [aircraft] then cancelled recall wasting thirty minutes. A/C forced to wait 20mins in vain over DZ awaiting signal + returned with full load contrary to pre flight calculation. FCO [Flight Control Officer] Harwell should have deployed Sandra lights [three searchlights used in cloud cover to provide a lock-on to aircraft] + given all assistance A/C in distress diverted to him. Landing attempted in fog – fog at base + other aerodromes necessitated diversion.

Son of Richard and Edie Ireland (née Targett) of Twickenham – Husband of Nellie Ireland of Gould Road, Twickenham – Brother of Jim and Arthur Ireland. After the war Taylor, who had gone on to operate with 2nd SAS in Italy, married Nellie bringing up Ireland's two boys as his own.
Age 30.
We miss him just as much today as in the hour he passed away
Plot K, row N, class C, grave 9, approximately 40 metres south-east of the Hospital Bridge Road entrance. Also commemorated within All Saints Church, Twickenham.

UNKNOWN LOCATION

The men listed in this section are all confirmed as casualties that fall under the remit of this Roll of Honour, but whose final resting place is currently unknown. Two are Frenchmen whose remains appear to have been moved from the area in which they were killed, most probably repatriated to wherever their next of kin were resident post-war, as with similar cases covered within the France section. The remains of a third, a Greek, are believed to have been moved to Egypt, even though his original grave on the island of Santorini is still maintained. Meanwhile, the graves of his fellow countrymen listed here, who fell whilst fighting in the North African Campaign as members of the Greek Sacred Squadron (1st SAS), were not recorded.

ANTHYPOLOCHAGOS IOANNIS **AGLAMISIS** [UNKNOWN S/N]
ROYAL HELLENIC ARMY ATT 1ST SAS (GREEK SACRED SQN)

In February 1943 sixteen Jeeps of the Greek Sacred Squadron, 1st SAS, set off from Nalut in western Libya. They reached Ksar Rhilane within Tunisia on the 21st having lost one vehicle to a mine, an officer being badly wounded in the explosion. Forming into three patrols the squadron joined French armoured cars of Général Leclerc's forces to recce Ksar Tarcine the following day. However, roughly twenty kilometres short of their objective the heavier French vehicles were brought to a halt by bad going, the Greeks pushing forward alone. Sergeant Govier, who was attached to them from the Special Boat Squadron, later reported:

> One patrol was following a track and about 6 miles [from] Ksar Tarcine they met a German Mk.3 tank and two A/Cs [armoured cars], which they immediately engaged. Opposition being heavy for the Jeeps, they started to withdraw, but owing to the bad nature of the ground on either side of the track (on one side was an escarpment, and the other side was very soft sand) they had great difficulty in turning round. One Jeep was hit and of the two occupants, one was killed and the other badly wounded and subsequently taken prisoner. Another Jeep turned over, but the two officers were picked up by a remaining Jeep. They then withdrew down the track, the enemy making no attempt to follow.
>
> One of the other patrols coming on later from the NE came across the crew of the A/Cs burying the Greek officer who had been killed. The four Jeeps formed up in cavalry fashion and with all guns firing, charged down on the enemy, who promptly jumped into their vehicles and turned tail, making no attempt at retaliation [WO 218/98].

Anthypolochagos (2nd Lieutenant) Ioannis Aglamisis (Γιάννης Αγλαμίσης) is commemorated on the Greek Sacred Regiment memorial within Ares Park (Pedion Areos), Athens, as having being killed in action on 22 February 1943 and must therefore be this officer. His current resting place is unknown.

ANTHYPOLOCHAGOS L. **ANAGNOSTIDIS** [UNKNOWN S/N]
ROYAL HELLENIC ARMY ATT 1ST SAS (GREEK SACRED SQN)

From mid February 1943 the Greek Sacred Squadron (1st SAS) was operating in western Libya. From Nalut it pushed forward in Jeeps and was operating with Free French Forces of Général Leclerc at Ksar Rhilane within Tunisia by the 22nd. Sergeant Govier who had been attached from the Special Boat Squadron (1st SAS) reported that on 10 March:

The attack [on Ksar Rhilane] started at first light. The enemy had brought some aty [artillery] up, and we came under some heavy shell fire. At 0800hrs twelve Stukas and fifteen ME109s came over and bombed and strafed for ten minutes … The sand dunes formed quite good protection from strafing. The air attack was repeated again about an hour later. About fifty enemy A/Cs [armoured cars] took part in the ground attack. The French very successfully and cleverly held their fire until the A/Cs came to within about 400 yards and then opened up causing considerable damage.

… Some of the A/Cs crept round the southern flank and engaged the Greek Squadron HQ with heavy MG fire. Things got pretty hot, and we were forced to withdraw to a hill. Fortunately some Spitfires and Hurricanes came over and bombed and MG the cars, knocking out three and two half tracked vehicles …

Towards dusk the Germans started to withdraw, having given up the attack. Altogether over fifty of their vehicles had been destroyed, four planes shot down and many wounded and dead Germans were left behind. A most successful day. Our losses in men were two French killed and seventeen wounded. At about 1100hrs the Greek Col's driver who was taking the staff car to B Boeuf [unknown] was hit in the leg and taken prisoner. The car was looted and left. Two Greek officers are also reported missing [WO 218/98].

Anthypolochagos (2nd Lieutenant) L. Anagnostidis (Λ. Αναγνωστίδης) is commemorated on the Greek Sacred Regiment memorial within Ares Park (Pedion Areos), Athens, as one of two officers and an other rank posted missing in action in Tunisia on 10 March 1943. He thus appears to be one of those described here (see entries for Astifilakas N. Pagonis and Anthipaspistis P. Tsaousopoulos within this section).

SOLDAT 'MARCEL **FAUCHOIS**' – REAL NAME MARCEL **FRIEDMANN** [35982]
1ER BATAILLON D'INFANTERIE DE L'AIR
AND 2E RÉGIMENT DE CHASSEURS PARACHUTISTES (4TH SAS) ATT 1ST SAS (C SQN)

Marcel Friedmann was born in Paris on 13 August 1923. In October 1942 he fled to Spain intending to reach the UK. However, en route he was interned at the infamous Miranda del Ebro Concentration Camp until the following May when released into British custody by Franco's men. Eventually arriving in England he joined the Forces aériennes françaises libres (FAFL) in July 1943 and was posted to the newly-formed 1er Bataillon d'infanterie de l'air at Camberley the following month. This was reorganised as the 4e Bataillon d'infanterie de l'air that November, Friedmann subsequently qualifying as a parachutist at No.1 PTS Ringway in January 1944. That April his unit was again renamed, this time to the 2e Régiment de chasseurs parachutistes, more commonly known within the SAS Brigade that it joined as 4th (French) SAS. Assigned to No.1 Squadron at Auchinleck he was involved in training until elements of the brigade were locked down in camps across southern England in the run up to D-Day operations.

Having been attached as an interpreter to C Squadron, 1st SAS, Friedmann and four others under Captain Derrick Harrison formed the advance party for OPERATION KIPLING. In the early hours of 14 August 1944 they parachuted into France, the DZ being a field at Les Placeaux on the edge of the Forêt de Merryvaux west of Auxerre. So as not to endanger his family in the event of capture, Friedmann was carrying a counterfeit Canadian passport under his alias of 'Fauchois'. Having been reinforced by two other sticks, a pair of Jeeps was dropped to the party on the night of the 18–19th. On the afternoon of the 23rd Friedmann's patrol was on its way to contact the Maquis at Aillant-sur-Tholon when it came across smoke and the sound of gunfire emanating from the village of Les Ormes. Driving their Jeeps into the square the patrol subsequently attacked an estimated force of 250 SS who were murdering local men. Whilst the majority of the hostages were able to escape, the enemy, who suffered fifty to sixty casualties, returned fire and killed Lance-corporal 'Curly' Hall. Friedmann retrieved his body under fire despite Harrison warning him of the danger (see Hall's entry within this volume under Les Ormes Communal Cemetery, France).

That evening Harrison's patrol met with the main KIPLING party, the combined group eventually concentrating with other elements at Cosne-sur-Loire to refit before reaching Brussels on 5 October for extensive maintenance. Friedmann was killed the following month, numerous dates of death being reported. On 7 November 1944 the squadron commander, Major Tony Marsh, DSO, signalled Brigade HQ: '35982 FRIEDMANN 4th French Bn att. C Squadron killed Jeep accident. Passenger Belgian injured' (AIR 20/8842). Although it is often reported that he was killed in Belgium it thought he was across the border at Panningen in Holland and that he was killed on the 6th. No further details can currently be located.

The citation that accompanied Friedmann's posthumous Medaille militaire, awarded on 16 January 1945, states:

> Detached to a regiment of British parachutists he took part in a number of Jeep patrols behind the enemy lines. The patrol fell into an ambush [*sic*] set by a company of German SS with the lead vehicle destroyed and the driver [Hall] killed. Completely disregarding the danger Friedmann rushed through enemy fire across 30 meters of open ground to his friend, pulled his body from the Jeep, and carried it to cover. Not wanting to abandon it he disregarded the patrol commander's orders. His bravery, his determination, and the force of character he showed were a living example of the spirit of sacrifice and devotion to duty worthy of the noble traditions of the French Army to which he belongs and the British Army with which he served.

Age 21.

A 'M. Friedmann' is commemorated on the war memorial within the Maisons-Laffitte Communal Cemetery in the north-west suburbs of Paris, although he is not buried at this location, or within the adjoining parish. No trace can be found of his family. Thought to be Jewish, they may have been deported only to perish in the concentration camp system.

CHASSEUR ROBERT <u>GUICHAOUA</u> [52241] 1ER COMPAGNIE DE CHASSEURS PARACHUTISTES ATT L DETACHMENT SAS BRIGADE (FRENCH SQN)

Robert Guichaoua was born on 16 August 1921 at Quimper in the Finistère department of Bretagne (Brittany), north-west France. Having joined the Forces françaises libres (FFL) in London during July 1940 he was posted to the 1er Compagnie d'infanterie de l'air the following January and subsequently qualified as a parachutist at No.1 PTS Ringway (Brevet No.438). After training at Exbury on the south coast he embarked for the Middle East on the SS *Cameronia* at Greenock in late July 1941, arriving at Suez in Egypt. From here the company moved via Haifa to Beirut in what was then Syria. Local training followed, as did a change of name, the unit being retitled the 1er Compagnie de chasseurs parachutistes from mid October. At the beginning of January 1942 this was absorbed into L Detachment, SAS Brigade, at Kabrit in Egypt as the Free French Squadron and thus fell under the overall command of Captain David Stirling.

Guichaoua was one of those captured on 12 June 1942 during an attack on Derna airfield in Libya. A German member of the Special Interrogation Group betrayed his group (see Private Eliahu Gottlieb's entry under Alamein Memorial, Egypt, Volume I, for full details). When discovered, Guichaoua threw a grenade and, despite being wounded, he initially escaped into the surrounding desert. He was taken prisoner 20 kilometres from Derna on the 17th and died in hospital in Bari, Italy, on 29 August 1942 (*Revue de la France Libre*, June 1953).

The French magazine, *Troupes d'Elites*, reported that when the French were betrayed:

Guichaoua threw a grenade and escaped with the Lieutenant [Jordan]. The others were quickly neutralised … Guichaoua used his last grenade on something that burnt. He was wounded in the head but escaped to the north-west. On the 17th he came across an Italian bivouac and was again wounded, this time in the hand, before fleeing. Lost in the desert he was captured on the 19th of June by an Italian patrol … Guichaoua died of disease in Italy during August of 1942 [Issue No.45].

Age 21.
His grave cannot currently be located. He is commemorated on the SAS Brigade Memorial at Sennecey-le-Grand and by the rue Robert Guichaoua in Quimper.

ANTHYPOLOCHAGOS STEPHANOS MICHALIS **KAZOULIS** [UNKNOWN S/N]
ROYAL HELLENIC ARMY ATT SBS (Z PATROL, S DET)

Stephanos Kazoulis (Στέφανος Καζούλης), or 'Stefan Casulli' as he was known within the Special Boat Squadron, was born during 1912 in Alexandria, Egypt. His parents had migrated from the Dodecanese island of Rhodes to trade in cotton under the company name 'M. S. Casulli & Co'. Educated at the Averofio Greek School in Alexandria he went on to read law at the University of Lausanne before studying at the London School of Economics. Although his service record cannot currently be located within Greek military archives he is said to have enlisted alongside his brothers Alexandros and Pavlos as soon as the Italian Army invaded Greece in October 1940. Having risen to the rank of lochias (sergeant) he was commissioned into the Greek Sacred Squadron, a Special Forces unit that had been attached 1st SAS Regiment and that later formed part of Raiding Forces (1st SAS). Presumably due to his language skills he was asked to join the Special Boat Squadron, the unit's War Diary noting that on 20 July 1943: 'Lt Hallett, Lt Clarke and 2Lt Casulli [the equivalent of the Greek rank Anthypolochagos] joined the Squadron from their respective Regts and are members of Raiding Forces'. It also notes that he was attached from the 'Greek War Ministry' as the 'Greek Liaison Officer' (WO 218/98). He subsequently reported for parachute course No.57 at Ramat David in Palestine on 30 July.

In September 1943 Italy signed an armistice, the SBS being rushed into the Aegean to seize Italian-held islands before German troops could do so. That month Kazoulis and a small party from S Detachment subsequently landed on Cos where he was paraded on the shoulders of the inhabitants and forced to give a speech. Having withdrawn first to Leros, and then to Calino, German parachutists landed on Cos at the beginning of October. Kazoulis' patrol, accompanied by that of Captain Walter Milner-Barry, returned soon after by caique of the Levant Schooner Flotilla. Having gathered over eighty British evaders, the group was hard pressed by German forces and attempted to reach neutral Turkey on rafts. These had been found abandoned on the shore but proved to be useless, the men losing much of their equipment when forced to swim back to the island. The LSF eventually ferried the whole party to Bodrum in two journeys (WO 210/793).

Having been re-equipped on Castelrosso, Kazoulis was back on Leros in November 1943, leaving for Gumushuk, a small Turkish fishing village, the night before the German airborne and naval invasion. In the days that followed he sailed to Lisso, a tiny island off Leros, to facilitate the extraction of at least sixteen British evaders.

At the beginning of March 1944 S Detachment deployed to the Aegean once more, this time for OPERATION FIREATER. Setting sail from Haifa it arrived, via Cyprus and Castelrosso, at Port Deremen on the Turkish coast. Here the SBS and the LSF had established a base at nearby Yedi Atala. After arranging supplies from Bodrum, Kazoulis took Z Patrol to the island of Nisiro at the end of the month where it gained valuable intelligence before ambushing and killing one German officer and three other ranks on the night of 11–12 April. It was picked up and returned to base the following night (WO 201/801).

A week later, on 19 April 1944, P and Z Patrols set sail for the island of Thira aboard two LSF caiques. On the evening of the 21st Kazoulis and Captain Andy Lassen, MC*, went ashore to gather information from a monastery near Perissa. As none was forthcoming they returned to the ship and lay-up camouflaged against the satellite island of Nea Kameni during the 22nd. Here a local fisherman informed them, having been lubricated with ouzo, that a mixed garrison of Germans and fascist Italians was billeted on the first floor of the Bank of Athens within Thira Town. Although tasked with capturing or destroying enemy shipping, no sign could be seen of any such vessels and the force fell back on its alternate objective of attacking opportunistic targets. That night both patrols therefore landed near Vourvoulos where Kazoulis disguised himself as a shepherd and wandered into Thira to gather further intelligence. From the information gained Lassen planned three simultaneous actions for the early hours of the 24th. One cut the island's communications, taking eight prisoners in an attack on a wireless station at Merovigli. Another attempted to kill the German commandant. Concurrently, at 0045hrs, Lassen, Kazoulis, and twelve other ranks, attacked the bank as outlined in Lassen's subsequent report:

> We succeeded in getting the main force into the billet unobserved, in spite of barking dogs and sentries. The living quarters comprised twelve rooms. It was our intention to take the troops there prisoner. This idea had to be abandoned, and will have to be abandoned in similar circumstances in the future, until raiding parties are issued with good torches. Casualties were sustained during the general mix-up in the dark. Instead, the doors of the rooms [were] kicked in, a grenade thrown into the room, and 2/3 magazines of TSMG [Thompson Sub-Machine Gun] and Bren emptied into each room.
>
> Lt Casulli was killed almost instantaneously [believed to be by gunfire whilst framed in a doorway], and Sgt [Frank] Kingston seriously wounded by shots fired either from the rooms or by the sentries outside.

Having killed or wounded every member of the garrison, Lassen retrieved Kazoulis' identity disc, gold chain and diary to give to his widow, before withdrawing his force at 0245hrs. Carrying the wounded Kingston they met the other two parties at a cave near Vourvoulos where the group had rested the previous evening.

Kingston died of his wounds the following day, Lassen later noting that: 'arrangements were made with the local doctor for him to be buried with full honours. The same request was made about Lt Casulli, and I have every reason to believe this was carried out' (see Kingston's entry under Phaleron War Cemetery, Greece, and Lassen's own entry under Argenta War Cemetery, Italy, both within Volume II). Kazoulis and Kingston were originally buried with full military honours by the Germans at Agios Gerasimos Kondohori Cemetery, local inhabitants being forbidden to attend. Although Kazoulis' grave

still exists and is tended by the local community it's believed that his remains were later moved to Egypt.

Five local men were shot by the Germans in retaliation for this raid and are commemorated on a memorial within Thira Town alongside the names of Kazoulis and Kingston. In addition, islanders were accidentally killed after they rushed into the wireless station at Merovigli to seek food. Without a Greek speaker it was not possible for the SBS party to convince them that delayed charges had been set to destroy the building and thirteen locals died when it subsequently collapsed. On 1 August 1944 the King of Greece awarded Kazoulis a posthumous Chryssoun Arition Andrias (Cross of Valour), the highest Greek military decoration of the time.

Son of Michail and Marika Kazoulis of Rhodes (his mother, the daughter of Greek Prime Minister Stefanos Dragoumis, having died pre-war) – Husband of Yvet Kazoulis (née Laskof, of Belgian descent living in Cairo) – Father of Stephanos Kazoulis – Younger brother of Alexandros and older brother of Elli, Pavlos, Ion, Daphni and Myrto.

A bronze bust of Kazoulis is located within Kiprou Square in Rhodes New Town alongside those of two guides used by the SBS on OPERATION ANGLO. His name also appears on the Greek Sacred Regiment memorial within Ares Park (Pedion Areos) in Athens. On Santorini he is commemorated as a hero and whether buried there or not his original grave is tended lovingly by the island's population.

Fallen for the Country

ANTHYPASPISTIS A. <u>LAFOGIANNIS</u> [UNKNOWN S/N]
ROYAL HELLENIC ARMY ATT 1ST SAS (GREEK SACRED SQN)

Anthypaspistis (Warrant Officer) A. Lafogiannis (Α. Λαφογιάννης) is commemorated on the Greek Sacred Regiment memorial within Ares Park (Pedion Areos), Athens, as having been killed in action on 19 March 1943. At this time Jeep patrols of what was then the Greek Sacred Squadron, 1st SAS, were harassing German troops on their withdraw in Tunisia, specifically in the area of El Outed. There are no further details.

ASTIFILAKAS N. <u>PAGONIS</u> [UNKNOWN S/N]
ROYAL HELLENIC ARMY ATT 1ST SAS (GREEK SACRED SQN)

Astifilakas (Police Constable) N. Pagonis (Ν. Παγώνης) is commemorated on the Greek Sacred Regiment memorial within Ares Park (Pedion Areos), Athens, as having been posted missing in action in Tunisia on 10 March 1943. On that day what was then the Greek Sacred Squadron, 1st SAS, was attacked by German air and ground forces at Ksar Rhilane whilst serving alongside Free French troops of Général Leclerc. Pagonis appears to have been the driver of the squadron's Commanding Officer, Colonel Christodoulos Tsigantes, and was reported as having been wounded and taken prisoner that day (see Anthypolochagos L. Anagnostidis' entry within this section for full details).

ANTHYPASPISTIS P. <u>TSAOUSOPOULOS</u> [UNKNOWN S/N]
ROYAL HELLENIC ARMY ATT 1ST SAS (GREEK SACRED SQN)

From mid February 1943 the Greek Sacred Squadron, 1st SAS, was operating in western Libya. From Nalut it pushed forward in Jeeps and by the 22nd was operating alongside Général Leclerc's Free French troops at Ksar Rhilane within Tunisia. Anthypaspistis (Warrant Officer) P. Tsaousopoulos (Π. Τσαουσόπουλος) is commemorated on the Greek Sacred Regiment memorial within Ares Park (Pedion Areos), Athens, as having been posted missing in action in Tunisia on 10 March and thus appears to be one of two officers reported as such that day (see Anthypolochagos L. Anagnostidis' entry within this section for full details).

UNKNOWN IDENTITY

The following servicemen are mentioned within either official or unofficial publications as casualties applicable to this Roll of Honour. However, whilst extensive research and the anecdotal evidence of various veterans have helped resolve similar cases, the identities of these individuals cannot currently be established. In addition to them, the Greek Sacred Regiment's memorial in Athens records seven officers and two other ranks, all unnamed, who died in service. Given the list inscribed above it, which identifies those members of the same unit who were killed in action, one can surmise that these nine men died of wounds or in training accidents. Unfortunately, bar a parachute fatality buried at Khayat Beach War Cemetery in Israel, it has not proved possible to find further details. Until these are forthcoming this must suffice as their sole mention.

'JOHNSON' [RANK, REAL NAME AND SERVICE NUMBER UNKNOWN]
L DETACHMENT SAS BRIGADE

After the war Malcolm Pleydell, MC, former Medical Officer of L Detachment, SAS Brigade, described how he had recruited two additional orderlies for OPERATION BIGAMY, a large-scale raid on the Libyan port of Benghazi, far behind enemy lines:

> I only had one medical orderly with me, a well-trained man called Ritchie who had been out on the last series of operations …
>
> From this visit [to the Royal Army Medical Corps depot] I obtained Shotton, a fair-haired Yorkshire lad whose common-sense came to our rescue more than once, and Johnson [name changed for publication], a spectacled Londoner, who soon earned the nickname of 'Razor-blade' through his evident surgical skill with this implement [*Born of the Desert*, by Malcolm 'James', Pleydell's nom de plume].

In late August 1942, 212 men of L Detachment, distributed amongst three columns of vehicles, subsequently set off from Kabrit, passing through Kharga, the Wadi Sura and Kufra Oasis. They regrouped at the Wadi Gamra south-east of Benghazi. Corporal James Webster and SQMS Arthur Sque, who had been injured en route, were left here under the care of one of the medical orderlies. On 13 September a small team including 'Johnson' moved forward to neutralise Fort Benito, a wireless station on an escarpment overlooking the port that might compromise that evening's attack. In the ensuing fight there were further casualties for the medics to deal with. The main force then descended the escarpment in Jeeps and gained the main road towards Benghazi. It was subsequently ambushed on this route and forced to retire to the hills, bringing with it further wounded.

Spotted by Axis aircraft, the SAS were bombed repeatedly, Pleydell and 'Johnson' attending to Captain Bob Mélot throughout (see his entry within this volume under Brussels War Cemetery, Belgium). Due to the amount of vehicles destroyed during this withdrawal, and the need for the party to move rapidly so as not to incur further casualties, it was decided that the stretcher cases would be left behind with two Italian prisoners, one of whom was a medic. According to Pleydell 'Johnson' was also allotted to stay with them having lost the spinning of a coin:

> Of the wounded, the four most serious cases:
> Capt [Chris] Bailey
> SQMS [Arthur] Skew [*sic* – Sque]
> Cpl [James] Webster and
> Cpl [Anthony] Drongin
> were left at the RV with a medical orderly ['Johnson'] who was sent into Benghazi [the following morning, the

16th] in a Bantam [Jeep] under a Red Cross flag with instructions to invite the enemy to bring them in with two of the Italian prisoners who had been captured; subsequent observation showed that this had been done [WO 201/748].

According to Pleydell Lt-Colonel David Stirling, DSO, stayed in the area for several days and reported seeing:

> An Italian ambulance on its way to our rendezvous to pick up our wounded …
>
> I have since learned, with deep sorrow, that the British party who were left behind at Benghazi, died later as a result of their wounds. I can understand why Dawson died [Drongin – all names changed for publication]; the outlook for Longland [Bailey] was uncertain; Cox [Webster], I had expected to recover; while the cause of Wilkinson's [Sque] death must remain a mystery. Finally Johnson, the medical orderly who accompanied them, also died some eighteen months later, although no reason for this is known [*Born of the Desert*].

Despite such accounts of the men having been picked up by the Italians, their fate remains unclear: a report within Drongin's file notes that a 'Private Watson' witnessed his burial at 'Sidi Moies (Jebel, Cyrenaica)' on 'about Sept 19th 1942'. Meanwhile, a similar note in Sque's file records that he had been 'left badly wounded at Sidi Moies, Jebel, Cyrenaica' and that Captain Arthur Duveen of L Detachment, who had gone missing during the withdrawal from the raid and subsequently met the wounded men, had gone to 'look for food and water. When he returned he was told by the Arabs that they [the four wounded, and therefore potentially 'Johnson'] had died. About 19.10.42'. There were no Italian forces manning Sidi Moies and foul play seems likely, the four being officially recorded as having died of wounds between 16 and 19 September 1942. They are now commemorated on the Alamein Memorial (see their entries under Egypt, Volume I, especially the quotes within Sque's in which Joe Plater suggests that the locals were unfriendly and Reg Seekings, DCM, MM, alleged that the wounded had been 'finished off').

This leaves 'Johnson'. Jim Smith, a veteran of Bigamy, recalled, contrary to Pleydell's' description:

> All I can tell you is that I'm not sure if it's Jakes, Jaques or Jakeman for a start. But he went to Barkers Butts Lane School, Coventry. There might be somebody who went to school with him at the time who remembers him. We knew him as Jakie. I met him at Kabrit. I'd never seen him since we left school, and he was a bit younger than us. I'm not sure whether Ronny Moore [another local resident and wartime veteran] married his sister, either Irene or Eileen, and whether her name was then Jakes, Jaques or Jakeman [personal interview, 2010].

Despite appeals in the Coventry press it has not proved possible to locate any next of kin or to access the records of Barkers Butts Lane School which has since been demolished. Although records show that an 'Irene Jackman' married Ronald A. Moore in Coventry during 1945, no birth certificate can be found for a brother.

None of the three Jackmans who were transported to Italy as POWs appear to have died during the war. The only men of this surname commemorated in Egypt are Royal Navy, Royal Air Force, or Commonwealth troops. Meanwhile, there are two Jackmans buried in Libya. One was an officer and can therefore be discounted. According to his service record the other died in June 1943 from wounds incurred two months previously, no mention being made of capture. Searches for this name, and variations of it, amongst general casualty and Royal Army Medical Corps records have proved inconclusive. Meanwhile, there were no Second World War casualties from the RAMC with the name Watson that fit. It is the unknown identity of 'Johnson' and uncertainty of his fate that warrant his inclusion within this section.

'**LARRY LAWRENCE**' [Rank, Real Name And Service Number Unknown]
L Detachment SAS Brigade or 1st SAS

During the course of a 2010 interview with Jim Smith, former L Detachment and 1st SAS, the author reminded him of a casualty that he had described the previous year as 'Larry Lawrence', killed at Gazala:

I went to see somebody in the tent [at Kabrit] and he [Lawrence] was in there and was talking about going on the next raid but I didn't now where it was all he said was that he was heading out with the next lot. I knew his name because I'd been out with him and when we were on the one [operation] when we were out together he was saying: 'Oh, I wish I was at home now. My mum makes the best rice pudding in the country.'

And he was always on about his mother and that's when the bit about the boxing come in. You know, that he was an amateur boxer, so anybody in the boxing world may know him from Reading. I mean he'd be a kid like boxing I suppose, as he was in his twenties in the army, 21, 22 …

I wanted to get to Newbury in case he's on a war memorial in Newbury because that's where he came from.

Although there is an 'L. C. Lawrence' on Newbury's memorial no such person is listed by the Commonwealth War Graves Commission and this individual may therefore have been a civilian casualty. Further research has proved inconclusive.

UNKNOWN CORPORAL L Detachment SAS Brigade

'Busty' Cooper, former member of L Detachment, SAS Brigade, wrote that during Operation Bigamy a corporal was wounded in the attack on Fort Benito, a wireless post on the escarpment that overlooked the approaches to Benghazi:

As the Belgian captain [Bob Mélot] got to the fort doors an Eyetie shouted 'Inglesi' but before he could shut the door the captain threw a grenade in and killed him. The captain was wounded, and also a corporal. There were bomb flashes and fighting inside the fort. A quarter of an hour and all were killed inside except one. We made him carry the captain back to his Jeep. The corporal died of his wounds, but we made the Eyetie dig his grave. He screamed, he thought that we were going to kill him. He was young, only sixteen and had been taken off his farm in Italy and drafted out to Algeria [see Mélot's entry within this volume under Brussels War Cemetery, Belgium].

There are no known casualties from this raid that fit the description given and further research has proved inconclusive.

'WILSON' [Rank, Real Name And Service Number Unknown] L Detachment SAS Brigade

An unknown member of L Detachment, SAS Brigade, died during a training exercise some time around May 1942. He was referred to as 'Wilson' by 'Busty' Cooper and Captain Douglas Smith. The latter, an American who had served with the Free French Squadron attached to the unit, later recalled:

On one occasion a big group started out on a daytime hike to nowhere and back. It was viciously hot that morning, and after some 15 miles of slogging through soft sand or stumbling along the rocky bottoms of dry wadis, one of the marchers had to give up. He was utterly exhausted. He kept going as long as he could, then reeled from the ranks and collapsed.

He had already drunk the quart of water with which he started. A little was taken from each of the other men's canteens to give him a full bottle. He was told the direction in which to walk back to camp, if he wished to make the effort after resting; or if still unequal to it, he was told to stay where he was and a car would be sent to bring him in. Satisfied all would be well, and advising him not to worry, the column moved on.

When it got back to the camp late that afternoon and discovered the straggler had not yet turned up, the promised car was promptly sent for him. However it was dark by the time the car reached the neighbourhood and the men in it could not locate their comrade; the headlights did not reveal him nor did anyone answer their shots. They cruised around for hours, thinking of the bitter cold the man must endure if they did not find him before morning. But all efforts were useless. They turned back.

We realised at camp the man's situation must be getting desperate. Several cars went out at dawn, drove to the area and searched it section by section. When they radioed failure, planes went up and made an exhaustive survey of the countryside. Training was suspended temporarily while all hands were driven to the place where the soldier had last been seen and turned out to hunt.

This may seem odd to people – if there are any left – who think of the desert as a flat sandy plain no rougher than a well-kept putting green. As a matter of fact, it is an endless succession of rolling and dunes with hollows between, all crisscrossed by innumerable dry river beds, or wadis, and dotted here and there with piles of rock and rubble.

He had left a trail, faint and difficult to pick up and follow, yet that is how we finally found him on the third day. He was unconscious, and he died shortly after we got him to the hospital. Careful estimate showed he had travelled nearly 50 miles from the place where he was left to the point where we found him – and he travelled that in a vast circle because, being a new recruit, he did not know how to use a compass. His fate was a tragic reminder of the importance of training men thoroughly [*American Guerrilla*, by Captain Douglas M. Smith and Cecil Carnes].

Meanwhile, Cooper recalled this first endurance test in which his section walked on compass bearings for set distances that they counted off by pacing:

Bad luck befell our section and it was my endurance test. One poor lad came to me and asked for a drink.
I said 'What have you done with yours?'
He said 'I've drunk it!'
We only had one bottle per man and we were told to conserve it, as there wasn't any water to be had anywhere.
I'm sorry I had to refuse him and the rest of the section did the same. Had I given him a drink I couldn't have told you this!
He said 'I can't go on.'
'All right, ' I said, 'stay put and don't move.'
We left him and carried on. We had to share the rest of the mileage between three of us. During the next morning the sun was getting up and I had drunk all of my water. We plodded on and saw the road from the escarpment. It would be about 2 miles away. As we carried on towards this rendezvous a Jeep came towards us, and I was glad to see it! A sergeant got out and said 'Are you alright?'

I could not speak. My tongue was beginning to swell. He gave me a swallow and I was sick. I do not want that experience again. The rest of the section were the same, but we managed to get to the rendezvous.

Our colonel was there and congratulated us. The whole lot of us had come within 200 yards of the rendezvous – a fine feat!
He said 'Are you alright?'
I said 'One man is missing.'
He said 'Who's that?'
I told him.

Straight away he got a Jeep and the MO [Medical Officer] asked when he dropped out. We told him what mileage we had done and the degree. Of course they would have to take a backward bearing. They went off and found him. He had tried to follow us. They found his pack, which he had discarded first. Then they found him. He lay there, his tongue had swollen like a banana. They took him to hospital, but he died. His tongue had choked him, but the MO tried to save him. Sorry to say we buried him the next morning and no more was said of him, but our duties were carried on as normal.

Service records for the most likely Wilsons, i.e. those buried near to Kabrit or near to a general hospital in Cairo, have been researched without any positive outcome.

UNCONFIRMED

Each casualty linked with units included within this Roll of Honour has been subject to careful research and cross-checking. Whilst this has also resulted in the discovery of some previously unattributed casualties, a small number have subsequently been proven to be unconnected. Meanwhile, those listed below can neither be confirmed nor negated owing to contradictory entries in regimental War Diaries or service records, further research having proved inconclusive.

[UNKNOWN RANK] ANDRÉ LUCIEN JULES **BELLANGER** [UNKNOWN S/N]
3ᴱ RÉGIMENT DE ZOUAVES AND 2ND SAS (FRENCH SQN)

André Bellanger is believed to have been born on 22 July 1924 at Ville Le Marclet in the Somme département of Picardie, northern France. Although it is not known when he joined 2nd SAS he was serving in the Regiment's French Squadron under Captain 'Raymond Lee', real name Raymond Couraud, by the time that it disembarked at the port of Taranto on mainland Italy (OPERATION SLAPSTICK). Coming ashore at dusk on 10 September 1943 the Regiment's Jeep patrols soon found that, although Italian forces had surrendered, German troops were intent on fighting rearguard actions, Sergent-chef Meronane noting:

> 11 Sep [1943]. At 0900hrs the Squadron patrolled in two troops along the railway [from Taranto] to Palagianello [south-east of Castellaneta], and on arrival at the railway bridge made contact with the enemy. This lasted two hours, during which the enemy opened fire with machine guns, and Pte Felger was slightly wounded by two bullets. Lt [Gabriel Saltet] de Sablet, on the right, had one of his men, Bellanger, killed by a burst of MG [machine-gun] fire [WO 218/176].

This 2nd SAS War Diary also notes that on the same day a troop from D Squadron under Lieutenant Peter Jackson, MC: 'patrolled north to "feel" the flanks of the German positions in front of Castellaneta. Made contact with the French Sqn, and discovered Castellaneta strongly held' (see Jackson's own entry under Bari War Cemetery, Italy, Volume II).

Although the remains of French casualties were often repatriated to their home towns, Bellanger is not buried at Ville Le Marclet. He is not commemorated on the village war memorial, nor on any of those nearby. A memorial at nearby Saint-Ouen does, however, record the names of two Bellangers killed in action during the First World War who may be relatives. Despite the War Diary entry, no other official references to Bellanger can be found. He is not commemorated on the Sennecey-le-Grand SAS Brigade Memorial. It is for these reasons that he is included within this particular section.

CAPTAIN ALEXANDER HENRY RICHARD MAULE **RAMSAY** [70727] SCOTS GUARDS
AND L DETACHMENT SAS BRIGADE (?)

Alec Ramsay was born on 20 February 1918 at the family home in Bryanstone Square, Central London. Educated at Eton he was selected as Captain of Oppidans, the senior Colleger next to the Captain of the School. In March 1937 he was commissioned onto the supplementary reserve of officers (Scots Guards) from the college OTC, attending annual training until being mobilised on 1 September 1939. Although proposed as the next ADC to the Governor of Madras the appointment was cancelled at the outbreak of war.

Posted to the 1st Battalion in February 1940 Ramsay was promoted to lieutenant the following month

and embarked for Norway at the beginning of April. By 11 May his battalion had taken up positions south of Mo with the intention of halting the German advance. However, the vessel transporting its Irish Guards reinforcement was bombed en route, the survivors being forced to turn back (see Guardsman Maurice Reynolds' entry under Bari War Cemetery, Italy, Volume II, for full details). A second reinforcement party consisting of the South Wales Borderers was also forced to return after the cruiser transporting it ran aground on an uncharted rock. Left alone to cover a wide area, enemy troops advanced into the battalion's arcs on the 17th. That evening German parachutists landed to the east in a flanking movement and were soon attacking No.16 Platoon under Ramsay. He was shot in his right forearm in the early hours of the following morning. Ordered to withdraw to the north, the battalion fell back from one defensive position to the next until Ramsay could eventually pause for treatment on the 26th. He was evacuated soon after and on discharge from Gleneagles Hospital was posted to the Holding Battalion before rejoining the 1st Battalion that October.

By this time Ramsay's father, a Scottish Unionist MP who was both vehemently anti-communist and anti-Semitic, was in trouble: The Right Club, an underground society that he had founded and whose members had included the future Lord Haw-Haw, William Joyce and the Duke of Wellington, had been infiltrated by MI5. Another member, Tyler Kent, was a cipher clerk at the US Embassy in London and was already under suspicion of selling secrets. Ramsay Senior entrusted him with the movement's membership book, this being discovered when Kent was arrested in May 1940 and his property searched. Ramsay's father was subsequently detained under Regulation 18b, the internment of those suspected to be Nazi sympathisers, and not released from Brixton Prison until the autumn of 1944.

Ramsay no doubt wanted to leave such issues behind and join his stepbrother and fellow Scots Guards officer, Michael Crichton-Stuart, who at the time was detached to the LRDG. He therefore applied to join the 2nd Battalion in the Middle East and subsequently embarked for Egypt at the beginning of 1941. He was soon at the frontline, the battalion forming part of the 22nd Guards Brigade positioned west of Sidi Barrani by mid April. In the early hours of 15 May Ramsay took part in a battalion attack, his company capturing over 320 prisoners and a large number of vehicles. On 16 June the battalion took further positions at Musaid during an unsupported bayonet charge. However, having been forced to retire in the face of Rommel's offensive it was transformed into a motor battalion at el Daba during July before taking up exposed positions near Buq Buq. The regimental War Diary notes: 'there has been a lot of sickness in the last month [August 1941], owing to the heat and general living conditions. Buq Buq has nothing to commend it from the hygienic point of view.' For Ramsay the statement was to be prophetic.

The battalion was in almost constant contact with the enemy and in November 1941 was badly mauled by German armour at the Battle of Sidi Razegh. However, there was to be no time to recuperate and it took an active role in the subsequent counter advance the following month. On 22 January 1942 it was in retreat once more, having been forced from its positions in Agedabia. On 6 February it settled on the Gazala Line, Ramsay subsequently being appointed acting captain and the battalion withdrawing to the unhealthy Buq Buq at the end of April.

Ramsay's service record is split and filed at two locations, one part within the Scots Guards archive and the other at the Army Personnel Centre in Glasgow. Whilst his Guards file notes that on an unspecified date he joined 'SAS, ME' his Glasgow record makes no mention of any such transfer. However, Sir Stephen Hastings, MC, noted in his autobiography:

It was at this juncture that Alec Ramsay and I learned that David Stirling, also a Scots Guards officer, was recruiting for his SAS Regiment, then known as L Detachment. We volunteered and were accepted …

From Buq Buq Alec and I got a lift to Cairo where, to my bewildered concern, Alec fell gravely ill. In just a few days his towering 7-foot frame began to buckle … It would have been hard indeed to support life in Right Flank Company for so long without his comradeship. We laughed, we sang, we cursed a lot and got drunk together. We were as close as two young men at war can be. Indeed he was like an elder brother … Intelligent, sensitive and brave, this was a happy warrior whose life promised much [*The Drums of Memory*, by Stephen Hastings].

In May 1942 Ramsay developed a persistent cough, experiencing chest pain and weight loss. He was admitted to No.9 General Hospital in Cairo on 8 June and diagnosed as suffering from tuberculosis. Later that month he was evacuated to South Africa where it was hoped the air would induce recovery, his mother reporting to a friend that he was 'very disappointed and rather appalled at the thought of being invalided for six months' (Scots Guards archive). Owing to the discrepancies in his service records it is unknown whether he was officially attached to the SAS before his relocation. He died at Baragwanath Military Hospital, Johannesburg, in the early hours of 19 August 1943, a local newspaper reporting:

Full military honours were accorded at the funeral of Captain Alexander Ramsay, of the Scots Guards, which took place yesterday at West Park Cemetery, Johannesburg …
The pall-bearers were officers from the hospital. The chief mourner was Captain Ramsay's sister-in-law, Mrs Crichton-Stuart [*Rand Daily Mail*, 21 August 1943].

Hastings later wrote:

Memory, even of one's friends, dims with the years, yet there are a very few who remain as vivid as ever they were. I hear his voice now, see him walk into the room as if it were yesterday, his face suffused with fun, enquiry and mischief. We laugh again, it seems to me. Perhaps in time, who knows, we will [*The Drums of Memory*].

Son of Captain Archibald Ramsay, MP, who was severely wounded during the First World War whilst serving with the Coldstream Guards, and of The Hon. Ismay Ramsay (née Preston) of Kellie Castle near Arbroath, Angus – Older brother to Robert, George (who also saw wartime service in the Scots Guards) and the Reverend John Ramsay – Stepbrother of Ninian, Ismay, Claudia and Michael Crichton-Stuart (who in addition to his LRDG service was married to Barbara Symes, the sister of Captain John Symes of 2nd SAS, whose entry can be found within this volume under Graffigny Communal Cemetery, France).
Age 25.
My Father which gave is greater than all. None can pluck them from his hand.
Johannesburg (West Park) Cemetery, Military Section, Grave 74.

LANCE-CORPORAL NATAN **ROSENSTEIN** [PAL/12479] AUXILIARY MILITARY PIONEER CORPS, NO.51 COMMANDO AND L DETACHMENT SAS BRIGADE (?)

Natan Rosenstein, an Austrian Jew, was born in Vienna on 28 November 1918. In September 1940 he enlisted into the Auxiliary Military Pioneer Corps at Sarafand in Palestine (modern-day Israel), declaring his trade as carpenter and his father's address as 'Unknown Manchester England'. Posted to No.6 Company, AMPC, he volunteered for the newly-formed No.51 (Middle East) Commando on 9 November, his service record noting that he was 'abroad' with this unit from that day until late the following January. At this time No.51 Commando was aboard Royal Navy vessels waiting to land behind Italian lines on the coast of Libya. Although the men were eventually put ashore at Sollum near to the Egyptian/Libyan border to prepare for an attack on Bardia, they were instead employed for three weeks unloading ships under artillery and air bombardment. With no further operations planned the Commando returned to Geneifa in the Canal Zone on 22 January 1941. The following day Rosenstein sailed from Port Suez to Port Sudan, seeing action against the Italians in Eritrea and Ethiopia during the East African Campaign and being promoted to lance-corporal in August. Returning to Egypt late that November, No.51 was reorganised into a new formation, the Middle East Commando (later retitled the 1st Special Service Regiment), at Geneifa.

Rosenstein was admitted to hospital on 20 July 1942, his service record noting that he 'died on active service 28/7/42' whilst serving with the '1st SS Regt', and that the cause of death was 'disease'. However, the following May *The Jewish Chronicle* announced his death whilst with the 'SAS Regt'. Although, given the date, this may well be a simple transcription error, many members of 1st Special Service Regiment (Middle East Commando) had transferred to L Detachment, SAS Brigade, by this time. As a German speaker the possibility also remains that he was a member of the Special Interrogation Group attached to L Detachment. Unfortunately, it has not been possible to conclusively ascertain which unit he was serving with at the time of his death.

Son of Moriz and Paula Rosenstein, of Paddington, London.
Age 22.
In loving memory
Fayid War Cemetery, Egypt. Grave 2.F.12.

Sergeant Philip **WILDING** [1345156] Royal Air Force Volunteer Reserve Att SAS (Brigade HQ) (?)

Phil Wilding joined the Royal Air Force Volunteer Reserve at Edinburgh in March 1941. The following month he reported to No.9 Recruitment Centre at Blackpool before being posted to RAF Kirkham and various other recruitment centres for further training. He was promoted to leading aircraftman that September and to corporal the following June. In July 1942 he qualified as a PTI and that September was posted to No.1 Parachute Training Centre (later School) at Ringway. Having been promoted to sergeant two months later he was briefly loaned to the 5th Parachute Brigade in November 1943 and to the 4th Parachute Brigade in April 1944. On 6 June his service record notes that he was attached to 'RAF Fairford (A)' (Army) where elements of the SAS Brigade were waiting at to embark on post D-Day operations. However, Group Captain Maurice Newnham, OBE, DFC, who had organised Britain's parachute training, later wrote:

> The attachment of PTS [Parachute Training School] instructors to the regular Airborne Divisions was proving so valuable that the Commander of the Special Air Service troops asked for similar assistance for his units … this small attachment commenced an association between the School and the SAS which developed into a remarkably friendly and efficient combination of forces …

1st SAS was keen to reiterate the close relationship between its men and their despatchers:

> Those known to us best of all were our Despatchers – those men who shout "Go!" in such a way that one just "Goes!" These Despatchers did a tour of operations consisting of fifteen trips before being grounded. Ask any officer or man in the Regiment what he thinks of these fellows, and the answer will always be "smashing blokes". They won the admiration of everyone … some were called upon to make the supreme sacrifice.

Newnham went on to suggest that Wilding was one of those called to do so whilst attached to the SAS Brigade:

> Finally when they set flight for the locality where they were to be dropped a PTS instructor would be in the aircraft with them to ensure that the parachuting equipment was in perfect order, to help them with their kitbags and other equipment, to tend their sickness and, by the confidence engendered by his presence, give them a good send-off upon their perilous adventures. After the men had jumped the instructor would despatch panniers and containers of additional equipment to the 'reception committees' that were usually waiting at the selected localities … it was inevitable that misfortune should sometimes overtake such perilous missions, and Sergeant Phil Wilding was the first of the Ringway men to lose his life in such circumstances [*Prelude to Glory: The Story of the Creation of Britain's Parachute Army*, by Group Captain Maurice Newnham, OBE, DFC].

On the night of 17 June 1944 a Stirling aircraft of 620 Squadron, 38 Group, took off from Fairford at 2320hrs. It was carrying Lieutenant Leslie Cairns' stick that was to parachute into the Morvan region of France for 1st SAS' Operation Houndsworth. Wilding was the despatcher. The post-operation report states: 'On the night of 17/18 June three Stirlings took off with reinforcements for A Squadron but were unable to find the DZ owing to thick cloud. Unfortunately one aircraft with Lt Cairns and his party failed to return' (WO 361/732). From a radio fix this aircraft, LJ850 Y for Yorker, captained by Warrant Officer Robert Crane of the Royal Australian Air Force, was last known to have been outbound over the Channel at 0050hrs and almost certainly went down into the sea.

The CWGC incorrectly records Wilding as a member of 620 Squadron, this unit omitting his name from the crew list it submitted in its report into the incident. It did, however, note him as the despatcher in its initial casualty signal. Unfortunately, it has not been possible to ascertain whether he was attached to the SAS Brigade as Newnham suggests or whether he was placed at the army's general disposal at Fairford, hence his inclusion within this section. He is, like Crane and the four other aircrew, commemorated on the Runnymede Memorial, their dates of death being correctly recorded as 18 June 1944. Bizarrely the sixteen SAS passengers are officially recorded as having lost their lives on the 17th and are commemorated on the Bayeux Memorial in France (see Cairns' entry within this volume for further details).

Son of John and Ethel Wilding of Glasgow.

Age 22.

Runnymede Memorial, panel 240.